SOCIAL PSYCHOLOGY

SOCIAL PSYCHOLOGY

4th Edition

Eliot R. Smith, *Indiana University, Bloomington*
Diane M. Mackie, *University of California, Santa Barbara*
Heather M. Claypool, *Miami University, Oxford, Ohio*

Routledge
Taylor & Francis Group

LONDON AND NEW YORK

First published 1995 by Worth

[Second edition published by Psychology Press in 1999]
[Third edition published by Psychology Press in 2007]
Fourth edition published in 2015
by Psychology Press

Published 2019 by Routledge
2 Park Square, Milton Park, Abingdon, Oxon OX14 4RN
52 Vanderbilt Avenue, New York, NY 10017

Routledge is an imprint of the Taylor & Francis Group, an informa business

Library of Congress Cataloguing in Publication Data
Smith, Eliot R.
    Social psychology / Eliot R. Smith, Diane M. Mackie, and Heather
    M. Claypool. — [Fourth edition].
        pages cm
    1. Social psychology. I. Mackie, Diane M.
    II. Claypool, Heather M. III. Title.
    HM1033.S55 2014
    302—dc23   2014016161

ISBN: 978–1–84872–894–3 (pbk)
ISBN: 978–1–84872–893–6 (hbk)
ISBN: 978–0–203–83369–8 (ebk)

Typeset in Berkeley
by Keystroke, Station Road, Codsall, Wolverhampton

Acquisitions Editor: Paul Dukes
Textbook Development Manager: Rebecca Pearce
Editorial Assistant: Lee Transue
Production Editor: Kristin Susser
Marketing Manager: Leo Cuellar
Text Design: Karl Hunt
Copy-editor: Susan Dunsmore
Proofreader: Alison Wertheimer
Indexer: Judith Reading
Cover Design: Nigel Turner

CONTENTS IN BRIEF

CONTENTS

6 SOCIAL IDENTITY   190

ABOUT THE AUTHORS

Eliot Smith is Chancellor's Professor of Psychological and Brain Sciences at Indiana University, Bloomington. His research interests range widely, including person perception, prejudice and intergroup relations, political and social opinions, and situated and embodied cognition. He has published more than 150 scientific articles and chapters on these and other topics, and his work has been supported by research grants from the National Institute of Mental Health and the National Science Foundation. Professor Smith earned his B.A. and Ph.D. at Harvard University, and before moving to Bloomington held positions at the University of California, Riverside and at Purdue University. Besides this textbook, he has authored *Beliefs about Inequality* (with James Kluegel) as well as editing *Beyond Prejudice: Differentiated Reactions to Social Groups* (with Diane Mackie). Among his professional honors are the Gordon Allport Intergroup Relations award in 1998, the Thomas M. Ostrom Award for contributions to social cognition in 2004, the Society of Social and Personality Psychology's Theoretical Innovation Prize in 2005, and the International Social Cognition Network's award for the best paper in 2009. He has been chair of a grant review committee at the National Institute of Mental Health, Editor of *Personality and Social Psychology Review,* and is currently Editor of *Journal of Personality and Social Psychology: Attitudes and Social Cognition.* These positions have given him tremendous appreciation for the best work in every area of social psychology. Professor Smith is married to Pamela Grenfell Smith, a poet and storyteller. They take great joy in their grown-up children, who share their passions for world music, science fiction, and good cooking, but the big deal for them is their astonishingly accomplished grandchildren, Griffin James Hassett and Iona Beatrice Hassett.

Diane Mackie is Professor and Chair of Psychological and Brain Sciences at the University of California, Santa Barbara, where she has been honored with a Distinguished Teaching Award and listed as one of "Ten Terrific Teachers" by UCSB students. Professor Mackie grew up in New Zealand, received her B.A. and M.A. at the University of Auckland, New Zealand, and then worked as a researcher at the University of Geneva, Switzerland. She received her Ph.D. in Social Psychology from Princeton University in 1984. These opportunities to become steeped in both European and North American traditions of social psychology are reflected in her interests in integrating different perspectives and approaches both in her research and in this textbook. The author of more than 100 articles, chapters, and books on persuasion, social influence, group interaction, and intergroup relations, Professor Mackie is also co-editor of *Affect, Cognition, and Stereotyping:*

Interactive Processes in Group Perception (with David Hamilton) as well as *Beyond Prejudice: Differentiated Reactions to Social Groups* (with Eliot Smith). Reflecting her broad interests, Professor Mackie has served as Associate Editor for *Personality and Social Psychology Review, Group Processes and Intergroup Relations,* and *Personality and Social Psychology Bulletin,* as well as on the editorial boards of almost all major social psychological journals. Both the National Science Foundation and the National Institutes of Health have funded her research. Professor Mackie counts among her honors fellow status in the Association for Psychological Science, the Society for Personality and Social Psychology, and the Society for the Psychological Study of Social Issues. However, by far her greatest (and busiest) honor is being Mom to college freshman Alex and high school freshman Nico, the two coolest kids on the planet.

Heather Claypool is Professor of Psychology at Miami University in Oxford, Ohio. Her research interests focus on how motivation, emotion, and mood influence and are influenced by cognitive processes. Specific topics of study have examined how processing ease (or fluency) shapes social perceptions and behaviors; how feelings of positivity trigger feelings of familiarity; and how feelings of belongingness and a lack of belongingness shape emotions, self-esteem, social perceptions, and social information processing. She has published more than 30 scientific articles and chapters on these and other topics, and her work has been supported by research grants from the National Science Foundation. Professor Claypool earned her Ph.D. at Purdue University in 2002 (where Eliot Smith served as one of her mentors), and then worked as a post-doctoral researcher at the University of California, Santa Barbara (with Diane Mackie). In 2003, she took a position at Miami University in Oxford, OH, where she continues on the faculty today. She has been an Associate Editor for *Basic and Applied Social Psychology*, is currently an Associate Editor at *Personality and Social Psychology Bulletin,* and serves on the editorial boards of several other journals. She has also served as a panelist for the National Science Foundation Graduate Research Fellowship Program. Professor Claypool is married to Eric Core, an engineer, and they share a love for travel, tennis, good food, and their two adorable cats, Abby and Murphy.

PREFACE

"No wise fish would go anywhere without a porpoise!" claims *Alice's Adventures in Wonderland*'s Mock Turtle. "Why, if a fish came to ME, and told me he was going on a journey, I should say 'With what porpoise?'" So, you may wonder, what's our "porpoise" in writing this social psychology textbook when there are many others? The answer is simple—we undertook this journey because we wanted to provide undergraduates the opportunity to share in our excitement about and our appreciation for the richness, variety, and interconnectedness of human social behavior in a more meaningful, unified, and logical way. The behaviors examined by social psychologists affect all of us every day in real life, so we wanted to equip our students to interpret and connect what they learn about in our text, applying it to the rest of their lives. While many books portray social behavior as a list of interesting but unrelated phenomena that are explained by numerous theories that are presented once (and then forgotten), we wanted to do something different. Our goal is to show students how all the topics that fall into the realm of "social psychology" are indeed related to one another in relevant and important ways. To do so, we decided to present social behavior and the science that studies it in a conceptually and thematically integrated approach. We want to show students the wonderfully diverse *what* of social behavior—but we also want to highlight the impressive (and sometimes surprising) orderliness and organization of the *how* and *why* of it.

THREE TYPES OF INTEGRATION

1. **Integration of diverse topics using unifying principles**: Eight basic principles of social behavior, introduced in Chapter 1, emerge and re-emerge throughout the text.

    1. People construct their own social reality.
    2. Social environments pervasively influence people.
    3. Motivational principle #1: People strive for mastery.
    4. Motivational principle #2: People seek connectedness.
    5. Motivational principle #3: People value "me and mine."
    6. Processing principle #1: Conservatism; established views are slow to change.
    7. Processing principle #2: Accessibility; the most readily available information has the most impact.
    8. Processing principle #3: Superficial or deep processing: People can process information to a greater or lesser extent.

2. **Integration of the social and the cognitive:** Social psychology branched off from other areas of psychology based on social psychologists' firm conviction that people's behavior depends on the cognitive processes through which they perceive and interpret social situations. But social psychologists are also aware that social motives, interpersonal relationships, and emotional attachments to group membership guide and direct everything people do. The intertwining of social processes with cognitive processes is the essential tension of human social behavior, and so we have made it a central theme of our book. To address the ways in which social behavior is similar or different across cultures, ethnicities, and nationalities, we have included many contributions from research beyond North America and Europe and included new *Social Psychology and Culture* boxes to highlight cultural differences and similarities.

SOCIAL PSYCHOLOGY AND CULTURE: AWARENESS OF PERSONAL MORTALITY AS A PSYCHOLOGICAL THREAT

Even those not facing a life-threatening illness, but who are simply subtly reminded of their own mortality, may choose to self-affirm as a means to cope. According to **Terror Management Theory** (Solomon and others, 2000), such a reminder leads us to cope by reaffirming our most basic cultural worldviews, such as religious beliefs or views about what is most important in life. Indeed, thoughts of one's own death may spark a host of positive, prosocial behaviors (Vail, Juhl, Arndt, Vess, Routledge, & Rutjens, 2012). But they also have a more negative side, generating intolerance and rejection for the deviant, the defiant, and the just "different"—anyone who fails to conform to the cultural worldview (Solomon and others, 2000).

---

3. **Integration of the science of psychology and its applications in real life**: Historically, social psychology has simultaneously focused its efforts on advancing theories to explain behavior while addressing important social problems. In our book, we demonstrate how research helps scientists explain phenomena that impact our everyday lives. For example, we include:

    ■ a discussion of polygraph usage next to a section on nonverbal cues to deception;
    ■ an overview of jury decision-making in the chapter on group influence;
    ■ a discussion of how stereotypes can create self-fulfilling prophecies in the classroom;
    ■ an account of why advertising might have especially strong effects on children.

TEXT ORGANIZATION AND PEDAGOGY

As people who care deeply about our field, we take pride in demonstrating social psychology's growth as a science and the accumulation of knowledge about social behavior. By showing students social psychology as an integrated whole, rather than as a list of topics that happen to share a label, our approach makes our field both easier to understand and more applicable to their daily lives. As the same principles emerge over and over among diverse topic areas, they serve as a useful organizing framework and a context for particular findings and theories.

After an introductory chapter and one focused on research methods, the main part of the book is organized into three broad topic areas: social perception (Chapters 3–6), social influence (Chapters 7–10), and social relations (Chapters 11–14). The section on social perception emphasizes the role of cognitive and motivational processes, but it also reinforces the idea that all such processes are socially influenced—even such basic and personal ideas as what we think about ourselves. The social influence chapters focus on the role of social processes, but stress that the effects of social processes are filtered through cognitive and motivational processes. For example, the amount of effort devoted to processing a persuasive argument may differ depending on whether it is delivered by a friend, a sales person, or a politician. The section on social relations illustrates the way social and cognitive processes are inextricably intertwined as they shape the ways we get to know and like other people, cooperate in groups, and help (or harm) others. While we have chosen to present the topics in this order, we recognize that this is not necessarily the way everyone would prefer to teach the course. Our integrated approach makes it easy for instructors to teach chapters in different sequences (some possibilities are described in the Instructor's Manual), since we apply the same themes consistently throughout the chapters.

You may observe that we have no separate chapters on law, business, or education. This is because, as part of our integration, examples of applications to real-world topics are woven throughout our text to reinforce the fact that what social psychologists study applies to the world beyond their labs. Further, we operate with a broad definition of what is "applied," considering not only major societal institutions like law and business, but also such topics as personal relationships and divorce, media violence and aggression, social support and health, cooperation in solving environmental problems, norms on eating and health, conflicts in international relations, and the effectiveness of advertising. These applications are easily spotted throughout the text as boxes labeled *Social Psychology in Practice*.

SOCIAL PSYCHOLOGY IN PRACTICE: PERSEVERANCE IN THE COURTROOM

When legally inadmissible evidence is introduced in courtroom proceedings, it can be stricken from the official trial record. The judge may even instruct jurors to disregard it. Unfortunately, jurors cannot wipe the information from their minds as easily as the court reporter can expunge the record. In fact, research has found that inadmissible evidence does influence jurors' deliberations and verdicts (Thompson, Fong, & Rosenhan, 1981). The same is true of discredited evidence. In one mock-trial study, for example, one group of participants saw minimal evidence against the defendant, and only 18 % voted for conviction. A second group saw the same evidence plus an eyewitness identification of the defendant; in that group, 72 % voted for conviction. A third group, after receiving all this information, learned that the eyewitness was legally blind and was not wearing his glasses at the time he claimed to have seen the defendant. This discrediting information had virtually no impact, however, reducing the conviction rate only to 68 % (Loftus, 1974). The perseverance bias means that, as in this example, information may have effects that persist even after the information is found to be false.

Throughout the text, we remind students of concepts and principles we've addressed and how they apply in other contexts—and even preview when a theory has applications that they'll read about in future chapters. At the end of each chapter, we devote space to *Concluding Comments*, which are our broader reflections on some of the larger issues raised by the chapters, on interrelations among the chapters, or on special aspects about how the principles play themselves out in that chapter.

Chapter 8 describes some of the many predictions that researchers have derived from cognitive dissonance theory and self-perception theory.

HOT TOPICS IN SOCIAL PSYCHOLOGY: IS FOLLOWING NORMS IN THE GENES?

Directives, environments, behavior, in-groups—we absorb these signals, learning—and being taught—over time what the relevant norms are and why we should follow them. There is little doubt that learning plays a role in acquiring a desire to follow norms. But because of their adaptive role in facilitating group living, humans may have evolved to give special attention to norms. Humans in our ancient past who followed norms likely would have been more likely to survive, and thus modern humans may be descendants of those norm-following relatives. Recent work offers some supportive evidence. In one set of studies, students in both America and the United Kingdom read about behaviors allegedly performed in an unfamiliar culture, whose norms they did not know and could not have previously learned. Part of the material was norm-related such as, "an unresolvable argument must be taken to the Ariki, as is dictated by custom." Other information did not describe norms. When the students' memory for the material was assessed, the norm-related information was better remembered than the norm-irrelevant information (O'Gorman, Wilson, & Miller, 2008). These researchers argue that these findings indicate an automatic readiness to perceive norm-relevant information, which may enable humans to pick up on norms and ultimately follow them. Other work suggests that people categorize others spontaneously as violators versus non-violators of moral norms, much as we spontaneously categorize others based on race, sex, and age. This again suggests that humans may come equipped with cognitive processes that facilitate the impact of norms (van Leeuwen, Park, & Penton-Voak, 2012).

Social psychology is a continuously evolving science. To highlight some new and important studies, we've included new *Hot Topics in Social Psychology* boxes.

To support students as they read through the text, we have incorporated several features with them in mind. Every chapter begins with a *Chapter Overview* so that they know what to expect to learn about in the chapter. Then, at the start of each new section within the chapter, we include a *Section Preview* (in blue text) to help them understand the materials the first time they read them. This allows students to distinguish the main concepts in each section from the less important supporting details. In addition, all key terms are included in a marginal glossary, so students can easily find them. The key terms are also located in a glossary at the end of the text. Lastly, *Chapter Summaries* at the end of each chapter highlight the key terms and concepts discussed in the chapter while the *Chapter Themes* box outlines the key themes discussed in the chapter.

social psychology
the scientific study of the effects of social and cognitive processes on the way individuals perceive, influence, and relate to others

---

Growth and Integration

Since the 1950s and 1960s, social psychology has grown and flourished, moving t[...] an integrated theoretical understanding of social and cognitive processes and t[...] further applications of social-psychological theory to important applied problems.

Both basic and applied social psychology flourished in the United States durin[...] prosperous 1950s and 1960s. Backed by expanding university enrollments and ge[...]

In line with our emphasis on the principles that underlie the diversity of behavior, explanations are often visually supported by graphs and flow-charts and study findings are visually summarized in easy-to-understand charts and graphs.

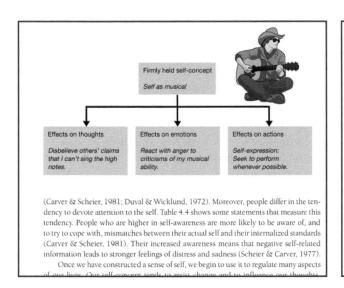

(Carver & Scheier, 1981; Duval & Wicklund, 1972). Moreover, people differ in the tendency to devote attention to the self. Table 4.4 shows some statements that measure this tendency. People who are higher in self-awareness are more likely to be aware of, and to try to cope with, mismatches between their actual self and their internalized standards (Carver & Scheier, 1981). Their increased awareness means that negative self-related information leads to stronger feelings of distress and sadness (Scheier & Carver, 1977).

    Once we have constructed a sense of self, we begin to use it to regulate many aspects of our lives. Our self-concept tends to resist change and to influence our thoughts

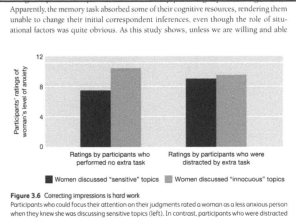

Apparently, the memory task absorbed some of their cognitive resources, rendering them unable to change their initial correspondent inferences, even though the role of situational factors was quite obvious. As this study shows, unless we are willing and able

Figure 3.6 Correcting impressions is hard work
Participants who could focus their attention on their judgments rated a woman as a less anxious person when they knew she was discussing sensitive topics (left). In contrast, participants who were distracted by an additional task failed to discount (right). Those who believed the topics were sensitive assigned approximately the same ratings as those assigned by participants who believed the topics were innocuous. (Based on Gilbert and others, 1988.)

ONLINE RESOURCES ACCOMPANYING THE TEXT

As innovations in teaching and technology continue to change the way courses are being taught in classrooms around the world, our online resources have been designed to support you and your students as you use our book. The companion website for the text is located at http://www.psypress.com/cw/smith. There, both instructors and students will find a wealth of resources to help with the teaching and learning of the materials covered in the book.

For Instructors:

- Instructor's Manual (revised by Sara Crump of Baker University)
- Ideas for in-class activities
- Editable test bank of questions
- PowerPoint lecture slides with images from text
- Sample Syllabi
- Annotated web links to videos

For Students:

- Practice quizzes
- Chapter summaries
- Research activities
- Annotated web links to additional resources

TO THE STUDENT: AN INTRODUCTION AND TIPS FOR SUCCESS IN YOUR COURSE

Have you ever wondered why some people seem willing to help a person in distress while others might blatantly ignore a person's cries for help? Or why another person's opinion can have such a huge impact on how you feel about yourself? Social psychology is a fascinating field that directly impacts your everyday existence. Our goal is to help you better understand your own and others' social behaviors—to get beyond the *what*, to the *how* and *why*. We do this by using an integrated approach in which we apply the same overarching principles that we introduce in Chapter 1 to all the topics that fall under the umbrella of the science of social psychology. By understanding just a few basic principles and seeing how they apply in different contexts, we hope you'll see how all social behavior is interrelated, and how social behaviors are all pieces of the same larger puzzle rather than a variety of separate puzzles. Therefore, we don't expect you to memorize lots of unrelated ideas; rather, we hope that our integrated approach helps you see, understand, remember, and apply these principles in your own life.

Some Study Tips

Our combined years of experience teaching (and studying) bring some insights that we'd like to share with you. We have included a number of features within the text to support learning and best practices for studying (such as Chapter Overviews, Section Previews, and Chapter Summaries), and here is some additional advice that will help you study more effectively and be better active readers.

- Start by reading the chapter title and Chapter Overview. Then read the introductory paragraph and browse through the images in the chapter. This will give you a general sense of the chapter's content.
- Within a chapter, work on one section at a time—this isn't a novel, so you shouldn't read it like one. Pay attention to the Section Previews before you read each section. This should help make the key material in that section easier to understand and prevent you from getting bogged down in details.
- Keep an eye out for those basic principles we introduce in Chapter 1 of the text. This will help you connect materials throughout the chapter and make the story of social psychology more coherent across what might sometimes seem like unrelated topics. We will always use the same key words or phrases whenever an example of the principles in action arises.
- We include marginal references that refer you back to previous chapters or ahead to future chapters so you can see how concepts and principles relate to topics elsewhere in the text. This will help you see similarities between topics and chapters so you can link the new material to things you may have already learned about— or remind you to keep an eye out for a certain concept later in the text as you know you'll encounter it elsewhere.
- Key terms are always in blue boldface type and the definitions appear in the margins as well as all together at the end of the text for easy reference. As scientists,

psychologists use technical terms for precision in writing. Don't try to memorize the definitions on first reading; it is more important to first understand the gist of what you are reading. After you have finished reading through the chapter, read through the definitions again and then try to learn them and review them for your exam.

■ Once you've finished reading the chapter's main sections, read the Concluding Comments, Chapter Themes, and Summary. If anything seems unfamiliar to you, go back to that section and re-read it.

Last, but not least, enjoy yourself! Ask questions! Think about all the social behaviors we still don't understand and how researchers might go about examining and explaining those behaviors. And then think about all you have learned in this book and how you can apply it to your everyday life—at school, at work, at home, and in your relationships.

ACKNOWLEDGMENTS

As the Mock Turtle no doubt knew, it takes more than just a porpoise to allow wise fish to complete a journey. We owe thanks to many, many people who have helped us not just to make the journey but to become wise fish. First, our friends, students, and colleagues over the years have provided advice and social support—Chris Agnew, Ishani Banaji, Jim Blascovich, Don Carlston, Nancy Collins, Riki Conrey, Alice Eagly, Amber Garcia, Shelly Gable, Dave Hamilton, Ed Hirt, Heejung Kim, Janice Kelly, Brenda Major, Dan Miller, Anthony Scroggins, Charlie Seger, David Sherman, Jim Sherman, Zak Tormala, Taylor Tuscherer, and Duane Wegener were particularly important to us. The many undergraduate students who participated in classroom tests of various drafts of the manuscript were also extremely helpful to us—even their occasional puzzled looks provided useful feedback. The all-engrossing process of writing a book always becomes an imposition on family, friends, and companions. We are grateful to Pamela Smith, Thomas Smith, Eric Core, Alex Mackie, and Nico Mackie for putting up with us and giving us perspective on our work. We promise to be in a better mood from now on, to talk about something else every once in a while, and to stop trying to use them as examples in the book.

We have been lucky indeed to have worked with the many dedicated and talented people at Psychology Press. We began with the conviction that a textbook taking an integrated approach to social psychology could be written. We thank J. George Owen, good friend and incomparable next-door neighbor, for encouraging us in this process and Gün Semin for steering us toward Psychology Press. Rebecca Pearce has applied her wisdom and experience to shaping and improving this fourth edition.

Many of our colleagues and friends generously gave their time to review portions of this text. We are particularly grateful to those who have used the previous editions in their classrooms over the years, and for the comments, suggestions, and encouragement that they have passed along to us. To all those who reviewed various portions of the manuscript, and whose insightful comments have often gently shaped and smoothed the ideas we present here, our heartfelt thanks:

Christopher Agnew, *Purdue University*
Craig Anderson, *Iowa State University*
Daniel Balliet, *Vilnius University*
John Bargh, *Yale University*
Mark Bennett, *University of Dundee*

Leonard Berkowitz, *University of Wisconsin-Madison*
Hart Blanton, *University of Connecticut*
William Michael Brown, *University of Bedfordshire*
Russell Clark, *University of North Texas*
Frederica Conrey, *Indiana University, Bloomington*
Leslie Croot, *University of Montana*
John F. Dovidio, *University of Connecticut*
Ann Duran, *California State University-Bakersfield*
Kai Epstude, *Groningen University*
Klaus Fiedler, *Heidelberg University*
Jens Förster, *University of Amsterdam*
Kentaro Fujita, *Ohio State University*
R. Michael Furr, *Wake Forest University*
Roger Giner-Sorolla, *University of Kent at Canterbury*
Rainer Greifeneder, *University of Mannheim*
Tom Grimwood, *University of Cumbria*
Rosanna E. Guadagno, *National Science Foundation*
P.J. Henry, *DePaul University*
Hubert J.M. Hermans, *Radboud University of Nijmegen*
Guido Hertel, *University of Würzburg*
Jolanda Jetten, *University of Queensland*
Eric Jones, *Southern Illinois University*
Shinobu Kitayama, *University of Michigan*
Barbara Krahé, *University of Potsdam*
Joachim Krueger, *Brown University*
Jurgita Lazauskaite-Zabielske, *Vilnius University*
Benjamin Le, *Haverford College*
Karlijn Massar, *Maastricht University*
Tom Postmes, *University of Groningen*
Ron Roberts, *Kingston University*
Miia Sainio, *University of Turku*
Fabio Sani, *University of Dundee*
Karl E. Scheibe, *Wesleyan University*
Steven J. Scher, *Eastern Illinois University*
Michelle See, *National University of Singapore*
Gün E. Semin, *Utrecht University*
John Skowronski, *University of Northern Illinois*
Steve Stroessner, *Columbia University*
Annette Thompson, *Open University, and University of Glasgow-Crichton Campus*
David Trafimow, *New Mexico State University*
Laura VanderDrift, *Syracuse University*
Mark Van Vugt, *University of Kent at Canterbury*
Eva Walther, *University of Trier*
Duane T. Wegener, *Ohio State University*
Emyr Williams, *Glyndwr University*

Heather Claypool joined us as a co-author for this fourth edition. She worked with Eliot during her Ph.D. studies and with Diane as a postdoctoral researcher, so she already knew our quirks and passions. She has brought fresh insights and novel ideas to this revision, as well as an endless supply of tennis examples, and she has Diane and Eliot's heartfelt gratitude for her many contributions. We would like to thank each other for the many benefits of co-authorship. Through our collaboration on each section and sometimes each sentence of the text, we believe we have accomplished a sort of integration through teamwork. We learned to respect and admire each other's different strengths and talents, to appreciate each other's different views of the field, and to blame each other when deadlines were missed! We also became much better friends in the process.

WHAT IS SOCIAL PSYCHOLOGY?

In the fall of 1951, Princeton University's undefeated football team played Dartmouth College in a particularly hard-fought game. The teams were long-term rivals, and the game started rough and went downhill from there. Penalties punctuated the game, and fights left players on both sides with serious injuries before Princeton finally won. One month later, two social psychologists asked Princeton and Dartmouth undergraduates to view a film of the game (Hastorf & Cantril, 1954). The responses were astonishing. Princeton fans and Dartmouth supporters reported seeing events so differently that they might have been watching different games. Princeton students saw a constant barrage of Dartmouth violence and poor sportsmanship, with Princeton players occasionally retaliating in self-defense. Dartmouth students rated the teams as equally aggressive but saw their battered team's infractions as understandable responses to brutal Princeton attacks. One Dartmouth alumnus who watched the film saw so few Dartmouth violations that he concluded he must have been sent an edited copy of the film.

Perhaps these findings are not really so astonishing if you consider that fans of opposing teams hardly ever agree on the impartiality of the umpiring. Similarly, partisan observers of political debates almost always proclaim their own candidate "the winner," and proud parents at the school music contest often disagree with the judges' decision. Yet consider the profound questions that these findings raise. If the world is objectively "out there" for all to see, how can observers reach such different conclusions about what seems to be the same event? Why do we so often end up seeing exactly what we expected to see, and how then can we decide what "really" happened? Can the same innocent feelings of belonging that make us see our team, our candidate, or our child in such positive terms also produce biased judgments, unfair decisions, and unequal treatment of others?

Thirty years after Hastorf and Cantril's study, researchers at Vanderbilt University asked two groups of students to consider the difficult issue of whether convicted criminals should be given probation as an alternative to imprisonment (Axsom, Yates, & Chaiken, 1987). One group of students had a special reason to be concerned with the issue: They had been led to believe that the probation policy might soon be introduced in their area. For the other group, the issue was merely academic—the policy was not being considered for their community. The researchers told the students that, to help them make up their minds, they would hear a tape of a local candidate speaking in favor of the issue at a political rally. What the students did not know was that the researchers had actually prepared four quite different tapes. On one tape, the candidate put forward compelling evidence in support of probation while an enthusiastic audience warmly applauded his words. On a second, the same effective presentation elicited scattered hisses, boos, and heckling from the audience. A third tape had the candidate giving rambling, specious, and disjointed arguments, which were met with enthusiastic applause from the audience. And on the fourth tape, the weak arguments were greeted by boos and hissing.

When the researchers polled the students whose interest in the probation issue was merely academic, the impact of the audience's taped response was clear. Students in this group who heard the audience greet the candidate's position with enthusiasm adopted the position themselves, and those who heard the audience voice disdain rejected the candidate's position. A completely different pattern of responses emerged among students who expected the issue to affect their community. These students focused on the content of the speech. They were swayed if they heard the candidate give cogent arguments but remained unpersuaded if the arguments were weak—regardless of the applause or hisses of the taped audience. Why were the reactions of other people so compelling to some students and so unimportant to others? Why did some participants "go with the flow" while others considered the issues carefully? Did some students care less than others about being right, or were all of the students trying to take different paths to the "truth?"

Like the Vanderbilt students, we are all bombarded daily by attempts to persuade us: advertising campaigns, paid political messages, even the cajoling of friends and family. Consider the last time you were persuaded by one of these attempts. What approach was used by the person who persuaded you? Did that person present you with the hard facts, or did he or she play on your emotions? If you were told that "everyone else" had already joined the parade, would you be more likely to go along or more likely to rebel? Or would it depend on the issue?

Questions like those raised by these studies lure social psychologists into their labs every day in search of reliable answers. Social psychology offers a special perspective on human behavior, because the social aspects of human behavior—the ways that people's thoughts and actions are affected by other people—can be both powerful and puzzling. Our goal in this book is to give you some insight into how people act, and why they act the way they do, by introducing you to some of the many questions social psychologists ask about social behavior, the ways they go about answering those questions, and the answers they have found. We know that you will find these questions intriguing and hope that the often surprising conclusions will make you want to delve more deeply into these compelling issues.

Our first step will be to provide a definition of social psychology: to chart out the territory we will be covering and to give you a glimpse of what makes the terrain so fascinating. We next describe how social psychology developed its special perspective on human behavior. Like other fields of human inquiry, contemporary social psychology is a product of its own history and of the history of the societies in which it developed. With a quick survey of the past behind us, we then map out the territory ahead. The final part of the chapter provides a sneak preview of the material we cover in the rest of this book. To help you find your way with confidence, we point out some signposts and landmarks to look for along the route.

A DEFINITION OF SOCIAL PSYCHOLOGY

Social psychology is the scientific study of the effects of social and cognitive processes on the way individuals perceive, influence, and relate to others. Notice that social psychology is defined as a science, that social psychologists are as keenly interested in underlying social and cognitive processes as they are in overt behavior, and that the central concern of social psychology is how people understand and interact with others. Let us consider each of these components in turn.

social psychology
the scientific study of the effects of social and cognitive processes on the way individuals perceive, influence, and relate to others

The Scientific Study . . .

Social psychologists, like other scientists, gather knowledge systematically by means of scientific methods. These methods help to produce knowledge that is less subject to the biases and distortions that often characterize common-sense knowledge.

This blue text is a brief preview of the section that follows. For advice on how you can use it to improve your efficiency in studying the text, turn back to the "To the Student" section in the Preface, pages xxx–xxxi.

Of course, you have been studying social behavior all your life. Everyone uses common sense and "street smarts" to make sense of the social world they inhabit because we all want to make good friends, reach mutually satisfying decisions, raise children properly, hire the best personnel, and live in peace and security rather than in conflict and fear. How does the social psychologist's approach differ from our everyday approaches? The answer is found in methods, not goals. Although scientific researchers and common-sense observers share many goals—both wish to understand, predict, and influence people's thoughts and behavior—their methods for achieving those goals differ greatly.

As common-sense observers, people often reach conclusions about social behavior based on limited samples from their own or others' experiences. Therefore common-sense knowledge is sometimes inconsistent, even contradictory. You may have heard, for example, that "opposites attract," and also the reverse, that "birds of a feather flock together." As scientists, on the other hand, social psychologists study social behavior systematically, seeking to avoid the misconceptions and distortions that so often afflict our common-sense knowledge. Of course, even scientific knowledge is not infallible. The history of science shows that some findings from individual studies cannot be confirmed by further observation, and many conclusions proposed as scientific truths are eventually overturned by new insights. But as you will see in Chapter 2, scientific conclusions are sounder and more resistant to challenge than common-sense knowledge because they are based on systematic methods of gathering information and are constructed with an awareness of the possibility of error.

. . . of the Effects of Social and Cognitive Processes . . .

The presence of other people, the knowledge and opinions they pass on to us, and our feelings about the groups to which we belong all deeply influence us through social processes, whether we are with other people or alone. Our perceptions, memories, emotions, and motives also exert a pervasive influence on us through cognitive processes. Effects of social and cognitive processes are not separate but inextricably intertwined.

A first date, a classroom presentation, a job interview, a problem-solving session with co-workers: What do these situations have in common? Each is a situation in which others observe us or interact with us, influencing our thoughts, feelings, and behavior. We try to make a good impression, to live up to the standards of the people we care about, to cooperate or compete with others as appropriate. These examples show the operation of social processes. **Social processes** are the ways in which our thoughts, feelings, and actions are influenced by the people around us, the groups to which we belong, our personal relationships, the teachings of our parents and culture, and the pressures we experience from others.

social processes
the ways in which input from the people and groups around us affect our thoughts, feelings, and actions

cognitive processes
the ways in which our memories, perceptions, thoughts, emotions, and motives influence our understanding of the world and guide our actions

Cognitive processes, on the other hand, are the ways in which our memories, perceptions, thoughts, emotions, and motives guide our understanding of the world and our actions. Note that emotion and motivation are intrinsic parts of every cognitive process, just as are memory and thought. Modern social psychology rejects the misleading opposition—dating back to ancient Greek philosophers—between pure, "rational" thought and irrational emotions. Cognitive processes affect every aspect of our lives, because the content of our thoughts, the goals toward which we strive, and the feelings we have about people and activities—all the ways we act and react in the social world—are based on what we believe the world is like.

Though we have defined them separately, in reality, social and cognitive processes are inextricably intertwined. To illustrate their intimate connections, consider these two points.

First, social processes affect us even when others are not physically present: We are social creatures even when alone. Faced with an important decision, we often stop to think about the possible reactions of absent friends, relatives, or fellow group members, and these thoughts can also influence us. Even during many of our most private activities—writing a term paper, practicing a musical instrument, exercising, or showering—we are motivated by our concern for what others think of us. Think about the last time you rode an elevator in which you were the only passenger. We bet you stood facing the doors, just as you would have if other people had been physically present. Because our group memberships become part of who we are, they influence us even when other group members are absent. Whether other supporters are present or not, we rise to the defense of our party's political platform and feel elated about our sports team's victory. We react in this way because our party or our team has become a basic part of our identity. In cases like these, by considering the group in the individual, social psychologists examine how people are affected by their knowledge of what is expected of them, that is, by their knowledge about the beliefs, attitudes, and actions that are considered appropriate for members of their group.

Second, the social processes that affect us even when others are physically present depend on how we interpret those others and their actions, and therefore on the operation of cognitive processes. The impact of other people's arguments or comments in a group discussion depends on how we think and feel about those people and their statements: Is the argument strong and compelling, or shaky and questionable? Is the person who makes a particular comment genuinely trying to help the group arrive at the right answer or just seeking to dominate others by belittling their ideas? By studying the individual in the group, researchers gain insights into how people are affected by others who are physically present, whether they offer friendly hugs or scornful glares, provide trustworthy information or try to deceive, lead by example or wait for someone to follow. But in all these cases, the way others affect us depends on our own thoughts and feelings.

Whether we are alone or together with others, then, both social and cognitive processes operate together to affect everything we think, feel, and do.

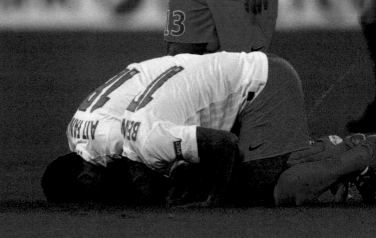

Photo 1.1 Group influence far from the group. These soccer players of Moroccan descent are celebrating a goal scored in a 2012 match in Germany. Although engaged in a sporting competition, and away from their homeland, they so thoroughly accept their Muslim faith that they stop and pray after the goal. For all of us, beliefs, attitudes, and practices endorsed by the groups to which we belong strongly affect our thoughts, feelings, and actions, even when we are far away from other group members.

. . . on the Way Individuals Perceive, Influence, and Relate to Others

Social psychology focuses on the effects of social and cognitive processes on the way individuals perceive, influence, and relate to others. Understanding these processes can help us comprehend why people act the way they do and may also help solve important social problems.

Social psychology seeks to understand the social behavior of individuals, a focus that distinguishes it from sociology, political science, and other social sciences. The cognitive and social processes we have just described affect individuals as they perceive, influence, and relate to others. Consequently, these processes shape all forms of social behavior, including some that are significant concerns in today's world. Here are some examples of social behaviors that are important concerns and some questions social psychologists might ask about them.

■ *Why do many marriages end in divorce?* A social psychologist might study divorce as an outcome of the social and cognitive processes of conflict in marriages. The research might focus on questions like the following: How do couples interpret events that put the relationship under stress? What alternatives to the relationship do they believe they have? What types of actions in the course of an argument determine whether one partner storms angrily out of the house or allow the couple to kiss and make up after a fight? Whereas sociologists might study the effects of unemployment on divorce rates in a society, social psychologists might instead examine the ways that being unemployed causes conflict and divorce, by affecting how the partners think about their relationship or how they try to influence one another.

■ *How do salespeople sell products?* Have you ever found yourself leaving a store carrying an item that was different from what you entered the store to buy, wondering how you were manipulated into purchasing it? A social psychologist would be interested in knowing the social and cognitive processes that induced you to make the purchase. For example, how can a sales pitch expertly play on the consumer's needs, desires, or feelings of guilt or obligation? Did the salesperson subtly hint that the product you asked about was unfashionable or outdated, while pushing a newer (and more expensive) item instead? In contrast, an economist might study whether TV advertisements or in-store promotions produce more total sales.

■ *What causes outbreaks of ethnic violence?* An historian or journalist might document the unique events that sparked a particular conflict. To the social psychologist, however, intergroup hostility stems from fundamental aspects of the ways people think about and interact with members of different groups. These include both competition for concrete resources (like jobs and political clout) and people's attitudes, emotions, and actions toward their own and other social groups. Social psychologists would ask whether the ways people categorize individuals into groups, the stereotypes they form about others, their preferences for people "just like them," or their feelings of power or powerlessness contribute to intergroup hostility.

Thus, social psychology seeks an understanding of the reasons people act the way they do in social situations. Such an understanding helps us explain events in our own lives: that disastrous first date, the successful job interview, the loneliness of being the new kid on the block, the hesitation we feel before making a major decision. It also helps us comprehend the factors that contribute to the complex events of our times: crime and violence, ethnic unrest and civil war, the spread of pandemic diseases, the destruction of the global environment. And if we understand how people are influenced by social and cognitive processes, we can begin developing solutions for such pressing social problems (Walton, 2014). For example, knowing that stereotypes and prejudice about members of other religious groups may have contributed to violent conflict in the Middle East or Northern Ireland suggests that changing those beliefs might help to prevent recurrences. In fact, social-psychological research has been instrumental in exposing workplace discrimination (Fiske, Bersoff, Borgida, Deaux, & Heilman, 1991) and investigating why innocent people sometimes confess to crimes they did not commit (Kassin & Gudjonsson, 2004). It has suggested policies to increase people's feelings of security and self-worth in their close relationships (Marigold, Holmes, & Ross, 2010) and to improve classroom environments and performance for minority students (Walton & Cohen, 2011). It has also been influential in developing programs to reduce tensions in situations of intense intergroup conflict (Gross, Halperin, & Porat, 2013). Thus the social-psychological perspective invites us not only to understand but also to act on that understanding.

HISTORICAL TRENDS AND CURRENT THEMES IN SOCIAL PSYCHOLOGY

How did social psychology come to develop its particular point of view? Like any field of knowledge, social psychology is a product of its past. The current focus of its research reflects historical events of the 20th and 21st centuries, changing societal concerns, and developments in other scientific fields, as well as changes in the techniques social psychologists have used in their research. This brief survey of the field's history will place the field in context and serve as a partial explanation for where social psychology stands today.

Social Psychology Becomes an Empirical Science

Soon after the emergence of scientific psychology in the late 19th century, researchers began considering questions about social influences on human thought and action.

From the time of the ancient Greeks, the study of the human condition was considered to be the domain of philosophy. Like social psychologists today, early philosophers recognized the impact that other people can have on individual behavior. Plato, for example, speculated about the "crowd mind," arguing that even the wisest individuals, if assembled into a crowd, might be transformed into an irrational mob. Through the ages, philosophers continued to theorize about the workings of the human mind—and they still do—but the development of social psychology had to await the emergence of its parent discipline, the science of psychology. This new field was born in the late 19th century, when a few researchers in Germany, impressed by laboratory methods being used by physiologists, began to employ experimental techniques to understand mental processes like sensation, memory, and judgment.

The experimental investigation of social-psychological issues began soon afterward, as researchers in North America, Britain, and France began systematically measuring how behavior is influenced by the presence of others. A study published in 1898 by an American researcher, Norman Triplett, is sometimes cited as the first research study in social psychology (G. W. Allport, 1954a). Triplett, having noticed that swimmers and cyclists performed better when competing against their rivals than when practicing by themselves, wondered whether the presence of other people has a generally beneficial effect on performance. To find out, he asked school children to wind fishing line onto reels as quickly as possible, with and without others present. Sure enough, the children's performance improved in the presence of others. This interesting finding, however, appeared to contradict a conclusion that Max Ringelmann, a French agricultural engineer, had reached in an even earlier study conducted in the 1880s. Ringelmann found that when people worked together to pull on a rope or push on a cart, they put less effort into the task than when they worked alone (Ringelmann, 1913). The study of group effects on performance still continues today, and we now know that Ringelmann's and Triplett's results are not necessarily inconsistent. As you will see in Chapter 11, the presence of others often facilitates performance when individual contributions are easily identified, but it reduces performance when people are "lost in a crowd."

As you will see in Chapters 2, 3 and 9, all these topics are still being actively researched today.

For the first social psychologists, this puzzle was just one among many questions about how people influence one another. Early researchers also tackled questions about how facial expressions and body movements reveal people's feelings, how people conform to the suggestions of others, and the role that experimenters might play in influencing the outcomes of research (Haines & Vaughan, 1979). The first two textbooks bearing the name Social Psychology both appeared in 1908. One of these, by psychologist William McDougall, argued that all social behavior stems from innate tendencies or instincts, an idea that was popular throughout psychology at the time. The other, by sociologist E. A. Ross, took up the theme that was soon to become social psychology's central concern: that people are heavily influenced by others, whether those others are physically present or not.

Social Psychology Splits from General Psychology Over What Causes Behavior

Throughout much of the 20th century, North American psychology was dominated by behaviorism, but social psychologists maintained an emphasis on the important effects of thoughts and feelings on behavior.

Although it arrived on the coattails of general psychology, social psychology soon developed an identity distinct from that of its parent discipline. Early in the 20th century, North American psychology as a whole became dominated by the behaviorist viewpoint. This perspective, exemplified by the work of John B. Watson and B. F. Skinner, denied the scientific validity of explanations for behavior that invoke mental events like thoughts, feelings, and emotions. For radical behaviorists, a legitimate science of human activity could be based only on the study of observable behavior as influenced by observable environmental stimuli.

Most social psychologists, however, resisted the behaviorist view that thoughts and feelings had no place in scientific explanations. They accepted the behaviorists' argument that the ultimate goal of science is to explain behavior, but their studies showed that behavior could not be explained without taking into account people's thoughts and feelings. Social psychologists learned that individuals often hold divergent views of, and react in different ways to, the same object or idea, be it a football game, a political candidate, or capitalism. Such findings could be explained only by differences in individuals' attitudes, personality traits, impressions of others, group identifications, emotions, goals, and so forth (F. H. Allport, 1924). Behaviorists were certainly right in their belief that external stimuli can influence behavior. However, social psychologists maintained that the effect of any stimulus depends on how individuals and groups interpret it. Right from the start, then, social psychology was distinctive in its conviction that understanding and measuring people's perceptions, beliefs, and feelings are essential to understanding their overt behavior (E. E. Jones, 1985).

The Rise of Nazism Shapes the Development of Social Psychology

In the 1930s and 1940s, many European social psychologists fled to North America, where they had a major influence on the field's direction. Significant questions generated by the rise of Nazism and the Second World War shaped research interests during this period.

It has been said that the one person who has had the most impact on the development of social psychology in North America is Adolf Hitler (Cartwright, 1979). Ironic though this observation is, it contains important elements of truth. In fact, both the events that precipitated the Second World War and the war itself had a dramatic and lasting impact on social psychology.

As Nazi domination spread across Europe in the 1930s, a number of psychologists fled their homelands to continue distinguished scientific careers in North America. One result was that the major growth in social psychology was concentrated in North America for the next few decades. In addition, this influx of European researchers consolidated social psychology's special emphasis on how people interpret the world and how they are influenced by others. Most European researchers were trained not in the behaviorist tradition that was prominent in North America but in Gestalt theory, which sought to understand the rules underlying the organization of perception. This school of thought took for granted the role cognitive processes play in our interpretations of the social world. Around the same time, researchers became increasingly impressed by anthropologists' accounts of the pervasiveness of cultural influences on people's thoughts and behavior. It fell to social psychologists to identify the mechanisms by which such influences occurred, and they soon developed techniques to perform realistic studies of complex social influences in the laboratory. Muzafer Sherif's (1936) elegant experiments, for example, showed that a social group can influence even a person's perception and interpretation of physical reality, as you will see in Chapter 9.

But the war's effect on social psychology went beyond bringing a new group of skilled researchers to North America. Revelations of Nazi genocide led a horrified world to ask questions about the roots of prejudice (Adorno, Frenkel-Brunswik, Levinson, & Sanford, 1950). How could people feel and act on such murderous hatred for Jews, homosexuals, and members of other groups? These questions still resonate today as the world contemplates ethnic conflicts in Rwanda, Iraq, Sri Lanka, and Syria, and "gay bashing" on streets around the world.

Conditions created by the Second World War also drew social psychologists to the search for solutions to immediate practical problems. With food in short supply and rationing in full swing, the U.S. government asked social psychologists how to convince civilians to change their eating habits: to eat less steak and more kidneys and liver, to drink more milk, and to feed their babies cod-liver oil and orange juice (Lewin, 1947). Social psychologists were also called on to help the military maintain troop morale, improve the performance of aircraft and tank crews (Stouffer, 1949), and teach troops to resist enemy propaganda—and even to brush their teeth regularly (Hovland, Janis, & Kelley, 1953).

Social psychologists flocked to applied research willingly, realizing that they would be able to develop and test general theories of behavior even as they solved practical problems. As we will see in Chapter 10, Kurt Lewin (1947) found that active participation in discussion groups, by establishing behavior in a social context, was more effective in changing what women fed their families than passive listening to lectures on the topic. Lewin's findings are still successfully applied in support groups like Weight Watchers, Gamblers Anonymous, and many other organizations. Samuel Stouffer's (1949) research on American soldiers' morale showed that it depended more on the soldiers' interpretations of how they were doing compared to other enlisted men than on how well they were actually doing. Satisfaction with the rate of promotion, for example, was sometimes lower in units with higher-than-average promotion rates. Stouffer suggested that in these units the soldiers' expectations of promotion were high, setting them up for disappointment if others were promoted but they were not. The importance of comparisons with others and ways comparisons can lead to feelings of relative deprivation are still important topics in current social-psychological research. And, though we may be amused by Carl Hovland's assignment of devising ways to persuade soldiers to brush their teeth regularly, current theories of persuasion build on his original demonstrations that persuasion depends on who delivers the message, who receives the message, and how the message is processed (Hovland and others, 1953).

During this crucial period of research and theory building, the work of one social psychologist in particular embodied the themes that characterized the young discipline. Kurt Lewin, one of the scientists who had fled Hitler, held that all behavior depends on the individual's life space, which he defined as a subjective map of the individual's current goals and his or her social environment (Lewin, 1936). Perhaps you can see how Lewin's ideas sum up two of social psychology's enduring themes: that people's subjective interpretation of reality is the key determinant of their beliefs and behaviors, and that social influences structure those interpretations and behaviors. Lewin's work also reflected the close link between research aimed at understanding the underlying social and cognitive causes of behavior and research aimed at solving important social problems, a link that will receive considerable attention throughout this book. Lewin had a gift for conducting research that combined the testing of theories with the solving of problems. As he put it, "There is nothing so practical as a good theory" (Lewin, 1951, p. 169).

Growth and Integration

Since the 1950s and 1960s, social psychology has grown and flourished, moving toward an integrated theoretical understanding of social and cognitive processes and toward further applications of social-psychological theory to important applied problems.

Both basic and applied social psychology flourished in the United States during the prosperous 1950s and 1960s. Backed by expanding university enrollments and generous government grants, researchers addressed a great variety of topics central to understanding social behavior. Research contributions during this period laid the foundations of what we now know about self-esteem, prejudice and stereotyping, conformity, persuasion and attitude change, impression formation, interpersonal attraction and intimate relationships, and intergroup relations, all still key topics within social psychology today.

During the same period, as Europe recovered and rebuilt from the destruction of the war, social psychologists in several countries developed theoretical and research approaches to a wide range of topics, particularly those involving group memberships, influence within groups, and the often-competitive relationships between groups (Doise, 1978; Moscovici, 1980; Tajfel, 1978). These emphases dated back to a European tradition of research on the psychology of the crowd (LeBon, 1895/1947) and "folk psychology" or the study of common products of human groups such as culture and religion (Wundt, 1916). By the 1970s, social psychology on both sides of the Atlantic had developed a set of reliable and repeatable findings, which is a mark of scientific maturity. The time was ripe for both internal integration, the melding of various specific topic areas into broader explanations of behavior, and external integration, increasing attention to neighboring scientific fields and to significant social concerns. And so the movement toward integration began.

Integration of Cognitive and Social Processes. The study of cognitive processes became a natural framework for integration both within and outside social psychology. As the tight grip of behaviorism on North American psychology was finally broken, a cognitive revolution got under way in the 1960s (Neisser, 1967). Cognitive themes and theories swiftly gained attention in experimental, developmental, personality, and even clinical psychology. Of course, the cognitive revolution was no revolution for social psychology. Cognitive themes such as the importance of people's interpretations in shaping their reactions to events were familiar to social psychologists because their foundations had been laid decades earlier in Allport's, Sherif's, and Lewin's work in the 1930s and in Stouffer's and Hovland's studies in the 1940s. Concepts such as attitudes, norms, and beliefs, already common currency in social psychology, began to be applied to new areas of study: personal relationships, aggression and altruism, stereotyping and discrimination. These applications were greatly facilitated during the 1970s and 1980s by the adoption of research techniques that had been found to be valuable by cognitive psychologists studying perception and memory. Thus, theoretical concerns and proven experimental methods converged as researchers in many areas of social psychology focused on the study of cognitive processes (E. E. Jones, 1985).

Concern with cognitive processes is only one side of the coin, however. Social psychologists have always been aware that social processes, including personal and group relationships and social influence, also impinge on everything people do. True, our behavior is a function of our perceptions and interpretations and our attitudes and beliefs, but those factors in turn are fundamentally shaped by our relationships to others, our thoughts about their reactions, and the group memberships that help us define who we are (Markus, Kitayama, & Heiman, 1996). Scientific understanding of the way social and cognitive processes work together to mold all social behavior has benefited from the increasing integration of North American social psychology with European social psychology, where the impact of social group memberships had long been a dominant theme. Today, researchers in all domains of social psychology are weaving together the effects of cognitive and social processes to provide explanations of people's experience and behavior.

Integration with Other Research Trends. As the world became more interconnected in the late 20th century and as social psychological research spread to many more regions of the globe, researchers were confronted with findings showing that even what had been regarded as "basic" processes differed strikingly in different nations and cultures (Henrich, Heine, & Norenzayan, 2010). For example, North Americans tend to explain behaviors by referring to characteristics of the actor, and this had been considered to be a fundamental human tendency. However, Chinese and other East Asians usually give explanations based on other people's social expectations (Morris & Peng, 1994). Even seemingly basic visual processes such as susceptibility to optical illusions can differ substantially from one culture to another (Henrich, 2008). Researchers have now advanced beyond merely cataloging such cultural differences in cognitive and social processes, to developing theories of when and why the differences occur (Kitayama & Uskul, 2011). As you will see at many points throughout the book, social psychologists are now integrating these theories with the principles of their own science to arrive at a fuller understanding of what aspects of social behavior are especially sensitive to cultural contexts, as well as why.

Other newer theoretical trends are also becoming incorporated into social psychological thinking (Kaschak & Maner, 2009). Evolutionary psychology emphasizes that humans as well as other animals have evolved processes for solving specific problems that have recurred over evolutionary timespans. These processes still affect our thoughts, feelings, and behaviors today, as we, for example, cooperate or compete in groups (Wilson, Van Vugt, & O'Gorman, 2008) or choose dating and mating partners (Todd, Penke, Fasolo, & Lenton, 2007). The embodiment perspective argues that people's thoughts and judgments are deeply intertwined with sensory experiences and bodily movements, rather than being based just on abstract knowledge. For example, researchers have found that when we perceive other people's emotional facial expressions, we subtly mimic those expressions with our own face—and if such mimicry is blocked, accuracy in perceiving the other's emotion decreases (Niedenthal, 2007). In other words, we use our own bodies in the process of perceiving others. A recent explosion of research on neuroscience has led to the development of powerful research methods yielding new insights into how our brains represent and process social information (Cacioppo, Berntson, & Decety, 2011). The future is likely to bring even more integration of social psychological theory with cultural psychology, evolutionary principles, embodiment, and neuroscience as well as other emerging perspectives.

Integration of Basic Science and Social Problems. Can technological advancement by itself offer solutions to such global threats as resource depletion, environmental pollution, war and ethnic conflict, and overpopulation? Many people believe the answer to that question is no. Instead, solving such massive problems requires profound changes in human behavior.

Social psychologists are attacking these and other crucial social problems, and this attack will require their best theoretical efforts. In this regard, social psychologists are lucky. Scientists in many other fields have to choose whether they will work on purely theoretical issues or apply their theoretical knowledge to practical problems. A materials scientist, for example, may seek to understand the nature of the molecular bonds that produce stronger materials, but it is the engineer who will use the new materials to design an improved wind-turbine blade. Social psychologists do not have to make this kind of choice. It is difficult to think of a single area of social-psychological research that does not have some application to significant social issues. Whether social psychologists are looking at close relationships or divorce, altruism or aggression, attitude change or the effectiveness of advertising, intergroup conflict or its resolution, they simultaneously address the basic theoretical questions that spur pure scientific curiosity and the important phenomena that affect our daily lives.

Traditionally, many psychologists have thought of basic and applied research as distinct, even opposite, areas, with applied research taking a back seat to basic research. This stance is foreign to contemporary social psychology. Because virtually all social-psychological research is relevant to significant social issues, it is simultaneously basic and applied. The same underlying social and cognitive processes operate wherever people perceive, influence, and interact with each other, both inside the research laboratory and outside it, in schools, factories, courtrooms, playgrounds, boardrooms, and neighborhoods. For this reason, as we describe theories and research areas throughout this text, we will also discuss their

Photo 1.2 Social psychology helps society. Social psychology is relevant to many important problems facing society. It can inform policy on issues related to health, environmental conservation, intergroup conflict, prejudice and discrimination, etc. Research conducted by social psychologists has even been used in important cases before the U.S. Supreme Court on issues including racial segregation in schools and overcrowding in prisons.

applied implications. As you will see, talented researchers are studying social-psychological processes in many applied settings, with a particular focus on major issues relevant to health, education, law, the environment, and business. We have created special section headings to help you locate discussions of particularly important applications to areas such as the following.

- **■ *Health*.** Good health is just a matter of good diet, regular exercise, and lucky genes, right? Wrong. The emotions we experience, the amount of stress we encounter from daily hassles, our ability to find love and acceptance in close relationships, and even the way we feel about ourselves can influence our bodies as well as our minds. When public health officials promote exercise and fight drug abuse, when hospitals allow patients more control over their treatments, and when support groups speed recovery from illness, addiction, and grief, social-psychological processes are playing a part in producing sound minds in sound bodies.

- **■ *Education*.** As teachers teach and students learn, more is being communicated than just Spanish and geography. Teachers' expectations can shape their pupils' self-esteem, self-confidence, and even their actual performance. Classroom activities can encourage competition or cooperation and can eliminate or exacerbate ethnic and gender stereotypes. No wonder that for some the classroom is an open field of opportunity, whereas for others it is a minefield of adversity and disappointment.

- **■ *Law*.** How do the police extract confessions? Do lie detectors really work? Is a defendant in suit and tie more credible to a jury than one in prison fatigues? How might leading questions and inadmissible evidence influence a juror's thinking? Does the minority opinion of a dissenting juror ever sway jury verdicts? From crime to conviction, social-psychological processes are at work as police enforce laws, juries weigh evidence, and societies try to distribute justice.

■ *Environment*. Japanese commuters buy whiffs of oxygen from coin-operated machines in subways, yields of Atlantic fisheries decline, and American motorists waste hours in traffic jams. These human dimensions of environmental change are among those motivating social psychologists to discover how individuals can be encouraged to conserve energy or to recycle used materials. Others are working hard to determine the ways groups can be convinced to cooperate in harvesting renewable resources instead of overexploiting and destroying them.

■ *Business*. From advertising and sales techniques to the pitfalls of managerial decision making and diversity in the workplace, social-psychological processes are the gears that drive the wheels of business. Consider, for example, the way effective leadership can mold diverse individuals into a smoothly functioning work team, whereas ineffective leadership generates only conflict, dissatisfaction, and low productivity.

In social psychology, the everyday world is not just a place to test discoveries made during laboratory research. Instead, social psychologists regard issues that are important outside the laboratory, such as those listed here, as both a source of theoretical ideas and a target for solutions (Walton, 2014).

HOW THE APPROACH OF THIS BOOK REFLECTS AN INTEGRATIVE PERSPECTIVE

Not surprisingly, given the way social psychology has developed, our conception of social psychology is an integrated one. In this text we share with you our view of social psychology as a field that integrates not only the cognitive and the social but also basic theory and applied research. We believe that all the diversity and richness of human social behavior can be understood in terms of a few fundamental social-psychological processes. These processes flow from eight principles: two fundamental axioms, three motivational principles, and three processing principles.

As the chapters in this book describe specific topics like attraction, aggression, altruism, and attitude change, we will show you how all these forms of social behavior flow from the interaction of these same fundamental principles. At the same time, seeing these principles at work in different settings, producing apparently different forms of social behavior, will enhance your understanding of their meanings and implications. Here we give you just a quick introduction to these basic principles and the processes that flow from them.

Two Fundamental Axioms of Social Psychology

Two fundamental axioms of social psychology are that people construct their own reality and that social influences are pervasive.

Two fundamental axioms, or most important principles, integrate all the topics in this text. The first is that people construct their own reality. The second is that social influence pervades all social life.

Construction of Reality. At first glance, studying social behavior may seem to be an exercise in the obvious. As we go through our daily routines, we trust that we are seeing the world around us as it is—that an objective reality exists "out there" for all to see. When we join friends to watch a ball game or to eat dinner in a restaurant, we assume that we all see the same game and hear the same enjoyable dinnertime conversation. When we meet someone new, we quickly form an impression of what he or she "is like." And when we see someone raise a fist, furrow a brow, or slump in a chair, we know what the behavior means because "actions speak louder than words." Because we assume that our impressions are accurate and true, we usually expect anyone else who meets the same person, goes on the same date, or sees the same action to share those impressions.

Every now and then, however, we are forced to think twice. Discovering how different the reactions of others can be to the "same" social event overturns our usual lack of awareness of the extent to which we construct our own reality. Try reminiscing with one of your parents about what happened on your first day of school, and you may discover that your memories of the details of that milestone in your lives are quite different. Or, if you are a sports fan, compare your recollection of an important game with the view of the opposing team's fans and see if you agree about what happened. At such times we discover that we do not, in fact, share the same experience. A fist can be raised in intimidation or triumph, and a furrowed brow can indicate depression or concentration. What is real for each of us is a **construction of reality**, shaped in part by cognitive processes (the way our minds work) and in part by social processes (input from others who are actually present or whose presence we imagine).

Cognitive processes operate as we piece together fragments of information, draw inferences from them, and try to weave them into a coherent whole. We may hear a speaker deliver a series of arguments, note the audience's response, draw inferences about how others feel, and decide whether the message is worth our close consideration. In this sense, a person's view of the world is certainly in the eye—or the ear—of the beholder.

Social processes enable us to influence and be influenced by the views of others as we pursue agreement about the nature of reality. Within the groups that are important to us, agreement is our standard for interpreting and responding to events. For example,

Photo 1.3 Who is this man? Is Vladimir Putin a greedy, power-hungry dictator or a patriotic president who simply wants the best for his country? An enemy of human rights or a concerned leader looking out for his own citizens? Or is he none of these? The answer depends on who is doing the perceiving—the Russian military, Ukrainians, gay and lesbian Russian citizens, or Putin himself. What seems real to us is socially constructed and, like beauty, is in the eye of the beholder.

construction of reality
the axiom that each person's view of reality is a construction, shaped both by cognitive processes (the ways our minds work) and by social processes (input from others either actually present or imagined)

most members of Western societies enjoy kissing, although the meaning of the kiss varies, depending on whom we kiss and how. But when the Thonga of southeast Africa first saw Europeans kissing, they were disgusted by what they regarded as "eating each other's saliva and dirt" (Hyde, 1979, p. 18). Whether we are Thonga cattle herders or German university students, we tune in to others' interpretations—our parent's views about kisses or the cheers or boos of an audience listening to a speech—and we use those interpretations as the basis for our own responses. In this sense, a person's view of the world is at least in part a reflection of what is seen in the eyes of others.

Pervasiveness of Social Influence. We could probably all agree that other people influence our public behavior and that our actions in turn can influence what others say and do. Having supporters at our back gives us a bit more courage to speak out; face-to-face confrontations with detractors may frighten us into silence.

pervasiveness of social influence
the axiom that other people influence virtually all of our thoughts, feelings, and behavior, whether those others are physically present or not

Recall, however, that we said earlier that others can influence us even when we are alone. The **pervasiveness of social influence** means that other people influence virtually all of our thoughts, feelings, and behavior, whether those others are physically present or not. Our thoughts about others' reactions and our identification with social groups mold our innermost perceptions, thoughts, feelings, motives, and even our sense of self. Do you proudly think of yourself as an Ajax fan, a member of your temple, a citizen of Canada? Our allegiances may be small-scale, such as membership in families, teams, and committees, or large-scale, including affiliations based on race, ethnicity, religion, gender, or the society and culture in which we live. But whether the group is large or small, our membership in it provides a frame and a filter through which we view social events. The Dartmouth–Princeton game described at the beginning of the chapter had a particular meaning for students from each school and a quite different meaning for people who felt no allegiance to either team. Even among those on the same side, the game meant different things to the team members and their fans.

We sometimes experience social influence as social pressure, as when we encounter an aggressive salesperson or are given the cold shoulder or ridiculed for holding a political opinion that differs from our friends. But social influence is most profound when it is least evident: when it shapes our most fundamental assumptions and beliefs about the world without our realizing it. The reactions of the Princeton and Dartmouth fans were certainly shaped and biased by their school allegiances, but were the fans aware of that influence? Probably not. We would not expect anyone to think, "I'd better interpret that tackle as vicious because my friends will reject me if I don't." Social influences have surrounded us since infancy, and it is therefore no surprise that we usually are unaware of their impact. Does the fish know it swims in water? Sometimes it takes a shift in perspective to make us aware of the impact of social influence. Such shifts are familiar to all of us: A rebellious teenager becomes a parent and imposes a curfew on his own teenagers; a die-hard Braves fan moves from Atlanta to Toronto and eventually joins with her new co-workers to support the local Blue Jays. Even then, such changes often seem so natural that we attribute them not to social influence but to simple reality, for example, the self-evident fact that the Blue Jays are just the best team. Throughout this text, you will see evidence of the powerful effect social influence has in molding the reality we construct for ourselves—and therefore our thoughts, feelings, and actions—whether we are together with others or alone with our thoughts.

Three Motivational Principles

As they construct reality and influence and are influenced by others, people have three basic motives: to strive for mastery, to seek connectedness with others, and to value themselves and others connected to them.

As individuals and groups construct reality while influencing and being influenced by others, they direct their thoughts, feelings, and behaviors toward three important goals.

People Strive for Mastery. Mastery refers to understanding ourselves and the world around us and applying that understanding to help us control outcomes and gain rewards in our lives. Each of us is **striving for mastery**: We seek to understand and predict events in the social world in order to obtain many types of rewards. Achieving mastery is an important incentive in our attempt to form and hold accurate opinions and beliefs about the world, because accurate beliefs can guide us to effective and satisfying actions. For example, if you want the last available part-time job at the campus bookstore, forming an accurate impression of the manager's needs and knowing yourself well enough to give a convincing account of your qualifications may help you get the job. Similarly, insightfully diagnosing business problems and successfully understanding students' and faculty members' needs may help you keep such a job. Our desire for long-term rewards can also show itself in seeking ways to enhance our skills and knowledge and to improve ourselves in other ways. In many everyday decisions, individuals and groups choose to act in ways that appear likely to lead to the most rewarding results, guided by the most reliable and accurate information we can muster.

> **striving for mastery**
> the motivational principle that people seek to understand and predict events in the social world in order to obtain rewards

People Seek Connectedness. In **seeking connectedness**, each person attempts to create and maintain feelings of mutual support, liking, and acceptance from those they care about and value. For members of groups in bitter conflict, such as Israelis and Palestinians, actions that benefit their group often seem even more important than civil peace and an end to conflict. Conforming to group standards, even standards that have destructive consequences for people outside the group, fulfills a need for belonging and connectedness. Fulfilling such needs does not always bring about destructive consequences, of course. This same fundamental motive cements the relationships that bring joy and meaning to our lives, linking us to our teammates, families, friends, and lovers.

> **seeking connectedness**
> the motivational principle that people seek support, liking, and acceptance from the people and groups they care about and value

People Value "Me and Mine." The motivational principle of **valuing "me and mine"** means that we are motivated to see ourselves and anything or anyone connected to us, such as our families, teams, nations, or even possessions, in a positive light. Even people with life-threatening illnesses can maintain a positive view of themselves by comparing themselves with others who are even worse off. Our biased views of those who are connected to us often explain why members of different groups see the same events in very different ways. A Princeton fan may view the Dartmouth quarterback's broken leg as an accident—unfortunate, but part of the game of football and certainly not something that reflects badly on the Princeton team. A Dartmouth supporter might blame the injury on a viciously dirty tackle, clear evidence that the Princeton team is incapable of good sportsmanship. Little wonder that these fans came away from the game with very

> **valuing "me and mine"**
> the motivational principle that people desire to see themselves, and other people and groups connected to themselves, in a positive light

different views of it, views that emphasized the positive characteristics of their own teams and let them feel good about themselves.

Three Processing Principles

The operation of social and cognitive processes is described by three processing principles: Established views are slow to change, accessible information has the most impact, and processing is sometimes superficial but at other times goes into great depth.

In seeking rewards and connectedness and in valuing me and mine, people and groups gather and interpret information about the world in which they live. Three principles govern the cognitive and social processes that operate as we construct a picture of reality, influence other people, and are influenced by them.

Conservatism: Established Views Are Slow to Change. The **conservatism principle** states that individuals' and groups' views of the world are slow to change and prone to perpetuate themselves. The Princeton supporters, convinced that their Tigers were the better team, interpreted what they saw through the filter of their beliefs. Their selective perceptions thus supported their views of reality, as did the influence of their group, the equally biased fans around them. Examples of conservatism are almost endless: the first impressions we form of job applicants, the stereotypes we harbor about other groups, or preferences we nurture for the brand of peanut butter Mom always bought. In all these cases and more, the principle is the same: established knowledge tends to perpetuate itself. In the chapters to come you will see why prior beliefs, expectations, and preferences are so hard to change, and you will become more aware of the consequences of their resiliency. You will also appreciate the enormous amount of effort needed to budge them at all.

Accessibility: Accessible Information Has the Most Impact. From football games to political debates, every social situation provides an incredibly rich array of information—so rich that we could not consider all its details. Consequently, we are likely to consider, remember, and use only a tiny fraction of the potentially relevant information when we make judgments or decisions. The **accessibility principle** states that whatever information is most readily available to us usually has the most impact on our thoughts, feelings, and behavior. In many situations, what comes most easily to mind is what we were already thinking. So, to return to the football example, Dartmouth stalwarts used their conviction that their team is good as a basis for their judgments of what happened. In other situations, we base our judgments on the information that is most easily noticed and interpreted. For many of the students who listened to the probation speech without expecting to be personally affected, enthusiastic applause or disapproving whistles were the most noticeable and had the most impact on their judgments.

Superficiality Versus Depth: People Can Process Superficially or In Depth. Much of the time, people seem to operate on automatic pilot, putting little effort into forming a superficial picture of reality and relying heavily on whatever information is most

conservatism principle
the processing principle that individuals' and groups' views of the world are slow to change and prone to perpetuate themselves

accessibility principle
the processing principle that the information that is most readily available generally has the most impact on thoughts, feelings, and behavior

accessible. But sometimes, particularly when we notice that events fail to match our expectations or when our important goals are threatened, we take the time and trouble to process information more extensively. These are examples of the principle of **superficiality versus depth**. Confronted with an opposing point of view—one that clearly contradicted their own—students who cared about probation reconsidered their positions. They reviewed the arguments and based their opinions on the content of the speeches rather than on the circumstances of their presentation. Disagreement or rejection challenges not only our sense of mastery and understanding but also our feelings of connectedness, triggering anxiety and uncertainty. Threats to any of our important goals may motivate us to consider information in more depth and to think hard about our own beliefs and actions.

The interrelationships among the eight basic principles of social psychology are summarized in Figure 1.1.

superficiality versus depth
the processing principle that people ordinarily put little effort into dealing with information, but at times are motivated to consider information in more depth

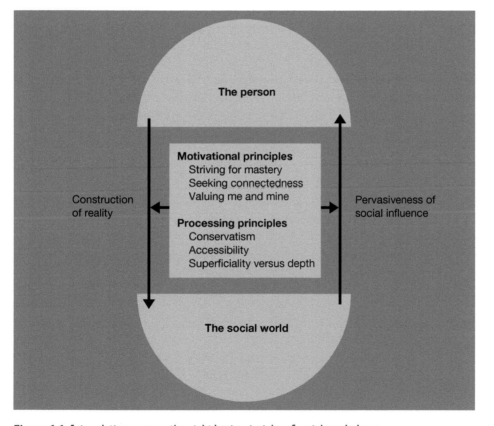

Figure 1.1 Interrelations among the eight basic principles of social psychology
Two fundamental axioms link the individual person to the social world. Each person constructs his or her own picture of social reality, which then guides all thoughts, feelings, and actions. At the same time, the pervasiveness of social influence also affects the person's thoughts, feelings, and behavior. Three motivational principles and three processing principles determine both the nature of the constructed reality and the nature of the social influence.

Common Processes, Diverse Behaviors

In combination, these eight principles account for all types of social behavior, including thoughts and actions that are useful and valuable as well as those that are misleading and destructive.

In combination, then, these eight principles account for all types of social behavior. This includes not only desirable outcomes such as accurate decisions, successful social interactions, and harmonious relationships between groups, but also more problematic and negative forms of behavior. As our examples demonstrate, exactly the same processes that produce useful and valuable outcomes in some situations produce misleading and destructive outcomes in others. Our ability to construct reality allows us to see our world as a coherent and meaningful place, but it also opens the door to bias and misinterpretation. Social influences sometimes provide us with safety in numbers, but they also may lead us like lambs to the slaughter. The drive for connectedness and the value we place on me and mine can give us the warm glow of belonging, but it can also prompt us to reject, devalue, and exclude others not in our chosen circle. Basing decisions on accessible information often produces extremely efficient decision making but sometimes leads to bad decisions. Even when we contemplate information as thoughtfully as possible, we are not always guaranteed an accurate decision. Sometimes the very act of thinking about things can slant our interpretations and introduce mistakes without our being aware of the problem.

Human behavior is not always as simple as it seems, but neither is it impenetrable to scientific inquiry or impossible to understand systematically. In fact, although social behavior is incredibly diverse, this diversity results from the operation of these same few processes. Thus, as you work through chapter by chapter in this text, watch for these principles at work. We offer some help by calling attention to the principles and general themes of the book. In addition, we make special efforts to present theories and research findings as interrelated sets of ideas by placing cross-references to related ideas in the margins. We know that disconnected items of information are hard to remember and do not contribute much to a real understanding of social behavior. We would like you to see this text as an integrated story of (1) the fundamental social and cognitive processes that operate as human beings perceive, influence, and interact with others; and (2) the way social psychologists learn about these processes, both in the laboratory and in the world of everyday life. It is a fascinating story, and we hope you will learn much about yourself and others as you follow it through the text.

PLAN OF THE BOOK

The first two chapters of this text are an introduction to social psychology, covering the "Why?" and the "How?" of our science. The remainder of the book explores the "What?" of social psychology—the topic areas that make up the discipline. In this chapter we have tried to convey why social psychologists ask the questions they do. Chapter 2 tells more about how they seek answers.

■ *Asking and Answering Research Questions.* Have we convinced you already that people's interpretive processes and social surroundings may bias what they know? Scientists are no exception. Chapter 2 describes the logical checks and balances built into the structure of science that help researchers guard against subjectivity and bias.

Chapters 3 through 14 explore what social psychologists study. Following our definition of social psychology, we deal in turn with how individuals perceive others (Chapters 3–6), influence others (Chapters 7–10), and relate to others (Chapters 11–14). Chapters 3 through 6 focus on social perception, the way we come to know and understand the basic elements of our social world: individuals and social groups.

■ *Perceiving Individuals.* From fleeting impressions of passing strangers to the intimate familiarity of our best friend, Chapter 3 deals with knowing and understanding other people.

■ *The Self.* What person is probably most important, most near and dear to each of us? Chapter 4 describes how we understand the self.

■ *Perceiving Groups.* In Chapter 5, we investigate the beliefs and feelings people develop about social groups like working women, Russians, schoolteachers, or Muslims.

■ *Social Identity.* Chapter 6 brings the topics of Chapters 4 and 5 together in a discussion of how we come to see ourselves as members of a social group and how a group can become part of the self.

Social influence is the impact each of us has on others, and it is the topic of Chapters 7 through 10. The elements of social psychology do not occur in isolation: Each of us is constantly influencing and being influenced by others. Others affect us whether they are in our face, like an aggressive salesperson, or on our minds even when we are alone.

■ *Attitudes and Attitude Change.* Advertisements aim at our pocketbooks, political campaigns play on our fears, debates appeal to our reason. Do they change our minds? If so, how? Chapter 7 gives some answers to questions like these.

■ *Attitudes and Behavior.* Under the right circumstances, attitudes both reflect and guide behaviors. Chapter 8 tells a tale of the mutual influence of attitudes and behaviors.

■ *Norms and Conformity.* A different kind of mutual influence is the focus of Chapter 9. Here we examine how groups reach agreement and why that agreement has such compelling effects on group members.

■ *Norms and Behavior.* Chapter 10 describes the effects of groups on what people do, not just on what they think. Bringing all the chapters of this section together, we describe how attitudes and group influences combine to affect behavior.

In the final four chapters we concentrate on social relations, the bonds that link us one to another, as individuals and as groups. Whether we are bound by attraction or cooperation, or shackled by aggression and conflict, our relations with others can pull us together or drive us apart.

■ *Interaction and Performance in Groups.* Small groups—management committees, paramedic teams, juries, and others—do most of society's work. Chapter 11's main topics are how we interact with others in small groups and how groups work to accomplish shared tasks.

■ *Attraction, Relationships, and Love.* Chapter 12 takes a close look at feelings of attraction to other people and the formation and development of close and loving relationships. We also review what social psychology can tell us about why relationships flourish or wither.

■ *Aggression and Conflict.* Who can watch the evening news without being struck by the many conflicts that pit person against person or group against group? In Chapter 13 we analyze the path of such conflicts: how they can arise, escalate, and, sometimes, be resolved.

■ *Helping and Cooperation.* Dramatic incidents of selfless heroism or more commonplace acts of cooperation that benefit others: Why do they occur? Chapter 14 examines the conditions under which we help other people and our reasons for doing so.

■ *Epilogue.* The text ends with an epilogue, a brief concluding comment that summarizes the major themes and reflects on some of their interrelationships and applications.

As you read this book, we invite you to join us in seeing social-psychological principles at work in people's actions and interactions. Seeing events around you in this framework is the first and most essential step toward becoming a social psychologist, having the fun of doing research that advances our knowledge of how social-psychological principles work, and of applying the principles to real and important problems. But you do not have to do research to use your new knowledge to understand why your friends act as they do, how other people influence you, or what accounts for group conflicts around the world. We hope you will come to appreciate both the usefulness and the excitement of social psychology.

SUMMARY

A Definition of Social Psychology. **Social psychology** is the scientific study of the effects of social and cognitive processes on the way individuals perceive, influence, and relate to others. Like other scientists, social psychologists gather knowledge systematically by means of scientific methods. These methods help produce knowledge that is less subject to the biases and distortions that often characterize common-sense knowledge.

The physical presence of other people, the knowledge and opinions that they pass on to us, and our feelings about the groups to which we belong all deeply influence us through **social processes**, whether we are with other people or alone. Our perceptions, memories, emotions, and motives also influence us through **cognitive processes**. Effects of social and cognitive processes are not separate but are inextricably intertwined.

All types of social behavior, including individuals' perceptions of, influences on, and relationships with others, reflect the operation of social and cognitive processes.

Understanding these processes can help us comprehend why people act the way they do, and it may also help solve important social problems.

Historical Trends and Current Themes in Social Psychology. Social psychology emerged soon after the beginning of scientific psychology in the late 19th century, when researchers began considering questions about social influences on human thought and action. Through much of the 20th century, North American psychology was dominated by behaviorism, but social psychologists maintained an emphasis on the important effects of thoughts and feelings on behavior.

In the 1930s and 1940s, many European social psychologists fled to North America, where they had a major influence on the field's direction. Throughout this period, significant questions inspired by the rise of Nazism and the Second World War shaped research interests.

Since the 1950s and 1960s, social psychology has grown and flourished, moving toward an integrated theoretical understanding of social and cognitive processes and toward further applications of social-psychological theory to important applied problems.

How the Approach of This Book Reflects an Integrative Perspective. Social psychology is a field that integrates not only the cognitive and the social but also basic theory and applied research. All the diversity and richness of human social behavior can be understood in terms of eight basic principles. Two fundamental axioms of social psychology are that people **construct their own reality** and that **social influences are pervasive**. Three motivational principles are that, as they construct reality and influence and are influenced by others, people **strive for mastery**, or understanding and control of their environment; **seek connectedness** with others; and **value "me and mine."** People's thoughts and actions are also influenced by three processing principles. One is the **conservatism principle**: Established views are slow to change. Another is the **accessibility principle**: Easily accessed information has the most impact. The final principle is **superficiality versus depth**: People can process superficially or in depth. In combination, these eight principles account for all types of social behavior, including thoughts and actions that are useful and valuable as well as those that are misleading and destructive.

Plan of the Book. This text has four main parts. Chapters 1 and 2 introduce social psychology and its typical research methods. Chapters 3 through 6 focus on social perception, the ways that people interpret and understand other people, themselves, and social groups. Chapters 7 through 10 deal with social influence, the ways that people and groups affect each other as they interact and communicate. Chapters 11 through 14 describe the social relations that lead people to form relationships, work together in groups, and help and hurt each other.

2

ASKING AND ANSWERING RESEARCH QUESTIONS

Imagine winning the lottery. Or receiving a promotion after only 5 months in your new position. Or getting a would-be buyer to meet your price on the sale of your used car. How do you think you would react to these events? Most people anticipate being very happy. Now imagine finding out that you have a life-threatening illness, that you have stayed in the same job for years and still have little hope of advancement, or that you got much less for your used car than you had hoped for. You probably would predict that you would be quite unhappy about these alternatives. It might surprise you to learn that social-psychological research has shown that these intuitively obvious conclusions are not always true. Lottery winners are soon no happier than the rest of us (Brickman, Coates, & Janoff-Bulman, 1978). Those receiving rapid promotions are often more dissatisfied than people with less chance of advancement (Stouffer, Suchman, DeVinney, Star, & Williams, 1949). Patients with serious illnesses often show remarkably good spirits (J. V. Wood, Taylor, & Lichtman, 1985). And the money actually gained or lost in negotiation with others has little to do with people's satisfaction about the outcome (Loewenstein, Thompson, & Bazerman, 1989).

Most people find these research findings pretty surprising. Common sense tells us that good outcomes make people feel happy, contented, and satisfied, and that negative events or failures make us unhappy. But conclusions based on scientific research are not always the same as those we reach using everyday common sense or intuition. When those conclusions differ, which should you trust: research findings or common sense? Are research findings really more dependable, trustworthy, or accurate than our everyday understanding of social behavior?

These kinds of questions are at the heart of this chapter. Social psychology is an empirical science, meaning that its theories and conclusions about social behavior rest on the results of research. Like other scientists, most social psychologists believe that scientific research methods produce answers that are more likely to be trustworthy and unbiased than those we arrive at through everyday common sense, hunches, and intuitions. Why? It is not that scientists are perfectly objective logicians like *Star Trek*'s Mr. Spock. On the contrary, scientists are human, too, and they are just as vulnerable as anyone else to preconceptions, prejudices, and wishful thinking. But this is exactly why scientific methods are so important! Most people are unaware of the biases in their everyday thinking and knowledge, and they therefore fail to guard against them. Because scientists know that biases can distort their reasoning and their findings, they use research methods specifically designed to counter such slips in thinking.

Most of this chapter is dedicated to describing the lengths to which social psychologists go to try to reach conclusions about human social behavior that are as trustworthy and general as possible. Understanding the practical and logical steps researchers take to reach this goal will help you grasp why social psychologists do the sorts of research you will read about in this book. It will also help you to judge which research findings should be taken seriously and when research you read about in magazines or on the web falls short of its goal.

But good science is about more than just producing trustworthy and general results. Social-psychological research is a human enterprise, in which people are both the investigators and the investigated. This situation inevitably raises issues of values and ethics. How should research participants be treated? Are there research questions that should not be pursued? Should the results of research be made known to everyone, no matter how they will use those results? No researcher can ignore these questions, and neither should any consumer of social-psychological research. As you read this chapter and the rest of this text, you may wish to reflect on the values implicit in social psychologists' work and on how your own values guide your reactions to the topics and results that we will discuss. Clarifying the ethics and values of research is just as important to good science as carefully following the rules of the scientific method.

A NOTE TO THE STUDENT ON HOW TO USE THIS CHAPTER

Research methods can seem dry and abstract, compared to the richness and excitement of the substance of social psychology. Although some familiarity with research methods is essential for understanding how social psychologists reach their conclusions about people's social behavior, instructors may use this chapter in different ways. Some may assign this chapter early in the course, corresponding to its place in the book. Others may ask you to read this chapter after two or three substantive chapters, so that your knowledge of some meaningful and important studies can serve as background for deeper understanding of research methods. Other instructors may not assign this chapter at all, preferring to describe research methods in lectures or handouts.

Whatever your instructor's approach, we add one piece of advice. Through the book, as you read about particular studies, you may wonder what justifies the research conclusions, or feel concerned about the well-being of participants in the study. When questions like these arise in your mind, it is a good idea to turn back to this chapter as a resource to help you think about the issues. So if you question a study's conclusion that violence in the media can actually *cause* people to become more aggressive, you might want to look at the section on experimental designs and the strength of causal inferences on pages 34–36. Or if you wonder whether the treatment of participants in a particular study meets current ethical standards, look at the description of how those standards have evolved, pages 47–51. These examples illustrate some ways this chapter can serve as a resource for understanding how and why research is conducted, throughout the entire course.

RESEARCH QUESTIONS AND THE ROLE OF THEORY

Origins of Research Questions

Research questions are provoked by curiosity about why people act the way they do. In turn, this curiosity often reflects concern about important social problems.

Research is almost always provoked by curiosity: the researcher's desire to know the answer to some question about events, ideas, and people. Some questions are provoked by unexpectedly negative or positive events. Well-publicized events such as the brutality of ethnic warfare in Syria and the global outpouring of aid for Asian tsunami victims provoke questions about hatred and altruism. The shocking acts of suicide bombers who give their lives to kill their group's perceived enemies cause social psychologists, like other observers, to ask what motivates these individuals. And the way rescuers work together to help victims of earthquakes, floods, hurricanes, and fires stimulates researchers' curiosity about processes leading to cooperation. But research ideas also stem from questioning the mundane and the accepted—the everyday events that affect the lives of all of us. Why do women still earn less than men performing the same jobs? How good are people at judging others' characters? How can city managers convince more motorists to carpool? Is breaking up really hard to do, even if you are the breaker-upper rather than the broken-up-with?

Part of what makes a person choose to become a social psychologist is a healthy store of curiosity about why people act the way they do. Notice, however, that many of these questions go beyond mere curiosity. Many social psychologists try to explain and solve social problems that have a major impact on many people's lives: racial or religious prejudice, gender discrimination, depletion of environmental resources, violence, unhealthy lifestyles, and depression. And although individual events and people may provoke their research questions, social psychologists do not strive merely to understand specific events or specific individuals. They seek instead to discover general principles that explain the behavior of many people in many situations. From those principles will flow an understanding of why behavior occurs and under what conditions.

What Is a Scientific Theory?

Social psychologists seek to develop scientific theories to explain social behavior. A scientific theory is a statement about the causal relationships among abstract constructs. It is a statement that holds for specified types of people, times, and settings.

To conduct their research, social psychologists have to translate specific questions about individuals and events into general statements about social behavior. Consider, for example, some of the research referred to at the beginning of this chapter. One study interviewed women diagnosed with breast cancer and noted whether they compared themselves to others who were adjusting better or worse to the disease (J. V. Wood and others, 1985). In another study, business school students engaged in a mock negotiation with an opponent, then learned that the opponent was happy or sad about the outcome

(Loewenstein and others, 1989). What was the point of these exercises? Were the researchers concerned only about the behavior of particular cancer patients, or about specific students involved in one set of negotiations? Not at all. The real goal of these studies was not to gauge the reactions of particular individuals in particular situations but rather to test a general social-psychological theory about human behavior. In fact, all the research referred to in the introduction to the chapter was testing some aspect of social comparison theory, the idea that people evaluate their abilities, opinions, and outcomes by comparing themselves to others (Festinger, 1954). All of our judgments about ourselves, as slow or smart, right or wrong, winners or losers, are affected by our comparisons of our own abilities, attitudes, and outcomes to those of others.

Theories provide general explanations for social behavior. More formally, a **scientific theory** satisfies three requirements:

- It is a statement about constructs.
- It describes causal relations.
- It is general in scope.

Let us look more closely at each part of this definition.

1. *Theories are about constructs.* **Constructs** are abstract concepts like "anxiety," "aggression," or "self-esteem." "The knowledge of others' attitudes" and "the evaluation of one's own attitudes" are two constructs that feature in social comparison theory. Each of these constructs is abstract, in that it cannot be directly observed. You cannot see knowledge or touch an evaluation.

2. *Theories describe causal relations.* Theories describe causal relations among constructs, stating that a change in one construct (the cause) produces a corresponding change in another construct (the effect). Social comparison theory is a theory about cause and effect: Our knowledge of other people's outcomes, performances, or opinions causes changes in how we evaluate our own outcomes, performances, or opinions.

   Because theories offer reasons to explain why events occur, they are very powerful. If we know that one state or event causes another, we can take practical steps, known as **interventions**, to change behavior or solve problems. The knowledge that people evaluate their own abilities, attitudes, and outcomes by reference to those of other people, for example, could have a variety of practical applications. Thus, medical personnel who work with cancer patients might encourage those patients not to compare themselves to media portrayals of "supercopers" who are presented as experiencing little stress from the disease. Refraining from such comparisons might help them to cope better with their illness. Such strategies are made possible by research showing that comparisons between our own experiences and those of other people actually cause us to feel and act in certain ways.

3. *Theories are general in scope.* Theories are intended to be general in scope, applying to many people in different settings and times. However, the range of applicability may vary from one theory to another. Social comparison theory, for example, is intended to be a broadly applicable statement about how all people evaluate many aspects of their life. And, indeed, judging one's own experience in the context of what happens to others does appear to be a general human characteristic, although

Information gleaned from comparison to others has a major impact on what people think and how they feel about themselves, as described in Chapter 4, pages 99–100.

scientific theory
a statement that satisfies three requirements: It is about constructs; it describes causal relations; and it is general in scope, although the range of generality differs for different theories

constructs
abstract and general concepts that are used in theories and that are not directly observable

interventions
practical steps taken to change people's behavior or to solve social problems

reactions to the comparison may differ in different cultures (Moghaddam, Taylor, & Wright, 1993).

Other theories, however, have a more limited scope. Perhaps they pertain only to males, or only to people in specific cultures. The more generally applicable a theory is, the more useful it is because it will hold for many different kinds of people in many different situations and at many different times. Currently, however, little is known about just how broadly many social-psychological theories can be applied (M. H. Bond, 1988; Markus, Kitayama, & Heiman, 1996). This important issue of the generality of theories is explored in more detail later in this chapter.

HOW RESEARCH TESTS THEORIES

The ultimate goal of research is to test whether a theory provides an accurate explanation of human behavior. Theories can be evaluated only on the basis of valid research: research that is trustworthy because the researcher has taken pains to exclude bias and error. How can researchers be sure their research is valid and can provide evidence for or against theories? It turns out that valid research is guided by the same three properties of theories just described (T. D. Cook & Campbell, 1979).

1. Because theories deal with *constructs*—abstract concepts—researchers have to be sure the specific observations they make in their studies are in fact relevant to those constructs. For example, researchers studying how social comparisons affect cancer patients' "adjustment to their illness" must have some way to accurately measure "adjustment."

2. Because theories describe *causal relations*, researchers have to be sure they know the causes of any changes in behavior they find in their studies. Research must allow the conclusion that the cancer patients' successful adjustment is due to the social comparisons they make, rather than to some other, extraneous cause.

3. Because theories are *general* in scope, researchers have to be sure they have learned something about how people in general, not just a few individuals, think, feel, and act. Conclusions about effects of social comparisons on people's attitudes or behaviors would be most valuable if they held for many types of people—not just for patients hospitalized for cancer treatment.

As we shall see, all three of these criteria are essential links in the logical chain by which research supports theory, and so we describe them in detail in the following three sections.

Construct Validity and Measurement

To provide a valid test of a theory, research must have construct validity, which means that the independent and dependent variables used in the research must correspond to the intended theoretical constructs. Construct validity is endangered if participants behave in ways they think are socially desirable. Researchers ensure construct validity by measuring independent and dependent variables in many different ways.

The researcher's first task is to make sure that the research has good **construct validity**, meaning that the events that occur in the research setting actually correspond to the theoretical constructs under investigation. This is not always easy because abstract concepts (like anxiety or social comparison) are not directly observable. Thus researchers have to infer their presence using observable variables (factors on which people can vary). Variables that are considered to be causal factors are called **independent variables**. Variables representing effects are called **dependent variables**, because they depend on the causal or independent variable.

An example can help clarify these terms. Let's consider a theory stating that direct competition for limited resources (an abstract construct assumed to be a cause) causes hostility between social groups (the construct assumed to be the effect). To infer whether "competition for limited resources" is present in a particular situation, researchers might measure people's belief that their department and another department are pitted against each other for a share of an organizational budget. These beliefs would be the independent variable in the study. To infer whether "hostility between social groups" occurs as a result of the competition, researchers can measure negative stereotypes, insults, refusal to help, and acts of aggression that rival groups direct toward each other. These would be the dependent variables in the research. If the independent and dependent variables correspond to the intended theoretical constructs, the researchers will be able to draw valid conclusions about those constructs.

Construct validity has two parts. First, independent and dependent variables must correspond to the intended cause and effect constructs, and, second, they must not correspond to other constructs. As you will see in the pages that follow, much of the ingenuity in social-psychological research goes into selecting and refining ways to measure important theoretical constructs that are unaffected by other, unintended constructs.

Threats to Construct Validity. Unfortunately, ensuring construct validity is a pretty tall order. A common problem is that an observed variable may be affected by unwanted influences, other than the construct that it is intended to measure. Suppose researchers

construct validity
the extent to which the independent and dependent variables used in research correspond to the theoretical constructs under investigation

independent variable
a concrete manipulation or measurement of a construct that is thought to cause other constructs

dependent variable
a concrete measurement of a construct that is thought to be an effect of other constructs

Chapter 13, pages 498–500, describes in more depth the negative effects of between-group competition for resources.

Photo 2.1 The Rattlers and the Eagles. These archival photographs show two groups of boys who participated in Muzafer Sherif's famous study testing realistic conflict theory, to be described in Chapter 13. On the left, the boys compete in a tug-of-war, an activity that corresponds to the construct of competition for limited resources because only the winning group received prizes. On the right, the boys cooperate to solve a problem with the water tank. This activity reflects the theoretical construct of cooperation for common goals, which the study found can reduce intergroup conflict.

social desirability response bias
people's tendency to act in ways that they believe others find acceptable and approve of

self-report measures
those based on asking the individual about his or her thoughts, feelings, or behaviors

observational measures
those based on directly watching and recording people's behavior, including online behavior

archival measures
those based on examining traces of past behavior

performance measures
those that ask participants to perform some task as well as they can

tried to measure intergroup hostility by asking workers in the organization how much they liked members of the competing department. Workers might be unwilling to admit that they hate their co-workers, so their ratings might not honestly reflect their feelings of hostility. This threat to construct validity is called **social desirability response bias**: people's tendency to act in ways that make them look good (M. J. Rosenberg, 1969). Social psychologists must be constantly on guard against the threat of social desirability as well as other biases in their measurements. This is particularly true when researchers are interested in attitudes or behaviors that might meet with some social disapproval, such as stereotyping, prejudice, aggression, or unusual opinions or lifestyles.

Ensuring Construct Validity by Using Appropriate Measures. Researchers try hard to choose measurement techniques that tap the construct under investigation but minimize other influences. There are a few distinct kinds of measures, each with its own strengths and weaknesses. **Self-report measures**, which rely on asking the individual about his or her thoughts, feelings, or behaviors, are the most direct source of information about beliefs, attitudes, and intentions. But they are also particularly susceptible to social desirability biases, especially if the topic is a sensitive one. Thus, asking people overt questions about their racial prejudice might not produce answers with high construct validity (Dunton & Fazio, 1997).

A researcher studying racial prejudice might decide, therefore, that a better technique for his particular study would be to use **observational measures**: those based on directly watching and recording people's behavior. The researcher could watch, for example, how close a participant stood or sat next to a person of another race and whether people participating in intergroup interactions displayed relaxed smiles or nervous fidgeting. Behavior that occurs online on blogs or social networking sites can also be observed. For example, researchers have sought to understand the relation between number of Facebook friends and psychological well-being (Manago, Taylor, & Greenfield, 2012), and have analyzed Facebook profile photographs to test hypothesized cultural differences in self-presentation (Chih-Mao & Park, 2013). Observational measures often have good construct validity, although if the research setting is public or if participants know they are being observed, social desirability biases could still undermine construct validity. Related to observational measures are **archival measures**, which examine traces of past behavior such as organizational or governmental records. Google's database of word usage in published books, for example, has been used to draw conclusions about changes over time in the concept of happiness (Oishi and others, 2013).

Performance measures are most appropriate for some research goals. Performance measures ask participants to perform some task as well as they can, for example, by answering questions as rapidly and accurately as possible or by recalling as much as they can about information presented earlier. A performance measure of prejudice might require participants to read a complicated description of a character's successes and failures and then to recall everything they could from the story. If participants recalled mostly successes when they believed the character was White but mostly failures if the same character was described as Hispanic, the researcher might conclude that the participants were biased against Hispanics. Because people usually just try to perform as well as they can on such tasks, social desirability tends to be less of a problem than it is with self-report or observational measures.

Physiological measures include measurements of heart rate, skin conductance (which reflects the amount of sweating), or small, visually unobservable muscle movements. They can also include measures of blood levels of certain substances such as stress hormones. Under the right circumstances these measures can give good evidence as to people's levels of stress or physiological arousal, and even their like or dislike for certain objects—such as prejudice against social groups—often in more valid ways compared to simple self-reports. In recent years neuroscience-based measures that indicate actual brain activity have been widely applied in research. **EEG (electro-encephalographic)** measures use electrical signals on the scalp to very accurately detect the times at which specific neural events occur (for example, in the processing of visual information) and can even suggest what general brain areas are active at specific times. **fMRI (functional magnetic resonance imaging)** indirectly measures the activation levels of specific brain regions, although with lower time accuracy compared to EEG. Much is known about what brain regions are active during specific types of processing such as visual imagery, memory retrieval, or person perception (Amodio & Frith, 2006). As a result, fMRI measures can provide important evidence regarding the mental processes that occur in research participants. For example, Elizabeth Phelps and her colleagues (2000) showed that activation in response to images of African-Americans in the amygdala, a brain region associated with negative emotional reactions, was stronger in White participants who scored higher on a measure of anti-Black prejudice.

Like any good carpenter or chef, a social psychology researcher must choose the right measurement tool for the job at hand. Measures that prove to be particularly precise

physiological measures those based on measurement of some physiological process such as heart rate or muscle movements

EEG (electro-encephalographic) measures use electrical signals on the scalp to very accurately detect the times at which specific neural events occur

fMRI (functional magnetic resonance imaging) indirectly measures the activation levels of specific brain regions

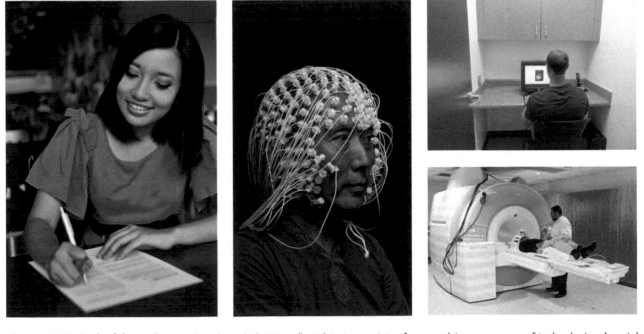

Photo 2.2 Methods of data collection. Social psychologists collect data in a variety of ways, relying on a range of technologies. A social psychologist might ask someone to respond to a questionnaire or survey; view stimuli while EEG measurements are taken (second photo from left); interact with others electronically during an experiment; or imagine intergroup contact in a functional magnetic resonance imager (bottom right photo).

and effective ways of assessing constructs often become quite popular in research, as ones with less construct validity fall by the wayside. But even the best available measure might not by itself guarantee construct validity.

Ensuring Construct Validity by Using Multiple Measures. Because different kinds of measures have different strengths, the best way a researcher can ensure construct validity is to use multiple measures. To understand why, imagine you want to be sure your boss is in a good mood before you ask her for time off. You check her expression for a smile and conclude she probably is feeling fine. Because you really are not sure, however, you ask a co-worker, who reports that the supervisor has been quite amicable. Still, you decide to see if she chooses to work out during her lunch hour—usually a good sign of a positive mood. Each of these very different means of gathering information has its own unique problems, but the accumulated evidence all points to the fact that your boss is feeling pretty upbeat. You can see how your conviction that you are actually reading the supervisor's mood accurately grows with each converging piece of evidence, even though no single piece of evidence can be conclusive alone. When different measures produce the same results it works the same way: Researchers can be reasonably confident that the measures reflect the intended construct and nothing else.

Now imagine for a moment that you are part of a research team trying to test the impact of positive or negative mood on helping. How could you assess the dependent variable construct, helping? You can probably think of a number of different possibilities. You might ask people about their intentions to help. Alternatively, you could count the number of spilled papers they retrieve or tally the dollars they donate to a worthy cause. A third possibility is to time how long it takes the research participants to come to another person's aid. These are diverse measures of willingness to help. Which should you use? Your best choice might be "all of the above." By using so many diverse measures of willingness to help, researchers increase the likelihood that the construct of helping is adequately measured.

Internal Validity and Types of Research Design

To provide a valid test of a theory, research must allow observers to conclude that changes in the independent variable actually caused changes in the dependent variable. If both the independent and dependent variables are measured, the research may lack internal validity because many other unknown factors could affect the research results. Random assignment of participants to groups followed by manipulation of independent variables allows the researcher to draw stronger conclusions about cause and effect.

internal validity
the extent to which it can be concluded that changes in the independent variable actually caused changes in the dependent variable in a research study

research design
a plan that specifies how research participants will be selected and treated

A good test of a theory provides solid evidence about cause and effect. Research has high **internal validity** if the researcher can confidently conclude that a change in the independent variable caused a change in the dependent variable. Whether or not such a conclusion can be drawn depends primarily on a study's **research design**, a plan that specifies how research participants will be selected and treated. Some types of research designs offer a higher level of internal validity than do others.

Threats to Internal Validity. The major threat to internal validity is that factors other than changes in the independent variable may be present and may be causing the observed changes in the dependent variable. Eliminating all such alternative factors is often very difficult, as you will see in the following example.

The contact hypothesis is a theory that states that casual, friendly contact with members of a different ethnic group increases liking for that group (G. W. Allport, 1954b). One obvious way of testing this idea is to investigate the impact of important, naturally occurring forms of contact, such as a person's everyday encounters with different groups in the neighborhood, on liking for various groups. Rudolf Kalin and J. W. Berry (1982) did just that, using data from a public opinion survey as the dependent variable. The survey asked how much Canadians liked English-speaking and French-speaking Canadians, Canadian Native Americans, and Canadians of German, Jewish, Italian, and Ukrainian descent. Kalin and Berry compared the survey results with official government data showing which ethnic groups lived in the same neighborhoods as the survey respondents. Their results showed that people who lived in areas with a relatively high percentage of a particular group liked that group more than did people who lived far away from members of the group. In other words, there was a correlation—a statistical association—between living near a group and liking for that group. Thus, this study is an example of a **nonexperimental research design**, sometimes called a correlational design, in which researchers simply measure both the independent variable (in this case, neighborhood ethnic composition) and the dependent variable (people's opinions of groups).

Unfortunately, nonexperimental or correlational designs are vulnerable to many threats to internal validity. For example, measurement of the independent variable in this survey does allow researchers to identify participants who live near many French-speaking Canadians and participants who do not. However, the nonexperimental design cannot rule out the possibility that these two groups of participants may differ in many other unknown ways. As a result, even if the groups differ in their favorability toward French-speaking Canadians, researchers cannot confidently state the cause of that difference. Indeed, if you have taken a class devoted entirely to research methods, you may have heard the adage "correlation does not equal causation." It is clear in this example why this is so. Although highly favorable responses may be due to the causal impact of frequent contact with the group in the participants' neighborhood, other factors besides increased contact could also be the cause. In fact, you can probably think of several alternative explanations. For example, rather than contact causing the liking, liking may cause the contact. That is, people who hold more positive views of a group might choose to move into or remain in

The conditions under which intergroup contact can undermine prejudice and help resolve intergroup conflict are described in Chapter 5, pages 184–186, and Chapter 13, pages 520–524.

nonexperimental research design
a research design in which both the independent and dependent variables are measured

Photo 2.3 Yes, but is it internally valid? Many nonexperimental studies find that children exposed to violent television or video games are more aggressive than those who are not. Unfortunately, these designs lack internal validity. Their results cannot tell us whether what the children are watching causes aggression, or whether aggressive children prefer such video games and television programs. To establish the causal role of TV and video game violence, social psychologists have turned to experimental research designs with high internal validity, as discussed in Chapter 13.

areas in which many members of that group live. Another explanation may be that people who live in a particular neighborhood share other personal characteristics, such as a particular type of social background, that influence both where the people live and how they feel about ethnic diversity. Each of these and other alternative explanations are possible because of the nonexperimental design, in which both independent and dependent variables are measured. When many other factors provide viable explanations for changes in the dependent variable, the research has low internal validity.

Ensuring Internal Validity. Given the vast number of differences that characterize humankind, is it possible for a research design to ensure that groups of people differ only in the way the researcher intends and that it is that difference that explains the behavior being studied? Amazingly, the answer is yes. This feat can be accomplished by using an **experimental research design**. Two aspects of experimental design are crucial for internal validity.

experimental research design
a research design in which researchers randomly assign participants to different groups and manipulate one or more independent variables

First, researchers divide participants into groups that are expected to be equivalent. To do so, they use a technique similar to a lottery or a flip of a coin to assign participants to different groups. **Random assignment** gives every participant in an experiment exactly the same chance of ending up in any given experimental group. The beauty of random assignment of participants is that it ensures that the groups are approximately equivalent in every way. Suppose you started out with 20 people, 10 men and 10 women, and randomly divided them into two groups by flipping a coin for each person. Would it be likely that all of the women would end up in one group and all the men in the other? It could happen, but it is extremely unlikely; in fact, this outcome would occur less often than once in 500,000 times. Because the coin has the same chance of landing head-up each time it is flipped, every person has an equal chance of being assigned to the "heads" group. In the end, each group will probably have a roughly even number of males and females. The same logic applies not just to gender but to all attributes of the individuals who are being assigned: their age, eye color, friendliness, shoe size, and even other characteristics the researcher would not think of or could not measure. So random assignment creates groups that are, on the average, approximately equivalent to one another.

random assignment
the procedure of assigning participants to different experimental groups so that every participant has exactly the same chance as every other participant of being in any given group

This sets the stage for the second important step in an experimental design: The researcher now **manipulates**, or intentionally varies, the independent variable so that participants in the different conditions are exposed to different treatments. For example, members of one group may be exposed to a treatment intended to create a positive mood, while nothing special is done to the other group (such a no-treatment group is often called a control group). Because the groups were expected to be equivalent to begin with, this procedure creates groups that differ only in terms of the independent variable. Finally, the researcher measures the dependent variable. Now it is reasonable to conclude that any observed group differences in the dependent variable were caused by the manipulated independent variable, simply because no other differences between the groups are expected to exist. Of course, manipulations as well as measures must have good construct validity for an experiment to be meaningful. That is, a good manipulation (like a good measure) must successfully cause changes in the desired theoretical construct, but not in other, unintended constructs.

manipulate
intentionally varying some factor as the independent variable in an experimental research design

Donna Desforges and her associates (1991) used an experimental design when they set out to test the contact hypothesis. These researchers randomly assigned some participants, U.S. college students, to work cooperatively with a person described as a former mental patient. (The "patient" was actually a **confederate**, a research assistant playing a specific role in the study.) Other participants simply sat in the same room with the person. The students who interacted with the individual came to hold more positive beliefs about former mental patients than did the students who simply worked in the same room. We can be confident that the interaction caused this difference because the groups of students who received these two treatments were created by random assignment and therefore can be expected to be equivalent in every other way.

confederate

a research assistant playing a specific role in the study, such as pretending to be just another participant

"Well, I guess we're the control group."

Experimental Versus Nonexperimental Research Designs. A researcher who wishes to test a theory may choose either an experimental or a nonexperimental design. In general, experimental designs offer higher internal validity and therefore permit stronger tests of the causal relations between constructs. A nonexperimental study could produce results that are consistent with a causal theory by showing that the dependent variable and independent variable are correlated, meaning they are statistically linked so that people who have high values on one variable tend systematically to have high (or low) values on the other. For example, Kalin and Berry's (1982) finding that people who lived in ethnically diverse neighborhoods are lower in ethnic prejudice is certainly consistent with the contact hypothesis. The result does not provide strong support for the theory, however, because factors other than the independent variable could also be causing the observed pattern of results. Experimental designs provide stronger tests of theory because the combination of random assignment and manipulation of the independent variable rules out virtually all alternative explanations.

TABLE 2.1 Advantages and Disadvantages of Nonexperimental and Experimental Designs

Type of validity	Nonexperimental design	Experimental design
Internal validity	*Low*, because the lack of random assignment and manipulation means that alternative explanations for results may be possible.	*High*, because random assignment and manipulation allow alternative causal explanations to be ruled out.
Construct validity	*High*, if powerful effects of real-life variables—including those that cannot practically or ethically be manipulated—can be studied in their natural contexts.	*Low*, when practical or ethical constraints render manipulations weak or artificial. *High*, when manipulations can adequately vary theoretically important constructs.

Why, then, would a researcher ever use a nonexperimental design? The reasons are quite straightforward. First, some theoretically important independent variables, like gender, ethnicity, or area of residence, obviously cannot be intentionally varied. Thus, Kalin and Berry could not practically have assigned people to live in neighborhoods near or far from members of other ethnic groups. Second, for ethical reasons, researchers must not manipulate variables like participants' relationships with their spouse, feelings of depression, or the degree of their ethnic prejudice. And, finally, most of the time research manipulations just cannot be as powerful as the natural variation in constructs found in everyday life. For example, no experimental study of the effects of intergroup contact on prejudice could reproduce the effects of working side by side with colleagues of another race for a period of 10 or 20 years. For all these reasons, nonexperimental designs are sometimes the most appropriate. Table 2.1 summarizes the advantages and disadvantages of experimental and nonexperimental designs.

External Validity and Research Populations and Settings

To provide a valid test of a theory, research must have external validity, meaning that its results can be generalized to other people, settings, and times. Some theories apply to many different kinds of people and places, whereas others apply more narrowly. When a theory is intended to apply to a particular population and setting, external validity is ensured by conducting studies using that population and setting. When a theory is intended to apply generally across different people, places, and times, external validity is ensured by conducting repeated tests of the theory in diverse populations, settings, and cultures.

external validity

the extent to which research results can be generalized to other appropriate people, times, and settings

A single research study is usually conducted with a single type of participant at a single time and in a single location. Research has **external validity** if its results can be assumed to generalize, that is, to hold for other types of participants, other times, or other places relevant to the theory.

The results of the study by Desforges and her associates (1991), for example, offer support for the contact hypothesis. But you might wonder whether these results would be found only if the participants were North American college students, or only if the contact group was former mental patients. One of the important functions of research is to determine just how broadly theories generalize. Recall from the earlier discussion in this chapter that the more generalizable a theory is, the more powerful it is because it explains the behavior of many different people in many different situations. But not all theories claim to hold true for all people in all places (T. D. Cook & Campbell, 1979; Kruglanski, 1975): Some research aims at generalizing *to* specific people in specific places. Most of the research you will read about in this text, however, seeks to generalize more broadly *across* various kinds of people, places, and times.

Generalizing to Versus Generalizing across People and Places. In some research, a specific target population and setting are the researcher's primary interest. Applied research, where the goal is to use scientific findings to solve immediate practical problems, often falls into this category. For example, researchers have long known that when people have a sense of control over their situation, they cope better with stress. A physician might wonder whether an increased sense of control could help seriously ill patients cope better when they are hospitalized. A study that attempts to answer this question has a specific and relevant population and setting. Only people hospitalized with serious illnesses can be used as participants if the goal is to answer this particular research question. In fact, as a result of such studies, giving hospitalized patients some control over their situation is now a widely used technique for helping them deal with stressful medical procedures (Pranulis, Dabbs, & Johnson, 1975).

Most research you will read about in this text does not attempt to generalize to a single, specific target population or setting. Instead, as you will see, the research goal is usually a broader sort of generalization across many types of people in various times and places. Does the research apply, for example, to women as well as men? To Israelis and Koreans, as well as North Americans? To people living in the year 2030 as well as those living today? A typical study is conducted with a limited number of participants of a particular type—often college students—in one location at one point in time. Few people would be interested in research results that applied only to those participants at that time and place. The key question therefore becomes: Exactly what aspects of the research conclusions will successfully generalize?

Let us return to the example of the North American college students who engaged in a cooperative learning task in the laboratory with a person they believed was a former mental patient. Those students came to hold more favorable beliefs about one group, former mental patients (Desforges and others, 1991). One could ask whether exactly the same finding would be obtained among Ethiopian college students, Israeli sixth graders, or adults in Papua New Guinea. But social-psychological researchers rarely study participant populations as diverse as these; indeed, the very concept of a "former mental patient" would be meaningless to some of these groups. This is because researchers are usually not concerned with whether a study's specific findings can be directly generalized.

What is the appropriate generalization? To answer that question, we need to recall the fundamental reason why a study like this was conducted. That study was not aimed at generalizing to some target population or setting. Nor was it intended to reveal some modestly interesting fact about people's opinions of former mental patients, that is, about the specific dependent variable used in the study. Instead, the goal was to test a theory about causal relations between abstract constructs. In this case, the theory states that

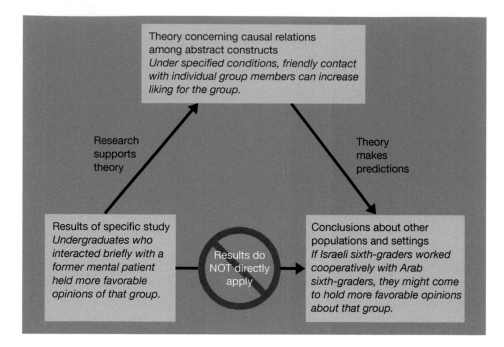

Figure 2.1 Research results generalize through theories
Most studies are conducted to test theories. The theory may then make predictions that apply to different people and places. The results of a particular study are not generalized *directly*, but they have implications for other people, times, and places to the extent that the results support a valid and general theory.

under specific conditions, friendly interaction with individual group members causes positive changes in people's attitudes and beliefs about the group. This theoretical level defines the generalization that is expected. So we would not expect all kinds of people around the world to hold the same views about former mental patients. We would, however, expect to find that similar processes of belief and attitude change are caused by friendly interaction with group members, and that is what the great majority of studies on the topic show (Pettigrew & Tropp, 2006).

Recall that we emphasized in Chapter 1 that you should seek to learn general principles about social psychology rather than a long list of findings of specific studies. In exactly the same way, researchers hope that the underlying principles, rather than the details of the findings, will generalize from one population and setting to other appropriate ones. Figure 2.1 illustrates this idea: The results of a study are not applied directly to another population or setting but are used to support a general theory, which in turn has implications for other people and places (Mook, 1980).

External Validity and Research Participants. External validity means that the results of research hold for other types of participants, other times, or other places relevant to the theory. The first major threat to such generalizations thus involves the types of people studied. One problem is the use of participants who are unrepresentative of all the people to whom a theory is intended to apply. College students differ in many ways from the average person (Henrich, Heine, & Norenzayan, 2010). For example, compared with the general population, they tend to be younger and more intelligent; they probably have less stable close relationships; they are still involved in forming new roles and images of themselves; they are less likely to have experienced serious illness, divorce, or parenthood. Can researchers assume that all research findings obtained with college student participants will generalize to all other types of people? Of course not.

As we have said, however, researchers ordinarily do not wish to generalize specific findings. Their usual goal is to generalize a broader conclusion about underlying causal relations between constructs. So one would not expect, for example, to find that the specific issues responsible for arguments and conflict were the same for both college dating couples and older married couples. Nevertheless, the causal effect of conflict on the partners' satisfaction with their relationships might be similar for both kinds of couples. Thus generalizing about causal explanations is more justifiable than generalizing about the specific content of thoughts and behavior.

Cultures and External Validity. People who have traveled outside their own country can testify that patterns of social behavior differ, and anthropologists' scientific observations confirm this conclusion. Since the findings of social psychologists come largely from Western countries, do the research conclusions of social psychologists generalize across the world's societies and cultures? It depends. We can answer this question only by examining the specific set of research conclusions that we expect to generalize. Consider the observation that people tend to have certain expectations, or stereotypes, about what other social groups are like. Though the stereotypes that French and Australian citizens (for example) have of the English will probably be very different, the way the two groups of people develop those stereotypes and how they use them are likely to be very similar. Culture strongly dictates the content of people's thoughts and actions. The processes by which that content is developed and used, however, are more likely to be generalizable.

If you are interested in how and why people form stereotypes, why they are so resistant to change, and what can be done to overcome that resistance, look at Chapter 5, where these topics are covered.

Sometimes, however, both content and processes can differ for members of different cultures. For example, members of Western cultures are particularly likely to think of themselves as separate from other people and to define themselves in terms of their uniqueness. For this reason, such cultures are often termed **individualist**. In **collectivist** cultures like Japan and many other Eastern nations, people tend to think of themselves as linked to others, and they define themselves in terms of their relationships to others (Markus, Kitayama, & Heiman, 1996). Such cultural differences influence the ways people process information about the self, respond to social conflict and disagreement, and experience emotions. Any theory on these topics that has been formulated and tested in only one type of culture may not generalize to members of other cultures.

The social-psychological processes that are most likely to operate in similar ways among diverse groups of people are the most basic processes. Research has shown

Photo 2.4 Cultural differences: When can research findings be generalized? These Chinese workers are participating in group exercises before the opening of a mall. Their notion of "working out" differs greatly from what someone from a Western culture would envision. Social psychologists—aware that not all research findings generalize across cultures—have started to integrate cultural effects into many scientific theories. These new findings are discussed throughout this book.

individualist cultures

those in which people are
particularly likely to think of
themselves as separate from other
people and to define themselves in
terms of their uniqueness

collectivist cultures

those in which people tend to think
of themselves as linked to others,
and to define themselves in terms
of their relationships to others

that these include the major principles that are the themes of this book, such as the ways people are influenced by others, use the most accessible information, and seek mastery over their environment and connectedness with other people. As you will see in later chapters, these are the sorts of processes many social psychologists have investigated, often using college students as participants because they are easily accessible. Still, the only way to be really sure that research conclusions generalize is to repeat the research with different types of participants because, as you will see, sometimes even conclusions about processes cannot be generalized (Jaffe, 2005).

External Validity and Laboratory Research. Another factor that can affect external validity is the setting or place in which the research is conducted. Each research setting, whether in the laboratory or outside it, has advantages and disadvantages that arise from its particular characteristics.

Most social-psychological research is conducted in the laboratory because the researcher can control this setting. In the laboratory, the researcher can randomly assign participants to different conditions, manipulate independent variables while keeping other factors constant, and measure dependent variables with high construct validity. The chief virtue of the laboratory setting is that experimental designs with high internal validity are most easily implemented there.

But the lab also has a down side. One disadvantage is the short time span of most studies, which usually last no more than a few hours. Another is the somewhat artificial quality of many laboratory manipulations and measures. A researcher may, for example, ask participants to donate to another student the points they earn in the experiment and then count those points and use them as a measure of the concept of helping. You might wonder how well such measures correspond to nonlaboratory examples of helping, like volunteering 3 hours a week at the church food pantry.

Another potential weakness of the laboratory for external validity is that participants probably pay much more attention to the information provided in the laboratory than they would in some other context. In laboratory research on persuasion, for example, participants read persuasive messages and their attitudes are measured. Different kinds of messages can then be shown to be more or less effective. But outside the laboratory people do not go around reading every persuasive communication they see! Do you read every ad for cold medicine in your bus or subway car? In everyday life outside the lab, the effectiveness of any persuasive message depends crucially on its ability to attract your attention. Thus, when processes operate in different ways in laboratory and nonlaboratory settings, theories supported by findings from the laboratory may not apply to nonlaboratory settings.

A final disadvantage of laboratory settings is that the knowledge that one is participating in research may itself elicit special motives. This can occur inside or outside the lab, but in lab studies such knowledge is virtually inescapable. Whenever people are aware that they are being studied, they may start to wonder, "What are they trying to get at here?" and their perceptions of the purpose of the research (whether the perceptions are accurate or wildly off base) may then affect their behaviors. Behaviors that are based on the participant's perceptions of the research purpose are said to be influenced by **demand characteristics**. Demand characteristics threaten construct validity because factors—the participants' impressions of what the researcher wants or expects—other

demand characteristics

cues in a research setting that lead
participants to make inferences
about what researchers expect or
desire and that therefore bias how
the participants act

than the intended construct may affect the participants' behavior (Orne, 1962; Rosenthal, 1969). When research takes place in a strange and novel environment like the laboratory, people are remarkably sensitive to subtle cues that tell them how they are expected to act. This effect was demonstrated in a study in which participants were asked to judge the degree of success or failure shown in a series of photographed faces (Rosenthal & Fode, 1963). One group of participants was guided through the study by a researcher who had been led to believe that the photos represented "successful" faces. The second group worked with a researcher led to believe that the same photos showed faces of "failure." Both researchers followed identical procedures and gave their participants identically worded instructions. Though participants were told nothing about the photos, they picked up clues about the expected responses from the researchers' subtle nonverbal behaviors. In each group, the participants' evaluations of the photos corresponded to the researcher's expectations. Because their responses reflected not only the intended construct (perceptions of the photos) but also demand characteristics (the responses the researcher seemed to expect), this study demonstrates how construct validity can be compromised.

To counteract demand characteristics, researchers often exercise extra precautions with members of the research team who will have contact with participants. These team members are prevented from knowing the responses that are expected from any particular participant, so they cannot subtly and unintentionally communicate those expectations to the participant. In addition, as you will see later in this chapter, researchers often attempt to conceal the true purpose of their research from participants and, in some cases, may even mislead participants about the purpose. Despite all these precautions, any research in which people are aware they are being studied always has to be carefully scrutinized for the potential impact of demand characteristics.

External Validity and Nonlaboratory Research. The strengths and weaknesses of **field research**—research that takes place outside the laboratory—complement those of laboratory research. Field researchers can study the long-term effects of such variables as relationship development or public health campaigns. They can measure concrete, powerful variables. For example, instead of counting the points students donate in experiments, they can count donations of blood as a measure of helping. They can study the effects of an earthquake prediction or other event that could not ethically or practically be reproduced in a laboratory. Thus, field research often has good construct validity. And if random assignment and manipulation of independent variables can be carried out in the field, the use of an experimental design can also provide good internal validity. When field experiments can be done they can produce impressive demonstrations of positive effects —such as long-term gains in minority schoolchildren's academic performance— that can occur from theoretically guided interventions in real-life settings (Walton & Cohen, 2011). However, for practical reasons, carrying out experiments outside the laboratory is often very difficult. As a result, most field studies are nonexperimental in design.

You should not make the mistake of assuming that research conducted in field settings always has more external validity than laboratory research. Diverse field settings, such as hospitals, airport departure lounges, and office cafeterias, also have particular characteristics that influence people's thoughts, motives, and actions in specific ways. Research conducted in one of these settings may or may not generalize to another, just as laboratory research may or may not generalize to a field setting.

field research
research that takes place outside the laboratory

Ensuring External Validity. The keys to achieving external validity, then, depend on the underlying research purpose.

1. *If the goal is to generalize to some specific target population and setting, the participants and setting must be representative of the target.* For example, if the goal is to see how assembly-line workers respond to changes in a supervisor's behavior, a study of assembly-line workers in their factory would be the most useful and appropriate.

2. *If the goal is to generalize across people, places, and times, the best way to do so is to repeat the research in multiple settings and with multiple populations, including people from different cultures.* Most of the research you will read about in this text is concerned with generalizing across people and places. Ultimately, as social psychology adopts a more integrative perspective and becomes less bound by Western culture, two important consequences will follow. Cultural variables, such as differences in self-conceptions, will be incorporated into theories so that cultural differences in social behavior can be explained rather than merely described. In addition, more research will be performed in diverse cultural settings, so that such broadly integrative theories can be developed and tested. Indeed, social psychology is currently moving in these directions (Nisbett, 2003; Markus, Kitayama, & Heiman, 1996; Henrich and others, 2010). Throughout this book, we will report the results of cross-cultural research whenever it throws new light on our understanding of the social and cognitive processes that influence human behavior.

Construct, internal, and external validity pertain to different aspects of the research process, are threatened by different factors, and are ensured by different types of strategies. Table 2.2 summarizes the most important characteristics of the three types of validity.

TABLE 2.2 Properties of Theories and Corresponding Characteristics of the Three Forms of Research Validity

Property of theory	Corresponding type of validity	Threats to validity	Relevant aspects of research	Ideal research characteristics
A theory deals with abstract constructs.	Construct validity: Observable variables used in research match the theoretical constructs.	Participants may respond in socially desirable ways or act in accordance with perceived demands.	Measures and manipulations	Multiple measures; multiple manipulations
A theory proposes causal relations among constructs.	Internal validity: Relationship among observable variables is due to postulated causal process.	Alternative causal explanations may be possible.	Designs	Experimental designs
A theory is general in scope, although the range varies across theories.	External validity: Research results can be obtained with many types of people, times, and settings.	Findings may apply to only limited types of people, times, or settings.	Populations and settings	Multiple replications in different settings

Evaluating Theories: The Bottom Line

Theories become generally accepted if the results of multiple valid studies show them to be superior to rival theories. Sometimes theories that seem to compete are in fact complementary explanations of events. Social-psychological research cannot help but be influenced by researchers' personal beliefs and cultural values. However, the rigorous use of research methods is our best hope for excluding the biases and errors that characterize everyday thinking.

Theories about social behavior ultimately stand or fall on the basis of how well they are supported by the results of valid research. As shown in Figure 2.2, the process involves a logical chain in which all three types of validity play a part. And just as a chain can be no stronger than its weakest link, each type of validity is crucial if research is to provide support for a theory.

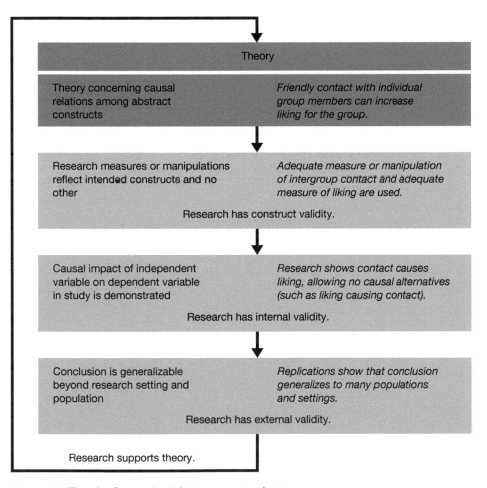

Figure 2.2 The role of research validity in supporting theory
To test a theory, researchers must follow a logical chain. Only if the research has high construct validity, strong internal validity, and good external validity can the theory be supported with confidence. Any weak link breaks the inferential chain.

Of course, no theory ultimately stands or falls on the basis of a single study. The results of any one study might have been influenced by simple mistakes by the researcher, the use of particular manipulations or measures, poor internal validity, special characteristics of the participants, or even chance variation. Indeed, researchers' attempts to increase one form of validity (for example, internal validity) often decrease other forms (external or construct validity). Kalin and Berry's (1982) survey testing the contact hypothesis in the field had high construct and external validity, as it measured long-term and powerful intergroup contact in the general population of Canada. But, as we pointed out earlier, that study had low internal validity because many differences other than degree of contact might explain the results. In contrast, the test of the same theory in a laboratory setting by Desforges and others (1991) had high internal validity because participants were randomly assigned to different levels of contact. But that study, in turn, had questionable external validity, given the artificial nature of the laboratory cooperative learning task.

replication

conducting new studies in an effort to provide evidence for the same theoretically predicted relations found in prior research

The Importance of Replication. Because no single study can be fully convincing by itself, researchers seek **replication**, or to reproduce the results of prior research. Indeed, scientists are required to report the procedures and methods used in their studies so that other researchers can repeat the research. The most important replications produce the same results by using different manipulations and measures of the theoretical constructs in studies carried out in different settings with different participant populations, because they help establish the generality of findings across differences in such specifics. Thus, for example, because studies as different as Kalin and Berry's (1982) survey and Desforges and her associates' (1991) laboratory tests show the same result, we can have greater confidence that intergroup contact does indeed increase liking.

The importance of replication in science means that when researchers are unable to replicate published findings, it is taken very seriously. In fact, in recent years increasing attention has been given to frequent reports of failures to replicate in many scientific fields ranging from psychology to the biomedical sciences (Pashler & Wagenmakers, 2012; McNutt, 2014). Some of these involve attempts at replicating a study using different manipulations or measures, suggesting that problems with construct validity may be responsible for the failure. More troubling are cases where researchers have sought to replicate the exact procedures (instructions, task materials, and so on) from a previous

Photo 2.5 The importance of replication. The Center for Open Science encourages and provides resources for scientists to conduct replications of studies. Initiatives like this underscore the importance of conducting replications in social psychology to ensure that theoretical insights from previous work are well supported and to identify possible ways in which theories may need to be refined.

C✽S   CENTER FOR OPEN SCIENCE   Home   About us ⌄   News   Jobs   Donate

WE FOSTER

OPENNESS

INTEGRITY

AND **REPRODUCIBILITY**

OF SCIENTIFIC RESEARCH

COS is dedicated to improving the alignment between scientific values and scientific practices. As a non-profit technology start-up, our team moves quickly from problem to solution, and continuously evaluates and improves our solutions. We blend science and technology in support of open science - transparency and inclusivity.

study, but still failed to obtain the same results. It is very difficult to know what such failures mean: did the effect depend on some highly specific aspect of the original research setting or population that cannot be reproduced in the replication attempt despite researchers' best efforts? Or was the effect not "real" in the first place, obtained originally by a mere fluke of chance?

The scientific response to the apparent difficulty of replicating many findings is still unfolding, but it will include greater emphasis on the importance and value of replication studies, and increased openness on the part of researchers about their exact methods and procedures, which is essential to permit others to attempt replications. Replication attempts, even those that fail to reproduce the original findings, can be of great scientific value if they help us understand problems with construct, internal, or external validity in specific studies. And repeated replication failures may point to weaknesses in the underlying theory itself. This may spur researchers to discard the theory and seek better explanations. Or it may encourage them to further elaborate the theory to describe more precisely the specific settings and contexts in which an effect is predicted to occur, as well as those in which it is not expected to replicate (Cesario & Jonas, in press). In this way, even failures to replicate can ultimately contribute to advancing scientific understanding.

Because replicated findings provide the most convincing support for theories, social psychologists often compare and combine the results of different tests of the same theory. They perform these comparisons using **meta-analysis**, a systematic technique for locating relevant studies and summarizing their results (H. Cooper, 1990; Rosenthal, 1991). Meta-analysis allows researchers to examine the generality of results across replications conducted by different researchers using diverse methods, settings, and participant populations. When many such studies all produce similar results, they provide stronger evidence for or against theories. Thus, for example, many studies of contact between groups, using widely varying participant populations and methods, have generally shown that it leads to increased liking. As a result we can have great confidence that intergroup contact does indeed increase liking (Pettigrew & Tropp, 2006). Because replication is so important, you will often see more than one study or the results of a meta-analysis cited to support conclusions reported in this text.

meta-analysis
a systematic technique for locating studies on a particular topic and summarizing their results

Competition with Other Theories. The theories that social psychologists propose to explain social events or processes sometimes compete with and contradict each other. Eventually, one theory may stand out among all the others as being more consistent with replicated research findings. This victory may be only temporary, however. Research in social psychology, like that in other sciences, is ongoing, and any day some psychologist may propose a new theory that is even better able to explain the set of research findings. For this reason scientists avoid applying the term proven to a theory. At best, a theory is generally accepted, a phrase that points to the importance of social consensus—the judgment made by the community of scientists.

In some cases, theories that first compete to explain research findings turn out to provide complementary explanations of events. Consider, for example, the competition that took place in the 1960s and 1970s between two theories that seemed to explain why attitudes often change to reflect people's behavior. In a series of studies, participants were assigned the task of writing an essay supporting a position they initially opposed. Researchers demonstrated that after the participants wrote the essay, their attitudes often became more similar to the view they had advocated in their writing (Goethals, Cooper, & Nacify, 1979; Linder, Cooper, & Jones, 1967). To explain these changes, one group of social psychologists, those who supported cognitive dissonance theory, argued that when people choose to act inconsistently (such as writing an essay they disagree with), the inconsistency creates psychological tension. The tension can be resolved, they proposed, if attitudes change to become consistent with behavior (moving toward the stand taken in the essay). In contrast, proponents of self-perception theory suggested that such changes occurred merely because people observed their own behavior and inferred their attitudes from their behavior. "I agreed to write the supportive essay, therefore I suppose I must have a supportive attitude."

Chapter 8 describes some of the many predictions that researchers have derived from cognitive dissonance theory and self-perception theory.

Although researchers conducted many studies and compared the predictions of the two theories, they were not able to settle the controversy. Cognitive dissonance theory and self-perception theory were each supported by some results, and neither theory gained general acceptance at the expense of the other. Finally, researchers Russell Fazio, Mark Zanna, and Joel Cooper (1977) noticed an interesting difference between the two sets of findings. Most successful tests of self-perception theory occurred when people behaved in ways not too inconsistent with their original attitudes. But the successful tests of cognitive dissonance theory seemed to be those in which people were induced to act in a way that directly opposed their initial convictions. This observation led Fazio, Zanna, and Cooper to suggest that the two theories offer a complementary understanding of the effect of behavior on attitudes. Perhaps self-perception processes operate to change attitudes when behavior is mildly different from initial attitudes. Cognitive dissonance processes, on the other hand, might kick in when behavior is so divergent from original attitudes that the discrepancy is upsetting. Further research confirmed their suggestions. Thus two theories that started out as seeming competitors now work together to provide a better understanding of the interplay between action and attitudes, as you will see in Chapter 8.

Getting the Bias Out. Perhaps you can see now why scientists prefer to believe well-supported theories, even if they sometimes conflict with common sense. Research methods are designed to exclude many biases and errors by maintaining concern with all three forms of validity. In contrast, common-sense conclusions often are invalid. Someone might fail to recognize that a friend's expressed admiration for their new hairstyle could be just a socially desirable response, and go on to incorrectly infer that the friend's true opinion is equally positive. Or a single encounter with a member of a new social group might be taken as evidence for what the group is like in general, ignoring the high probability of error in such an overgeneralization. In fact, common-sense ideas conveyed in sayings such as "birds of a feather flock together" and "opposites attract" can even be directly contradictory.

But scientists do not always successfully achieve their objective of excluding bias and error from their research methods. On the contrary, the scientific enterprise is full of judgment calls that open the door to such influences as researchers' personal attitudes and beliefs, cultural beliefs, educational background, scientific training, or religious, moral, and political views. Scientists, after all, are human beings and are no more able than anyone else to stand outside their culture and society and evaluate theories with a pure, detached rationality (Gould, 1978). Thus, they tend to prefer theories that are consistent with their culture's generally accepted beliefs and values. For example, the 1935 *Handbook of Social Psychology* contained chapters on the "negro," the "red man," the "white man," and the "yellow man." The contents reflected the unquestioned assumptions of that time—assumptions that most people today would regard as offensively racist and sexist. In addition, feminist psychologists have pointed out some cultural assumptions about women and men that have crept unnoticed into scientific practice (Hare-Mustin & Marecek, 1988; McGrath, Kelly, & Rhodes, 1993; Peplau & Conrad, 1989; C. W. Sherif, 1979). For example, in some areas of research such as the study of achievement motivation, conclusions were based almost entirely on responses of male participants. But unique aspects of women's behavior may never be discovered if results from men are assumed to generalize to all humans. And even if such differences are discovered, they may be inappropriately interpreted as mere deviations from the male "standard" rather than legitimate parts of the human standard (Cundiff, 2012).

Nevertheless, their fundamental reliance on research findings has often enabled social psychologists to expose and overturn generally accepted myths and falsehoods. For example, many social psychologists participated in preparing a statement presented to the U.S. Supreme Court in the 1954 *Brown v. Board of Education* case. Challenging the prevailing acceptance of "separate but equal" education for Whites and Blacks, the statement summarized research evidence showing that racially segregated schools could never be equal. That statement contributed to the Court's landmark decision to overturn legally enforced school segregation (Klineberg, 1986). Science is a human enterprise with no guarantees of objectivity. Nevertheless, its research techniques are the best ways yet devised to limit the effects of bias.

THE ROLE OF ETHICS AND VALUES IN RESEARCH

Social psychology is both similar to and different from other scientific disciplines. Like all scientists, psychologists have responsibilities to the scientific community. Scientists must not falsify or misrepresent their procedures or data. They must avoid personal attacks in scientific controversies, while engaging in full, no-holds-barred debates on theoretical and empirical issues. And they must allocate credit fairly for scientific work. They must not plagiarize other scholars' work, and in publications, they must give credit to all who earned it by working on the research project. Good science depends on the integrity of each researcher, and serious violations of these rules of conduct are not tolerated.

But social psychology shares with the other social and behavioral sciences a special element: humans are both the investigators and the investigated. In social-psychological research, there are people filling out questionnaires as well as devising them, people exposed to independent variables as well as manipulating them, and people in front of the camera as well as at the controls. Especially because of the inherently people-packed nature of social-psychological research, researchers must grapple not only with research problems and scientific responsibility but also with issues of values and ethics. When designing and conducting studies that might provide answers to questions about human behavior, researchers must always ask whether the end justifies the means. Do the research results justify the experiences of the research participants? And when the results are in hand, another question must be answered. If those findings can easily be applied to society as a whole, will the results of research be used in a socially responsible way? The issues of fairness to research participants and of social responsibility are a special part of social psychologists' scientific training (Ethical Principles of Psychologists and Code of Conduct, 2010, available at http://www.apa.org/ethics/code/principles.pdf).

Being Fair to Participants

Researchers seek to treat their participants fairly, often ensuring that participants know what they will experience in the study and agree to it in advance. However, to avoid biases when sensitive topics are investigated, researchers sometimes deceive participants about various aspects of the study. If deception is used, participants must be given information about research procedures and purposes at the conclusion of the study.

One of social psychology's best-known experiments began about 50 years ago when Stanley Milgram of Yale University sought to study the extent to which people would obey authoritative commands, even if other people would be harmed. In this famous research, which we will discuss in detail in Chapter 10, participants were led to believe that they were giving increasingly strong electric shocks to another person. That individual cried out in pain, demanded that the procedure be stopped because he had a heart condition, and ultimately fell silent, suggesting that he might be unconscious or even dead. Of course, none of this was true, but because participants believed it, the entire experience was extremely stressful for them.

Milgram's findings were no doubt important; perhaps, by extension, destructive obedience could occur in many real-life settings such as the military or the workplace. But did the results justify the research participants' experiences, which were far more difficult and stressful than they had expected? Many people now believe that the study violated a number of the special obligations psychologists have to their research participants.

Primary among those obligations, of course, is to avoid harming participants. Potential harm can come from several different sources. Self-reports or observations may reveal things about participants that they would not wish to have publicly known. In most studies, this threat is routinely averted by keeping participants' responses completely anonymous and unidentifiable. Another source of harm is that people can be upset or distressed by their participation in research, as in Milgram's research. Participants may experience intense distress when they are involved in potentially doing harm, are required to make difficult decisions, or are placed in situations over which they have no control.

Research participants also may be upset by their own reactions to events, as Milgram's participants may have been when they realized how readily they had agreed to give potentially fatal shocks. In fact, research on topics as divergent as helping and stereotyping often causes distress when participants later realize that their actions were socially undesirable. This is a dilemma social psychologists face: They want their research to address many important issues, but in such research some participants may discover potentially damaging information about themselves or others. How, then, can researchers ethically proceed with their studies? The answer is by obtaining participants' **informed**

informed consent

consent voluntarily given by an individual who decides to participate in a study after being told what will be involved in participation

consent, and social psychologists arrived at that answer partly in response to concern over research like Milgram's. Researchers must now help protect participants against the possibility of harm by telling participants they can withdraw from a study without penalty at any time. And they must give any volunteer enough information about the research to allow the person to make an informed decision about participating. "Without penalty" means that participants (often college students) cannot be coerced into participating, and any rewards resulting from participation, such as earning course credit, must be made available in alternative ways, such as through conducting library research. "Informed consent" does not mean participants are told everything about the research. They do not need to know the specific theory being tested, the rationale for the procedures, or other technical details. Participants must, however, be informed about and consent to the experiences they personally will undergo, such as filling out personality questionnaires, watching a videotape of erotic scenes, or participating in a group discussion. People who know they are free to participate and know what will happen to them if they do participate can freely choose to avoid any procedure they consider potentially harmful. How many of Milgram's participants do you think would have agreed to the experiment had they been informed in advance?

The Use of Deception in Research. Because of the importance of informed consent, ethical questions arise when researchers use **deception** to keep participants in the dark about various aspects of the research. Most instances of deception are relatively trivial. Participants are often told in advance what they will experience during the study (for example, watching a brief video clip and filling out a questionnaire) without being told the exact purpose of the study or the details of the procedure until their participation is complete.

deception
keeping participants uninformed or actively misleading them about particular aspects of a study

In other cases participants are actually misled about what will happen to them. Charles Hardy and Bibb Latané constructed an elaborate ruse to compare people's efforts on a task when they thought they were working alone versus their efforts in the presence of others. The researchers told participants the study concerned the effects of sensory deprivation on noise production. This explanation provided a rationale for having the participants wear earphones and blindfolds so that they had to rely on a researcher's word as to whether they were alone or with others. When told to yell and clap as loudly as they could, participants made less noise when they thought a second person was performing with them, compared to when they thought they were working alone (Hardy & Latané, 1986). Although deception was involved, its consequences were rather minor. But not all deception is this benign, as illustrated by examples like Milgram's research or the Stanford Prison Experiment, also described in Chapter 10.

This drop-off in individual effort often found in groups, called social loafing, is discussed in detail in Chapter 11.

Why would social psychologists engage in such practices? The point of deception, whether trivial or consequential, is to combat demand characteristics and social desirability biases while gathering information about socially important topics. Think honestly about how you would act if a researcher told you, "This study concerns the effects of racial prejudice on reactions to requests for help," or "We are testing the ways failure at an important task can affect people's self-esteem." Perhaps you and everyone else would refuse to participate, and thus these topics could never be studied. Even if you did agree to participate, how could you prevent your knowledge of the topic from affecting your responses? Perhaps you might try, with the best of intentions, to help confirm the researcher's expectations. Or you might act in the most socially acceptable way you could think of. Either of these reactions, which are responses to factors other than the researcher's intended causal construct, would invalidate the research findings.

Most researchers believe that many social-psychological topics, such as helping, aggression, racial and gender prejudice, and conformity, are so sensitive that deception is often necessary to produce valid results. Yet the use of deception frequently makes it impossible to obtain truly informed consent, and it runs counter to most people's ideas about honest and fair treatment of others. Once again the question arises: Does the end justify the means? Most researchers are willing to use deception as a last resort when they judge the research topic to be highly important and when no other alternatives are feasible. Even then, they try to keep deception to a minimum, and they inform participants of the deception as soon as possible through **debriefing**. Debriefing has several goals:

- The participant can raise questions and concerns about the research, and the researcher can address them.
- The researcher can fully explain any necessary deception.
- The researcher and participant can discuss the overall purpose and methods of the study, thereby enhancing the educational value of research participation.
- The researcher can detect and deal with any possible negative effects of the research.

Because most of these goals are important even for nondeceptive research, debriefing is now customary in most research. When deception is involved, however, debriefing is particularly important. If a participant is led to believe that he or she has failed at an important task, for example, the deception is carefully explained and every effort is made to ensure that participants leave the study feeling no worse than when they entered (L. Ross, Lepper, & Hubbard, 1975). In response to a heightened concern with ethical issues, the studies that social psychologists perform today usually have little potential for long-lasting harm. That was not always true of earlier studies. Consider Milgram's work again, for example. The researchers offered their participants extensive debriefing, but you may wonder whether any after-the-fact explanations could fully eliminate lasting ill effects of such powerful experiences (Baumrind, 1964; Milgram, 1964). Fortunately, most research shows that debriefing can provide deceived participants with more positive attitudes both about themselves and about research activities (Y. M. Epstein, Suedfeld, & Silverstein, 1973; S. S. Smith & Richardson, 1983; W. C. Thompson, Cohen, & Rosenhan, 1980). To do so, the debriefing must be thorough and professional, emphasize the importance of the research, and treat participants with respect.

When it comes to making difficult decisions about research ethics, a researcher is not forced to rely solely on his or her individual judgment. Since the mid-1970s, universities and other research institutions in the United States have established Institutional Review Boards. These committees, whose members include both scientists and members of the community, review and approve research plans before the research is conducted. They have the power to ask for changes in the plan or even to deny approval if they believe a study may harm participants. The greater ethical sensitivity that exists today, which was sparked largely by controversy over a few well-publicized studies like Milgram's, means that some types of study can probably no longer be performed. Take

debriefing
informing research participants—as soon as possible after the completion of their participation in research—about the purposes, procedures, and scientific value of the study, and discussing any questions participants may have

a moment to think about how you, as a member of a review board, would weigh the social and scientific importance of a study like Milgram's against the undoubted stress it would cause to participants.

Being Helpful to Society

Researchers have obligations as citizens and members of society to make choices about what topics to study and how their findings should be applied. Although social-psychological research cannot decide moral or ethical questions, valid research can provide relevant evidence to inform individual and societal decision making about such issues.

Like every individual, each scientist has his or her own conception of responsibility to society and to humanity. Social psychologists have long focused on major social issues like poverty, prejudice, pollution, and peace because we believe that our discipline can contribute to solving these problems. As you read this book, you will see some of the results of this research.

Of course, psychologists often disagree about social and political issues. In the area of research, these differences often show up as disagreements over how science can best serve society. For instance, one researcher who studies persuasion may firmly believe that advertising offers major economic benefits by informing consumers about available products and services. Another researcher may believe just as firmly that advertising manipulates and exploits consumers, encouraging people to spend money on products they do not truly need. Given their differences, these two researchers would presumably also disagree on the appropriate application of social-psychological research on persuasion. The first might act as a consultant, assisting companies that want to use the research to make their advertising more effective. The second might instead use the same research findings to develop ways to teach children to resist the lure of ads for faddish toys. And a third researcher might take a middle ground, endorsing the use of knowledge of persuasion processes in public health campaigns to encourage healthier lifestyles, but opposing their use in selling consumer products. These three views represent disagreements about how science can best serve society.

In practice, every researcher must come to her or his own decisions about how research findings should be applied. Psychologists can refuse to participate in research they find morally objectionable and can encourage others to do the same. Many researchers, for example, question the benefit of conducting research designed to show gender or ethnic differences, especially in politically and legally sensitive areas like leadership potential or propensity for aggression.

Social psychology is an empirical science, and as such it is designed to answer empirical questions. The results of research will not answer questions of morality and ethics: whether abortion is right or wrong, whether or when aggression is justified, or how much our individual freedoms should be curtailed by a government's concern for the population as a whole. Such issues must be decided by every individual—scientist and nonscientist alike—through the democratic political process. But we can hope that this political process is informed by the results of valid scientific research where it is relevant. This is one role that social psychology can play in the larger society. Although research cannot tell us whether abortion is right or wrong, it can tell us who has abortions and why, how women make such difficult decisions, how they adjust to the experience, and whether it has effects on their later emotions, attitudes, and behaviors. These are all issues that may enter into individuals' moral judgments.

CONCLUDING COMMENTS

Chapter 1 described how each of us, individually and as a member of social groups, constructs his or her own picture of reality. Scientists are no different from anybody else in this respect, even as they ply their trade. Relying on inference, deduction, and generalization, they draw on fragmentary, incomplete, and sometimes contradictory bits of research evidence to construct a coherent picture of reality. A scientific theory—a statement about unobservable causal relationships among abstract constructs—is intended to be such a picture.

Because scientific theories are invented rather than discovered, the scientific enterprise draws on its practitioners' creativity and imagination. The greatest contributions of Galileo, Newton, Darwin, and Einstein were not new data, but deep insights into new conceptions of reality that organized and explained existing evidence. On a more mundane level, creativity is also a crucial ingredient as scientists devise ways to test existing theories. A clever study, like a novel theory, is a product of creative imagination as well as disciplined hard work. As any social psychologist will tell you, this is one of the main reasons why doing research is fun.

Science is a human activity. Needless to say, then, it cannot be completely logical and unbiased. Just as scientists, like all humans, construct a version of reality based on bits and pieces of evidence, so scientists, like all humans, are subject to biases. Cultural values, political and religious views, and personal preferences may influence the problems that scientists choose to study or the theories they find congenial or abhorrent. Further, once a scientist creates or endorses a theory, it is likely to influence the way he or she evaluates research. A researcher may uncritically applaud some studies because their results support a "pet" theory, while dismissing less supportive studies as methodologically flawed or inadequately generalizable. Still, the standards and procedures of science, especially its public nature and its emphasis on the possibility of bias, limit the effects of such biases. And the danger of bias recedes even further when a number of studies conducted by scientists with diverse theoretical orientations in various places converge to support a theory.

This text now turns from "how we find out" to "what we know" about social behavior. However, the transition is not as drastic as you might think. As Chapter 1 pointed out, all of us, scientists and nonscientists alike, are constantly constructing theories to help explain what we experience. As you will see throughout this text, these processes are at work when people watch a football game, read a political advertisement, or deal with conflict in a relationship. One of the most important applications of these processes occurs when we get to know someone, when we form impressions of what others are "really like." Just as scientists try to explain "the facts" theoretically, we all gather information about others and try to make sense of it by forming a coherent impression.

The information we gather and the way we put it together can have a dramatic impact on how we act and react to the others around us.

SUMMARY

Research Questions and the Role of Theory. Research questions are provoked by curiosity about why people act the way they do. In turn, this curiosity often reflects concern about important social problems. Social psychologists seek to develop scientific theories to provide explanations for social behavior. A **scientific theory** is a statement about causal relationships among abstract, general **constructs**. It is a statement that holds for specified types of people, times, and settings. Because it specifies a causal relationship, theories are useful for designing **interventions**.

How Research Tests Theories. To provide a valid test of a theory, research must have three types of validity. **Construct validity** means that the **independent variables** and **dependent variables**—the concrete manipulations or measures used in the research—must correspond to the intended theoretical constructs. Construct validity is threatened by **social desirability response bias** if participants act in ways they think are socially desirable. Researchers ensure construct validity by manipulating and measuring independent and dependent variables in many different ways. Examples include **self-report measures**, **observational** and **archival measures**, as well as **performance measures**. More recently developed techniques include **physiological measures** and neuroscience-based measures such as **EEG** and **fMRI**.

To provide a valid test of a theory, research must also have **internal validity** so that observers can conclude that changes in the independent variable actually caused changes in the dependent variable. Internal validity depends mainly on a study's **research design**. In **nonexperimental research designs** (also called correlational designs) in which both independent and dependent variables are measured, the research may lack internal validity because many other unknown causal factors could affect the research results. **Random assignment** of participants to groups, followed by **manipulation** of independent variables, defines **experimental research designs**. Sometimes a **confederate** is used to administer a manipulation. Experiments allow researchers to draw stronger conclusions about cause and effect.

Finally, research must have **external validity**, meaning that its results can be generalized to other people, settings, and times, for example to both **individualist** and **collectivist** cultures. Some theories apply to many different kinds of people and places, whereas others apply more narrowly. When a theory is intended to apply to a particular population and setting, external validity is ensured by conducting studies using that population and setting. For example, **field research** may be conducted in specific settings, often limiting the potential effects of **demand characteristics**. When a theory is intended to apply more generally across different people, places, and times, external validity is ensured by conducting **replications**, repeated tests of the theory in diverse populations, settings, and cultures. Difficulties in replicating a finding may point to problems in specific studies, or to shortcomings in the underlying theory.

CHAPTER 2 THEMES

■ **Construction of Reality**
Scientific theories are developed to summarize and explain observed patterns of behavior.

■ **Pervasiveness of Social Influence**
Scientists are influenced not only by the rules and customs of science but also by personal and cultural values and goals.

■ **Striving for Mastery**
Scientists attempt to understand and predict nature.

Theories become generally accepted if the results of multiple valid studies, often summarized in a **meta-analysis**, show them to be superior to rival theories. Sometimes theories that seem to compete are in fact complementary explanations of events. Social-psychological research cannot help but be influenced by researchers' personal beliefs and cultural values. However, striving to maximize all three forms of validity is our best hope for excluding the biases and errors that characterize everyday thinking.

The Role of Ethics and Values in Research. Researchers seek to treat their participants fairly, often ensuring that participants know what they will experience in the study and agree to it in advance, a procedure called **informed consent**. However, to avoid biases when sensitive topics are investigated, researchers sometimes use **deception** or fail to inform participants about various aspects of the study. If deception is used, participants must be given information about research procedures and purposes in a **debriefing** at the conclusion of the study.

Researchers have obligations as citizens and members of society to make choices about what topics to study and how their findings should be applied. Although social-psychological research cannot decide moral or ethical questions, valid research can provide relevant evidence to inform individual and societal decision making about such questions.

PERCEIVING INDIVIDUALS

SALIENCE AUTOMATIC CONSERVATISM
SUPERFICIAL DISCOUNTING ACCESSIBILITY
MENTAL REPRESENTATION MASTERY
PRIMING PROCESSES SYSTEMATIC ASSOCIATION
CONNECTEDNES ATTRIBUTION

The summer before you entered college, perhaps you got in touch with your future roommate—did you email, text, IM, or friend her on Facebook? If you did exchange some information, post photos, and make plans for furnishing your room, you probably formed an impression of what your future roommate was like—whether a partier, a serious and studious person, or a committed social activist. Thinking back, did that impression match what you learned when you actually met your roommate? Interestingly, impressions formed online often turn out to be quite accurate. For example, people can make fairly accurate judgments about strangers' extraversion, conscientiousness, and likability from scanning their social-networking profiles (Back, Stopfer, Vazire, Gaddis, Schmukle, Egloff, & Gosling, 2010; Weisbuch, Ivcevic, & Ambady, 2009). And we can accurately assess someone's poise, warmth, and sociability after watching them even for just a few minutes (Ambady, Bernieri, & Richeson, 2000; Funder & Colvin, 1988).

What processes allow us to form accurate impressions based on such minimal information? Why do we immediately like some people and dislike others, sometimes without even knowing the reasons? This chapter explores the ways that people construct, maintain, and change their impressions of others. First, we describe how people rely on general knowledge plus some convenient principles to form first impressions of strangers. Surprisingly, these judgments are often quite accurate, at least accurate enough to let people move smoothly through most everyday social encounters.

Sometimes, however, we need to go beyond snap judgments to form detailed impressions of others. Employers must decide which job applicants are right for their business needs, and parents must decide which daycare providers would be the best fit for their child. And, of course, if we are deciding whom we want to befriend or work closely with, we might want to give the matter some extra thought. Does giving more thought to impressions increase their accuracy? Not necessarily, because, as this chapter explains, our motives and expectations can slant our judgments. Although Juliet may spend a lot of time thinking about Romeo, you probably would ask someone else if you wanted an impartial picture of his personality. As you will see, once our minds are made up, we find it hard to see, let alone accept, evidence that contradicts our views.

This chapter describes these processes of forming, maintaining, and changing impressions in the context of person perception, but as we will see throughout the text, fundamentally similar processes operate in all areas of social psychology.

Of course, sometimes we have to face facts that are clearly inconsistent with our impressions. What happens then? Our discussion concludes with a description of the ways we can change impressions to accommodate contradictory evidence. How we handle inconsistency has important consequences for the accuracy of our impressions— and therefore for the success of our dealings with others.

FORMING FIRST IMPRESSIONS: CUES, INTERPRETATIONS, AND INFERENCES

Try to answer a few questions about the people in Photo 3.1. Who would rather read the philosophical works of Jean-Paul Sartre than the latest Tom Clancy thriller? Who would prefer season tickets to the Metropolitan Opera and who to the Oakland A's baseball team? Which person would you choose to get together with for lunch? You can probably answer such questions fairly readily and with some confidence, because you formed a quick first impression of each person. Impressions include many elements, such as the person's physical appearance and behaviors (Carlston, 1994). However, the core elements are how much we like the person and what we think the person is "really like," including their underlying personality characteristics, personal goals, and values.

mental representation
a body of knowledge that an individual has stored in memory

Our knowledge about people's characteristics and the ways they are related to one another is one type of **mental representation**, a term for a body of knowledge an individual has stored in his or her memory (E. R. Smith, 1998). We have mental representations of objects, situations, people, and social groups. For example, our knowledge of chocolate, including what it looks, smells, and tastes like, is a mental representation. Our beliefs

Photo 3.1 Physical appearance offers many cues to people's personality and preferences, but these cues are interpreted through our own prior beliefs. Which of these people would you predict listens to country music? Who do you think reads up on stock market trends? What impression might you form of the woman second in line?

and impressions about members of particular occupations, nationalities, and ethnic groups are also mental representations. Because our stored knowledge influences virtually all of our social beliefs and behaviors, the effects of various types of mental representations are described throughout this text.

Why do we form and remember impressions of individuals? The answer is that impressions guide our actions in ways that meet our needs for both concrete rewards and connectedness to other people. An impression that someone is generous might lead you to approach her (rather than someone else) for a loan until payday. An impression that someone else is smart might encourage you to choose that person as a study partner. And general positive or negative impressions—our liking for some people and distaste for others—influence our choices of companions to spend time with or share our personal thoughts and feelings with, and ultimately, what close relationships we form. Thus, the impressions that we construct guide us along the paths of our social lives.

The Raw Materials of First Impressions

Perceptions of other people begin with visible cues, including the person's physical appearance, nonverbal communication, environments, and behavior. Familiarity also affects impressions, leading to increased liking. Cues that stand out and attract attention in the particular context in which they occur are particularly influential.

The raw materials of first impressions are the way people look, what they do, how they present themselves, such as in their online profiles, and the environments they choose, including their living spaces (Gosling, Gaddis, & Vazire, 2008; Vazire & Gosling, 2004). These cues are informative because we believe that appearance, behavior, and choices reflect personality characteristics, preferences, and lifestyles. This section considers these cues and the kinds of personal characteristics people believe they convey.

Impressions from Physical Appearance. According to tennis star Andre Agassi, "Image is everything." It may not be everything to everyone, but physical appearance certainly influences our impressions of other people, as it probably influenced your reactions to the people in Photo 3.1. After all, the way people look is usually our first and sometimes our only cue to what they are like. Our ideas about the meaning of physical appearance are endless. Blondes are sociable and fun-loving, but redheads are fiery and quick-tempered. People who wear glasses are scholarly and those with silvery hair are distinguished. People rely on many beliefs like these when they meet a stranger, even though many are unsupported by research.

Physical beauty, particularly a beautiful face, calls up a variety of positive expectations. Apparently people assume that "what is beautiful is good" (Dion, Berscheid, & Walster, 1972) or, as the German poet and philosopher Johann Schiller wrote over a century ago: "Physical beauty is the sign of an interior beauty, a spiritual and moral beauty" (1882). We expect highly attractive people to be more interesting, warm, outgoing, and socially skilled than less attractive people (Eagly & Makhijani, 1991; Feingold, 1992b). Moreover, this attractive-is-good belief transcends specific cultures: people from different cultures generally agree about who is physically attractive and about the traits attractiveness conveys (Dion, 2002).

For these reasons, physical appearance is an important element in people's attraction to strangers. In a classic study, Elaine Walster and her colleagues (Walster, Aronson, Abrahams, & Rottman, 1966) randomly paired college men and women for an evening of talking and dancing. The researchers unobtrusively rated each student's attractiveness and social skills, and they also obtained their grades and their scores on intelligence and personality tests. After the evening ended, the researchers asked the students how satisfied they were with their dates. The partner's physical attractiveness was by far the most important influence on both men's and women's satisfaction. It also strongly influenced the likelihood that the men would contact their partners to seek another date. None of the other variables measured in this study—intelligence, social skills, or personality differences—had a similar influence on liking for the partner.

Well, you may say, physical attractiveness may be important to college students in a dating context, but does it have more general effects? The answer is yes. People are more likely to imitate the behavior of an attractive stranger seen in a photograph, someone they never expect to meet, than a less attractive one (van Leeuwen, Veling, van Baaren, & Dijksterhuis, 2009). Elementary school teachers rate more physically attractive children as having more intelligence and greater academic potential (Clifford, 1975). More attractive defendants have lower bail set in misdemeanor cases (Downs & Lyons, 1991), and if they are convicted, they receive lighter prison sentences (Stewart, 1985). Apparently justice is not blind, after all! Attractiveness also shapes voting, with recent experiments showing that college students, especially those with little political knowledge, prefer more attractive fictitious candidates (Hart, Ottati, & Krumdick, 2011). No wonder then that taller candidates are more likely to be elected than their shorter rivals (McCann, 2001). Clearly, physical beauty has a pervasive influence on our impressions of other people, even when dating and romance are not at issue.

Beauty is not the only physical characteristic that influences perceptions of other people. Certain patterns of facial features also work this way. Some people have baby-faced features: large, round eyes, high eyebrows, and a small chin. In studies conducted in both the United States and Korea, Diane Berry and Leslie McArthur found that baby-faced adult males were viewed as more naive, honest, kind, and warm than males of more mature facial appearance (Berry & McArthur, 1985; McArthur & Berry, 1987). Because of these perceptions, baby-faced adults are more likely to be chosen as dates by people who like to dominate others, but are less likely to be recommended for jobs that require mature characteristics like competence or leadership ability (Zebrowitz, Tenenbaum, & Goldstein, 1991). A fascinating study by Alexander Todorov and his colleagues (Todorov, Mandisodza, Goren, & Hall, 2005) showed that impressions of competence based on facial appearance, much like physical attractiveness, can influence voting. The researchers showed people facial photos of two candidates running for office in distant states, and asked those people (who did not recognize any of the candidates) which one appeared more competent. Amazingly, the candidates chosen by the participants as appearing more competent were actually more likely to win their elections! In contrast, candidates whose faces looked more threatening were less likely to win (Mattes, Spezio, Kim, Todorov, Adolphs, & Alvarez, 2010). Although voters in elections often know the candidates' party affiliations, stand on issues, and how much experience they have, the results of these studies suggest that initial impressions based on physical appearance also contribute to voting choices.

SOCIAL PSYCHOLOGY IN PRACTICE: PHYSICAL APPEARANCE IN THE WORKPLACE

Impressions based on physical appearance can impact everyday work lives. Good news for tall men: One researcher found that newly hired professional men taller than 6 feet 2 inches received starting salaries 10 % higher than those given to men under 6 feet (Knapp, 1978). And a study by economists found that in both the United States and Canada, workers with below-average looks earned as much as 10 % less than their average-looking counterparts, whereas those with above-average looks earned about 5 % more than average (Hamermesh & Biddle, 1993). These findings were not limited to occupations such as sales or customer service, where good looks might naturally help attract customers. The benefits of particular physical attributes don't just accrue to their holders. Consider the outcome of a study in which Nicholas Rule and Nalini Ambady (2008) asked students to rate the traits of CEOs of some U.S. corporations after seeing only their photos. Judgments of the CEOs' "power-related traits" like competence and maturity predicted the company's actual profits! Perhaps this is because their facial features gave the CEOs an advantage in negotiations or in influencing other people.

Interestingly, the benefits of being attractive in the workplace may not be as universal for women as they are for men. One study showed that being attractive is equally helpful for men regardless of whether they are applying for jobs thought of as masculine or as feminine; however, attractiveness helped women more when they applied for feminine jobs than when they applied for masculine ones (Johnson, Podratz, Dipboye, & Gibbons, 2010). Furthermore, the same study showed that being attractive might actually be harmful for women applying for masculine jobs for which good physical appearance is not valued (e.g., mechanical engineer).

Impressions from Nonverbal Communication. Did your mother tell you that the proper way to greet people was to "stand up straight, look them in the eye, smile, and shake hands firmly"? If so, she knew how much information is communicated by facial expressions, eye contact, and body language. Nonverbal communication influences whether we like people, how we think they are feeling, and what we think they are like. In general, we like people who express their feelings nonverbally more than less expressive individuals (Friedman, Riggio, & Casella, 1988). Specific nonverbal cues also affect liking, even when we're not aware of them. In individualist cultures like the United States, we like people who orient their bodies toward us—facing us directly, leaning toward us, nodding while we speak—and we believe that they like us (Mehrabian, 1972). We also tend to like people who look at us with dilated pupils—a sign of interest and attention—even though we typically don't consciously notice this feature (Niedenthal & Cantor, 1986).

Body language offers a special insight into people's moods and emotions (Ekman, Friesen, & Ellsworth, 1972). In such diverse cultures as those of Germany, Hong Kong, Japan, Turkey, and the United States, people express sadness and happiness, fear and anger, surprise and disgust with similar bodily postures and facial expressions (Ekman and others, 1987). Based on such findings, researchers concluded that emotional expression is a kind of universal language. However, other findings show that despite some general agreement, interpretations of emotional expressions often differ between cultures, particularly for the emotions of surprise, sadness, and disgust (Markus, Kitayama, & Heiman, 1996; Russell, 1994).

Impressions from nonverbal behavior can be formed quickly and are often quite accurate. For example, Nalini Ambady and Robert Rosenthal (1993) asked individuals

As we will see in Chapter 4, p. 117, the very basis of emotions—whether they arise from a person's private feelings or from a network of social relationships—also differs from one culture to another.

to watch three 10-second, silent videos of teachers giving a class lecture and to rate the teachers on traits such as warmth, honesty, confidence, and enthusiasm. Even with only these 30 seconds of visual information, watchers' impressions agreed quite substantially with how the teachers' own students rated them in end-of-semester evaluations! Nonverbal behavior also conveys status information equally accurately. When researchers showed participants photos of a brief interaction between two co-workers they didn't know, participants could nevertheless accurately judge which co-worker had higher status (Mast & Hall, 2004). Visual cues aren't the only ones that convey information. In one study, students listened to the recorded voice of a person reading text and then tried to judge which of two same-sex photos showed the person they had just heard. Surprisingly, they were accurate over 75% of the time, suggesting that voice cues alone convey a great deal about a communicator (Krauss, Freyberg, & Morsella, 2002). Thus, individuals can form clear and often quite accurate impressions by observing "thin slices" of even strangers' nonverbal behaviors (Ambady & Rosenthal, 1993).

Detection of Deception. Have you ever wondered how people can be gullible enough to lose their savings to a con artist who has told them some outrageous lie? Or how an instructor could believe some far-fetched excuse spun by one of your classmates? Perhaps you told yourself that you could never be so easily deceived. Maybe not, but detecting lies is not always easy. Indeed, a review of over 200 lie-detection studies suggests that perceivers are, on average, correct in classifying statements as lies or truths only about 54% of the time, a percentage just slightly better than chance (Bond & DePaulo, 2006). Isn't this surprising, given that initial impressions can sometimes be so accurate? One answer to this puzzle is that although liars often give themselves away with nonverbal cues, people don't watch for the right ones (Ekman & Friesen, 1974). Most people look for evidence of deception

HOT TOPICS IN SOCIAL PSYCHOLOGY: CAN YOU JUDGE A BOOK BY ITS COVER?

Recent research illustrates the accuracy of some judgments based on facial appearance, alongside inaccuracy in judgments of trustworthiness or deception. Nicholas Rule and his colleagues (2013) gave students a test under conditions that tempted them to cheat by working longer than the allotted 5 minutes on a set of problems, on which the highest scorer would be given a prize. They also obtained the students' self-reports of their level of extraversion. Raters from a different university were shown photos of these individuals and rated their intelligence, extraversion, and trustworthiness. Were these ratings accurate? Intelligence as judged from a photo was related to the students' actual performance on the test, and ratings of extraversion related to the students' self-reports on this personality dimension. However, ratings of trustworthiness told a different story. Although the raters tended to agree on who looked more trustworthy and who looked less so, these ratings were completely unrelated to whether the students had cheated on the test. A separate group of raters made judgments of trustworthiness about the same photos, while in an fMRI scanner. Activity in the amygdala, a brain region that is central for person perception, was found to relate to judgments of trustworthiness. However, once again both the judgments and the measured amygdala activation were unrelated to the students' actual honesty. It remains for further research to determine what specific facial-appearance cues are responsible for the agreement among raters on who looks trustworthy, in the absence of any relation between that appearance and actual trustworthiness or honesty.

in a liar's face or words, when in fact these are what the liar can easily control to lead observers astray (DePaulo, Lassiter, & Stone, 1982). Paying attention instead to the diagnostic hints of deception, such as a quivering or high-pitched tone of voice, can increase successful detection of lies from those within our own culture, as well as from those from other cultures (Bond & Atoum, 2000). The fact that people use the wrong cues to assess truthfulness helps explain why initial impressions based on nonverbal cues can be accurate but detecting deception is hard. When people are focused on the "thin slices" of behavior that actually betray deception, they become much better at detecting it.

Impressions from Familiarity. Most of us tend to develop positive feelings about the people we encounter frequently in our everyday lives (Festinger, Schachter, & Back, 1950; Zajonc, 1968). Of course, such encounters may lead to an acquaintanceship or even friendship, as we will discuss in Chapter 12. But even when little or no interaction takes place, **mere exposure** to another person increases liking. Richard Moreland and Scott Beach (1992) demonstrated this effect when they arranged for four women to attend varying numbers of sessions of a large college lecture course. The women sat quietly and took notes without interacting with any of the students. At the end of the semester, students in the course viewed photos of the women and answered questions about their impressions of them. The students thought the women they had seen more often were more interesting, attractive, warm, and intelligent than the women who had attended fewer class sessions. The students also thought they would like the more familiar women better and would enjoy spending time with them. As you can see, familiarity

mere exposure
exposure to a stimulus without any external reward, which creates familiarity with the stimulus and generally makes people feel more positively about it

---

SOCIAL PSYCHOLOGY IN PRACTICE: LIE DETECTION IN THE LEGAL SYSTEM

Given the difficulty of detecting deception, perhaps it is not surprising that some people have looked for more mechanical means of exposing dishonesty. The most widely used "lie detector" is a polygraph, a device that measures signs of physiological arousal, such as rapid breathing, increased heart rate, and sweating, as the test taker answers questions. Because people cannot completely control these responses, increased arousal is assumed to reveal the extra stress and effort of lying. However, research evidence suggests that polygraph examinations are not precise enough to warrant their widespread use. In one study, for example, polygraph examiners correctly detected 75 % of guilty suspects, but they also declared guilty 37 % of those who were actually innocent (Lykken, 1985; Saxe, Dougherty, & Cross, 1985). Most scientists are skeptical about the accuracy of polygraph testing (National Research Council, 2003).

Nevertheless, polygraph tests continue to be widely used. Much of their apparent effectiveness may derive from superstitions about the device rather than from its inherent accuracy. Some criminal suspects who anticipate that their lies will be detected may decide to confess when confronted with a polygraph examination (Lykken, 1985). Similarly, some dishonest job seekers may avoid employers who use the polygraph to screen applicants. Yet, because of the lack of evidence in support of the accuracy of polygraphs, some scholars have advocated for the development of other technology-based lie detection systems (Iacono, 2008). Some, like those based on functional magnetic resonance imaging (fMRI), are already emerging (e.g., Wolpe, Foster, & Langleben, 2010) and have been shown to reliably separate truth tellers from liars in laboratory-based settings. The effectiveness of these methods in real-world criminal cases awaits rigorous empirical testing.

alone can be one basis for developing a positive impression and feelings of liking for another person.

Impressions from Environments. Clues to others' personality, behavior, and values can be seen in the real and virtual environments they inhabit and create. For example, your dorm room might feature a poster of Martin Luther King or a large collection of science-fiction books; your work area might be well organized or messy; your Facebook profile might denote that you "like" Barcelona football and cats. Can observers form impressions of you from these types of cues? To find out, Samuel Gosling and his colleagues (Gosling, Ko, Mannarelli, & Morris, 2002) had a number of observers look around bedrooms in apartments or college dorms (with the occupants' permission, of course!) and then rate their impressions of the person who lived there. The observers never met the occupants, and photos and any references to the occupant's name were covered up. Yet the impressions the observers formed based on the rooms were quite similar to the way the occupants of the rooms rated themselves. Remarkably, similar levels of accuracy were obtained in another study in which observers looked at single-person offices or cubicles in a bank, a real estate agency, and other businesses—even though office decor is much more restricted than that in a bedroom.

Thus, perceivers seem capable of forming fairly accurate impressions of others by observing the physical spaces they occupy. But today, virtual environments also serve as a reflection of people's identities and personalities. Nowhere is this more evident than on social-networking sites like Facebook, where users can list their interests, upload pictures and videos of themselves and their friends, as well as post "status updates" to convey their thoughts and opinions on matters both trivial and serious. As with real-world environments, perceivers seem capable of accurately forming impressions from these virtual representations. To illustrate this, Mitja Back and colleagues (2010) obtained personality ratings of social-networking users in the U.S. and Germany from both the users themselves and from their close friends. Then, other participants examined the social-networking profiles of the users and made personality judgments about them. Results showed that participants' impressions correlated highly with the users' personalities on nearly every dimension measured. Because we select and create physical and virtual environments that both reflect and reinforce who we are, observers can evidently learn a lot about us from those environments.

Photo 3.2 What type of person do you think lives in this room? Do you think the person who lives here is trustworthy or unreliable? Studious or lazy? We often infer a great deal about people based simply on what's in their living quarters, and often with good accuracy.

Impressions from Behavior. By far the most useful resource for developing an impression of another person is the individual's behavior (Gilbert, 1998). If you know that someone donates hours of free time working in a local food bank, you may reasonably conclude that the person is caring, altruistic, and philanthropic. If you find out that someone stole money from a cash register at work, you can probably assume that he or she is dishonest. As in these examples, many behaviors are strongly linked to particular personality traits. Indeed, people are often advised to judge others by their deeds, not by their appearance or their words. The processes by which people draw inferences from others' behaviors will be described in detail shortly.

Which Cues Capture Attention? Imagine sitting in the cafeteria idly watching those around you. What cues attract your attention? You might notice that one person makes nasty comments to the clerk at the cash register, that another drinks three cups of coffee in quick succession, and that a third towers over all the other people in the room. Characteristics that are different stand out, and this is true for all kinds of characteristics, including behaviors such as making rude comments or physical cues like tallness. Or suppose you learn that someone has two hobbies: playing tennis and keeping snakes as pets. You will probably find the person's unusual taste in pets more revealing than the more commonplace athletic interests. If you were going to buy this person a book as a gift, would you be more likely to choose one on snakes or one on tennis? Research suggests you'd go for herpetology (Nelson & Miller, 1995).

In cases like this, what makes a characteristic stand out is its rarity or uniqueness. **Salience** refers to a cue's ability to attract attention in its context. Of course, a cue that is unusual or unexpected in one context may be quite normal in another, as Figure 3.1 shows. The person who towered over everyone might be salient in the cafeteria but not on the basketball court, surrounded by equally tall team members. Thus, attributes that stand out in one context may be quite normal in another. When we have information about a person's physical appearance, their nonverbal communication, their chosen environments, and some of their behavior, those aspects that are salient are likely to grab our attention and provide the basis for first impressions.

salience
the ability of a cue to attract attention in its context

Unusual and salient characteristics not only make a difference in our impressions of others, but also help us define ourselves, as you will see in Chapter 4, page 100.

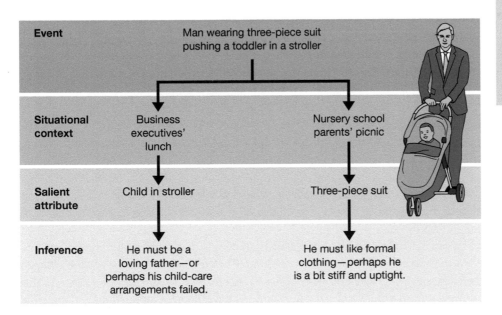

Figure 3.1 Salient cues dominate impressions
Our impression of the same individual may differ greatly from one situation to another because attributes that stand out in one context may go unnoticed in another. An attribute that is salient in its context may give rise to inferences that become part of our first impression of a person.

Automatic Interpretations of Cues

Cues have no meaning in themselves. Instead, they are interpreted in light of our stored knowledge about people, behaviors, traits, and social situations. Stored knowledge that is linked to the cue itself or is easy to bring to mind is most likely to be used in interpreting cues.

We seem to leap effortlessly from the cues of appearance, body language, familiarity, environments, and behavior to liking or disliking a person, and to conclusions about his or her inner characteristics. Yet none of the cues we use in perceiving people have much meaning in themselves. No behavior, appearance, gesture, or expression indicates a person's inner qualities directly. Instead, even our first impressions rely on rapid but seemingly effortless cognitive processes (Chun, Spiegel, & Kruglanski, 2002; Gilbert, 1998). Termed **automatic**, these processes operate spontaneously even when we are not specifically trying to make sense of another individual. They operate efficiently, that is, even when we are processing superficially rather than devoting a lot of thought to the issue. And they often operate without our awareness of them occurring at all (Bargh, 1994).

> **automatic**
> refers to processes that operate spontaneously (without the perceiver's deliberate intent) and often efficiently and without awareness

The first step in processing is interpreting the cues themselves: deciding whether a wrinkled brow reflects menace or puzzlement or whether a lie is an act of deceit or of loyalty. Two crucial kinds of stored knowledge help us make these decisions: the **associations** we have already learned and the thoughts that are currently in our mind.

> **association**
> a link between two or more mental representations

The Role of Associations in Interpretation. On learning that someone was caught stealing money from the cash register at the local convenience store, most people immediately conclude that the person is dishonest. Why do we jump to that conclusion? The answer has to do with the strong link that exists between two mental representations. Our concept of stealing money is associated, or linked, to our knowledge about the trait of dishonesty. When we think about stealing, the associated trait of dishonesty is activated, or brought to mind. To understand why association is important, imagine a child's toy box containing a jumble of all kinds of toys, among them a paddle connected by a string to a rubber ball. If you pull the paddle out of the box (think of this as hearing about the behavior of stealing), you can be sure the ball (the associated trait of dishonesty) will soon follow.

Associations can arise from similarity in meanings between two mental representations, like the similarity between the act of stealing and the concept of dishonesty. However, even unrelated ideas can become associated if they are repeatedly thought about together. Thus, Brad and Angelina, cops and robbers, and Windows and Microsoft have become associated concepts for most of us. Of course, these learned connections depend on the culture that surrounds us. Suppose a co-worker expresses agreement when you voice objections to his new plans, but then goes ahead with the plans anyway. A North American might decide that this kind of behavior signals insincerity, but in Japan the same behavior, agreeing with criticism, is regarded as simple politeness. As this example suggests, members of different cultures have different associations and therefore arrive at different interpretations for the same behavior (Markus and others, 1996).

Once we form an association, it links the two mental representations just as the string links the paddle to the ball. If either of the linked representations comes to mind, the other will usually come to mind also. Because of these patterns of stored associations, some cues are easier to interpret than others. For example, the act of turning in money that was found in a lonely spot with no witnesses is so closely connected with our idea of honesty that we would be hard pressed to interpret the behavior in any other way. Similarly, superior performance in the decathlon immediately conjures up the idea of athleticism. In cases like these, people spontaneously think of the associated trait when they comprehend a behavior, even if they are not specifically trying to form an impression of the person (Uleman, Saribay, & Gonzalez, 2008).

The Role of Accessibility in Interpretation. The meaning of a behavior is not always so clear. Imagine discovering that someone you know had shared test answers with a classmate. How would you interpret that behavior? The act of sharing could reflect either helpfulness or dishonesty, and you might have difficulty choosing one interpretation over the other. In such cases, we tend to rely on relevant information we currently have in mind. The **accessibility** of knowledge—the ease and speed with which it comes to mind and is used—exerts a powerful influence on the interpretation of behavior or other cues. Going back to our toybox metaphor, accessible toys are those near the top of the pile, whereas the less accessible ones are buried near the bottom.

accessibility
the ease and speed with which information comes to mind and is used.

The more accessible the knowledge, the more likely it is to come to mind automatically, without our consciously trying to retrieve it, and the more likely it is to guide our interpretation of cues (Ford & Thompson, 2000; Higgins, 1996a). Thus, someone whose ideas about helpfulness are highly accessible may interpret the act of sharing answers as a helpful act. Another person, perhaps an instructor for whom the concept of academic dishonesty is more accessible, might see the same behavior as dishonest—a quite different interpretation. Knowledge becomes accessible and influences how we interpret cues in three main ways. First, it can be activated by some other cause concurrently—at the same time—that the cue occurs. Second, knowledge can be accessible because it has recently been activated. Third, knowledge can be accessible because it is frequently or chronically activated.

Accessibility from Concurrent Activation. Whatever thoughts are in our mind when we are interpreting cues activate related mental representations, making them highly accessible and thus likely to affect our interpretations. For instance, moods have a well-documented impact on how we react to others. People in a happy and cheerful mood see both their own and others' behavior through rose-colored glasses, evaluating all behavior more positively than do people in neutral moods (Isen, 1987; Williamson & Clark, 1989). This is because how good or bad we feel activates other positive or negative information, and makes it more accessible when we interpret cues.

Sometimes already activated concepts can have very subtle influences on interpretations and therefore impressions. In English-speaking countries, we often use metaphors of physical weight to describe concepts that are serious or important—a weighty issue is an important one, for example. As a result, physical sensations of heaviness may in turn activate concepts of importance or seriousness. In one recent study illustrating this possibility, people were asked to judge a job candidate whose résumé was placed on either a heavy or a light clipboard (Ackerman, Nocera, & Bargh, 2010). Those holding the heavier clipboard judged the candidate as more serious about the job than did those holding the lighter clipboard.

An important source of expectations about other people is their social group memberships (age, gender, ethnicity, occupation, and the like). The powerful effects of such expectations will be discussed in detail in Chapter 5.

Our current expectations also act as accessible knowledge that can powerfully influence our interpretations. In a classic demonstration of the effects of expectations, Harold Kelley (1950) arranged for a guest instructor to conduct 20-minute discussions in psychology courses. Before his appearance, the students were given background information about the guest instructor. Different students were given different background information and thus had different concepts already activated. Some students learned that the guest instructor was "a very warm person, industrious, critical, practical, and determined." Others were informed that he was "a rather cold person, industrious, critical, practical, and determined." All students then had an extensive opportunity to observe the instructor's actual behavior during the discussion. When the students later rated his personality, the results clearly demonstrated the effects of expectation. Students who had the expectation of warmth activated interpreted the instructor's behaviors in light of this, seeing him as more considerate, informal, sociable, popular, good-natured, humorous, and humane than did those who expected a colder individual.

The effects of expectations on social perception are pervasive (Harris, 1991; Rosenthal, 1985). Supporters of opposing candidates in presidential debates expect that their own candidate will show statesmanlike behavior and leadership potential and will win the debate. And when the debate is over, each group of supporters is usually sure that they saw just that (Kinder & Sears, 1985). And because doctors and staff in psychiatric hospitals expect their patients to display disturbed behavior, one study found that they were unable to detect perfectly normal people who had themselves admitted to a hospital under a ruse (Rosenhan, 1973).

Our expectations about situations also activate related information, which we then use to help interpret behavior. Look at Photo 3.3a, for example. Is the man expressing grim determination or anger? Yaacov Trope (1986) found that people answer such questions in different ways, depending on what has already been activated by the situation. Trope showed students photos of people wearing ambiguous facial expressions together with information about the context. The same expression looked grief-stricken to students who were told the photographed person was attending a funeral, but was interpreted as tearful laughter by those who thought the person was at a comedy performance. Indeed, situational information can override even relatively unambiguous facial expressions when people interpret others' emotions (Carroll & Russell, 1996).

Accessibility from Recent Activation. A toy that a child has recently used can be found near the top of the toy chest. Similarly, a mental representation that has recently been brought to mind also remains accessible for a time (Wyer & Srull, 1989). Therefore, anything that brings an idea to mind—even coincidental, irrelevant events—can make it accessible and influence our interpretations of behavior. Imagine walking down the street with a friend and noticing in passing a *Die Hard* movie poster featuring Bruce Willis in an aggressive pose holding a handgun. Could the poster increase the accessibility of your mental representations related to hostility and aggression? If so, might it influence your interpretations, leading you to see hostility in an ambiguous remark made by your friend when none was intended?

The answer to both of these questions is yes. To demonstrate this effect, Tory Higgins and his colleagues (Higgins, Rholes, & Jones, 1977) asked students to memorize several words. One group memorized words related to the positive trait *adventurous*, whereas another group learned words related to the negative trait reckless. This procedure was intended to activate stored knowledge about one or the other of these two traits, thereby making that knowledge accessible for a time. Then, in what students thought was an unrelated experiment, they read a description of Donald, who had climbed Mount McKinley, gone white-water kayaking, and driven in a demolition derby. Later, the two groups were asked to describe Donald's activities. Their descriptions showed that the first group of students, for whom adventurous was accessible, saw Donald's behavior as daring, whereas those who had focused on words relating to reckless saw his behavior as foolhardy and rash. Correspondingly, the "adventurous" students evaluated Donald more positively than the "reckless" group.

Activating a mental representation to increase its accessibility and make it more likely to be used is called **priming**. Naturally, the effects of an activated representation will decrease with the passage of time. However, the effects of priming can be long-lasting: Concepts that have been primed have been shown to remain accessible and influence later interpretations for as long as 24 hours (Was, 2010). The impact of priming does not even depend on people's awareness of the activation! To demonstrate this, John Bargh and Paula Pietromonaco (1982) showed some participants neutral words, whereas others saw words related to the trait of hostility. Then both groups read a description of a character's ambiguous behaviors. When the groups' responses were compared, those primed with the hostility-related words interpreted the behaviors as more hostile and aggressive. The interesting twist is that the presentation of the priming words was **subliminal**—a very brief flash on a computer screen—so the participants could not say what the words were. Even when people are unable to identify a word consciously, encountering the word can still make mental representations accessible and influence the interpretation of later information. Other similar studies have confirmed this remarkable finding (DeCoster & Claypool, 2004). So even if you just glimpse the Bruce Willis poster out of the corner of your eye without consciously registering it, it might make you interpret someone's behaviors as aggressive.

priming
the activation of a mental representation to increase its accessibility and thus the likelihood that it will be used

subliminal
presentation of stimuli in such a way (usually with a very brief duration) that perceivers are not consciously aware of them

Chapter 7, especially page 244, will discuss the thought-provoking possibility that our attitudes might similarly be influenced without our awareness.

Accessibility from Frequent Activation.

What toys are usually found lying at the top of the toy box? The ones that get dragged out and played with every day. The same is true of thoughts. The frequent use of a mental representation over days, months, or years can make it chronically accessible (Bargh, Bond, Lombardi, & Tota, 1986; Higgins, 1996a). When this happens, people repeatedly use the same concepts in interpreting others' behavior. For example, intelligence might always be important in one person's judgments, whereas friendliness or helpfulness might matter more to someone else. In fact, people can more easily recognize information relevant to their "favorite" traits and can

Photo 3.3a Emotional expressions are some of the easiest signals for humans to understand. But before you come to a firm conclusion, turn the page.

Photo 3.3b The social context of interpretation. Even our understanding of emotional expression is influenced by the social context. Now that you know that Novak Djokovic is reacting to having just won a set in a quarterfinal match at the Australian Open, his look is not one of anger or pain, but of celebration and determination.

remember it better than unrelated information (Bargh & Thein, 1985; Higgins, King, & Mavin, 1982). Imagine, for instance, that you observed someone performing many behaviors: greeting friends, going to a party, studying in the library, and working at a part-time job. If friendliness is chronically accessible for you, you would be more likely to notice and later remember the first two of these behaviors. Another observer for whom intelligence is a chronically accessible concept would more easily notice and remember the time the person spent in the library.

As you have seen, then, accessibility has many sources, and it works in many ways to alter the interpretation of a given behavior, as summarized in Figure 3.2. In fact, as you will see throughout this book, the principle of accessibility has implications for many of our thoughts and actions, not only for our impressions of others.

SOCIAL PSYCHOLOGY IN PRACTICE: ACCESSIBILITY OF SEXISM FROM THE MEDIA

Television, the Internet, and print advertisements often use sex to sell products like beer and automobiles, implicitly promising the intended heterosexual male consumers that attractive women will flock around them if they purchase the correct product. Do such ads make thoughts about women as sex objects more accessible? Might this priming even affect the way men treat women they meet? Laurie Rudman and Eugene Borgida (1995) showed one group of male students a series of TV commercials that the researchers felt portrayed women as sex objects, whereas another group saw commercials for similar products (such as beer or cars) that lacked sexist imagery. The students then were asked, as a favor to the experimenter, to interview a female student (actually a confederate) for a job as a research assistant. The students who had viewed the sexist ads (compared to the nonsexist ones) sat closer to the interviewee and asked her more personal and inappropriate questions. After the interview, they recalled more about her physical appearance, but less about the information she had revealed in the interview. They also rated her as more friendly, but as less competent! Finally, the interviewee, who did not know which priming video each man had viewed, rated how much she felt the interviewer had been looking at her body and how sexually motivated he was. These ratings were also higher for the men who had watched the sexist commercials. It seems that the concept of viewing women as sex objects can be primed, affecting men's judgments and behavior toward real women over whom they may hold power. It is worth pondering the fact that in this study, these effects were produced by typical, everyday TV commercials, not extreme or pornographic materials.

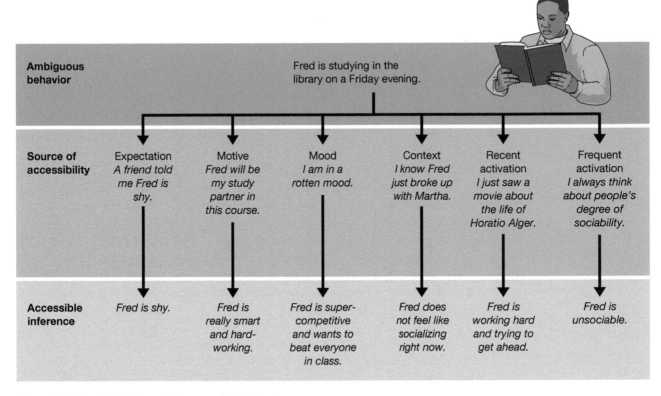

Ambiguous behavior	Fred is studying in the library on a Friday evening.					
Source of accessibility	Expectation *A friend told me Fred is shy.*	Motive *Fred will be my study partner in this course.*	Mood *I am in a rotten mood.*	Context *I know Fred just broke up with Martha.*	Recent activation *I just saw a movie about the life of Horatio Alger.*	Frequent activation *I always think about people's degree of sociability.*
Accessible inference	*Fred is shy.*	*Fred is really smart and hard-working.*	*Fred is super-competitive and wants to beat everyone in class.*	*Fred does not feel like socializing right now.*	*Fred is working hard and trying to get ahead.*	*Fred is unsociable.*

Figure 3.2 Accessibility shapes inferences about behavior
The same behavior can give rise to a variety of inferences, depending on what mental representations are accessible for the observer. Expectations, motives, and moods are just some of the many factors that can influence accessibility.

Characterizing the Behaving Person: Correspondent Inferences

People often assume that others have inner qualities that correspond to their observable behaviors. This assumption is frequently made even when external factors could have influenced the behaviors.

Sometimes automatic interpretations shaped by associations and accessible mental representations are enough for us. If we never expect to interact with a person again, we may not go beyond interpreting their looks or their behaviors. Sometimes circumstances require us to take a second step: using the behavior to decide what the person is really like. Does a menacing expression reveal a dangerous person? Does deceitful behavior imply that the person is untrustworthy? Characterizing someone as having a personality trait that corresponds to his or her behavior is called making a **correspondent inference**. When a correspondent inference follows the initial interpretation of a behavior, it completes a first impression, an initial mental representation of what the other person is like (Gilbert, Pelham, & Krull, 1988; Trope, 1986). Research shows that this can occur spontaneously. In one study, participants examined photos of people together with written descriptions of behaviors that strongly implied a trait. Even if instructed simply

correspondent inference
the process of characterizing someone as having a personality trait that corresponds to his or her observed behavior

to familiarize themselves with these materials rather than to form impressions of the pictured individuals, the participants associated the traits with the people (Carlston & Skowronski, 1994).

When Is a Correspondent Inference Justified? According to Edward Jones and Keith Davis (1965), correspondent inferences are justified when three conditions hold true:

- ■ *The individual freely chooses to perform the behavior.* No one should conclude that a child forced to write a pleasant thank-you note for an unloved birthday gift actually feels grateful.
- ■ *The behavior has unique effects that other behaviors do not.* The fewer effects that a behavior shares with other possible choices, the easier it is to decide which effect motivated the behavior. For example, if a person chooses a college in the sunny state of Florida over an identical campus in the chilly U.S. Midwest, we would be justified in seeing the choice as reflecting a love of warm weather. However, if the Florida school also has a better reputation, that muddies the inferential waters—it is no longer clear whether the person loves sunshine or status.
- ■ *The behavior is unexpected rather than expected or typical.* When it is not fashionable to be patriotic, one can reasonably assume that neighbors who fly their country's flag outside their home feel strongly about the issue. The unexpectedness of the behavior increases our confidence in the leap from behavior to a trait inference.

The Correspondence Bias: People Are What They Do. In a study designed to test these ideas about correspondent inferences, Edward Jones and Victor Harris (1967) found some unexpected results. Each participant in the study read an essay favoring or opposing Fidel Castro's communist regime in Cuba. Some were told that the writer of the essay had freely chosen what position to take. When asked to guess the writer's real opinion, these participants naturally assumed that it mirrored the position taken in the essay.

Other participants learned that the writer was given no choice: The position had been assigned. You might expect these individuals to realize that a required essay, like a dictated thank-you note, carries no information whatsoever about the writer's actual opinion. But they did not. Instead, like those who thought the essay writer had a choice, the second group of participants concluded that the writer actually held the views expressed in the essay, as Figure 3.3 shows. In other words, they made an unjustified correspondent inference when they inferred that the writer's opinion corresponded with the writer's behavior.

Our tendency to draw correspondent inferences even when they are not justified, for example, when other possible causes of the behavior exist, is known as the **correspondence bias**. The correspondence bias has been demonstrated repeatedly, both inside and outside the social psychology laboratory (Gilbert, 1998; Jones, 1990b). People tend to assume that the behaviors they observe must reflect the actors' inner characteristics even though other aspects of the situation could explain those behaviors.

Limits on the Correspondence Bias. Despite its power and pervasiveness, the correspondence bias does not inevitably affect our impressions of other people. Consider the following situation: You are waiting in line at a movie theater to see the latest comedy

It is the correspondence bias—our belief that people's acts reflect their inner qualities rather than situational pressures—that makes some of the most central and important research results in social psychology so unexpected and therefore compelling. For example, it is this bias that makes it seem paradoxical that perfectly ordinary people often follow orders to carry out actions that injure innocent victims (Chapter 10, pages 371–381).

correspondence bias
the tendency to infer an actor's personal characteristics from observed behaviors, even when the inference is unjustified because other possible causes of the behavior exist

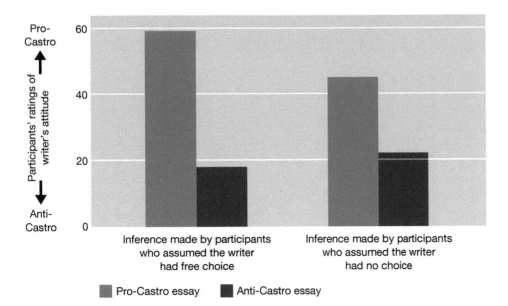

Figure 3.3 The correspondence bias: People are what they do
Participants who read an essay and thought the writer had freely chosen the position were likely to infer that the writer's true position corresponded to that advocated in the essay (left bars). However, they were nearly as likely to make the same inference when they knew that the writer had no choice about the position (right). People often leap to the conclusion that behaviors reflect inner characteristics, when situational forces are truly responsible. (Based on Jones & Harris, 1967.)

hit. As the audience from the previous showing streams out of the theater, you notice someone grinning broadly and chuckling. The correspondence bias would suggest that you should see him as a jolly person—but do you think that is what you would do? You would more likely take his reactions as evidence that the movie is funny, drawing an inference about the situation rather than the person. This is what Douglas Krull (1993) found. As in this example, when people pay specific attention to the situation, the correspondence bias is reduced or reversed. Perhaps in the Jones and Harris (1967) study, the correspondence bias emerged because the research participants assumed that they were supposed to draw conclusions about the person (the writer's true attitude toward Castro) rather than the situation (being instructed to write an essay).

Culture also sets limits on the correspondence bias. In individualist cultures, like those found in many Western countries, individuals are seen as independent and autonomous, responsible for their own thoughts, feelings, and actions (Markus and others, 1996; Nisbett, 1987). Thus, such observers naturally tend to assume that people's inner dispositions cause their behaviors, leading to the correspondence bias. Collectivist cultures, like those found in many Eastern countries, portray individuals as interdependent with their groups and social contexts, rather than as separate from them (Markus and others, 1996). As a result, a larger number of potential causes of behavior, including causes outside the individual, must be considered. Therefore collectivists, compared to individualists, consider a wider range of causal alternatives—including situational as well as personal factors—when explaining behaviors (Choi, Dalal, Kim-Prieto, & Park, 2003). And as a result, in collectivist cultures the correspondence bias

SOCIAL PSYCHOLOGY IN PRACTICE: CORRESPONDENCE BIAS IN THE WORKPLACE

The correspondence bias has serious implications for fairness in the workplace. If others see us as having personal characteristics that fit with our behaviors, their impressions of us can be shaped by behaviors we are instructed to perform (Ross, Amabile, & Steinmetz, 1977). Consider the results of a study in which groups of five participants were assigned in an obviously random way to two "manager" and three "clerk" positions (Humphrey, 1985). For a couple of hours, the managers made decisions, read documents, dictated letters to customers, and performed other varied and challenging tasks. Meanwhile the clerks filed papers, alphabetized cards, and filled out forms in triplicate, with little opportunity to make decisions or display initiative. When the participants rated each other at the end of the study, they did not recognize that the randomly assigned roles conveyed no information about their personal characteristics or abilities. Managers and clerks alike believed that managers were assertive and decisive, with real leadership potential. Even the clerks predicted that managers would be more successful than clerks in their real-life future careers.

When the correspondence bias occurs, roles make the person. Given this bias, how likely is it that even a highly competent secretary will ever be seen as having what it takes to be an effective manager?

is less prevalent (Fiske, Kitayama, Markus, & Nisbett, 1998). When observers pay attention to potential situational causes of a behavior, they are less likely to immediately leap to an inference that the actor possesses the corresponding trait (Trope & Gaunt, 2000).

Other factors also limit our tendency to characterize others' behaviors in trait terms. Indeed, recent work suggests that distance in time or space may be one such factor. In a study illustrating this point, participants were shown a video of two individuals having a conversation. Some participants were told the conversation took place in a nearby location, whereas others believed it took place in a far-away city. Participants were then asked to describe in their own words what they saw in the video. Their descriptions indicated stronger correspondent inferences when perceivers believed the conversation took place far away compared to when it allegedly took place nearby (Fujita, Henderson, Eng, Trope, & Liberman, 2006). This is just one instance of a general tendency, that greater perceived distance from a behavior or other event leads perceivers to focus on the causes of the behavior or event—such as the correspondent inference in this case—rather than on their effects (Rim, Hansen, & Trope, 2013).

Though our first impressions of other people seem to just "come to us," in reality we actively construct them, though this happens without our effort, intention, or even our control. The construction follows the steps summarized in Figure 3.4, proceeding from initial cues to correspondent inferences.

Photo 3.4 Systematic processing and impressions. We are sometimes motivated to put lots of thought into the impressions we form of others. For instance, if we believe we may have to work with another person, we may put in lots of effort to form an accurate impression of her. But, if not, we may form an impression in a more superficial way.

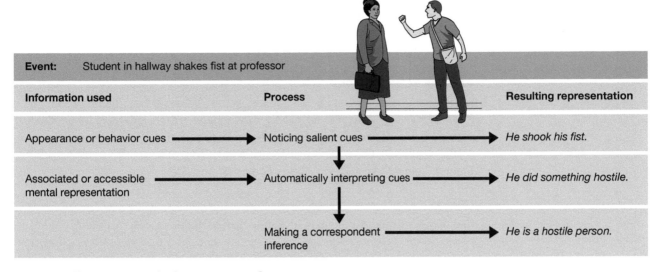

Event:	Student in hallway shakes fist at professor	
Information used	**Process**	**Resulting representation**
Appearance or behavior cues ⟶	Noticing salient cues ⟶	*He shook his fist.*
Associated or accessible mental representation ⟶	Automatically interpreting cues ⟶	*He did something hostile.*
	Making a correspondent inference ⟶	*He is a hostile person.*

Figure 3.4 The processes involved in constructing a first impression
Although forming a first impression seems immediate and effortless, it involves processes of noticing salient cues, interpreting them, and making correspondent inferences about the person's characteristics.

BEYOND FIRST IMPRESSIONS: SYSTEMATIC PROCESSING

Think back to the last time someone paid you a particularly outrageous compliment. Did you buy it? Perhaps you took the compliment at face value and, drawing a correspondent inference, decided that the person had a particularly high opinion of you. Probably, however, you were not quite so naive. Astute observers know that people say and do things for many reasons: the desire to flatter others, the demands of social situations, or the wish to receive something in return. Because we know that actions do not always reflect the inner person, we sometimes try to avoid the correspondence bias, correcting our first impressions by considering other possible causes of behaviors (Gilbert and others, 1988).

Initial impressions formed with minimal effort and thought on the basis of just one or two obvious attributes—such as impressions based on the assumption that inner characteristics correspond directly to observed behavior—are one example of **superficial processing**. But sometimes a quick glance at another person does not tell us all we want to know. Then we may think more deeply and take more information into account—a process termed **systematic processing**. We do this in the hope of forming a more adequate impression, although as we will see this hope is not always realized.

Processing systematically requires two ingredients. One is motivation. Only when people have some reason to form a deeper or more complex impression will they generally expend the effort to go beyond superficial processing. The second ingredient is the ability to process thoroughly: adequate time to think, freedom from distractions, and so on. When both motivation and ability to process are in the mix, systematic processing is likely to result. And as we will see throughout this book, this is true not only when people are forming impressions of others. In many different areas of life—

superficial processing
relying on accessible information to make inferences or judgments, while expending little effort in processing

systematic processing
giving thorough, effortful consideration to a wide range of information relevant to a judgment

when we are reading advertisements and thinking about buying a new product, or when we are interacting with a member of a stereotyped group—the extent to which people think systematically can be crucial in determining the outcomes.

Causal Attributions

To go beyond a first impression, people must engage in more extensive thought, particularly to explain others' behaviors. People are likely to consider potential causes that are salient in context, generally accessible, or suggested by the pattern of available information. Cultural learning also influences attributions.

causal attribution
a judgment about the cause of a behavior or other event

In the process of person perception, the systematic processing that people perform when they are willing and able includes making **causal attributions**: judgments about the cause of a behavior or an event. In fact, making inferences about the causes of people's behaviors is central to our perception of other people, for example, when we try to interpret an unexpected compliment by thinking about whether it reflects the speaker's true opinion or an effort at flattery. As we will see next, people draw on many types of information as they think about others' actions and attempt to understand why they have occurred.

Sources of Attribution. Attributions are more likely to be made to whatever possible cause is salient and thus draws our attention. Features such as bright colors, moving images, loud voices, or any other features that stand out draw our attention and thus become probable causes of behavior (McArthur & Post, 1977; Robinson & McArthur,

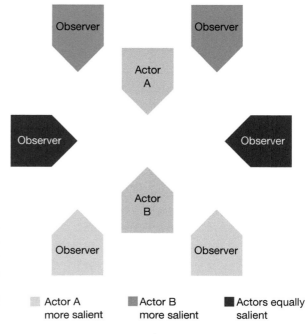

Figure 3.5 *Salient causes dominate impressions*
In this study, two people held a conversation as six others watched. The observers were seated so two could most easily see participant *A*, two faced participant *B*, and two could see both participants equally well. The results? The observers attributed a greater causal role to the participant they were directly watching than to the other participant. (Adapted from Taylor & Fiske, 1975, copyright © 1975 by the American Psychological Association. Adapted with permission.)

Actor A more salient   ·   Actor B more salient   ·   Actors equally salient

1982). To demonstrate the impact of salience on attribution, Shelley Taylor and Susan Fiske (1975) arranged an experiment in which six students watched a two-person conversation from different viewing positions, as Figure 3.5 shows. When questioned about what they had seen, the students attributed a greater causal role to the person they were directly watching. They gave that person higher ratings for dominating the conversation and dictating its tone and outcome.

Consider the implications of these findings for courtroom proceedings. Jurors may watch a videotape of a suspect confessing while being interrogated by police. When the video camera is focused on the suspect, jurors might believe the confession was given voluntarily, but when their attention is directed mainly to the interrogating detective, they might think he coerced the suspect to confess (Lassiter, Geers, Munhall, Handley, & Beers, 2001).

Attributions can also be based on accessible causes, that is, those that are already activated in our minds. In one study illustrating this, students were first exposed to words like aviator or rug, to make those concepts more accessible in memory. They then explained hypothetical events, such as "The pilot liked the carpet." Those who had been primed with aviator attributed the behavior to the actor, whereas those who had seen rug attributed the behavior to the stimulus object (Rholes & Pryor, 1982).

Finally, covariation information, or information about potential causal factors that are present when the event occurs and absent when it does not, may also shape attributions. Consider observing a behavior, such as a graduate student flattering a professor.

TABLE 3.1 Information About the Presence or Absence of Potential Causes Influences Attributions

Event *The graduate student flatters a professor*

	Situation A	Situation B	Situation C
Consensus	High	Low	Low
	Almost everyone flatters this professor.	*Almost nobody flatters this professor.*	*Almost nobody flatters this professor.*
Distinctiveness	High	Low	High
	The graduate student does not flatter anyone else.	*The graduate student flatters almost everyone.*	*The graduate student does not flatter anyone else.*
Consistency	High	High	Low
	The graduate student flatters this professor almost all the time.	*The graduate student flatters this professor almost all the time.*	*The graduate student does not flatter this professor on most occasions.*
	↓	↓	↓
Attribution	*Something about the professor (stimulus)*	*Something about the graduate student (person)*	*Something about the particular time or situation (circumstances)*

SOCIAL PSYCHOLOGY AND CULTURE: CULTURAL DIFFERENCES IN ATTRIBUTIONS

People from different cultures learn to consider different types of causes for many behaviors. Whereas individualists attribute behavior to the actor's general personality traits, those from collectivist cultures place more emphasis on the actor's social roles and relationships (Miller, 1984). In one study, researchers described a murder case to Americans and Chinese and asked them to explain the event (Morris & Peng, 1994). The Americans tended to say things like, "He was a psycho." In contrast, Chinese perceivers did not attribute the event to causes within the actor, but located the cause in the social relationships between the murderer, his victim, and the larger social context. Similarly, Chiu and colleagues (2000) showed that Americans were more likely to blame a pharmaceutical error on the person who filled the prescription rather than the pharmacy at which the person worked, whereas Chinese participants did the opposite.

Harold Kelley (1967) argued that the behavior might be explained by something about the actor (the graduate student), the target of the behavior (the professor), or the particular situation or circumstances. Then, an observer would seek out information about whether the student flatters other people, about whether other people flatter the professor, and about whether the student flatters the professor in other circumstances. Different patterns of such information will encourage one type of attribution over the other, as shown in Table 3.1. For example, if virtually no one flatters the professor, the graduate student does not flatter anyone else, and the graduate student does not flatter this professor on most occasions, an observer would likely attribute the flattery to something about the particular situation (e.g., the student is "buttering up" the professor for a letter of recommendation request).

Using Attributions to Correct First Impressions

When external factors appear to have caused behavior, people may attempt to correct an initial inference about the actor's characteristics. This correction takes time and cognitive effort, however, so it often does not occur.

discounting

reducing a belief in one potential cause of behavior because there is another viable cause

Attributional thinking may lead us to revise our initial correspondent inferences; that is, we may become less confident that the actor's inner characteristics correspond to his or her behavior. This process is termed **discounting**, which refers to reducing a belief in one potential cause of behavior, such as the flatterer's true opinion, because there is another viable cause, his need for a favor (Kelley, 1972). When you see your classmates sweating and biting their fingernails as they await the calculus exam, the associated trait of anxiety immediately springs to mind. Processing superficially, you may go on to draw a correspondent inference—to form a first impression that the students are nervous people. However, if you think more systematically about the circumstances in which the behavior is occurring—the looming examination—you might take a third step and correct your initial impression by discounting, concluding that the nail biters may not be such nervous Nellies after all.

This third step seems so logical and sensible that one might wonder why people so often fall prey to the correspondence bias, even when situational causes are quite obvious. The answer lies in the fact that the first two steps, interpreting the behavior and characterizing the person, are relatively easy, and frequently occur automatically, without any conscious effort. In contrast, the third step, using causal reasoning to correct the impression, is difficult unless a situational cause is quite salient or accessible (Gilbert, 1991; Trope & Gaunt, 2000). Causal reasoning usually takes time and effort and, as we all can testify, things that take more time and effort often do not get done at all.

Daniel Gilbert and his colleagues (1988) illustrated this point in a classic experiment, in which students watched a silent, videotaped interview of an obviously nervous woman. The topics she was allegedly discussing were displayed as subtitles. One group of students believed the interview concerned highly anxiety-provoking topics, such as "My most embarrassing moment." Another group thought she was discussing innocuous matters like "My favorite vacation." After seeing the interview, all students rated how anxious a person the woman was in general. A correspondent inference would suggest that because the woman showed signs of nervousness, she must be a nervous type. However, those who knew of a situational cause for her anxiety—the personal topics— should engage in discounting. And, indeed, their ratings of her general level of anxiety were lower than those of the students who thought the topics were mundane.

Two additional groups of students in the experiment went through the same procedure with one exception: The researchers required them to memorize the topics the woman was allegedly discussing. The researchers predicted that this distracting activity would leave them with insufficient cognitive resources to engage in effortful discounting, which is precisely what they found. They rated the woman as an anxious type even though they successfully memorized the anxiety-provoking topics (see Figure 3.6). Apparently, the memory task absorbed some of their cognitive resources, rendering them unable to change

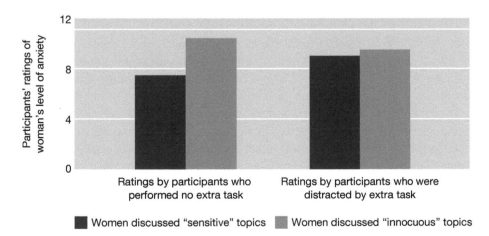

Figure 3.6 Correcting impressions is hard work
Participants who could focus their attention on their judgments rated a woman as a less anxious person when they knew she was discussing sensitive topics (left). In contrast, participants who were distracted by an additional task failed to discount (right). Those who believed the topics were sensitive assigned approximately the same ratings as those assigned by participants who believed the topics were innocuous. (Based on Gilbert and others, 1988.)

their initial correspondent inferences, even though the role of situational factors was quite obvious. As this study shows, unless we are willing and able to process information systematically, the principle of conservatism applies: We stick with our first impressions.

All the typical demands of everyday interaction—trying to remember other people's names and faces, planning what we want to say, or working to create a good impression—also use up considerable cognitive capacity. Thus, interaction itself may limit our ability to form accurate impressions of the people with whom we interact, leaving our impressions very much at the mercy of the behaviors we happen to see people perform first.

Putting It All Together: Forming Complex Impressions

Impressions usually include multiple traits or characteristics as well as liking. People may infer additional traits based on their knowledge or observations of the individual. The multiple components of an impression may become linked as people attempt to infer causal connections among them. People also integrate the good and bad qualities of others to arrive at an overall impression.

Our everyday encounters with other people are likely to reveal more about them than just a single characteristic. How, then, do we develop coherent overall impressions? Imagine being introduced to Paul at a city council meeting. As you chat, you find that in addition to his involvement in city politics, Paul sells salad dressing and popcorn, acts in movies, contributes to newspaper advertisements for political causes, writes to his congressional representative regularly, and drives race cars. How would you put together all this information into an overall impression of Paul? We form our overall impressions by integrating multiple characteristics of the person.

Integrating Multiple Traits. We usually expect certain traits to go together. Knowing that an acquaintance is generous, for example, often leads us to expect that he will be warm as well. These patterns of associations among traits, called implicit personality theories (Schneider, 1973), can guide the development and elaboration of complex impressions of others. For example, if you conclude that Paul is daring because he drives race cars, you might immediately conclude that he also is reckless or dominating because most people associate these traits with the trait daring (Rosenberg, Nelson, & Vivekananthan, 1968). People seem to think that most positive traits are related to each other and that negative traits form another distinct group. When people rely on their implicit personality theories, they may infer that a person has many positive qualities on the basis of a single good one, and they may expect a lot of negative characteristics if they learn about one bad quality. Learning that someone is pessimistic, for example, most people would expect him or her to also be irritable, cold, vain, and finicky.

As we observe or infer more and more characteristics of an individual, we try to organize what we know and create an overall impression that is a complex and inter-linked whole. For example, if you notice that several behaviors have similar trait implications, you may think about them together. This reflection, in turn, may cause the behaviors to become associated in your mind. For example, you may realize that Paul's behaviors of attending the council meeting, supporting the political ad campaigns, and writing letters to his congressional representative all reflect political activism. David Hamilton and his colleagues (Hamilton, Katz, & Leirer, 1980) suggest that behaviors that represent the same trait are linked into associated clusters in memory as people mentally organize their impressions of others. Supporting this idea, these researchers found that when people were asked to recall behaviors of a person they had earlier read about, they often recalled a number of behaviors reflecting the same trait in sequence, followed by behaviors linked to a different trait, and so on.

We may also make sense of a person's diverse behaviors and traits by creating causal links among them (Park, 1986; Prentice, 1990). You may know, for example, that a star athlete is quick-tempered. You might assume that she has a burning competitive drive that causes both her athletic successes and her outbursts of temper. These processes of inferring additional traits and linking multiple traits and behaviors into an integrated whole thus allow us to build impressions that are unified and coherent, not just lists of seemingly unrelated characteristics.

Integrating the Good and the Bad. Most of the people we meet in everyday life are neither saints nor axe murderers, but have some positive and some negative characteristics. How do we put together our admiration for someone's artistic talents, positive feelings about their attractive appearance, and dismay at their occasional rude behavior? We could simply average these and conclude that, overall, two positives and one negative lead to a mildly positive impression. However, we tend to give negative information more weight than positive information when we integrate impressions in this way (Baumeister, Bratslavsky, Finkenauer, & Vohs, 2001; Skowronski & Carlston, 1989). We do this partly because negative information is generally surprising and unexpected—after all, more people are generally polite than rude. Therefore, the negative information seems more extreme and informative than comparable positive information. In addition, negative aspects of an object can sometimes "contaminate" or spoil positive aspects (Rozin & Royzman, 2001)—just imagine finding a fly in your bowl of delicious soup. Rarely if ever does a single positive item have the power to reverse our evaluation of a generally negative object. Negativity biases develop early in life and can be found even in young children's impressions (e.g., Aloise, 1993), suggesting that this bias is adaptive in helping individuals deal successfully with their environments (Vaish, Grossmann, & Woodward, 2008). Thus, negativity biases may reflect our motivation for mastery in the domain of person perception. We may make better decisions about who to approach and avoid and who to like and dislike if we heavily weight negative information in our impressions of others.

Chapter 7 will go into more detail on how items of information that may have different evaluations are integrated into an overall judgment, and the resulting effects.

The Accuracy of Considered Impressions

Considered impressions may not be completely accurate. When people devote extra thought to forming an impression, biases may still limit their accuracy, and the extra efforts may only confirm an existing positive or negative view. Unless people are aware of such biases in social perception, they are unlikely to try to correct them.

Earlier we noted that first impressions based on little information and simple cues can sometimes be fairly accurate. Intuitively, you might suspect that, when we go beyond such first impressions, making attributions and integrating multiple behaviors and traits, we would be even more accurate. After all, making attributions and integrating multiple pieces of information about another person requires considerable thought. What might motivate the expenditure of all this cognitive effort? And will the extra effort guarantee that considered impressions are unbiased, valid conceptions of what the person is really like?

Motive for Accuracy. Accuracy is one of the strongest motivations for working hard on forming an impression. Suppose you have a new acquaintance, Tom, and you are sure your friend will like him. You realize that your friend might hold you responsible if you bring Tom along to a party and he turns out to be rude or boring. If it is important to be accurate because you will be held accountable, you will probably make an extra effort to gather information (Kruglanski & Freund, 1983).

We can also be particularly motivated to form accurate perceptions of people when we will have to work with them (Flink & Park, 1991; Srull & Brand, 1983). In one study, students learned that they would shortly meet a man who had previously been hospitalized for schizophrenia. Some of the students were told they would simply meet him, but others believed that they would work cooperatively with him on a joint task (Neuberg & Fiske, 1987). The students then received an information sheet describing the man's personal background, hobbies, and so on. Those who expected to cooperate with him spent more time reading about his personal characteristics, and used that additional information in forming their impressions. In contrast, the others spent less time reading about the man's attributes and formed an impression that was based almost entirely on the schizophrenia diagnosis.

Finally, suspicion about the information we obtain may also cause us to think carefully about the impressions we form. For example, we often acquire information about others from a third party. Such exchange of information between two people about another person who is not present, termed gossip, can play an important role in shaping our views of others (Smith & Collins, 2009). But we may need to consider whether such sources of information are biased before we take at face value what they communicate. In recent work showing that perceivers are sensitive to possible biases of this sort, participants read about a manager who was considering two candidates for a position (Brandt and colleagues, 2011). The manager felt they were about equally suited for the position and was having difficulty selecting one over the other. So the manager asked a former colleague of both candidates, named John, who praised one target and provided a fairly negative opinion about the other. But participants further learned that John's recommendations may have been biased by personal relationships. Some participants were told that John was friends with the person he praised and enemies with the person he denounced, and others were told the opposite. Participants' competency ratings of the candidates clearly showed that the perceived bias of the source mattered. When John recommended his enemy over his friend, participants rated the recommended person more favorably. But, when John's personal friendships might have accounted for his recommendations, participants rated the recommended person as less competent than the non-recommended one. Thus, participants evidently "didn't buy" a recommendation from someone they perceived as biased.

As you can see, there are multiple factors that may encourage us to be accurate in our impressions. Feeling accountable, anticipating future interaction, and being suspicious of the information we obtain may make us think more carefully and go beyond a first impression to a more fully considered one.

Motives for Connectedness and Valuing Me and Mine. Accuracy is not the only motive that drives people to devote extra efforts to processing information about others. People also care about connections with others, and sometimes maintaining relationships is more important than being accurate. Jeffry Simpson and his colleagues (Simpson, Ickes, & Blackstone, 1995) had members of dating couples evaluate photographs of highly attractive opposite-sex individuals and then attempt to guess each other's thoughts and feelings about the task. When the situation posed a threat to the couple's relationship because the relationship was insecure, these guesses were relatively inaccurate. Accuracy is not always the primary goal of person perception!

Another goal that may supersede accuracy considerations is our desire to see the world in a way that will result in a good outcome for ourselves (Kruglanski & Freund, 1983; Kunda, 1990). In one study, for example, students evaluated the trivia knowledge of a man whom they expected to be either their competitor or their partner in a contest. All students watched him answer a few practice questions correctly. Those who expected to be the man's future partner rated his trivia ability higher than did those who expected to compete with him (Klein & Kunda, 1992). When he will be our teammate, we want the man to be gifted, as this will be good for us!

In other research, individuals interacted with another person whom they believed either would or would not be evaluating their performance for a possible monetary prize. Those whose fate was controlled by their partner were motivated to see this partner as competent, whereas those who were not dependent upon the partner did not show this bias (Stevens & Fiske, 2000). When others have control over our outcomes, we hope that they are fair and competent people, and this hope may bias the impressions that we actually form.

As such studies show, our approach to perceiving other people or the world in general is sometimes like that of an attorney constructing the best possible case for a client (Baumeister & Newman, 1994). Rather than conducting an unbiased search with accuracy as the only goal, we hunt for evidence that supports other motives like connectedness or seeing ourselves in a positive light. And because behavior is often ambiguous, we often find just the evidence that we are seeking. If the trivia player is to be our partner, we focus on how much knowledge his answers displayed; if we will have to compete with him, we instead emphasize how easy the practice questions were. When our search succeeds, we remain unaware of the biases in the search process and we blissfully forget that, had we searched with different goals, we might have unearthed a very different body of evidence.

Attempting to Undo Biases. Most of the time we remain blind to the processes that underlie our impressions, accepting the world we perceive at face value. We think that what we see is what actually is, because we are so good at constructing a coherent representation of reality (Gilbert, 1998). And we ordinarily get along well enough relying on the picture we've built up (Fiske, 1993). But sometimes an important motive makes us try to correct our impressions. Even when this happens, however, a lack of time or cognitive resources may undermine our best intentions and leave us unable to correct

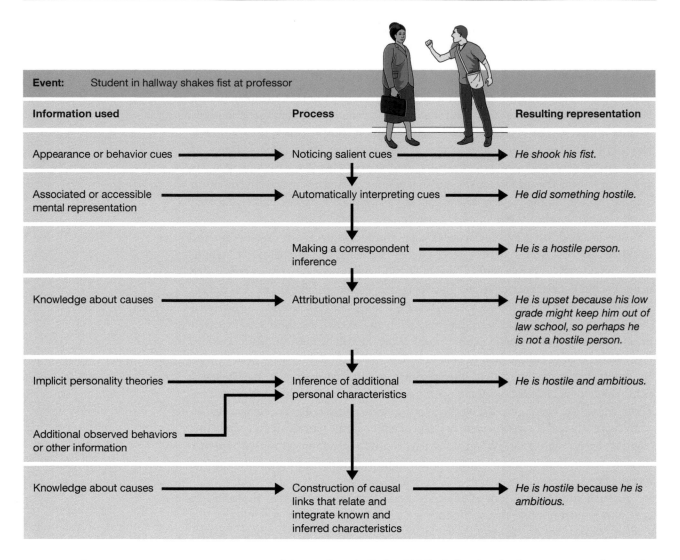

Event: Student in hallway shakes fist at professor

Information used	Process	Resulting representation
Appearance or behavior cues	Noticing salient cues	*He shook his fist.*
Associated or accessible mental representation	Automatically interpreting cues	*He did something hostile.*
	Making a correspondent inference	*He is a hostile person.*
Knowledge about causes	Attributional processing	*He is upset because his low grade might keep him out of law school, so perhaps he is not a hostile person.*
Implicit personality theories Additional observed behaviors or other information	Inference of additional personal characteristics	*He is hostile and ambitious.*
Knowledge about causes	Construction of causal links that relate and integrate known and inferred characteristics	*He is hostile because he is ambitious.*

Figure 3.7 From snap judgments to complex impressions

our impressions (Martin, Seta, & Crelia, 1990). Only when both motivation and cognitive ability are available will we attempt to counteract potential biases in how we see others. At that point, our attempted correction will depend on our beliefs about the nature and direction of the bias (Wegener & Petty, 1995). For instance, in the previous example where someone recommended a friend over an enemy, participants were likely aware that individuals are biased positively toward friends. Thus perceivers should and did adjust their opinions downward when sources praised friends, trying to cancel out the assumed bias (Wegener & Petty, 2001). The net result of this process may be a more accurate judgment, but only if your theory about the direction and size of the bias is relatively correct.

Figure 3.7 summarizes all the processes involved in impression formation, from noticing cues to interpreting them, inferring traits, and integrating multiple traits to form an overall impression. What is surprising is how little we are usually aware of all this processing. Our impressions of others seem to be formed immediately, rarely requiring much thought. But in fact, this sense of immediacy actually reflects the unobtrusive efficiency with which our interpretive processes construct our picture of reality.

THE IMPACT OF IMPRESSIONS: USING, DEFENDING, AND CHANGING IMPRESSIONS

Once we have formed an impression of another person, whether it is a snap judgment or a thoughtful construction, and whether it is biased or accurate, we use it to guide our decisions and social interactions. Thus, once we have concluded that the next-door neighbor is a generous fellow, we trust that our interpretation represents objective reality. And even if these impressions are biased, they take on reality as we act on them.

Using Impressions

Once an impression is formed, it becomes a basis for decisions and behaviors. Sometimes decisions about others rest on simple, superficial processing; at other times people engage in extensive processing, attempting to put together the implications of all relevant information.

Imagine that you need to find several housemates. As you interview a few candidates, you may develop complex, well-articulated impressions of each of them. Whom should you pick? What aspects of your impressions will influence your decision? Sometimes only a single aspect of an impression really matters. If the only thing you care about is a compatible lifestyle (similar tastes in music, similar preferences for late hours), the happy-go-lucky night person may seem to be your best bet. If a shared interest in animal rights is your most important criterion, you certainly will not choose the woman in the fur coat. Often, however, more than one aspect of your impression seems important. You want someone you like, who has a compatible lifestyle, but you also want that person to be financially responsible—someone who will not stick you with bills for unpaid rent and utilities each month. How do we make judgments about others on the basis of our impressions of them?

Superficial Processing: Using a Single Attribute. Decisions based on a single accessible or salient characteristic require minimal effort and thought. You might pick the best-looking person who turns up to see your apartment or base your decision on some other equally obvious characteristic, ignoring all other considerations. Having to make a decision quickly or without full attention might force such superficial processing even if you would prefer a more systematic approach.

When people process quickly and superficially, they generally rely on their past judgments of an individual, rather than on the underlying evidence that led to those judgments in the first place (Carlston & Skowronski, 1986). For example, on learning that your city's mayor takes conservative positions on several issues, you may form the judgment that she is a conservative. If a new issue, such as capital punishment, becomes a topic for political discussion, you probably will assume that she will take an equally conservative stand. If you make this assumption, you will be relying on your past judgment rather than on specific statements the representative may have made about capital punishment. In fact, when we use our past judgments we may not even bother to retrieve from memory or reconsider the specific facts on which those judgments were based (Hastie & Park, 1986; Sherman & Klein, 1994).

Our tendency to rely on our past judgments makes us slow to change our thinking and can lead us into trouble. For example, people tend to rely on their past judgments even if those judgments were made in circumstances that create bias. If a doting mother asked us for an opinion of her rather ordinary son, most of us would find it difficult to describe him in anything except positive terms. Interestingly, giving such a slanted description may affect our private impressions of the son (Echterhoff, Higgins, & Levine, 2009; Higgins & McCann, 1984). Rather than thinking again about the evidence, people tend to draw on their previous descriptions of others—forgetting or ignoring the fact that these descriptions were shaped by the demands of an audience.

Systematic Processing: Integrating Multiple Factors. When we apply for jobs or loans, we all hope that those evaluating us as part of the application process think carefully and deeply about us, taking account of the complexity of our true selves. As noted earlier, when people know their decisions matter and when accuracy is extremely important to them, they often do carry out such systematic processing (Neuberg, 1989; Neuberg & Fiske, 1987). When people integrate multiple items of information, instead of evaluating each attribute independently, they may attempt to fit the information together into a meaningful whole. In this integration process, one item may subtly change the meaning of others (Asch, 1946; Asch & Zukier, 1984). For example, suppose one person is described as intelligent and cold, and another as intelligent and warm. The very meaning of intelligent seems to differ in these two descriptions, connoting something like "calculating" or "sly" when combined with cold, but taking on the meaning of "wise" in the context of warm. As mentioned earlier in this chapter, integrating multiple characteristics often involves causal reasoning, as when we infer that coldness leads people to use their intelligence in self-centered ways, making them seem calculating.

Defending Impressions

Impressions resist change, partly because a first impression can alter the interpretation of later information. As a result, impressions may survive even the discrediting of the information on which they were based. Impressions shape overt interaction as well as judgments. They often lead people to seek consistent information or even to elicit confirming actions from others.

Once formed, our impressions of others can influence both our private judgments about those individuals and our interactions with them. As we obtain further information, we may slant our interpretations to maintain our first impressions. And as we treat people in ways that reflect our existing impressions, we may produce in them the very behavior we expect to see. The principle of conservatism is at work here: Once formed, our beliefs about other people are slow to change, in part because they tend to maintain themselves.

Impressions Shape Interpretations. Suppose you are watching a TV quiz show. One contestant gives quick correct answers early but cools off as the questions continue. Another contestant starts out with a series of wrong answers and then improves. By the first commercial break, they have an equal number of right and wrong answers. Which

Photo 3.5 It's hard to shake a first impression. Take a look at the man on the left. Now imagine this same man, shown again on the right, is applying for a job in your organization. Do you find it difficult to take this person seriously as a candidate? If you are like most people, you may, because the first impression of him as a "partier" is hard to overcome.

contestant seems more intelligent to you? If you are like most people, you will give the edge to the one who started strongly (Jones, Rock, Shaver, Goethals, & Ward, 1968). Our initial impressions can set up an expectation that shapes our interpretations of later information—letting the early information have a greater impact, in what is called a **primacy effect** (Asch, 1946). This is an example of conservatism. The initial information shapes our impression, which then resists change.

In an illustration of the lasting effects of initial impressions, Bernadette Park (1986) arranged for small groups of strangers to meet together over a 7-week period. After the first meeting, and periodically after that, participants wrote descriptions of one another. Week after week, first impressions dominated these profiles. The characteristics noted after the very first meeting turned up repeatedly, even though the first impressions were based on little information. Apparently initial impressions biased the participants' interpretations of later behavior. So when you meet new people, putting your best foot forward right from the start is much easier than trying to change opinions once you have put your foot in it.

Impressions Resist Rebuttal. Because our impressions shape the interpretation of later information, their effects can persist even if we find out the initial impression is false. This distortion is called the **perseverance bias** (Lord, Lepper, & Preston, 1984). To investigate this bias, Lee Ross and his colleagues (1975) arranged for female students to observe others performing a decision-making task. Some observers received false feedback that made it

primacy effect
a pattern in which early-encountered information has a greater impact than subsequent information; an example of the principle of cognitive conservatism

perseverance bias
the tendency for information to have a persisting effect on our judgments even after it has been discredited

SOCIAL PSYCHOLOGY IN PRACTICE: PERSEVERANCE IN THE COURTROOM

When legally inadmissible evidence is introduced in courtroom proceedings, it can be stricken from the official trial record. The judge may even instruct jurors to disregard it. Unfortunately, jurors cannot wipe the information from their minds as easily as the court reporter can expunge the record. In fact, research has found that inadmissible evidence does influence jurors' deliberations and verdicts (Thompson, Fong, & Rosenhan, 1981). The same is true of discredited evidence. In one mock-trial study, for example, one group of participants saw minimal evidence against the defendant, and only 18 % voted for conviction. A second group saw the same evidence plus an eyewitness identification of the defendant; in that group, 72 % voted for conviction. A third group, after receiving all this information, learned that the eyewitness was legally blind and was not wearing his glasses at the time he claimed to have seen the defendant. This discrediting information had virtually no impact, however, reducing the conviction rate only to 68 % (Loftus, 1974). The perseverance bias means that, as in this example, information may have effects that persist even after the information is found to be false.

appear that the decision maker performed quite well, getting nearly all items correct. Others learned that the decision maker performed poorly. The experimenter then revealed that the feedback had been randomly determined and had no relation to the decision maker's actual performance. However, even after the observers learned of this deception, their ratings of the decision maker's ability and their predictions of future performance still showed the effects of the now-discredited feedback. As this experiment shows, once beliefs have influenced our interpretation of other information, it is difficult to undo their effects completely if we later learn the beliefs are false (Gilbert, Krull, & Malone, 1990; Gilbert & Osborne, 1989). No wonder that it is notoriously difficult to counteract a rumor or other misinformation after it is initially spread (Lewandowsky and others, 2012).

The most effective way to reduce or eliminate the perseverance bias is to explicitly consider the opposite possibility (Lord, Lepper, & Preston, 1984). Learning that the supposed high score was false had little effect on the observers in Ross's study. However, considering the possibility that the individual might have actually performed quite poorly could have reduced the bias.

Selectively Seeking Impression-Consistent Behavior. Most of us are somewhat inconsistent in our behaviors, for instance, we may act shy at some times and outgoing at others. What would happen if someone expected you to be outgoing and attempted to test that belief? He or she might ask you leading questions about occasions when you were outgoing, for example, when you were the center of attention at a large party or particularly enjoyed a social gathering (Snyder & Swann, 1978). As you recounted such instances, the questioner's initial hypothesis would seem to be confirmed. But was it? If the questions had focused on the times you felt shy and avoided other people, you would have been able to report on those equally well. Any hypothesis about another person could probably be confirmed if tested in this way.

"Thank God we're cute. You only get one chance to make a good first impression."

Actually, people do not always ask biased or leading questions to test their beliefs about others. Given a choice, they often prefer questions that are diagnostic—that is, questions whose answers will provide information about the truth or falsity of the hypothesis (Trope, Bassok, & Alon, 1984). For example, a diagnostic question to assess whether someone is outgoing could take the following form: "Would you rather attend a large party or have a quiet get-together with one or two close friends?" Unlike the earlier example, this question would not necessarily produce a false confirmation of an initial hypothesis. However, coming up with properly diagnostic questions is often difficult unless the questioner is aware of alternatives to the given hypothesis (Higgins & Bargh, 1987; Hodgins & Zuckerman, 1993). As we have already seen, a strategy of "considering the opposite"—thinking about the possibility that the person might be quiet and retiring rather than outgoing—can reduce biases (Trope & Mackie, 1987).

Creating Impression-Consistent Behavior: The Self-Fulfilling Prophecy. Suppose you believe, for whatever reason, that people from the southern United States tend to be gracious and friendly. When you meet a Southerner, you will probably act warmly, and the person will naturally reciprocate. You will probably end up liking the person, just as you thought you would. Of course, the outcome might be quite different if your initial expectation was that Southerners would be hostile and unfriendly. As this example demonstrates, we do more than just ask other people about their behaviors. Our initial impressions may actually create corresponding behaviors (Synder, Tanke, & Berscheid, 1977; Zebrowitz, Hall, Murphy, & Rhodes, 2002). When a person's expectation about another causes that person to act in ways that confirm the expectation, the process is called a **self-fulfilling prophecy** (Darley & Fazio, 1980; Merton, 1948). Figure 3.8 portrays an example of this process.

Of course, if people were aware of their influence on others, they might try to discount that influence to improve the accuracy of their impressions. However, people sometimes fail to recognize even their clear and overt influences on others. To demonstrate this point, researchers set up an interview situation in which interviewers and interviewees read questions and answers from fixed scripts (Gilbert & Jones, 1986). The questions concerned politics; the prepared answers reflected a conservative or liberal viewpoint. The interviewer read each question and then pushed a "Liberal" or "Conservative" button, as specified by the script, to signal which answer the interviewee should read. Of course, by pushing the buttons, the interviewers themselves controlled the answers they heard. But did they recognize their own influence? No. They rated the

self-fulfilling prophecy
the process by which one person's expectations about another become reality by eliciting behaviors that confirm the expectations

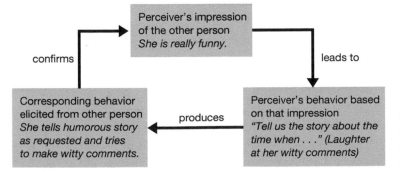

Figure 3.8 Expectations create confirmation: The self-fulfilling prophecy
Once we have formed an impression of another person, our expectations often lead us to behave in ways that elicit expectation-confirming behaviors.

SOCIAL PSYCHOLOGY IN PRACTICE: SELF-FULFILLING PROPHECY IN THE CLASSROOM

Self-fulfilling prophecies can operate anywhere: at home, on the job, and in the classroom. In studies pioneered by Robert Rosenthal and his colleagues, researchers gave schoolteachers the names of some pupils in their classes who were expected to "bloom" intellectually over the next few months (Rosenthal, 1985; Rosenthal & Jacobson, 1968). Actually, the students had been selected at random. Later in the school year all the students were tested. Multiple studies using this technique have shown that children identified as "bloomers" tend to perform better than their classmates—on objective tests, not just in the teachers' own estimation. The teachers' high expectations for these children are somehow translated into actual achievement over the course of a few months. The reason may be that teachers give students more attention and more challenging assignments when they expect them to perform at a high level (Cooper & Good, 1983). These types of teacher behaviors improve students' performance. Similar processes operate in the workplace, where supervisors' impressions shape subordinates' actual performance (Kierein & Gold, 2000; McNatt, 2000), an effect that is particularly strong when the worker's initial performance level is low.

interviewees as conservative when most of their answers were conservative, and liberal when most answers were liberal. It is surprisingly difficult for people to recognize the effects of their own actions on others, and without such awareness we cannot correct our impressions to improve their validity.

Limits on the Self-Fulfilling Prophecy. How vulnerable are we to the effects of other people's expectations, particularly those of people such as teachers or employers, who have some power over us? To some extent, the answer to that question is determined by our views of our self, our awareness of the views others have of us, and our social motives in the situation.

First, when the person being perceived has strong views about him- or herself, the self-fulfilling effects of a perceiver's expectations become weaker, as demonstrated by William Swann and Robin Ely (1984). They paired previously unacquainted female students, and had one member (the perceiver) interview the other (the target). Despite being given a false expectation about the target's personality beforehand, perceivers usually changed their original impression to match the target's own view of her personality. A self-fulfilling prophecy emerged only when the target was uncertain about whether she was extroverted, for example, and the perceiver was highly confident in her expectation. In such cases, the self-fulfilling prophecy influenced both the target's overt behavior and her view of herself.

Second, self-fulfilling prophecies can also be foiled when targets are aware of the perceivers' expectations. If you met someone whom you knew expected you to be uncertain and naive, would you make a special effort to show your independence and sophistication? Many people would react just this way. Indeed, research shows that people who are aware of others' unfavorable expectations about them often succeed in disconfirming those expectations (Hilton & Darley, 1985).

Third, self-fulfilling prophecy effects are weaker when the targets are more concerned about conveying an accurate impression than making the interaction go smoothly and pleasantly (Snyder & Haugen, 1995). This finding suggests that when targets do confirm perceivers' expectations, it is often out of their desire for social acceptance and connectedness.

Thus, the self-fulfilling prophecy does not affect everyone equally. Like the schoolchildren in Rosenthal's studies, some people—those who are uncertain about their self-views, are unaware of others' beliefs, or are focused on making interactions run smoothly—are especially vulnerable to shaping by others' expectations.

Dealing with Inconsistent Information

People sometimes encounter information that is clearly inconsistent with an impression. They may attempt to explain it away in various ways, or they may take it into account and assume that the other person has changed. Most of the time, however, impressions of others' personal characteristics are stable and difficult to change.

Consider the many mental tricks you may use to sustain your impression of another person. Believing that Albert is intelligent, you notice only his ground-breaking discoveries in physics. When his behavior is ambiguous, you interpret it as being smart rather than stupid. Sometimes you seek out evidence of his intelligence, questioning him about his latest ideas on relativity rather than about the times he forgot where he parked his car. You may even create the opportunity for Albert to be smart by giving him his own lab, a supply of freshly sharpened pencils, a supercomputer, and all the coffee he can drink. Then, one day, Albert does something so remarkably stupid—so unambiguously inconsistent with your belief—that there can be no denying it. How would you handle this conflict? You could explain away this inconsistency, defending your original impression to the death. Or you could take account of the information in ways that make your impression of Albert more accurate.

Reconciling Inconsistencies. When we encounter inconsistent and contradictory information about someone, it challenges two central social motives. Our sense of mastery and understanding is threatened by the unexpected information, and our ability to maintain a relationship or social interaction with the person may also be thrown into doubt. Inconsistent information is therefore generally unwelcome (Olson, Roese, & Zanna, 1996). This is why we often prefer to gloss over and ignore it, continuing to process superficially rather than paying attention to the inconsistency. However, important inconsistencies are likely to trigger systematic processing, at least when people have adequate time and resources to devote to the task (Hamilton, Driscoll, & Worth, 1989; Srull, Lichtenstein, & Rothbart, 1985).

How would you react, for example, if one friend told you that a classmate is kind and another friend said that the same person is hostile? When people in one study were presented with such contradictory trait descriptions and asked to describe their impressions in their own words, they creatively integrated the seemingly inconsistent traits (Asch & Zukier, 1984). They decided, for example, that the person was hostile to most people but kind to family members, or that the person masked a hostile disposition with an appearance of kindness.

When people make the effort to reconcile inconsistent and contradictory information, it has several effects on cognitive processing and impressions. First, people spend more time thinking about unexpected behaviors than about expected ones. For example, if you read that your liberal mayor is fighting for a conservative position such as a reduction in the minimum wage for young workers, you might pay extra attention, although you might quickly pass over more expected news of his support of several liberal causes (Belmore & Hubbard, 1987). Second, people try to explain unexpected behaviors—to make sense of them. Thus, you might begin to wonder why the mayor supports reducing the minimum wage. Perhaps you will decide that he supports this measure because it will provide more jobs for the poor and disadvantaged, whose cause he generally favors. As we noted earlier, people are more likely to make causal attributions about unexpected events than about events that are normal and expected (Hastie, 1984). Finally, extra processing improves people's ability to recall inconsistent behaviors. The special attributional processing that we give to inconsistent behaviors may help us remember them better than the behaviors consistent with our expectations (Hastie & Kumar, 1979; Srull, 1981). In fact, any behaviors that people explain can be better recalled at a later time, compared with behaviors that people read but do not explain (Hastie, 1984). This is true whether the behaviors are consistent or inconsistent with the person's expectations.

Even when people make an effort at reconciliation, their impressions of others do not always change. For example, in a study conducted in the Netherlands, inconsistent behaviors sometimes had no effect on people's impressions (Vonk, 1995). One reason is that the extensive processing may be directed at explaining away the inconsistency. If unexpected behaviors can be attributed to situational factors, the initial impression can be maintained intact (Crocker, Hannah, & Weber, 1983). Thus, a battered woman might defend her impression that her abusive partner is basically a good person by attributing his occasional violence to external factors, such as the effects of alcohol or, sadly, even some behavior of her own.

Integrating Inconsistencies. Still, as you get to know someone well over a period of time, encounters with more and more potential inconsistencies should lead you to develop a more complex impression of the person. In these circumstances, research shows that impressions do indeed become less consistent and also more complex and elaborated, featuring a larger number of causal links (Welbourne, 2001). The causal attributions may reflect the perceiver's attempts to interpret and reconcile inconsistencies, as we just discussed. Interestingly, the most complex impressions were not necessarily of those individuals the perceiver had known for the longest time, but of individuals who were encountered in a number of different contexts. If you only see someone in the classroom day after day, week after week, your impression may remain quite simple and consistent. It is when you also get to know that person in the context of her family, performing in the community theater, and in her part-time job that impressions grow more multi-faceted and complex.

Altering Impressions: Is Fundamental Change Possible? By now, you may be pretty pessimistic about the possibility of ever changing an established impression. Because so many processes tend to maintain our views, it is not surprising that even long weeks of interaction can leave people's initial impressions largely intact (Kenny, 1991; Park, 1986). Is fundamental change in impressions ever possible? Linda Silka's (1989) research offers some reason for optimism. Silka's participants read the life history of a young woman

SOCIAL PSYCHOLOGY AND CULTURE: CULTURE AND PERCEPTIONS OF CHANGE

Like many other aspects of person perception, perceptions of change differ for different perceivers and in different cultures. Some people are ready to believe that an individual's personality or abilities have changed over time, whereas others seem to see such psychological attributes as fixed and unchanging (Dweck & Leggett, 1988). And collectivists (compared to individualists) are more likely to view people's behavior as changing with circumstances and social contexts. As we have said, this is one reason that in explaining behaviors collectivists are less affected by the correspondence bias (Norenzayan & Nisbett, 2000). In fact, this tendency appears to be just one facet of a much more general readiness of collectivists to perceive change (Spencer-Rodgers, Williams, & Peng, 2010). Researchers gave simple scenarios to American (individualist) and Chinese (collectivist) college students (Ji, Nisbett, & Su, 2001). The scenarios described a situation and asked about the possibility that it would change to the reverse; for example, "Richard grew up in a poor family but he managed to go to college. How likely is it that he will become rich some day?" or "Two children are fighting in kindergarten. How likely is it that they will ever become lovers?" Across five different scenarios, the Chinese rated the possibility of change higher than Americans. The general emphasis on change in collectivist cultures means that people from these places may be more willing than individualists to see people as changing in fundamental ways, or as simultaneously possessing opposite characteristics.

who appeared, at least on the surface, to change greatly. Lany Tyler was a high school cheerleader who, although she initially failed to win admission to college, eventually obtained a Ph.D. and became a Princeton University professor of history. Those asked to write about how Lany had changed had no trouble identifying examples, noting that she changed "from the stereotypical 'social butterfly' to an intellectually geared individual" (p. 126). This finding suggests that when people are actively looking for change in an individual, they are able to perceive it. Indeed, faced with inconsistent information for which no situational explanations are obvious, people often make sense of the behaviors by assuming that the person's beliefs, attitudes, motivation, or ability have changed (Allison, Mackie, Muller, & Worth, 1993; Silka, 1989).

CONCLUDING COMMENTS

As you reflect on the evidence presented in this chapter, you may conclude that biases in impressions are pretty hard to overcome. Most of the time that is true. We get a lot of mileage out of the simple general principle that behavior reflects personality. Sometimes this principle is valid, and our impressions based on just a few seconds of someone else's behavior can be accurate. Yet we also know that human nature is more complicated than this rule would indicate. When accuracy is of the utmost importance, we attend fully, process carefully, and are sometimes rewarded with even more accurate impressions of other people. But why are simple principles, with all their possibilities of bias, usually more than adequate for our needs?

First, in many cases, our needs for accuracy in day-to-day life are modest. Correspondent inferences work perfectly well if our encounters with people are limited to particular situations or roles. For example, your assumption that the office bookkeeper is a quiet and restrained person on the basis of his office demeanor will not create problems if the office is the only place the two of you interact—though you might be surprised to see how he acts at a wild party. We can ignore people's individual personalities and still interact successfully with them if their behaviors are governed largely by the power of social situations and roles.

Second, people's behavior in particular situations often accurately reflects their personalities because they choose to be in those situations. Suppose you watch someone telling jokes at a comedy try-out. Technically, it might be correct that her provocative, lively, and funny behaviors are called for by this situation. But since the would-be comedian chose the situation, it is probably reasonable to assume that she is a lively, funny person. Thus, a correspondent inference works just fine.

Third, correspondent inferences are often accurate because other people offer us accurate cues to their true nature, at least as they themselves perceive it. As you will see in the next chapter, being perceived accurately by others is rewarding and being misperceived is frustrating and uncomfortable. So the lover of baroque music might wear a J. S. Bach T-shirt to let us know. Even if the cues a new acquaintance offers do not ring quite true, it is often wise to go along for the ride, accepting rather than challenging the person. Certainly the interaction will go more smoothly if we save the other's face.

Thus, people's tendency to take others' behaviors or observable cues at face value can grease the wheels of social interaction, and this tendency usually lets us get along quite well. Still, going beyond first impressions to seek greater accuracy in person perception is sometimes important. When choosing a housemate, we want to predict a variety of compatible behaviors accurately on the basis of a few items of background information and a brief conversation. Serving on a jury, we want to decide whether the defendant or the accuser is telling the truth.

In the final analysis, both accurate and inaccurate impressions flow from the same underlying processes that people use as they attempt to understand others. Therefore, it is these processes that social psychologists seek to understand. They include tapping our stored knowledge to make quick inferences about observed behaviors, thinking about the causes of behaviors or other events, integrating multiple items of information to make a decision and reconciling inconsistencies. People use these basic processes not only to understand other people, but also to understand other social objects. In the chapters that follow we will discuss how similar processes operate as we perceive and interpret ourselves (Chapter 4), our own and other social groups (Chapter 5), consumer products and social issues (Chapter 7), our loved ones (Chapter 12), even our enemies (Chapter 13). Nothing in the nature of these processes necessarily leads to either accurate or inaccurate judgments. Accuracy depends more on the circumstances in which the processes are applied: the amount of useful information available, the applicability of the person's knowledge, the amount of effort the person is willing and able to put in, and whether the goal is to be accurate or to form a particular impression. Our perceptions of all social objects—including other people—are not determined solely by their observable characteristics. Instead, they also reflect our own individuality and uniqueness as perceivers: our motives and biases, our cognitive limitations, and the content and accessibility of our pre-existing knowledge.

SUMMARY

Forming First Impressions: Cues, Interpretations, and Inferences. Perceptions of other people begin with visible cues, including physical appearance, nonverbal communication, the environments they create and occupy, and overt behavior. Familiarity arising from **mere exposure** also affects impressions, generally leading to increased liking. Cues that are **salient**—that stand out and attract attention in the context in which they occur—are particularly influential.

These cues have no meaning in themselves, but are **automatically** interpreted in the light of our existing knowledge or **mental representations** of people, behaviors, traits, and social situations. A representation that is **associated** with the cue itself or is **accessible** and easy to bring to mind is most likely to be used in interpreting cues. Accessibility can stem from the person's expectations, moods, the situational context, recent activation (termed **priming**)—even if the priming was **subliminal**, or from frequent activation of the representation.

When processing **superficially**, people often make **correspondent inferences**, assuming that others have inner qualities that correspond to their observable behaviors. In fact, people often make correspondent inferences even when situational causes actually account for behaviors, a pattern termed the **correspondence bias**.

Beyond First Impressions: Systematic Processing. To go beyond a first impression, people must engage in more **systematic** thought, particularly to make **causal attributions** for behavior. People usually consider potential causes that are associated with the behavior, generally accessible, salient in context, or suggested by the pattern of available information.

When external factors appear to have caused behavior, people may attempt to **discount** or correct their initial correspondent inference about the actor's characteristics. This correction takes time and cognitive effort, however, so it often does not occur.

An impression of another person usually includes several characteristics. People may infer additional traits based on their knowledge or observations of the individual. The multiple components of an impression may become linked as people attempt to infer causal connections among them. Overall impressions, too, are usually constructed by integrating the good and bad features of others.

Even considered impressions may not be completely accurate. When people devote extra thought to forming an impression, biases may still limit their accuracy, and the extra efforts may only confirm an existing positive or negative view. Unless people are aware of such biases in social perception, they are unlikely to try to correct them.

The Impact of Impressions: Using, Defending, and Changing Impressions. Once an impression is formed, it becomes a basis for judgments and behaviors. Sometimes decisions about others rest on simple, superficial processing; at other times, people engage in systematic processing, attempting to put together the implications of all relevant information.

Impressions tend to resist change, partly because an initial impression can alter the interpretation of later information in a pattern termed the **primacy effect**. As a result,

CHAPTER 3 THEMES

■ **Construction of Reality**
Our impressions of others are constructions based on our own selection and interpretation of cues.

■ **Pervasiveness of Social Influence**
General knowledge shaped by our culture and past experiences enters into our impressions of others.

■ **Striving for Mastery**
Accurate understanding of others helps us deal successfully with them.

■ **Conservatism**
Once formed, an impression of another person tends to perpetuate itself by affecting our interpretations and our interactions.

■ **Accessibility**
The most salient cues and our most accessible knowledge contribute the most to our impressions.

■ **Superficiality Versus Depth**
Sometimes we are content with first impressions and snap judgments, but sometimes we strive to understand others more deeply.

impressions may survive even the discrediting of the information on which they were based, creating a **perseverance bias**. Impressions shape overt interaction as well as judgments. They often lead people to seek consistent information or even to elicit confirming actions from others, creating a **self-fulfilling prophecy**.

Still, sometimes people encounter information that is clearly inconsistent with an impression. They may attempt to explain it away in various ways, or they may take it into account and assume that the other person has changed. Most of the time, however, people's impressions of others' personal characteristics are stable and difficult to change.

THE SELF

How do you rate your driving skills? Your honesty, social sensitivity, and leadership skills? Are you about average, below average, or above average on these qualities? It turns out that most people think of themselves as above average on a wide range of desirable characteristics like these (Larwood & Whittaker, 1977; Svenson, 1981; Weinstein, 1987), and perhaps you do too. But think about it. When nearly one million high school students were surveyed in one study, 89% said they were above average in getting along with others—and they can't all be right. The same goes for the 70% who rated themselves above average on leadership, and the 60% who said the same thing about their athletic skills (College Board, 1976–77). This self-enhancing tendency has been termed the "Lake Wobegon effect," after the humorist Garrison Keillor's mythical town where "all the children are above average." How do people arrive at these inflated views of themselves and then defend them in the face of inevitable negative evidence? How does our tendency to see ourselves in a highly positive light co-exist with our need to perceive ourselves accurately? Questions like these are important because what you think of yourself, how you feel about yourself, and the ways you choose to express yourself influence virtually all aspects of your life. One indication of the importance of the self to almost everyone is that a Google search for the term "self" in 2013 turned up almost a billion hits.

What is this "self" anyway? Since ancient times philosophers have admonished: "Know thyself," for the self is an object of knowledge. What we call the self has two components: the self-concept, what we know about ourselves, and self-esteem, how we feel about ourselves. You may be confident that you are shy or honest or intelligent or attractive. You may feel that, all things considered, you are a pretty decent human being. Although these parts of our self seem as familiar and comfortable as a favorite pair of jeans, both develop and change as our experiences, life circumstances, and social surroundings do. So how do you come to know what you are like? The first part of this chapter looks at the way we form our impressions of the self, how we come to know what qualities and characteristics we have. In many ways, forming impressions of the self is very similar to the way we perceive other people. However, as you will see in the second part of the chapter, where we discuss how we feel about ourselves, we bring more biases to the process of self-perception. For most of us, although the self-portraits we paint are accurate in a general way, they are also colored by powerful motivational pressures to think well of ourselves.

Why do we need to know who we are? The reason is that self-knowledge is crucial in directing and regulating our thoughts, feelings, and behaviors. Self-knowledge lets us seek out situations that match our capabilities: Knowing ourselves to be good at tennis, we welcome the opportunity to compete on the court. Goals that are important in defining who we are dictate our emotional responses to events. For example, valued accomplishments arouse pride and joy, whereas events that threaten or thwart us evoke fear or anger. And when we choose to coach Little League on the weekends or volunteer for Habitat for Humanity, our sense of self guides our behavior as we try to show others the kind of person we are. In the third part of the chapter we see the self in action, regulating and directing our interpretations and interactions with the social world.

In the final section of this chapter we consider what happens when our sense of self is challenged—when what happens is not what we planned, hoped for, or expected. Will juggling school work and a social life or failing admission to your preferred sorority be too much for you? How do people cope with sudden illness, the loss of a job, or moving away from all one's childhood friends and family? The last part of the chapter examines our attempts to cope with stresses, failures, and inconsistencies. As you will see, the way we defend ourselves against threats and disappointments influences not only our emotional well-being but also our physical health.

CONSTRUCTING THE SELF-CONCEPT: LEARNING WHO WE ARE

self-concept
all of an individual's knowledge about his or her personal qualities

The **self-concept** is the set of all an individual's beliefs about his or her personal qualities. You might think that because we are dealing with ourselves that the self-concept is just simply or directly "known" to us. But, just as our impressions of other people are constructions based on available cues and our general knowledge, our self-concepts are also actively constructed. Indeed, if complete self-understanding were easily attained, philosophers would not have to advise us to seek the self, therapists would not spend hours helping people get in touch with themselves, and "self-help" books would not be necessary.

Sources of the Self-Concept

People construct the self-concept in much the same way they form impressions of others, by interpreting various types of cues. People often learn their own characteristics from their observed behaviors. They also use thoughts and feelings and other people's reactions to form impressions of themselves. Finally, people compare themselves to others to learn what characteristics make them unique.

If asked to describe yourself, you might report being a good organizer, talkative, just a little obsessed with being punctual, and scrupulously honest. How did you come to see yourself this way? Recall from Chapter 3 that we learn about and form impressions of others based on our interpretations of different sorts of cues. It turns out that we engage in a similar process when learning about and forming an impression of ourselves. That is, we piece together our self-concept over time from interpretations of many different kinds of cues. Some important cues originate from the self: we can interpret our own behaviors, thoughts, and feelings to learn who we are. But cues to our self-concept also come from others, as we can learn who we are by considering how other people react to us or by comparing ourselves to them.

Learning Who We Are from Our Own Behavior. British author E. M. Forster quipped, "How do I know what I think until I see what I say?" This tongue-in-cheek comment conveys the key idea of Daryl Bem's (1967) **self-perception theory**: We can learn things about ourselves by observing our own behavior. For example, when we star in a community theater production and decide we are extroverted, self-perception is at work (Rhodewalt & Agustsdottir, 1986; Salancik & Conway, 1975). According to the theory, people rely on their behavior to draw inferences about themselves, and this is especially true when we are first developing a self-concept or when we do not have a good sense of who we are in a particular domain.

self-perception theory
the theory that we make inferences about our personal characteristics on the basis of our overt behaviors when internal cues are weak or ambiguous

In addition, people are especially likely to draw self-inferences from behaviors that they see as having freely chosen. These behaviors are driven by intrinsic motivation. We are doing what we want to do rather than what we have to do. In contrast, when a behavior is performed as a means to some external end, it is governed by extrinsic motivation. Not only does such a behavior reveal less about our inner qualities, but we often lose pleasure in performing it (Deci, 1971; Harackiewicz, 1979).

Accordingly, providing external rewards often undermines intrinsic motivation, as Mark Lepper and his colleagues (Lepper, Greene, & Nisbett, 1973) have demonstrated. They introduced children to an attractive new activity: drawing with colorful markers. After drawing for a while, some children received a previously promised "Good Player" certificate, others unexpectedly received the same certificate, and still others received nothing. One to two weeks later, the markers were placed in the children's regular classroom. The amount of free time each child spent playing with the markers was recorded as a measure of their intrinsic motivation. The children who had not been rewarded and those who had received the unexpected reward retained their motivation, drawing for about 16% of the time. In contrast, children who expected and received an award used the markers for an average of only 8.6% of their free time.

Self-perception processes explain this drop in motivation. Children who saw themselves drawing pictures when a reward had been promised must have concluded that they drew for the reward, not just for the pleasure of creating the picture. In contrast, drawing with no anticipation of reward allowed other youngsters to infer that the activity must be interesting and enjoyable.

Even imagined behaviors can be input for self-perception processes. Take a moment to picture yourself doing various things to preserve the environment, perhaps recycling aluminum cans. Do you now see yourself as a more environmentally aware person? Self-perception processes again suggest that you will (C. A. Anderson & Godfrey, 1987). Thinking about actual or imagined behavior increases the accessibility of related personal characteristics. You might imagine solving a puzzle and then reflect on your good spatial memory, recalling that you loved playing with puzzles as a child. As thoughts like these come to mind, they become the basis for a self-inference: "I am very good at solving puzzles." Seeing the self as possessing relevant traits may improve not only your confidence, persistence, and effort, but also your actual performance on the task (Campbell & Fairey, 1985). Athletes and sports psychologists have put such findings to work. For example, in one study, some junior gymnasts were assigned to physically practice a new balance-beam move, and others to imagine doing the same move, trying to form a realistic image of every detail (D. Smith and others, 2007). After practicing these tasks three times a week for six weeks, the imagery group performed just as well as those who physically practiced, and both of these groups performed better than control gymnasts who just did stretching exercises.

Learning Who We Are from Thoughts and Feelings. Another important cue to learning who we are comes from an interpretation of our own thoughts and feelings. In fact, when it comes to knowing who we are, our own thoughts and feelings might have more impact than our behaviors. After all, we are often aware of the gap between what we think and feel and how we have to behave in the world. Attending your best friend's wedding may prompt you to act like the life of the party, but your inner feelings of envy and loss tell you more about yourself. One study underlines the importance of thoughts and feelings for self-knowledge (Andersen, 1984). Some observers in the study heard participants talk about their thoughts and feelings in various everyday situations, whereas others heard participants describe only their behaviors in those situations. The observers then wrote down their impressions. Observers who listened to descriptions of thoughts and feelings formed impressions that matched the participants' own self-concept more accurately than the impressions recorded by observers who heard only about behaviors. This finding suggests that our thoughts and feelings can play a bigger role than behaviors in our inferences about what we are like.

Learning Who We Are from Other People's Reactions. Other people's views of us also serve as a cue in the development of the self-concept. In 1902, the sociologist Charles H. Cooley coined the phrase the "looking-glass self" to indicate that one source of our self-knowledge is other people's reactions to us. These reactions serve as a kind of mirror, reflecting our image so that we, too, can see it (Felson, 1989). Parents coo over us. Peers belittle us. Relatives note with pleasure that we remind them of devout Aunt Agatha. These reactions tell us we are cute, clumsy, or religious.

One study supported the concept of the looking-glass self when it compared the behaviors of three groups of schoolchildren. Teachers and others repeatedly told some of the children that they were tidy. Children in another group were repeatedly instructed that they should be tidy, and the third group was not told anything special. The researchers then observed how much litter each group spread around. The tidiest youngsters were those in the first group. Labeled as tidy, they behaved accordingly, reflecting their new self-concept (R. L. Miller, Brickman, & Bolen, 1975).

Being explicitly labeled with a trait, like tidy, may shape your self-concept. But, others need not explicitly announce "you are tidy" to produce the same result. Indeed, other people's more subtle reactions may do the trick. For example, when your parents consistently enlist you, and not your sister, to run important errands, they are implicitly communicating that you are more helpful and reliable. You may then begin to see yourself in these ways.

Other people's reactions have the largest effects on people whose self-concepts are uncertain or are still developing (as with the "tidy" children in the study just described). For most adults, in contrast, self-views rely more on other types of evidence, such as comparisons with other people, as we will see next.

Learning Who We Are from Social Comparison. If you, as a moderately skilled chess player, want to know how good you really are, your best approach is not to listen to what other people tell you about your playing skills, but to play a lot of games and see how many you win. This is the idea behind **social comparison theory**, which states that the self-concept is often shaped by comparisons between ourselves and others. This theory was initially proposed by Leon Festinger (1954), who assumed that people would gain the most accurate information about themselves by seeking out similar others for comparison. According to this view, you learn more by comparing your chess game with that of opponents with similar skills than by judging yourself against either world chess champion Viswanathan Anand or a rank beginner.

It might be intuitively obvious that comparing your own average chess abilities to one of the most skilled players of all time or to a beginner could lead to inaccurate self-views. Indeed, research has shown that when we compare our own average skills to those who are extremely good or bad, we often see ourselves in the opposite way, termed a **contrast effect** (Mussweiler, Ruter, & Epstude, 2004). Thus, when comparing yourself to Anand, you might conclude that you are lousy, but when comparing yourself to a beginner, you might surmise that you are a chess wizard. Perhaps for this reason, Festinger contended that comparisons with similar others should lead to fairly accurate self-knowledge. Although this seems quite sensible, it turns out that comparisons to similar others may also bias self-views. Even if you compared your average chess-playing self with someone who is only moderately good or moderately bad at chess, your self-views will move slightly in that same direction, termed an **assimilation effect** (Mussweiler and others, 2004). That is, you will see your own chess skills as a little bit better when comparing to someone who is slightly more skilled than you, and a little bit worse when comparing to someone who is slightly less skilled.

Like the self-fulfilling prophecy (discussed in Chapter 3), the looking-glass self involves an observer's reactions that influence someone else's behavior and self-concept (D. T. Miller & Turnbull, 1986). Chapter 3 noted that self-fulfilling prophecies mainly affect people who are uncertain of their actual self-concept, and the same is true with the looking-glass self.

social comparison theory
the theory that people learn about and evaluate their personal qualities by comparing themselves to others

contrast effect
an effect of a comparison standard or prime that makes the perceiver's judgment more different from the standard

assimilation effect
an effect of a comparison standard or prime that makes the perceiver's judgment more similar to the standard

Photo 4.1 Social comparisons and the self. The male tennis player may infer that he is very unskilled if he watches the female tennis player perform extremely well during drills. Indeed, we often learn who we are by comparing ourselves to others.

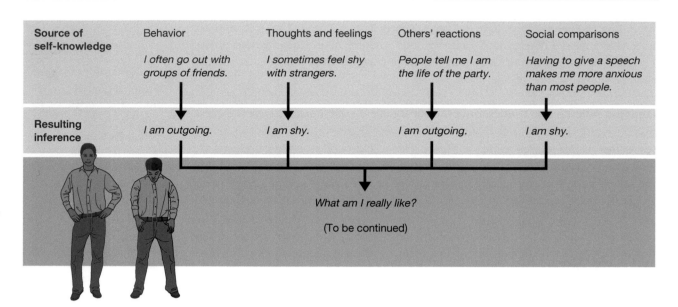

Figure 4.1 Sources of self-knowledge
Because no one is totally consistent all the time, multiple sources of information about ourselves may lead to potentially conflicting inferences, which will eventually have to be integrated.

Chapter 6 will deal with the aspects of self-knowledge, such as our membership in social groups, that we share in common with other people.

Of course, people have multiple motives for comparing themselves to others (Suls, Martin, & Wheeler, 2002), and these spring from our fundamental motivational principles. As just described, people may seek accurate self-knowledge (mastery), but they might also make comparisons to show solidarity with others (connectedness), or to feel better about themselves (valuing me and mine; Helgeson & Mickelson, 1995).

Besides affording shifts in our self-views, social comparisons are important in helping us shape our sense of uniqueness. The attributes that distinguish us from most others often become defining features of the self. Children writing self-descriptions are likely to mention characteristics, such as being left-handed or having red hair, that mark them as unusual in their family or classroom (W. J. McGuire & McGuire, 1981; W. J. McGuire & Padawer-Singer, 1978). By summarizing the ways in which we differ from others, social comparison permits us to construct a self-concept that gives each of us a strong sense of being unique and distinctive.

Figure 4.1 shows the many sources of the self-concept. Note that social influences are pervasive even as we are constructing the self and learning what makes us unique.

Learning about Self and Others: The Same or Different?

Despite the general similarity between the ways people learn about themselves and others, self-knowledge is richer and more detailed than knowledge about others. People can observe themselves in more situations and have better access to private thoughts and feelings. People also tend to explain their own and other people's behaviors differently. However, these differences do not guarantee that our self views are more insightful than others' views of us.

Most of the time, the cues we use to learn about ourselves are the same sorts of cues we use to learn about others. Our reliance on similar sorts of cues creates important similarities between our knowledge about the self and about others, but there are differences as well, particularly in the number of cues we have and in the type of knowledge we draw from them.

Differences in Cues and Knowledge. We usually have a greater quantity and variety of cues about ourselves than we have about others. For example, we see ourselves in a wider range of situations and for more time than we do anyone else. This fact probably explains why we view ourselves as quite variable and flexible, whereas we view other people as more set in their ways (T. L. Baxter & Goldberg, 1987). Asked to state whether they are serious or carefree, for example, most people will describe themselves by saying, "In-between" or "It depends." But they freely characterize strangers as closer to the extremes (Prentice, 1990; Sande, Goethals, & Radloff, 1988). Interestingly, the number of cues and type of knowledge we have about close others fall somewhere between the richness of self-knowledge and the paucity of stranger knowledge. A best friend, a long-time romantic partner, a sibling, or a parent is a person who, like ourselves, we have observed over a long period of time across many contexts. Thus, like the self, we may characterize close others as variable and flexible.

In addition to observing ourselves across more situations than we observe others, we also have special access to one type of cue about ourselves that we rarely, if ever, have about others: inner thoughts. This simple fact can lead to a host of inferences that differ for the self compared to other people (Pronin, 2008). For instance, we may see ourselves, relative to others, as less conformist because we are aware of our thoughts like "Isn't this silly?" even as we go along with the latest fashion trend. However, we typically do not know the inner thoughts of others and thus may make judgments of them based on their outward conformity (Pronin, Berger, & Molouki, 2007). Of course, sometimes other people, especially close others, divulge their inner thoughts to us. In these cases, we may have good access to this information, making self and other perceptions quite similar.

Just because we lack direct access to others' inner thoughts does not stop us from trying to surmise what they might be. But, as we shall see, these efforts can lead to erroneous conclusions. One common strategy we employ to infer others' thoughts is to consider our own thoughts, assume that others have similar thoughts, and then adjust them, if necessary, to reflect specific information we know about that other person (Epley, 2008). For example, if trying to guess what a co-worker thinks of a new television comedy, you may start with your own positive reaction to the show. You then assume your co-worker also likes the show, but may guess that her evaluation may be slightly less favorable than yours, as you believe her humor style differs somewhat from yours. If your co-worker had a completely different reaction to the show than you did, this strategy will obviously fail. Thus, our efforts to determine others' inner thoughts may lead us astray.

Differences in Inferences. Because we have greater access to our own reactions, we are more aware of the impact people, places, and events have on us than of the impact they have on others. As a result, we may draw different inferences about the causes of behaviors. Recall for a moment the last time you became really angry and yelled at someone. Why did you act the way you did? Try to answer the same question about the last person who became irate at you. Why did he or she do that?

You may have answered these similar questions in very different ways. In explaining your own aggressive actions, you may have pointed to external factors, perhaps saying that the person you became angry with had been really annoying and provocative. Answering the same question about someone else, you may have cited that person's personal characteristics: He or she is just an aggressive type who boils over easily. These different answers reflect an **actor-observer effect**, the idea that people tend to attribute their own choices and actions to situational factors but to attribute others' choices and actions to internal characteristics. E. E. Jones and Richard Nisbett proposed this idea in 1972, and there are a few reasons that these actor–observer differences could occur.

First, when we witness another person's behavior, that person is salient: He or she is the focus of attention and stands out against the background (Heider, 1958; Storms, 1973). In contrast, when we act, we literally look out at the world, so the stimulus or trigger for our action is the salient factor. You see the snake in the grass as causing your sudden jump, whereas a passerby focuses mainly on your startle response and may conclude that you are an easily frightened person. Second, when asked why something occurred, people consider alternative causes, but they consider different alternatives for the self and for others (Kahneman & Miller, 1986; McGill, 1989). For example, if someone asks you why you liked the latest John Grisham thriller, you will probably assume that the questioner means why you liked it as compared to other books you've read. Obviously, then, it would be reasonable to cite the aspects of the novel that distinguish it from others, providing a situational cause for your behavior. But if someone asks why a friend of yours liked the same book, you might assume that the questioner seeks to learn why this friend among all other people liked the book, and so you might cite some of your friend's unique personal characteristics, leading you to provide internal causes for your friend's behavior (McGill, 1989; Wells & Gavanski, 1989).

At one time, the actor-observer effect was considered a robust and pervasive phenomenon (e.g., Watson, 1982), but recent insights suggest this effect is much smaller than once assumed and occurs in much more limited circumstances (Malle, 2006). For example, actor-observer effects may operate differently depending on whether the to-be-explained action is positive or negative (Malle, 2006). The classic actor-observer effect emerges reliably for negative actions (for example, an academic failure), but it may reverse for positive behaviors (for example, an academic success)—partly to boost self-esteem, people like to take personal credit for their successes. Moreover, the actor-observer effect is more likely when a behavior is seen as deviating widely from what most others do in a particular circumstance, compared to behaviors that seem more typical. Malle (1999) suggests that the most fundamental difference between actors and observers is that actors usually explain their behaviors by their own beliefs and goals, whereas observers more often cite more remote causes of those beliefs or goals. Thus, you might say you tried out for the track team because you wanted an activity that would help you stay fit (your goal) and believed you would be able to make the team. In contrast, a friend might explain your behavior by noting that one of your close relatives was overweight and died of heart disease: a potential cause that presumably contributed to your goal of keeping fit.

actor-observer effect
the idea that we attribute our own behaviors to situational causes while seeing others' acts as due to their inner characteristics

Similar Shortcomings: More Is Not Always Better. When considering other people, we sometimes devote a great deal of careful thought to forming our impressions of them. As discussed in Chapter 3, thinking more about others does not always lead to better or more insightful impressions. Similarly, although we know a great deal more about ourselves than we do about others, having all this extra knowledge does not necessarily mean we have better or more insightful self impressions. In fact, being the leading authority on the topic does not guarantee that we are always aware of why we think, feel, and act the way we do (Nisbett & Wilson, 1977). Consider the efforts of 50 students who for 5 weeks kept diaries of their positive and negative moods and tried to identify the sources of those moods. They recorded many potential causes, such as whether the weather was sunny or wet and whether it was a Monday or a weekend day. Another group of students was simply asked to describe how these factors generally affect people's moods. Despite their efforts at self-analysis, the diary keepers' reports about the causes of their own moods were no different than the blind guesses of people who did not know them (Wilson, Laser, & Stone, 1982). Apparently, all the participants relied on general causal theories, like the idea that rainy days and Mondays cause blue moods, even if they were explaining their own moods. Thus, the vast wealth of self-knowledge we possess does not guarantee that we can generate unique insights into our own behavior, beyond what strangers may be able to guess.

Sometimes people's judgments about the self are influenced not by the content of self-knowledge but by motives that will increase or decrease their accuracy in making those judgments (like the motive to value me and mine), a subject we will turn to later.

Multiple Selves

Because people see themselves in a wide range of situations and roles, self-knowledge is organized around multiple roles, activities, and relationships. People vary in the number and diversity of "selves" that they believe they possess.

As information about the self accumulates from all these different sources, we become aware that we have many different "selves." We begin to see that some of our behaviors, thoughts, and feelings depend on what we are doing and who our companions are (Markus & Wurf, 1987). For instance, most of us probably act and feel differently when we are working with our office mates—perhaps more responsibly and less playfully—than we do when we are with family and close friends. Social comparisons also vary from situation to situation. Someone who is one of the least polite people at work may be the most polite family member at home. Others' reactions also differ. Older relatives may view a 40-year-old physician as a youngster, but his co-workers may see him as a mature leader in the field of transplant surgery.

How do we deal with all this varying and potentially confusing information? We organize it according to our various roles, activities, and relationships (Carver & Scheier, 1981; T. B. Rogers, 1981). Thus, a woman might consider herself studious in academic situations, hard-working at the office, and fun-loving when relaxing with a group of friends. Each of these different **self-aspects** summarizes what she believes she is like in a particular domain, role, or activity (McConnell, 2011). Other self-aspects may reflect

self-aspects
Summaries of a person's beliefs about the **self** in specific domains, roles, or activities

additional roles and activities such as sister, lover, chess player, or jogger (Hoelter, 1985). Distinct self-aspects in our mental representation of the self are the inner reflection of the fact that we actually do think, feel, and behave differently when we are in different social roles, groups, and relationships.

Putting It All Together: Constructing a Coherent Self-Concept

People try to fit the diverse elements of the self-concept together in a way that seems coherent and stable. Coherence can be attained by focusing on a few central traits, making accessible only limited aspects of the self at any given time, and by selectively remembering past acts.

Self-knowledge is assembled from disparate pieces of self-knowledge derived from our multiple roles and social interactions, and the pieces may not fit together very well. You may be an eager participant in one class but unmotivated in another. You may be a vociferous team leader but reserved off the field. And yet, individuals come to have a sense of unity and constancy about themselves. People typically feel that they have always been a certain way. Indeed, few people describe themselves as chameleon-like, constantly changing. People achieve this coherence through various strategies (Baumeister, 1998), and, as we shall see, culture strongly affects their choice of strategies.

self-schema
core characteristics that a person believes characterize him or her across situations

First, people can construct a unified and enduring sense of self by noting a few core attributes they believe characterize them uniquely among people and consistently across situations. These personal characteristics form the **self-schema** (Markus, 1977). Once a particular characteristic is incorporated into the self-schema, people notice and process information about it very efficiently. For example, people whose self-schema includes a trait like helpful can answer questions like "Are you helpful?" more quickly than other individuals (Markus, 1977). People tend to see evidence for these core traits even in their most mundane behaviors, thereby reinforcing their sense of a stable and unitary self (Cantor & Kihlstrom, 1987). Thus, you might see confirmation for your view of yourself as helpful even in a trivial interaction like giving directions to a stranger on campus. Though people may view themselves as variable in some ways, the key traits that comprise the self-schema are seen as stable, contributing to our sense of a coherent self.

Second, self-coherence can be achieved by making accessible at any one time only a subset of our self-knowledge and self-aspects. Your loud and fun self at your roommate's party may seem quite inconsistent with your quiet and serious self in the classroom. But, if only one of these selves is accessible at a particular moment, you may not experience or notice this contradiction. In one study, researchers asked biased questions to induce students to reflect on either their past introverted or extraverted behaviors (Fazio, Effrein, & Falender, 1981). Increasing the accessibility of a biased subset of the self-concept in this way not only caused the students to rate themselves as more introverted or extraverted (depending on their experimental condition), but even made them behave accordingly. As this experiment demonstrates, different self-aspects will be accessible in different situations, so at any given time you will rarely be uncomfortably aware of potential inconsistencies.

Finally, self-coherence can be created and maintained through selective memory. As people think about their past, they reconstruct an autobiography or life story (e.g.,

McAdams, 2001) that integrates their various self-aspects and characteristics. For example, people whose behavior has changed from shy to outgoing may retrieve a biased set of autobiographical memories in which they were always outgoing (M. Ross & Conway, 1986). Reconstruction may shape the basic materials drawn from memory in a way that suits the person's current goals (Conway & Pleydell-Pearce, 2000), as inconvenient or inconsistent bits of information are simply forgotten (Greenwald, 1980). This strategy gives the person a sense of self that feels coherent over time, even if it fails to accurately record the facts of personal history.

As we saw earlier, different sources often provide mixed information about the self. But Figure 4.2 illustrates the several ways that people can construct a self-concept that is coherent and meaningful.

Across all cultures the primary function of the self-concept is the same. For people to survive and flourish, they must adapt successfully to their environment, particularly the social environment consisting of other people. The self-concept is a crucial aid in that adaptation. Knowing our unique configuration of personal talents and social ties allows us to choose goals that we can reasonably attain, avoid situations that make us miserable, and act in ways that play up our strong points while compensating for our shortcomings (Higgins, 1996b). One might intuitively expect that the self-concept is most helpful in

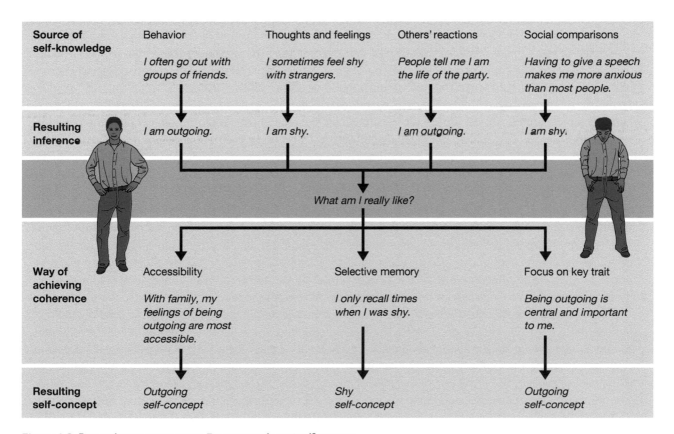

Figure 4.2 Reconciling inconsistencies: Forming a coherent self-concept
We have several ways to reconcile inconsistencies in the process of forming a stable and coherent self-concept. Different people select different strategies from among these alternatives.

SOCIAL PSYCHOLOGY AND CULTURE: CULTURAL DIFFERENCES IN THE SELF-CONCEPT

Imagine two stubborn 4-year-olds, each steadfastly refusing to taste the carrots. "Just try them," coaxes one mother, "vegetables help you grow up big and strong. You want to be big and strong, don't you?" The other caregiver tries a different tactic: "Think of the farmer who grew the carrots so you could have them to eat. He will be so disappointed if you don't like them. Just a taste, to make the farmer happy!" Perhaps you recognize one or the other of these strategies. In fact, the first "you-oriented" approach is more often used by parents in individualist cultures, whereas the second strategy reflects the "other-directed" concerns of collectivist cultures. Do cultures with such different emphases also foster different conceptions of the self?

Although members of all cultures seek a coherent sense of the self, Hazel Markus and Shinobu Kitayama (1991; Markus, Kitayama, & VandenBos, 1996) suggest that cultures emphasize different ways of constructing a coherent sense of self. In individualist cultures, typical of many of the countries of North America and Western Europe, people tend to see the self as independent, separate from other people, and revealed primarily in inner thoughts and feelings. North American students describing themselves tend to list general attributes that mark them as unique or distinctive individuals, such as "I am intelligent" or "I am musical"—the sort of characteristics that make up the self-schema. In contrast, people in collectivist cultures found in many parts of Asia, Africa, and South America tend to see the self as connected with others and revealed primarily in social roles and relationships, not in unique personal characteristics. Chinese students are more likely than those from individualist cultures to define themselves in terms of relationships, roles, or attributes they share with others, such as "I am a daughter" or "I am Buddhist" (Trafimow, Triandis, & Goto, 1991). The importance of social connections is so great that in one study where Asian people were asked to recall memories from their own past, they often reported visualizing them from a "third person" perspective—as if looking at themselves from an observer's viewpoint. Americans, in contrast, typically report experiencing such memories from their own visual perspective (Cohen & Gunz, 2002).

Because relationships with others are so important in collectivist cultures, members of those cultures place relatively more emphasis on self-aspects—their social roles and relationships with others—to define the self, than they do on self-schemata (Cousins, 1989; Markus & Kitayama, 1991). Because different social roles and relationships may call for quite different behaviors and traits, collectivists may have self-concepts that incorporate more variability, inconsistencies, and even contradictions than individualists do (Choi & Choi, 2002). In fact, greater contextual self-variation is seen among those from collectivist cultures, especially when considering relationship contexts (English & Chen, 2007). In one study, East Asian American and European American students were asked to rate themselves in either a pair of settings, like being at the gym or the cafeteria, or in a pair of relationships, like friends and roommates. European American students reported self-trait ratings that were quite consistent across different settings and relationships. On the other hand, the East Asian American students showed substantial trait rating variability across relationship types, but judged themselves consistently across settings. Table 4.1 shows some of the contrasts between individualist and collectivist cultural views of the self.

Across all cultures, though, there are similarities in self-knowledge. First, each of us has the capacity to think of ourselves in both individualist and collectivist ways. Gardner and others (Gardner, Gabriel, & Lee, 1999) found that priming American students with individualism or collectivism caused them to display the types of values and judgments characteristic of those respective cultures. Thus, our everyday cultural surroundings or more transitory influences like priming can make one or the other more accessible. Second, though there appears to be greater variation in self-concept across relationship types in collectivist samples, those from both types of cultures appear to show similar degrees of self-concept consistency over time within a particular context (English & Chen, 2007).

■■■

■■■

TABLE 4.1 Some Differences Between Construction of the Self in Individualist and Collectivist Cultures

Feature	Individualist culture	Collectivist culture
Definition of the self	Unique individual, separate from social context	Connected with others in mesh of social roles and relationships
Structure of the self	Unitary and stable, constant across situations and relationships	Fluid and variable, changing from one situation or relationship to another
Important features	Internal, private self (abilities, thoughts, feelings, traits)	External, public self (statuses, roles, relationships)
Significant tasks	Being unique Expressing yourself Promoting your own goals Being direct (saying what's on your mind)	Belonging, fitting in Acting appropriately Promoting group goals Being indirect (reading others' minds)

Source: Adapted from "Culture and the self: Implications for cognition, emotion, and motivation," by H. Markus and S. Kitayama, *Psychological Review, 98,* p. 230. Copyright © 1991 by the American Psychological Association. Adapted with permission.

guiding our adaptation if it is accurate. After all, if we held inflated ideas of our own capabilities, we might be tempted into situations that demanded more than we could produce, setting ourselves up for disappointment and failure. Nevertheless, accuracy is but only one important goal we pursue in constructing our self-knowledge. As we shall soon see, other goals are important as well.

CONSTRUCTING SELF-ESTEEM: HOW WE FEEL ABOUT OURSELVES

The self-concept is what we think about the self; **self-esteem**, the positive or negative evaluation of the self, is how we feel about it (E. E. Jones, 1990a). Trait self-esteem captures a person's relatively chronic feelings about the self. It is reflected in people's agreement or disagreement with statements like: "I feel I'm a person of worth," or "On the whole, I am satisfied with myself" (M. Rosenberg, 1965). State self-esteem, on the other hand, captures a person's relatively fleeting feelings about the self in a particular moment. It is reflected in people's agreement or disagreement with statements like: "I feel inferior to others at this moment," "I am pleased with my appearance right now," and "I feel as smart as others" (Heatherton & Polivy, 1991). Thus, a person might have generally high trait self-esteem, but her state self-esteem might plummet temporarily right after failing an exam or a romantic break-up. As these examples underscore, our feelings of mastery (Baumeister and colleagues, 2003) and connectedness to others (Leary and others, 1995) play crucial roles in our self-esteem; that is, when we feel we are performing well or are included by others, our self-esteem is high.

self-esteem

an individual's positive or negative evaluation of himself or herself

Balancing Accuracy and Enhancement

Accurate self-knowledge regarding our capabilities and preferences is important for guiding us through our lives. But accuracy is not the only consideration in evaluating the self: We are also greatly influenced by motivational pressures to think well of the self.

Self-esteem summarizes how we are doing at using our self-knowledge to navigate the social world. To see how this works, consider that to successfully regulate anything, such as your financial life, it is important to keep track of your current standing, for example, with a bank statement showing your balance at the end of each month. Like a bank statement that shows how well you are managing your income and expenses, self-esteem is a signal of how well you are doing in successfully adapting to your own social world (Leary, Tambor, Terdal, & Downs, 1995). It tracks the net result of your successes and failures, achievements and difficulties, as well as your acclaim or rejection by important other people (Baldwin & Sinclair, 1996). But to serve its proper role, self-esteem should be a relatively accurate reflection of how you are doing. What use would be an inaccurate bank statement that showed you with hundreds of dollars more than you really have? It would only encourage you to overspend and leave you with an empty account.

Yet here is a puzzle. Despite the clear value of accurate knowledge, people generally tend to inflate their own abilities and accomplishments, seeking to elevate their self-esteem. For example, consider the "Lake Wobegon" effect that we discussed at the beginning of this chapter. Pick a few traits—honesty, social sensitivity, and leadership, for example—and ask some people to rate themselves on each. You will probably find few people who rate themselves below average on any one (let alone on all) of these qualities (Svenson, 1981; Weinstein, 1987). You may find a few people who show a worse-than-average effect when they think they are pretty incompetent at something (Kruger, 1999; Moore & Small, 2007), but most of the time, most people rate themselves above average on the majority of these qualities.

People's high views of themselves even extend to things they own or are attached to in some way (Beggan, 1992). In fact, if you're like most people, you probably even prefer letters that occur in your name to other letters (Nuttin, 1987). The tendency to prefer the letters in our own name occurs most strongly for those with high self-esteem, suggesting that it is due to a general tendency to favorably evaluate ourselves and things linked with ourselves (Koole, Dijksterhuis, & van Knippenberg, 2001).

Linking the self with other people can even make us like those others more. In an interesting demonstration of this, students in one study viewed an image of an alleged male politician whose face had (in some conditions) been digitally blended with the participant's own face (Bailenson, Garland, Iyengar, & Yee, 2006). Results showed that male participants preferred the politician whose image resembled themselves more than the unaltered one. (Female participants showed the reverse, perhaps because the blending of a female with a male face produced a less realistic or attractive face.) For male participants, making another person resemble the self resulted in better evaluations of him.

Such findings reflect our desire to view ourselves in a positive light. Thus, as we will see in the next few sections, our level of self-esteem often reflects compromises between accurate self-evaluation and self-enhancement. Though an objective assessment of self-relevant information could allow us to form reasonably accurate views of where we stand, **self-enhancing biases** sneak into the processes of gathering and interpreting such information (Kunda, 1990).

self-enhancing bias
any tendency to gather or interpret information concerning the self in a way that leads to overly positive evaluations

Evaluating Personal Experiences: Some Pain but Mainly Gain

Events that affect us positively or negatively influence our self-esteem, but we try in several ways to accumulate more positive than negative experiences.

Remember how happy you felt the first time you beat your regular opponent at tennis? And how your image of yourself plunged on the day you broke up with your first love? Experiences like these can raise or lower self-esteem at a moment's notice. However, self-enhancing biases can color the impact of our experiences on self-esteem. Almost without thinking about it, most of us stack the deck so that life produces more gain and less pain.

One obvious way we do this is to choose situations in which we can shine. One of the authors of this text is a member of two choirs and regularly chooses to sing in public; the other two take care to avoid embarrassment by putting a great distance between themselves, choirs, and even occasional invitations to Karaoke nights. Most of us tend to abandon relationships that make us miserable, hobbies that we are unskilled at, and careers that do not allow us to flourish. Instead, our life choices often move us into domains that let us be all that we can be.

We not only select areas of life in which we can succeed, but also tend to remember our successes more than our failures. For one thing, we inflate our own contributions to joint efforts or projects. This may stem from the unbiased workings of memory. It is easy to remember one's own contributions to a joint project; the hours others worked are naturally less vivid. However, people inflate their own contributions to a lesser extent when a project ends in failure (M. Ross & Sicoly, 1979). If overestimating were due only to superior memory for one's own actions, then the overestimate should occur to an equal extent when a project fails. Since it does not, we can infer the tendency occurs, in part, from a self-enhancing motive.

Even when we try to retrieve memories of our past performances in an unbiased fashion, we tend to end up with a sample that is slanted in our favor. In one demonstration of this self-enhancing bias in memory, students were led to believe that either extroversion or introversion was a desirable characteristic (Sanitioso, Kunda, & Fong, 1990). When the students then recalled relevant past behaviors, they described more memories of the sort they believed to be desirable. Success and failure do not have to be very important to bias our recall. People who were led to believe that tooth-brushing has negative effects on health remembered brushing their teeth less frequently in the past than others who thought brushing was a healthy practice (M. Ross, McFarland, & Fletcher, 1981). For reasons like these, most of us amass more positive experiences than negative ones, both in reality and in memory.

On the other hand, the impact of those experiences is not the same for everyone. As described above, some people organize their self-knowledge around multiple

self-complexity
the extent to which a person possesses many and diverse self-aspects

self-aspects. People who have many and diverse self-aspects have a high level of **self-complexity** (Linville, 1985). Because a given event, such as a career success, tends to directly impact only one or two self-aspects (such as an employee self), it should have a more dramatic positive effect overall on a person with low self-complexity. This is because the uplifting effect of the event on mood and well-being will not be diluted by many other, unaffected self-aspects. This hypothesis has been confirmed by a meta-analysis summarizing over 70 studies on the issue (Rafaeli-Mor & Steinberg, 2002). However, the meta-analysis found that negative events or failures seem to have about the same negative impact on people regardless of their level of self-complexity. This may be because negative events, overall, have more powerful effects on us than do positive events (Baumeister and others, 2001).

Social Comparisons: Better or Worse Than Others?

We also evaluate ourselves by making comparisons with others. These comparisons are sometimes self-enhancing, but sometimes self-deprecating.

Self-esteem, like the self-concept, depends on social comparisons. Consider, for example, the plight of a young man who recently enrolled in one of our universities with a basketball scholarship. He is an athlete of above-average talent who is expected, in time, to make real contributions to the team. The problem is that his older brother, who played at the same school 2 years earlier, was a major star and is now beginning a career as a professional. It seems inevitable that the young man will be compared to his older brother.

self-evaluation maintenance
a theory outlining the conditions under which people's self-esteem will be maintained or will suffer based on social comparisons to close or distant others

How might these comparisons influence the player's self-esteem if his performance is not equal to his brother's? Abraham Tesser's (1988) model of **self-evaluation maintenance** suggests two possible reactions. They both depend on the closeness of the other person, for example, the fact that the star player was a brother rather than a cousin, as well as the importance or centrality of the attribute in question for the person's self-concept. Suppose the young man was planning to compete in track and field instead of basketball. Then he would be likely to feel good because of the reflected glory of his brother's impressive accomplishments. But if playing basketball is an important and central part of the younger brother's self-concept, disappointment stemming from the comparison could overwhelm his pleasure in his brother's success. In fact, being outperformed by a sibling or close friend may be even more painful than being beaten by a stranger, because the likelihood of social comparison is greater. Sometimes we want to bask in a loved one's reflected glory; at other times the glare of his or her achievement is just too painfully illuminating.

Chapter 6, pages 197–199, will discuss in more detail the ways in which connections with other people can help us feel good or bad about ourselves.

As this example illustrates, we cannot always choose whom to compare ourselves with (J. V. Wood, 1989). Most of us have probably had the unfortunate experience of performing in public, for example, at a track meet, immediately after the local superstar turned in a superb performance. This kind of inescapable comparison can induce feelings of envy and resentment and can lower self-esteem (Salovey & Rodin, 1984; Tesser & Collins, 1988). However, forced comparisons can have positive as well as negative consequences. Consider the top three competitors in an Olympic event, all of whom are awarded medals. The silver medalist naturally compares him- or herself to the winner, and probably doesn't feel good about coming in second. However, for the bronze medalist, the most natural comparison is to the fourth-place competitor, who gets no medal at all! Based on these ideas about social comparison, Victoria Medvec and her colleagues (Medvec, Madey, & Gilovich, 1995) coded videotapes of Olympic Games medal winners. They found that the facial expressions of the bronze medal winners—who had performed less well in absolute terms—were happier than those of the silver medal winners.

Sometimes, however, we can try to avoid comparisons that make us look bad or feel unhappy. One common tactic we employ is establishing distance between ourselves and those who are successful. We do this by either downplaying our similarities to them or backing off from our relationships with them (Tesser, 1988). Another form of protection involves comparing ourselves with others who are less fortunate or less successful. For example, Bram Buunk and his colleagues (Buunk, Oldersma, & de Dreu, 2001) found that when people were asked to list aspects of their relationships that were "better than most people's," eliciting favorable social comparisons, they felt more positive about their relationships, compared to other

"Of course you're going to be depressed if you keep comparing yourself with successful people."

people who just listed good aspects of their relationships without making social comparisons. Similarly, an average grade on the calculus final looks better in the light of the failing grades some students received. A not-so-exciting home life sure beats the misery experienced by friends with recently divorced parents. In fact, people who learn that they have some positive attribute tend to underestimate the number of others who share the same characteristic—a bias that fosters a sense of superiority (Goethals, Messick, & Allison, 1991).

Even when the situation is objectively pretty grim, it can help to know that life could be worse. Interviews with breast-cancer patients, for example, found that they compared themselves with others who were worse off: people whose disease was not responding to treatments, or those who lacked social support or contracted the disease at a comparatively young age (S. E. Taylor & Lobel, 1989). Buoyed by such comparisons, most cancer patients think they are better off than their peers (S. E. Taylor, Falke, Shoptaw, & Lichtman, 1986).

Why Self-Enhance?

Despite the value of accurate self-knowledge, self-enhancement occurs for two primary reasons. Some actions that appear self-enhancing are aimed at actual self-improvement, reflecting the successful use of the self to guide our behavior adaptively. And high self-esteem can be an important resource that protects us against stress and threats to the self.

We noted earlier that successful dealings with the social world can be aided with some degree of accurate self-knowledge. But if that is true, why are we so prone to biases that create and maintain positively biased views of ourselves? The answer has two parts.

First, some of the ways people strive for high self-esteem really amount to efforts at self-improvement. For example, you might work hard to learn to play a musical instrument to ensure that your public performances will be successful, earning you applause and boosted self-esteem. To return to our earlier analogy of self-esteem as a statement giving your bank balance, people may try to increase their income or reduce their spending as a way to increase their balance. In fact, this is simply an example of successful **self-regulation**, with self-esteem (or the bank balance) telling us how well we are doing in attaining our valued goals.

self-regulation
efforts to control one's behavior in line with internal standards (self-guides) or external standards

Second, self-esteem has value above and beyond its usefulness as an indicator of our level of success in our commerce with the world. People prefer to feel good about themselves—to value "me and mine." For example, high self-esteem is associated with generally positive emotions and a lower likelihood of depression (J. D. Campbell, Chew, & Scratchley, 1991; Tennen & Affleck, 1993). And, as we will see later in this chapter, high self-esteem not only feels good but has real positive effects on our lives, acting as a kind of resource that can buffer us from some of the blows of fortune. For both of these reasons, people often process information about the self in ways that favor a positive view. In other words, despite the clear usefulness of knowing one's bank balance accurately, we suspect that if people guessed how much they had in the bank on any given day, more estimates would be high than low. Despite these positive points, we will see later in the chapter that high self-esteem is not an unmixed blessing.

Thus, as Figure 4.3 summarizes, self-esteem reflects a compromise between the stern mirror of accurate self-assessment and some self-enhancing biases that give our image a positive tilt and a rosy glow. We often avoid situations in which we do not perform

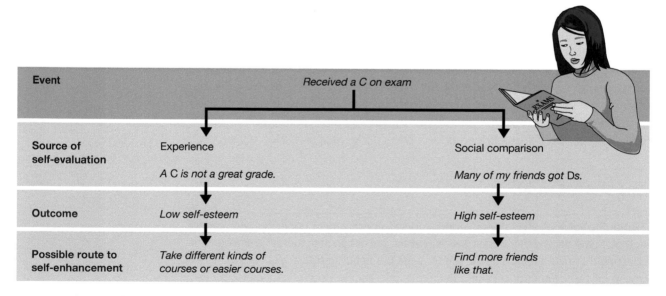

Figure 4.3 Events, self-evaluation, and self-enhancement
Many self-relevant events are neither intrinsically positive nor intrinsically negative. Instead, they must be interpreted and evaluated. The evaluation process may lead to increases or decreases in self-esteem, and it almost always leaves room for operation of self-enhancing biases.

SOCIAL PSYCHOLOGY AND CULTURE: SELF-ESTEEM AND SELF-ENHANCEMENT IN CULTURAL CONTEXT

Since so many aspects of the self differ between individualist and collectivist cultures, you may be wondering whether levels of self-esteem and biases related to self-esteem are universal or whether they vary cross-culturally. Though there is on-going debate about the answers to these questions (see Heine, 2005; Heine, Kitayama, & Hamamura, 2007; Sedikides, Gaertner, & Vevea, 2007), many scholars believe that people from collectivist Asian cultures show intriguing differences from those in North America and Western Europe. For example, Japanese students (whether in Japan or studying in America) score lower on self-esteem questionnaires than American students do (Kitayama, Markus, Matsumoto, & Norasakkunkit, 1997). Japanese people may even reverse the self-enhancing bias, showing a greater tendency to accept negative rather than positive information about the self (Kitayama, Takagi, & Matsumoto, 1995).

Does this mean that members of collectivist cultures are psychologically unhealthy? Kitayama and his colleagues (1997) argue otherwise. They propose that the sensitivity to negative information about the self that is found in collectivist cultures actually serves as a form of self-criticism, which is ultimately meant to improve one's actions and ability to fit in harmoniously with others. In North America and other individualist cultures, the view of the self as autonomous and separate from others means that positive personal attributes are the fundamental source of personal worth. In this cultural setting, self-enhancement is natural. In contrast, in collectivist cultures, connectedness among individuals and groups is emphasized over personal autonomy. The value of the self is measured not by outstanding individual characteristics, but by adjustment to others' expectations and shared ideals. Thus, in Japanese schools, it is common for classes to take time at the end of a day to reflect on the ways they have failed to meet class goals, either as individuals or as a group (Lewis, 1995). Such self-criticism is both a way of affirming one's acceptance of shared social standards and a way of seeking to remedy deviations from those standards. From this perspective, self-criticism is just as natural a way of enhancing the value of the self in collectivist cultures as overt self-enhancement is in individualist cultures.

Another reason that self-enhancement may take different forms in different cultural contexts is that people may self-enhance on the specific types of characteristics that are particularly valued in their culture. Thus, North Americans might be expected to see themselves as outstandingly intelligent, independent, and fit for leadership— the very attributes that are valued in an individualist culture (Kurman, 2001; Sedikides, Gaertner, & Toguchi, 2003). But members of more collectivist cultures may see themselves as particularly good at fitting in with others or suiting their actions to social situations. Self-enhancement might exist in all cultures, then, but be directed at whatever traits are most culturally valued (Sedikides and others, 2003; Sedikides, Gaertner, & Vevea, 2005).

well, refuse to compare ourselves with more successful others, and fail to notice that we are not all that we could or should be. Even if our inadequacies become obvious, however, we are not without resources. Later in the chapter you will see that failures, inconsistencies, and shortcomings set off some of the self's best defense mechanisms.

Despite cultural variations (described in the box), the function of self-esteem is the same for everyone. The ups and downs of self-esteem are not just meaningless fluctuations. Rather, self-esteem serves a crucial function as the self regulates our thoughts, feelings, and behavior: It signals how well we are doing in fulfilling our fundamental social motives for mastery of our environment and connectedness with others (Leary and others, 1995). People differ in their relative sensitivity to these two motives, with men's self-esteem more influenced by successes or failures involving mastery and women's self-esteem more affected by connectedness (Josephs, Markus, & Tafarodi, 1992). Cultural differences are important as well, as just described. For everyone, though, success and acceptance (that is, events that help us feel in control and connected to others) make us feel particularly good about ourselves, whereas failure, rejection, and loss can knock us to our knees. And, as you will see later, people with high and low self-esteem differ significantly in the ways they respond to and cope with all kinds of life experiences.

EFFECTS OF THE SELF: SELF-REGULATION

What is the fundamental purpose of having a self? The answer is that what we know about ourselves functions to regulate—to control and govern—many important aspects of our lives, including our thoughts, emotions and behavior.

The Self and Thoughts about Ourselves and Others

Self-knowledge serves as a framework for perceiving other people and processing social information in general.

Once we have constructed a self-concept, the familiar principle of conservatism comes into operation, and we become much less open to new information about the self. A young child might begin to think of himself as tidy after noticing that he neatens up his room a few times, but once the self-concept is firmly established, people are less likely to make inferences from their behaviors to decide who they are (S. B. Klein & Loftus, 1993; Schell, Klein, & Babey, 1996). This is important in creating our sense of a stable personal identity.

An established self-concept influences both the way we think about ourselves and the way we perceive and remember social information in general. For example, when we perceive others we tend to notice and use information that is important in our own self-concept (Markus, Smith, & Moreland, 1985; Sedikides & Skowronski, 1993). So if you think of yourself as honest, you may be particularly likely to note others' honest or dishonest behaviors and to use that information in making judgments about them. The self-concept also affects memory. For example, if we make judgments about whether a series of traits are self-descriptive or not, we remember those traits better than we do if we make other judgments, such as whether the traits are positive or negative (Symons & Johnson, 1997). The self-concept tells us what types of social information are particularly important to us, so it serves as an organizing framework for perceiving and remembering information about people in general.

The Self and Emotions

Emotions are sparked by interpretations of self-relevant events and their causes. Emotions signal the occurrence of significant events and motivate us to act in response, for example, to flee from danger. As they perform this self-regulation function, emotions involve the whole self, body, and mind: They involve facial expressions, physiological responses, subjective feelings, and overt behaviors.

Emotions mark the most meaningful moments of our lives. Feelings like pride, anxiety, joy, fear, or anger signal that something important to the self is happening (Zajonc, 1998). Fear signals that a danger must be escaped; joy lets us know that a positive outcome should be celebrated. The intrusive quality of emotions forces us to pay attention to significant events, even as the positive or negative quality of the emotion indicates the nature of the event. Emotions also direct behavior toward a goal. For example, fear turns our efforts toward escaping from threat, and anger toward harming the target. Because of their intrusiveness, emotions often seem to "just happen" to us, but as we shall see, they actually depend on the perceiver's interpretation of events.

How Do Emotions Arise? Emotions are complex and multifaceted and involve the entire self, body, and mind. When you feel angry, your heart pounds and blood rushes to your face. You believe deeply that someone injured you without cause. You want to strike out at the target of your anger. Thoughts, feelings, bodily reactions, and desires for action are tied together in patterns that characterize different emotions. Which of these many components is primary in causing the emotion? Psychologists have offered different answers to this question over the years. A century ago, William James (1884) argued that sensations from the skin and muscles were the chief causes of the experience of emotion. A generation ago, Stanley Schachter and Jerome Singer (1962) identified emotion as the product of physiological arousal plus a belief concerning its cause.

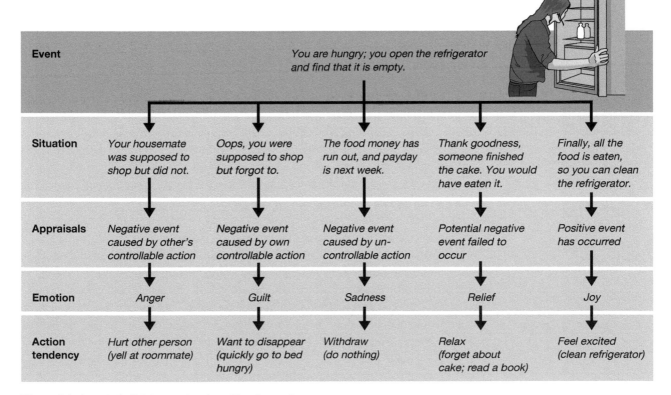

Figure 4.4 Appraisals dictate emotional reactions to events
Here are examples of different emotions and action tendencies arising from different appraisals of the same event—in this case, opening the refrigerator and finding that it is empty.

appraisal
an individual's interpretation of a self-relevant event or situation that directs emotional responses and behavior

In Chapter 3, page 66, we explained that our interpretations of others' emotional expressions depend on context. The same smiling facial expression might be labeled as happiness or anxiety, depending whether you think the person was just given a raise or was about to give an important speech. As we see here, the interpretation of our own emotions can similarly be influenced by context.

The prevailing view today is that emotions are caused by appraisals of a self-relevant object or event (Arnold, 1960; Frijda, 1986; Roseman, Spindel, & Jose, 1990; Tomaka, Blascovich, Kibler, & Ernst, 1997). An **appraisal** is an interpretation of an event, including both the causes of the event and how the event affects the self. Different appraisals of the same situation can produce different emotions, as is illustrated in Figure 4.4 for the everyday event of feeling hungry and finding the refrigerator empty.

As illustrated in Figure 4.4, appraisals can involve a host of considerations, such as whether an action or event is positive or negative for the self, whether an event or action was caused by the self, caused by another person, or caused by circumstance, and whether the action or event is seen as controllable or uncontrollable. Various combinations of these can produce quite different emotions. For example, perhaps the refrigerator is empty because you decided to play basketball with your friends, rather than go shopping. In this situation, the refrigerator is empty (and you are hungry) because of your own controllable actions, which resulted in a negative outcome. In this case, you likely feel guilty. Imagine, instead, that the refrigerator is empty because your housemate failed to contribute his share of the grocery money and shopping chores. The result is the same negative outcome for you, but it was caused by another person's controllable actions. This may lead to anger. Thus, as you can see, our emotional reactions can vary widely for the same event, depending on our appraisal of it. Understanding appraisals is important, not only because it helps us predict what one's emotional reactions will be, but also what behaviors may spring from those emotions. As shown in Figure 4.4, when we feel responsible for the refrigerator being empty, and feel guilt, we may want to "hide," but when we blame our roommate for the same outcome, and feel anger, we may want to lash out at him.

Like all interpretations, appraisals are flexible, not cut and dried. As we saw in Chapter 3, many factors can influence how we appraise events, including the context, accessible thoughts, and transient moods. And, as always, other people's reactions play a large role in our appraisals. A toddler who trips over her feet may burst into either tears or giggles, depending on whether others gasp with concern or laugh. When other people seem to judge that a situation warrants calmness or dejection or goofy light-heartedness, we often follow suit (Schachter & Singer, 1962).

As these examples illustrate, we can be misled about the emotions we are feeling and about their causes. Our appraisals and the labels we apply to our own inner feelings are often based on salient cues: conspicuous features, people, or events that may or may not correspond to the true causes of our emotions (Reisenzein, 1983; Russell, 2003). In many cases, of course, the salient object that we identify as the cause of our emotion—the wasp buzzing around your head and threatening to sting, for example—is truly the cause of our fearful feelings. But in other cases the salient object may not be the real cause. You might believe you are angry with your child because of her annoying behavior, when the true cause of your anger is your run-in with your boss earlier in the day. An experiment by James Olson (1990) demonstrated this point by misleading participants about the cause of their anxiety. Everyone in the experiment expected to be exposed to "subliminal noise" as they were videotaped while delivering a speech. Some people were told the noise would arouse them physiologically, and others were told it would relax them. Although no noise was actually played, the participants' beliefs about it still influenced their emotions. Those who thought the noise would arouse them rated themselves as less anxious and made fewer speech errors than those who expected to be relaxed by the noise. Apparently those who expected arousal attributed their stage fright to the "noise," whereas those who expected relaxation had no such excuse.

Thus, like other aspects of self-knowledge, the emotions we experience and our beliefs about their causes actually reflect our interpretations. And, of course, culture can strongly affect the ways we interpret events and therefore the kinds of emotions we feel. Japanese people, for example, are more likely than Westerners to report feeling emotions like connectedness, indebtedness, and familiarity, which tie the self to important others (Markus & Kitayama, 1991; Mesquita, 2001). In fact, in any culture the emotions that are most common and most intense are those that fit culturally valued types of relationships. These emotions not only are favored by individuals' patterns of appraisals, but are also reinforced by close others and by common social situations (Leersnyder, Boiger, & Mesquita, 2013). For example, in cultures that highly value politeness, people often structure their interactions to avoid angry confrontations, making polite rather than negative interactions more common. Despite such cultural differences, researchers assume that at least a few "basic" emotions are common to all human cultures, although there is not full consensus on what these emotions are (Russell, 2003; Wierzbicka, 1994; Zajonc, 1998). Findings also show not only that facial expressions of the "basic" emotions are universally (cross-culturally) understood, but even vocalizations of these same emotions are as well (Sauter, Eisner, Ekman, & Scott, 2010).

Appraisals, Emotions, Bodily Responses: All Together Now. Our appraisals of events not only cause our emotions but also affect many aspects of our body and mind. People in many different cultures smile when they feel happy, frown when they feel sad, and wrinkle their brow when they feel angry (Ekman and others, 1987). Physiological systems come on line, revving us up or calming us down. We are motivated to act: to strike back in anger, escape in fear, or move closer in happiness. Some of these action tendencies, like attack and flight, appear to be universal and biologically determined. Other emotional behaviors are, of course, learned and differ from one culture to another (Frijda, Kuipers, & ter Schure, 1989; Markus & Kitayama, 1991).

Emotions also affect thinking, focusing us on the content of our appraisals. Thus, in the grip of extreme rage you may be totally focused on the thought of how your antagonist mistreated you and how he deserves to have his lights punched out (Keltner, Ellsworth, & Edwards, 1993; Tiedens & Linton, 2001). Strong emotions of any sort, positive or negative, can create intense arousal that limits people's ability to pay attention to other events (Easterbrook, 1959).

These components—appraisals, bodily responses, subjective feelings, and emotionally driven behavior—are frequently activated together. As a result, they become associated so that any one aspect can engage all the rest. If your heart is pounding, your face is contorted in a snarl, and your fists are tightly clenched, you are likely to feel anger, just as anger provokes those same responses. Because our inner feelings and outward expressions of emotion are linked, bodily signs of emotion often intensify emotional feelings (Adelmann & Zajonc, 1989; Ekman, 1992). Fritz Strack and his colleagues (Strack, Martin, & Stepper, 1988) ingeniously demonstrated this point by having participants write with a pen either clenched tightly between their teeth or held loosely between pursed lips. These maneuvers force expressions resembling a smile and a scowl, respectively, although participants were unaware of this fact. (Try it yourself.) The experimenters then asked both groups to assign ratings to a series of cartoons, telling how funny they were. The participants holding the pen between their teeth in a "smile" assigned higher ratings than did those holding the pen "scowlingly" between their lips.

If an emotional facial expression promotes emotional experience, it stands to reason that an inconsistent expression will reduce the intensity of the emotion. Have you ever been in a clutch situation and been terrified you might fail? Perhaps you were about to speak to a large audience. Did you take a couple of long deep breaths to calm yourself down or lock your face in a determined grin? If so, you were trying to take advantage of the way emotions often follow bodily expressions, and research suggests that your actions may produce the intended effect. For example, David Havas and his colleagues (2010) asked women to comprehend sentences describing happy-, sad- and anger-inducing actions. They did this exercise twice, before and after receiving a botox injection. Such injections paralyze the muscles used for frowning and thus help reduce and prevent wrinkles. The researchers wondered if blocking one's ability to move facial muscles involved in negative emotions might also slow access to emotional content. In support of this idea, women were slower to understand the sadness- and anger-inducing sentences after receiving the injection than before. Because botox does not paralyze the muscles involved in smiling, comprehension of happiness sentences was unaffected.

Another example illustrates that physical actions can block access to emotions, which then reduces emotion-consistent judgments (Schnall, Benton, & Harvey, 2008). In this study, students were shown a film clip of a disgust-inducing scene, an emotion that can underlie our judgments of moral outrage (Wheatley & Haidt, 2005). After viewing the clip, some participants were asked to wash their hands, to symbolically clean

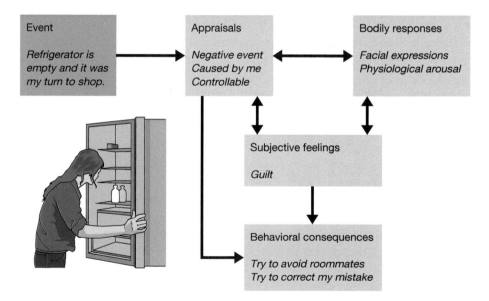

Figure 4.5 Components of emotions
When events are appraised as self-relevant, the resulting emotion has many components: cognitive appraisals, physiological responses, and subjective feelings. Each component can affect the others, and all may contribute to emotionally driven behaviors.

themselves of the disgusting feeling, whereas others were not. Finally, the students read descriptions of actions that might be considered immoral, such as falsifying one's résumé. Results showed that those who washed their hands (who thus presumably felt less disgusted) rated these scenarios as less morally wrong than those who did not wash their hands.

As Figure 4.5 shows, emotions tie together aspects of body, action, and thought (De Rivera, 1977; Shaver, Schwartz, Kirson, & O'Connor, 1987).

The Self in Action: Regulating Behavior

We sometimes control our behavior in a manner that allows us to communicate our true selves to others. Other times we manipulate our behavior to craft a desired impression from others. Finally, we sometimes control our behavior in ways that help us achieve a desired self. No matter why we regulate our behaviors, doing so may shape our self-views to be consistent with those behaviors.

Photo 4.2 Self-expression in action. This protester is revealing important parts of his self-concept as he publicly protests war.

Once we have an established self, we use this self to control and direct our behavior in important ways. Sometimes our behaviors help us show the world who we think we really are. Other times, we behave in ways to shape a particular impression of ourselves from others. Individuals differ in which type of behavioral control they favor.

Self-Expression and Self-Presentation. When people engage in **self-expression**, they attempt to demonstrate or reveal their self-concept through their actions. Self-expression confirms and reinforces the individual's sense of self and also conveys it to other people. If you think of yourself as a committed supporter of animal welfare, you may see many of your behaviors—volunteering at the Humane Society or campaigning to stop unnecessary cosmetics testing—as expressions and affirmations of that self-concept. Research shows that, if given a choice, most people prefer to enter social situations that allow them to act in a way consistent with their self-concept (M. Snyder & Gangestad, 1982), and prefer relationship partners who agree with their own self-images (Swann, Hixon, & de la Ronde, 1992). Thus, an outgoing man may accept invitations to parties, and an organized woman may take a job that offers clearly structured tasks.

Sometimes we try to create a desirable impression, whether we believe the impression is accurate or not. Thus, another motive for choosing particular behaviors is **self-presentation**, trying to shape other people's impressions of us in order to gain power, influence, or approval (Jones & Pittman, 1982; Tedeschi, 1981). Most people care about conveying a positive impression to others. After all, attracting a desirable date or impressing a job interviewer can have a real impact on the course of our lives. Even in less crucial situations, we usually want to show the world a face it can like, admire, and respect. In fact, ingratiation, trying to convey the impression we are likable, and self-promotion, trying to convey an impression of competence, are two of the most common goals of social interaction (Arkin, 1981; Leary, 1995).

We all have had so much practice trying to win approval and respect that ingratiation and self-promotion should be easy. To be seen as likable, we go out of our way to help, to fit in with the other person's wishes, and to deliver charming compliments. To be

self-expression
a motive for choosing behaviors that are intended to reflect and express the self-concept

self-presentation
a motive for choosing behaviors intended to create in observers a desired impression of the self

seen as competent, we play up our strong points, mention our accomplishments, and display our knowledge. But self-presentation is fraught with potential pitfalls; taken too far, these qualities become blatant flattery or unseemly boasting. For advice on how to ingratiate yourself smoothly and subtly, look at Table 4.2.

self-monitoring

a personality characteristic defined as the degree to which people are sensitive to the demands of social situations and shape their behaviors accordingly

Personality Differences in Preference for Self-Expression and Self-Presentation: Self-Monitoring. Although everyone engages in both self-expression and self-presentation, people show stable preferences for one or the other. This individual difference is called **self-monitoring** (M. Snyder, 1974). High self-monitors typically shape their behaviors to project the impression they think their current audience or situation demands. These behavioral patterns may be motivated by a desire to obtain status within social groups (Flynn, Reagans, Amanatullah, & Ames, 2006; Fuglestad & Snyder, 2010). Low self-monitors, on the other hand, behave in ways that express their internal attitudes and dispositions, and they therefore behave more consistently from audience to audience and situation to situation (Gangestad & Snyder, 2000). You might like to answer the questions in Table 4.3 to see whether you tend to be high or low in self-monitoring.

The importance of personality differences in self-monitoring was demonstrated by a study of people's reactions to success or failure at a rather peculiar task: portraying themselves as corrupt and immoral individuals (E. E. Jones, Brenner, & Knight, 1990). In a simulated job interview, each participant pretended to be an ambitious, selfish person who would be suitable for a "cutthroat position in a dog-eat-dog environment." Some participants learned that their act was convincing by overhearing comments like

TABLE 4.2   The Self-Presenter's Handbook, Lesson 1: How to Make Others Like You Without Being Obvious

Don't let others notice that you are conforming to their opinions. (Or, if you are going to try to get in someone's good books, keep it credible.)

- Disagree on trivial issues, agree on important ones.
- Be wish-washy when you disagree, forceful when you agree.

Be modest (selectively).

- Make gentle fun of your standing on unimportant traits.
- Put yourself down in areas that don't make much difference.

Keep your need for others' approval under wraps.

- Don't conform or flatter someone in a situation where it is expected—for example, when talking to your boss just before annual raises are handed out.
- Use these tactics only when you really need to.
- Get others to do the self-presentation for you—for example, in letters of reference.

Bask in others' reflected glory if you can.

- Make casual references to connections with winners.
- Link yourself to losers only when it cannot be used against you.

Source: Adapted from *Interpersonal perception,* by E. E. Jones, 1990, San Francisco: Freeman, p. 184.

TABLE 4.3 Examples of Items Used to Measure Self-Monitoring

1. I have considered being an entertainer.
2. In a group of people I am rarely the center of attention.
3. I have trouble changing my behavior to suit different people and different situations.
4. I guess I put on a show to impress or entertain people.
5. I may deceive people by being friendly when I really dislike them.

Note: People who agree with items 1, 4, and 5 and disagree with items 2 and 3 are probably high in self-monitoring. The actual scale contains many more than five items, so it can more accurately classify people as high or low in self-monitoring.

Source: From "The self-monitoring of expressive behavior," by M. Snyder, 1974, *Journal of Personality and Social Psychology, 30,* p. 531. Copyright © 1974 by the American Psychological Association. Reprinted with permission.

"He wouldn't mind selling his mother down the river." Others learned they had failed in their portrayals. High self-monitors felt better about themselves when they succeeded at the task, even though success meant convincing others that they were corrupt. Apparently creating an "appropriate" impression was more important than being true to who they really were. In contrast, low self-monitors felt better about themselves after failing at this task. They prefer being seen as they truly are instead of successfully, even profitably, putting on a false face.

Regulating Behavior to Achieve a Desired Self. One of the most fundamental aspects of self-regulation involves the way self-knowledge motivates our behavior toward important goals or standards. This is because our self-knowledge includes not only conceptions of what we are currently like, but also significant personal standards toward which we strive. Tory Higgins (1987) calls these personal standards self-guides. Self-guides come in two flavors: the **ideal self** (the person we would like to be) and the **ought self** (the person we feel we should be; Higgins, 1987; Markus & Nurius, 1986). Ideal self-guides include the traits that help you match your aspirations; ought self-guides include those that help you meet your obligations. Self-guides are the part of the self-concept most closely and directly tied to the self-regulatory function (Higgins, 1996b).

According to Higgins's **regulatory focus theory**, people may have a promotion focus, in which self-regulation is guided primarily by the ideal self or other standards that represent ideals, or a prevention focus, in which self-regulation is guided primarily by the ought self or other standards representing duties or obligations (Higgins, 1997). Those with a promotion focus seek opportunities to obtain positive outcomes relevant to goals. When they succeed in achieving these favorable outcomes, they feel happiness, and when they fail, they feel sadness. On the other hand, those with a prevention focus seek to avoid negative outcomes relevant to goals. When they succeed in avoiding these unfortunate outcomes, they feel relief, and when they fail, they feel anxiety.

Let's illustrate with an example. Two individuals might have the same goal—to stay married. A person who is sensitive to ideal self-guides ("I want to be happily married") and thus has a promotion focus, will take action to make his marriage a happy one, perhaps by surprising his wife with romantic dinners and frequently complimenting her sense of humor. When these dinners and compliments result in pleasant reactions, he

ideal self
a person's sense of what he or she would ideally like to be

ought self
a person's sense of what he or she is obligated to be, or should be

regulatory focus theory
a theory that people typically have either a promotion or prevention focus, shaping the ways they self-regulate to attain positive outcomes versus avoiding negative outcomes

is happy. When these efforts misfire, he will be sad. On the other hand, a person who is sensitive to ought self-guides ("I should avoid being unhappy and divorced") and thus has a prevention focus, will avoid actions that might cause marital strife, perhaps by changing the topic when a sensitive matter is discussed or by refraining from engaging in behaviors he knows annoy his spouse, like leaving dirty dishes in the sink. When these behaviors are successful, in that no discord occurs, he will feel relieved. But when these behaviors are not enough to avoid discord, he will feel anxiety.

Not surprisingly, people prefer behavioral strategies that match their regulatory focus. In one example illustrating this, students were induced to think of their ideal selves (making a promotion focus salient) or their ought selves (making a prevention focus salient; Freitas & Higgins, 2002). Then, they were presented with strategies one could employ to obtain a high grade point average. Some strategies had a promotion frame ("Attend all classes") and others had a prevention frame ("Avoid missing any classes"). Those who had thought about ideal selves rated the strategies as more enjoyable if framed in promotion (rather than prevention) terms compared to those who had thought about ought selves. In a follow-up study, students were asked to list an ideal or ought goal. They were then asked to list strategies that could help them achieve the goal or avoid failing at the goal. As expected, ideal-primed students believed the strategies they generated would be more enjoyable if they were promotion focused rather than prevention focused. Ought-primed students showed the reverse pattern.

From Self to Behavior, and Back Again. As we have seen, people have many reasons for regulating their behavior. They may behave in ways that express their self-concepts to others, that create a desired impression, or that achieve a self they personally desire. Regardless of the reason, such regulation can have lasting effects because our behavior often ends up impressing ourselves just as much as our audience. Remember self-perception theory from earlier in the chapter? It says that we can infer information about ourselves from an examination of our own behavior. So, when we act out a particular self, we may infer that it is actually reflective of who we are. For example, when people are instructed to present themselves as extraverted, they later give themselves higher ratings on that dimension (Jones, Rhodewalt, Berglas, & Skelton, 1981; Schlenker, 1985). Even just recalling past extraverted actions may be enough to alter the self-concept (C. A. Anderson & Godfrey, 1987).

Interestingly, the presence of an audience strengthens these outcomes, illustrating the fundamentally social nature of the self. In one study, students were asked to present themselves in particular ways in two videotaped segments that they believed would be viewed by others (Kelly & Rodriguez, 2006). In one, they portrayed themselves as introverted, and in the other, as extroverted. Afterwards, they were informed that only one of the tapes was needed, and, in the participant's presence, either the introverted or extroverted tape was erased. Those whose introversion tape was erased, and thus believed that only their extroversion tape would be seen by others, subsequently sat closer to a confederate, a measure of extroverted behavior, than did those whose extroversion tape was erased. So just displaying introverted or extroverted behaviors may not have strong effects on the self; the effects depend on knowing that others will see the behaviors.

These studies show that even a single self-presentation has effects on the private self, but sorting out the portrayal from the self may be even more difficult if the performance becomes routine. We would do well to heed sociologist Erving Goffman's warning: Choose your self-presentations carefully, for what starts out as a mask may become your face (Goffman, 1959).

Temptations that May Derail Self-Regulation

When situations offer us short-term benefits that detract from our longer-term goals, we may face challenges in regulating our behavior. We can actively and effortfully choose strategies to overcome these temptations. But, if we fail to reach our goals, negative consequences ensue.

Every dieter knows what it is like to stroll past a batch of delicious doughnuts in a shop window; every student knows how it feels to be invited out for the evening by friends when a term paper is due the next day. Temptations like these are obvious threats to self-regulation, for they force us to choose between immediately appealing short-term benefits and the more abstract longer-term gains of sticking with our diets or our schoolwork. Thus, temptations thwart our commitment to pursuing our ideal and ought selves; for instance, whether you ideally want to be a good student·or think you should lose weight, temptations can get us off track. How do we deal with such temptations?

According to Yaacov Trope and Ayelet Fishbach (2000), several strategies can weaken the effects of temptations and allow us to better accomplish our long-term goals. We can self-administer penalties or rewards to encourage ourselves to stick with our goals. For example, a dieter may decide to buy himself a new smartphone app every week he successfully resists off-limits snack foods. Or we can pay a non-refundable annual membership fee at the health club to encourage ourselves to stick with our exercise and fitness program. We can also try to think of the acts that contribute to our long-term goals in especially positive ways, linking them to our central values (such as being healthy and fit or getting good grades and a good job after graduation). Note that this second strategy has the effect of turning those actions (dieting or studying) from things that we feel we ought to do into things we want to do. We can also view temptations in more abstract ways, which should highlight the temptation's incompatibility with our central goals (Fujita, Trope, Liberman, & Levin-Sagi, 2006). Research suggests that each of these three approaches can effectively help people resist short-term temptations and engage in better self control.

For example, female students in one study were presented with different objects, like a car (Fujita & Han, 2009). Some were asked to generate a superordinate category for the object (like a transportation vehicle), whereas others were asked to generate a subordinate example of the object (like a Ford). Producing broad categories should prime more abstract thinking than producing specific examples. After this task,

Photo 4.3 Is a cell phone a way to text friends, surf the web, and play games? Or, is it a "study killer"—something that will distract a student from studying for tomorrow's test? Thinking of this tempting object in a more abstract way should help this student put down her phone and pick up her books.

participants were asked to evaluate two objects, a healthy apple and a tempting candy bar. Which would they rather have? Those primed with abstract thinking not only rated the candy bars more negatively, but also opted for the apple more often. Thus, approaching temptations with abstract thinking appears to enable effective self-control.

Even with strategies like these, self-regulation can be hard work. In fact, Roy Baumeister and his colleagues (Baumeister, Muraven, & Tice, 2000) liken self-regulation to exercising a muscle. At first, the exercise may be easy, but with repetitions it becomes harder and harder. And after the muscle is fatigued, it may be difficult to use it for some time until it recovers. Similarly, exerting self-control in one task (such as trying to suppress thoughts about a particular object, or having to wait in a room with a plate full of tempting cookies) weakens people's ability to exercise control in a completely different task, such as persisting in a difficult figure-drawing or anagram-solving task. The fact that self-regulation depletes some inner resource in this way may even account for the observation that people who are fatigued, under stress, or are low in regulatory resources for other reasons often turn to binge eating, alcohol consumption, or other tempting behaviors that are damaging in the long run (Tice, Bratslavsky, & Baumeister, 2001). These outcomes are not inevitable, however; recent studies suggest that at times, a cognitive load may reduce attention to, and feelings of temptation by, attractive stimuli such as calorie-rich treat foods (Van Dillen, Papies, & Hofmann, 2013). The reason appears to be that some cognitive resources are required to recognize the tempting nature of such stimuli, so at times a demanding cognitive task may actually facilitate self-regulation.

self-affirmation

any action or event that enhances or highlights one's own sense of personal integrity, such as affirming one's most important values

Self-affirmation can also restore self-control when one is low on inner resources. Self-affirmation is any action or event that enhances or highlights one's own sense of personal integrity (Steele, 1988). In one study, students engaged in an initial task that either required or did not require self-control (Schmeichel & Vohs, 2009). Then, some participants wrote about their most important personal value, a common self-affirmation task. Subsequently, all students engaged in a task that required self-control, keeping their hand in a bucket of painfully cold water. Those who did not self-affirm showed the typical detrimental effect of initial self-control. That is, those who had engaged in self-control earlier, who presumably had some of their inner resources drained, kept their hand in the cold water for a shorter period of time than those who had not initially engaged in self-control. This effect was eliminated, however, for those who had engaged in self-affirmation. .

Negative Effects of Not Reaching Goals.

When our actual self does not match our ideal or ought selves, this motivates us to meet personal goals, but at a price: awareness of the ways in which we fall short is painful! In extreme cases, we may experience negative emotions that lead to a cycle of sadness and anxiety, lowered self-esteem, and even depression (Csikszentmihalyi & Figurski, 1982; Pyszczynski & Greenberg, 1987). Certain situations can exaggerate our awareness of our failures to meet our self-guides.

self-awareness

a state of heightened awareness of the self, including our internal standards and whether we measure up to them

For example, being photographed, placed in front of a mirror, or standing before an audience are all situations that create **self-awareness**, directing our attention to our internal standards and heightening our awareness of whether we measure up to them. According to self-awareness theory, focusing attention on the self highlights the distance between our current self and our actual or ideal selves, which is why it is often unpleasant

TABLE 4.4 Examples of Items Used to Measure Private Self-Consciousness

1. I'm always trying to figure myself out.
2. I reflect about myself a lot.
3. I never scrutinize myself.
4. I'm alert to changes in my mood.
5. I'm constantly examining my motives.

Note: A person who agrees with items like 1, 2, 4, and 5, and disagrees with item 3 and similar items is probably high in private self-consciousness. The actual scale contains many more than five items, so it can more accurately classify people as high or low in private self-consciousness.

Source: From "Public and private self-consciousness: Assessment and theory," by A. Fenigstein, M. F. Scheier, & A. H. Buss, *Journal of Consulting and Clinical Psychology, 43,* p. 524. Copyright © 1975 by the American Psychological Association. Reprinted with permission.

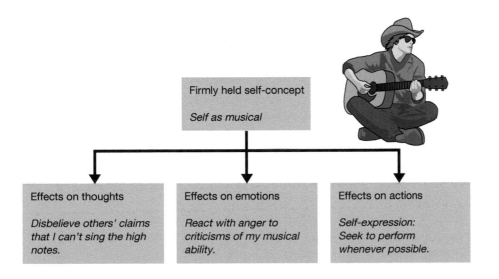

Figure 4.6 What a difference a self makes
Once formed, a person's self-concept influences his or her thoughts, feelings, and actions.

(Carver & Scheier, 1981; Duval & Wicklund, 1972). Moreover, people differ in the tendency to devote attention to the self. Table 4.4 shows some statements that measure this tendency. People who are higher in self-awareness are more likely to be aware of, and to try to cope with, mismatches between their actual self and their internalized standards (Carver & Scheier, 1981). Their increased awareness means that negative self-related information leads to stronger feelings of distress and sadness (Scheier & Carver, 1977).

Once we have constructed a sense of self, we begin to use it to regulate many aspects of our lives. Our self-concept tends to resist change and to influence our thoughts, emotions, and behavior. Figure 4.6 summarizes some of the effects of the self.

DEFENDING THE SELF: COPING WITH STRESSES, INCONSISTENCIES, AND FAILURES

Our sense of self is our most valued possession, and we certainly treat it that way. We use it continually, as both a guide for action and an aid in interpreting others' reactions to us. We keep it polished and in good repair as we enhance our self-esteem and present our best face to others. And, as we shall see, we strive to defend our sense of self against all comers. When events set off our security alarms, we may respond in two different ways. We may attempt to deal with what set off the alarm, or we may try to change the way it makes us feel.

Threats to the Well-Being of the Self

When threatened by external events or negative feedback, people must defend their sense of who and what they are. Major failures and disasters obviously threaten the self, but so do inconsistent information and daily hassles and stresses. Threats to the self affect not only emotional well-being but also physical health. The most damaging threats are those we appraise as uncontrollable.

Anything that contradicts our sense of who we are and how we feel can cause negative implications for the self. Because of this, feedback inconsistent with an established self-concept is avoided, distrusted, or resisted—even if it is flattering (Markus, 1977; Swann & Read, 1981). Many types of events can pose significant threats. Failures—flubbing the driver's test, ending a marriage in divorce—expose us to negative feedback about who we are and what we do. Inconsistencies—illness in a usually healthy person, an empty nest for an at-home mom—provide us with information that contradicts who and what we thought we were. Events do not have to be negative to be inconsistent. Because they change our lives, even joyous occasions like getting married or becoming a parent also require difficult changes in the self-concept. Finally, stress also arises from daily events: the small but relentless grind-you-down frustrations and hassles of everyday life, the boredom of routine, the pressures of the rat-race. All these types of events call our sense of self into question.

Emotional and Physical Effects of Threat. Threats to the self arouse the gamut of negative emotions. Experiences like losing a loved one to illness or being fired from a job for poor performance activate the most intense emotions: terror, crushing depression. However, people with high self-esteem are at least in part protected from the negative effects of such events (Taylor, Kemeny, Reed, Bower, & Gruenwald, 2000). The protective effect is found even when the events are extreme, as found in a study of people affected by the brutal civil war in Bosnia (Bonnanno, Field, Kovacevic, & Kaltman, 2002). In contrast, when people's self-esteem is overinflated or unstable, the impact of negative events may be magnified (Kernis & Goldman, 2003). People with unrealistically inflated self-views, which may be especially unstable and highly vulnerable to negative information, are the most likely to turn to violence and aggression (Baumeister, Smart, & Boden, 1996; Bushman & Baumeister, 1998). Similarly, people whose self-concept is much higher than their friends' ratings of them—those who are most likely to have their lofty views challenged periodically—tend to have poor social skills, and the negative effects on mental health may last for years (Colvin, Block, & Funder, 1995).

Threats to the self have effects beyond our emotions: they also contribute to physical illness (Salovey, Rothman, & Rodin, 1998). Major setbacks adversely affect our health, but so do everyday minor hassles, like arguing with a best friend or receiving a parking ticket. Threats to the self bring us down, tick us off, and also alter our immune responses, nervous-system activity, and blood pressure—the kinds of physiological changes that contribute to illness (S. Cohen, Doyle, Skoner, & Fireman, 1995; Miller, Chen, & Cole, 2009; J. Rodin & Salovey, 1989). For example, one study found that when people were reminded of significant mismatches between their current self and their self-guides, levels of "natural killer" cell activity in their bloodstream decreased (Strauman, Lemieux, & Coe, 1993). These immune-system cells are important in defending the body against viral infections and cancers. Moreover, threats to the self elevate the stress hormone cortisol which, in the short term, may aid in dealing with the threat; but, if such reactions occur over the long haul, they may lead to a host of physical health ailments (Dickerson, Gruenewald, & Kemeny, 2009).

Photo 4.4 The self under threat. Threats to the self—like feeling like one can't "hack it" as a student—can cause a host of negative emotional reactions and harm physical health.

The negative emotions that we experience in response to threats put physical health at risk. People who habitually respond to failures, setbacks, and stresses with negative emotions are the most likely to suffer physically (Watson & Pennebaker, 1989). One of the best-known examples of this finding is the Type A behavior pattern, which is associated with risks of heart disease (Booth-Kewley & Friedman, 1987; Thoresen & Low, 1990). The Type A pattern includes ambitiousness, competitiveness, rapid speech style, hostility, and anger, but not all of these characteristics are harmful to health. Anger and hostility appear to be the most important risk factors (Booth-Kewley & Friedman, 1987). People who react with rage to everyday annoyances, such as noticing that the person before them in the 10-items-or-fewer line at the supermarket has 11 items in the shopping cart, may be at greatest risk for heart disease (Angier, 1990). Another type of negative emotion, shame, also appears highly important. Multiple findings suggest that self-threats trigger feelings of shame and that these feelings could dictate subsequent physiological changes relevant to physical health (Dickerson, Gruenewald, & Kemeny, 2004).

Several remarkable studies have now demonstrated that the effects of positive emotions endure across major portions of a lifetime. One study (Harker & Keltner, 2001) had observers rate the amount of positive emotion evident in women's college yearbook photos, and found that the ratings predicted positive outcomes in the women's marriages and their personal well-being, as much as 30 years after the photos were taken. Another study examined autobiographical statements written by Roman Catholic nuns when they entered their religious order at an average age of 22 years, early in the 1900s. Although all these nuns lived in quite similar objective circumstances, those whose youthful statements had more positive emotional content turned out to be longer-lived. The death rates of those with the most positive statements were 2.5 times lower than those showing the least positive emotion (Danner, Snowdon, & Friesen, 2001). These and other similar results (e.g., Martin and others, 2002) show that positive emotion is strongly associated with better health across many years or even decades.

Threat and Appraisals of Control. By far the most threatening events are those we judge to be out of our control (Rodin & Salovey, 1989). Think about how the perception of control might affect some of your own responses. Do you feel more comfortable driving a car or riding in an airplane? Most people choose driving even though flying is as much as 10 times safer than driving, as measured in deaths per mile. Our deep-seated preference for control is one reason for this perverse response. When our basic motive to master our environment is called into question, a vital part of our sense of self is threatened. Feeling that events are beyond one's control increases the likelihood of many kinds of negative outcomes, including worker "burnout" and the perception of overcrowding in dormitories and prisons (Paulus, 1988; Pines, Aronson, & Kafry, 1981). For example, if you were assigned roommates in a dormitory suite, you would probably feel more crowded than if you roomed with the same number of individuals whom you had picked yourself. Not surprisingly, the anxiety and frustration that accompany lack of control take their toll on physical well-being. Uncontrollable stressful events are much more hazardous to health than controllable ones (Fleming, Baum, & Weiss, 1987; Kiecolt-Glaser & Glaser, 1988; Salovey and others, 1998).

SOCIAL PSYCHOLOGY IN PRACTICE: CONTROL AND DEPRESSION

Perhaps the most negative result of repeated experiences of lack of control is learned helplessness (Abramson, Seligman, & Teasdale, 1978; Seligman, 1975). Animals and humans that have endured uncontrollable outcomes often give up attempting to control their fate (M. E. P. Seligman & Maier, 1967). In one study, people were exposed to inescapable bursts of noise and later failed to protect themselves from noises they could easily have stopped (Hiroto, 1974). Learned helplessness can undermine people's efforts to master their situations. For example, people who experience uncontrollable failures may give up trying, even when their efforts might be of use. Part of the reason may be that repeated thoughts, such as "I can't do anything," and the associated sad and hopeless emotions interfere with thought processes that would help people actually gain control (Sedek & Kofta, 1990).

Such findings have triggered speculation that appraisals of events as uncontrollable contribute to clinical depression, a psychological disorder characterized by negative moods, low self-esteem, pessimism, and a disruption of thinking, sleeping, eating, and activity patterns (Abramson and others, 1978). Figure 4.7 shows how the process works. A negative event or situation that occurs is appraised as both uncontrollable and laden with widespread implications for many areas of the person's life. The expectation of lack of control produces learned helplessness.

But learned helplessness is only part of depression. If global, enduring, uncontrollable events are also attributed to internal causes, that is, perceived to be "my fault," depression is the likely result (Abramson and others, 1978). For instance, in explaining a romantic break-up, a person might conclude that he is completely and totally unlovable. This explanation robs him of control and of any hope of finding a future loving relationship. Research shows that people who use this depressive attributional style are more likely than others to become depressed when things go wrong (C. A. Anderson, Jennings, & Arnoult, 1988). The effects can last for years and can damage physical and mental health. Peterson and his colleagues (C. Peterson, Seligman, & Vaillant, 1988) examined interviews of men recorded when they were college students in the early 1940s, coding their attributions about negative events as depressive or not. The men were medically examined periodically over the ensuing decades, with highly consistent results: Those who had explained negative events more pessimistically in their early 20s experienced poorer physical and mental health even into their 60s.

■ ■ ■

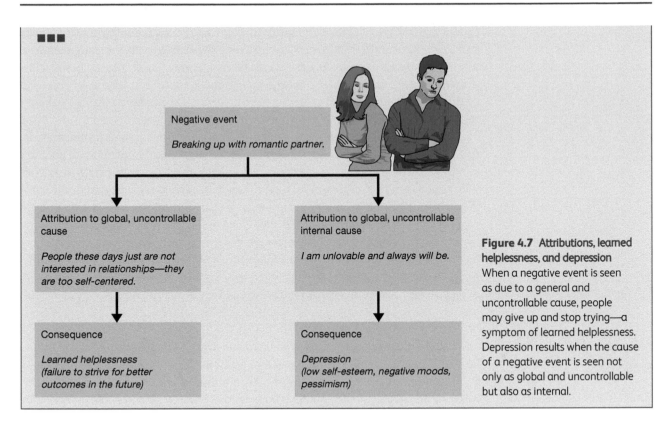

Figure 4.7 Attributions, learned helplessness, and depression When a negative event is seen as due to a general and uncontrollable cause, people may give up and stop trying—a symptom of learned helplessness. Depression results when the cause of a negative event is seen not only as global and uncontrollable but also as internal.

Defending Against Threat: Emotion-Focused Coping

To defend against threats, people sometimes try to manage their emotional responses through escape, distraction, focusing on more positive (less threatened) aspects of the self, writing about the threat, or tending to the self and important relationships.

Though learned helplessness may keep people from doing anything about events that are appraised as threats to the self, people ordinarily respond with coping strategies, efforts to reduce the negative consequences produced by threatening events. In one common type of coping response, **emotion-focused coping**, people attempt to deal with the negative emotions associated with the event, perhaps by escaping or avoiding the threatening situation. Faced with family discord, for example, a person could ignore the problem or become immersed in some distracting hobby or activity. How do these strategies of emotion-focused coping work?

emotion-focused coping
dealing with the negative emotions aroused by threats or stressors, often by suppressing emotions or distraction

Escaping from Threat. When events conspire to bring home our failures and short-comings, a common first impulse is to ship out rather than shape up. After all, escape mercifully terminates the painful awareness of inadequacies (Gibbons & Wicklund, 1982). Experimental evidence bears out the idea that people who have fallen short of a personal standard will make a quick exit from the stressful situation—if they can. In one study, an experimenter told participants that they had scored very well or very poorly on a test of intelligence and creativity and then asked them to wait 5 minutes for a second experimenter. For half of the participants, the waiting room was equipped with a mirror and video camera, both designed to induce self-awareness. Did the combination of scoring poorly on the test and self-awareness make escape look like the best option? Apparently so. The people who scored poorly and were told to wait in the specially equipped room left significantly sooner than did other participants (Duval & Wicklund, 1972).

Even as mundane a behavior as watching TV may be a way for some people to escape painful self-awareness through distraction. To test this idea, Sophia Moskalenko and Steven Heine (2003) gave participants false feedback about their test performance, and then seated each one in front of a TV set to watch a video as the next part of the study. When the video came on, showing nature scenes with a musical soundtrack, the experimenter exclaimed that this was the wrong video and went supposedly to get the correct one, leaving the participant alone as the video played. The participants who had received failure feedback watched the video much longer than those who thought they had succeeded. The researchers concluded that distraction through television viewing can effectively relieve the discomfort associated with painful failures or mismatches between the self and self-guides. In contrast, successful participants had little wish to be distracted from their self-related thoughts!

Escape can take other forms as well. People drink, take drugs, and engage in "just for kicks" risky behavior for many reasons, but sometimes these activities are attempts at blotting out the self, eliminating the uncomfortable consequences of mismatches between the self and our self-guides (Paquette, Bergeron, & Lacourse, 2012). For example, Jay Hull (1981) found that people really can "drown their sorrows" with alcohol: Alcohol consumption temporarily reduces self-awareness.

Downplaying Threat by Focusing on the More Positive Aspects of the Self. Besides escape through drinking or distraction, another way to manage the negative consequences of poor performances is to downplay their importance in comparison to other domains of life. Expressing the personal characteristics we see as most important and value most highly through self-affirmation can help us cope with failure, uncertainty, and stress in other areas (Steele, 1988). Shelley Taylor (1983) found that breast-cancer patients who were facing the possibility of death often expressed and reaffirmed what

terror management theory
a theory stating that reminders of one's own mortality lead individuals to reaffirm basic cultural worldviews, which can have both positive and negative effects

HOT TOPICS IN SOCIAL PSYCHOLOGY: AWARENESS OF PERSONAL MORTALITY AS A PSYCHOLOGICAL THREAT

Even those not facing a life-threatening illness, but who are simply subtly reminded of their own mortality, may choose to self-affirm as a means to cope. According to **Terror Management Theory** (Solomon and others, 2000), such a reminder leads us to cope by reaffirming our most basic cultural worldviews, such as religious beliefs or views about what is most important in life. Indeed, thoughts of one's own death may spark a host of positive, prosocial behaviors (Vail, Juhl, Arndt, Vess, Routledge, & Rutjens, 2012). But they also have a more negative side, generating intolerance and rejection for the deviant, the defiant, and the just "different"—anyone who fails to conform to the cultural worldview (Solomon and others, 2000).

they regarded as their most basic self-aspects. Some individuals quit dead-end jobs, whereas others turned to writing poetry or reaffirmed significant relationships.

Thus, when faced with irrefutable evidence of our couch-potato behavior and our selfish motives, we may downplay the importance of those topics, deciding that slimness and generosity are not all they are cracked up to be—compared to other areas of life. Research shows, for example, that the more highly skilled people are on dimensions like academic ability, social skills, or artistic ability, the more important they think those dimensions are; conversely, the less skilled, the less importance they attach to the dimensions (Pelham, 1991).

Working Through Threat by Writing About It.

"Sometimes I wonder how all those who do not write, compose, or paint can manage to escape the madness, the melancholia, the panic fear which is inherent in the human situation." As novelist Graham Greene realized (1980, p. 285), artistic expression helps people cope emotionally. Even such simple forms of expression such as writing or talking about the feelings produced by threatening events can help overcome some of their emotional and physical costs (Bulman & Wortman, 1977; Tait & Silver, 1989).

James Pennebaker (1997) has championed the idea that bringing to the surface deeply buried stressful events can help alleviate some of their negative effects. In one dramatic illustration of this idea, he and his colleagues asked some students to write about personally traumatic life events that they had never before discussed, and they asked others to write about trivial topics (Pennebaker, Kiecolt-Glaser, & Glaser, 1988). The students were assured that their names would not be connected to what they wrote. On the 4 successive days of the experiment, the first group dealt with extremely significant events in their lives, including such traumas as the sudden death of a sibling or childhood sexual abuse. Not surprisingly, they reported more negative emotions and more physical discomforts (headaches, muscle tension, pounding heart) at the time, compared with participants who wrote about unimportant topics. However, physiological measures showed that immune-system functioning was superior among students who wrote about traumas. This health benefit persisted for 6 weeks, during which these students visited the university health center less often than did the other participants. Other studies have replicated these types of powerful effects (Frattaroli, 2006; Sexton & Pennebaker, 2009).

Of course, although these participants benefited in the long run, the immediate impact of writing about traumatic events was negative. Before agreeing to participate in this study, the students were warned that they might be asked to write about extremely upsetting events. In addition, researchers conducting studies of this type are always prepared to refer for counseling any participants who become overly distressed. Traumatic events do, of course, harm the victim in many ways, and merely thinking and writing about the event cannot remove all its negative effects. But writing about them can at least help reduce the costs of suppressing and inhibiting

Photo 4.5 Coping with threat. Writing about threatening events in a diary can help us cope with those events and improve our health in the long term.

painful thoughts, and it is often the first step toward appraising negative events differently (Horowitz, 1987; Lepore, Ragan, & Jones, 2000). As you will see, reappraising events is one way to cope directly with problems.

Tend and Befriend. One means to cope emotionally with stress is by nurturing one's self, one's kin, and other people, and by creating and maintaining social networks of close others. Shelly Taylor has named this pattern "tend and befriend" (Taylor, Klein, Lewis, Gruenewald, Gurung, & Updegraff, 2000). Though this coping strategy could be effective for anyone, women are more likely to use it than are men (Taylor and others, 2000). Men are instead more likely to display "fight or flight" responses when under stress. This sex difference is so stable and robust that of 26 studies examining people's tendency to affiliate with others under stress, 25 found that women were more likely than men to do so (Luckow, Reifman, & McIntosh, 1998).

Tend and befriend deals primarily with seeking out and giving support to others. In Chapter 12, we will discuss the benefits of receiving support from others.

Attacking Threat Head-On: Problem-Focused Coping

Sometimes people respond to threats directly, attempting to reinterpret or remove the negative threat or situation itself. Strategies include making excuses, seeking to take control, or directly attacking the problem.

Focusing on the emotional responses produced by threats to the self can help us to feel good about ourselves, but sometimes we prefer tackling events head-on. If emotion-focused coping is so effective, why would we ever opt to use other strategies? The reason may be that suppressing emotional feelings comes with costs (Baumeister and others, 2000). Illustrating this point, one study found that when students watched an emotionally evocative film under instructions to suppress their emotions, the effortful suppression actually reduced their ability to remember details from the film (Richards & Gross, 2000). Instead of trying to suppress emotional responses, the alternative strategy of **problem-focused coping** directs people's cognitive, emotional, and behavioral resources toward reinterpreting the event as nonthreatening (rather than just trying to manage emotional reactions to the threat) or toward physically removing the threat.

problem-focused coping
dealing with threats or stressors directly, often by reappraising the situation or by directly removing the threat

Making Excuses: It's Not My Fault. What happens when our worst fears are realized and we do fail a test, get caught in a lie, or get pulled over for speeding on the expressway? Although we have all wished the earth would open up and swallow us in such circumstances, our usual recourse is to apologize, offer excuses, and try to pick up where we left off. Whenever an action ends in disaster and threatens our self-concept, a good excuse is worth its weight in gold.

Why are excuses so important? The answer has to do with self-enhancing attributions that distort people's explanations for successes and failures (Mullen & Riordan, 1988). Most people like to take credit for their successes and notable accomplishments and to attribute failure to external causes. A good grade on an exam reflects well on our intelligence and motivation, whereas a failing grade is surely due to poorly written test items, an emergency at home, a sudden bout of the flu, or even loud music playing down the hall (D. T. Miller & Ross, 1975).

Self-Handicapping. A good excuse can be even more valuable if it is lined up before the performance: If we do fail, our defense is already in place. Charles Snyder and his colleagues found that people often use disclaimers like shyness, anxiety, ill health, or disruptive events when they anticipate failing at an important task (C. R. Snyder & Higgins, 1988; C. R. Snyder, Smith, Augelli, & Ingram, 1985). Letting others think we are shy, sick, or under stress seems preferable to conveying the impression that we are unlikable or incompetent.

If verbal excuses help us save face, could the creation of actual barriers to successful performance do the same? Strange as it may seem, some people actually sabotage their own performances to provide excuses for subsequent failures. The strategy is called **self-handicapping** (Berglas & Jones, 1978). To see how and why self-handicapping might work, imagine that you have been bragging for months about your chicken curry, and now your friends are finally coming over for dinner. It suddenly occurs to you that your culinary skills may not quite match those you have advertised. Is there any way out? One possibility is self-handicapping: You could intentionally arrange to run out of a crucial ingredient for the curry. In attributional terms, self-handicapping is a no-lose proposition: Observers' impressions of your skill will be even more positive than they otherwise would be, regardless of the dinner's failure or success. If the curry is not so great, your reputation as a great cook will be saved as your friends blame the disaster on the missing ingredient rather than on your poor skills. If the dinner is wonderful anyway, your culinary expertise will appear even more impressive.

But remember, the attributional benefit of self-handicapping comes with costs. Self-handicapping can lower the real probability of good performance (Baumgardner & Brownlee, 1987). Moreover, it may undercut one's desire to improve on a task following failure (McCrea, 2008). It may come with social costs, as well: observers—especially women—dislike those who self-handicap and rate them negatively on a wide range of traits (Hirt, McCrea, & Boris, 2003). The reason seems to be that women, more than men, value effort for itself, and have little respect for those who make excuses rather than trying hard in performance situations. All in all, these interpersonal costs mean that self-handicapping is usually counterproductive.

self-handicapping
seeking to avoid blame for an expected poor performance, either by claiming an excuse in advance or by actively sabotaging one's own performance (for example, by failing to practice)

Taking Control of the Problem. If external attributions usually help us to save face, what do you make of the following finding? In one survey of U.S. residents, people who regarded themselves as poor or economically struggling were questioned about their attributions for their situation and about their general emotional well-being. Poor people who believed they had had a fair chance to achieve felt more pride and joy and less guilt and disappointment about their lives than those who believed that external forces had held them back (E. R. Smith & Kluegel, 1982). That is, even when their outcomes are negative, people often feel better if they think they have control. Blaming external factors for failures might let you off the hook momentarily, but interpreting the forces that influence your life as controllable will put you back in charge for the long term. Feelings of control are so important that we attempt to exert control whenever we can (R. W. White, 1959), and when we feel in control we try harder and often perform better (Dweck, 1986). A recent study showed that when people felt in control, their self-regulatory abilities improved. Those who felt they had control were more sensitive to their own errors (indicated by a larger neural signal associated with self-regulation, termed error-related negativity), explaining their superior self-regulation performance (Legault & Inzlicht, 2013). In fact, we often exaggerate the amount of control we possess, even in situations actually ruled by chance (Langer, 1975). For example, most people who play the state lottery prefer to pick their "lucky number," even though any number would have an equal chance of winning.

What gives people the feeling that they can control events in their lives? One crucial ingredient is their confidence in their ability to deal with a particular area, such as passing exams in psychology or successfully managing their social life. This confidence in our ability to produce the outcomes we desire is termed self-efficacy (Bandura, 1986). Self-efficacy is particularly strongly linked with the way people explain their failures: whether they explain them in terms of controllable or uncontrollable causes. If the bank bounces one of your checks for the third time this month and you explain it by saying, "Oh, I just can't keep a checkbook balanced; I'm no good at finance," you are pointing to your supposed lack of ability—an uncontrollable cause. If you blame the situation on your lack of effort or attention, you are pointing to a potentially controllable cause. Such an explanation for a failure should lead you to try harder to keep track of your deposits and withdrawals, which may result in fewer overdraft fees in the future.

Another crucial ingredient in eliciting control is counterfactual thinking, or thoughts about how an outcome might have turned out differently (Epstude & Roese, 2008). When we fail at something, for example, when we score poorly on an exam, we may

SOCIAL PSYCHOLOGY IN PRACTICE: CONTROL AND LIFE GOALS

The issue of who is in control is central even when people set overall directions for their lives. Take a moment to contemplate your most important long-term objectives and goals. Do these aspirations reflect your own internally guided choices, or are they goals that other people have selected for you? Consistent with the general benefits of control, actions and goals that we choose for ourselves benefit us psychologically more than those that are externally imposed. Tim Kasser and Richard Ryan (1996) asked people to rate the importance they personally attached to several different life goals. These goals included some that the researchers classified as intrinsic or self-chosen, such as positive relationships with friends and family, community service, or health, as well as some goals the researchers viewed as involving external approval or rewards, such as financial success, fame, and physical attractiveness. The researchers also measured several forms of physical and psychological well-being, including physical symptoms and depression. Consistent results emerged in separate studies of undergraduate students and of adults from 18 to 79 years old. Those who attached more importance to the intrinsic goals tended to have better well-being and lower levels of depression and psychological distress, compared to those whose aspirations were classified as more extrinsic. It seems that striving for wealth, fame, and beauty is not a sure route to happiness. Instead, people whose most important goals reflect intrinsic values, goals involving such things as relatedness to others and community service, have the best life outcomes overall.

Moreover, there may be benefits of deciding to cease pursuing a goal if it seems (or becomes) unreachable and to choose to adopt new ones (Wrosch, Scheier, Miller, Schulz, & Carver, 2003). If you have a goal to be a professional athlete, but injury, small stature, and/or lack of access to effective coaching make achieving this goal impossible, data suggest that multiple indicators of your well-being will be enhanced if you can "let go" of that goal.

consider ways the score could have been better ("If only I had studied more, I would have scored a B+ instead of a D"). Though focusing on these "if-only" thoughts may make us feel badly, it may also be functional in helping us improve by suggesting appropriate tactics we can execute when next faced with the same circumstance or by highlighting what to avoid. In the case of the poor exam performance, this kind of counterfactual thought might make salient to us that we should avoid going to a party the night before the test and should instead review our notes and re-read the textbook chapters. Indeed, work has shown that counterfactuals that focus on better outcomes appear to elicit positive changes in our future behavior, which enhances our perceived sense of control over the outcome, which subsequently results in future improvements (Nasco & Marsh, 1999).

How to Cope?

The individual's resources as well as characteristics of the threatening situation dictate the best response to threats. No single type of response is always best, but many types of coping can help overcome the threat, preserve psychological well-being, and protect physical health.

As we have seen, there are many ways to cope with threats to the self. Both problem-focused and emotion-focused coping can improve psychological well-being and lessen the health damage caused by threatening events (F. Cohen, 1984; Kiecolt-Glaser, Fisher, & Ogrocki, 1987). But which type works better? The answer depends on who is being threatened—the individual and the resources she or he brings to the situation—and also on the nature of the threat, particularly its controllability.

Self-Esteem as a Resource for Coping. People vary in the cognitive and emotional resources they have to aid in coping. Self-esteem is not only an indicator of how well we are meeting our fundamental social motives for mastery and connectedness, but also an important resource for coping with threats to the self. Indeed, those with high self-esteem respond to such threats with far fewer emotional and physical symptoms than do those with low self-esteem (J. D. Brown & Smart, 1991), and they even respond better physiologically in the face of the most pressing social threat, social exclusion (Ford & Collins, 2010). These beneficial outcomes occur because those with high self-esteem roll out a formidable arsenal of weapons to defend against threats. For example, they fight negative feedback, setbacks, or stress with an aggressive use of self-enhancing biases and problem-focused coping (J. D. Brown, 1986; S. Epstein, 1992; Josephs, Larrick, Steele, & Nisbett, 1992). They are largely unaffected emotionally by negative feedback (J. D. Brown, 2010). They compare themselves with others who are worse off and make self-enhancing attributions for their failures and shortcomings. Finally, a strong sense of control lets people with high self-esteem tackle problems head-on. The successful use of this impressive array of self-enhancing biases and coping strategies restores and maintains high self-esteem so the whole cycle can begin again (S. E. Taylor & Brown, 1988). Like a reflection in a series of fun-house mirrors, high self-esteem leads to self-enhancement and successful coping, which restores high self-esteem, which triggers self-enhancement, and so on. No wonder, then, that people with high self-esteem have more stable levels of self-esteem and clearer self-concepts (J. D. Campbell, 1990).

If you have ever interacted with someone who has low self-esteem, however, you may have noticed a very different set of reactions (vanDellen, Campbell, Hoyle, & Bradfield, 2011). Rather than predicting that the rain clouds will be followed by spring flowers, people with low self-esteem seem resigned to permanent flood conditions. Indeed, depressed people and those with low self-esteem are much less likely to self-enhance than others (Alloy & Abramson, 1979; S. E. Taylor & Brown, 1988). They make downward comparisons less often, remember more negative things about themselves, and assume they have less control over events.

So it is clear that everyday decisions—whether to apply for graduate school, try out for the band, or ask a popular classmate for a date—are very different proposals for different individuals, depending on their level of self-esteem. Great rewards might follow from taking these actions, but individuals with low self-esteem may be unable to take the risk because they are highly sensitive to the possibility of failure and embarrassment (Leary, Barners, & Griebel, 1986). "To the person high in self-esteem . . . the world is an oyster bed of opportunities to enhance themselves, but to the person low in self-esteem, it is a minefield that can humiliate and depress" (Josephs, Larrick, and others, 1992, p. 35). The differences between the ways people with high or low self-esteem approach events can compound across a lifetime, affecting the ways we deal with daily threats and ultimately our physical health.

Controllability and Coping. The best way to cope depends on the characteristics of the threat as well as on those of the threatened person. Depending on their appraisals of the threat and their own resources, people can choose among many possible coping strategies, as Figure 4.8 shows. Every style of coping, however, has costs as well as benefits. The most important appraisal is of a threat's controllability. Controllable threats, those that one is confident in being able to handle, really represent challenges rather than threats (Blascovich & Tomaka, 1996). People's emotional responses to challenges are generally positive or only mildly negative, and physiological responses (including heart-rate changes, for instance) are geared toward successful mobilization and effective action. With challenges, problem-focused coping might work best, even if it increases immediate distress (S. M. Miller & Mangan, 1983). In contrast, when threats are appraised as uncontrollable, escape, distraction, and other forms of emotion-focused coping may be the only effective ways to deal with them (Folkman, 1984). Unlike challenges, threats elicit negative feelings and physiological responses that are ineffective and perhaps even health-damaging (Blascovich, 2008).

But the difference between a threat and a challenge is not so much in the event itself as in the way one looks at it. In one study, Joe Tomaka and his colleagues (1997) gave students a mental arithmetic task, introducing the task for some students by stressing the need for both speed and accuracy (making the task somewhat threatening) and for others by asking them to think of the task as "a challenge" and to think of themselves as "someone capable of meeting that challenge." This simple difference in instructions for the very same task elicited the physiological response patterns characteristic of threats versus challenges. Thus, once again, as we have seen so many times in this chapter, the way people appraise a stressful event is crucial.

Aid in fighting stress also comes from external sources. The presence of others who give support, advice, and assistance can help ward off the negative consequences of threat. We see how this happens in Chapter 12, pages 458–460.

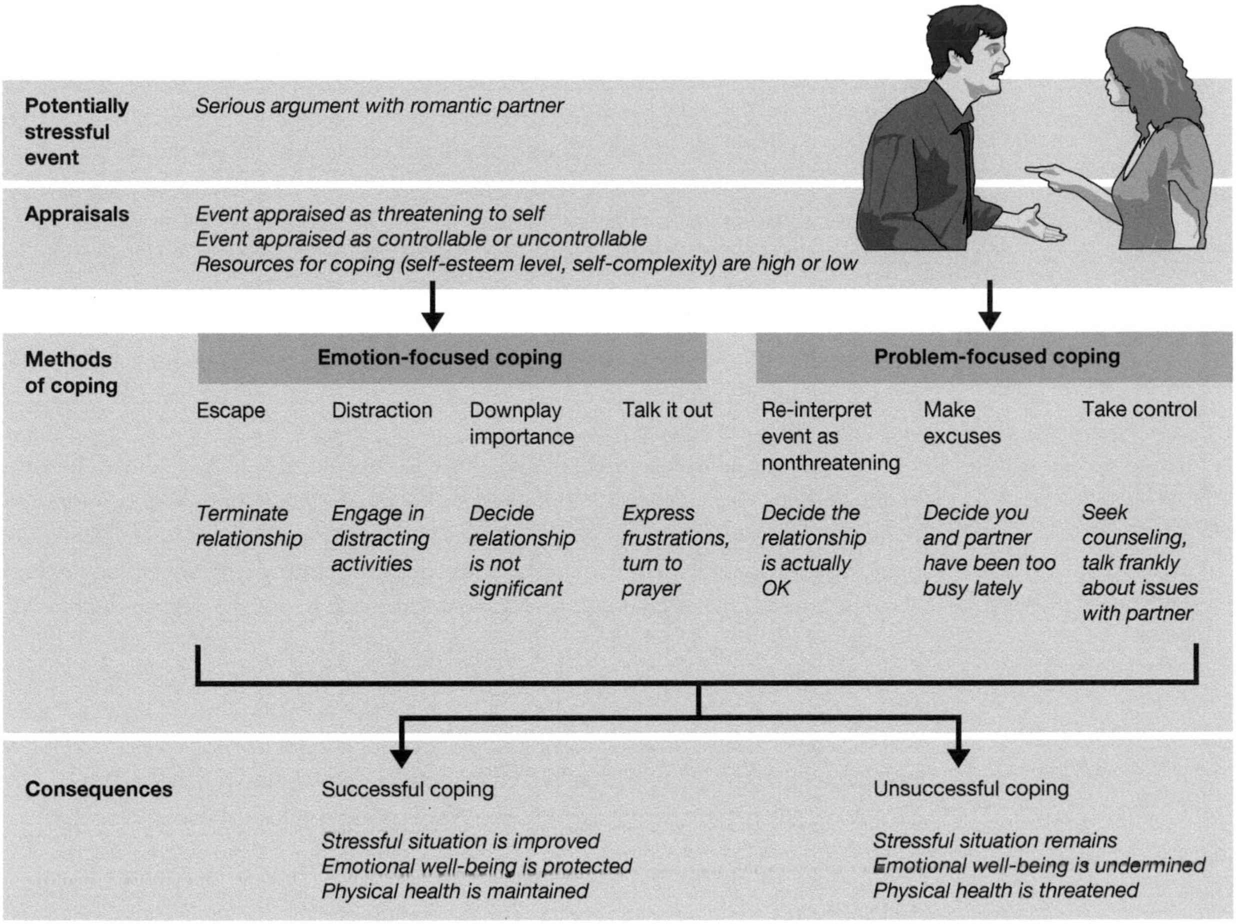

Potentially stressful event	Serious argument with romantic partner						
Appraisals	Event appraised as threatening to self Event appraised as controllable or uncontrollable Resources for coping (self-esteem level, self-complexity) are high or low						

Methods of coping	**Emotion-focused coping**				**Problem-focused coping**		
	Escape	Distraction	Downplay importance	Talk it out	Re-interpret event as nonthreatening	Make excuses	Take control
	Terminate relationship	Engage in distracting activities	Decide relationship is not significant	Express frustrations, turn to prayer	Decide the relationship is actually OK	Decide you and partner have been too busy lately	Seek counseling, talk frankly about issues with partner

Consequences	Successful coping	Unsuccessful coping
	Stressful situation is improved Emotional well-being is protected Physical health is maintained	Stressful situation remains Emotional well-being is undermined Physical health is threatened

Figure 4.8 Ways of coping and their effects
Appraisals of a self-threatening event—particularly of its controllability—and of one's coping resources influence the selection of coping strategies. Successful or unsuccessful coping may influence emotional well-being and physical health—as well as affecting the concrete stressful situation itself.

CONCLUDING COMMENTS

We started the chapter by saying that one of the most important life tasks each of us faces is understanding both who we are and how we feel about ourselves. Philosophers have long admonished us to "know thyself," the first aspect of this important task. An accurate understanding of our individual abilities, preferences, and talents enables us to choose the partners, pastimes, and professions that suit us best. It lets us know where we fit in the social world and provides a starting point in any attempt at change or improvement. But psychologists know that it is not enough to "know thyself." Self-esteem is equally central in our lives. Viewing the self as both good and in control—even in exaggerated ways—protects our emotional and physical well-being as we cope with inconsistencies, failures, and stress. Whenever we think about the self, we are faced with two, sometimes conflicting, motives: enhancing the self and accurately evaluating the self.

The dual needs for accurate self-knowledge and positive self-esteem play themselves out in a variety of ways that were discussed throughout this chapter. Sometimes we seek accurate assessments of the self; at other times we engage in biased searches or interpretations to come up with self-enhancing information. Sometimes we compare ourselves with similar others and sometimes with others who are worse off than we are. Sometimes we choose our behaviors to accurately reflect the person we believe we are, but at other times we try to create a positive impression of ourselves. Even the ways we defend ourselves against such threats as negative feedback, obvious shortcomings, and large and small stressors provoke the same dilemma. The warm glow of positive thinking infuses us with strength to clear life's many hurdles, but escaping into a fantasy world of self-enhancement can just as easily set us up for a fall. Taking negative feedback at face value can help us to deal constructively with, and possibly to overcome, our failures and shortcomings. But it can also be painful.

Does this mean we are caught in a no-win situation, forced to make trade-offs between reality and illusion, happiness and depression? Are our choices limited to being eternal optimists, happy but out of touch, or hard realists, on top of the facts but miserable because of it? Fortunately, we have other options. The recipe for a healthy sense of self calls for both accurate self-knowledge and protective self-enhancement, in just the right amounts at just the right times. Weighing these ingredients may be the most important aspect of constructing and maintaining the self. The correct measure of self-enhancement keeps our spirits high and our body healthy, whereas a judicious amount of self-assessment keeps our goals realistic and our efforts focused in the best direction. A good dollop of self-evaluation tells us what we need to do, a splash of self-enhancement gives us the courage to do it.

SUMMARY

Constructing the Self-Concept: Learning Who We Are. People construct the **self-concept** in much the same way that they form impressions of others, drawing knowledge from similar types of cues using similar interpretive processes. People often infer their own characteristics from their observed behaviors, as **self-perception theory** notes. They also use thoughts and feelings and other people's reactions to form opinions about themselves. Finally, **social comparison theory** describes how people compare themselves to others to learn what characteristics make them unique. These comparisons can result either in **contrast effects** or **assimilation effects**.

Despite the general similarity of the ways people learn about themselves and others, self-knowledge is richer and more detailed than knowledge about others. People can observe themselves in more situations and have better access to private thoughts and feelings. People also sometimes explain their own and other people's behaviors differently, producing **actor–observer differences in attribution**. However, having all this rich and detailed self knowledge does not guarantee that our self views are more insightful than others' views of us.

Because people see themselves in a wide range of situations and roles, self-knowledge is organized around multiple **self-aspects** representing roles, activities, and relationships. The number and diversity of self-aspects constitutes the individual's **self-complexity**.

CHAPTER 4 THEMES

■ **Construction of Reality**
We construct an impression of the self, based on a multitude of cues.

■ **Pervasiveness of Social Influence**
Our perceptions of other people and their reactions to us pervasively influence our self-concept and self-esteem.

■ **Striving for Mastery**
Perceiving that we control our environment helps mental well-being and physical health.

■ **Valuing Me and Mine**
Self-enhancing biases shape our self-concept and elevate self-esteem.

■ **Conservatism**
Once formed, the self-concept is resistant to change and well defended against threats.

■ **Accessibility**
The self-concept and self-esteem depend on information and experiences that come readily to mind.

People try to fit the diverse elements of the self-concept together in a way that seems coherent and stable. Coherence can be attained by focusing on a few central traits that people believe characterize them uniquely among people and consistently across situations, which forms the basis of the **self-schema**. They can also attain coherence by making accessible only limited aspects of the self at any given time and by selectively remembering past acts. Culture influences the ways in which people seek coherence. Members of individualist cultures stress the self-schema, traits that generally describe them across situations, whereas those in collectivist cultures emphasize self-aspects, their roles and relationships with others.

Constructing Self-Esteem: How We Feel About Ourselves. Accurate self-knowledge regarding our capabilities and preferences is important for guiding us through our lives in ways that suit our needs and abilities. But accuracy is not the only consideration in evaluating the self: **Self-esteem** is also greatly influenced by motivational pressures to think well of the self. These motivations color many of our thoughts and feelings about the self through **self-enhancing biases**.

Events that affect us positively or negatively influence our self-esteem, but we try in several ways to accumulate more positive than negative experiences. We also evaluate ourselves by making comparisons with others, as described by **self-evaluation maintenance** theory. These comparisons also are sometimes self-enhancing, though at times are self-deprecating. Despite the value of accurate self-knowledge, self-enhancement occurs for two primary reasons. Some actions that appear self-enhancing are aimed at actual self-improvement, reflecting successful **self-regulation**. And high self-esteem can be an important resource that protects us against stress and threats to the self.

Like most other aspects of the self, self-enhancing biases operate somewhat differently in different cultures. Individualist cultures emphasize positive individual characteristics as the source of self-esteem, whereas collectivist cultures stress connectedness to others. Despite these differences, self-esteem functions in all cultures to indicate how well we are meeting our most important motives for mastery and connectedness.

Effects of the Self: Self-Regulation. Self-knowledge serves as a framework for perceiving other people and influences what types of social information we will remember.

The self regulates many aspects of our lives. Emotions are sparked by **appraisals** of self-relevant events and their causes or controllability. Emotions signal the occurrence of significant events and motivate us to act in response, for example, to flee from danger. As they perform this self-regulation function, emotions involve the whole self, body and mind: They activate facial expressions, physiological responses, subjective feelings, and overt behaviors.

The self also directs behavior. Sometimes people engage in **self-expression**, acting in ways that express their true inner selves. At other times, people are concerned with **self-presentation**, attempting to shape others' opinions in order to gain power, influence, or approval. The personality variable of **self-monitoring** reflects the degree to which people seek one or the other of these two general goals. Finally, people sometimes control their behavior in ways that help achieve desired internal standards or goals. **Regulatory focus theory** describes how people seek to attain desired states or avoid undesired ones, for example when they compare the self with the internal standards of their **ideal selves** or their **ought selves**. No matter why we choose to control our behavior, these actions may end up influencing people's private views of themselves.

When temptations arise, they offer us short-term benefits that detract from our longer-term goals, challenging people's ability to regulate their behavior. People can actively and effortfully choose strategies to overcome these temptations. Yet, efforts at self-regulation can be hard work and can deplete our resources, though acts of **self-affirmation** can help us restore self-control. But, if we fail to reach our goals, negative consequences ensue. Some situations, such as when **self-awareness** is high, can cause people to realize that their current state falls short of their desired goals.

Defending the Self: Coping with Stresses, Inconsistencies, and Failures. When threatened by external events or negative feedback, people must defend their sense of who and what they are. Major failures and disasters obviously threaten the self, but so do inconsistent information, daily hassles, and stresses. Threats to the self affect not only emotional well-being but also physical health. The most damaging threats are those we appraise as uncontrollable, which can lead to learned helplessness.

Faced with threats, people respond with coping strategies. Sometimes they engage in **emotion-focused coping**, regulating emotional responses to threat through escape, distraction, focusing on more positive (less threatened) aspects of the self, writing about the threat, or tending to the self and important relationships. At other times, people respond to threats directly with **problem-focused coping**, trying to reduce the negative consequences of self-threatening events. Possible strategies are making excuses (such as through **self-handicapping**), seeking to take control, or directly attacking the problem. Reminders of mortality also constitute threats, as described by **Terror Management Theory**.

The individual's resources, including self-esteem, as well as characteristics of the threatening situation, dictate the best response to threats. No single type of response is always best, but many types of coping can help overcome the threat, preserve psychological well-being, and protect physical health.

PERCEIVING GROUPS

STEREOTYPE PREJUDICE
CONTACT HYPOTHESIS
CONNECTEDNESS ACCESSIBILITY CONDITIONING
NORMS CATEGORIZATION
CONSTRUCTION REALITY DISCRIMINATION
SOCIAL GROUP IMPLICIT MEASURES

Biology, chemistry, and physics professors at universities around the United States recently received an undergraduate student application for a science lab manager job (Moss-Racusin, Dovidio, Brescoll, Graham, & Handelsman, 2012). The student had graduate-school aspirations and qualifications that were promising, but somewhat ambiguous. The professors were asked to evaluate the student's application, believing that the student would receive this feedback. Unbeknownst to these professors, however, this application did not represent a real person, but was created by a team of researchers, who assigned the applicant a female name in some cases and a male name in others. Thus, one professor might have seen a particular job application under the name Jennifer, whereas another saw exactly the same application with the name John. Because Jennifer and John had identical credentials, they were evaluated identically, right? Sadly, no: the results showed dramatic sex bias. The equally qualified female applicant was judged as less competent and less employable than the male applicant. Moreover, the professors indicated that, if they were to hire the woman, they would provide her less professional mentoring and pay her roughly $3700 less than they would pay the man. These findings held whether the professor making the judgments was male or female!

The evidence provided by this study, as well as other studies in which matched Black and White candidates apply for the same job (Krueger, 2002), strongly suggests that some employers engage in racial and sex discrimination. The term **discrimination** refers to positive or negative behavior directed toward a social group and its members. Of course, people are usually concerned with negative behaviors—with discrimination against a specific group—but discrimination against one group inevitably amounts to discrimination in favor of others. For example, the former South African system of apartheid—legally enforced segregation—victimized Blacks while preserving the power and wealth of the small White minority.

Though apartheid and many other forms of discrimination are illegal in the United States and many other countries, people still find themselves ill-treated because of their group memberships. The forms of discrimination and the types of groups affected by it are many. Economic discrimination victimizes women and people of color when they

discrimination
any positive or negative behavior directed toward a social group and its members

prejudice
a positive or negative evaluation of a social group and its members

stereotype
a mental representation or impression of a social group that people form by associating particular characteristics and emotions with the group

try to purchase a used car, rent or purchase a home, or negotiate a salary (Abrams, 1991; Goldin, 1990; W. E. Schmidt, 1990; Seidel, Polzer, & Stewart, 2000). Black men's experiences with the criminal justice system often differ substantially from those of most Whites (D. A. Bell, 1973; Silverstein, 1965). Turks and other foreigners living in Germany have been victims of verbal abuse, beatings, arson, and murder by neo-Nazis and teenage "skinheads" (Moseley, 1998). In Europe, Black soccer players—even major stars of their teams—are frequently subjected to racist chants (Vecsey, 2003). Indeed, in 2012, Chelsea captain John Terry, who is White, was banned for four games and given a hefty fine for racially insulting a Black soccer player on another team, Anton Ferdinand. French Canadians feel oppressed by the English-speaking majority; Canadian Mohawk Indians feel oppressed by French Canadians. Tamils in Sri Lanka, women in Afghanistan, and Blacks in South Africa have little access to adequate schooling, health care, or political power. And Shia and Sunni Muslims attack each other violently in places like Pakistan.

What leads one group of people to victimize another? Religious thinkers, political leaders, social scientists, and others have searched for an answer to this important question. Social psychologists believe that the underlying processes leading to discrimination usually include **prejudice**, positive or negative evaluations of a social group and its members. Once again, people's concern is most often with negative reactions, which range from mild dislike to blind hatred. As you will see in the first part of this chapter, prejudice is complex and multifaceted, and its roots can be traced to the kinds of motivational and cognitive processes that guide our every interaction with groups.

Prejudice can be "hot" or "cold." Virulent and emotional hatred for other groups, such as that espoused by the Nazis or the Ku Klux Klan, is easy to recognize. It shows itself in burning crosses, the use of ethnic slurs and other types of "hate speech," and campaigns of "ethnic cleansing," pogroms, and massacres. Unfortunately, the very obviousness of this type of bigotry and hatred may blind us to a more insidious type of prejudice based on the calm assumption that certain groups just "do not have what it takes" and should therefore be excluded from desirable positions, wealth, or power. This quieter, cooler form of prejudice is at work when sports team owners profit from the performance of Black athletes on the field but can never find a "qualified" Black for a managerial or front-office job. And it is present when a construction union maintains an all-male membership by keeping women out of apprenticeship programs, or when a real estate agent steers prospective home buyers who are Hispanic to particular neighborhoods. Such discriminatory actions are carried out calmly, routinely, and without any of the familiar overt signs of bigotry. But even though no hooded robes or swastika armbands are anywhere in sight, very real harm is suffered by those on the receiving end. As we will see, prejudice, like most social psychological phenomena, is affected both by how we think and feel about others, and also by how we think and feel about ourselves. In this chapter we focus more on how we come to view other groups the way we do. In Chapter 6, we'll see that the fact that we ourselves belong to groups plays a huge role in prejudice and discrimination.

We start this chapter with the very basis of prejudice: the way in which people divide the world into social groups. We then consider the **stereotypes**, or impressions that people form of groups by associating the groups with particular characteristics (Eagly & Mladinic, 1989; D. L. Hamilton, 1981). The sometimes biased and often sketchy impressions we form of groups can permeate our thinking and become a basis for both prejudice and discrimination. For example, many associate women with characteristics like a lack of math and science acumen (Nosek and others, 2009). In the case of a female applicant for a science or math related job, this stereotype may translate into prejudice (negative reactions to the information on her résumé) and discrimination (a failure to offer her an interview).

Is it possible to eliminate the stereotypical thinking that contributes to prejudice? Will female job-seekers ever have their credentials evaluated fairly, by the same standards as their male counterparts? The answer is a cautious but optimistic yes. Stereotypes can be changed, though it does not happen easily. Remember the idea of conservatism: Initial impressions of groups, like first impressions of individuals, tend to have lasting power. Established stereotypes often influence thoughts and actions in ways that make stereotypes resistant to modification. But as you will see in the final section of this chapter, the defenses protecting stereotypes from change can be breached, under the right conditions. Negative stereotypes can then be replaced by more favorable impressions, and prejudice can be replaced by more unbiased evaluations.

"Let me guess. You want French and you want ranch?"

Targets of Prejudice: Social Groups

Any group that shares a socially meaningful common characteristic can be a target for prejudice. Different cultures emphasize different types of groups, but race, religion, gender, age, social status, and cultural background are important dividing lines in many societies.

Stereotypes, prejudice, discrimination: All these processes depend on identifying people as members of social groups. But what is it that turns "people" into "members of social groups"? A **social group** is two or more people who share some common characteristic that is socially meaningful for themselves or for others (Shaw, 1976; Tajfel & Turner, 1979; J. C. Turner, 1981). The key phrase here is socially meaningful. People who share just any attribute, such as pedestrians who happen to be waiting in the same place to cross the same street, do not qualify as a social group (D. L. Hamilton & Sherman, 1996). Categories of people who share socially meaningful attributes—college students, Quakers, the "working poor," white-collar criminals, environmentalists—are groups, however. So are members of smaller groups who interact face-to-face while performing shared tasks, such as the cast of a play or members of a committee. So groups can be of many types (Lickel, Hamilton, & Sherman, 2001). In fact, individuals who believe they share socially significant attributes are a group even if others do not think of them that way. Likewise, people who are seen by others as sharing meaningful similarities are a group even if they themselves do not hold that view. Recent immigrants who see

social group
two or more people who share some common characteristic that is socially meaningful for themselves or for others

Members of some groups have much more in common than shared features. Interaction and shared goals also affect group members' beliefs, feelings, and behaviors in important ways, as you will see in Chapters 9 and 11.

themselves as blending into their new culture are often disappointed when their new compatriots think of them as "foreigners." Social groups exist very much in the eyes of their beholders.

Socially meaningful characteristics, of course, can change from time to time and from culture to culture. If several heterosexual British and French men and women are discussing dating, they will probably think of themselves and each other primarily as members of the groups "men" or "women." If the topic shifts to the Euro currency, however, the implicit lines of group membership will probably shift as well. These people may now see themselves and each other as members of national groups that are affected differently by European economic union.

Even though rapid changes in perceptions of group membership are possible, each society and culture generally emphasizes particular group distinctions. In most North American and European countries today, discussion of stereotypes and prejudice is likely to make people think of racial and ethnic groups. And because most research on these issues has been conducted in North America and Europe, it displays a strong focus on racial stereotypes and prejudice, particularly on Whites' perceptions and reactions to Blacks. But often through history, not race but religion has been the characteristic that elicited the most prejudice and discrimination, and this is still true today in many parts of the world. In Lebanon, for example, the characteristic that matters is whether a person is Muslim or Christian.

In Chapter 6 we will discuss many additional consequences of dividing the world into in-groups and out-groups through social categorization.

Social Categorization: Dividing the World into Social Groups

People identify individuals as members of social groups because they share socially meaningful features. Social categorization is helpful because it allows people to deal with others efficiently and appropriately. Social categorization also helps us feel connected to other people. However, social categorization also exaggerates similarities within groups and differences between groups, and hence it forms the basis for stereotyping.

social categorization

the process of identifying individual people as members of a social group because they share certain features that are typical of the group

"Doggie," says the 2-year-old, pointing to a horse. "Doggie," she says again as she spies a cat. This common mistake reflects an attempt at categorization, the process of recognizing individual objects as members of a category because they share certain features. Categorization is the process by which we group things or people, and it is an intrinsic part of the way we think about and try to understand the nonsocial world. In the same way, we divide the enormous number of individuals we meet into groups, lumping them together on the basis of their shared socially relevant features. Instead of individuals, they become men, women, Whites, Flemish, Jews, elderly persons, single mothers, or blue-collar workers. **Social categorization** occurs when people are perceived as members of social groups rather than unique individuals. Gender, ethnicity, and age are obvious bases for social categorization, but they are not the only attributes we use. Name tags, uniforms, or tools of the trade, for example, help us categorize people by occupation, whereas accent and speech dialect may identify an individual's nationality, regional background, or social class.

Why does social categorization occur? First, it is a useful tool, enabling us to master our environment and function effectively in society (S. E. Taylor, 1981; Wilder, 1986).

Think, for example, what you gain when you categorize the man standing by the library stacks as a librarian (Andersen & Klatsky, 1987; C. F. Bond & Brockett, 1987). You can infer that he will help you locate a book and check it out. That is, knowing that this individual is a member of the group "librarians" tells you he has many characteristics shared by members of that group, even if they are not immediately obvious. Also, categorization allows you to ignore unimportant information. You can focus on what is relevant—his knowledge of books and where they are kept—without having to notice the color of his suit or his lifestyle. Social categorization saves you the effort of having to deal with all the unique aspects of every individual you meet, when they are irrelevant to your interaction.

Second, we socially categorize because it allows us to feel connected to others. If you are a Portuguese, female, college student, majoring in psychology, other Portuguese, females, college students, and psychology majors share one of these social categories with you. Using social categories, then, can allow you to divide the world up into those who are like you (are in "your group") and those who are not. By simply categorizing some individuals as part of your group, you will feel closer to them than you do those not categorized in your group.

Photo 5.1 Multiple group memberships. Sitting in the stands, watching the game, and cheering on their team, these people share the socially meaningful characteristics of "sports fans." But all are members of other social groups as well. Thus, under different circumstances, they could be categorized in terms of their family membership, age, ethnicity, or gender.

Despite these benefits, as victims of prejudice and discrimination know well, categorization also has negative side effects. Social categorization makes all members of a group seem more similar to each other than they would be if they were not categorized (Hugenberg & Sacco, 2008; Tajfel & Wilkes, 1963). This is true whether people sort others into groups on the basis of real differences or arbitrary and trivial characteristics. The librarian who breeds cocker spaniels and the librarian who writes movie scripts seem more similar if we focus only on their shared group membership as librarians. Because of this focus on similarity, people often overestimate group members' uniformity and overlook their diversity (G. W. Allport, 1954b; Brigham, 1971; Wilder, 1981). Thus, we go from a world in which some professors are forgetful to one in which all professors are absent-minded, and we move beyond the news that a majority of the voters have cast their ballots for a right-wing Republican to the idea that the electorate is uniformly conservative (Allison & Messick, 1985).

Just as it exaggerates similarities within groups, social categorization exaggerates differences between groups. If librarians are all alike, and if tennis players are all alike, the difference between tennis players and librarians gets exaggerated. In fact, once we categorize people into groups, we become more aware of the characteristics that make one group different from another rather than of those that make them similar (Krueger & Rothbart, 1990). Thus, social categorization makes individuals seem more similar or more different, depending on whether you are focusing on a shared group membership or not. Serena Williams and Roger Federer seem more similar if we think about both of them as champion tennis players, but if we think about them as members of different gender or ethnic or national groups they seem more different. Thus, social categorization brings the world into sharper focus, but the exaggeration of similarities within groups and differences between groups is the price we pay for better resolution.

FORMING IMPRESSIONS OF GROUPS: ESTABLISHING STEREOTYPES

There are many similarities between the ways we form impressions of individuals (as described in Chapter 3) and the ways we form impressions of groups. Yet there are also subtle differences that contribute to the special properties of group stereotypes (D. L. Hamilton & Sherman, 1996). To understand these special properties we must first answer two questions: What kinds of characteristics are included in stereotypes? What motivates people to form stereotypes?

The Content of Stereotypes

Many different kinds of characteristics are included in stereotypes, which can be positive or negative. Some stereotypes accurately reflect actual differences between groups, though in exaggerated form. Other stereotypes are completely inaccurate.

Photo 5.2 What are these two people like? What traits do they have? What behaviors do they perform? What is their relationship like? What are their values? The mental representation of the social group gay men may include information about these sorts of characteristics and many others.

Stereotypes Include Many Types of Characteristics. Walter Lippmann, a journalist who introduced the current meaning of the term stereotype in 1922, saw stereotypes as "pictures in the head," simplified mental images of what groups look like and what they do. Stereotypes often do incorporate physical appearance, typical interests and goals, preferred activities and occupations, and similar characteristics (Andersen & Klatzky, 1987; Brewer, 1988; Deaux & Lewis, 1983, 1984). Yet they usually go well beyond what groups look like or act like, to include the personality traits group members are believed to share and the positive or negative emotions or feelings group members arouse in others.

Early research on stereotypes found that college students held well-developed beliefs about the traits characterizing various ethnic groups (D. Katz & Braly, 1933). Considerable social pressure now exists against the public expression of such beliefs, but stereotypes have not disappeared. Do you have an image of what the "typical" college professor, accountant, or truck driver is like? Or, if you are an English Canadian, what is your view of French Canadians? Research suggests you may think of them as talkative, excitable, and proud (Gardner, Lalone, Nero, & Young, 1988), whereas French Canadians may describe you as educated, dominant, and ambitious (Aboud & Taylor, 1971). Russians view men of Caucasian nationalities—

Georgians, Armenians, and others from the mountainous Caucasus region—as brazen, flashy, criminally inclined, and likely to accost respectable women in the street (Bohlen, 1992). And though such views appear to have improved over time, White adults in the U.S. still associate Hispanics and Blacks with a propensity to commit acts of violence (Unnever & Cullen, 2012).

Gender stereotypes are just as pervasive. Men are more likely than women to be viewed as leaders (Koenig, Eagly, Mitchell, & Ristikari, 2011), and most people describe women as sensitive, warm, weak, and interested in children, whereas men are considered forceful, self-reliant, ambitious, and aggressive (Prentice & Carranza, 2002). In fact, gender stereotypes have been found in similar forms among adults and children in North and South America, Asia, Africa, Europe, and Australia (J. E. Williams & Best, 1982).

Group stereotypes also incorporate the positive or negative emotions that group members arouse in others. For example, observers may regard members of one group with feelings of disgust and repulsion, a second group with fear and apprehension, and yet a third with respect and admiration (Fiske, Cuddy, Glick, & Xu, 2002; Mackie & Hamilton, 1993; E. R. Smith & Mackie, 2005). As a result, the first group may be labeled "disgusting," the second "hostile," and the third "admirable." As we will see shortly, our emotions can have important effects on our actual face-to-face interactions with members of stereotyped groups.

Stereotypes Can Be Either Positive or Negative. As these examples make clear, stereotypes can include positive as well as negative characteristics (Rudman, 2005). You may wonder, though, why we should be concerned with positive beliefs about groups. After all, positive stereotypes may represent attributes, such as women's sensitivity, that group members themselves value and take pride in claiming. Still, even positive stereotypes can have negative consequences. Consider the belief, widespread among White American college students, that Asian Americans are straight-A students. One problem with that stereotype is its implication that everyone in the group is the same, and, therefore, it ignores people's individuality.

A second problem is that positive stereotypes may set unreasonably high standards, so that an Asian-American student who gets average grades may be regarded as particularly dull (E. R. Smith & Ho, 1999). Finally, positive stereotypes may be part of an overall pattern of paternalistic attitudes toward a social group that actually reinforces the group's weakness and dependence. For example, a common set of beliefs about women includes the idea that they are pure, moral, delicate, and in need of men's protection. This pattern has been termed "benevolent sexism," measured by agreement with statements like, "Many women have a quality of purity that few men possess" and "Women should be cherished and protected by men" (Glick & Fiske, 1996). Despite their apparent positive tone, these beliefs tend to be held by people who also hold more hostile beliefs about women, including the ideas that women attempt to manipulate men or are overly ready to claim discrimination. In fact, a study examining 19 nations shows that nations whose citizens have higher average scores on benevolent sexism also tend to have more gender inequality, for example, lower representation of women in powerful and well-paying jobs (Glick and others, 2000). As these findings suggest, then, positive stereotypes can be just as problematic as negative ones.

Thus, stereotypes lead to perceived uniformity among group members and rigid expectations. These can contribute to prejudice and discrimination, even when the stereotypes themselves are positive.

Stereotypes Can Be Accurate or Inaccurate. Perhaps even more important than whether stereotypes are positive or negative is the issue of whether they are accurate or inaccurate. No good yardstick is available for measuring the accuracy or inaccuracy of most stereotypes. There is no solid evidence, for example, on the relative frequency with which Georgian versus Russian men accost female passers-by. In addition, many concepts included in common stereotypes, for example, "clannish," "lazy," or "dirty," are so subjective as to be virtually meaningless.

Nevertheless, some stereotypes have some accuracy at least in the sense that they reflect small differences that exist between groups (Judd & Park, 2005; Jussim, 2005) or small differences that group members themselves feel to be true about their groups. For example, as Table 5.1 shows, many gender stereotypes accurately describe the direction of differences that research has identified between men's behavior and women's behavior, although often in exaggerated form (Eagly, 1995; C. L. Martin, 1987). Similarly, Black and White college students' stereotypes of their respective groups on attributes such as "dance well," "have high SAT math scores," and "self-centered" generally differ in the same direction as the group members' self-descriptions (C. S. Ryan, 1996). The fact that some stereotypes are somewhat accurate is not surprising because people often join together in clubs, political parties, professional associations, and other groups precisely because they share attitudes, feelings, and beliefs. This self-sorting process creates real group differences that may be reflected in stereotypes. Moreover, social norms and customs help create accurate stereotypes by prescribing what men and women, teenagers and retirees, and different racial groups can or should think, feel, and do.

Chapter 9 will describe in detail how social norms form, and Chapter 10 covers how they influence group members' behavior.

TABLE 5.1 Do Gender Stereotypes Reflect Actual Gender Differences? Results from Meta-Analyses

Gender stereotypes	*Differences identified by research*
Aggressiveness: (male) aggressive (female) soft-hearted	Men are more aggressive than women overall. The difference is larger for physical than for psychological aggression, and in situations in which aggression may be dangerous.
Influenceability: (male) independent (female) submissive, dependent	Women are more influenceable than men. The difference is larger for influence exerted by a group than for persuasive messages, and larger when the topic is regarded as "masculine."
Emotionality: (male) strong, tough (female) affectionate, anxious, emotional, sensitive, sentimental	Women are more nonverbally expressive and more nonverbally sensitive than men.
Leadership style: (male) autocratic, dominant (female) sensitive, emotional	As leaders, women are more democratic and men are more autocratic. The difference is larger in laboratory studies than in studies of leadership in real, ongoing organizations.

Sources: Stereotypes—J. E. Williams and Best (1982); Meta-analyses of research on gender differences—Eagly (1987), Eagly and Johnson (1990).

Yet stereotypes can also be inaccurate. Consider an early study of Californians' stereotypes of Armenian Americans (LaPiere, 1936). The researcher compared official statistics on this small, segregated minority with popular stereotypes about their behavior. Whereas Californians claimed that Armenians were constantly in trouble with the law, records showed that only about 1.5% had arrest records, compared with about 6% of the rest of the population. Similarly, Californians believed Armenians were more likely to be on welfare than working. In fact, only 1 of every 500 Armenians had applied for welfare, whereas the proportion for all Californians was five times higher. As another example, many people hold the stereotype that men are more effective leaders than are women. A meta-analysis of the research, in contrast, found no sex differences (or even small differences favoring women) in leadership effectiveness in business, educational, or government organizations (Eagly, Karau, & Makhijani, 1995).

Finally, there is one sense in which every stereotype is inaccurate: when it is viewed as applying to every member of a group. Not every French Canadian is talkative; not every woman is emotional; not every Asian American is a straight-A student. So it is an error for anyone to confidently assume that an individual member of a group possesses all of the group's stereotypic qualities.

But whatever their content—positive characteristics or negative ones, accurate descriptions or inaccurate distortions—stereotypes are a very real part of our daily lives. Each of us could reel off dozens of well-known stereotypes. Used-car dealers cannot be trusted; the French are great lovers. Nobel-winning physicist Leon Lederman, in advocating a TV series to humanize the image of physicists, said: "Scientists fall in love. But when was the last time you saw a physicist on TV galloping off into the sunset with a beautiful woman?" (*The New York Times Magazine,* 1995). Think about this for a moment. Did you notice Lederman's stereotypic assumption that a physicist is both male and heterosexual?

Why do people form and use stereotypes? Many different social motives have been suggested to account for them, including some people's need to resolve intense inner psychological conflicts as well as more everyday social and cognitive processes.

Seeking the Motives behind Stereotyping

Early theorists traced prejudice and extreme negative stereotypes to deep inner conflicts in a few disturbed individuals, rather than to more normal social motives such as mastery and connectedness.

Social psychologists' first systematic attempts to explain stereotypes and prejudice were triggered by the genocidal policies of the Nazis during the Third Reich (Ashmore & Del Boca, 1981). The unprecedented nature of the Nazis' actions seemed to call for equally extreme explanations, and led to the idea that hatred of other groups is abnormal. Drawing on the work of Sigmund Freud, Theodor Adorno and his colleagues (Adorno, Frenkel-Brunswik, Levinson, & Sanford, 1950) argued that hatred for social groups, as well as the accompanying extreme negative stereotypes, has its roots in the inner conflicts of those with **authoritarian personalities**. These are people who cannot accept their own hostility, believe uncritically in the legitimacy of authority, and see their own inadequacies

authoritarian personality
based on Freudian ideas, people who are prejudiced because they cannot accept their own hostility, believe uncritically in the legitimacy of authority, and see their own inadequacies in others

in others. The theorists argued that prejudice and rigid negative stereotypes against other groups serve to protect such individuals from an awareness of their painful inner conflicts and self-doubts.

There is something psychologically satisfying about the authoritarian personality explanation of prejudice and stereotyping. We would like to see the mental and emotional deviance of certain individuals as responsible for prejudice and the extreme stereotypes that accompany and justify that prejudice. These phenomena then become the exception rather than the rule, problems that other people have. Unfortunately, despite its appeal, this explanation does not stand up against the accumulated evidence (Altemeyer, 1981; Billig, 1976). Some individuals' extreme prejudice may in fact flow from deep inner conflicts (Esses, Haddock, & Zanna, 1993). However, as the examples cited at the beginning of the chapter suggest, prejudice and stereotypes seem to be the rule and not the exception. In fact, they are so pervasive that social psychologists have come to a more mundane, but also more consequential, conclusion: Prejudice and stereotypes most often grow out of the same social and cognitive processes that affect all aspects of our lives—such as our desires to understand our social environments and to connect with other people.

Motives for Forming Stereotypes: Mastery through Summarizing Personal Experiences

---

Stereotypes can be learned through personal experience with group members, but may still be biased because of emotions that arise during cross-group interactions and because people pay attention to extremes or inaccurately perceive groups' characteristics. Social roles often shape group members' behaviors, but people attribute the behaviors to group members' inner characteristics. Learning about groups can also take place through media portrayals as well as firsthand experiences.

The world is getting smaller. Throughout Europe, boundaries between nations and peoples are becoming more permeable with increasing economic integration. Residents of Germany, France, and Italy are more often coming face to face with immigrants about whom they once knew little: Albanians, Mozambicans, Arabs, and Turks. Changes in U.S. immigration patterns have created a similar situation. The new family moving into the apartment across the hall might be Vietnamese Hmong, or the new sales representative joining your company might be from El Salvador.

As people encounter group members, they try to make sense of their world by summarizing the information they get about those groups. Thus, these encounters can serve as building blocks to forming stereotypes, so even a single encounter can have an impact. In one illustration of this, White students in one study observed a confederate, who was pretending to be another experimental participant (Henderson-King & Nisbett, 1996). This confederate behaved in a rude and hostile manner toward the experimenter. In some cases, the confederate was Black and in other cases White, whereas in a third condition no hostile interaction took place. The participants were then asked to conduct a mock interview of another student for a position of residence hall counselor. They were given a list of suggested questions and told that the interview could last up to 20 minutes.

The student to be interviewed turned out to be Black. The participants who had previously seen another Black's negative behavior ended the interview much sooner (after an average of just 8 minutes) compared to those who had seen a White behaving in the same obnoxious fashion or who had seen no negative behavior at all (about 10 minutes). Evidently, a single group member's negative acts can activate negative thoughts about the entire group.

Fortunately, bringing to mind positively evaluated group members can make feelings about a group more positive as well. Galen Bodenhausen and his colleagues (Bodenhausen, Schwarz, Bless, & Wänke, 1995) demonstrated that when people have recently thought about well-liked Blacks (such as Oprah Winfrey), their opinions on issues related to Blacks' position in American society become more positive. Findings like these suggest that positive or negative impressions of individual group members are important contributors to people's overall impressions of a group (E. R. Smith & Zárate, 1992).

But this fact raises a puzzle. Why does trying to summarize the information we receive about group members during interactions—seemingly the most trustworthy form of information—lead to bias and exaggeration? There are several reasons.

Between-Group Interactions Generate Emotion. Feelings of uncertainty and concern often arise when people interact with novel groups, and these feelings can influence the stereotypes people form. Dutch adults described just these feelings when asked about their everyday dealings with Surinamers, Turks, and Moroccans, groups that have immigrated in large numbers to the Netherlands (Dijker, 1987). According to the respondents, interactions with these groups produced anxiety, and the interactions with Moroccans and Turks—the groups culturally most different from the native-born Dutch—also provoked feelings of irritation. North American college students responded the same way when asked to imagine what emotions they might experience in a casual conversation with someone of a different race (Vanman & Miller, 1993). The most frequently reported emotion was irritation, followed closely by dislike, apprehension, and anxiety. Other research shows that the presence of another man they know to be homosexual can make heterosexual men nervous and uncomfortable (L. A. Jackson & Sullivan, 1989).

Why are interactions across group lines so often tinged with arousal and anxiety? The first reason is a lack of knowledge of or familiarity with members of other groups. For example, the less Asian Americans and Whites in Hawaii knew about each other's groups, the more anxious and irritated they felt when they met (Stephan & Stephan, 1985). The same researchers obtained similar results when they investigated interactions between Latinos and Whites in New Mexico. Not knowing what to do or say and not knowing how another person will react usually creates awkwardness, frustration, and impatience.

A second reason concerns the fact that members of different groups may be pursuing different sorts of goals during cross-group interactions, and these goals are associated with negative emotions like anger and irritation. In the U.S., for example, Blacks are often stereotyped as incompetent, but Whites are stereotyped as prejudiced. Research suggests, therefore, that when Whites and Blacks in the U.S. interact, each is hoping to create an impression that counters these stereotypes, with Blacks hoping to be respected and seen as competent, and Whites wanting to be liked and seen as unbiased (Bergsieker, Shelton, & Richeson, 2010). These differing goals result in negative emotional consequences.

HOT TOPICS IN SOCIAL PSYCHOLOGY: STRESSFUL EFFECTS OF CROSS-RACIAL INTERACTION

Recent research finds that the desire to appear non-prejudiced, in and of itself, may become salient during cross-group interactions, creating stress and discomfort. In one study, for example, White U.S. college students interacted with either a White or a Black research assistant (Trawalter, Adam, Chase-Lansdale, & Richeson, 2012). Those highly motivated to appear non-prejudiced for external reasons, for example, to avoid being judged negatively by society, showed greater cortisol activity, a physiological indicator of stress, while speaking with the Black (other race) compared to the White (same race) partner. Similar stress effects appear in more real-life contexts and can have long-term consequences. In a second study, White U.S. college students provided saliva samples early in the fall term and again in the spring term, from which measurements of cortisol (the stress hormone) were taken (Trawalter and others, 2012). In addition, for one week during the fall, winter, and spring terms, participants completed a nightly questionnaire regarding that day's social interactions, from which the researchers could gauge how much cross-racial interaction the person experienced. The primary question was whether interracial interaction might disrupt normal, healthy cortisol patterns over time. Consistent with the first study, results indicated that externally motivated individuals who had more interracial contact over the academic year showed cortisol patterns that diverged from what is typical and healthy at the end of that year.

Specifically, this research found that the more Blacks prefer to be seen as competent (rather than likable) and the more Whites prefer to be seen as likable (rather than competent) during a cross-group interaction, the more they feel emotions like anger and irritation with their interaction partner.

When even relatively benign cross-group interactions cause anxiety and irritation, imagine the strength of emotion that is generated when groups threaten one another, compete for scarce resources, and violate one another's values (Neuberg & Cottrell, 2002; Stephan & Renfro, 2002). In these circumstances, powerful emotions become associated with group encounters. The emotions provoked by uncomfortable intergroup encounters then become an integral part of a stereotype (Devos, Silver, Mackie, & Smith, 2002; Olson & Fazio, 2002; E. R. Smith, 1993). When interaction with a group is repeatedly accompanied by negative emotion, bad feelings are soon transferred to the group itself through the process of **classical conditioning**. Classical conditioning occurs when a person or object that has been repeatedly paired with a particular emotion or other response begins itself to elicit the emotion. Thus, after several uncomfortable interactions, the emotions arising from the encounter become associated with the group, so that seeing group members, hearing the group mentioned, or even thinking about the group will itself reactivate the emotion. An individual who repeatedly experiences disgust, fear, or hatred in interactions with group members eventually will view the group as intrinsically disgusting, threatening, or loathsome.

classical conditioning
a form of learning in which a previously neutral stimulus, when paired with a stimulus that elicits an emotion or other response, itself comes to generate that response

People Notice Some Members More than Others. The next time you are at a party, glance around the room. Whom are you most likely to notice? The guest in the tuxedo, when everyone else is wearing blue jeans? Or the very tall woman standing over by the window? If these people stand out, it is because our attention is typically drawn to what is unusual, unexpected, or salient (L. Z. McArthur, 1981). For this reason, distinctive individuals can have a disproportionate impact on the formation of group stereotypes, as a classic study by Myron Rothbart and his colleagues (Rothbart, Fulero, Jensen, Howard, & Birrel, 1978) demonstrated. Some participants in their experiment read a list of the actions of 50 men, 10 of whom had committed nonviolent crimes. Other participants read the same list, but the criminal actions of the 10 men were violent and therefore salient. The participants were later asked how many men from each group had committed crimes. Compared with those exposed to the nonviolent crimes, participants exposed to the violent crimes thought that more group members had committed crimes.

Some Information Attracts More Attention than Other Information. Even if a few extremes stand out, why do our impressions of groups remain unchanged when we encounter other group members whose appearance or actions are quite ordinary? The answer is that biases in processing lead us to form an association between unusual or distinctive characteristics and rare or infrequently encountered groups. These processes can operate even if we have no prior stereotype of a group, so they can generate a stereotype more or less out of thin air.

Suppose you move to a new city and discover that the residents there classify themselves as Eastsiders or Westsiders, but you have no idea what characteristics are associated with these categories. As you read the "Police Blotter" column in the local newspaper, you notice that more Eastsiders than Westsiders are mentioned. Most members of each group are named for innocent reasons, such as reporting a mysteriously broken car window or having a cat stranded in a tree, but about a third of each group are named as crime suspects. What impressions would you form of the two groups?

According to David Hamilton and Robert Gifford (1976), you might overestimate the incidence of crime among the Westsiders, the smaller group. Your overestimate would illustrate the creation of an **illusory correlation**, a perceived association between two characteristics that are not actually related. In a demonstration of the illusory correlation, Hamilton and Gifford asked participants to read a series of sentences, each describing a desirable or undesirable behavior performed by a member of Group A or Group B. For both groups, more desirable behaviors were reported than undesirable ones: The ratio was about two positive behaviors for every negative one. Overall, participants saw more sentences about Group A than about Group B. When participants were asked their impressions of the groups, they liked Group B less. They had formed an illusory correlation by perceiving a link between the two relatively infrequent and distinctive characteristics: undesirable behavior, and membership in the group about which they had read less often.

What explains this surprising bias in our perceptions of groups? Researchers have found that when something occurs infrequently, it becomes distinctive and people pay attention to it. When one of the behavior descriptions involves two distinctive characteristics occurring together—a Group B member doing something antisocial—it really stands out. These behaviors may attract special attention when people encounter them (D. L. Hamilton & Sherman, 1989). Or they may have a disproportionate impact when people combine what they know into judgments about the groups (Fiedler, 1991; E. R. Smith, 1991). Either way, these doubly distinctive behaviors have the greatest impact on the impressions we form of groups. So suppose that people have only limited encounters with members of a group that is numerically small or segregated. Even if

Salient characteristics have more impact when we form impressions of individuals (Chapter 3, page 63), just as salient group members have more impact when we form impressions of groups.

illusory correlation

a perceived association between two characteristics that are not actually related

How and why people fall prey to the correspondence bias when making inferences was discussed in Chapter 3, pages 69–72.

criminal acts are equally rare among members of a large group and those of the small group, observers may form an illusory correlation, judging the small group to be more criminal than the larger group.

Social Roles Trigger Correspondence Biases. Regardless of how often we encounter a group, what we see the group doing has a big impact on our impressions. Yet even this kind of firsthand observation can lead to biased stereotypes when a group's social role shapes the behavior that can be observed. For example, most of us form our impressions of doctors by watching a doctor care for us or for a loved one, or of ministers or rabbis by watching one perform a religious ceremony. As a result, our stereotypes of particular groups often come to reflect the social roles occupied by those groups (D. T. Campbell, 1967; Eagly, 1987). Consider the following facts:

- In the Middle Ages, money handling was one of very few occupations open to Jews, who soon came to be seen as excelling in this occupation for reasons of personality, that is, because they were inherently "sharp" and "frugal." These same traits have been attributed to many other groups: the Chinese in Indonesia and Malaysia, Muslim merchants in eastern and southern Africa, and Korean merchants in Black neighborhoods in the United States. What do these wildly diverse groups have in common? They all fill the same "middleman" economic niche in their societies (Pettigrew, 1968). Apparently the role produces the assumed personality characteristics, rather than the other way around.

- In virtually every society, socioeconomically disadvantaged groups, regardless of their ethnicity, are seen as ignorant, lazy, loud, dirty, and carefree. In the United States this stereotype has been applied to a number of groups in the last century: first, to poor Irish immigrants, then to the first wave of Italian immigrants, and more recently to Puerto Rican and Mexican Americans (Pettigrew, 1968; L. Ross & Nisbett, 1990). As the economic position of a group rises, stereotypes about them change and, like hand-me-down clothing, the lower-class stereotype is passed on to some new and less fortunate group.

- Stereotypes adapt rapidly as a group's roles change. Such changes are especially obvious in times of war or hardship, as we shall see in Chapter 13. As peace is replaced by war, the Germans become "Huns" and the Japanese "Japs." And as war is replaced by peace, German ruthlessness becomes German efficiency, and Japanese cunning becomes Japanese ingenuity.

As all these facts suggest, stereotypes may not reflect what groups are actually like. Instead, they reflect the roles groups play in society relative to the perceiver (Fiske and others, 2002). The correspondence bias leads people to see behavior as reflecting others' inner dispositions, even if roles or situational contingencies truly cause the behavior. As can be seen in Figure 5.1, the outcome is the formation of a stereotype.

Social Roles and Gender Stereotypes. Males' and females' differing social roles also contribute to gender stereotypes (Eagly, 1987). (Look back at Table 5.1 for some examples.) The process works like this: Virtually all societies assign men and women to somewhat different roles and occupations (Wood & Eagly, 2002). In Western cultures,

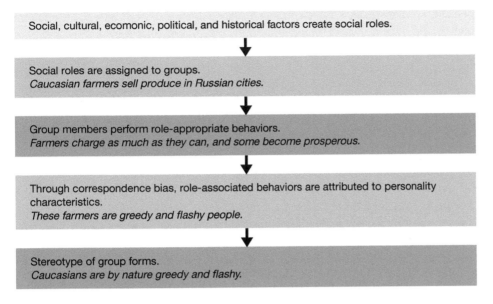

Social, cultural, ecomonic, political, and historical factors create social roles.

Social roles are assigned to groups.
Caucasian farmers sell produce in Russian cities.

Group members perform role-appropriate behaviors.
Farmers charge as much as they can, and some become prosperous.

Through correspondence bias, role-associated behaviors are attributed to personality characteristics.
These farmers are greedy and flashy people.

Stereotype of group forms.
Caucasians are by nature greedy and flashy.

Figure 5.1 Social roles shape stereotypes
The roles allocated to a particular group influence group members' behavior. Based on that behavior, observers are likely to be influenced by the correspondence bias— ignoring the effects of the roles and attributing the behavior to the group members' personality characteristics. These characteristics then become part of the stereotype of the group.

Photo 5.3 Career roles and stereotypes. When people repeatedly see group members in particular roles, they link the traits necessary for those roles with that group. For instance, seeing many more women than men as elementary school teachers may lead to and reinforce the stereotype that women have nurturing traits like patience and kindness.

for example, men are more often employed outside the home, whereas women are more likely to be responsible for home and family. Employee roles demand the kinds of traits—task-orientation, assertiveness, rationality—that characterize the traditional male stereotype. In contrast, the role of homemaker requires those qualities—interpersonal orientation, sensitivity, warmth—that characterize the female stereotype (Eagly & Steffen, 1984). Thus, men and women tend to act in ways that are appropriate for their roles. And if observers note those differences and fail to make allowances for the effects of roles, they may conclude that men are by nature task oriented, and women interpersonally oriented.

A clever laboratory study by Curt Hoffman and Nancy Hurst (1990) demonstrated this process. Students read descriptions of fictitious groups of "Orinthians" and "Ackmians" who supposedly inhabit a distant planet. Most Orinthians were described as involved in child care, whereas Ackmians were mainly employed outside the home. All child-care workers (regardless of group membership) were described as typically nurturant, affectionate, and gentle, and all employees as typically competitive and ambitious. However, participants asked to guess these creatures' typical psychological characteristics attached traits to the groups rather than to the roles, and assumed that Orinthians (not child-care workers) were nurturant and Ackmians (not employees) were competitive (see Figure 5.2). That is, each group was seen as having psychological characteristics appropriate for the group's typical role. Once the stereotype was formed, participants applied it even to individual group members whose occupations clashed with the stereotype: they saw an employed Ackmian as more competitive and ambitious than an employed Orinthian. This finding suggests that the different typical social roles of men and women contribute to shaping earthly gender stereotypes.

Learning Stereotypes from the Media.

People's experience with members of particular social groups comes not only from direct personal interactions: we also learn about others from art, literature, popular music, television, film, and the Internet. Not surprisingly, media portrayals of groups often reflect stereotypes that are deeply ingrained in a culture (Jost & Hamilton, 2005). This pattern is found in modern-day rap music and other forms of confrontational art (Nields, 1991), but it also occurred in William Shakespeare's plays, written over 400 years ago. Othello is called "thick lips" because he is Black. Shylock is spat on because he is a Jew. Richard III attributes his evil to his physical deformity, and King Lear is reviled because he is old.

Mainstream media including television also help convey stereotypes. On an average day, North American children watch 3 hours of television, and during those hours children receive a mixed message. Some prime-time entertainment shows have reversed the traditional invisibility of people of color. *The Cosby Show,* which portrayed the family life of a Black doctor and lawyer and their children, ranked as the most popular show in the United States from 1985 to 1990. However, representation of Black characters in prime-time TV declined between 2000 and 2008. Representation of Whites correspondingly increased, with other minority groups seldom portrayed at all (Signorielli, 2009). And compared to entertainment shows, news programs send different messages. Studies of Philadelphia and Los Angeles local TV news both found that in comparison to actual crime statistics, Blacks are overrepresented as crime suspects whereas Whites are underrepresented (Romer, Jamieson, & de Coteau, 1998; Dixon & Linz, 2000). Video

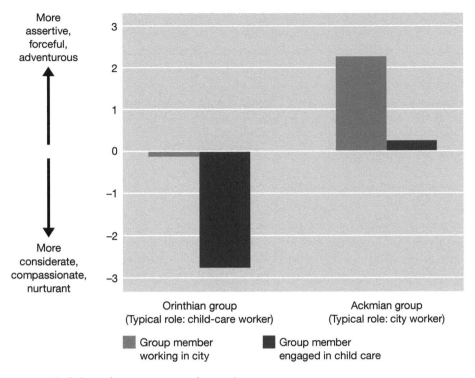

Figure 5.2 Roles and stereotypes on a distant planet
Participants viewed group members who performed their group's typical roles as possessing psychological characteristics appropriate for that role. They then generalized those characteristics to all group members. Thus, they saw an Ackmian engaged in child care as more assertive than an Orinthian city worker. (Based on Hoffman & Hurst, 1990.)

games, a popular new media form, also fail to accurately represent the population, according to a large-scale study by Williams and others (2009). Their analysis, which gave more weight to the best-selling games, found systematic overrepresentation of Whites, males, and adults and underrepresentation of females, Hispanics, Native Americans, children, and the elderly, a pattern resembling that found with TV.

Media portrayals of other groups are no better. Asian Americans appear frequently in television ads (in over 8% of commercials, compared to their 3.6% of the U.S. population), but are usually cast in stereotypic ways. Consistent with the "work ethic" stereotype, Asian Americans are generally portrayed in business settings and only rarely in home or family settings (C. R. Taylor & Stern, 1997). Differences between Chinese, Japanese, and Koreans are minimized or ignored. Latinos fare equally poorly. Though they constituted 12.5% of the U.S. population at the time, when researchers analyzed prime-time shows on U.S. channels in 2002, only about 4% of the characters were Latino (Mastro & Behm-Morawitz, 2005). This same work reported that though some Latino stereotypes are fading from television, many still persist. For example, Latino men, more than their other-race counterparts, were depicted as unintelligent and inarticulate.

Homosexuals, too, are often underrepresented or portrayed in stereotypical ways on television. A report from the Gay and Lesbian Alliance Against Defamation (2011) found that only 2.9% of characters on U.S. prime-time network shows in the 2011–12 television season were homosexual or bisexual. However, recent estimates suggest that 3.5% of the adult U.S. population identifies as gay, lesbian, or bisexual, and over 8% report having participated in sexual behavior with a person of the same sex (Gates, 2011). In England, much the same is true. In one study, researchers examined roughly 126 hours of popular television shows in England and found that roughly 4.5% (about 5.75 hours) of this time depicted gay, lesbian, or bisexual characters. Of the time they were on screen, the report concluded that such characters were depicted "positively and realistically" for only 46 minutes, less than 15% of their screen time (Stonewall, n.d.). All in all, then, media stereotyping and underrepresentation is quite pervasive.

Gender Stereotypes and the Media. Media messages about women can be summed up in a single word: contradictory. On the one hand, television programming increasingly has portrayed women in realistic or counterstereotypic roles. Popular dramatic and comedy series often feature strong female characters who are competent, assertive, independent, and successful in their careers. However, during the commercial breaks a different type of message comes through. Analyses of French-language television ads in Quebec and radio ads in Australia replicate findings from the U.S.: Commercials typically reinforce gender stereotypes (Dalcourt, 1996; Hurtz & Durkin, 1997). For example, male voice-overs predominate when the voice of an "expert" is required. Men and women generally sell gender-stereotypic products: Men sell lawnmowers and computers, women sell shoes and toilet bowl cleaners. Ads that appear on the Internet suffer from similar problems, with research showing that nearly 70% of examined ads portrayed women in stereotypic ways, most often as being concerned with their appearance, as sex objects, or as housewives (Plakoyiannaki, Mathioudaki, Dimitratos, & Zotos, 2008). Children's cartoons also convey gender stereotypes (Chu & McIntyre, 1995; T. L. Thompson & Zerbinos, 1995). In one analysis, for example, female cartoon characters were more likely than male cartoon characters to show fear, be supportive, and behave romantically and politely (Leaper, Breed, Hoffman, & Perlman, 2002).

Do biased media portrayals of men and women matter? Experimental studies suggest that the answer is yes. Florence Geis and her colleagues (Geis, Brown, Jennings, & Porter, 1984; Jennings, Geis, & Brown, 1980) showed college women one of two sets of television commercials. One set depicted men and women in traditional roles, with the woman playing an alluring and subordinate role. In the other set the roles were reversed, with the man shown as subordinate and seductive. The young women who watched the traditional commercials later expressed lower self-confidence, less independence, and fewer career aspirations than did those who watched the nontraditional commercials. Meta-analyses summarizing many studies support the conclusion that media content increases viewers' acceptance of gender stereotypes (Herrett-Skjellum & Allen, 1996). If media portrayals can subtly influence viewers' thinking about themselves as men and women, it is undoubtedly true that they become part of our thinking about members of other groups as well.

Motives for Forming Stereotypes: Connectedness to Others

Social learning contributes to stereotypes. Stereotypes and discriminatory behavior are often accepted and endorsed as right and proper by members of a particular group. Group members learn such stereotypes from family and peers. As stereotypes are communicated, they may become even stronger.

Stereotypes can be formed as summaries of our experiences with members of social groups, and as we have seen, whether those experiences are direct or through the media they can give rise to biased perceptions. But our desire to master the world by summarizing our experiences is not the only motive behind the formation of stereotypes. Stereotypes also serve our desire to establish connections with similar others, when we adopt the same stereotypes that those others hold. Thus, stereotypes often are communicated to us in prepackaged form, and we learn them in particular social, economic, cultural, religious, and political contexts (Stangor & Schaller, 1996). Our desire to connect with others may encourage us to adopt these prepackaged stereotypes.

Learning Stereotypes from Others. Parents, teachers, and peers offer us our first lessons about group differences. By age 5, for example, most children have begun to develop clear-cut racial attitudes (Goodman, 1952; Rosenfield & Stephan, 1981). Parents and teachers do not have to teach stereotypes explicitly, although they sometimes do. Children can pick up stereotypes simply by observing and imitating their elders: listening to disparaging group labels or derogatory jokes that elicit approving laughter, or following family rules against playing with those "other" children.

What other people say and do typically reflects **social norms**, generally accepted ways of thinking, feeling, or behaving that people in a group agree on and endorse as right and proper (Thibaut & Kelley, 1959). When stereotypes are deeply embedded in the social norms of a culture, people learn them naturally as part of growing up (Crandall & Stangor, 2005). In one study, students rated numerous groups (such as ethnic and religious groups, political groups, as well as other groups such as murderers and thieves) in terms of how socially acceptable it would be to hold negative views of the groups. They also rated their own personal views of the same groups. Answers to these two questions were almost perfectly related, suggesting that people's actual opinions of the groups were strongly driven by their perceptions of social norms—that is, by the acceptability of holding negative views of each group (Crandall & Eshleman, 2003).

Social Communication of Stereotypes. Stereotypes may even become stronger through the process of social communication. When people form impressions of a group by being told about them secondhand, their impressions are more stereotypic than those of people who learn about the group through firsthand experience (Thompson, Judd, & Park, 2000). These secondhand impressions, once formed, remain highly stereotypic even after later direct experience with the group itself. Discussion of group members' behaviors among several people also tends to make their impressions more stereotypic (Brauer, Judd, & Jacquelin, 2001). Conversations between individuals tend to focus on stereotypic information because such information is thought to bring people closer together (Clark & Kashima, 2007).

social norms
generally accepted ways of thinking, feeling, or behaving that people in a group agree on and endorse as right and proper

We discuss the formation and effects of social norms in greater depth in both Chapters 9 and 10.

Motives for Forming Stereotypes: Justifying Inequalities

The stereotypes prevalent in a society often serve to justify existing social inequalities. They do so by portraying groups as deserving their social roles and positions on the basis of their own characteristics.

Our direct or indirect experiences with members of other groups, and the beliefs and norms prevalent in our own groups, usually work together to reinforce each other and, ultimately, to reinforce the perception that members of different groups are naturally suited for the roles they play. Most cultures, for example, assign nurturing roles to women, so perceivers see women as "naturally" nurturing. This stereotype is further strengthened as people learn what society teaches about women. Soon, it becomes the basis for an inference with even more serious consequences. The belief that women have the right stuff to care for others then becomes a justification for retaining them in that role: They have the perfect qualifications. Most stereotypes, like this example, justify groups' existing places and roles in society as right, natural, and inevitable (Jost & Banaji, 1994; Jost, Kivetz, Rubini, Guermandi, & Mosso, 2005; Yzerbyt, Rocher, & Schadron, 1997).

Every society maintains inequalities that benefit some groups and hurt others. In Taiwan, people from mainland China who fled the Communists in 1949 still dominate native Taiwanese. Gaps in income and opportunity between men and women and between Whites and people of color persist in the United States. As stereotypes reflecting these differences have developed, they have justified and rationalized the underlying inequalities (Pettigrew, 1980). For example, historically, women and people of color have often been viewed in ways that justified their treatment as childlike, unintelligent, and weak, and thus in need of direction and guidance (Hacker, 1951). And in fact, people who believe inequality is natural and right—views that are more often found among members of dominant groups, such as Whites and males—are particularly likely to be prejudiced against others (Pratto, Sidanius, Stallworth, & Malle, 1994). Moreover, high-status groups are stereotyped as more competent than are low-status groups, providing apparent justification for the status differences (Caprariello, Cuddy, & Fiske, 2009). Thus, as these examples illustrate, inequalities can produce different opportunities for different groups in a society, and then perceivers form stereotypes of those groups that will help perpetuate and maintain those same inequalities.

Why do we slide so quickly down the slope from behavior to stereotype to justification of inequality? One reason may be the widespread belief that the world is just and that people therefore deserve what they get and get what they deserve. This just-world belief (Lerner, 1980) leads people to blame victims for their misfortunes. This effect was demonstrated by one study in which students watched a woman apparently receive painful electric shocks (Lerner & Simmons, 1966). Did they react with sympathy toward this unfortunate victim? On the contrary, most derogated the victim, concluding that she must have done something to deserve her suffering. Rape victims, victims of spouse abuse, and people with AIDS often suffer the same fate (Carli & Leonard, 1989; Hunter & Ross, 1991), as do those whose social roles confine them to subordinate positions. It is no surprise, then, that people who believe more strongly that the world is just also tend to be prejudiced against gays and other groups (Crandall & Cohen,

1994). It is comforting to believe that bad things happen only to bad people: that AIDS is a punishment for taking drugs or for a gay lifestyle, or that poor people are lazy and shiftless (Furnham & Gunter, 1984; R. Robinson & Bell, 1978). Believing that groups' positions in society are somehow deserved, fitting, or justified lets us off the hook morally, as Martin Luther King (1967) observed so astutely:

> It seems to be a fact of life that human beings cannot continue to do wrong without eventually reaching out for some rationalization to clothe their acts in the garments of righteousness. And so, with the growth of slavery, men had to convince themselves that a system which was so economically profitable was morally justifiable. The attempt to give moral sanction to a profitable system gave birth to the doctrine of white supremacy. (p. 72)

Bit by bit, our personal experiences and the influence of others help us construct a coherent impression of the social groups around us. As Figure 5.3 shows, the information we weave together is a product both of our own personal interactions and of the influence of others, and biases can enter into the process in several ways. And as we will see in Chapter 6, our own group memberships provide additional scope for stereotypes and biases in the ways we view others.

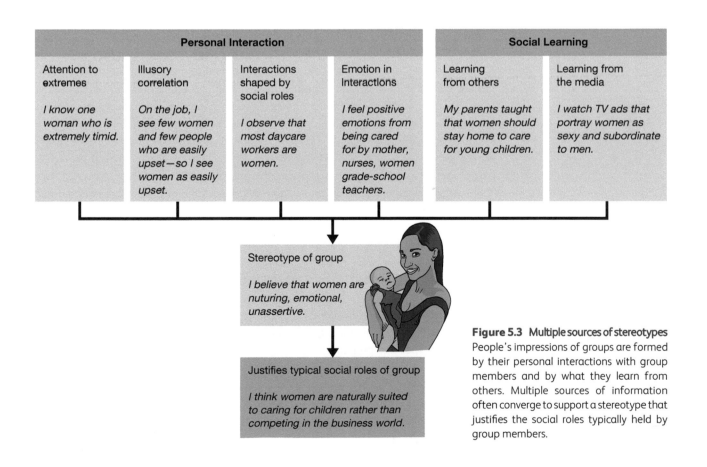

Figure 5.3 Multiple sources of stereotypes People's impressions of groups are formed by their personal interactions with group members and by what they learn from others. Multiple sources of information often converge to support a stereotype that justifies the social roles typically held by group members.

USING STEREOTYPES: FROM PRECONCEPTIONS TO PREJUDICE

For all the reasons just described, group stereotypes are rarely just neutral descriptions, but often have a strong evaluative tinge. When we think of men as aggressive, of immigrants as cliquish, or of Scots as thrifty, those terms have evaluative implications, whether positive or negative, mild or extreme. Moreover, stereotypes often incorporate emotions we associate with groups. We see some groups not only as hostile, stubborn, aggressive, and deviant but also as frightening, frustrating, threatening, and repulsive. Once these beliefs and feelings are firmly established, they take on a life of their own, provoking prejudiced judgments and directing discriminatory behavior.

The notion that group stereotypes can spawn prejudice and discrimination is captured in a conference experience described by Stephen Carter, a professor at Yale Law School who is Black.

> *A dapper, buttoned-down young white man glanced at my nametag, evidently ignored the name but noted the school, and said, "If you're at Yale, you must know this Carter fellow who wrote that article about thus-and-so." Well, yes, I admitted. I did know that Carter fellow slightly. An awkward pause ensued. And then the young man, realizing his error, apologized . . . . "Oh," he said, "you're Carter."* (Carter, 1991, p. 56)

The young man's assumptions about race and academic excellence had been embarrassingly revealed. As Carter notes, "Since this young man liked the article, its author could not, in his initial evaluation, have been a person of color. He had not even conceived of that possibility, or he would have glanced twice at my name tag" (p. 57).

Once a stereotype exists, it influences what people think and how they behave toward members of stereotyped groups. In fact, stereotype effects are so pervasive that they can even affect our judgments of inanimate objects! When computers are programmed to "talk" with synthesized male voices, people take their evaluations more seriously than if they use female voices; on matters related to relationships, people prefer advice given by a computer in a female voice. This is true even when people are specifically told that a male programmer created the software in the first place (Reeves & Nass, 1996). Stereotypes can have this impact whether we are making snap judgments of others quickly and with minimal thought—like the young man at the conference—or making considered judgments involving extensive processing of information.

Activation of Stereotypes and Prejudice

Once established, stereotypes and prejudice can be activated by obvious cues, use of group labels, or the presence of a group member, especially a minority in a social situation. Some stereotypes and prejudices come to mind automatically.

A stereotype can influence judgments or actions only if it comes to mind. Does this happen frequently? You bet it does! The very first thing we notice about other people is often their group memberships, and once a category is activated, the associated stereotype comes to mind as well. In fact, some categories seem so important that we use them to classify people even when they appear irrelevant to the social context. Consider the first thing most people ask the parents of a newborn: Is it a girl or a boy? In almost every social situation, perceivers note general categories like gender, race, and age (Brewer, 1988; Stangor, Lynch, Duan, & Glass, 1992).

What Activates Stereotypes? The more obvious and salient the cues to category membership, the more likely it is that the category and its related stereotypes will come to mind. Indeed, women with a highly feminine physical appearance and dress are perceived as also having highly feminine natures (Deaux & Lewis, 1984; Forsyth, Schlenker, Leary, & McCown, 1985). The deliberate use of pejorative group labels, ethnic or sexist jokes, or slurs can bring stereotypes to a listener's mind at once (Ford, 2000; Greenberg & Pyszczynski, 1985).

A category often becomes particularly salient when only a single member of the group is present among multiple members of another group. Consider an increasingly common occurrence: A woman is hired as a member of a previously all-male work crew, or a single Latino student joins a class or seminar. Because of their salience, such solo appearances draw much more attention, and the extra attention usually leads to particularly stereotypic perceptions. A solo male seems more masculine and a solo female more feminine than they would in a more evenly split group (S. E. Taylor, 1981; S. E. Taylor, Fiske, Etcoff, & Ruderman, 1978). Field studies in work organizations have recorded the same effects (Kanter, 1977). "Token" integration of a workplace or other social setting—admitting a single member of a previously excluded group—can thus increase the likelihood of stereotyped thinking rather than decrease it.

Stereotypes Can Be Activated Automatically. If reminders of group membership surround us, the ease with which race, gender, age, or other categories come to mind can set off a vicious cycle. The more often a category is used, the more accessible it becomes; the more accessible it is, the more it is used (Higgins, 1996a; Stangor and others, 1992). In fact, a stereotype sometimes becomes so well learned and so often used that its activation becomes automatic. Cues that relate to group membership can bring stereotypic information to mind, even if the perceiver does not consciously notice the group membership at all!

Multiple studies have illustrated such effects. In one, participants engaged in several trials during which they saw XXXXX on a computer screen, followed by either a word or a nonsense letter string (Wittenbrink, Judd, & Park, 2001). Some of the words were related to Black or White stereotypes. Participants had to press one of two keys to indicate whether or not the letters on the screen spelled an English word. Unknown to the participants, on some trials the word BLACK or WHITE was also flashed on the screen before the XXXXX—so briefly that it could not be consciously registered. However, as studies we have already described show, such subliminally presented words can still act as a prime. Results showed that participants responded to negative Black stereotypic words (such as poor, dishonest, and violent) more quickly on trials where the word BLACK had been flashed as a prime. The same was true of positive White stereotypic words (such as intelligent, successful, and wealthy) on trials with WHITE primes. Thus, this study shows that exposure to labels for different social groups can automatically active stereotypic traits of those groups. The automatic nature of this stereotype activation is

demonstrated by the occurrence of the effect when the participants could not consciously read the prime words. Other studies have obtained similar results (Blair & Banaji, 1996; Gawronski, Deutsch, Mbirkou, Seibt, & Strack, 2008; Lepore & Brown, 1997).

In Chapter 3, page 67 we described evidence that words that could not be consciously read nevertheless could bring related beliefs to mind, without the perceiver's awareness.

Prejudice Can Be Activated Automatically. Can general positive or negative prejudicial feelings about a group, as well as the specific trait information contained in stereotypes, also be activated automatically? The answer appears to be yes. One approach

Sequence	Task Name Instructions: For specific type of stimulus, press left or right response button	Examples of stimuli and correct responses
1	**Black-White Names** Black name - Left White name - Right	Meredith - Right Tashika - Left Betsy - Right
2	**Pleasant-Unpleasant Words** Pleasant word - Left Unpleasant word - Right	poison - Right gift - Left disaster - Right
3	**Initial Combined Task** Black name or pleasant word - Left White name or unpleasant word - Right	Peggy - Right evil - Right Ebony - Left miracle - Left
4	**Reversed Black-White Names** Black name - Right White name - Left	Courtney - Left Shereen - Right Tia - Right
5	**Reversed Combined Task** Black name or unpleasant word - Right White name or pleasant word - Left	peace - Left Latisha - Right filth - Right Nancy - Left

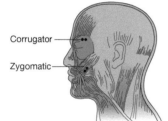

Corrugator

Zygomatic

Figure 5.4 Facial electromyography (EMG): An indirect measure of attitudes
When people react positively to an attitude object, activity in the zygomatic muscles increases, whereas negative responses are accompanied by increased activity in the corrugator muscles. Although this activity cannot be observed with the naked eye, it can be measured by electrodes placed at the indicated positions. (Adapted from Petty & Cacioppo, 1986, p. 42.)

Figure 5.5 The Implicit Association Test
The Implicit Association Test (IAT; Greenwald, McGhee, & Schwartz, 1998) involves a series of tasks, performed in the indicated order. Each task involves making a response by pressing one of two buttons (labeled Left and Right in this figure) for each of a number of names or words presented on a computer screen. The computer records how long it takes to complete a fixed number of trials of each task. This figure shows the use of the IAT to measure people's evaluations of Blacks versus Whites as an example, but the same approach can be adapted to measure evaluations of any two groups. The first two tasks (sequence numbers 1 and 2) are quite easy, and participants are able to respond rapidly. When responses to both names and words are required (as in the combined tasks 3 and 5), however, performance may be easy or difficult, depending on the way the responses go together. For most White participants, the combination shown as sequence number 3 (where Black names and pleasant words require the same response) is much more difficult than the combination in sequence number 5 (where White names and pleasant words are given the same response). By measuring how much longer it takes participants to complete the more difficult combination task compared to the other one, researchers are able to assess how strongly the participants associate the Black category with negative evaluations and the White category with positive ones. It is difficult for participants to intentionally alter their patterns of responses in order to conceal their evaluations of the categories. To read more about the Implicit Association Test or to try it for yourself, visit the Project Implicit website, http://projectimplicit.net

illustrating this involves physiological measurement (Cacioppo, Petty, Losch, & Kim, 1986). Facial electromyography (EMG) measures electrical activity in the facial muscles that create expressions such as smiles or frowns, as shown in Figure 5.4. Electrical activity can be measured even when changes in facial expressions are not visible, and evidence suggests that these measurements can accurately assess people's automatically activated positive or negative feelings about social groups (Vanman, Paul, Ito, & Miller, 1997). However, this approach requires specialized equipment, a carefully controlled environment, and extremely cooperative research participants.

Another approach uses methods similar to the study by Wittenbrink and his colleagues (2001). Russell Fazio and his colleagues (Fazio, Jackson, Dunton, & Williams, 1995) used a priming technique in which participants saw images of Black or White faces on a computer screen, followed by words (like *sunshine* or *disease*) that were clearly positive or negative but unrelated to racial stereotypes. Their task was simply to press one of two keys as rapidly as possible to categorize the word as positive or negative. For most participants, responses to positive words were faster following a White person's face, and responses to negative words were faster following a Black face (Fazio and others, 1995). These differences in response speed, which indicate the individual's relative evaluation of Blacks and Whites, are very difficult if not impossible for the person to control or conceal.

Another technique, the Implicit Association Test (IAT), has also been used to demonstrate that people automatically associate social groups with positive or negative evaluations (Greenwald, McGhee, & Schwartz, 1998). The IAT is described in Figure 5.5. Both the IAT and traditional self-report measures of prejudice contribute to predicting judgments and behavior toward social groups (Greenwald, Poehlman, Uhlmann, & Banaji, 2009).

Measuring Stereotypes and Prejudice

Stereotypes and prejudice can be measured by asking plain questions or in more subtle ways that make it difficult for people to hide their stereotypes or prejudiced feelings. However, people who reveal stereotypes or prejudice in subtle ways while overtly denying them may not be dishonest; they may actually hold conflicting views.

We have just described some of the sophisticated techniques that researchers have used to demonstrate that stereotypes or prejudiced evaluations of social groups can be automatically activated, without people's intention or even awareness. As you may have realized, these techniques offer a means to measure people's stereotypes and prejudice. And indeed, the measurement of stereotypes and prejudice has been a continuing problem affecting research in this area. A generation or two ago, measuring stereotypes or prejudice was a relatively easy task: Researchers could just ask, and generally received honest answers because social norms were much more accepting of group-based biases (D. Katz & Braly, 1933). However, more recently, people have become less likely to endorse group stereotypes or to openly reveal prejudice against racial or other groups (Devine, 1989; Dovidio & Fazio, 1992). Does this mean that stereotyping and prejudice have actually declined over time? Or only that people are now less likely to be honest about such socially sensitive matters? Or, perhaps most intriguingly, that people still harbor group stereotypes or prejudices of which they are not consciously aware?

In fact, many people who deny harboring stereotypes or prejudice, apparently with great sincerity, nevertheless show telltale signs of these phenomena when tested with modern **implicit measures**. Implicit measures, like the priming measures and IAT just discussed, are based on some difficult-to-control aspect of people's performance, such as their response speed or accuracy, and thus do not rely on people's ability or willingness to report their beliefs or feelings (Fazio & Olson, 2003). The underlying question is how we should interpret this pattern. At first glance, it is tempting to assume that implicit measures offer a direct route to people's unchanging, "true" inner beliefs and feelings, in contrast to explicit self-report measures, which can be distorted by social desirability biases and other transitory effects. In this view, people who show prejudice on an implicit measure like the IAT yet deny it when asked are simply lying to make themselves look good (to others or to themselves). However appealing it may be, this view is not correct. Implicit measures of group prejudice are now known to be affected by many situational factors, including recent encounters with liked or disliked group members, and even the race of the experimenter who administers the tasks (Blair, 2002; Lowery, Hardin, & Sinclair, 2001). Moreover, people can "fake" IAT responses to some extent, to make themselves appear as unprejudiced (Fiedler and others, 2006; Fiedler & Bluemke, 2005). We have to conclude, then, that implicit measures are not a direct "pipeline" to the person's true inner attitudes, free of distortions by situational or social factors.

A clear understanding of the differences between self-reports and implicit measures begins with the assumption that at least some people are perfectly honest and sincere in saying they reject group stereotypes and prejudice. If implicit measures nevertheless show that they display automatic activation of stereotypes and prejudiced feelings, perhaps these individuals can be accused of lacking insight into what these sophisticated research techniques reveal about them, but not of dishonestly denying prejudices that they secretly realize they maintain. To get a personal sense of what this means, take the IAT yourself (at http://projectimplicit.net/) and see what you think! If you regard yourself as a generally unprejudiced person, you may, like your authors, be upset and perhaps even ashamed at the biases that the IAT may suggest you have. The common pattern of overt denials combined with subtle indications of the activation of stereotypes and prejudice may reflect the fact that many people have learned stereotypes from an early age—from parents, the media, the culture in general—despite honestly attempting to escape their influence (Devine, 1989). Unfortunately, as we will see shortly, their good intentions cannot always be carried out.

Thus, current research does not support the view that implicit measures give the "true" picture whereas self-report measures are systematically misleading. Instead, implicit and explicit measures of stereotypes and prejudice may simply measure different aspects of an individual's overall views of a social group. If this is the case, implicit and explicit stereotypes and prejudice should predict different sorts of consequences. And this is what is often found. Consider, for example, the findings of one study that implicit measures of prejudice are related to White students' subtle nonverbal friendliness toward a Black confederate—a type of response that is relatively spontaneous (Dovidio, Kawakami, & Gaertner, 2002). In contrast, that same study showed that the students' levels of overtly reported racial prejudice were related to the positivity of their verbal

implicit measures
alternatives to self-report measures, such as priming measures or the IAT, which are based on difficult-to-control aspects of people's performance, such as their response speed or accuracy

statements toward the Black confederate, an aspect of their behavior that was likely more deliberately considered. Similarly, researchers have found that Black students' implicit preference for Whites versus Blacks, as measured by an IAT, influenced their choice to work with a White or Black partner for a challenging task (Ashbum-Nardo, Knowles, & Monteith, 2003). Other work has shown that implicit racial prejudice influences how quickly one perceives anger on Black male faces, while explicit racial prejudice has no effect on this outcome (Hugenberg & Bodenhausen, 2003). Thus, current researchers often use both implicit and explicit measures of stereotyping and prejudice in their studies, to produce the fullest possible picture of people's impressions and reactions to other groups (e.g., Son Hing, Chung-Yan, Hamilton, & Zanna, 2008).

Impact of Stereotypes on Judgments and Actions

Stereotypes can affect our interpretations of behaviors performed by members of groups, and also our actions toward them. In extreme cases, stereotypes may even affect life-or-death judgments. Stereotypes have greater effects when judgments must be made under time pressure and when emotions are intense. Feelings of power can also impact stereotype usage.

Once activated, stereotypes can serve as a basis for making judgments or guiding action toward a group. For one thing, stereotypes can cause us to focus on one group membership (whether an occupational, racial, or gender group) and therefore to ignore other, competing group memberships (Macrae, Bodenhausen, Milne, & Jetten, 1994). As a result, all members of the stereotyped group become just the same. Being treated as an anonymous, interchangeable group member is a common experience for victims of stereotyping. Virtually every woman professor or business manager can tell stories about being mistaken for the secretary; many a male Hispanic homeowner can recall times when he was out working in his yard, and passersby assumed he was the hired gardener.

Stereotypes can change people's interpretations of behaviors performed by members of different groups. For example, suppose a man and a woman both succeed in some difficult task, such as selling $1,000,000 of residential real estate in a month. For an observer who has stereotypic ideas about gender differences in abilities, the success might be attributed to a man's great skills—but to the woman's luck (Deaux & Emswiller, 1974). Obviously, such attributions would lead to lower expectations that the woman (compared to the man) would continue her successful ways in the future.

Stereotypes can also affect more consequential judgments about others, as recent studies have compellingly demonstrated. Imagine a police officer, patrolling in a dangerous neighborhood. If a stranger suddenly appears on the street holding a metal object in his hand, the officer may have only moments to decide whether the object is a weapon or something perfectly innocent, like a cell phone. In a well-publicized event in February 1999, Amadou Diallo was shot to death in New York City in a hail of 41 police bullets. The officers thought he was holding a gun, but investigation showed that he had only his wallet in his hand. Diallo was Black; might racial stereotypes have influenced the police officers' judgments? According to research by Keith Payne (2001), the answer may be yes. In his study, Black or White faces were shown on a computer screen as primes, followed by a photo of either a handgun or a tool such as pliers or a screwdriver. The participants had to press one of two keys to indicate whether the object was a weapon or a tool. They identified guns faster, and in a second study actually misidentified tools as guns more often, when primed with a Black face rather than a White one. These results suggest that common stereotypes of Blacks as violent or crime-prone could have real implications for the way Black people are treated in threatening situations.

Another study by Joshua Correll and his colleagues (Correll, Park, Judd, & Wittenbrink, 2002) took the idea a step further. In their study, students were instructed to push a button to "shoot" if a person pictured on the computer screen held a gun, but to press a second, "don't shoot" button if the person was unarmed. The pictured person was sometimes White and sometimes Black, and some members of each group were shown holding guns. When the photo showed someone holding a gun, participants were substantially quicker to "pull the trigger" if the person was Black than if he was White. Even more thought-provoking was the result in a second study: when participants were forced to make decisions under great time pressure, unarmed Blacks were "shot" 16% of the time, compared to only 12% for unarmed Whites. Conversely, the students failed to shoot at an armed Black only 7% of the time, whereas they made such errors 12% of the time for armed Whites. A final study that recruited community members from bus stations and malls as participants replicated the results of the college student participants—and revealed that the bias was just as large and in the same direction for Black participants as for Whites.

You may be wondering whether these results apply to actual police officers, and Correll and his associates (2007) have investigated this issue. The promising news: in comparison to non-officers, police officers showed noticeably less racial bias in the decision to shoot Blacks. However, officers and non-officers alike showed the same pattern of racial bias on their reaction times. That is, both officers and non-officers were faster to shoot an armed Black (versus a White) target and to refrain from shooting an unarmed White (compared to Black) target. Therefore, officers appear to display racial bias in the speed with which they make correct decisions. But, fortunately, these findings also suggest that racial bias does not impact their actual shoot/don't shoot decisions. Though these findings provide some optimism that police officers might not allow race to impact the life-and-death reactions they have in the line of duty, questions still remain whether these results would hold under intense stress or fatigue.

Effects of Cognitive Capacity. Indeed, research shows that time pressure or other conditions that limit people's cognitive capacity generally increase the effects of stereotypes on their judgments. For example, people who must make quick decisions about others are more likely to rely on stereotypes than are those who can take their time (Freund, Kruglanski, & Shpitzajzen, 1985; Kruglanski & Freund, 1983). In one study, the less time people had, the more likely they were to rely on gender stereotypes in deciding among male and female job candidates (Bechtold, Naccarato, & Zanna, 1986). And in a study using the same priming method as Payne (2001), people's tendency to misidentify tools as weapons when primed by Black faces was magnified by time pressure (Payne, Lambert, & Jacoby, 2002).

Lack of time is not the only factor that can increase the impact of stereotypes. Sometimes information is just too complex to process adequately. In such circumstances, people may rely on stereotypes as their best bet for making the judgments, even if they have plenty of time and the consequences of their decisions are important. In one mock jury trial, for example, participants role-playing jurors based their decisions on their unfavorable stereotypes of the Latino defendant when the information relevant to making the judgment was complex. They did not show stereotypic biases when the information was presented in a simpler way (Bodenhausen & Lichtenstein, 1987).

Almost anything that diminishes an individual's cognitive capacity can also increase the impact of stereotypes on judgment. Are you a morning person or a night person? In either case, you probably realize that at certain times of day your thinking is not at its best. Galen Bodenhausen (1990) wondered whether time of day could have an impact on stereotyping. He used a questionnaire to measure whether participants were "morning types" or "evening types" and then assigned them randomly to experimental sessions that met at 9 a.m., 3 p.m., or 8 p.m. Their task was to read several items of evidence about a fictitious character named either Roberto Garcia or Robert Garner, who was accused of assault. After reading the evidence, participants were asked about Garcia/Garner's guilt. When people were scheduled for their worst times, they were more prone to rely on their stereotypic expectations that Latinos are aggressive and to assert that the Latino individual had committed the crime (see Figure 5.6). So morning people: Beware of stereotyping others after lunch. And night people: Watch what you think in the morning!

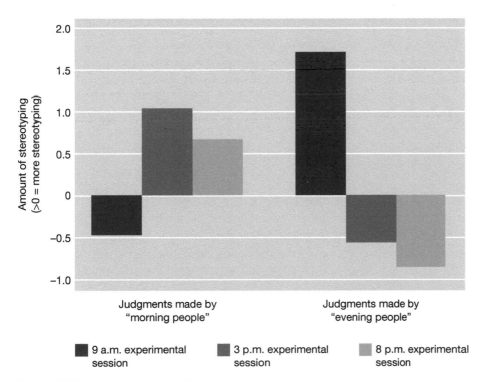

Figure 5.6 Stereotyping by the clock?
At people's nonpreferred times of day, they were more likely to fall back on ethnic stereotyping. For morning people, the stereotype of Latinos as aggressive had its greatest effect on their judgments of guilt in the afternoon and evening. For night owls, the effect of the stereotype was greatest in the morning. (Based on Bodenhausen, 1990.)

Even familiarity can impact stereotype usage because people have a sense that they do not need to think carefully about previously encountered material which, presumably, they already thought about deeply and carefully in the past. So, when information feels familiar, it is often processed fairly superficially, leading to greater usage of stereotypes. In one study showing this, students read about several pictured targets described with various occupational labels (E. R. Smith and others, 2006). Some of the information presented about these people countered a prevailing stereotype about those types of workers. Importantly, photos of some of these targets had been shown to participants earlier in the study. For targets seen just one time, participants seemed to pay attention to these counter-stereotypic descriptions and rated them fairly low on stereotypic attributes. But, for targets that were familiar from the earlier presentation, participants seemed to not process this information carefully, leading to much higher stereotypic ratings.

Effects of Emotion. If the impact of stereotypes is magnified when decision making is difficult, what happens when emotions like anxiety, irritation, or anger cloud our judgment? If you suspect that stereotyping will get worse, you are right (Mackie & Hamilton, 1993). By disrupting careful processing and short-circuiting attention, strong emotions increase our reliance on stereotypes (Dijker, 1987; C. W. Stephan & Stephan, 1984). For example, fear, anxiety, and sadness increase the impact of stereotypic expectations on perceptions of individual group members (D. L. Hamilton, Stroessner, & Mackie, 1993; H.-S. Kim & Baron, 1988; Wilder & Shapiro, 1988), and they decrease recognition of differences among group members (Stroessner & Mackie, 1992). In one study of the effect of anger on stereotyping, students playing mock jurors were asked to decide the guilt or innocence of a defendant whom some believed to be a Latino and others thought was ethnically nondescript (Bodenhausen & Kramer, 1990, cited in Bodenhausen, 1993). Students who were made to feel angry by an experimental manipulation before reading the evidence were more likely to deliver a guilty verdict against the Latino defendant than against the other defendant. In contrast, those who were not angered treated the two defendants the same.

Effects of Power. Suppose a male Latino boss interacts with a female subordinate. Which of the two individuals is more likely to perceive the other in stereotypic ways? The answer, it turns out, is "it depends." Some work shows that those who hold power stereotype more than less powerful individuals (Fiske, 1993; Goodwin, Gubin, Fiske, & Yzerbyt, 2000). Other work, though, shows the reverse: that powerful people stereotype less (Overbeck & Park, 2001). Why the contradiction? Ana Guinote (2007c) has argued that powerful people are highly attuned to their goals and will pay the most attention to information that helps them pursue those goals. Thus, when stereotyping others serves a goal, powerful people will do it more readily; whereas, when avoiding stereotypes will serve a goal, powerful people will be more apt to avoid their use.

HOT TOPICS IN SOCIAL PSYCHOLOGY: INTERSECTIONS OF RACE AND GENDER CATEGORIES

Most research on the impact of stereotyping and prejudice deals with a single dimension of social categorization, such as gender, race/ethnicity, or age. And in many cases, a single group membership largely determines people's perceptions and responses to another individual. However, at times multiple dimensions of categorization become relevant at the same time, a phenomenon termed intersectionality (Goff, Thomas, & Jackson, 2008). Early work by Eagly and Kite (1987) found that stereotypes of ethnic groups and national groups (such as Spanish people) are usually very similar to stereotypes of men of that group (such as Spanish men). In contrast, stereotypes of women of various ethnicities or nationalities were all rather similar to each other, and to stereotypes of women in general. This strongly suggests that when people think of an ethnic or national group, they think mostly of the men in that group. More recent work has examined overlaps between racial and gender stereotypes (Johnson, Freeman, & Pauker, 2011). One such study found that the Black stereotype held by U.S. students overlaps more with the male stereotype, while the Asian stereotype overlaps more with the female stereotype (Galinsky, Hall, & Cuddy, 2013). This fact has several consequences. The researchers found that heterosexual White men generally preferred Asian women over Black women as romantic partners, while heterosexual White women generally preferred Black men over Asian men. In addition, Blacks were more likely than Asians to be selected for leadership positions, and are more heavily represented in college sports that are considered more masculine. The fact that gender and racial stereotypes have some overlapping content may have notable implications in the real world.

Trying to Overcome Prejudice and Stereotype Effects

People may try to overcome the effects of stereotypes and prejudice by suppressing stereotypic thoughts or prejudicial feelings, correcting for their impact on judgments, or exposing themselves to counterstereotypic information. However, all these tactics require motivation and cognitive capacity.

Evidently, we are often in danger of making stereotypic snap judgments because common and well-learned stereotypes can be activated automatically. If the content of stereotypes comes to mind unbidden, and can influence our thoughts, feelings, and behaviors every time we encounter a group member, can people do anything to overcome stereotype effects?

Fortunately, the answer is yes. Even though negative stereotypic information may be activated whenever a particular category comes to mind—at the mere sight or sound of a group member—negative judgments about the group or its members are not inevitable. The activation of a category brings certain information to mind, but we do not have to rely on this information alone. Instead, people can make conscious efforts to avoid thinking of stereotypes, can revise and correct any judgments that they suspect may have been influenced by stereotypes, or can intentionally expose themselves to counterstereotypic information.

Suppressing Stereotypes and Prejudice. Think back to the last time you had a conversation with a member of a group about which you had well-learned negative stereotypes. Naturally, during the conversation you probably worked hard to avoid expressing any stereotypic thoughts or feelings. However, your well-intentioned efforts at suppressing the stereotype might have had negative results later! This conclusion rests on fascinating research by Neil Macrae and his colleagues (1994). The British students who participated in this study were shown a photograph of a skinhead, a member of a social group linked to extremely negative stereotypes, and were asked to write a paragraph about a day in this person's life. Half were told to avoid using any stereotypes or preconceptions, whereas the other half were not given any special instructions. Those who were told to suppress the stereotype clearly were able to do so: Their paragraphs were less stereotypic than those written by the other participants. Next, the participants were told that they would meet the skinhead in person, and were taken into another room where a coat and other items (evidently belonging to the skinhead) were draped over a chair, making it appear that he had left the room momentarily. Participants selected a seat for themselves, and the distance from the skinhead's supposed seat was measured. Those who had earlier suppressed the negative skinhead stereotype now chose to sit farther away from the skinhead!

Other studies found similar results when people suppressed stereotypes on their own because they believed that using stereotypes was inappropriate, rather than because of an experimenter's instruction (Macrae, Bodenhausen, & Milne, 1998). Consistent with other research suggesting that once-suppressed thoughts often rebound and become even more accessible (Wegner, 1994), suppressing a stereotype may make its content more likely to influence our thoughts and feelings later. Suppressing stereotypes may

HOT TOPICS IN SOCIAL PSYCHOLOGY: WHO CAN SUPPRESS STEREOTYPE ACTIVATION?

Do findings such as these mean we are all doomed to activate and use stereotypes, despite our desires to avoid these biases and behave in an egalitarian fashion? Fortunately, the answer is no. Certain people, namely those with particular types of motivations to avoid prejudice, seem capable of controlling their stereotypic responses. People may want to avoid prejudice for internally-driven reasons such as the personal desire to be egalitarian, or for externally-driven reasons, such as a wish to appear politically correct (Plant & Devine, 1998). Individuals who are high on internal motivation and low on external motivation actually exhibit better stereotype control, even in the gun-versus-tool task described previously. People completed this task while electroencephalographic (EEG) measurements were taken from various locations on their scalps (Amodio, Devine, & Harmon-Jones, 2008). These EEG readings allow researchers to measure the activity of large groups of neurons and therefore provide clues about what happens at a neurological level during different sorts of tasks. Such measurements during the gun-versus-tool task suggest that people high on internal and low on external motivation to control prejudice show high levels of conflict monitoring, meaning that they are especially apt to notice when competing responses are activated so that behavior control is necessary. This was especially evident in trials with a Black face as the prime and a tool as the target, so the correct answer is tool, but the conflicting stereotypic tendency is to reply with gun. Furthermore, analyses of the responses in this study revealed that high internal-low external motivated respondents showed less activation of the stereotypic response in the first place (Sherman and others, 2008). It is interesting that only these specific individuals show this pattern of conflict monitoring and reduced stereotype activation. Why, for example, do people who are high on both internal and external motivation to control prejudice not do the same thing? Research to date does not answer this question.

not always be possible, either. Consider the studies by Payne and his colleagues (2002) on tool versus weapon judgments primed by Black or White faces, described earlier. Results in those studies were virtually identical for participants who were specifically instructed to avoid using race as for those who were instructed to use race in making their judgments. Thus, suppressing or simply trying to avoid using stereotypes may not be the best approach to eliminating stereotype effects on our thoughts and judgments (Monteith, Sherman, & Devine, 1998).

Correcting Biased Judgments. A different approach to trying to overcome stereotypes and prejudice involves correction rather than suppression. If we think that an unwanted stereotype may have influenced our thinking, we can try to correct for its effects, for example, by trying hard to be pleasant (Wegener & Petty, 1997). A half-century ago Gordon Allport (1958) quoted two college students writing anonymously about their feelings about groups:

> *Intellectually, I am firmly convinced that this prejudice against Italians is unjustified. And in my present behavior to Italian friends I try to lean over backwards to counteract the attitude. But it is remarkable how strong a hold it has on me.* (p. 310)

> *These prejudices make me feel narrow-minded and intolerant and therefore I try to be as pleasant as possible. I get so angry with myself for having such feelings, but somehow I do not seem to be able to quench them.* (p. 311)

Patricia Devine (1989) argues that these quotations capture exactly what most non-prejudiced people do. She believes that virtually everyone is affected by the negative content of early learned and deeply ingrained stereotypes, but that some people try to overcome their insidious consequences by correcting their judgments. Thus, being unprejudiced does not mean never having stereotypic thoughts or feelings, but rather acknowledging them and making a conscious effort to avoid being influenced by them. Like trying to break any bad habit, this work is not easy, for it requires people to wrestle with inner conflicts between the negative stereotypes they have learned and the non-prejudiced views they also hold (I. Katz & Hass, 1988).

When well-intentioned people try to correct judgments that they suspect may have been affected by stereotypes, they may even make overly positive judgments of stereo-typed group members. This outcome was observed in studies by Kent Harber (1998). In these studies, White college students read essays that were intentionally filled with major stylistic flaws and content errors, and gave feedback to the supposed essay writers. When the participants believed the writer was a Black student, the feedback was more positive and supportive than when the writer was believed to be White. In cases like this, people may alter their judgments to avoid appearing prejudiced—not only to others, but even more important, to themselves. But doing this can have negative effects and be difficult to pull off. For one thing, withholding honest feedback on major flaws in students' work deprives the students of an opportunity to learn and improve. And in addition, intentionally correcting our judgments can take time and mental resources. The inability to make corrections is undoubtedly one reason that a lack of time and cognitive capacity leads to judgments that are more stereotypic, as we described earlier.

Activating Counterstereotypic Information. Potentially even more effective than correction is a strategy of intentionally exposing oneself to counterstereotypic information. Irene Blair and her colleagues (Blair, Ma, & Lenton, 2001) asked people to self-generate counterstereotypical mental images. They used the stereotype that men are stronger than women, and instructed some participants to form a mental image of a strong woman. Different participants, of course, interpreted this idea differently, with some visualizing a body-builder type who is physically strong, whereas others thought of a grandmotherly woman who was a strong source of emotional support for her family. This imaging task reduced the tendency to stereotype women as weak, according to an implicit measure (a version of the IAT), compared to participants who formed an irrelevant mental image. In a related approach, Bertram Gawronski and his associates (Gawronski and others, 2008) put participants through a long series of trials in which they pressed a "yes" button to counterstereotypical pairings of names and traits. For example, in one study, when participants saw a female name and strong word or a male name and a weak word, they were to respond with "yes." Like Blair's counterstereotypic mental imagery, this task also reduced implicit stereotypes.

Beyond Simple Activation: Effects of Stereotypes on Considered Judgments

Even when people make considered judgments, established stereotypes exert an effect. People tend to look for stereotype-confirming, not disconfirming, evidence and to interpret ambiguous information as stereotype-consistent. People may even elicit stereotype-consistent information from others by the way they interact with them.

We have seen that people often use stereotypes when they are in a hurry, when they make judgments without much thought, or when they are emotionally upset. Unfortunately, stereotypes also leave their mark even when people try to gather more information. Stereotypes often guide our decisions because we generally believe they are accurate—for two main reasons. First, when we learn information that appears consistent with our expectations, we will leap to the conclusion that those expectations were correct. And, as you will see, stereotypes can bias the information people process, producing apparent consistency. Second, confidence also flows from consensus. A stereotype that is socially shared—as most stereotypes are—boosts our confidence by letting us know that other people agree with our beliefs and react in the same way we do.

In many situations, of course, confidence in a stereotype is not enough. We need to see beyond group membership and consider personal characteristics, reactions, or emotions. For example, in choosing an employee, competency is more important than gender, and in choosing a friend, shared tastes and preferences are more important than race. So in some situations—when the judgment is important and when we choose to devote attention to the task—we may try to go beyond group stereotypes and collect further information about people as individuals (Fiske & Neuberg, 1990; M. L. Hoffman, 1986; M. J. Rodin, 1987). When we do this, stereotypic information is less likely to come to mind (Macrae, Bodenhausen, Milne, Thorn, & Castelli, 1997). Even when we collect additional information, however, stereotypes can subtly bias the way we see other people.

We discussed the conditions that lead people to go beyond their initial expectations to consider others as individuals in Chapter 3, pages 73–78.

Seeking Evidence to Confirm the Stereotype: Just Tell Me Where to Look. How do stereotypes distort our considered judgments about others? One source of bias is our stereotypic expectations: We tend to notice and remember what we expect to see. For one thing, when people are given both stereotypic and stereotype-inconsistent information about a person, they tend to spend more time reading and thinking about the stereotypic information (Neuberg & Fiske, 1987). If they are allowed to select what information they will receive, they are likely to ask for more stereotype-consistent information (L. Johnston & Macrae, 1994).

Stereotypic biases affect not only the information we seek out and attend to, but also what we remember. Recall from Chapter 3's discussion of person perception that when we are especially motivated to pay attention to an individual, we carefully process unexpected information and remember it particularly well (Hastie & Kumar, 1979). For example, suppose you have an impression of an individual as generally self-centered, but then observe the person volunteering four consecutive weekends to work on building a Habitat for Humanity house. As we described in Chapter 3, you are likely to think hard about this unexpected behavior, and you will probably remember it particularly well when you think about the person again. However, this special processing of unexpected behaviors is less likely to occur with groups (D. L. Hamilton & Sherman, 1996). That is, if you think of a group as self-centered but learn that a group member volunteered for Habitat, you are unlikely to devote the same kind of special processing to the inconsistent behavior or to remember it well. In fact, you may remember mostly stereotype-consistent information about the group (D. L. Hamilton & Rose, 1980; Rothbart, Evans, & Fulero, 1979). This memory bias means that once a stereotype is in place, people may falsely recall that the stereotype was confirmed in their actual encounters with group members. As D. L. Hamilton and Rose (1980) concluded, believing is seeing. When bias molds people's observations and memories so that they fit their stereotypes, the stereotypes grow even stronger (Rothbart & John, 1985; Wilder & Shapiro, 1984).

Chapter 3, pages 89–90, described why people tend to better remember unexpected rather than expected information about an individual when forming an impression.

Interpreting Evidence to Fit the Stereotype: Well, If You Look at It That Way. The implications of a good deal of the information we gather are not immediately obvious. As a person on a lonely street at night reaches for an object in his pocket, who is to say whether he is pulling out a handgun or just a cell phone or a pack of cigarettes? When information is ambiguous, activation of a stereotype influences our interpretation of the behavior (or of the individual performing the behavior), making it seem consistent with the stereotype (Darley & Gross, 1983).

In an early study demonstrating this point, Andrew Sagar and Janet Schofield (1980) showed schoolchildren stick-figure drawings of children who were identified as Black or White, and described each stick-child's behavior. For example, a picture of two students sitting one behind the other in a classroom was accompanied by the following description: "Mark was sitting at his desk, working on his social studies assignment, when David started poking him in the back with the eraser end of his pencil. Mark just kept on working. David kept poking him for a while and then he finally stopped." When David was Black, the children saw his behavior as more mean and threatening than when he was White. Thus, the same behavior was interpreted differently depending on who the actor was and what stereotype his group membership evoked.

Stereotypes can similarly influence our interpretations of others' behavior in everyday situations, as an episode recounted to author Studs Terkel (1992) demonstrates. A White man described how his wife, driving down the street in a Black neighborhood, noticed that the people on the street corners were all gesturing at her forcefully. Frightened, she closed the car windows and drove very determinedly through the area. Only after several blocks did she discover that she was going the wrong way on a one-way street and that the pedestrians had merely been trying to help her. If stereotypes can bend our interpretation of behaviors in one direction or another, some group impressions may be almost impossible to counteract (Rothbart & Park, 1986).

Comparing Information to Stereotypic Standards: That Looks Good, for a Group Member.

At 5 feet 10 inches, Sarah is more likely to be called "tall" than Samuel, who is also 5 feet 10. This is just common sense; Sarah is indeed tall for a woman. But this example illustrates one additional way stereotypes can affect our judgments: by shifting our standards for judgments, at least on characteristics like "tall" or "smart" or "athletic" that involve a strong subjective element. For example, student judges gave an essay on a feminine topic a better letter grade when they believed it was written by Joan, a woman, than by John, a man. Yet the students' ratings of the essays on a subjective scale (for example, from "poor" to "excellent") showed no differences by the author's supposed gender. Evidently the students believed that John's essay on the feminine topic, while not as good as Joan's, was still "good" for a man (Biernat & Manis, 1994).

The fact that people use different standards to judge different groups shows up in how they communicate about group members, and recipients of those communications seem capable of detecting this. In one study, student communicators reviewed the academic transcript of an alleged male student with fairly average credentials, who was either Black or White (Collins, Biernat, & Eidelman, 2009). The communicators wrote their impressions of the student and rated him on several response scales, such as "This person's GPA is strong." There were three groups of "interpreters." One read the communicator's impressions and ratings of the target, learned of the target's race, and estimated the student's GPA from this information. Another made the same estimate after receiving the same information, but without knowing the target's race. A final group was given no information and simply guessed the GPA of a Black male and White male student. Results showed that communicators described more positive impressions of the Black student than they did for the White student. This may be evidence of the use of shifting standards— an average set of academic credentials seems "really good" for a Black student, who is stereotyped to be less academically gifted. But how were these communications interpreted? Interpreters who knew the race of the student actually estimated his GPA as lower when they thought he was Black (versus White), despite receiving a more positive description of the Black student! This effect did not show up in the other two groups of interpreters.

Constraining Evidence to Fit the Stereotype: The Self-Fulfilling Prophecy.

Not only do people seek out stereotype-consistent behavior, they may even elicit it. One of us observed just such a situation when he was in graduate school. Two of his fellow students who had co-authored a paper ran into the professor who had given them their assignment. The professor immediately engaged the male student co-author in conversation, spending several minutes complimenting him on the paper and discussing a few of its fine points. The woman student stood by, silently fuming. So did the observer, because he knew that the woman was by far the more talented student and suspected that three-quarters of the work on the paper was hers. Yet the professor, stereotypically assuming that the male student was the primary author, was holding a conversation that reinforced his opinion that the male student could talk intelligently on the topic while the female student had nothing to say.

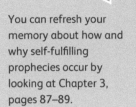

You can refresh your memory about how and why self-fulfilling prophecies occur by looking at Chapter 3, pages 87–89.

When stereotypes lead us to act in ways that produce the very behaviors that confirm our expectations, the stereotype becomes a self-fulfilling prophecy. Recall from Chapter 3 that when people interact with someone about whom they hold a particular expectation, they often induce that person to confirm the expectation (M. Snyder, Tanke, & Berscheid, 1977). Similarly, people's actions often elicit information that confirms and maintains their group stereotypes. When we ask women about their family and men about their job, our behavior produces responses that are likely to tell us what we already

SOCIAL PSYCHOLOGY IN PRACTICE: SELF-FULFILLING PROPHECIES IN SCHOOL AND AT WORK

The self-fulfilling nature of stereotypes can set up a chain reaction in which not only the perceiver's beliefs but also the actual behavior of members of the stereotyped groups are affected (Word, Zanna, & Cooper, 1974). In the classroom, the consequences can be devastating. For this reason, researchers have intensively studied the effects of teachers' expectations on student performance. Expectations may be based on social categorizations like gender, race, or social class, or on personal characteristics like physical attractiveness (M. J. Harris, 1991). When teachers' expectations for students are high, they tend to treat them with more warmth, teach them more material, and give them more chances to contribute to discussions and answer questions in class. These differences translate directly into differences in student achievement (M. J. Harris & Rosenthal, 1985). Such findings make it clear why we should be concerned about studies like one showing that classroom teachers generally give more attention and encouragement to boys than to girls (Wellesley College Center for Research on Women, 1992). Another study undertaken in a New York City suburb indicated that teachers' expectations for Black children are consistently lower than for White children, regardless of the children's actual abilities (S. I. Ross & Jackson, 1991). And a recent review, though it argued that self-fulfilling prophecy effects in classrooms are generally small, acknowledged that they can have powerful effects on students from generally negatively stereotyped groups (Jussim & Harber, 2005).

Self-fulfilling prophecies operate in the workplace, too. An employer's preconceptions can predetermine the outcome of applications for job openings. For example, interviewers who believe that a particular candidate is not suitable for a position are likely to probe for negative information (Binning, Goldstein, Garcia, & Scatteregia, 1988), whereas those with positive preconceptions tend to spend time gaining and giving positive information (Phillips & Dipboye, 1989). In one study, White participants interviewed Black or White applicants. When dealing with Blacks, they conducted briefer interviews and sat farther away, causing the applicants to react in a less confident and effective manner (Word and others, 1974). Self-fulfilling prophecies also restrict the opportunities of employees already on the job. Employers can generate confirmations of their stereotypes in a number of subtle ways. A supervisor who regularly interrupts his female subordinates is clearly communicating to them that their contributions are unimportant, damaging their self-confidence. A boss who delegates responsibilities to his female staff but then checks up on every detail is not only advertising his distrust but also denying the women the opportunity to prove their competence.

know. Alternatively, we may simply not bother to gather much specific information from people who are members of a stereotyped group. In one study, perceivers who held a stereotypic expectation about someone sought less information from them in an interview, asking fewer questions than when the target person was not described as a member of a stereotyped group (Trope & Thompson, 1997).

No wonder then that group stereotypes, like other mental representations, tend to perpetuate themselves and to be slow to change. When people process superficially, stereotypes alone can dictate their judgments. When people process more extensively, stereotypes influence what they see and how they interpret it. Either way, the outcome is likely to be a judgment consistent with the stereotype, as Figure 5.7 demonstrates.

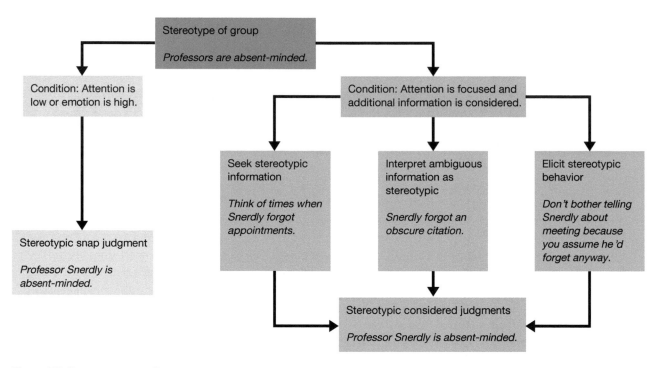

Figure 5.7 Stereotypes are self-perpetuating
Whether people make snap judgments or attempt to process information more carefully, stereotypes shape their thoughts and actions. In most cases, the result seems to confirm and perpetuate the stereotype.

CHANGING STEREOTYPES AND REDUCING PREJUDICE

Even though people sometimes selectively gather, interpret, and elicit information so that their stereotypes are confirmed, they may eventually have an experience that unambiguously contradicts their impression of a group. For example, a member of a group regarded as hostile and clannish may move into the neighborhood and turn out to be unobjectionable, even pleasant. Could getting to know likable individual group members change negative stereotypes of the entire group and lead to less prejudice? Somehow, we like to think that stereotypes and prejudices are born out of ignorance, so that simply learning more about a group will put them to rest.

That simple idea—that contact with individual members who violate the group stereotype should bring about its downfall—is the basis of one of the oldest and most researched theories of stereotype change. The **contact hypothesis** suggests that under certain conditions, direct contact between members of different groups can reduce intergroup stereotyping, prejudice, and discrimination (G. W. Allport, 1954b). When members of different groups socialize, perhaps they can exchange the kind of information that undermines stereotypic thinking. Getting to know group members on a one-to-one-basis should make it obvious that they do not fit the group stereotype. In the face of this inconsistent information, common sense says that the stereotype should change.

contact hypothesis

the theory that certain types of direct contact between members of hostile groups will reduce stereotyping and prejudice

Barriers to Stereotype Change

Even when people obtain information that is blatantly inconsistent with a stereotype, stereotypes may remain unchanged. This is because people can explain away the inconsistency, create a new category for exceptions to the rule, and see the behavior of unusual group members as being irrelevant to the group stereotype.

Unfortunately, reality is not as straightforward as common sense. Consider, for example, the high level of contact between men and women, police officers and gang members, Palestinians and Israelis. None of these contact situations has been a stereotype-reduction success story. The problem lies in the fact that contact in and of itself—even contact that contradicts a stereotype—may not undermine a stereotype (G. W. Allport, 1954b; Amir, 1969; W. G. Stephan, 1987). In fact, exposure to inconsistent information can trigger powerful mechanisms that protect established stereotypes from change.

Explaining Away Inconsistent Information. Well-intentioned authors of uplifting stories for young people sometimes devise plots in which the hero holds a negative stereotype about Group X, meets an X, after some initial misunderstandings gets to know the X as a person, and finally decides the stereotype was wrong and Xs are as likable as anybody else. The idea that a stereotype can be changed by a single inconsistent experience, a process called conversion (Rothbart, 1981), is appealing. But the plot somehow seems contrived. Does true conversion occur so easily?

One barrier to stereotype change is the fact that when people even notice information that fails to fit their expectations, they often just explain it away. Information that is in some way discrepant often makes us look hard for its causes, and thus makes it likely that we will find some "special circumstances" to explain it. If we interpret friendly and positive behaviors performed by a member of a disliked group as just the result of special circumstances, we will not accept the behaviors as a reflection of the actor's true nature (Crocker, Hannah, & Weber, 1983; Gordon & Anderson, 1995). Similarly, women who succeed in a "man's world" are often viewed as highly motivated or very lucky, rather than as very able (Deaux & Emswiller, 1974; Heilman & Stopek, 1985). Encountering a few successful women, or individuals who violate other stereotypes, generally does not change observers' stereotypes.

subtype

a narrower and more specific social group, such as housewife or feminist, that is included within a broad social group, like women

Compartmentalizing Inconsistent Information. Even when inconsistent information is too plentiful to be explained away, people can still defend their stereotypes by resorting to specific **subtypes**: social categories that are narrower than broad groups like men or Latinos. For example, German students have different stereotypes for subtypes of women, such as "chick," housewife, career woman, and "woman's libber" (Eckes, 1994). Older people are also categorized into common subtypes such as respected elder statesman, sweet grandmother, and inactive senior citizen (Brewer, Dull, & Lui, 1981).

Although these differentiated categories permit the perceiver to formulate fine-grained expectations about different group members, they also protect stereotyped beliefs from change. If we place a group of people who are exceptions to the rule in a new category, the old rule can remain inviolate. Male executives who work alongside highly competent female colleagues can form a "career woman" subtype that allows them to maintain a more general belief that most women cannot succeed in business (Rothbart & John, 1985; Weber & Crocker, 1983). Similarly, we can maintain our view that outstanding physical feats are the province of the young if we compartmentalize stereotype-inconsistent older people in special subtypes. We merely create an exceptions-to-the-rule category for people like John Glenn, who at age 76 took another space trip 38 years after he became the first American to orbit the earth, or Johnny Kelly, who completed his 57th Boston marathon at age 83.

Differentiating Atypical Group Members: Contrast Effects. Stereotype-inconsistent information can be defused in yet a third way. If we cannot explain away inconsistencies or create new subtypes, we may defend our stereotypes by seeing stereotype-disconfirming individuals as remarkable or exceptional people. When stereotypic expectations serve as a background against which individual group members are judged, people who do not behave as expected seem even more different, creating what is called a contrast effect. In one study, for example, researchers created stereotypes of patients in a mental hospital. They had college students read statements, supposedly written by the hospital's patients that revealed the patients as either severely disturbed or only mildly disturbed (Manis, Nelson, & Shedler, 1988). The students then read statements by other patients who showed a moderate level of pathology. Because of the contrast with their expectations, those who had been led to expect severe disturbance judged these new patients to be only mildly ill, whereas those who expected only mild disturbance thought the new patients were extremely ill. Similar processes probably explain why people's stereotypes of an employed woman are quite different from those for a "typical woman" and are very similar to their impression of an employed man. People apparently assume that employed women have actively chosen that role and that only the

Photo 5.4 Subtypes. Even exposure to people who clearly violate stereotypes might not lead to stereotype change because of the use of subtypes. What subtype comes to mind to describe this man?

most ambitious and independent women—the ones most unlike the rest of their group—would so choose (Eagly & Steffen, 1984).

Through contrast effects, members who deviate from expectations for their group seem even more different from the rest of the group than they really are. As a result, perceivers can easily decide that these unusual people are not true group members at all: Their difference makes them exceptions to the rule. As such, they have little bearing on people's impressions of the group as a whole (Rasinski, Crocker, & Hastie, 1985; Rothbart & John, 1985).

Overcoming Stereotype Defenses: The Kind of Contact That Works

Effective contact has to provide stereotype-inconsistent information that is repeated (so that it cannot be explained away), that involves many group members (so that subtyping is prevented), and that comes from typical group members (so that contrast will not occur). Under these conditions, contact does reduce stereotypes.

Given all the barriers to stereotype change, it might seem that contact between groups is not a very useful remedy for altering stereotypes. And, because stereotypes are one cause of prejudice, contact, by extension, may also not seem an effective means to reduce prejudicial feelings. Yet across an incredibly wide range of situations, contact does have generally positive effects. A meta-analysis of literally hundreds of studies shows that people with more intergroup contact tend to be less prejudiced, whether the contact occurs in public housing units, schoolrooms, workplaces, or in shorter-term interactions (Pettigrew & Tropp, 2006). What about the possibility that low prejudice produces contact rather than the reverse? Perhaps only people who were unprejudiced in the first place chose to be in situations where they would encounter members of other groups. The meta-analysis convincingly shows that this process, however plausible it is, cannot be responsible for the total effect. For example, contact that is forced rather than voluntary actually has stronger effects on reducing prejudice (Pettigrew & Tropp, 2006). However, even though contact is generally helpful, some types of contact are more effective than others (S. W. Cook, 1985; Kenworthy, Turner, Hewstone, & Voci, 2005; W. G. Stephan, 1987). To allow the kind of information exchange that undermines stereotypic thinking and reduces prejudice, contact situations must expose people to information that cannot be explained away, subtyped, or contrasted.

Positive and cooperative intergroup contact can not only change stereotypes, but also help resolve ongoing conflict between groups. Thus, we will return to the question of what kinds of contact are most effective when we consider intergroup conflict in Chapter 13, pages 520–524.

Repeated Inconsistency: An Antidote for "Explaining Away." One counterstereotypic act can easily be explained away. The sales manager who expects inferior performances from women might attribute a woman sales rep's single week of outstanding sales just to extra effort or sheer luck. However, if the strong performance continues week after week, these attributions become harder to support (Kelley, 1967). When behavior remains stable over time and circumstances, attributions to the person are warranted. Thus, stereotype change requires counterstereotypic behaviors to be performed more than once or twice. Of course, this places a special burden on members of stereotyped groups. They cannot afford to perform poorly, even once, for fear that a failure will reinforce rather than change others' stereotypes (Steele, 1992).

Widespread Inconsistency: An Antidote for Subtyping. Even if the sales manager in the previous example changes his impression of that particular woman sales rep, he may still maintain his stereotype by simply compartmentalizing her as a member of a small subgroup of highly competent women. When behaviors are performed by just a few individual group members, perceivers may create a subtype to insulate their general stereotype from change. To illustrate how this defense can be overcome, Reneé Weber and Jennifer Crocker (1983) gave people information about many behaviors performed by members of a group. Some learned that just a few group members performed stereotype-inconsistent behaviors; the other members' actions were all in line with the stereotype. These participants did not change their overall stereotype of the group, presumably because they categorized the few inconsistent individuals into a new subtype (Johnston & Hewstone, 1992). In contrast, other participants who learned that the same number of inconsistent behaviors were spread out over a large number of group members were more likely to change their stereotype. In the latter case, the inconsistent individuals could not be considered a subtype: Too many group members had unusual, counter-stereotypic features.

Being Typical as Well as Inconsistent: An Antidote for Contrast Effects. People have other weapons besides subtypes to use in defense of their stereotypes. Recall that group members who violate the stereotype may simply be considered highly unusual individuals—so atypical that their characteristics have no impact on impressions of "typical" group members (Johnston & Hewstone, 1992). This defense can be overcome if individual stereotype violators provide strong and consistent reminders of their group membership. In one study, college students interacted with a confederate posing as a student from a rival college. The students initially disliked people from the other school, but this particular interaction was positive and friendly. The students' general beliefs about those attending the rival school, however, became more positive only if the confederate acted and dressed in ways perceived to be "typical" of the rival college (Wilder, 1984). If the confederate did not display such highly typical characteristics, the friendly interaction had no impact on students' general views about the other college.

These effects extend to racial perceptions as well (Wolsko, Park, Judd, & Bachelor, 2003). White students interacted with a male Latino student (a confederate) in a group task. Both before and during the group task, participants learned information about the Latino confederate that either confirmed the stereotype of his group or disconfirmed it. After the task, participants were asked to judge how "typical" they thought he was of Latinos. Results indicated that stereotypic judgments of Latinos decreased only for those who interacted with the stereotype disconfirming Latino confederate and perceived him as typical of that group.

This finding poses a dilemma for group members who wish to change others' negative stereotypes by being a positive example of their group. The very accomplishments and valued attributes that make you a positive example may make you less of an example, by making you less typical of the group in the eyes of an observer who holds negative stereotypes (Desforges and others, 1991; Rothbart & John, 1985). Indeed, any sort of extensive personal information about you, whether positive or negative, can make you seem less of a group member (Fein & Hilton, 1992). As others get to know you as an individual, they may fail to generalize their positive feelings about you to other members of your group. If your goal is stereotype change, therefore, you should repeatedly remind others of your group membership, so that they cannot treat you as an exception to the rule.

Before we review the bottom line for changing stereotypes, we should pause to consider for a moment whether all stereotypes ought to be changed. If you have a stereotype that neo-Nazis are evil, but meet a member of that group who smiles politely and acts pleasant, should this experience alter your stereotype? Many of us might say no. And a Frenchman may not want to change the stereotype that the French are good cooks, any more than a Marine would disavow his group's stereotype of toughness and bravery.

Many individuals, though, in keeping with today's social norms, have decided that they do not endorse or wish to use stereotypes of racial, gender, religious, or ethnic groups of the sort that were commonly accepted in past decades. In such cases changing stereotypes is possible, but not easy. Although many factors conspire to keep stereotypes in place, exposure to the right kinds of information can eventually beat down the defense mechanisms that protect stereotypes from change. Even when old stereotypes are activated, people can choose to counter them with unbiased thoughts, feelings, and behaviors. Figure 5.8 shows both the factors that make stereotypes resistant to change and the factors that can finally overcome that resistance. Although it is sometimes difficult to find situations that have all the necessary ingredients working together, contact of the right type can break down negative stereotypes.

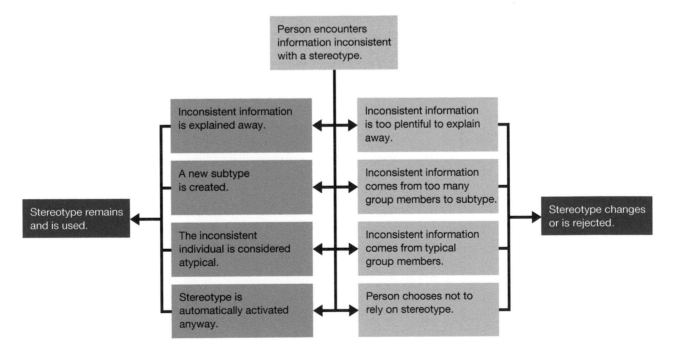

Figure 5.8 Possible fates of stereotype-inconsistent information
Inconsistent information will not always lead people to change or reject their stereotypes, because people have many ways to defend stereotypes against such information (shown on the left side of figure). However, these defenses can be overcome if the inconsistent information appears in the right patterns, or if the individual intentionally chooses not to rely on the stereotype (right side). In some circumstances, stereotypes can be changed.

Reducing Prejudice Through Contact

Pleasant contact with members of other groups can reduce prejudice, even when that same contact does not alter stereotypes. Contact that involves the formation of actual friendships across group lines is especially effective in reducing prejudice.

As just described, stereotypes can be changed through the right kind of contact—contact that blocks attribution, subtyping, and contrast effects. But what about prejudice—can contact reduce negative evaluations of and feelings about groups as well? As with stereotypes, the answer appears to be yes. Because stereotypes are one underlying cause of prejudice, the types of contact that eliminate stereotyping might also reduce prejudice. But, prejudice is sometimes triggered by things other than stereotypes, as we'll discuss in Chapter 6. So, contact experiences might be effective in knocking out prejudice, even when they do not eliminate stereotypes.

In fact, a single positive encounter with a member of another group may be sufficient to reduce prejudicial evaluations, even if it cannot alter stereotypes. Earlier we described a study in which White students interacted pleasantly with a male Latino student (a confederate) who either did or did not confirm the stereotype of his group. Stereotypic judgments of Latinos decreased only when the Latino disconfirmed the stereotype and was perceived as very typical of his group. Nevertheless, in that same study, this brief, pleasant contact did improve White students' evaluations of Latinos, regardless of whether or not the student fit common stereotypes of that group (Wolsko and others, 2003). In general, then, positive face-to-face interaction may be effective in creating warm and positive feelings about another group, even if it does not change specific stereotypes of the group (Tropp & Pettigrew, 2005).

Even more minimal forms of contact can create positive feelings about group members. For instance, simply imagining a positive interaction with a member of another social group can reduce prejudice toward that group (Turner, Crisp, & Lambert, 2007). Also, simple exposure to faces of group members can enhance our liking for them. For example, one study showed that exposing White students to photos of Black strangers increased their liking of other (non-exposed) Black faces (Zebrowitz, White, & Wieneke, 2008). Thus, pleasant or even neutral contact of a variety of forms can reduce prejudice toward others.

Of course, extended, positive interactions that encourage the development of a real personal relationship involving positive feelings and sharing of thoughts and feelings—in other words, a friendship—may be especially effective in reducing prejudice (Pettigrew, 1998). Stephen Wright and his colleagues (S. C. Wright, Aron, McLaughlin-Volpe, & Ropp, 1997) illustrated this idea in a laboratory study, by first creating conflict between experimentally created groups and then trying friendly contact as a way of reducing it. College students were randomly assigned to two teams that then participated in a series of problem-solving and creativity competitions. Though this procedure alone often suffices to build conflict, as you will see in Chapter 13, the experimenters helped it along in various ways. For example, each team was asked to provide an evaluation of the other team's problem solutions, and the experimenters covertly edited these comments to make them more negative before delivering them to the other team. After steps like these had built up negative feelings between the groups, one member from each group was selected,

This study loosely adapted the methods used by Muzafer Sherif in his famous summer camp study, to be discussed in Chapter 13, pages 520–524.

ostensibly as part of an unrelated study, to participate in a dyadic getting-to-know-you task that established feelings of personal closeness. Finally, all members of both groups, after learning about the experimentally created friendship between these individual members, again rated both groups.

The results of this experimentally created contact were clear. The individual members who built up a close relationship with the opposite-group partner rated that group more positively. Perhaps of greater importance, the other group members did so as well! It seems that not only having a member of another group as a friend, but even knowing that someone else from your group has a member of the other group as a friend, is sufficient to reduce negative feelings about that group. This optimistic conclusion has been confirmed in additional studies (S. C. Wright and others, 1997).

Other laboratory research has demonstrated similar positive effects of intergroup contact. Donna Desforges and her associates (1991) set up a 1-hour laboratory session in which participants interacted with a confederate posing as a former mental patient, a member of a group about which the participants had negative stereotypes. The contact was structured to be cooperative

Photo 5.5 The benefits of cross-group friendships. The formation of cross-group friendships, like the one depicted here between these Black and White young women, is one powerful way to reduce prejudice.

in nature, and as a result friendship budded, and the students came to like their partners. They also developed improved attitudes toward former mental patients in general.

SOCIAL PSYCHOLOGY IN PRACTICE: INTERGROUP CONTACT IN THE WILD

Finding that positive contact breaks down prejudice in the controlled conditions of the laboratory is one thing, but can the right kind of contact break down prejudice in other settings, too? Several studies suggest that reductions in prejudice are associated with increased everyday contact.

The 1950s were a period of large-scale desegregation of public housing units in the United States, creating the conditions for research on the effects of living near members of other groups. Morton Deutsch and Mary Collins (1951) studied the responses of White families assigned to live alongside Black families as well as Whites living in all-White buildings. When the groups were compared, those living in desegregated housing, and particularly those who lived closest to Black families, had more positive feelings about Blacks. Two Canadian researchers obtained similar results when they matched national survey data on prejudice with census information on the racial composition of residential neighborhoods (Kalin & Berry, 1982). People felt relatively positive about the groups that lived nearby, suggesting again that informal, everyday contact reduces prejudice.

More recent surveys tell the same story. Thomas Pettigrew (1997) analyzed survey data from Britain, France, the Netherlands, and Germany. People were asked whether they had any friends who were members of minority racial groups with common negative stereotypes (such as Turkish immigrants in Germany or North Africans in France). Those with such friendships were less prejudiced against the minority group, to a greater extent than could

■■■

■■■

be explained by the simple fact that less prejudiced individuals would be more likely to form such friendships in the first place. The effects of a cross-group friendship were not even limited to the specific group: A French person who had an Algerian friend became less prejudiced not only against Algerians, but against other groups as well (Pettigrew, 1997). Pettigrew (2009) later examined a German sample and found that the more positive contact the German respondents had with foreigners, the less prejudice they had toward foreigners and several other groups, including Muslims, the homeless, gays and lesbians, non-traditional women, and Jews.

Not surprisingly, closer more intimate contact also has beneficial effects. Natalie Shook and Russell Fazio (2008) examined White, first-year college students who were randomly assigned to live with either a White or a Black roommate. Both near the beginning and near the end of the first academic term, these students completed a variety of measures, including one that tapped implicit racial evaluations. Results showed that White students who lived with other Whites showed no improvement in these racial attitudes over time, whereas Whites who lived with a Black roommate did.

Chapter 2, page 42, describes why replication of findings inside and outside the laboratory increases researchers' confidence that contact of the right kind does in fact reduce prejudice.

Thus, the results of non-experimental and field studies of contact and friendship "in the wild" converge with experimental findings from the laboratory. Contact can reduce group prejudice.

CONCLUDING COMMENTS

One theme that has surfaced repeatedly in this book is that our social knowledge is slow to change and tends to perpetuate itself. Stereotypes offer perhaps the most dramatic illustration of this principle, for they perpetuate themselves in two different ways.

First, within each individual, the effects of stereotypes mean that believing is seeing. Stereotypes color our perceptions so that unclear or ambiguous events are quickly interpreted in line with the stereotype. If we think politicians are self-serving, we might decide that any action they take is made only for its publicity value. When we read in the newspaper that our member of Congress donated $100 to the local orphanage, for example, we then conclude that the donation was meant to attract media attention. Even when we try to think hard and process carefully, stereotypes shape the information we seek out, remember, and use to make judgments. We might question the politician about foreign junkets rather than efforts on behalf of the district, or we might remember negative campaign tactics rather than sponsorship of important legislation. Even when inconsistent information comes our way, we are likely to defend our stereotypes by explaining away inconsistencies, forming subtypes, or contrasting a particular individual as a praiseworthy exception to the rule.

Of course, none of these self-fulfilling and defensive tendencies are intentional. No one consciously decides, "I want to maintain my biased and stereotypic view of politicians, so don't confuse me with the facts!" Instead, our stereotypes, like our other mental representations, constitute the picture of reality we have constructed for ourselves. And for this reason, their effects are below the level of our awareness. We don't try to defend and maintain our stereotypic beliefs, it just happens that way most of the time.

Second, stereotypes perpetuate themselves and resist change in society as well. As we have seen, stereotypes generally reflect the roles society allocates to members of the stereotyped group. If more women than men care for children, if members of one ethnic group tend to be small shopkeepers whereas most members of another group hold unrewarding jobs as menial laborers, those roles will become the raw material of stereotypes. People are likely to end up believing that women are nurturant, that the first ethnic group is greedy and grasping, and that the second group is lazy and dirty. Stereotypes track social roles both because the roles limit the behaviors that we observe individual group members performing, and because the culture and media generally foster the idea that personal characteristics fit roles. Thus the circle is closed. Because people believe groups are naturally suited for the roles they play, those beliefs become the justification for keeping the groups in those roles. Social change that would alter groups' roles is seen as a violation of the natural order of things, becoming morally wrong as well as impractical.

Thus stereotypes have self-fulfilling force not only in an individual's head but also in society. Because stereotypes operate on two levels, changing them will demand alterations not only in the way we think, but also in the way we live. We need to consciously reflect on the extent to which social roles and other external constraints determine not only other people's actions but also our own. Equally, we need to interact with members of all groups in more varied contexts, to see them in more diverse roles, and to work toward change in social inequalities that are reflected in and rationalized by stereotypes.

Could changes like these allow us to retain the benefits of social categorization while eliminating the costs of stereotypes? We would still perceive groups, but we would know each group for its positive and valued characteristics. Perhaps all groups would respect and value all other groups, a goal that is implicit in the concept of multiculturalism. Unfortunately, another factor stands in the way of developing a society in which all groups are equally valued and respected: We all show strong preferences for the groups to which we belong. In Chapter 6 we consider the consequences of this preference for the way we think about and act toward others and ourselves.

SUMMARY

Discrimination, or treatment of individuals based on their group memberships, and **prejudice**, evaluations of individuals as group members, or evaluations of social groups, are significant problems in the world today. Both social and cognitive factors contribute to prejudice. One important source is people's **stereotypes**: positive or negative beliefs about a group's characteristics.

Any **social group** that shares a socially meaningful common characteristic can be a target for prejudice. Different cultures emphasize different types of groups, but race, religion, gender, age, social status, and cultural background are important dividing lines in many societies. People identify individuals as members of social groups because they share socially meaningful features. This process of **social categorization** is helpful because

CHAPTER 5 THEMES

■ **Construction of Reality**
We construct impressions of social groups based on our interactions with group members and what we learn from others.

■ **Pervasiveness of Social Influence**
These interactions and the things we learn are shaped by society and culture.

■ **Striving for Mastery**
Stereotypes often reflect individuals' actual social experiences.

■ **Conservatism**
Stereotypes perpetuate themselves by shaping both the way we think and the way we act.

■ **Superficiality Versus Depth**
Stereotypes influence judgments made quickly with little thought and also judgments made by collecting further information.

it allows people to deal with others efficiently and appropriately. Social categorization also helps us feel connected to other people. However, it also exaggerates similarities within groups and differences between groups, and hence it forms the basis for stereotyping.

Forming Impressions of Groups: Establishing Stereotypes. Many different kinds of characteristics are included in stereotypes, which can be positive or negative. Some stereotypes accurately reflect actual differences between groups, though in exaggerated form. Other stereotypes are completely inaccurate.

Early theorists traced prejudice and negative stereotypes to deep inner conflicts in a few disturbed individuals, such as the **authoritarian personality**, rather than to more normal social motives such as mastery and connectedness. Stereotypes can be learned through personal experience with group members, but may still be biased because of emotions that arise during cross-group interactions and become associated with the group through **classical conditioning**, and because people pay attention to extremes or inaccurately perceive groups' characteristics, sometimes creating an **illusory correlation**. Social roles often shape group members' behaviors, but people attribute the behaviors to group members' inner characteristics. Learning about groups can take place through media portrayals as well as firsthand experiences.

Social learning also contributes to stereotypes. Stereotypes and discrimination are often accepted and endorsed as right and proper by members of a particular group, becoming **social norms**. Group members then learn these beliefs and behaviors from family and peers. As stereotypes are communicated, they may become even stronger.

The stereotypes prevalent in a society often serve to justify existing social inequalities. They do so by portraying groups as deserving their social roles and positions on the basis of their own characteristics.

Using Stereotypes: From Preconceptions to Prejudice. Once established, stereotypes and prejudice can be activated by obvious cues, use of group labels, or the presence of a group member, especially as a minority in a social situation. Some stereotypes and prejudices come to mind automatically.

The same research techniques that demonstrate stereotypes and prejudices are automatically activated offer subtle ways to measure stereotypes and prejudice, termed **implicit measures**, which make it difficult for people to hide biases that they could readily conceal in answers to plain questions. However, people who reveal stereotypes or prejudice in subtle ways while overtly denying them may actually hold conflicting views rather than being dishonest.

Once activated, stereotypes can affect our interpretations of behaviors performed by members of groups, and also our actions toward them. In extreme cases, stereotypes may even affect life-or-death judgments. Stereotypes have greater effects when judgments must be made under time pressure and when emotions are intense. Stereotype usage is also influenced by power.

People may try to overcome the effects of stereotypes or prejudice by suppressing stereotypic thoughts and prejudicial feelings, correcting for their impact on judgments, or exposing themselves to counterstereotypic information. However, all these tactics require motivation and cognitive capacity.

Even when people make considered judgments, established stereotypes exert an effect. People tend to look for stereotype-confirming, not disconfirming, evidence and to interpret ambiguous information as stereotype-consistent. People may even elicit stereotype-consistent information from others by the way they interact with them.

Changing Stereotypes and Reducing Prejudice. Research on how stereotypes and prejudice may be changed in society has focused on the **contact hypothesis**, the idea that under certain conditions, contact with members of a stereotyped group may reduce stereotyping and prejudice. But contact is not always sufficient. Even when people obtain information that is blatantly inconsistent with a stereotype, stereotypes may remain unchanged because people explain away the inconsistency, create a new **subtype** for exceptions to the rule, and see the behavior of unusual group members as irrelevant to the group stereotype.

To be effective in changing stereotypes, contact has to provide stereotype-inconsistent information that is repeated (so it cannot be explained away), that involves many group members (so subtyping is prevented), and that comes from typical group members (so contrast will not occur). Pleasant contact with members of other groups can reduce prejudice, even when that same contact does not alter stereotypes. Contact that involves the formation of actual friendships across group lines is especially effective in reducing prejudice.

SOCIAL IDENTITY

STIGMATIZED **SOCIAL IDENTITY**
CONNECTEDNESS   CONSERVATISM   MORAL EXCLUSION
SELF-CATEGORIZATION
SOCIAL CREATIVITY   MASTERY SOCIAL INFLUENCE
STEREOTYPE THREAT

As part of your participation in a psychological experiment, you learn that you will be videotaped being interviewed about various social and academic aspects of your life as a student. The experimenter shows you a sample videotape, which shows a student who appears incredibly successful: earning straight A's in premed courses, well dressed and attractive, full of self-confidence—yet still coming across as likable. Now you are given a questionnaire asking you to rate your own academic ability, social competence, and so on. With the superstar interview still echoing in your mind, wouldn't your ratings perhaps be a little below the top of the scale? In contrast, suppose you saw a real loser instead of the superstar. The same actor (for the interviews were staged, of course) portrays a sloppily dressed, unmotivated individual who comes across as socially awkward and not terribly intelligent. Wouldn't your self-ratings go up a bit in this case? Many studies similar to this have established that making social comparisons to another person's outstanding performance lowers people's self-ratings, whereas witnessing a poor performance raises them.

Marilynn Brewer and Joseph Weber (1994), though, added a new twist to their study when they also manipulated group membership. Before seeing the videotape, each participant took a bogus test classifying him or her into one of two personality types, one said to include 80% of college students and the other only 20%. The videotaped actor was also said to belong to one or the other group. These group memberships fundamentally shifted the outcomes of the social comparison. When the videotaped interviewee was a member of the larger group, social comparison had its typical effect: Participants felt bad if the performance was great and good if it was terrible, regardless of their own group membership. But consider what happened when the videotaped student belonged to the minority group:

■ For a majority group participant, a videotape of a minority interviewee had no effect whatever on the participant's self-concept. It seems that majority group members simply do not compare themselves to minorities.

■ Even more striking, minority group participants who saw a minority interviewee reacted in the opposite way from the usual social comparison process. They felt good if their fellow group member gave a great performance, and bad if he or she looked terrible! Could it be that people in this situation do not compare themselves as individuals against other individuals, but psychologically share in the positive or negative image the other person's performance gives to their group?

We described the effects of social comparison on the self in Chapter 4, pages 99–100.

As these findings show, being a member of a group influences many of our thoughts, feelings, and actions. You may feel good or bad about yourself depending on the specific groups that come to your mind. Being part of and identifying with a group such as the Filipino community or the swim team, being a woman or a member of any other group can boost or lower self-esteem. Group memberships are an essential part of the self.

Group membership can confer tremendous benefits. It gives us a sense of belonging and worth, of being valued for who we are (Tajfel, 1972). As group members, we can bask in the glow of achievements other than our own and feel at home in a haven of similarity and understanding. A sense of group membership that connects us to others is the basis for our participation in social life. It even protects our mental well-being and physical health, as you will see in Chapter 12. Group membership supports our needs for mastery as well as connectedness. Our groups can offer us support and confidence in our ways of understanding the world (Festinger, 1954; Hogg & Abrams, 1993), a topic that will receive much more attention in Chapter 9.

The many benefits of group belonging come at a cost, however. Because our groups are so important for defining the self, we need to see them as attractive, valued, and successful. Unfortunately, valuing our own groups often entails preferring them over other groups. Regard, esteem, and liking for in-groups—groups to which we belong—at times become coupled with disregard, derogation, and dislike for out-groups. When this occurs, as sociologist William Graham Sumner (1906) said long ago, "loyalty to the in-group . . . [and] hatred and contempt for outsiders . . . all grow together" (p. 13). From school rivalries to ethnic prejudice to national patriotism, both the exaltation of in-groups and the belittling of out-groups reflect the importance of group membership for each of us.

These positive and negative sides of our group memberships will both be explored throughout this chapter. The chapter first describes the way people come to view social groups as aspects of the self: how we learn what our group memberships mean, and what factors conspire to make a particular membership significant at any given time. The chapter then turns to the consequences of placing ourselves and others in social categories. Once a group membership is activated, it affects the way we see and respond to ourselves and others. Shared group membership tends to make us view other in-group members as similar to ourselves and as likable, so we try to treat them justly and fairly. But we often respond to out-group members with indifference, active dislike, or even overt discrimination.

The chapter concludes with a discussion of the effects of belonging to a group that others look down on. From playgrounds to boardrooms, being Muslim, speaking with an accent, using a wheelchair, being gay or lesbian, or being on welfare can provoke scorn, dislike, and avoidance. Such negative group identities can take their toll on individuals and groups. But this outcome is not inevitable, and the chapter concludes by describing how people resist the implications of a negative identity and even work to change society's evaluation of their groups.

CATEGORIZING ONESELF AS A GROUP MEMBER

Some group memberships are so important that they become a basic part of our view of ourselves. Try asking a friend to take a piece of paper and write 10 different sentences beginning "I am . . ." When people perform this task they typically list some individual characteristics such as "I am outgoing" or "I am tall," but they also list group memberships: "I am a woman," "I am German." In fact, most people list more group than individual characteristics (M. H. Kuhn & McPartland, 1954). The process of seeing oneself as a member of a group is known as **self-categorization** (J. C. Turner, Hogg, Oakes, Reicher, & Wetherell, 1987). Self-categorization is flexible and can readily shift (Mussweiler, Gabriel, & Bodenhausen, 2000). Depending on the social context, for example, sometimes you may see yourself as a Mexican-American, other times as a student, and still other times as a unique individual, with group memberships temporarily receding into the background. The term **social identity** refers to the way we feel about the group memberships that we share with others (M. Rosenberg, 1979; Tajfel, 1972). Social identity turns "I" into "we"; it extends the self out beyond the skin to include other members of our groups—and, as we will see, it generally involves positive feelings about both ourselves, and those others.

Although some group memberships are only fleetingly important—being part of the "white shirts" team in a lunch-hour basketball game, for example—most group memberships are stable and enduring. Membership in gender and ethnic groups lasts a lifetime. Being a member of the Kardashian or the Hilton family, or being Muslim, Roman Catholic, or Buddhist can be just as long-lasting. How do we learn what characteristics are associated with our groups?

self-categorization

the process of seeing oneself as a member of a social group

social identity

those aspects of the self-concept that derive from an individual's knowledge and feelings about the group memberships he or she shares with others

Learning about Our Groups

People learn about the groups to which they belong in the same ways that they learn the characteristics of other groups: by observing other group members or from the culture.

These are, of course, the same ways we learn about the stereotypic characteristics of groups to which we do not belong, as Chapter 5 (pages 149—161) discussed.

We learn about our own groups in the same ways that we learn stereotypes of other groups: Lessons come from parents, teachers, peers, and the media. However, our most important lessons generally come from fellow group members and what they do (Postmes, Haslam, & Swaab, 2005; Prentice & Miller, 2002). Consider your first job. What did it mean to become part of the team in the service department, on the factory floor, or in corporate headquarters? Did people joke around, or was the atmosphere pretty serious? Probably you figured out what it meant to be an employee in your company primarily—maybe only—by watching others. To illustrate the importance of interaction with group members, one study tracked sorority pledges' perceptions of their groups over an academic year and found that as they got to know them better, these women saw their groups in increasingly stereotypic terms—in other words, they learned the stereotypes (C. S. Ryan & Bogart, 1997).

In this way, what we and other group members do often becomes the basis for group stereotypes. But what we do is strongly influenced by our roles. In any society, members of a group may occupy particular roles that influence who they are. In the United States, for example, women are less than 2% of mechanics, 4.5% of mechanical engineers, and 8% of computer network architects, compared to 72% of cashiers, 81% of elementary and middle school teachers, and 90% of registered nurses (Bureau of Labor Statistics, 2012). Do a group's common roles and occupations influence group members' views of themselves? The answer is a qualified yes. People may not make direct inferences about their own characteristics on the basis of role-constrained behaviors as readily as observers do. Still, roles affect the individuals who hold them because as people enact their roles, they acquire role-related skills and develop tendencies to behave in certain ways. These skills and tendencies in turn make those behaviors, and correspondent self-inferences, more likely. For instance, a woman's experiences raising young children may leave her better able to interpret nonverbal behaviors or to comfort people when they are distressed. Thus, performing a role based on gender or on membership in some other group can shape our future behaviors and, ultimately, our self-knowledge (Eagly, 1987).

Chapter 3, pages 69–72, discussed how and why we often draw personality inferences about others, even when their behaviors are driven by their roles.

Feeling Like a Group Member

Knowledge about group memberships may be activated by direct reminders, such as group labels; by the presence of out-group members; by being a minority; or by intergroup conflict. Group membership is particularly significant in some cultures and for some individuals, who tend to see the world in terms of that group membership.

No matter how extensive our knowledge about the characteristics of our groups, that knowledge will have little impact unless the group membership comes to mind. Imagine you are a male Midwestern feminist, or a female Canadian conservative. Perhaps you are also musically talented, near-sighted, and love Cajun food. In what circumstances will your gender, politics, or other group memberships be more important than your individual attributes? And which group membership will matter? A variety of social and cognitive factors can conspire to make a particular group membership accessible. These range from temporary situational factors, to more enduring aspects of social structure or culture, to stable individual differences.

Direct Reminders of Membership. If someone calls you "jock," or "nerd," or uses an ethnic slur, you are reminded directly, though perhaps temporarily, about your social identity. Honorary titles or pejorative labels bring group membership home in a hurry (Billig & Tajfel, 1973; Charters & Newcomb, 1958). Being offered a "senior citizen" discount at a restaurant or movie theater may be an unwelcome reminder of one's age (Stock, 1995). Often, however, the process is more subtle. Circumstances remind us of our similarities with others, and this activates knowledge of group membership. The mere presence of other in-group members can be a potent reminder (Doise & Sinclair, 1973; Wilder & Shapiro, 1991). Just hearing another New Zealand accent is enough to make one of the authors of this text "feel" like a New Zealander, seeing someone in a Harvard T-shirt reminds another author of his New England background, and spying a person carrying a tennis racquet reminds another of her tennis player identity. When group similarities are highlighted, as when a team wears uniforms or when members coordinate their actions for a common goal, membership and all it entails becomes even more accessible. This process is powerful enough to overcome alternative categorizations that might be important in other circumstances (Cosmides, Tooby, & Kurzban, 2003). So White and Surinamese soccer players join together on the Dutch national team, and Republicans and Democrats coordinate their talents on a town planning committee.

Presence of Out-Group Members. The presence of out-group members can also be a forcible reminder of shared group membership, as demonstrated in a study conducted in Belgium. Belgian university students were asked to write descriptions of typical students of Belgian and North African origin. For some, the experimenter who made this request was a North African; for others, the experimenter was Belgian. The responses of the students who wrote in the presence of an out-group member, the North African experimenter, revealed greater identification with their Belgian in-group (Marques, Yzerbyt, & Rijsman, 1988). Apparently, the presence of even a single out-group member is enough to increase our sense of in-group membership.

When outsiders are present, resourceful group members sometimes put their mouth where their membership is, using language to emphasize their identification with their group. For example, when French-speaking Canadians were confronted with English-speaking Canadians in one experiment, the French speakers either broadened their accents or switched to their native language altogether (Bourhis, Giles, Leyens, & Tajfel, 1978). Ethnic languages are important sources of social identity, as efforts by French speakers in Canada, Catalans in Spain, and Welsh nationalists in Britain to preserve their languages all attest.

Being a Minority. If a few out-group members arriving on the scene can make in-group membership accessible, imagine the impact when they actually outnumber the in-group. In Chapter 4, we noted that people are more likely to think of themselves in terms of individual characteristics that are unusual or distinctive in their social group (W. J. McGuire & Padawer-Singer, 1978). The same principle operates at the group level: People are more likely to think of themselves in terms of their memberships in smaller groups than in larger ones (Brewer, 1991; S. E. Taylor and others, 1978), and especially when they are solo representatives of their group in a situation (Sekaquaptewa, Waldman, & Thompson, 2007). The study by Brewer and Weber (1994) described at the beginning of this chapter illustrated this point, showing that members of a minority group were more likely than members of a majority to base their self-esteem on the performance of a fellow group member.

Consider the results obtained when William McGuire and his colleagues (W. J. McGuire, McGuire, & Winton, 1979) asked grade-school children to talk for 5 minutes about themselves and carefully coded these self-descriptions. As can be seen in Figure 6.1, the researchers found that boys and girls from households where their gender was in the minority were more likely to mention gender than were children from households where their gender made up the majority. Similarly, children whose ethnic group constituted a minority at school were more likely to mention their ethnicity in informal self-descriptions than were children who were part of the ethnic majority (W. J. McGuire, McGuire, Child, & Fujioka, 1978).

You may recall a similar point from Chapter 5, page 163: A solo member of a group tends to be perceived by observers in terms of that group membership.

Conflict or Rivalry. Although all of these transitory circumstances can make a social identity accessible, probably the most potent factor that brings group membership to

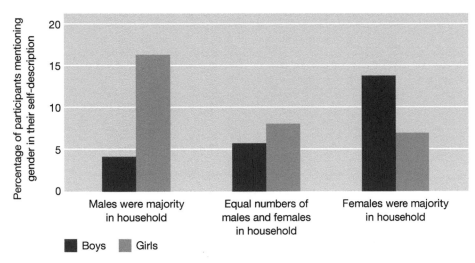

Figure 6.1 Being in the minority matters
In this study, grade-school children spoke for five minutes in response to the instruction "Tell us about yourself." Notice that both boys and girls were more likely to mention their gender if their gender was a minority at home. (Based on W. J. McGuire and others, 1979.)

mind is ongoing conflict or rivalry between groups (Doise & Weinberger, 1973; Ryen & Kahn, 1975). One experiment set up a discussion on a social issue, either between a male and a female participant who disagreed on the issue or between two men and two women, who disagreed along gender lines (Hogg & Turner, 1987). In the second

Chapter 13 will describe the several vivid demonstrations of the effects of intergroup conflict on group identification, including the famed "Robbers Cave" study.

SOCIAL PSYCHOLOGY AND CULTURE: CULTURAL DIFFERENCES IN THE IMPORTANCE OF GROUP MEMBERSHIP

Group membership does not exist in a vacuum, of course, but has an importance that depends on the cultural context (Oyserman, Coon, & Kemmelmeier, 2002). Collectivist cultures, like most in Asia, South America, and Africa, foster and reinforce views of the self in group terms (Markus, Kitayama, & Heiman, 1996; Trafimow & Finlay, 2001). People from these cultures tend to see themselves as members of groups or categories—perhaps as workers at a particular plant, graduates of a certain school, or inhabitants of a specific village. In such societies, family units are often multigenerational and employment relationships may last a lifetime.

In contrast, people who live in the United States, Canada, Northern Europe, and other individualist cultures are encouraged to think of themselves in comparatively idiosyncratic terms, for example, as tall, dark, and handsome. They tend to value freedom, personal enjoyment, and the achievement of individual goals, while viewing group memberships as temporary and changeable (Bellah, Madsen, Sullivan, Tipton, & Swidler, 1985). Members of these societies have high divorce rates and often seem comfortable switching churches or employers. Thus, cultural differences can affect whether people think of themselves more often as individuals or as members of groups, and by so doing, they can create corresponding differences in social behavior (Markus & Kitayama, 1991). But as we will see throughout this chapter, even in individualist cultures in which group memberships are seen as more fluid and less omnipresent, group memberships make a big difference to people's ways of thinking about themselves and those around them (Jetten, Postmes, & McAuliffe, 2002).

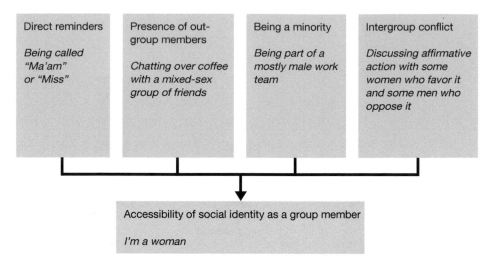

Figure 6.2 Factors that make a social identity accessible
Many factors can increase the accessibility of a particular group membership. Not only obvious reminders, like group labels or intergroup conflict, but even relatively subtle factors like the presence of out-group members can activate our knowledge of group membership.

condition, because the conflict was along group lines, participants identified more strongly with their groups, for example, by rating themselves as more typical of their sex. Even a news report of rivalry can remind us of group loyalties. In one study, exposure to a campus newspaper headline like "Humanities, Science Majors at Odds over Core Program" was enough to increase the accessibility of students' identity as scientists or humanists (V. Price, 1989). The importance of conflict also means that people identify more strongly with groups that they learn are targets of discrimination from the society at large (Jetten, Branscombe, Schmitt, & Spears, 2001). All in all, conflict is perhaps the most powerful factor in making a group membership accessible. Figure 6.2 summarizes the many factors that can have this effect.

ME, YOU, AND THEM: EFFECTS OF SOCIAL CATEGORIZATION

Does it really make a difference if we see ourselves as Belgians, Californians, socialists, or libertarians? It certainly does! When group memberships surface, they influence the way we see ourselves and others, making a huge difference in how we think, feel, and act. The reason is that group memberships not only help define our self and tell us who we are, but they also connect us to some people (fellow in-group members) at the same time as they divide us from others (out-group members). As we discuss these three effects of group memberships in turn, you will see that they are all interconnected.

"I" Becomes "We": Social Categorization and the Self

Activated knowledge about a group membership has multiple effects on people's self-concept and self-esteem. The group's typical characteristics become standards for members' behavior. Group memberships also influence people's moods and self-esteem as they feel bad about their group's failures or good about their successes. Relatively small groups typically have the greatest effects.

Seeing Oneself as a Group Member. Seeing oneself as a group member means that the group's typical characteristics become norms or standards for one's own behavior (J. C. Turner, Hogg, Oakes, Reicher, & Wetherell, 1987). As a result, people tend to think and act in group-typical ways. One experiment demonstrated this effect by having some students listen to a discussion in which one group presented pro-environmental attitudes. Some of the students were about to join the group voicing the positive attitudes, whereas others knew they would not be joining. The students who were going to join the group rated themselves as higher in environmental awareness than did the other students who heard the same discussion (Mackie, 1986). In other words, their own opinions moved toward the group's position. In another study, Dutch university students were presented with a comparison that was potentially threatening to their group; for example, psychology students were asked to compare their own group to physics students on intelligence (Spears, Doosje, & Ellemers, 1997). The way students responded to this threat depended on their initial level of identification with their group. Students who identified only weakly avoided the threat by dissociating themselves from the in-group. But students who strongly identified with their group tended to show group solidarity by rating themselves as highly typical of their group. As this result shows, factors that activate people's group identity—even social comparisons that are threatening to the group—can cause people to see themselves as typical group members.

The same process is responsible for the finding that when laboratory groups include men, women speak more tentatively than they do in all-female groups (Carli, 1990). The presence of men apparently makes the women's identity as females accessible, causing them to act in ways that they regard as typical of women, such as by avoiding assertive speech. In fact, gender group norms are usually highly valued, so acting in accordance with those norms tends to make people feel good about themselves (W. Wood, Christensen, Hebl, & Rothgerber, 1997).

Liking Ourselves: Social Identity and Self-Esteem. We have all experienced it: We feel great when our team wins. When Germany won soccer's World Cup championship in 2014, defeating Argentina by scoring a winning goal in the last few minutes of the game, hundreds of thousands of their fans celebrated in the streets, waving flags, tooting horns, and setting off fireworks. Why? Because our groups are part of ourselves, when good things happen to our team, our school, or our city, we feel good—about life and about ourselves. Recall that in the experiment described at the outset of this chapter, the same process made members of a minority group feel good or bad depending on the performance of a fellow group member (Brewer & Weber, 1994).

Photo 6.1 Basking in reflected glory. When we identify with a group, their emotional ups and downs become our own. Like these New York Giants fans, we are not only happy to join in a victory celebration, we are happy *because* our team has won.

You may recall from Chapter 4, pages 109–110, that, in the same way, people tend to play up the idiosyncratic characteristics they feel good about.

BIRG (bask in reflected glory)
a way of boosting self-esteem by identifying oneself with the accomplishments or good qualities of fellow in-group members

Strivers for positive self-esteem that we are, we play up group memberships that make us feel good about ourselves (Mussweiler, Gabriel, & Bodenhausen, 2000; Tesser, 1988). Robert Cialdini and his co-workers (1976) investigated this tendency to **BIRG** (pronounced to rhyme with "surge"), or bask in the reflected glory of a positive group identification, by counting "in-group" clothing worn on school days following football games. At seven universities they found that students wore more school sweatshirts, baseball caps, scarves, and pins if the football team won than if it lost.

To test their hypothesis that links to a positive group membership serve to raise self-esteem, Cialdini and his colleagues (1976) gave students a brief general-knowledge test and temporarily raised or lowered their self-esteem by manipulating the results. Some randomly selected students were told falsely that they had performed poorly on the test, and others were told that they had done well. The students were then asked, seemingly incidentally, to describe the outcome of a recent game. In their descriptions, the students who thought they had failed the test were more likely to associate themselves with winning teams (referring to them as "we") and to dissociate themselves from losing teams (referring to them as "they"), than were students who believed they had done well and whose self-esteem was intact. Thus, people BIRG as a way of restoring positive self-regard, and they do so particularly when self-esteem is threatened.

Social Identity and Emotions. Group memberships lead us to experience emotions on behalf of our groups, as well as affecting our self-esteem (E. R. Smith, 1993). In one study demonstrating this point, psychology students were told about another psychology student at a different university who had been treated unfairly by authorities. In one condition where the participants were subtly reminded of their common identity with the victim, they reported feeling less happy and more angry—despite the fact that they themselves remained totally unaffected by the events (Gordijn, Wigboldus, & Yzerbyt, 2001). People experience anger, fear, pride, guilt, or other emotions in response to events that affect their groups because identification with a group makes the group part of the self, giving the group emotional significance (Iyer, Leach, & Crosby, 2003; Mackie, Devos, & Smith, 2000). Importantly, these emotional reactions are not just a form of empathy—feeling an emotion on behalf of another person. Rather, they appear to be truly an integral part of group membership as evidenced, in part, by the fact that highly identified group members feel stronger emotions in response to group-relevant events (Smith, Seger, & Mackie, 2007). For example, in one study, students reported how much they felt emotions as an individual and as a member of various groups (e.g., as an American; Smith and others, 2007). They also reported their feelings about other groups and the actions they would like to enact toward them, such as to argue with or oppose them. Much more reliably than their individual-level emotions, participants' group-level emotions predicted their feelings and desires for action toward other groups. Thus, we experience emotions as group members, which influence how we feel about and behave toward out-groups.

Balancing Individuality and Connectedness. As we saw in Chapter 4, members of individualist cultures like to see themselves as unique individuals, distinct from others. Yet they are also motivated to seek connectedness and similarity with others. Can people balance these two seemingly incompatible needs? In fact, group membership can simultaneously satisfy both. Perceiving the differences between our group and other groups provides feelings of being unique and special, whereas seeing the similarity among members within our group can help us feel connected and similar (Brewer, 1991). Though individual and cultural differences influence the relative strengths of these opposing motives, the best balance for most people most of the time involves membership in relatively small groups. A group that is too small might not be an adequate basis for group pride, but in a group that is too large, the person might be too anonymous to attain much respect. Studies have confirmed this idea by showing that people's identification with small groups increases when experimental manipulations increase their desires either for connectedness or for uniqueness (Leonardelli, Pickett, & Brewer, 2010).

Additional evidence comes from an examination of how college-aged students identify with musical styles (Abrams, 2009). A large survey asked United Kingdom residents aged 18–21 to pick their three favorite musical styles from a lengthy list of options that included things like pop/rock, Motown, and ska. They were also asked about how much they expressed their favored musical styles, for example, by buying the music or adopting clothing or hair styles associated with that music. Fans of the musical styles that were objectively most and least popular showed fewer of these behaviors than fans of music in the middle range. Engaging with a form of music that is not popular might make one feel too distinct, while engaging with one that is extremely popular may not offer enough distinctiveness. The "just right" groups in the middle appear best for expressing one's group identity. Thus, relatively small groups seem to provide the best balance between similarity and group identification, on the one hand, and uniqueness and recognition for one's individual qualities, on the other (Hornsey & Jetten, 2004).

Others Become "We": Social Categorization and the In-Group

When group membership is highly accessible, people see other in-group members as similar in their central group-linked characteristics. However, extensive personal interaction (when group membership is not activated) also provides knowledge about their unique and diverse personal characteristics. People like fellow in-group members and tend to treat them in fair, humane, and altruistic ways, seeing the other members as similar to themselves in their goals and interests.

An accessible group membership is not just an aspect of the individual self, like one's height or chess-playing ability. Instead, a social identity links the individual to others and therefore influences the way the person thinks, feels, and acts toward other in-group members.

Perceiving Fellow In-Group Members. When we think about fellow in-group members, what is uppermost in our minds? When group membership is accessible, we think mostly about the features we believe we share with the group, thereby causing us to see other in-group members as similar to ourselves (Krueger, 2007; Gramzow, Gaertner, & Sedikides, 2001). In one demonstration of this effect, students were assigned to groups ostensibly on the basis of their artistic preferences. They were then asked to guess the extent to which other in-group members shared their own personal characteristics and preferences (V. L. Allen & Wilder, 1979). As expected, the students assumed that all members of the group would be very similar in art preferences. Surprisingly, they also thought that in-group members' interests, activities, and even personality traits would match their own. Anything that increases the accessibility of group membership—being a minority, engaging in competition, even just making judgments about another group, for example—further enhances this assumed similarity (Haslam, Oakes, Turner, & McGarty, 1995; Mussweiler & Bodenhausen, 2002; B. Simon, 1992).

Although a highly accessible shared group membership leads us to focus on our similarities with other in-group members, we also manage to learn quite a lot about other in-group members' personal qualities—the things that make them unique as individuals. This awareness of specific, personal attributes develops as we interact with other members in a variety of contexts and situations (J. C. Turner and others, 1987). It is particularly acute when personal rather than group identities are most salient, as when a group of close friends chat together over dinner.

HOT TOPICS IN SOCIAL PSYCHOLOGY: IS THE SELF SIMILAR TO THE IN-GROUP, OR IS THE IN-GROUP SIMILAR TO THE SELF?

We just described how people perceive fellow in-group members as similar to themselves, using their self-knowledge as a basis for inferring what the in-group is like (Krueger, 2007). However, earlier we stated that when they are socially categorized, people think of themselves in terms of in-group norms and stereotypes—using group knowledge as a basis for inferring what the self is like (Turner and others, 1987). Are these processes competitors, or could both of them operate simultaneously? A recent study by Jeff Cho and Eric Knowles (2013) demonstrated both, within the same sample of participants and the same set of traits. For each of 90 traits, participants rated whether the trait described them personally and whether it described their gender group, on 5-point scales. In a later task, they made yes/no responses for each trait, again judging whether or not it described both the self and the in-group, while the response times were recorded. Patterns of response times provided evidence that both processes were operating. When participants were relatively certain that a trait characterized (or did not characterize) the in-group but were uncertain about whether it described themselves personally—as indicated by extreme ratings on the 1–5 scale for the group but midrange ratings for the self—they used their group knowledge as a basis for their response for the self. This amounts to assuming that the self shares the group's typical characteristics. But conversely, when participants were relatively certain that a trait characterized (or did not characterize) the self but were uncertain about whether it described the in-group, they used their self-knowledge to generate their response for the in-group. This amounts to assuming that the in-group shares the self's typical characteristics. In summary, knowledge about the self and the in-group mutually influence each other, with both processes contributing to convergence or overlap between perceptions of the self and the group (Smith and others, 1999).

Knowing about others' unique characteristics helps us to find our own place in the group. As Chapter 4 noted, we define our personal selves in terms of what makes us distinct from others (W. J. McGuire and others, 1978; Park & Rothbart, 1982). Among your fellow students, you may be the serious one, the conservationist, the lover of country music. Of course, to make these differentiations you have to pay attention to the personality, passions, and preferences of your fellow in-group members. In doing so, you learn a lot about them—so much that when group membership is not highly accessible, you are likely to see your group as quite diverse in characteristics not related to group membership (Park & Judd, 1990).

Liking In-Group Members: To Be Us Is to Be Lovable. Because they share our attributes, fellow in-group members become part of "me and mine" and so we like them, usually much more than we like out-group members (Otten & Wentura, 2001). Asked to evaluate essays or creative solutions to problems, people treat their own group's work more generously than out-group products. They choose to interact with and to befriend members of their own rather than of another group (Brewer, 1979; Brewer & Silver, 1978). Even people assigned to groups on a trivial or random basis evaluate their own group as more positive and desirable than other groups, and the in-group bias is stronger yet when the groups are real and meaningful (Mullen, Brown, & Smith, 1992).

Indeed, the very concept "we" seems to have positive connotations, as compared with the concept "they" (Perdue, Dovidio, Gurtman, & Tyler, 1990). When people have seen nonsense syllables (like xeh) paired with the word "we," they have more positive feelings about them, compared to syllables paired with the word "they." Participants also respond more quickly to positive words that follow the prime "we" than to those that follow "they." This is true even when the prime words are flashed too quickly to be consciously read. Both of these findings suggest that the label "we" automatically activates positive associations that facilitate the recognition of other positive words. In a clever study of the consequences of these effects for intergroup behavior, students were asked to read a description of the task that they were to perform with other individuals. For one group of participants, this task was described as "something we all have to do our best on"; for other participants it was "something they have to do their best on." When asked to imagine the quality of the interaction and the likability of the other participants, those who had been exposed to the in-group pronouns had more positive expectations than those who had read out-group pronouns (Dovidio & Gaertner, 1993).

It may have occurred to you that attraction to other in-group members is somehow different from "ordinary" feelings of liking for another individual. After all, attraction usually depends on getting to know someone—on recognizing their desirable personal characteristics and your common interests. In contrast, attraction in group situations seems to depend merely on the knowledge of shared group membership (J. C. Turner, Sachdev, & Hogg, 1983; Gaertner, Iuzzini, Witt, & Orina, 2006). Indeed, people often prefer others who are typical members of an in-group even if those people would not be especially likable on the merits of their individual characteristics alone. This pattern has been observed in many types of groups, including work groups and the members of an Australian football team (Hogg, Cooper-Shaw, & Holzworth, 1993; Hogg & Hardie, 1991; Schmitt & Branscombe, 2001). In a sense, in-group members are liked not as individuals but as representatives of the liked group (Clement & Krueger, 1998).

You might have noticed that the attributions we make about our groups are just like the self-enhancing attributions we make as individuals. To check the parallels for yourself, see Chapter 4, page 132.

The fact that we like our groups so much even shows up in the very language people use to describe others' actions (Maass, 1999). Anne Maass and her colleagues (Maass, Salvi, Arcuri, & Semin, 1989) prepared cartoon drawings depicting positive actions by in-group and out-group members. Asked to describe the actions, participants gave relatively concrete and specific descriptions of out-group behavior, whereas the in-group descriptions were more abstract and general. If an out-group member comforted a lost child on a crowded street, participants said "he talked to the child," or some similarly specific statement. The same action by an in-group member elicited "he helped" or "cared for the child." The concreteness of the out-group descriptions implicitly casts the behaviors as ungeneralizable, one-of-a-kind instances, whereas the more abstract terms used for in-group actions emphasize their links to the actor's positive general characteristics, such as helpfulness or caring (Maass and others, 1989).

Treating the In-Group Right: Justice and Altruism. If in-group members are lovable and similar to us, we will want to treat them as we ourselves would like to be treated. Indeed, people sometimes act in ways that seem to make no sense from the perspective of individual costs and benefits. Parents scrimp and save to leave an inheritance for their children. Soldiers sacrifice their lives for their comrades or their country. From the perspective of a social group, however, actions like these make a great deal of sense. Groups prosper when their members are willing to subordinate personal interests to the group and to help other members in times of need. This has been true since members of many early hunting societies shared the meat from large animals among the whole group (A. P. Fiske, 1992). When group memberships are uppermost in people's minds, they often act in these altruistic ways, showing more concern for treating others fairly than for getting the largest share of rewards (Tyler, Lind, Ohbuchi, Sugawara, & Huo, 1998; Wenzel, 2004).

It is this unification of self-interest and group-interest that makes altruistic and self-sacrificing behavior possible, as we will see in Chapter 14. It is also the basis of effective functioning of small interacting groups, a topic discussed in detail in Chapter 11.

When people see the world through the lens of their group memberships, what is best for the group blurs together with what is best for the individual. As "I" becomes "we," the distinction between self-interest and group interest vanishes (J. C. Turner and others, 1987). This merging of perceived individual and group interests constitutes the psychological basis for fair and altruistic behavior. Over a century ago, Charles Darwin (1871/1909) argued that morality derives originally "from the social instincts": Actions are judged good or bad "solely as they obviously affect the welfare of the tribe." When people think of themselves as members of a family, community, ethnic group, or nation, they feel like and feel for fellow in-group members. As a result, treating those others with fairness and compassion—indeed, treating others as they themselves would like to be treated—becomes easy, natural, and the right thing to do (Deutsch, 1973, 1990; Staub, 1978; Struch & Schwartz, 1989).

An accessible group membership makes other in-group members part of "me and mine." Shared group membership has dramatic effects on the way we think about, evaluate, and behave toward other members, as shown in Figure 6.3.

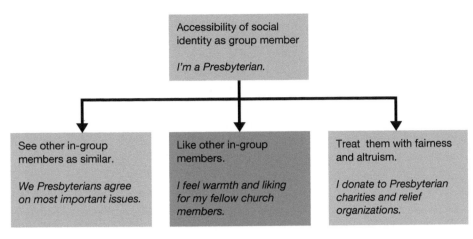

Figure 6.3 Social identity turns others into "we"

When a shared group membership is accessible, it has positive effects on the way we see, evaluate, and treat other group members.

Others Become "They": Social Categorization and the Out-Group

People see out-groups as uniform and homogeneous. People also dislike, devalue, and discriminate against out-group members, depending on the extent to which they are seen as threatening to the in-group. When the out-group is simply different, it elicits mild dislike. When the out-group is seen as outdoing the in-group, this more serious threat results in resentment, dislike, and overt discrimination. Out-groups that are seen as severe threats to the in-group elicit murderous hatred, severe discrimination, aggression, or moral exclusion.

The comedian Emo Phillips (cited in D. L. Hamilton & Mackie, 1990) describes a conversation with a suicidal man threatening to jump off a bridge:

> I said, "Are you a Christian or a Jew?" He said, "A Christian." I said, "Me too. Protestant or Catholic?" He said, "Protestant." I said, "Me too. What franchise?" He says, "Baptist." I said, "Me too. Northern Baptist or Southern Baptist?" He says, "Northern Baptist." I said, "Me too. Northern Conservative Baptist or Northern Liberal Baptist?" He says, "Northern Conservative Baptist." I said, "Me too. Northern Conservative Fundamentalist Baptist or Northern Conservative Reformed Baptist?" He says, "Northern Conservative Fundamentalist Baptist." I said, "Me too. Northern Conservative Fundamentalist Baptist, Great Lakes Region, or Northern Conservative Fundamentalist Baptist, Eastern Region?" He says, "Northern Conservative Fundamentalist Baptist, Great Lakes Region." I said, "Me too. Northern Conservative Fundamentalist Baptist, Great Lakes Region, Council of 1879 or Northern Conservative Fundamentalist Baptist, Great Lakes Region, Council of 1912?" He says, "Northern Conservative Fundamentalist Baptist, Great Lakes Region, Council of 1912." I said, "Die, heretic!" and I pushed him over. (D. L. Hamilton & Mackie, 1990, p. 110)

Emo Phillips makes comic what more often is tragic: the tendency to hate and mistreat those who are not members of our in-group, regardless of how similar to us they may seem to outsiders. We have seen that people generally feel good about their own groups, and while this tendency may be benign, all too often bringing one group up in the world also means putting others down. Unfortunately, anthropological evidence suggests that hostility toward out-groups is common in intergroup relations. Throughout human history and in every human culture, esteem, consideration, and favoritism await in-group members, whereas disdain, discrimination, and domination are often the fate of those categorized as out-group members (LeVine & Campbell, 1972). In short, categorization into an out-group has a range of negative consequences.

Perceiving the Out-Group as Homogeneous: "They're All Alike!" A member of an Isla Vista, California, band explained, "Los Angeles bands are all homogeneous. Seattle bands all sound like Seattle bands. But Isla Vista music is more original. Bands here play all kinds of music!" (Lagerquist, 1992). You should have no difficulty finding other examples of this **out-group homogeneity effect**: the tendency to perceive out-group members as "all the same" compared to the relatively more diverse in-group. People of European origin typically see the widely diverse groups of Native Americans as "all the same" while finding great diversity and variety among those of European descent. Members of one fraternity find members of other houses just as they expected them, but do not think they themselves fit their own group's stereotype (Linville, Fisher, & Salorey, 1989; Mullen & Hu, 1989). Thus the tendency to see out-groups as relatively homogeneous is quite widespread. What accounts for this effect?

> **out-group homogeneity effect**
> the tendency to see the out-group as relatively more homogeneous and less diverse than the in-group

One obvious potential explanation involves familiarity: We usually know more in-group members than out-group members, and we are therefore more aware of their diversity. Because we are less familiar with out-group members, we do not observe their diversity, which gives the impression that they are very similar to one another (Linville and others, 1989). But lack of familiarity with the out-group is not the whole story. Another important factor is the relatively constrained nature of typical interactions with out-group members. People's exposure to out-groups often takes place in settings where no individual interaction is even possible, for example, when students from a rival school attend a sports event en masse. In such settings, one can easily gain the impression that out-group members are pretty much all alike. In contrast, interactions with in-group members are likely to be relatively more varied, relaxed, and informal (Rothbart, Dawes, & Park, 1984). Finally, as we noted earlier, people habitually focus on the personal characteristics that make them unique and different from others. Within the in-group, this means that we learn a lot about others' characteristics in the process of finding out what differentiates us from them. But we can feel unique and different from out-group members just by noting their group-defining characteristics, such as ethnicity, gender, nationality, or university affiliation (J. C. Turner and others, 1987). In a study demonstrating this effect, Bernadette Park and Myron Rothbart (1982) asked students to read brief newspaper stories about men and women. When they later were asked to recall as much as they could about the protagonists, they remembered more personal details, such as occupation, about same-sex than about opposite-sex individuals (see Figure 6.4).

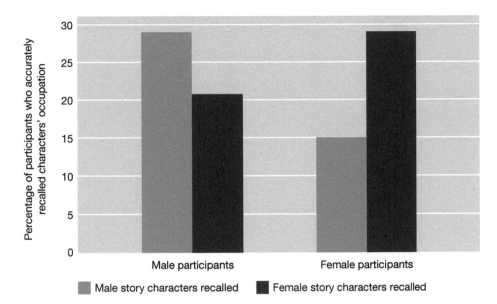

Figure 6.4 It is easier to remember us than them

In this study, men and women were asked to read a "newspaper story" and, at a later time, to recall information about the main characters. As you can see, men more easily recalled the occupations of male characters, whereas women more easily recalled female characters' occupations. (Based on Park & Rothbart, 1982.)

SOCIAL PSYCHOLOGY IN PRACTICE: OUT-GROUP HOMOGENEITY IN EYEWITNESS IDENTIFICATION

Seeing members of an out-group as all alike can set the stage for harmful effects, perhaps most strikingly in the realm of witness misidentification. This happens because the out-group homogeneity effect extends even to the perception of physical characteristics. Apparently, members of other groups "all look alike." A consequence of this is that people can recognize the faces of members of their own ethnic group more easily than the faces of members of other groups, an effect called the cross-race identification bias (Anthony, Copper, & Mullen, 1992; Bothwell, Brigham, & Malpass, 1989; Hugenberg, Young, Bernstein, & Sacco, 2010). In one study illustrating this, Texas convenience store clerks were asked to identify three male customers—actually experimental confederates—who had stopped by to make a purchase earlier in the day. One confederate was Black, another was Mexican-American, and the third was Anglo-American. The shop clerks were also members of these three ethnic groups. As Figure 6.5 shows, the clerks made more accurate identifications of the customer belonging to their own group than they did of the customers from the other two groups (Platz & Hosch, 1988).

This cross-race identification bias appears to result in part because people typically do not have the motivation to pay close attention to the distinguishing features of other-race faces (Hugenberg, Miller, & Claypool, 2007). In one study supporting this notion, White students were shown pictures of White and Black faces during an initial exposure task and later tried to recognize these faces. Before the initial exposure, some students were warned about the cross-race identification bias and instructed to pay close attention to the distinguishing features of faces, especially those of a different race. Those given no special instructions showed the standard bias: White perceivers recognized White faces with greater accuracy than Black faces. But those told to pay close attention to individual

■■■

■■■

faces were able to identify Black and White faces equally accurately. Thus, unless people are aware of the bias and motivated to distinguish one other-race face from another, the bias appears. No wonder, then, that criminal defendants and their attorneys often question the accuracy of eyewitness identifications across ethnic group lines.

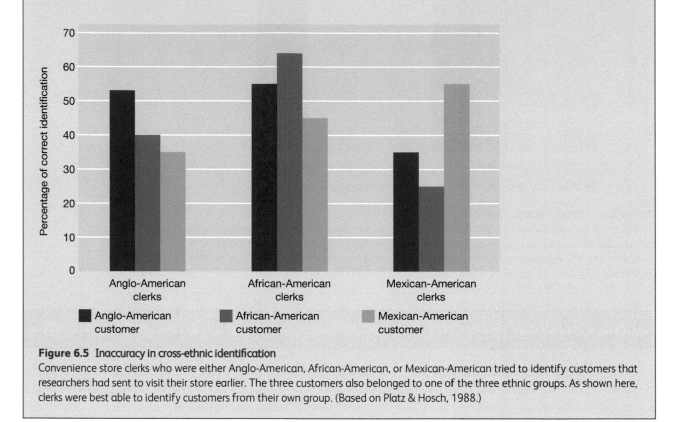

Figure 6.5 Inaccuracy in cross-ethnic identification
Convenience store clerks who were either Anglo-American, African-American, or Mexican-American tried to identify customers that researchers had sent to visit their store earlier. The three customers also belonged to one of the three ethnic groups. As shown here, clerks were best able to identify customers from their own group. (Based on Platz & Hosch, 1988.)

Effects of Mere Categorization: Minimal Groups. As we just described, people usually have poor memory for racial out-group faces. But, consider a recent intriguing study: White students were given an alleged personality test and told that they were a "green" or a "red" personality type (Bernstein, Young, & Hugenberg, 2007). In actuality, these personality types do not exist and were assigned to participants at random. Students then saw a series of White faces appearing on red or green backgrounds that supposedly identified the personality type of the pictured individual. Results showed that the students had better memory for faces that matched their own personality types. "Red" students remembered "red" faces more than "green" faces, and "green" students remembered "green" faces better than "red" ones. It seems people show an effect akin to the cross-race identification bias, even when race isn't involved!

These results suggest that we think differently about in-group versus out-group members, even when the groups are not real or meaningful. Memory confusions are one thing, but might we actually treat others differently simply because they are in another group, even a seemingly inconsequential one? When we consider ethnic conflict in the

Sudan or Iraq, or any of the other manifold examples of one group's maltreatment of another, multiple explanations can be offered. These include negative stereotypes, mutual ignorance and fear, unjust distribution of resources, and a history of conflict. However, perhaps the most sobering body of social-psychological research on the issue reaches a startling conclusion: Explanations like these are not always necessary. Discrimination can occur when a dividing line simply creates two groups, even in the absence of these common sources of antagonism.

In one of the initial experiments illustrating this point, a number of English boys aged 14 to 16 were assigned to Group X or Group W on the basis of a coin toss (Billig & Tajfel, 1973). The groups had no defining characteristics, and members did not know which other individuals were in each group. There was no basis for in-group or out-group stereotypes, and the groups had no history of conflict or antagonism—indeed, no history at all. For all these reasons, this situation was appropriately labeled a **minimal intergroup situation**. After being assigned to a group, each boy was given the opportunity to distribute rewards worth a small amount of money to two other individuals. For example, he might be asked to divide, in any way he wanted, 15 points between two other boys, who were identified only as "Member number 49 of the W group" and "Member number 72 of the X group."

The late European social psychologist Henri Tajfel devised this procedure as a baseline for further comparisons. He planned to go beyond merely categorizing participants into groups, and to add other ingredients, such as negative stereotypes or conflict over resources, one at a time until prejudice and discrimination developed. However, the results in the baseline situation confounded the researchers' expectations. Even in this minimal situation, the boys favored their own group: They awarded more points to members of their in-group than to boys in the outgroup. They were not always blatantly unfair; for example, of the 15 points, boys awarded an average of 8.08 to the in-group and 6.92 to the out-group. However, the bias in favor of the in-group was consistent, and this finding was replicated in many other similar studies (Brewer, 1979; Mullen and others, 1992). Simple categorization into groups seems to be sufficient reason for people to dispense valued rewards in ways that favor in-group members over those who are "different."

Discrimination and Social Identity. What explains the favoritism found in minimal intergroup situations? Were people simply seeking material gain for the in-group? Tajfel was not so sure. His further explorations of behavior in minimal intergroup situations revealed a startling tendency: Participants

minimal intergroup situation
a research situation in which people are categorized, on an arbitrary or trivial basis, into groups that have no history, no conflicts of interest, and no stereotypes

"GOOD NEWS - WE CAN ENTER AN APPEAL! I JUST FOUND OUT THAT THE JUDGE AS WELL AS THE JURY WERE VEGETARIANS!"

often favor the in-group over the out-group even when doing so costs the in-group in absolute terms. For example, Tajfel gave some of his participants a choice between option A, which allocates 11 points to an in-group member and 7 to an out-group member, and option B, which gives 17 points to each. Many preferred option A, which gave the in-group an edge over the out-group, even though choosing A instead of B cost the in-group 6 points (Tajfel, Billig, Bundy, & Flament, 1971). These results and others show that the expectation of rewards is not the driving force behind intergroup discrimination (Gagnon & Bourhis, 1996). A host of studies of minimal groups showed that members give their own group higher ratings on positive traits, evaluations of performance, and inferences of morality (Brewer, 1979). Apparently, group members want to make their groups better, stronger, and more lovable in any way available to them.

These findings led Tajfel to propose that just as we strive to view our individual selves positively, we also want to view our social identities in positive terms. This idea was the basis for **social identity theory**, which argues that people's motivation to derive positive self-esteem from their group memberships is one driving force behind in-group bias (Tajfel and others, 1971). Preferring the in-group over the out-group becomes a way of expressing regard for the in-group, and it is therefore a way of feeling good about oneself, of valuing me and mine (M. Rubin & Hewstone, 1998). Interestingly, studies show that people in minimal intergroup situations do not discriminate when allocating negative outcomes (like unpleasant blasts of noise) as they do when handing out praise or money (Otten & Mummendey, 2000). This finding illustrates the important distinction between in-group favoritism (which occurs even in minimal intergroup situations) and out-group hostility, which as we will see requires other ingredients such as threat or direct intergroup conflict. Only when in-group preference is joined by threat or conflict do people shift from simply rewarding the in-group to actively punishing the out-group.

Effects of Perceived Mild Threat. One type of threat people sometimes face is a threat to their self-esteem. One of the many benefits of group membership is that it can serve to enhance self-esteem, as social identity theory holds. In fact, the finding that people can increase their self-esteem by discriminating against out-groups has been repeatedly confirmed (Lemyre & Smith, 1985; Hewstone, Rubin, & Willis, 2002; M. Rubin & Hewstone, 1998). And people are particularly likely to choose this tactic when their self-esteem is threatened. In a study by Steven Fein and Steven Spencer (1997), for example, some participants (who were assumed to be mostly heterosexual) were given false negative feedback on a supposed intelligence test. They then read a detailed description about a young actor's struggles to begin a career in New York City. If the description of the actor implied that he was probably gay, participants who had been made to feel bad about themselves rated the actor in highly negative and stereotypic terms. The ratings were more positive if the actor was described as heterosexual, or if the participant had received no negative feedback.

So, we may discriminate against out-groups if we experience a threat to our individual self-esteem. But, what if the out-group posed a mild threat to the in-group itself? If an out-group is perceived to be competing with us or outdoing us, this can trigger intergroup discrimination. The effects differ, however, depending on the relative status positions of the groups (Ellemers & van Knippenberg, 1997; Bettencourt, Charlton, Dorr, & Hume, 2001). When higher-status groups are threatened, they tend to discriminate

social identity theory
the theory that people's motivation to derive self-esteem from their group memberships is one driving force behind in-group bias

on dimensions that are centrally relevant to the group distinction. Thus, the economically successful tend to view their own groups as superior to out-groups on dimensions such as hard work, ambition, and intelligence—traits seen as quite relevant to economic position and success. In contrast, lower-status groups show more discrimination on other dimensions that are less directly relevant to status. So lower-status groups frequently evaluate themselves more favorably than higher-status out-groups on dimensions like friendliness, cooperativeness, or likability (Sachdev & Bourhis, 1991).

In general, unequal status amplifies intergroup discrimination. If groups perceive themselves as losing out to an out-group that is gaining in status, power, or prosperity, they often turn from mild dislike to stronger emotions (Fiske, 2002). Anger, resentment, and support for overt discrimination against the out-group are frequent outcomes.

Effects of Perceived Extreme Threat: Moral Exclusion and Hate Crimes.

In June 2011, a group of White teenagers came upon James Craig Anderson, a middle-aged African-American, in a parking lot. They beat him and eventually ran over him with a truck, killing him. The attackers did not know Anderson personally, and they had no history of disagreement or conflict with him. Their only motive for this brutal crime was that Anderson was Black. What can explain this kind of behavior? Stereotypes can produce group prejudice, as we discussed in Chapter 5, and Anderson's attackers probably believed that Black men have a variety of negative characteristics. But can stereotypes fully account for such murderous actions? It seems more likely that extreme forms of prejudice—going beyond mere dislike to outright hatred—may be the cause. Where does such hatred come from?

When prejudice turns from dislike to extreme hatred, it usually reflects the perception that what "they" stand for threatens everything that "we" stand for (Brewer, 2001). At times, we may perceive our in-group as especially virtuous and an out-group as posing a threat to our group (Reicher and colleagues, 2008). This can set the stage for particularly destructive clashes with the out-group. Indeed, if we perceive our in-group as especially good and an out-group is perceived to threaten our existence, it becomes imperative that we get rid of them. For our virtuous group to remain, we must eliminate this threat.

When people perceive such extreme threat, they usually respond in two interrelated ways. First, they exalt in-group symbols and values. Past or present group leaders, flags, slogans, and the group's historical accomplishments are glorified and cast in a totally positive light (Castano, 2008). Second, they begin to hate the out-group. Thus, hatred for outsiders often arises in connection with the exaltation of in-group symbols, whether the hatred is directed against homosexuals, women, immigrants, or racial, ethnic, or religious groups (Kinder, 1986; Sears, 1988). Recall that in the minimal intergroup situation, preferences for the in-group are relatively mild, taking the form of favoring the in-group with good things but usually not giving the out-group an unfair share of punishments (Otten & Mummendey, 2000). However, extreme group threat ties together glorification of the in-group and hatred for the out-group into an ominous package (Branscombe & Wann, 1994).

In these situations, out-groups may also be viewed as fundamentally inferior to the in-group—as subhuman and outside the domain in which the rules of morality apply (Opotow, 1990). **Moral exclusion** can begin with symptoms that appear relatively benign,

moral exclusion
viewing out-groups as subhuman and outside the domain in which the rules of morality apply

Photo 6.2 Less than human. Group hatred is sometimes so strong that the in-group portrays the out-group as less than human, as seen here in this World War I poster trying to entice Americans to enlist in the military to fight the "gorilla like" Germans.

such as a belief in the in-group's moral superiority. The disease quickly spreads, however. In-group members may portray the out-group in subhuman terms, often by labeling them as vermin, barbarians, or even germs "infecting" the pure in-group, or by dismissing their ability to experience human sentiments like joy or grief (Paladino and others, 2002; Vaes, Paladino, Castelli, Leyens, & Giovanazzi, 2003). This attitude allows us to suspend behaviors we usually consider both human and humane, such as helping others and treating them fairly and justly. Thus, when in-group members commit atrocities against an out-group, in-group members who are especially inclined to glorify their group respond by dehumanizing the out-group and resisting demands that the perpetrators be brought to justice (Leidner, Castano, Zaiser, & Giner-Sorolla, 2010). When a powerful in-group excludes members of relatively powerless groups from the scope of moral principles, the stage may be set for extreme intergroup oppression, massacre, or genocide (Opotow, 1990; Sachdev & Bourhis, 1991).

Destructive actions against the out-group may be rationalized by the idea that "they brought it on themselves" or by self-justifying comparisons with horrible atrocities committed by others. The actions may be given euphemistic and misleading labels, like Hitler's genocidal "final solution" or the Serbian "ethnic cleansing." Finally, group members reject personal responsibility for hateful or destructive acts by appealing to the in-group's welfare as a source of higher moral authority (Reicher and others, 2008). These aspects of moral exclusion often play a role in the dynamics of intergroup conflict, which we will discuss in Chapter 13.

Sadly, examples of prejudice and discrimination fueled by perceptions of extreme threat are easy to find. One took place when the Communist regime in the former Yugoslavia began to fail around 1990. People of Serbian descent felt themselves threatened by Croatians and Muslims, and under a strongly nationalist leader, Slobodan Milošević, they launched military campaigns aimed at "ethnic cleansing," creating a new, larger homeland by killing members of other groups or driving them from their homes and lands. Similar patterns were found in the genocidal attacks in Rwanda launched in 1994 by Hutu extremists against Tutsi and moderate Hutus, and in the attacks beginning in 2003 by ethnically Arab militias against Black residents in the Darfur region of the Sudan. Beginning in 2011, the Syrian government slaughtered many of its own civilians who were engaged in peaceful protests in the country. These actions led to the formation of an armed opposition group, prompting a civil war. This war was fueled, in part, by religious differences, as the Syrian government is primarily Alawites, whereas a majority of the opposition is Sunni Muslims. In all these cases, the victimized out-group was perceived, because of cultural, ethnic, or religious differences, as threatening the valued in-group's control of the government or other major societal symbols and institutions.

People's reactions to out-groups usually stop short of virulent hatred, moral exclusion, and violent hate crimes. Still, as shown in Figure 6.6, the reactions, though they range from mild to intense, are always negative. Moreover, prejudice and discrimination against out-groups are found in all cultures (LeVine & Campbell, 1972), and they may be even stronger in the collectivist cultures of Asia and Africa than in Western, individualist

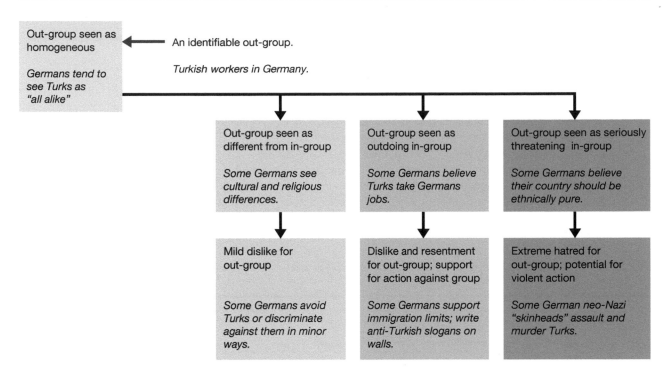

Figure 6.6 Social identity turns others into "them"

Out-group members tend to be seen as "all alike." In addition, they are often disliked and victimized by discrimination, depending on the magnitude of threat they are seen as posing to the in-group. Negative reactions may range from mild dislike, due to the simple perception of difference, to extreme hatred or even genocide when the in-group's very existence is believed to be threatened.

cultures (Hsu, 1983; Moghaddam, Taylor, & Wright, 1993). Those high in collectivism care deeply about their own groups and have been shown to favor them in various ways more strongly than those scoring lower in collectivism (e.g., Yoo & Donthu, 2005). Thus, those in collectivist cultures may be even more likely to discriminate against out-groups. Dislike, distrust, and discrimination seem to be intrinsic parts of the way people respond to out-groups: When intergroup threats emerge, negative treatment of the out-group is inextricably linked to the esteem and favor that in-groups enjoy.

THEY DON'T LIKE US: CONSEQUENCES OF BELONGING TO NEGATIVELY PERCEIVED GROUPS

What are the costs of belonging to a group that is disliked, discriminated against, or excluded from the scope of moral principles? Out-group discrimination does not always escalate to out-group genocide or other hate-motivated violence, but it can have insidious effects even when it does stop short of these extreme acts. For example, members of such groups are likely to suffer from unequal economic opportunity, lack of access to quality education and medical care, and poor living conditions. In the United States, for example, the infant mortality rate for Blacks is more than twice the average for Whites; in fact, it is worse than the rate in Malaysia. Moreover, 43 of every 100 Black children live in poverty.

TABLE 6.1 Turning the Tables: Questions Implying that Group Membership is Abnormal and Devalued

1. What do you think caused your heterosexuality?
2. When and how did you decide you were a heterosexual?
3. Is it possible that heterosexuality is just a phase you may grow out of?
4. Is it possible your heterosexuality stems from a neurotic fear of others of the same sex?
5. If you've never slept with a person of the same sex, is it possible that all you need is a good same-sex lover?
6. To whom have you disclosed your heterosexual tendencies?
7. Why do heterosexuals feel compelled to seduce others into their lifestyle?
8. Why do you insist on flaunting your heterosexuality? Why can't you just be who you are and keep quiet about it?
9. Why do heterosexuals place so much emphasis on sex?
10. There seem to be very few happy heterosexuals. Techniques have been developed that might enable you to change. Have you considered aversion therapy?
11. Considering the menace of hunger and overpopulation, can the human race survive if everyone were heterosexual like yourself?
12. Despite social support of marriage, the divorce rate is still 50 percent. Why are there so few stable relationships among heterosexuals?

Note: This questionnaire has been used in sensitivity-training workshops to provoke discussion. Does it give you a sense of what it might feel like to belong to a group that most people dislike and regard as abnormal?

Source: From *Working It Out: The Newsletter for Gay and Lesbian Employment Issues.*

stigmatized
negatively evaluated by others

Membership in disliked groups can impose other important costs as well, and the price is paid in decreased self-esteem and emotional well-being. If a group becomes part of the member's view of the self, the effects of belonging to a **stigmatized**, or negatively evaluated, group may be pervasive (Crocker, Major, & Steele, 1998). Brian Mullen and Joshua Smyth (2004) found that specific immigrant groups in the United States that were more frequently targeted by negative ethnic slurs actually had higher suicide rates—a tragic reminder of the power of hateful speech in people's lives. Does being stigmatized inevitably drag down the individual, as this finding suggests? Or can a group become a source of pride for its members even when others look down on them? What kinds of strategies can people use, either as individuals or on behalf of an entire group, to escape or overcome their stigmatization? This part of the chapter will consider all these questions.

Most of us belong to one or more groups that society devalues and stigmatizes, at least in certain contexts—women, people of color, the elderly, recent immigrants, people with AIDS, the overweight, disabled people, the unemployed, the addicted; the list seems endless. If you cannot think of any negatively regarded groups that you belong to yourself, perhaps reading the questions in Table 6.1 will give you a sense of what others experience.

We Are Stigmatized: Effects on What We Do and How We Feel

Negative stereotypes about the abilities of a group's members can become self-fulfilling, actually harming the members' performances. Belonging to a devalued group also poses a threat to self-esteem.

Effects on Performance. Realizing that others think that your group does not have what it takes to perform well is a psychological burden in itself. However, research shows that this **stereotype threat** can actually act as a self-fulfilling prophecy, bringing about confirmation of the stereotype. To examine this process, Claude Steele and Joshua Aronson (1995) used the common stereotype that Black Americans are unintelligent and academically untalented. They gave Black and White students a difficult test, telling some that it was highly related to intellectual ability and telling others that the test was "just a laboratory exercise." When the test was described as an unimportant exercise, or when the research participants were not asked to record their race on the experimental materials, Black students performed as well as White students (when appropriate statistical adjustments were made for the students' individual levels of academic preparation, as measured by their SAT scores). But in the condition that posed a stereotype threat—when the test was said to tap intellectual ability and the student's race was explicitly identified—Black students scored more poorly than Whites. Similar effects have been found with a different group with a different stereotype about performance: women, and the idea that women are less capable than men at math (Spencer, 1994). Women perform worse than men when presented with very difficult math tests under standard instructions, but this difference vanishes if the participants are simply told that on "this particular test" research has found that there is no gender difference in performance! Stereotype threat harms performance even for members of generally high-status and nonstigmatized groups, like White males, in specific domains, such as "natural athletic ability," where negative stereotypes exist about them (Stone, 2002).

What accounts for these unsettling effects? Steele and his colleagues believe that the very knowledge that other people hold a negative stereotype about your group's performance can bring the stereotype to mind, even if you do not personally believe it. The result may be anxiety and reduced performance (Steele & Aronson, 1995). You may worry, for example, that any mistake you make will not only harm you personally, but will reflect negatively on your whole group, confirming the stereotype in the minds of observers. Simone Young, one of the first women to conduct major symphony orchestras around the world, said: "Somehow, if a man gets in front of an orchestra and does a bad job, people say 'Well, we won't have him back again.' But if a woman fails, they say, 'See what happens when you have a woman conductor'" (Tommasini, 1996). Such worries about the impact of failure on the entire group may be the underlying reason that stereotype threat reduces people's ability to hold information in memory, which can harm performance on many types of tasks (Croizet and others, 2004; Schmader & Johns, 2003; Schmader, Johns, & Forbes, 2008).

Fortunately, several potential interventions have been developed that can reduce or eliminate entirely the effects of stereotype threat on performance. One intervention involves self-affirmation. One study had White

stereotype threat
the fear of confirming others' negative stereotype of your group

Photo 6.3 Stereotype threat. Realizing that others think that your group does not have what it takes to perform well can cause stereotype threat. A number of situational factors may increase this threat. For example, being in a small minority—like being the only female student in a math class—may increase risk for stereotype threat, because one's group membership (and the associated stereotypes) are quite salient.

and Black seventh-graders complete writing assignments early in the academic year that asked them to describe either a personal value and its importance to them (the self-affirmation condition) or neutral information (Cohen & Garcia, 2008). Black students who self-affirmed, compared to those who did not, had better grade point averages in that semester. Moreover, self-affirmation reduced by half the percentage of Black students receiving a grade of D or worse, to levels that did not differ from White students. These positive effects on Black students' grade point averages were observed even two years later.

Additionally, some individuals can avoid the negative effects of stereotype threat by focusing on other group identities that are stereotyped positively in that same domain. Consider female college students, as one example. There is a prevailing stereotype that women are bad at math, but also a stereotype that college students are good at math. Thus perhaps female college students might be able to avoid stereotype threat effects on math performance if their college identity is highlighted. In one study showing this, female college students took a math test after having no identity highlighted, only their female identity highlighted, only their college student identity highlighted, or after both their college and female identities were highlighted. Women whose female identity only was highlighted performed worse than those in the no-identity condition: a classic stereotype threat effect. But, women who had their college student identity highlighted (either alone or in conjunction with their female identity) showed no deficits in their performance, as the stereotype threat effect was eliminated (Rydell, McConnell, & Beilock, 2009).

Protection against stereotype threat can also be provided by the presence of role models who exemplify high performance by members of the stereotyped group. For example, the presence of a female experimenter who is a math expert safeguards women's performance on a difficult test, although the same test elicits stereotype threat effects when the experimenter is male (Marx & Roman, 2002). For a woman, seeing a female math expert might activate her female identity, but also improves her perception of her own math ability, helping her overcome stereotype threat effects.

Finally, people are protected from stereotype threat when stereotype-relevant tasks are framed as a challenge. Recall from Chapter 4 that stressful events that are seen as controllable are perceived as challenges, rather than threats, and people's reactions to them are more productive. Thus, might framing a stereotype-threatening task as a challenge eliminate its typically negative impact on performance? The answer appears to be yes. In one study, Black schoolchildren took a math test and either reported their race before starting or after finishing. Reporting one's membership in a negatively stereotyped group can elicit threat if done before taking an intellectual test. The researchers also varied how they framed the test. Some were told that the test would accurately assess their abilities (threat), whereas others were told it would be a helpful learning opportunity (challenge). Among those who reported their race prior to taking the test, the condition that normally elicits stereotype threat effects, students scored significantly higher if the exam was framed in challenging rather than in threatening terms (Alter, Aronson, Darley, Rodriguez, & Ruble, 2010).

Effects on Self-Esteem. However negative the effects on task performance, belonging to a socially devalued group can have effects on self-esteem that are more subtle, but perhaps ultimately even more severe. Because social group membership contributes so directly to individual self-identity, belonging to a negatively regarded group can take its toll on the individual. Kenneth Clark, a distinguished social psychologist whose research contributed to the 1954 U.S. Supreme Court decision mandating school desegregation, commented, "Human beings . . . whose daily experience tells them that almost nowhere in society are they respected and granted the ordinary dignity and courtesy accorded to others, will, as a matter of course, begin to doubt their self worth" (K. B. Clark, 1965, p. 64).

Clark was right to be worried, for feelings about group membership do have a major impact on the emotional and physical well-being of members of stigmatized groups (Twenge & Crocker, 2002). One group of researchers measured Black and White students' personal self-esteem, their feelings about their group memberships, and symptoms of depression (Luhtanen & Crocker, 1992). For Whites, low personal self-esteem was the key factor that increased the risk of depression. For Blacks, in contrast, not personal but collective self-esteem—positive or negative feelings about group membership—was more strongly related to depression (Luhtanen, Blaine, & Crocker, 1991). Negative feelings arising from group membership are not limited to socially disadvantaged groups. Even members of dominant groups like men, when reminded of their group's privileges and advantages over women, can have their self-esteem lowered by feelings of guilt (Branscombe, 1998; Doosje, Branscombe, Spears, & Manstead, 1998).

Wouldn't you expect that belonging to a group that many people look down on, despise, and discriminate against would bring you down? Then consider this puzzle: Individual members of many stigmatized groups, including Blacks, people with developmental disabilities, and people who are facially disfigured, have self-esteem that is just as high as that of individuals who are not members of these groups (Crocker & Major, 1989). Clearly, at least some members of negatively regarded groups can defend and enhance their self-esteem. How are they able to value themselves in a society that devalues their groups?

HOT TOPICS IN SOCIAL PSYCHOLOGY: SPORTS DEFEATS, COLLECTIVE SELF-ESTEEM, AND UNHEALTHY BEHAVIOR

Blows to self-esteem due to an in-group's failures——even symbolic failures such as a sports defeat——can lead to unhealthy behavior as well as depression. Cornil and Chandon (2013) recently drew on food-diary data collected in a survey to demonstrate that on the day following a game in the U.S. National Football League, consumption of fatty and high-calorie foods increased in cities whose teams lost, compared to cities whose teams won or cities without an NFL team. The effect was strongest in cities whose teams were ranked as having the most devoted fan bases. A second study examined French adults who were experimentally assigned to write about either a victory or defeat of their favorite athlete or sports team. Subsequently, while completing a filler task they were invited to snack from bowls of healthy and unhealthy foods set before them. Those who had written about a defeat (compared to those who wrote about a victory) were more likely to chow down on potato chips and chocolate, rather than grapes or cherry tomatoes. In a third study, a self-affirmation manipulation eliminated the effect of a sports defeat on unhealthy eating, just as it eliminates stereotype threat effects as described earlier. All these results suggest that for sports fans, team losses can undermine collective self-esteem and cause unhealthy eating (potentially damaging their health in the long term), but that self-affirmation can protect against this threat.

Defending Individual Self-Esteem

Belonging to a group that is disliked and discriminated against by others can have a major impact on the individual. But this experience does not inevitably lead to lowered self-esteem, because people can attribute negative reactions to others' prejudice or compare themselves to fellow in-group members.

Using Attributions to Advantage. A Black person described a common dilemma to a White reporter:

> *If you go into a restaurant and get totally lousy service, you know it's for one reason. They do totally lousy service. I go into a restaurant and I get totally lousy service, I don't know why . . . Is it because we're black or is it because . . . it's a bad service person?* (Duke & Morin, 1992.)

When a member of a devalued group is treated badly, attributional ambiguity is created: The treatment might have been due to group membership. The same uncertainty arises in more significant form when group members are rejected for jobs, promotions, or bank loans. People in these situations are free to attribute others' behavior to prejudice against their group.

Attributing negative outcomes to others' prejudice against one's group instead of to one's personal failings can protect self-esteem against the negative psychological effects of failure (Crocker & Major, 1989; Crocker and others, 1998; Major, Kaiser, & McCoy, 2003). Interestingly, making attributions to group-based prejudice appears to be uniquely effective, more than attributions to other external factors. To demonstrate this point, Christian Crandall and his colleagues put male students into a brief conversation with an attractive woman (Crandall, Tsang, Harvey, & Britt, 2000). Before the conversation, the men had to eat either a mint candy or an entire clove of raw garlic. When the woman (by prearrangement) gave them negative feedback after the interaction, the men who had eaten garlic naturally tended to attribute their rejection to their breath rather than, say, their lack of social skills. Strikingly, though, making these attributions did not elevate their self-esteem. Only when participants were able to attribute others' negative feedback to prejudice against a meaningful group, rather than to a purely individual characteristic like garlic breath, did such self-protective attributions actually elevate self-esteem.

Despite its potential benefits for self-esteem, attributing negative outcomes to prejudice against one's group, like many of the self-enhancing biases described in Chapter 4, also carries important costs. First, negative feedback is sometimes realistic, and discounting it can prevent accurate self-assessment and self-improvement. Second, the strategy may breed a sense of hopelessness and a loss of control: If one always expects to be treated primarily as a group member, no personal action will make any difference. Third, members of stigmatized groups who attribute their outcomes to others' prejudice may face social penalties, a topic we will return to later (Kaiser & Miller, 2001).

Finally, attributing other people's reactions to group membership can destroy trust in positive feedback. Are praise and promotions signs of respect and admiration for one's accomplishments, or are they due to sympathy, pity, and resigned affirmative action? Research suggests that members of stigmatized groups are likely to suspect the latter— to discount positive feedback and attribute honors and accomplishments to others' efforts to appear unprejudiced. Unfortunately, these cynical views are sometimes right. Leaning over backwards to avoid seeming prejudiced, people sometimes inflate their evaluations of members of disliked out-groups compared to their ratings of in-group members who turn in the same performance (Crocker, Voelkl, Testa, & Major, 1991).

Thus, belonging to a stigmatized group can be a buffer against the chill of negative feedback, but it also barricades you from the warm pleasure usually derived from positive feedback. Perhaps it is awareness of these costs that keeps some members of stigmatized groups from making attributions to others' prejudice unless the evidence is virtually unavoidable. As we will see shortly, even people who accurately view their group as a target of societal discrimination sometimes deny that they themselves have been affected.

Making the Most of Intragroup Comparisons. Chapter 4 showed that social comparisons are an important source of self-evaluation. Thus, is it any wonder that a female middle manager in a large firm might choose to think of herself as "one of the highest-ranking women here at Acme Corporation" rather than to compare herself to the male members of top corporate management (Major, 1994)? This kind of in-group comparison

---

SOCIAL PSYCHOLOGY IN PRACTICE: ATTRIBUTIONAL AMBIGUITY IN THE WORKPLACE

Not knowing how to interpret feedback can create serious workplace problems for people with disabilities, women, and other groups. For example, if a few wheelchair users are hired at a typical business, they draw more than their fair share of attention. Like members of other groups, they may feel that their every move is scrutinized and that their behavior reflects not only on themselves but on all people with disabilities (Pettigrew & Martin, 1987).

In some cases, an employee may suspect that he or she is a token, a single group member hired in order to avoid more thoroughgoing change. Consider the dilemma this suspicion creates: In these circumstances, people find it hard to trust feedback because outcomes seem to be determined by group membership. For example, women managers who believe they were hired because of their gender show lower organizational commitment and job satisfaction and higher role stress than women who believe they were hired for their abilities (Chacko, 1982).

In an experimental demonstration of this effect, one group of men and women were told that they were selected for a leadership role because they had scored well on leadership potential tests. Another group learned that they had been selected because the experimenter "needed more" of their gender in leadership positions (Heilman, Simon, & Repper, 1987). Later, the participants learned that they had either succeeded or failed on the leadership task. As can be seen in Figure 6.7, women who thought they had been selected on the basis of gender rather than merit devalued their own leadership ability, regardless of whether they performed well or poorly as leaders. The women in this condition also reported less interest in persisting as leaders. In contrast, men did not show such self-doubts, whether they believed their selection reflected merit or gender-based preference. Members of groups that are typically devalued and discriminated against are the most at risk from attributional ambiguities involving performance feedback. Fortunately, these negative effects of group-based selection can be overcome when the role of merit (and not solely group membership) in the selection process is emphasized (Heilman, Battle, Keller, & Lee, 1998)

■■■

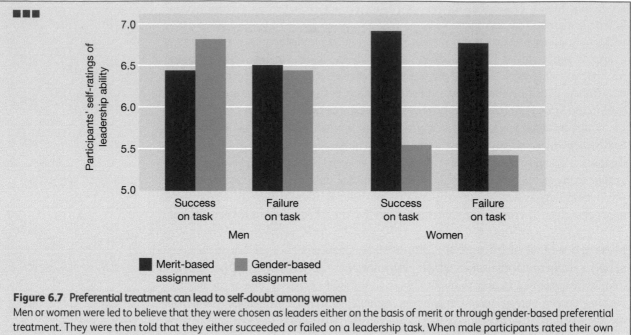

Figure 6.7 Preferential treatment can lead to self-doubt among women

Men or women were led to believe that they were chosen as leaders either on the basis of merit or through gender-based preferential treatment. They were then told that they either succeeded or failed on a leadership task. When male participants rated their own leadership ability, as the left bars show, their ratings were about equal in all conditions. However, women who thought that they had been chosen on the basis of gender doubted their own leadership ability—whether they had succeeded or failed. (Based on Heilman and others, 1987.)

is also typical of ethnic groups. One study found that Black schoolchildren who compared themselves mainly with other Blacks had higher self-esteem than those who compared themselves with White children (M. Rosenberg & Simmons, 1971). Intragroup comparisons not only boost self-esteem by showing us that we are better off than some others, they also remind us of in-group members who are doing particularly well—even if we are not. When given the opportunity to choose others for comparisons, schoolchildren from low-status groups in both New Zealand and the United States often name other in-group members who are high performers in the social, academic, or athletic domains (Aboud, 1976; Mackie, 1984). And recall that in the social comparison study cited at the beginning of this chapter, members of an artificial "minority group" got a boost from a fellow group member's good performance (Brewer & Weber, 1994); similar patterns are displayed by members of an actual minority group, African-American college students (Blanton, Crocker, & Miller, 2000).

Individual Mobility: Escaping Negative Group Membership

If self-protective strategies are insufficient, people can attempt to escape from membership in a negatively regarded group. They can psychologically disidentify with the group, for example, by playing down group memberships that reflect badly on them or by regarding themselves as atypical group members. Another option is to dissociate, to escape physically by "passing" or keeping group membership hidden "in the closet."

When strategies intended to buffer self-esteem against the implications of negative group membership prove ineffective, people may turn to more long-term solutions involving individual mobility, social creativity, or social change (Ellemers, Spears, & Doosje, 2002; Tajfel & Turner, 1979). **Individual mobility** is a strategy involving individual escape from membership in a negative group, either through disidentification (creating a psychological distance between oneself and the group) or through dissociation (physically escaping the group). Escape frees the individual from many of the costs of group membership and leaves the group's situation as a whole unchanged in the short run. Social creativity and social change strategies, in contrast, involve direct efforts to improve society's evaluation of the entire group. Note, however, that large amounts of individual mobility may also create social change over time. For example, as increasing numbers of women overcome stereotypes and discrimination to enter previously male-dominated occupations, their actions may, over time, alter societal stereotypes of women. This is because that the roles typically held by group members often shape stereotypes of the group (Eagly, 1987).

individual mobility
the strategy of individual escape, either physical or psychological, from a stigmatized group

Disidentification: Putting the Group at a Psychological Distance.

Individual mobility can be purely psychological, as when people disidentify, or minimize their personal connections to the group. One strategy is to avoid reminders of membership in a stigmatized group, as a laboratory study demonstrated (C. R. Snyder, Lassegard, & Ford, 1986). Students participated in a group problem-solving session and each group received success feedback, failure feedback, or no feedback at all. The experimenter then announced that they could take home team badges that advertised their group membership. Would team performance influence pride of membership? Apparently so. Over half of the members of groups that succeeded or received no feedback took badges home. But only 9% of those on a losing team welcomed the opportunity to announce their membership in it.

People can also disidentify from a group by publicly criticizing and devaluing an in-group member's poor performance. This reaction, termed the black sheep effect (Marques & Yzerbyt, 1988), makes it clear that the critic regards the poor performance as unrepresentative of the group. For example, imagine that you (a law student) have to evaluate speeches given by a fellow law student and by a philosophy student. If the law student's speech was third-rate, your self-categorization with him would put you in an uncomfortable situation. In these circumstances, you might be inclined to downgrade the in-group speaker, rating him even more negatively than an out-group member who performed equally poorly. By doing so, you will make it clear that this in-group member's performance is not representative of your group. Marques and Yzerbyt (1988) obtained exactly this pattern of results. People rated successful in-group members higher, and poorly performing in-group members lower, compared with out-group members. When the previously cheering fans turn to booing and hissing the home team's losses with even more enthusiasm, perhaps part of their motivation is to psychologically distance themselves from poor performance (Branscombe, Wann, Noel, & Coleman, 1993; Lewis & Sherman, 2010).

Yet a third way of disidentifying is to consider oneself to be an exception rather than a typical group member. For example, many women acknowledge that women in general are discriminated against but insist that discrimination does not affect them personally

(Crosby, Pufall, Snyder, O'Connell, & Whalen, 1989; Ellemers, 2001). The same pattern of beliefs is found among many other groups, including French-speakers in Quebec and immigrants to Canada from Haiti and India (D. M. Taylor, Wright, Moghaddam, & Lalonde, 1990). Of course, there could be many reasons for this belief, and it is certainly possible that some individual group members are fortunate enough to escape discrimination personally. But the belief is held most often by those who identify least strongly with their groups, suggesting that the belief serves, at least in part, as a psychological distancing mechanism (H. J. Smith & Spears, 1996).

Dissociation: Putting the Group at a Physical Distance. Whereas disidentifying takes place in the mind, dissociating involves actual escape from a disadvantaged group or concealment of group membership. This form of individual mobility occurs, for example, when immigrants cast off their cultural and linguistic heritage and become indistinguishable members of a new nationality. Gays or lesbians who are "in the closet" are concealing their group membership. A related strategy of some historical importance is "passing," a pattern in which light-skinned individuals of African ancestry adopted a White identity, or American Jews adopted anglicized names and the customs of Gentile society (K. Lewin, 1948).

How successful is escape as a solution to membership in a negatively evaluated group? The answer seems to be that it is a mixed blessing. The individual does reap some personal benefits, such as freedom from discrimination, but for some, these benefits may be outweighed by the strategy's potential costs. New members of a group often suffer the isolation of not being thought quite the same as those "born to it." In addition, concealing group membership can be lonely and dangerous. The heartache of having to join in the laughter at antigay or racist jokes might be surpassed only by anxiety at being "outed." To deal with the problems of living with a concealed stigmatized identity, a study suggests that the potential anonymity provided by the internet can help. Results found that online discussions on sites devoted to group support can be an important source of identity for those with concealable stigmatized group memberships (such as drug addiction or homosexuality). Comparing people who participate in such groups with those in similar support groups for nonconcealable stigmas (such as stuttering or being overweight), Katelyn McKenna and John Bargh (1998) found that online support groups involving concealable characteristics were more important to the lives of their members and had greater impact on their members' emotions and behavior. In effect, participation in the discussions increased members' acceptance of their identity, replacing feelings of isolation and just being different.

Finally, those who conceal their group membership give up opportunities to influence others' thinking about their group. Long-time U.S. Representative Barney Frank kept his homosexuality secret when he was first elected to Congress. He recalls that when he lobbied his colleagues on gay issues, "They would say 'Ah, you're right. But you know, it's not that important.' The pain gay people felt was unknown. We were hiding it from them. How the hell are they supposed to know when we were making damn sure they didn't?" (Schmalz, 1992).

Disidentification and dissociation are not viable options for many group members. Instead of separating from the group, either psychologically or physically, group members can directly seek to change society's negative evaluation of their group.

Social Creativity: Redefining Group Membership as Positive

Sometimes group members attempt to change society's evaluation of their in-group, through redefining group characteristics in positive terms.

When individual escape is difficult, a group that is faced with a negative identity can introduce and emphasize alternative dimensions on which the in-group is superior. A group of French boys at a summer camp showed this kind of **social creativity** when they found themselves in a hut-building contest with another team that had better construction materials (Lemaine, 1974). Realizing their inability to construct a large and sturdy structure, they created an elaborate garden around their mediocre cabin and asked the judges to consider them the garden-building winners. By introducing a new dimension of competition, the group maintained its superiority and distinctiveness. Similarly, players on the last-place team in an ice hockey league cannot make a claim on skill and competitiveness, but they may be able to think of themselves as "cleaner" and more sportsmanlike than other teams. For one team, adopting this belief served to maintain the players' self-esteem, even though it seemed to correspond very little with reality— observers and coaches viewed the last-place team as one of the "dirtiest" in the league (Lalonde, 1992). In studies involving both laboratory-created and real-life groups, Jackson and others (L. A. Jackson, Sullivan, Harnish, & Hodge, 1996) found that social creativity strategies were used more when the group boundaries were relatively fixed. When boundaries were permeable, individual mobility became a preferred strategy.

Some women show social creativity by accepting society's definition of femininity and seeking a positive group identity through its distinctive positive characteristics. For example, they may emphasize dimensions of achievement that they view as specifically feminine, such as nurturing or peacemaking (Branscombe, 1998). Along the same lines, a gay pride movement has emerged, with an emphasis on celebrating the accomplishments of gays and lesbians, particularly in artistic and cultural fields. "Black is beautiful!" was one group's statement that distinctive characteristics that have been derogated by the majority, such as skin color, language, or cultural heritage, can be redefined as a source of pride (Bourhis and others, 1978). These social creativity strategies, however, may not lead in any direct way to lasting changes in a group's position in society. For example, emphasizing women's positive qualities as nurturers or peacemakers may proclaim the value of feminine qualities and strengthen collective self-esteem, but it does not directly challenge social definitions of gender roles. It may even unintentionally provide rationales and justifications for the continued exclusion of women from positions of economic or political power. Moreover, those who successfully redefine their group memberships as positive may, ironically, then see little need to fight against or protest problems their groups face. For example, in one study, women were reminded of their economic disadvantages in comparison to men. Then, some women answered questions about how women compared to men in terms of their social warmth. A common social stereotype is that women are warmer than men, and thus, this gave these women a chance to see their own group in a positive way relative to men. Results showed that, indeed, women in this condition reported that women were warmer than men. Importantly, though, answering this question led them to report fewer intentions to engage in actions to eliminate women's inequality—like attend a demonstration or sign a petition (Becker,

social creativity

the strategy of introducing and emphasizing new dimensions of social comparison, on which a negatively regarded group can see itself as superior

2012). Thus, those who engage in social creativity may be less motivated to engage in direct challenges to group discrimination, the strategy of social change.

Social Change: Changing the Intergroup Context

Finally, group members may engage in direct intergroup conflict or struggle to achieve equitable treatment. Strategies that reduce prejudice do not necessarily lead to better objective outcomes for groups, and strategies that improve outcomes often increase prejudice.

social change
the strategy of improving the overall societal situation of a stigmatized group

social competition
the strategy of directly seeking to change the conditions that disadvantage the in-group, for example by building group solidarity and challenging the out-group

As we have discussed in this chapter, members of devalued and stigmatized groups are often disliked and subjected to discrimination. Not surprisingly, members of such social groups often want to eliminate the negative prejudice and stigma they face. But, being liked is not the final goal. Ultimately, being treated equally and fairly is just as important, if not more so. To achieve better and more equitable treatment, groups may engage in various strategies to better their positions in society.

Strikes, protest marches, and struggles in the courts and legislatures to outlaw discrimination are familiar tactics of such groups. These actions reflect a strategy of confronting and challenging the hierarchy of group domination. **Social change** refers to the strategy of improving the overall societal situation of a group held in low esteem. Social change is generally preferred by people who identify strongly with their group, see individual mobility as impossible, and respond with anger to the unjust situation of their group (van Zomeren, Postmes, & Spears, 2008). Rather than changing only their personal situation, they wish to, and believe they can, change the way society regards their group as a whole (Ellemers, Spears, & Doosje, 2002; Tajfel & Turner, 1979). The main tactic employed by these determined group members is social competition.

Social Competition. Sometimes groups attempt to build in-group solidarity and oppose domination by the out-group, by taking direct action to improve the relative position, status, power, and resources of the in-group. When they do so, they are engaging in **social competition** by directly seeking to change the conditions that disadvantage them. This is the strategy that leads to in-group bias, when a group member gives the in-group an edge over the out-group by allocating his or her group more resources, evaluating in-group products more positively, and judging the in-group to be morally and socially superior. Of course, what looks like opportunity for advancement to disadvantaged groups often appears as a threat to a dominant group. Earlier, we saw that dominant groups respond with increased

Photo 6.4 Fighting for social change. A gay rights activist in Hong Kong protests Russia's anti-gay laws at the start of the Sochi Olympics. Protests like this attempt to improve the status of entire groups, in this case, gays and lesbians.

levels of prejudice and discrimination against out-groups when they see those groups as threats. Thus, social competition strategies are likely to provoke a backlash from powerful groups.

A frequent form of backlash is that when disadvantaged group members do push for change, they are often penalized. Indeed, even claiming that one has been subject to discrimination can lead to bad treatment. In one study, for example, perceivers labeled those who claimed they had been discriminated against as "complainers," even when there was good evidence to support such a claim (Kaiser & Miller, 2001). Calling attention to unfair treatment seems to be a necessary first step in engagement in social competition tactics. Yet, doing so may increase intergroup hostility.

Groups may be undeterred by backlash and engage in these strategies when they believe they can make a difference and improve their situation in concrete ways (Tajfel & Turner, 1979), when their members strongly identify with the group (Ellemers and others, 2002; B. Simon and others, 1998), and when they feel the group-based emotion of anger (van Zomeren, Leach, & Spears, 2012). Collective actions to advance a group's interests are often most effective when group members stick together, emphasizing their homogeneity in attitudes and values (Doosje, Ellemers, & Spears, 1995; Simon & Brown, 1987).

Social competition strategies take many forms, including drives for self-sufficiency, autonomy, and separatism among racial or ethnic minorities such as French Canadians or Basques in Spain. Everywhere in society, lobbies and advocacy organizations seek social changes that will benefit particular groups. The American Association of Retired Persons and Gray Panthers mobilize efforts on behalf of seniors. Groups such as the Coalition of Citizens with Disabilities and Mainstream, Inc. lead "wheelchair rebellions." Organizations such as the Gay and Lesbian Alliance Against Defamation actively combat negative portrayals of homosexuals in the media while lobbying for open and equal opportunities for their group. Individuals as well as organizations can engage in social competition strategies, for example, by creating informal associations of group members aimed at community building and mutual support. Individuals can also speak out against stereotypes, prejudice, and discrimination whenever they encounter them: in ethnic slurs, sexist jokes, or "old boy" hiring practices in organizations.

Social Competition or Prejudice Reduction: Mutually Exclusive Goals? Members of devalued groups face a difficult dilemma. They want to be liked and free from negative prejudice, but also want to be treated fairly—having equal access to educational opportunities, equal pay, and so forth. This is why they often engage in various forms of social competition. Unfortunately, research shows that strategies that can reduce prejudice toward groups often undermine desires for social competition, and conversely engagement in social competition often increases group dislike.

For example, as discussed in Chapter 5, positive contact between groups can improve intergroup attitudes and reduce prejudice (Pettigrew & Tropp, 2006). But doing so, it turns out, may also smooth over perceptions of group inequality. Tamar Saguy and colleagues (2009) argue that positive intergroup interactions are effective, in part, because they encourage the interacting groups to re-conceptualize themselves as members of one common group that share similarities. Though this is helpful in improving attitudes between the two groups, it comes with a potential cost: focusing on similarities may mean ignoring true differences between groups, such as one group's socially disadvantaged position, relative lack of access to resources, and so forth. Thus, while positive contact can improve attitudes, it may simultaneously shift attention away from the inequitable conditions facing the disadvantaged group. If the disadvantaged group perceives greater equity between the groups than is real, their motivation to agitate for social change will be diminished.

In a study illustrating this process, these researchers (Saguy and others, 2009) created two three-person groups in the lab. One group was randomly assigned to an advantaged position, able to decide how an important resource, extra research credits, would be allocated between the groups. The other group lacked such power. Members of the two groups then interacted with each other in one of two ways. Some were told to discuss "similar steps the groups went through in this study;" in other words, ways the two groups were alike. Others discussed "differences between the tasks the groups will do next," discussions that would highlight one group's advantage over the other. After interaction, members of both groups rated how they felt about the out-group and how much they thought about the inequality of the groups during the interaction. Similarity-focused group interaction led to better intergroup attitudes but also fewer thoughts about group inequality, compared to difference-focused interaction. Moreover, in the similarity-focused condition, disadvantaged group members expected to be treated fairly in the distribution of credits. But confounding these favorable expectations, the advantaged group discriminated against the out-group by assigning more credits to themselves than to the out-group, equally in both interaction conditions. Thus, positive intergroup interaction improved intergroup attitudes, but also created unrealistic expectations of fairness.

A follow-up study used real groups in a real conflict: Israeli Arabs and Jews (Saguy and others, 2009). Arabs living in Israel were asked to rate how much contact they had with Jews, how they felt about Jews, how fair they perceived Jews to be, how unjust they considered the inequality between the groups, and how much they supported various social change initiatives to create more equitable treatment for Arabs living in Israel. More contact went along with better attitudes toward Jews and greater perceptions that Jews are fair, and less intense feelings that the inequality between the groups was unjust. Perhaps most importantly, because greater contact reduced feelings of injustice, it also resulted in less desire to work for social change. Thus, as we can see from these studies, contact may reduce prejudice, but might simultaneously undermine a disadvantaged group's support for social change initiatives.

Results like these bear on the types of policies that might be supported by members of disadvantaged groups and those who want to support them by fostering greater equality in society. For example, some advocate for a "color-blind" ideology, the idea that race should not affect the way people are treated, and should therefore be disregarded and even actively ignored (Schofield, 1986). This ideology fits well with the emphasis on individual achievement that prevails in individualist cultures, so it has a strong appeal to many people. It may be an appropriate and desirable approach in organizations where job performance can be objectively measured and used to rank and reward people independent of their race or other group memberships. However, some have argued that the use of this ideology is simply a means to reduce conflict between groups and ignore real group inequities (Dovidio and others, 2009). This fear may be well founded given the findings just described. Focusing on similarities between groups, which is what a color-blind ideology encourages, does seem to improve intergroup feelings, and might ease intergroup conflict, a topic we will discuss further in Chapter 13. But these approaches may also impede the desire or ability of disadvantaged group members to achieve real changes in their standing in society.

One Goal, Many Strategies

Those who most strongly identify with a group and see group boundaries as fixed tend to choose social change rather than individual mobility strategies. However, no single approach is always best for dealing with a negatively evaluated group membership, just as no single coping strategy is uniformly the best way to handle threats to the individual self.

As you can see in Figure 6.8, there is more than one way to cope with the threat to social identity posed by negative group memberships. No one way is always better or worse than others; like the strategies for coping with threats to the individual self that were described in Chapter 4, the effectiveness of each method depends on many factors. The

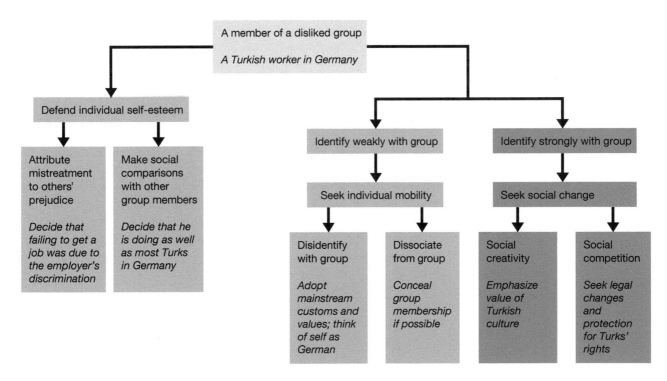

Figure 6.8 How can I value myself when others devalue my group?
Members of groups that suffer dislike and discrimination try to defend their individual self-esteem. In addition, they may seek escape from their group through individual mobility or seek to improve the whole group's situation through social change, depending on the strength of their identification with the group.

size of a group, the resources its members control, the ease or difficulty of concealing or changing group membership, and the personal significance of group membership for each individual will all influence how people respond (Eberhard & Fiske, 1996; Ellemers and others, 2002). It is no surprise, then, that different groups tend to prefer distinct strategies for coping when others disdain and discriminate against them (Frable, 1997).

The two most important factors that affect people's choices among strategies are the strength of their group identification and their perceptions of the possibility of individual mobility (Tajfel & Turner, 1979; Wright, Taylor, & Moghaddam, 1990). The importance of group identification was illustrated in studies with Dutch university students conducted by Naomi Ellemers and her colleagues (Ellemers, Spears, & Doosje, 1997). Students who were led to identify strongly with a low-status group were less likely to seek individual mobility out of the group. They also perceived their group as homogeneous, a display of group solidarity that is associated with collective action such as social competition. Other work replicates these sorts of effects. For example, French students watched a video clip of their national rugby team losing. Those who highly identified with the team were more apt to endorse social competition responses, whereas those who were less identified were more apt to endorse individual mobility (Bernache-Assollant and others, 2010). The key role of the perceived possibility of individual mobility was underlined in studies showing that people prefer to seek individual mobility out of a disadvantaged group whenever they see that as possible (Wright and others, 1990). They do this even if they knew that only a trivial or token number of individuals would be permitted to escape from their original group. Only when the group members realized that absolutely no mobility was possible did they turn to more disruptive social competition strategies.

At times, multiple forces push and pull people in different directions. For example, many African Americans feel a fundamental tension between the desire to maintain in-group solidarity and the desire for individual advancement in White-dominated society. Deep, often emotional disagreements have sprung up between advocates of various strategies. It seems to some that "in order to be accepted by Whites they must give up everything that is Black; that if they played basketball before they now have to play golf" (L. Williams, 1991). Yet those who seek professional advancement sometimes "fear that if you are successful you will be too alienated from Black people," according to Cornel West, a Princeton University professor (Cary, 1992). The different strategies of individual mobility, social creativity, and social change often contradict each other. Nevertheless, all aim at improving the group's situation and any one of them may be appropriate for a particular individual or group, given the unique social situation.

In thinking about the ways in which people cope with being a likable member of a devalued group, you may have noticed some similarities with the ways in which people deal with meeting a likable member of a disliked group (discussed in Chapter 5). For example, if you are a member of a disliked group, you might want to distance yourself from it psychologically or physically; similarly, if you meet a likeable member of a disliked group, you might psychologically distance them from their group, perhaps by seeing them as part of a subtype. These parallels, detailed in Table 6.2, are no accident. They reflect the fundamental principle that group memberships influence our thoughts and feelings about individual group members, whether the individual is someone else or the self.

TABLE 6.2   Three Types of Responses to a Likable Member of a Disliked Group

Response	Knowing a likable member of a disliked group	Being a likable member of a disliked group
See the individual as unrepresentative of the group; separate beliefs about the group from beliefs about the individual.	Exclude the individual from the group by seeing him or her as a special type of the general category (*subtyping*) or by seeing him or her as extremely different from typical category members (*contrasting*).	Remove the self from the group, either psychologically by down-playing group membership as an aspect of the self (*disidentification*) or physically by escaping from or concealing group membership (*dissociation*).
See the individual as representative of the group; use beliefs about the individual to modify beliefs about the group.	See the likable individual as a typical group member, improving the evaluation of the group (*stereotype change* and *prejudice reduction*).	Attempt to make society's evaluation of the group more positive (*social change*). Interpret the group and its history, culture, and other distinctive aspects in positive terms (*social creativity*) or struggle to change the group's generally low status and power in society (*social competition*).

CONCLUDING COMMENTS

Social identity is central to every aspect of social behavior, just as this chapter occupies a central place in this text. The concept of social identity, as discussed in this chapter, makes clear how intertwined are people's knowledge about groups, their conceptions of themselves, and their impressions of others. Group memberships not only shape the ways we perceive our own and other groups, but also fundamentally affect the ways we perceive other individuals and ourselves. Not only do we see ourselves in group terms and act in accordance with in-group standards and norms, but as in-groups become part of the self, we think about our groups in many of the same ways that we think about ourselves as individuals. For example, various biases lead us to value me and mine—to view not only ourselves but also our groups through rose-colored glasses.

Social identities anchor us in the social world by connecting us to other people— people we otherwise might have little reason to trust, to like, or even to know at all. Because relationships are encouraged and even made possible by our assumptions about what we have in common, group belonging and identification provide a truly social basis for thinking, feeling, and acting. Thus, understanding group membership is vital for understanding many aspects of social behavior. As you will see in later chapters, the effects of our groups on our beliefs, opinions, and behavior; on our close and loving relationships with other individuals; and on the ways we act in face-to-face groups all depend crucially on the ways we accept and identify with in-groups. No wonder, then, that we often feel lost and adrift when we lose important social identities, as when we are expelled or fired, or when our social identities are threatened, for example, when we experience discrimination and realize that others devalue our group. We may still be the individuals we always were, but important parts of our whole selves have been damaged or have disappeared because our place in the social world is lost or threatened.

Negative views of out-groups sprout from the same roots as people's positive views of themselves and their own kind. The biased stereotypes of groups that were discussed in Chapter 5 are only part of the underpinning of prejudice and discrimination. Disregard and maltreatment of others are supported by our social and psychological investment in our own groups as well. When group membership is most important, out-group members are only faceless outsiders; their individuality is of little concern to us. We see "them" as all the same and as totally different from us in their goals, values, and beliefs. As we will see, this way of thinking is an important basis for both aggression and inter-group conflict.

Perhaps understanding how group membership can contribute to hurtful and destructive human behavior will help provide solutions to some of these problems by redefining in-groups and out-groups. Whether the effects of social identity are good or bad, the fundamental fact remains that our sense of self extends beyond our skin to encompass some people and exclude others, with powerful implications for how we see and treat others and ourselves.

SUMMARY

Categorizing Oneself as a Group Member. Group membership can turn into a **social identity** that links individuals with others, when the group becomes a significant part of a person's self-concept through the process of **self-categorization**. People learn about the groups to which they belong in the same ways that they learn the characteristics of other groups: through observation of other group members or from the culture.

Knowledge about group memberships may be activated by direct reminders, such as group labels; by the presence of out-group members; by being a minority; or by inter-group conflict. Group membership is particularly significant in some cultures and for some individuals, who tend to see the world in terms of that group membership.

Me, You, and Them: Effects of Social Categorization. Activated knowledge about a group membership has multiple effects on people's self-concept and self-esteem. The group's typical characteristics become standards for members' behavior. Group member-ship also influences people's moods and self-esteem, as they feel bad about their group's failures or **BIRG (bask in reflected glory)** when their group succeeds. Relatively small groups typically have the greatest effects on their members' feelings.

When group membership is highly accessible, people see other in-group members as similar in their central group-linked characteristics. However, extensive personal interaction (when group membership is not salient) also provides knowledge about their unique and diverse personal characteristics. People like in-group members and tend to treat them in fair, humane, and altruistic ways because people see them as similar to themselves in their goals and interests.

In contrast, the **out-group homogeneity effect** causes people to see out-groups as uniform and homogeneous. People also dislike, devalue, and discriminate against

CHAPTER 6 THEMES

■ **Construction of Reality**
We construct the self using our knowledge about our social groups.

■ **Pervasiveness of Social Influence**
This construction process imports social influences into the very core of the self.

■ **Seeking Connectedness**
Group memberships that we share with others are rewarding.

■ **Valuing Me and Mine**
We positively value the groups to which we belong as well as our individual self.

out-group members, depending on the extent to which they are seen as threatening the in-group. When the out-group is simply different, it elicits mild dislike. This effect can be demonstrated even in the **minimal intergroup situation,** in which mere categorization results in mild discrimination against the out-group. **Social identity theory** argues that people's motivation to derive positive self-esteem from their group memberships is one driving force behind in-group bias in these settings.

When the out-group is seen as outdoing the in-group, this more serious threat results in resentment, dislike, and overt discrimination. Out-groups that are seen as severe threats to the in-group elicit murderous hatred, severe discrimination, aggression, or **moral exclusion**.

They Don't Like Us: Consequences of Belonging to Negatively Perceived Groups.

Negative stereotypes about a group's ability can become self-fulfilling, actually harming the group members' performances when **stereotype threat** is present. In addition, belonging to a **stigmatized** group that others dislike or discriminate against poses a threat to self-esteem. However, people can defend self-esteem by attributing negative reactions to others' prejudice or by making most of their social comparisons against fellow in-group members.

If these strategies are insufficient to protect individual self-esteem, people can use **individual mobility** strategies: attempting to escape their membership in a stigmatized group. They can psychologically disidentify with the group, for example, by playing down group membership, by regarding themselves as atypical group members, or by strongly criticizing poorly performing in-group members. Another option is to dissociate: to escape physically, by "passing" or keeping group membership hidden "in the closet."

Sometimes group members adopt **social creativity** strategies, attempting to alter society's evaluation of their in-group by redefining group characteristics in positive terms. Finally, they may seek **social change** by engaging in **social competition**, direct intergroup conflict or struggle to achieve equitable treatment. Strategies that reduce prejudice do not necessarily lead to better objective outcomes for groups, and strategies that improve outcomes often increase prejudice. Those who most strongly identify with a group and see group boundaries as fixed tend to choose social change rather than individual mobility strategies. However, no single approach is always best for dealing with a negatively evaluated group membership, just as no single coping strategy is uniformly the best way to handle threats to the individual self.

ATTITUDES AND ATTITUDE CHANGE

attitude
a mental representation that summarizes an individual's evaluation of a particular person, group, thing, action, or idea

What do the following events have in common? In countries from every continent, committees campaign to make sure that their nation is chosen as the host for the next World Cup soccer championships. In Spain, fast food franchise McDonald's pays for pop-up internet ads featuring videos of basketball star Ricky Rubio to promote its EuroAhorro menu items. In Guangzhou, China, and Seattle, USA, worried parents enroll their teenage sons in "internet addiction" programs to try to change their children's fascination with social media. And on street corners, classrooms, and cafes near you, religious groups seek converts, scientists dispute evidence for a well-established theory, and friends argue over the best movie to see.

In all these cases someone is trying to develop, strengthen, or change the attitudes of others. An **attitude** is a summary evaluation of an attitude object. Attitude objects include the self, others, things, actions, events, or ideas: any aspect of the social world (W. J. McGuire, 1985; Zanna & Rempel, 1988). People can—and do—hold attitudes about just about anything. You may realize from this definition that we have already dealt with attitudes in earlier chapters. Liking for others, discussed in Chapter 3, is an attitude about other individuals; self-esteem (Chapter 4) is an attitude about ourselves; and prejudice (Chapters 5 and 6) is an attitude toward our own or other groups. Although Chapters 7 and 8 focus on attitudes about objects, issues, events, ideas, and actions, what we say in these two chapters can also be applied to evaluations of ourselves, other people, and social groups. Because attitudes are so pervasive, the study of attitudes and **attitude change**—the process by which attitudes form and change by the association of positive or negative information with the attitude object—has been a central concern in social psychology since the discipline began. Both this chapter and the next focus on how attitudes form and change, and on the important impact attitudes can have on what we think, feel, and do.

This chapter begins by describing how social psychologists measure attitudes, and then why and how we form them. Knowing the kind of information attitudes are based on gives us clues about how to create, strengthen, or change attitudes through persuasion. **Persuasion** is the deliberate attempt to bring about attitude change by communication. As you will see, persuasion attempts can be so subtle that they fly under our radar or so obviously direct that we know we are being manipulated. They may appeal to cold logic or play on emotions, elicit a knee-jerk response or require careful thought. What makes some attempts to persuade us effective while others fail to change our minds? It won't surprise you to know that the answer lies in the way people process persuasive communications. As you will see in the second section of the chapter, how we consider persuasive information can affect what kinds of appeals are effective, for what kinds of people, and under what kinds of conditions. And as you will see in the final section of the chapter, because what makes a persuasive appeal effective depends on how we process it, whether we are persuaded or whether we resist is often largely up to us.

attitude change
the process by which attitudes form and change by the association of positive or negative information with the attitude object

persuasion
the process of forming, strengthening, or changing attitudes by communication

ATTITUDES AND THEIR ORIGINS

Do you agree with laws that ban women from serving in military combat units? Should more Eastern European countries be allowed to join the European Union? Do you think people should be allowed to talk on their cell phones while driving? The answers people give to these kinds of questions reveal their attitudes, or evaluations of attitude objects. Researchers have developed a number of measurement techniques to do the same thing. Assessing attitudes leads to one clear conclusion: people have attitudes about pretty much everything! Why do we make these kinds of judgments? And how do we come to have attitudes in the first place?

In Chapter 9 we will discuss conformity, which also brings about attitude change, but doesn't require deliberate communication.

Measuring Attitudes

Researchers infer attitudes from people's reactions to attitude objects. Such reactions can range from subtle uncontrollable evaluative reactions that people are unaware of, to more deliberate and controllable expressions of support or opposition. Assessing these different reactions shows that implicit attitudes can sometimes differ from explicit attitudes.

Because attitudes are mental representations, they cannot be weighed, watched, or observed under microscopes. Attitude researchers infer attitudes from how people react to attitude objects. Two aspects of people's reactions are important: attitude direction —whether the attitude is favorable, neutral, or unfavorable—and attitude intensity— whether the attitude is moderate or extreme.

The most straightforward way to measure attitudes is through self-report: asking people to say what they think. Consumer surveys, political polls, and even our daily exchange of opinions with friends and family are forms of self-reports. Social psychologists usually get people to report their attitudes using attitude scales. An attitude scale is a series of questions that provides precise and reliable information about how strongly people agree or disagree with, favor or oppose, or like or dislike any attitude object (Dawes & Smith, 1985). Respondents choose among options that range from an extreme negative evaluation through a neutral point to an extreme positive evaluation, thus assessing direction and intensity. Researchers have to be careful constructing such scales. The attitudes that people report can be easily influenced by how such questions are worded. In the United States, for example, where freedom to do as one chooses is an

You'll remember that a mental representation, first discussed in Chapter 3, page 56, is a body of knowledge—about people, the self, other groups, or an attitude object, that an individual has stored in memory.

important concern, asking "Should students be allowed to pray in public schools?" might well yield different responses than asking "Should students be forbidden to pray in public schools?" Expressed attitudes can also be influenced by the response alternatives people are given. For example, if asked to rate a particular politician on a scale from 0 to 10, many more people report an evaluation on the negative half of the scale (using the numbers 0–4) than they do if asked to rate the same politician on a scale ranging from –5 to +5 (apparently no one wants to use those negative numbers). Researchers need to keep in mind that the words they use and the response options they offer can subtly change the attitudes people report (Schwarz, 1999).

Social psychologists also use observations of behavior to gauge attitudes. For example, they might infer attitude direction from whether people volunteer to stuff envelopes for a campaign to save the spotted owl, and intensity from how many envelopes they are willing to stuff (Deci, 1975; Wilson & Dunn, 1986). Many kinds of behaviors can tell researchers about attitudes: how closely people approach attitude objects, how often they choose or use them, how much they are willing to risk or spend for them, how much time or effort they expend to promote or obtain them, and whether they are willing to try to persuade another person in favor of or against a given attitude object.

explicit attitude

the attitude that people openly and deliberately express about an attitude object in self-report or by behavior

The attitudes that people openly and deliberately express in self-report or by behavior are **explicit attitudes**. When people suspect that their attitudes differ from what most other people think, or from what other people think is good, they can control their explicit attitudes to hide or deny their true attitudes (D. T. Campbell, 1963). Just as people might not want to admit that they have a negative attitude—a prejudice—against some social group, they typically don't like to admit that they favor underage drinking and unprotected sex, or that they think it's just fine to illegally download music and movies from the internet.

Attitude researchers have developed a number of techniques to get around people's desire to hide what they really think. Some self-report techniques guarantee anonymity, so participants can be honest because the opinions they express won't be linked to them. Other techniques increase the honesty of participants' explicit attitude reports by convincing them that their "real" physiological reactions about issues such as drug and alcohol use, for example, are being measured, even when that's not true (Quigley-Fernandez & Tedeschi, 1978; Werch, Lundstrum, & Moore, 1989). Here's how this technique works. Experimenters secretly find out the participant's attitude on one not-so-sensitive topic, perhaps from a previous attitude questionnaire. They then instruct the participant to try to trick the "attitude detection" machinery about that topic and show that the "equipment" can catch the participant in the lie. Convinced that their real attitudes can be detected, participants tend to tell the truth about sensitive topics. Other techniques assess attitudes so subtly that participants are not aware of revealing their opinions (Hammond, 1948; Vargas, von Hippel, & Petty, 2004). Supposed tests of obscure general knowledge ("Did Russian President Vladimir Putin gain an A or a C grade average at Leningrad State University?) often reflect attitudes (supporters of Mr. Putin might guess that he earned the higher grade, for example).

implicit attitude

automatic and uncontrollable positive or negative evaluation of an attitude object

Researchers have also come up with implicit measures to reveal people's **implicit attitudes**—their automatic and uncontrollable evaluations of objects as positive or negative. One kind of implicit measure assesses muscle activity around the mouth and brows using facial electromyography (EMG). Because such muscle activity is involuntary, researchers can gauge both the intensity and the direction of attitudes on such sensitive issues as alcohol abuse or pre-marital sex regardless of respondents' overt reactions (Cacioppo & Petty, 1979; Cacioppo, Petty, Losch, & Kim, 1986). Other implicit measures use the time people take to make a particular response to an attitude object to tell researchers whether people see the object as positive or negative, regardless of what they say about it (Greenwald, McGhee, & Schwartz, 1998). If an object is evaluated positively, for example, people automatically take longer to respond to it if it is seen with or associated to something negative, even though they are not aware of doing so. These subtle and difficult-to-control differences in response time are seen in priming and IAT measures, and reveal implicit attitudes.

Implicit measures sometimes reveal that people's implicit attitudes—their automatic evaluations of objects—are different from their explicit attitudes—the attitudes they overtly express about them (Fazio & Olson, 2003). We discussed these same discrepancies in Chapter 5, when we discussed the notion that people sometimes verbally report liking a social group on an explicit measure, but then show negative associations with that group on an implicit measure (such as the IAT). Differences between implicit and explicit attitudes can emerge for any attitude object, not just for social groups. For example, almost everyone has negative implicit attitudes toward spiders, yet many people may say they feel "just fine" about them (de Jong, van den Hout, Rietbroek, & Huijding, 2003). So different versions of attitudes (one negative, one "just fine," for example) about the same object might exist at the same time.

Such differences don't mean that implicit attitudes are pure measures of what people "really" think about attitude objects, while their explicit attitudes are designed to dissemble or distort. Implicit attitudes simply reflect the positive or negative associations that people have—for whatever reason—to an object. People might be unaware that they have these associations, and the valence of the associations, positive or negative, might be unwanted. Explicit attitudes are more likely to reflect the evaluations that people deliberately endorse, and these include the attitudes they want to have, not just the ones they want to be seen as having. For example, a positive "just fine" explicit attitude might reflect a commendable real overcoming of a negative implicit phobia or prejudice and not just an insincere expression of a socially desirable position (Greenwald, Poehlman, Uhlmann, & Banaji, 2009; Han, Czellar, Olson, & Fazio, 2010; Rydell & McConnell, 2010). So both implicit and explicit measures of attitudes have important things to tell us about how and why evaluations form and how and why they change, the topics of concern in this chapter. It turns out that implicit and explicit attitudes can also have different effects on behavior, a topic covered in the next chapter. By learning more about when and why implicit and explicit attitudes differ, social psychologists learn much more about the causes and consequences of attitudes.

The ways that subtle techniques such as facial EMG, priming, and the IAT are used to measure implicit attitudes about other groups—the potentially unpopular evaluations that people might want to hide or deny—were discussed in more detail in Chapter 5. To refresh your memory about these implicit measures, how implicit and explicit measures might differ, and what that means, see Chapter 5, pages 163–167.

Attitude Function

People form attitudes about almost everything they encounter because attitudes are useful. The knowledge function and instrumental function of attitudes help people master the environment. The social identity and impression management function of attitudes express important connections with others.

knowledge function
the way an attitude contributes to mastery by organizing, summarizing, and simplifying experience with an attitude object

instrumental function
the way an attitude contributes to mastery by guiding our approach to positive objects and our avoidance of negative objects

Forming attitudes comes naturally to humans. Research including studies measuring brain activity shows that people evaluate almost everything they encounter and do so very quickly (Bargh, Chaiken, Raymond, & Hymes, 1996; Duckworth, Bargh, Garcia, & Chaiken, 2002; Stanley, Phelps, & Banaji, 2008). This is because attitudes are so useful (Katz, 1960; Maio & Olson, 2000; Smith, Bruner, & White, 1956).

First, attitudes help people master the environment, in two different ways. Attitudes serve a **knowledge function** by organizing, summarizing, and simplifying our experience, orienting us to the important characteristics of an attitude object, and providing a summary of its pluses and minuses. If we have a positive attitude toward chocolate ice cream, we can focus quickly on the positive taste and texture of any chocolate ice cream we encounter and know we'll like it (Fazio, 2000). We don't have to worry about the myriad of ways in which different chocolate ice creams might differ, or wonder how to evaluate each one. Attitudes also serve an **instrumental function**, steering us toward things that will help us achieve our goals and keeping us away from things that will hurt us (Ennis & Zanna, 2000). Inborn preferences often work this way, with positive attitudes toward sweet tastes guiding us toward sources of high nutrition and negative attitudes toward bitter tasting foods steering us away from poisonous or toxic substances. So attitudes are a quick and handy guide to whether to approach or avoid attitude objects. A positive attitude toward chocolate ice cream makes us more likely to choose it at the store, whereas a negative attitude makes us pass it over. Both the knowledge function and the instrumental function of attitudes help us master the environment.

Photo 7.1 The social identity function of attitudes. We can probably guess some of the attitudes that the owner of this vehicle has about politics and the environment. Like the symbols of peace on this Volkswagen, attitudes can communicate who a person is and what he or she values. Attitudes like this illustrate the social identity function, communicating our true selves to others.

Second, attitudes are useful because they help us gain and maintain connectedness with others. Because other people's impressions of us are influenced by the attitudes we hold (Shavitt & Nelson, 2000), attitudes serve a **social identity function** (sometimes called the value expressive function) by helping us define ourselves. Holding a particular attitude lets people express their true selves, affirm the groups they belong to, and show what they stand for (Berger & Heath, 2008; Smith & Hogg, 2008). For example, those who see themselves as traditionalists are more likely to prefer well-established brand-name products to new or generic ones (Khan, Misra, & Singh, 2013). Environmentalists prefer a Prius to a Hummer, and no one cool would be caught using a flip-phone. At the same time, expressing the "right" views can smooth interactions and allow us to make a good impression (Chaiken, Giner-Sorolla, & Chen, 1996). When this **impression management function** is uppermost, people try to adopt and support the attitude that they think their audience also endorses (Nienhuis, Manstead, & Spears, 2001). Both the social identity function and the impression management function of attitudes help us stay connected to others.

social identity function
the way an attitude contributes to connectedness by expressing important self and group identities and functions

impression management function
the way an attitude contributes to connectedness by smoothing interactions and relationships

Any attitude can serve both mastery and connectedness functions. It's easy to see the instrumental functions of attitudes. Whether the attitude object is as practical as rain boots, or as symbolic an idea as environmentalism, all attitudes summarize our experience with the object and quickly let us know whether we should approach and support or avoid and oppose it. But every attitude can serve connectedness functions as well: wearing rain boots covered with peace symbols reveals just as much about you as wearing organic cotton does. Because attitudes serve different functions, we can form multiple attitudes about one and the same object (Wilson and others, 2000; Petty, Tormala, Briñol, & Jarvis, 2006). We may have a different attitude about our local club's cap, for example, when our team loses the football final (when the hat serves an identity function) than when the hat keeps off the sun on a hot day (serving an instrumental function).

SOCIAL PSYCHOLOGY IN PRACTICE: ATTITUDE FUNCTIONS AND THE ENVIRONMENT

The social identity or value expressive function of attitudes allows people to express their underlying values through the attitudes they hold. Nowhere is this truer than in attitudes toward the environment. Political orientation, from conservative to liberal, is a major factor in determining attitudes about the environment. For example, more politically conservative individuals are less supportive of investment in energy-efficient technology than are more politically liberal individuals. This expression of underlying values makes them less likely to choose energy-saving products like light bulbs labeled as "green" than products not so labeled (Gromet, Kunreuther, & Larrick, 2013). Individuals who place an especially high value on the status quo and on meritocracy are also less likely to believe in global warming and less willing to engage in activities designed to reduce it. This seems to be because their belief that some groups deserve to dominate others extends to the belief that humans deserve to dominate the natural world (Milfont, Richter, Sibley, Wilson, & Fischer, 2013). Can understanding that attitudes reflect values help environmental activists convert conservatives into conservationists? When protecting the environment is couched in terms of conservative values—patriotism, protecting the status quo, keeping nature pure—both conservatives and those who endorse social inequalities adopt more pro-environmental attitudes (Feinberg & Willer, 2013; Feygina, Jost, & Goldsmith, 2010).

SOCIAL PSYCHOLOGY AND CULTURE: CULTURAL DIFFERENCES AND ATTITUDE FUNCTIONS

Cultural differences demonstrate the important influence of social identity functions on why particular attitudes form. As first pointed out in Chapter 3, people in individualist cultures, like those found in North America, see themselves as independent and tend to hold attitudes that both show who they are and how they are distinct from others. People in collectivist cultures, such as those found in many parts of Asia, on the other hand, are more concerned with group harmony and belongingness. People in those countries see themselves in more interdependent terms, are less concerned with individual self expression (Kim & Sherman, 2007), and are more likely to hold attitudes that demonstrate similarity with their peers (Aaker & Schmitt, 2001). So it's not surprising that persuaders use different appeals to help members of these different cultures express the values important to them. American ads emphasize rugged individualism, personal success, and independence with slogans like: "The art of being unique," or "You, only better" (Han & Shavitt, 1993). Japanese and Korean ads emphasize group benefits, interpersonal harmony, and family integrity with slogans like: "We have a way of bringing people together," and "Sharing is beautiful" (Morling & Lamoreaux, 2008). These strategies work: Ads that suggest a product can help its owner express cultural ideals are more persuasive (Shavitt, Lee, & Johnson, 2008). Such values might be changing, however. In more recent studies, Chinese Generation-X consumers with high income and extensive education were equally persuaded by individualist and collectivist ad appeals, even as their older counterparts still found collectivist appeals more persuasive (Zhang, 2010). As cultural values shift, so too do the social identity functions that drive attitude formation and change.

Attitude Formation

People combine the important, salient, and accessible positive and negative pieces of cognitive, affective, and behavioral information they acquire about an attitude object to form an attitude. That combination determines the direction and intensity of the attitude toward the object and can produce strong attitudes or ambivalent attitudes. Once an attitude is formed, it is associated with the attitude object.

Are you for or against democracy? Spiders: love them or hate them? We expect that you can answer these questions without much thought. Many attitudes are so well established and so frequently used that people can express them and act on them without a second thought. But even familiar things that now elicit almost a knee-jerk response were once evaluated for the first time. How do we come to like or support one attitude object and dislike or oppose another?

The Informational Base of Attitudes. When it comes to forming attitudes, association is everything. As people encounter information about an attitude object—by seeing the object together with other liked or disliked objects, interacting with it, or by hearing about it from friends, family, teachers, or the media—they form a mental representation of the object and everything they associate with it. This representation includes cognitive, affective, and behavioral information linked with or related to the object (Ostrom, 1969; Zanna & Rempel, 1988).

1. *Cognitive information includes the facts people know and the beliefs they have about an attitude object.* Perhaps the high incidence of lung cancer among smokers has convinced you that cigarette smoking causes disease. This belief is cognitive information linked to this attitude object, cigarette smoking.

2. *Affective information consists of people's feelings and emotions about the object.* Experiencing nausea or anger when you are in a smoky closed area are pieces of affective information associated with cigarette smoking.

3. *Behavioral information is knowledge about people's past, present, or future interactions with the attitude object.* Knowing that you've never even been tempted to try smoking, and that you leave a space when someone lights up is behavioral information related to cigarette smoking.

Because impressions of ourselves, others, and other groups discussed in earlier chapters are also attitudes, they too are based on cognitive, affective, and behavioral information. In Chapter 5, for example, we saw that what we think group members are like, how we feel about them, and our actions toward them could all contribute to prejudice.

Attitudes can be based on just one type of information, or on any combination of these types of information (Breckler & Wiggins, 1989; Zanna & Rempel, 1988). Many attitudes reflect mainly cognitive information—beliefs and facts—about attitude objects (Fishbein & Ajzen, 1975), especially if that information comes from hearsay rather than direct experience (Millar & Millar, 1996). We might read about the low fuel consumption, the smooth responsiveness, and the aerodynamic shape of a new model automobile in a magazine, for example.

Other attitudes are based primarily on affective information (Abelson, Kinder, Peters, & Fiske, 1982; Edwards & von Hippel, 1995; Zajonc, 1980). There are several reasons why this can happen. First, we often get affective information before encountering cognitive information. Imagine you see someone new across the room at a club. If she's dancing with a detested ex-boyfriend, you may have a negative gut reaction before even getting to know what she is like. Second, affective information can be very strong and simply overwhelm cognitions. Needles and blood often trigger strong negative emotional reactions that can determine attitudes toward donating blood, for example, regardless of supportive cognitions about this altruistic act (Breckler & Wiggins, 1989). Finally, some affective reactions may reflect inborn or genetic predispositions. For example, reactions to sensory information like tastes, smells, loud noises, or repugnant sights reflect an inborn preference for pleasure over pain and play a big role in determining attitudes. People also differ genetically by temperament and disposition in ways that contribute to their attitudes. You may recognize yourself or some of your friends as having one of those sunny dispositions that typically reacts warmly to most things most of the time—such people tend to have positive attitudes to most things compared to people who have sadder or darker personalities. People who are bold and fearless in interacting with new things tend to have more positive attitudes than those who are more timid and cautious, aware of possible danger and uncertainty in the environment. Both inherited preferences for pleasure over pain and inherited differences in temperament and disposition probably help explain why some attitudes are linked to our genes (Kandler, Bleidorn, & Riemann, 2012; Tesser, 1993). For example, the attitudes of identical twins are more likely to be similar than the attitudes of nonidentical twins, even when the identical twins are reared apart (Olson, Vernon, Harris, & Jang, 2001).

Information about behavior can also dominate our attitudes, particularly if that behavior is habitual. Knowing that you donate to the Multiple Sclerosis Fund year after year, for example, is likely to have a powerful influence on your attitudes toward the charity (Fazio & Zanna, 1981). Most people are surprised to find that behavior has the sizeable impact on attitudes that it does. Because of the varied and important influence that behavior can have on attitudes, we discuss this topic in much more detail in Chapter 8.

Putting It All Together. How do evaluative summaries—attitudes—emerge from all the information that accumulates about attitude objects? Almost every piece of information reflects something good or bad about the attitude object: Thinking that smoking makes people look cool is positive but feeling sick at the smell of smoke is negative. How might an attitude emerge from such mixed information? People form attitudes that reflect the evaluative worth of what they know, feel, and experience, as Figure 7.1 shows. Having lots of positive information about an attitude object typically results in a positive attitude, whereas having negative beliefs, feelings, or behaviors produces a negative attitude (Festinger, 1957; Heider, 1944; M. Rosenberg, 1956).

But not all information counts equally in determining an attitude. First, important information usually out-muscles unimportant information. By definition, important information is anything that matters to you. For example, negative information has an edge over positive information, probably because its consequences are potentially more

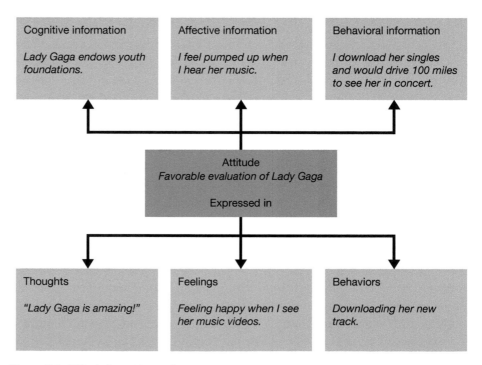

Figure 7.1 Attitude formation and measurement
If you learn that Lady Gaga endows the Born This Way Foundation for youth, feel energized when you listen to her music, and know that you would drive over one hundred miles to see her in concert, you are likely to form a positive attitude toward the popular recording artist. The attitude in turn will influence thoughts, feelings, and observable behaviors, which researchers can use to measure the underlying attitude.

dangerous. Negative information is more likely to be noticed, weighted more heavily when we combine information, and is harder to "cancel out" than positive information (Baumeister and others, 2001; Eiser, Fazio, Stafford, & Prescott, 2003; Ito, Larsen, Smith, & Cacioppo, 1998). Similarly, information that speaks to your personal needs, goals, and motives counts a lot more than cognitions, emotions, and behaviors that don't. If you are buying a car for utilitarian reasons, one model's excellent fuel economy and sound maintenance record will count more, and your attitude toward the car will be positive. On the other hand, if being stylish is important to you, and you think that what you drive reflects who you are, the fact that the car has unattractive vinyl seats and inexpensive plastic accessories will outweigh its good points, making your attitude negative.

Second, information that is accessible (comes to mind easily) or is salient (grabs attention and stands out in its context) dominates attitude judgments. For example, their obvious and salient smell and taste tends to determine whether we like or dislike foods, rather than their hidden nutritional benefits or drawbacks. Information that is accessible because it has just been brought to mind plays a similarly dominant role. People who have just been led to focus on conservative values like the importance of hard work, for example, have less favorable attitudes toward government spending on welfare programs than do people who have just been led to focus on government responsibility (Tourangeau & Rasinski, 1988).

People combine the important, salient, and accessible positive and negative cognitive, affective, and behavioral information they acquire about objects to form attitudes that differ in direction and intensity. If most of the important, salient, and accessible information is positive, your attitude will be favorable; if most of it is negative, your attitude will be unfavorable. Lots of important, salient, or accessible negative or positive information produces a more extreme attitude, whereas just a few such items produces a more moderate attitude. Different mixes of information produce different attitudes.

More often than not, the information that we gather about any given object will be largely one-sided: the bad will outweigh the good, or vice versa. How does this happen? Most people interact with a majority of people who share their opinions (Brooks, 2004). So if everyone in your home, club, and church group is politically conservative, for example, your day-to-day interactions will provide a one-sided view of the issues. Moreover, with a variety of TV, magazines, newspapers, and internet sites available, people can choose to be exposed to only the conservative or only the liberal side of an issue, and never learn anything that contradicts their view. In addition, our first reactions to an attitude object can also make exposure to inconsistent information less likely. After all, if your first early encounter with lima beans, bean sprouts, or guavas is largely negative, you probably avoid them from then on. This prevents you from gathering further information that might contradict your lopsidedly negative information base (Eiser & Fazio, 2008). For these reasons, most attitudes we hold are decidedly positive or negative.

Strong attitudes are attitudes that are based on lots of personally important, confidently held, and quite lopsidedly positive or negative information—which also, of course, makes them intense or extreme (DeMarree, Petty, & Brinol, 2007). Because their information base is so lopsided, it is very hard to change strong attitudes. Strong attitudes meet mastery needs and connectedness needs very easily. Because they provide such clear-cut and confidently held evaluative summaries, strong attitudes direct thinking and

strong attitude
a confidently-held extremely positive or negative evaluation that is persistent and resistant and that influences information processing and behavior

determine behavior much more reliably than weak attitudes (Krosnick and others, 1993), so they have good knowledge and utilitarian functions. And as you can imagine, holding strong attitudes like these about particular issues can be like wearing a badge proclaiming who you are or what you stand for.

Of course, the information that accumulates does not always imply a consistently positive or negative evaluation of an attitude object. For example, although a 2009 poll about abortion in the United States revealed that 16% of respondents felt unreservedly in favor of legal abortion and 17% were unilaterally opposed to it, 58% reported having conflicted favorable and unfavorable reactions toward abortion (Pew Research Center, 2009). In fact, having contradictory cognitions, emotions, and behaviors is a common reaction to some major social issues, such as the death penalty and environmental conservation, and to very personal health-related concerns, like donating blood or practicing safe sex.

ambivalent attitude
an attitude based on conflicting negative and positive information

Ambivalent attitudes reflect the presence of conflicting positive and negative reactions to an attitude object (I. Katz, 1981; Priester & Petty, 2001; van Harreveld, van der Pligt, & de Liver, 2009). Although some people might find it important to be even-handed or open-minded about both sides of a controversial issue, ambivalent attitudes do not help much with connectedness functions, because they do not really show what you stand for. And because they do not provide a clear-cut summary of the positivity or negativity of an attitude object, ambivalent attitudes do not serve mastery functions as well as other attitudes, as they do not direct information processing or guide behavior very well.

Linking Attitudes to Their Objects. Once we form an attitude about an attitude object, it becomes part of our mental representation of the object, as seen in Figure 7.2. The more tightly coupled the attitude and attitude object are, the more accessible the attitude is—encountering the attitude object brings its associated attitude immediately to mind as well (Bargh and others, 1996; Ito and others, 1998; Fazio, 1986, 2001). For example, we don't come across just a spider, but a repulsive spider. When this happens, our attitude will become a shorthand substitute for all the information we have about the object. We know how we feel about spiders, without having to review the cognitions, feelings, and behaviors that initially generated our reaction (Lingle & Ostrom, 1979). Accessible attitudes are confidently held and harder to change. Not surprisingly, strong attitudes are especially accessible (Fazio, 1995).

SUPERFICIAL AND SYSTEMATIC ROUTES TO PERSUASION: FROM SNAP JUDGMENTS TO CONSIDERED OPINIONS

We form attitudes because they are useful to us. But other people also find our attitudes useful. In the marketplace, political arena, or doctor's office—wherever you go these days—people try to influence you to develop new attitudes or change old ones. Understanding how attitudes form provides the basis for trying to change them. If positive beliefs, feelings, or behaviors produce positive attitudes, and negative beliefs, feelings, and behaviors produce negative attitudes, anyone trying to create or change an attitude knows what to do: provide the right building blocks for the desired attitude.

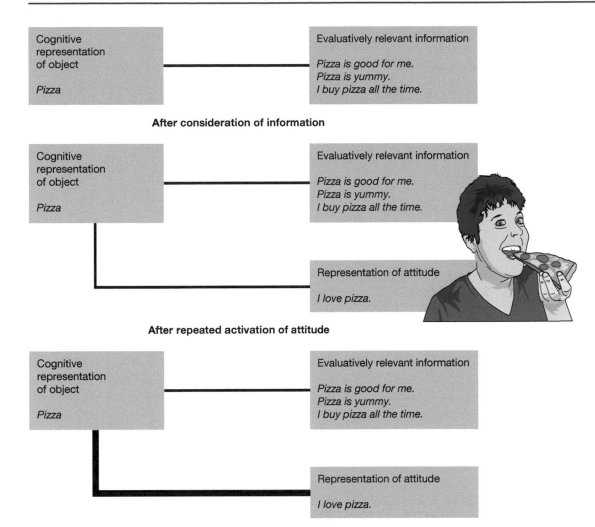

Figure 7.2 Linking an attitude to the object
People form an attitude based on cognitive, affective, and behavioral information about an attitude object, top panel. That evaluative summary also becomes associated with the mental representation of the attitude object and can come to mind when the object is encountered, center panel. As the attitude is repeatedly activated, perhaps because the attitude object is thought about or encountered frequently, the link between the object and the attitude strengthens, bottom panel.

To ensure that you will love their product, scorn drug use, or support immigration restrictions, all persuaders need to do is connect important information consistent with the attitude they want you to develop. Right?

Marketers, advertisers, and political handlers certainly seem to think so, as they surround us with an overwhelming barrage of information that could potentially change our attitudes. But actually, it's not that simple. Regardless of what is provided, people often do not go any further than superficial processing of information, so attitudes are often based on automatic associations or on accessible or salient information that triggers simple evaluative inferences about the attitude object. More rarely—usually because mastery or connectedness or me and mine motives are engaged—people take more

These two types of processing should sound familiar, because superficial and systematic processing also come into play when we make judgments about other individuals as we saw in Chapter 3, and about members of groups, as we saw in Chapter 5.

notice of attitude-relevant evidence and engage in systematic processing, going beyond simple cues to also consider the validity and importance of all attitude-relevant information and sometimes even going so far as to reflect upon their own reactions to the information. As we will see, these different means of dealing with information can all change attitudes, but they do so in different ways and under different conditions. Thus, when it comes to persuasion, how people deal with information can make as much difference as what information they deal with.

Superficial Processing: Persuasion Shortcuts

When people do not give persuasive communications much thought, various superficial aspects of the persuasive appeal can lead to attitude change. For example, people might be influenced by positive or negative objects or events associated with the attitude object, or by other feelings they are experiencing. They might also agree with messages from familiar, attractive, or expert sources or with familiar or long messages.

When you thumb absentmindedly through a magazine, you probably pay very little attention to the ads. Nevertheless, even as you superficially skim over them, some aspects of the images or words in ads may filter in. Even at a glance, you may notice the beautiful people using a product, the amount of evidence that supports an advertising claim, or find a photo accompanying a request for donations appealingly familiar. An advertisement may evoke feelings of joy, nostalgia, disgust, or fear. A persuasive setting—a store or a mall—may feature inviting smells and cheerful music or glaring lights and uncomfortable temperatures. Even if you are not aware of it, any of this information can get linked to the attitude object. When people process superficially, such simple pieces of information can act as persuasion heuristics, making attitudes more positive or negative. A **persuasion heuristic** is a cue that can make people like or dislike an attitude object without thinking about it in any depth (Chaiken, 1980, 1987). Forming attitudes based on persuasion heuristics rather than thinking about the attitude object itself is sometimes described as taking a peripheral route to persuasion (Petty & Cacioppo, 1981, 1986). When people are processing superficially, a wide range of cues can automatically influence their attitudes.

persuasion heuristic
association of a cue that is positively or negatively evaluated with the attitude object, allowing the attitude object to be evaluated quickly and without much thought

Attitudes by Association. A couple of cute toddlers type at a computer in an ad for an internet trading company. Bus shelters in San Francisco emit the smell of freshly baked cookies to go with ads for milk. Delibes' "Flower Duet" accompanies British Airways ads, and United Airlines visuals are accompanied by Gershwin's *Rhapsody in Blue*. Why do advertisers want adorable babies, the smell of home-baked cookies, and well-loved music in their ads?

If other objects are repeatedly associated with an attitude object, the attitude object soon comes to elicit the evaluation associated with those other objects. This process is called **evaluative conditioning** (Walther, 2002), and it is illustrated in Figure 7.3. To demonstrate this effect, female students watched a series of slides that included pairings of novel objects with clearly positive or negative words or images (Olson & Fazio, 2002). A later test showed that these subtle associations had created attitudes: objects earlier

evaluative conditioning
the process by which positive or negative attitudes are formed or changed by association with other positively or negatively valued objects

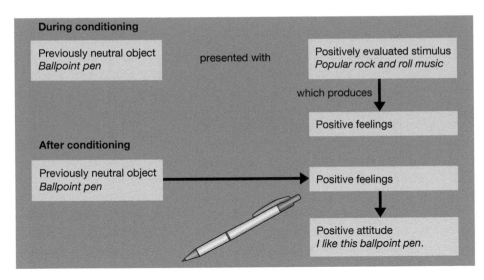

Figure 7.3 Evaluative conditioning and attitude formation
Suppose that people encounter a neutral object associated with a stimulus that they evaluate positively or negatively. After this happens a few times, the feelings produced by the stimulus become associated with the object, resulting in the formation of an attitude about the object.

Photo 7.2 Attitudes by association. This bus shelter in San Francisco emitted the smell of cookies to accompany an ad for milk. This tactic of trying to shape an attitude (in this case toward milk) by associating it with something positive (the smell of delicious cookies) is an example of evaluative conditioning.

paired with positive images or words were now seen as positive, and objects paired with negative images or words were seen as negative.

Evaluative conditioning can create powerful attitudes with only a few pairings. As part of a class exercise, students saw a fictitious brand of mouthwash paired with either positive images—a beautiful beach, a cute panda bear—or neutral images—a table or a book. Although students saw only six such pairings during the class, they reported liking the brand much better if it had been seen with the positive images. This preference for the item associated with the positive images was still present three weeks later (Grossman & Till, 1998), showing the power of evaluative conditioning in creating attitudes.

Just as positive evaluative conditioning makes attitudes more positive, negative evaluative conditioning can be particularly useful if you want to make people feel more negatively about things that are unhealthy or illegal. For example, researchers showed college students alcohol-related words, like beer and wine, paired with negative images (like a snarling animal) or with neutral images. Compared to those who saw neutral images, students who saw alcohol paired with such negative images reported more negative implicit attitudes about alcohol (measured using an IAT) and reduced drinking (Houben, Havermans, & Wiers, 2010).

People don't even have to be aware of the associated positive or negative cues for evaluative conditioning to work. Consider what happened when students were shown several photos of a woman and asked how much they liked her. Although they did not realize it, the students were at the same time also shown other photos presented so rapidly that no one could actually detect their presence or their content (such presentations are called subliminal because they are below the threshold of people's conscious perceptual awareness). One group saw the woman preceded by subliminal photos that showed puppies, cute babies, a happy couple at their wedding, and a birthday cake. Another group saw photos of the woman preceded by subliminal images of a snake about to strike, a scary mask, a face consumed by flame, and the jaws of a shark. Although none of the people were aware of the extra photos, their influence was very clear. When positive photos were associated with the woman, people liked her more, without knowing why, than when negative photos were linked to her (Krosnick, Betz, Jussim, & Lynn, 1992). Not surprisingly then, people also like, consume, and are more willing to pay for objects they see accompanied by a subliminal "smiley face" than objects accompanied by a subliminal frowning face (Niedenthal, 1990; Winkielman, Berridge, & Wilbarger, 2005). What you don't know can certainly influence your attitudes!

Evaluative conditioning is the backbone of many persuasion campaigns that try to make their attitude objects wonderful by surrounding them with as many pleasant associations as possible. Evaluative conditioning probably explains the popularity of the business lunch and the fund-raising dinner. Associating a sales pitch or an appeal for a donation with good food may well increase its persuasiveness (Janis, Kaye, & Kirschner, 1965). Music can work the same way. In one study, students in a management class much preferred a ball-point pen ad that featured popular rock-and-roll music compared to one that featured unpopular classical music (Gorn, 1982). Smells also have powerful evaluative associations. Students rated a simulated store and its merchandise more favorably when it was filled with a pleasing scent than in a no scent condition (Spangenberg, Crowley, & Henderson, 1996) and littered less in Dutch train compartments scented with cleaning products rather than in compartments with no smell (de Lange, Debets, Ruitenberg, & Holland, 2012).

In all of these examples, a researcher, advertiser, or retailer is deliberately creating an association between an attitude object and a cue. But, sometimes associations form coincidentally, because our feelings about one object or experience get mixed up with the attitude object. People might feel good, perhaps because the sun is shining, or feel bad, perhaps because they failed a test. When people are feeling good or bad for another reason, asking "How do I feel?" about an attitude object might mistakenly make the object look good when they're feeling good and look bad when they're not (Schwarz & Clore, 1988). Indeed, students evaluate their lives more positively when interviewed on sunny, upbeat days than they do on rainy, downbeat days for example. Gentle reminders of the real source of their feelings are usually enough to make people realize that what they

We first saw some of the effects subliminal stimuli can have when we discussed priming in Chapter 3, page 67.

are feeling is not relevant to the attitude object and adjust their attitude appropriately (Albarracin & Kumkale, 2003). Like other heuristics, the "How do I feel about it?" cue is most powerful when people process only superficially.

The Familiarity Heuristic: Familiarity Makes the Heart Grow Fonder.
There's nothing more comforting than the presence of old friends, repeated rituals, or familiar surroundings. In fact, repeated exposure to a stimulus increases people's liking for it. Consider what happened, for example, when Robert Zajonc (1968) showed college students unfamiliar "Turkish words" like *saracik* and *dilikli* different numbers of times and asked them to pronounce the word. When they were later asked to guess how positive or negative each word was, people rated the words they had seen more often as positive. This mere exposure effect, the finding that people prefer things to which they have been more frequently exposed, is one of the most replicated findings in social psychology (Bornstein, 1989) and occurs in all kinds of settings. For example, recent research showed that contestants did better in the final of the Eurovision Song Contest if they had previously appeared in a semifinal that was seen by voters than if they had not (Verrier, 2012). This association between familiarity and goodness is so powerful that it operates even when people are unaware of whether or how often they have seen the stimulus before. In fact, the mere exposure effect is even stronger when people are unaware of how frequently they have been exposed to the stimuli (Bornstein, Leone, & Galley, 1987; Hansen & Wanke, 2009). Familiarity may have these effects because things we've encountered before are easier to process the second time around and easy is good (Reber, Schwarz, & Winkielman, 2004) or because things we've encountered before and are still around to see again are inferred to be safe (Zajonc, 2001; Song & Schwarz, 2009).

Recall from Chapter 3, page 61, that frequent exposure to a person similarly increases liking for that person.

Because of the positive feelings associated with familiarity, familiar stimuli can also be more persuasive. A familiar spokesperson is more persuasive than one being seen for the first time (Weisbuch & Mackie, 2009). In one study, for example, researchers arranged for students to participate with two experimental confederates in making what was supposed to be a series of group decisions. Following instructions, the confederates disagreed on most of the judgments, leaving the real participant in the uncomfortable position of casting the tie-breaking vote by siding with one of the two confederates. Students in a control condition agreed with each confederate about half the time. But a different pattern emerged among people in the experimental condition. They formed coalitions with one confederate much more often than with the other. Which confederate did they go along with? During a slide show just before the discussion session, participants in the experimental condition had been exposed to subliminal photographs of one of the confederates. Although they were not aware of their exposure to the photos, participants were much more likely to side with this "familiar" face (Bornstein and others, 1987).

Familiarity makes other aspects of a persuasive appeal more effective too. A repeated argument, claim, or persuasive appeal is more credible and persuasive the second time people hear it than it is the first, and repetition strengthens weak arguments even more than it does strong ones (Arkes, Hackett, & Boehm, 1989; Moons, Mackie, & Garcia-Marques, 2009). Even framing arguments in terms of familiar idioms and metaphors makes arguments more convincing than phrases conveying the same information in more literal form. In one study, college students were presented with a message urging them

SOCIAL PSYCHOLOGY IN PRACTICE: FAMILIARITY EFFECTS AND HEALTH WARNINGS

The persuasive effects of familiarity can create some unexpected outcomes. Medical researchers and consumer advocates often try to correct misperceptions about health issues by publicizing corrective messages such as "vaccinations don't cause autism" or "shark cartilage doesn't help arthritis." But when you tell someone that something they've heard before isn't true, the part they've heard before (vaccinations . . . cause autism; shark cartilage . . . helps arthritis) becomes more familiar. And as we've just seen, familiar claims, messages, and arguments seem even truer. Ironically, then, the more often the misinformation is denied or corrected, the more familiar, and the more accurate, it seems (Allport & Lepkin, 1945). For the same reasons, consumer warnings can become consumer recommendations. In one study, repeatedly telling older adults that a consumer claim was false helped them remember it as false in the short term, but after a three-day delay, the repeated claim was more likely to be remembered as true! Younger adults showed the same effect, although it took them longer—seven days, rather than three—before they began to remember the claim as true rather than false. Over time, the claim itself ("People say that shark cartilage is good for arthritis") became more familiar and thus seemed more valid, but the contradictory evidence ("It's not true!") got lost (Johar & Roggeveen, 2007; Skurnik, Yoon, Park, & Schwarz, 2005). Adding to the familiarity of the original claim might make it even more persuasive as time goes on. How can such unintended effects be avoided? Researchers working in this area recommend going with the positive "Vaccinations are safe" rather than the negative "Vaccinations don't . . ." and repeating those positive statements to enhance their familiarity (Lewandowsky, Ecker, Seifert, Schwarz, & Cook, 2012).

to begin financial planning for retirement soon (Howard, 1997). The content of the persuasive message was summarized using either familiar phrases or more literal arguments. For example, some students received the advice: "Don't bury your head in the sand" and "Don't put all your eggs in one basket." Others were told: "Don't pretend a problem doesn't exist" and "Don't risk everything on a single venture." Use of the familiar phrases was more effective: Those hearing the more commonplace advice developed more positive attitudes toward financial planning. Since familiar stimuli are more easily processed (Reber and others, 2004) and make people feel good about them (Monahan, Murphy, & Zajonc, 2000), both of these consequences can help familiarity increase persuasion.

The Attractiveness Heuristic: Agreeing with Those We Like. If surrounding an attitude object with positive associations makes it seem more positive, no wonder advertisements often pair an attitude object with a popular or attractive figure. Often these communicators make no claim to expertise, so why does someone who turns our head also change our minds? Evaluative conditioning tells us that associating someone we like with the attitude object makes us think that it too is likable. No wonder that Roger Ailes (1988), an adviser to several former U.S. presidents, called likability a persuasive "magic bullet": "If you could master one element of personal communication that is more powerful than anything, it is the quality of being likable. If your audience likes you, they'll forgive just about everything else" (p. 81).

He seems to be right. Attractive people are well liked, and others are more likely to agree with them (Byrne, 1971; Insko, 1981). No wonder then that attractive people are more likely to get their way. In one study, attractive confederates were able to get many more people to agree to sign a petition than were less attractive ones (Chaiken, 1979), and attractive people have a persuasive edge even if they are upfront about using their good looks to get their way (Messner, Reinhard, & Sporer, 2008). So attractiveness serves as a persuasion cue: If Ricky Rubio eats at McDonald's and Megan Fox wears Armani jeans, consumers will want those products too.

Though we typically think of attractiveness as a feature of a person's physical attributes, such as one's muscular body or beautiful skin, communicators can be attractive or likable for other reasons. For instance, those who subtly mimic us, that is, copy our speech patterns, gestures, and other bodily movements, are perceived as quite likable (Chartrand & Bargh, 1999). It turns out that mimickers can be more persuasive as well, as research is beginning to document (Chartrand & van Baaren, 2009). For example, students in a virtual environment who encountered a computer-generated avatar programmed to mimic their head movements were more persuaded by the avatar's persuasive appeal than students confronted with an avatar whose head movements were random (Bailenson & Yee, 2005). Preferences for and consumption of a novel sports drink also increased when consumers were mimicked by an investigator posing as a market researcher compared to when they were not mimicked (Tanner, Ferraro, Chartrand, Bettman, & Van Baaren, 2009). Restaurant servers who verbally mimic their customers' order even get bigger tips (Jacob & Gueguen, 2013). Therefore, the attractiveness or likability of a communicator, whether that likability is from their physical features or from things like mimicry, can make them more persuasive.

When advertisers use attractive communicators, they usually make them the most prominent feature of the appeal. Does emphasizing a communicator's attractiveness increase our reliance on the attractiveness heuristic? Apparently so. Suzanne Pallak (1983) showed two groups of women the same article, which urged donations in support of the arts. One of the groups also saw a vivid color photo of an attractive man who had supposedly written the article. Others students saw only a blurred photocopy of the man's photograph. Although the arguments were exactly the same, women for whom the communicator's attractiveness was made most accessible were much more persuaded than were women for whom the man's appearance was not so obvious. Surveys show that voters prefer candidates they find attractive, and the more accessible that attractiveness is, the more it dominates attitudes. No wonder then that media like television and the internet make attractiveness even more of an advantage for good looking politicians than do radio and newsprint (Patterson, Churchill, Burger, & Powell, 1992).

These aren't the only advantages that attractive people have over the rest of the population. See Chapter 3, pages 57–58 and Chapter 12, page 441–444.

Photo 7.3 The attractiveness heuristic. Gillette knows that ads like this one featuring David Beckham, a celebrity known for his good looks as well as his soccer abilities, use the persuasive power of an attractive source to get consumers to buy Gillette razors without having to think carefully about their benefits.

The Expertise Heuristic: Agreeing with Those Who Know. "Life exists elsewhere in our galaxy!" Imagine that this sentence catches your attention as you flip through the television channels on a Sunday afternoon. You soon discover that the source of the intriguing statement is a talk-show guest, a farmer who claims he has been taken for multiple rides on a spaceship. Would you nod in agreement or snort with derision? Imagine now that you hear this same claim from European Space Agency General Director, Jean-Jacques Dordain, a member of the French Académie des Technologies and the National Air and Space Academy. Would your reaction be different? Research suggests that it would.

Because communicators with excellent credentials usually offer compelling arguments, people often associate them with opinions that should be respected: Experts know what they are talking about. On the basis of this association, the credibility or expertise heuristic leads people to accept the validity of a claim on the basis of who says it, not what is said (Hovland & Weiss, 1951; Sternthal, Dholakia, & Leavitt, 1978). This is true not only for claims about space aliens, but for more earthly and serious concerns. For instance, health experts, such as medical doctors, are more persuasive when advocating for increased condom use to prevent contraction of HIV than are laypersons, such as community leaders (Durantini, Albarracin, Mitchell, Earl, & Gillette, 2006). Expertise effects like these are most pronounced when the recipient has little knowledge or no strong pre-existing attitude on the topic (Kumkale, Albarracin, & Seignourel, 2010).

Why is a European Space Agency administrator or a medical doctor an expert source whereas the space-traveling farmer or the community leader is not? First, to be an expert, communicators must be competent. Competence refers to proof of the communicator's accomplishment or status in a particular field. When an ad features Ronaldo in action on the soccer field, a robed judge banging a gavel in a wood-paneled courtroom, or a stethoscope-bedecked doctor writing prescriptions, its creators are hoping to capitalize on the expertise heuristic. One early demonstration of this simple association between occupation and competence compared the persuasive powers of a judge and a drug dealer (Kelman & Hovland, 1953). Participants were told that one or the other had recommended relatively lenient treatment of a juvenile delinquent. As you might expect, they found the judge more persuasive than the drug dealer.

Occupation is not the only cue that suggests competence. Research findings indicate that fast talkers also convey an image of expertise. Witnesses who give quick confident replies to lawyers' questions appear more credible and competent than those who don't (Erickson, Lind, Johnson, & O'Barr, 1978). As long as people can understand the gist of a message, the faster the message is delivered, the more objective, intelligent, and knowledgeable the communicator is seen to be, and the more willing listeners are to buy, learn about, and recommend the attitude object to others (Chebat, El Hedhli, Gelinas-Chebat, & Boivin, 2007; MacLachlan & Siegel, 1980). Rapid delivery makes it harder for listeners to tell a strong appeal from a weak one and boosts the weak ones' persuasiveness (Moore, Hausknecht, & Thamodaran, 1986; S. M. Smith & Shaffer, 1995). There are limits, however. If delivery is so rapid that the meaning of the message is lost, persuasion is undermined. And when listeners really care about the topic, they are less likely to let a fast talker influence their attitudes (S. M. Smith & Shaffer, 1995).

After competence, trustworthiness is the most important characteristic a credible communicator can have. People expect expert communicators not only to know the facts but also to tell the truth (Eagly, Wood, & Chaiken, 1978). That is why communicators sometimes earn persuasion points by presenting both sides of an issue; the strategy makes them seem well-informed, fair-minded, and credible (Bohner, Einwiller, Erb, & Siebler, 2003; R. A. Jones & Brehm, 1970). Trustworthiness is also the goal when advertisers arrange for their audience to "sit in on" or "overhear" product testimonials and "slice of life" endorsements. If the communication seems to happen by accident, rather than being tailored specifically for the listener's ears, the casual observer is likely to think it is true and is more easily persuaded (Walster & Festinger, 1962).

Of course, we are likely to be taken in by these ploys only if we are processing very minimally. If we devote even a little more attention to the communication, we might be prompted to ask why a particular source is advocating a particular position (Eagly, Chaiken, & Wood, 1981). Such attributional processing can undermine a communicator's apparent trustworthiness. Imagine, for example, that an advertisement for Nike athletic sportswear featuring tennis star Maria Sharapova prompts you to wonder why Sharapova endorses the product. Does she promote that brand because of the quality of the product? Could it be that this particular line of sportswear is so terrific that Sharapova cannot help but recommend it? If the ad leads to the belief that the communicator's position reflects the stimulus object's actual qualities—deciding that Sharapova endorses Nike because the clothing is so good—such a stimulus attribution produces persuasion (Eagly and others, 1978). If the advocate seems to have ulterior motives, however, people become suspicious. If they recognize that Sharapova—like Kim Clijsters with Fila clothing, Novak Djokovic with Uniqlo clothing, and Andy Murray with Adidas clothing—is well paid for such an endorsement, they may find the ad less persuasive: Maybe it's the money talking, not the quality of the product. Attributional processing may explain why people are particularly impressed when communicators seem to speak or act against their own best interests (Eagly, Wood, & Chaiken, 1978).

Attributional processing (processing concerned with discovering the causes for behavior) and the conditions that lead to stimulus attributions were discussed in Chapter 3, pages 74–76.

HOT TOPICS IN SOCIAL PSYCHOLOGY: COMPETENCE AND TRUSTWORTHINESS

What makes someone competent and trustworthy? In Chapter 3, we noted that people make consistent judgments of competence and trustworthiness within the first 100 milliseconds of seeing a face and that these almost instantaneous judgments are good predictors of the outcomes of political elections (Olivola & Todorov, 2010). It turns out that children as young as 5 and adults as old as 85 make similar judgments of competence equally quickly (Zebrowitz, Franklin, Hillman, & Boc, 2013) and regardless of whether they are looking at faces from their own culture or from another (Antonakis & Dalgas, 2009; Chen, Jing, & Lee, 2012). To find out what drives such judgments, Oosterhof and Todorov (2008) had participants judge hundreds of computer-generated faces that varied systematically on multiple dimensions. They found that mature-looking faces were judged to be more competent—faces that had higher cheekbones, more angular jaws, squarer shape, and less distance between eyebrows and eyes were seen as more competent than faces without those features. Current research is focused on identifying the specific visual cues that people use when they draw inferences of competence and trustworthiness and which cues are actually associated with behaviors demonstrating these traits. Perhaps political parties and advertising agencies will soon be using social psychological research to specify the facial structure of candidates and commercial spokespeople to maximize their persuasiveness.

We would probably be persuaded if we learned that Maria Sharapova owns stock in a competing clothing company but feels compelled to recommend Nike because of its quality.

The Message-Length Heuristic: Length Equals Strength. If we are processing superficially, even the form of a persuasive appeal can help persuade us. Perhaps you have noticed over the years that longer campaign speeches seem more convincing than briefer ones. Such observations might produce a simple message-length heuristic: The longer the message, the more valid it appears to be. Ads that pointedly list "the 25 best reasons" to prefer a product are trying to invoke this heuristic. Table 7.1 describes another persuasion technique that encourages people to rely on the sheer number of arguments supporting a particular position.

Of course, quantity does not always mean quality, and the focus on numbers can blind us to the inadequacy of the reasoning. Imagine the following scenario. You are waiting in line at the photocopy machine when you are approached by someone wanting to cut ahead of you. Her request is relatively small: She wants to make only five copies. Would you find her simple request persuasive? About 60% of students waiting in line to use the copy machine at the City University of New York did (Langer, Blank, & Chanowitz, 1978). Now imagine that the would-be line cutter not only made the same request but also explained that she was in a rush. Would this legitimate argument in favor of letting her go ahead be even more persuasive? If you say yes, you agree with the New York students, 94% of whom agreed to the request when given a good reason.

These findings suggest that the quality of a message increases persuasiveness, but is that always the case? If people are processing superficially—relying on whether the request is long or not, for example—maybe anything that just sounds like an argument or reason will do. In fact, other people were approached by the woman with a request

TABLE 7.1 Length Equals Strength: The Ben Franklin Close

A *close* is a persuasive technique that "closes a deal." A salesperson using the Ben Franklin close would begin with a story like this:

> As you know, Ben Franklin has always been considered one of the wisest men America has ever had. Whenever he felt himself in a situation where he couldn't quite make up his mind, he felt pretty much as you do now. If it was the right thing, he wanted to be sure he did it. If it was the wrong thing, he wanted to be just as sure that he avoided it. Isn't that about the way you feel?

> So here's what he would do to arrive at a decision. He would take a clean sheet of paper and draw a line down the middle, like this. On one side of the line he would list all the reasons why he should make a "yes" decision and on the other side of the line he would list all the reasons against making this decision. When he was through, he would count the reasons that he was able to tally on each side, and his decision was made for him. Why don't we try it here and see what happens?

As the customer attempts to come up with reasons for buying the product, the salesperson helps suggest and list reasons. When it comes to producing reasons for the other side, however, the salesperson leaves the customer to work alone. Often it will be difficult for one person to generate more reasons than two people can. With the sheet of paper showing more reasons "for" than "against," the customer can be influenced by the message-length heuristic.

Source: Adapted with permission of Lexington Books, a division of Rowmans & Littlefield Publishers, Inc., from J. Jacoby (1984). Some social psychological perspectives on closing. In J. Jacoby & C. S. Craig (Eds.), *Personal selling* (pp. 73–92). Copyright © 1984 by Lexington Books.

and an empty explanation that only sounded like a reason: "Excuse me, I have five pages. May I use the Xerox machine, because I have to make some copies?" Ninety-three percent of those approached this way agreed to let her go ahead! When people rely on the message-length heuristic, a longer message, no matter what it says, seems compelling (Petty & Cacioppo, 1984). As you will see later, however, when a request is substantial enough to provoke more extensive processing, for example, if the person had to make fifty copies instead of five, people will think more carefully about the reason.

Much of the time, the associations that underlie persuasion heuristics allow us to effectively evaluate the attitude objects we encounter. Experts usually know what they are talking about, and a long message often yields more relevant information than a short one. If the attitude object makes us feel good, it probably is good. After all, it is the usefulness of these cues that led people to develop the heuristics in the first place. Sometimes, however, superficial processing just doesn't cut it. An advertiser might pay an expert to provide a biased opinion about a product, longer messages are some-

times "padded" and full of non-informative "fluff," and we might feel good about an attitude object simply because it is presented in the presence of pleasing music. Thus, though basing our attitudes on these heuristic cues is often good enough, we may want or need to know more about the attitude object than superficial processing provides. In these circumstances we move into high gear, and we process information in depth.

Systematic Processing: Thinking Persuasion Through

Sometimes people carefully consider the content of arguments presented in a persuasive communication. When people pay attention to a message, understand its content, and react to it, a process called elaboration, systematic processing changes attitudes. Sometimes systematic processing also includes metacognition, or thinking about what those elaborations mean. Attitudes resulting from systematic processing last longer and are more resistant to later change than most attitudes produced by superficial processing.

When people process systematically, they begin to think about aspects of the attitude object that go beyond the immediate evaluations associated with communicators and messages. They turn their attention to evaluating the quality of the information provided about the attitude object and to thinking about what they are being told in relation to what they already know. It is not that systematic processors do not notice or are not immediately affected by the presence of heuristic cues in the persuasion setting; they are. But as they start to take notice of other information as well, the impact of superficial factors on attitudes becomes less important. How does this increase in thinking affect persuasion?

Processing Information about the Attitude Object. Systematic processing involves paying increased attention to the strength and quality of information about the attitude object (Chaiken, 1980, 1987; Petty & Cacioppo, 1981, 1986; Petty & Wegener, 1999). Because systematic processing means thinking carefully about the central merits of the attitude object, Petty and Cacioppo (1981, 1986) have called it the central route to persuasion. Over the years, researchers have learned a lot about the steps involved in systematic processing and how those steps influence persuasion (W. J. McGuire, 1969).

1. *Attending to information.* In one popular French commercial, a desperate car owner attacks his old jalopy with hammers, a blowtorch, and even an elephant to beat it into the stylish shape of a late model Peugeot. In a recent North American ad, two women mud wrestle to decide a dispute about a particular brand of beer. Advertisers go to such lengths because they realize that getting the audience's attention is the first crucial step in bringing about persuasion, a fact persuasion researchers recognized long ago (Hovland, Janis, & Kelley, 1953; Hovland, Lumsdaine, & Sheffield, 1949). It is also a step that is easier said than done. Because people are bombarded by hundreds of persuasive messages a day—from the mass media, computers, billboards, friends, on packaging, even in public restrooms—most messages receive at best a superficial once-over. Television advertisers have the upper hand here: The use of both vision and sound makes their ads more attention grabbing than messages delivered on radio or in print (Andreoli & Worchel, 1978), especially if they stand out from the program they are placed in (Russell, 2002). Online advertisers, perhaps trying to capitalize on some of these same attention-grabbing features of television, now regularly use ads that are colorful and animated, such as ads that slowly "creep" across the online news article you are trying to read! But all professional persuaders know that, if they are to keep their candidate in the spotlight or make their product's packaging stand out from the rest, they must quickly snare the audience's attention, giving them a reason to watch and listen. As one successful adman concluded from his years of advertising experience, "People screen out a lot of commercials because they start with something dull. When you advertise fire extinguishers, open with the fire" (Ogilvy, 1983, p. 111).

   Although attention is crucial for persuasion, uninformed attempts to attract attention to a persuasive message can backfire. Research suggests that people pay more attention to violent than nonviolent media and to sexually explicit media than to nonsexual media (Geer, Judice, & Jackson, 1994; Lang, Newhagen, & Reeves, 1996). Advertisers have often taken this to mean that ads featured in such shows will receive a lot of attention. They are wrong, however. The more attention viewers direct to television content, the less they seem to have for the persuasive appeals broadcast during breaks in programming. Memory for products advertised during shows featuring sex and violence is actually much worse than memory for products advertised during nonsexual and nonviolent programming (Bushman, 2005). So for most persuasion attempts: make sure attention is drawn to the message, not away from it!

2. *Comprehending information.* Although getting the audience's attention is a critical first step in communicating, attention does not guarantee comprehension. Reading or hearing an argument does not mean we understand it. Research indicates, in fact, that much of the persuasive information aimed at us goes right over our heads (Morgan & Reichart, 1999). In one survey, for example, consumer psychologist Jacob Jacoby and his colleagues found that adults misunderstood 30–40% of the information presented in 30-second television segments (Jacoby, Hoyer, & Sheluga, 1980). When messages are easy to comprehend, people can recognize compelling or weak content and react accordingly (Eagly, 1974). But when messages are complex and difficult, people can miss the true attributes of the attitude object and fall prey to superficial heuristics (Hafer, Reynolds, & Obertynski, 1996).

In fact, some advertisers might use this information to their advantage. Consider the case of commercials for prescription drugs. Such drugs provide benefits to people, like curing diseases and easing pain, but also typically come with a host of possible harmful side effects. Advertising companies attempting to sell such drugs to consumers might want to make the beneficial aspects obvious and easy to understand, while simultaneously making it hard to understand the side effects. Indeed, Ruth Day (2006) examined several drug commercials that aired in 2000 and 2001, she found just this effect. The language used to describe the benefits of the drugs required comprehension skills typical of 12-year-olds, whereas the side effect language required typical 15-year-old comprehension skills (Pickert, 2008)!

3. *Reacting to information.* People do not just passively soak up information; they react to it, sometimes favorably and sometimes unfavorably. Whether the persuasive communication is your doctor's recommendation regarding a treatment regimen or your best friend's pitch to sign you up as an exercise buddy, you will do more than just listen to it if it has engaged your attention and you understand it. You will react to the persuader's arguments. You might even generate arguments of your own on one side of the issue or the other. Favorable reactions might include merely registering agreement ("Walking for a half hour per day sounds good to me") or developing the supportive information even further ("Yes, and didn't I also read somewhere that daily exercise cuts the likelihood you'll get diabetes in half?"). Negative reactions may range from simply disagreeing with some point ("Oh, pleeease!") to developing a detailed set of counterarguments ("I'm so busy now, I couldn't possibly!"). The process of generating such favorable and unfavorable reactions to the content of a message is called **elaboration**. These reactions can be affective as well as cognitive, reflecting feelings associated with the attitude object as well as additional characteristics that the object might have. One study presented messages favoring the use of animals in medical experiments to students who opposed their use. Faced with such a message, participants produced as many affective responses (like "Children dying unnecessarily makes me want to cry") as cognitive ones ("I realize now that some drug effects can't be modeled by computers"; Rosselli, Skelly, & Mackie, 1995).

Sometimes people engaged in systematic processing go even further than elaborating on information about an attitude object—they also think about what those elaborations mean. This "thinking about thinking" is called **metacognition**, and metacognition can also affect whether or not a persuasion appeal is accepted (Wagner, Brinol, & Petty, 2012). For example, people who are led to feel they have

elaboration
the generation of favorable or unfavorable reactions to the content of a persuasive appeal

metacognition
thoughts about thoughts or about thought processes

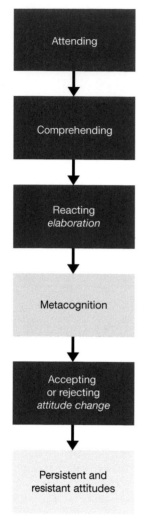

Figure 7.4 Systematic processing involves paying attention to information about the attitude object, comprehending its meaning, and elaborating it, reacting in positive and negative ways. Sometimes people even engage in metacognition—reacting to their reactions to the information. The number and valence of elaborations determines attitude change. Attitudes changed via systematic processing are long-lasting and hard to change.

produced a lot of reactions to a persuasive appeal are more persuaded than people who—even though they generated the same actual number of responses—are made to think they produced only a few. And the more confident about their reactions people are, the more swayed they are by the valence of those reactions. So people producing positive elaborations in which they are confident are more persuaded than those having equal numbers of not-so-confidently held positive reactions (Barden & Petty, 2008; Brinol & Petty, 2009).

4. ***Accepting or rejecting the advocated position.*** If systematically processed information about the attitude object stimulates favorable cognitive or affective elaborations, it will be persuasive. If the arguments evoke unfavorable reactions, the message will fail to persuade (Greenwald, 1968; Petty, Cacioppo, & Goldman, 1981). If arguments are carefully processed and provoke positive elaborations, the more arguments there are, the more attitude change there will be. By the same token, greater numbers of carefully processed weak arguments will produce more negative responses than would result from only a few silly arguments. To assess the impact of systematic thinking about strong and weak arguments on persuasion, researchers presented students with different numbers of arguments in favor of instituting comprehensive examinations for graduating college students—a popular attitude issue in persuasion research (Petty & Cacioppo, 1984). Strong arguments—ones that typically prompt favorable elaborations—in this experiment included statements like the following: "Graduate schools and law and medical schools are beginning to show clear and significant preferences for students who received their undergraduate degrees from institutions with comprehensive exams." Weak arguments, which typically elicit unfavorable elaborations, included such statements as, "Graduate students have always had to take a comprehensive exam in their major area before receiving their degrees, and it is only fair that undergraduates should have to take them also." Some students heard three weak arguments and others heard nine weak arguments. A third group heard three strong arguments, and a fourth group, nine strong ones. All students then gave their own opinions on the comprehensive exams issue. The results indicated that when students were processing systematically, they found three strong arguments persuasive and nine even more so. In contrast, a few weak arguments were unimpressive, and many weak arguments were a real turn-off. When communicators attempt to influence us with really bad arguments, we may even respond by moving in a direction opposite the one intended. This change is called a boomerang effect.

Thus when systematic processing occurs, people's reactions to information about the attitude object can be even more important than the content of the information itself. In effect, people persuade themselves.

The Consequences of Systematic Processing.
Attitudes that result from systematic thinking are both persistent and resistant. When attitudes change because information is carefully attended, comprehended, and elaborated, all this mental work helps write the resulting attitudes almost indelibly in memory. In fact, the new attitudes become so firmly fixed that they are less likely to change with time (Chaiken, 1980; Petty, Haugtvedt, & Smith, 1995). Compared with attitudes produced by heuristic processing, attitudes based on systematic processing are also resistant in the face of new persuasion attempts. In one demonstration of this advantage, individuals first read a message promoting

nuclear power plants, and then an equally strong message arguing against them. Those individuals who reacted to the first message with lots of issue-relevant thinking were less influenced by the second message (Haugtvedt & Wegener, 1994). Trial lawyers, political candidates engaged in debate, and disputing siblings arguing their case to a parent should all find these results very useful. If the audience is going to hear both sides of an issue, is it better to present your case first or last? If you have strong arguments and you expect people to do a lot of thinking about them, it's best to go first. If people put a lot of thought into changing their mind on the basis of your appeal, they are much more likely to resist the opposite point of view. The processes involved in systematic processing and their likely outcome are illustrated in Figure 7.4.

Superficial and Systematic Processing: Which Strategy, When?

People process messages systematically only when they have both the motivation and the cognitive capacity to do so. Motivation is high when the message is relevant to important goals. Cognitive capacity is available when people have the ability to process and can do so without distraction. People differ in their levels of motivation and capacity to process different kinds of messages. Messages that match people's motivation and capacity are most persuasive. Positive and negative emotions influence persuasion because they have consequences for motivation and capacity. People often use a mix of superficial and systematic processing, meaning that cues and content can interact in some interesting ways.

So what is the best strategy if you want to change someone's mind about something? Whether you are addressing your constituents, launching a new business, trying to get your family to adopt a sensible diet, or trying to convince your friends to start a study group to prepare for final exams, any strategy that evokes systematic processing seems to be the best bet for both persuader and persuadee. For the persuader, systematic processing guarantees long-term and resistant attitude change: Once you have won their minds, you will keep their allegiance. For the consumer of persuasive communications, careful processing gives us greater confidence in the validity of our attitudes.

Why, then, don't people process systematically all the time? Here's the catch: Systematic processing of persuasive appeals requires a big investment of effort and ability. In fact, whether communications are processed superficially or systematically depends on two factors: people's motivation and their cognitive capacity to think carefully about the content of the message. The idea that systematic processing requires both motivation and capacity, whereas superficial processing can occur without them, is central to many prominent theories of attitude formation and change (Chaiken & Trope, 1999). One of the most well known and influential of these theories is the **Elaboration Likelihood Model (ELM)** (Petty & Cacioppo, 1986). As you know, elaboration, a key process in systematic processing, occurs when people consider the merits of a persuasive message and generate favorable or unfavorable responses to it. The ELM argues that the likelihood of elaboration occurring depends on whether someone has sufficient motivation and capacity. Let's see how motivation and capacity affect superficial and systematic processing.

Elaboration Likelihood Model (ELM)

a model of persuasion that claims that attitude change occurs through either a peripheral route or a central route that involves elaboration, and that the extent of elaboration depends on motivation and capacity

How Motivation Influences Superficial and Systematic Processing. Motives like mastery, connectedness, and protecting a positive view of ourselves play an important role in how we approach persuasive communications. Imagine the plight of a small company's purchasing manager given the responsibility of selecting and purchasing new computer equipment to be used for product design. The decision is a crucial one: The company needs to upgrade to stay competitive, but if it goes over budget there could be a real problem with cash flow; this decision has serious consequences. It's also the supervisor's first real test as purchasing manager, and so her reputation for mixing technical smarts with an eye for a bargain is also on the line. How will she decide which product line uses her company's money most effectively? When the attitudes and opinions we form have consequences for ourselves and others, and when those attitudes and opinions reflect directly on us, systematic processing is our greatest ally.

1.   *Mastery motivation: The importance of being accurate.* When we are being held accountable for our preferences and are concerned about making the correct decision, mastery motives will predominate and issues of accuracy will be central. The product manager will need solid evidence to justify her choice of computer system, because others will hold her accountable. She may also fear that if she chooses a faulty piece of equipment, the costs of being incorrect could be severe. Compared with people who have no one to answer to, accountable message processors and those anxious to avoid being wrong process persuasive communications more thoroughly, think more about the information, and are more concerned with integrating new information as it comes to light (Chaiken, 1980; Kim & Paek, 2009).

     Some people just naturally seem to prefer puzzling over difficult problems, resolving inconsistencies, and searching for the right answers, regardless of the situation. Those who enjoy such activities are said to have high need for cognition (Cacioppo & Petty, 1982; A. Cohen, 1957). This need is indicated by people's responses to statements like the ones in Table 7.2. Research has found that individuals with a high need for cognition are more likely than others to put effort into processing persuasive communications. In one study demonstrating this point, participants read a strongly or weakly argued editorial. The higher their need for cognition, the more likely they

TABLE 7.2   The Need for Cognition Scale: Sample Items

1. I find satisfaction in deliberating hard for long hours.
2. Learning new ways to think doesn't excite me very much.
3. I like tasks that require little thought once I've learned them.
4. I would prefer complex to simple problems.
5. The notion of thinking abstractly is appealing to me.
6. More often than not, more thinking just leads to more errors.

Note: These are sample items from the Need for Cognition Scale, which assesses how much people enjoy engaging in effortful cognitive activities. People who agree with items 1, 4, and 5 and disagree with items 2, 3, and 6 would be regarded as high in need for cognition. The actual scale used in research contains many more than six items, so it can more accurately classify people as high or low in need for cognition.

Source: From "The need for cognition" by J. T. Cacioppo & R. E. Petty, 1982, *Journal of Personality and Social Psychology, 42,* pp. 116–131. Copyright © 1982 by the American Psychological Association. Reprinted with permission.

were to respond favorably to strong arguments and to be unmoved by weak ones, indicating that they had carefully processed the content of the editorial (Cacioppo, Petty, Feinstein, Jarvis, & Blair, 1996). In contrast, people with a low need for cognition tend to rely more on heuristic cues that require little processing, like the expertise of a communicator (Cacioppo & Petty, 1984; Petty, Brinol, Loersch, & McCaslin, 2009).

Accuracy concerns are often triggered when the evidence seems mixed. Imagine that you are looking forward to seeing a newly released movie that one of your friends says is the best movie he's seen in a long time. But then your local paper pans it and movie critics hate it. Now your confidence in your judgment wavers, and you start looking for new input. Perhaps you ask your friend about the plot and characters, or you seek out several additional reviews. When persuasive communications advocate inconsistent positions, as they do in this example, people often move from casual to careful processing. People are motivated to undertake a detailed analysis of all aspects of the communication when they encounter arguments that do not fit or conclusions that do not follow (Festinger, 1957; Maheswaran & Chaiken, 1991; Petty, Tormala, Brinol, & Jarvis, 2006).

2. *Connectedness motivation: The importance of relations with others.* Of course, many of our most cherished goals have to do with other people and our connections to them. You might recall from Chapter 4 that high self-monitors are conscious of how others evaluate them, whereas low self-monitors, on the other hand, are more focused on expressing who they really are. Howard Lavine and Mark Snyder (1996) showed what a difference this could make to attitudes about voting in local and presidential elections. They presented high and low self-monitors either image-focused appeals (which argued that voting enhances a person's status, popularity, and attractiveness) or value-expressive appeals (which pointed out that voting affords the opportunity to confirm and act on values and beliefs). As the researchers expected, high self-monitors had more positive attitudes toward voting when the message appealed to image. In contrast, low self-monitors were more positive when the message focused on value expression. Importantly, those exposed to messages tuned to their individual motivational preferences were also more likely to ask for information about the candidates and more likely to actually vote. Why did such motivationally matched appeals produce these persuasive benefits? First, both high and low self-monitors pay more attention to and spend more time carefully processing information that furthers their goals (DeBono & Harnish, 1988; Petty & Wegener, 1998b). Second, both groups see those functionally relevant arguments as more compelling than arguments that do not speak to their goals (Lavine & Snyder, 1996).

Even transitory goals that highlight our connections to others can have similar effects. When students were given the goal of having a pleasant interaction with others, they were particularly likely to express opinions similar to those of their interaction partners. But this outcome was not the result of a lack of thought. In fact, the students put quite a lot of effort into thinking about their partner's point of view. But the fact that they were motivated to agree with the partner biased this extra thinking toward positive elaboration of the partner's position (Chen, Shechter, & Chaiken, 1996).

3. *Me and mine motivation: The importance of self-relevance.* An old Chinese proverb says, "Tell me and I'll forget; involve me and I'll understand." When information is relevant to something that affects us, we want to know all about it. The product manager,

To remind yourself of characteristics of typical high and low self-monitors, reread Chapter 4, pages 120–121.

for example, knows her decision will affect more than the company's bottom line. With her own reputation at stake, she will be motivated to pay careful attention to the information presented by the competing systems manufacturers.

In a classic demonstration of the influence of self-relevance on persuasion, researchers asked groups of students to listen to a speech dealing with the issue of whether comprehensive exams should be required for graduation (Petty and others, 1981). Some groups heard a speech composed of strong and valid arguments advocating the exams, whereas other groups were given rather weak and silly arguments. Some groups were led to believe the speech had been delivered by an expert communicator—a Princeton University professor of education—whereas others were told the source was a nonexpert—a local high school junior "interested" in such issues. The most important manipulation was one of self-relevance. Some groups of students were told the exam would be implemented at their own school, which meant that they personally would be affected. Other groups were told the exams were planned for another institution, and thus they were personally less relevant. Perhaps you can guess how this manipulation of relevance influenced students' reactions. Those who thought the plan would not affect them processed the communication superficially. Relying on the expertise heuristic, they responded favorably to the expert communicator and unfavorably to the nonexpert, regardless of the message's content. As you can see in Figure 7.5, however, the message had quite a different impact on students who thought the exam proposal would affect them

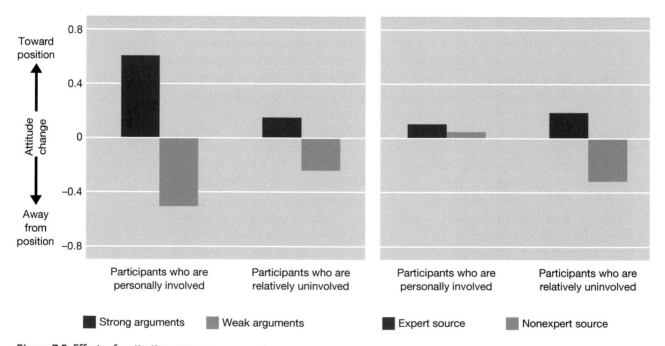

Figure 7.5 Effects of motivation on message processing
In this study, some participants were highly involved in the issue and others were uninvolved. They heard strong or weak arguments, presented by an expert or nonexpert source. Notice that the strength of the arguments made more difference to highly involved participants (graph on left). In contrast, the expertise of the source had more influence on the less involved participants (graph on right). (Data from Petty and others, 1981.)

personally. These students were motivated to pay careful attention to the quality of the arguments. This systematic processing led them to accept strong and compelling arguments and to reject weak and silly ones, regardless of who espoused them.

The relevance of personal goals almost always increases systematic processing of relevant information. Appeals that advocate positions or provide product benefits that match people's needs or their views of themselves are more carefully processed and more compelling than those that don't (Evans & Petty, 2003; Lee & Aaker, 2004). For example, some people are more concerned that their situation gets no worse (they have a prevention focus), whereas others are more concerned about improving their lot (they are promotion focused). Prevention-focused folk find messages that talk about avoiding losses much more compelling, whereas promotion-focused types are more persuaded by gain-oriented appeals (Cesario, Corker, & Jelinek, 2013; Mannetti, Brizi, Giacomantonio, & Higgins, 2013). Similarly, people who approach an issue from a predominately cognitive perspective find a persuasive message on that issue more convincing if it is cognitively versus emotionally focused; and the reverse is true for those with a predominately emotional perspective on the issue (Mayer & Tormala, 2010; See, Petty, & Fabrigar, 2013).

Other consequences of having either a prevention or a promotion focus were discussed in Chapter 4, pages 121–122.

How Capacity Influences Superficial and Systematic Processing. Even when we are highly motivated, we may encounter obstacles to systematic processing. Imagine the product manager spreading the dozen or so computer brochures out on her desk. Each describes different product lines in different ways; each computer system offers different features for different prices. Will she be able to understand and evaluate every claim? Even when people want to process systematically, they are not always able to do so.

1. *The ability to process.* Sometimes, people just do not have the mental resources to take in and evaluate all the available information. Even the most motivated processors

---

SOCIAL PSYCHOLOGY AND CULTURE: CULTURE AND CONNECTEDNESS MATCHING

Given the importance of connectedness motivations, it will come as no surprise that emphasizing the kind of connectedness that makes sense in a culture makes appeals more persuasive. Ayse Uskul and Daphna Oyserman (2010) asked European Americans and Asian Americans who regularly consumed caffeinated drinks to read a message about the health risks of such products. European Americans found especially relevant and were especially persuaded by a message that focused on the personal self—and even more so if they were first reminded of individualist values. As you might expect, Asian Americans, who tend to value collectivist connections, were in contrast more likely to find the health warning more relevant and to accept the health warning when it focused on relational obligations—the effects on other people. Again this cultural value and message framing match was further enhanced if they were first primed with collectivist values. These findings are excellent evidence for the persuasive benefits of matching message content to both the situational and the chronic long-term motivations of recipients. The findings also illustrate that although the content of what motivates people—in this case relevance of the self versus connection to others—differs by culture, the process—matching message and motivation to increase processing and persuasion—is the same across cultures.

of persuasive communications occasionally have difficulty understanding all the complex and rapidly presented information offered in print, radio, and television commercials. This is particularly true when, as in the product manager's case, the information is technical, there is too much of it, or it has multiple dimensions on which alternatives differ.

Consider, for example, a group of college students from a community rocked both by the murders of two local teenage girls and the reduced sentence given one of those convicted as the result of a plea bargain (in plea bargaining, an accused person agrees to plead guilty to a less serious charge, usually in exchange for information that will convict another, or in exchange for a particular sentence). When presented with strong or weak arguments supporting the wider use of plea-bargaining to reduce court backlogs, the students were highly motivated to evaluate them thoroughly and probably to disagree with them (Hafer, Reynolds, & Obertynski, 1996). Why then, did some of them end up agreeing with the position advocated by a judge with a Harvard Law School pedigree and 15 years of experience, regardless of whether his arguments were weak or strong?

The answer lay in the complexity of the legal arguments used to support plea bargaining. In some conditions, the arguments used layperson's terms, common terms, and simple grammatical structures. Indicating their high motivation and thorough evaluation of the messages, students in this condition who read strong arguments were somewhat persuaded, whereas those presented with weak arguments completely dismissed them. But in other conditions, the same strong and weak arguments were framed in legal jargon and complex grammar. Despite their motivation, the students just could not comprehend and evaluate the information, and their attitudes ended up reflecting the expertise heuristic.

SOCIAL PSYCHOLOGY IN PRACTICE: COGNITIVE ABILITY AND ADVERTISING AIMED AT CHILDREN

Children are at a special disadvantage in scrutinizing persuasive messages. Young children often have enough ability to understand a message but lack the critical capacity to evaluate it. Many of them trust television to tell the truth, and they do not always know when programs stop and advertisements begin. Even if they understand the difference between the ad and the television program itself, they may not realize that the intent of the ad is to get them (or their parents) to buy something specific. Indeed, when asked about the purpose of ads placed in a cartoon, none of the children of age 6 in one particular study mentioned persuasion, with most instead suggesting the ads were to offer them a break from the program or to provide information (Oates, Blades, & Gunter, 2002). Though awareness of the persuasive intent of ads increased with age, still only 36 % of 10-year-olds could recognize its true purpose. If children do not realize that an ad is attempting to persuade them, they may have limited ability to resist those messages (Calvert, 2008). Indeed, research has repeatedly shown that children are easily persuaded by television ads. For example, some children watched a television program without commercials and another set of children watched the same show with advertisements for a particular toy. The children who had seen the advertised toy were more likely to ask their parents for it, more likely to have a negative view of a parent who refused to buy the toy, and more likely to play with a "not so nice" boy who had the toy than a "nice boy" who didn't have it (Liebert & Sprafkin, 1988). Moreover, the more commercial TV they watched, the more items young children requested in their letters to "Father Christmas" (Pine & Nash, 2002).

As you might imagine, there are many things that can impact capacity and, thus the ability to systematically process. Indeed, even the liquids we ingest can have an effect. For example, caffeine, a stimulant known to facilitate attention and concentration, seems to increase systematic processing. In one study, students consumed a drink with or without caffeine and then read a persuasive message comprised of strong or weak arguments. Though both groups were more persuaded by the strong message than the weak one, showing systematic processing was occurring, this difference was much more pronounced in the caffeine condition (Martin, Laing, Martin, & Mitchell, 2005). Thus, the common student practice of drinking a cup of coffee or caffeinated soda before taking a test or working on a paper might be effective!

Unfortunately, not everything we drink is so beneficial for processing. Intoxication from alcohol and other drugs can reduce cognitive capacity and lower people's ability to carefully and critically evaluate information. Research shows, for example, that intoxicated individuals have more favorable attitudes than sober individuals toward drinking and driving, and are more likely to report engaging in unprotected sex, partially because they fail to critically evaluate information for and against the action (MacDonald, Zanna, & Fong, 1995, 1996). Some researchers refer to the impact of alcohol on processing as "alcohol myopia:" alcohol reduces people's capacity to systematically process and focuses them on superficial cues in the environment (Steele & Josephs, 1990). Of course, if this is true, alcohol myopia might promote safe sex if the right cues are made salient. In fact, alcohol intake actually encouraged condom use if people at a nightclub had AIDS KILLS stamped on their hands (MacDonald, Fong, Zanna, & Martineau, 2003).

In Chapter 13, page 495, you will see that alcohol has a similar limiting effect on cognitive processing, which can increase emotional aggression.

2. *The opportunity to concentrate.* Even if we have the ability, we cannot process systematically if we cannot concentrate those resources on the job at hand. Ready and willing to understand and evaluate all the relevant material, our hapless manager is suddenly interrupted by the phone. As she hangs up, a co-worker stops by wanting to discuss a purchase order. Then her boss reminds her that the departmental meeting begins in an hour. These continual distractions, as you undoubtedly know from your own experience, will reduce her ability to process information carefully.

By reducing our critical ability, distractions can decrease the effectiveness of strongly persuasive communications because we are not able to elaborate them favorably. To make matters worse, distraction exerts the opposite effect on weak communications. By reducing people's cognitive capacity, distraction makes it difficult for them to counter flawed arguments or demolish shaky logic, and weak communications become more persuasive (Petty, Wells, & Brock, 1976). And as careful processing of message content goes down, people are more influenced by superficial cues. Distracted people are more influenced for example by the expertise heuristic: Their attitudes reflect the presence of a credible source more than their nondistracted counterparts (Baron, Baron, & Miller, 1973). No wonder the old advertising motto recommends: "If you have nothing to say, distract them!"

How Moods and Emotions Influence Superficial and Systematic Persuasive Processing.

Are people in good moods easier to persuade? Most of us think so—perhaps you can recall a time when you cooked someone a special dinner or offered a little gift to create a good mood, before trying to convince that person to do something you wanted. But unless people just rely on their current mood to make the judgment, the role that feeling good plays in persuasion is a little more complicated. Being in a good mood sometimes increases persuasion, but sometimes makes persuasion less likely to occur (Isen & Levin, 1972; Petty, Schumann, Richman, & Strathman, 1993; Wegener, Petty, & Smith, 1995). And obviously, all persuasive appeals don't just try to make people feel good. What about an antismoking appeal that shows a premature baby screaming in an incubator? Or a toothpaste ad showing diseased gums and decaying teeth? Do scenes and ideas that make us feel bad also have persuasive power? In fact, the answer is that both feeling good and feeling bad (or anxious or angry or guilty) can sometimes increase and sometimes decrease persuasion because they can all affect capacity and motivation (Forgas, 1995; Giner-Sorolla, 1999).

Emotional reactions can be triggered directly from a persuasive appeal, as in the case when a commercial features a heart-warming scene, or from events unrelated to the appeal, as in the case when you eat an enjoyable meal right before viewing a television ad. Regardless of their origins, emotions affect capacity because almost all emotions involve some physiological arousal. Arousal and systematic processing are related in a curvilinear way. As arousal increases from low to moderate levels, consideration of persuasive appeals also increases from superficial to some optimal level of systematic processing. But as arousal levels continue to climb, the resources necessary for extensive processing become less and less available. Systematic processing is no longer possible, although superficial processing may well be. Finally, as arousal levels become extreme, no processing at all is possible. Compared to moderate emotions, extreme emotions—terror versus alarm, euphoria versus happiness, misery versus sadness, fury versus irritation, for example—reduce capacity and interfere with the ability to process persuasive information carefully. The experience of abject terror or blind fury leaves little capacity left over for carefully thinking about the pros and cons of a particular attitude object.

By definition, emotions have motivational consequences and thus can facilitate or impede persuasive processing. Some researchers have pointed out that emotions are like the proverbial canary in the coalmine—they tell you if everything is just fine or if danger is imminent. According to the affect as information model (Schwarz & Clore, 1983), positive emotions such as happiness, pride, or joy signal a benign environment about which no additional processing is necessary (Bless and others, 1996; Schwarz, Bless, & Bohner, 1991). Negative emotions like sadness, anger, or fear, on the other hand, convey that something is wrong, and that the situation requires additional processing. According to the affect as information model then, positive emotions will diminish processing of persuasive messages and negative emotions will amplify it. Other theorists have argued that the quality of perceived certainty or control that accompanies an emotion is the crucial motivational driver of emotions (E. J. Johnson & Tversky, 1983; Tiedens & Linton, 2001). Despite both being positive, for example, happiness and surprise differ in whether they are accompanied by feelings of confidence and assuredness (happiness is, surprise isn't), as do anger (a certainty emotion) and fear (an uncertainty emotion). According to this view, people feeling certainty emotions will deal with persuasive appeals superficially, whereas people feeling uncertainty emotions will deal with them systematically.

Notice that both these views suggest that people feeling happy are less likely than people who feel neutral to process the content of persuasive appeals systematically and

SOCIAL PSYCHOLOGY IN PRACTICE: MOTIVATION AND CAPACITY CONSEQUENCES OF FEAR-INDUCING HEALTH MESSAGES

Fear is by far the most common negative emotion that influence agents exploit. Advertisements remind us that body odor or bad breath could make us social pariahs, and public health campaigns show addicted babies, skin cancer wounds, and horribly smashed cars to warn us about smoking during pregnancy, sunbathing, and drinking before driving. Can the scare tactics in these fear appeals really help change our minds?

The answer is yes, under certain conditions.

Fear is evoked by a personally relevant threat that creates anxiety—uncertainty and lack of control. For a fear appeal to be effective, it must increase motivation by triggering concerns for mastery, connectedness, or me and mine. When recipients believe that the threatened negative consequences will happen to them (Leventhal, 1970; R. W. Rogers, 1983), people are motivated to pay attention and start processing. Compared to students who thought they weren't at risk, for example, laptop-using college students told they were likely to suffer repetitive strain injuries (and thus were faced with a personally relevant threat) were better able to distinguish between appeals with strong and weak arguments, showing that they carefully processed the information (de Hoog, Stroebe, & de Wit, 2005).

When a message includes reassuring instructions on how to eliminate the threat, people can adopt its recommendations to reduce fear (Hovland, Janis, & Kelley, 1953; Robberson & Rogers, 1988). A classic study found, for example, that students who received messages about the potentially life-threatening disease tetanus that included specific information about how to get inoculated were more likely than other students to do so (Leventhal, Singer, & Jones, 1965).

Anxiety also influences people's ability to process persuasive information. Consider what happened when college students read a message advocating regular cancer check-ups that contained a number of reasoning errors (Jepson & Chaiken, 1990). Participants who were very fearful of getting cancer showed several signs of superficial processing. They detected fewer errors, recalled fewer arguments, and elaborated message content less than did readers with little fear. It wasn't that fearful participants were avoiding the message; they just didn't seem to be able to do a very good job of dealing with it. As fear increases in intensity, concentrating on complex cognitive tasks like systematic processing becomes harder and harder.

The bottom line? If fear increases motivation without eliminating capacity, it can get people to change stress-causing work habits, get vaccinations, and schedule cancer check-ups.

Photo 7.4 The fear factor. Government health warnings like this one harness fear to provoke changes in attitudes. To be successful, fear appeals must arouse just the right amount of anxiety by showing the negative consequences— like damaged lungs—that will follow if behavior doesn't change. The provision of an explicit avenue of action—like calling a "quit now" hotline for help—eliminates the anxiety by showing how the negative consequences can be avoided.

more likely to rely on persuasion heuristics. The evidence bears this out—happy people faced with persuasive appeals are not impressed by strong compared to weak messages, but they are persuaded by expert compared to nonexpert sources (Mackie, Asuncion, & Rosselli, 1992; Worth & Mackie, 1987). Sadness seems to work in exactly the opposite way—most studies show that sad people process very carefully (Schwarz, Bless, & Bohner, 1991). But what about emotions like anger, which is negative (increasing processing) and certain (reducing processing)? In the few existing studies on anger and persuasive processing, evidence is mixed. Sometimes anger seems to induce superficial processing, making angry people more susceptible to heuristic cues like the expertise or credibility of a source (Bodenhausen, Sheppard, & Kramer, 1994; Tiedens, 2001), and sometimes it triggers systematic processing (Moons & Mackie, 2007).

Apart from suggesting that more research needs to be done, such findings probably mean that multiple motivational and capacity factors are at work when emotions are experienced. Some researchers have suggested, for example, that the key motivating factor of emotions is their "hedonic" value, or how good or bad they make you feel. People feeling good may not want anything to interfere with their good spirits—not even the effort of careful thought (Isen & Levin, 1972)—whereas people feeling bad might want to do anything they can—even processing hard—to replace their bad feelings with good ones. It's true that a good mood can also be harnessed to make people process more. For example, if processors are led to believe that their good mood shows how much they enjoy the task (rather than showing that they are doing fine on it), they process more deeply (L. L. Martin, Ward, Achee, & Wyer, 1993). And if people think that particular information will put them or keep them in a good mood, they think about that material much more (Wegener and others, 1995; see also Hullett, 2005).

Thus, both positive and negative emotions can increase or interfere with persuasion, depending on their motivational and capacity consequences in particular circumstances. If moods reduce either motivation or capacity, persuasion is more likely to depend on superficial processes and less on systematic processing.

The Interplay of Cues and Content.

As you have been reading about systematic and superficial processing, you may have wondered if people use only one or the other when they look at an ad or hear a commercial. It turns out that people often use a mix of superficial and systematic processing and that means that cues and content can interact in some interesting ways.

First, persuasion-relevant information can play multiple roles when it comes to changing attitudes. When you see a famous supermodel endorsing a particular brand of shampoo, for example, the model's attractiveness can operate as a heuristic cue, but it can also act as evidence for the effectiveness of the product. In the same way, a long message might be particularly compelling because of the "length equals strength" heuristic. But those same lengthy arguments might provide ammunition for attitude change if they are processed systematically. Any piece of information in a persuasion setting can be processed superficially or systematically (Kruglanski, Thompson, & Spiegal, 1999; Petty & Wegener, 1998a).

Second, people might engage in both types of processing about the same persuasive message simultaneously and so superficial and systematic processing can work together or at cross-purposes. When a heuristic cue and careful processing suggest the same attitude, the two types of processing can have additive effects (Chen & Chaiken, 1999). For example, if an expert endorses a product and careful consideration of the product's features confirms the product's high quality, then both types of processing may result in your having a very favorable attitude toward the product. Sometimes, however, content processing is at odds with the cue. This can lead to attenuation (Chen & Chaiken, 1999), whereby the impact of the heuristic cue on your attitudes may be weakened considerably by careful processing. For example, if a likable person provides a weak argument, the attractiveness heuristic and careful processing of message content tilt us in different attitudinal directions. In these cases, careful processing of the argument typically overwhelms the influence of the cue, and attitudes will be based more on message content (Maheswaran, Mackie, & Chaiken, 1992).

Finally, when message content is not so convincingly strong or weak, processing can be biased by heuristic cues. The presence of an expert or attractive source might bias reactions to an ambiguous message, making elaborations more favorable. Having a nonexpert or unattractive source deliver the same message might bias reactions in the opposite direction. In these cases lots of thinking goes on, but the thinking is tilted in one direction more than the other, and a similarly slanted attitude results (Chaiken & Maheswaran, 1994). Extensive thinking does not guarantee unbiased attitudes: if thinking is biased, attitudes will be biased in the same way. Thus, cues and content can interplay in interesting ways, having complex effects on persuasion.

In summary, people can be persuaded whether they process superficially or systematically. Both motivation, which is highest when a message taps into the important mastery, connectedness, and me and mine goals, and capacity, which depends on ability and freedom from distraction, are required for systematic processing. Situational factors, personality differences, and emotional states can all influence motivation, capacity, or both, and thus determine whether persuasive appeals are dealt with superficially or systematically. These influences are shown in Figure 7.6. Given all the constraints on motivation and capacity, perhaps you can see now why most persuasive communications are processed superficially.

Photo 7.5 Relying on both heuristic and systematic processing. This ad demonstrates how cues and content might work together at the same time. This ad for the organization Doctors Without Borders allows people to rely on heuristic processing. For example, activation of the length equals strength heuristic makes a positive evaluation of the organization likely. But if, in addition, the ad attracts sustained attention from motivated readers, it also provides lots of strong arguments so that systematic processing will also produce a positive attitude toward Doctors Without Borders.

Figure 7.6 How motivation and capacity influence superficial and systematic processing of persuasive communications If an individual exposed to a persuasive communication has motivation and capacity, a persuasive appeal can be systematically processed and persuasion depends on elaboration of content. If motivation or capacity are lacking, persuasion can still occur but will depend on associations and heuristics.

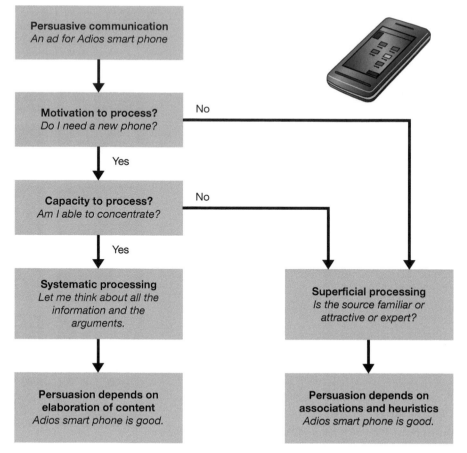

DEFENDING ATTITUDES: RESISTING PERSUASION

Strong arguments compel us; familiarity reassures us; expert and attractive sources inspire us; fear and happiness move us. When it comes to filling our heads or emptying our pockets, communicators have a number of powerful persuasion tools at their disposal. Yet one of the reasons that social psychologists study attitude change so closely, and one of the reasons that persuasion professionals spend so much money and effort on advertising, is that attitudes don't always change willy-nilly. We don't have a complete change of heart and mind with every ad, every appeal, every communication. How do we resist these ever-present inducements to change our attitudes? In fact, established attitudes have a number of built-in defense mechanisms.

Ignoring, Reinterpreting, and Countering Attitude-Inconsistent Information

People protect established attitudes by ignoring, reinterpreting, or resisting information that is inconsistent with them. Being forewarned of a persuasion attempt and having previous experience with related arguments makes persuasion easier to resist, and resisting attitude change can make established attitudes even stronger.

People protect established attitudes by ignoring, reinterpreting, and resisting information that is inconsistent with them. First, we often try to ignore information that challenges our preferred views and deal only with information that supports them. Remember that we mentioned that people usually choose to interact with others who think as they do, and seek out media sources that also confirm their opinions—think about how seldom you read newspaper editorials or internet blogs that oppose rather than support your views (Fischer & Greitemeyer, 2010). By ignoring or evading inconsistent information, we protect our current attitudes.

When we do encounter such information, a second line of defense comes into action: reinterpretation. Any information that is close to an established attitude is often viewed as resembling the attitude exactly, a process called assimilation. So if a newspaper article ranked your school or college as the second most prestigious in the state, you might in fact see this as further confirmation of your view that yours is the best college around. On the other hand, information that is quite discrepant with your view—perhaps the article ranked your institution way down on the list—is often seen as even more inconsistent with the attitude than it actually is, a process called contrast. Such discrepant information is usually ignored as totally invalid and irrelevant.

Finally, attitudes themselves create biases in how information is processed, so that inconsistent information is resisted. Consider what happened, for example, when Charles Lord and his colleagues (C. G. Lord, Ross, & Lepper, 1979) showed Stanford undergraduates who supported or opposed capital punishment two supposed research studies about the issue. One study provided evidence that capital punishment deters crime, a position consistent with an attitude supporting the death penalty. The second study contradicted the first and confirmed the views of the death penalty opponents. Both studies had several strong points but also some obvious weaknesses. As can be seen in Figure 7.7, both the supporters and the opponents of capital punishment judged whichever study was consistent with their own views to be much more convincing than the other one. They favored supportive information by accepting it at face value, while criticizing and rejecting the opposing arguments (Ledgerwood, Mandisodza, Jost, & Pohl, 2011). And this bias toward supportive information is long lasting: people typically remember compelling arguments that support their attitudes but can recall only weak (and easily dismissed) arguments that oppose it (Edwards & Smith, 1996).

This tendency to see attitude-supporting information as especially convincing can be found in many realms, including politics. In one study, students were brought to a lab shortly before a U.S. Presidential debate between Bill Clinton and Bob Dole was to air live on television (Munro, Ditto, Lockhart, Fagerlin, Gready, & Peterson, 2002). Before the debate was shown, the students completed some initial measures, including which candidate they favored. After watching the debate in the lab, the students were

Remember assimilation and contrast effects work the same when it comes to self-evaluations, as discussed in Chapter 4, page 99. If you compare yourself to someone who is similar in ability, you see an assimilation effect, but if you compare yourself to some quite different, then contrast occurs.

These processes contribute to conservatism: well-established attitudes influence thoughts and behaviors in ways that confirm the attitude. We saw the same thing in Chapter 3, why first impressions can be so lasting, and in Chapter 5, why stereotypes are so persistent.

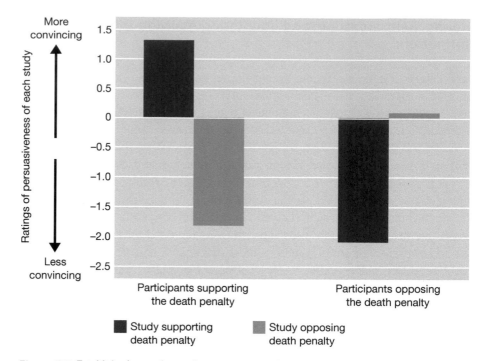

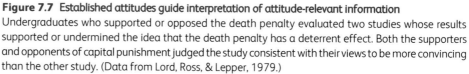

Figure 7.7 Established attitudes guide interpretation of attitude-relevant information
Undergraduates who supported or opposed the death penalty evaluated two studies whose results supported or undermined the idea that the death penalty has a deterrent effect. Both the supporters and opponents of capital punishment judged the study consistent with their views to be more convincing than the other study. (Data from Lord, Ross, & Lepper, 1979.)

asked to assess the quality of the candidates' arguments and to assess which candidate prevailed. Results showed that the students found their pre-debate favored candidate to have "won" and that his arguments were more compelling.

Inoculation: Practice Can Be the Best Resistance Medicine. People do an even better job of protecting their opinion if they are forewarned, or know in advance they are going to be attacked. When people expect others to try to change attitudes that are important to them, they marshal arguments to mount a good defense (Wood & Quinn, 2003) and the more time they have to prepare a defense, the more successfully they resist persuasion (Freedman & Sears, 1965).

William McGuire (1964) in fact suggested that the most effective way to resist persuasion is to practice arguing against a persuasive appeal. He drew an analogy to medical inoculations, which stimulate the body's defenses by exposing the person to weak doses of an infection. According to McGuire, immunity to arguments can be obtained in the same way. The strategy seems to work (McAlister, Perry, Killen, Slinkard, & Maccoby, 1980). Indeed, in one study, some young adults with positive attitudes about condom use and negative ones about binge drinking were initially presented with arguments against the use of condoms. But, along with these attacks, they were given strong counter-arguments to refute each one, allowing them to potentially inoculate themselves against them. Other young adults were not given this inoculation opportunity. Later, the young adults encountered two persuasive messages that attacked their pre-existing attitudes concerning binge drinking and condom use. The results indicated the effectiveness of the inoculation. Compared to those in the control group, those in the inoculation group were better able to resist the persuasive attack not only on the inoculated topic (condom use) but also on the non-inoculated one (on binge drinking; Parker, Ivanov, & Compton, 2012). Thus, inoculation might provide "umbrella protection" against not only the target attitude, but other related ones as well.

Finally, the effectiveness of inoculation can also be seen indirectly when examining attitudes that we rarely defend. If we rarely practice defending a particular attitude, it should be quite vulnerable to change when attacked. Recent work shows that attitudes that rest on values, like those about affirmative action, are more effectively changed when the value, rather than the attitude itself, is targeted, perhaps because we rarely defend values (Blankenship, Wegener, & Murray, 2012).

Working hard to counter or argue against a persuasive attempt can have some important consequences. When we process information to defend our established views—accepting consistent information, criticizing discrepant information—we can end up with more extreme views. In the death penalty study we described earlier, for example, reading the same body of conflicting information actually increased the disagreement between the two groups after each had processed it in a biased manner. Supporters of the death penalty now believed even more intensely in capital punishment, whereas its opponents were even more firmly opposed. The processes we engage in to defend our attitudes can also make them even more extreme (Munro & Ditto, 1997).

We might also come to hold an opinion with more certainty. When college students were told to resist a persuasive message, everyone was able to do so (no one's attitudes changed; Tormala & Petty, 2004). Although everyone saw the same message, some students were led to believe that the arguments they had resisted had been strong and compelling, whereas others were told that the arguments had not been very convincing anyway. When students believed that they had resisted strong rather than weak arguments, they felt much more certain about their original opinion—they must feel strongly about it, since they had overcome such persuasive arguments! Of course the flip side is also true—when people believe they did a poor job of defending their views, they lose confidence in them, and are more vulnerable to changing their minds in the face of subsequent persuasive attacks (Tormala, Clarkson, & Petty, 2006).

What It Takes to Resist Persuasion

Because it involves careful thinking, resisting attitude change depends on having the motivation and capacity to fight off a persuasion attempt. Many people overestimate their ability to resist persuasive appeals.

Resisting attitude change depends on having the motivation and capacity to fight off a persuasion attempt. When people don't care about a particular attitude issue, they are less likely to resist claims about it—if they even bother to listen to the persuasive appeal in the first place. But attitudes related to important personal goals are much harder to change (Johnson & Eagly, 1989), as are strong attitudes about which we are both certain and confident (Clarkson, Tormala, & Rucker, 2008). When attitudes are important, people are motivated to resist the threat to self-image and self-interest that changing them entails (Darke & Chaiken, 2005; Wood & Quinn, 2003). They are also motivated to build up an informational base that supports their views and gives them ammunition to fight off challenges to those views (Holbrook, Berent, Krosnick, Visser, & Boninger, 2005). Similarly, people need capacity to counteract a persuasive attempt. Forewarning may help people resist attitude change attempts, in part, because it alerts them to conserve necessary resources to engage in counter-arguing (Janssen, Fennis, & Pruyn, 2010). Without the ability, time, or opportunity to marshal arguments for the defense, people are more vulnerable to appeals that try to change their minds.

The take-home message from this research is clear: careful thinking and practice with counter-arguing can make us less vulnerable to persuasion attempts. But what happens if we don't even know we are being persuaded? As we've already seen, research shows that evaluative conditioning, familiarity effects, and some heuristic cues operate whether we see the stimuli or not. But those same research findings make clear the limits on such influence. Importantly, the influence of subliminal cues can also be overcome by conscious processing, just as we saw that systematic processing often overturns superficial processing. For example, subliminal effects on our attitudes and behavior seem to occur only when they are consistent with consciously held goals. Consider one study where students arrived at a study fairly thirsty, having not had anything to drink for three hours (Strahan, Spencer, & Zanna, 2002). Some of these students were then allowed to drink some water, quenching their thirst, but others were not. Next, all students were subliminally exposed to words related or unrelated to thirst. Afterward, participants were given the opportunity to drink. Did everyone primed with thirst drink more? No. As can be seen in Figure 7.8, results showed that only the still thirsty students drank more if thirst-primed than non-thirst primed. The priming had no impact on students who

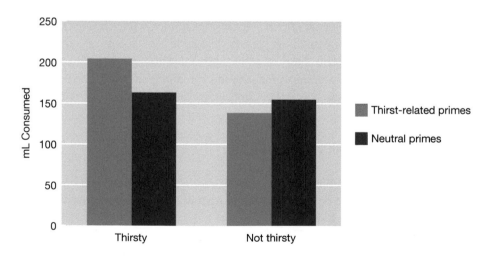

Figure 7.8 Effects of subliminal processing depend on conscious goals
Canadian male and female undergraduates who were thirsty or who had just quenched their thirst were exposed to subliminally presented words. Some of the words were related to thirst and some were not. Only the thirsty students drank more if primed with thirst-related words compared to when they were not. (Data from Strahan, Zanna, & Spencer, 2002.)

were no longer thirsty. In other words, the subliminal cues nudged participants to do what they already wanted to do, but had no effect on people who did not already have the goal.

Other research showed the same thing when students were subliminally exposed to words related or unrelated to achievement and then expressed their preferences for activities such as "I would rather spend my time at the library than at a party" and "I think that I am more motivated to achieve than have fun." Was it the case the subliminal exposure to achievement words prompted all students to prefer achievement over fun? Again, the answer is no. Only those students who were high in achievement motivation showed this effect. That is, achievement priming (compared to non-achievement priming) led to more preference for achievement only for those who consciously cared about achievement (Hart & Albarracin, 2009; Milyavsky, Hassin, & Schul, 2012). So just as systematic processing can redirect or reverse the attitudes that superficial processing inclines us to, conscious processing can resist the influence of subliminally processed cues.

Interestingly, people tend to overestimate both their invulnerability to persuasive appeals and their ability to generate effective arguments to counter them (Wilson, Gilbert, & Wheatley, 1998; Wilson, Houston, & Meyers, 1998). Such beliefs make the task of the professional persuader much easier! Most people think they possess special skills—"strong-mindedness" and "willingness to engage in careful processing"—that stop them personally falling prey to persuasive appeals even as "weaker-minded" others succumb to unwanted influence (Douglas, Sutton, & Stathi, 2010; Xu & Wyer, 2010). So other people might get fooled, but they certainly won't! No wonder then that just telling people that deceptive ads can fool people does not reduce their impact. What does work? One study of resistance effects found that only a personal demonstration to each participant that he or she had been duped was enough to bring the targets of deceptive ads to their senses (Sagarin, Cialdini, Rice, & Serna, 2002). A recent meta-analysis indicated that interventions designed to make people think critically about media-based persuasive appeals were largely successful in making both adults and children more skeptical about what they were told and more resistant to it. Interestingly, however, such interventions were more effective the more sessions they included; the more practice people got in actively resisting, the better they were at it (Jeong, Cho, & Hwang, 2012).

So if you think, as most people do, that you are immune to the influence of persuasive appeals, take a lesson from the research findings: get over it! Whether the appeal is subliminal or conscious, thinking is the key: To resist persuasion on important issues, we must put time and effort into our judgments.

CONCLUDING COMMENTS

Persuasion has a pretty bad reputation. We often associate advertising with attempts to make us buy products we do not want or cannot afford. Political campaigns often seem little more than attempts to package and sell candidates who might not prevail if considered on their merits. Classic literature like George Orwell's *1984* warns us that by controlling information and playing on feelings, totalitarian governments may even persuade their citizens that the history they remember never really happened.

CHAPTER 7 THEMES

■ **Construction of Reality**
We construct attitudes based on our beliefs, feelings, and behaviors about objects.

■ **Pervasiveness of Social Influence**
In this construction process, we draw heavily on persuasive communications from others.

■ **Striving for Mastery**
Attitudes help us master our environment and obtain rewards.

■ **Seeking Connectedness**
Attitudes also help us express our connectedness with groups or ideas we value.

■ **Conservatism**
An existing attitude shapes our interpretations in ways that confirm the attitude.

■ **Accessibility**
Attitudes are formed and changed on the basis of whatever attributes of or associations with the attitude object come to mind most readily.

■ **Superficiality Versus Depth**
Attitude change may result when we process persuasive messages superficially or when we think about them in more depth.

Realizing that persuaders do not always have our best interests at heart is healthy: It pays to remember that we can be misled. And it helps if we know what we are up against. The citizens of ancient Greece and Rome were schooled in the art—and artifice—of argumentation. But most of today's citizens, unless they take classes in social psychology or communication, are taught little about the different ways in which attitude change can come about. Perhaps the most important lesson to be learned from the research discussed in this chapter is that influence is not something that others do to us: Whether we are persuaded or not lies largely in our own hands, or at least in our own heads.

When we do not care about or cannot cope with persuasive messages, we may well be influenced by emotional appeals, celebrity endorsements, and the use of complicated statistics. Of course, such simple cues work pretty well for us most of the time. But sometimes circumstances demand careful evaluation of a communication. When we are motivated by concerns about mastery and connectedness, we pay attention, try to make sense of the information presented to us, and think it through carefully. This kind of careful thinking, responding, and reacting can help a persuasion attempt to flourish or can let it wither away. Just as careful thought can flesh out a first impression into a coherent and balanced view of another individual, or take us beyond stereotypes and prejudices to more individualized conceptions of groups and their members, so careful thinking can prove a persuasion cue wrong and show a tear-jerker to be nothing more than a manipulative tug on the heartstrings. Systematic processing does not always mean we get things right—as we have seen, processing can be biased too, and more biased processing just means more bias. Regardless of whether we are superficially or systematically processing, it's what and how we process that determines whether or not our attitudes change. It's important to remember: we quite literally persuade ourselves.

Realizing our role in attitude change enables us to view persuasion as an empowering process rather than an overpowering one. In ancient Greece, the Sophists believed that persuasion was needed to lay bare the advantages and disadvantages of any object, and Aristotle argued that persuasion was needed to ensure that everyone came to see what was true and good. Persuasion does not have to involve deception, confusion, and trickery. The same processes that sometimes sell us inferior products and disreputable politicians are also at work when charitable organizations raise money for worthy causes, when public service messages improve the population's health and wellbeing, and when parents pass their values along to a new generation.

SUMMARY

Attitudes and Their Origins. To understand **attitude change**—the process by which evaluations of objects are altered, attitude researchers infer **attitudes** from how people react to attitude objects. Such reactions can range from subtle uncontrollable evaluative reactions that people are unaware of, to more deliberate and controllable expressions of support or opposition. Assessing these different reactions shows that **implicit attitudes** can sometimes differ from **explicit attitudes**.

People form attitudes because attitudes are useful. Attitudes help people master the environment, via the **knowledge** and **instrumental functions**, and express important connections with others, via the **social identity** and **impression management functions**. People combine the important, salient, and accessible positive and negative pieces of cognitive, affective, and behavioral information they acquire about an attitude object to form an attitude. That combination determines the direction and intensity of the attitude toward the object and can produce **strong attitudes** or **ambivalent attitudes**. Once an attitude is formed, it is associated with the attitude object.

Superficial and Systematic Routes to Persuasion: From Snap Judgments to Considered Opinions.

When people are targets of **persuasion**, they often do not give persuasive communications much thought. In this case, various superficial aspects of the persuasive appeal can lead to attitude change. For example, people might form a positive or negative attitude because positive or negative objects or events become associated with the attitude object, via a process called **evaluative conditioning**. The mere exposure effect can make people feel more positively about objects they have frequently encountered. People might also be influenced by **persuasion heuristics** to agree with messages from familiar, attractive, or expert sources or with familiar or long messages.

Sometimes people carefully consider the content of arguments presented in a persuasive communication. When people pay attention to a message, understand its content, and react to it, a process called **elaboration**, systematic processing changes attitudes. Attitudes resulting from such systematic processing last longer and are more resistant to later change than most attitudes produced by superficial processing. Sometimes people engaged in systematic processing not only elaborate on information, they might also think about what those elaborations mean. Such **metacognition** can also affect whether or not a persuasion appeal is accepted.

According to the **Elaboration Likelihood Model** and other similar theories, people process messages systematically only when they have both the motivation and the cognitive capacity to do so. Motivation is high when the message is relevant to important goals. Cognitive capacity is available when people have the ability to process and can do so without distraction. People differ in their levels of motivation and capacity to process different kinds of messages. Messages that match people's motivation and capacity are most persuasive. Positive and negative emotions influence persuasion because they have motivational and capacity consequences. People often use a mix of superficial and systematic processing, meaning that cues and content can interact in some interesting ways.

Defending Attitudes: Resisting Persuasion.

People protect established attitudes by ignoring, reinterpreting, or resisting information that is inconsistent with them. Being forewarned of a persuasion attempt and having previous experience with related arguments makes persuasion easier to resist, and resisting attitude change can make established attitudes even stronger. Because it involves careful thinking, resisting attitude change depends on having the motivation and capacity to fight off a persuasion attempt. Many people overestimate their ability to resist persuasive appeals.

8

ATTITUDES AND BEHAVIOR

ACCESSIBILITY
COGNITIVE DISSONANCE
HABIT
CONSERVATISM FOOT-IN-THE-DOOR
CHOICE HYPOCRISY SELF-PERCEPTION INTENTION
INSUFFICIENT JUSTIFICATION REASONED ACTION
ACTION EFFORT

Most of us assume that what we think and feel on the inside goes along with what we do on the outside—that attitudes and behaviors go hand in hand. Recall from Chapter 7 that an attitude is any mental representation that summarizes our evaluation of an attitude object. We take for granted that our political attitudes (the candidates we prefer, for example) are related to our political behaviors (the candidates we vote for). We assume that we eat what we like and like what we eat, and that we spend time with people we like and like the people we spend time with. Social psychology provides considerable evidence for this comfortable consistency between attitudes and behaviors. As pointed out in previous chapters, we typically treat attitude objects, including other people and other groups, in ways consistent with our attitudes toward them, approaching, accepting, and supporting those we like while avoiding, rejecting, or victimizing those we don't.

Attitudes and behaviors are often related like this for two very good reasons. The first is that actions influence attitudes. Recall from Chapter 7 that attitudes are constructed on the basis of behavioral information, as well as cognitive and affective information. So although we might not always be aware of it, what we do can affect our attitudes. Collecting cans for recycling can help develop caring attitudes toward environmental conservation; donating some loose change to a panhandler can generate positive attitudes toward the homeless. In the first part of this chapter, we consider two different ways in which behaviors become building blocks for attitudes. Sometimes people's behavior impacts their attitudes directly, because an action is simply associated with or implies an attitude. At other times, when behavior has more serious consequences, for example, people work hard to justify or rationalize their actions, and this too can result in attitude change. When our attitudes are changed by our actions, it's not surprising that actions and attitudes go hand in hand.

The second reason attitudes and behaviors are often predictably related is that given the right conditions, attitudes influence actions. Attitudes dictate how we look at attitude objects, and this in turn determines how we act toward them. You may recall examples of this from earlier chapters: Seeing their team as the most talented, the fans turn out for every game. Noticing only the immigrant's differences, the bigot refuses to hire him.

Focusing on their child's positive qualities, the doting parents pamper and indulge him. Attitudes sometimes trigger action in an almost knee-jerk fashion, with very little forethought. On other occasions, the process is more deliberate. When this happens, our attitudes produce intentions to act in particular ways, and much time, effort, and thought is exerted to follow through on those intentions. The means by which attitudes shape and direct behavior are the topic of the second part of the chapter.

Just because attitudes and behaviors are predictably related does not mean, however, that they will always be consistent. We sometimes act against our personal convictions. We raid the children's Halloween candy when we mean to diet. We watch action movies even though we hate media violence. We buy trucks for our nephews and dolls for our nieces despite our long-standing opposition to gender stereotypes. Why don't we always act in line with our attitudes? First, some important conditions have to be in place for attitudes to guide behavior, and we review these conditions in the final section of this chapter. Second, attitudes are only one of several factors that can affect behavior. As we have already seen in several chapters, social norms can also have powerful effects on behavior, and sometimes they, rather than attitudes, direct behavior. The impact of norms on behavior is so important that we will cover that topic in Chapters 9 and 10.

CHANGING ATTITUDES WITH ACTIONS

Have you ever found yourself in a brand new role? Perhaps you just started a job as a cashier or were elected president of a student organization dedicated to increasing conservation on campus. A new position demands new actions and new ways of interacting with people, and these new actions soon spawn new attitudes. When Seymour Lieberman (1956) followed the careers of male factory workers, he found just such a change. Workers promoted to foremen soon showed increased sympathy for management's viewpoint; in contrast, those newly elected to union offices adopted more hard-line union positions. Lieberman's findings show the tremendous impact of career choices: Careers can dictate conduct, which in turn can determine character. So choose carefully! Even playing a part can change attitudes. For example, students playing the role of U.S. advisers in international negotiation games often develop hard-line pro-U.S. positions (Trost, Cialdini, & Maass, 1989). If such transitory roles can exert this influence, it's no wonder that "taking on" the preferences of the roles they play is an occupational hazard for some actors and actresses (Magnusson, 1981). From Richard Burton and Elizabeth Taylor to Angelina Jolie and Brad Pitt, how many actresses and actors seem to get romantically involved in real life with their on-screen romantic interests?

As these examples illustrate, behavior can be an important part of the information on which we base our attitudes: new actions contribute to new attitudes. How does information about our actions exert an influence on our attitudes? By now, you know that people deal with information either superficially or

Photo 8.1 Actions changing attitudes. This grandfather is getting help with a laptop. The action of trying out the laptop and learning to use its features may lead him to develop positive attitudes about laptop usage.

systematically. We deal with information about our own behavior the same ways. Sometimes people take what they do at face value and make simple action-to-attitude associations and inferences. Especially if the behavior has serious consequences, however, people consider the implications of their actions more deeply.

From Action to Attitude via Superficial Processing

Behavior is an important part of the information on which people base attitudes. If behaviors change, attitudes can also change. When people process superficially, attitudes can be based on associations with actions or on inferences from actions. Like other forms of superficial processing, actions are more likely to affect attitudes in this way when people lack the motivation or ability to process more thoroughly.

At the most superficial level of processing, attitudes can be based on associations with actions. This is because some actions, even simple muscle movements, are associated with agreement, pleasure, and approach whereas other actions are associated with their opposites. When they like something, people tend to smile, nod their heads, and move the object toward them. When they don't, they frown, shake their head, and push disliked objects away. Even ambivalence is associated with movement—people standing on a Wii balance board moved from side to side, rather than leaning forward in approach or back in rejection, more often when they had mixed reactions to a newspaper article they were reading (Schneider and others, 2013).

Associations with Action. Because of these associations, movements that are strongly associated with liking and disliking can rub off when they occur in the presence of an attitude object. This is what happened in a study in which participants were told to pull up or push down on a bar while they were evaluating "foreign" (actually nonsense) words like *begrid*, *plicen*, and *triwen* (Priester, Cacioppo, & Petty, 1996). Pulling up on the bar used muscle movements that typically bring objects closer, whereas pushing down on the bar required the muscle extension used in pushing objects away. Those who pulled up on the bar liked the words more than those who pushed down on it: the associated positivity or negativity of the muscle movement affected the perceived positivity and negativity of the words. Cultural rituals of greeting like gripping a hand, inclining the head forward, or hugging someone to you, may work to give attitudes toward fellow group members a subtly positive boost.

The impact of such activity is also seen in an ingenious study that demonstrated how nodding and shaking the head affects attitudes (Wells & Petty, 1980). To see if participants would infer their attitudes from such head movements, the researchers led them to believe they were testing the sound quality of stereo headphones during jogging or bike riding. To simulate jogging, some participants were asked to move their heads up and down; to simulate bicycling, others moved their heads from side to side. These actions were carried out as they listened through headphones to an editorial, supposedly broadcast from the campus radio station, that advocated increases or decreases in college tuition. As you can see in Figure 8.1, the gestures had an impact. Head nodders were more supportive of the position advocated in the broadcast, whereas head shakers opposed the position.

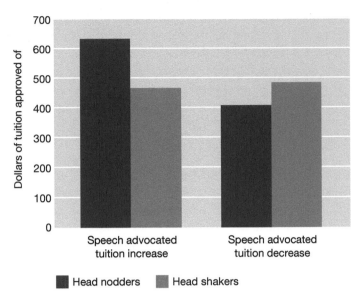

Figure 8.1 Head movements and opinions: Inferring attitudes from actions
In this study, participants nodded their heads up and down or shook them from side to side while listening to a speech calling for raised or lowered tuition. As you can see, their gestures influenced their attitudes. The nodders (darker bars) were more supportive of the position taken in the message than the shakers (lighter bars). (Data from Wells & Petty, 1980.)

Does this mean evaluations are literally in your muscles? Because the association between some muscle movements and positive or negative evaluation is very strong, activating those muscles and movements makes particular attitudes more likely. But this effect depends upon what such movements mean to us. People believe that actions reflect intention and motivation. Just as we think that others' actions reflect their inner states, we are used to assuming our own do too, unless something tells us otherwise (Preston, Ritter, & Wegner, 2011). This is what happened in a series of studies in which students moved a computer mouse either toward an object or away from it, muscle movements that typically facilitate positive or negative evaluations, respectively. The twist in this study was that some students' muscles moved like this because their hands were passively resting on the hands of other students who actually controlled whether an approach or avoidant movement was made (Taylor, Lord, & Bond, 2009). Only the students who intended their movements came to like what they approached and dislike what they avoided. Although the passively guided students made the same movements, the automatically assumed meaning of these movements (liking or disliking) was apparently disrupted, undermining the action-to-attitude effect. Consistent with the idea that it is the associated meaning of the movements that affects attitudes, head nodders are more confident that the evaluative reactions they have while nodding are correct, whereas head shakers have more doubts about their reactions. People who write evaluations with their confident dominant hand are more likely to adopt those evaluations than when they write the same thing with their shakier, less confident non-dominant hand (Briñol & Petty, 2003).

You might remember from Chapter 3, pages 69–72, that this process of assuming that someone has a quality that corresponds to his or her behavior is called a correspondent inference.

Inferences from Action: Self-Perception Theory. Because actions and evaluations are associated, people often make straightforward inferences from their actions to their attitudes. Smiling indicates being amused. Eating something indicates liking it. Signing a petition means you support the position it advocates. Darryl Bem's (1972) theory of self-perception explains the impact of actions on attitudes by suggesting that people infer

Chapter 4, pages 97–98, described this process at work as people infer their own personal characteristics, like traits and dispositions, from their actions.

their attitudes by observing their own behaviors and the situations in which those actions occur. You may have experienced self-perception processes yourself. Have you ever contemplated the growing presence of Lorde on your playlist, and suddenly realized you had developed a taste for indie music? Or, noting that you are spending more and more time at the gym, have you decided that you are committed to the benefits of regular exercise?

Researchers have mimicked such situations experimentally by making particular aspects of participants' previous behavior salient and then measuring their attitudes (Salancik & Conway, 1975). Dolores Albarracin and Robert Wyer (2000) led some students to believe, falsely, that they had expressed support for instituting comprehensive exams for graduating seniors, and others to believe that they had expressed opposition to the exams. They managed this clever ruse by telling students that various attitude issues were being subliminally presented on a computer screen, and asking them to let their "unconscious impulses" guide them to press a "yes" or "no" button to support or oppose the issue. Of course, no subliminal stimuli were presented, but students believed the experimenters' false feedback that they had either supported or opposed having comprehensive exams. When later asked about their attitudes, the group that believed they had already expressed support was much more favorable toward the exams than was the group who thought they had expressed opposition.

Here's an equally subtle but much more everyday demonstration of the same effect: saying what you think someone else wants to hear. When students were asked to describe a man to someone who supposedly either liked or disliked him, they said—perhaps not surprisingly—more good things about the man when they believed the listener liked him than when the listener did not (Hausmann, Levine, & Higgins, 2008; Higgins & Rholes, 1978). More surprisingly, what participants said colored their own attitudes. Those who had given glowing descriptions ended up liking the man better than those who had described him less favorably. How can you use this "saying is believing" effect in your favor? If you want to improve your professor's or boss's opinion of you, ask her to write a strongly positive letter of recommendation for you, especially if that letter is going to someone she knows already thinks highly of you.

Consistent with self-perception theory, people often infer their attitudes from their behavior. However, Bem was very clear that self-perception was likely only when people chose their own behaviors freely rather than being forced to do them. As we saw in Chapter 4, people are quick to see their own behavior as determined by environmental forces. Not surprisingly, this tendency undermines the operation of self-perception processes. If attending religious services or donating to a cause is forced on you by parental insistence or by social pressure from your co-workers, you are unlikely to infer that your actions really had implications for something about your own attitudes (Burger & Caldwell, 2003; DeJong, 1979). You may recognize some irony here. Although we are used to thinking that we like what we are rewarded for, it is often the case that behaviors undertaken for external rewards fail to translate into internal preferences.

Advertisers and sales personnel have been quick to take advantage of the connection between behavior and attitude change. They sponsor slogan-writing contests that induce thousands of people to describe the benefits of particular products. They offer their products to game shows, assuming that having contestants compete for their goods will make those products seem valuable. Sales personnel are content with a small purchase from their customer, knowing that one small commitment to a product will often result

In Chapter 4, page 97, we discussed extrinsically motivated behavior, behaviors performed as a means to some external end. Such behaviors often do not reflect our attitudes, and external rewards usually stop us from inferring action-consistent attitudes.

HOT TOPICS IN SOCIAL PSYCHOLOGY: SELF-PERCEPTION AND CHOICE

Self-perception theory suggests that making an active behavioral choice is more reflective of internal states than performing the same behavior without choice. If so, offering particular choices might be an especially effective way to bring about long-term and sustained behavioral change in important domains. For example, researchers have shown that actively choosing a particular course of action over the alternative of doing nothing increases people's persistence with the chosen option (Schrift & Parker, 2014). In these studies, participants were given a word-search task. Some were allowed to choose between two options as the topic for the word-search puzzle. Others were given this same choice, as well as the choice of not completing the task at all. Consistent with the idea that making the choice to act is important, participants who could choose not to complete the task spent significantly longer on the word-search puzzle than did those in the other condition. In another study showing the practical benefits of such an effect, researchers had some patients receive instructions to call and schedule an appointment for a colonoscopy (a cancer-screening procedure that many people avoid despite its effectiveness). These patients were more likely to actually show up for the appointment compared to others who were notified that an appointment had been scheduled for them at the same date and time. Those who actively chose an option were more likely to follow through than those who were passively given the option (Narula, Ramprasad, Ruggs, & Hebl, 2014). Thus managing alternatives so that people make the "right" choices can help change attitudes and help trigger persistent attitude-consistent behavior.

in larger and larger sales. Thus, the simple process of self-perception has become a popular—and effective—social influence technique.

The Foot-in-the-Door Technique: Could You Do This Small Thing (First)? A particularly clever ploy that takes advantage of people's tendency to judge their own behavior at face value is called the **foot-in-the-door technique**. As the name implies, this social influence technique is like the tactics of door-to-door salespeople who try to get their foot in a customer's door, so the customer has to listen. To use the foot-in-the-door technique, you get people to perform a small act consistent with an intended goal, and this "foot in the door" makes them open to further influence. Jonathan Freedman and Scott Fraser (1966) demonstrated the technique's effectiveness when they approached female householders in California and asked them to sign a petition supporting safe driving. Nearly all complied. Then, about 2 weeks later, they contacted the same women, and some who had never been approached before, with a big request: Would they agree to let the experimenters place a large, ugly "Drive Safely" sign in their front yards? Three times as many people who had gone along with the first small request agreed to do so compared to those who had not received the first request. The fact that people are more likely to agree to a large request if they have first made a small consistent commitment has been demonstrated over and over again, including when the requests are made by email rather than face to face (Guéguen, 2002) and by an avatar in a virtual world (Eastwick & Gardner, 2009). The foot-in-the-door technique might even get you more dates! In one study, a man approached a young woman in public and asked her to join him for a drink. In some conditions, however, the man first asked her for directions or to light his cigarette. Women agreed to the drink much more in the foot-in-the-door conditions (Guéguen, Marchand, Pascual, & Lourel, 2008).

foot-in-the-door technique
a technique for increasing compliance with a large request by first asking people to go along with a smaller request, engaging self-perception processes

Photo 8.2 The foot-in-the-door. Beware of taking actions consistent with an attitude if you aren't prepared to perform even more costly and effortful actions in service of the same attitude. The simple act of signing a petition in favor of some cause may make this man susceptible to agreeing to make a monetary donation later, demonstrating the foot-in-the-door technique at work.

Of course, when you make a commitment, even a small one, you might worry about what it means for your reputation, as well as what it means for your opinions. We look at how commitments change behaviors in Chapter 10, pages 368–370.

How does the foot-in-the-door technique work? Why would a small inconsequential act of signing a petition translate into a costly commitment to obscure one's house behind an unattractive billboard? The answer is that performance of the initial behavior triggers self-perception processes, and the presence of an action-consistent attitude is inferred. This new attitude then makes agreement with the second request more likely, but only if all the conditions for self perception are met (Burger, 1999). First, of course, the initial behavior must be freely chosen—only when the initial choice seems ours alone are we likely to infer that we hold an action-consistent attitude. Second, the initial action must be significant or distinctive enough to allow people to draw an inference about themselves and their attitudes (Dolinski, 2012). Performing the first request can be made meaningful if the person using the foot-in-the-door technique draws the self-perception inference for the target. When people who donated to a charity after a first request were explicitly told: "You are the kind of person who supports charitable causes," they were even more likely to give a second generous donation than were donors whose first gift was received without comment (Burger & Caldwell, 2003). But as long as people try to comply with the first request (even if they fail in the end), they seem to make the self-perception connection (Dolinski, 2000). Of course, initial requests cannot be so large that people will refuse them. In this case, self-perception processes can backfire and work against further change.

SOCIAL PSYCHOLOGY IN PRACTICE: SELF-PERCEPTION PROCESSES AND HEALTH

With its ability to turn small commitments into large convictions, the foot-in-the-door technique is particularly helpful to those trying to improve people's health-related behaviors. Paul Bloom and his colleagues (Bloom, McBride, Pollak, Schwartz-Bloom, & Lipkus, 2006) used the technique to persuade teen smokers to volunteer for a smoking-cessation program. Teen smokers were approached at malls and some were asked to answer a few questions or watch a short video about the negative effects of nicotine. The fact that they agreed to do so apparently led at least some of these teens to believe they had negative attitudes toward smoking that opened the way for further influence. When the teens were called back by telephone several weeks later and asked to join a smoking cessation program, the 12% signup rate—significantly higher than the rate of teens who had not been approached before—was credited to the foot-in-the-door technique. Other research-practitioners have used the same small-agreement-followed-by-large-request technique to increase HIV vaccinations (Cox, Cox, Sturm, & Zimet, 2010) and willingness to be an organ donor (Girandola, 2002). These effects are even stronger when people can easily imagine themselves performing the health behaviors in question (Levav & Fitzsimons, 2006). When they affect self-perception, small health-oriented behaviors produce staunch health-invested individuals.

When Do Action-to-Attitude Inferences Change Attitudes? So actions, from muscle movements to activities that reflect the self, can lead us to adopt consistent attitudes. Such action-to-attitude associations and inferences are most likely to occur, however, when people don't have capacity or motivation to take much notice of or think very much about these changes. First, foot-in-the-door effects are strongest when people's cognitive resources have been exhausted, and they are less likely to show the same effects when given the opportunity to think about the situation (Janssen, Fennis, Pruyn, & Vohs, 2008).

Second, action-to-attitude inferences are most likely when attitudes are unformed or unimportant. Although approach and avoidance arm movements can change positive and negative ratings of unknown objects like nonsense words, they don't have this dramatic effect on evaluative judgments of real words about which students have a well-established evaluation (Priester and others, 1996). For example, approach body movements can make a well-established positive attitude (say, liking for a candy bar) more positive, but avoidance movements cannot undermine it (Centerbar & Clore, 2006). Similarly, avoidance movements make evaluations of disgusting foods (like cow lungs, for example) more negative, but approach behaviors have no influence (Förster, 2004).

The same effect was demonstrated when researchers measured students' environmental attitudes, gave the students the opportunity to donate money to the environmental organization Greenpeace, and later measured their attitudes again. Students who did not at first have strongly or clearly defined attitudes on the issue changed their later attitudes in the direction of their behavior: those who donated money supported the environment more strongly, whereas those who didn't donate later reported more anti-conservation attitudes. Self-perception processes seemed to be at work. But behavior did not change the opinions of students with well-established environmental attitudes—whether they donated or not, they did not use their behavior to infer new attitudes (Holland, Verplanken, & van Knippenberg, 2002; Chaiken & Baldwin, 1981).

As these studies show, actions are likely to lead us to adopt consistent attitudes when people think rather superficially. When attitudes are well established and important, and the consequences of changing them are serious and significant to the self, people tend to think much more systematically about behavior that contradicts them. Just as high motivation increases systematic processing of persuasive communications, high stakes also cause us to think much more about our behavior and our attitudes. Often the very importance of the attitude that is contradicted makes that attitude hard to change. But in the right circumstances, thinking about the implications of attitude inconsistent behavior can change even important attitudes.

Cognitive Dissonance: Changing Attitudes to Justify Behavior

When freely chosen actions violate important self-relevant attitudes, the inconsistency produces an uncomfortable state of tension and arousal called cognitive dissonance, which can motivate people to change their attitudes to make them consistent with their behavior. Because this kind of attitude change involves extensive processing, it is often long-lasting. However, there are alternatives to reducing dissonance besides changing our attitudes. While minor discrepancies between action and attitudes might trigger self-perception processes, conflicts between actions and attitudes that are important enough to cause unpleasant tension trigger dissonance reduction processes.

Actions sometimes contradict important attitudes. Especially when they first come to school, most students at universities in the U.S. are firmly opposed to cheating. But anonymous surveys reveal that many of them actually end up cheating in one way or another during their college careers (Storch & Storch, 2003). The ones who do certainly don't act in line with their attitudes. Among Europeans given a description of an electric car and a traditional car, roughly 40% stated a preference to buy the electric one (Thiel, Alemanno, Scarcella, Zubaryeva, & Pasaoglu, 2012). Yet, in most European countries today, electric vehicles represent a tiny fraction of the market, suggesting a substantial disconnect between what these consumers say they prefer and what they actually buy. Although 99% of Americans have strongly negative attitudes toward cigarette smoking, 20% are regular smokers, a contradiction between attitude and action for a significant portion of them (McMillen, Ritchie, Frese, & Cosby, 2000). When such conflicts occur, does the fact that attitudes are important mean that behavior has no impact?

The importance of the attitude certainly means that people reflect more deeply on their attitude-inconsistent behavior. Does this careful thinking prevent their actions from having any impact on their attitudes? On the contrary. Under the right conditions, there is often dramatic evidence of attitude change. For example, the number of times that students have engaged in a particular form of academic dishonesty predicts their acceptance of the behavior (Storch & Storch, 2003). So the more they act dishonestly, the less negative their attitude toward cheating becomes. In both Europe and the United States, consumers' car purchases are heavily influenced by price and convenience and those factors may undermine further support for electric cars. Heavy smokers who try to quit and don't succeed actually come to see the health consequences of smoking as much less negative (Gibbons, Eggleston, & Benthin, 1997). When even life-threatening behavior continues, attitudes can change to make the threat seem less. Let's see how such change in important attitudes might occur in the face of conflicting behavior.

The Theory of Cognitive Dissonance. In 1957, Leon Festinger, a brilliant young social psychologist, argued that when people become aware that their important beliefs, attitudes, and knowledge of their actions ("cognitions") are inconsistent with one another, this realization brings with it an uncomfortable state of tension ("dissonance"). **Cognitive dissonance** is an unpleasant state caused by people's awareness of inconsistency among important beliefs, attitudes, or actions. Festinger did more than just reiterate a long and widely held belief that inconsistencies cause discomfort. He also offered a bold new proposal: that people's motivation to reduce the unpleasant side effects of inconsistency often produces change. Festinger was particularly interested in the conflict that arises when behavior conflicts with a prior attitude: when, for example, people think of themselves as honest but cheat on an exam; think of themselves as environmentally conscious, but then buy a gas-guzzling vehicle; or say they care about their health, but then smoke. Because behavior is often difficult to undo, Festinger argued that the tension caused by differences between important actions and attitudes is often reduced by adjustments we make to our thinking, not to our behavior.

In the decades following Festinger's proposal, literally hundreds of experiments have verified the existence and effects of dissonance, and recent work has even begun to uncover the possible neurological basis of dissonance effects, identifying specific brain regions that activate when experiencing dissonance (van Veen, Krug, Schooler, & Carter,

cognitive dissonance
an unpleasant state caused by people's awareness of inconsistency among important beliefs, attitudes, or actions

2009). Those experiments have also helped clarify the conditions under which dissonance arises, the nature of dissonance itself, and the way dissonance drives attitude change (Cooper & Fazio, 1984; Harmon-Jones, Schmeichel, Inzlicht, & Harmon-Jones, 2011; Petty & Wegener, 1998a). According to the accumulated research, four steps are necessary for actions to produce cognitive dissonance and in turn attitude change.

1. *The individual perceives the action as inconsistent.* In Festinger's view, inconsistency in and of itself is enough to cause discomfort, and more recent research confirms this (Gawronski, 2012; Harmon-Jones, Amodio, & Harmon-Jones, 2009; Proulx and others, 2012). Not all inconsistencies are created equal, however. Dissonance is most likely to be provoked when actions are inconsistent with positive and important images of ourselves (E. Aronson, 1961; Greenwald & Ronis, 1978; Steele, 1988; Stone & Cooper, 2001). Actions that violate our sense of self-integrity (like lying or cheating) or value-laden attitudes (like believing that pesticide use pollutes the planet for profit) or personal standards (like caring for one's health) are most likely to produce discomfort. All of these situations involve inconsistency with attitudes, self-concepts, or standards that are important to the individual. It is this inconsistency, regardless of its exact source, that is the first step on the road to dissonance arousal.

2. *The individual perceives the action as freely chosen.* Dissonance is aroused only when an internal attribution is made, that is, when we perceive ourselves as having freely engaged in the attitude-discrepant behavior. When we are coerced by severe threat or driven by large rewards, we can attribute the action to an external cause, which will forestall dissonance arousal. If, for example, people were forced to cheat on an exam by a gun-wielding madman or agreed to smoke a cigarette to win a new car, such behavior would not arouse dissonance. But typically, deciding to peek at someone else's work during an exam or smoking a cigarette during a break are matters of free choice. Even when we are seduced into such behaviors by very small reinforcements, dissonance will still occur if we see the final decision to act as ours. Studies show, for example, that participants freely choosing one item when they really like another or agreeing to write an essay inconsistent with their personal beliefs experience considerable dissonance, whereas those forced to make a choice, required to write an essay, or promised large rewards for behavior show no signs of dissonance arousal (Egan, Santos, & Bloom, 2007; Linder, Cooper, & Jones, 1967). The more choice individuals think they have, and the more they see their behavior as internally motivated, the more likely they are to experience dissonance (Galinsky, Magee, Gruenfeld, Whitson, & Liljenquist, 2008; Guadagno & Cialdini, 2010; Heitland & Bohner, 2010).

3. *The individual experiences uncomfortable physiological arousal.* Just as Festinger suggested, dissonance seems to be experienced as an uncomfortable state of arousal. Robert Croyle and Joel Cooper (1983) measured this arousal by attaching electrodes to participants' fingers while they participated in an essay-writing study. Students who freely agreed to write essays that were inconsistent with their personal opinions showed increased physiological arousal compared to those who were required to write an inconsistent essay or who wrote an essay consistent with their beliefs. Only when a freely chosen behavior conflicted with prior beliefs was dissonance aroused. Inconsistency between behavior and belief also improves performance on simple

tasks but impairs performance on difficult tasks (Martinie, Olive, & Milland, 2010), the classic impact of arousal on performance. Self-reports also confirm that dissonance is experienced as a feeling of unpleasant arousal (Elliot & Devine, 1994). Although Festinger described this feeling merely as "discomfort," more recent researchers have argued that this uncomfortable arousal feels a lot like what most of us would describe as guilt (Kenworthy, Miller, Collins, Read, & Earleywine, 2011).

4. ***The individual attributes the arousal to the inconsistency between attitude and action.*** People have to believe they are feeling unpleasantly aroused because of their inconsistency (Cooper & Fazio, 1984). This point has been demonstrated by studies in which people were tricked into believing that the discomfort they felt was due to something else: fluorescent lights that malfunctioned, a pill they ingested, electric shocks they were anticipating, or prism goggles they had to wear (Fazio, Zanna, & Cooper, 1977; Losch & Cacioppo, 1990; Pittman, 1975). In such cases, the discomfort has no implications for the inconsistencies between attitudes and actions. But when people correctly attribute their discomfort to the inconsistency between attitude and action, their attention is focused on that inconsistency.

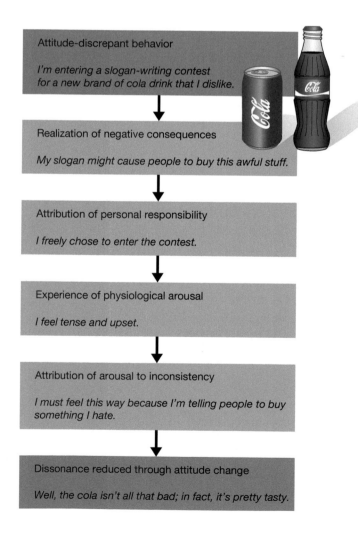

Just as people are motivated to eliminate uncomfortable physiological states like hunger and thirst, they want to reduce the discomfort of dissonance. When attitudes and behaviors are uncomfortably inconsistent, something has to change. Because freely chosen behavior and its negative consequences are often hard to take back or deny, we can restore consistency most easily by changing our attitude. It is only when attitudes are brought into line with actions—when inconsistency between cognitions is eliminated—that dissonance is finally eliminated. This whole process of dissonance arousal and its eventual reduction through attitude change is summarized in Figure 8.2.

In summary, then, people who behave in an attitude-discrepant way can change even important attitudes to conform to their actions if the circumstances are right. The theory of cognitive dissonance provides a simple explanation for a wide variety of day-to-day situations in which people perform behaviors that are inconsistent

Figure 8.2 Four steps to dissonance arousal and reduction For dissonance to result in physiological arousal and ultimately in dissonance-reducing attitude change, four steps must occur.

with important attitudes and dissonance triggers justification processes that produce attitude change. Let's see how.

Justifying Attitude-Discrepant Behavior: I Have My Reasons! Imagine that you are a participant in a very boring experiment. For what seems like hours, you perform meaningless and repetitive tasks. First, the experimenter gives you a pegboard containing 48 square pegs and asks you to give them a quarter turn to the left, a quarter turn back to the right, a quarter turn to the left again, back to the right, and so on, again and again. Just as you are sure you will die of boredom, you are instructed to change tasks. But the next task is no better: Now you are instructed to remove pegs from the board, put them back, take them off, put them back on. Finally (mercifully) the experiment is over. But just as you are about to leave, the experimenter requests your help. A graduate student assistant who was supposed to motivate participants in a different condition of the experiment has not arrived on time. Will you fill in and tell the next participant how much you enjoyed the experiment? The experimenter even offers to pay you $1 for doing so.

If you agree, the classic conditions for dissonance have been set up. An attitude-discrepant behavior (lying about the experiment) with potentially negative consequences (the next person's unrealistic expectations about the study) has been performed with insufficient external justification (the payment of only $1). Dissonance will be aroused. But by changing attitudes about the task ("Well, actually, the experiment was a challenge, I quite enjoyed it") to match the behavior ("And that's what I told the next participant"), dissonance can be eliminated. In their classic study of just such a situation, Festinger and J. Merrill Carlsmith (1959) confirmed this prediction. As you can see in Figure 8.3, control participants who were not asked to mislead the next participant rated the experimental task as pretty boring. So did participants paid $20 to lie about the experimental task: They had plenty of external justification for what they said to the next participant.

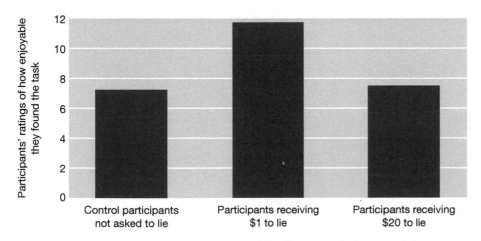

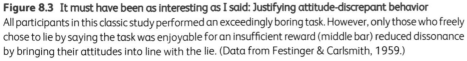

Figure 8.3 It must have been as interesting as I said: Justifying attitude-discrepant behavior
All participants in this classic study performed an exceedingly boring task. However, only those who freely chose to lie by saying the task was enjoyable for an insufficient reward (middle bar) reduced dissonance by bringing their attitudes into line with the lie. (Data from Festinger & Carlsmith, 1959.)

insufficient justification effect
attitude change that occurs to
reduce dissonance caused by
attitude-discrepant behavior that
cannot be attributed to external
reward or punishment

In contrast, those who agreed to mislead others for only a single dollar showed an **insufficient justification effect**—they reduced the dissonance caused by performing an insufficiently justified behavior by changing their attitudes about the experiment.

Note that in this experimental demonstration of the power of dissonance, the attitude that was the source of the dissonance was probably not the same attitude that ultimately changed. To cause uncomfortable tension, behavior has to contradict an important attitude—in this case, a positive attitude about the self. Most students didn't see themselves as immoral people who would tell lies for only a dollar, so when they did exactly this, their inconsistent behavior created a lot of dissonance. But the dissonance did not lead to change in the important attitude (the students did not decide that they were immoral deceivers)! Instead, it set in motion the processes that caused other attitudes to change (the experiment now seemed more valuable, an attitude change that made the behavior less of a lie).

Justifying Effort: I Suffered for It, So I Like It.

Perhaps you have a friend caught up in a bad relationship. You notice that as the relationship worsens, your friend makes even more sacrifices, and as the partner grows more hurtful, your friend becomes more committed. Why do people sometimes come to like what they suffer for? Cognitive dissonance provides an explanation: People change their attitudes to justify their suffering.

effort justification effect
attitude change that occurs to
reduce the dissonance caused
by freely choosing to exert
considerable effort or suffering
to achieve a goal

This **effort justification effect** explains why members of groups who undergo severe initiation rituals value their groups more highly than those accepted without initiation

Photo 8.3 Attitudes shaped by hazing. Hazing rituals that ask new group members to do embarrassing, aversive, or difficult things often lead to very strong and positive attitudes about the group through an effort justification process. Here, new students in France undergo hazing, being covered with eggs and other food products, by older students.

(E. Aronson & Mills, 1959). They also support the current group hierarchy and feel more dependence on the group (Keating and others, 2005). No wonder then that from high school cliques to elite military groups, hazing—the practice of making new members experience difficult, humiliating, and unfortunately often dangerous experiences—seems impossible to eliminate.

Effort justification helps trigger change in a wide range of attitudes. People prefer difficult experimental tasks they perform for rude instructors over those they perform for personable ones, and workers whose jobs require challenging and difficult situations much prefer them to those who have easy routine assignments (Rosenfeld, Giacalone, & Tedeschi, 1984). Students prefer candy bars after having had to rate them by combining 12 attributes versus having to combine only 4 attributes (Cunha & Caldieraro, 2009). The more salient the financial cost of having children, the more parents say they enjoy their offspring (Eibach & Mock, 2011). Those who go through more extreme religious rituals are more generous than those who go through less extreme ones (Xygalatas and others, 2013). People lose more weight if their weight reduction program involves more effort—even if this effort is not related to exercise or calorie usage (Axsom & Cooper, 1985). In these cases people have freely chosen to act in ways that cause them suffering (surely an example of inconsistent behavior for someone with positive self-esteem). Realization of this fact no doubt triggers uncomfortable tension, which is resolved by valuing more and more the goal for which you suffered.

More recently, pigeons and rats have also been found to value rewards (such as a food source) for which they have had to work harder—that is, when they have to peck or push a lever harder or more often to receive rewards (Lydall, Gilmour, & Dwyer, 2010; Zentall, 2010), raising the question of whether cognitive dissonance (with all its assumptions about thinking in the pursuit of justification) is necessary to explain such effects. Some researchers have seen such findings as welcome evidence that the drive for consistency at the heart of cognitive dissonance theory is in fact universal. Others have seen them as evidence that mechanisms that humans share with other animals also contribute to our preference for a hard-earned goal. In the animal studies, for example, a contrast between the aversiveness of earning the goal and the pleasure of achieving the goal seems likely to contribute to the preference for high effort rewards. Perhaps this contributes in humans too—although they are of course likely to feel an inconsistency between these two states—which might well arouse dissonance!

In experimental situations, the attitudes that are changed toward made-up groups or pointless tasks may not seem that important. But if you've ever noted with dismay how wonderful an abusive spouse or parent or friendship group can seem to their victim, you've seen that dissonance processes can change very important and consequential attitudes. Even more disturbing is the possibility that dissonance might be reduced by changing the really important attitude that one is a good person, as when victims of abuse come to see themselves as somehow "deserving it."

Justifying Decisions: Of Course I Was Right! Every difficult decision we make—to return to work or to stay at home with our children, to major in science or in the humanities, to expand our business into a new district or to consolidate local gains—has advantages and drawbacks. Whenever we make decisions, we give up some things in order to gain others. By definition, then, decisions involve tension between the chosen

post-decisional regret effect
attitude change that occurs to
reduce the dissonance caused by
freely making a choice or decision

alternative and all the attractive features of the alternatives given up. A **post-decisional regret effect** occurs when people try to reduce such dissonance by evaluating the chosen option even more positively and disparaging the unchosen alternative.

In the classic demonstration of this process, Jack Brehm (1956) asked women to evaluate several small appliances as part of a supposed study of consumer preferences. After they rated a toaster, a coffee pot, a radio, and other products, the women were allowed to choose one product as payment for their participation. Some participants had a chance to choose between two products they had found almost equally desirable— a dissonance-invoking dilemma. When the women were later asked to evaluate all the products again, their ratings offered strong support for dissonance theory: The women now evaluated the product they had chosen much more positively than the item they rejected.

Unfortunately, there are some aspects of this task—particularly that people are treated differently depending what they choose, making their initial preference even more salient—that make it hard to say that the results are due to dissonance (Chen & Risen, 2010). With this critique in mind, more recent studies have nevertheless shown that dissonance is at work when decisions are made. In decision-making situations where choice between two options is not salient, the number of choices and the more different the choices, the more post-decisional regret is felt, just as dissonance theory would predict (Sagi & Friedland, 2007). Using both self-report and measures of brain activity, Izuma and colleagues (2010) showed strong evidence for choice-induced preference change accompanied by activity in brain regions associated with conflict detection and resolution. Another set of studies assessed people's preferences for alternatives that they had never directly compared, also avoiding the problems of earlier studies. Choices again altered preferences, and the choice itself triggered reappraisal of the chosen and rejected alternatives almost immediately (Alos-Ferrer, Granic, Shi, & Wagner, 2012). Consistent with dissonance theory, it is making the choice to have one thing and give up another that triggers dissonance and the need to reduce it.

In a variety of important decision-making situations, dissonance processes help people convince themselves that what they chose was right. In one U.S. Presidential election after another, voters are more positive about their preferred candidate and more negative about the other candidate after voting than before (Beasley & Joslyn, 2001). Compared to their initial views, students' moral standards become more lenient after imagining themselves cheating (Shu, Gino, & Bazerman, 2011). And people who start to smoke again after quitting for a while perceive smoking to be less dangerous to their health, compared to their views when they decided to stop and to the views of those who stay nonsmokers (Gibbons, Eggleston, & Benthin, 1997).

The Processing Payoff: Justifying Inconsistent Actions Creates Persistent Attitudes. As we saw in Chapter 7, attitudes that result from extensive processing last longer than attitudes changed with little thought. Trying to justify inconsistent behavior prompts people to consider arguments they might otherwise have ignored, generate new evidence, interpret their behavior in new ways, evaluate the consequences of their actions, and think about why they feel the way they do (Albarracin & McNatt, 2005). Given the extensive processing required to reduce dissonance, then, it is no surprise that attitude change brought about by dissonance reduction can be long-lasting. In a

---

SOCIAL PSYCHOLOGY IN PRACTICE: DISSONANCE PROCESSES AND HEALTH INTERVENTIONS

These same dissonance-reduction processes can be used to give adolescent girls with body image dissatisfaction long-term protection against eating disorders. In one study, girls with body image concerns were randomly assigned to a control condition with no intervention or to one of three treatment conditions (Stice, Marti, Spoor, Presnell, & Shaw, 2008). In the healthy-weight treatment group, the girls learned how to make changes in their diet and exercise patterns that would facilitate healthy living. In the expressive-writing treatment group, the girls wrote about emotional events from their own lives. In the dissonance group, the girls voluntarily completed activities such as writing essays or participating in role plays that countered the thin-body ideal. The researchers measured several variables that are risk factors for eating disorders, such as body image satisfaction, and actual eating disorder symptoms over time. Along with the healthy-weight treatment, the dissonance treatment was effective over time. For example, compared to the no-treatment control group, the girls in the dissonance and healthy-weight groups had a lower risk of eating disorder onset three years later.

---

recent demonstration of this point, undergraduate students wrote essays that conflicted with their own attitudes with or without free choice and reported their attitudes either immediately or after a one month delay. Only participants in the free choice condition changed their attitudes immediately, and that attitude change persisted throughout the month (Sénémeaud & Somat, 2009). Even more tellingly, business students made hypothetical decisions between vacation destinations and then rated the alternatives again. Consistent with dissonance theory, their chosen destination was rated much more positively than their rejected one. But amazingly, the results were the same when the participants rated the same vacation spots 2.5 to 3 years later (Sharot, Fleming, Yu, Koster, & Dolan, 2012)! With its underpinning of extensive processing, dissonance-provoked attitude change is durable over time.

Alternatives to Attitude Change. You may have noticed that many experimental tests of dissonance theory set up situations in which attitude change is the easiest avenue by which cognitive dissonance can be reduced and consistency reestablished. Festinger (1957) was the first to point out, however, that people can reduce dissonance in other ways if they have the opportunity. Imagine that you have just broken a month-long diet by eating an entire bag of chocolate chip cookies. Rather than changing your pro-dieting attitude, you could dissipate dissonance at any point in the four steps of the arousal and reduction process. One strategy would be to minimize the inconsistency by trivializing the attitude-discrepant behavior ("A few cookies won't make any difference, and besides, they were low fat") or adding cognitions to make it consonant ("Actually, you have to treat yourself once in a while or you just can't stay on a diet"). For example, students in one study performed a high effort activity—propelling themselves up hill sitting on a skateboard! They then underestimated the steepness of the hill, trivializing the behavior ("No big deal, wasn't that hard") if they freely chose the activity (classic dissonance provoking conditions) but not if they had no choice (Balcetis & Dunning, 2007).

As an alternative, you might try minimizing perceptions of free choice ("The cookies were a gift; not eating them would be rude"). Or you could attribute your

HOT TOPICS IN SOCIAL PSYCHOLOGY: DISSONANCE AND DIET

Many people eat meat as part of their diet, yet most people feel it is wrong to harm things, like animals, that possess a "mind." Thus, eating meat might trigger an uncomfortable sense of inconsistency. This is the perspective of a group of researchers who examined whether meat eaters might avoid attributing a "mind" to animals in order to reduce the dissonance that eating those animals might arouse (Bastian and others, 2012). In support of this notion, self-identified meat-eating students at an Australian university were shown two animals, a cow and a sheep. For one of them, the animal was shown in a field, and the accompanying description noted that the animal grazed on grass in different parts of a farm. The other animal was shown in a similar setting, but the description noted that the animal was being bred for food production and would later be killed. The students were asked to rate each animal's possession of a number of "mind" features, such as the degree to which it had goals and plans and experienced things like fear, joy, pain, etc. As expected, the animal in the food production condition was ascribed fewer mind qualities than the one in the other condition. Thus, even a fairly routine daily event for many people, eating a meal with meat, might prompt dissonance reduction efforts.

You may recall a similar point from Chapter 4, page 130: Some people seem to drink alcohol to reduce the awareness of unpleasant discrepancies between their current selves and their ideal or ought selves.

As described in Chapter 4, page 124, self-affirmation involves enhancing or highlighting one's own sense of personal integrity.

dissonance-induced arousal to something other than your inconsistent behavior ("All this food deprivation is making me feel grouchy"), thereby feeling no need to reestablish consistency between word and deed.

Measures taken to reduce the uncomfortable tension of dissonance-induced arousal can sometimes be harmful. Claude Steele and his colleagues (Steele, Southwick, & Critchlow, 1981) have demonstrated that people may reduce dissonance by using alcohol. These researchers induced students to write an essay favoring a big tuition increase—an action clearly inconsistent with their attitudes. Displaying the usual dissonance-induced attitude change, participants given free choice to write the essay became more supportive of the fee hike, except in one condition. Right after writing the essay, some students participated in a "taste-test" in which they drank beer or vodka. These participants showed none of the usual signs of dissonance and failed to change their attitudes. The researchers believe that drinking alcohol eliminated the unpleasant tension of dissonance, so attitude change never occurred. Their conclusion was that alcohol and drug use may be habitual and health-damaging ways in which some people avoid or reduce the tension cognitive dissonance creates in their lives (Steele, 1988; Steele & Southwick, 1985).

Fortunately, a more constructive avenue of dissipating dissonance is often available. Because the actions and attitudes that trigger dissonance are usually important or self-relevant, people can reduce the uncomfortable tension associated with such inconsistencies by reaffirming their positive sense of self-worth and integrity. Perhaps offering people who have just committed an attitude-discrepant act the opportunity to say: "Hey, I really am a good person, you know" could eliminate attitude change.

Researchers have tested this idea by asking college students, some of whom were science majors and some of whom were not, to rate 10 popular musical recordings, and then to choose to keep either their fifth- or sixth-ranked one—a classic post-decisional regret situation (Steele, 1988). Participants were then asked to prepare for a second experiment, in which about half of them would be required to don white lab coats. Then came a surprise task: Everyone was asked to rate all the recordings again. Consistent with dissonance theory, most participants reduced the dissonance created by their earlier difficult choice by evaluating their chosen recording more highly than the one they had not chosen. But different results were found for one particular group of students, the science majors who had been asked to wear lab coats, a symbol of their values and training. Science students given this opportunity to reaffirm their positive self-identity showed no signs of the usual dissonance-induced attitude change. The potential distress aroused by performing actions inconsistent with a positive view of ourselves can apparently be dissolved by an act that underscores our sense of identity.

Perhaps the most obvious alternative to changing attitudes to reduce dissonance is to change behavior (Harmon-Jones & Harmon-Jones, 2008). Although past behavior might be impossible to change, tension between important attitudes and behavior can sometimes be reduced by changing future behavior. Imagine being asked to tell a group of high school students the dangers of having unprotected sexual intercourse in an attempt to persuade them to use condoms to prevent the spread of AIDS. Now imagine that just having taken such action, you are asked to make a list of the occasions in which you yourself might not have used a condom. Having just advocated their use, being reminded of your own failure to use condoms might produce a high state of dissonance. Preaching what you might not be practicing is one recipe for hypocrisy, and a considerable threat to self-esteem (Fointiat, Somat, & Grosbras, 2011). What's the best way to restore your faith in yourself? Perhaps it is starting to practice what you preached. That's just what researchers find when they put participants in such a position. Compared to people who merely write or think about a health-related behavior, people who publicly promote a health behavior but then are reminded that they have failed to perform it show a **hypocrisy effect**: they are much more likely to actually start performing the behavior (Freijy & Kothe, 2013; Stone & Focella, 2011). The dissonance created by making hypocritical behavior salient has also been used to improve water conservation and increase donations to homeless shelters.

hypocrisy effect
change in behavior that occurs to reduce the dissonance caused by freely choosing to publicly advocate a behavior that one does not actually perform oneself

Which Dissonance Reduction Strategy Is Used? With many alternatives available, how do people decide how to reduce dissonance? Opportunity and motivation typically determine the avenue of dissonance reduction. Given that dissonance is an unpleasant state, people tend to use the first reduction opportunity that presents itself. Perhaps this is why misattribution of negative feelings to some cause other than the inconsistent behavior occurs most frequently—this strategy makes any tension seem unrelated to the inconsistent behavior, resolving any need to change either attitude or behavior (Joule & Martinie, 2008). Once dissonance is aroused and attributed to the inconsistency, trivialization of the behavior is a popular tension-reducing strategy, especially if a change in attitude would conflict with social norms (Voisin, Stone, & Becker, 2013). Such direct ways of reducing dissonance (changing or trivializing inconsistent cognitions) are preferred over indirect ways, such as self-affirmation (Stone and others, 1997). Self-affirmation is easier for individuals who have many "affirmational resources," such as a large number of alternative positive self-concepts that can be at the ready when one's self-image is threatened (Steele, Spencer, & Lynch, 1993), whereas individuals with fewer such resources might end up changing attitudes (McConnell & Brown, 2010). Motivational factors can also influence how dissonance is resolved. For example, although

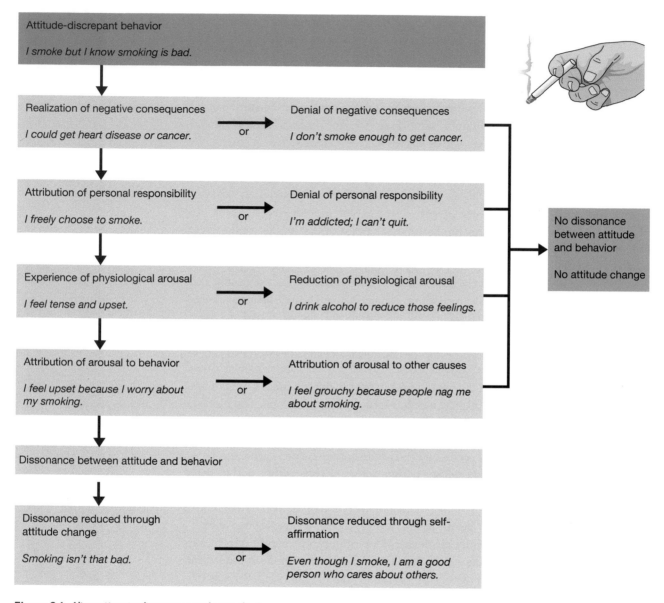

Figure 8.4 Alternatives to dissonance and attitude change

An attitude-discrepant behavior may lead to dissonance arousal through the four steps described earlier in the chapter. However, at each step alternatives exist that will block the arousal of dissonance. Even if dissonance is aroused, it can be reduced by self-affirmation instead of by attitude change.

violations of important attitudes trigger dissonance, the very importance of those attitudes makes them unlikely to change in the service of dissonance reduction (Devine, Tauer, Barron, Elliot, & Vance, 1999; Starzyk, Fabrigar, Soryal, & Fanning, 2009).

Figure 8.4 shows the entire sequence of steps by which dissonance arousal leads to attitude change and the alternative processes that can either block the arousal of dissonance or reduce dissonance through self-affirmation rather than attitude change. As you can see, behavior that is inconsistent with attitudes can lead to many outcomes, not only to attitude change.

SOCIAL PSYCHOLOGY AND CULTURE: CULTURAL DIFFERENCES AND DISSONANCE

Dissonance seems to arise when something important to the self—a valued attitude, a central self-definition, a well-established standard of behavior—is violated. Such violations, and the dissonance that results from them, can be found in almost every country (Beauvois & Joule, 1996; Joule & Beauvois, 1998; Sakai, 1999). But because the self and the social world are viewed differently in different cultures, you might expect that dissonance would be aroused differently in different cultures. Recall that in collectivist cultures, the self is more contextualized—who the self is varies depending on specific social relationships that are salient. That fact suggests three differences in when and how dissonance might work across cultures. First, those in collectivist cultures might have an overall higher tolerance for inconsistency, so that the apparent contradictions that arouse individualists might be serenely accepted as sometimes true, sometimes false (Peng & Nisbett, 1999). Second, the greater tendency of those in collectivist cultures to explain behavior in situational terms (Morris & Peng, 1994) may make them immune to situations that create dissonance for individualists sensitive to individual freedom of choice. Finally, whereas inconsistencies that reflect on the self might be more problematic for individualists, inconsistencies that have consequences for others might be more arousing for those from collectivist cultures.

All of these propositions appear true. When members of individualist cultures and members of collectivist cultures are asked to rate a number of alternatives and then choose among fairly equally rated alternatives, they act quite differently. Individualists appear to be resolving dissonance—after the choice they rate the chosen alternative more positively than they did before. Those from collectivist cultures don't show this effect. Their rerating of the alternatives shows no tendency to justify their choice (Heine & Lehman, 1997). But consider what happens when the choice has implications for important others like friends or family. Shinobu Kitayama and his colleagues (2004) had European American students and Japanese students rate CDs and then asked some in each group to choose CDs in the usual way and others to think about what others would think of their choices. Regardless of condition, American students justified their choices by re-evaluating the chosen CD more positively. Japanese students did so only when the social implications of their decision had been made obvious. The crucial role of relationships in this effect has been further demonstrated by studies that make members of one culture act as if they are members of the other. That is, members of collectivist cultures who are chronically individualist justify their individual choices (Kitayama, Ishii, Imada, Takemura, & Ramaswamy, 2006), and individualists who are subtly primed with relationships justify only choices that have significance for others (Kimel, Grossmann, & Kitayama, 2012). Thus, it seems that behaviors that violate important attitudes about the self cause dissonance across cultures, but what constitutes such a violation is culturally sensitive (Hoshino-Browne, 2012).

As we have seen, behaviors can have an impact on attitudes whether we engage in superficial processing or extensive processing. Whenever behaviors are inconsistent with previously established attitudes, self-perception processes or dissonance-reduction processes can come into play to change attitudes in the direction of actions. As you read about studies conducted to test the operation of self-perception and dissonance processes, and thought about the kinds of behaviors they were trying to explain, you may have realized that, in many cases, both processes provided viable explanations. In fact, whether self-perception or dissonance was the correct explanation for the changes that followed attitude-inconsistent behavior was a source of great controversy among social psychologists. The resolution began to become clear when Russell Fazio and his colleagues (1977) compared the conditions under which attitudes changed in response to

You may recall that Fazio and his colleagues' study was first discussed in Chapter 2, page 46, as an example of how theories might complement rather than compete with each other.

behaviors that were either mildly or more severely discrepant with previous attitudes (see also Wakslak, 2012). They concluded that when freely chosen actions are relatively trivial—when they do not violate cherished self-images or important attitudes—changed attitudes are inferred with little or no effort. Under these conditions, self-perception processes explain the change. In contrast, freely chosen actions that run counter to well-established and important attitudes trigger emotional arousal and cause extensive thinking as people work to justify their actions. In these cases, attitudes change in the service of dissonance reduction. Under different conditions and via different processes, both superficial and systematic thinking provide means by which behaviors (as well as the thoughts and feelings discussed in Chapter 7) determine our attitudes.

CHANGING ACTIONS WITH ATTITUDES

"Attitudes determine for each individual what he [or she] will do," wrote Gordon Allport more than half a century ago (Allport, 1935, p. 806). This basic tenet of social psychology—that attitudes direct behavior—is the driving force behind decades of research on how attitudes can be formed and changed. After all, if attitudes guide actions, then knowing something about people's attitudes permits the prediction of behavior. And if attitudes guide actions, changing attitudes—about ourselves, others, objects, events, and issues—permits behavioral change. If we convince the patient that the drug is a good one, she will take it as prescribed; if we convert the atheist to our religion, he will act on the teachings of the faith; if we persuade the consumer that vehicle emissions are causing global warming, she will buy the suggested hybrid vehicle. Research has provided a lot of evidence to justify these optimistic statements. Attitudes influence behaviors that range from breastfeeding and organ donation to use of contraception, cheating in a relationship, illegal drug use, participating in psychology experiments, voting in elections, and cleaning up the environment (Glasman & Albarracin, 2006).

But this is not always the case. Perhaps because attitudes and behavior often go hand in hand, we are jolted when they seem glaringly inconsistent. Plenty of people might note the inconsistency of the fact that roughly 80% of surveyed men said they welcomed fatherhood (Agiesta, 2013), yet the latest data from the U.S. Census Bureau shows that about 1 of every 3 U.S. children grow up in a home without his or her biological father. But social psychologists have been documenting attitude–action mismatches for some time. In a classic study completed in 1934, Robert LaPiere found that despite treating a Chinese couple who visited their hotel and restaurant quite courteously, an overwhelming majority of the hotel and restaurant managers later expressed negative attitudes toward serving Chinese customers at all (LaPiere, 1934). Other studies have shown similar gaps between attitudes and behavior. So the answer to the question: "Do attitudes guide behavior?" seemed to be a very unsatisfactory: "Sometimes!"

Faced with the fact that attitudes often did not seem to reliably predict behavior either inside or outside the laboratory, some social psychologists suggested that the concept of attitudes should be abandoned altogether (Wicker, 1969). This was clearly an overreaction. But it did cause social psychologists to think carefully about the role of attitudes in eliciting, modifying, and inhibiting behavior. Rather than asking: "Do attitudes guide behavior?" researchers began asking: "How do attitudes guide behavior?"

By understanding how behavior was influenced by attitudes, they hoped to learn when attitudes would influence behavior. This change in tactics led to a new understanding of the processes by which attitudes are translated into action.

How Attitudes Guide Behavior

Established attitudes can guide behaviors in a very direct way. Attitudes bias perceptions, thereby making attitude-consistent information about objects, people, and events more obvious and attitude-consistent behavior more likely. Attitudes also influence behavior in a more considered way by prompting intentions to act in certain ways. Intentions in turn can trigger planning that makes attitude-consistent behavior more likely.

What is it about attitudes that makes attitude-consistent behavior more likely? How does preferring a particular politician translate into voting for him or her? Or having a negative attitude toward drinking dictate lifelong abstinence? It might not surprise you to learn that attitude researchers have come to see that attitudes can have an impact on behaviors in two different ways. One way in which attitudes influence behavior is to trigger consistent behaviors quite directly, with very little thinking. When the attitude comes to mind, it sets in motion certain processes that quite straightforwardly make an attitude-consistent course of action more likely than any other, just as seeing the well-loved face of a spouse might almost automatically cause us to lean forward for an embrace. At the same time, however, attitudes can also influence behaviors after extensive and deliberate consideration. This type of deliberative processing focuses on the formation of intentions to perform the behavior and plans for how to do so. Imagine that you have formed a very positive evaluation of the young stranger who sits a few rows down from you in the lecture hall. You may well agonize over all the advantages and disadvantages of acting before forming an intention to ask him to join you for a coffee after the lecture, and then agonize once again about how to actually carry out the request. In this case, extensive processing occurs before the attitude is translated into attitude-consistent behavior.

Attitudes Guide Behavior Without Much Thought. Sometimes attitude–behavior connections occur without any effortful thought. Attitudes offer handy evaluative summaries of their attitude objects, and those evaluations predispose a positive or negative response so that behavior follows evaluation automatically (Hofmann, Friese, & Roefs, 2009). The better established the attitude, the better guide to behavior. Consider, for example, the way participants responded to the opportunity to choose five small snacks (such as a Mounds candy bar, Dentyne gum, a packet of raisins) as payment for participation in an experiment (Fazio, Blascovich, & Driscoll, 1992). Earlier in the session, participants had indicated whether they liked or disliked a large number of products, including the offered snacks. Participants who held highly-accessible attitudes about the snacks (as indicated by their speedy responses) were much more likely to make choices consistent with their attitudes than were the participants who were uncertain of their likes and dislikes (as indicated by their slow responses). Preferred snacks were chosen and less-favored snacks were left on the table. What is it about the activation of an attitude that can guide behavior in this automatic fashion?

The answer is that attitudes can bias perceptions, literally changing what people see in ways that make attitude-consistent behavior more likely. First, attitudes orient people to the attitude object, so that they're ready to act on it. When people's attitudes toward flying, for example, are activated because they have been repeatedly expressed, people are slower to identify a target object if the sought-after object appears with an image of an airplane than when it appears without it. The object associated with the activated attitude—the plane —appears to automatically attract attention, making it harder to identify the other object (Roskos-Ewoldsen & Fazio, 1992).

Second, attitudes focus attention on some characteristics of the stimulus and away from others, changing the object that people perceive (Fazio, 1986, 1990). A favorable attitude makes the positive qualities of the object more obvious: For those who love ice cream, a scoop brings to mind its delicious flavor and smooth, creamy taste. A negative attitude, on the other hand, makes the object's unfavorable attributes most salient: Those who dislike it are likely to see its many calories and high fat content. Attitudes can even change the apparent physical properties of objects. Thirsty people see a bottle of water as closer than do already sated perceivers. Perceivers also judge reports pinned on a wall across the room to be closer if they think the reports describe them as possessing positive qualities rather than revealing negative ones (Balcetis & Dunning, 2010).

Amazingly, attitudes dictate the perception of objects to such an extent that people have a tough time realizing that the objects have changed. In one clever experiment showing this effect, some students repeatedly expressed (rehearsed) their attitudes toward photos of other people whereas other students saw the photos an equal number of times but didn't rehearse attitudes toward the photographed targets (Fazio, Ledbetter, & Towles-Schwen, 2000). Everyone was then shown pictures of the targets that differed in subtle ways from the original snapshots. People who had rehearsed attitudes were

If you're thinking that these processes are similar to ones that occur when attitudes are defended, you're right. Recall from Chapter 7, especially page 267–268, that people often focus on attitude-consistent information and distort and reinterpret information inconsistent with their attitudes.

HOT TOPICS IN SOCIAL PSYCHOLOGY: EVALUATING IS SEEING

Building on the idea that attitudes bias perceptions of objects, Alison Young, Kyle Ratner, and Russell Fazio demonstrated that citizens with different political attitudes might actually see the world differently. They showed U.S. college students 450 pairs of photos and asked them to choose which one from each pair looked more like 2012 Republican presidential candidate Mitt Romney. Each pair of photos showed the same facial shot of Romney, but each individual photo was masked or degraded by a different random pattern of noise. After making their choices, students identified themselves as Republicans or Democrats and as supporters of Romney or not. The researchers then averaged all 450 of a participant's chosen faces, to construct a likeness of what each participant thought Romney looked like. In a second phase of the study, other raters evaluated these averaged faces and rated them for trustworthiness. The results were revealing. The more an individual supported Romney, the more trustworthy his or her constructed Romney face was judged to be. When researchers averaged all the faces constructed by Republican supporters and had raters compare them to the average of all the faces constructed by Democrats, they found that Romney supporters had constructed a more positive and a more trustworthy-looking image of Romney than did his opponents. This method of getting people to reveal their mental representations is an ingenious way to demonstrate that attitudes can fundamentally change people's perception of the world. No wonder that we describe people with conflicting attitudes as not seeing eye to eye.

less likely to notice the differences, took longer to accurately identify what was different, and were convinced that the differences were smaller than people who had not rehearsed their attitudes! Having an accessible attitude made the objects look a certain way, and that's the way people saw them.

Thus, our attitudes typically bias our perceptions of the attitude object. This process increases the likelihood that behavior consistent with the attitude will be elicited in a rather straightforward way. Favorable attitudes make the positive qualities of the object more obvious (mmm, that delicious flavor and creamy taste), whereas negative attitudes make the object's unfavorable attributes salient (yuck, all that fat and calories). If people then respond to the most salient qualities of the objects, attitude-consistent behaviors are likely to follow. For example, if participants' attitudes toward fitness are activated, their decisions about eating specific foods depend on the healthiness of the foods (Young & Fazio, 2013). In sum, attitudes about objects can directly influence actions, in a relatively simple and straightforward manner. At other times, however, attitudes play a role in a more complex sequence of action-producing events.

Attitudes Guide Behavior Through Considered Intentions. Attitudes can also guide behavior in a much more considered and thoughtful way. When people deliberately attempt to make their behavior consistent with their attitudes, they usually put considerable effort into forming an **intention** to act in a particular way. Intentions typically specify a behavior that will help achieve a goal. For example, if your old clunker keeps breaking down and you have formed a positive attitude toward buying a new car, you may thoughtfully consider a great deal of information as you form an intention to buy a new one. How does having an intention help? According to the **theory of reasoned action**, attitudes are an important source of intentions, which in turn produce behavior. In fact, intentions are the single most important predictor of actual behavior (Fishbein & Ajzen, 1975; Fitzsimmons, 2004). Intentions to act have been found to be good predictors of a wide variety of important social behaviors, including donating blood, voting, using family planning techniques, attending church, eating out, practicing dental hygiene, having an abortion, smoking cigarettes, and participating in on-the-job training (Sheeran, 2002).

Intentions can range from the very general to the very specific, and the level at which we think about our intentions determines the potential behaviors that will be activated (Wegner & Vallacher, 1986). For example, a very general intention—"Time to lose some weight!"—brings to mind various options by which this intention can be carried out, whereas a very specific intention—"I intend to reduce my fat intake to no more than 30% of my daily calories"—is likely to activate more specific goal-focused behaviors. Although broad intentions allow us more flexibility to adopt alternative plans, forming specific intentions better achieves the behavioral goal (Gollwitzer & Sheeran, 2006). It is perhaps not surprising, then, that thinking about behaviors that have to be performed in the near future tends to be more specific, whereas thinking about distant actions tends to be more abstract and general. Making plans as if they had to be carried out tomorrow makes it more likely that we will in fact see them through (Trope & Liberman, 2010).

Once intentions have been formed and relevant behavioral information has been activated, the next step is planning (Gollwitzer & Moskowitz, 1996), deciding the when, where, and how of carrying through on the intention. **Implementation intentions** help

intention
a commitment to reach a desired outcome or desired behavior

theory of reasoned action
the theory that attitudes and social norms combine to produce behavioral intentions, which in turn influence behavior

We return to discuss the theory of reasoned action in Chapter 10, pages 389–391, where we see how social norms also work with attitudes to trigger intentions.

implementation intention
a plan to carry out a specific goal-directed behavior in a specific situation

in this regard: they are "if-then" plans that link a critical situational or environmental cue to a specific goal-directed behavior (Gollwitzer, 1999). For a procrastinating author, an implementation intention might take the form "At 9:00am, I will write for two hours." For a weak-willed dieter "If I see chocolate, I will go and read for 30 minutes" might work. Perhaps because they are so simple, specific, and associated with the kinds of cues that typically disrupt goal-directed behavior, implementation intentions are more likely than general intentions to produce desired behavior. In two field studies, participants who formed implementation intentions were more successful with long-term dieting and performed better in tennis matches (Achtziger, Gollwitzer, & Sheeran, 2008).

The power of implementation intentions was demonstrated in one study that compared people's ability to achieve the goal of controlling their typical emotional reaction to frightening or disgusting stimuli. Participants were told either to "believe you will not get frightened" or to implement the intention "When I see a spider, I will stay calm and relaxed." People were much better able to reach their goal when they were given the implementation intention (Gallo, Keil, McCulloch, Rockstroh, & Gollwitzer, 2009). Other studies showed that implementation intentions were particularly successful in getting people to engage in physical activity when exercise was difficult rather than easy (Hall, Zehr, Ng, & Zanna, 2012) and when dieters were faced with particularly tempting snack foods (Kroese, Adriaanse, Evers, & De Ridder, 2011). And the effects are not just short-term. Adolescent smokers trained to form implementation intentions had reduced rates of smoking compared to control participants even 24 months later (Conner & Higgins, 2010).

With intentions in place, behavioral knowledge activated, and plans selected, we are ready to carry out intended behavior if an opportunity presents itself. Of course, once we start acting, our actions may or may not accomplish our intention. For this reason, people monitor their behavior against their intentions: If the behavior seems to reduce the gap between the present state and the desired state, the behavior continues until the goal is attained. If, on the other hand, the action seems ineffective, it may be increased in intensity, replaced by a new plan, or eventually abandoned altogether (Carver & Scheier, 1990; Gollwitzer, 1996). As part of this monitoring process, people mentally keep track of intentions and goals that they haven't yet made good on. From finishing experimental tasks to climbing up the corporate ladder, focusing on those actions still to go increases motivation to keep on, whereas focusing on already completed actions increases satisfaction, but slows accomplishment (Fishbach, Dhar, & Zhang, 2006; Koo & Fishbach, 2010).

By influencing intentions and plans, then, attitudes can guide attitude-consistent behavior in a more considered and thoughtful way. This does not mean that attitudes, intentions, and plans are deliberately formed anew each time you enter a new situation (Ajzen & Fishbein, 1980). An intention, and a plan to carry it out, may have been formed quite deliberately and systematically at some time in the past, but might later pop into mind almost automatically whenever a relevant attitude object or particular situation is confronted (Gollwitzer & Schaal, 1998). A patriotic attitude, for example, may at one point have led to the conscious intention of singing a national song before a sporting match, but that behavior may now, after many repetitions, be performed virtually without thought.

When do attitudes trigger consistent behaviors automatically versus deliberately? It is probably obvious that thinking about attitudes in relation to intentions, and about intentions in relation to behavior, involves much more systematic processing than the superficial processing that occurs when attitudes guide behaviors more directly, the two routes shown in Figure 8.5. Because systematic processing requires a lot more effort and concentration than responding in a knee-jerk fashion to salient features of an attitude object, motivation and opportunity to engage in thinking dictate whether attitudes affect behavior with either little thought or considerable thought (Fazio, 1990; Hofmann and others, 2009). So when people aren't motivated to think carefully or when attitudes aren't important, behavior may follow quite automatically from how the attitude object is viewed. Compared to people feeling sad, people experiencing a good mood—a state that often motivates reduced processing—tend to act in ways that reflect an object's associated evaluation (Holland, deVries, Hermsen, & van Knippenberg, 2012). The same thing happens when careful consideration is not possible (because the behavior has to occur immediately, for example) or when people's cognitive and emotional resources—those resources necessary to think actions through—have been used up: Behavior follows quite automatically from how the attitude object is viewed. The more students in one study said they were mentally exhausted by final exams or by performing a difficult task,

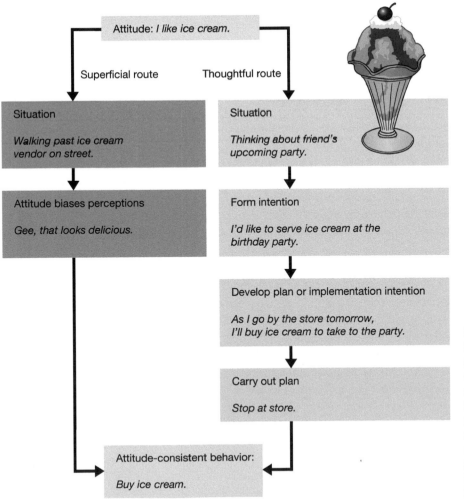

Figure 8.5 Superficial and thoughtful routes from attitude to behavior

Attitudes can influence behavior relatively automatically by influencing people's immediate perceptions. At other times, the effect of attitudes on behavior occurs with more thought when people plan and carry out intentions that results in attitude-consistent behavior.

the more automatically they snacked on comforting and familiar foods, both healthy and unhealthy (Neal, Wood, & Drolet, 2013). Just as we saw that persuasion in routine situations was more likely to occur through superficial than systematic processing, most routine behavior is undoubtedly the result of less thoughtful reliance on activated attitudes. When the stakes are high and extensive thinking is possible, however, attitudes may influence behavior through their impact on intentions.

Did you notice that this is the same kind of effect that occurs when the resources we need to regulate our behavior are depleted, as we discussed in Chapter 4, page 124?

When Do Attitudes Influence Action?

The more accessible the attitude and the more closely the attitude corresponds to the intended behavior, the more attitudes will guide actions. Attitudes can be made accessible by deliberate thought, self-awareness, or frequent use. Only attitudes that correspond to a particular behavior will be able to guide that behavior. Implicit attitudes predict uncontrollable behaviors better and explicit attitudes predict controllable behaviors better. Finally, behavior is more likely to reflect attitudes if people both believe they have control and actually do have control over behavior.

What has to happen for an attitude to guide behavior either directly or indirectly? How can we increase the likelihood that people will act on their socially useful and constructive attitudes? Answering the question of how attitudes guide actions has helped social psychologists specify two conditions that increase the extent to which attitudes guide behaviors.

Attitude Accessibility. If it is the attitude that changes perception of the object, and the attitude that triggers plans and intentions, we need to make sure that the attitude is brought to mind if attitude-consistent behavior is to occur. We're not likely to focus on the positive features of the latest fuel-efficient sedan or form intentions to start checking prices at local dealerships unless we are aware of our positive attitude toward such vehicles. So to have the maximal effect on behavior, attitudes about objects, events, people, or ideas have to be accessible at the right time (Fazio, 1990; Lord & Lepper, 1999). Some people's inner convictions seem to come to mind more easily most of the time. Low self-monitors, for example, for whom expressing the true self is important, have more accessible attitudes than high self-monitors (DeBono and Snyder, 1995; Kardes, Sanbonmatsu, Voss, & Fazio, 1986). Not surprisingly, then, low self-monitors are more likely to practice what they preach (Kraus, 1995). But you don't have to be a low self-monitor to show such consistency.

After all, attitudes can be brought to mind by deliberate effort. Before taking action, you might think about a relevant attitude for a few minutes, and thus ensure that the attitude has more impact on your behavior. Mark Snyder and William Swann (1976) demonstrated this idea in a study of attitudes toward affirmative action employment policies. Undergraduate men served as jurors in mock sex-discrimination trials. Some of the men were given "a few minutes to organize your thoughts and views on the affirmative action issue" before hearing the case, whereas others were not. Only those who were first encouraged to bring their attitude to mind reached verdicts consistent with their attitudes (which had been measured in a separate session 2 weeks earlier).

The opposite result—decreased consistency between attitude and behavior—may occur when factors other than their attitudes are made salient right before people make a choice. Imagine, for example, that you have always loved posters of August Macke's prints because the vivid colors make you feel so cheerful. If allowed to choose a poster to take home as a reward for participation in an experiment, your positive attitude would probably guide you to pick a Macke print. But what if right before you made the choice, you were required to think about aspects of the poster other than your attitude toward it—to focus on its artistic merit or its fit with the color scheme in your living room, for example? In one experiment that tested this idea, one group of students was asked to spend time analyzing their thoughts about various art posters before choosing one to take home. Compared with students who were not required to do so (and presumably just relied on their attitudes to pick their poster), the students required to take other considerations into account were more likely to take home a poster they originally had not liked. They also were more likely to regret their choice (Millar & Tesser, 1986; Wilson and others, 1993). When the relevant attitude is not uppermost in the actor's mind at the time action is called for, its impact on behavior is reduced.

Think how much more powerful an influence an attitude could have on behavior if the attitude came to mind automatically in the right situation, rather than having to be deliberately brought to mind. The more often an attitude is activated, the more the link between attitude object and attitude is strengthened. When that happens, the attitude will come to mind whenever the attitude object is encountered (Fazio, 1989; Fazio, Chen, McDonel, & Sherman, 1982). Many factors can strengthen attitude–object links. Some such connections might be partially innate, for example, to help us take immediate action whenever we perceive a dangerous or nurturing stimulus (Frijda, Kuipers, & ter Schure, 1989; Tesser, 1993). Others are built up through constant activation, deliberation, discussion, and action (Fazio, 1989). Not surprisingly, then, attitudes that come to mind frequently and easily are more likely to produce consistent behavior (Fazio and others, 1982; Glasman & Albarracin, 2006).

What kinds of attitudes have these qualities? First, attitudes built up by direct interaction and practice with attitude objects—ones frequently activated along with the attitude object—are more likely to direct consistent behavior than more abstract "hearsay"-based attitudes (Fazio & Zanna, 1981). Second, attitudes formed on the basis of systematic processing both come to mind more readily and are more likely to be followed by attitude-consistent behavior (Petty, Haugtvedt, & Smith, 1995; Pierro, Mannetti, Kruglanski, Klein, & Orehek, 2012). Third, attitudes that are personally important—ones that people are concerned about and believe to be significant—are also more likely to be spontaneously activated in a wide variety of information-processing and decision-making situations. As you might predict, then, they are also more likely to be used as guides for a wide range of attitude-relevant actions (Boninger, Krosnick, & Berent, 1995). Fourth, strong attitudes, intense attitudes that we hold with great confidence and certainty, usually have a long history of activation. Strong attitudes have high attitude-behavior consistency, whereas ambivalent attitudes do not (Cooke & Sheeran, 2004; Costarelli & Colloca, 2007; Rucker & Petty, 2004). Thus, whenever attitudes have features that make them well-established and frequently used, they are much more likely than less accessible attitudes to predict behaviors.

Refer to Figure 7.2 on page 241 for a quick refresher on the link between an attitude object and the attitude associated with it. Because of that link, thinking about almost any object also brings to mind the positive or negative evaluation associated with it.

We described the nature of strong attitudes in Chapter 7, pages 239–240, and noted some of their consequences for persuasion, pages 269–270.

Attitude Correspondence. If attitudes dictate perceptions of and intentions toward a particular attitude object, they will have their greatest effect on behavior toward that particular attitude object (Ajzen & Cote, 2008). If we are busy thinking about our attitude toward recycling, it's probably not going to have much impact on how we see the newest fuel-efficient vehicle or what intentions we form about it. For an attitude to guide behavior, the right attitude must come to mind at the right time. Think about the issue of environmental conservation. You may favor conservation as a general principle, but that is not your only environmental attitude. You probably have several related and increasingly specific attitudes toward implementation, for example, toward downsizing landfills, using recycled aluminum cans versus glass or plastic bottles, or cutting down on automobile emissions. It isn't enough if just any vaguely related attitude comes to mind when we contemplate action—how we feel about glass bottles is irrelevant at the gas pump. Only an attitude that corresponds to a particular behavior can be expected to influence that behavior strongly (Glasman & Albarracin, 2006; Schwarz, Groves, & Schuman, 1998).

To influence a specific behavior, specific attitudes must come to mind (Eckes & Six, 1994; Kraus, 1995). When researchers tried to predict whether women would use birth-control pills during a 2-year period, they found that the women's specific attitudes about birth-control pills were better predictors than their attitudes toward birth control in general (Davidson & Jaccard, 1979). An attitude about performing the behavior in question ("What's your opinion on curbside recycling?") is the best predictor of whether or not the behavior occurs (Eagly & Chaiken, 1993; McIntyre, Paulson, Lord, & Lepper, 2004). Whether you want to improve health habits, change environmental practices, or increase support for worthy causes, it is important to bring an attitude that corresponds with the desired behavior to mind.

Research by Charles Lord and his colleagues (Lord, Lepper, & Mackie, 1984; Sia, Lord, Blessum, Ratcliff, & Lepper, 1997) makes a similar point. These researchers asked male undergraduates whether they would be willing to show a hypothetical transferring student, John B., around the Princeton campus. John was identified (ostensibly by a counseling psychologist at his current school) as being gay. Would participants' attitudes about gays influence their willingness to spend time with John? The researchers hypothesized that this would be true only if John matched the students' expectations of typical gay men. To test this idea, participants were asked to read a description of John that either closely matched or largely disconfirmed their stereotype. When John's description matched students' preconceptions, their attitudes (whether positive or negative) toward gays were highly correlated with their willingness to interact with him. Participants acted in line with their attitudes: if John seemed to be a "typical" gay man, students who disliked gays wanted to have nothing to do with him whereas students with positive attitudes toward gays were quite happy to show him around. When John did not appear to match the preconception, participants' attitudes, whether positive or negative, had no impact. Attitude–behavior consistency can only be expected when the attitude object (what or whom you think about when asked your opinion) and the target of behavior (what or whom you act toward when given the opportunity) are the same (Ajzen, 1996).

Such findings might help explain one of the classic studies that made social psychologists wonder if attitudes did guide behavior at all (LaPiere, 1934). Recall the study in which managers' attitudes toward serving Chinese customers were not at all consistent with treatment of a well-dressed Chinese couple who asked to dine or stay at their hotel or restaurant? Given the stereotypes of the day, it is likely that the managers' attitudes were based on images of and experiences with Chinese laborers. Faced with a target of behavior (the well-dressed couple) that was very different from the attitude object (the uneducated laborer) they had no doubt thought about when asked their opinion, no wonder the managers' attitudes did not predict their behavior.

Correspondence of activity levels has also been shown to predict greater attitude-behavior consistency (Paulson and others, 2012). An active behavior is fairly overt and effortful to perform, whereas a passive one is less so (Cuddy, Fiske, & Glick, 2007). In one study, participants were shown a list of either active positive and negative behaviors they could perform relevant to the social group gay men, like "have a rally for them" and "beat them up," or passive behaviors, like "take them for who they are" and "not stand close to them" (Paulson and others, 2012). Participants circled the behaviors they had personally enacted toward gay men and then reported their attitudes toward gay men. About 1–2 weeks later, these same participants learned about a gay transfer student and were given a list of both active and passive behaviors they might be asked to perform with this student during the semester, and they rated their willingness to perform each. Attitudes towards gay men predicted willingness to engage in behaviors with a gay man best when there was an activity match. In other words, those who had considered active behaviors earlier were more likely to have attitudes that later predicted active behaviors; whereas those who had considered passive behaviors earlier had attitudes that were more likely to predict their passive behaviors. Having attitudes that corresponded to particular behaviors made it more likely that attitudes guided those particular behaviors.

Even one's physical actions may help bring the corresponding attitude to mind and increase attitude-behavior consistency. In one study, students were asked to watch an exercise demonstration video. Some did this while imagining doing the same exercises, whereas others both imagined doing the exercises and simultaneously walked in place. Over the next week, those who had walked in place exercised more than those who had not. Also, their reported intentions to exercise (reported in the same session in which the exercise video was viewed) predicted subsequent exercise behavior more in the "walking in place" condition. Walking in place while viewing the exercise video might have made people's exercise-related attitudes more accessible, which may have made them guide subsequent behavior more reliably (Sherman, Gangi, & White, 2010).

Implicit and Explicit Attitudes as Guides for Behavior. If only an activated attitude that is appropriate and relevant for a particular behavior can be expected to influence that behavior, what does that say about when implicit attitudes will affect behaviors? Recall from Chapter 7 that people's implicit attitudes, ones that reflect their automatic evaluations of objects, can diverge from their explicit attitudes, the ones they consciously endorse and overtly express (Fazio & Olson, 2003). As we noted, most people have an implicit automatic negative evaluation of spiders and snakes, for example, even though many people's explicit attitudes toward these same objects are neutral or even positive. These differences can arise because implicit and explicit attitudes reflect different kinds of information about an object. Implicit attitudes might reflect more automatic, less controllable aspects of evaluations, like hard-wired positive and negative affective reactions, or associations built up from frequent pairing of the attitude object with positive

To remind yourself about the IAT, and how it provides a measure of implicit attitudes, re-read Chapter 5, pages 163–165.

Recall that just the same kinds of findings were reported in Chapter 5, pages 166–167: Implicit measures of prejudice are more closely related to subtle nonverbal behaviors toward out-groups, whereas explicit attitudes are better predictors of more deliberative verbal behavior toward out-groups.

theory of planned behavior
the theory that attitudes, social norms, and perceived control combine to influence intentions and thus behavior

or negative events. In contrast, explicit attitudes reflect our conscious thoughts and considered reactions to the object.

If all this is true, then we might expect implicit and explicit attitudes to guide different kinds of behaviors, and that is just what some researchers have found. In one study, student participants completed both an Implicit Association Test (a measure of implicit attitudes) and an explicit questionnaire about their attitudes toward the soda brands Coke and Pepsi (Karpinski, Steinman, & Hilton, 2005). They were then asked how they thought they would act if offered a free Pepsi or Coke product. The students' explicit attitudes toward the sodas were a much better predictor than the implicit measure of this highly deliberate and controllable behavior. In contrast, in another study, soda drinkers also completed implicit and explicit measures of their attitudes toward Coke and Pepsi, but their behavioral preference for the sodas was measured in a blind taste-test (Maison, Greenwald, & Bruin, 2004). Perhaps because reactions to tastes are much less controllable and deliberate, the participants' responses in the taste-test were better predicted by their implicit attitudes. Thus, findings like these suggest that implicit attitudes are especially good predictors of less controllable sorts of behaviors and explicit attitudes are good predictors of more controllable actions.

Yet, the story may be more complicated than this. One recent meta-analysis suggests that implicit attitudes are equally good at predicting controllable behaviors (like purchasing) and less controllable behaviors (like body language; Greenwald and others, 2009). Another recent meta-analysis concludes that implicit attitudes are fairly weak predictors of behaviors, whether controllable or not (Oswald and others, 2013). Therefore, though individual studies suggest that implicit and explicit attitudes may predict different sorts of behaviors, more research is needed to identify the sorts of behaviors for which this is true, and to test whether certain types of implicit measures do a better job predicting behaviors than other sorts of implicit measures.

Despite the need for more research to clarify these issues, the fact that implicit and explicit attitudes often do influence different kinds of behaviors may help explain why strong attitudes are such good predictors of a wide range of attitude relevant behaviors, as we mentioned above. For strong attitudes, implicit and explicit attitudes tend to be consistent, so both work together to guide both spontaneous and more controlled behaviors (Karpinski and others, 2005). But when implicit and explicit attitudes differ, either one might be a more influential guide for action, depending on just what the action is. Thus, whether an attitude is general or specific, and whether it is implicit or explicit, the same principle applies: the right attitude has to come to mind to guide behavior.

When Attitudes Are Not Enough. Even though the right attitude may come to mind at the right time, it still may not be enough to dictate behavior (Kaiser, Byrka, & Hartig, 2010). People do not act on attitudes if they think they cannot perform the required behavior (Liska, 1984). According to the **theory of planned behavior**, perceptions of personal control—whether people feel capable of action—thus have a big influence on intentions and thus on behavior (Ajzen, 1991; Armitage & Conner, 2001). When people think they can control their behavior, attitudes can become highly effective in mobilizing and sustaining effective action (Armitage & Reidy, 2008). A sense of control has been shown to facilitate effective weight loss (Sheppard, Hartwick, & Warshaw, 1988), reduce binge drinking in college females (Todd & Mullan, 2011), and increase the expectation and achievement of success at stopping smoking (Eiser & Sutton, 1977; Eiser, van der Pligt, Raw, & Sutton, 1985). In contrast, overeaters who believe obesity is due to hormonal factors, smokers who attribute their behavior to addiction, and drivers who believe being in a car wreck is a matter of fate have no reason to follow through on even a relevant attitude and therefore do not do so (Ajzen & Madden, 1986; Bandura, 1982; Eiser & van der Pligt, 1986; Ronis & Kaiser, 1989).

Of course, even when our attitudes are positive, our intentions are firm, and we perceive ourselves to be in control, unforeseen circumstances or lack of ability can prevent us from following through on behavior. A would-be voter who cannot get transportation to the polls cannot translate his political attitudes into action. Many useful and much-wanted consumer products are so expensive that desire cannot be translated into ownership. So even when we think we have control, we don't always actually have the objective control to carry through on our attitudes and intentions. This is particularly true when attitude-consistent behavior requires social interaction, that is, when we need other people to help us act on our attitudes. An uncooperative spouse may sabotage the best-laid plans to discipline the children. An old-fashioned boss may squash attempts to introduce a parental-leave policy in a company. Intentions to conserve energy and lower utility bills may be undermined by family members who leave on lights and open windows in air-conditioned rooms. Although attitudes are personal, we often need interpersonal cooperation to carry through on them.

Another factor that limits the impact of attitudes on behaviors is the power of habit. It has become increasingly clear to social psychologists that many of the behaviors they are most interested in—healthy or unhealthy lifestyle choices, social and political behaviors, patterns of consumption—are influenced as much by sheer habit as by anything else. A **habit** is a repeated behavior that is automatically triggered in a particular situation (Neal, Wood, & Quinn, 2006). Habits result from associations that develop between an often-repeated or well-practiced action and particular features of the environment, such as a particular location or a recognizable body state. Habitual behaviors—like reaching for a snack when you read the paper, turning on the TV when you walk in the house, or lighting up a cigarette after a meal—are performed quite independently of attitudes, norms, motives, or even goals—indeed with little conscious input of any kind (Neal, Wood, Labrecque, & Lally, 2012; Wood, Quinn, & Kashy, 2002). Imagine you were asked to watch a movie during an experiment and were offered popcorn to munch on while you did so. In this situation, people who described themselves as habitually eating popcorn while watching movies not only ate more than other viewers, but they ate the same amount of popcorn regardless of whether it was fresh or stale and regardless of whether they were hungry or had just eaten! In the context of movie watching, they simply, and apparently mindlessly, ate

We have already seen in Chapter 4, pages 128–129 how important perceived control is to individual striving for mastery. The impact that perceiving control has on individual action will be discussed again in Chapter 10, page 390.

habit
a repeated behavior automatically triggered in a particular situation

Photo 8.4 Habits. Habits are often triggered by particular environmental cues. Do you pick up coffee every day while walking to campus or sip from a coffee mug while studying or doing school work, like the woman shown here? If so, drinking coffee is a habit for you, triggered by campus or studying cues.

popcorn. Importantly, it took only a small change to disrupt this habitual behavior—when study participants were told they had to eat with their nondominant hand, the amount of popcorn they ate depended on hunger and taste, rather than on mindless routine (Neal, Wood, Wu, & Kurlander, 2011).

Habits are triggered in particular situations so automatically that people "find themselves" in the middle of acting before they realize they have acted (Triandis, 1980; Wood, Tam, & Witt, 2005). Smokers, for example, often notice they are smoking but do not recall having decided to smoke or lighting the cigarette. Of course habits can be positive, like automatically fastening the seat belt as soon as you sit down in a car, locking a door as soon as you close it, or flossing right after brushing, and so habit formation can be a powerful means of making sure behavior happens (Neal, Wood, & Drolet, 2013). But many habitual behaviors like nail biting, overeating, excessive television watching, and smoking continue even in the face of people's obvious desire to stop them. For all of us frustrated by the failure of our latest crop of New Year's Resolutions, it's clear that bad habits can be quite resistant to our good attitudes and intentions.

No wonder, then, that it's a long step from having an attitude to acting on it. Whether we are deciding what to eat for breakfast or whether to join the armed forces, a behavioral decision, like all judgments large and small, depends on the information that goes into it. Attitudes are an important element in the behavioral equation, but they are seldom the only source of information relevant to action. Indeed, as we will discuss next in Chapters 9 and 10, powerful constraints on our behavior, like the pressures we may feel to follow social norms—the ways of thinking, feeling, or behaving that people in a group agree upon as right and proper—can greatly undermine the degree to which our personally held attitudes guide our behavior.

As Figure 8.6 shows, attitudes are most likely to influence actions when the attitude comes to mind, when the attitude is appropriate, and when attitude-consistent behavior is not constrained in any other way. When we understand how attitudes influence behaviors, we come to see some of the complexities involved in getting attitudes to influence behavior in everyday situations.

CONCLUDING COMMENTS

A greater understanding of how our inner selves fit with our outer selves—of how behaviors can shape attitudes and attitudes can shape behaviors—is one of the most significant contributions that social-psychological research offers us. Research on attitudes and behaviors often goes against the accepted wisdom. Consider these counterintuitive findings.

■ Most people would never guess that behavior has an impact on our attitudes. Yet when we casually give money to the homeless person on the corner, or murmur support for the boss's unworkable plan, we may be helping to change our own opinions. As the research discussed in this chapter has demonstrated, subtle situational and interpersonal pressures that produce behaviors can trigger changes in our attitudes.

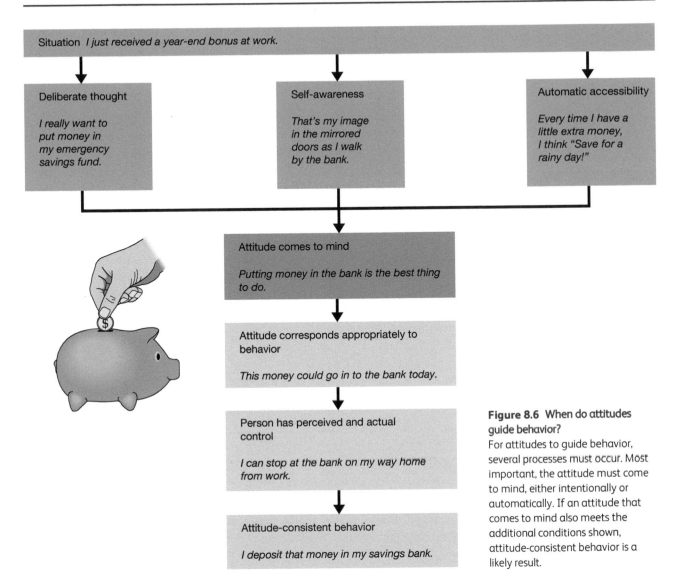

Figure 8.6 When do attitudes guide behavior?
For attitudes to guide behavior, several processes must occur. Most important, the attitude must come to mind, either intentionally or automatically. If an attitude that comes to mind also meets the additional conditions shown, attitude-consistent behavior is a likely result.

- Most of us would probably guess that what we are rewarded for, we will come to like. Yet self-perception and dissonance theory teach us that sometimes less is more. It is when external rewards are missing, when we suffer pains to reach our goals, and when we give up alternatives with many positive benefits that we are likely to form the most positive attitudes toward what we choose.

- Most of us would certainly guess that, by and large, we act on our attitudes. Much of human activity is marked by a motive for consistency—why else would we experience dissonance when our attitudes and behaviors are inconsistent? We certainly expect other people to follow through on their convictions. After all, we work hard to change customers' minds in order to change their purchases. We try to raise employees' morale in order to boost their productivity; we take pains to eliminate prejudice in order to eliminate discrimination. All of these efforts assume that there is an attitude–action connection, and there is good reason to assume it. Yet this relationship is not one on which we can routinely rely. Attitudes are just one of the factors that have to come to mind to influence perceptions, intentions, plans, and, ultimately, behavior.

As researchers continue to specify the conditions under which attitudes do influence behavior, however, their findings also reaffirm their optimism. Knowing how attitudes influence behavior means that we can have some control over when they do. Such knowledge has important personal and societal consequences. Recall from Chapter 5 that in their battle against prejudice and discrimination, some individuals try to inhibit the impact of their initial responses and consciously bring to bear more egalitarian attitudes. Similar processes could be involved when managers evaluate workers' performance and when jury members form impressions on which they acquit or convict defendants. The research described in this chapter suggests ways both to suppress the influence of some attitudes and to increase the influence of others. When we want attitudes to be potent, they must come to mind readily and be related to the behavioral options at hand. Weak connections between attitude and object, competition from other attitudes, and a lack of control over the desired behavior will all reduce the impact of attitudes on behaviors.

Of course, the influence of social norms can also reduce this impact. Social norms often conflict with people's personal inclinations. Yet, information about others' standards of appropriateness is vital for effective social functioning—so vital that these standards often override personal attitudes to determine social behavior. The development of social norms and the impact they have on behavior are the focus of the next two chapters.

CHAPTER 8 THEMES

■ **Construction of Reality**
Our actions are guided by the attitudes we have constructed toward the world.

■ **Pervasiveness of Social Influence**
Both our attitudes and our behavior are shaped by other people and by our social surroundings.

■ **Conservatism**
Once an attitude is strongly established it changes perceptions and guides the development of intentions and plans, leading to behavior that further strengthens the attitude.

■ **Accessibility**
Attitudes can guide behavior only when they come to mind.

■ **Superficiality Versus Depth**
The effect of behavior on attitudes, and also the effect of attitudes on behavior, can reflect either superficial processing or more thoughtful systematic processing.

SUMMARY

Changing Attitudes with Actions. Behavior is an important part of the information on which people base attitudes. If behaviors change, attitudes can also change. When people process superficially, attitudes can be based on associations with actions or on inferences from actions. In the **foot-in-the-door technique**, people who are induced to comply with a small request come to view themselves as having corresponding attitudes. If they are later faced with a larger request from the same source, they are more likely to grant it than are people who never received the initial request. Like other forms of superficial processing, associations with and inferences from actions are more likely to occur when people lack the motivation or ability to process more thoroughly.

When freely chosen actions violate important self-relevant attitudes, the inconsistency produces an uncomfortable state of tension and arousal termed **cognitive dissonance**. This can motivate people to change their attitudes to make them consistent with their behavior. This might occur, for example, following attitude-discrepant behavior that cannot be attributed to an external cause, producing an **insufficient justification** effect. Dissonance might also motivate people to change their attitudes to value highly what they have worked hard for (an **effort justification effect**) or to emphasize the positive aspects of options they have chosen, a **post-decisional regret effect**. Because this kind of attitude change involves extensive processing, it is often long-lasting. However, there are alternatives to reducing dissonance besides changing our attitudes. For example, a

hypocrisy effect occurs when future behavior is changed to reduce dissonance aroused by publicly advocating a non-performed behavior. While minor discrepancies between action and attitudes might trigger self-perception processes, conflicts between actions and attitudes that are important enough to cause unpleasant tension trigger dissonance reduction processes.

Changing Actions with Attitudes. Established attitudes can guide behaviors in a very direct way. Attitudes bias perceptions, thereby making attitude-consistent information about attitude objects more obvious and attitude-consistent behavior more likely. Attitudes also influence behavior in a more considered way by prompting **intentions** to reach desired goals or perform desired behaviors. According to the **theory of reasoned action**, attitudes are an important source of intentions. Intentions in turn can trigger planning and the development of **implementation intentions** to act in certain ways in certain situations, that makes attitude-consistent behavior more likely.

The more accessible the attitude and the more closely the attitude corresponds to the intended behavior, the more attitudes will guide actions. Attitudes can be made accessible by deliberate thought, self-awareness, or frequent use. Only attitudes that correspond to a particular behavior will guide that behavior. Implicit attitudes predict uncontrollable behaviors better and explicit attitudes predict controllable behaviors better. Sometimes attitudes are not enough to influence behavior. According to the **theory of planned behavior**, perceptions of personal control have a big influence on intentions and thus on behavior. Behavior is more likely to reflect attitudes if people both believe they have control and actually do have control over their behavior. Some behaviors are **habits**, which are automatically triggered by situations and performed quite independently of attitudes, norms, motives, or even goals.

NORMS AND CONFORMITY

Like it on Facebook. View it on YouTube. Tweet your vote to **#voteAGT** to tell the judges who you think should win *America's Got Talent*, or the UK's *X Factor*, or *Idols* in the Netherlands. Make a blog post to share your views on a vacation spot, a political policy, which headphones have the best sound isolation. Modern social media make sharing your views, and finding out what others think, only a click away. While the media might be new, the message is as old as social interaction itself. What others think, feel, and do is vitally important to humans, and we are profoundly influenced by others' reactions.

Social influence affects every aspect of our lives. Songs become hits because teens think other teens like the song, more than because of any inherent quality of the music itself (Salganik, Dodds, & Watts, 2006). When jokes and slapstick routines are accompanied by canned laughter, people find them funnier and laugh longer (Martin & Gray, 1996): the fake laughter makes it seem that other people find the jokes funny. Bartenders, street musicians, church ushers, and collectors for charitable agencies use a similar ploy. They know that putting dollar bills in their tip jars and collection boxes will increase what they get, because people will be led to believe that leaving a sizable amount of money is

Photo 9.1 Social media and the communication of norms. Social media platforms make it easier than ever to learn what others are thinking, feeling, and doing. We can even learn what is "trending" on Twitter—learning what topics are being discussed most.

the right thing to do. What we eat and whether we eat too much of it are closely tied to the eating habits and weight of our friends (Christakis & Fowler, 2011). And because a company's financial future can depend on the successful launch of a new product, some companies have started "manufacturing" popularity by giving new products away to thousands of specially selected consumers. They know that when tech-savvy 18–24-year-olds are seen tapping on iPads or busy working moms pull denim-style Huggies onto their toddlers before dropping them at day care, the potential success of the products skyrocket as others discover that "everyone is doing it" (Friess, 2002). Companies launching products aren't the only ones creating consensus. *Situations Matter* author Sam Sommers (Sommers, 2011) reports that Cameron Hughes, a self-styled "crowd whisperer," is able to make a comfortable living hiring himself out to whip otherwise less-than-inspired crowds into a frenzy by acting half-crazy himself. What we think, feel, and do is often closely dependent on what others think, feel, and do.

Although influencing and being influenced by others may seem silly when the result is only going along with the latest fad, such influence plays a crucial role in social behavior. In fact, a basic premise of social life is that many heads are better than one (Mannes, Larrick, & Soll, 2012; Surowiecki, 2004). In countries such as the United Kingdom, the United States, France, Russia, and Iran, such beliefs have been institutionalized so that a jury—a group of people—rather than a judge can decide the fate of people accused of crimes. We trust executive committees and boards of directors to run schools, businesses, and charitable organizations, and we respect the decisions of the panels of judges at art events, talent shows, and disciplinary hearings. All these arrangements reflect our trust that collective wisdom will emerge from the mutual interaction and influence of multiple individuals in a group.

In this chapter, we explore the processes that occur when groups of individuals influence each other and reach agreement. We begin by considering two related questions: Why do groups seek to reach agreement, and why do people accept influence from others? You will see that part of the answer to these questions is that people want to master their social worlds—to see things the right way, hold correct opinions, and do the right thing. People also want to be connected to others, to be liked and valued by those whose opinions they respect, and achieving such a connection to in-groups—which promotes a sense of me and mine—counts the most. Thus, when a group comes to an agreement, it leaves people with feelings of both mastery and connectedness.

We then turn to the question of how agreement is reached. For example, how are the differing opinions of 12 individual jury members forged into a verdict that all can accept? As you will see, the processes of social influence are reciprocal. Individuals contribute their views to the group position, and what the group thinks influences each individual's views. When the group decision-making process is at its most effective, the consensus reached by the group incorporates multiple views and reflects the best available evidence.

Agreement in and of itself does not guarantee a positive outcome, however. Sometimes groups reach agreements that don't rest on careful consideration of information, openness to divergent opinions, or true conviction. When groups make such decisions and act on them, the consequences can be disastrous. In the final two sections, we consider how such negative outcomes occur and how they can be avoided. Groups that foster dissent rather than squelch it often reach agreements that are worthy guides for their members' thoughts, feelings, and behavior.

CONFORMITY TO SOCIAL NORMS

What Are Social Norms?

Because people are profoundly influenced by others' ideas and actions, interaction or communication causes group members' thoughts, feelings, and behaviors to become more alike. Whether a judgment task is clear-cut or ambiguous, trivial or important, individual members' views converge to form a social norm. Norms reflect the group's generally accepted way of thinking, feeling, or acting. Descriptive social norms are what people think, feel, or do whereas injunctive social norms specify what people should think, feel, or do.

Face-to-face and social category groups were first discussed in Chapter 5, page 143.

All types of groups have the power to dramatically affect group members' thoughts, feelings, and behaviors. Remember that some social groups share socially relevant features (like gender, age, or an interest in the environment). Members of such social categories may or may not interact much. Other social groups form because they share a common goal, such as the members of a jury, a sports team, or lab groups assigned to work on a particular problem. Such face-to-face groups interact and influence each other to reach that goal or complete a task. These face-to-face groups have the advantage of direct communication with one another. When people interact in a group, their thoughts, emotions, and actions tend to converge, becoming more and more alike.

Consider, for example, Muzafer Sherif's (1936) classic demonstration of a group's power to affect its members' beliefs. Each participant in Sherif's experiment first sat alone in a totally dark room and focused on a single point of light. As the participant watched, the light seemed to jump erratically and then disappear. Seconds later the light again appeared, moved, and disappeared. Each time the light appeared, the observer had to estimate how far it moved. In fact, the light did not move at all. Because a dark room provides no points of reference, a stationary point of light appears to careen in a jagged circle, but this is just an optical illusion. Given the ambiguity of the situation, it is not surprising that the participants' original distance estimates differed, ranging from barely an inch to nearly a foot.

These numbers changed dramatically, however, when participants returned to the lab in the following days to judge the light's movement, this time as members of three-person groups. As they heard one another's estimates of the light's movement, group members' responses began to converge until they were nearly identical (see Figure 9.1). And these shared estimates had lasting power: As much as a year later, these participants continued to use the common response when judging the light, even when alone (Rohrer, Baron, Hoffman, & Schwander, 1954).

In coming to this collective agreement, group members established a social norm, or consensus, about the movement of the light. As you may recall from Chapter 5, a social norm is a generally accepted way of thinking, feeling, or behaving that most people in a group agree on and endorse as right and proper (Thibaut & Kelley, 1959). When people talk about "a well-known fact," "public opinion," "the way we do things," "the way things are," they are really talking about social norms. Social norms are similar to attitudes in that both are mental representations of appropriate ways of thinking, feeling, and acting. But whereas attitudes represent an individual's positive or negative evaluations, norms

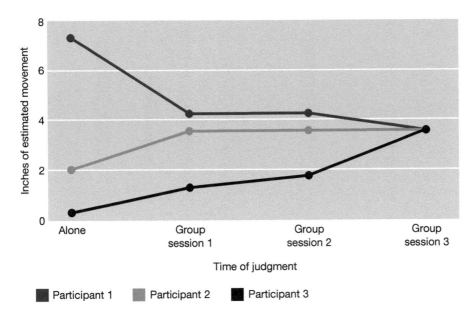

Figure 9.1 How consensus develops

These three typical individuals in Muzafer Sherif's experiment entered the group with varied views about the apparent movement of the light, as indicated by their initial judgments. Note how their estimates in the group sessions gradually converged until they were identical. (Data from Sherif, 1936.)

reflect shared group evaluations of what is true or false, good or bad, appropriate or inappropriate. Thus, for example, a parent's love for his or her children is an attitude, whereas the idea that parents do—and should—love their offspring is a social norm. **Descriptive social norms**—what a group of people think, feel, or do—are sometimes contrasted with **injunctive social norms**—what people should think, feel, or do. The idea that parents do love their children is a descriptive norm, whereas the idea that people should love their children is an injunctive norm. But most norms have both qualities—it is because most people do think, feel, or behave in a certain way that we think they should. When many people act in the same way over and over again, they begin to think that they should act that way, and descriptive norms morph into injunctive ones (Guala & Mittone, 2010). And this intertwining holds for social norms that range from the trivial, such as what a group finds funny, to the profound, such as a group's standards of morality.

You may be thinking that Sherif stacked the deck in favor of social influence and against individual independence. After all, the experimental situation was highly ambiguous, the light's movement could not be measured, and participants were not told if they were right or wrong. Under these conditions, what else could the participants do but rely on the responses of others? What about decisions that are not ambiguous? Do groups still have such influence? The answer is yes. Worried by how easily influenced Sherif's participants seemed to be, Solomon Asch (1951, 1955) set out to show that if a judgment task were unambiguous, social influence would be eliminated. In fact, his now famous experiment demonstrated just the opposite.

Imagine being a participant in Asch's experiment. With eight other people, you are shown lines like those in Figure 9.2. A single straight line, called the standard line,

descriptive social norms
agreed upon mental representations of what a group of people think, feel, or do

injunctive social norms
agreed upon mental representations of what a group of people should think, feel, or do

Figure 9.2 Asch's line judgment task
Participants had to decide which comparison line—
A, B, or *C*—was identical to the standard line for 18
different sets of lines. On certain trials, confederates
agreed on obviously wrong answers—in this case, *A*
or *C.* Participants conformed to this incorrect consensus about a third of the time. (Adapted from Asch,
1955.)

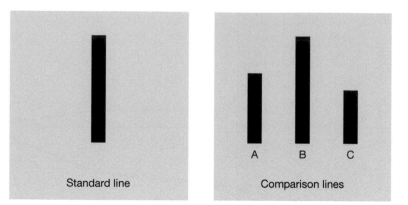

Standard line   Comparison lines

appears with three comparison lines of different lengths. There are 18 different sets of
comparison lines, and your task is merely to say which of the three comparison lines is
the same length as the standard line. You all answer in order of seating, and you are next
to last. The task seems simple: The test lines clearly differ from one another, and for the
first few trials everyone agrees on the correct line. But on the next trial, all of the other
participants, who were actually confederates, each unanimously picked an obviously
wrong answer, creating a strong descriptive norm of which line to select. Now it's your
turn. Faced with a conflict between the evidence of your senses and the opinions of your
peers, how do you respond?

If you are like most of Asch's participants, you are likely to agree with this wrong
answer. Despite the ease of the task, the confederates' wrong answers caused a great deal
of anxiety, and they also had a considerable impact on the real participants' responses.

Three-quarters of the participants echoed the confederates' choice on at least 1 trial, and half agreed with an
obviously wrong answer on 50% or more trials. Only
25% ignored everyone else's answers on all the critical
trials. Why did so many change their answers? When
questioned later, some participants told Asch they were
concerned about looking ridiculous and just went along
with the group. Others said they quite literally "couldn't
believe their eyes" and assumed that the group was
correct. Even those who stuck with their original answers
were still looking for ways to reconcile their judgments
with those of the majority when the experiment ended.

The essential results of Sherif's and Asch's studies—
that people are influenced by and often adopt the opinions
of other group members—have been replicated many
times. In case you're wondering, such conformity is not
just a thing of the past: demonstrations of individuals
changing their own responses to match those of others
continue to accumulate (Campbell-Meiklejohn and others,
2010; Haun, van Leeuwen, & Edelson, 2013; Rosander &
Eriksson, 2012). Nor is conformity to the views of others

Photo 9.2 Huh? Why don't we agree? It's not hard to identify the real
participant in this photograph from one of Solomon Asch's original
experiments on conformity. Faced unexpectedly with unanimous disagreement from the rest of the group, participant Number 6 peers
anxiously at the line matching task. What powerful social influences
might make him accept the group norm over the evidence of his
senses?

limited to judgments about relatively trivial things—the movement of lights, the length of lines. In fact, social influence is so powerful it can even make us question our own guilt or innocence (Perillo & Kassin 2011). Saul Kassin and Katherine Kiechel (1996) had college students type letters either relatively quickly or at a more leisurely pace on a computer keyboard, ostensibly to show their reflex speed. All participants were warned not to hit the ALT key, as doing so could crash the computer. When the computer malfunctioned a minute later, the distressed experimenter accused the student of hitting the forbidden key. The student initially denied the charge, but the experimenter turned to a confederate and asked, "Did you see anything?" In one condition, the confederate reported seeing nothing, but in another condition, the confederate agreed that she had seen the student press the forbidden key, apparently confirming the experimenter's suggestion of guilt. The experimenter then demanded that the students sign a handwritten confession ("I hit the ALT key and caused the computer to crash. Data were lost"). Sixty-nine percent agreed to do so! Even more revealingly, 28% privately came to see themselves as guilty. Participants were more likely to believe themselves guilty when the confederate agreed with the experimenter and especially if the speed at which they were typing made them uncertain about what had actually happened. Just as in the classic conformity studies, uncertain participants were particularly likely to accept the responses of multiple others—the apparent descriptive norm—even if it meant confessing to a "crime" that initially they were all sure they hadn't committed!

These dramatic results reveal the powerful impact of others' reactions that goes on as groups all around us make judgments and decisions. Whether the judgment task is clear-cut or ambiguous, and whether prior opinions are held with more or less conviction, group members offer, exchange, and accept various points of view until consensus evolves.

Public Versus Private Conformity

Conformity is the convergence of individual responses toward group norms. Conformity occurs for two important reasons: because people believe that the group is right and because they want the group to accept and approve of them. Most of the time people privately accept group norms as their own, believing them to be correct and appropriate. Sometimes, however, people publicly go along with norms they do not privately accept.

The convergence of individuals' thoughts, feelings, and behavior toward a group norm is called **conformity** (Allen, 1965; Deutsch & Gerard, 1955; Kiesler & Kiesler, 1969). Most of the time, this tendency to let other people's reactions and responses guide our own occurs because we privately accept the group's view, believing it to be both a correct and an appropriate guide for our own position. **Private conformity** occurs when people are truly persuaded that the group is right, when they willingly and privately accept group norms as their own beliefs, even if the group is no longer physically present. When participants in Sherif's study adopted their group's standard opinion regarding the movement of the light, even though there was no pressure to do so, they showed private conformity. Remember that they used the group norm as their personal standard as much

conformity
the convergence of individuals' thoughts, feelings, or behavior toward a social norm

private conformity
private acceptance of social norms

as a year later, when they were asked to judge the light movements in the absence of other group members.

Sometimes, however, conformity occurs because we feel we have no choice but to go along with social norms. **Public conformity** occurs when people respond to real or imagined pressure and behave consistently with norms that they do not privately accept as correct. Public conformity produces only a surface change: People pretend to go along with the group norm in what they say or do, but privately they do not think the group is right. People publicly conform because they fear ridicule, rejection, incarceration, or worse. Those of Asch's participants who went along with the incorrect majority view to avoid seeming ridiculous were publicly conforming, as are political dissidents who survive by paying lip service to the party line even though they do not agree with it.

public conformity

overt behavior consistent with social norms that are not privately accepted

HOT TOPICS IN SOCIAL PSYCHOLOGY: THE SOCIAL NEUROSCIENCE OF CONFORMITY

New technologies in social neuroscience are revealing what social influence looks like in the brain. Such studies typically assess activity in different parts of the brain while or after participants are exposed to information about others' responses, views, or opinions. Such studies show the profound effects of conformity on the way we view the world. In one illustrative study, Jamil Zaki, Jessica Schirmer, and Jason Mitchell (2011) had participants rate the attractiveness of multiple faces and then learn how other students like them had allegedly evaluated each face. Participants then rated the faces for a second time, this time while in an fMRI scanner. The second set of ratings showed a typical conformity effect: participants' own ratings of each face moved toward their peers' judgments. The brain activity that accompanied these new judgments indicated that exposure to descriptive social norms actually changed participants' neural representation of the stimuli's value—good evidence of private acceptance, a change in the way the world was viewed because of social input (see also Edelson, Sharot, Dolan, & Dudai, 2011). Recent evidence from studies using EEG technology similarly shows that social influence appears to impact early unconscious visual perceptual processing, essentially changing the world that recipients of social input see (Trautmann-Lengsfeld & Herrmann, 2013). Social neuroscientists are also attempting to track the perspective taking and affective processes that underlie adoption of other people's points of view (Stallen, Smidts, & Sanfey, 2013).

SOCIAL PSYCHOLOGY AND CULTURE: CONFORMITY AND CULTURE

Because the results of Sherif's and Asch's studies tell us so much about the relationship between individual and group, attempts have been made to replicate their results in many different cultures and countries. The relatively high levels of conformity found in the original studies were surprising partly because individualist cultures (like the predominant cultures in the United States and Europe) put such a high value on individual autonomy. In such cultures, both public and private conformity have somewhat negative overtones. Nonetheless, more than a hundred replications of Asch's procedure in the United States confirm that even individualist North Americans are profoundly influenced by others' reactions. The power of conformity can lead to an ironic outcome: when people who strongly identify as North Americans are reminded of their group's norm of individualism, they conform more strongly to that norm—by conforming less in other ways (Jetten, Postmes, & McAuliffe, 2002)!

■■■

Conformity is seen much more positively in collectivist cultures such as those found in India or Japan. In such cultures, individuals see themselves as an integral part of the group and view conformity as a kind of social glue (Kim & Markus, 1999). Thus, one might expect conformity to readily occur in such settings. In fact, a meta-analysis of 133 studies conducted in 17 different countries provided evidence that the more collectivist the culture, the more conformity to the responses of others occurs (Bond & Smith, 1996). These effects are mimicked at the individual level—when given the choice, people who see themselves as collectivist-oriented conform more than those whose self-construals are individualist (Täuber & Sassenberg, 2012). Nevertheless, such results should be interpreted with caution, as many of the early cross-cultural studies did not differentiate between public and private conformity—perhaps only public conformity is stronger in collectivist cultures (Oh, 2013). As the evidence stands now, it's clear that conformity occurs in all cultural contexts—those that are individualist, collectivist, or somewhere in between.

Although public conformity in the face of heavy-handed group pressure does occur, private acceptance of group norms is far more prevalent and powerful. Because we usually see others as valid and valued sources of knowledge about the world, we often privately conform to social norms without even realizing we are doing so.

MOTIVATIONAL FUNCTIONS OF CONFORMITY TO NORMS

Advertisers, market specialists, and campaign managers have been quick to use the idea that people rely on others' views and often adopt others' behaviors. Slice-of-life scenes—the hidden camera recording family breakfasts with Kellogg's Corn Flakes, the testimonial from the schoolteacher with the headache that only Advil pain medication can relieve—provide us with models of people "just like us" who are solving problems and improving their lives. Headlines that shout: "Only two left at this price!" or "Get yours now while supplies last!" convey just how desirable such sought-after products must be. In one demonstration of such effects, college students preferred cookies they thought were in short supply because they were popular with others over the same cookies described as being in plentiful supply. And putting their money where their mouths were, students were willing to pay more for the scarce cookies (Ku, Kuo, & Kuo, 2012; Worchel, Lee, & Adewole, 1975). Why are we so influenced by these descriptive norms of what others are thinking, feeling, and presumably eating? Why do we conform to others' views at all? And what makes the views of others "just like us" particularly important? Why do we seem to care more what some people think and not worry too much about others?

Expecting Consensus

Private conformity comes about because we expect to see the world the same way similar others see it. In fact, we often assume that most other people share our own opinions and preferences. Agreement with others increases our confidence that our views are correct, whereas disagreement undermines that certainty.

false consensus effect

the tendency to overestimate
others' agreement with one's own
opinions, characteristics, and
behaviors

The key reason people conform to norms is that we expect everyone to see the world the same way. This expectation has two parts. First, we usually expect others to see the world the way we do. In fact, people tend to overestimate the extent to which others agree with their views of the world, a phenomenon called the **false consensus effect** (Ross, Greene, & House, 1977). The more important the connection to those others is, the stronger this false consensus effect is (Morrison & Matthes, 2011). To see the effect in action, researchers used the social networking platform Facebook to ask participants about their own political beliefs as well as their perceptions of their friends' attitudes (Goel, Mason, & Watts, 2010). Although friends' attitudes were more similar to their own than different, participants significantly over-estimated the extent to which they and their friends agreed politically. This over-estimation resulted from a false consensus at both the individual and group level—participants thought that everyone thought the same way they did, especially other "people like us."

Second, we usually expect to see the world the same way others do. When other people share our views, their agreement increases our confidence that we see things the right way. When people make judgments or hold opinions that are consistent with what most people think, they do so more quickly and with more confidence, even when making judgments in private (Horcajo, Petty, & Briñol, 2010; Koriat & Adiv, 2011). Our expectation of consensus is fulfilled. In contrast, disagreement with others, and especially disagreement with a consensus, can be a startling disconfirmation of our view of the world and our place in it. Disagreement leaves us uncertain, uncomfortable, and, as Sherif and Asch demonstrated, vulnerable to social influence until a new consensus is formed. How does the consensus represented in a norm help us to avoid that uncertainty and discomfort?

Norms Fulfill Mastery Motives

Agreeing with others assures people that they are in contact with a common reality. When people privately conform because they believe a group's norms reflect reality, the group has informational influence.

Norms are important because we need other people to help us construct an appropriate view of reality. Other people's reactions tell us what the world is like. Imagine, for example, that you made both an apple pie and a peach pie for a family get-together. If everyone came back for seconds on the peach pie but there were no repeats on the apple, it would be natural to infer that your peach pie was a success but your apple was not as good as usual. When everyone prefers the peach pie, we make the attribution that the characteristics of the pie itself, rather than any idiosyncrasy of the eaters, determine its positive reception. That is, consensus tells us something about reality. In fact, descriptive norms are such powerful guides to reality that we are often unaware of their influence and take them for granted (Zou and others, 2009). For example, we often see our country's monetary system as operating quite independently of social norms. On the contrary, it depends heavily on them. The more money people invest, the more the price of stocks and shares goes up, and the more money people invest in the market. Thus, economic good times are at least partially the result of a descriptive norm: the common perception and expectation that economic times are good. But when enough people start to question the system's assumptions—for example, that money deposited in a bank will be safe—and to act on their doubts—by making mass withdrawals—the system collapses. These examples show that something that we think of as "objective reality" actually depends on social conformity processes. Conformity to those norms helps to actually create the reality that the norm is seen as reflecting.

If we believe that group norms reflect reality, then conforming to them satisfies our need for mastery (Crano, Gorenflo, & Shackelford, 1988). We believe the group has more knowledge than we do, so accepting their input makes sense if we want to make better decisions. **Informational influence** occurs when people privately conform because they believe a group's norms reflect reality (Deutsch & Gerard, 1955). If people conform because they believe input from others increases their chances of making an accurate decision, then they should be particularly likely to conform when the stakes are high. That's exactly what happens. In Asch's task, participants given incentives to be as accurate as possible relied even more heavily on the (inaccurate) views of confederates (Baron, Vandello, & Brunsman, 1996). Individuals who are strongly motivated to acquire a clear and accurate view of the world conform more to others (Lun, Sinclair, Whitchurch, & Glenn, 2007). Decades of research bears out the advantages of such beliefs. Across a wide range of judgment tasks, the responses that groups converge upon are typically more accurate than the judgments of any one group member (Mannes, Larrick, & Soll, 2012). In fact, people would be more accurate if they relied more on the group response and less on their own. In one cunning study, participants judged the calorie value of some food after hearing others also make the same estimates (Yaniv & Choshen-Hillel, 2012). The twist came in that some participants could see the food that everyone was judging, whereas others made their judgments about an unknown "food item X" while wearing blindfolds. Participants were much more accurate when they could rely only on others' responses; when they could also see the food, they were overly swayed by their own idiosyncratic judgment. The motivation for accuracy thus leads to greater reliance on the social input of descriptive norms, and such confidence is well placed.

Some of the most convincing demonstrations of the importance of a consensus in shaping beliefs about reality come from variations on Asch's experimental procedure. Asch found that the amount of influence the confederate group exerted increased as the size of the group increased, but only up to a point. As you can see in Figure 9.3, adding more than three confederates, did not lead to further increases in conformity. Perhaps this is the origin of the old Spanish proverb: "If three men call you a donkey, put on a bridle!" Once an adequate consensus has formed, adding to the size of that consensus apparently has no further effect (Insko and others, 1983). The exact size of the consensus needed for maximal influence can differ from one judgment to another, but people share a good idea of what the burden of proof for a particular judgment should be (MacCoun, 2012).

If consensus exerts such an important influence on an individual's views, breaking the consensus should undermine the group's influence. To test this idea, Asch arranged for one of the confederates to agree with the real participant. He found that the presence of an ally dramatically decreased conformity to only about 10% of responses. This was true even when the dissenter gave a different incorrect answer or dropped out after a few responses (Allen & Bragg, 1965; Allen & Wilder, 1972; both cited in V. L. Allen, 1975). As the size of the dissenting minority increases, the majority's opinion seems more

You may recognize this effect from earlier chapters—the power of social norms to either maintain or disrupt behavior is an example of a self-fulfilling prophecy at work, see Chapter 5, pages 176–178.

informational influence
the process by which group norms are privately accepted to achieve or maintain mastery of reality

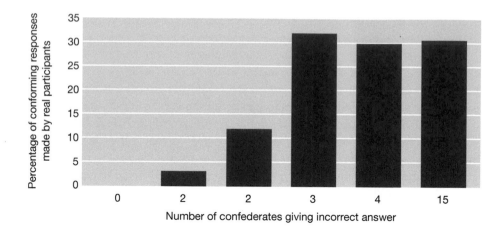

Figure 9.3 The importance of consensus
Amassing a consensus of three people around an obviously incorrect answer caused considerable conformity among real participants in this variation on Asch's procedure. Once the consensus was established, however, adding to it did not make much difference. A unanimous group of 15 confederates caused no more conformity than a unanimous group of three. (Data from Asch, 1955.)

and more open to question, and is less and less likely to be adopted (Gordijn, De Vries, & De Dreu, 2002). When there is no longer a consensus about reality—when the descriptive norm is not uniformly held—the group loses its power to persuade.

Because we depend so much on agreement with others, disagreement causes surprise, confusion, and, eventually, uncertainty, and self-doubt (Asch, 1956). Disagreement undermines our confidence in our view of reality. Thus, there is a potential for informational influence whenever people find themselves at odds with others with whom they expect to agree. Under these conditions, agreeing with the group consensus helps re-establish our confidence that we are indeed in touch with reality.

Norms Fulfill Connectedness Motives

Agreeing with others also gives people the feeling of belonging with others. A group has normative influence when members conform to it to attain a positive and valued social identity.

As discussed in Chapter 6, pages 197–199, feeling like a group member can bring us many benefits, including increased self-esteem.

In many religious communities, children who have reached an appropriate age go through some kind of ceremony, such as the Christian First Communion, the Jewish Bar or Bat Mitzvah, or the Hindu Sacred Thread ceremony. After these rituals, they are considered ready to participate fully in the rites of their community. The new members learn, through formal instruction or by observing others, how to speak, what thoughts and feelings are appropriate, and how to act. Knowing and following these standards allows them to take their place and fulfill their roles in the group. They experience a proud sense of belonging, as full members of their religious community.

What people learn in such situations are descriptive and injunctive group norms. By adopting such norms, we demonstrate our commitment and connections to our new associates and our pride in "who we are" and "what we stand for." A group has **normative influence** when members privately conform to it to attain a positive and valued social identity and to win respect from other group members (Turner, 1991). Normative influence thus satisfies our needs for connectedness because consensus provides and expresses our identity and values. Not surprisingly, then, the presence of the hormone oxytocin, which plays a significant role in human bonding, increases conformity to one's group (Stallen, De Dreu, Shalvi, Smidts, & Sanfey, 2012). The desire to be a valued member of a group is so strong that people typically adopt group norms whenever they are reminded of their membership in a group that is important to them (Ledgerwood & Chaiken, 2007; Livingstone, Haslam, Postmes, & Jetten, 2011).

And with good reason: there are many connectedness benefits of conformity to group norms. Conforming to in-group norms makes people feel good, whereas finding out you disagree with a group you value, identify with, and feel connected to lowers self-esteem and well-being (Matz & Wood, 2005; Pool, Wood, & Leck, 1998; Sassenberg, Matschke, & Scholl, 2011). To demonstrate this effect, researchers had single participants work on a puzzle at the same time as a confederate did. Perhaps because the study seemed to be about individual problem solving, the participants did not help the confederate, even though the confederate obviously could not solve the puzzle. Experimenters then told the participants that they had either conformed to or violated an in-group norm by not offering help. Participants whose lack of help was labeled as conforming to the group norm reported feeling more positive emotions than students whose lack of help was labeled as violating group norms. And as we might expect if conformity confers connectedness, these effects were stronger for people who identified more closely with the group (Christensen, Rothgerber, Wood, & Matz, 2004). Those who do endorse group norms are admired by fellow group members and accorded more influence in the group (Levinger & Schneider, 1969; Oakes, Haslam, & Turner, 1998; Rubin, 2012). No wonder then that marginal members of a group—those whose connectedness is called into question or whose sense of belonging has been threatened by feelings of exclusion or ostracism—are more likely to conform when given the opportunity (DeWall, 2010; Heerdink, van Kleef, Homan, & Fischer, 2013; Tam, Lee, Kim, Li, & Chao, 2012).

So, just as disagreement undermines our confidence that we view reality correctly, being out of step with group norms undermines the secure social identity we derive from belonging to a group. And just as moving toward the group consensus helps reestablish the perceived accuracy of our views, conforming to group norms helps maintain and reconfirm our sense of identity.

Whose Consensus? Me and Mine Norms Are the Ones that Count

People expect to agree with those who share attributes relevant to the judgment at hand. In-groups often serve as reference groups, and people are much more influenced by in-group than out-group others. Other in-group members do not have to be present for conformity to occur, but having other group members present increases conformity even more. The more highly members identify with the group, the greater the reference group's impact.

normative influence
the process by which group norms are privately accepted to achieve or maintain connectedness and a valued social identity

Do you expect to agree with everyone about everything? Of course not. Rather, if you need support for a decision or evaluation, you turn to the people you believe are an appropriate source of information for the particular judgment (Abrams, Wetherell, Cochrane, Hogg, & Turner, 2001; J. C. Turner and others, 1987). These people are called a **reference group**.

reference group
those people accepted as an appropriate source of information for a judgment because they share the attributes relevant for making that judgment

The reference group you turn to depends on the kind of judgment or evaluation you are making. When physical judgments or statements of fact are required, most other people can serve as a reference group, because many people have the knowledge and skills to verify the solutions to such tasks. If the task involves, for example, visual judgments, as Sherif's and Asch's experimental tasks did, people expect to agree with any other people who have reasonably good eyesight. The expectation that most other people will agree on such tasks is very strong (S. A. Insko and others, 1983; Kaplan & Miller, 1987).

The appropriate reference groups for a value-laden or opinion-based judgment are somewhat different—they are groups who share similar values, attitudes, and relationships. In such cases, people usually expect to agree with others who share their pastimes, tastes, and values (Goethals & Nelson, 1973; Gorenflo & Crano, 1989). If others don't appear to have the qualifications for consensus on value-laden issues, their opinions hold no sway. For example, in multiple studies involving students in Australia, China, and the United States, researchers have shown that students whose opinions about issues were rooted in strong religious or moral grounds were not swayed by the opinions of average college students who did not share those values (Aramovich, Lytle, & Skitka, 2012; Skitka and others, 2013).

Because of all the things we share with them, our long-standing memberships in national, ethnic, religious, age, or political in-groups can provide ready-made reference groups, whether we are Flemish, Muslims, "Millennials," or Conservatives. Because they are like us and liked by us, we often use in-groups as reference groups, regardless of the judgments to be made. We expect to agree with members of the groups to which we belong and many of our most cherished and fiercely held convictions are descriptive and injunctive norms rooted in and shared by members of those groups (Boninger, Krosnick, & Berent, 1995; Christensen and others, 2004). In contrast, we do not expect to agree with out-group members: we don't have much in common with them, and don't care that we don't (Robbins & Krueger, 2005).

It is not surprising, then, that people are far more affected by social influence from in-group than from out-group members (Turner, 1982). Remember the finding that people laugh longer and harder if jokes are accompanied by canned laughter? Australian and British social psychologists have shown that this is only true if participants think that the laughter is coming from other in-group members. The participants seemed to be saying: "It's not

Photo 9.3 All for one and one for all. Here Marine recruits are learning physical skills and developing total devotion to group norms at the same time. Conforming to group norms will help the recruits master harsh environments and also provides a strong sense of belonging: The group has both informational and normative influence.

funny if they (rather than we) are laughing!" (Platow and others, 2005). Similarly, the finding that members of collectivist cultures show more conformity holds only if the sources of influence are other in-group members (P. B. Smith & Bond, 1993). Such acceptance of in-group norms and rejection of out-group norms isn't just public conformity. In one study, liberal and conservative students formed favorable attitudes toward a social policy if the political party they identified with expressed support for it, but failed to support it if a political out-group did so (Cohen, 2003). When asked about the issue, these students gave responses that showed that in-group endorsement had changed the very way they saw the issue and its moral implications.

Persuasive appeals from in-group members are also treated differently than those from out-group members. The in-group membership of the message source can act as a persuasion heuristic ("If my group thinks this, it must be right!"), especially if motivation or opportunity to process are in short supply (Mackie, Gastardo-Conaco, & Skelly, 1992; Verkuyten & Maliepaard, 2013). But because the information they provide is usually important to group memberships, persuasive appeals from in-group members are typically processed more systematically than appeals from out-group members, and the more important the group, the more processing the in-group message receives (Mackie, Worth, & Asuncion, 1990; Maitner, Mackie, Claypool, & Crisp, 2010). In contrast, messages from out-group members have little impact, regardless of argument quality (Esposo, Hornsey, & Spoor, 2013). The finding that in-group communications receive more systematic processing than out-group messages has been confirmed many times (Fleming, 2009).

The power of persuasive appeals from the in-group shows that you do not need to have other group members present to conform to group norms. Because the group is part of the individual—as a social identity that is part of the self—conformity can occur whenever group belonging becomes salient, even in one's head. But because the physical

Membership in even a minimal in-group can affect our thoughts and actions, as we saw in Chapter 6, especially pages 206–207.

Like other persuasion heuristics discussed in Chapter 7, pages 242–251, an in-group or out-group source is a cue that people can use to accept or reject a message without thinking systematically.

SOCIAL PSYCHOLOGY IN PRACTICE: REFERENCE GROUP EFFECTS IN FOOD PREFERENCE

We're used to thinking that what we eat—at least as adults—is just a matter of personal preference, dependent upon our own particular palate. But in fact, when it comes to food choice, descriptive norms determine consumption. In laboratory settings, female undergraduates say they dislike orange juice if they find out that others don't like it, but only if those others are in-group members (Robinson & Higgs, 2012). And it's not just liking: Experimental participants actually eat more or less popcorn or cookies if they believe that someone else has just eaten a lot or a little of the snack food—but again, only if that someone else was a student from their own, but not another, university (Cruwys and others, 2012). How closely fruit intake in another study mirrored the intake of other in-group members depended on how much the individuals identified with the group (Stok, de Ridder, de Vet, & de Wit, 2012). Such effects are not limited to the laboratory. The likes and dislikes of close others influence acceptance of novel foods in 2–5-year-olds, and in-group descriptive norms dictate the habitual food choices of adolescents (Addessi, Galloway, Visalberghi, & Birch, 2005; Lally, Bartle, & Wardle, 2011). In fact, longitudinal studies of public health information show that the consumption patterns—especially of alcohol and snacks—and weight of spouses and friends is likely to be closely matched (Christakis & Fowler, 2007; Pachucki, Jacques, & Christakis, 2011). We aren't just what we eat, but whom we eat it with.

presence of the group makes group membership both cognitively and physically salient, having other group members present can increase conformity to group norms even more (Crutchfield, 1955; Bond, 2005). The more highly members identify with the group, and the more closely and frequently the group interacts, the greater the reference group's impact (Livingstone, Haslam, Postmes, & Jetten, 2011).

Mastery, Connectedness, or Me and Mine?

Although particular circumstances can make one motive more important than another, agreeing with in-groups fulfills mastery, connectedness, and me and mine motives.

Particular circumstances can tip the balance in motives for conformity toward mastery or connectedness concerns (Kaplan & Wilke, 2001). Mastery concerns are particularly closely associated with descriptive norms, for example, and connectedness concerns are particularly associated with injunctive norms (Jacobson, Mortensen, & Cialdini, 2011). Whenever connectedness concerns are activated, it is the norms of "me and mine" in-groups that impact what people think, feel and do.

Most of the time, agreement with in-group others fulfills all three motives simultaneously. We adopt group norms of people like us not only because we think they reflect reality but also because we want to express our connectedness with groups we value (Kelman, 1961). Reaching consensus about the reality of our world is often the way we establish a connection with valued others. These multiple functions make conformity to norms centrally important to the success of social life. In fact, Nobel Prize-winner Herbert Simon (1990) argues that the tendency to adopt in-group norms is the product of evolution. Because norms convey knowledge about how to cope effectively with the social and physical world, and because norms connect people together, individuals who adopt group norms are probably at a survival advantage. That certainly seemed to be the case in one of the most compelling demonstrations of the power of in-group norms: one that came to light after a 1972 plane crash in the Andes mountains stranded the starving survivors of a soccer team among dead victims for 70 days. Despite their individual repugnance at the idea, the small group of crash survivors developed in-group injunctive and descriptive norms that governed their cannibalism of some of the victims. According to survivors' accounts, the development of and conformity to such norms were crucial to ensuring not only their physical but also their psychological survival (Henslin, 2003).

Although they may not be so dramatic, adherence to in-group norms on a day-to-day basis provides us with just the same motivational benefits. When other people like us share our views, their agreement fulfills our need for mastery of the world: It increases our confidence that we hold correct opinions, experience appropriate feelings, and do the right things. And because we depend on valued others to define and endorse the ideas, values, and expectations that are the basis for the smooth operation of the social system, their agreement also strengthens our feelings of connectedness with those whose opinions we respect. Conformity to in-group norms helps us achieve mastery, connectedness, and the positivity of groups connected to us simultaneously.

The formation and transmission of group norms are powerful examples of how we work together with others to socially construct a shared view of reality. As can be seen

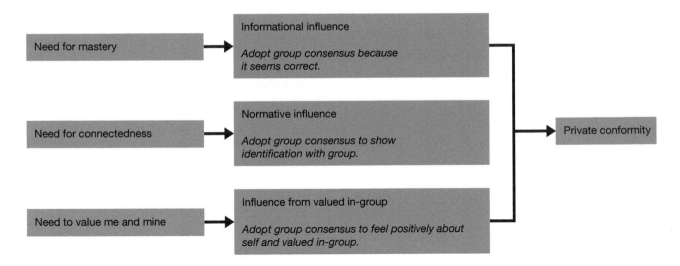

in Figure 9.4, motivational needs guide our reactions to informational and normative influence from our in-groups as we try to reach consensus on a multitude of judgments and decisions.

Figure 9.4 Motives behind private conformity
People adopt a group consensus as their own private belief because they wish to hold correct opinions and to show their identification with a group they value and respect. These two processes are termed *informational influence* and *normative influence*. Influence from valued in-groups is especially likely and powerful.

HOW GROUPS FORM NORMS: PROCESSES OF SOCIAL INFLUENCE

Every day in boardrooms, personnel offices, and employment agencies around the world, groups of people gather to make decisions about which of the many applicants for a position should be hired. Such decisions are obviously of importance not only to those wanting to be hired but also to those doing the hiring: good decisions increase productivity and the bottom line, whereas poor decisions waste the company's financial and human resources. Candidates are interviewed, applications are reviewed, and the evaluations of others sought. But the final decisions are often made socially, with members of a hiring committee or personnel team contributing some of their views and ideas to the group, while listening to what others think and seeing how they react. Gradually the group forms a consensus, agreeing on which candidates should be hired and which will be rejected. How does this happen, and how does the pursuit of mastery and connectedness influence the norms that are forged from this kind of give and take?

You might expect that a middle-of-the-road compromise would be the most likely outcome when people share their views. For example, just as Sherif's participants converged on a middling estimate of how far the light moved in the darkened room, people with extremely positive or negative evaluations of a particular job candidate might move toward more moderate views when faced with arguments that oppose their original evaluations. Surprisingly, though, this outcome is rare in group discussions. Such compromise usually happens only when a group's views are evenly split, with roughly half the members supporting an issue and half opposing it (Burnstein & Vinokur, 1977; Wetherell, 1987). More commonly, most groups lean one way or the other on an issue, and when that happens, the communication and consideration of individual input focuses and accentuates that view.

Group Polarization: Going to Normative Extremes

When a majority of group members initially favor one side of the issue, communication and interaction usually move the group to an even more extreme position.

Most of the time, a majority of group members initially favor a particular point of view. Why do groups initially lean in one direction or another? Recall from Chapter 7 that people tend to associate with others who share their views, and that groups often form because of shared interests and shared views. Individual members of the local Greenpeace organization probably joined because they favor conservation and thus share similar opinions on the endangered spotted owl. Similarly, members of a neighborhood watch committee can be expected to share views about local law enforcement. Even representative or appointed groups typically have a majority opinion. In these cases, the majority views might reflect the weight of the evidence. An applicant with good academic preparation, relevant work experience, and impeccable references from reliable sources will appeal to the majority of hiring committee members, for example. If the evidence leans in one direction, a majority of jurors might initially favor one verdict over another. In fact, one large-scale study of jury proceedings found that a majority initially favored acquittal or conviction in all but 10 of 225 trials studied (Kalven & Zeisel, 1966). As a rule, then, most groups will lean one way or the other before discussion even begins.

How do group norms develop when most members of a group initially share an opinion? If you participated in or studied hiring discussions long enough, you would begin to notice a reliable pattern. Imagine that a candidate with some potential is being discussed. Someone points out her solid but not startling academic credentials. Another notes that while her first position was with a mediocre organization, she is currently employed by a well-regarded firm that has a reputation for excellent employee development. A third mentions that the candidate is on his "accept" list, at which point a fourth chimes in with "Uh huh, I gave her a high rating, too." One of her stronger letters of reference is reread, her solid performance at the interview recalled, and the group agrees enthusiastically to hire her: She is excellent. Seen at first as merely having potential, the candidate is now a superior applicant. And, of course, movement in the opposite direction can also happen. When the majority of committee members lean toward rejection, talking about credentials and interview performance and lack of experience seems only to doom the applicant further. In the context of group discussion, the good gets better and the bad gets worse.

The first to study this unexpected effect of group discussion was a young graduate student named James Stoner (1961). Stoner asked business school students to respond to a series of fictitious "choice dilemmas," in which they had to decide between a cautious course of action with a small potential benefit (staying in a secure job with moderate yearly raises) and a risky option with a large payoff (moving to a start-up company with the potential of boom—or bust). Stoner found that when people work together in groups on this kind of problem, they opt for more risky actions than when they make decisions alone.

It soon became clear that this effect had nothing to do with risk itself—regardless of what is being discussed, what matters is what most people in the group prefer to begin with. If most people initially prefer risk, group discussions produce more risk. If most people favor caution, group discussion produces a more cautious outcome. If most members of a group initially are racially prejudiced, group interaction and discussion tends to increase their prejudice. If most members initially are not prejudiced, then group discussion shifts them further in the direction of egalitarian views (Myers & Bishop, 1971).

Such **group polarization** occurs when the group's initial average position becomes more extreme following face-to-face group interaction (Moscovici & Zavalloni, 1969). This extremitization of initial views following group discussion has been found multiple times in many different countries and cultures and in field studies as well as laboratory experiments (DiFonzo and others, 2013; Paluck, 2010; Wojcieszak, 2011). For example, group polarization in jury deliberations has been found to influence judgments of guilt and innocence both in laboratories and when real jurors decide real cases (Devine, 2012; Kalven & Zeisel, 1966; Myers & Kaplan, 1976).

group polarization
the process by which a group's initial average position becomes more extreme following group interaction

Explaining Polarized Norm Formation

When people process superficially, merely relying on others' positions can produce polarization of group norms as undecided or moderate group members move toward the group position and try to show that they are good group members. When people process systematically, both others' positions and arguments work together to polarize group norms. Majority arguments are more numerous, receive more discussion, seem more compelling, and are presented more persuasively. All these factors give majority views a persuasive advantage.

What explains the formation of polarized group norms? The answer has to do with how information is processed and what motives people have in mind as they process. Remember from Chapters 7 and 8 that in forming or changing attitudes, people sometimes process available information quite superficially but on other occasions process it quite extensively. Both superficial and systematic processing also characterize our reactions to information about others' opinions during norm formation and change. Sometimes we notice where others stand and go along with the majority without worrying about their reasons. If, for example, you and some friends are choosing a restaurant and you do not particularly care what you eat, you may pay no attention to claims about the quality of the food and service and simply throw your support behind the majority. But if you are in a situation in which your decision will matter a great deal (for example, as a member of a personnel committee or a jury), you probably will consider more than just the other members' positions. You will also want to understand their reasons, evidence, and arguments. In this case, the persuasive effects of the majority of others' opinions can be even stronger. Regardless of whether superficial or systematic processing occurs, more extreme group norms are the likely result. Let's see why.

Superficial Processing: Relying on Others' Positions. People often know the group's position, but not why they came to such a position (Baron & Roper, 1976). Many overt and subtle cues can signal or communicate what the group thinks. First, group interactions often open with some exchange of views, during which the group members' positions are directly voiced. Second, people can guess the group norm from who the members of the group are. For example, knowing that the group consists of science majors or retirees can make us assume that the group will all think alike and tend to agree on a group-relevant issue (Postmes, Spears, Lee, & Novak, 2005). Finally, people can reveal their preferences by the kinds of questions they ask or by their body language (Willard, Madon, Guyll, Scherr, & Buller, 2012).

In cases like these, people can use the group position alone as a guide to what their own position should be. That is, consensus is used as a heuristic: It provides a short cut to the position that people believe to be both correct and appropriate, without their having to do a lot of hard work figuring out the right answer. In fact, hearing what people think before a discussion begins makes group members less likely to pay attention to the information later exchanged (Mojzisch & Schulz-Hardt, 2010). The fact that people tend to conform more when they are happy rather than sad is also consistent with the idea that reliance on consensus provides a quick and easy guide to appropriate decisions—happy people often avoid systematic thinking (Tong, Tan, Latheef, Selamat, & Tan, 2008).

How might a superficial reliance on consensus as a heuristic lead to extreme positions? First, when undecided or dissenting members of a group adopt the majority consensus, the group's average position moves toward the extreme. Imagine that there are pros and cons about a particular restaurant, but on the whole it has become very popular. Wanting to choose the best restaurant for an important guest, imagine that you rely on the consensus and patronize the restaurant yourself. In doing so, of course, you have added to its popularity by endorsing the consensus, even though a careful review of the eatery's attributes might have resulted in a less extreme evaluation. So superficial acceptance of group descriptive norms—even when motivated by mastery concerns—can move the group toward the extreme (Bohner, Dykema-Engblade, Tindale, & Meisenhelder, 2008).

Second, heuristic reliance on others' views can lead to extreme positions because people often want to be the best possible members of their group (Codol, 1975). Most members of cohesive groups think of themselves not as average but as superior representatives of their groups. Thus, for example, most business executives think of themselves as more ethical than the average executive, and most editors think their grasp of grammar is better than that of their average colleague (Allison, Messick, & Goethals, 1989; Guenther & Alicke, 2010). However, others' views may not support the opinions we hold of ourselves. Sometimes hearing what others think reveals that we are not as far above average as we thought we were. This social comparison may in turn prompt a speedy adoption of a more extreme position so that we can again become above average on important dimensions within the group (Pool, Wood, & Leck, 1998). As more and more group members adopt this strategy, the group norm grows more extreme.

Even when others' positions are all we know, our desire for mastery and our wish to be valued by important others encourage us to move toward, or even beyond, the majority's view. Group members who hold the minority position shift to adopt the majority consensus. Members of the majority may move even farther toward the extreme. Together, these two processes make group polarization a likely outcome of norm formation as the average position in the group grows more extreme.

Recall from Chapter 4, page 108, that we all tend to believe that we are above average on almost every positive dimension, so it's a surprise if we find out we are not.

Systematic Processing: Attending to Both Positions and Arguments. When the evaluations that a group makes are important or affect the group directly, group members shift their processing into high gear. They consider not just the preferences of others but in addition their supporting arguments and evidence. You might think that such careful processing would never produce the exaggerated or extreme norms that occur in group polarization. In fact, however, systematic processing makes group polarization even more likely.

In the lively interchange that characterizes most group discussions, preferences and the arguments for those preferences are aired simultaneously. Imagine, for example, that you are a jury member listening to another juror argue, "Well, if the defendant was at work, as his foreman testified, he could not possibly have arrived home before 6:30, and the doctors said that the victim was already dead by then." Although this statement reviews relevant evidence, it also reveals the juror's opinion. If, instead of laying out her position, the juror had merely voiced her opinion that the defendant was innocent, you might still have been able to figure out the unstated arguments supporting that view. When a jury or another group is deeply engaged in resolving a dilemma, both what other group members believe and why they believe it become important considerations. The resulting attention given to both arguments and positions gives even more of a persuasive edge to the position initially favored by the majority of other group members, which moves the norm towards polarization. Several forces join together to make this happen.

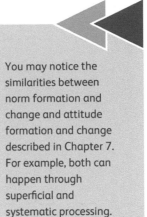

You may notice the similarities between norm formation and change and attitude formation and change described in Chapter 7. For example, both can happen through superficial and systematic processing.

1. *Majority arguments are more numerous.* The greater the number of people who hold a particular viewpoint, the more numerous the arguments favoring that position are likely to be. So there are not only more people sharing a viewpoint, but more people expressing evidence in support of it. Thus initial preferences bias the kinds of arguments discussed and this preponderance of evidence in turn makes the group's view more extreme (Burnstein & Vinokur, 1977; Kaplan & Miller, 1987). Especially when group members hear novel and compelling persuasive arguments that they had not previously considered, they move toward the majority position and the group norm becomes more extreme (Hinsz & Davis, 1984).

2. *Majority arguments are discussed more.* When people think that others share their views, they are more likely to express them (Glynn, Hayes, & Shanahan, 1997). Information and evidence endorsed by more than one group member is more likely to be raised and discussed than ideas endorsed by only a single person. In a compelling demonstration of this, Garold Stasser and his colleagues (Stasser, Taylor, & Hanna, 1989) asked students to read different sets of information about candidates for president of a student body. Some information was given to all members of the group, but other information was given to just one person (because all the relevant information is not immediately available to everyone in the group, this is sometimes called a "hidden profile"). When the group met to evaluate the candidates, they discussed 46% of the shared information but only 18% of the unshared information. Not only was the unshared information less likely to be raised with the group, but even when it was, it was less likely to be discussed and evaluated. This bias toward what everyone already knows has been replicated in dozens of studies (Lu, Yuan, & McLeod 2012; Miller & Morrison, 2009; Mojzisch, Grouneva,

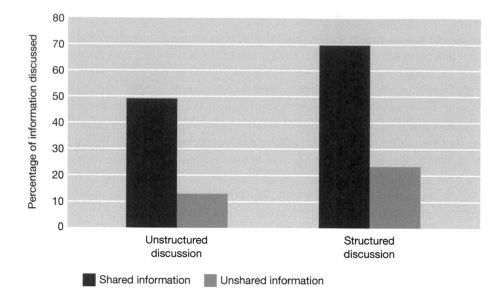

Figure 9.5 Let's talk about something we all know
Students asked to evaluate candidates were much more likely to discuss information that everyone in the group shared than they were to discuss information known to only one member of the group. When rules were instituted to structure the discussion, the shared information was even *more* likely to be discussed. (Data from Stasser and others, 1989.)

& Schulz-Hardt, 2010). It occurs even when researchers institute rules that encourage the group to discuss all the facts available to them. In fact, such instructions result in an even more intense focus on the shared information (see Figure 9.5). Group members apparently believe that the information on which they all agree is the information most relevant to the issue under discussion. The bias toward discussing shared rather than individually held information is bound to strengthen the majority's case—after all, by definition, majority arguments are shared viewpoints, whereas minority arguments are likely to be unique, dissenting views. Such biased discussions confirm the majority position and convince some minority members, making the group norm more extreme.

3. ***Majority arguments seem more compelling.*** When several people make the same argument, it has extra impact. First, any argument we hear over and over again gains a persuasive advantage through familiarity, and we also assume that familiar, oft-repeated arguments are endorsed by many more people (Weaver, Garcia, Schwarz, & Miller, 2007). Second, three different people voicing an identical argument is more persuasive than a single person who repeats the same argument three times (Harkins & Petty, 1983). The fact that different people with different perspectives reach the same conclusion makes that conclusion seem particularly compelling: one person's information gets "confirmed" by another group member who also has that information (Stewart & Stasser, 1995). In fact, any group member whose information is widely shared (and can thus be confirmed again and again by other group members) exerts considerable influence in the group (Kameda, Ohtsubo, & Takezawa, 1997; Stasser, Abele, & Parsons, 2012). Consistent with this bias is the finding that people rate as more persuasive, and respond more favorably to,

those arguments with which "most people" or "a majority" agree: If most people buy the argument, it must be a good one (Erb & Bohner, 2001). In fact, people expect strong arguments from a majority and weak ones from a minority (Tormala & DeSensi, 2009). Thus, the arguments put forward by a majority in a group discussion seem particularly persuasive, and their influence moves the group further toward the extreme.

4. *Majority arguments are presented more compellingly.* Majority arguments are presented in ways that make them particularly persuasive. First, perhaps in an attempt to find common ground, most people turn first in discussions to information that they believe to be shared and familiar (Fast, Heath, & Wu, 2009; Larson and others, 1996). This gives majority arguments a persuasive head start. After all, information that is considered at the beginning of a discussion has more impact than information presented later on, and if a discussion is cut short, unshared or minority information may not be heard at all. Second, majority views are expressed faster, whereas those with minority views often hesitate—if only for a second—before expressing them (Bassili, 2003). This difference in speed of expression grows as the difference between the size of the majority and the size of the minority grows, so that minority views are most slowly expressed when the majority is very large. Third, people surrounded by others who feel the same way they do are most likely to be confident about their views (Huckfeldt & Sprague, 2000) and this seems to show in how they express them. Group members, especially males, use a less cautious and more argumentative style of advocacy when they are members of the majority than when they are in the minority (N. L. Kerr, MacCoun, Hansen, & Hymes, 1987). On the other hand, hesitating before expressing a view might make minority adherents seem uncertain or lacking in commitment to their views.

> The greater impact of information presented early in a discussion reflects primacy effects (Chapter 3, page 85). Arguments presented first capture more attention and can subtly change the meaning or importance of later information.

Thus, when group members engage in systematic processing, the existence of consensus means that they are likely to hear and discuss more arguments, and more confidently presented arguments, in favor of the majority view. The result once again is that majority arguments are more persuasive, and this persuasive advantage in turn strengthens the consensus. As members of the minority are won over to the majority view, the group consensus becomes more extreme, and polarization is the consequence. The process is summarized in Figure 9.6.

UNDERMINING TRUE CONSENSUS

Because people place such a high value on group consensus, there are powerful forces that underpin conformity to group norms. As we have seen, relying on one another when we make judgments and decisions—when we do so in a way that avoids personal bias, provides reassuring replication, and considers all information thoroughly—can give us a handle on reality and connect us firmly to our groups. But groups sometimes short-circuit such processes, coercing their members and ignoring dissenting voices no matter how worthy these opinions might be. When that happens, group consensus can lead to invalid and unreliable decisions, even when individual members have the knowledge and skills to come up with the right ones.

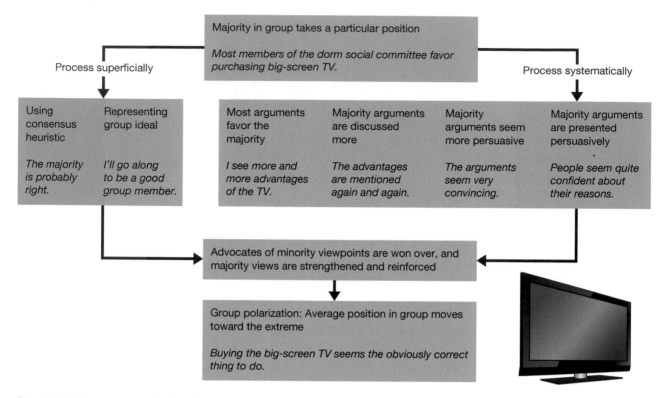

Figure 9.6 Why a consensus is influential: Processes underlying group polarization

When a majority in a group initially lean in a particular direction, their consensus tends to influence others in a variety of ways—whether the group members process superficially or think about the issues in more depth. As the majority position attracts converts from the other side and majority members find their beliefs further strengthened and reinforced, the group's average position moves in the direction initially favored by the majority. Group polarization has occurred.

When Consensus Seeking Goes Awry

Consensus implies that opinions are valid, but this inference is true only when consensus is achieved in the right way. A consensus cannot be trusted if it arises from unthinking reliance on others' positions, contamination by shared biases, or public conformity. Such a consensus offers only the illusion of mastery and connectedness and can lead to situations of pluralistic ignorance, where everyone is publicly conforming to a norm that nobody privately endorses.

A decision is not necessarily valid merely because it is based on a consensus. Plenty of decisions reached through group agreement turn out to be seriously flawed. How does this happen, if two heads are supposedly better than one?

Consensus Without Consideration: Unthinking Reliance on Consensus. If we merely rely on the presence of consensus, we can be influenced by an unreliable or even a manipulated consensus. If you've ever had someone flirt with you in a bar and hand you their state-of-the-art phone to take down their number, it may have been an example of stealth marketing. Such marketing tactics create an apparent consensus or descriptive norm—everyone's using this; the coolest people all have this—for a product or a service, knowing full well that conformity to those apparent norms will positively impact a company's bottom line. Marketers do so by making and posting messages and videos to social networking sites as if they were actual users, sending samples of products to thousands of "alpha users" recruited and paid to talk the product up to friends, and paying people to post fake reviews and "likes" of products and services on the internet. Similar tactics are used in politics—reports of biased polls (where only true supporters were sampled) or thousands of letters to representatives generated by hired services can exercise considerable political influence. In these cases, unthinking adoption of the consensus can lead us astray.

Photo 9.4 Consensus without consideration. Have you ever wondered how an entire audience often manages to express its approval by applauding simultaneously, just at the right moment? The power of the consensus heuristic is clearly illustrated by this fact, as individuals in the audience rely on and conform to the apparent endorsement by the surrounding audience members, and may quite unthinkingly clap along in unison. Applause may even be orchestrated by people planted in the audience by performers or management.

Consider what happened when researchers had students listen to arguments that were presented in a speech supporting probation as an alternative to imprisonment (Axsom, Yates, & Chaiken, 1987). During the presentation, one group of students heard several bouts of loud clapping and cheers from the audience listening to the speech; another group of students heard only scattered applause and occasional jeering. When asked what they thought, the students who heard cheering—a supportive consensus – agreed with the probation policy, whereas the students who heard jeering—consensus leaning against the proposal—opposed it. What was the problem with relying on the responses of others? In addition to manipulating consensus, the researchers had also included weak arguments in some speeches and strong arguments in others. So students relying only on consensus sometimes ended up making poor judgments—supporting an apparently popular proposal for which there was really very little evidence, or ignoring an apparently forgettable proposal for which strong arguments existed. Just like stealth marketers, the researchers in this experiment made the proposal (regardless of its actual quality) look good or bad by manufacturing a false consensus. Compared to students motivated to carefully consider evidence for the policies, the students who followed the apparent descriptive norm without carefully considering the relevant information themselves not only ended up on the wrong side of the issue, but also further strengthened the false consensus by adding their support to it. Part of the strength of a consensus is that if different people come to the same conclusion after reviewing the available evidence, the conclusion is likely to be valid (Festinger, 1950; Kelley, 1967). But if people skip careful consideration of the evidence, then the consensus they contribute to is not trustworthy.

You may recall that this experiment was cited in Chapter 1, pages 1–2, as an interesting example of pervasive social influence.

Consensus Without Independence: Contamination. The idea that a consensus provides reality insurance rests on an assumption: We think we can trust the consensus because multiple individuals considered the evidence independently and from diverse perspectives, and came to the same conclusion. One person might be influenced by a particular bias and thus see things incorrectly, make the wrong decision, or come to a false conclusion. But it seems unlikely that many people with many different perspectives will all make the same mistake (Allen, 1965, 1975; Asch, 1951; Vala, Drozda-Senkowska, Oberlé, Lopes, & Silva, 2011).

Given the importance of this assumption, it's not surprising that people understand that shared biases might contaminate group decisions. For example, a consensus reached by a very diverse group is more compelling and persuasive than a consensus reached by a very homogeneous group (Lopes, Vala, & Garcia-Marques, 2007). Any hint that the people reaching the consensus might have influenced and thus contaminated one another's views also reduces the power of consensus. For example, people are less persuaded by the views of others if the same number of others are described as a committee rather than not being given a group label, as "one group" rather than "two subgroups", or as two groups rather than separate individuals (Harkins & Petty, 1987; Hofmann & Windschitl, 2008; Wilder, 1977). Why? Perhaps whenever the people forming a consensus are lumped together in some way, perceivers suspect contamination, thinking that the group members might have shared a bias or influenced each other. Consistent with this interpretation, the consensus presented by a "committee" was persuasive only when it was made clear that the committee members represented diverse perspectives—that their individual views had not been contaminated by undue influence or a shared bias (Harkins & Petty, 1987).

You may sense a contradiction here. On the one hand, we trust a consensus when independent and separate individuals endorse it; the convergence of their differing perspectives on the same position confirms the validity of that position. On the other hand, as you may recall from the discussion earlier in this chapter, we really expect to agree only with those who share our characteristics. If we disagree with people who are different from us, it is easy to write them off as confused, ignorant, or just plain wrong. We seem simultaneously to demand that group members be different and independent (so their consensus indicates validity) and similar and in accord (so that they are an appropriate reference group).

In fact, simultaneous similarity and difference is just what we need. We need others to be similar to us in terms of the features relevant to making the judgment so that agreement with them will tell us about reality. But we need them to be different from us in many other possible ways so that it is unlikely that any other shared feature could bias everyone's judgment. Remember that people usually see members of their own group as similar on characteristics that define the group but as variable and different in other ways, whereas out-groups "all look alike." This simultaneous similarity and difference is part of what makes an in-group consensus so much more persuasive than an out-group consensus.

David Wilder (1990) devised a clever demonstration of this effect by getting participants to listen to in-group or out-group members presenting their views on an issue while a photo of the speaker's face was presented. Later the arguments were repeated and participants were asked to match each speaker's picture with his or her arguments. Participants also indicated how much they agreed with the views expressed by the group. The results showed that participants could accurately match in-group members' faces

To refresh your memory about the reasons people see in-groups as more diverse than out-groups, review Chapter 6, pages 200 and 201.

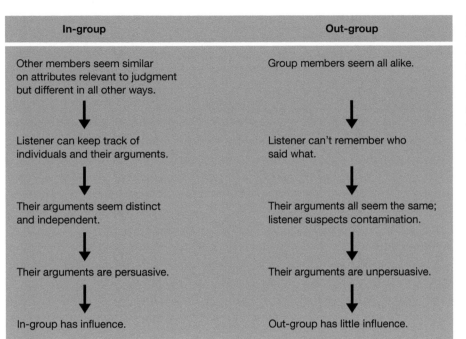

Figure 9.7 How in-groups become more persuasive than out-groups
In-groups offer simultaneous similarity and difference. They are viewed as similar on attributes that are crucial for the judgment but as diverse in other ways. As a result, in-groups are more persuasive than out-groups.

to their arguments: They seemed able to keep track of each in-group member as a distinct and separate individual making distinct and separate arguments. In contrast, students could not match the out-group members with their arguments: they knew that an argument came from an out-group member, but not which one. These different perceptions of in-group and out-group members translated into very different amounts of influence. Since participants saw in-group members as distinct individuals putting forward independent arguments and coming to the same conclusion, they were persuaded by the replicated and validated in-group consensus. In contrast, seeing the out-group as faceless figures droning the party line over and over again made it easy to ignore them. As summarized in Figure 9.7, thinking of the in-group as simultaneously similar and diverse makes their individual views seem independent and in turn renders their shared consensus persuasive. In contrast, the sameness of the out-group heightens the perception that their views might be contaminated, and it decreases their ability to exert influence.

Consensus Without Acceptance: Public Conformity. The most dangerous threat to the ideal of consensus formation is public conformity, which we earlier defined as people publicly supporting or endorsing norms that they do not privately accept as correct. When some of Asch's participants went along with norms that they did not believe were correct, they were demonstrating public conformity. Motivated by the desire to avoid wrath or ridicule, these students followed the motto, "go along to get along" (Deutsch & Gerard, 1955; H. H. Kelley, 1952), and their public conformity destroyed the reliability of the consensus.

Public conformity reflects people's recognition that groups can both reward and punish their members. People who disagree with other group members often anticipate negative reactions (Gerard & Rabbie, 1961), and their fears are well founded. In a classic study, Stanley Schachter (1951) arranged for a confederate to persistently disagree with other group members. At first, the group tried hard to win over the deviant. When this failed, the group ignored his views, assigned him to undesirable tasks, and suggested that he be excluded from the group. Those who don't agree with popular positions are often criticized and disparaged, especially if their failure to adhere to the group norm makes those who do agree feel bad about themselves (Minson & Monin, 2012). Even jurors experience this pressure to publicly conform. In a 2009 New York trial against pharmaceutical giant Merck over its osteoporosis drug Fosamax, one juror sent the judge a plea for help: "I am being intimidated, threatened, screamed at, as well as verbally insulted that I am stupid because I do not agree. I have had 2 physical threats against me, a chair thrown and a verbal threat to beat me up. I need a police escort out of here . . ." (Renaud, 2010).

Such heavy-handed tactics often work. Group members who are bullied or threatened with exclusion from the group often change their behavior and comply to regain the group's favor (Carter-Sowell, Chen, & Williams, 2008). Group members whose deviant views trigger anger from others are more likely to publicly conform unless they have an alternative group to move to (Heerdink and others, 2013). Unfortunately, because public conformity brought about by fear, exhaustion, or the desire to please cannot easily be distinguished from real acceptance, it can still influence others. People follow a group norm that doesn't really reflect reality.

pluralistic ignorance

occurs when everyone publicly conforms to an apparent norm that no one in fact privately accepts

When everyone publicly adheres to a descriptive or injunctive norm that no one privately endorses, **pluralistic ignorance** exists. Such a situation can arise in many areas of daily life, even in the classroom. Have you ever been afraid to ask a question because the silence of your classmates led you to believe that everyone but you understood the

SOCIAL PSYCHOLOGY IN PRACTICE: PLURALISTIC IGNORANCE AND HEALTH RISK BEHAVIOR

Pluralistic ignorance may contribute to such significant social and health problems as alcohol abuse, risky sexual behavior, illegal drug use, and smoking. Many studies supporting this idea have shown, for example, that many students drink more excessively than they personally feel comfortable doing. Why? Pluralistic ignorance seems partly to blame. Most students report believing that everyone else is more comfortable with heavy drinking (the (mis)perceived norm) than everyone else actually is (the actual descriptive norm; Prentice & Miller, 1993). Heavy drinkers are particularly likely to show this effect. In studies of New Zealand 16–29-year-olds, for example, the majority of both men and women overestimated the incidence of binge drinking among their peers (Kypri and others, 2009). Anti-alcohol campaigns that focus on extreme cases of alcohol abuse, and social networking posts that feature excessive drinking have unwittingly made the situation worse, again making everyone think that everyone else is drinking more than they are (Fournier, Hall, Ricke, & Storey, 2013; Haines & Spear, 1996). The upshot is that everyone might be drinking more than they actually want to because they think that others approve of excessive drinking! Other studies have shown similar conformity to misperceived group norms about substance abuse (Henry, Kobus, & Schoeny, 2011), "hooking up"—agreeing to engage in sexual behavior with no future commitment—and other risky sexual behaviors (Reiber & Garcia, 2010). Although there is some disagreement about the extent to which group norms are over-estimated, it is clear that there is considerable conformity to whatever people believe the norms to be (Pape, 2012).

teacher? Many of the other students undoubtedly were feeling exactly the same way but made the same false assumption you did (Miller & McFarland, 1987).

So consensus itself is not enough—conformity to a consensus fulfills mastery and connectedness needs only when that consensus reflects careful consideration, is free from contamination, and is privately accepted rather than reflecting mere public conformity. When decisions are made based on unthinking reliance on what others do, or when what looks like a consensus is actually the result of people having mutually influenced each other, especially in ways that result in outward shows of yielding rather than inner acceptance of the relevant evidence, being influenced by others can decrease rather than increase the quality of our judgments.

Consensus Seeking at Its Worst: Groupthink

Groupthink occurs when groups become more concerned with reaching consensus than with reaching consensus in a way that ensures its validity. Groupthink can be avoided by safeguarding consideration of alternatives, independence of views, and private acceptance.

Sometimes, the desire to reach a consensus becomes more important than the desire to reach a consensus the right way. When this is the case, norm formation goes terribly wrong—norms are created without careful consideration of the evidence, the convergence of different perspectives on a shared point of view is dispensed with, and false norms are created as group members publicly agree with the norm despite their private doubts. Under these circumstances, achieving group consensus hinders rather than helps good decision-making.

Over forty years ago, Irving Janis (1972, 1982) coined the term **groupthink** for situations in which the desire to reach consensus interferes with effective decision-making. Groupthink can influence "high command" decisions to pursue ill-advised military offensives, corporate decisions to market products despite concerns about their side effects or safety, organizational decisions that risk the entity's financial soundness, and institutional decisions to block public exposure of revered figures suspected of sexual abuse. Social psychologists have studied these and other group decisions to try and understand the antecedents of groupthink, since its consequences are almost always a poor decision which, when acted upon, can lead to disaster. These studies suggest that such ill-fated decision-making situations start out as ordinary situations in which groups try to seek consensus, and end up being special instances of consensus being reached in the wrong way (Tindale, Smith, Dykema-Engblade, & Kluwe, 2012). This typically occurs when groups feel overwhelming pressure for agreement to maintain a positive view of the group in the face of threat (Baron, 2005; Janis, 2007; Turner, Pratkanis, & Struckman, 2007).

Under such circumstances, for example, groups short-circuit the careful consideration of available evidence. Compared to people working alone, people making decisions together are more likely to ignore or under-weight external points of view (Minson & Mueller, 2012). If groups overestimate their abilities and effectiveness, premature confidence reduces both the healthy debate of alternatives within the group and seeking input from outside (De Dreu & Beersma, 2010; Goncalo, Polman, & Maslach, 2010).

groupthink
group decision making that is impaired by the drive to reach consensus regardless of how the consensus is formed

Doubting members engage in self-censorship, voluntarily suppressing their concerns and criticisms, whereas confident members might shield other members from unwelcome information that might destroy confidence in the consensus. Lack of independence among members' views makes this situation worse. Groups whose members are very similar and who are very focused on "who we are and what we stand for"—as groups under threat often are—are particularly likely to fall prey to groupthink because they also share many biases (Alderfer, 2011; Mok & Morris, 2010). When the stakes are high and groups anxiously stick together in the face of threat, pressures toward public conformity can be intense (Chapman, 2006). Dissenters might be brought into line or "cut out of the loop." Failure to consider information, contamination of views, and public conformity are all more likely if powerful and respected members of the group state their opinions before discussion takes place (Magee, Gruenfeld, Keltner, & Galinsky, 2005; Peterson, 1997). If a majority of the group falls into line, of course, any dissenter is then faced with a situation very much like that of Asch's participants in the line-matching task, under pressure to go along in public without being privately convinced.

As shown in Figure 9.8, groupthink processes produce an illusion of unanimity, rather than a true consensus. Everyone thinks that everyone else accepts the group position, so pluralistic ignorance also reigns. The apparent consensus in turn validates the group's judgment: "All reasonable people" would have reached the same conclusion. In fact, the process producing consensus has gone horribly awry. Relevant information has not been processed, shared biases have produced contamination, and a group decision that should be based in fact actually reflects fantasy.

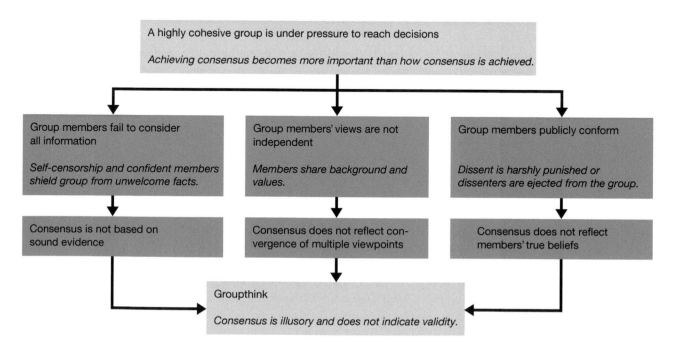

Figure 9.8 Groupthink undermines the validity of consensus
For consensus to be valid, it has to be attained in the right way. Groupthink produces a biased and inaccurate consensus that is not based on consideration of alternatives, independence of views, or private acceptance.

Remedies for Faulty Consensus Seeking. How can the dangers of achieving consensus in the wrong way be combated? If groupthink is just a special case of faulty consensus seeking, the solution lies in making sure that consensus is reached the right way. To avoid consensus without consideration, groups need to engage in open inquiry, carefully processing available evidence and alternatives, and to encourage dissenting perspectives and points of view. To ensure that consensus is not contaminated by shared biases, group membership can be intentionally selected for diversity. Members with different backgrounds and experience are likely to see problems in different ways and advocate different solutions which can then be considered. And to reduce pressures toward public conformity that contribute to apparent consensus, public votes should be the exception rather than the rule. The role of the leader should be minimized in favor of equally valued contributions from all members, and the voicing of doubts and objections—which should make everyone consider the pros and cons of alternatives more deeply—should be encouraged. What do all these recommendations have in common? The key is to ensure that all views, and not just the majority view, are thoroughly considered when groups form a consensus. The best way to achieve this goal is to ensure that minority views are given their due. Although appointing a "devil's advocate" to point out flaws in majority positions can help (Waddell, Roberto, & Yoon, 2013), including true proponents of other views in groups, especially if it's clear that they represent the minority, ensures authentic dissent —a situation in which real alternative positions are advanced by their true adherents, pushing for their careful consideration (Nemeth, Connell, Rogers, & Brown, 2001; Smith, 2008). Although they might not be a "magic bullet" for all the problems that can occur when groups try to reach consensus, inclusion and consideration of minority points of view are crucial to achieving valid judgments and good decisions in groups. Let's see how.

MINORITY INFLUENCE: THE VALUE OF DISSENT

Consider the fact that the tenets of Christianity, now accepted by thousands of millions around the world, were once the scandalous heresy of a small group of dissenters from the Jewish tradition. Similarly, the now widely (although not universally) accepted norm that women should have the right to vote and own property was once championed by only a few hardy women and even fewer men. Despite the strength of majorities, minority opinions sometimes ultimately win the day. Under the right conditions, exposure to minority dissent plays a crucial role in ensuring the mastery and connectedness functions of social norms.

Successful Minority Influence

Minority views can sway the majority. To be influential, the minority must offer an alternative consensus, remain consistent, strike the right balance between similarity to and difference from the majority, and promote systematic processing.

When minorities find themselves disadvantaged, they may try to change the minds of the majority or they might engage in a strategy of social change—confronting or challenging the minority-majority hierarchy as described in Chapter 6, pages 222–223.

Minority viewpoints can alter the consensus reached in a group. But to achieve their victories and convince the majority to reconsider, minorities must turn the processes of social influence to their own advantage.

Offering an Alternative Consensus. Just as a majority's power lies in its command of consensus, the main source of a minority's power is its potential to undermine the majority's consensus and to promote an alternative view. Because group members expect to agree, a minority can exert influence by undermining confidence in the correctness of the majority consensus or majority norm (Asch, 1956; Moscovici, 1980). Sometimes the exceptional credentials or charisma of a single person like Galileo or Martin Luther King may be able to sway others to the cause. But most of the time a lone dissenter has little impact on the group. To make the majority sit up and take notice, the alternative view must be a consensus in its own right. That is, it must be supported by more than one person. It must also be presented in such a way that the majority takes it seriously.

First, minorities are most influential when they agree among themselves. Just as Asch found that influence began when majorities of two or three formed, so researchers have shown that minority factions of two or three are more influential than a lone dissenter in allowing the minority position to be heard (Gardikiotis, Martin, & Hewstone, 2004; Levine & Prislin, 2013). Asch found, for example, that as soon as real participants—who wanted to espouse a minority position compared to the majority of confederates—were joined by just a single other dissenter from the majority position, they were able to maintain their own position. Increasing numbers espousing the minority position (especially if they defect from the majority) engender more minority influence. The agreement of multiple group members on a single position apparently signals that the position is a viable alternative to the majority position (Gardikiotis, 2011; Moscovici & Lage, 1976; Nemeth, Wachtler, & Endicott, 1977).

Second, minorities are most influential when they are consistent. Because majorities are hardly ever swayed immediately, a minority must remain loyal to its consensus over time (Moscovici, 1980; Nemeth & Wachtler, 1983). Many researchers have demonstrated that behavioral consistency is essential in giving a minority clout across a wide range of judgments and topics (Wood and others, 1994). The first to do so were Serge Moscovici and his colleagues (Moscovici, Lage, & Naffrechoux, 1969), who devised a mirror image of Asch's line-matching task. They asked groups of six (four participants and two confederates) to judge the color of a series of unambiguously blue slides. When the confederates insisted on all 36 trials that the slides were green, a small but significant number of participants joined them in this error. However, when the minority wavered, calling the slides green on only 24 of the 36 trials, they had no influence on the majority. Consistency is important because it conveys commitment to the viability of an alternative position. Proponents of a minority view walk a fine line, however. Taken too far, consistency may be interpreted as rigidity or intractability, which leads to a rapid decline of the minority's influence (Mugny, 1975; Mugny & Papastamous, 1980).

When a minority successfully challenges the majority view, the effect can extend beyond the single immediate issue, pushing majority group members to be more open-minded in the future. In fact, seeing a minority express opposition in one situation might even give majority members the courage of their convictions in other situations. One study looked at the effects of hearing a minority point of view on people's later ability to resist conformity pressure (Nemeth & Chiles, 1988). Students made color perception judgments in the presence of a confederate who made dissenting judgments—calling a blue slide green—all the time, some of the time, or not at all. They later participated in a study like the Asch line-matching task, in which the majority agreed on an obviously incorrect response. Up against this unanimous majority, students who had not been exposed to any prior dissent conformed to the majority 70% of the time. But those who had viewed minority dissent in an earlier experiment were much more likely to insist on the correct response. In fact, as can be seen in Figure 9.9, the more consistent the earlier observed dissent had been, the less students later conformed to the group norm.

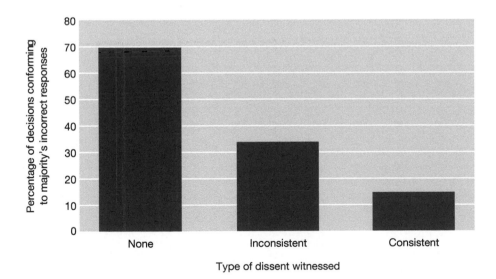

Figure 9.9 Learning dissent from dissent
In the presence of confederates who made unanimous but obviously incorrect judgments on a line-matching task, participants who had not been exposed to a dissenting minority in a previous study conformed 70% of the time. But those who had previously witnessed minority dissent conformed much less often. The more consistent the earlier dissent had been, the less participants conformed. (Data from Nemeth & Chiles, 1988.)

Negotiating Similarity and Difference. Advocates of minority views face a dilemma. To influence the majority viewpoint, they must offer a consensus that clearly differs from the majority position. At the same time, however, dissenters will not be heard if they are perceived as too different from the majority, lacking in the qualifications for making the judgment, and therefore not an appropriate reference group. How can minorities successfully navigate this fine line? According to John Turner (1982; David & Turner, 1996) and William Crano (Alvaro & Crano, 1996; Crano & Alvaro, 1998), the most effective way is for the minority to first establish itself as psychologically part of the in-group. Research confirms this advice. In-group members with minority views have much greater social influence success than out-group members with the same views (Bohner, Dykema-Engblade, Tindale, & Meisenhelder, 2008; Rios, 2012). And confirming one's in-group credentials by first agreeing with the majority before dissenting is a particularly effective way to promote minority influence (Bray, Johnson, & Chilstrom, 1982; Hollander, 1958).

Even when minorities have negotiated their in-group identity as best they can, their views might still not be embraced publicly the way majority views are. For many people, the very label "minority" has more negative associations than the label "majority" (Mucchi-Faina, Pacilli, & Pagliaro, 2011; Seyranian, Atuel, & Crano, 2008). And given the powerful mastery and connectedness functions of the majority norm, group members may often resist openly agreeing with the deviant viewpoint (Alvaro & Crano, 1997; Wood and others, 1996).

Fortunately, however, seeing the minority's in-group credentials makes most in-group majority members wonder why the in-group minority—others just like them—thinks the way it does, producing the uncertainty that is the first step to influence (Martin & Hewstone, 2001). This unleashes a powerful minority influence weapon.

HOT TOPICS IN SOCIAL PSYCHOLOGY: CONSEQUENCES OF NORM MISMATCH

We follow social norms because doing so fulfills our desires for mastery and connectedness. It may come as no surprise, then, that when our norms clash with the norms of communities or organizations we want to join, we may find this upsetting. Recent research shows evidence for this at a physiological level. In this work, researchers focused on first-generation college students in the U.S. (Stephens and others, 2012). These students often come from backgrounds that foster and promote interdependent norms, such as relying on others or the community. American universities, however, tend to emphasize independent norms—like having and expressing one's own ideas. To investigate whether this clash in norms might be troubling for these students, the researchers showed first- and continuing-generation U.S. college students a letter supposedly written by their university's president, characterizing the college in either interdependent or independent terms. After reading this letter, students were asked to give a brief speech about their college goals. The speeches were analyzed by judges for emotional content, and the stress hormone cortisol was measured. When the college was described as independent, first-generation students showed more negative emotions and a larger increase in cortisol than did continuing-generation students. But, in the interdependent condition, the two types of students did not differ. This pattern suggests that it is the clash between the norms and values of first-generation students and the independent norms of college that generates stress and negative emotions.

Promoting Systematic Processing. Serge Moscovici (1980) was the first to suggest that when minorities manage their dissent effectively, other group members are more likely to systematically process their arguments. He argued that their plausible alternative creates uncertainty about reality and that this stimulates thinking among majority members. The majority seeks additional information about the issue and processes it in greater depth (Nemeth, 1995). That is, minority dissent promotes systematic processing.

A minority made the majority process carefully in a study in which first-year British undergraduates were told that administrators had decided to try out oral exams in one of the colleges in the university system, but they were not told which college. The students were then confronted with either strong or weak arguments in favor of instituting oral exams and also given the information that a focus group had shown that either 9 of 11 (a majority) or only 2 of 11 (a minority) of their peers supported the proposal (Martin, Hewstone, & Martin, 2007). When asked later what they thought of the idea, participants in the minority condition had been persuaded if they had been exposed to strong arguments but not if they had been exposed to weak arguments—classic evidence that they had systematically processed the arguments supportive of the minority. In contrast, students were persuaded by the majority position regardless of whether they saw strong or weak arguments—equally classic evidence that the majority position was adopted without careful thought. Such systematic processing of minority information is particularly likely if the minority is consistent (Crano, 2012; Martin & Hewstone, 2008; Nemeth, 2012). Another sure sign that minority messages trigger systematic processing comes from studies showing that minority-induced attitude change is more likely to translate into consistent behavioral action (Martin, Martin, Smith, & Hewstone, 2007). Recall from Chapter 7 that consistency between attitudes and behavior is one of the hallmarks of attitudes formed on the basis of systematic processing. Such extensive processing of minority arguments in the face of reluctance to openly endorse minority views produces another well-established characteristic of minority influence: minorities often produce more private than public change in majority members' opinions and behaviors (Codaccioni & Tafani, 2011; Sinaceur, Thomas-Hunt, Neale, O'Neill, & Haag, 2010).

Of course, hearing minority views makes majority members look more deeply at issues outside the laboratory as well. From top management teams at British Airways to the U.S. Supreme Court, organizational decision-making groups that are faced with minority dissent also look at more information, make more integrative decisions, and solve problems better (van Dijk, van Engen, & van Knippenberg, 2012; de Wit, Greer, & Jehn, 2012; Gruenfeld, Thomas-Hunt, & Kim, 1998; Phillips, Liljenquist, & Neale, 2009). For example, compared to situations in which there was no dissent, exposure to minority points of view was able to prevent groups from continuing to pursue a losing course of action, a self–destructive path that tempts many cohesive decision-making groups (Greitemeyer, Schulz-Hardt, & Frey, 2009). Such findings provide further evidence that minority influence might indeed be an antidote for groupthink. Confronting minority views prompts the majority to develop deeper and more considered judgments, compared to when such opposition is lacking.

Because minority dissent encourages people to consider alternatives, it also encourages people to be more creative. People hearing minority messages think more broadly, go beyond the information given, and diverge from the topic at hand (Erb, Bohner,

Photo 9.5 Hanging tough to make others think. When those holding minority views take a clear, consistent stand—even when opposed by others—they can make the majority think deeply about the issues involved. When members of the environmental group Greenpeace engage in repeated dangerous acts, like those depicted here, they demonstrate solid commitment to their cause in a way that can promote systematic thinking, and attitude change, in the majority.

Schmalzle, & Rank, 1998; Nemeth & Kwan, 1987). This may allow them to see novel connections and to look at things from a fresh perspective. Minority dissent can thus be a facilitator of creativity and innovation (Clevering, 2009; De Dreu, Nijstad, Baas, & Bechtoldt, 2008; Schulz-Hardt, Mojzisch, & Vogelgesang, 2008).

SOCIAL PSYCHOLOGY IN PRACTICE: MINORITY INFLUENCE IN THE COURTROOM

As we have seen, the expression and consideration of minority views can be vital to forming a valid consensus. And this principle has important implications for jury deliberations. In 1972, the U.S. Supreme Court ruled that states could allow juries to give verdicts that command only majority support, holding that there is neither legal nor historical basis for requiring unanimity. This ruling makes it possible for a majority to ignore minority views. An initial majority would have no need to convince the minority to go along with its position, nor any strong reason to listen to the minority's arguments. Could loosening the requirement of unanimity have weakened minority influence and perhaps even have lessened the quality of jury decisions?

   To investigate these issues, Charlan Nemeth (1977) divided University of Virginia students into mock juries and asked them to reach a verdict about the guilt or innocence of a defendant charged with murder. Nemeth made sure that each group included some students who initially favored acquittal and others who favored conviction. Some of the juries were forced to deliberate until they reached a unanimous verdict, whereas others were allowed

■ ■ ■

■■■

to bring in a verdict with only a two-thirds majority. The groups forced to consider and respond to minority points of view not only deliberated longer but also were more confident about their eventual decisions. These mock jurors recalled more of the evidence, suggesting that they had considered it more thoroughly than those in the non-unanimous juries. Even more importantly, they were more likely to change their initial views on the case than were members of groups allowed to bring in a two-thirds majority opinion. A similar outcome—that mock juries took minority views into account only when there was a unanimity rule—was found with Japanese students (Ohtsubo, Miller, Hayashi, & Masuchi, 2004). And when more than 800 Massachusetts citizens recruited from the jury rolls participated in mock jury discussions after watching a videotaped trial, they terminated discussion of the evidence as soon as a majority was reached if unanimity was not required (Hastie, Penrod, & Pennington, 1983).

These findings suggest that relaxing the unanimity requirement does weaken minority influence and thus may reduce the quality of jury deliberations. Of course, it is possible that real jurors, knowing that their judgments will affect the lives of real people, would give careful consideration to each juror's point of view even if a unanimity rule did not force them to do so. The authors of the Supreme Court decision assumed that they would. And of course many of the deliberation benefits of unanimity might accrue if even a 'supermajority"—say, 10 of 12—of the jury had to agree. Detractors of this research also point out that unanimity means nothing if pressures toward unanimity cause public conformity, falsely inflating the apparent strength of the unanimous consensus. Still, it appears that a unanimity rule both increases the likelihood that minority views will contribute to the final group consensus and improves the quality of group consensus formation, particularly if the evidence is mixed (Devine, 2012).

Processes of Minority and Majority Influence

By and large, majorities and minorities influence others by the same processes. Both majorities and minorities can satisfy concerns about mastery and connectedness, encourage heuristic or systematic processing of the evidence, and elicit public compliance or private acceptance.

By and large, majority and minorities influence each other for the same reasons and by the same processes. First, although majority agreement usually helps people master reality, consistent disagreement from a minority can trigger concerns about the validity of the majority position. Thus, it seems that both majority and minority influence can occur to satisfy concerns about mastery. Second, although majorities offer group members positive identities as good team players, not everybody wants to be a member of the establishment team. A minority identity of independent-mindedness, deviance, and rebellion can also be appealing. When being avant-garde, innovative, or socially progressive is important, minority opinions offer all the benefits of a positive identity (Nemeth, 2012; Rios, 2012). And especially in times of change, a remaining conservative minority is frequently the defender of the status quo (Mucchi-Faina, Pacilli, & Pagliaro, 2010). Thus despite the generally positive glow that majorities enjoy, either majority or minority influence can provide positive connectedness. Finally, as we have seen, both majority and minority messages are reacted to in knee-jerk fashion in some circum-stances. At other times, both types of appeal apparently provoke extensive thinking. So it seems that both majority and minority influence can come about through superficial

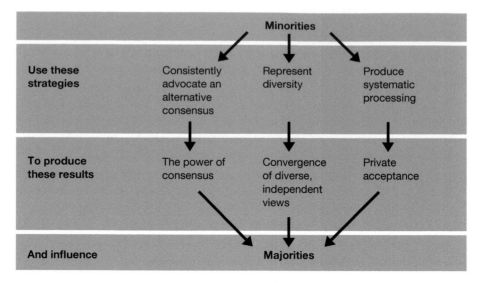

Figure 9.10 Minorities use consensus to influence others
Minorities as well as majorities can influence others when they offer a consensus that represents the convergence of diverse views and is built on systematic processing of relevant evidence.

or systematic processing depending on the circumstances (Gardikiotis, 2011; Kruglanski & Mackie, 1990; Martin & Hewstone, 2008). Not surprisingly then, majority positions and arguments, as well as minority views, can both be privately accepted. At the same time, it is easy to find examples of situations in which minorities, just like majorities, elicit mere public conformity. Majorities may control rewards, but minorities can often dispense punishments. One need only listen to the screaming 4-year-old who helps the family decide not to eat out that night. So both majorities and minorities can produce both public and private conformity. In fact, as can be seen in Figure 9.10, minorities are influential when their dissent offers a consensus, avoids contamination, and triggers private acceptance—the same processes by which all groups achieve influence. By and large, majorities and minorities achieve influence by pulling the same levers.

Beyond Minority Influence: Using Norms to Strengthen Consensus

The best way to promote effective group norm formation and consensus seeking is to set up norms that make group members more critical thinkers as a group rather than as individuals. When group members are united behind norms of seeking consensus with systematic consideration of alternatives, independence from contamination, and the conviction of private acceptance, the desire for mastery and for connectedness work together to produce a valid consensus.

The careful consideration of minority as well as majority viewpoints in the context of group discussion can help ensure that the consensus reached by the group is one that can be relied on. Clearly, consensus will have the greatest chance to be accurate when groups overcome tendencies to accept shared and majority arguments at face value. They can do this by systematically processing all information, counteracting the powerful persuasive impact of majority views by including persistent and committed minority voices. Do these findings mean that group decision making can be improved simply by making group members better information processors as individuals? Studies assessing this idea have produced some surprising results.

In one such study, a group of participants had to solve a murder mystery together—that is, they had to come to a group consensus as to "whodunit" (Liljenquist, Galinsky, & Kray, 2004). The study used a hidden profile paradigm, so some clues to the murderer's identity were shared by all participants, whereas some pieces of relevant information were known only to single members of the group. Remember that in such situations group discussion usually emphasizes the shared information, reducing the likelihood of solving the mystery. After the participants had read their information about the murder mystery but before discussing it as a group, they were led through a short exercise. Some of them performed a task designed to make them engage in counterfactual thinking—that is, to consider what might happen in various sets of circumstances. The researchers used this task because the consideration of "what if?" scenarios has been found to promote systematic processing of information (Galinsky & Moskowitz, 2000). The most important aspect of the experiment was that some participants performed this task separately, as individuals, whereas others completed the exercise together as a group before going on to the murder mystery task. The results showed that far from improving group performance, making group members better individual information processors by encouraging them to think counterfactually actually hurt the group's chances of solving the murder mystery. In contrast, encouraging the group as a whole to think counterfactually together improved their ability to identify the culprit.

Thus, the best way to promote effective group norm formation and consensus seeking is to make group members more critical and systematic thinkers as a group rather than as individuals (Postmes, Spears, & Cihangir, 2001; Thomas, McGarty, & Mavor, 2009). These findings demonstrate that the power of the group situation can be harnessed to improve group consensus seeking (Postmes, Haslam, & Swaab, 2005; Rink & Ellemers, 2010; Swaab, Phillips, Diermeier, & Medvec, 2008). If the power of norms can make groups susceptible to poor decision making in the first place, why not use that power to improve decision making? The key to successful consensus seeking is setting up norms to govern norm formation itself. When group members are united behind norms of seeking consensus with systematic consideration of alternatives, independence from contamination, and the conviction of private acceptance, the desire for mastery and for connectedness work together to produce a valid consensus.

CONCLUDING COMMENTS

Among the most important characteristics of group interaction are the formation, transmission, and change of group norms. When group members interact, they offer opinions and arguments and listen to others voicing their views, until finally a consensus emerges. Individuals are highly motivated to have their beliefs, feelings, and actions reflect reality. When participating in a discussion with similar others who share the same information, they fully expect to agree with one another. When such agreement fails to materialize, people are puzzled, distressed, and uncertain. Thus social dissent opens the way for social influence.

This view of group influence makes clear that both social and cognitive processes confer validity on group norms. The social process is the give-and-take interaction that occurs as the group works out a consensus. The cognitive process is the independent evaluation of information carried out by group members. Maximal validity—maximal certainty about our view of reality—depends on both processes.

In many important ways, scientists are engaged in a reality-construction enterprise that is just like everyone's day-to-day attempts to understand social and physical reality. Recall our discussion of scientific method in Chapter 2. Just as people try to construct social reality by forging agreement with fellow group members, social psychologists use many of the same strategies to ascertain the truth about social behavior. Every individual researcher has his or her own personal biases that, despite all efforts to be objective, might influence research strategies, results, and interpretations.

Scientists often come to an experimental test as partisan adherents of a favorite theory. How to discover the truth? The scientific community's solution, like that of other social groups, is to seek consensus. Regardless of researchers' different theoretical perspectives, tests of theories and evaluations of information should ultimately converge on the same outcome. And reaching the same conclusion from different theoretical starting points, using different techniques, and with different participants, offers strong evidence for the validity of the shared conclusion. Such convergence increases our certainty that we are learning about a phenomenon that is real to all of us and independent of our preconceived views. All the norms and procedures of science are intended to promote systematic processing and the acceptance of positions based on the underlying evidence rather than on public conformity. This in turn means that minority influence should be maximized, allowing for the acceptance of new insights and innovations.

True consensus is achieved only when a variety of opinions are processed from multiple points of view and are accepted only after being proved valid by such processing. When we think about how consensus is forged, we can see that true consensus should be constantly undergoing revision. The current norm should be constantly open to new ideas that might challenge the status quo. We should listen to minority opinions instead of closing our minds and finding comfort in majority support for our existing view. When new ideas become too threatening to the status quo, groups often try to expel the deviants from the group. But as we have seen, the expression and consideration of minority views is crucial to the development of reliable group norms. Thus, it is important to nurture diverse and different voices in any group: The validity of a group's norms depends on their being forged from the consideration of many points of view.

SUMMARY

Conformity to Social Norms. Because people are profoundly influenced by others' ideas and actions, interaction or communication causes group members' thoughts, feelings, and behaviors to become more alike. Whether a judgment task is clear-cut or ambiguous, trivial or important, individual members' views converge to form a social norm. Social norms reflect the group's generally accepted way of thinking, feeling, or acting. **Descriptive social norms** are what people think, feel, or do whereas **injunctive social norms** specify what people should think, feel, or do.

Conformity is the convergence of individual responses toward group norms. Conformity occurs for two important reasons: because people believe that the group is right and because they want the group to accept and approve of them. Most of the time people show **private conformity** to group norms, accepting them as their own, because they believe them to be correct and appropriate. Sometimes, however, people engage in **public conformity** to norms they do not privately accept.

Motivational Functions of Conformity to Norms. Private conformity comes about because we expect to see the world the same way similar others see it. In fact, we often assume that most other people share our own opinions and preferences, a tendency called the **false consensus effect**. Agreement with others increases our confidence that our views are correct, whereas disagreement undermines that certainty.

Agreeing with others assures people that they are in contact with a common reality. When people privately conform because they believe a group's norms reflect reality, the group is said to have **informational influence**. Agreeing with others also gives people the feeling of belonging with others. A group has **normative influence** when members conform to it to attain a positive and valued social identity. People expect to agree with **reference groups**, those who share attributes relevant to the judgment at hand. In-groups often serve as reference groups and people are much more influenced by in-group than out-group others. Other in-group members do not have to be present for conformity to occur, but having other group members present increases conformity even more. The more highly members identify with the group, the greater the reference group's impact. Although particular circumstances can make one goal more important than the other, usually agreement with an in-group of similar others simultaneously fulfills the mastery, connectedness, and me and mine motives.

How Groups Form Norms: Processes of Social Influence. Although sometimes group discussion results in convergence on a moderate position, whenever a majority of group members initially favors one side of the issue, communication and interaction results in **group polarization**, in which the group norm becomes more extreme.

When people process superficially, merely relying on others' positions can produce polarization of group norms as undecided or moderate group members move toward the group position and try to show that they are good group members. When people process systematically, others' positions and arguments both work together to polarize group norms. Majority arguments are more numerous, receive more discussion, seem

CHAPTER 9 THEMES

■ **Construction of Reality**
Individuals and groups construct consensus about what is true and good.

■ **Pervasiveness of Social Influence**
This construction process involves conformity and mutual influence among group members.

■ **Striving for Mastery**
Conformity helps us to hold valid opinions because the convergence of many opinions often means correctness.

■ **Seeking Connectedness**
Conformity helps us feel connected to and valued by other group members.

■ **Valuing Me and Mine**
The views of other in-group members are the ones to which we conform most.

■ **Conservatism**
Positions supported by a majority in a group usually attract more supporters and do not readily change.

■ **Superficiality Versus Depth**
People process the opinions of other group members either in superficial ways or with careful consideration.

more compelling, and are presented more persuasively. All these factors give majority views a persuasive advantage.

Undermining True Consensus. Consensus implies that opinions are valid only when consensus is achieved in the right way. A consensus cannot be trusted if it arises from unthinking reliance on others' positions, contamination by shared biases, or public conformity. Such a consensus offers only the illusion of mastery and connectedness and can lead to situations of **pluralistic ignorance**, where everyone is publicly conforming to a norm that no one privately endorses.

Groupthink occurs when groups become more concerned with reaching consensus than with reaching consensus in a way that ensures its validity. Groupthink can be avoided by safeguarding consideration of alternatives, independence of views, and private acceptance.

Minority Influence: The Value of Dissent. Minority views can sway the majority. To be influential, the minority must offer an alternative consensus, remain consistent, strike the right balance between similarity to and difference from the majority, and promote systematic processing. By and large, majorities and minorities influence others by the same processes. Both majorities and minorities can satisfy concerns about mastery and connectedness, encourage heuristic or systematic processing of the evidence, and elicit public compliance or private acceptance.

The best way to promote effective group norm formation and consensus seeking is to set up norms that make group members more critical thinkers as a group rather than as individuals. When group members are united behind norms of seeking consensus with systematic consideration of alternatives, independence from contamination, and the conviction of private acceptance, the desire for mastery and for connectedness work together to produce a valid consensus.

NORMS AND BEHAVIOR

NORMS OBEDIENCE TO AUTHORITY RESISTANCE SOCIAL RECIPROCITY POLARIZATION DOOR-IN-THE-FACE TECHNIQUE SOCIAL COMMITMENT SOCIAL INFLUENCE ACCESSIBILITY DEINDIVIDUATION REACTANCE

10

Consider the following three seemingly unrelated events:

■ In June 2013, the United States Supreme Court struck down the Defense of Marriage Act, a federal statute aimed at limiting the rights of gays and lesbians. As word of the ruling spread a type of behavioral contagion occurred as well: millions of Facebook users professed their support for the ruling and changed their profile pictures to a rainbow-colored flag or an equal sign, both symbols of support for marriage equality for gays and lesbians (Stern, 2013).

■ When Henrietta and Dennis Taylor allowed two door-to-door salesmen into their Florida home, the elderly couple ended up buying a $1749 vacuum cleaner. Because their monthly income was only $1100, the salesmen arranged a loan that brought their total payments to over $2500 (Cahill, 1999).

■ The caller to a Wendy's fast food restaurant in Texas claimed to be from corporate headquarters and instructed employees to conduct an immediate test of the restaurant's fire-suppression system. When they did so, flooding the building with foam, they were ordered to evacuate, breaking the front windows as they went to vent the toxic fumes. One employee was badly cut (Powell, 2009).

What do the Facebook updates of millions of users, the cautionary tale of an elderly couple who paid too much for a household appliance, and the willingness of people to damage a business and injure themselves on command from an unidentified caller have in common? As you will see in this chapter, each involves people following social norms.

Through the processes we described in Chapter 9, all human groups—even fleeting ones—establish social norms: generally accepted ways of thinking, feeling, and behaving that people agree on and endorse as right and proper. In this chapter, we focus on when and how those norms guide our behavior. Because social norms reflect a group's view of the world, itself, and others, they have a powerful effect on almost all aspects of our behavior. Of course, established groups create laws and sanctions—systems of reward and punishment—to enforce appropriate standards of behavior among their members. But as you will see in the first part of this chapter, norms are powerful precisely because they usually control group members' behavior without any kind of outside enforcement. Spurred to change our status or profile picture simply because we see that our Facebook friends are also doing it, no one makes us conform. We just do it. For members of important and abiding groups, norms are so well learned and privately accepted that when a norm is activated its standards automatically govern behavior. Thus, most of the time people do what the social customs and conventions of their group prescribe because they want to, not because they have to.

Some of the most powerful norms reflect deeply held beliefs about how people should treat one another. Norms about reciprocity dictate that people should repay others' kindnesses or favors, even if repayment comes at a cost to us. Norms about interpersonal commitment direct us to keep our word, stand by our promises, and be trustworthy and reliable, even when others are not. Norms about obedience command us to obey those to whom society has given legitimate authority. Because norms like reciprocity, commitment, and obedience are so important in regulating human interaction, we discuss them in detail in major sections of the chapter.

What happens when others exploit our tendency to follow our groups' rules? Like the Taylors, we may find ourselves in trouble. If a salesperson appears to do us an unasked-for favor (cleaning a carpet for free), or makes a meaningless concession (reduces an over-inflated price tag by a small percentage), our impulse to reciprocate can trap us into giving up something of real value (our hard earned money). And just as the employees at the Wendy's restaurant dutifully obeyed an apparently legitimate authority, throughout history malevolent authorities have used norms to make people act obediently in the service of great evil. Hitler's death camps, Stalin's secret police, Argentinean dictators' death squads, and the infamous U.S. military detention center at Abu Ghraib all could not have functioned without the norm of obedience.

If norms have such power, can people successfully resist and rebel against them? We saw in Chapter 9 that considering diverse points of view can sometimes change group norms, even those that are initially fully accepted and widely endorsed. The same strategy of careful thinking can help us resist inappropriate attempts to use norms against us. Because we are subject to a variety of norms that offer sometimes contradictory suggestions about how we should act, every influence situation is open to interpretation. By understanding how norms influence our actions, by questioning the norms that others assume should guide our behavior, and by deliberately considering which norms apply to each situation, people can successfully resist normative pressure.

Of course, norms are not the only mental representation that helps guide behavior. As you may recall from Chapter 8, attitudes also have a potent influence on what we do. The final section of this chapter shows that norms and attitudes usually operate together to guide behavior. Because so many of our attitudes are also a product of our

Photo 10.1 Norms are powerful. At public meetings, sporting events, even in many schools and businesses in the United States, the opening notes of the national anthem or the opening words of the Pledge of Allegiance are enough to bring people to their feet with hands over their hearts. Although such norm-driven behavior is sometimes maintained by reward and punishment, most of the time people behave in line with group norms because they want to, not because they have to.

memberships in groups, these attitudes rarely conflict with norms. Sometimes, however, norms and attitudes suggest different courses of action, and then the outcome depends on which of them comes to mind more easily. Whether or not an employee's personal attitudes lead her to "blow the whistle" on a company's way of doing business or whether a young man's personal convictions cause him to challenge the state's authority to draft him into the military will depend on the mix of social norms and individual attitudes that are brought to bear in the situation. To understand how all these forces affect our actions, however, we have to begin at the beginning. How do norms influence our behavior, and why do they have such a powerful effect on what we do?

NORMS: EFFECTIVE GUIDES FOR SOCIAL BEHAVIOR

Kurt Lewin (1943) was one of the first social psychologists to demonstrate the powerful effect of group norms on behavior. During the Second World War, traditional cuts of meat like steaks and chops were scarce and, when available, very expensive. To keep the civilian population healthy, the U.S. government wanted people to consume more liver, kidneys, and other unfamiliar organ meats. Commendable as this goal was, U.S. citizens found it hard to swallow at the dinner table. Pamphlets extolling the nutritional value of these meats and public lectures by expert nutritionists—both of which might have changed attitudes—had little impact on well-entrenched food-buying and eating habits. Lewin believed that changes in behavior could best be accomplished by changing the prevailing norms. That is, he suspected that only a shared consensus about what was appropriate to eat would change this kind of behavior. To test this idea, he brought homemakers together in small groups to discuss in depth such questions as how to cook the new cuts and how to overcome family members' resistance. In the course of these discussions, group members' willingness to try the new foods increased, and this produced a shift in norms. A follow-up survey showed that over 30% of the discussion group members actually tried the unusual foods, compared with only 3% of homemakers who listened to a lecture advocating the same course of action (but who had no idea how other people just like them reacted to the new foods). Norms thus had an impact on behavior that information alone could not achieve.

Based on this impressive finding, one might conclude that norms always prevail. But, just as we know that a number of conditions have to be in place for attitudes to predict behavior, the same is true for norms (Harries, Eslambolchilar, Stride, Rettie, & Walton, 2013; Thombs and others, 2004, 2007).

Activating Norms to Guide Behavior

Norms must be activated before they can guide behavior. They can be activated by direct reminders, environmental cues, or observations of other people's behavior. When people see themselves purely in terms of group identity, their behavior is likely to be guided by group norms alone.

No norm, attitude, or other mental representation can influence behavior unless it comes to mind. Thus, whichever norm happens to be most activated is often followed (Jonas,

Sullivan, & Greenberg, 2013). Moreover, if a norm is activated in one situation, it can carry over into another situation, because it has been made accessible (Hertel & Kerr, 2001; Kallgren, Reno, & Cialdini, 2000). Norms, like attitudes, can be made accessible by several means.

Direct Reminders of Norms. Deliberate and direct reminders of appropriate norms are all around us. The sign in the library requests, "Quiet, please." The reluctant child is instructed, "Do as you're told!" And the announcer at the Olympic medal award ceremony states, "Please rise for the playing of the national anthem." Not surprisingly, this direct approach pays off in norm-based behavior. In one demonstration of this effect, Robert Cialdini and his colleagues (Cialdini, Reno, & Kallgren, 1990) placed handbills on the windshields of cars parked at their campus library. Some handbills activated antilittering norms in a straightforward way, announcing, "April Is Keep Arizona Beautiful Month. Please Do Not Litter." Others delivered a message irrelevant to littering: "April Is Arizona's Fine Arts Month. Please Visit Your Local Art Museum." Unobtrusive observers counted (and we hope picked up) the handbills thrown to the ground. Twenty-five percent of those receiving the irrelevant message discarded it before getting into the car, compared with only 10% of those receiving the direct reminder about antilittering norms.

Environments Activate Norms. Descriptive and injunctive norms are also activated by cues in the environment. The silence in libraries and churches keeps our voices hushed. We slow down at the sight of flashing lights and pull over at the sound of a siren. The first few notes of the national anthem bring us to our feet, and the dimming of lights at a concert settles us down.

What empirical evidence supports the notion that environments can activate norms and guide behavior? Let's again consider littering. Most of us have had the experience of having someone drop trash on the floor or the ground near us. When this happens, probably the first things that spring to mind are norms about such actions: Is littering acceptable behavior or not? Your surroundings may offer clues about the prevailing descriptive or injunctive norm. Heaps of discarded trash suggest that other people have found it acceptable to litter, whereas a pristine environment implies norms against such behavior. One study demonstrating this point placed participants in one of two settings: One was littered, the other was clean (Cialdini and others, 1990). The researchers found that more participants littered in the dirty environment than in the clean one. These actions are evidence that prevailing norms have a big impact on behavior. For other participants in the same environments, researchers drew attention to the norms regarding littering by having a confederate walk by and drop a piece of trash. Those who saw the confederate litter the clean environment littered even less than those in the same environment with no confederate. In contrast, the confederate's littering made participants throw even more trash into the dirty environment (see Figure 10.1). Evidently, the confederate's behavior made the norm implied by the state of the environment—whether neatness or messiness—even more accessible, and, in doing so, it increased behavior consistent with the norm.

As we encounter particular environments over and over again, we can build up mental associations between the environment and the norms that apply there. Every time

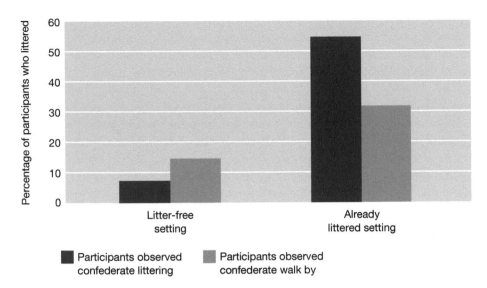

Figure 10.1 Effect of activated norms on littering
In this study, people littered least when they observed someone messing up a clean environment, and they littered most when they saw trash being thrown into an already dirty environment. Researchers explain this paradox in terms of norm accessibility: The litterer's behavior called attention to the prevailing norm, whether cleanliness or messiness, and the norm, in turn, influenced behavior. (Data from Cialdini and others, 1990.)

we enter a house of worship, step onto the platform at a train station, or take our seat in an exclusive restaurant, we make a mental connection between the place and what others are doing there. Over time, these connections become so well learned that the environment itself can automatically activate the appropriate behavior. Compared to students shown photos of a railway station, Dutch students shown pictures of a library not only recognized words like silent, quiet, and whisper more quickly, but also used softer voices in a later speech task (Aarts & Dijksterhuis, 2003). When U.S. citizens voted in churches (compared to other polling places such as schools or firehouses), they cast more votes for the more conservative (versus the more liberal) political candidate and were more likely to support a state constitutional amendment defining marriage as excluding same-sex couples (Rutchick, 2010). Thus, as all these examples illustrate, environmental cues can communicate the norms appropriate in that environment, which can powerfully direct behavior.

You may notice that normative behaviors become associated with and activated by environments just as individual behaviors like habits also become associated with particular situations and contexts, see Chapter 8, pages 305–306.

Groups Activate Norms. The most powerful and frequent activator of norms is actually learning or seeing what other people do. How people behave tells us what the norm is. And just as norms can become joined to environments, we learn over time what different people or groups do, and so seeing those people then activates the norm automatically.

The people we care about most are in-group members, those with whom we share group identity, and numerous findings suggest that we are especially likely to follow norms associated with them. One clever study illustrated this (Goldstein, Cialdini, & Griskevicius, 2008). Over a roughly 2-month span, researchers collected data on towel re-usage at a hotel. Some guests received a message in their room asking them to "HELP SAVE THE ENVIRONMENT. You can show your respect for nature and help save the environment by reusing your towels during your stay." Other guests received a similar message, but with an important twist. These alternative messages noted that 75% of other sorts of people in the past had reused towels. Depending on condition, the message referred to "your fellow guests," "fellow guests who stayed in this room," "your fellow citizens," or people of their same gender. All of the in-group norm messages yielded more towel re-usage than did the control message, which did not reference any in-group at all. The closest in-group, the "guests in this room" was the most effective of all. Other studies show similar effects. College students drink more alcohol the more they believe a key in-group (such as their friends, fellow university students, or fraternity/sorority group) endorses such behavior, and this is especially the case among those for whom the group is most important (Reed, Lange, Ketchie, & Clapp, 2007). Even just wishing to belong to a group makes people more likely to act in line with the group's norms (Litt, Stock, & Lewis, 2012).

What factors make in-group norms more accessible and effective? Whatever makes the group more salient activates its norms. For example, the more group members who are present, the more accessible and effective the group norm is. One study had college students report their drinking in various situations such as while socializing or at parties. Findings showed that when others in the setting drank a lot, participants also did so, and this effect was bigger when more other group members were present (Cullum, O'Grady, Armeli, & Tennen, 2012).

When groups are salient, some group members are more likely than others to activate and communicate norms and in turn to have the greatest impact on the group's behavior. Drawing on this principle to try to reduce bullying in a school, researchers had the most socially connected and popular children publicly denounce bullying and harassment, hoping that other kids would take their cue from these key players. It seems to have worked: the more contact students had with these norm leaders, the better they behaved, as indicated by teacher reports and disciplinary records (Paluck & Shepherd, 2012).

Finally, there is nothing like a little "compare and contrast" with another group to bring in-group norms to mind. Researchers demonstrated this effect by asking British students to write a brief essay about "what it means to be British." In other conditions, they compared being British to being American (who pretesting showed were viewed as low in environmental consciousness) or Swedish (viewed as highly environmentally conscious). Results showed that British students perceived their own in-group as more environmentally conscious after comparing themselves to Americans rather than to Swedes. When perceptions about their group's norm shifted depending on the nature of an out-group comparison, behavior followed this newly activated norm. British students picked up more fliers about sustainability and showed more willingness to contact a government official about the issue if they had earlier compared themselves to Americans rather than Swedes (Rabinovich, Morton, Postmes, & Verplanken, 2012). As all these findings illustrate, the more accessible the in-group norm, the more likely we are to use it to guide our behavior.

Deindividuation. Perhaps the most dramatic circumstance that can make group norms accessible is one where we find ourselves totally embedded in the group, to the point that we don't even think of ourselves as individuals. Have you had such an experience?

Perhaps you've been in a stadium full of fans, decked out in your team's colors, singing their song, jumping to your feet to applaud a particularly fine play, and surrounded by hundreds of others looking the same way and behaving identically.

Deindividuation refers to the state in which group or social identity dominates personal or individual identity: your identity as a "fan" is way more important in that moment than your unique individual identity. Being present among others just like you, particularly if you are anonymous and indistinguishable from them, only increases feelings of shared group membership. Under these conditions, group norms become maximally accessible; the only thing group members think about is what the other group members around them are thinking, saying, and doing (Reicher, 1987).

deindividuation
the psychological state in which group or social identity completely dominates personal or individual identity so that group norms become maximally accessible

Because experiences like this of being lost in the crowd are sometimes associated with violent behavior—riots, soccer hooliganism, out-of-control parties—some social psychologists speculate that being anonymous and indistinguishable in a group changes the rules of human behavior, making it "antisocial"—less rational, more volatile, and often more violent (LeBon, 1895/1947). This is the way a particularly famous study, the Stanford Prison Experiment, is often interpreted (Haney, Banks, & Zimbardo, 1973). The researchers in this study randomly assigned 24 psychologically and physically healthy young men to be either mock guards or mock prisoners in a simulated prison constructed in the basement of the Stanford University Psychology Building. The researchers took great pains to make the situation psychologically compelling. "Prisoners" were stripped, searched, and given identical shapeless uniforms that identified them only by number, whereas guards wore identical military style uniforms, carried a billyclub, and sported reflective glasses that hid their eyes. The power the guards wielded over the prisoners was reinforced by the prison "superintendent," and then the researchers observed how both groups behaved. Although the study was intended to run for two weeks, the researchers halted it after six days to protect the well-being of the participants. Guards, especially after a rebellion by the prisoners, became abusive and degrading, depriving the prisoners of food, humiliating them, and placing them in solitary confinement. As a group the prisoners were at first defiant but later became passive; some became so emotionally troubled that they had to be released early.

These findings are often interpreted as showing that stripping people of their individual identities triggers extreme, violent, and antisocial behavior, especially when one group has power over another. But understanding deindividuation as extreme group salience suggests a different view. From this perspective, deindividuation should maximally increase the tendency of individual members to join in whatever behavior the group is performing, whether that behavior is tearing down goal posts or rescuing earthquake victims. Research evidence supports this idea. In a meta-analysis of 60 studies, Tom Postmes and Russell Spears (1998) found that deindividuation increased normative behavior rather than antisocial behavior. That is, deindividuation increases whatever behavior is typical of the group (Postmes, Spears, Sakhel, & de Groot, 2001; Sassenberg & Boos, 2003).

Consider, for example, the results of a classic study that varied the accessible norms in a situation in which people's anonymity was also manipulated (R. D. Johnson & Downing, 1979). Some groups of participants in this study dressed in robes and hoods designed to activate negative and aggressive associations, such as thoughts about the disguises worn by the racist Ku Klux Klan organization or the hoods worn by executioners. Other groups of participants dressed in nurse's uniforms, outfits that activated positive associations with helping and caring. In addition, some participants were anonymous—their outfits covered their faces—whereas others were identifiable. All participants had to decide the level of shock to deliver to another person for failing a task. As can be seen in Figure 10.2, anonymous participants in the executioner costume delivered higher levels of shock than those who were identifiable. This could be either because anonymous individuals are free to behave badly, or because the prevailing group norm was one of aggression, and norm adherence was increased by anonymity. The "helper" conditions are the ones that really tell us what is going on. The anonymous participants in nurses' uniforms delivered lower levels of shock when they were unidentifiable than when their faces and name tags were visible. Far from being more aggressive when they were anonymous, these participants acted more in line with the group's prosocial norms when they felt less like identifiable individuals. When social identity is uppermost, people are more likely to do what the group norm tells them they should.

Seen in this light, the responses of the participants in the simulated prison experiment are thus better explained as classic examples of norm-driven behavior. First, the guards received direct reminders of appropriate guard behavior from both the

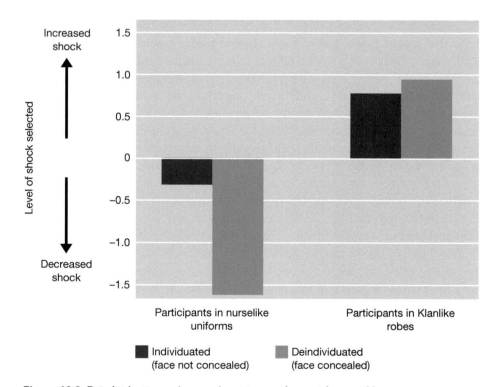

Figure 10.2 Deindividuation makes people act in accordance with accessible group norms
Participants in this experiment could increase or decrease the levels of shock by 1, 2, or 3 units. When dressed in nurselike uniforms, participants selected lower levels of shock, and deindividuation magnified this tendency. In contrast, participants dressed in Klanlike robes tended to increase shock levels, and deindividuation increased this tendency still further. Deindividuation does not always lead to antisocial behavior, but it does make people more likely to follow currently salient norms. (Data from R. D. Johnson & Downing, 1979.)

superintendent and a prison consultant involved in the study. In fact the direct nature of these instructions have led some to credit the results not to the power of the situation but to blatant demand characteristics (Banuazizi & Movahedi, 1975; Reicher & Haslam, 2006). Second, the realistic environment provided multiple cues to normative behavior, such as military style uniforms and billyclubs for the guards versus "feminine" smocks and ankle chains for the prisoners. Third, the researchers set up a classic norm conformity situation by arraying one group against another. At least some of the behaviors of both groups were designed to establish in-group solidarity and to break the cohesion of the out-group, and intergroup conflicts almost always make norm conformity more extreme. Finally, the use of identical uniforms among prisoners and guards, making the prisoners anonymous by referring to them as numbers, and doing much the same for the guards by making them wear expression-hiding glasses, created the classic conditions for deindividuation. Group identities were purposefully made more salient than individual identities, with the result that behavior followed group norms.

These findings suggest that deindividuation does not universally "free" people to follow their "basic" antisocial impulses. Instead, deindividuation makes people act in accordance with whatever group identification is accessible at the time: being a member of a disaster-response relief team, a Manchester United supporter, a sadistic prison guard, or even a nurse.

You might notice some parallels between deindividuation effects and group polarization, discussed in Chapter 9, pages 326–331. The more people see themselves in terms of their group membership, the more they adopt both the norms and behaviors that define the group, as seen in these studies.

Which Norms Guide Behavior?

Both descriptive norms and injunctive norms influence behavior, and these norms may sometimes interact with each other in interesting ways. One type of normative information may be more important than another, depending on our motivation and ability to think carefully.

It is clear that accessible norms are likely to direct behavior. But, as we first discussed in Chapter 9, there are two broad classes of norms: descriptive norms—what a group of people think, feel, or do—and injunctive norms—what group members believe people should think, feel, or do. In some situations, these norms may be one and the same: most parents do love their children (the descriptive norm) and believe that parents should love their children (the injunctive norm). But these types of norms can sometimes be in conflict: what most people are actually doing may deviate from what we think most people should be doing (Cialdini, 2003). And both of these types of norms can guide behavior.

Descriptive Norms as Guides for Behavior. As many findings in this chapter have already illustrated, what other people are actually doing (descriptive norms) frequently influences what we do, too. For example, when we see others around us drinking alcohol, we are more likely to drink alcohol as well (Cullum and others, 2012). Social media may play an important role in communicating descriptive norms. With networking sites like Facebook, it is easier than ever to learn what our friends are doing. If we see Facebook photos suggestive of a particular behavior, research suggests that we may infer that "everyone is doing it," which may increase our likelihood of doing it too. In one study,

SOCIAL PSYCHOLOGY IN PRACTICE: USING NORMS TO INFLUENCE HEALTH BEHAVIORS

Many behaviors that benefit our health are unpleasant, painful, or inconvenient—walking up those flights of stairs instead of taking the elevator, finding time to go to the gym, applying sunscreen, eating flavorless (but nutritious) foods, or undergoing that mildly uncomfortable cancer screening. Governments and policy makers wanting to encourage citizens to behave in healthier ways might draw on research illustrating that the proper use of norms can be quite effective. For example, researchers in one study counted how many people used the elevator instead of the stairs and then posted signs indicating that a majority of people used the stairs or simply stating that using the stairs was a good form of exercise. Elevator usage dropped by more than 46 % in the week following the posting of the signs, but only in the norm condition (Burger & Shelton, 2011). Thus, telling would-be elevator riders that most people take the stairs (giving them descriptive normative information) was effective in getting them to forego the elevator, whereas simply reminding people that stair walking is healthy was much less so.

But using descriptive norms in health messages can sometimes backfire. Health messages often bemoan the low number of people who get a flu shot, floss after meals, or exercise every day. The intention of these messages is, of course, to raise awareness that those behaviors should be changed. Can you see the problem with this strategy? In fact, given the power of norms, telling people that most others don't do something is likely to reduce, rather than increase, performance of that behavior (Sieverding, Decker, & Zimmermann, 2010).

people were randomly assigned to look at Facebook photos from people of their same age group that were sexually-suggestive or not (Young & Jordan, 2013). Viewing the suggestive photos led participants to think that more of their peers had unprotected sex and sex with strangers. That is, perception of the descriptive norm for these types of sexual activities was influenced by seeing others on Facebook engaged in sexually-suggestive behavior. Moreover, participants in this condition thought they themselves would be more likely to perform these behaviors as well.

Although we may sometimes be given accurate information about what others are doing, we are usually left to estimate this on our own. Do most people eat sushi, go to parties, or wear seatbelts? Unfortunately, our estimates can be quite inaccurate—we are led astray by attention-grabbing instances of extreme behavior, or forget that we interact only with a small number of in-group members, or are influenced by media depictions that don't reflect reality. Biased estimates can lead us to "follow the crowd," even though we are mistaken about what the crowd is really doing! Remember from Chapter 9 that people often overestimate how much others are performing particular behaviors ("everyone's drinking like a fish!") and that these overestimations predict their own behavior ("so I'll just have another drink myself"). Findings like these again illustrate the power of descriptive norms: even the perception of what others do can guide our own actions. Fortunately, we can also use that power to correct the situation: providing more accurate descriptive norms has been shown to reduce drinking and driving and to increase the use of designated drivers (Perkins, Linkenbach, Lewis, & Neighbors, 2010). In one such study, large numbers of students at regularly scheduled meetings of various campus organizations anonymously responded on handheld keyboards to questions about their own actual alcohol consumption or about their perceptions of normative group behavior. In the intervention conditions, these data were then immediately presented to the groups in graphical form, making the discrepancy between perceived and actual group norms obvious. Anonymous follow-up surveys one and two months later that also collected data about personal alcohol use showed less misperception of norms and, more importantly, reduced alcohol use in the intervention conditions (LaBrie, Hummer, Neighbors, & Pedersen, 2008; Neighbors and others, 2011). Giving people more accurate views of what their reference groups are doing changes behavior—more evidence for the power of norms.

To remind yourself about the concept of pluralistic ignorance and how it might arise, take a look at pages 336–337 in Chapter 9.

Injunctive Norms as Guides for Behavior. Injunctive norms, shared beliefs about what should be done, can also influence behavior. However, as with descriptive norms, we sometimes misperceive injunctive norms. When asked whether tanning and sunscreen use were good or bad, women participants first reported their own views, and then reported their perceptions of other women's views (Reid & Aiken, 2013). Consistent with findings on descriptive norms, most women misperceived injunctive norms—they believed more women thought tanning was good and use of sunscreen was bad than was actually the case. The women were then assigned either to a control group or a norm group. Those in the control group received a standard pamphlet advocating the use of sun protection. Those in the norm condition got this pamphlet plus information about the actual injunctive norm from the sample and how their estimates compared to the true norm. This norm intervention proved effective. Four weeks later, those in the norm condition not only reported greater intentions to use sun protection but were also actually wearing a hat and using sunscreen more frequently than those in the control group.

The Interplay of Descriptive and Injunctive Norms. It is clear that both descriptive and injunctive norms can shape our behavioral intentions and choices. But how do these types of norms work together? If you learned that most students think plagiarism is "no big deal" (injunctive norm) and that most do it (descriptive norm), would the combination of these norms, more so than either alone, make you especially likely to plagiarize? Or what if injunctive and descriptive norms are in disagreement: if most students think plagiarism is bad, but most do it anyway, how would this impact your behavior?

To tackle such questions, researchers gave students both injunctive and descriptive norm information regarding energy conservation (Smith and others, 2012). Specifically, the students learned that most other students (1) approved of and enacted energy conservation; (2) approved of, but did not enact, energy conservation; (3) disapproved of, but enacted, energy conservation; or (4) disapproved of, and did not enact, energy conservation. Only when both injunctive and descriptive norms were favorable—that is, when students approved of and enacted energy conservation—did participants report strong intentions to conserve energy themselves. This means that when injunctive and descriptive norms mismatched, behavioral intentions were as low as they were when there was no support from either type of norm. These findings, which held true with both British and Chinese students, thus suggest that endorsement of injunctive norms is more effective when it is seen as sincere rather than as mere lip service—that is, when norm endorsers also actually follow the norm. They also suggest that when people get information about just one type of norm, they assume that the other norm is in line—that's why providing people with just one type of norm typically changes behavior, as we have repeatedly seen. Only when a possible mismatch is made obvious is behavior undermined.

These findings shed light on how people respond to combinations of descriptive and injunctive norm information when they are fully motivated and able to do so. But we know that people do not always process information in depth, raising the possibility that different results occur when cognitive motivation and ability are taxed. Some researchers have suggested that using and following descriptive norms should be rather easy—one need only notice what others are doing—but that following injunctive norms might require more cognitive resources, as one has to think about the values and morals involved with an injunctive norm (Cialdini, 2003; Jacobson, Mortensen, & Cialdini, 2011). In a test of this idea, students learned about a potential health program on campus. Participants learned either that many students intended to sign up for it (the descriptive norm), or that many students favored the program and its goals (the injunctive norm). Participants' motivation and ability to engage in cognitive elaboration were also manipulated. In the high elaboration condition, students thought the program would be offered at their university within a year. In the low elaboration condition, students thought the program would be available at a different university, and they also had to hold an 8-digit number in their memory while reading the message. When students did not have much motivation or ability to think, they had stronger intentions to join the health program if presented with a supportive descriptive (rather than injunctive) norm (Kredentser, Fabrigar, Smith, & Fulton, 2012). This supports the idea that using descriptive norms may be cognitively easier. However, when students had the ability and motivation to think carefully, the injunctive norm information had stronger effects on their intentions to join the health program.

Thus, both descriptive and injunctive norms can guide behavior and these norms may sometimes interact with each other in interesting ways. Moreover, one type of normative information may be more important than another, depending on our motivation and ability to think carefully. So, it's clear that norms can be very effective. We next explain why this is so.

Perhaps you realized from these results that descriptive norms act as "action heuristics" just as attractiveness and expertise act as persuasion heuristics (described on pages 246–249 in Chapter 7), letting you know how to act or think without too much processing.

Why Norms Guide Behavior So Effectively

Norms are sometimes enforced by rewards and punishments. More often, however, people follow norms simply because they seem right. Following norms may also be in our genetic makeup.

Why do we resist the impulse to litter a clean environment, return a favor rather than profiting from someone's generosity, eat more fruit and vegetables because we learn others are doing so, or drink more alcohol because we imagine others are drinking more? Why does our behavior follow social norms at all?

Enforcement: Do It, Or Else. The most obvious reason is that groups sometimes use a carrot-and-stick approach—rewards and punishments—to motivate people to adhere to group standards. Norms are important, often vital, to the smooth functioning of

"What's wrong with you?"

groups, and groups take quite seriously their need to identify and stop norm violators. Indeed, even children as young as 3 years old appear to enforce norms (Schmidt & Tomasello, 2012), and people are better at detecting violations of social norms (which often have more serious social consequences) than they are at detecting violations of logic (Cosmides, 1989). You soon notice the colleague who never puts money into the office coffee fund while you dutifully pay for your daily mug of java.

Norm enforcement can occur through various means. Some groups handle norm violations by embodying their norms in legal statutes or moral canons: by specifying behaviors that are legitimate and those that are not. Societies take such action not only out of concern for any particular wronged individual but also to reinforce the importance of the norm to the group as a whole. And, as we saw in Chapter 9, groups often attempt to maintain conformity to social norms by withdrawing social acceptance and support from norm violators. Thus, we sometimes use subtle social behavioral signals to get people "back in line." For example, short silences in conversation following norm-violating statements make the violator uncomfortable and can put him or her back on the right normative track, especially if he or she really cares about belonging to the group (Koudenburg, Postmes, & Gordijn, 2013). Moreover, expressing disapproval of other's norm violations appears to be even more effective in encouraging long-lasting norm-consistent behavior than are financial punishments (Nelissen & Mulder, 2013). And, group members are also more likely to gossip about fellow group members if they violate a group norm (Beersma & Van Kleef, 2012). Bucking social convention can be both a lonely and a painful activity.

Private Acceptance: It's Right and Proper, So I Do It. Behavior usually matches norms for a much more powerful reason: Most norms are privately accepted, and they thus seem to be both the right thing and the proper thing to do. As we saw in Chapter 9, social norms are accepted because people accept group consensus as truly reflecting reality and expressing the kind of people they are. Acting in line with group norms is not an unpleasant obligation, but a way of maintaining a shared reality and expressing group identity. Most of the time, acting in line with group norms is the same as acting in line with one's own preferences. Typically, rules that benefit the group also benefit the

HOT TOPICS IN SOCIAL PSYCHOLOGY: IS FOLLOWING NORMS IN THE GENES?

Directives, environments, behavior, in-groups—we absorb these signals, learning over time what the relevant norms are and why we should follow them. There is little doubt that learning plays a role in acquiring a desire to follow norms. But because of their adaptive role in facilitating group living, humans may have evolved to give special attention to norms. Humans in our ancient past who followed norms would have been more likely to survive, and thus modern humans may be descendants of those norm-following relatives. Recent work offers some supportive evidence. In one set of studies, students in both the United States and the United Kingdom read about behaviors allegedly performed in an unfamiliar culture, whose norms they did not know and could not have previously learned. Part of the material was norm-related such as, "an unresolvable argument must be taken to the Ariki, as is dictated by custom." Other information did not describe norms. When the students' memory for the material was assessed, the norm-related information was better remembered than the norm-irrelevant information (O'Gorman, Wilson, & Miller, 2008). These researchers argue that these findings indicate an automatic readiness to perceive norm-relevant information, which may enable humans to pick up on norms and ultimately follow them. Other work suggests that people categorize others spontaneously as violators versus non-violators of moral norms, much as we spontaneously categorize others based on race, sex, and age. This again suggests that humans may come equipped with cognitive processes that facilitate the impact of norms (van Leeuwen, Park, & Penton-Voak, 2012).

individual, another reason that makes internalization of norms functional. The North American immigrant to England, for example, accepts with little resistance the norm that he must drive on the left side of the road to avoid injuring himself and others. Of course, the individual benefits of social rules are not always so immediately clear. Nevertheless, these norms—the norm of obedience, for example, or the norm of reciprocity—become deeply ingrained through the process of socialization as new group members absorb group norms as relevant to and benefiting the self (Bandura, 1977). Adhering to such norms not only feels like the right and proper thing to do, but also makes people feel respected by others whose opinions they value. In fact, surveillance can undermine compliance if people feel that doing the right and proper thing is just part of group membership—when people want to act in line with norms because they feel it's the right and proper thing to do, finding out that they are being watched as well undermines group identity and decreases conformity (O'Donnell, Jetten, & Ryan, 2010).

NORMS FOR MASTERY AND CONNECTEDNESS: RECIPROCITY AND COMMITMENT

Because the dual motives of mastering our environment and making close connections with others are so basic to human life, it is not surprising that two of the most powerful norms that guide behavior—the norm of reciprocity and the norm of commitment—facilitate these goals. Almost all societies endorse some form of these norms, because they benefit both individual group members and the group as a whole, and because they harness the power of group members to get things done, while drawing them closer together.

The Norm of Reciprocity

Reciprocity, one of the most prevalent social norms, directs us to return to others favors, goods, services, and concessions they offer to us. This norm can sometimes be activated to our disadvantage.

Winnie the Pooh, hero of the much-loved British children's stories, gently instructs one of his fellow inhabitants of the Hundred Acre Wood: "When someone does something nice for you, you're supposed to do something nice for them in return. That's called friendship." Actually, it's called the norm of reciprocity. The **norm of reciprocity** directs us to return to others the goods, services, and concessions they offer to us. According to the sociologist Alvin Gouldner (1960), this norm is nearly universal, and only a few members of society—the very young, the sick, or the old—are exempt from it. And for good reason. The exchange of benefits spreads resources more generally throughout a group, and any resources shared in good times will be returned by others when times are lean. At the same time, adherence to the norm of reciprocity builds trust, strengthening the bonds that hold the group together.

norm of reciprocity
the shared view that people are obligated to return to others the goods, services, and concessions they offer to us

Returning Favors. The offer of some valued resource triggers the norm of reciprocity, which directs us to give something in return. This means we are obliged to return gifts, favors, and compliments, even if they are unsolicited (H. Wilke & Lanzetta, 1970, 1982). Consider the power of a small, unsolicited favor to increase giving, as demonstrated by one laboratory study (D. T. Regan, 1971). As each male participant settled to his supposed task of making aesthetic judgments, he was joined by a confederate who was trained to be either particularly friendly or rather rude. In one condition, the confederate returned from a break with two bottles of cola and offered one to the participant; in another condition he returned empty-handed. The confederate later asked the participants to purchase some 25-cent raffle tickets. As you can see from Figure 10.3, participants bought the most raffle tickets when the confederate had done them an unsolicited favor, even though at the time a bottle of cola cost much less than the 25-cent ticket. Notice also that the norm of reciprocity was so strong that it prevailed even when the confederate was unlikable. In fact, the power of the norm of reciprocity is so great that people even feel compelled to return the favors of a stranger who has been forced to help them out (Goranson & Berkowitz, 1966).

Salespeople, market managers, and survey researchers are well aware of the power of unsolicited gifts. When was the last time you received a free sample of a product in the mail, were offered a free aerobics session at a newly opened health club, or were sent an online coupon code as an incentive to fill out a long questionnaire? These techniques activate the feeling that you should do something in return: buy the product, enroll at the health club, or complete and return the questionnaire. And the technique seems to work. Door-to-door sales increase when households receive products to try for a day or two without charge. When a salesperson eventually follows up with a call, customers typically buy as many as half the products they have sampled (Cialdini, 1984). The vacuum cleaner buying Taylors, described at the beginning of this chapter, felt obligated because the salesperson had shampooed their rug for free.

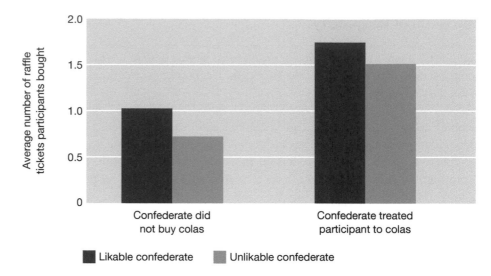

Figure 10.3 Banking on the norm of reciprocity
In this experiment, some participants were treated to a bottle of cola by a likable or an unlikable confederate. Later, the confederate tried to sell participants raffle tickets. Participants who had received the unsolicited favor from the confederate bought more raffle tickets, even though they cost more than the drinks. They honored the norm of reciprocity—returning favors, goods, and services that others offered them—even when they did not like the confederate much. As these results show, honoring the norm of reciprocity can sometimes lead to returning a favor more valuable than the one received. (Data from D. T. Regan, 1971.)

Photo 10.2 The norm of reciprocity. A worker offers customers samples of food. Offering free samples serves to increase sales, as people then feel obligated to buy the product.

What happens once you have "repaid" a favor done for you? Once you have reciprocated, that should let you off the hook for future requests from the favor giver, right? Perhaps not. Consider what happened when students were placed into one of four different groups: (1) they exchanged favors with a confederate; (2) the confederate did a favor for them, but they did not reciprocate; (3) they did a favor for the confederate, but the confederate did not reciprocate; or (4) no favors were done, which served as the control condition (Burger, Ehrlichman, Raymond, Ishikawa, & Sandoval, 2006). At the end of the study, the confederate asked the participants if they would mind reading and providing feedback on an essay. In the control condition and when only the participant had performed an earlier favor, agreement rates were fairly low. Not surprisingly, when the confederate had done the participant a favor earlier, agreement rates were very high, reflecting basic reciprocity. Perhaps most interestingly, when favors had been previously exchanged, agreement rates were again very high, just as high as when only the confederate had earlier performed the favor! Thus, even after paying back a favor, a situation in which no further need for reciprocation would seem warranted, participants were very likely to agree to another request from the confederate. This further underscores the power of reciprocity.

Reciprocating Concessions: The Door-in-the-Face Technique.

Concessions are also supposed to be reciprocated. This can leave us vulnerable to a common ploy called the **door-in-the-face technique**, which consists of making a large request and following its refusal with a concession that invokes the norm of reciprocity (Cialdini and others, 1975). The ploy gets its name from the fact that the requester wants the door to be slammed so that he or she can retreat from the initial request. In fact, the first request is always for something much greater than requesters actually want, leaving room for them to back down, thereby putting pressure on the other person to reciprocate with a concession.

door-in-the-face technique
a technique in which the influencer makes an initial request so large that it will be rejected, and follows it with a smaller request that looks like a concession, making it more likely that the other person will concede in turn

The door-in-the-face technique is extremely effective (Pascual & Gueguen, 2005). In one investigation of the technique, researchers asked two groups of students to volunteer for a worthy cause (Cialdini and others, 1975). The researchers approached some students as they walked across campus and asked if they would be willing to accompany a group of teenage delinquents on a 2-hour trip to the local zoo. Not surprisingly, the idea of spending several hours with an unspecified number of potentially uncooperative teenagers had little appeal, and only 17% agreed. Other students were first asked to spend 2 years serving as personal counselors to juvenile delinquents. When all refused this long-term commitment, the request was downgraded to the 2-hour zoo trip. This technique induced 51% of the participants to agree—more than three times the number in the control group. The door-in-the-face technique is also effective in getting young children to complete school work (Chan & Au, 2011). Second graders in an afterschool program in Hong Kong were asked first to do 100 math problems, a large request. After refusing, they were then asked if they would do 20 problems instead. Ninety percent of them agreed, compared to only 35% of students who were simply asked to do the 20 problems.

The door-in-the-face technique will activate the norm of reciprocity when three conditions exist (Cialdini and others, 1975). First, the initial request must be large enough that it is sure to be refused but not so large that it will breed resentment or suspicion.

Second, the target must be given the chance to compromise by refusing the initial request and complying with the second request. Finally, the second request must be related to the first request and come from the same person, who must be seen as making a personal concession (O'Keefe & Hale, 2001).

Once it is clear that the requester has made a concession, the target is on the spot, and acting in accordance with the norm is the most likely outcome. The sense that the other person is really giving something up makes the target of the request feel guilty—am I acting appropriately? Am I creating a negative impression? How can I make up for it? (Millar, 2002a; O'Keefe & Figgé, 1999). Agreeing to the second request gives the target an opportunity to repair a damaged sense of self (Millar, 2002b; Pendleton & Bateson, 1979). Perhaps this is why people who comply with the door-in-the-face technique are more likely to carry out the agreed-on behaviors than are those who make the same commitment without refusing a prior request. In one study in which the commitment involved 2 hours of work without pay in a community mental health agency, 85% of those in the door-in-the-face group actually reported for duty, compared with only 50% of the volunteers from the control group (R. L. Miller, Seligman, Clark, & Bush, 1976). Once again, privately accepted norms have a powerful effect on actual behavior.

The Norm of Social Commitment

The norm of social commitment encourages people to stand by their agreements and fulfill their obligations. Like the norm of reciprocity, it can be used by others to one's disadvantage.

---

norm of social commitment
the shared view that people are required to honor their agreements and obligations

"You're only as good as your word." "Don't make promises you cannot keep." "Put your money where your mouth is." These nuggets of folk wisdom reflect a key component of social life: the **norm of social commitment**. This norm requires us to stand by our agreements and fulfill our obligations. If your friend agrees to save your seat while you buy popcorn, she is obligated to protect it from encroachment. If you agree to subscribe to the Sunday paper, you must pay the delivery person when he or she comes to collect.

One study demonstrated the lengths to which people will go to maintain a commitment (Moriarty, 1975). The scene was a crowded New York beach. In one condition, the researcher made an explicit social contract with neighboring sunbathers: He asked them to keep an eye on his radio while he was away for a short time. In the control condition, the researcher only interacted socially with his neighbors; he asked them for the time before leaving. A few minutes later, a confederate pretended to steal the radio. Did the norm of social commitment affect behavior? Indeed it did. Ninety-five percent of the people who agreed to watch the radio tried to stop the thief, with some even running after the thief to retrieve it. In contrast, only 20% of the uncommitted bystanders bothered to intervene. In a replication of the study, a pocketbook was left for a few minutes in a booth at a fast-food restaurant, with similar results. The bystanders who helped were those who had made a prior commitment to do so.

The norm of social commitment is as important and near universal as the norm of reciprocity, and for the same reasons. Social contracts help ensure that members of a group or society play their part when coordinated behavior is required to achieve goals, and thus allow groups and societies to function effectively. At the same time, because social commitment is all about trust—the value of one's reputation—adherence to the norm also binds group members together.

The Low-Ball Technique. Our tendency to honor interpersonal commitments, and the corresponding expectation that others will honor their commitments to us, are so ingrained that we stand by agreements even when the deal has changed to our disadvantage. Imagine the following scenario. An acquaintance asks if you will help her move her few belongings to a small apartment in your neighborhood on Saturday morning. You agree, but when you turn up, you find that she has a new plan. She is now moving into a house with one of her friends in a new location across town, so each trip will take about 2 hours. And the deal seems to include collecting her friend's belongings and helping her move in as well. Suddenly, a couple of hours work on a Saturday morning has turned into a mammoth moving experience that will probably take all day. You have been low-balled. The **low-ball technique** is used when an influencer secures an agreement with a request but then increases the size of that request by revealing hidden costs. How would you respond in such a situation?

low-ball technique
a technique in which the influencer secures agreement with a request but then increases the cost of honoring the commitment

If the findings of social-psychological research are any indication, you would probably spend the day helping your acquaintance move. In one study demonstrating the low-ball technique, experimenters phoned students and asked them to participate in an experiment for extra credit. Some students were told the bad news up front: The experiment was to start at 7 a.m. Knowing that, only 31% were willing to participate. Other students were low-balled: They were first asked to make a commitment to participate, and those who agreed were then told about the early starting time. Yet, 56% of these students agreed to participate, a significantly higher percentage than in the other group. Having made a deal, the students were reluctant to break the commitment, even though the deal had changed (Cialdini, Cacioppo, Bassett, & Miller, 1978). When people agreed with a complete stranger's request to look after a dog on a leash, most of them honored their commitment—even when they were later told that the owner would be away for over half an hour (Guéguen, Pascual, & Dagot, 2002)!

The norms of reciprocity and social commitment can sometimes be used to our detriment, pushing us to buy things we don't need or want, to spend more money than we should, to do favors that pose a burden on us, and to make decisions that are outright foolish. Yet, despite this, following these norms gives us tremendous benefits overall. People who reciprocate and keep their social commitments make cooperation and coordinated behavior in groups possible, increasing everyone's ability to master their environment. At the same time, they are the basis of positive social reputation, fostering social connectedness. Thus, without such norms, people might never help one another or develop close relationships. And, as you will see later, we can protect ourselves against misuse of these norms and can, at least sometimes, simply enjoy the positive benefits they offer.

SOCIAL PSYCHOLOGY AND CULTURE: NORM-CONSISTENT BEHAVIOR ACROSS CULTURES

Although norms of reciprocity and social commitment are important in all cultures, they appear to have even stronger effects in collectivist cultures (Boer & Fischer, 2013; Triandis, 1994; Vauclair & Fischer, 2011). Usually this means that members of such cultures bring their behavior closely in line with social norms. For example, members of collectivist cultures are more sensitive to the norm of reciprocity, and are therefore more likely to reciprocate a gift or favor from an acquaintance than their individualist counterparts (Shen, Wan, & Wyer, 2011; Singelis, 1994). Similarly, the norm of social commitment may be stronger in collectivist cultures. One study, for example, found that participants in India regarded social commitment as a moral imperative rather than a choice. U.S. participants were more likely to think that the norm could be avoided, unless it involved life-threatening need or immediate family (J. G. Miller, Bersoff, & Harwood, 1997).

This extra sensitivity to group norms may lead to some unexpected behavior. In a situation where reciprocity may be expected, members of collectivist cultures sometimes seek to avoid the pressure to return a favor by avoiding receiving the favor in the first place. Thus, Chinese people are more likely to refuse offers or gifts than are people from Canada and the United States (Shen, Wan, & Wyer, 2011). These researchers argue that those from collectivist cultures, like China, may be more aware of their social connections to others and thus more likely to consider, in advance, the possibility that receiving a gift might obligate them to reciprocate. In one study, students from Hong Kong and Canada imagined that they were offered a sample of free food in a grocery store. They were asked the likelihood they would sample the food, how much appreciation they felt for the offer, and how much they would feel indebted if they accepted it. The students from Hong Kong were less likely to agree to taste the free food than the students from Canada, due to their greater feelings of indebtedness and lower levels of appreciation. Follow-up experiments replicated these findings conceptually and underscored the role of reciprocity in these effects. In another study, Asian and Canadian students were approached around campus before a holiday and offered some free candy. Next, the researcher asked if the person would fill out a survey. Asian students accepted less candy than did the Canadian students. Moreover, willingness to complete the survey was related to how much candy the student had accepted, but only for the Asian students and not the Canadians. Thus, it seems that those from collectivist cultures experience the norm of reciprocity as stronger than those from more individualist cultures, to the point that they sometimes avoid even putting themselves in situations in which it applies.

THE NORM OF OBEDIENCE: SUBMITTING TO AUTHORITY

For millions of people around the world, the war-crimes trial of Adolf Eichmann raised deep questions about human nature (Arendt, 1965). As one of Hitler's top officials during the Second World War, Eichmann sent millions of European Jews, Gypsies, homosexuals, Communists, mental patients, and Christian Scientists to their deaths in Nazi concentration camps. To his Israeli captors and to the worldwide audience, Eichmann's behavior seemed incomprehensibly evil. Yet, like countless people who have slaughtered others in the line of "duty" before and since, Eichmann appeared quite normal, even boring. He described himself as a good family man who had lived quite blamelessly before the rise of the Nazi regime. He said he had nothing in particular against the Jews. Over and over again, he claimed he was "just following orders." Eichmann's defense did not save his life: He was found guilty and hanged for crimes against the Jewish people and humanity. But genocidal policies are still with us today, and so the questions about human nature raised by Eichmann's actions and his trial still linger. Is torture or murder something that any of us might do on command?

Among those fascinated by the trial was the North American social psychologist Stanley Milgram. A firm believer in cultural differences, Milgram doubted that behavior like Eichmann's could occur in cultures where rugged individualism and independence were valued. He believed that members of such cultures would resist group pressure to obey orders that would involve hurting someone. Once he had finalized the procedures for a control condition—a situation in which participants were merely instructed to harm another without any group pressure to do so—Milgram planned to test his hypotheses about conformity and obedience in many different countries. But the startling responses of participants in this control condition put Milgram's plans on hold. Understanding when and why people obeyed authority, even if doing so harmed others, became Milgram's main concern, and his findings became perhaps the best known and most controversial in social psychology.

Milgram's Studies of Obedience

In one of the best-known experiments in psychology, people obeyed orders to deliver shocks to an unwilling and clearly suffering victim. They obeyed these orders even though they were not forced to do so.

Using advertisements in a New Haven, Connecticut, newspaper, Milgram recruited men from all walks of life to participate in his experiment in return for a small payment. When each volunteer arrived in the laboratory on the Yale University campus, he was introduced to a middle-aged man, a confederate pretending to be another participant. The experimenter explained that the study concerned the effects of punishment on learning, and that one of the participants would serve as teacher and the other as the learner for the session. A rigged draw assigned the real participant to the role of teacher. His job was to teach the pupil word pairs and to punish any incorrect response by delivering an electric shock to the pupil's wrist. As the teacher watched, the pupil was strapped without protest into a chair in an adjoining room and electrodes were taped to his wrist. To "test the equipment," the experimenter gave the teacher a low-voltage shock, enabling him to experience the small, mildly unpleasant feeling that the learner would be subjected to in the early stages of the experiment.

Back in the experimental room, the experimenter explained the operation of the equipment. To deliver a shock, the teacher merely had to flick one of the switches on the shock generator. There were 30 switches, in 15-volt increments ranging from 15 volts (labeled "slight shock") to 450 volts (ominously marked only with XXX). The teacher was to start with the lowest level of shock and move to the next higher level with each mistake. The shocks may be "painful," the experimenter said, "but do not cause permanent tissue damage." The experimenter stood beside the teacher as the experiment began.

The pupil's initial mistakes were met with only low levels of shock. But as incorrect responses mounted, so did the voltage. Soon, grunts of pain came from the pupil's room, but he continued trying to learn the word pairs. At this stage, the teachers typically showed visible signs of distress and tried to stop the experiment. But the experimenter

Photo 10.3a The victim in Milgram's experiment. In a simple experiment with powerful implications, Stanley Milgram studied obedience by asking participants acting as "teachers" to deliver electric shocks to a "learner," shown here being fitted with electrodes and strapped into a chair. The results of the experiment demonstrated the often startling power of widely accepted social norms on behavior.

Photo 10.3b Obedience rules.
Even when the learner's pain and distress were obvious, teachers often went along with the experimenter's implacable demands that they continue giving shocks. Why did so many people obey?

was unrelenting, repeating that the teacher must continue. Finally, at the 300-volt level, the learner pounded on the wall in protest and refused to answer further questions. Most teachers sighed with relief at this point, believing the experiment was over. Instead, the experimenter announced that silence was to be considered an incorrect answer and punished. Teachers' protests were met with the response: "The experiment requires that you continue." As the shocks increased and the learner pounded ever more feebly on the wall, the experimenter urged the teacher onward, saying, "You have no choice, you must go on." Finally, even the pounding stopped. Anguished teachers typically raised the possibility of injury, but the experimenter never wavered, insisting, "The responsibility is mine. Please continue."

As is now widely known, most of the participants did continue. In one study, 65% of them delivered shocks all the way to the 450-volt level (Milgram, 1963). Far from demonstrating that ordinary people would resist the dictates of authority, the experiment showed the opposite. The results astounded scientists and nonscientists alike. When Milgram described his experimental procedure to middle-class adults, college students, and psychiatrists, most guessed that only a few people in a thousand would obey the experimenter to the end. Yet more than two-thirds of the participants agreed to perform actions they found repulsive.

Attempting to Explain Obedience

The destructive obedience of Milgram's participants was not due to hard-hearted unconcern about the victim or suspicion that the experiment was rigged. In fact, obedience in nonexperimental settings can be just as high, and authorities command as much obedience in recent studies as they did 50 years ago in Milgram's experiments.

Why did so many people obey? Were Milgram's participants particularly heartless and uncaring individuals? Could they have seen through the deception and realized that no shocks were actually delivered? These explanations seem implausible in the face of the reactions of the participants themselves. Milgram's teachers experienced extraordinary distress as the experiment progressed. They trembled, pleaded to be allowed to stop, muttered to themselves, stuttered when they spoke, laughed nervously, dug their nails into their flesh, and offered to take the learner's place. Clearly, not only did they fully believe that the shocks were real, but they also cared deeply about the learner's suffering. In fact, the potential harm to the hapless participants in Milgram's experiments attracted severe ethical criticism when the results were published (Baumrind, 1964).

The ethical complexities of Milgram's experiment, and the ethical guidelines that were instituted by social psychologists in response to it, were discussed in detail in Chapter 2, pages 48–49.

The fact that Milgram's participants felt so badly about the punishments they believed they were inflicting makes it unlikely that they obeyed because they were cruel or heartless. And obedience is not limited to adult men in the U.S. Milgram's procedure has been replicated in several different countries with women as well as men, and children as well as adults, in the role of teacher (Askenasy, 1978; Blass, 2000; V. L. Hamilton & Sanders, 1992, 1995; Meeus & Raaijmakers, 1986; Shanab & Yahra, 1977). A recent meta-analysis concluded that obedience rates in U.S. studies do not differ significantly from the average of non-U.S. countries, which included Italy, South Africa, Germany, Jordan, India, and Austria (Blass, 2012).

SOCIAL PSYCHOLOGY IN PRACTICE: OBEDIENCE IN ORGANIZATIONS

If high levels of obedience cannot be attributed to the participants' character, might the results of the original studies be a consequence of the nature of the experimental setting itself? Perhaps people who feel that obedience is appropriate in a protected laboratory environment would never dream of carrying out harmful orders in settings outside the laboratory. Unfortunately, obedience to authority occurs in many other settings. In most medical settings, unquestioning obedience to the physician is the normal state of affairs. No one overrules the doctor—not the patient, not nurses, and not interns. What happens, then, when doctors make mistakes? Does anyone question them?

To find out, researchers looked at nurses' responses when a "doctor" gave an unreasonable order (Hofling, Brotzman, Dalrymple, Graves, & Pierce, 1966). A researcher posing as a doctor phoned 22 different nurses' stations at different hospitals, identifying himself as a physician at the hospital. He instructed the nurse, who was alone at the station, to deliver 20 milligrams of the drug Astrogen to a specific patient. Such an instruction violated hospital policy in several ways. Prescriptions were supposed to be given in person, not over the phone. The drug had not been cleared for use on the particular ward. The requested dosage was twice the maximum listed on the container. Finally, the "doctor" giving the order was unknown to the nurse. Despite all these red flags, all but one of the nurses immediately prepared to obey. The norm of obedience overpowered their considerable medical training. In a 1995 study, 46 % of nurses reported having complied with an order from a doctor that they thought would harm the patient (Krackow & Blass, 1995).

As our chapter-opening example of obedience at fast food restaurants makes clear, hospitals are not the only other settings in which obedience is the norm. In fact, many recent studies indicate that "organizational obedience"— obedience that occurs in hierarchical bureaucratic organizations—may occur at even higher levels than suggested by Milgram's studies. In one study, for example, North American business students derogated the credentials of qualified African-American job applicants and recommended against interviewing them, if given "instructions from the company's president" that favored giving the job to a White American (Brief, Dietz, Cohen, Pugh, & Vaslow, 2000).

Another study with Dutch undergraduate students was designed to determine if people will engage in "whistle blowing," alerting a regulatory body about improper behavior. Participants arrived at the lab and were asked to give the researcher the names of some fellow students. Participants were then told that the researcher had previously conducted a study in another country on the effects of sensory deprivation, with very aversive effects on the participants (Bocchiaro, Zimbardo, & Van Lange, 2012). The researcher asked the current participants to write a letter to the students they had named earlier, urging them to take part in a replication of the sensory deprivation study, praising it as an exciting experience, and avoiding any mention of its negative effects. The results were dramatic. Seventy-six percent of students obeyed, and wrote the letter as instructed. Moreover, only about 10 % "blew the whistle" when they had the opportunity to do so by dropping a form anonymously into a box to alert the research ethics committee about concerns with the sensory deprivation study. Thus, despite the researcher's apparent dubious actions, students largely seemed unwilling to alert university authorities to his questionable tactics.

Might the high level of obedience be due to something about the particular historic era? Most of the Milgram studies and their replications took place in the 1960s and 1970s. But Jerry Burger (2009) recently conducted a replication of the Milgram experiment, with modifications to comply with current ethical requirements. In his sample of men and women 70% obeyed past the 150-volt level, including 67% of the men. These rates are slightly lower than the 80% of Milgram's male participants who went to that level, but are still startlingly high.

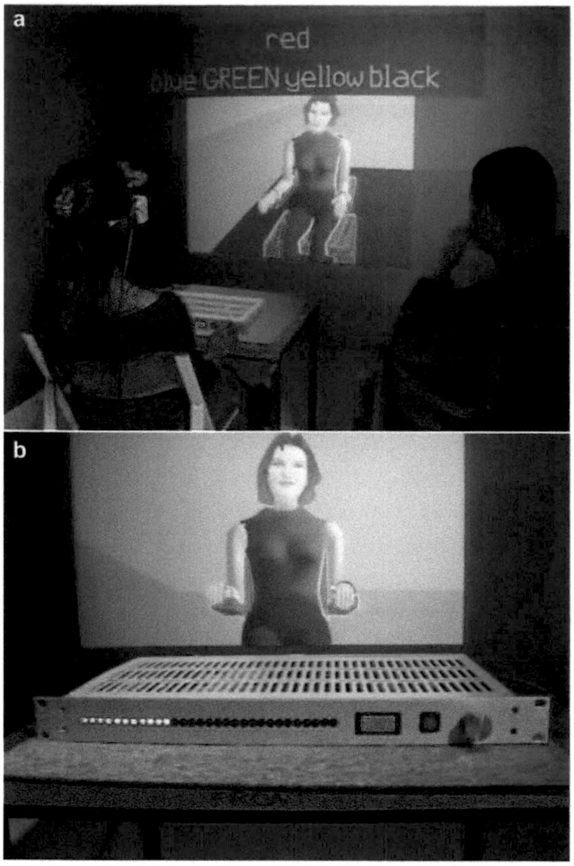

Photo 10.4 Obedience in virtual reality. In these images, you see the experimental setup of the virtual obedience study conducted by Slater and colleagues (2006). In the top image, the participant, shown on the left, observes the virtual learner who appears as if through a window. On this trial, the participant reads 5 words: "red" (the cue word), followed by "blue," "green," "yellow," and "black" (the possible associated words). The virtual learner is instructed to give the correct associated word ("Green," shown in capital letters), which the virtual learner supposedly had a chance to memorize earlier. If the learner gives the wrong answer, the participant is ordered to give her a shock, using the machine shown in the bottom image.

Thus, when authority figures ask us to do improper things, most of us go along. Even when there is an anonymous and easy way to tell on them, we often do not. These findings again show that obedience to authority is just as likely today as it was 50 years ago; people were not just more obedient back then. All in all, the research record indicates that obedience to authority can occur regardless of participant, culture, setting, or time: Milgram's results cannot be explained away by the time, the place, or the people involved (Blass, 2000).

HOT TOPICS IN SOCIAL PSYCHOLOGY: OBEDIENCE IN VIRTUAL REALITY

Advances in technology since the Milgram days have opened up new ways to study obedience that minimize, to some degree, the ethical concerns regarding the original work. These advances, therefore, may allow for new and exciting opportunities for research exploration in this area. One study has used virtual reality, attempting to replicate the original Milgram study with a virtual character as the learner. Participants in the "visible" condition could see and hear the virtual character react painfully to the shocks, while those in the "hidden" condition could neither see nor hear the virtual character during the shocks. In the "hidden" condition, 100% of participants gave the highest shock, and in the "visible" condition, nearly 75% did the same (Slater and others, 2006). Physiological measures during the study indicated that in the visible condition, participants reacted to the situation as if it were completely real. A subsequent study used a similar procedure with participants in an fMRI machine. Even though the learner was virtual, and thus suffered no real pain, scans of participants' brains revealed activity consistent with personal distress when viewing the avatar apparently in pain (Cheetham, Pedroni, Antley, Slater, & Jancke, 2009). These virtual reality results add further support to the notion that rates of obedience today are still high, but also support the conclusion discussed earlier that these participants are not heartless. They clearly show signs of distress, even when the pain they inflict isn't real.

The Norm of Obedience to Authority

The norm of obedience to authority had a powerful effect on behavior in Milgram's experiment and has a similar effect on behavior outside the lab. Authorities must be legitimate and accept responsibility. Both in Milgram's studies and in everyday situations, conditions that increase the accessibility of the obedience norm or decrease attention to other norms increase obedience. Because legitimacy of authority derives from the group, people who identify more with the authority or the group the authority represents are more likely to follow the authority's directives. Once obedience occurs, it can be maintained or escalated by gradual entrapment and the impact of justification processes.

If none of these factors (character, culture, or time) can explain the obedience Milgram found, what does? When he observed participants' responses to the systematic manipulation of various features of the experimental procedure, Milgram became convinced that the explanation lay in the power of the social situation to activate a norm of obedience (Milgram, 1963, 1974). The **norm of obedience to authority** is the shared view that people should obey commands given by a person with legitimate authority. "Legitimate" and "authority" are important parts of this definition. Legitimacy derives from the group: The group endows the authority figure with the might and right to give orders, and the group assigns to its members the responsibility of obeying. Authority derives from status, not from any particular person. When a soldier salutes an officer in the army, for example, he or she is saluting the senior officer's rank, a gesture symbolizing the authority the officer holds over the ordinary soldier.

> **norm of obedience to authority** the shared view that people should obey those with legitimate authority

Obedience to authority is sometimes enforced, as when military courts stand ready to enforce obedience to authoritative orders. Most often, however, obedience is motivated by private feelings that legitimate authority should be obeyed. This seemed to be the case in Milgram's experiment. The experimenter represented legitimate authority: participants believed the experimenter had the legitimate right to tell them what to do and that they had an equal duty to obey him. Other norms that supported the norm of authority were brought into play; norms incompatible with obedience were excluded. The end result was overwhelming obedience. Let's see how the activation of the norm of legitimate authority can lead to obedience in Milgram's laboratory and beyond.

Authority Must Be Legitimate. When news reports stated that employees of Wendy's fast food restaurants had flooded their own workplace with foam and been injured breaking windows on the orders of someone posing as corporate management, many people wondered how those carrying out the orders could have been so gullible. But the employees thought they were dutifully and appropriately following orders of someone—a boss—who had the right to give orders. People don't obey just anyone who tells them to do something. To achieve obedience, an authority must convey that he or she is the person who should be obeyed. Although the Wendy's caller was apparently convincing over the phone, a person's physical presence usually gives lots of cues to authority. Larissa Tiedens and her colleagues (Tiedens, 2001; Tiedens & Fragale, 2003) have demonstrated that facial expression, tone of voice, posture, and emotional expression can all convey status and power. Height and spatial superiority also convey power, so tall people and people occupying higher ground are seen as having power—no wonder that leaders of groups are often placed up high on thrones and referred to as "Your Highness" for example (Schubert, 2005). When people send the right authority signals, other people see them as having legitimate authority and are much more likely to fall into line with their commands.

An especially obvious cue to authority is a uniform. The lab-coat-wearing experimenter in Milgram's experiments was seen, then and now, as embodying a combination of legitimate authority and scientific expertise—someone with the right to give orders in the experimental setting. Police officers, firefighters, and paramedics wear uniforms and badges, which are usually enough to activate the norm of obedience to authority. In one experiment demonstrating the power of a uniform, a stranger—actually an experimental confederate—asked passersby on a busy city street to comply with an unusual request, for example, to pick up garbage or move to the other side of a bus-stop sign (Bickman, 1974). Half the time, the stranger wore ordinary clothes; the rest of the time he wore a security guard's uniform. Clothes made the authority figure: Many more people did his bidding when he was dressed in a uniform than when he wore street clothes. More recent work with children shows the power—and the danger—that uniforms, and the authority that comes with them, can cause. Nine- and 10-year-olds saw a staged crime and were later asked by a uniformed or non-uniformed person to pick the perpetrator out of a lineup if they thought he was there. Children picked out a perpetrator more often in the uniform condition. Perhaps more frighteningly, when the real perpetrator was not in the lineup, children were more likely to pick an innocent man in the uniform condition as well (Lowenstein, Blank, & Sauer, 2010).

Authority Must Accept Responsibility. Recall that when some of the "teachers" in Milgram's experiments had qualms about continuing, the experimenter reminded them that he took full responsibility, and this was often enough to maintain obedience. When all responsibility is ceded to the authority, people enter what Milgram called the agentic state: They see themselves as merely the agent of the authority figure. When this displacement of responsibility occurs, people don't think of themselves as agents of their own action, and thus, other attitudes, norms, or values that might usually guide their behavior are not consulted (Bandura, Barbaranelli, Caprara, & Pastorelli, 1996). Responsibility can sometimes be diffused as well, as when authorities divide reprehensible behavior into small subtasks, each of which may be performed by a different person and each of which may in and of itself seem harmless (Kelman, 1973). In fact, when Milgram ran a variant of his study in which another person actually delivered the shocks and the participant only had to administer the learning, fully 83% of the participants carried out their orders to the letter. When responsibility is displaced or diffused, people ignore the possibility that they could or should control their own behavior. In fact, the assumption of responsibility is crucial to the power of the authority figure. Both people who obey and observers who view obedient subordinates attribute responsibility for obedience to the authority figure (V. L. Hamilton & Sanders, 1995; Meeus & Raaijmakers, 1995). Indeed, during the debriefing of Burger's (2009) Milgram replication, participants who had refused to obey were more likely to make statements about personal responsibility compared to those who had been fully obedient (Burger, Girgis, & Manning, 2011).

The Norm of Obedience Must Be Activated. In one experiment, Milgram had a confederate posing as a participant deliver the instructions to obey. With no legitimate authority present, the results were dramatically different from those in the original experiment. Teachers ignored the confederate and refused to deliver the shocks. When the confederate tried to deliver the shocks himself, the teachers protested vigorously. Some went so far as to unplug the shock generator so it could not be used. Thus, without a legitimate authority, no norm of obedience was activated. Of course the authority figure does not need to be physically present for the norm to be accessible—merely thinking about the authority figure would probably be enough. However, as can be seen in Figure 10.4, the more obvious the authority figure in Milgram's experiments, the more likely the norm is to be accessible, and the more likely people are to obey. The presence of the experimenter kept participants focused exclusively on the norm of legitimate authority even when some of them questioned what was happening. His prompts—"You must continue," "The experiment requires that you continue," "You have no choice"—made obedience seem an appropriate response to the situation. His calm confidence in the face of both the teacher's indecision and the learner's apparent suffering further reinforced the idea that obedience was typical, normal, and expected behavior. With the norm of authority fully, forcefully, and repeatedly activated, most participants fell into line, following the experimenter's directions.

Of course other norms must have been activated in the situation as well. The participants were clearly distressed by the apparent suffering of the learner consistent with in-group norms that require us to help, care for, cooperate with, and have compassion for others like us. In fact, Milgram deliberately provoked a conflict between norms when, for example, he had the pupil cry out and bang on the wall in distress. Bringing the suffering learner up close and personal made norms that conflict with the

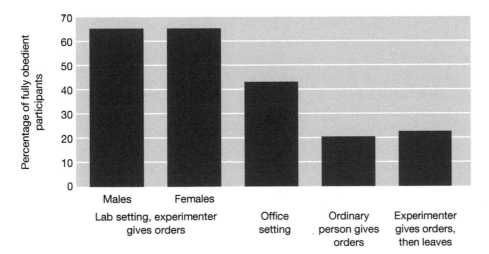

Figure 10.4 Conditions for obedience
By changing experimental conditions to make the norm of obedience more or less accessible, Milgram showed the power of the norm on behavior. In the laboratory, in the presence of the authoritative experimenter, fully 65% of men and women followed his orders. But in conditions that reduced the salience of the norm—such as a less "official" location, or a nonlegitimate authority giving orders, or the absence of any authority figure—obedience was reduced. (Data from Milgram, 1974.)

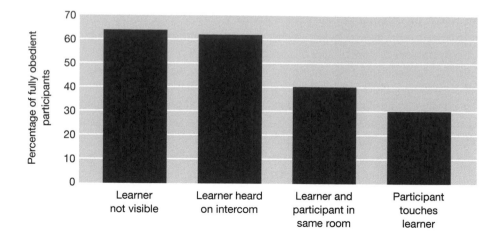

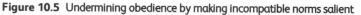

Figure 10.5 Undermining obedience by making incompatible norms salient
The norm governing obedience to legitimate authority held tremendous sway in Milgram's experimental situation. But it was not the only norm brought into play in the situation. When experimental variations focused participants' attention on the suffering of the learner, norms that dictate the good treatment of other in-group members became salient, reducing the level of obedience. (Data from Milgram, 1974.)

norm of obedience even more accessible, and as the balance tipped from one norm to another, so too did obedience decline (see Figure 10.5). When the learner and the teacher were in the same room, only 40% of participants obeyed. As Milgram gradually brought teacher and pupil closer together, the pupil's suffering became less avoidable and obedience decreased. Milgram's experiment mimicked life: It is easier to drop a bomb from a plane than to kill a person with a bayonet, and it is easier to shuffle papers decreeing a death than to actually torture or kill someone (Bandura, Barbaranelli, Caprara, & Pastorelli, 1996; Silver & Geller, 1978). The same Eichmann who sat in his office dispassionately consigning people to their deaths, reportedly was sickened when he was actually forced to tour the concentration camps.

You may see the similarity here to the processes of moral exclusion described in Chapter 6, pages 209–211. In the context of extreme intergroup hatred, groups dehumanize out-groups so that norm that govern cooperation, compassion, and caring don't apply to them, justifying acts of savagery, repression, and brutality.

Physically distancing oneself is not the only way to suppress other norms that are incompatible with obedience—psychologically distancing the victim works too. Blaming the victim means that people come to believe that those being hurt somehow deserve to be punished. The tendency to blame victims stems from a widely held belief in a "just world," the idea that the universe is a just and orderly place where people "get what they deserve" (Lerner, 1980). Such beliefs prompt thoughts that victims must in some way have "asked for trouble," provoked it, or brought it on themselves (Hafer & Begue, 2005; Lerner & Miller, 1978). Of course, such beliefs are meant to protect the perpetrator, and the tendency to blame the victim is strongest when we ourselves are the instrument of another person's pain. Indeed, Milgram (1974) reported that many of his participants, after delivering the maximum amount of shock, cruelly criticized the pupil with comments like "He was so stupid and stubborn, he deserved to get shocked." As Milgram noted, "Once having acted against the victim, these subjects found it necessary to view him as an unworthy individual whose punishment was made inevitable by his own deficiencies of intellect and character" (p. 10). Blaming the victim may be the most potentially dangerous consequence of obeying commands that hurt others.

As it occurs, the target—once an innocent victim harmed only reluctantly—becomes a person deserving of abuse.

Social Identification and Obedience. As we noted above, legitimacy of authority derives from the group: the right of the authority to command and the responsibility of others to obey is part of the group norm. It stands to reason then, as we have seen so many times before, that people who care more about the group are more likely to follow group norms. Thus people who identify more with the authority or the group the authority represents might be more likely to follow the authority's directives (Haslam & Reicher, 2012a; Reicher, Haslam, & Smith, 2012).

To test these ideas, Reicher and colleagues (2012) had raters read about several different versions of Milgram's experiments. For each version, they judged the degree to which the situation would encourage participants to identify with either the experimenter and the scientific community, or with the learner or the general community. The researchers then examined how these judgments related to rates of obedience in those studies. The results were clear: As perceived identification with the experimenter and scientific community increased, rates of obedience also increased, but as perceived identification with the learner and the general community increased, obedience decreased.

The power of identification with the authority may also help explain a set of recent findings showing that "being in sync" with an authority can increase obedience (Wiltermuth, 2012). In this work, individual participants were asked to walk behind an experimenter. Some were asked to walk in step with the experimenter. Just like in a marching band, when the experimenter stepped with his right or left foot, so too would the participant. In a second condition, the participant matched the timing of the experimenter's steps, but when the experimenter stepped with his right foot, the participant would step with his/her left, and vice versa. In the control condition, the participant just walked behind the experimenter, with no other specific instructions. Those who synchronized in step felt more of a connection with the experimenter than those in the other two conditions. Everyone was later asked by the experimenter to perform the distasteful task of putting bugs into a grinder as part of the study. Those in the synchrony condition obeyed more (killed more bugs) than those in the other conditions. (Of course, the bug-killing machine was bogus and no bugs were actually harmed in the study.)

Maintaining and Escalating Obedience. Once obedience begins, other processes help maintain or even escalate it. Notice that at first the consequences of obedience were not very negative for Milgram's participants. In fact, they were asked to do something quite benign; the shocks were very weak and had a positive goal, to improve learning. Only gradually were his participants asked to act in a way that might cause harm to the learner. But by this point, they had already obeyed, confirming in their own minds the experimenter's right and authority to direct their actions, and activating the norm of commitment to follow through on their agreement to participate in the study. Having acknowledged the experimenter as a legitimate authority, and already obeyed, participants found it increasingly difficult to refuse his gradually escalating demands.

In this way, participants in obedience experiments, and many others who commit crimes of politically and socially sanctioned evil, are led from the acceptable to the unthinkable, gradually (Kelman & Hamilton, 1989; Staub, 1989). Torturers are often trained this way, at first just delivering occasional pain, then watching while others do so, then participating in group infliction of suffering and finally carrying out the torture alone (Haritos-Fatouros, 1988). The gradual escalation of obedience reinforces the legitimacy of the authority and acceptance of the norm of obedience.

To remind yourself of the nature and consequences of cognitive dissonance, refer to Chapter 8, especially pages 282–285.

Dissonance processes also help maintain obedience once it occurs. Like the participants in Milgram's study, most of us see ourselves as kind, caring, decent people. But as the consequences of obedience become more negative, the inconsistency between this self-concept and actual behavior increases, triggering unpleasant arousal and an increasing motivation to reduce that arousal by providing justifications for their behavior. Of course these processes tend to maintain obedience. To reduce their dissonance, people might, for example, focus on the positive implications of being a reliable and obedient agent, or on the superior knowledge and wisdom of the authority to direct their behavior. Denying their own free choice will of course reduce dissonance, as we saw in Chapter 7, and as we saw in Chapter 4, people tend to attribute their own behavior to situational factors, especially if they behave badly. Unfortunately this denial of free choice and admiration of the authority figure, while it might reduce dissonance, only makes obedience more likely. Another way to reduce dissonance might be to change the meaning of obedience, interpreting it as promoting a positive goal. (Milgram helped his participants do this by claiming the shocks would "promote learning.") Many acts of aggression are justified in terms of defending honor and reputation, for example (D. Cohen & Nisbett, 1994). Such moral justifications are often cloaked in euphemistic language, such as "the final solution" or "ethnic cleansing" (Bandura and others, 1996). And as we have already seen, derogating victims as "deserving it" or dehumanizing sufferers with beliefs that "they don't have feelings like us" is one of the most chilling ways that we try to justify hurting others.

In Chapter 13, pages 510–513, we will see how these processes of obedience, escalation, and justification can combine with the intergroup hostility described in Chapter 6, to make extreme forms of intergroup violence—massacres, atrocities, torture, and extermination—more likely.

Thus, many social psychological processes combine to set the stage for and help maintain obedience not only inside the lab but outside it. Obedience to authorities, the entrapment that results from increasingly inhumane acts, and the tendency to justify one's own and one's group's actions can combine to make truly destructive obedience far more widespread than we might like to acknowledge.

Normative Trade-Offs: The Pluses and Minuses of Obedience

Like all norms, the obligation to obey authority figures can be used for good or evil purposes.

Although the norm of obedience can be exploited for great evil, acceptance of legitimate authority is essential for the optimal functioning of society. Almost every group, whether an informal group of friends or a complex society, develops roles and functions that give some members authority over others. Imagine what would happen if people made individual and independent decisions about which side of the road they would drive on, what language they would speak, whether they would contribute to the defense of their group, or what principles of justice they would uphold. As Milgram points out, obeying legitimate authority has many advantages for every individual.

Perhaps the most important lesson we can take away from Milgram's studies is just how hard it is to resist the power of deeply ingrained and widely shared norms. Indeed, his findings make clear the often unexpected and unanticipated power of social situations. Obedience works well most of the time and, for that reason, resisting authority is very difficult. Neither Milgram himself nor any of those who read descriptions of his studies had any idea of the degree of obedience he would find. You may find it difficult to imagine that in similar circumstances you could act the same way Milgram's participants did. Yet the social-psychological processes invoked in this situation—activation of the norm of obedience, exclusion of other norms that might guide behavior, gradual commitment to a particular course of behavior, and justification of it—can be an overpowering combination.

RESISTING, REJECTING, AND REBELLING AGAINST NORMS

An ad in the newspapers of a small southeastern Michigan town sought paid participants for "market research involving group discussion of community standards" (Gamson, Fireman, & Rytina, 1982). Those who responded met in groups of nine with the representatives of Manufacturer's Human Relations Consultants, Inc. (MHRC) at a local Holiday Inn. The coordinator, a young man in a business suit, explained that MHRC was conducting research for a major oil company involved in legal action against the manager of a local gas station. To give the court a picture of "community standards"— what local people believed to be right and wrong—MHRC would videotape the group while it discussed various issues relevant to the case. After signing a consent form and being paid for their participation, participants learned that the oil company had terminated the manager because he was living with a woman to whom he was not married. The company claimed that this behavior offended community standards. For his part, the manager stated that his private life was none of the company's business, and that the company had sent investigators after him because he had criticized their pricing policies in a televised interview. After starting the video camera, the coordinator instructed the group to discuss the manager's behavior, and then left the room for 5 minutes.

When the coordinator returned, he stopped the camera and gave the group a second discussion topic: Would they be reluctant to do business with the manager because of his lifestyle? This time, he asked three of the nine group members to take a stand against the manager's behavior. Two more filming sessions followed: In the first, three additional people were asked to criticize the manager's behavior, and in the last, all nine of the participants were asked to take a stand against the manager. Participants were then given an affidavit to sign, permitting MHRC to edit the videotape and use it in court. Only then were they free to leave.

How do you think participants responded? On the basis of Milgram's findings, we might expect them to obey the researchers' instructions about what to discuss and what position to take. But they didn't. Only 1 of the 33 groups of participants in the study allowed the procedure to be completed. In all the other cases, group members challenged the coordinator's authority to make them act in a blatantly unfair and potentially harmful manner. Rather than attacking the manager as instructed, some participants remained silent during the videotaping sessions. When they were not openly defying the coordinator—refusing to participate or to sign the final affidavit—they were arguing with him, calling into question the rationale and justification for the procedure. In 25 of the 33 groups, a majority of members refused to sign the final affidavit. Nine groups threatened action against MHRC, such as publicizing the abuse in the local newspaper. Even in the 8 groups in which most people signed, participants refused to cooperate with some parts of the procedure.

Why were the participants in this study able to take a stand, while many of Milgram's participants seemed unable to resist the norm of obedience to authority? Why and how does anyone resist the power of a norm? Children sometimes disobey their parents, students sometimes disobey their teachers, and employees sometimes disobey their supervisors. By examining what happened when groups rebelled, researchers have found that three processes—reactance, systematic processing, and using norms against norms —lead to resistance rather than capitulation.

Reactance

People can resist being manipulated by norms. People fight against threats to freedom of action when norms are not privately accepted or seen as appropriate.

---

reactance
the motive to protect or restore a threatened sense of behavioral freedom

Turn back to Chapter 7 right now and review the information about resisting persuasion. If you decided not to do this, you've just demonstrated reactance. People often respond to attempts to limit their choice with **reactance**, a desire to restore threatened freedom of action (Brehm, 1966; Rains, 2013). Reactance is common when people lose the opportunity to choose goods, services, or products. Banning a book or some music in one part of the country ensures record-breaking sales elsewhere; reports that a movie is censored abroad is a sure-fire boost to domestic box office receipts. And every parent knows that the best strategy is sometimes "reverse psychology": telling children to stay in the house when you really want them to go outside to play.

Heavy-handed social pressure often raises the red flag of reactance. It certainly did so in the MHRC study. Some individuals, feeling that their behavioral freedom was being threatened, simply walked out of the experiment. This also means that well-intentioned messages can backfire if they seem too heavy-handed. For instance, cigarette packaging with vivid and alarming pictures of the damages of smoking elicit much higher levels of reactance in smokers than do written warnings, like "Smoking Kills," perhaps because the former seem so extreme (Erceg-Hurn & Steed, 2011).

Why do people respond with reactance to a simple request but not to an order to shock another person? In this case, the answer has to do with perceptions of legitimacy of authority. If we accept a norm as legitimate and appropriate and relevant, we are likely to comply, even if it used in a heavy-handed way: its imposition is not seen as an infringement on our freedom. Such norms bypass the reactance aroused by inappropriate threats to our freedom. But when normative pressure is perceived to be inappropriate or illegitimate, reactance is triggered. In Milgram's experiments, the experimenter was perceived to be a legitimate authority. In the MHRC study, however, some participants disputed a "market consultant's" right to tell them what they should say and do. When authority is not appropriate or legitimate, reactance can push us to say "Enough is enough!"

Reactance also is less likely when the threat to our freedom is a "done deal" versus when we perceive it as potentially changeable. In one study, students read a message

SOCIAL PSYCHOLOGY AND CULTURE: PERCEPTIONS OF ILLEGITIMACY AND DISOBEDIENCE ACROSS CULTURE

The power of the norm of obedience lies in the legitimacy of the authority, but perceptions of what constitutes legitimacy apparently differ across cultures, along with different levels of readiness to disobey. In the individualist United States and the more collectivist Poland, researchers ran a field study of workers' willingness to obey instructions from a manager. U.S. workers were more resistant to managers perceived as lacking in expertise, whereas Poles were more resistant to managers perceived as lacking in relational skills. Why the difference? U.S. workers believe expertise to be a key aspect of legitimate authority, part of the attributes that someone must have to be entitled to be in charge in a particular domain. Poles, on the other hand, value in a boss the relational skills necessary to bring everyone together to get a task completed, and a manager lacking those skills has no legitimate authority to be giving orders. In both cultures, the differences in obedience held only in well-established workplaces, suggesting that group identity triggered the motivation to adhere to the predominant culture norms in the first place (Wosinska and others, 2009). The same factor—perception of legitimate authority—dictated whether or not obedience occurred, but cultural differences in that perception meant that in different cultures different bosses were disobeyed more often.

about the dangers of high speed limits. Some also learned that a law would definitely be passed lowering speed limits, while others learned that such a law would probably (but not definitely) pass. Attitudes about the law were then assessed. When the law change was definite, participants accepted it and rated the law more favorably than those in the control condition. But, when the law was only a possibility, reactance occurred: participants had more unfavorable attitudes than in the control condition (Laurin, Kay, & Fitzsimons, 2012).

Resisting and Rejecting Norms Using Systematic Processing

One defense against normative pressure on behavior is to think things through to make sure that any norm made accessible in the situation is actually applicable.

By now you may not be surprised to learn that thinking is one of your best defenses against normative pressure. During the breaks in which the experimenter left the room, the participants in the MHRC study were given the opportunity to step back from the situation and consider what was going on, and many of them realized that unfair normative pressures were being applied. Thinking things through is not always easy, of course. Situations involving normative pressure often create anxiety and stress, and as anxiety mounts, we may be unable to think clearly. The attempt to resist social influence of various sorts is itself mentally depleting, which may leave one more susceptible to later influence attempts (Burkley, Anderson, & Curtis, 2011). To avoid undue pressure, it's often a good idea to try to give yourself a "cooling off" period before you make a commitment, reciprocate a favor, or obey an order. Even then, systematic thinking about the situation is important. Several strategies can help you fend off unfair normative pressure.

Recall from Chapter 7, pages 267–271, that systematic processing plays the same role in helping people resist persuasion.

1. *Question how norms are being used.* Recognizing how norms operate and how they can be used against you is a good starting point. When you realize that a norm is being used against you, it loses its power (Cialdini, 1993). In fact, explicitly drawing attention to the other side's questionable tactics helps prevent their recurrence (R. Fisher & Ury, 1981). So if you believe you are being low-balled, let the culprit know you understand the tactic. By doing so, you may embarrass the other person and encourage forthright negotiation. Even more important, you will free yourself from forced feelings of obligation. Realizing that "the boss's" change in the terms of a sale is part of a low-ball plan frees you from the norm of social commitment: The agreement the salesperson made with you was just part of a strategy, not an honest deal. Thus, the very knowledge of how norms work is a strong defense against their influence.

2. *Question claims about relationships.* Norms are powerful because of the connections between people. So you might stop to think: Is the person invoking the norm really one with whom you share that connection? Does the person giving orders really have the authority to command you? Maybe not. Is the salesperson really your ally and advocate, fighting against an intractable "boss" who won't approve the deal? Probably not. And make sure that you are both abiding by the same rules of normative behavior. As part of the low-ball tactic, the salesperson often claims to be unable to make the deal without consulting the boss. This setup means that you have the power to make concessions, but the other person does not and so is freed from the obligation. As the old saying goes, "What's mine is mine; what's yours is negotiable!" In cases like this, insist on dealing directly with the person who can make a binding agreement (R. Fisher & Ury, 1981). This is also a good reminder to think twice about whether you want to be part of the group whose norms you are being pressured about. One tactic that lowers the pull of norms is to re-assert an individual identity. When researchers had some people think about their own personal values, their behavior was less likely to follow group norms (Binning, Sherman, Cohen, & Heitland, 2010).

3. *Question others' views of the situation.* One of the most important lessons that social psychology can teach is that all situations are open to multiple interpretations. Your definition of what happened may be just as valid as the other person's. Did she really do you a favor? Do you really owe one in return? Before buying into someone else's view of how you should behave, consider all the norms and attitudes that might be relevant. Balance such norms as obedience and social commitment against other possible views of the situation. The willingness of participants in the MHRC study to question others' views of the situation was central to their successful resistance. The coordinator used the norm of legitimate obedience to authority to get participants to sign the documents. In response, group members who resisted argued that the authority was not legitimate, and therefore the norms didn't apply. Remember from Chapter 9 that the best group norms grow out of consideration of multiple points of view. If your interpretation of a situation differs from the one being presented, suggest some alternatives. Others may agree with you, or, at the very least, the person trying to influence the group will have to defend his or her interpretation. The sooner you offer an alternative the better, because the longer you buy into the other person's definition of the situation, the harder it will be to resist, and the sooner

you suggest a different interpretation, the freer others will feel to resist the social pressure (Gamson and others, 1982).

Using Norms Against Norms

An effective defense is to use norms against norms: to break down an existing norm and forge or exploit an alternative consensus that makes a different course of behavior the appropriate one.

The strength of a norm lies in the consensus that it represents. When people start to break away from a consensus, it becomes easier for others to do the same thing. The same is true when the norm of obedience—or any other norm—is in play. When Milgram provided his otherwise solitary participants with an ally, obedience was immediately reduced (Rochat & Modigliani, 1995) and it can be reduced even further when an alternative norm is forged. When nurses given inappropriate orders were allowed to talk with one another, disobedience rose dramatically (Rank & Jacobsen, 1977). The biggest resistance advantage that participants in the MHRC study had was the presence of social support for alternatives. The presence of others and the opportunity this affords to form and affirm group norms of resistance—especially in the form of group endorsed alternatives—is the most crucial factor in creating rebellion (Gamson, 1992; Haslam & Reicher, 2004; B. Simon, 1998). In every MHRC group in which discussion produced a consensus against compliance, group resistance to the coordinator followed. The coordinator's absence during taping sessions gave the group an opportunity to air their doubts and to find out that others felt the same way they did. To help build and strengthen the norm of resistance, participants stressed their shared views and bolstered their solidarity by telling the coordinator: ". . . we don't want to go on the record . . . We don't. All three of us feel the same way. I think every one of us feels that way here." (Gamson and others, 1982, p. 102).

Such findings show that forging a social identity is crucial among people trying to engage in resistance. Researchers Alexander Haslam and Stephen Reicher (2012b) recount case studies of successful resistance among different prisoner groups, including at the infamous Robben Island Prison in South Africa that housed political prisoners, including Nelson Mandela. In this case, as in others, a group of prisoners banded together with a common identity that enabled them to eventually secure important short-term or long-term victories.

Group identity is also central to recent models of how people can take collective action to combat or resist established social norms. Martijn van Zomeren, Russell Spears, Agneta Fischer, and Colin Leach (2004) argue that many types of civil or collective disobedience such as demonstrations and protest marches result from the simultaneous development of two group norms. One is the shared group-based emotion of anger, which arises from a shared perception of injustice and which motivates action. The other is a shared belief in the group's efficacy, that is, the ability of collective action to achieve its goals and bring about change. Extensive research supports the idea that group-based anger and high group efficacy help instigate resistance to and rebellion from established norms in the form of demonstrations and protests, as well as the formation of social

Recall from Chapter 9, pages 340–341, that the power of a norm depends on its representing consenus—the agreement of multiple others. When consensus is broken and alternative views are endorsed, established norms weaken and new norms can form to guide behavior.

We discussed the antecedents and powerful consequences for prejudice of group-based emotions in Chapter 5, pages 147, 151–152 and 170.

Photo 10.5 Resistance is a collective act. An estimated 50,000 people in Moscow protest Russia's actions in Crimea. The protest is an example of people banding together to reject a perceived norm in their society, in this case, of governmental aggression.

movements (van Zomeren, Leach, & Spears, 2012). Other research shows that shared emotion and efficacy norms also predict participation in more extreme group action such as violent protests and terrorism as means to overturning established norms (Tausch and others, 2011). Interestingly, however, the emotions and efficacy norms for more violent protest differ from those that are influential in less extreme protest. Whereas shared anger and efficacy norms motivate collective protest, shared contempt and shared low efficacy—agreement that nothing can be done—predicts extreme forms of rejecting and rebelling against established norms.

Thus the best way to resist norms is to form new norms that can guide changed behavior. The idea that effective resistance is often facilitated by group identity and group norms is reflected in historian Michael Walzer's observation: "Disobedience . . . is always a collective act" (Walzer, 1970, p. 4).

In some cases, inappropriate norms may not originate from an illegitimate authority, but from inside an important in-group itself. What then? It seems that issues of social identity again matter in who attempts to change and resist those group norms. In one study, students were given normative information about a group they belonged to: they were told that most students at their university had lenient attitudes about plagiarism. Afterwards, some students were asked to think about why plagiarism might hurt the group (the university); others were asked to think about why plagiarism might hurt people within the group; yet others were not asked to think about the norm at all. When asked to think about why the lenient norm about plagiarism might be bad for their group, those who highly identified with the group expressed the most willingness to combat the norm by, for example, endorsing the use of anti-plagiarism technologies (Packer & Chasteen, 2010). Thus, those who really care about the group may operate by the global norm to do what's best for the group, rather than simply agreeing with group norms that may be damaging to its interests.

In terms of cause and cure, destructive obedience is like groupthink, described in Chapter 9. In each case a natural and usually beneficial process—obedience to authority or conformity to a group decision —goes awry. You may recall that the way to prevent or cure groupthink is to create conditions that enhance careful, systematic processing of alternative views. In the same way, the key to the prevention or cure of destructive obedience lies in creating alternatives. In particular, it consists of forming or reaffirming a more appropriate and applicable group norm.

HOT TOPICS IN SOCIAL PSYCHOLOGY: RESISTING NORMS SOMETIMES HAS REWARDS

Resisting norms is difficult for all the reasons discussed in this chapter and Chapter 9. Yet people can and do resist and outright disobey norms. Even in one of Milgram's (1963) famous studies described in this chapter, where 65 % of participants delivered the maximum shock to the learner, 35 % did not fully obey. The desire to follow norms is strong because doing so helps us gain mastery and connectedness with others. But might there be rewards for not following norms, at least under some circumstances? Recent findings suggest the answer is yes.

The authors of one set of studies argued that people may deliberately disobey a norm to signal to others that they have high status and ability and therefore can follow their own rules (Bellezza, Gino, & Keinan, 2014). One study asked women who worked at luxury fashion boutiques in Milan and women recruited in a train station in Milan to read about a female shopper who entered a luxury store wearing either norm-consistent clothes—a dress and a fur coat—or norm-inconsistent clothes—gym clothes. Participants rated the shopper's status by judging the likelihood that this woman would buy something and how much she would spend. They also indicated whether they thought this woman might be a celebrity or a "very important person." Participants who themselves worked in luxury fashion stores, who were familiar with that environment, judged the norm-inconsistent shopper as having higher status and as more likely to be a celebrity or VIP than the norm-consistent one. But participants recruited from a train station, who were less familiar with the relevant environment, showed the opposite pattern. A follow-up study showed that status was attributed to those who disobeyed norms when the norm violation seemed to be deliberate, and it was driven by perceptions that norm violators had high levels of autonomy. Thus, although norms have powerful effects on our behavior, people do disobey them at times and doing so may come with its own rewards.

From norms that instruct us to use hushed voices in the library, to honor our social contracts, and to obey persons in authority, norms have a powerful influence on almost every aspect of human behavior. Their influence on behavior helps us achieve mastery—by telling us how to act appropriately to achieve our goals—and connectedness—as when the norm of reciprocity binds us together. Norms, like attitudes, can only influence behavior when they are accessible. For norms to help prevent littering or improve your manners in an exclusive restaurant, they must first be brought to mind. Once established, the power of norms on behavior is hard to change—we defer to the norms of reciprocity and commitment even if we end up getting a bad deal, and the power of a legitimate authority can be hard to resist. As the examples in this chapter also demonstrate, norms, like attitudes, can influence behavior in a direct and superficial way, or through much more systematic thought. Sometimes mere activation of the norm of equality will facilitate an easy division of resources without much thought. At other times, the appropriateness of the norm of obedience might be questioned in depth and weighed against other norms before having any impact. Thus, norms direct behavior in much the same way that attitudes do.

PUTTING IT ALL TOGETHER: MULTIPLE GUIDES FOR BEHAVIOR

Most of the behaviors that are important to human interaction are voluntary; that is, people can decide whether to perform them. In these cases behavior is usually a product of the way people define situations and of social influence exerted by others. How situations are perceived—both by the individual and by his or her groups—is enormously influential in determining what behaviors occur. In most situations, attitudes and norms work together to exert a combined influence on our actions.

Both Attitudes and Norms Influence Behavior

Attitudes and norms typically work together to influence behavior, either by triggering behavior superficially or by being combined to influence intentions to act, which in turn direct behavior. People's perception of control over the behavior is also an important influence on intentions and thus on behavior.

If you think this sounds similar to the ways in which attitudes direct behavior, you're right. As you read these sections, flip back to Chapter 8, pages 295 to 300 and especially Figure 8.5, to see the parallels.

Whenever we act or interact in socially important ways—voting for a political leader or protesting university policies, using birth control or following a vegetarian diet, deciding whom to hire or accept for training, egging on our team at a soccer match or jeering the other side—multiple sources of influence can potentially mold our behavior. Most of the time, both attitudes and norms relevant to any given behavior are present. At the soccer game, loud partisanship is the norm, but you might prefer quiet environments. In the voting booth, you have your own preferences, but are also very aware of the choices of your friends and the expectations of your group. How do these multiple potential forces work together to influence behavior? Just as was the case with attitudes and norms separately, attitudes and norms can combine to influence behavior by two different routes. They may trigger behavior directly and almost automatically, or they may operate indirectly, by influencing our intentions to act (Fazio, 1986; Ouellette & Wood, 1998).

The Superficial Route. Attitudes and norms can guide behavior rather simply and directly, especially when we do not give matters much systematic thought. At such times, accessible attitudes may affect our perceptions of attitude objects, and accessible norms may serve as decision heuristics. Together, the attitudes and norms can color our perceptions and influence our behavior in an immediate and automatic way. For example, a person who holds a negative attitude toward an out-group member may be more aware of the out-group member's hostility-provoking characteristics. At the same time, a norm that says "protect the in-group" may be activated, and the attitude and norm together may lead directly to aggressive behavior. Attitudes and norms are especially likely to affect behavior directly when the resources and motivation to process deeply are not available. As Figure 10.6 illustrates, behavior may then follow quite simply and without much thought.

Providing further support to these ideas, we know (from Chapter 8) that automatic evaluations of objects, called implicit attitudes, can guide behavior directly and without careful thought. People also appear to possess implicit norms—automatically activated views of what most others favor and don't favor (Yoshida, Peach, Zanna, & Spencer, 2012). Remember the Implicit Association Test (IAT) from Chapter 5? In it, people complete a computerized task in which they respond to words like "good" or "bad" using the same response keys as they use to categorize some objects. If a person responds faster when an attitude object like "movies" is paired with the "good" rather than the

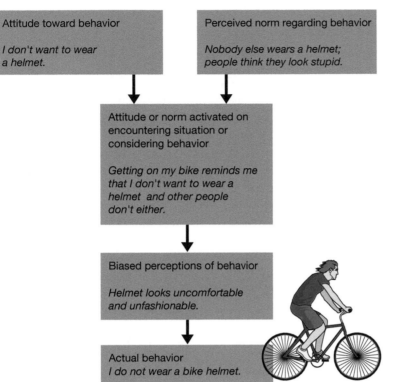

Attitude toward behavior

I don't want to wear a helmet.

Perceived norm regarding behavior

Nobody else wears a helmet; people think they look stupid.

Attitude or norm activated on encountering situation or considering behavior

Getting on my bike reminds me that I don't want to wear a helmet and other people don't either.

Biased perceptions of behavior

Helmet looks uncomfortable and unfashionable.

Actual behavior
I do not wear a bike helmet.

Figure 10.6 Attitudes and norms affect behavior without much thought
When we do not give matters much systematic thought, both attitudes and norms can color our perceptions, influencing behavior in a relatively immediate and automatic way.

"bad" response, it suggests that the person's implicit attitude about movies is favorable. In the emerging work on implicit norms, people complete a modified IAT in which they respond to objects using response keys that are also paired with "most people like" or "most people don't like." If people respond faster when an object, such as "smoking," is paired with "most people don't like," then the person has an anti-smoking implicit norm. Studies have shown that these implicit norms are distinct from implicit attitudes, and also that they can predict important behaviors (Yoshida and others, 2012). Thus, attitudes and norms, both explicit and implicit, can guide behavior directly, especially when people aren't thinking deeply.

The Thoughtful Route. Sometimes norms combine with other factors in a much more deliberate way as we form our intentions to act and then try to follow through on these intentions. Remember that according to the theory of reasoned action and the theory of planned behavior (Ajzen & Fishbein, 1977, 1980; Armitage & Conner, 2001), introduced in Chapter 8, intentions are a function of multiple factors that can be thought about in the situation.

One such factor is the individual's attitude toward the behavior. For example, if a college student believes that organ donation is an effective way to save lives, her attitude toward organ donation is likely to be positive. Social norms would also have an influence in such a situation, because people care about what significant reference groups, such as close friends, co-workers, experts, and family, would like or expect them to do. If, for example, the student knows that her cousin donated a kidney to a stranger, and that most of her friends have stated their desires to be donors, she will perceive social norms

We discussed the theory of reasoned action and the theory of planned behavior while focusing on attitudes leading to intentions in Chapter 8, pages 297–298 and 304–305. Here we see that attitudes actually combine with norms and perceptions of control to produce intentions.

In Chapter 4, pages 128 and 133–135, we saw that a sense of control, fulfilling the need for mastery, was an important component of a healthy sense of self. Here we see it is an important prerequisite to effective behavior in the world.

as supporting organ donation. Finally, the theory of planned behavior suggests that people additionally take into account their perceived control over behavior: A sense of control is necessary before positive attitudes and supportive norms translate into first intentions and then action. Only if this student has confidence in her ability to register as an organ donor and perceives herself as being able to control the outcome of her actions by her efforts will she perceive herself as having control over organ donation (Manstead & van Eekelen, 1998). With attitudes, norms, and perceived control in place, she will form the intention to donate her organs (Rocheleau, 2013).

Figure 10.7 illustrates the way behavior is influenced by attitudes, perceived norms, and perceptions of control associated with particular behaviors. By carefully measuring these three factors, researchers have used the theory of planned behavior to predict occupational choice, consumer purchasing decisions, blood donations, dietary changes, attendance at religious services, compliance with speed limits, use of public transportation, and participation in psychotherapy. In one study of attitudes and norms relating to the use of alcohol, marijuana, and hard drugs, researchers found that both attitudes

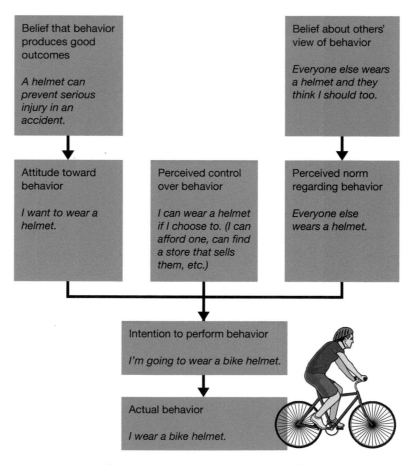

Figure 10.7 Attitudes and norms affect thoughtfully planned behavior
According to the theory of planned behavior, people's attitudes, perceived norms, and their perception of their own control combine to produce a considered intention to act. This intention, in turn, guides behavior. (Based on Ajzen & Fishbein, 1977, 1980.)

and norms influenced students' intentions, which in turn influenced their self-reported behavior (Bentler & Speckart, 1979). Consistent with the theory, attitudes and norms influence only the behaviors that people consider to be under their control. If a smoker sees his behavior as due to an uncontrollable addiction, for example, norms and attitudes will have little effect on the behavior (Ajzen & Madden, 1986). Moreover, the theory of planned behavior effectively predicts behavior in different cultural contexts (Aguilar-Luzon, Garcia-Martinez, Calvo-Salguero, & Salinas, 2012; Mullan, Wong, & Kothe, 2013; Sieverding, Matterne, & Ciccarello, 2010).

You may have noticed that in discussing both the superficial and more thoughtful impact of norms and attitudes on behavior, we have used examples in which attitudes and norms suggest the same action. Although attitudes and norms often converge, this is not always the case, of course. Milgram's participants obviously hated what they did, even as they bowed to the norm of obedience. You may earnestly desire a quiet Saturday afternoon by yourself but nevertheless fulfill your social commitment to help your friend move. How do we behave when attitudes and norms are at odds?

When Attitudes and Norms Conflict: Accessibility Determines Behavior

Whether attitudes or norms have more influence on behavior depends on their relative accessibility for a particular behavior, in a particular situation, and for a particular person.

When a relevant attitude is very accessible, it comes to mind easily, and behavior falls in line with it, as we saw in Chapter 8. And, as the research described in this chapter has demonstrated, this fundamental principle applies to norms as well: Accessible norms have a powerful influence on behavior. When attitudes and norms disagree, their impact on behavior, whether superficial or thoughtful, depends on their relative accessibility: Whichever is more accessible will have the greater influence on behavior. Consider, for example, experiments designed to independently manipulate the accessibility of attitudes and norms (Trafimow & Fishbein, 1994a, 1994b). One study showed that accessibility is a function of who is watching your behavior (Froming, Walker, & Lopyan, 1982). Students completed a questionnaire twice, first giving their own attitudes toward punishment, and then indicating what they thought their peers thought, that is, what they perceived as the relevant social norms. Later in the term, they participated as "teachers" in a learning experiment similar to Milgram's, in which they believed they were delivering electric shocks to a failing "pupil." There were three conditions in the experiment. Some participants delivered the shocks in front of a mirror, some before an audience of their classmates, and others before an audience of advanced psychology students. In the presence of their own image in the mirror, which increases self-awareness and activates people's private attitudes, the participants' behavior was relatively consistent with their attitudes. But in the presence of the audiences, their behavior was more consistent with norms.

Not surprisingly, then, norms might be more accessible and have more sway on behaviors that are performed in public, involve others, and are crucial to the well-being of the group. Most groups, for example, have rules about safeguarding food and water, protecting others' property, controlling aggression and sex, exchanging social resources, keeping social commitments, and respecting authority (Maccoby, 1980). Individual attitudes tend to have more influence over private, individual behaviors: whether or not you cut the tags off clothes to make them more comfortable, what you wear around the house, and whether you have a strawberry or a chocolate ice cream cone.

For the same reasons, individuals can differ in the extent to which they are responsive to social norms versus private attitudes. As you might expect, people who identify closely with membership in a particular group are more sensitive to and more influenced by the social norms of that group (Terry & Hogg, 1996; Trafimow & Finlay, 1996). This finding can also be generalized to cultures. As we noted above members of collective cultures tend to have group identities that are more accessible, and thus are more typically attuned to group norms. Moreover, individualism and collectivism themselves can be conceived of as descriptive and injunctive social norms: ways that people do and should act in different cultures (Chiu, Gelfand, Yamagishi, Shteynberg, & Wan, 2010). In one study, U.S. and Indonesian participants reported their levels of individualism and collectivism as well as their national identification (Jetten, Postmes, & McAuliffe, 2002). Indonesians who were strongly identified with their nationality were more collectivist than those who weakly identified with their nationality. In contrast, U.S. citizens who strongly identified with their nationality were more individualist than those who weakly identified. Such findings show that people who feel more connected to a group tend to pick up group norms and also that individualism and collectivism can become norms for a culture or a group, like other beliefs or behaviors. Thus, for some people, attitudes are more likely to guide behavior because these people are constantly aware of their attitudes. For others, social norms are uppermost in their minds and tend to guide their behavior.

Neither attitudes nor norms predominate for all behaviors, for all people, in all situations. Whether their impact is superficial or thoughtful, relevant attitudes can limit or modify the powerful influence of norms on behavior. Similarly, norms that are activated and considered can block individual attitudes from being expressed in behavior. In our daily lives, multiple social norms and a variety of personal attitudes contribute to how we perceive a given set of circumstances and, thus, to the way we behave. Will an employee blow the whistle on his company's illegal dumping of chemical waste? Will a young mother nurse her baby or use formula? Will a soldier carry out orders she suspects are illegal? When the behavior is perceived as controllable, the answer will depend on the particular mix of norms and attitudes that are brought to mind as each individual interprets his or her situation.

CONCLUDING COMMENTS

Social psychology has always aimed at understanding the intricate interplay between social thoughts, social feelings, and social behavior. One thing that makes achieving such a goal difficult is the incredible diversity of human behavior. On the one hand are behaviors like stepping on the brake when the traffic light turns red—behaviors so automatic that they take no conscious thought. On the other hand are decisions about choosing a particular career or voting for a particular candidate—behaviors that often involve an agonizingly careful scrutiny of available information. As we hope you have seen in this and the three previous chapters, the differences between these two types of behaviors are more apparent than real. It is easy to see how cognitive processes and social influences contribute to the kinds of carefully reasoned actions that follow the consideration of a variety of relevant attitudes and norms. But even automatic behaviors are influenced by the way we and others interpret and define social situations. You won't stop at the traffic signal unless you recognize the red light and interpret its meaning appropriately. And how you interpret the red light is governed to a large degree by social conventions and norms: Must you stay motionless until the light changes to green, or can you turn right if the way is clear? Even your knowledge that the color red means "stop" is a cultural norm. Like carefully considered behaviors, apparently automatic actions are also influenced by both cognitive and social processes. Whether automatic or carefully thought through, then, all behavior is susceptible to the same principle of accessibility: The more readily the relevant attitude or norm comes to mind, the more impact it will have on behavior.

Although norms and attitudes affect behavior in the same ways, norms have a slight edge over attitudes. Indeed, if you think about it, you will probably be surprised to find how much more often when norms and attitudes conflict, you follow norms rather than your attitudes. You do what you should do rather than what you want to do. Part of the impact of norms comes from the fact that they are group-based, and thus the presence of group members is a cue that activates them. And because norms come from the group, norm-consistent behavior is likely to be supported and rewarded, rather than undermined. Although norm-consistent behavior can be maintained by threats or rejection, the pressure to conform usually comes from the inside: from our acceptance of group norms as the right and proper way to think, feel, and act. Thus, we construct a world of right and wrong, good and bad, that is reflected in the norms and attitudes we develop and maintain. Effective social influence really stems from the ability to create and then make accessible the mental representations that make desired behavior more likely to occur.

Businesses and other organizations have begun to reap the benefits of encouraging groups to form and maintain their own standards of behavior, as have individuals joining self-help support groups. The power of social norms might be used with equal success in other social areas, not as rules imposed from above but as a grass-roots movement that builds from the small group level. In neighborhoods, for example, norms involving energy conservation through bicycle commuting might be established and made effective, just as block organizations and neighborhood watch groups have successfully developed standards of pride and caring for property and protection from crime. Standards of curiosity and respect for learning might be reinforced in classrooms if students themselves participated in establishing norms for classroom behavior. As social and environmental problems escalate, such techniques could help produce much-needed change.

SUMMARY

Norms: Effective Guides for Social Behavior. Norms must be activated before they can guide behavior. They can be activated by direct reminders, environmental cues, or observations of other people's behavior. When in a state of **deindividuation**, group norms may be especially highly activated. In this state, people see themselves purely in terms of group identity, and their behavior is likely to be guided by group norms alone. Both descriptive norms and injunctive norms influence behavior, and these norms may sometimes interact with each other in interesting ways. One type of normative information may be more important than another, depending on our motivation and ability to think carefully. Norms are sometimes enforced by rewards and punishments. More often, however, people follow norms simply because they seem right. Following norms may also be in our genetic makeup.

Norms for Mastery and Connectedness: Reciprocity and Social Commitment. The **norm of reciprocity**, one of the most prevalent social norms, directs us to return to others favors, goods, services, and concessions they offer to us. This norm can sometimes be activated to our disadvantage, such as when people give us small favors to induce us to return something of greater value. Because concessions are also supposed to be reciprocated, this can leave us vulnerable when others use the **door-in-the-face technique**, making a concession following our refusal to comply with a large demand. We feel obligated to make a concession in return.

The **norm of social commitment** encourages people to stand by their agreements and fulfill their obligations. Like the norm of reciprocity, it can be used by others to one's disadvantage. It can make people vulnerable through the **low-ball technique**, when they make a deal and then discover there are hidden costs. People usually stick to the deal even though it has changed for the worse.

The Norm of Obedience: Submitting to Authority. In one of the best-known experiments in psychology, people obeyed orders to deliver shocks to an unwilling and clearly suffering victim. They obeyed these orders even though they were not forced to do so. The destructive obedience of Milgram's participants was not due to hard-hearted unconcern about the victim or suspicion that the experiment was rigged. In fact, obedience in nonexperimental settings can be just as high, and authorities command as much obedience in recent studies as they did 50 years ago in Milgram's experiments. The **norm of obedience to authority** had a powerful effect on behavior in Milgram's experiment and has a similar effect on behavior outside the lab. Authorities must be legitimate and accept responsibility. Both in Milgram's studies and in everyday situations, conditions that increase the accessibility of the obedience norm or decrease attention to other norms, increase obedience. Because legitimacy of authority derives from the group, people who identify more with the authority or the group the authority represents are more likely to follow the authority's directives. Once obedience occurs it can be maintained or escalated by gradual entrapment and the impact of justification processes. Like all norms, the obligation to obey authority figures can be used for good or evil purposes.

Resisting, Rejecting, and Rebelling Against Norms. People can resist being manipulated by norms. People display **reactance** by fighting against threats to their freedom
of action when they do not privately accept norms or when they believe they are inappropriate. One defense against normative pressure on behavior is to think things through
to make sure that any norm made accessible in the situation is actually applicable. The
most effective defense is to use norms against norms: to break down an existing norm
and forge or exploit an alternative consensus that makes a different course of behavior
the appropriate one.

Putting It All Together: Multiple Guides for Behavior. Attitudes and norms typically
work together to influence behavior, either by triggering behavior superficially or by
being combined more thoughtfully to influence intentions to act, which in turn direct
behavior. People's perception of control over the behavior is also an important influence
on intentions and thus on behavior. Whether attitudes or norms have more influence
on behavior depends on their relative accessibility for a particular behavior, in a particular
situation, and for a particular person.

11

INTERACTION AND PERFORMANCE IN GROUPS

osting the Olympics. Winning the World Cup. Coordinating a humanitarian response to a hurricane. Starting a business. Completing a group project for a class. These seemingly unrelated events have one thing in common—they all involve a group of people working together as a team to accomplish a shared goal. If you have ever been part of such a group, you know that groups can sometimes achieve great things, but sometimes they instead fall into disarray. Issues with leadership, coordination, or morale can lead to missed deadlines, substandard products, defeats, and loss of money and time. But when groups function smoothly, profits soar, innovative projects are designed, and matches are won. When people put their heads together—and their muscle and drive—their individual efforts are sometimes multiplied in astonishing ways, and the group can achieve goals far beyond the reach of any one member. Scientists at CERN, the European Organization for Nuclear Research, who built the Large Hadron Collider in Geneva, baseball's 2013 Boston Red Sox who came back from a last-place finish in their division the previous year to take the World Series championship, and the legions of volunteers who staff the Red Cross to help respond to disasters like Typhoon Haiyan in the Philippines in 2013, Hurricane Sandy in the United States in 2012, and the massive earthquake in Haiti in 2010 are just a few examples of the remarkable achievements of group action.

Our aim in this chapter is to understand the consequences of group membership for behavior. To some extent, this topic has been woven throughout the earlier chapters. In Chapter 6, for example, we examined the many effects of a shared group identity on people's thoughts, feelings, and actions. In Chapter 9, we looked at the ways juries and other groups make decisions. But decision making is often only a first step. Most groups act on their decisions as they win or lose games, manufacture products, build roads, fight fires, complete group term projects, and throw a surprise party for their roommate.

Because the outcomes of group action are often strikingly different from the inputs of individual members—and sometimes very different from what is desired and intended—early theorists concluded that the behavior of a group has almost nothing to do with the individual characteristics of its members (Durkheim, 1898; LeBon, 1895/1947). Rather, they argued, people lose their individuality in a group and, swept along by the crowd, no longer have a mind of their own. Although contemporary social scientists do not agree that individuals give up their autonomy to the group, they do recognize that being part of a group affects individual behavior in distinctive and sometimes dramatic ways. Groups differ in the degree of interaction and interdependence they share. **Interdependence** means that each group member's thoughts, emotions, and behaviors influence the others' (H. H. Kelley and others, 1983). At one extreme are a group of people who, like passengers on an airplane, are physically in the same place but who hardly interact and are only minimally interdependent. We saw in several earlier chapters that membership in groups defined by shared, socially significant features—such as Roman Catholics, socialists, or Mexican-Americans—can influence people's thoughts, feelings, and behavior. Such groups may or may not interact face to face but are often at least somewhat interdependent, because what happens to one member of the group often affects others.

interdependence
each group member's thoughts, emotions, and behaviors influence the others'

However, the impact of group membership is most obvious when people not only identify with a group but also interact and depend on one another, relying on other members' actions as well as their own for mastery of material rewards and feelings of connectedness. Most of this chapter focuses on such face-to-face groups, like the decision-making groups we discussed in Chapter 9. Like the CERN scientists and the Red Sox players, members of face-to-face groups share values and coordinate their efforts to get things done. Their attempts to reach their goals are marked by intense communication and extensive interaction. The group's success often depends on just how well its leaders and members can manage the problems of interdependence.

To study the processes that shape interaction and performance in face-to-face groups, scientists can create groups in lab settings and examine outcomes like how well they communicate with each other, how well they coordinate their work, and their performance in achieving their goals. Other researchers examine already established groups that exist outside the lab—a sports team, a student project group, a volunteer organization, or employees of a business. Regardless of which type of group is studied, the most basic processes operate in similar ways. Thus, what you learn in this chapter, even from studies of employee groups, is likely to be relevant to the operation of your soccer team, study group, sorority planning committee, or debate club.

SOCIAL FACILITATION: EFFECTS OF MINIMAL INTERDEPENDENCE

Imagine that, as you jog along your usual route, you catch up with another jogger who runs alongside you for a couple of blocks. You greet each other with a friendly nod and perhaps check out each other's brand of running shoe, but otherwise you have no contact before you go your separate ways. A block later, you pass by a half-dozen people gathered on a front porch, and they look up and follow your progress down the street. Although your contact with your fellow jogger and with your temporary audience is minimal, their mere presence can influence your behavior in quite predictable ways.

Social Facilitation: Improvement and Impairment

Even when interdependence is minimal, the mere presence of others can produce arousal, either because the other people are highly evaluative or because they are distracting. Arousal improves performance of easy, well-learned behaviors, but often interferes with performance of novel or complex tasks.

If you are like most people, you will run slightly faster in the presence of others than when you are alone (Worringham & Messick, 1983). This facilitating effect of other people on individual performance may seem familiar. In our discussion of the history of social psychology in Chapter 1, we described Norman Triplett's (1898) observation that children winding line onto fishing reels worked more quickly in the presence of others than when they were alone. Other research confirms the idea that the presence of others improves performance on a variety of simple tasks, from running to solving easy arithmetic problems (Aiello & Douthitt, 2001; Grant & Dajee, 2003; Guerin, 1986).

But is having others around always helpful? You may doubt this if you can remember standing in the glare of the footlights desperately trying to remember your lines or stumbling through a complex new dance routine in front of your fellow dance students. And your answer would be correct, for research also shows that the presence of others often interferes with performance. On many complicated and difficult tasks, from mazes to math problems to a newly learned tennis serve, our performance often declines when others are present (Aiello & Douthitt, 2001; Guerin, 1986). How can the presence of others both help and hurt performance?

In 1965, Robert Zajonc proposed an explanation of these apparently contradictory effects of the presence of others. According to Zajonc, **social facilitation** occurs because the presence of others increases an individual's level of arousal, which in turn makes some behaviors easier and others more difficult. (Although the term "facilitation" suggests that the presence of others improves performance, social facilitation also refers to the decrease in performance in other circumstances.) Arousal improves the performance of behaviors that are very accessible because they are simple, well learned, and highly practiced (often termed dominant responses), but it impairs the performance of behaviors that are complex or new (nondominant responses). Accessibility should be a familiar concept by now. Accessible thoughts and feelings are more likely to come to mind than are less accessible ones; similarly, accessible behaviors are more likely to be performed than are less accessible ones. Thus, the arousal caused by an audience may help a jogger to run faster and an entrant in a math contest to ace the easy problems. That same arousal may make it more difficult for a novice skier to complete a difficult course or for the math contestant to answer the tough final questions that will determine the winner. When behaviors are

social facilitation

an increase in the likelihood of highly accessible responses, and a decrease in the likelihood of less accessible responses, due to the presence of others

Photo 11.1 Presence and performance. Perhaps the runner checking out the competition is aware of the dramatic effects of the presence of others. When the responses necessary for success are well learned and highly accessible, others' presence can trigger superior performance.

complicated or not well learned, the arousal caused by the presence of others will detract from performance. Interestingly, even the virtual presence of fictional others can cause these same effects. In one study, participants completed difficult and easy tasks with a picture of either their favorite TV character or a non-favored character on a nearby computer screen (Gardner & Knowles, 2008). Participants performed better on the easy task when in the presence of the favored TV character, compared to the non-favored one, but they showed the opposite pattern on the difficult task. Because the favored character seemed more "real" to the participants, it created the classic pattern of social facilitation effects.

Because of the contradictory effects of arousal, the presence of an audience can even affect two people in quite opposite ways when they are performing the same task. For example, expert pool players, for whom good shots are highly accessible responses, performed better when an interested audience was close by than when they thought no one was watching. In contrast, poor players, for whom miscues were most accessible, succeeded on fewer shots when others watched (Michaels, Blommel, Brocato, Linkous, & Rowe, 1982). Zajonc's idea (1965) that other people cause arousal and that arousal improves performance of simple tasks but interferes with performance of difficult tasks, makes sense of these findings and has been confirmed by most subsequent research (Aiello & Douthitt, 2001; Guerin, 1986).

Of course, these findings leave one question unanswered: Why does the presence of others lead to arousal? Zajonc (1965) believed that humans and other animals have an innate tendency to be aroused by other members of their species. But why is this so? Subsequent research points to two underlying causes: evaluation apprehension and distraction (Geen, 1991; Nijstad, 2013).

Evaluation Apprehension

When we focus on what other people think about us, it creates arousal, with sometimes positive and sometimes negative effects on performance.

Most of the time, we want other people to value, include, and like us. In fact, our self-esteem is greatly affected by what others think of us. For these reasons, we may worry about whether onlookers are judging us in some way. As you jog past people, for example, you may suddenly be concerned about whether you look out of shape, and you may pull in your stomach and step up your pace. Research has confirmed that the presence of others who are in a position to judge us produces evaluation apprehension (M. Rosenberg, 1969), which changes our performance in the way predicted by social facilitation theory. One study, for example, demonstrated that apprehension can improve performance on simple aspects of a task and hinder it on complex aspects of the same task. Scott Bartis and his colleagues (Bartis, Szymanski, & Harkins, 1988) asked groups of participants to list various uses for a knife. Some participants were given the simple task of coming up with as many uses as possible. Others had the relatively challenging task of being as creative as possible. In each group, some participants believed the experimenter would evaluate their individual performance and others knew their responses would go into a common pool (where they could not be individually evaluated). As

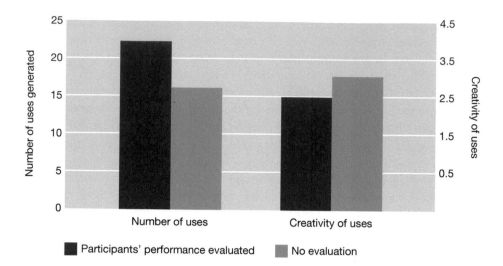

Figure 11.1 Effects of evaluation on simple and complex tasks
Some participants (*dark bars*) knew their individual task performance would be evaluated by the experimenter, whereas others (*light bars*) did not expect individual evaluations. When the task was fairly simple—generating as many suggestions as possible for ways to use a knife—evaluation improved performance, as shown by the bars on the left. However, when participants were given a much harder task—being as creative as possible in devising uses for the knife—evaluation had the opposite effect; it decreased their creativity (see scale on the right). (Data from Bartis and others, 1988.)

Figure 11.1 illustrates, the possibility of evaluation increased output on the simple task, and it decreased output on the intellectually more difficult task.

It's no wonder, then, that if you expect to succeed at a task (because it is easy, or it involves an accessible response, or you have succeeded at this task in the past), you will do better when you are observed, whereas the opposite is true if you expect to fail (Sanna

SOCIAL PSYCHOLOGY IN PRACTICE: EVALUATION APPREHENSION IN THE WORKPLACE AND THE CLASSROOM: MONITORING AND PERFORMANCE

In this technological age, observation and evaluation do not require the physical presence of an observer. Some employers monitor their employees' performances, for example, by automatically recording the number of keystrokes per minute made by clerical workers as they enter data into computers. Students in some online courses have their coursework tracked, with such measures as time spent doing readings or numbers of sample problems attempted. The goal is presumably to increase the work effort and performance of those who are monitored, but if electronic monitoring has the same effects as the physical presence of observers, it may sometimes decrease rather than increase performance. In an experiment by Jack Aiello and Kathryn Kolb (1995), highly skilled workers performed better when they knew they were being monitored than when they were unmonitored. On the other hand, monitoring decreased the performance of relatively unskilled workers. Monitoring also increased workers' feelings of stress. And in a study of people participating in an online training program, monitoring of their activities reduced both their satisfaction and their performance (Thompson, Sebastianelli, & Murray, 2009). Thus, monitoring and evaluation may have similar effects whether the observers are actually present or are recording performance from afar.

& Shotland, 1990). Other researchers have provided evidence that evaluation, not mere presence, is the critical factor that affects behavior. For example, the presence of actively supportive, nonevaluative observers—humans or even pets— neither provokes arousal nor interferes with performance (K. M. Allen, Blascovich, Tomaka, & Kelsey, 1991).

Distraction

The presence of others can also distract us from our task, also creating arousal and impacting performance. However, with specific types of tasks, distraction can focus us on task-relevant cues, potentially improving performance.

Other people can affect our performance not only by observing and evaluating us but also by creating distraction. Their mere presence causes us to think about them, to react to them, or to monitor what they are doing, and thereby deflects attention from the task at hand (Aiello & Douthitt, 2001; R. S. Baron, 1986; Guerin, 1986). Researchers in one study, for example, had someone sit behind the participant in a location in which he or she could not monitor the participant's performance. The presence of this person nevertheless improved the participant's performance on easy tasks and interfered with it on difficult ones (Schmitt, Gilovich, Goore, & Joseph, 1986).

It is easy to understand why evaluation apprehension can create arousal, but how does distraction do so? The answer seems to be that as our impulses to do two different things at once—concentrate on the task and react to others—start to conflict with each other, we become agitated and aroused (Geen, 1991; Muller, Atzeni, & Butera, 2004). This arousal, like that caused by evaluation apprehension, will typically improve performance on simple tasks and interfere with it on difficult ones.

The presence of distracting others not only causes arousal, but also requires people to split their attention between the other people and the task at hand (Baron, 1986). The result is that the scope of attention for the task becomes narrowed. But if it narrows attention, distraction may improve performance on difficult tasks that require picking up a task-relevant cue amongst other, irrelevant cues that compete with the relevant one. Huguet and colleagues (1999) tested this hypothesis and found that on such a difficult task, people performed better in the presence of distracting others who could not witness the participant's performance (ruling out the possibility of evaluation apprehension) than they did when alone. Thus, in some cases, the presence of others may improve performance on difficult tasks. Figure 11.2 summarizes how the presence of others, even those with whom we do not interact, can make us worry about evaluation or can distract us.

In much of the work on social facilitation, the "audience" is one person or a small number of others, often at some distance from the actor. But, what about being surrounded or engulfed by others, in a large crowd? If you have ever been packed into a busy metro station at rush hour or in a standing-room only auditorium, you may know that feeling crowded is often aversive. This is because being crowded, like having an audience, is arousing because crowds create many opportunities for evaluation and distraction. One study found, for example, that 10 strangers who were crammed into an 8-by-12-foot room had higher blood pressure and greater increases in other physiological indicators of arousal than did those occupying a larger room (Evans, 1979). Like the arousal

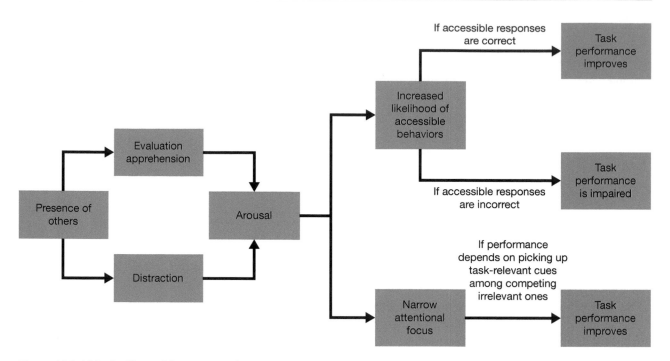

Figure 11.2 Multiple effects of the presence of others

The presence of others can produce arousal, through either evaluation apprehension or simple distraction. Arousal increases the likelihood that people will perform the most accessible actions. With a simple or well-practiced task, highly accessible responses are likely to be correct and arousal improves performance. But if the task is complex or novel, accessible responses will not help much and arousal will impair task performance. Arousal can also narrow attentional focus. If performance depends on picking up task-relevant cues among competing irrelevant ones, then performance can improve.

produced by an audience, arousal induced by crowding can energize effort, thereby improving performance on simple tasks, such as cheering loudly at a football game, and impairing performance on complex tasks, such as making difficult judgments about the star player's scoring abilities (Paulus, Annis, Seta, Schkade, & Matthews, 1976). With these powerful effects, it is no wonder that the home crowd is a key part of the home-field advantage in sports such as soccer (Goumas, 2013).

PERFORMANCE IN FACE-TO-FACE GROUPS: INTERACTION AND INTERDEPENDENCE

task interdependence
reliance on other members of a group for mastery of material outcomes that arise from the group's task

social interdependence
reliance on other members of the group for feelings of connectedness, social and emotional rewards, and a positive social identity

If the minimal influence of other people who are present can influence our behavior, consider how much more potent is the effect of a face-to-face group. Members of such groups—families, flight crews, rock bands, government commissions, and others—are highly interdependent. They are characterized by **task interdependence** because their mastery of material outcomes depends on working together to perform some collective task: a successful flight, the negotiation of teachers' contracts, or the completion of a group presentation for class. They also face **social interdependence** because they rely on one another for feelings of connectedness and positive emotional outcomes, such as respect, caring, and positive social identity. Large or small, all face-to-face groups are characterized by some combination of task and social interdependence (J. M. Levine & Moreland, 1998).

Face-to-face groups have widely differing goals and purposes. For businesses, the group goal is profit; for university faculties, it is the production of new knowledge and well-rounded graduates; for high school bands, it is the performance of harmonious music. Depending on their goals, groups demand different amounts of social or task interdependence. Social interdependence or connectedness is particularly important for primary or intimacy groups, like families and close friends, which value their members just because they are members. Of course, these groups are also frequently task interdependent, as when they work together to care for the yard, balance the budget, or organize vacations. Secondary groups, such as those found in most work settings, often exist for a specific purpose involving the mastery of rewards, so task interdependence is their defining feature. But as we all know, roles, status hierarchies, and friendships are inevitable in work settings, which means that work groups are always also somewhat socially interdependent.

Indeed, every group faces the challenge of successfully managing both forms of interdependence to achieve high levels of productivity (in other words, mastery goals) and positive relationships among group members (connectedness goals). Managing these two forms of interdependence is a challenge because they sometimes conflict. Fostering task interdependence, for example, can interfere with feeling good about being in the group, as when the study group organizer prohibits idle chit-chat in an effort to keep the group focused on their preparation for the upcoming test. Social interdependence can similarly detract from task performance if classmates socialize so much that their work on the team project falls behind schedule. To understand how such problems arise and how they can be solved, we need to look at what happens as groups come together and work toward their goals. Although most of our examples involve work groups because they have been the focus of most research, the same processes operate in all groups working together to produce something.

Of course these properties were also true of the groups forming norms we discussed back in Chapter 9. They were socially interdependent because forming norms helps achieve connectedness, and they were task interdependent because they relied on one another to form norms that appropriately reflect reality.

How Groups Change: Stages of Group Development

Face-to-face groups usually go through different stages of relationship with their members. During group socialization, groups and individuals can become committed to each other, through processes that guide members' entry, socialization, role maintenance, and sometimes exit, from the group. At the same time, groups go through formation, conflict, development of norms, performance, and dissolution as they try to maximize social and task interdependence to develop an identity and reach their goals. Time pressure can affect how groups solve these problems.

The Ashland Corporation, a manufacturer of air conditioners, decided to assemble a special task group to propose and produce innovative new products. The team, composed of a team leader, "team advisers," and several production-line employees, was asked to turn a huge, empty factory building into a functioning production line for a newly designed series of compressors. The team had to select, order, and arrange for the installation of production machinery. It also was responsible for organizing and training the production-line workers in a way that maximized their efficiency and maintained extremely high quality standards. As the different members came together, their first task was simply to become a group. Then as the group began to work toward its goals over a period of months, it confronted a series of problems and challenges, which in turn influenced the group's structure and operation. Finally, when the team's goals had been reached, the team was disbanded (Eisenstat, 1990).

These changes were not unique to the Ashland team. All groups, whether short-term, ad hoc groups created to solve isolated problems or long-term groups that might take years to reach their goals, go through different stages as they try to maximize task and social interdependence (Eisenstat, 1990; McGrath & Tschan, 2004; Moreland & Levine, 1988; Tuckman, 1965; Wheelan, 1994). Part of this process has to do with evolving relationships between individual members and the group, as each individual begins, continues, and perhaps ends his or her participation. The other part of the process is the changing concerns the group as a whole must deal with to achieve the kind of interaction and interdependence that will get the job done.

Group Socialization: Mutual Evaluation by Members and Groups.

Richard Moreland and John Levine (1988) coined the term **group socialization** to describe the cognitive, affective, and behavioral changes that occur as individuals join—and leave—such diverse groups as sports teams, social clubs, or religious sects. Group socialization is an ongoing process of mutual evaluation from both the individual member's and the group's perspectives. When the individual feels that the group offers a better chance of meeting his or her needs than alternative group memberships, the individual becomes committed to the group. Conversely, when the group feels that the individual offers a better chance of fulfilling group goals than other potential members, the group is also committed to the individual. These processes of evaluation and mutual commitment define the various stages of relationship that members can have with their groups.

Initially, groups try to size up potential members who might contribute to the group good and help the group succeed, while individuals at the same time assess the extent to which groups help satisfy personal needs for mastery and connectedness. If this initial evaluation leads the individual to commit to the group and vice versa, the individual becomes a new member of the group. Of course groups and individuals may not always have control over this process—sometimes membership in a group or team is dictated by outside forces, as it was in the case of the Ashland team.

Regardless of how membership comes about, entry into the group triggers the second phase of group membership, socialization. The group now tries to mold the individual into a "team player" who can help achieve group goals. The Ashland team needed several different kinds of expertise to solve its problems, and so it needed specific team members to fill those various kinds of roles. At the same time, the individual tries to shape the group so that it meets as many of his or her needs as possible, both for task mastery and for social connections. To the extent that individuals and groups like what they see in each other at this stage, their mutual commitment may rise again. Such commitment to the group makes individuals adopt group values, feel good about fellow members, and work hard to achieve group goals and maintain membership in the group. Similarly, commitment to the individual makes the group value, like, and seek to keep the individual as a member.

group socialization

the cognitive, affective, and behavioral changes that occur as individuals join and leave groups

People select a particular romantic partner because that partner seems better than alternatives, as we will describe in Chapter 12, pages 460–461. The same happens when selecting groups.

Sometimes groups might be reluctant to commit to a new group member, especially if they know that the newcomer isn't permanent. One study found that, if group members believe that a newly assigned member will be part of the group only temporarily, they perceive that person as less similar to the group, which makes it harder to accept him or her (Rink & Ellemers, 2009). Moreover, though temporary members seemed to make group decision making better, they also created more conflict in the group, compared to new permanent members.

Once the individual is a fully committed member, the relationship enters the maintenance phase. During this time, the group tries to find a specific role for the individual that maximizes his or her contribution, and the individual tries to find a role that maximizes the satisfaction he or she can obtain from the group. If this role negotiation succeeds, mutual commitment remains high and membership works well from both perspectives. Such mutually beneficial memberships might go on indefinitely, and might only be severed when the group disbands, as the Ashland group did once its work was complete. But if the mutual evaluation that occurs during this phase lowers commitment, an individual can become a marginal member of the group. Unless corrective efforts succeed, commitment is likely to continue to fall until the individual leaves or is ousted from the group.

Because the group and its members must be mutually committed to one another, those who want to join and remain in the group must be careful not to upset the group in ways that might lead to their ousting. This raises interesting dilemmas when one's fellow group members misbehave. If you see a member of your group violate a group rule, what would you do? The answer might depend on whether you are new or a veteran group member. In one study, female rugby players were presented with descriptions of various rugby rule violations that involved inappropriate behavior during games, and asked whether they would confront members of their own team who performed these behaviors. Those who reported feeling like veteran players were more likely to confront in-group rule-violators than those who felt like novices. Veterans feel more secure in their standing in the group than do newcomers, and are thus more free to "rock the boat" (Jetten and others, 2010).

Several studies find that individuals' passages into and out of groups are marked by the kinds of stages described by the group socialization model (Chen & Klimoski, 2003; Moreland & Levine, 2001). The group socialization model is also important because it makes clear that groups don't just change individuals: individuals change groups as well. From sports teams and hobby clubs to service organizations and work teams, the formation and development of a group is a mutual interaction between individual pursuit of mastery and connectedness, and group pursuit of successful task and social interdependence.

Group Development: Coming Together, Falling Apart. Just as the relationship between each individual and the group goes through different stages, so too do the overall interaction patterns among all the members of the group go through different stages as they try to coordinate task interdependence and enhance social interdependence. Although some groups go through all five of the stages described here, many others skip steps, repeat steps, recycle through many of the steps, or dissolve before they ever reach the later stages (Ilgen, Hollenbeck, Johnson, & Jundt, 2005).

1. *Forming.* In the initial stage of group development, when initial processes of evaluation and mutual selection are occurring, members attempt to understand where other individuals stand in the group and what the group as a whole stands for (Moreland, 1987). For both these reasons, there is usually an intense focus on the group's leader who both has the highest status in the group and is expected to articulate the group's goals (Hogg, van Knippenberg, & Rast, 2012). Managers facilitated the Ashland group's progress through this stage by giving group members time to get acquainted and by stressing the special nature of their task—a task that could not be completed without everyone's full cooperation.

2. *Storming.* Conflict is often evident in the second stage, and disagreements can be intense and emotional (Bales, Cohen, & Williamson, 1979; Tuckman, 1965). At this point, as the group socialization model describes, the group and individual members are attempting to shape and negotiate specific roles. But conflicts can arise for multiple reasons (de Wit, Greer, & Jehn, 2012). Relationship conflicts arise from interpersonal incompatibilities, such as personality differences. Task conflicts arise from differing opinions about the content of the tasks the group is performing and the results of those tasks. Process conflicts arise from diverging opinions concerning the mechanics of task pursuit, such as conflicts over task delegation. A recent meta-analysis revealed that all three of these types of conflicts harm group commitment and trust within the group. Both relationship and process conflict reduce group performance. In contrast, task conflict is not reliably related to group performance overall, and in fact under some conditions, it can actually lead to better group performance (de Wit and others, 2012). Thus, conflict can be problematic for groups, but certain types of conflict under some conditions may be beneficial.

HOT TOPICS IN SOCIAL PSYCHOLOGY: PREFERENCE FOR HIERARCHY

Groups can be formed and organized in different ways. Some groups are relatively "flat" or egalitarian, with all group members having equal power, status, etc. But most groups take on a hierarchical structure—where some group members are "above" others, possessing more resources, power, sway in decision making, and so forth. Recent research suggests that humans may generally prefer hierarchical structure in their groups (Friesen, Kay, Eibach, & Galinsky, 2014). These studies showed that people perceive hierarchical groups as more structured than egalitarian groups and that employees who feel their workplaces are more hierarchical also feel more able to achieve their goals, at least if the workplace seems fair. The authors speculate that hierarchies are viewed positively in these ways because they offer people a sense of control. In one of their experimental studies, participants first wrote about a time they felt high or low levels of control. They then read about a small group whose structure was not clear. Those who wrote about a lack of control perceived more hierarchy in that group than those who had written about having control. In another experiment, some participants read an article that described the economy or the world more broadly as lacking control, whereas others read an article unrelated to control. Then all rated their preference for hierarchy, measured with items like, "Every company needs a boss who is in charge of everyone else" and "Businesses are most effective when there are a few people who have the influence to get things done." Those who had previously read about a lack of control reported a greater preference for hierarchy than those in the neutral condition. Thus, groups may take hierarchical form because hierarchies help satisfy the need for mastery and control.

Indeed, some research suggests that task conflict is helpful for group performance specifically when group members feel that it is safe to state their ideas without fear of interpersonal attack (Bradley, Postlethwaite, Klotz, Hamdani, & Brown, 2012).

Conflict may die down when a majority forms and persuades the rest of the group to adopt its views. However, many companies deliberately build in protection for "screwball" ideas, so that "storming" works to keep them on the cutting edge. In a classic case of persistent and effective dissent, a market researcher at Compaq Computer Corporation persuaded management to disregard surveys that predicted a limited market for a briefcase-size portable computer. Like other organizations that allow their members to express their doubts and differences of opinion in a context that does not pressure them to compromise too soon, Compaq introduced the product, which became highly successful. Compaq reaped big benefits because it did not simply try to suppress conflict, but allowed minority influence to prevail (Kotkin, 1986; Ilgen and others, 2005).

3. ***Norming.*** If the group survives the storming stage, harmony and unity usually emerge as consensus, cohesion, and a positive group identity develop. A sense of security and trust emerges when conflict declines as members' disagreements are resolved into a unified purpose (Wheelan, Davidson, & Tilin, 2003). In this stage most members tend to be highly satisfied with the group and to agree about the group's purpose and the role and responsibilities of individual members. Group commitment is high, with group members who more strongly identify with their group being more likely to remain an active part of it (Van Vugt & Hart, 2004). As one member of the Ashland team described the norming stage: "Then everyone jelled together . . . Nobody said no, everybody said yes . . . It was smooth, and people [were] in a good mood" (Eisenstat, 1990).

4. ***Performing.*** With norms established, the group moves into the performance stage. Members cooperate to solve problems, make decisions, and generate output. They exchange information freely, handle disagreements productively, and maintain mutual allegiance to the group goals. Groups that have developed open communication about and support for task interdependence in the norming stage are better able to adapt to changing task demands in the performing stage than groups whose members value independence (Moon and others, 2004). At this stage of the Ashland group's development, employees worked long hours, helped wherever they needed to, and operated as a team. Their product was declared a success, further enhancing group morale (Eisenstat, 1990).

5. ***Adjourning.*** Most groups, especially ad hoc groups put together for a specific purpose, eventually reach the end of their life span, the adjourning stage. Some, like the new factory team at Ashland, know from the outset that their lifetime is limited. Others dissolve because they have accomplished their goals. Still others fall apart when members lose interest, move away, or flee conflict (Rusbult, 1983; Thibaut & Kelley, 1959). At a group's endpoint, members often gather to evaluate their work, give feedback to each other, and express their feelings about the group (Lundgren & Knight, 1978). The dissolution of a cohesive group can be stressful for members if group identification has taken place, because loss of the group entails a change in social identity. Members lose the benefits of others' skills and contributions and the security of others' support and companionship. When cohesion and

If you think these conditions for a good decision sound familiar, you're right. We described the importance of including minority viewpoints so a group can make valid judgments in Chapter 9, pages 339–346.

Chapter 6 described these and the many other effects of group identification.

TABLE 11.1 Stages of Group Development

Stage	Task Processes	Social Processes
Forming	Exchange of information, task exploration	Getting to know each other, self-disclosure, dependence on leader
Storming	Disagreement over goals and procedures	Disagreement over status, criticism of ideas, hostility, coalition formation
Norming	Formation of consensus and norms	Growth of cohesion and unity, positive group identity and connectedness
Performing	Goal-focused efforts, orientation toward mastery and task performance	Social influence, cooperation
Adjourning	Completion of tasks, dissolution of roles	Withdrawal, emotional expressions, reminiscence

Sources: D. R. Forsyth, *Group dynamics,* 3rd ed., 1999, Pacific Grove, CA: Brooks/Cole; S. A. Wheelan, *Group processes: A developmental perspective,* 1994, Boston, MA: Allyn & Bacon.

interaction are particularly intense, the psychological impact of the adjourning of a group can be similar to that of a break-up of a close relationship, leaving the same feelings of grief and loneliness. Group members can prevent some of this stress if they prepare themselves for the adjournment by reducing group cohesion, stressing individual independence, and searching for new groups to join (Mayadas & Glasser, 1985).

Table 11.1 summarizes these five typical stages of group development, along with the task and social processes that characterize each stage.

Time and Group Development. Besides the typical progression through these developmental stages, time has other effects on the ways groups interact and deal with their tasks. Perhaps you have had the experience of working with a group on a long-term project for a class. If so, you may recall that at a certain point, after getting to know each other in a relaxed way and developing and discarding various tentative plans, your group suddenly realized that time was passing and little concrete progress had been made. Connie Gersick (1989) proposed that many groups go through this process, which she termed the "mid-life crisis" because she found that it often occurred when about half of the group's total time remained. The reorientation spurred by the realization that time is growing short may trigger a radically different approach to the group's task, shifts in strategies, and a greater emphasis on productive work. Research suggests that groups that spend part of their early planning on timing issues—considering when tasks will be performed, how much time to allot for them, and other timing constraints—will perform better (Janicik & Bartel, 2003).

Janice Kelly and her colleagues (J. R. Kelly, Jackson, & Hutson-Comeaux, 1997; J. R. Kelly & Karau, 1999; J. R. Kelly & Loving, 2004) also found that time pressure alters the way groups approach their tasks. Groups under time pressure devote more of their interaction to clearly task-focused matters and differ from less pressured groups in the ways they share information and seek to influence each other. In some ways they perform better than groups with more time available. For example, because of their increased task focus, groups that have to write a proposal for a new program write more words per minute when they are under a tight deadline. Still, time pressure has its costs. Proposals that are written in a rush tend to be less creative and original than those written with more adequate time (Karau & Kelly, 1992), and groups under time pressure tend to find worse solutions in decision-making tasks than those who do not feel rushed (Bowman & Wittenbaum, 2012).

Being Pushed Out of Groups: Rejection and Ostracism.
Group members sometimes leave groups under amicable circumstances. Perhaps they decide to change jobs to pursue new opportunities, voluntarily leaving a current work group. Or perhaps a group member simply loses interest in a hobby group—like a book club, poker group, or tennis league—and takes up other hobbies instead. But sometimes group members are pushed out because they are no longer wanted by the remaining members. When existing group members decide to actively remove someone from a group, social rejection has occurred. Sometimes people are not only excluded but also ignored, a type of treatment called **ostracism** (Williams, 2007). Research has compellingly demonstrated that being rejected or ostracized from groups can have profound effects on a person (Williams, 2009).

ostracism
being ignored and excluded from a group

One of the most commonly used methods to study ostracism experimentally is called Cyberball (Williams, Cheung, & Choi, 2000). In this paradigm, participants believe they are playing a virtual ball-tossing game for a few minutes with two others on a computer. In reality, the other "players" in the game are controlled by a computer program. In the inclusion version of this game, the real participant receives the ball regularly from the others, with each player being thrown the ball roughly one-third of the time. In the ostracism condition, though, the real player is thrown the virtual ball a few times at the beginning of the game, but after that the other two "players" toss the ball back and forth between them, leaving the participant out. See Figure 11.3 for how Cyberball appears to participants.

Chapter 9, pages 335–336, described how groups regularly try to exclude or to punish deviants.

On the face of it, you might not expect this treatment to have much of an effect on people. After all, the game lasts for only a short while and involves other people that you cannot see and probably will never meet. Anyway, who cares if they don't throw you a virtual ball? There are no real, tangible negative consequences. Yet despite its seeming triviality, even this form of ostracism affects people. Compared to being included, being ostracized in Cyberball leads people to report lower levels of belonging, self-esteem, control, and a sense of a meaningful existence (Zadro, Williams, & Richardson, 2004). Even ostracism by others we deplore, such as members of the racist KKK, can have the same effect (Gonsalkorale & Williams, 2007). What's more, when people play a modified version of the game called Cyberbomb, when they believe they are tossing a virtual bomb that could "explode" and "kill" them, people still feel bad if they are ostracized (van Beest, Williams, & van Dijk, 2011)! People not only report feeling bad following ostracism in Cyberball, but areas of the brain that activate in response to physical pain are also activated during this type of ostracism (Eisenberger, Lieberman, & Williams, 2003), and their sensitivity to physical pain changes (Bernstein & Claypool, 2012). If people are affected in this way following ostracism in brief lab-based games, imagine how upset people likely feel when they are ostracized in real life from groups that matter to them.

Figure 11.3 Cyberball paradigm
In Cyberball participants throw a virtual ball to each other. The real participant is represented by a "hand" at the bottom, and the two other "players" (actually controlled by a computer program) are represented by the figures shown at the top-right and top-left. In the included version of the game, the real participant receives the virtual ball regularly from the other "players." In the ostracism version, the real participant receives the ball a few times at the start of the game, but then never again. (Reprinted with permission from Williams, 2009.)

Ostracism and rejection have potent effects on people's perceptions, motivations, and behaviors (Williams, 2007). Using Cyberball and other manipulations, researchers have discovered that those who are rejected or ostracized want to recapture affiliation with other people (Maner and others, 2007). Perhaps for this reason, they seem highly attuned to social cues in the environment that might help them secure good social interactions. They have especially good memory for social information (Gardner, Pickett, & Brewer, 2000), can quickly spot a smiling face in an array of faces (DeWall, Maner, & Rouby, 2009), and can more accurately discriminate "real" from "fake" smiles (Bernstein and others, 2008). Though these sound like adaptive and positive responses to rejection and ostracism, not all responses are so constructive. Indeed, rejection and ostracism can at times make people highly aggressive (Gaertner, Iuzzini, & O'Mara, 2008; Twenge and others, 2001; Warburton, Williams, & Cairns, 2006). Based on a case study of school shootings in the U.S., some scholars have even argued that rejection and ostracism may play a role in causing these tragedies (Leary and others, 2003).

Recent work has examined a more subtle form of ostracism that occurs in task groups, sometimes called being "out of the loop," where a group member finds it difficult to participate in a group discussion due to a lack of relevant information (Jones, Carter-Sowell, Kelly, & Williams, 2009). Imagine being appointed to a committee on planning a charity fundraiser. You are new to this committee and have no experience or expertise in fundraising. The other group members, though, have served on similar committees in the past and "know the ropes." You may find yourself unable to contribute to the group discussion and may feel left out as the other group members discuss issues that you don't understand. A recent study examined what happens in these situations by bringing students together in groups of three (Wittenbaum, Shulman, & Braz, 2010). First, each member was given two documents to read alone, but not all were given the same documents. Next, the experimenter announced that the group would be discussing one of those documents. The situation was rigged such that two members had read the document but one, the "uninformed member," had not. The group discussed the details of the selected document and wrote a response to it. As expected, coders who viewed the videotaped interaction judged the uninformed member to be less involved in the conversation than the informed ones, suggesting that subtle ostracism of the uninformed member occurred. Moreover, mirroring other ostracism findings, on a questionnaire that followed the group interaction the uninformed members reported worse mood and lower levels of belonging, meaningful existence, control, and self-esteem compared to the informed members.

Getting the Job Done: Group Performance

To achieve their performance goals, groups must maintain their motivation and avoid problems of coordination. Processes including communication within the group and shared emotions can influence group performance. Training and accountability can improve performance, but perhaps most important is developing a common social identity, which helps avoid performance problems by attracting and keeping valuable group members and by encouraging acceptance of group goals and normative cooperation.

For most groups, performing is the crucial stage because the work of the group must be accomplished during this period. Whether the group carries through with a flawless performance or collapses into disarray will depend on the kinds of tasks it faces, the quality of the group effort, and the resources available for reaching goals and repairing damage to the group (Kerr & Tindale, 2004).

Forms of Task Interdependence. According to Ivan Steiner (1972), group tasks differ in terms of the type of interdependence they require. With additive tasks, the potential performance of the group is approximately equal to the sum of the performances of the individual members and is generally better than any one member's performance. A tug-of-war is an additive task, as is joining others to push a stalled car out of an intersection. In additive tasks, individual effort is the key because the final outcome is roughly proportional to the number of individuals contributing and how much they give (Littlepage, 1991). But coordination is also important: One person tugging on the rope when all the others are resting will not ensure tug-of-war victory.

In disjunctive tasks, a group's performance is expected to be as good as the performance of its best individual member (Laughlin, VanderStoep, & Hollingshead, 1991). When one member of a student group comes up with a terrific concept for the term project and everyone else recognizes its merit, the task is disjunctive. In this case, interdependence means that the outcome will be a function of the individual skills and talents of the group members. Thus, education or training of individual members can improve group performance, as can the selection of members with the right mix of skills (Hackman, 1987). Coordination is important, too, because other members have to be careful not to get in the way of any individual member who can complete the task (Diehl & Stroebe, 1991; Littlepage, 1991).

Conjunctive tasks depend on every member playing his or her part. In this case, the group's performance is only as good as the performance of its worst member. Groups of mountain climbers or assembly-line teams are engaged in conjunctive tasks: Their slowest or weakest member determines whether and how quickly they achieve their goal. If three students agree that one will do the research for a report, a second will write it, and the third will deliver it in class, their grade will depend on how well each of them performs his or her part of the task. Coordination is very important in conjunctive tasks, so the group has to organize its members' activities (Hertel, Kerr, & Messe, 2000). If coordination fails, so that two people do the research but nobody writes the presentation, the total task will remain undone.

Compensatory tasks involve each group member contributing a judgment or estimate, which are averaged to produce the group's product. In this case, if each group member provides an independent input, not influenced by others, their individual errors can often cancel each other out, leading to a good overall performance. Imagine that a work group is trying to estimate the cost of creating a new product for its business. Some group members will likely guess too high, whereas others will guess too low. As these errors are averaged together, they compensate for each other. Under the right circumstances, the result is often a good final judgment that reflects the collective wisdom of the group as a whole (Surowiecki, 2004).

Most tasks are complex tasks, which consist of subtasks that involve all forms of interdependence. In playing football, for example, some tasks are disjunctive (any of several players can block the opposing defensive end), whereas others are conjunctive (the quarterback must throw the pass and the receiver must catch it). Of course, the more complicated the task, the greater the need for planning and coordination to ensure that members' skills and efforts are appropriately allocated. And the more complicated the task, the greater the opportunity will be for the group's performance to multiply and surpass any possible effort by a single individual. At the same time, unfortunately, putting individuals' efforts together in complicated group tasks also provides many opportunities for things to go wrong.

Photo 11.2 Task interdependence at work. Most complex tasks require multiple forms of interdependence. The assembly of automobiles, as shown in this photo of a Porsche factory, requires workers to complete specialized tasks within precisely specified times. The task is a conjunctive one. A worker who does not finish his or her task on time can undermine productivity for everyone on the line.

Gains and Losses in Group Performance. "Two heads are better than one," and two sets of hands are better than one too. That is certainly one reason so much work is performed by groups. Groups do perform many tasks better than an individual could. Groups can multiply individual effort, provide a variety of skills that no one person possesses, and work together to complete tasks in parallel, rather than serial, fashion. Perhaps each Amish farmer has all the skills necessary to build a barn alone, but when all the members of his community pool their skills, labor, and enthusiasm, a barn can be raised in a day or two. The advantages of group effort are also evident in many cognitive tasks (Kerr & Tindale, 2004; Laughlin, Hatch, Silver, & Boh, 2006). For example, groups solve puzzles more quickly than individuals do (Laughlin, 1980). Members of the surgical team in an operating room can correct an error by one group member quickly, before its consequences become severe (Azar, 1994). And collective memory is often better than individual memory: After watching a video-tape portraying a police interrogation, groups of participants offered more accurate and detailed accounts of the event than did individuals who worked alone (N. K. Clark, Stephenson, & Kniveton, 1990; Wegner, 1987). However, groups do not always have more accurate memory. In one study, interacting groups were more likely to mistakenly recall an item that had never been presented compared to the same number of people working individually (Thorley & Dewhurst, 2009).

Another reason that dyads or groups often perform better than lone individuals is that they can observe each other's levels of confidence. The group member who has the better or more correct answer is also likely to be more confident, and others in the dyad or group use that person's confidence as a cue to go with his or her answer (Koriat, 2012). This results in the group or dyad performing better. But this same research shows that two heads can sometimes be worse than one for the same reason. The researchers gave dyads tricky general-knowledge questions that most people answer incorrectly. On such questions, the individual who gave the more common (but incorrect) answer was often more confident. This misplaced confidence often led others to go along with the wrong answer, leading to poorer group decisions.

Two sets of hands and heads may often be better than one, but are they twice as good? That is, do groups perform as well as the same number of individuals working alone? Frequently the answer is no. Much research has focused on the popular technique known as brainstorming, in which a group of people try to generate a large number of ideas without criticizing or evaluating them, at least initially. The premise is that one person's idea, even if wild and unworkable, may be built on and improved by other group members (Osborn, 1953). The evidence indicates that although brainstorming groups do better than a single person, they usually come up with fewer ideas and ideas of poorer quality than those produced by the same number of individuals working separately (Paulus & Coskun, 2013). The same is true for memory tasks: Although a group can remember more than a single individual, group performance is inferior to the combined information that can be recalled by an equal number of individuals working on their own (Wegner, 1987). Finally, groups sometimes display greater biases in judgment or decision-making tasks than do individuals provided with the same information (Boyle, Hanlon, & Russo, 2012; N. L. Kerr, MacCoun, & Kramer, 1996).

In cases like these, when groups do not amplify but actually diminish the sum of individual efforts, the cause is often a loss of either motivation or coordination among group members (Kerr & Tindale, 2004; J. M. Levine & Moreland, 1998; Nijstad, 2013).

Losses from Decreased Motivation: Social Loafing.
Sometimes working in a group leads people to slack off—to put less effort into the task than they would if working alone. As we noted in Chapter 1, this loss of motivation, termed **social loafing**, was first studied in the 1880s by Max Ringelmann, a French agricultural engineer who was interested in group performance on very simple additive tasks (Kravitz & Martin, 1986). Over a century later, Ringelmann's early insights have been confirmed by laboratory experiments. In the study of social loafing illustrated in Figure 11.4 for example, college students were told to clap and cheer as loudly as they could. The amount of sound generated by each

social loafing
the tendency to exert less effort on a task when an individual's efforts are an unidentifiable part of a group than when the same task is performed alone

If you reflect on the social facilitation research described on pages 398–399, you may realize that the mere presence of others should create arousal and therefore increase performance on simple tasks like clapping. The fact that declines in performance sometimes occur suggests that declines in motivation and coordination can sometimes outweigh the effects of arousal.

student's efforts decreased as the size of the group increased. Individual efforts seem quite literally to get lost in the crowd, and the degree of loss is substantial. In this study, an individual in a group of six made less than half the noise he or she made when clapping alone.

Social loafing is not restricted to simple motor tasks. When performance on cognitive tasks was measured, individuals in three-person brainstorming groups generated only 75% as many uses for a common object as they did when working alone. And working in groups, they made more than twice as many errors on a "vigilance" task of detecting brief flashes on a computer screen than they did when working alone (Harkins & Szymanski, 1989). Sharing responsibility can reduce effort no matter the task (Karau & Williams, 1993). People may even "preloaf" by preparing less for an upcoming group task than they do for an upcoming individual one (Ohlert & Kleinert, 2013).

Why do people loaf on group tasks? To some extent, the nature of the task itself is a factor. Social loafing occurs less often when tasks are interesting and involving (Brickner, Harkins, & Ostrom, 1986). The perceived features of one's group partners also matter. When a person's partner in a group task seems stereotypically well suited for the task, the person is more likely to loaf, believing that the partner is perfectly capable of doing the work well without much help (Plaks & Higgins, 2000). Interdependence also plays a role. For example, when interdependence is minimal and individual roles are unimportant, as when the crowd sings the national anthem before a ball game begins, it is easy to let others pick up the slack (Karau & Williams, 1993; N. L. Kerr & Bruun, 1983). In contrast, social loafing is reduced when individual contributions are essential for success (Kerr & Hertel, 2011; Weldon & Mustari, 1988) or when group members know that their individual contributions can be monitored (K. D. Williams, Harkins, &

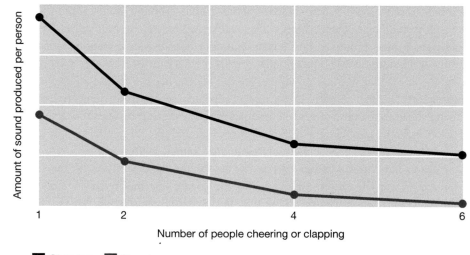

Figure 11.4 Effects of social loafing

In this experiment, college students were told to clap or cheer as loudly as they could. Note that the noise produced by each person decreased as the number of people clapping or cheering together increased. Social loafing is most likely to occur if the task is unchallenging, if individual performances cannot be monitored, or if the individual's contribution to the group is dispensable. (Data from Latané, Williams, & Harkins, 1979.)

SOCIAL PSYCHOLOGY AND CULTURE: SOCIAL LOAFING ACROSS CULTURES

Because people who identify more strongly with a group are less likely to socially loaf, it is perhaps not surprising that social loafing is less prevalent in collectivist cultures, which tend to be more group oriented than individualist cultures. A meta-analysis of social loafing found that participants from collectivist cultures showed less tendency to socially loaf than participants from individualist ones (Karau & Williams, 1993). One specific experiment used both American and Chinese manager trainees as participants (Earley, 1989). The Americans and Chinese participated individually on a work-simulation task, in which they completed as many work-related tasks as possible within an hour. In a key condition, participants believed they were working as part of a group to achieve a group productivity goal. Some of these participants faced high accountability for individual effort, because they had to put their names on the tasks they completed. In the low accountability condition, names were not attached and group efforts were pooled, creating conditions favorable to social loafing. Results showed that accountability had a big effect on Americans—they completed more tasks when they were accountable than when they were not. However, accountability had no effect on the Chinese participants, indicating that they worked equally hard no matter what.

Latané, 1981; Zaccaro, 1984). Moreover, those who are highly motivated to achieve are also unlikely to loaf (Hart, Karau, Stasson, & Kerr, 2004). Social loafing may be partly caused by an illusion of group productivity, people's tendency to believe that a group's performance is better than an individual's performance, even when it is not (Nijstad, Stroebe, & Lodewijkx, 2006). If you think your group is performing at an extremely high level, you may conclude that you do not have to push yourself hard to make

SOCIAL PSYCHOLOGY IN PRACTICE: SOCIAL LOAFING IN THE CLASSROOM

Imagine showing up on the first day of your social psychology class and reading over the syllabus. You notice that a lengthy research proposal is due at the end of the term and that it is to be done in small groups. Do you celebrate, knowing that you'll have fellow classmates to help you with this daunting assignment? Or do you mutter to yourself that you "hate group work?" If you are like many students, you probably are uneasy or unenthusiastic about the prospect of a group project in part because you may fear that you may do all the work while others "slack off," that is, socially loaf (e.g., Pfaff & Huddleston, 2003; Walker, 2001). Students commonly believe that others loaf on group work because the others simply do not care about the assignment or do not feel socially connected to group members (Jassawalla, Sashittal, & Malshe, 2009). Working well in groups is an important skill and can foster learning, which is why many instructors incorporate group assignments and projects in their classes. Is there a way to structure group assignments so that students don't loaf? One obvious way is to make each student feel more accountable for his or her input (Karau & Williams, 1993). Allowing students multiple opportunities to evaluate each other on the basis of their input into the project appears to both reduce rates of social loafing and make students feel more positively about group work (Brooks & Ammons, 2003). So do not despair. If you are allowed to evaluate your project team members, you may find you not only learn something while doing your group project, but you might even enjoy the experience!

contributions, so social loafing may result. Finally, people's orientation toward the group also influences the tendency to loaf, with strong group identification decreasing social loafing (Hogg, Abrams, Otten, & Hinkle, 2004; Karau & Williams, 1997).

As these findings indicate, to loaf or not to loaf seems to depend on motivation. When individual performance is important for task mastery, social loafing declines. And when an individual's performance has implications for connectedness to the group, for example, when others can praise or condemn individual efforts, social loafing declines. In fact, **social compensation** is sometimes observed, as one group member works extra hard to compensate for the weakness or lack of ability of another member (Hart, Bridgett, & Karau, 2001; Karau & Williams, 1997). In addition, sometimes the weakest or least capable group members work harder in groups than they do alone (Weber & Hertel, 2007), possibly because social comparison with other, better-performing group members inspires more effort. This seems to occur most often on a conjunctive task. As you remember, in this sort of task the group's performance is only as good as the performance of its worst member. Thus, the weakest member may feel that his group's fate rests on him, motivating especially hard work (Weber & Hertel, 2007).

social compensation

one group member working especially hard to compensate for another's low level of effort or performance

Losses from Poor Coordination. Even when group members are trying hard, the group needs to be organized if it is to do the best possible work. As John Ruskin (1907/1963) observed, "Failure is less frequently attributable to either insufficiency of means or impatience of labor than to a confused understanding of the thing to be done" (p. 1). Members need assigned roles and a clear sense of their resources. They also need to be aware of one another's strengths and weaknesses, of how their actions contribute to group goals, and of who has a right to command and who has a duty to obey. Group performance suffers when group members leave crucial tasks undone, duplicate others' efforts, compete for personal resources and status, or get in each other's way—literally or figuratively. On brainstorming tasks, interference caused by other group members' contributions appears to be a major reason for the inferior performance of groups compared to individuals working separately. Listening to others talk may distract group members from thinking up superior ideas or may even cause them to forget some ideas before they can be verbalized (Nijstad & Stroebe, 2006; Stroebe & Diehl, 1991).

Coordination in groups is often achieved via explicit communication, when group members directly spell out who should do what tasks. But, coordination can also be tacit, occurring without explicit communication (de Kwaadsteniet & van Dijk, 2012). Even when communication is difficult or impossible, group members may be able to

SOCIAL PSYCHOLOGY IN PRACTICE: POOR COORDINATION IN THE WORKPLACE

Poor coordination on group tasks can be disastrous in some circumstances. Consider, for example, the life-and-death responsibilities of cockpit crews on commercial airliners. If these small groups fail to work well together in an emergency, the results can be tragic. An investigation of one crash found that the pilot failed to pay attention to the copilot's repeated but timid comments that the takeoff was not proceeding normally. In another incident, a flight engineer manually silenced a noisy alarm, leaving the pilot with the impression that it was a false warning (Foushee, 1984).

Airlines typically select pilots and copilots almost exclusively for their outstanding individual skills and knowledge, paying less attention to their interpersonal or communication skills. Unfortunately, as Hackman (1993) concluded, "It is the team, not the aircraft or the individual pilot, that is at the root of most accidents." This insight has led to training aimed specifically at teamwork skills, rather than individual technical skills, which is now routine in both commercial and military aviation (Salas and others, 2006). As is the case with flight crews, errors made by teams of surgeons, anesthesiologists, and nurses in hospital operating rooms often reflect communication and coordination failures rather than deficiencies in individual skills. As a result, training of medical-care teams is now drawing on the lessons learned from decades of experience in aviation (Hamman, 2004).

anticipate what other group members will do and then plan their own behaviors accordingly (Wittenbaum, Stasser, & Merry, 1996). But how are members able to successfully anticipate each other's actions and decisions and, therefore, successfully coordinate in this fashion?

Shared social knowledge is especially important for tacit coordination (Abele & Stasser, 2008). Consider a simple coordination decision used in one study (de Kwaadsteniet & van Dijk, 2010). Participants imagined a scenario where they and a co-worker were going to travel by train together to a conference. However, they had not discussed at which train station they would meet. One station is close to the participant's house and one close to the co-worker's house, and each person would naturally prefer the closer station. The question is, without explicit pre-arrangement could the participant pick the same station as the co-worker? People were successful in conditions where the scenario included valuable social information: participants were told that they were the boss and their co-worker was a low-status intern, or that these roles were reversed. In these conditions there was a clear preference to pick the station closer to the boss. Thus, information about the status of the group members helped coordination. If no social information was given, participants selected both train stations at about equal rates and thus would often have failed to coordinate. Other types of social information, like whether a group member is similar or different to us, can also aid in tacit coordination decisions (de Kwaadsteniet and others, 2011).

Processes that Affect Performance: Group Communication. Regardless of what the task is, groups have one primary weapon in the struggle to achieve high task efficiency while maintaining cohesion: communication. It is no wonder, then, that as group members share and exchange information, most of the talk is about getting the job done and feeling good while doing it. In general—not surprisingly—a high level of open communication does contribute to overall group performance (Hyatt & Ruddy, 1997).

Beyond the overall level of communication, the balance between task-focused and socially-focused communications is also crucial if a group is to be effective (McGrath, 1984). If a group's performance suffers because of ineffective strategies or inadequate skills, the group must seek task-focused remedies, such as repeated instructions, new directions, or reminders of goals (Schachter, 1951). But when low cohesion is to blame for poor performance, remedies must have a social focus aimed at increasing positive interpersonal relationships and group identification. A pattern identified very early in the history of group research is that groups often alternate between a cluster of instrumental communications ("No, do it this way") and a cluster of social ones ("Yes, you're doing a great job"), nurturing both task and social interdependence (Bales, 1953). However, the optimal type and amount of communication depend on several factors. For example, if tasks are complex and standards for performance are unclear, high levels of task-focused communication such as problem analysis, planning, and evaluation of potential solutions become crucial (Hirokawa, 1990).

Technology and Communication. Before the days of audio and video conference calls, web-based instant messaging, email, and electronic discussion boards, if a group wanted to communicate, meeting face-to-face was its only option. But, today is a different world, and groups often interact through technology instead of in person. Not surprisingly, these new technologies influence both how tasks are completed and how group members feel as they complete them (Hollingshead, 2004).

Is technology-mediated communication better overall than face-to-face communication? The answer is complicated. Some findings—especially from studies in the 1980s and 1990s, earlier in the development of electronic communication technology—point to advantages of technology-mediated communication. When groups perform brainstorming tasks via computer, they perform better than face-to-face groups, partly because members are not interrupted by others' contributions yet are still able to see them on the screen (Gallupe and others, 1994). Computer-mediated group decision making may also be less vulnerable to problems like the premature consensus of groupthink and biases that polarize majority views. In one comparison of three-member groups of university administrators reaching decisions, group polarization was less likely after computer-mediated discussion than when the groups met face-to-face (T. W. McGuire, Kiesler, & Siegel, 1987).

Moreover, electronic communication seems to promote more equal participation among members. When groups meet face-to-face, high-status members typically dominate the discussion (Rutter & Robinson, 1981; E. Williams, 1977). This was certainly the case when researchers arranged for university students of different levels to make decisions together: High-status group members like graduate students took up much more "air time" than lower-status first-year undergraduates. When the same groups made comparable decisions using email, however, status inequalities in participation were reduced (Dubrovsky, Kiesler, & Sethna, 1991). Remember that if everyone participates, the group has a better chance of maximizing the potential of all its members to get the job done right.

On the other hand, technology-mediated communication has pitfalls, which became more evident as research accumulated over the years. One such problem is evident in a study of students who worked cooperatively on large-scale projects, either in face-to-face

HOT TOPICS IN SOCIAL PSYCHOLOGY: VIRTUAL MINORITY INFLUENCE

One advantage of technology-mediated communication is the promotion of minority influence. As we discussed in Chapter 9, minorities can often get groups to think in new and helpful ways. Emerging findings suggest that minorities arguing their point of view electronically can be influential in ways that improve group performance, as long as they claim in-group affiliation and maintain their views consistently (Bazarova, Walther, & McLeod, 2012). Several fascinating studies have also demonstrated a persuasive and performance advantage for remote or geographically removed minorities (O'Leary & Mortensen, 2010). In these cases, groups with a minority advocate who is geographically remote seemed to perform better because the minority was able to play devil's advocate, effectively inducing the majority to think about alternatives. Perhaps being removed from the anxiety and discomfort of face-to-face disagreements makes it easier for the minority to assert a deviant view without fear of reprisal, and makes it easier for majorities to accept minority input without worrying about the identity consequences of publicly accepting it. Thus increased opportunity for minority points of view to improve group decisions should be counted among the benefits of electronic or technology-mediated communication.

groups or by interactive videoconferencing (Storck & Sproull, 1995). After considerable collaborative work, each student rated how much he or she would like to work together in the future with other members of his or her group. The ratings in the face-to-face condition reflected mainly the other student's actual competence and task performance. Evidently it is easy to gain a solid impression of another's skills when interacting in person. In contrast, the ratings made by students in the videoconference condition were less influenced by the other individual's task skills and more by task-irrelevant characteristics, such as physical appearance and how effectively the person used the video medium. The effectiveness of real-world organizations may suffer if people are selected for collaborations based on such irrelevant factors rather than their task-related skills.

A meta-analysis found that overall, technology-mediated groups took longer to reach a decision, made poorer quality decisions, and group members were less satisfied with their decisions compared to groups who communicated face-to-face (Baltes, Dickson, Sherman, Bauer, & LaGanke, 2002). It may not feel very good to interact in technology-mediated groups either. One study asked students to write about a present or recent work group and to estimate the amount of time they spent interacting with team members in computer-mediated ways. Their reported levels of positive feelings and their commitment to the team were both lower when there was more computer-mediated interaction (Johnson, Bettenhausen, & Gibbons, 2009). These findings are nonexperimental, but they nevertheless suggest that computer-mediated communication may damage group commitment and reduce positive emotions in groups. Finally, different types of computer-mediated communication may have unique problems. For example, email cannot communicate important non-verbal signals like tone or emphasis, although these sorts of signals might readily be noticed on a voice or video conference. Not surprisingly then, email messages are misinterpreted more often than voice messages (Kruger and others, 2005). Therefore, even within different forms of computer-mediated technology, important differences may exist.

When and why researchers might use nonexperimental designs, and why caution might be needed in interpreting results from such studies, was discussed in more detail in Chapter 2, pages 35–36.

Given the downsides of technology-mediated communication, face-to-face communication is still preferred in many instances. For example, face-to-face gatherings like scientific conventions continue to thrive despite scientists' ready access to email and other forms of electronic communication. Also important is the informal exchange of information, summed up by the maxim that conference attendees generally learn more in the coffee breaks and hallway conversations than in the formal sessions.

Perhaps most important, the emotional ties that develop from actual interaction seem essential for the growth of interpersonal trust and commitment, as well as group solidarity. Some purely electronic collaborations may fail because their members cannot develop the same level of trust as when they exchange jokes and gossip over lunch or trade idle chit-chat (Goldberg, 1997). Physical proximity seems to be essential for this type of frequent, informal interaction.

Processes that Affect Performance: Emotions and Mood in Groups. The emotional ties that form between group members, as just noted, can be a force for good, helping to develop trust and commitment. In fact, just as individual moods affect performance in many ways, a group's emotional climate or mood can have similar effects (Barsade & Gibson, 2012; Bartel & Saavedra, 2000; Kelly & Spoor, 2013). These group moods may arise through contagion, with the moods of one or more members spreading to many other group members. One clever study by Sigal Barsade not only shows the effect of group mood on group outcomes, but also shows how moods can be transferred within a group (Barsade, 2002). Barsade had a trained confederate pretend to be in a good or bad mood during a group activity. Emotional contagion occurred, with other members exposed to a negative mood showing decreases in cooperation and perceived task performance, compared to those who were exposed to a positive mood. These consequences were evident to outside observers as well as to the group members themselves. So keeping your negative emotions in check at work, during group study sessions, or with fellow volunteers at an event may be a wise move, to avoid negative impacts on motivation and ultimately on group performance (Wong, Tschan, Messerli, & Semmer, 2013).

Besides examining how group mood shapes group outcomes, research has also examined what perceivers infer about groups displaying different types of emotions. In one study, participants were shown four-person groups, with each person displaying either a sad or happy facial expression (Magee & Tiedens, 2006). Some participants saw groups with members all showing sad or all showing happy expressions. Other participants saw a group with two happy and two sad members. As shown in Figure 11.5, happy expressions increased impressions of group cohesion—the all happy group was thought to be the most cohesive, the mixed group in the middle, and the all sad group was thought to be least cohesive. Perceivers also thought the group, more than the individual members, was responsible for a group outcome when emotions were shared (all happy or all sad), but the opposite was true in the mixed condition. Therefore, both the content of group emotions and the consistency of emotions across members shape observers' impressions.

Cures for Group Performance Losses. Communication and shared emotions do not always do the trick. Loss of motivation and failures of coordination can undermine a

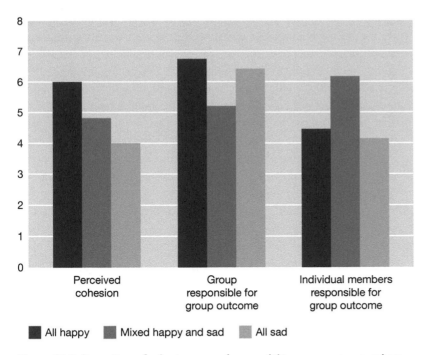

Figure 11.5 Perceptions of cohesiveness and responsibility among group members
In this experiment, participants saw four-person groups. Some saw groups with members all showing sad or all showing happy expressions. Other participants saw a group with two happy and two sad members. The more happy members there were, the more cohesive the group seemed. Perceived responsibility for the group's outcome varied based on group emotion, too. The group itself seemed responsible when all members shared the same emotions. But individual members seemed responsible when emotions were mixed. (Graph adapted from data in Magee & Tiedens, 2006.)

group's ability to achieve its goals and can frustrate individual members as well. Nipping such problems in the bud seems a wise step for any organization, and available research evidence indicates that multiple strategies can help.

First, group training can improve performance. A meta-analysis has shown that training that instructs groups on how to alter their coordination efforts is particularly effective (Salas, Nichols, & Driskell, 2007). Teaching groups how to be flexible in their approach, altering their strategies as the environment changes, also seems very fruitful (Burke and others, 2006).

Second, making groups feel accountable for their process can help. In one study, groups were asked to choose the best among three candidates for a job. However, not all members of the group received the same information about the three candidates. If all information was shared, one particular candidate would have stood out as the best. Before discussing the candidates and reaching a group decision about who to hire, half the groups were told that they would take part in an interview later and describe how the group came to their decision. The other half were not told about this interview. Results indicated that the groups expecting an interview were more likely to pick the best candidate. Thus, feeling accountable, such as by being required to explain the decision process, can lead to better group decisions (Scholten, van Knippenberg, Nijstad, & De Dreu, 2007).

A third successful strategy to improve group performance is making group membership a positive part of members' social identity. Organizations often try to achieve this goal by selling the "corporate culture," the set of values, beliefs, understandings, and norms shared by members of the organization (J. M. Levine & Moreland, 1991; Tellis, Prabhu, & Chandy, 2009). To build a sense of group identity and cohesion, organizations create slogans and symbols, develop and distribute literature describing the principles that embody the company's ideals and goals, and introduce rituals, ceremonies, and awards (Sadri & Lees, 2001). For example, the online retailer Zappos emphasizes ten "core values" to its employees, such as "create fun and a little weirdness" and "deliver WOW through service," hoping to build a strong and thriving work culture (zappos.com). In sports, teams have uniforms, mascots, and team activities and rituals to promote players' cohesiveness and dedication to their teammates (Hogg & Abrams, 1988). All of these tactics are designed to give group members a strong sense of shared social identity.

But even if corporate culture makes people feel good, can it help reach the organization's goals? The answer is yes. Building positive social interdependence often helps solve some of the problems of task interdependence (De Dreu & Weingart, 2003; Ellemers, de Gilder, & Haslam, 2004). Organizations sell the corporate culture because it encourages group cohesion, and group cohesion increases group performance (Beal, Cohen, Burke, & McLendon, 2003). Indeed, a recent meta-analysis finds a reliable relationship between group cohesion and better performance (Gully, Devine, & Whitney, 2012). In part, this is likely because high performance improves cohesion. But in addition, a strong sense of group identity can be a remedy for many of the motivational and coordination losses that can render groups ineffective.

To review the many effects of shared group identity, see Chapter 6.

1. ***Cohesive groups encourage cooperation.*** Cohesive groups foster cooperation in the service of group goals, rather than competition for individual ones (Turner and others, 1987). Cooperation leads to positive feelings among group members and helps them work together to achieve group goals (Deutsch, 1949; Sherif, 1966). For example, those who identify with a cohesive group are more likely to participate in and contribute to group activities than are members of noncohesive groups (Brawley, Carron, & Widmeyer, 1988).

   One practical way to promote group goals is to make rewards clearly contingent on group outcomes. For example, students in "cooperative classrooms" work together to help each other learn and are graded on the basis of the entire group's performance, in contrast to "competitive classrooms" where grades are based on individual performance in comparison to other group members. In the classroom as in the laboratory, mutual cooperation leads to positive feelings: Compared with members of competitive groups, cooperative group members generally like each other better. They also learn more. A meta-analysis of over 100 studies concluded that cooperative learning results in better classroom performance than is found in either competitive or individualist situations (D. W. Johnson, Maruyama, Johnson, Nelson, & Skon, 1981).

   Employers sometimes adopt a similar cooperative reward arrangement: a system in which employees receive bonuses only when certain group goals (such as production levels) are met. One study of 66 large U.S. firms compared compensation packages among low-performing and high-performing companies. The study found that the companies with high performance records more often had packages that emphasized teamwork rather than individual competition (Schuster, 1985). More recent research suggests that rewards that are based on a combination of individual and group output may be even more effective than purely group-based rewards (Pearsall, Christian, & Ellis, 2010). These researchers suggest that the combined awards may motivate people to work together to maximize team output, but also keep up their own individual efforts because they know that they will be rewarded too.

2. ***Cohesive groups follow norms.*** A sense of group belonging usually helps members reach consensus about the group's goals and its strategies for accomplishing those goals (Abrams, 2013). And what a cohesive group decides, its members usually do. Once consensus has been reached, those who identify with the group are likely to adhere to its norms (McGrath, 1984), and new members quickly absorb the group's "way of doing things" (Forsyth, 1999; J. R. Levine & Moreland, 1991). In one study of male junior soccer players, for example, they found that the more players perceived team cohesion, the more strongly they believed the team also had competition norms (Hoigaard, Safvenbom, & Tonnessen, 2006). If a group is cohesive and has high-performance norms, its members will be highly productive (Keller, 1986). And the specific dimension of performance that is emphasized by the norms—such as creativity or feasibility—will be especially improved (Bechtoldt, De Dreu, Nijstad, & Choi, 2010). Of course, if group norms are inconsistent with high performance, productivity will be low (Roethlisberger & Dickson, 1939).

The reasons why group norms are such effective guides for group behavior were described in Chapter 10.

Reaching consensus also means the group no longer needs to spend time repeatedly renegotiating the issues. Members know what the group is set up to do and they know how to do it, so consensus on how the group should proceed has a positive impact on group performance (Kellermanns, Walter, Floyd, Lechner, & Shaw, 2011). Consider, for example, the effect of norms on the goal of preparing a community meal. If the group has not reached a consensus, members may feel they have a right to work on the task they enjoy most; no one will do the dirty work, and there will be no dinner. Group norms, however, can specify that all the jobs must be done, that certain members have the right or obligation to do specific tasks, and that the tasks should be performed at certain times and in specific ways. Given these conditions, the community meal should proceed on schedule: When group norms match task demands, groups operate more smoothly.

3. ***Cohesive groups attract and keep valued members.*** When tasks are difficult, rewards are few, and conflict is frequent, potentially productive group members may slack off or drop out altogether. Member turnover can lessen a group's chances of achieving its goals, and it often represents the loss of a huge investment in training and skill development. Shared social identity acts as a counterforce by boosting people's liking for the group, their commitment, and their morale (Abrams, 2013; Hackman, 1992). Belonging to a cohesive group even helps people cope with stress, perhaps by offering them effective social support (Bowers, Weaver, & Morgan, 1996; Christensen, Schmidt, Budtz-Jorgensen, & Avlund, 2006). You may recall that members of groups—even groups formed on the basis of arbitrary categorizations—tend to hold in-group members in higher esteem than out-group members (Hogg, 1987, 2012).

To review the many ways in which membership in a social group increases preference for in-group over out-group members, see Chapter 6, pages 199–203.

This tendency is even stronger in cohesive face-to-face groups. Many Japanese businesses see group cohesion as a way to keep their workers productive and happy. They are famous for their efforts to ensure that employee morale is high and that performance is rewarded. Companies foster friendships between members; sponsor picnics, parties, and sports teams; and promise long-term employment. Company-sponsored computer dating services even encourage employees to marry within the company. Their efforts no doubt contribute to the fact that Japanese workers seldom change companies. In one study illustrating the power of cohesion to keep groups together, researchers asked junior male hockey players to report feelings of team cohesion. During the subsequent season, the researchers checked to see which members returned to the team. Those who had reported greater cohesion during the previous season were more likely to return (Spink, Wilson, & Odnokon, 2010).

Social identity can be such a powerful tool that it sometimes holds groups together when no material benefits are forthcoming (Van Vugt & Hart, 2004). For example, groups with strong social identity often preserve (or even strengthen) their cohesion even when they lose or fail at important tasks (Brawley, Carron, & Widmeyer, 1987; D. M. Taylor, Doria, & Tyler, 1983). This occurred during the closing stages of the Second World War, when units of the German army, outnumbered, undersupplied, and with no chance of victory, continued to fight against all odds. They did so not because they believed deeply in Nazi ideology but because they were motivated by group loyalty forged by shared identity (Shils & Janowitz,

Source of productivity loss in groups	Motivation loss Individuals diminish personal efforts, engage in social loafing.	Coordination loss Individuals interfere with each other's actions. Individuals fail to communicate effectively about group tasks.
Remedy for productivity loss in groups	Cooperation: Individuals work toward group goals. Individuals maintain efforts even when contributions are not identifiable.	Consensus: Individuals agree on goals and strategies. Individuals follow group norms. If norms are appropriate, high productivity results.
Contribution of group cohesion to remedy	Individuals adopt group goals as their own.	Group exercises social influence over individuals.
Contribution of training to remedy	Group can learn how to keep its members motivated.	Group can learn better coordination strategies and how to be flexible in its approach.
Contribution of accountability to remedy	Making groups feel accountable may keep them motivated to process carefully and come to reasoned decisions.	Making groups feel accountable may focus their efforts and help them communicate effectively.

Figure 11.6 Causes and cures of group productivity loss
Group productivity declines when individual members do not try hard to accomplish group goals—for example, when they engage in social loafing—or when the members' efforts are poorly coordinated. Group cohesion, training, and accountability can help remedy both of these problems.

1948). Studies of U.S. soldiers in Europe and Vietnam tell a similar story of social interdependence motivating performance (Moskos, 1969; Stouffer and others, 1949).

We have seen that group performance can suffer from two basic types of problems. The first occurs when members stop trying or drop out because they do not care about group goals or are unwilling to waste their efforts while others slack off. The second problem arises when members try hard but cannot coordinate their efforts effectively because members do not share common goals or interfere with each other. These motivational and coordination losses may be remedied with training, by making groups feel accountable, or by making people identify with the group and follow its norms, at least when those norms favor high productivity (see Figure 11.6). Thus, multiple strategies offer remedies for motivational and coordination losses in groups.

Leadership and Power

Effective leaders enhance task performance and maintain social interdependence. The ways they do this must differ from situation to situation. Sometimes, however, stereo-typical thinking prevents the most effective leaders from emerging in groups. Some types of leadership are particularly likely to help align individual and group goals and these leaders may help groups be particularly successful. Of course, such extraordinary influence can be used in destructive as well as constructive ways. Formal group leaders as well as others (such as parents) usually can control other people's outcomes, and such power has a number of psychological effects.

Whose job is it to make sure that groups fulfill their mastery and connectedness goals? As former U.S. President Dwight D. Eisenhower once wrote, "Leadership is the ability to decide what is to be done, and then to get others to want to do it." Leaders are crucial to the attainment of group goals (Goethals, 2005). In fact, **leadership** can be defined formally as a process in which one or more group members are permitted to influence and motivate others to help attain group goals (Forsyth, 1999; Reicher, Haslam, & Hopkins, 2005; Hogg, 2013). Notice that in this definition the group grants the leader his or her power; as we noted in Chapter 10, legitimate authority works only if the group accepts and agrees with it. The definition does not specify the route to power: Leaders may be appointed by an outside authority, elected by group members themselves, or simply emerge as a group interacts. Leaders may or may not be effective, but before we explore that issue, let's examine what leaders do.

leadership
a process in which one or more group members are permitted to influence and motivate others to help attain group goals

What Do Leaders Do? The exercise of leadership generally involves two distinct types of behavior: those focused on decision making and task performance and those aimed at enhancing cohesion and liking among group members (Misumi, 1995; Stogdill, 1963). This pattern is understandable. Because people draw on groups both for mastery and concrete rewards stemming from task performance and for feelings of connectedness and belonging, groups require both task and social leadership. Task-related leader behaviors include telling group members what to do, criticizing poor performance, and coordinating others' activities. In contrast, relationship-oriented leadership involves being open, friendly, and approachable, treating group members as equals, and listening to group members' opinions. Both of these functions are vital to effective groups, and together they account for most of what leaders do (Mintzberg, 1980).

Relationship-oriented leadership appears to be especially important when work groups are diverse rather than homogeneous (Homan & Greer, 2013). In general, diversity can have both positive and negative effects on groups, whether diversity is defined by racial and ethnic categories, gender differences, or even differences between veteran group members and newcomers. Diversity can reduce interpersonal liking and trust and increase conflict within the group. On the other hand, a diverse group can also bring to bear multiple perspectives, viewing work problems from many angles and increasing performance and satisfaction (van Knippenberg and others, 2004). Leader behavior strongly influences whether group diversity will hurt or help in these ways. Astrid Homan and Lindred Greer (2013) hypothesized that relationship-oriented leader behavior would be especially helpful to a diverse group because it would help defuse the potential interpersonal problems, while acknowledging and appreciating differences in group members' perspectives. In two studies, they showed that members prefer relationship-oriented leadership more when working in a diverse rather than a homogeneous group, and that such leadership benefits actual performance by diverse groups.

We described earlier how moods and emotions can influence group performance. Naturally, the mood of a group's leader has especially significant effects on group mood and group performance (Johnson, 2008, 2009). In one study, groups were created as part of an experiment and one person was singled out to be the group leader. Before the group performed a task together, the leader was asked to watch a funny or an upsetting video clip, to manipulate mood. Results showed that members with leaders in a positive mood were happier and coordinated better, but put forth less effort, compared to members with leaders in a negative mood (Sy, Cote, & Saavedra, 2005). However, other research suggests that a match between leader mood and follower characteristics may be important. For example, in one study, four-person groups completed a task with a leader who displayed happiness or anger (Van Kleef and others, 2010). Groups whose members had high levels of the personality trait of agreeableness performed better with a happy leader than an angry one, but the opposite was true for groups with low levels of agreeableness.

Chapter 9 (pages 339–345) discussed the many effects of diversity in groups.

Leadership Effectiveness: Person or Situation? Effective leaders can make or break countries, businesses, organizations, religions, clubs, sports teams, and even families. It is not surprising, then, that literally thousands of studies have tried to understand why some leaders have the capacity to inspire followers and others do not (Goethals, 2005). When one considers the lives of Mohandas Gandhi or Martin Luther King, Jr., there is a strong temptation to attribute their influence to their unique personal attributes. This tendency may be one more example of the correspondence bias at work, leading us to attribute behavior to individual traits rather than to situational demands.

Despite the appeal of the idea that effective leadership depends on characteristics of the leader, researchers have had little success in identifying specific personality traits that universally characterize effective leaders. Indeed, studies have revealed that the same person could be an effective leader in one context (for example, in a cockpit crew) but ineffective in another (such as a community service organization). When researchers

To remind yourself about the correspondence bias, and what might be done to undermine it, check out Chapter 3, pages 70–72.

examined the relation of leader behaviors to group outcomes, they found that giving social and emotional support consistently helps improve group morale, motivation, and job satisfaction. However, task-focused leader behaviors are not as consistently related to improved group task performance; their effect varies more for different types of groups and situations (Judge, Piccolo, & Ilies, 2004; Vroom, 1976). This suggests that group success depends less on who the leader is than on what kind of leadership is needed in a particular situation.

This insight about the importance of the situation led to the development of **contingency theories of leadership** (Fiedler, 1964; Vroom & Jago, 2007). That is, leaders differ in whether they are task-oriented or relationship-oriented, and leadership situations also differ in the opportunities and limitations they offer for influence on tasks and group morale. Contingency theories focus on "matching": To maximize leadership effectiveness,

contingency theories of leadership
theories holding that leader behaviors can differ and that different behaviors are most effective in specific leadership situations

SOCIAL PSYCHOLOGY IN PRACTICE: COACHING LEADERSHIP IN YOUTH SPORTS

Swimming teams, Little League baseball, youth soccer . . . if you have the impression that today's youngsters are heavily involved in sports activities, you would be right! Estimates are that over 25 million children and 3 million adult supervisors and coaches are involved in the United States alone. Proponents of youth sports argue that they teach the benefits of cooperation and teamwork, self-control and discipline, and important lessons about dealing with success and failure, not to mention promoting physical fitness and other positive health habits. But the leadership of coaches is crucial if these worthy goals are to be attained. Ronald Smith and Frank Smoll (1996) studied coaches' behaviors and their effects on young athletes. They found that the children enjoyed their athletic experiences and teammates most and had the highest self-esteem when coaches gave positive feedback for good efforts as well as good performances, responded to mistakes with instruction about proper technique, and emphasized fun and personal improvement more than winning matches. In other words, a good mix of relationship-oriented leadership (encouragement) and task-oriented leadership (instruction, especially after a poor performance) carries the day. Unfortunately, along with these types of positive behaviors, coaches sometimes engaged in more negative acts, being punitive and critical toward the children. Though these behaviors occurred only rarely, when they did they had a dramatic negative impact on the children's attitudes and enjoyment.

These same researchers also demonstrated that the behaviors that produce positive effects on young team members can be taught to coaches in brief workshops. Compared to children who played for coaches attending workshops focused on the technical aspects of sport, the children who played for coaches graduating from Smith and Smoll's program enjoyed sport more, were less anxious about performing, and had higher self-esteem. Perhaps the most important indicator of the effectiveness of the program was that only 5% of the athletes who played for the workshop-trained coaches failed to return for the sports program the next season, compared to about 26% for the other coaches.

Even though everyone presumably agrees that the chief goal of youth sports programs should be enjoyment, learning, and building positive attitudes rather than winning, you may still have one question about these results: Do the workshop-trained coaches, like other proverbial "nice guys," end up finishing last? No. They did not differ from the other coaches in their overall win/loss percentages in any of Smith and Smoll's studies (1997). So coaches do not have to choose between one leadership style that increases athletes' enjoyment and another style that wins matches. Instead, a single approach can attain the first (and more important) of these goals without sacrificing the second.

the leader's style should match the type of leadership demanded by the situation. If a skilled and experienced group takes on a task that requires lots of interpersonal interaction and cooperation, a relationship-oriented leader may be most effective. Such a group does not need task instruction, but a leader who can maintain positive feelings, group cohesion, and motivation. If, on the other hand, an already cohesive group takes on a difficult and complex task, group performance may be maximized by a task-oriented leader. The group climate is not a concern, so in this case leadership resources can be focused primarily on improving task performance. The effectiveness of matching leader to task has been supported by a number of studies that have looked at such diverse groups as military units and basketball teams (Strube & Garcia, 1981).

Although some specific tasks may be best matched by a task-focused or relationship-oriented leader, most complex tasks require both leadership styles. In terms of group success, the leader's skill at handling one particular type of task may be less important than his or her ability to balance the two crucial elements of leadership as tasks and situations change (Hersey & Blanchard, 1982; Zaccaro, Foti, & Kenny, 1991). In fact, the essence of good leadership may be the flexibility to adjust the mix of social and task motivation that a group needs in a particular situation. So wouldn't a person who is high in both relationship and task concerns be the best leader for every situation (Blake & Mouton, 1980)? Most of the time, this is true. The most effective supervisors in settings as diverse as banks, factories, coal mines, and government offices are in fact those who score well in both task and social leadership and have the ability to develop the skills the group needs at the time the group needs them (Bass, 1985; P. B. Smith & Tayeb, 1989). In short, leadership is about the flexible exercise of social influence: Given a particular group performing a particular task, a good leader simultaneously maximizes both successful task performance and positive social identity.

Who Becomes Leader? Contingency theories make it clear that groups should choose leaders whose styles match the demands of the situation. But people seem to have ideas about who is "leader material" regardless of the task at hand. One clue they use is how much group members talk. Laboratory studies show that group members who talk a lot tend to be viewed as leaders (Littlepage, Schmidt, Whisler, & Frost, 1995; Sorrentino & Field, 1986). Group success can depend on a leader who offers advice and guidance, so choosing a talker is not necessarily a bad idea. However, the amount a group member talks doesn't always reflect actual expertise. Fortunately, recent work has shown that the quality of what group members say also can play a significant role in judging who is "leader material" and, in some cases, quality of remarks can trump their quantity (Jones & Kelly, 2007). And the association between talkativeness and leadership may be limited to individualist cultures; other cultures may be more inclined to believe that silence indicates thoughtfulness, an important attribute of a leader (Kim, 2002).

People also use nonverbal signs of dominance and assertiveness to make leadership judgments. In studies of groups of business school students, Tiedens and Fragale (2003) examined how group members respond to another member who has assumed either a dominant posture (e.g., with arm draped on back of an adjacent chair) or a submissive posture (e.g., with hands in lap). The other members tended to take on complementary body positions, with those exposed to another's assertive postures assuming a more submissive stance and vice versa. When questioned afterwards, study participants were unaware that the posture of their interaction partner influenced their own behavior. Such findings highlight some of the subtle ways in which aspects of our social environment may influence leadership emergence. It is no wonder then that people also tend to confer leadership on those who exercise less subtle signs of dominance—like taking the seat at the head of the table, or picking up the microphone.

Groups also seem to prefer leaders who embody the group's stereotypes, norms, or central defining attributes (Hogg, 1996; Hogg, van Knippenberg, & Rast, 2012). For example, a quiet, book-loving English literature major might be considered an appropriate leader for a literary discussion group, whereas a loud, tough, physically strong individual might be expected to captain a rugby football team. By the same token, a leader who matches the group's norms should be seen as particularly effective by group members. One study of college students who met in groups to discuss a social issue illustrated this point. The study did show an effect of general leader stereotypes: Leaders who were described as performing stereotypical leader behaviors, such as emphasizing group goals and letting other members know what was expected of them, were rated as more effective. But group leaders who were close to the group's typical position on the issue were also rated as more effective leaders (Hains, Hogg, & Duck, 1997). Perhaps these findings help explain why group members prefer, and perform better for, elected leaders who embody the group's norms and goals compared to appointed leaders who do not (De Cremer & Van Vugt, 2002; Van Vugt & De Cremer, 1999). These effects are especially strong for members who strongly identify with the group. Thus, members who highly identify with a group, who see the group as a potential basis for their

Photo 11.3a and 11.3b Who will lead? Suppose both of these people are members of the pre-law student organization and a fraternity on your campus. Which one do you think is better suited to lead the pre-law organization and which a campus fraternity? If you are like most people, you will see the professionally dressed person as the pre-law leader because he matches the stereotype of a pre-professional student. On the other hand, the more casually dressed person stereotypically resembles the leader of a social organization, like a fraternity. Research suggests that leaders who embody the stereotypes of their groups will be seen as "leader material."

As you may recall from Chapter 9, pages 322–324, when people identify with a group, they especially like the other group members who most strongly personify group norms.

self-definition, will view leaders who most strongly embody the group's norms as the most acceptable and as the most effective leaders (Cicero, Bonaiuto, Pierro, & van Knippenberg, 2008; Hirst, van Dick, & van Knippenberg, 2009). These sorts of leaders tend to be viewed positively by group members even following failure. That is, when stereotypic leaders failed, they were rated as more effective than non-stereotypic leaders who failed, an effect that appeared to result because stereotypic leaders are trusted more (Giessner, van Knippenberg, & Sleebos, 2009).

Stereotypes and Leadership. Common stereotypes about gender, ethnicity, age, or other social characteristics also influence people's perceptions of leadership. Thus, as you might expect, group members who are male, taller, or older than others tend to be treated as leaders (Judge & Cable, 2004; Schein, Mueller, Lituchy, & Liu, 1996). In fact, individuals who look masculine, regardless of gender, are often judged to be more competent leaders. People seem unaware of this appearance bias, so even when they are reminded of the possible impact of stereotypes on their judgments, they still choose masculine-looking men and women as leaders, and rate masculine-looking leaders of either gender as more effective (Sczesny & Kühnen, 2004). These effects are not universal, however. Masculine-looking men who say competitive things and feminine-looking men who say cooperative things are perceived as leaders more than the opposite pairings (Spisak, Homan, Grabo, & van Vugt, 2012). This finding suggests that people are seen as leaders when their appearance fits stereotypically with what they say.

The effects of stereotypes on perceptions of leadership may help explain the preference for and preponderance of men in leadership positions in business, government, religious, and military institutions. For example, in a recent survey of U.S. citizens, most respondents said they preferred a male political candidate over a female one (Dolan, 2010). If people believe that competence and assertiveness are associated with leadership and that men are competent and assertive, they may turn to men for leadership (Eagly & Carli, 2003; Scott & Brown, 2006). Even women themselves, after serving as leaders in a laboratory group interaction, rate their leadership skills less positively if they were previously exposed to gender stereotypic (rather than counterstereotypic) advertisements (Simon & Hoyt, 2013). Thus, the expectation that men make good leaders creates a self-fulfilling prophecy in which men assume most leadership roles. A wealth of research data support this point. For example, a meta-analysis summarized 75 laboratory studies of mixed-sex informal groups that interacted without an appointed leader. When the group members later identified who had emerged as leaders, men were perceived as playing leadership roles more often than women were (Eagly & Karau, 1991). Other researchers examined job ads for a variety of occupations, and found that ads for jobs held mostly by men included many more words associated with leadership, such as leader, competitive, or dominant. This pattern creates a self-fulfilling prophecy: When students read experimentally constructed ads, high frequencies of such words made the jobs less appealing to women (Gaucher, Friesen, & Kay, 2011). A recent meta-analysis confirms that leader stereotypes are generally masculine, but also provides hopeful evidence that this effect has been weakening over time (Koenig, Eagly, Mitchell, & Ristikari, 2011).

Groups do turn to or prefer women leaders in certain situations, for example, when their tasks require extensive social interaction as in consensus-seeking tasks or negotiations (Eagly & Carli, 2003). Women are preferred as leaders more when the group experiences intragroup competition for resources—which threatens group cohesion and requires seeking consensus—but men are preferred under conditions of intergroup competition (Van Vugt & Spisak, 2008). Finally, when people feel threatened, they often desire a change in leadership, and women are more associated with change than are men. Thus, in times of threat, women are preferred as much or more than men as leaders (Brown, Diekman, & Schneider, 2011).

Stereotypes also limit ethnic minorities' chances of rising to leadership positions. One set of studies showed that Whites fit the "business leader prototype" and that White CEOs were rated more favorably than were African-American CEOs (Rosette, Leonardelli, & Phillips, 2008). These sorts of biases against racial minority leaders may help account for the relative infrequency with which racial minorities occupy leadership positions in various settings. For example, in 2013, only 6 of the top 500 U.S. companies were currently headed (as a chief executive officer or chairperson) by African-Americans (BlackEntrepreneurProfile.com). In sports, there is a similar disproportion. For example, in American football, African-Americans made up about 67% of the players but held only about 20% of the head coaching positions in 2005. Political leadership demonstrates the same pattern. Only 4% of the members elected to the U.K. Parliament in 2010 were members of ethnic minorities, compared to over 10% of the population. In the French Parliament elected in 2012, the figures were 1.5% and 15%. As you might expect, ethnic minority women leaders are in particular jeopardy. One study found that African-American women leaders are evaluated much more negatively than others, especially under conditions of organizational failure (Rosette & Livingston, 2012).

Are groups hurting themselves by using stereotypes to choose their leaders? Little research has examined ethnic differences, but meta-analyses of research on gender differences in leader effectiveness have looked at two key questions. First, who holds the group together? In creating connectedness and cohesion, women leaders beat men hands down (Eagly, Makhijani, & Klonsky, 1992). Both groups and individual group members are happier when their boss is a woman. One reason may be that in a wide range of leadership situations women leaders show more concern with morale and encourage more participation in decision making than men do (Eagly & Johnson, 1990; van Engen & Willemsen, 2004), although consistent with contingency theories, certain types of organizations encourage this type of leadership from both men and women. Second, who gets the job done? When it comes to mastery and task performance, studies of leaders in organizations show that, in general, women perform just as well as men on objective measures. However, the type of organization makes a substantial difference. In business, educational, and government organizations, women leaders slightly outperform men on the average. In contrast, in the military, men have been found to be much more effective leaders than women (Eagly and others, 1995).

Despite these research findings, as we have seen, many people still doubt women's ability to lead, perhaps because women do not fit their stereotype of a leader (Eagly & Carli, 2003; Hoyt, 2010). The power of stereotypic thinking to obstruct the selection of the best leader for the job becomes clear. Perhaps this is why so many of us have worked for an incompetent boss, an unlikable coach, or a disorganized chairperson at some point in our lives. Recent data confirm that poor management is one of the leading causes of employee dissatisfaction (Gallup, 2013). Given the central role leaders play in coordinating both task and social interdependence in groups, perhaps it is time that stereotypical thinking about leadership went the way of the dinosaur.

Putting the Group First: Transformational Leadership. Jesus of Nazareth, Mohammad, and Gautama Buddha founded religious movements that have changed the lives of literally billions of followers over many centuries and that remain among the most powerful forces shaping our world today. What can we learn about leadership from the way these and other individuals have been able to transform other people? The sociologist Max Weber (1921/1946), writing in the early part of the last century, considered this question. He defined charismatic leaders as those who inspire extreme devotion and emotional identification on the part of their followers. This devotion allows these leaders to have profound effects on their followers. Whereas most leaders help followers reach existing goals, charismatic leaders may actually change their followers' goals, for example, turning them from seekers of worldly success into religious devotees practicing self-denial.

transformational leadership
leaders who inspire extreme devotion and emotional identification on the part of their followers, allowing them to have profound effects on their followers

If the key to this kind of leadership lies in being able to refocus people's goals, can such leadership also be exercised in the everyday world of business offices and sports teams? In fact, the crucial aspect of such leadership, now more often called **transformational leadership**, seems to be the re-focusing of group members' individual and personal concerns toward community- or group-centered goals (Burns, 2003; Burns & Sorenson, 2000; De Cremer, 2002). Transformational leaders articulate an inspiring vision for the group, motivating their followers to pursue collective goals that transcend self-interest, and to make personal sacrifices for the collective good (Bass, 1990, 1997; Halverson, Holladay, Kazama, & Quiñones, 2004; House & Shamir, 1993). To have these profound effects, transformational leaders must be self-confident and determined, as well as skilled and inspiring communicators. They take clear and strong stands that emphasize commitment to goals, optimistically express an attractive vision of the future, question old assumptions and traditions, and are highly caring toward group members (Bass, 1997; Shamir, House, & Arthur, 1993). When successful, such leaders can indeed be transformational as they bring about social and organizational change (Bass & Riggio, 2006).

Studies of leaders who exhibit these kinds of behaviors suggest that they are successful in promoting not only organizational commitment and work satisfaction, but also group performance (Huang, 2013; Judge & Piccolo, 2004). Both setting clear group goals and self-sacrifice have been found to increase group morale and group performance under transformational leaders (De Cremer & van Knippenberg, 2004; Gillespie & Mann, 2004; Whittington, Goodwin, & Murray, 2004). Transformational practices tend to empower followers, creating a sense of control that helps explain the success of such leadership (Avolio, Zhu, Koh, & Bhatia, 2004; de Hoogh and others, 2004; Walumbwa, Wang, Lawler, & Shi, 2004). Other studies have confirmed the importance of a leader's ability to communicate and inspire a shared vision for the group, as well as the leader's ability to stimulate the group intellectually and recognize and support individual group members (Rafferty & Griffin, 2004). These studies also caution, however, that transformational leadership is, as contingency theories suggest, dependent on both the leader and the group's situation. For example, the ability of transformational leadership practices to improve group performance seems to be greater in times of uncertainty and change than in the case of "business as usual."

Perhaps the results of these studies should come as no surprise. Transformational leaders are effective for exactly the same reasons as other leaders: because they nurture cohesion among group members and inspire them to adopt the group's goals as their own. These factors in turn inspire group members to look beyond themselves and adopt new collective goals for the group, eliminating potential coordination and motivation losses in the process.

The Dark Side of Leadership. The quest to understand what makes a good leader is driven not just by theoretical curiosity. Groups and group members can pay a high cost for poor leadership. Inept leadership can cost businesses, communities, and citizens not only millions of dollars but also millions of lives. Just as a bad coach can lower self-esteem and enjoyment of sport, a short-sighted national leader can take countries down the path to war. When leaders lead the wrong way, group members who can do so will withdraw from the group, hurting their own, the group's, and the leader's chances of achieving the goal that brought the group together in the first place (Van Vugt, Jepson, Hart, & De Cremer, 2004). Under bad leaders, task motivation ebbs away and group members not only fail to perform, but can actively attempt to undermine the leader's agenda and the group's goals (Hogan, Curphy, & Hogan, 1994). When leadership has life-and-death consequences, as it does for military leaders, incompetence is not counted in deficits and lost profits, but in body bags and lost generations (Dixon, 1976). Even the life-changing potential of charismatic or transformational leadership can have a dark side. In 1978, over 900 members of the People's Temple group committed mass suicide at the urging of their leader, the Rev. Jim Jones. In a scenario eerily reminiscent of that earlier tragedy, Marshall Applewhite and nearly 40 other members of his Heaven's Gate group committed mass suicide in March 1997. They were following Applewhite's teaching that they had reached a new evolutionary stage in which their earthly "vehicles" or bodies would no longer be required, and that after shedding their bodies they would be picked up by a spaceship. Tragedies like these remind us that charismatic leaders may use their extraordinary influence over their followers in destructive as well as positive ways.

Power. Formal or informal leaders including bosses, managers, or supervisors usually have the ability to determine the outcomes of those in the group, deciding who gets promoted, who gets a raise (and how much of one), who has to do the undesirable tasks, who should be fired, and so forth. Thus, leaders often have **power** or a "relative capacity to modify others' states by providing or withholding resources or administering punishments" (Keltner, Gruenfeld, & Anderson, 2003, p. 265). Though formal leaders usually have power, others can have power, too. For example, an administrative assistant for a department may control who gets on the department chair's meeting schedule, and parents can give their children extra treats or make them take a time-out. Though it can have many facets (status, official positions of leadership, competence, and so on), by its very definition power is a relational state, in which one person has more ability to control the resources or outcomes of another person or persons (Schmid Mast, 2010). Certainly, someone can feel powerful when alone—at times when he or she is not interacting in a group. But, because power is relational, power rests on the real or imagined presence of other people, so it has important consequences for how people interact in groups.

power
the ability to provide or withhold rewards or punishments from others

Photo 11.4 Power poses. The man shown here is adopting a power pose. Recent research suggests that merely adopting poses like this makes one feel powerful and act in powerful ways.

Having power or even just feeling powerful—for example, due to recalling a past event in which one had power—has a number of effects on people's perceptions and behaviors. For example, powerful people can better direct their attention, focusing on important elements in the environment and ignoring less relevant, peripheral ones (Guinote, 2007b). Moreover, powerful people show a better ability to persist at and pursue goals. For example, in one study, participants completed a psychological test that ostensibly measured their leadership abilities. The researchers told them either that they had the profile of a leader (powerful condition) or a subordinate (non-powerful condition). In actuality, these roles were randomly assigned. While they waited for an upcoming task with another person in which they would be the leader or subordinate, they were asked to work on a visual puzzle. The puzzle was unsolvable, and the researchers measured how long people persisted in trying to solve it. Those in the powerful condition persisted longer than those in the non-powerful condition (Guinote, 2007c). Not only do powerful people seem to pursue goals differently, but they prefer to pursue certain types of goals more than others, especially those focused on rewards and those that help maintain their power (Willis & Guinote, 2011).

It is clear that individuals who feel powerful often feel and act differently than those without power. But what effect does power have within groups? Recent research suggests

HOT TOPICS IN SOCIAL PSYCHOLOGY: POWER POSES

Research on nonverbal behavior has shown that humans adopt certain body postures and positions when they feel powerful. Recent work shows that the opposite is also true—simply adopting "power poses" can make one feel powerful, causing some of the same physiological and behavioral effects associated with actual power (Carney, Cuddy, & Yap, 2010). In this study, some participants were asked to assume "power poses," one of which involved propping the feet up on a desk while leaning backwards in a chair. The hands were interlocked behind the head, with elbows flaring out from the body. Other participants assumed low-power poses such as sitting in a chair while taking up very little space—feet flat on the floor close together, arms tucked close to the body, hands clasped on the lap. After posing in either a low- or high-power manner, participants reported how powerful they felt and completed a gambling task, where they were given $2 but told they could roll a die with the possibility of losing or doubling their money. Saliva samples were also collected to assess levels of cortisol, the stress hormone, and testosterone, a dominance-related hormone. The study found that high-power posers had more testosterone and less cortisol than did low-power posers. High-power posers said they felt more powerful than the low-power posers, and they also acted more powerfully—being more likely to take the gamble to earn the reward. Thus, the simple act of looking powerful seems capable of making one feel and act like a person who is actually in charge.

that either too much power or too little power within a group can harm performance (Ronay and others, 2012). According to this research, when a group needs to perform a highly interdependent task—when group members need to coordinate and work together—having too many high-power people is problematic. The high-power people spend too much time squabbling about who should be in charge and too little time contributing to the group's work. If there are no powerful people, there may be problems because no one takes the lead to coordinate the group's efforts. Thus, the researchers argue that a clear hierarchy—with one clear leader and other followers—should enhance performance in these situations. To test these ideas, they had three-person groups complete two tasks, one highly interdependent and one not. Before the group interaction, individuals were asked to write about a time from their own lives when they had power (creating feelings of high power), a time they lacked power (low power), or about a mundane topic (baseline). Groups were then assembled with either 3 members with high power; 3 members with low power; or 1 high power, 1 low power, and 1 baseline member. On the highly interdependent task, the groups that had a clear hierarchy, with one powerful person and two less powerful ones, performed better than both the other types of groups. On the less interdependent task, group composition had no effect on performance. Thus, at least when groups need to coordinate their efforts for success, it seems that either too many or too few powerful people harm what the group can achieve. Having a clear hierarchy in these cases appears quite beneficial.

Because of the profound implications of good or poor group performance for every aspect of modern society, the quest to understand how power is wielded by leaders and what makes a good leader has huge practical importance. Theories of leadership wax and wane in popularity outside the laboratory (as evidenced by the dozens of competing books on the topic published each year), driven by many forces besides the scientific evidence for their effectiveness. As the evidence accumulates, however, it becomes clear that group effectiveness depends on whether the positive potential of social and task interdependence can be unleashed, while the negative consequences of social and task interdependence can be avoided. An effective leader is one who uses his or her skills to solve the problems of social and task interdependence in the best way for a given group in a given situation. Because a shared social identity makes it possible for leaders to motivate and organize groups, the most effective leaders provide both the identity and the structure that groups need to satisfy their members' mastery and connectedness needs, and to solve the twin problems of social and task interdependence.

CONCLUDING COMMENTS

Social life centers on groups, so by understanding how they work we can better understand ourselves as social beings. Interdependence, the sharing of common experiences and of a common fate, is the key to all group processes. Most common-sense ideas about group interaction focus on task interdependence: on the need to coordinate individual skills, roles, and efforts so that the group contributes to mastery goals and obtains concrete rewards for members. This is certainly the focus that drives human-engineering approaches to personnel management, organizational behavior, and management science. Our message in this chapter is slightly different. Task interdependence is important, of course, but social interdependence may be even more important. Our need for a shared understanding of the social world and of our place in it, and our concern for being positively connected to others, manifest themselves in almost every aspect of our social behavior, and particularly our behavior in face-to-face groups.

The impact of social interdependence and the desire for group membership has been evident since the earliest research on group interaction and leadership. In much of that research, however, investigations viewed these social influences mainly as an impediment to the successful and efficient completion of group tasks. Thus, the social rewards of group membership and the development of group norms were seen as elements that interfered with the goals of production. Today's social psychology offers a different point of view. Far from working against effective task interdependence, social interdependence can exert a positive influence on group behavior. Social, not technological, solutions may be our best bet for eliminating many apparently task-related problems, such as failures of coordination, social loafing, and low productivity. A positive social identity can provide the consensus, cohesion, and cooperation needed to get the job done.

However, we must add a word of caution here. As Chapter 6 made clear, cohesion and cooperation within the in-group often come at the cost of antagonism and hostility toward out-groups. And as Chapter 9 pointed out, a group can be so intent on feeling good about itself that its decisions and actions are vulnerable to groupthink. Thus, as we have argued before, the optimal solution is always one of balance. The sales group needs enough cohesion to keep morale high and attention focused on their sales goals, but not so much that they are in constant conflict with the production team. The local school board needs enough group identity to maintain its members' enthusiasm about solving the district's problems, but not so much that they suppress doubts and support one another in unrealistic and ill-advised decisions. The student team needs enough positive feelings of social connection that they want to meet frequently to work on the project, but not so much that they spend all their time having fun and no time doing the work. In situations like these we all need to learn how to use a shared group identity to promote both positive feelings and effective group performance. Under ideal conditions, working together in groups can help us to see what we have in common and to cooperate to solve the problems that threaten us all.

CHAPTER 11 THEMES

■ **Construction of Reality**
Groups define for their members what their tasks are and how to perform them.

■ **Pervasiveness of Social Influence**
Interaction and interdependence in face-to-face groups affects performance on many tasks.

■ **Striving for Mastery**
Face-to-face groups bring their members rewards of many kinds.

■ **Seeking Connectedness**
Face-to-face groups provide their members with strong feelings of belonging and identity.

■ **Valuing Me and Mine**
When we value group membership, we frequently seek to act in the group's interest.

SUMMARY

Social Facilitation: Effects of Minimal Interdependence. **Interdependence** means that each group member's thoughts, emotions, and behaviors influence the others'. Even when interdependence is minimal, the mere presence of others can produce arousal. Arousal improves the performance of easy, well-learned behaviors, but often interferes with performance of novel or complex tasks. This pattern is termed **social facilitation.** The arousal can occur when we focus on other people's evaluation of us. And the presence of others can also distract us, also leading to arousal and impacting performance.

However, with specific types of tasks, distraction can focus us on task-relevant cues, potentially improving performance.

Performance in Face-to-Face Groups: Interaction and Interdependence. The members of face-to-face groups interact with one another and share both **task interdependence** and **social interdependence**. Face-to-face groups usually go through different stages of relationship with their members. During **group socialization**, mutual evaluation can lead groups and individuals to become committed to each other, through processes that guide entry, socialization, role maintenance, and sometimes exit, from the group. At the same time groups go through formation, conflict, development of norms, performance, and dissolution as they try to maximize social and task interdependence to develop an identity and reach their goals. Time pressure can affect how groups solve these problems. Sometimes members exit groups voluntarily, but sometimes they are rejected and even subjected to **ostracism**, with significant negative effects on their well-being.

To achieve their performance goals, groups must maintain their motivation and avoid problems of coordination. For example, groups must ensure that their members work hard and avoid **social loafing**. Processes including communication within the group and shared emotions can influence group performance. Training and accountability can improve performance, but perhaps most important is developing a common social identity, which helps avoid performance problems by attracting and keeping valuable group members and by encouraging acceptance of group goals and normative cooperation. On occasion the opposite of social loafing, **social compensation**, can even occur.

Effective **leadership** enhances task performance and maintains social interdependence. The ways leaders do this must differ from situation to situation, the core insight of **contingency theories of leadership**. Sometimes, however, stereotypical thinking prevents the most effective leaders from emerging in groups. Some types of leadership are particularly likely to help align individual and group goals and these leaders may help groups be particularly successful. Of course the extraordinary influence of such **transformational leadership** can be used in destructive as well as constructive ways. Formal group leaders as well as others (such as parents) usually have **power** to control other people's outcomes, which has a number of psychological effects.

12

ATTRACTION, RELATIONSHIPS, AND LOVE

For most people, a happy marriage, a good family life, and a network of close friends are among the most important elements of their lives. And for good reasons: Research findings suggest that relationships with other people can make us healthy as well as happy. Consider the following:

■ Compared to people in troubled marriages, those who are happily married are healthier in a variety of ways, having, for example, lower blood pressure and better immune functioning (Robies, Slatcher, Trombello, & McGinn, 2014; Slatcher, 2010).
■ The more friends elderly individuals have, the less likely they are to die during a subsequent 10-year period (Giles, Glonek, Luszcz, & Andrews, 2005).
■ People who have coronary heart disease are less likely to die if they see themselves as having more social support (Barth, Schneider, & von Känel, 2010).

It is no wonder, then, that people's feelings about their relationships have a bigger impact on their overall satisfaction with their lives than do their job, income, community, or even physical health (A. Campbell, Converse, & Rodgers, 1976). In fact, close relationships are so important to people's well-being that the end of a relationship can be psychologically and physically devastating (Agnew, 2000; Hemstrom, 1996).

Why are relationships so important? Well, when you have to move all your worldly belongings from one apartment to another in a single afternoon, who can you rely on to help? When you need to confirm that the boss who kept you working well into the evening is a jerk, who do you call first? We bet that the answer to questions such as these is "a good friend" or "a family member." These responses illustrate why relationships matter: whether the help we need is material—food, safety, a pickup truck—or emotional—support, reassurance, the opportunity to express our true selves—the people we turn to are typically those with whom we share close relationships. Friends and families sometimes operate by different rules, but it's surprising how much they overlap. For example, people tend to have more choice about their friends than their relatives, but in many societies your closest friends are likely to be genetically related to you (Daly,

Salmon, & Wilson, 1997). Romantic partnerships typically involve sexual feelings, and marriage in almost all societies includes legal or consensual adherence to rules that friendships do not (Ackerman, Kenrick, & Schaller, 2007). And yet at least in the United States, most married people name their spouse as their best friend (Myers, 2000). These overlaps remind us that all relationship bonds, from family ties to friendship to long term romantic partnerships, help meet our needs for both mastery and connectedness. Because of this, they have many things in common.

In this chapter, we consider what research tells us about the properties and processes of relationship formation, maintenance, and dissolution that are common to many kinds of loving relationships—between best friends, parents and children, romantic partners, and spouses. What factors spark initial attraction between people and motivate them to try to know each other better? You will see that once two people begin interacting on a regular basis—chatting on the phone and sharing meals and other activities—feelings of liking based on personal characteristics become less important than feelings about the relationship itself and about what each partner gets out of it.

As two people's lives become interlinked and each comes to know the other more deeply, casual acquaintanceship is transformed into a close relationship, whether between friends or partners. We also discuss what is special about romantic and sexual relationships: Sexual feelings, like hot peppers in an antipasto salad, are powerful additional ingredients that spice some relationships.

Of course, difficulties eventually arise in any relationship. When conflicts are handled constructively, relationships can endure and deepen over the years. If conflict leads to a break-up, however, the pain can be swift and sure. In the final section of the chapter we consider the causes of problems in relationships and the ways people deal with them.

Challenges in Studying Attraction, Relationships, and Love

By necessity, most research on close relationships uses nonexperimental designs that leave some ambiguity about causal relations among variables, and most studies have focused on romantic attachments between heterosexual couples in individualist cultures.

Studying attraction, relationships, and love scientifically can be a challenge. We've seen in earlier chapters that there are many experiences about which people can't or won't express their thoughts and feelings very accurately, and so studying these topics with self-report measures seems fraught with risk. And yet observation of behaviors that many believe to be private and personal is also tricky. As you will see in this chapter, relationship researchers have had to be particularly creative in mixing multiple methods to try and converge on reliable patterns and processes that underlie who is attracted to whom, how relationships begin, develop, and end, and what love is all about. One of the most difficult problems that researchers face in studying real relationships is establishing cause and effect. For obvious reasons, people cannot be randomly assigned to have high or low levels of variables like commitment to their friends or partners, nor can relationships be randomly assigned to last for years or break up quickly. The impracticality of random assignment sometimes rules out experimental designs and weakens conclusions about the direction of cause and effect. For example, researchers have found that in romantic relationships, the frequency of sexual intercourse is higher among couples who are generally satisfied with their relationship. This observation may mean that sexual activity increases relationship satisfaction, but it could also mean that couples who are generally satisfied with their relationship tend to have sex more often.

Researchers are sometimes able to overcome such ambiguities by studying relationships over time, which may allow them to determine the order in which processes occur. For example, researchers can ask friends or couples to come to a lab and discuss a particular topic. These conversations can be coded for various features to determine which ones predict relationship stability or breakup in the future (e.g., Gottman, 1993). In one study, newlyweds described their relationship history, marriage philosophy, and how their marriage compared to their parents' marriage. By coding how these topics were discussed and delivered, the researchers could predict with great accuracy which couples would still be married five years later (Carrere and others, 2000)! Research in speed dating paradigms is also increasingly being used to examine relationship processes over time (Finkel & Eastwick, 2008). In these studies, researchers can measure people's impressions of a potential partner at their first (speed) date and follow them over time to see what factors predict a romantic spark or fizzle.

Other challenges to researchers include the relative lack of cross-cultural research on some relationship-oriented topics and the fact that certain types of relationships have been studied more than others. Although some of the topics dealt with in this chapter, such as physical attractiveness, have been studied in many countries and cultures, much of the research on close relationships has been conducted in individualist countries. As you'll see below, however, this emphasis is starting to change. Social psychological research has also tended to focus far more on romantic relationships than on friendships or relations among family members. And even the research on romantic relationships has been conducted disproportionately using heterosexual couples, and often young college-aged couples. This focus reflects an easily available pool of research participants: dating and married college students. Research examining gay and lesbian relationships is emerging, however (Peplau & Fingerhut, 2007), and available evidence suggests that heterosexual and same-sex romantic relationships are much more alike than different (Kurdek, 1991; Leigh, 1989; Roisman and others, 2008). One of the fascinating lessons of studying relationships is the recognition that the motivations and processes underlying our relationships are similar regardless of relationship type or culture (Goodwin, 1999). Because psychologists are now making great strides in expanding our knowledge of how relationships form and function across culture and relationship types, a fuller and more nuanced picture of relationship processes is coming into focus.

FROM ATTRACTION TO LIKING

Newly arrived in a strange city or on a college campus, you look at the strangers around you and wonder: "Who will I get to know better?" How do we form new connections and turn nodding acquaintances into pals and partners? Especially in cultures that emphasize voluntary relationships instead of lifelong, unchangeable group memberships, we are first drawn to people on the basis of their immediately obvious appearance or behavior (Berscheid & Reis, 1998). Despite the many available choices, attraction follows rules: an alluring face, a pleasant interaction, or the perception of similarity might spark an intial attraction. As those factors draw two people together, liking can develop, as each individual goes beyond surface features to start knowing the other better.

Physical Attractiveness

Attraction to strangers is strongly influenced by perceptions of physical attractiveness. Some features, such as signs of genetic health and access to resources, are regarded as attractive across cultures. Other features that make people attractive are more dependent on experience, exposure, and expectation.

Everyone likes to look at beautiful people. Beyonce, Ryan Gosling, and Aishwarya Rai Bachchan are celebrities because of their good looks as well as their acting and singing talents. In fact, we know that Ryan Gosling is attractive immediately upon seeing him, whereas our appreciation of his acting talent might develop only after we watch several of his films. Because physical appearance is so immediately visible, it affects our initial reaction to anyone we meet for the first time. As we noted in Chapter 3, everyone makes rapid inferences about the kind of personality traits that lie under the surface of physical appearance, and one of the most strongly and widely held beliefs is "what is beautiful is good" (Dion and others, 1972; Dion, 2002). Compared to unattractive people, attractive people are rated as more friendly, sociable, and trustworthy, and these judgments can be made within 100 milliseconds (Locher, Unger, Sociedade, & Wahl, 1993). It is no wonder, then, that physical attractiveness is a powerful first cue to who we might like. So what makes people look good?

Biological Bases of Physical Attractiveness. Regardless of whether you're male or female, younger or older, living in a post-industrial individualist culture or a pre-industrial interdependent one, there are some immediately obvious physical features that almost everyone agrees are attractive (Langlois and colleagues, 2000; Rhodes, 2006; Xu and colleagues, 2012).

First, faces and bodies that are symmetrical are judged to be more attractive and likeable by both men and women (Perrett and colleagues, 1999; Scheib, Gangestad, & Thornhill, 1999) and in both western populations and in African hunter-gatherers (Little & Jones, 2006). Since damaged genes, injury, or exposure to disease often produce facial and bodily features that are markedly lopsided or unusual, symmetrical faces appear to signal good health, good genes, and freedom from disease (Penke and others, 2009; Thornhill & Gangestad, 2006; Zebrowitz & Montepare, 2006). Consistent with this idea that symmetry reflects good health, symmetry has an even greater impact on judgments of attractiveness when concerns about disease are uppermost in people's minds, for example, after they view slides of sick individuals or infected wounds (Duncan, Schaller, & Park, 2009; Young, Sacco, & Hugenberg, 2011). Although the preference for symmetrical faces is cross-cultural, the fact that it reflects concerns about health can underlie cultural differences. For example, Hadza hunter-gatherers, who face considerable threat from communicable diseases, prefer symmetrical faces even more than British participants, who live in a culture with much lower rates of such disease (Little and others,

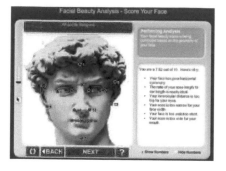

Photo 12.1 Symmetry and facial attractiveness. Anaface.com allows users to upload photos of faces (their own or others') and calculate a facial beauty score based on things like facial symmetry. Here, a user subjected Michelangelo's David, a statue frequently regarded as representing an ideal of masculine beauty, to this procedure.

2007). Other physical features such as clear rosy skin, average weight, and shiny hair also seem to signal good health.

Second, faces and bodies that suggest access to resources are attractive. It is not surprising that humans show preferences for others who look as if they have adequate food, or the wealth, power, or status to get it. The value of access to resources probably lies behind some of the attractiveness of male physical strength and cues to dominance such as height (Fink, Neave, & Seydel, 2007). As we saw in Chapter 3, taller men actually have greater access to resources even in industrialized societies. But taller men are not preferred in pre-industrial societies unless height predicts productivity or hunting success (Sear & Marlowe, 2009). Access to resources can also dictate other aspects of preference for body type. Almost universally, men and women living in cultures with scarce resources find heavier women more attractive, whereas in cultures with more resources, they find thinner women more attractive (Furnham & Baguma, 1994; Swami and colleagues, 2010). The same is true within cultures. In one recent survey of more than 7,000 individuals in 10 world regions, people in areas with low socio-economic indicators reported heavier ideal body weights compared to those in areas with high socio-economic indices (Swami and others, 2010). Such concerns can even be experimentally induced: hungry men, and men made to feel poor, prefer heavier women than do men who have food in their bellies and cash in their pockets (Nelson & Morrison, 2005). Thus physical signs of access to resources can make both males and females attractive.

Experiential Bases of Physical Attractiveness. Despite the generally universal nature of cues of health and wealth, individuals and groups can also differ greatly in some of the physical characteristics they find attractive (compare the Photos 12.2–12.4 of what makes Goth chic, the perfect bodybuilder physique, and a symbol of feminine beauty and purity in Tajikistan). This is because judgments of what is physically attractive are also strongly influenced by our experience and expectations.

First, we like what we see most. Studies that expose participants to novel sets of faces typically find that standards of attractiveness drift toward the features most common in those stimuli (Anzures, Mondloch, & Lackner, 2009; Cooper & Maurer, 2008). Long-term exposure makes even more difference. Studies have shown that people are attracted to others whose eyes and hair color match those of their opposite-sex parent (Little and others, 2003). And remember the large multi-country study that showed that ideal body weight depended on socio-economic conditions? That study also found that women's dissatisfaction with their own bodies and desire for thinness were widespread

Photo 12.2–12.4 Differences in attractiveness. As you can see, despite some cross-cultural similarities, there can be great variability in what different groups, such as Goths, body builders, and those from Tajikistan, consider attractive.

in high socio-economic areas, due to their greater exposure to Western media standards (Hausenblas and others, 2013; Swami and others, 2010).

Second, although we like people who are physically attractive, the opposite is also true. People find others they like more physically attractive than others they don't like (Kniffin & Wilson, 2004). Both men and women rate members of the opposite sex who display positive personality characteristics as more physically attractive than when no personality information is given (Jensen-Campbell, Graziano, & West, 1995). For example, both males and females find faces that they believe convey desirable traits to be particularly attractive (Little, Burt, & Perrett, 2006), and men rate a much wider range of body types as attractive if the female targets are described as having a positive personality (Swami and others, 2010). A man whom women initially find physically attractive becomes less so if the women find out he is flirtatious or has been unfaithful (Quist, DeBruine, Little, & Jones, 2012). Finally, members of happy couples perceive their partners as physically attractive even if others do not (Murray & Holmes, 1997). As these studies show, liking increases perceived physical attractiveness, just as physical attractiveness increases liking.

Similarity

Similarity of many kinds increases attraction and liking because of our natural tendency to see anything connected to the self as positive, because similarity makes things seem familiar, and because similarity also contributes to fulfilling needs for mastery and connectedness.

At any mixer, meet-and-greet, or new member orientation, you probably make a beeline for someone who seems similar to you. Perhaps they wear a pin suggesting they support the same candidate in the local election, recommend an event that indicates that they share your love of opera, or have an accent from the part of the country you call home.

Once you find someone who is "your type," chances are that you will end up liking this person. Though we all have heard that, like the north and south poles of magnets, "opposites attract," research shows that this is not true for people (Berscheid & Reis, 1998; Byrne, 1971). On the contrary, similarity breeds attraction and the better people get to know one another, the more their liking depends on similarity (Newcomb, 1961). Similarity does not have to be deep. People prefer others who physically look like them, favoring computer-generated faces that resemble their own face over those that do not (DeBruine, 2004; Laeng, Vermeer, & Sulutvedt, 2013). People tend to choose dates whose physical attractiveness matches their own (Montoya, 2008). People even prefer others who have the same initials as theirs (Jones, Pelham, Carvallo, & Mirenberg, 2004)! However, the content of getting-acquainted conversations typically revolves around finding out things that the conversationalists have in common (Insko & Wilson, 1977), providing an opportunity to find out about deeper types of similarities, such as attitudes, values, or experiences.

Chapter 2, pages 46–47, describes why common-sense principles such as this are less trustworthy than the results of scientific research.

Regardless of whether similarity is in looks, attitudes, personality, or activities, the conclusion from more than 300 studies is that the more similar they are, the more people like each other (Montoya, Horton, & Kirchner, 2008). Liking is even greater if the qualities we share with others are important to us, and if they are very salient (Montoya & Horton, 2013).

Why Similarity Increases Liking. Similarity helps us move from initial attraction to liking for a number of reasons.

1. *Similarity signals who is "me and mine."* One reason we like similar others is that we tend to view our own characteristics as desirable. This holds at the interpersonal level just as it does at the group level. Similarity is usually a significant cue to in-group membership, and as we have seen so often, we tend to prefer in-group members (who are just like me) to out-group members (who are not at all my

"type"). Perhaps this is one reason why "average" faces—computer-generated faces that resemble the majority of many other faces in a particular population—are seen as more attractive than faces that have extreme or non-representative characteristics (Galton, 1879; Langlois & Roggman, 1990). This effect holds above and beyond the effects of symmetry, which is higher for average faces and is independently associated with attractiveness. Interestingly, averageness predicts attraction in individualist cultures like the U.S., the U.K., and Australia just as much as it does in more collectivist cultures such as Japan and among African hunter-gatherers (Apicella, Little, & Marlowe, 2007; Rhodes and colleagues, 2001). And just as we like similar others, if we know that someone is similar to us, we usually assume that person will like us (E. Aronson & Worchel, 1966; Singh, Yeo, Lin, & Tan, 2007). Being liked by someone is one of the strongest reasons for liking that person (Condon & Crano, 1988; Montoya & Insko, 2008).

The ways our interactions with people can cause them to become what we expect them to be— creating a self-fulfilling prophecy— were detailed in Chapter 3, pages 87–89.

2. ***Similarity signals familiarity.*** Similarity and feelings of familiarity are closely intertwined (Cleary, Ryals, & Nomi, 2009) and, as first discussed in Chapter 3, feelings of familiarity trigger liking. So, when others seem similar to us, this may also make them seem familiar, which will make us like them. These effects were found in one study in which students made judgments about a set of other people who were said to have similar or different preferences for various activities. The more similar the others appeared, the more familiar and the more likeable they were judged (Moreland & Zajonc, 1982). So close is the connection between similarity and familiarity that even exposure to pronouns that reference similar others ("we") triggers feelings of familiarity (Housley, Claypool, Garcia-Marques, & Mackie, 2010).

3. ***Similarity contributes to mastery.*** "Birds of a feather flock together" is one of those old sayings that actually holds true: People tend to interact with similar others. Shared interests obviously create opportunities for interaction: Academically motivated students meet others of their kind at the library, fanatical golfers find their like at the golf course, and environmentalists find one another at Sierra Club meetings. Similarity makes it more likely that those interactions will be positive. First, similarity makes mimicry more likely (Miles and others, 2011), which as we will discuss later makes interactions with similar others even easier, leading to liking. Second, similarity is a key predictor of cooperation, trust, and helping (Krupp, DeBruine, & Barclay, 2008) increasing the rewards of interaction with similar others and again increasing liking.

4. ***Similarity validates connectedness.*** When other people share our attitudes, values, favorite activities, or even something as seemingly trivial as a birth date, it gives us a sense of connection with them (Walton, Cohen, Cwir, & Spencer, 2012). People expect similar others to accept and understand them, whereas a partner who is less similar is assumed to be less able to see and support who they really are (Murray and others, 2002).

The powerful effects of similarity on liking can be seen in its long-lasting influence on relationships. Friendship dyads tend to be more similar than randomly paired individuals, and the greater the variety of people available, the more similar friendship pairs are. Such findings show that people seek out more similar others to the extent that their environment allows them to. Thus, ironically, if you attend a large diverse school or work for a large diverse company, your friends in those settings will be more similar to you than if fewer people were available to befriend (Bahns, Pickett, & Crandall, 2012). Similarity is also important in romantic relationships. The members of married couples are more similar to one another on a wide range of variables than are the members of randomly paired couples (Buss, 1984; Rushton & Bons, 2005). Although couples can grow similar by being together (Gonzaga and others, 2007), the evidence shows the powerful influence of similarity on people's choices of partners, and suggests that relationships last when they are based on similarity—particularly in political and religious attitudes (Bleske-Rechek, Remiker, & Baker, 2009).

Similarity draws people toward each other, and gives them both the expectation and the reality of productive and enjoyable interactions, a reassuring sense of who they are, and mutual liking.

Positive Interaction

People are attracted to those with whom they have positive interactions. Interaction makes people familiar, provides opportunity for mimicry, helps people master the world, and helps people find connectedness.

Suppose you begin a new job, and you are assigned a desk near another worker. As the days pass, your neighbor shows you the ropes and you begin eating lunch together. You will probably end up liking this person better than your other co-workers. Or imagine you participate in a psychology experiment that pairs you up with a same-sex stranger and asks you to interact via an online "chat" system for either 1, 2, 4, 6, or 8 occasions. The more you interact with this randomly chosen stranger, the more you will probably like her (Reis and others, 2011). These facts reflect a surprisingly simple principle: People often come to like people they interact with, even if they are thrown together by chance.

One factor that promotes frequent interaction is physical proximity. A classic study of residents in a married-student housing complex found that friendships tended to form among those who lived near one another (Festinger, Schachter, & Back, 1950). The most popular residents were those whose apartments were located near the stairs or close to the mailbox area, where they had extra opportunities to interact with others. The benefits of proximity are particularly important if there are no other reasons why people might come together. In another housing study, researchers found that proximity had even more effect on friendships with others of different ages or races than on friendships with more similar others (Nahemow & Lawton, 1975). College roommates also tend to like each other, even if they do not initially share the kinds of characteristics that usually lead to attraction (Newcomb, 1961). Regardless of the reason,

Photo 12.5 The closeness of connectedness. Relationships need not involve romantic feelings to provide us with feelings of connectedness. More commonly we gain support, closeness, and a sense of identity from those with whom we share enjoyable activities or intimate revelations.

bringing people physically together often leads to friendships. That annoying habit that some teachers have of seating you alphabetically in classrooms? Students whose teachers use that technique typically form friendships with classmates whose names are in their part of the alphabet (Back, Schmukle, & Egloff, 2008; Segal, 1974).

Why Interaction Increases Liking. Of course, interactions can vary, from the simple nodding in recognition as your paths cross, through multiple 15-minute online chat sessions in an experiment, to the complex interactions between a veteran and the new worker being trained. Even minimal interactions can increase liking, and as interaction becomes more frequent or complex, additional processes contribute to the effect.

1. *Interaction makes others familiar.* Familiarity doesn't breed contempt. Instead, the familiarity that results from merely seeing something over and over again increases liking (Bornstein and others, 1987). Richard Moreland and Scott Beach (1992) demonstrated its powerful effect when they had women sit in on varying numbers of lectures in a large class. The other students in the class thought the women who had attended more often were more likeable and attractive. Familiarity is also important when interaction is more complex—the positive effects that the multiple computer chats had on liking were also due to the increased familiarity participants felt about their partners.

This study was initially discussed in Chapter 3, pages 61–62, because it illustrates a process that could influence the impressions we form of others in many circumstances, not just in the formation of a personal relationship.

2. *Interaction contributes to mastery.* If you stop to think about why you enjoy being with other people, your first reason will probably be that it's often just plain rewarding. Debating politics far into the night, listening to an inspiring lecture, and sharing what you know in joint study sessions are activities that meet our personal needs in many ways. Some ways are obvious: The study session may help improve test grades. Other benefits are not quite so obvious. Discussing a personal worry with a close friend can help us understand and cope with trying circumstances and with our own reactions to them (Buunk, Gibbons, & Visser, 2002). When interacting with someone is rewarding in any of these ways, the result is the same: We tend to like the person (Rusbult, Arriaga, & Agnew, 2001).

3. *Interaction helps us feel connected.* Interacting with someone who treats us with warmth, acceptance, and respect can confirm our sense of being connected to others (McAdams & Bryant, 1987; Reis & Patrick, 1996). This sense of relatedness and attachment to the other person is another important reward of interaction—one that, as we shall see, increases in importance as relationships deepen. An important contributor to these feelings of connectedness is mimicry. When two people interact, they start mimicking each other's speech patterns, posture, mannerisms and so forth, usually without either person realizing that it is happening (Chartrand & van Baaren, 2009). Even complete strangers will mimic each other during a brief interaction, with one following suit when the other shakes a foot or puts hands to the face (Chartrand & Bargh, 1999). Mimicry makes interactions feel comfortable and enhances liking (Lakin, Jefferis, Cheng, & Chartrand, 2003).

Chapter 7 described some of the effects of mimicry on liking for other people, page 247.

At this point you may be remembering a particularly obnoxious roommate or next-door neighbor and thinking that frequent interaction certainly does not always lead to liking. You're right: When interaction fails to meet our needs or even harms us, it will lead to

Figure 12.1 Interaction leads to attraction
Interacting with someone increases attraction to that person through three different processes.

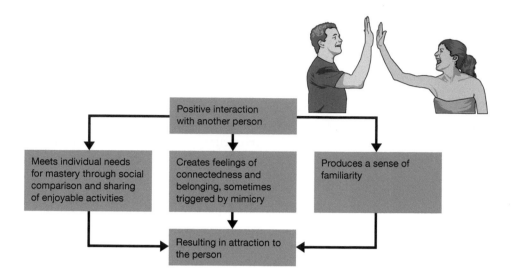

disliking. More negative interaction just spells more annoyance if you have to spend time with someone who holds offensive political views, or share a dorm room with someone who constantly plays classic rock music while you like only hip-hop (or vice versa). Incompatible musical tastes are one of the most important reasons for dissension between college roommates, so much so that one college application form asks students to "cross out any music you cannot tolerate" so that rooms can be assigned accordingly (Abramovitch, 1997). In fact, the very first contact between two people often sets the tone for future positive or negative interactions, with a marked impact on whether the relationship even exists nine weeks later (Sunnafrank & Ramirez, 2004). If interaction does continue, the effects of familiarity, mastery, and connectedness help increase attraction, as Figure 12.1 suggests (Rosenbaum, 1986).

Figure 12.2 The mutually reinforcing effects of interaction, similarity, perceived attractiveness, and liking
Interaction, similarity, perceived attractiveness, and liking all tend to influence one another. These mutually reinforcing processes move acquaintanceship toward friendship.

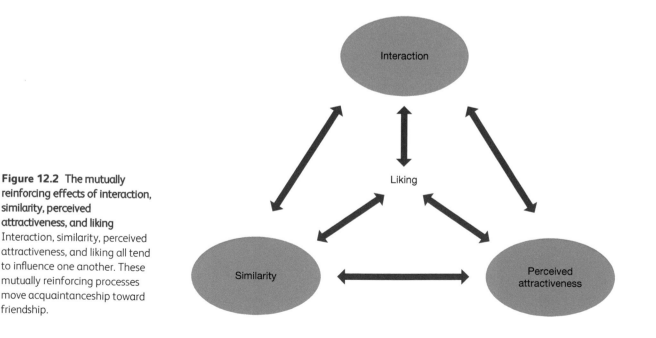

Initial attraction can be sparked by the draw of an attractive face, shared attitudes, or chance proximity, but as these factors all start to work together, liking quickly develops (Berscheid & Reis, 1998). Similarity encourages interaction, and when people interact, they discover more similarities, finding out what they have in common. The more we interact with someone, the more attractive we typically find them, and the more attractive they are, the more we are drawn to interact with them. We find those similar to us physically attractive and the more attractive people are, the more we want to be like them. And once liking develops, it feeds back on the other factors to develop and reinforce the connections. We find physically attractive people appealing, but we also find the people we like more physically attractive. Interaction creates liking, and liking leads to more interaction because we seek out the company of those we enjoy. Similarity triggers liking, and the more we like someone, the more motivated we are to find other similarities we share. Once liking, attractiveness, interaction, and similarity become mutually reinforcing processes as portrayed in Figure 12.2, acquaintanceship will progress toward friendship.

FROM ACQUAINTANCE TO FRIEND: RELATIONSHIP DEVELOPMENT

As we have just seen, strangers meeting for the first time will show some clear patterns of attraction. Almost everyone will find a few individuals likable, perhaps the especially attractive or friendly ones, those who seem similar to them, or the ones they first interact with. Some people will also have idiosyncratic preferences: Erica may be especially attracted to people with red hair, and Miguel may find Joe's sense of humor objectionable. On such short acquaintance, however, the factors that make Miguel dislike Joe will have little to do with Joe's feelings about Miguel.

If the same people interacted for weeks, months, or years, the patterns of liking would be very different (Kenny, 1994). Although initial attractions might have some lingering footprint, preferences will mostly reflect the unique history of the interactions between specific pairs of individuals. People's feelings will have become mutual. Erica and Miguel share a mutual passion for science fiction and will like each other, regardless of whether other people like Miguel because of his science fiction fixation or whether other people with whom she has nothing in common like Erica. Patterns like this demonstrate the existence of relationships, meaning that the purely individual characteristics that might have initially influenced others' feelings about each member of the couple become less important than the unique set of mutual associations and interactions between two people. What turns acquaintances into friends and partners? The answer involves both of the key motives we have already discussed: the need to master the environment and the need for connectedness with others (Baumeister & Leary, 1995; Cantor & Malley, 1991). Friendship develops through interactions that fulfill these two needs. Partners exchange rewards, helping each other find satisfaction, and they exchange self-disclosures, getting to know each other in increasingly intimate ways.

Exchanges of Rewards: What's in It for Me and for You?

As a relationship begins to develop, the partners exchange rewards.

For voluntary relationships such as friendships or romances to develop and deepen, each partner must receive benefits and rewards. Perhaps you have known someone who was always asking for a loan of a few dollars but never paid you back, or someone who always wanted to tell you his troubles without ever asking in return if you had had a good or a bad day yourself. If so, you probably tried to escape from those relationships unless they provided you with other types of rewards—maybe the chronic borrower was a witty raconteur, always fun to be around. As these examples illustrate, the rewards that each partner gets from interaction are key in determining the course of the relationship (Rusbult, Arriaga, & Agnew, 2001). People who know each other casually typically share activities that directly reward both partners. For example, two acquaintances may frequently play tennis because they both enjoy the game. Or two people may directly exchange benefits. For example, one may cook a gourmet dinner for a classmate in return for an evening's tutoring help with a tough calculus assignment. The kinds of relationships that work this way are termed **exchange relationships**, because people offer benefits to their partners in order to receive benefits in return (M. S. Clark & Mills, 1979).

exchange relationship
a relationship in which people offer rewards in order to receive benefits in return

Different kinds of relationships have different exchange rules (Fiske, 1992; Haslam & Fiske, 1999). As relationships develop, the rules about who gets what de-emphasize concerns about what the self gets and start to reflect the growing importance of the other person. For example, relationships among casual acquaintances are typically characterized by equity-based exchange. In this kind of exchange, people are given rewards based on how much they contribute to the relationship—people only contribute to the other if they believe that he or she deserves it and careful track is kept of the benefits to the self. But when relationships develop into friendships, people often share benefits equally, keep less track of who deserves what, and assume that their partner will do the same (Pataki, Shapiro, & Clark, 1994).

Thus changes in how rewards are exchanged signal important transitions in the development and deepening of a relationship. If you regard an acquaintance as a potential friend or partner, you may signal your desire for a closer relationship by offering a favor or picking up the check for a shared restaurant dinner (Lydon, Jamieson, & Holmes, 1997; Clark & Mills, 1979). But such gestures often leave the recipient uncertain about the individual's desires and intentions. Is the offered favor a genuine invitation to a closer relationship or something else, even an attempt at manipulation? Uncertainty and anxiety may cloud both partners' feelings about the transition (Lydon and others, 1997). If all goes well, the partner may read the intended meaning correctly and the relationship may progress further toward closeness. In contrast, if the partner refuses to accept the favor or insists on paying it back at the first available opportunity, that amounts to a statement that a closer relationship is not desired. In either case, actions take on special meanings in the context of the transition from acquaintanceship to a close friendship.

Self-Disclosure: Let's Talk About Me and You

Relationship development also includes exchanges of self-disclosures as the partners come to know each other better. Self-disclosures increase liking and offer opportunities for sympathetic, supportive responses.

"I hate this cold weather." "I can't believe how much money I just spent on groceries." Relatively impersonal topics like these are the kinds of things you might discuss with acquaintances. On the other hand, "My alcoholic father used to beat me," or "I don't know if I'm smart enough to make it in grad school" are the kinds of intimate disclosures we usually share only with close and trusted friends. Self-disclosures include facts about one's life and situation, as well as inner thoughts, feelings, and emotions (Morton, 1978). Both the depth of self-disclosure (the level of intimacy of the information) and the breadth (the range of topics) increase as a relationship develops (Altman & Taylor, 1973; Gore, Cross, & Morris, 2006; Z. Rubin, Hill, Peplau, & Dunkel-Schetter, 1980).

Effects of Self-Disclosure. Disclosing something about yourself makes both strangers and friends like you more (Collins & Miller, 1994). This fact probably explains why salespeople often self-disclose to their customers, offering cute stories about their children or pets. It may also explain why people who readily express their feelings nonverbally are liked more than less expressive individuals (Friedman, Riggio, & Casella, 1988). But self-disclosure can go too far: Those who disclose more than is appropriate for the closeness of the relationship make others uncomfortable (Wortman, Adesman, Herman, & Greenberg, 1976). Just as when an acquaintance offers a favor, the reason for such a revealing self-disclosure is uncertain: Does it express a desire to deepen the relationship?

When people are entrusted with a self-disclosure, the norm of reciprocity prescribes that they should respond in kind. For example, when someone describes sad personal experiences to you, you might recount similar events from your own life. Thus self-disclosures, like rewards, are often exchanged in a relationship (R. L. Archer, 1980) and doing so makes both giver and receiver like the other (Sprecher, Treger, Wondra, Hilaire, & Wallpe, 2013).

You may recall our discussion of other implications of the norm of reciprocity from Chapter 10, pages 364–368.

Self-disclosures can have many positive effects that work to deepen a relationship. Receiving as well as giving emotional disclosures fulfills a listener's need for connectedness (Hackenbracht & Gasper, 2013). Coordinating mutual activities is easier when each partner knows something of the other's abilities and preferences. And deeper mutual understanding lets each partner meet the other's needs more easily. Self-disclosure also signals trust, because in a particular relationship we may disclose things that we would not want the whole world to know.

There is a strong gender difference in the intimacy level of self-disclosure. Both in person and online, women self-disclose more than men, particularly by revealing their feelings and emotions (Dindia & Allen, 1992; Morton, 1978; Special & Li-Barber, 2012). As Figure 12.3 shows, the difference is largest in same-sex friendships: Women disclose much more to other women than men do to other men (Reis, 1986). But self-disclosure functions the same way for men and women: When men do engage in self-disclosure early in a heterosexual relationship, it can be part of an effort to make the relationship

Figure 12.3 Gender and the intimacy of interaction
In this study, college students filled out brief questionnaires rating the intimacy of all their social interactions within a given time period. As the figure shows, interactions involving a female participant or a male participant and a female partner—that is, any interaction that involved a female—tended to be more intimate and self-disclosing than interactions between two males. (Data from Reis, 1986.)

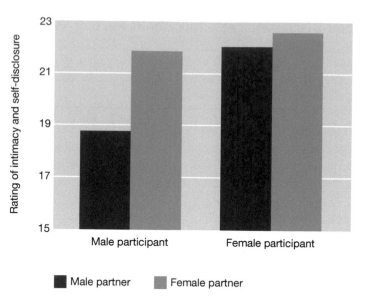

more intimate (Ackerman, Griskevicius, & Li, 2011; Derlega, Winstead, Wong, & Hunter, 1985).

As a relationship starts to deepen, the give and take of self-disclosures starts to be less about the discloser, and more about the partner. Whereas a typical response to a self-disclosure early on might be "Wow, something like that happened to me too!", later disclosures are more likely to be met with interest and concern about the disclosing

SOCIAL PSYCHOLOGY AND CULTURE: SELF-DISCLOSURE AND CULTURE

People from individualist cultures tend to self-disclose more than those from collectivist ones (Ting-Toomey, 1991; Kito, 2005). This is perhaps not surprising when one reflects on the many ways that the self differs in individualist and collectivist cultures. Much more than those in collectivist cultures, those in individualist cultures care about their own uniqueness and seek to express themselves, often communicating about their internal states, such as their own traits, goals, and opinions (Markus & Kitayama, 1991). These concerns might naturally encourage those from individualist cultures to self-disclose about their inner thoughts, feelings, and emotions more frequently.

Individualist cultures also encourage greater self-disclosure because they have higher relational mobility (Schug, Yuki, & Maddux, 2010). Cultures with greater relational mobility are ones where it is fairly easy to form new relationships and to dissolve unwanted old ones. Because it is easy for poor relationships to be terminated in these settings, maintaining a relationship takes more effort, and self-disclosure may be one strategy people use to help keep relationships intact. On the other hand, where terminating poor relationships is harder, people may not work as hard to maintain them, and thus might not self-disclose very often. To test these ideas, researchers asked students from Japan and the United States how likely they would be to disclose various types of information to a close friend or family member. The students also rated their relational mobility, responding to items like, "They (i.e., people in my immediate society) have many chances to get to know other people." U.S. students reported greater relational mobility and higher levels of self-disclosure than did the Japanese students. Moreover, the cultural difference in self-disclosure was due to the cultural difference in perceived relational mobility.

partner. As you will soon see, reacting to disclosures with sympathetic concern is a crucial means of building greater intimacy and closeness in relationships (Reis & Patrick, 1996).

As two people interact over time, the course of the relationship comes to depend on the way they treat each other. As they exchange rewards, they feel good about themselves and each other. As they share intimate information, they grow in mutual understanding, demonstrate trust, and obtain support and self-validation. Each partner's liking for the other now depends on the way the exchanges of rewards and self-disclosures starts to reflect the relationship, rather than its separate members. If the processes continue smoothly, casual friendship may be transformed into a close relationship. When that happens, psychological closeness transforms the nature of the self-disclosure and exchange processes that produced closeness in the first place.

CLOSE RELATIONSHIPS

Of your hundreds of relationships with other people, only a handful truly count as close. Are they the relationships that evoke the most positive feelings? Not necessarily. For example, you may have felt high regard and strong attraction for someone who will always remain distant, such as a teacher or movie star. Or you may have been in a close relationship with a sibling or a romantic partner that at times was so filled with conflict that your feelings were mostly negative. For reasons like these, researchers define a **close relationship** not in terms of positive feelings but as a connection involving strong and frequent interdependence in many different areas of life. Interdependence in a relationship means that each partner's thoughts, emotions, and behaviors influence the other's (H. H. Kelley and others, 1983; Rusbult and others, 2001). When we talk about close and interdependent relationships are we talking about love? Although many researchers have avoided the issue, Arthur Aron and Elaine Aron (1991) defined **love** as the "thoughts, feelings, and actions that are associated with a desire to enter or maintain a close relationship with a specific person" (p. 26). This definition emphasizes the desire for closeness or interdependence, and, like our everyday use of the word love, covers relationships with kin and friendships as well as romantic relationships (Meyers & Berscheid, 1997). That is, a close relationship can involve the secure, trusting attachment between parent and child, the one-for-all and all-for-one closeness of best friends, as well as the intense sexual attraction of romantic love (Hatfield, 1988). Because all close relationships share the basic properties of interdependence, we consider what research tells us about those common processes before discussing what is special about romantic and sexual relationships. Close relationships involve three forms of interdependence: cognitive, behavioral, and affective.

close relationship
a relationship involving strong and frequent interdependence in many domains of life

We defined interdependence in Chapter 11, page 397, because it applies to people's relations with their groups as well as with dyadic partners.

love
thoughts, feelings, and actions that occur when a person wishes to enter or maintain a close relationship with a specific person

Cognitive Interdependence: The Partner Becomes Part of the Self

In a close relationship, the partner is incorporated into the self-concept. Partner knowledge becomes more like self-knowledge, and we start to make attributions about our partners as if they were us.

Cognitive interdependence means thinking about the self and partner as inextricably linked parts of a whole—a couple—rather than as separate individuals (Agnew, van Lange, Rusbult, & Langston, 1998). In the intense and frequent interaction that marks a close relationship, partners learn a lot about each other: She can repair her car; he once cheated on an important exam. As each partner becomes increasingly familiar with intimate and varied information about the other, something important happens: The differences that typically exist between self-knowledge and knowledge about the partner are erased. Consider some of the self–other differences that melt away in a close relationship.

The differences that usually exist between knowledge of the self and knowledge of another person were described in Chapter 4, pages 101–102.

1. People know their own thoughts and feelings but are usually unaware of others' thoughts and feelings. Self-disclosure and extensive interaction, however, gives a person access to his or her partner's inner life. In a close relationship, people often have the sense that they know just what their partners are thinking. (Ickes & Simpson, 1997).

2. People perceive themselves in a wide range of situations, whereas their opportunities to observe others are relatively restricted. The shared intimacy of a close relationship changes that, as each partner learns about almost every aspect of the other person's life.

3. People have a different perspective on themselves (as actors) than on others (as observers). In a close relationship, however, self-disclosure allows each partner to share the other person's perspective and to know the reasons behind the other person's behaviors and preferences.

To remind yourself of how a group can similarly become part of the self, refer to Chapter 6.

As the typical differences between the mental representations of the self and the partner are reduced or eliminated, knowledge of the partner becomes more like self-knowledge. This process represents a sort of expansion of the self beyond the individual to incorporate the partner (Aron, Paris, & Aron, 1995). Indeed, people's desires to grow and expand themselves in new ways may be a motivating factor in initiating romantic relationships, as the members of a recently paired couple can explore new experiences with their partner and incorporate parts of the other person into the self (Aron & Aron, 1996). Moreover, continued efforts at self-expansion may help maintain the relationship. Couples who reported that their joint activities were more "exciting" (activities that allow for greater self-expansion) reported being less bored in their relationships, which in turn predicted relationship satisfaction even nine years later (Aron and others, 2000; Tsapelas, Aron, & Orbuch, 2009).

As the boundaries between self and other break down, mental representations of the self and partner become a single unit, the defining feature of cognitive interdependence (Agnew and others, 1998; Mashek, Aron, & Boncimino, 2003). For example, people use "we" to refer to themselves and the partner, just as they do with an in-group with which they identify. In one study demonstrating the linkage of partner and self, people rated whether each of a number of trait words terms described themselves, while a computer recorded the amount of time they took to respond to each item. The researchers then compared the speed of responding for those traits on which participants had previously rated themselves as similar to their spouses, versus those on which participants had rated themselves as different from their spouses. Participants were slower in responding on the traits where they thought they differed from their spouses (Aron, Aron, Tudor, & Nelson, 1991). The researchers concluded that people's representations of themselves and their partners become so intertwined that each partner is slowed down when having to report, for instance, that he is not assertive when his wife is, or she is extraverted but her boyfriend is the quiet one. The closer the relationship, the slower are these responses that require differentiation of the two partners (E. R. Smith, Coats, & Walling, 1999).

When the other becomes part of the self, we also start to make attributions about our partners as if they were, well, us. As we saw in Chapter 4, attributions for our own behaviors are often self-serving, and when a close relationship partner becomes part of "me and mine," the same self-serving biases apply to the partner. We inflate the significance of our partner's positive behaviors, linking them to his or her sterling qualities or loving feelings: "How much he must care about me!" We usually minimize the partner's negative behaviors, explaining them away as due to situational causes like a bad day at work or minor failings like a poor memory (Fletcher & Fincham, 1991). In fact, idealized, highly positive views of the partner—perceptions that are even more positive than the partner's own self-views—are typical of relationships that are deeply satisfying and long-lasting (Barelds & Dijkstra, 2011; S. L. Murray, Holmes, & Griffin, 1996). Though it may strike you that holding overly positive views of your partner might be troublesome, as we will discuss later, these positive biases may actually help relationship partners manage stress.

In a close relationship, processes of cognitive interdependence mean that the partner —whether a best friend, parent, or romantic partner—becomes part of the self. Self-definition as a member of the twosome, and the support and validation provided by the partner, become important to the person's identity, just as a significant group membership becomes important. Although convential wisdom has women more dependent for self-worth on relationships than men are, research shows that both men and women derive identity and value from their relationships, although from different aspects of them (Kwang, Crockett, Sanchez, & Swann, 2013), as we'll see shortly.

Behavioral Interdependence: Transformations in Exchange

Relationship closeness alters the way partners exchange rewards. In a close relationship, partners reward each other to show affection and because they want to make the partner happy.

Behavioral interdependence means that each person has a great deal of influence on the partner's decisions, activities, and plans. Partners spend a lot of time together, and they share a number of different activities. More importantly, the reason why they share decisions, activities, and plans changes. In close relationships, the exchange of rewards that characterizes casual relationships gives way to providing rewards that benefit the relationship itself.

Caring about the partner's feelings—wanting to make him or her feel good—can complicate decisions about what to do. Suppose, for example, you have a yen to take in a classic Federico Fellini film on a Friday night. If your partner prefers the latest

Hollywood action movie, you have to consider that preference as well as your own in deciding on the evening's entertainment. In a relationship, we solve minor coordination problems like this easily because the nature of exchange is transformed in a close relationship (H. H. Kelley, 1979; Rusbult and others, 2001). People do not just do whatever they would prefer as individuals and ignore the partner's wishes, or give in to the partner while expecting direct reciprocation in the future. Instead, close friends or others who have **communal relationships** are directly concerned for each other's welfare, and they provide benefits to demonstrate that they care about the relationship rather than to receive benefits in exchange. After all, if your partner is part of yourself, his or her needs and desires become indistinguishable from your own. The shift from an exchange to a communal orientation marks an important transition point to a close relationship (Mills, Clark, Ford, & Johnson, 2004).

In a study demonstrating this point, participants divided up a set amount of money between themselves and another person (Aron and others, 1991). As Figure 12.4 shows, people gave themselves considerably more than they gave to a stranger. When the other person was their best friend, however, they gave the friend just about the same amount as they gave themselves, even when the experimenter arranged that the friend would not know the source of the money. People really want to benefit a close friend just as much as they want to benefit themselves. Indeed, one's best friend is part of "me and mine."

Potential romantic relationships show the same changes from exchange to communal patterns—and if they don't, they often don't survive. An interesting study by Steven

communal relationship

a relationship in which people reward their partner out of direct concern and to show caring

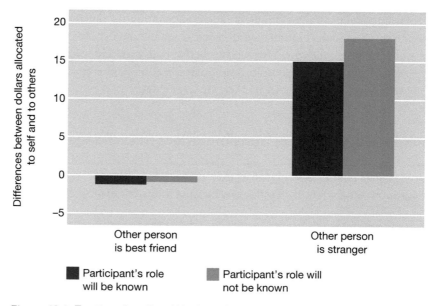

Figure 12.4 Treating a best friend like the self
In this study, participants were given a sum of money to divide between themselves and another person. As the left bars show, when the other person was their best friend, the participants gave that person slightly more than they gave themselves—regardless of whether the friend would know of their role in the allocation. In contrast, when the other person was a stranger, the right bars show that participants gave considerably more to themselves than to that person. (Data from Aron and others, 1991.)

Beach and his colleagues (1998) shows that when rewards are seen as accruing to one partner more than the other, social comparisons may stop the forward progress of the relationship. Have you and your partner ever worked for the same company, enrolled in the same course, or tried out for roles in the same play? If so, you know that you don't always feel great when your partner gets a glowing job evaluation, top grade, or starring role—if you didn't get as good an outcome yourself. With dating partners, this inequality in outcomes can become a kind of "romantic battleground" undermining the relationship. Married couples, in contrast, show concern for their partner's feelings and outcomes as well as for the damage to their own egos when performance comparisons arise. Their "relationship first" communal thinking lets them handle performance comparisons in ways that allow the relationship to survive.

Different people get different benefits from relationships. Men and women place different emphases on the various rewards that relationships offer (Tannen, 1990; P. H. Wright, 1982). Men prefer participating in enjoyable activities with their friends and partners, and the more time men spend with friends and partners in activities they enjoy, the more satisfied with those relationships they are. Men, more than women, also value relationships as a source of social standing and mastery, whereas women value relationships for the sharing, intimacy, and connectedness they provide (Kwang and others, 2013). Perhaps this is why women are happiest when their relationships are going well and conflict is avoided (H. H. Kelley, 1979; Surra & Longstreth, 1990; P. H. Wright, 1982). But closeness affects both men and women similarly in that it changes the types of benefits the partners bestow on each other. Material rewards are typically exchanged in relationships that are not close, whereas love and emotional support are more often the coin of close relationships (Foa & Foa, 1974; Goodfriend & Agnew, 2008; Hays, 1984). The more deeply the participants know one another, the more finely the rewards can be tuned to the other's specific needs and preferences. For example, new roommates who have just met seek a rough balance in the total amount of rewards they exchange, regardless of type. But as time passes and their relationship deepens to that of close friends, they are more likely to give each other the specific types of benefits that each values most: help with math homework, companionship for an evening at the movies (Berg, 1984).

Behavioral interdependence is thus a key factor in relationship development and maintenance: When people make decisions and take action that reflects the other rather than the self, relationships tend to endure over time (Berscheid, Snyder, & Omoto, 1989).

Affective Interdependence: Intimacy and Commitment

Intimacy, a positive emotional bond that includes understanding and support, is a key component of close relationships. Commitment, a dedication to maintaining the relationship for the long term, helps keep the relationship going.

Affective interdependence refers to the affective bond that links close relationship partners. Interdependence means that each partner's emotional well-being is deeply affected by what the other does. Usually, although not always, close relationships are marked by deepening feelings of warmth and positivity.

intimacy
a positive emotional bond that
includes understanding and
support

Intimacy. Perhaps the most important component of close relationships is **intimacy**. Intimacy is a positive emotional bond that includes understanding, acceptance, and support (Hatfield, 1988; Reis, Clark, & Holmes, 2004). You feel happy when you are with the partner and may feel low or even distressed when you are apart (Bowlby, 1969). You want to share with and help the partner (Sternberg & Grajek, 1984). Such feelings develop slowly over time, which is why it is difficult to imagine a truly intimate relationship springing up between two people "at first sight," no matter how strong their mutual attraction might be.

How does intimacy develop? Remember that the first step in deepening a relationship is reciprocating self-disclosures, particularly personal and emotional ones. Arriving home in the evening, you might tell your partner, "My computer crashed today and then the boss chewed me out because some important files got lost. I don't know how much longer I can handle this job." Instead of simply reciprocating with another self-disclosure, imagine that your partner now responds in a way that conveys acceptance, acknowledgment, and understanding of your feelings (Derlega, Wilson, & Chaikin, 1976; Reis, Clark, & Holmes, 2004).

This type of responsiveness is the second step in the process. It is important that the partner responds to the emotional content of the self-disclosure rather than to the surface issues. For example, you probably wouldn't find it very satisfying if the partner started talking about ways to keep your computer from crashing. The most effective responses not only incorporate the content of the self-disclosure (to show understanding) but go beyond it to express validation and caring (Reis, Clark, & Holmes, 2004). Perhaps because women are often better at the skills of understanding, empathy, and emotional responsiveness that build intimacy, women's close relationships, particularly with same-sex friends, tend to be more intimate than men's (Oswald, Clark, & Kelly, 2004; Reis, Senchak, & Solomon, 1985).

Although women tend to be more empathetic on average than men, it does not mean that men lack empathy (Carothers & Reis, 2013)—and for both women and men, increased responsiveness leads to the third step in the intimacy process. When you disclose, you feel understood when your partner correctly perceives your feelings. You also feel valued and esteemed by your partner's acceptance and acknowledgment. And you feel cared for by your partner's responsiveness and support. As an added bonus, such interactions may give you the strength to go back to work the next day and face your temperamental computer and curmudgeonly boss (Berg & Archer, 1980).

social support
emotional and physical coping
resources provided by other people

SOCIAL PSYCHOLOGY IN PRACTICE: INTIMATE INTERACTIONS AND HEALTH

Interactions that make close relationship partners feel understood, valued, and worthy don't just make people psychologically happier, they also make them physically healthier (S. Cohen, 2004; Uchino, 2009; Uchino, Cacioppo, & Kiecolt-Glaser, 1996). Such interactions are an important aspect of what relationship researchers call **social support**—the responsiveness of close others to one's needs (Cutrona, 1996). Of course, responsiveness can be in the form of material help like money, or informational help like advice, but close relationships are particularly

■■■

■■■

important in providing the resources that make us feel emotionally supported. And even apart from tangible benefits, social support has striking effects on physical health (Robies and others, 2014). For example, a recent review of studies indicated that people coping with cancer were 25% less likely to die from the disease if they felt they had good social support than if they did not (Pinquart & Duberstein, 2010). A meta-analysis of 148 studies of social support and mortality risk found a large effect of having stronger versus weaker social relationships overall, an effect that became even stronger when the analysis focused on those with high versus low levels of social support (Holt-Lunstad and others, 2010; see Figure 12.5). These effects are comparable to those of such well-known health risks as cigarette smoking or obesity.

Women seem to benefit even more from receiving social support than men do (Schwarzer & Leppin, 1989), but once again, it's a matter of degree: both gay and straight men and women fare better when they are in intimate relationships that allow them to give and receive emotional social support (Burleson, 2003; Graham & Barnow, 2013). Indeed, social support seems to be an all-purpose benefit in many ways. For example, believing that you have social support can have positive effects whether or not you actually receive the help. At the same time, receiving social support has benefits even if the support is provided so subtly and indirectly that recipients don't realize they are receiving it (Bolger, Zuckerman, & Kessler, 2000; Howland & Simpson, 2010)!

How does social support produce these striking benefits? Several theories have been offered. Some suggest that social support helps buffer people from stress, and that this is why it improves health. In one study supporting this idea, men with prostate cancer had better "health-related quality of life" if they had more social support, and this effect was due, in part, to perceived lower stress (Zhou and others, 2010). Other factors also contribute to social support's beneficial effects. For example, those in a social network or support group might encourage each other to seek out treatment or engage in healthier lifestyle practices, resulting in better health. Those with great support might feel like they have "more to live for," and thus be more willing to seek out and endure potentially costly or uncomfortable forms of treatment, which might be more effective. Or support might offer psychological benefits, like lower levels of depression or greater happiness, that then translate to better health (Cacioppo, Hughes, Waite, Hawkley, & Thisted, 2006; Pinquart & Duberstein, 2010.)

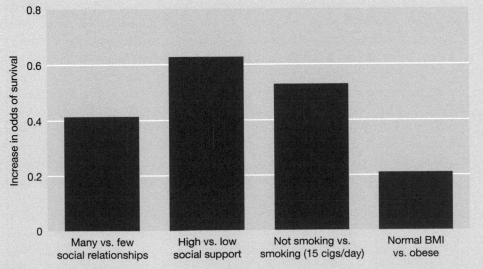

Figure 12.5 Social support and mortality risk A meta-analysis found that social support has as much of a positive influence on mortality risk as does not smoking or having a healthy weight. (Data from Holt-Lunstad and others, 2010.)

Don't think that closeness depends only on lending a shoulder to cry on. Just as people count on others for social support during times of trouble, people benefit from others' responsiveness when they have successes to share. Being able to tell another person about our triumphs and joys multiplies our good feelings about the events, and this is another important benefit of close relationships (Reis & Gable, 2003). In a series of studies, Shelly Gable and her colleagues have found that when people recounted positive events to others, they experienced more positive emotions and increased satisfaction with life, above and beyond the effects due to the event itself. Moreover, the more others they told, the more they benefited (Gable, Reis, Impett, & Asher, 2004). And the psychological and physical benefits are greatest when the other person reacts in that same validating, valuing, and understanding way that helps when partners share troubles (Uchino and others, 2013). Sharing a positive event with one's partner creates an opportunity to deepen the intimacy of the relationship, with subsequent benefits for psychological well-being.

Intimate interactions are therefore deeply linked with positive emotions of warmth, connectedness, and caring. Such feelings are so important to people that psychological intimacy is perhaps the most central reward of a close relationship (Harvey & Omarzu, 1997; Reis & Patrick, 1996).

commitment

the combined forces that hold the partners together in an enduring relationship

Commitment. Intimacy may draw people closer, but it is commitment that holds a relationship together over time (Rusbult, 1983). **Commitment** involves not only a strong emotional bond to the partner but also dedication to maintaining the relationship for the long term (Agnew and others, 1998). Committed partners know that the other is trustworthy, responsive, and available when needed, and that his or her support can bring comfort in times of distress. But committed partners also think, feel, and act with the best interest of the relationship in mind, dedicating their abilities and efforts to keeping it intact (Arriaga & Agnew, 2001; Rusbult, Martz, & Agnew, 1998).

What creates and maintains commitment to a relationship? Caryl Rusbult (1983) argues that it emerges from three factors. As Figure 12.6 shows, one factor is personal satisfaction with the relationship: recognition of the cognitive, affective, and behavioral rewards it offers (Drigotas & Rusbult, 1992). A second factor is the realization that equivalent rewards would not be available in alternative relationships (Thibaut & Kelley, 1959). If you see your relationship as offering unique rewards that you think would be unavailable from other relationships, you are likely to be strongly committed to it. The third factor is the number of barriers that make leaving a relationship difficult (Levinger, 1991). Once a relationship has developed, there is much to lose. People contemplating divorce must cope with the emotional, financial, and legal difficulties of breaking up a home and family, deal with the loss of other relationships associated with the disintegrating one, face the embarrassment of having to admit that the relationship failed, and confront the loss of their investments of time, energy, and emotion. Barriers like these can help maintain a relationship even if satisfaction is low.

Commitment usually grows as a relationship continues. As the partners' intimacy increases, they are likely to derive increasing satisfaction from the relationship, and they begin to perceive alternative relationships as less desirable and less available. In fact, compared with those who are dating casually, heterosexual college students who are committed to a dating relationship see their partner as relatively more attractive (Miller,

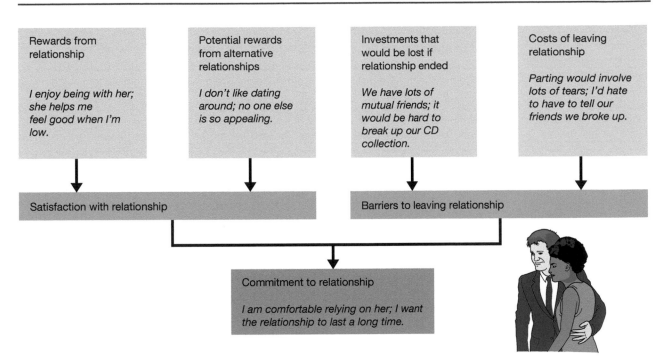

Figure 12.6 Factors influencing commitment to a relationship
Commitment depends on satisfaction with the relationship relative to its potential alternatives. Commitment is also strengthened by perceived barriers to leaving the relationship. (Based on Rusbult, 1983.)

1997) and opposite-sex others as less so (Simpson, Gangestad, & Lerma, 1990). Relationships that involve stronger feelings of commitment last longer, even when they are studied over a period of 15 years (Bui, Peplau, & Hill, 1996; Le & Agnew, 2003).

Cognitive, behavioral, and affective interdependence thus reflect the special ways that relationships help people meet their fundamental needs for connectedness with others and for mastery and rewards. Though they are all important aspects of relationship closeness, they are somewhat separate; a particular relationship may be higher on one dimension and lower on others.

Individual Differences in Close Relationships: Attachment Styles

People have different attachment styles in close relationships. Securely attached individuals are comfortable relying on the partner for support and acceptance. In contrast, some individuals avoid reliance on other people, and some individuals worry that the partner will not be available and responsive.

In a committed close relationship, psychological intimacy allows caring partners to share self-disclosures and to comfort and support each other. However, some people are more comfortable than others with intimacy, trust, reliance on, and commitment to, a partner.

Take a look at the self-descriptions in Table 12.1 and decide which one most closely fits you. Descriptions like these are used to classify adults as having distinct

attachment styles

people's basic securely attached, avoidant, or anxious orientation toward others in close relationships

attachment styles (Bartholomew & Horowitz, 1991; Brennan, Clark, & Shaver, 1998). The idea of attachment styles is based on the assumption that people have built-in tendencies to form emotional attachments to others, beginning in infancy (Bowlby, 1969). This innate mechanism binds infants emotionally to caregivers by leading them to feel good when in contact with the caregiver and anxious or distressed when apart, thus operating to keep helpless infants close to those who can ensure their survival. Although this psychological mechanism is common across all people, our differing lifetime experiences teach us different lessons about what to expect from close partners. If caregivers are attentive and responsive to our needs, we will come to hold different beliefs about ourselves, others, and therefore relationships, than if we find other people unresponsive or inconsistent.

Today relationship researchers tend to think of attachment styles not in terms of categories but as two continuous dimensions, the extent to which people seek or avoid intimacy with others, and the extent to which they are anxious about being abandoned by others (Shaver & Mikulincer, 2009). However, it is often convenient to talk in terms of discrete types of attachment, just as we often refer to people who are high or low in empathy or other individual differences—even though empathy actually defines a continuous dimension. As the descriptions in Table 12.1 show, secure individuals (description numbered 1), who make up a majority of the adult population (Mickelson, Kessler, & Shaver, 1997), feel good about themselves and others, are unafraid of intimacy, and unworried about abandonment. Dismissing individuals (description numbered 2) tend to feel good about themselves but do not trust others: they avoid intimacy and are not worried by the lack of it. Preoccupied individuals (description numbered 3) want to be intimate with others but worry that others don't want to be as close or as caring as they do. They are uneasy in their relationships and constantly anticipate threats and problems with them (Murray, Derrick, Leder, & Holmes, 2008; Murray, Holmes, & Collins, 2006). Finally, fearful attachment (description numbered 4) is characterized by anxiety about abandonment and a fear of intimacy. Individuals who are particularly sensitive to rejection, for example, may miss out on the benefits that most relationships offer because they are reluctant to open up or share (Downey & Feldman, 1996; Lemay & Clark, 2008).

TABLE 12.1   An Example of Statements Measuring Attachment Styles in Adult Close Relationships

1. It is easy for me to become emotionally close to others. I am comfortable depending on others and having others depend on me. I don't worry about being alone or having others not accept me.

2. I am comfortable without close emotional relationships. It is very important to me to feel independent and self-sufficient, and I prefer not to depend on others or have others depend on me.

3. I want to be completely emotionally intimate with others, but I often find that others are reluctant to get as close as I would like. I am uncomfortable being without close relationships, but I sometimes worry that others don't value me as much as I value them.

4. I am uncomfortable getting close to others. I want emotionally close relationships, but I find it difficult to trust others completely, or to depend on them. I worry that I will be hurt if I allow myself to become too close to others.

Source: From Bartholomew and Horowitz (1991). Copyright © 1991 by the American Psychological Association. Adapted with permission.

Research has convincingly confirmed Bowlby's ideas about attachment. Not only do infants display different types of attachment to their mothers (Ainsworth, Blehar, Waters, & Wall, 1978), but longitudinal studies show that maternal experiences at 18 months predict how people form attachments with romantic partners and peers about 20 years later (Fraley and others, 2013; Zayas, Mischel, Shoda, & Aber, 2011). So attachment-related experiences as an infant have strong implications for later attachment experiences as an adult. Still, attachment styles can and do change as a result of relationship experiences over a lifetime; evidence suggests that as many as 30% of people show different attachment styles when measured twice over a period of weeks or a few months (Baldwin & Fehr, 1995).

One specific effect of attachment styles is the way close partners give and receive social support. Jeffry Simpson and his colleagues (Simpson, Rholes, & Nelligan, 1992) separated the members of heterosexual dating couples and led each woman to a waiting room, where she was told that she would soon undergo "experimental procedures that arouse considerable anxiety and distress." To underline this warning, the researchers showed her a darkened room resembling an isolation chamber, filled with complex electronic equipment. Each man, unaware of his partner's experience, was then brought into the waiting room and the couple's ensuing interaction was covertly videotaped for 5 minutes.

People with different attachment styles showed distinct variations in their patterns of seeking and giving support. Among secure and preoccupied women, both of whom seek intimacy, those who were extremely upset sought more support from their partners than did those who were less frightened. In contrast, among women in the dismissing and fearful categories, who prefer to avoid intimacy, participants who were extremely upset actually sought less support than did their less frightened counterparts. Almost one-fifth of these women did not even mention the stressful event to their partners! The men's attachment styles also played a role in the amount of support they offered. Securely attached men tended to offer more support to a partner who displayed more fear than to a partner who was less frightened. But among men in the dismissing and fearful categories, a different pattern emerged. The more fear their partners displayed, the less support they offered them. Regardless of their attachment styles, all the women in this upsetting situation were calmed if their partners made supportive comments.

This study illustrates how attachment styles influence both people's trust in their partners' support and responsiveness and their own willingness to offer support. As a result of these processes, attachment styles influence the ways people attain intimacy and experience love in all close relationships (Collins & Read, 1990; Simpson, 1990). Because securely attached individuals are unafraid of intimacy and unworried about abandonment, they can both give comfort and support to and receive comfort and support from their partners. It is no wonder then that secure people have more satisfying romantic relationships, whether opposite-sex or same-sex (Elizur & Mintzer, 2003; Feeney, 2002). They also enjoy better friendships (Kafetsios & Nezlek, 2002) because attachment styles work the same way in friendships as they do in romantic relationships (Pietromonaco & Feldman Barrett, 1997). Because of the relationship advantages that secure attachments bestow in terms of responsive social support, securely attached individuals also enjoy better health outcomes (Pietromonaco, Uchino, & Dunkel-Schetter, 2013).

SOCIAL PSYCHOLOGY AND CULTURE: RELATIONSHIPS IN CULTURAL PERSPECTIVE

Much research on relationships, even studies of processes common to all types of close relationships, such as how people handle conflicts, has taken place in North America or other Western individualist cultures. Relationships in such cultures tend to be voluntary and often temporary. Perhaps the focus on voluntary relationships is responsible for the strong theoretical focus on rewards—on what each partner gets from the relationship—in many theories of relationship formation and development (Rusbult and others, 2001). At the same time, researchers have largely neglected relationships that are permanent and unchosen, such as ties to kin and other social groups, which in collectivist cultures are even more important than dyadic romantic connections (Moghaddam and others, 1993).

When researchers cast their net beyond North America, many differences between cultures are found (Goodwin, 1999; Markus, Kitayama, & Heiman, 1996). For example, the nature of the early bond between mother and infant, which is central to conceptions of adult attachment, differs considerably in other industrialized nations from its patterns in the United States (LeVine and others, 1994; Morelli & Rothbaum, 2007). East Asians, from collectivist cultures, are better able to read the emotions of close others but are worse at reading the emotions of strangers than are those from European (primarily individualist) nations, perhaps because connections with close others are so highly valued in such cultures (Ma-Kellams & Blascovich, 2012). Moreover, feeling that one is accurately understood is an important factor in building relationship closeness, but the situations that give rise to this feeling differ across individualist and collectivist cultures (Oishi, Krochik, & Akimoto, 2010).

The lesser importance accorded to individual choice in collectivist cultures is also reflected in the different ways cultures view the mysterious and powerful force of passion. Most North Americans believe that romantic love is natural, desirable, and necessary for marriage (Simpson, Campbell, & Berscheid, 1986). However, most Chinese words for love have negative connotations, like infatuation, unrequited love, and sorrow (Hatfield & Rapson, 1993). In some cultures, of course, marriages arranged by the parents or other relatives of the couple are common and passion is not seen as important at all (Merali, 2012). One study in India compared such arranged marriages to marriages chosen by the partners themselves, and found that love tended to increase over time in the arranged marriages, while decreasing in the other couples (Gupta & Singh, 1982). Our understanding of the full range of human relationships will be further enriched by more cross-cultural research and by theories that are sensitive to cultural assumptions and blind spots (Fiske, 1992).

ROMANTIC LOVE, PASSION, AND SEXUALITY

Romeo and Juliet, Rhett Butler and Scarlett O'Hara, Brad Pitt and Angelina Jolie—famous lovers of legend and lore feed our ideas about passionate romantic relationships. Although the development of attraction and liking, the interlinking of affective, cognitive, and behavioral interdependence, and the deepening of intimacy and commitment hold true for close relationships of every sort, relationships that involve passion and sexuality often provide an added spice or twist to the mix. What are these mysterious forces we call sexual attraction and passion? And how are they tied up with our ideas about sexuality and relationships?

Passionate Feelings

Some relationships involve passionate feelings and emotions. Passionate emotions can arise quickly and are closely linked to sexual desires and behavior.

"I want my partner, physically, emotionally, mentally." "Sometimes I feel I can't control my thoughts; they are obsessively on my partner." "I eagerly look for signs indicating my partner's desire for me." These statements capture the nature of **romantic love**: in addition to sexual feelings, there is a sense of intense longing for the partner, euphoric feelings of fulfillment and ecstasy when the relationship goes well, and anxiety and despair when it does not (Hatfield, 1988; Hatfield & Rapson, 1993). Other components of love, such as commitment, trust, intimacy, and attachment, are relatively quiet. But when people talk about passionate or romantic feelings, they use words like stormy, roller coaster, head-over-heels, and obsession. They also add one crucial preposition to the word love: being "in" love means feeling not only warmth and affection for the partner, but also sexual attraction (Meyers & Berscheid, 1997).

romantic love
involves sexual feelings, a sense of intense longing for the partner, euphoric feelings of fulfillment and ecstasy when the relationship goes well, and anxiety and despair when it does not

Romantic love is quite different from liking (Z. Rubin, 1970). Sometimes we realize that the object of our hopeless adoration is someone totally unsuitable, a person we don't know very well or even like very much. As Ellen Berscheid (1988) has noted, the intransigent independence of passionate feelings from the other components of love

> can be testified to by anyone who has earnestly desired to be in love with another, often because the other is so likable, or because they do have all those qualities one desires (or ought to desire) in a mate, or because it would please one's parents, friends, or the other person; one can like the other so hard one's nose bleeds, but that—still—does not, and seemingly cannot, cause the liking state to be transcended and romantic love to appear. (p. 369)

Like all strong emotions, passion is linked to a set of beliefs about the beloved and motivations for specific types of action. The beliefs often idealize the partner, especially as one's "perfect partner" (Hatfield, 1988). The desired actions include physical and sexual closeness and contact with the beloved. The high emotional value that lovers place on close contact may stem from the same innate attachment system that also serves to keep helpless infants in close proximity to their mothers (Bowlby, 1969; Hazan & Shaver, 1987).

Like all emotions, and like a roller coaster, passion has its peaks and valleys. When couples proclaim that they fell in love "at first sight," you can be sure that passion rather than commitment or intimacy is what they are describing. In fact, people often view passion as something that happens to them, as though they were struck by Cupid's arrow. Perhaps this helps explain why individuals who believe that external forces drive their lives are more likely to experience passion than are people who think they control their own fate (K. L. Dion & Dion, 1988). Even emotional arousal due to an extraneous reason such as a few minutes of exercise can intensify passionate feelings toward attractive others (G. L. White, Fishbein, & Rutstein, 1981; Zuckerman, 1979). However, after drawing people together, that first high peak of passion tends to fade as the relationship matures (R. J. Sternberg, 1988). Intimacy and commitment develop more slowly but become more important over time, giving a long-term close partnership quite a different character from the turbulent and frenzied feelings of its beginning.

So what is the source of the arousal that underlies and strengthens passion? Ellen Berscheid (1988), who has been studying love for three decades, answered this question by saying: "If forced against a brick wall to face a firing squad who would shoot if not given the correct answer, I would whisper 'It's about 90 percent sexual desire as yet not sated'" (p. 373).

Mate Preference: Who's Looking for What?

The social context of a relationship, especially whether it is short-term or long-term, determines the qualities people look for in mates.

As we discussed earlier, some aspects of physical appearance—signs of good health and access to resources—are initially attractive to almost everyone. Those same features make people sexually attractive, too, but with some interesting twists. Signs of good health and access to resources aren't equally important to everyone all the time.

Most research shows that men attach more importance to physical attractiveness than women do, whereas women care more about qualities related to a partner's status, ambition, and financial success (Feingold, 1990, 1992a). When people advertise for partners online or in personal columns, for example, more men than women specify that they are looking for physically attractive partners. This difference is found consistently across cultures (Shackelford and others, 2005), across the lifespan (Alterovitz & Mendelsohn, 2011), and regardless of whether the men seeking partners are gay or straight (Deaux & Hanna, 1984; Russock, 2011). As is typical of research in this domain, women's preferences are more variable: for example, in some of these studies the preferences of lesbian women are just like those of heterosexual women, whereas in other studies, lesbian women seem not to worry about resources at all (Russock, 2011; Smith, Konik, & Tuve, 2011).

What might explain the differences between men's and women's preferences about their partners? Evolutionary psychologists have advanced an explanation based in the much higher cost of successful reproduction for women (because of pregnancy, nursing, and childrearing) than for men (Trivers, 1972). Men can maximize their reproductive success simply by having a large number of healthy children, and so their best bet is to focus on the physical cues that signal a partner's good genetic health (D. M. Buss, 1994). Although women also seek attractive mates with good genes to pass on, their greater parental investment makes it important for them to seek men who are also able and willing to commit resources to support them and their children. From this perspective, it makes sense that men seek physical attractiveness and women seek dominance, social status, and wealth.

It turns out, however, that when researchers specify a social context for judgments of attractiveness—a short-term sexual encounter versus a long-term, committed relationship—what men and women want is not as different as it first might appear (Berscheid & Reis, 1998). When thinking about or anticipating short-term sexual encounters, such as "hooking up" or "a one-night stand," both men and women, whether gay or straight, are particularly attuned to physical attractiveness (Lucas, Koff, Grossmith, & Migliorini, 2011). With just sex on their minds, both men and women find individuals of the opposite sex who have signs of good genetic health physically attractive, especially when they themselves are biologically best prepared to reproduce (Gangestad, Garver-Apgar, Simpson, & Cousins, 2007; Li & Kenrick, 2006).

When thinking about long-term committed relationships, however, both sexes report personality traits to be among the most important factors in partner choice, a finding that holds across cultures (Buss, 1989; Buss & Barnes, 1986; Regan, Levin, Sprecher, Christopher, & Cate, 2000). Perhaps this is because the survival of human children has always depended on the shared resources of parents, making it reasonable that we have evolved preferences for either male or female partners with desirable personality traits and access to resources (Geary, 2007; Salmon & Shackelford, 2007). High among these important attributes are agreeableness, trustworthiness, honesty, and warmth. In one series of studies, for example, physical attractiveness predicted desirability for a one-night stand, whereas agreeableness was the strongest predictor of current and future long-term relationship satisfaction (Bryan, Webster, & Mahaffey, 2011). Thus both sexes seem to value physical attractiveness more for short-term encounters but have a wider range of concerns for long-term relationships.

The fact that specifying the relationship context diminishes gender differences suggests that in many attraction studies, men may be thinking about short-term encounters and women about longer-term relationships. This may be because men are much more willing than women to engage in casual sex with virtually unknown partners (de Jong and others, 2012; Li & Kenrick, 2006; Schmitt and others, 2012), a difference found across cultures (Greitemeyer, 2005). Biological factors such as men's higher testosterone levels contribute to this difference (McIntyre and others, 2006), but women also receive extensive socialization from parents, schools, and the media encouraging their role as

HOT TOPICS IN SOCIAL PSYCHOLOGY: FINDING AND MEETING ROMANTIC PARTNERS ONLINE

An important sexuality-related behavior is rapidly changing: the ways we meet possible romantic partners. Though people traditionally met their future spouse in person, at work, a bar, in church, or by chance at a supermarket, today we are increasingly likely to meet potential partners online, such as at a dating website. While convenient, online dating is not without its challenges. Recent research finds that people are often dissatisfied with online dating, perhaps because dating sites typically allow one to find and select a date primarily by examining "searchable" features. These are characteristics such as height, weight, or religion that can be ascertained by simply looking at a profile of a person. This is problematic because the information we usually want and need in deciding who to date is more "experiential," like the degree of rapport we feel when interacting with someone (Frost, Chance, Norton, & Ariely, 2008). Despite such challenges, overall outcomes of relationships that originate online are relatively positive. In a representative survey of nearly twenty thousand U.S. citizens who were married between 2005–2012, researchers found that roughly 35% of them had met their spouse online (Cacioppo and others, 2013). Compared to those who met offline, online couples were more likely to stay together rather than to be divorced or separated, and, if still married, had slightly better relationship satisfaction. Thus, newer means of meeting others appear, if anything, to produce more, not less, stable romantic relationships.

sexual "gatekeeper" rather than sexual initiator in relationships (Aubrey, 2004; Farvid & Braun, 2006). And times might be changing. One recent survey found that just over 50% of both male and female college students had "hooked up" during the last year (Barriger & Velez-Blasini, 2013; Owen and others, 2010).

While much research on relationship preferences has relied on self-report measures, recent research has compared what men and women think they might find attractive in the abstract, with what they actually find attractive in the flesh. In one study, researchers set up a "speed dating" event at which people could meet several other individuals for a short 4-minute "date" (Eastwick & Finkel, 2008). A week or two before this event, the student participants rated how much they desired attractiveness and earning potential in their speed-dating partners. At the speed-dating event itself, they rated each partner on these same dimensions, and recorded their degree of romantic interest. In the pre-event survey men said that attractiveness was more important in a speed-dating partner than women did, and women said that earning potential was more important than men did. Did these sex differences hold up when examining how they felt about their actual speed dates? No! Ratings of attractiveness and earnings potential predicted interest in actual dates equally for men and women (see also Todd, Penke, Fasolo, & Lenton, 2007). Indeed, a recent meta-analysis of several studies examining romantic interest in real potential partners (not hypothetical ones) showed that both physical attractiveness and earnings potential were important, and equally so for men and women (Eastwick and others, in press).

Thus a wide variety of factors contribute to humans' mate preferences (Buller, 2005; Said & Todorov, 2011). It is beyond question that evolved differences can affect men's and women's orientations toward both short-term and long-term mate selection. But cultural and social factors matter as well: In cultures in which women control more resources themselves, they also place less emphasis on men's resources relative to physical attractiveness (De Jong, Pieters, & Stremersch, 2012). As is always true, theories and perspectives that elucidate the interplay of all of these factors offer the best chance of helping us understand all close relationships, not just those involving sex (Eagly & Wood, 2011; Sutcliffe, Dunbar, Binder, & Arrow, 2012).

Sex in the Context of a Romantic Relationship

Like other mutually enjoyable activities, sexual activity can strengthen a relationship. But it can also be a focus of conflict.

Sexual intimacy is associated with increased stability within romantic relationships. Jeffry Simpson (1987) studied the stability of relationships among dating couples who were not having sex and among dating couples who were. He found that couples having sex were more likely to stay together over the course of 3 months. Another study of 101 heterosexual young dating couples over several years confirmed that sexual satisfaction was associated with relationship stability, at least for this age group (Sprecher, 2002).

Satisfaction with sex is also closely tied to relationship satisfaction (Reiss & Lee, 1988; Smith and others, 2011). One study, which compared happily married couples and troubled couples who had sought marital counseling, found that the happily married

HOT TOPICS IN SOCIAL PSYCHOLOGY: SEXUAL ORIENTATION, SEXUAL ATTRACTION, AND ROMANTIC LOVE

Lisa Diamond (2003) reviewed research evidence on sexual orientation and drew several provocative conclusions. One is that distinct psychological systems govern the preference for sexual partners and the other components of romantic love such as attachment and intimacy. An important implication is that people can experience romantic love in the absence of sexual desire. Indeed, Tennov (1979) found that over 60% of women and 35% of men reported experiencing infatuation with another without any desire for sex. This also means that a heterosexual person might fall in love with a same-gender other. The second point is that an individual's sexual orientation, which causes most people to prefer sexual partners of the same gender, the opposite gender, or both genders, does not limit possible romantic attachments. Supporting this idea is the fact that attachment is believed to result from a system that bonds infants to their caregivers (whether they are same-gender or opposite-gender).

Third, Diamond concludes that the links between sexual desire and romantic love can run both ways. We often assume that sexual attraction will cause two individuals to spend a lot of time together, building interdependence and intimacy, which will ultimately trigger attachment and affectional bonds. But the reverse process may also occur: people can develop sexual desires as a result of falling in love, even if those desires differ from their general sexual orientation. Evidence suggests this process is more likely in women than in men, because the links between sexual desire and love are stronger in women, both psychologically and culturally. Diamond's work points to some of the complexities in the interactions between sexuality and other components of romantic love.

couples had sex more frequently (Birchler & Webb, 1977). This pattern was not unique to sexual activity, however: These satisfied couples did many things together more frequently, including participating in sports and social events. The more rewarding and mutually enjoyable the activities in a relationship, the warmer the partners' feelings are likely to be. Conversely, when a couple are dissatisfied with sex or other major components of the relationship, satisfaction with the relationship is also likely to decline.

The reasons for sexual dissatisfaction tend to differ for women and men. Women become dissatisfied if they see their sexual relationships as lacking warmth, love, and caring, whereas men who are dissatisfied want more frequent and varied sexual activity (Hatfield and others, 1989; Laumann and others, 1994). This gender difference seems to diminish among older adults (Oliver & Hyde, 1993; Sprague & Quadagno, 1989). Sexual activity and satisfaction, however, need not decline. Although the frequency of sexual activity is lower among older adults than among younger adults, one study interviewed healthy adults ranging in age from 80 to over 100 and found that most were still sexually active (Neto & Pinto, 2013).

Why is sex such a unique and appropriate expression of love and intimacy in a close relationship? At least part of the answer is that sex uniquely combines the two fundamental processes that motivate people to form and maintain close relationships in the first place: mutual pleasure and enjoyment, and intimate self-disclosure (Reiss, 1986). These processes—giving and receiving pleasure, and knowing and being known—both flow from and reinforce the psychological link of partner to self, which is the foundation of an intimate relationship.

WHEN RELATIONSHIPS GO WRONG

In the course of most relationships, periods of calm are interspersed with troubled times. How relationship partners react to those troubled times determines whether togetherness can be maintained or whether the relationship falls apart. How does trouble start, and what resources help people handle conflict constructively and avoid relationship meltdown? When cognitive, behavioral, and affective interdependence unravels, breaking up is almost inevitable. Although most research has focused on the dissolution of romantic relationships, many of the same processes contribute to declines in friendship as well.

Threats to Relationships

Relationships can be threatened because interdependence inevitably leads to disagreements and because external factors, social norms, and the real or perceived presence of rivals can trigger relationship difficulties as well.

In Disney movies, acquaintances become best friends forever and lovers live happily ever after. Not so in real life, where interdependence inevitably breeds conflicts and relationships come under many pressures. Some pressures come from within: A change of interests or preferences, illness, or disability in either partner can reduce the other partner's willingness or ability to maintain the relationship. Both men and women frequently report that the desire for more autonomy or the lack of psychological support are reasons for relationship breakdown. But at least in one study some problems were mentioned more often by one sex than by the other. A lack of openness and intimacy was a problem for more women (31%) than men (8%), whereas the absence of romance or passion—feeling that "the magic has gone"—was an issue for more men (19%) than women (3%) (Baxter, 1986).

External factors also place stresses on relationships. If one person's job or family responsibilities increase, the resulting demands leave less time and energy for the partner. The birth of a couple's first child is a common source of stress for this reason: Children bring their parents love and joy, but they also force substantial changes in a couple's activities, which might breed conflict (Don & Mickelson, 2012). Of course, losing a job, with its financial and emotional consequences, also puts relationships at risk (Song, Foo, Uy, & Sun, 2011).

Social norms can also create stress and conflict, by dictating that one partner should perform a particular task regardless of individual preferences or abilities. For example, though gender roles have changed over the years, there remains a persistent difference in the amount of housekeeping that women do relative to men. A recent study of over 17,000 people in married or co-habiting heterosexual relationships in 28 different countries found that women do about 21 hours per week of housework, compared to about 9.5 hours for men (Davis, Greenstein, & Marks, 2007). The imbalance in household responsibility is reinforced by economic factors. Women across the globe are paid less on average than men. In the United States, for example, women are paid on average only about 81% as much as men for full-time work (U.S. Department of Labor, 2011), which tends to force men into the "breadwinner" role. Conflicts about who does what, such as how to share responsibility for housework, are among the most important causes of break-ups of both married and unmarried heterosexual relationships (Blumstein & Schwartz, 1983; Nettles & Loevinger, 1983).

Finally, when real or imagined rivals appear on the scene, most people experience a twinge of jealousy that can put a relationship to the test (Scheinkman & Werneck, 2010). Any sign of a friend's or partner's interest in other people may seem to be a dress rehearsal for impending rejection and the end of the relationship. Feelings of depression, anxiety, and anger may accompany jealousy. The depression and anxiety arise from the threatened loss of the valued relationship. Thus, they are similar to the feelings that would be aroused by other possible sources of loss, such as a serious illness. Anger, in contrast, is due to the loss of self-esteem from being rejected by the partner in favor of someone else. People's reactions to jealousy can run the gamut from talking to violence against the partner or rival (Kaighobadi, Shackelford, & Goetz, 2009; Salwen & O'Leary, 2013). In fact, jealousy can be so destructive that it is a common motive for homicide (Harris, 2004; Salovey & Rodin, 1989).

Every relationship will eventually run into some bumps in the road, such as disagreements about activities, performance comparisons, or a potential rival. Regardless of what goes wrong, such inevitable threats and pressures may damage relationship satisfaction and stability.

Handling Conflict: Maintaining Relationships in the Face of Threat

Conflicts can be handled constructively or destructively. There are many resources that afford constructive responses, and such responses lead to better relationship outcomes. If attempts to respond constructively fail, conflict escalates, which can lead to declining intimacy and commitment.

When problems arise, relationships require maintenance to repair the damage if they are to continue functioning. Both satisfaction and the survival of the relationship depend on how the relationship members respond to these problems. Problems can lead to a cycle of dissatisfaction and decline. However, if relationship participants have the resources to handle conflicts constructively, the relationship may survive its inevitable bad times and problems.

Constructive and Destructive Accommodation to Negative Acts. Even in the happiest of relationships, one partner's actions will occasionally annoy or hurt the other. Rusbult and her colleagues (1991) investigated couples' patterns of **accommodation**, the processes of responding to a negative action by the partner. Constructive accommodation involves actions that help maintain the relationship, including actively discussing problems, loyally waiting for the situation to improve, or forgiving the partner (McCullough, Worthington, & Rachal, 1997). Forgiveness involves a decrease in negative feelings and an increase in positive feelings toward a partner who has acted badly (Kachadourian, Fincham, & Davila, 2004). Forgiveness is more likely to be offered by partners who are generally high in self-control, and it has a strong impact on relationship

accommodation
the processes of responding to a negative action by the partner

**"Don't take this the wrong way, Howard, but I'd like
to go back to having an <u>on-line</u> relationship."**

well-being (Burnette and others, 2014; Fincham & Beach, 2001). It makes sense that the ability to "let it go" and "put it in the past" helps couples move past conflicts.

In contrast, destructive responses, such as screaming at the partner or refusing to spend time together, actively endanger the relationship. Actively misunderstanding and misinterpreting a partner's goals and feelings are also relationship-destroying reactions to negative events. As we have already seen, minor annoyances usually do not have major consequences in close relationships because attributions about the partner are positively biased. In contrast, a shift toward negative attributions often precedes other indications of marital conflict, suggesting that attributions are a basic cause of relationship dissatisfaction (Bradbury & Fincham, 1990; McNulty & Karney, 2001). In addition, the nature of a couple's conversations about conflict is extremely important. Happy couples are likely to nod and smile at each other, to make eye contact, and to agree, whereas unhappy couples sneer, scowl, and shout, reciprocating each other's negative acts (Gottman and others, 1976). Based on John Gottman's relationship studies, Lisitsa (2013) described four especially problematic types of communication often used in conflict, which may foreshadow the end of a relationship. One is criticism that goes beyond complaining about a specific act to characterize the person as a whole; for example "You never think about other people!" rather than "You left the kitchen really messy today!" A second is contempt, or a lack of respect for the partner conveyed by ridicule, sarcasm, or name-calling. A third is defensiveness, a response to criticism that makes excuses or conveys to the partner that a complaint is not being taken seriously, in contrast to a non-defensive response that often includes an apology. The fourth problematic type of communication is stonewalling, tuning out or withdrawing from interaction. Because responsiveness to the partner is key to building intimacy, one of the chief rewards of relationships, non-responsive behavior such as stonewalling can be especially problematic.

You may recall that attributing problems to global and stable causes can also lead to trouble of another sort. It is a recipe for learned helplessness and depression, as we discussed in Chapter 4, pages 128–129.

SOCIAL PSYCHOLOGY IN PRACTICE: RELATIONSHIP CONFLICT AND SOCIAL PROBLEMS

Several significant social problems have their ultimate roots in conflicts in intimate relationships. Violent assaults are estimated to occur in about one in ten marriages in the U.S. (Dutton, 1996), and 80 % of intimate partner violence victims are women (U.S. Department of Justice, 2012). Violence and spousal abuse are related to the same factors that lead to relationship conflict and break-up in general, underlining their origin in fundamental relationship processes (Berscheid & Reis, 1998).

Severe conflict in families can lead not only to violence but also to psychological problems for children. Large-scale studies of children in the United States and Britain examined the negative effects that are typically found in children whose parents have divorced (Cherlin and others, 1991). Like other research, these studies found that although most children of divorced parents turn out just fine, they do display more behavior problems and have lower school achievement than children from intact families. However, these researchers found that the problems usually appeared before the parents separated. Thus, these problems are not due to the trauma of divorce itself, as many people assume, but to conditions within intact but troubled families. As these studies indicate, the immediate costs of ending a conflict-filled relationship are sometimes easier to bear than the longer term costs of perpetuating it.

Given the costs to victims and to other family members, researchers are seeking the factors that trigger relationship violence and looking for ways to prevent it. One fruitful line of work shows the role that self-control plays in whether a person engages in intimate partner violence (Finkel and others, 2009) and how self-control might be bolstered to reduce such violence. In session one at the beginning of the study, all participants completed a task known to reduce levels of self-control and then completed a survey which asked their likelihood of responding with physical violence to a partner's negative act. Participants were then randomly assigned to a control group or to one of two experimental conditions designed to give participants practice engaging in self-control. Those in the "physical regulation practice" condition had to use their nondominant hand to perform several routine activities (like brushing their teeth) every other day for the next two weeks. Those in the "verbal regulation practice" condition had to talk in specified ways between 8 a.m. and 6 p.m. each day for the next two weeks. For example, they had to say "yes" rather than "yeah." At the end of the two-week period, all participants returned to the lab and repeated the same tasks they did in session one. The results were quite encouraging. Those in both self-control practice conditions reported a lower likelihood of responding with physical violence to their partners' (imagined) negative actions. Those in the no-intervention group showed no such reduction. Thus, practice with self-control might help prevent relationship violence and reduce its prevalence.

Resources for Constructive Accommodation. A couple's patterns of accommodation influence their satisfaction and the relationship's longevity. Some relationships and some relationship partners have more resources to bring to bear to maintain relationships in the face of threats.

1. *Attachment style.* Couples with secure attachment styles tend to accommodate more positively than other couples (Kobak & Hazan, 1991; Simpson, 1990), a pattern that holds in gay and lesbian couples as well as heterosexual pairings (Gaines & Henderson, 2002). They easily overlook a partner's faults or change their own behavior. Because they deal with conflict constructively, secure individuals see both their partner and their relationship more positively after discussing a major problem (Simpson, Rholes, & Phillips, 1996). Securely attached people are less likely to experience jealousy, but

even when they do, they are more likely to be open about it with their partner and to try to maintain the relationship (Collins & Read, 1990; Sharpsteen & Kirkpatrick, 1997). In fact, episodes of jealousy can end up strengthening a relationship in this case, a surprising outcome reported by many couples (Fitness & Fletcher, 1993).

Unfortunately, those with other attachment styles may react to conflict in ways that leave their relationships more vulnerable (see Figure 12.7). Partners with preoccupied or fearful attachment tend to deal with conflict in less constructive ways—for example, with outbursts of negative emotion and even violence (Downey, Feldman, & Ayduk, 2000). They are also quick to interpret negative behaviors in a relationship-threatening way and to respond in ways that trigger conflict (Collins, Ford, Guichard, & Allard, 2006). Dismissing individuals, in contrast, tend not to display distress or anger during conflict but can be distant and nonsupportive, reacting to discussion of a relationship-threatening behavior with relationship-threatening behavior of their own (Simpson and others, 1996).

2. **Commitment.** Constructive accommodation is also more likely when people are committed to the relationship (Rusbult, Yovetich, & Verette, 1996). Strong feelings of commitment can motivate people to overlook their partners' flaws, to communicate about their needs, even to change their own behaviors in ways that help the relationship (Rusbult, Verette, Whitney, Slovik, & Lipkus, 1991; van Lange and others, 1997). Committed partners are more likely to forgive transgressions (Karremans & Aarts, 2007) and the more committed to the relationship they are, the more forgiveness of the partner pays off for the forgiver's own mental and physical well-being (Karremans & Van Lange, 2008). As you might imagine, dating couples who perform more of the sorts of constructive accommodations that are linked to

Attachment style of member of the couple	During relationship conflict	Longer-term effects
Secure attachment	Overlook partner's faults Change own behavior	Perceive partner and relationship positively
Preoccupied or fearful attachment	Feel negative emotion, anger Interpret partner's behaviors as threatening relationship	Experience less love and commitment Experience damage to relationship
Dismissing attachment	Display little distress or emotion Fail to provide support to partner	Experience damage to relationship

Figure 12.7 Attachment styles and responses to conflict
Attachment style predicts how couple members respond during relationship conflicts and the long-term effects of those responses.

commitment are more likely to stay together than couples who perform fewer of them (Berg & McQuinn, 1986; Paleari, Regalia, & Fincham, 2005).

3. *Idealization of partner and relationship.* As we described earlier, romantic partners often idealize each other; that is, they hold images of the partner that are even more positive than the partner's self-image. You might think that idealization could set the relationship up for a fall when inevitable conflicts destroy the romantic illusions, but in fact idealization helps people deal with conflict. Sandra Murray and John Holmes (1997) found that among both dating and married couples, individuals who held more positive illusions about the partner reported less overt conflict and fewer destructive ways of handling conflicts (such as avoidance or returning criticism for criticism). Even among couples with equivalent levels of overall satisfaction with their relationship, illusions had these positive effects. Favorable beliefs about the partner, then, even if they are so biased as to exceed reality, are one important resource that can help couples either avoid conflict or deal with it in useful and productive ways. Perceiving your relationship as superior works the same way. People who see their relationship as having more positive features and fewer negative features than other relationships are particularly likely to boost this perceived superiority even more when the relationship is threatened. The strategy apparently works: In one longitudinal study, partners who saw their relationship as superior were more likely to still be together nearly two years later (Rusbult, Van Lange, Wildschut, Yovetich, & Verette, 2000).

4. *Beliefs about relationships.* Different people have different views, or implicit theories, of what it takes to make a relationship succeed (Knee & Bush, 2008; Knee, Patrick, & Lonsbary, 2003). For example, we all know people who claim that they and their current romantic partner were "destined to be together." But there are also people who view relationships as not destined but achieved, as something that one must work on for success. These individuals believe that with any partner, occasional conflicts are to be expected and can be overcome. They tend to date a partner for

SOCIAL PSYCHOLOGY IN PRACTICE: RELATIONSHIP CONFLICT AND CLINICAL PSYCHOLOGY

Fortunately, constructive ways to handle conflict can be taught to couples, with a positive impact on satisfaction and divorce rates. One study in Germany, for example, examined couples who completed a 6-session program on effective communication and problem solving and comparable couples who did not receive the training. Three years later, the trained couples not only reported more satisfaction and more positive communications in their relationship, but also had a lower rate of divorce (Hahlweg, Markman, Thurmaier, Engl, & Eckert, 1998). More recent work confirms that a variety of training methods can be helpful. During the first year of one study, married couples periodically reported various indicators of relationship quality. After one year, some couples were randomly assigned to receive training, which involved practice thinking about conflicts with their partner from a third-party perspective, to help them deal with such conflicts from a calmer, less angry frame of mind. Other couples received no special training. The results were clear and encouraging. During year 1, before the training, couples in both groups saw a steady decline in relationship quality. For those in the no-training group, this decline worsened during year 2 of the study. But for those who underwent the training, this slide in quality halted (Finkel and others, 2013).

longer periods of time, have fewer "one-night stands" during the first month of college (Knee, 1998), and are more likely to constructively discuss relationship conflicts with their partners (Kammrath & Dweck, 2006). In contrast, people who hold destiny beliefs, the idea that a particular romantic partner is inherently compatible or not, are more likely to be influenced by their initial satisfaction in the relationship. If initial satisfaction is high, the relationship is more likely to last a significant period of time. If initial satisfaction is low, the relationship tends to end quickly, as the partners conclude that "it was not meant to be" (Knee, 1998).

Declining Intimacy and Commitment. If attempts to respond constructively to relationship threats fail, conflict escalates. Partners spend less time together and become less open about their inner—now largely negative—feelings. Although the relationship may continue to satisfy some needs, it no longer provides the feelings of self-validation and acceptance that spring from deeply intimate partnerships. In fact, low levels of intimacy, reflected in limited self-disclosure and low levels of attachment and love, characterize relationships that are destined for disintegration (Hendrick, Hendrick, & Adler, 1988; C. T. Hill and others, 1976).

Even strong commitment, the glue that holds relationships together, can break down under the stress of conflict and dissatisfaction. Satisfaction declines, partners begin to perceive alternatives as more attractive, and accumulated investments may no longer seem to be important barriers to leaving (Rusbult and others, 2001). Unfortunately, this process feeds on itself: As you begin to view others as potential partners, those others note your potential availability and may in turn begin to pay you more attention. In other words, you will have a growing sense that the grass might be greener on the other side of the relationship fence.

Break-up, Bereavement, and Loneliness

All relationships end, either because of break-up or death. If a relationship breaks up, each partner usually blames the other for its general decline. Individuals cope more effectively if they feel they controlled the final separation. The end of a relationship because of partner death is particularly painful, in part because death is typically beyond our control. After the end of a close relationship, loneliness and other negative feelings are common.

All relationships eventually come to an end. This ending comes whether one or both members decide to break up a bad relationship, or whether a member of a lasting relationship dies. In either case, the ending is often quite painful emotionally. In the case of a break-up, in dating couples as well as married ones, women terminate heterosexual relationships more often than men do (Amato & Previti, 2003; C. T. Hill and others, 1976). Women are more distressed by relationship conflict and more focused on lost intimacy than men, and these facts may explain why they more often pull the plug (Surra & Longstreth, 1990). But no matter who delivers the final word, the break-up is often a lengthy and complex process, with repeated episodes of conflict and reconciliation (Cate & Lloyd, 1988). A longitudinal study by Susan Sprecher (1999) underlines the fact that breaking up is usually not an easy decision. This research found that in couples that would later break up, self-reports of various aspects of their relationship, such as satisfaction and commitment, became less positive before the final break. Interestingly, while satisfaction tended to diminish most, reports of love diminished least. This pattern means that for many couples, break-ups occur not because the partners "fall out of love," but because rising dissatisfaction and frustration with the relationship eventually outweigh the loving feelings that are still present.

After the Break-Up: Grief and Distress for Two. Most of us have been observers or participants in the break-up of more than one relationship and have seen first-hand that the psychological consequences of breaking up can vary. One sample of student dating couples found that the more depressed, lonely, and unhappy one partner felt after the break-up, the less the other partner did (Hill and others, 1976). Evidently, being the "breaker-upper" feels different from being the "broken-up-with" (Agnew, 2000). Each partner may feel wronged, and blaming the other for the break-up can be self-protective: those who attribute the cause of a divorce to the relationship, rather than to themselves, tend to adjust better (Amato & Previti, 2003). Despite this, the experience of ending a relationship almost always has more negative than positive consequences. On average, those who divorce suffer significant declines in mental and physical health (Richards, Hardy, & Wadsworth, 1997). If the partners cared deeply and helped each other in many ways, grief and distress are bound to occur. Such feelings arise even if the relationship's rewards were taken for granted before the break-up or if the interactions in the relationship were mostly negative (Berscheid, 1988; Simpson, 1987).

The cognitive and emotional consequences of the end of a close relationship can be long-lasting. People may reflect often and intensively on why the relationship ended, just as they think long and hard about other important negative events (Harvey, Wells, & Alvarez, 1978). Because failures of relationships often leave the partners baffled about what went wrong, the search for causes may become somewhat obsessive as the person repeatedly reviews past events, and unresolved longing for a recent ex-partner contributes to dissatisfaction with new relationships (Spielmann, Joel, MacDonald, & Kogan, 2013). Feelings of control, for example, knowing that you decided to end the relationship, or believing that you understand what happened, may influence the course of this stage (L. F. Clark & Collins, 1993). And understanding the causes of a relationship's end is an important learning experience that is likely to increase the chances of success in future relationships.

Till Death Do Us Part. Some close relationships are ended by death rather than break-up. The death of a spouse is regarded as the most stressful major life event (McCrae & Costa, 1988). It is also a particularly common one: Almost half of the population will experience it. The first year or two following the death of a spouse are marked by serious threats to mental and physical health (Hansson, Stroebe, & Stroebe, 1988). Indeed, grief over the death of a relationship partner increases the remaining partner's mortality risk, even after controlling for a number of factors (Stroebe, Schut, & Stroebe, 2007). Most people eventually make it through this period and recover their previous levels of well-being, but a minority fail to recover even after several years. The most serious problems are likely to befall those whose spouses died unexpectedly and who believe that they have little control over their future (Stroebe, Stroebe, & Domittner, 1988), a belief that may

Photo 12.6 Social support and health. Researchers now know that supportive relationships can be just as important to good physical health as medical treatment and healthy living. Group therapy, as shown here, offers people support for a variety of issues, such as dealing with illness, grief, or addiction.

cripple their ability to cope effectively. Social support from friends, self-help groups, or professional counselors can help the bereaved cope. Social support offers some of the rewards, such as opportunities to express inner feelings and to receive understanding and acceptance, that were part of the lost relationship (Vachon and others, 1982). Moreover, those who provide help to others appear to recover faster after the death of a spouse, which may occur because helping others is itself generally a positive experience that allows one to connect with others in a meaningful way (Brown, Brown, House, & Smith, 2008).

Loneliness. No matter what terminates a close relationship—death, conflict, or simple geographical separation—the end usually brings loneliness. Intense feelings of loneliness are common not only after the end of a relationship but also when people move to a new area and are separated from their existing close relationships. Feeling lonely is not the same as being alone: Sometimes you can feel loneliest in the middle of a crowd. Rather, loneliness is an emotion arising from unmet needs for affection and self-validation from a psychologically intimate relationship (Hawkley & Cacioppo, 2010; Shaver & Hazan, 1985). Loneliness not only involves feelings of distress, desperation, disconnectedness, and depression, but lonely people are at risk for a myriad of negative health conditions, cognitive decline, and impaired executive functioning (Cacioppo & Patrick, 2008; Hawkley, Preacher, & Cacioppo, 2010; Miller, 2011; Steptoe, Shankar, Demakakos, & Wardle, 2013). Constructive responses to loneliness include embracing opportunities to improve social skills, enhancing social support, or increasing opportunities for social interaction, such as trying to find new ways to meet people. Some of these goals may be attained by posting more frequently on social networking sites; a recent experiment showed that those encouraged to post more on Facebook showed less loneliness than those not given this instruction (Deters & Mehl, 2013). Trying to make something valuable out of solitude—learning a new skill or hobby, studying or working, or listening to music—also helps. But the most pernicious aspects of loneliness are its effects on how people see themselves and the world. Lonely individuals become increasingly focused on social threats and the possibility of rejection, until they hold negative social expectations for themselves and begin to behave in ways that confirm their negative views of themselves (Cacioppo & Hawkley, 2005). Interventions that break up this negative loop are the most effective in reducing loneliness (Masi, Chen, Hawkley, & Cacioppo, 2011). Consistent with this idea that changing how you view the social world is the best cure for loneliness, Carolyn Cutrona (1982) found that those who thought of loneliness as arising from transitory, potentially controllable causes most easily overcame it. Students who saw their loneliness as resulting from stable, negative personal qualities, such as unattractiveness or shyness, were more likely to remain lonely for long periods of time. Cutrona also found that lonely people who downplayed the importance

As we saw in Chapter 4, pages 128–129, stable internal explanations for negative events may even turn an episode of loneliness into severe depression.

Photo 12.7 Loneliness. Though this person is surrounded by others, she appears to feel quite lonely. Loneliness involves a lack of close relationships, rather than being physically separated from other people.

of friendship and thought that only a romantic relationship could help them had a more difficult time. Perhaps this is because friends are easier to find than "that perfect someone." After all, as we have seen in this chapter, a close friendship can meet our needs for self-validation and psychological intimacy (Rook & Peplau, 1982). These, rather than the sexual expression found in a romantic relationship, bring most of the benefits of relationships.

CONCLUDING COMMENTS

In concluding the chapter, we turn from conflict, break-up, and loneliness to something more positive: relationships that survive the challenges of time. Two factors are common to strong relationships in which the partners maintain and increase their love.

1. *The relationship satisfies many of the partners' individual needs.* Other people benefit us in many ways: as companions for leisure activities, as sources of social comparisons that help us understand ourselves, and as sources of validation for our beliefs and opinions. Relationships are most likely to meet our mastery needs in these ways when the partners are similar in their needs and desires, and when they reward each other to show love and caring.
2. *The relationship provides the partners with a sense of relatedness and connectedness.* As we indicated in Chapter 6, belonging to a group can give people the sense that they have a special place in the social world and that others value their thoughts, feelings, and behaviors—their very presence. As you have seen, intimacy and self-disclosure in a close relationship with another individual can also fulfill this need.

The dual motives of seeking individual satisfaction and interdependent relatedness run as two parallel threads throughout many of the topics we have discussed in this chapter.

- Relationship development proceeds through the exchange of rewards as the partners satisfy each other's needs, and through the exchange of self-disclosures as the partners build the intimate linkage of partner to self.
- Gifts given and favors performed in a relationship have a dual meaning. The concrete act may be pleasant and rewarding in itself. The underlying messages of love and relatedness that each partner sends the other by kind and thoughtful acts become equally crucial.

- Gender differences in relationships reflect the dual motives of individual satisfaction and interdependent relatedness. Men generally emphasize rewards, such as participating in enjoyable activities with the partner, and women often care more about intimacy, the self-disclosure of feelings, and intimate talks.
- Sexual behavior is particularly appropriate as an expression of relationship closeness because it fits with both motives: It is enjoyable and intimately self-disclosing.

The combination of these two powerful motives—the fact that at their best, close relationships can both help us find ourselves as individuals and find connection to valued others—makes relationships the most important components of our lives. As Charles Darwin wrote long ago (cited in Gould, 1991, p. 401): "Talk of fame, honor, pleasure, wealth, all are dirt compared to affection."

CHAPTER 12 THEMES

- **Construction of Reality**
We use biased attributions to construct an idealized impression of a relationship partner.

- **Pervasiveness of Social Influence**
In a close relationship, the partner becomes part of the self, influencing all aspects of thoughts, feelings, and behavior.

- **Striving for Mastery**
Relationships with others help us obtain rewards and individual satisfactions.

- **Seeking Connectedness**
Relationships with others help give us feelings of connectedness and belonging.

- **Valuing Me and Mine**
We are biased to view relationship partners favorably when they become part of the self.

SUMMARY

Challenges in Studying Attraction, Relationships, and Love. By necessity, most research on close relationships uses nonexperimental designs that leave some ambiguity about causal relations among variables, and most studies have focused on romantic attachments between young heterosexual couples in individulist cultures.

From Attraction to Liking. Attraction to strangers is strongly influenced by perceptions of physical attractiveness. Some features, such as signs of genetic health and access to resources, are regarded as attractive across cultures. Other features that make people attractive are more dependent on experience, exposure, and expectation. Similarity of many kinds also increases attraction and liking because of our natural tendency to see anything connected to the self as positive, because similiarity makes things seem familiar, and because similarity also contributes to fulfilling needs for mastery and connectedness. People are also attracted to those with whom they have positive interactions. Interaction makes people familiar, provides opportunity for mimicry, helps people master the world, and helps people find connectedness.

From Acquaintance to Friend: Relationship Development. Most newly developing relationships are **exchange relationships**, in which people offer benefits to their partners in order to receive benefits in return. Relationship development also involves exchanges of self-disclosures as the partners come to know each other better. Self-disclosures increase liking and offer opportunities for sympathetic, supportive responses.

Close Relationships. Love is thoughts, feelings, and actions that are associated with a desire to enter or maintain a **close relationship** with a specific person, a connection involving strong and frequent interdependence in many different areas of life. Interdependence in a relationship means that each partner's thoughts, emotions, and behaviors influence the other's. Cognitive interdependence means that the partner is incorporated into the self-concept. Partner knowledge becomes more like self-knowledge, and we start to make attributions about our partners as if they were us. Behavioral interdependence is reflected in the change to a **communal relationship**, in which partners provide benefits to demonstrate that they care about the partner and the relationship. Affective interdependence is reflected in intimacy and commitment.

Intimacy, a positive emotional bond that includes understanding and **social support**, is a key component of close relationships. **Commitment**, a dedication to maintaining the relationship for the long term, helps keep the relationship going.

People have different **attachment styles** that affect their close relationships. Securely attached individuals are comfortable relying on the partner for support and acceptance. In contrast, some individuals avoid reliance on other people, and some individuals worry that the partner will not be available and responsive.

Romantic Love, Passion, and Sexuality. Relationships involving **romantic love** include passionate feelings and emotions. Passionate emotions can arise quickly and are closely linked to sexual desires and behavior. The social context of a romantic relationship, especially whether it is short-term or long-term, determines the qualities people look for in mates. Like other mutually enjoyable activities, sexual activity can strengthen a relationship. But it can also be a focus of conflict.

When Relationships Go Wrong. Relationships can be threatened because interdependence inevitably leads to disagreements and because external factors, social norms, and the real or perceived presence of rivals can trigger relationship difficulties as well. People show different patterns of **accommodation** in how they deal with conflict or negative behavior by the partner.

There are many resources that promote constructive responses, and such responses lead to better relationship outcomes. If attempts to respond constructively fail, conflict escalates, which can lead to declining intimacy and commitment. All relationships end, either because of break-up or death. Individuals cope more effectively if they feel they controlled the final separation. The end of a relationship because of partner death is particularly painful, in part because death is typically beyond our control. After the end of a close relationship, loneliness and other negative feelings are common.

AGGRESSION AND CONFLICT

On June 19, 1954, two groups of 11-year-old boys tumbled out of buses to start summer camp in the Sans Bois Mountains near Oklahoma City, Oklahoma. Robbers Cave State Park, named for the hideout of the notorious outlaw Jesse James, offered a 200-acre site with fishing, swimming, canoeing, hiking, and the usual camp games and sports. The new arrivals were ordinary White, middle-class boys with no record of school, psychological, or behavioral problems. They had nothing on their minds except high hopes for a fun-filled 3-week vacation.

The camp was more than it seemed, however. Unknown to the boys, their parents had agreed to let them participate in a field study of intergroup conflict set up by Muzafer Sherif and his colleagues—a study that came to be known as the Robbers Cave experiment (Sherif, Harvey, White, Hood, & Sherif, 1961). The boys did not know that the camp counselors and directors were social psychologists and research assistants. Nor, at first, did members of each group know that another group was sharing the campsite.

During the first week, as they took part in separate activities designed to promote group cohesion, each group developed norms and leaders. They gave themselves names, the Eagles and the Rattlers, and each group designed a flag. Toward the end of the week, the groups discovered each other. Seeing "those guys" using "our ball field" and "our hiking trails" sparked demands for a competition. The staff were only too pleased to arrange a 4-day tournament including baseball, tug-of-war, a treasure hunt, and other events. The experimenters even promised the winners a fancy trophy, shiny badges, and four-bladed pocketknives. Both groups practiced hard, cheered their teammates, and roundly booed and insulted the competition. Hostilities escalated as the tournament progressed, culminating in a flag burning when the Eagles lost the tug-of-war.

The Eagles ultimately won the tournament, collecting the trophy and the coveted pocketknives. But while they were taking a celebratory swim, the Rattlers raided their cabins and stole the prizes. The rivalry had turned into full-blown war, and the staff was kept busy silencing name calling, breaking up fist fights, and cleaning up after cabin raids and food fights. The experiment had transformed 22 perfectly normal boys into two gangs of brawling troublemakers, full of hostility and intent on exacting revenge for every real or imagined slight.

As you may have guessed, Sherif and his colleagues set up this situation to understand how intergroup hostilities develop and how they can be resolved. This issue is one of the most significant facing the world today: As of 2011, there were 37 armed, ongoing conflicts in various parts of the world (Themnèr & Wallensteen, 2012). Unrest and hostility mar not only international relations but also interactions between ethnic, political, and religious groups. And conflict and violence occur among individuals as well as groups. Newspaper headlines scream of drive-by shootings, street crimes, spouse and child abuse, bar-room fights, even, tragically, shootings in schools by young students themselves.

This chapter examines the social and cognitive processes that underlie aggression—behavior intended to hurt other people—at both individual and intergroup levels. First, we discuss whether the seeming pervasiveness of aggression means that it is fundamentally part of human nature, built in by evolution and therefore unalterable. Then we describe the reasons that individuals act aggressively as well as the factors that can turn groups into rivals or deadly enemies. Finally, we consider what social psychology tells us about ways to reduce interpersonal or intergroup aggression, based on our understanding of their causes and dynamics. As we will see, the goal of reducing aggression draws on virtually everything we know about how people perceive and interact with each other, and requires not only stopping open hostilities but moving beyond that to resolve differences in ways that benefit all parties.

Resolving Conflict Through Negotiation
Intergroup Cooperation: Changing Social Identity

THE NATURE OF AGGRESSION AND CONFLICT

Defining Aggression and Conflict

Aggression, defined by people's immediate intention to hurt each other, is often set in motion by incompatible goals. There are two types of aggression—hostile and instrumental. Hostile aggression is often driven by anger due to insult, disrespect, or other threats to self-esteem or identity. Instrumental aggression is in the service of mastery needs.

The term aggression is used in a variety of imprecise ways in everyday language: You might apply the term to a fast-talking salesperson or a stalwart defensive player in a team sport. For social psychologists, the term is defined by the actor's motive: **Aggression** is behavior whose immediate intent is to hurt someone. Accidentally injuring someone in a soccer game is not aggression, but cursing out the referee is. Even doing nothing at all, such as intentionally failing to warn a rival of impending danger, could be aggressive. Aggression is defined by a behavior's immediate goal, even if the longer-range goal may be different: thus, trying to injure an opposing player is aggression, even if the ultimate goal of the act is not to harm the player but to win the game or to earn increased playing time by impressing the coach (Bushman & Anderson, 2001a).

Aggression often has its roots in **conflict**, which is defined as a perceived incompatibility of goals: What one party wants, the other party sees as harmful to its interests. Conflict between individuals and groups is acted out in many forums: complaints between neighbors about loud parties, protracted litigation in courtrooms, bloody battles in war zones. Whether the conflict is between Coke and Pepsi, labor and management,

aggression
behavior intended to harm someone else

conflict
a perceived incompatibility of goals between two or more parties

or candidates competing for a desirable promotion on the job, individuals and groups in conflict try to belittle, outdo, or frustrate the opponent and to extend and protect their own interests. The conflicts at the heart of these disputes frequently focus on mastery of material resources and social rewards.

Aggression and conflict between individuals and groups are found throughout the world. On a big-city street, a mugger displays a knife and demands that a tourist hand over his wallet. In a bar, a beer-fueled argument between two acquaintances suddenly turns from shouted insults to shoves and punches. Provoked by an incursion into its territory, one nation launches a military offensive at another. Despite the range and variety of aggressive behaviors, they generally fall into two distinct categories. Threatening harm and demanding a wallet is an instance of **instrumental aggression**, or aggression serving mastery needs—aggression used as a means to an end, to control other people or to obtain valuable resources. Punching someone in an escalating barroom argument is **hostile aggression**, which is often driven by spontaneous anger due to insult, disrespect, or other threats to self-esteem or social identity. Instrumental and hostile forms of aggression show somewhat different patterns, although the dividing line between these two is not always completely clear. For example, if someone who is insulted in public punches the provoker in the nose, that aggressive act is likely driven both by anger and by consideration of the act's concrete effects—such as deterring that person and others from future provocations (Bushman & Anderson, 2001a).

instrumental aggression
aggression serving mastery needs, used as a means to an end, to control other people, or to obtain valuable resources

hostile aggression
aggression that is driven by anger due to insult, disrespect, or other threats to self-esteem or social identity

Origins of Aggression

Humans have evolved to compete effectively for food and mates. Although the capacity to act aggressively may have helped, aggression has no special place in "human nature." Aggression is just one strategy among many others that humans use to attain rewards and respect, and it too is influenced by cognitive processes and social forces.

One popular view about human aggression holds that evolution has shaped humans to be fundamentally and unalterably selfish. According to this "beast within" view (Klama, 1988), "survival of the fittest" has bred aggressive impulses into human brain and bone (Lorenz, 1966). From this perspective, it is "human nature" to be aggressive, and aggression might seem both inevitable and uncontrollable. If this is so, you might be wondering whether social psychology, with its emphasis on emotions, interpretations of the situation, and norms, can really explain aggression.

However, modern evolutionary psychology offers a considerably more sophisticated view (Archer, 2013; Maner & Kenrick, 2010). According to this more recent perspective, "human nature" includes a wide variety of psychological mechanisms and motives that have contributed to survival and reproduction over the millennia. Competition for food and mates, especially among males, really means competition for status and resources, which are key to attracting mates and providing for offspring. Aggression is one means of competition that might help secure these important outcomes. Recent experimental work supports these ideas. In one study, when mating was made salient (versus when it was not), men behaved aggressively toward other men, who represent their "competition" in the search for mates, but not toward women (Ainsworth & Maner, 2012).

But in human groups, at least, such evolutionary influences do not mean that only the most aggressive men have had the evolutionary advantage. In human societies, competition, like all other human behaviors, has taken many forms. Any behavior that promoted and maintained status and resources, including the ability to form alliances with others, to learn from others, and to cooperate to overcome hardships, is likely to have become part of our genetic inheritance (D. M. Buss & Kenrick, 1998; Caporael, 1997; H. A. Simon, 1990). Far from concluding that aggression is the defining aspect of human nature, evolutionary psychology actually tells us that aggression is one technique among many others that humans may use as they strive for mastery of material resources as well as respect and connectedness to others.

You will recognize these as the fundamental motives that we have discussed throughout this text. The specific techniques that people use in the service of those motives in any particular situation depend, of course, on the relevant norms as well as the individual's assessment of a technique's likely success and effectiveness. In other words, both individual thought processes and social influence affect the experience and the expression of aggression, just as they do for other biologically based motives. Think about hunger, for example. Experiencing hunger does not inevitably lead to eating. Unsocialized infants may get away with stuffing into their mouths any food (or nonfood) within reach, but adults in most societies satisfy their hunger in more socially acceptable ways. The ways we experience hunger, the items we define as food, and the ways we act when hungry are all strongly influenced by what and how we think, as well as the norms of the groups we live in. The triggering of aggressive impulses, and our decisions about whether to act on those impulses, are influenced by the same cognitive processes and the same social forces that have played such a big role in every other form of social behavior discussed in this text.

Research on Aggression

Aggression can be difficult to study experimentally because people are often unwilling to act aggressively when they are being observed. Researchers have used a variety of techniques to get around these problems.

Aggression in everyday life is, unfortunately, easy to observe. Researchers have watched as schoolchildren pushed, shoved, and punched each other on the playground, as professional sports teams crossed the boundary from rough play to violence, and as urban street gangs fought over territory and bragging rights. Some researchers have even used official records of violent crimes to test hypotheses about aggression.

Studying aggression in the laboratory is much more difficult than observing it elsewhere. For ethical reasons, researchers cannot set up situations in which people actually harm one another. In addition, adults are reluctant to act aggressively in a research setting where they know they are being observed. As a result, laboratory researchers have been forced to develop cleverly disguised techniques. In one frequently used procedure, developed by Arnold Buss (1961), participants are told that they and another participant are in a study of the effects of punishment on learning. A rigged drawing assigns the participant to the "teacher" role, and the other participant, actually a confederate, is given the role of "learner." The teacher is instructed to deliver electric

You may recall from Chapter 10, pages 371–372, that Stanley Milgram adapted this method for his famous study of obedience to authority.

shocks to punish the learner for wrong answers. The intensity and duration of the shocks selected by the teacher on the "aggression machine" serve as measures of aggression. The learner, of course, never actually receives any shocks. Another laboratory measure involves a fake "taste test," in which the participant is allowed to select how much strong hot sauce another person will be required to consume (McGregor and others, 1998). Because people assume that the hot sauce will be painful, allocating more of it is assumed to indicate the intent to harm the other person.

You might worry that measures like these lack construct validity. Do they really measure aggression as the researchers intend? What if participants deliver the shocks not with the intent to harm—the definition of aggression—but because they believe the shocks will facilitate learning? In response to such questions, researchers have demonstrated that people who are highly aggressive outside the laboratory also score the highest on laboratory measures, indicating that those measures possess some construct validity (Anderson & Bushman, 1997; Carlson, Marcus-Newhall, & Miller, 1989; Giancola & Parrott, 2008). And as you will see throughout this chapter, most key findings have been confirmed both in laboratory and non-laboratory studies. It is interesting to note, too, that one common, everyday form of aggression, verbal assaults such as insults, curses, or ethnic slurs, is beginning to receive attention from researchers (Hamilton, 2012). As we all realized as children, sticks and stones may break our bones, but names can also hurt us. Adults as well as children hurt one another with acts such as name-calling, spreading vicious gossip, and employing the silent treatment, which are often termed relational aggression (Archer & Coyne, 2005; Williams, 2007).

Despite the difficulties researchers face in investigating aggression, a number of clear patterns emerge from their studies. As you will see, many of these patterns appear consistently across different types of research, both in the lab and in the field. They show that whether aggression is between individuals or between groups, it is usually triggered by perceptions and interpretations of some event or situation.

INTERPERSONAL AGGRESSION

Interpersonal aggression always involves the intention to harm someone. The road from intention to action is a long one, however, and it is posted with cognitive and social signs that can either halt our aggressive impulses or hurry us along the path. What factors motivate one person to hurt another? How do norms regulate aggression? Social psychologists have tried to answer these and other questions in their research on aggression.

What Causes Interpersonal Aggression? The Role of Rewards and Respect

Aggression is triggered by a variety of factors. Some aggression is a result of mastery needs. Potential rewards make this kind of aggression more likely and costs or risks make it less likely. Sometimes, however, perceived provocation such as a threat to self-esteem or connectedness produces anger, which can also set off aggression. Many negative emotions, in fact, can make aggression more likely. Norms too can promote aggressive behavior.

As we have seen many times, people strive for mastery of their environment and for connections with others, and in particular want to feel good about themselves and what they stand for. These fundamental needs are primary causes of interpersonal aggression as well.

Counting Rewards and Costs. When aggression pays, it becomes more likely (Bandura, 1973; Carnagey & Anderson, 2005). When people see an opportunity for gain, they may aggress: a person alone withdrawing money from a cash machine, or an opponent blocking the goal as the referee looks the other way (Tedeschi & Felson, 1994). Perhaps it's no surprise, then, that children who believe aggression will lead to rewards or will prevent other kids from hurting them are the most aggressive in school (Perry, Perry, & Rasmussen, 1986). Conversely, when rewards are withdrawn, aggression usually subsides. Even the possibility of punishment can deter aggression, if the threat is believed (R. A. Baron, 1983a; Zillmann, 1979). Rewards and costs are especially relevant for instrumental aggression, and often involve more systematic thinking about the situation, as opposed to an immediate emotional reaction.

One factor that enters into the cost-benefit equation of aggression is the aggressor's personal abilities. For someone who is large and muscular or knows how to fight or to wield a weapon, aggression becomes easier—and a low perceived cost increases aggression. Indeed, children and adolescents who believe they have the ability to carry out aggressive acts are more aggressive (Barchia & Bussey, 2011; Erdley & Asher, 1996). Of course, it is the perception of rewards and costs that trigger aggression. Some people may perceive that they lack non-aggressive ways of securing rewards. They may believe that they simply have to accept the possible costs that come with aggression because they believe it is the only way to get ahead. For someone lacking education or living in an area without employment opportunities, for example, aggression and crime may appear to be the only available means to resources and respect, even if they are accurately viewed as not very promising means (Gottfredson & Hirschi, 1990).

HOT TOPICS IN SOCIAL PSYCHOLOGY: GENDER AND AGGRESSION

A consistently endorsed gender stereotype is that men are aggressive and women are not. Supporting these beliefs, early work found that males were indeed more aggressive than females (Hyde, 1984). But more recent work suggests that this overall conclusion is too simplistic. When considering physical forms of aggression, men do appear, on average, to be more aggressive than women (Archer, 2004). This might in part be explained by men's greater size and physical strength than women, factors that increase men's ability to aggress and therefore reduce its costs. Another contributing factor is men's relatively higher level of testosterone, a hormone linked to aggressive behavior (Carré and others, 2009). But the general sex difference may hide important complexities. For example, within heterosexual romantic relationships, women are more likely to engage in specific types of physical aggression than men, such as slapping, kicking, biting, and punching. Men are more likely to choke, strangle, and "beat up" their partners (Archer, 2002). With regard to relational aggression, like spreading gossip or excluding someone from a group, the evidence is quite mixed. Some reviews suggest that girls exhibit this aggression more than boys (Archer, 2004) and others find little or no gender difference (Lansford and others, 2012). Clearly, more research is needed to understand the complex relations between gender and various forms of aggressive behavior.

Photo 13.1 Self-esteem threat and aggression. When a child is being laughed at, made fun of, or teased, this may harm self-esteem, potentially triggering an aggressive reaction.

Responding to Threats. Interpersonal aggression frequently occurs in response to threats to self-esteem or connections to valued people or groups, threats such as insult, derogation, or disrespect (Baumeister, 1997). Being coldly turned down when you ask someone for a date or being berated by an angry co-worker who believes you have messed up an important job can lead to aggressive action. Moreover, any blow to self-esteem is worse if it is public, because it is harder to just let an insult go by if others have witnessed the event. Thus, paradoxically, the presence of an audience may make aggressive responses to self-esteem threats more likely. One study found that more than half of murders were committed in front of an audience (Luckinbill, 1977).

Perhaps the most extreme threat to self-esteem is the reminder that the self doesn't last forever. Anything that reminds people of their own mortality is threatening, and people often respond to such threats by reaffirming their basic worldviews, such as ideological or religious beliefs (Solomon and others, 2000). Hence, such a threat can also lead to aggression, specifically against someone who attacks one's worldview. Testing this idea, McGregor and others (1998) gave politically liberal or conservative students information about someone of the opposite political persuasion who attacked the students' ideological position. They were then asked to decide how much of a fiery hot sauce the opponent should consume for a taste test, a frequently-used laboratory measure of aggression. Students who were reminded of their mortality (compared to those who were not) chose to give more of the painfully hot sauce to the ideological opponent.

Though any threat to self-esteem can trigger aggression, different people react in different ways to potential loss of respect. You may have heard that people who act aggressively typically have low self-esteem, and some research bears this out (Donnellan, Trzesniewski, Robins, Moffitt, & Caspi, 2005). Since people with low self-esteem might not have the inner resources to cope with frustrations, they might be more likely to react to everyday setbacks or social challenges with aggression. But certain other individuals are also highly likely to commit aggression: narcissists or people with very high but insecure self-esteem (Baumeister, 1997; Donnellan and others, 2005; Kernis, Grannemann, & Barclay, 1989). The self-esteem of these individuals is fragile and unstable, fluctuating with each new episode of social praise or rejection (Jordan, Spencer, Zanna, Hoshino-Browne, & Correll, 2003). Someone with stable and secure high self-esteem may brush off an insult or rejection, knowing that it is off target. But narcissists are more likely to respond to social rejection with aggression, sometimes even lashing out against others who are not responsible for the slight (Twenge & Campbell, 2003). So low self-esteem and high but unstable self-esteem might both lead to aggression, but for different reasons.

Some individuals are also more likely than others to interpret others' acts as provocations. In fact, children who are especially likely to interpret ambiguous acts as intentional disrespect and thus as threats to self-esteem tend to become chronically aggressive (Camodeca & Goossens, 2005; Crick & Dodge, 1994). They may interpret accidental collisions on the playground as intentional and may then retaliate, possibly starting a cycle of violence. Although this perceptual bias has a strong role in hostile aggression, it has no impact on instrumental aggression, such as bullying a younger child out of his lunch money (Dodge & Coie, 1987). Findings such as this support the idea that hostile and instrumental aggression are two somewhat distinct forms.

Thus, threats to one's sense of self, self-worth, or sense of belonging often trigger hostile aggression, fueled by a negative emotional reaction to the provocation. Such provocations sometimes lead people to act aggressively without regard for the likelihood of reward or punishment (R. A. Baron, 1983a). For example, in a seemingly impulsive act of violent aggression, Andrew Engeldinger shot and killed six at his workplace, moments after being fired in September 2012. He then turned the gun on himself and died at the scene. As this tragic example illustrates, hostile aggression often is not limited to striking back at a provoker.

SOCIAL PSYCHOLOGY AND CULTURE: CULTURAL NORMS AND RESPONSES TO THREAT

In some regions of the world, norms have developed that support aggression in response to perceived insults or threats of material loss. These "culture of honor" norms specify that men should be tough, loyal, and ready to fight. In regions characterized by these norms, "crimes of passion" such as killing a romantic rival are judged leniently by public opinion and may even draw light sentences from the courts. People may feel justified in murdering even family members if they believe the person has brought dishonor to the family. Though precise estimates are difficult to obtain, some suggest that at least 5,000 people die annually in such attacks (Honour Based Violence Awareness Network, 2013).

Richard Nisbett and Dov Cohen (1996) argue that such a culture of honor is more widespread in the generally rural and agricultural southern part of the United States. This might partially explain why homicide rates in the United States tend to be highest in those areas. In 2003, for example, the rate of violent crime in South Carolina (a mostly rural state) was the highest in the United States at 793.5 per 100,000 inhabitants, more than twice as high as that of densely populated Connecticut at 308.2 per 100,000 (Federal Bureau of Investigation, 2003). School violence also seems to be affected by the culture of honor. One study showed that high-school students from culture-of-honor states reported bringing a weapon to school in the past month at much greater rates than those from other states, and 75% of the 108 cases of U.S. school shootings between 1988 and 2008 took place in culture-of-honor states. These findings held even when controlling for a number of important factors—such as a state's average temperature, divorce rates, and poverty levels—that might possibly explain this effect (Brown, Osterman, & Barnes, 2009).

Some Mediterranean, Middle Eastern, and Latin American cultures similarly endorse culture-of-honor norms and their support for aggression under specific circumstances (Baldry, Pagliaro, & Porcaro, 2013; van Osch, Breugelmans, Zeelenberg, & Boluk, 2013). In one study, participants from Brazil (classified as an honor culture) and the Northern United States read about a couple that had been married for 7 years when the husband discovered that his wife had been unfaithful (Vandello & Cohen, 2003). In one version of the scenario, the husband yelled at his wife, while in the other version, the husband yelled at her and hit her. After reading the scenario, participants answered questions about how much the husband loved his wife and to what extent his actions were justified. U.S. participants thought the husband who hit his wife loved her less than did the husband who only yelled at his wife. However, Brazilian participants did not see hitting as reflecting less love for his spouse, and overall they saw aggression as more justified than U.S. participants did. Thus, the culture of honor illustrates one type of cultural influence on when and whether people turn to aggression (M. H. Bond, 2004).

frustration-aggression theory
a theory holding that any
frustration—defined as the
blocking of an important goal—
inevitably triggers aggression

The Role of Negative Emotions. When people's important mastery or connectedness goals are blocked or threatened, they generally feel negative emotions, which are strongly associated with aggression (DeWall, Anderson, & Bushman, 2011). In fact, one of the most influential early theories of aggression, **frustration-aggression theory**, held that any frustration—defined as the blocking of an important goal—inevitably triggers aggression (Dollard, Doob, Miller, Mowrer, & Sears, 1939). Early research evidence supported frustration-aggression theory, but critiques and conflicting data soon started to accumulate (N. E. Miller, 1941). More recently, Leonard Berkowitz (1989) advanced a broader idea that also accounts for the original evidence linking frustration and aggression. According to Berkowitz, aggression is set off not so much by the blocking of a goal, but by the negative feelings that result. Such negative feelings include anger, pain, fear, and irritation. As Berkowitz (1993) put it, "We're nasty when we feel bad."

Berkowitz seems to be right. We now know that a variety of conditions that create negative feelings—unpleasant heat or painful cold, stressful noises, crowding, even noxious odors and air pollution—can trigger aggression (Berkowitz & Harmon-Jones, 2004; Geen, 1998; Graham, Bernards, Osgood, & Wells, 2006; Lindsay & Anderson, 2000). The relationship between heat and aggression, for example, has been established in both field and laboratory studies (Anderson, 2001; R. A. Baron, 1972; Larrick, Timmerman, Carton, & Abrevaya, 2011). Examination of weather and crime records reveals that when the outdoor temperature is high, there is an increase in the incidence of assault (Bushman, Wang, & Anderson, 2005). Findings like these have led scholars to speculate that aggression may increase with global warming (Anderson & DeLisi, 2011).

HOT TOPICS IN SOCIAL PSYCHOLOGY: DISGUST AND AGGRESSION

Though the relation between various negative emotions (like anger) and aggression has been investigated for decades, recent work has focused on another emotion: disgust. Disgust is an emotion that encourages avoidance: disgust reactions help us avoid exposure to contaminants that might make us ill, such as rotting garbage, spoiled food, or others' bodily fluids. Recently, scholars have argued that because aggression is an approach-oriented behavior, but disgust is an avoidance-oriented emotion, disgust might discourage, rather than encourage, aggressive responses (Pond and others, 2012). In one study illustrating this, participants' levels of disgust sensitivity were first assessed with a questionnaire. Then in a later lab study, they played a computer game, supposedly against a same-sex partner. On each trial of this game, the two competitors were in a race to press a button. Whoever responded first was the winner and could select the level of aversive noise the partner would have to endure. The higher in disgust sensitivity a person was, the less frequently he or she displayed extreme levels of aggression by subjecting his or her partner to the highest levels of noise. This basic finding was replicated in four additional studies. Thus, not all negative emotions prompt aggression. Disgust, in contrast to anger, appears to reduce aggressive responding.

Increasing Aggression: Models and Cues

Other people's aggressive actions, including portrayals in the media, may indicate that aggression is appropriate. Cues in a specific situation, such as the presence of guns or other weapons, may also increase the accessibility of thoughts related to aggression. Both of these types of factors therefore make aggression more likely to occur.

Potential rewards, as well as threats that lead to negative emotions, may be the fundamental driving forces behind interpersonal aggression. However, external influences can push us further along the path to actual harmful action. Both the actions of other people that we observe, and cues in the environment that make thoughts about aggression accessible, can have this effect.

Models of Aggression. As we have seen many times, other people's actions offer clues to the behavior that is appropriate in a situation. Observing others who react to blocked goals, threats, or provocation with nonviolent solutions can reduce aggression. Unfortunately, aggressive models not only show people ways to act aggressively but also send the message that an aggressive response is right, correct, and acceptable, and others soon imitate them (Bandura, Ross, & Ross, 1961, 1963). For example, at many sporting events, violence among fans is often preceded by aggressive play on the field (J. H. Goldstein, 1982).

To review these and other effects of inferring norms from other people's behavior, refer back to Chapter 9.

Laboratory studies confirm the powerful impact that models have on aggressive behavior. Compared with those who had watched an innocuous film, people who had watched a film of a highly aggressive boxing match gave other participants stronger shocks on Buss's "aggression machine" (Bushman & Geen, 1990). Exposure to aggressive models makes violent behavior seem more appropriate because it stimulates aggressive thoughts and feelings (Bargh & Gollwitzer, 1994; Fischer & Greitemeyer, 2006).

"Your father kicked in the screen and threw the set out the window. He feels violence on TV is a bad influence."

Photo 13.2 Violence in video games. Increasing numbers of studies show that playing violent video games can increase aggressive behavior.

Tragically, people often encounter aggressive models in their own homes. Children of abusive parents learn at an early age that aggression is both appropriate and acceptable. Indeed, until recently, surveys in the United States indicated that public opinion supported the physical punishment of children as legitimate and necessary (Gelles, 1972). Yet in the home, as elsewhere, aggressive acts teach aggressive norms. Children who have been maltreated are more likely to aggress in social situations (Shields & Cicchetti, 1998), and as adults are more likely than others to abuse their own children or spouses (Sugarman & Hotaling, 1989; Widom, 1989).

SOCIAL PSYCHOLOGY IN PRACTICE: AGGRESSIVE MODELS IN THE MEDIA

Even children from peaceful homes are exposed to an enormous amount of violence because of the amount of time they spend watching television. By the seventh grade, the average American child has seen more than 8000 television murders and 100,000 acts of violence in the media (Bushman & Anderson, 2001b). Adults too see a lot of violence on television; one study found that 61 % of television programs depicted violence (Anderson and others, 2003). Media violence also reaches children and adults through video games. In one survey of 7th and 8th grade students in U.S. schools, 93 % reported having played a video or computer game in the prior six months (Olson and others, 2007). Of those who did play, about one-third of boys and about 10 % of girls reported playing 6 or 7 days per week. When these children were asked to name game titles they played frequently, nearly half of them listed at least one violent game.

Does aggressive media content stimulate viewers' aggression? Some people believe that watching aggressive TV shows, playing violent video games, or engaging in low-level aggression in sports can actually make people less aggressive over time. The idea of catharsis—that expressing an emotion can keep it from "building up"—has been around for a long time, and if it were true, then "letting out" aggressive impulses in relatively harmless ways might prevent or diminish later aggression. Unfortunately, the evidence consistently disconfirms the catharsis idea. Aggressing or witnessing aggression not only does not make people feel calmer, it makes them more angry (Anderson and others, 2004; Bushman, Baumeister, & Stack, 1999). Aggressive media content can also lead people to interpret other people's behavior as hostile (Bushman & Anderson, 2002) and to expect hostility from others (Hasan, Begue, & Bushman, 2012).

These results suggest that violent media content might have the effect of making people more aggressive, and that is what the evidence generally shows. Many studies have demonstrated that people who view more hours of violent television, listen to music with violent lyrics, or play violent video games tend to be more aggressive (Anderson, Carnagey, & Eubanks, 2003; Anderson & Dill, 2000; Anderson and others, 2010; Fischer & Greitemeyer, 2006; Singer & Singer, 1981). Even a single exposure to violent media is linked with more aggressive behavior. For example, those who played a violent video game for only 20 minutes were more aggressive one day later, if the game player was induced to ruminate on the game (Bushman & Gibson, 2011). Importantly, though, some of the accumulated evidence on the link between violent media exposure and aggressive behavior comes from nonexperimental designs that are weak on internal validity and cannot show that violent media causes aggression. Other causal relationships could lead to the same pattern of results. For example, parental neglect could both make children aggressive and cause them to spend a lot of time watching violent TV or playing violent video games.

Experimental research can overcome this weakness. In one classic experiment, incarcerated delinquent boys were randomly assigned to view aggressive films or nonaggressive films every evening for a week (Parke, Berkowitz,

■■■

Leyens, West, & Sebastian, 1977). Their aggressive behavior was observed both before and after the "film week," and boys who saw aggressive films committed more physical attacks than those who viewed neutral films. We can conclude that film viewing caused aggression because of the high internal validity of the experimental design, and this conclusion is supported by a meta-analysis of 28 different field experiments (W. Wood, Wong, & Chachere, 1991). However, most of these studies were relatively short term, examining the effects of only days or weeks of viewing.

Perhaps the most powerful findings on the issue come from longitudinal studies, which assess television viewing and aggressiveness over a long period of time to attempt to determine which variable causes the other. One ambitious study followed a group of participants for 22 years, finding that those who watched more TV violence at age 8 were more likely to have been convicted for violent crimes by age 30 (Huesmann, 1986). These findings were confirmed in a 3-year multination study in the United States, Finland, Israel, and Poland (Huesmann & Eron, 1986). Long-term impacts have been found for violent video games as well; that is, the more violent video games a person plays initially, the more aggressive he or she is up to a couple of years later (Anderson and others, 2010). Though time-consuming and costly to carry out, longitudinal research has important strengths: The variables can be measured in natural settings and strong causal conclusions can be drawn.

A consistent conclusion can be drawn from all these different studies: aggressive media content does increase viewers' aggressive behavior (Anderson and others, 2004; Liebert & Sprafkin, 1988). Perhaps even more ominously, the effect seems to be long-lasting. Studies indicate that witnessing violence dulls our perceptions and numbs our reactions, eventually leading to indifference and acceptance. For example, frequent viewers of "slasher" movies are relatively unconcerned about violence toward women (Donnerstein, Linz, & Penrod, 1987). And among those who do not frequently play violent video games, playing one for just 25 minutes led them to show less neurological reaction to violent images than those who played a non-violent game. The more they showed this neurological desensitization, the more aggressively they behaved in a later task (Engelhardt, Bartholow, Kerr, & Bushman, 2011). Moreover, those who reported frequently playing violent video games showed neurological desenitization to violent images regardless of what game they were asked to play in the lab. Perhaps their chronic violent game play had already made them "numb."

Some critics have questioned the link between violent media content and aggressive behavior (Ferguson, 2013). Still, the preponderance of evidence shows consistent effects, as indicated by meta-analyses including considerable cross-cultural research (Anderson and others, 2010).

Learned Cues to Aggression. Weapons, and especially guns, are strongly associated with the idea of aggression (Huesmann & Eron, 1984). If seeing a weapon cues thoughts of aggression, this in turn should make aggressive behavior more likely—and so it does, in an outcome termed the weapons effect (C. A. Anderson, Anderson, & Deuser, 1996; Berkowitz & LePage, 1967). In one nonlaboratory study of this effect, Charles Turner and his associates set up a booth at a campus carnival and invited students to throw sponges at a target person. Passersby threw more sponges when they could see a rifle that had been placed nearby than when no rifle was present (C. W. Turner, Simons, Berkowitz, & Frodi, 1977). Another study showed that motorists stopped by police officers acted more aggressively when the officers carried a holstered pistol than when they did not (Boyanowsky & Griffiths, 1982). Thus, the presence of a gun may not only make aggression more deadly, it may also make it more likely in the first place. Of course, it is a person's thoughts and feelings about guns or other cues that shape their effects, and people may differ in this way. For example, one study found that experienced hunters did not become more aggressive when shown images of hunting rifles, because their associations with those guns did not involve aggression against other people (Bartholow, Anderson, Carnagey, & Benjamin, 2005). Like other individuals, though, the hunters' aggressiveness was increased by images of nonhunting guns, such as military assault rifles.

Thus, perceiving a weapon can make aggression more likely. This gives special importance to the fact that common stereotypes can make observers more ready to see—or to imagine they see—a gun in the hands of members of some groups than of others. In a study that we discussed in Chapter 5, Keith Payne (2001) found that students were more likely to miscategorize images of common tools (such as a hammer or pliers) as guns when they were preceded by a photo of a Black male (compared to a White male) on the computer screen. These effects occurred automatically, even when the research participants were told to ignore the photos of faces, and generally take place outside the perceiver's conscious awareness. If you're wondering what this laboratory study has to do with real life, consider the case of Jordan Davis, a Black teenager. On November 23, 2012, Davis was in a Sport Utility Vehicle at a Florida gas station with friends. A White passenger in a nearby car argued with the SUV occupants about the loudness of their stereo, claimed he saw a gun, and then shot at them, killing Davis. However, no guns were found in the SUV.

Different countries' norms about the acceptability of owning firearms may also influence incidents of aggressive behavior. The United States, for example, has the highest gun ownership rate per capita in the world, perhaps because of the norm, enshrined in the U.S. Constitution, that its citizens have the right to bear arms. Along with this high gun ownership rate, though, comes great risk of gun violence. Indeed, the United States ranks first in the developed world in murders with firearms (Fisher, 2012).

Deciding Whether or Not to Aggress

Situations that favor superficial thinking often favor aggression. Thinking carefully can reduce aggression, but many factors interfere with people's motivation and ability to process information carefully and evenhandedly, increasing the likelihood of aggression.

What if you really want to smack your roommate, but know it would be wrong? What happens when the messages we get from environmental cues, feelings, anticipated rewards and punishments, and social norms conflict? Whether and how we turn to aggression in such circumstances depends on how we deal with the relevant information.

When people are processing superficially, the most salient aspect of the environment or the most accessible attitude or norm "wins": Whatever grabs our attention most easily has the greatest impact on our behavior. The salience of costs or rewards, the behavior of models, and situational cues can all trigger aggressive behavior in a person who is processing superficially. In anger-inducing situations, the self-esteem threat or other provocation that produced the anger is usually foremost in our attention. Thus, when people are thinking superficially, angry feelings and negative thoughts are likely to lead to aggression.

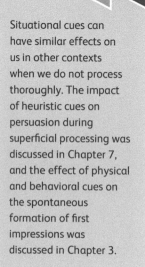

Situational cues can have similar effects on us in other contexts when we do not process thoroughly. The impact of heuristic cues on persuasion during superficial processing was discussed in Chapter 7, and the effect of physical and behavioral cues on the spontaneous formation of first impressions was discussed in Chapter 3.

To overcome the initial tendency to smack your roommate, you must engage in some systematic thinking about the situation and as a result might refrain from aggressing—but, as always, you need both motivation and capacity to find ways to resolve your conflict peacefully. When people have the time and ability to consider deeply, they can intentionally try to activate the most appropriate, rather than the most accessible, interpretations of the situation that they face (Yovetich & Rusbult, 1994). Given the opportunity, they can come up with alternatives to aggression: talking over a conflict, weighing the costs and benefits of retaliation, compromising on a solution, realizing that an apparent provocation may have been accidental. However, several factors may limit people's capacity to process deeply even when they are motivated to do so—often increasing the odds of aggression.

1. ***Emotional arousal.*** Threat, trauma, and intense emotions can reduce people's capacity to process information carefully, as we have seen many times throughout this text. Because strong emotions often accompany conflict, they temporarily interfere with careful processing just when it is most needed. The presence of weapons increases aggression even more strongly when people are already aroused and angered (Berkowitz, 1993). In the same way, aggressive boys' tendency to see any bump or jostle as an act of aggression is magnified when they are very anxious (Dodge & Somberg, 1987). Sadly, there is evidence that the physical and emotional trauma of child abuse may diminish a child's ability to interpret social cues correctly and to generate imaginative responses to conflict situations (Dodge, Bates, & Pettit, 1990). These deficits in turn increase the child's own tendency to turn to aggression, which may be one important reason why abused children sometimes grow up to perpetuate abuse against their own spouses or children (Geen, 1998; Sugarman & Hotaling, 1989).

2. ***Alchohol use.*** Alcohol can also diminish people's ability to think systematically. You may not be surprised to learn that drinking and violence often coincide (Bushman & Cooper, 1990; Felson & Staff, 2010; Ito, Miller, & Pollock, 1996). Alcohol is a factor in almost two-thirds of homicides and in one-third of rapes, burglaries, and assaults (Desmond, 1987; Wolfgang & Strohm, 1956). Moreover, a survey across 13 countries showed that violence between romantic partners was rated as more extreme when either or both parties had been drinking compared to when neither had (Graham, Bernards, Wilsnack, & Gmel, 2011). The statistics are less surprising, though no less shocking, when you realize that alcohol reduces people's capacity to process a wide range of information. Perceiving a restricted range of cues, a person under the influence of alcohol is likely to base his or her actions on whatever is most immediately obvious (Giancola, Josephs, Parrott, & Duke, 2010; Steele & Josephs, 1990). So alcohol by itself does not invariably lead to aggression: People sometimes become jolly or weepy when they drink if they happen to focus on cues that push them in those directions. However, alcohol plus anger or threat is a surefire recipe for aggression (S. P. Taylor, Gammon, & Capasso, 1976). In addition to reducing our capacity to process a wide range of cues, alcohol exerts a second and equally dangerous influence. It lessens people's concern for factors that ordinarily restrain aggression: the potential costs and dangers of aggressive acts, the social norms that constrain aggression, and the cues that ordinarily inhibit aggression, such as expressions of pain from the victim (Baumeister, 1997; Schmutte & Taylor, 1980).

3. **Time pressure.** Strong emotions and alcohol can reduce our ability to avoid aggression, but other factors that limit our ability to come up with alternatives to aggression can have the same effects. When a decision must be made quickly, an initial tendency to aggress may win more often. Police officers frequently must make snap judgments about whether to use force, and they sometimes make the wrong decision.

Putting It All Together: The General Aggression Model. What explains interpersonal aggression? We have seen that many factors can cause aggression, such as feeling too hot or cold, drinking a beer, or watching a violent movie. It is true that many different factors can push us in the direction of aggression, but all their effects can be understood in terms of the principles that we have described again and again as influencing people's social behavior. These include their appraisals and interpretations of the situation (that is, their construction of reality); the importance of accessible cognitions or emotions; the social context in which behavior occurs; and whether people engage in superficial or more systematic processing. These principles have been integrated into a broad theory of interpersonal aggression, portrayed in Figure 13.1. The **General Aggression Model** (Anderson & Bushman, 2002; Anderson, Deuser, & DeNeve, 1995; DeWall, Anderson, & Bushman, 2011) assumes that person factors (such as an individual's abilities or previous experiences with aggression) and situation factors (such as provocation from another person or cues in the environment) are the starting point. The desire to hurt increases when thoughts about potential rewards outweigh potential costs, or when anger and other negative emotions are present. The desire to act aggressively is not always carried out, however, because social norms and the actions of others also play a major role in the decision to initiate or restrain aggression. Aggressive models can show that violence is rewarded, offer evidence that aggression is normatively acceptable, and serve as a cue that makes aggressive thoughts and feelings more accessible. No wonder aggressive models are so potent in producing further aggression and that those aiming at reducing aggression in society have criticized the media for presenting so many aggressive models for public consumption.

General Aggression Model
a theory that person and situation factors influence people's cognition, emotions, and arousal, which in turn influence interpretations of the situation and decisions about aggression

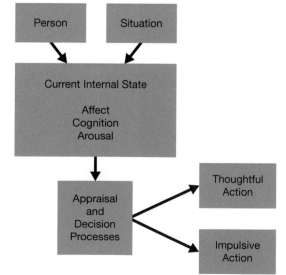

Figure 13.1 Processes in the General Aggression Model
The core processes in the General Aggression Model are depicted in this figure. Both personal and situational factors influence the individual's internal state, including emotions, thoughts, and level of arousal. As the individual interprets the situation and decides what to do, aggression may result either as a thoughtfully considered action or as a quick, impulsive action.

But appropriate norms and models can also reduce aggression, if they are brought to mind at the right time. This is one reason why it is so important to go beyond the immediate situation, and to think carefully about other cues, attitudes, and norms that oppose aggression. Unfortunately, this careful thought requires time, effort, and ability, resources that might not be available when people are pressed to make instant decisions, or are stressed by anger or other strong negative emotions. And although we have talked mostly about immediate and impulsive forms of aggression, it is important to remember (as the General Aggression Model states) that aggression can also result from thoughtful decisions – for example, crimes may be the result of deliberate planning and careful weighing of potential rewards and costs. A section at the end of this chapter will discuss approaches that have been successful in reducing aggression, based on scientific understanding of all of these processes.

Thus interpersonal aggression is guided by fundamental cognitive and social processes. It is motivated by desires for mastery, connectedness, and esteem. It can be directed by firmly established or situationally accessible attitudes and norms, depending on whether or not we have the ability and motivation to think things through thoroughly. Not surprisingly, these same points apply also to aggression and conflict that pit group against group.

INTERGROUP CONFLICT

As we have seen, individuals all too frequently act to harm others. Unfortunately, groups also harm other groups. Indeed, many of the same factors that promote interpersonal aggression can promote intergroup aggression. In addition, some extra factors can make groups even more aggressive than individuals! Nabith Berri, chief of one militia group in conflict-torn Lebanon, once stated, "When we deal with each other individually, we can be civilized . . . but when we deal with each other as groups, we are like savage tribes in the Middle Ages" (*Indianapolis Star*, 1989).

The greater aggressiveness of groups can be observed in the laboratory as well as in wars and civil conflicts around the world (Insko & Schopler, 1998). For example, in one study the researchers had either two individuals or two three-member groups allocate hot sauce for each other to consume (Meier & Hinsz, 2004). The researchers provided sauce that was extremely spicy, and students thought consuming it would be painful. When participants arrived in the lab for what they thought was a study of personality and taste, they learned that another individual or group had doled out quite a bit of hot sauce for them to consume. Then they were asked in turn to allocate some hot sauce for the other individual or group. Groups allocated an average of 93 grams for each member of the other group to consume. Individuals, on the other hand, gave the other individual only 58 grams.

Other studies similarly show that groups are more competitive than individuals. For example, when participants are asked to allocate valuable points to themselves and to others, they make more competitive choices when playing in teams of two or three than they do when playing as individuals (Wildschut & Insko, 2007), an effect found in both individualist societies like the United States and in collectivist cultures like Japan (Takemura & Yuki, 2007). In fact, anything that increases a group's feeling of identity can boost its competitiveness (L. Gaertner & Schopler, 1998). To demonstrate this point, one group of researchers gave young members of informal handball teams bright orange jerseys to wear—emphasizing their identity as a group. This symbol of group solidarity was enough to increase their aggressiveness, compared to their opponents who wore their usual street clothes (Rehm, Steinleitner, & Lilli, 1987).

Why are groups generally more aggressive than individuals? Like a jigsaw puzzle, the answer to this question has several pieces. We will discuss the reasons for the special competitiveness of groups as we describe the reasons and processes that underlie intergroup conflict.

Sources of Intergroup Conflict: The Battle for Riches and Respect

Most group conflict stems from competition for valued material resources or for social rewards such as respect and esteem. People use social comparisons to determine acceptable levels of resources. Groups in conflict are often more attuned to social rewards than to material ones.

Although groups are often more competitive and aggressive than individuals, groups and individuals turn to aggression for the same basic reasons: valued material resources or respect and esteem.

Photo 13.3 Realistic conflict in action. According to realistic conflict theory, intergroup hostility, conflict, and aggression arise from competition among groups for mastery of scarce but valued material resources. In early 2014, such a conflict erupted between Russia and Ukraine, as Russia moved to annex Crimea, a peninsula that was, at the time, Ukrainian territory. Here we see part of that conflict unfolding, as a Ukrainian military base in Crimea is surrounded by the Russian military.

Realistic Conflict Theory: Getting the Goods. In the conflict between the Eagles and the Rattlers at Robbers Cave State Park, each group defended its swimming and playing territory, stole the other's prized possessions, and engaged in athletic competition spiced by the knowledge that only the winners would receive new pocketknives. The resulting dramatic escalation of hostilities provided good evidence for **realistic conflict theory**. This theory argues that intergroup hostility, conflict, and aggression arise from competition among groups for mastery of scarce but valued material resources (D. T. Campbell, 1965; LeVine & Campbell, 1972; M. Sherif, 1966). Just as the calculation of material costs and rewards motivates instrumental aggression by individuals, the potential gain or loss of material resources motivates intergroup aggression.

> **realistic conflict theory**
> the theory that intergroup hostility arises from competition among groups for scarce but valued material resources

Laboratory research has confirmed that competition for scarce resources sours intergroup relations. Consider the way in which the potential for one group to win a reward can change intergroup interactions, for example. In one study two groups of students worked on tasks such as recommending a therapy program for a troubled adolescent or creating an advertising slogan for a new brand of toothpaste (D. A. Taylor & Moriarty, 1987). To set up a cooperative or a competitive environment, researchers gave different instructions to the participants. To create a cooperative environment, researchers told participants that proposals from the two groups would be combined to produce the best solution, and that both groups would be rewarded. In the competitive condition, participants heard that only the one group that came up with the best idea would receive the reward. Consistent with predictions from realistic conflict theory, the groups in competition for the scarce and valued resource liked in-group members better and disliked out-group members more (see Figure 13.2).

As the Rattlers and the Eagles demonstrated, group competition can quickly escalate from dislike into hostility and aggression (Horwitz & Rabbie, 1982; Rapoport &

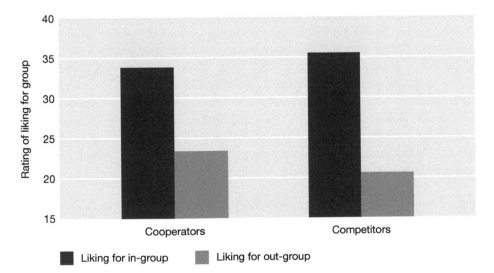

Figure 13.2 Competition increases solidarity and intergroup hostility
Two groups of participants either competed against one another or cooperated for rewards. Compared with the cooperators, those who competed liked their fellow in-group members better and disliked out-group members more. (Data from D. A. Taylor and Moriarty, 1987.)

Bornstein, 1987). Competition for real resources, such as land, jobs, and natural resources, is clearly one cause of the many conflicts that pit nation against nation and ethnic group against ethnic group (Brewer & Campbell, 1976; Gurr, 1970; Streufert & Streufert, 1986). When countries battle over the right to control strategic waterways or land rich in oil and minerals, realistic conflict is probably at the root of the conflict.

Relative Deprivation: When Is Enough Enough? Perhaps conflict is understandable when material resources are scarce. But even when people or groups seem to have adequate resources, they often continue to compete. Apparently, once people have the basic necessities of life, it becomes difficult to determine objectively how they are faring, and so they turn to comparisons with others to help them decide. This idea is central to **relative deprivation theory**, which suggests that social comparison, not objective reality, determines how satisfied or dissatisfied people are with what they have (Bernstein & Crosby, 1980; Crosby, 1976; Smith, Pettigrew, Pippin, & Bialosiewicz, 2012; Stouffer and others, 1949). It's not hard to see how this idea might apply in real life. If you had just bought a shiny new Chevrolet, you probably would feel pretty good about it—until your next-door neighbor proudly rolled his shiny new BMW into his driveway. Your Chevy is still exactly the same car, but suddenly you may not feel quite so proud of it. In fact, you may experience egoistic relative deprivation, a sense that you are doing less well than other individuals (Runciman, 1966).

In many circumstances, however, the crucial comparison people make is not between themselves and other individuals, but between their group and other groups. Fraternal relative deprivation is the sense that one's group is not doing as well as other groups (Runciman, 1966). Like egoistic deprivation, fraternal deprivation has little to do with objective levels of adequacy or success. A group with little may be content if those around them also have little. Conversely, a group whose situation is improving may feel discontent if other groups seem to be improving at a faster rate. During the economic boom of the 1960s, for example, most people in the United States achieved substantial economic gains. Yet the 1960s were also a period of some of the worst racial violence in U.S. history, in part because African-Americans saw their economic situation lagging behind that of Whites (Sears & McConahay, 1973). Fraternal deprivation is much more likely to cause intergroup conflict than is egoistic deprivation. Feelings of fraternal deprivation have been implicated in conflicts between unemployed youths and the authorities in Australia (Walker & Mann, 1987), gay and lesbian groups and straight groups in Toronto (Birt & Dion, 1987), French and English speakers in Canada (Guimond & Dube-Simard, 1983), Muslims and Hindus in India (Tripathi & Srivasta, 1981), and landowners and the landless within Nepal (Macours, 2010).

Social Competition: Getting a Little Respect. Groups, like individuals, fight not only over jobs, resources, and other material rewards but also over social goods: respect, esteem, and "bragging rights" (D. Katz, 1965; Tajfel & Turner, 1979). Consider a series of studies in which two groups of corporate executives attending a training program were assigned problem-solving tasks (Blake & Mouton, 1979, 1984). Researchers told the executives that experts would evaluate each team's performance, but they never mentioned competition, nor did they promise concrete rewards for performance. Nevertheless, the experience of being divided into groups and anticipating evaluation was apparently

---

relative deprivation theory
the theory that feelings of discontent arise from the belief that other individuals or other groups are better off

enough to produce conflict. Team spirit soared and intergroup antagonism emerged as group members huddled together during breaks and meals to plan strategies, analyze successful performances, and even hold pep rallies. In one version of the experiment, researchers asked representatives from each group to meet to evaluate the groups' products. These meetings almost always resulted in a deadlock, with each representative insisting his or her own group's work was best. When a neutral judge broke the deadlock, the losing team accused him of bias and incompetence. At one point the researchers had to break off the experiment to calm tempers and restore order.

What drives competition when no material resources whatever are at stake? If you think the answer has something to do with social identity, you're right. You may recall that people's desire to see their own groups as better than other groups can lead to intergroup bias. The same process can also contribute to outright conflict (Brewer, 1979). People can even identify with groups formed on the basis of an arbitrary toss of a coin: They don't need to interact with other group members or even to know them, and they don't need to feel that their access to material resources is at risk. Research indicates that members of such "minimal groups" nevertheless act as if they were at odds with other groups, treating them in ways that fuel conflict. They downgrade the out-group's products, dislike out-group members as individuals, and discriminate against the out-group in allocating rewards (Brewer, 1979; J. C. Turner, 1980). Thus, people's strivings for positive social identity may plant the seeds of intergroup conflict.

Social identity theory and studies that demonstrate people's readiness to identify even with arbitrary, transient groups were discussed in Chapter 6, especially pages 206–208.

The Special Competitiveness of Groups: Groups Often Value Respect over Riches.
One reason for the greater competitiveness of groups than individuals is this: When groups vie to be "Number One," social competition and the effort to outdo one's opponent frequently overshadow competition for material resources (L. Gaertner & Schopler, 1998; C. A. Insko & Schopler, 1987). If the boys at summer camp had cared only about the badges and pocketknives, the researchers could have given those prizes to everyone. But do you think that would have satisfied the boys or reduced their desire to outdo the other group? Chester Insko and John Schopler (1998) have documented the way groups seek respect over riches. In their studies, participants choose among several alternative ways to distribute points worth a small amount of money to their own group and to another group. Usually groups start by choosing alternatives that maximize the in-group's profit, paying little attention to the out-group's situation. As the play continues, however, the players' choices become more competitive—maximizing the advantage of the in-group over the out-group. In a display of supercompetitiveness, groups sometimes give up absolute gain in order to dominate their rivals (Brewer, 1979). And, of course, as soon as one side makes a competitive choice, the other retaliates.

In these laboratory studies, the actual cash value of the "points" is trivial, so perhaps it is no surprise that groups care more about the symbolic value of winning than about a dollar or two of prize money. Still, similar patterns occur in real organizational and international conflicts. For example, nations begin wars knowing that either victory or defeat will exact an enormous cost in physical pain, economic ruin, and ecological devastation. Yet they sound the war drums anyway, accepting huge costs in exchange for the chance of victory over their opponent. When competition for riches turns into competition for respect, winning becomes everything.

Escalating Conflict: Group Communication and Interaction

Once conflict starts, poor communication can make it worse. In-group interaction hardens in-group opinion, threats are directed at the out-group, each group retaliates more and more harshly, and other parties choose sides. All of these processes tend to escalate the conflict.

Once conflict catches fire, the flames spread quickly. Persuasion, promises, and verbal sparring are replaced by attempted coercion, threats, and physical assault. And as new issues and disagreements come to light and inhibitions about breaking the peace dissolve, the scope of conflict broadens. The Rattlers and the Eagles certainly followed this pattern. Name-calling soon moved on to flag burning and brawling, accompanied by food fights and midnight cabin raids.

What causes this pattern of escalating conflict? By now our answer should be familiar: The same social and cognitive processes responsible for other forms of social behavior play a role in conflict situations, too. Those processes, which can affect even the most well-intentioned individuals and groups, intensify conflict and cause opinions to harden.

We discussed why group polarization occurs and the many ways in which group discussion can make the majority opinion more extreme in Chapter 9, pages 326–332.

Talking to the In-Group: Polarization and Commitment. Discussion won't help if the only people you talk to are those who take your side. Talking things over with like-minded others pushes group members toward extreme views, a process called group polarization. As a result of group discussion, then, people may see their group's position as even more valid and valuable, and they may become even more firmly attached to it.

During discussion, we also become more committed to our views. As we explain and defend them, we marshal the best evidence, cite the strongest precedents, and organize every shred of support we can muster. We may pound the table for emphasis as we pick holes in the opposition's reasoning, seize on their slightest hesitations, and counter their every argument. These actions are unlikely to convince the opponents, but they can strengthen our own confidence and commitment (Binder, Dalrymple, Brossard, & Scheufele, 2009; Brauer, Judd, & Gliner, 1995; Hovland and others, 1953). As group members see themselves getting worked up, they conclude that they must care a lot about the issues. At the same time, dissonance-reduction processes ensure that their private attitudes line up with public positions, even if at first those public positions were just argued for effect without being fully believed. The very public nature of advocacy constitutes a commitment, which makes it even more difficult for group members to back down or change their minds.

To remind yourselves of the ways that self-perception processes and dissonance reduction can bring attitudes into lockstep with actions, review Chapter 8.

Of course, the same processes are also at work in the other group, so positions harden into extreme opposition. As in-group views are confirmed and out-group arguments demolished, each group's position becomes entrenched at the extreme and each group's commitment intensifies (Staw & Ross, 1987). Now the battle lines between groups are drawn even more clearly.

The Special Competitiveness of Groups: When Conflict Arises, Groups Close Ranks. Processes of commitment and polarization also help explain the special competitiveness of groups. In situations of conflict, groups demand loyalty, solidarity, and strict adherence to group norms (Ariyanto and others, 2010). The Eagles and Rattlers did this, forbidding any friendly contact or fraternization with the "enemy." This tight discipline permits no interaction or empathy with the out-group, widening the gap between the groups and making further conflict almost inevitable.

Leaders sometimes take advantage of the unifying effect of conflict to strengthen their hold on power. In a demonstration of this process, Jacob Rabbie and Frits Bekkers (1978) simulated a labor–management conflict in their laboratory at the University of Utrecht in the Netherlands. Some participants took the role of a union leader who could be removed from power by an election at any stage during the negotiations. Some students were in an unstable leadership position; just two negative votes could have removed them from office. Others held more stable positions; only a unanimous negative vote could have deposed them. Leaders whose jobs were shaky behaved more competitively in their negotiations with management, apparently to rally the rank and file around them. These laboratory findings remind us of a grim roster of real-world leaders who have taken their nations into wars and other misadventures to shore up power that was threatened by political rivals, economic troubles, or declining prestige.

Talking to the Out-Group: Back Off, or Else! As positions harden, groups find it increasingly difficult to communicate productively, so persuasion and discussion often give way to threats and attempted coercion. Most people believe that threats—describing punishments that will follow unwanted behavior—increase their bargaining power and their chances of getting their way (Falbo & Peplau, 1980; Rothbart & Hallmark, 1988). As a result both groups tend to use threats, leaving neither group with an advantage. Each is thinking exactly the same thing, cursing the other's unwillingness to listen to reason, deciding that the language of force is the only language the opponent can understand. The reality, unfortunately, is that threats provoke counterthreats, diminish people's willingness to compromise, and in the end generate hostility.

To see how counterproductive threats can be, consider the findings from a classic study by Morton Deutsch and Robert Krauss (1960). They asked pairs of female participants to imagine themselves as owners of two rival trucking companies, named Acme and Bolt, whose profits were based on the speed with which they carried merchandise over roads to specific destinations. The most profit could be attained by taking the short central road rather than the long and winding bypass (see Figure 13.3). As the map shows, a potential source of conflict is built into the road layout: One section of the central road is only one lane wide. If both players reach this section at the same time, one must back up and let the other proceed. This problem was not insurmountable, however. Participants soon worked out a cooperative solution: They took turns making deliveries along the central road, each earning close to the maximum profit from the experimenter.

So far, so good. But then researchers introduced conditions that allowed the players to control something that could be used to threaten their opponent: a gate on the central road. By closing the gate, a player could force the opponent's truck to back up and take the bypass, costing extra time and lowering profits. In the unilateral threat condition, Acme controlled the only gate at one end of the one-lane stretch of road. In the bilateral threat condition, each player controlled a gate. As before, the players were free to communicate to try to solve their differences.

How did the would-be trucking company operators react? When Acme could threaten Bolt with a gate closing, Bolt suffered quite a large loss, but Acme lost money,

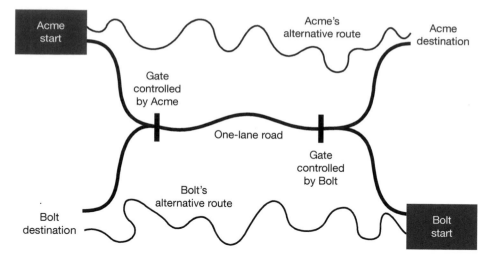

Figure 13.3 Routes to conflict

In this study, each participant had to move her company's trucks from a starting point to a destination. Participants could save time and earn more money by going over the central road, but conflict arose because only one truck could pass through the one-lane section at a time. When one or both parties controlled gates on the central road and threatened to close them, the trucks had to take a long alternate route, losing money. (Adapted from Deutsch & Krauss, 1960.)

too, as her trucks sat idle on the road during confrontations. When both players could use the threat, matters were even worse: Both consistently lost money. And whether the threat was unilateral or bilateral, players' communications focused on the use and consequences of the threat rather than on ways of cooperating to resolve the conflict.

It may have occurred to you that nothing in the rules of the trucking game forced the players to threaten one another. They could have worked together, taking turns and happily raking in the money just like the players in the condition without any gates. But these findings indicate that the mere availability of a potential threat appears to be enough to bring about its use. Once people have coercive means at their disposal, they shift from reward-seeking to socially competitive behavior.

The irony is that, as we said earlier, threats usually are counterproductive. The threatened group may assume that aggression is inevitable no matter how it responds. And if it responds with a counterthreat, the first group's belief in the opponent's hostility and unwillingness to compromise will be confirmed (North, Brody, & Holsti, 1964). Threats and counterthreats almost invariably escalate in intensity rather than staying at the same level (Tedeschi, Gaes, & Rivera, 1997). In laboratory simulations of international conflict, for example, other groups follow suit when one group stockpiles arms, and an arms race usually results (Kramer, 1989). In real-world conflicts, just perceiving a threat from an out-group appears to bolster support for highly aggressive actions. Jews in Israel, for example, were more likely to support several human rights violations against Palestinians, including the use of torture, if they perceived greater threat from Palestinians (Maoz & McCauley, 2008). Finally, when threats dominate communication, as they did when players controlled gates in the trucking game, they crowd out messages about cooperative solutions (Knudson, Sommers, & Golding, 1980). Communication can effectively deter and resolve conflict only when threats are not permitted, or when

SOCIAL PSYCHOLOGY IN PRACTICE: THREAT AND DETERRENCE IN INTERNATIONAL AFFAIRS

What can laboratory research tell us about policies of deterrence between nations? Deterrence is a political strategy in which one side threatens to use force in the hope of preventing an adversary's use of force (P. M. Morgan, 1983). Its central principle is that dangers arise when a potential aggressor believes its opponents are weak or vulnerable (Jervis, 1976). Proponents of these policies follow the maxim that "if you want peace, prepare for war." The lesson of history, however, suggests that if you prepare for war, you get war (Lebow & Stein, 1987). An analysis of two thousand years of international relations suggests that attempting to deter war by threats usually makes war more, not less, likely (Naroll, Bullough, & Naroll, 1974). Groups that stockpile resources in an effort at deterrence are often perceived as attempting to acquire an offensive edge in preparation for aggression. As a result, they often face escalating conflict from others who fear them (Hornstein, 1975). Speeches proclaiming defensive intentions are unlikely to persuade adversaries who feel threatened by an arms build-up.

Thus, deterrence, like other uses of threats, can backfire, eliciting counterthreats and escalation. This does not mean that it is wise for groups to neglect their defenses. As we have seen, intergroup conflict can stem from greed, and a group without power may appear as easy prey for strong aggressors who have little fear of retaliation. Such large differences in power leave the door open for those who would impose deadly "final solutions" to group conflict. Research indicates that groups roughly equal in power and ability use threats and coercion less often and achieve agreements more often than do parties with unequal power (Lawler and others, 1988; Sell, Lovaglia, Mannix, Samuelson, & Wilson, 2004). But even equality in power and command of threats cannot guarantee an absence of conflict: Recall that in the Acme–Bolt trucking game, the parties fared worst when they both controlled gates they could use as threats.

opponents learn to avoid making threats that spark retaliation (Lawler, Ford, & Bleger, 1988; W. P. Smith & Anderson, 1975).

Vicarious Retribution: They Hurt Us, Now I Hurt Them. Another reason conflicts between groups can quickly escalate is because the direct victims of a real or perceived intergroup attack or insult are not the only ones who want to retaliate. Members of a group who were not themselves directly harmed by an attack may lash out at members of the offending group, who themselves need not be the ones who committed the original attack. This process is termed **vicarious retribution** (Lickel, Miller, Stenstrom, Denson, & Schmader, 2006). This seems to be what occurred in May 2013, when several Muslim perpetrators struck a British soldier, Lee Rigby, with a car and then brutally stabbed him to death in broad daylight in a London neighborhood. One of the murderers then coldly approached a video camera, still wielding a bloody knife, and declared that the stabbing was revenge for the killing of Muslims by the British military. The stabbers probably had no idea whether Lee Rigby had himself killed any Muslims during his military service, but the answer likely would have made little difference to them. The specific victim needed only to be a member of the hated out-group—a British soldier. Thus, any intergroup insult, provocation, or attack may motivate not just the direct victims, but their group as a whole, to retaliate. With so many new potential perpetrators, further incidents between groups become likely. It is easy to see how just a single intergroup assault can trigger a spiraling series of attacks and counter-attacks.

vicarious retribution
members of a group who were not themselves directly harmed by an attack retaliating against members of the offending group

coalition formation

occurs when two or more parties pool their resources to obtain a mutual goal they probably could not achieve alone

Coalition Formation: Escalation as Others Choose Sides. Conflicts often begin as one-on-one confrontations, but as positions harden, the participants—particularly the weaker side—may call on outside parties for help. **Coalition formation** occurs when two or more parties pool their resources to obtain a mutual goal they probably could not achieve alone (Komorita & Meek, 1978). Coalition formation tends to polarize multiple parties into two opposing sides (Mack & Snyder, 1957). When groups are in conflict, coalition formation is usually seen as a threatening action that, like most threats, only intensifies competition. Those excluded from the coalition may react with fear and anger, and they often form their own coalitions. As unaffiliated groups ally with one side or the other, differences become polarized and the dangerous allure of consensus convinces each side that it is right.

For all these reasons, the formation of coalitions and alliances between nations usually increases the possibility of armed hostility (Q. Wright, 1965). This point, as well as the failure of threats and deterrence, is illustrated by the beginning of the First World War. The scene was set when Austrian Archduke Francis Ferdinand was assassinated by a Serbian nationalist; leaders of the Austro-Hungarian Empire retaliated by attacking Serbia. Even then, the conflict might have remained relatively localized, but the two parties' powerful allies stepped in. Serbia's ally Russia, viewing the Austrian attack as a pretext for a German–Austrian conquest of Europe, responded with military mobilization. Germany, feeling endangered, threatened war if Russia did not halt its mobilization. Russia's rejection of this demand led Germany to declare war, first on Russia and then on Russia's ally, France. The escalating hostilities finally drew another ally, Great Britain, into the war (Holsti & North, 1965; North and others, 1964). Not only did the build-up of opposed coalitions make the conflict more rather than less likely, but it resulted in the deaths of more than 8 million soldiers from more than 19 countries.

Perceptions in Conflict: What Else Could You Expect from Them?

As escalation continues, the in-group sees the out-group as totally evil and sees itself in unrealistically positive terms. Emotion and arousal make these biases even worse.

As conflict escalates, groups' views of themselves and of their opponents change. These conflict-driven perceptions may have little basis in reality, but they affect the group's understanding of what is happening and why. This skewed understanding in turn becomes a guide for group behavior (R. K. White, 1965, 1977, 1984). When perceptions are negative, distrust and suspicion cast every action in the worst possible light. And self-fulfilling prophecies exert their own pressure: If one side expects the other to be hostile and devious, a vicious cycle can begin in which the other is made to be more hostile and devious.

Polarized Perceptions of In-Group and Out-Group. If mere categorization—with no hint of conflict or competition—can make people evaluate their own group more positively than the out-group, imagine how much stronger perceptual biases become in the midst of bloody conflict. In fact, groups enmeshed in conflict tend to develop three blind spots in their thinking.

1. ***The in-group can do no wrong.*** Biased perceptions cause members of the in-group to see their group as righteous and morally superior. Its every intention seems pure hearted, its every action justifiable. Not surprisingly, groups in conflict almost always invoke religion to support their view. Leaders of warring parties in the Middle East have characterized their struggles as holy wars, and both the Germans and the Allies in the two World Wars were confident that God was on their side.

   Because of a desire to see the in-group so favorably and righteously, members engage in what has been called moral disengagement to help explain away the wrong-doing of their own group. We see the victims of violence perpetrated by our own group as less than human and we minimize their suffering, and this tendency is stronger for those who glorify the in-group (Castano, 2008; Leidner, Castano, Zaiser, & Giner-Sorolla, 2010). Through these psychological proceses, it becomes easier for us to see our violent actions in ways that make them seem more palatable and justifiable, thereby helping to maintain the image of our group as good.

2. ***The out-group can do no right.*** In contrast, the out-group is seen as evil, even diabolical. In the ongoing civil war in Syria, ethnic and religious divisions have sharpened, as members of each community perceive themselves as victims of inhuman and outrageous attacks by the other side. Omar Bakri, a Sunni Muslim cleric, asserted "There's a lot of blood now. A lot of people being killed. In Syria, 150,000 people have been killed and they're all Sunnis" (Workman, 2013). Of course, the other warring factions also see themselves as overwhelmingly the victims of the conflict. Perceptions like these support the idea that the enemy is capable of committing any evil, and therefore justify any action taken against them.

   Even when one group proposes a solution to a conflict, the other side automatically views it less favorably, reasoning that "if it's good for them it must be bad for us." This process is termed **reactive devaluation** (Curhan, Neale, & Ross, 2004; L. Ross & Nisbett, 1990). One set of studies used the Palestinian–Israeli conflict to demonstrate political antagonists' tendency to devalue each other's proposals (Maoz, Ward, Katz, & Ross, 2002). Both Israeli Jews and Israeli Arabs devalued peace plans that were described to them if the plan was attributed to the other side. The negative reactions were largely due to shifts in the perceivers' interpretations of what was being proposed—which differed dramatically depending on whether the proposal was attributed to an in-group or an out-group. Apparently, when we view the out-group as thoroughly evil, even a peace proposal that they advance is assumed to serve only their interests.

   reactive devaluation
   perceiving a proposed solution to a conflict negatively simply because the out-group offers it

3. ***The in-group is all-powerful.*** The in-group soon sees itself as having might as well as right on its side, leading to a preoccupation with appearing powerful, prestigious, tough, and courageous. This aggressive posturing, or what journalist Ross Barnet (1971) termed the "hairy chest syndrome," has dangerous side effects. The focus on winning may crowd out consideration of the merits or morals of in-group actions. The boasts of power may be seen as threats that deserve a response in kind (Lebow & Stein, 1987). Finally, the overconfident in-group may fall for its own rhetoric, just as it hopes the enemy will. The disastrous U.S. policy in Vietnam offered many examples of overconfidence, as military and political leaders repeatedly promised that the next minor escalation, the next 25,000 troops, would be enough to do the job.

Biased Attributions for Behavior. Groups in conflict frequently attribute identical behaviors by the in-group and the out-group to diametrically opposed causes. One study carried out during the Cold War contrasted American students' responses to similar military actions supposedly carried out by the United States or the Soviets (Oskamp & Hartry, 1968). Students considered, for example, sending aircraft carriers to patrol international waters off the coast of the other country. Participants who thought the United States had taken the actions against the Soviet Union saw them as more positive and more justifiable than did those who thought the Soviets had acted against the United States. In the context of conflict, attributions for in-group and out-group actions are biased in two different ways.

First, in-group motives are perceived as positive, whereas out-group motives are perceived as negative. An in-group action is correct and justified: a protection of our rights, a measured defense against their hostile intentions. When the out-group carries out exactly the same action, it is seen as provocative: a clear instance of aggression. We offer concessions, but they attempt to lure us with ploys. We are steadfast and courageous, but they are unyielding, irrational, stubborn, and blinded by ideology.

Second, we perceive in-group actions as dictated by situations, but out-group actions as dictated by character flaws. Our own military's actions, for example, reflect reasonable responses to difficult situations like defending us from attack or restraining internal unrest. Their military's moves instead reflect aggressiveness, and their harassment of dissidents reflects inhumanity, intolerance, and insecurity. In particular, groups often fail to recognize how often fear motivates out-group actions (R. K. White, 1987). During the Cold War, fear of powerful Soviet forces largely motivated the U.S. arms build-up. Failing to understand this motivation, however, the Soviets saw the build-up as threatening and responded with increased military production of their own. The U.S. side similarly reacted to their increase but not to the underlying Soviet fear. And so the cycle continued.

The Impact of Emotion and Arousal: More Heat, Less Light. As conflict rises, people experience tension, anxiety, anger, frustration, and fear. Even participants in competitive games in the laboratory show obvious signs of stress, such as accelerated heart rate (Cooke, Kavussanu, McIntyre, & Ring, 2011; Van Egeren, 1979). Not surprisingly, this emotional arousal affects processes of perception and communication and produces simplistic thinking. As complex thinking shuts down, decisions are based on simple stereotypes, snap judgments, and automatic reactions. If laboratory studies can generate such stress, imagine the pressure decision makers in real intergroup conflicts must experience (Milburn, 1977).

Recall from Chapter 5 that these were just the circumstances that cause people to rely more on stereotypic views of others.

Philip Tetlock and his colleagues found evidence of a simplistic pattern of thinking when they analyzed former U.S. and Soviet leaders' portrayals of each other in several decades of public speeches (Suedfeld & Tetlock, 1977; P. E. Tetlock, 1988). During times of East–West crisis—the Berlin blockade, the Korean War, the Soviet invasion of Afghanistan—both sides' political statements reflected simplistic and stereotypic thinking about the out-group. The United States was seen as an imperialist aggressor and the Soviet Union as an "evil empire." Editorials appearing in major newspapers in the United States, Canada, and the Soviet Union reflected these oversimplifications (Suedfeld, 1992). When tensions relaxed, each side's statements about the other became

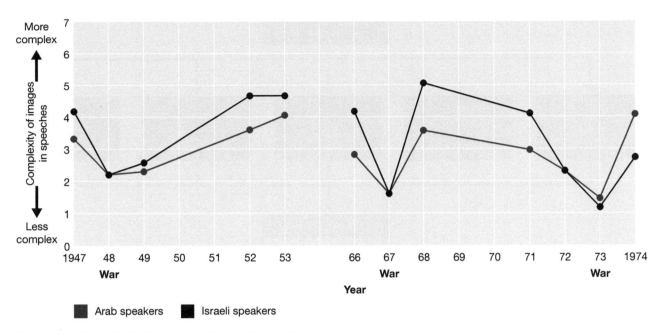

Figure 13.4 Simplistic thinking appears when conflict escalates
This study tracked the degree of complex thinking in verbal images of the opponent used in speeches by Arab and Israeli leaders in the United Nations. Note that the scores hit their lowest points in the years Arab–Israeli wars occurred. (Data from Suedfeld, Tetlock, & Ramirez, 1977.)

more complex, acknowledging areas of agreement and common interests as well as continuing disputes. A study of United Nations speeches, shown in Figure 13.4, showed a similar pattern of simplification in the images used in Arab–Israeli exchanges during years in which war occurred.

Emotions can not only lead to oversimple thinking about an opposing group, but also direct behavior toward that group—often in negative ways. Of particular importance are the emotions that people feel when they are thinking of themselves as members of their group (rather than emotions that they happen to feel as individuals; Mackie, Smith, & Ray, 2008). Group-based emotions depend on the particular nature of the threats that an out-group is seen as posing (Cottrell & Neuberg, 2005), whether a threat to the in-group's physical safety, territory, or cherished values and symbols. In turn, distinct emotions can motivate different types of action toward an out-group (E. R. Smith, Seger, & Mackie, 2007). Anger at the out-group, for example, is associated with increased desire to confront that group aggressively (Mackie and others, 2008). Indeed, Americans more strongly supported military action against terrorists after the Sept, 11th attacks the more they felt anger at that group (Huddy & Feldman, 2011). A more extreme group-based emotion, hatred, also predicts desires to aggress against the out-group, often with the intent of causing the group suffering (Halperin, 2008). Thus, group-based emotions may well play a role in group conflicts that is comparable to that played by individuals' feelings of anger and frustration in instances of individual hostile aggression. There is an important lesson in all of this. People tend to perceive members of out-groups negatively, and anxiety, perceived threats, and emotion strengthen this tendency. In stressful conflict situations, we may leap to the erroneous conclusion that our opponents are ignorant, are willfully misinterpreting evidence, and are fools whose self-interest or pernicious

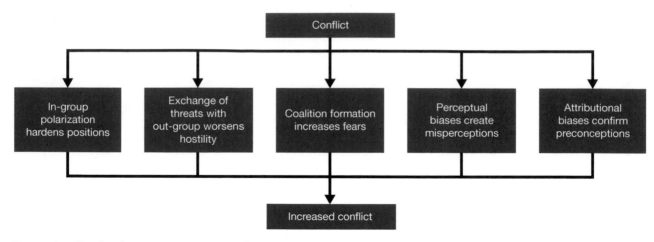

Figure 13.5 Social and cognitive processes in conflict escalation
Conflict between groups sets in motion a series of social and cognitive processes. Unfortunately, these processes usually harden each side's position and reinforce mutual negative views.

Why does an expectation often elicit behavior that confirms it? To review the ways self-fulfilling prophecies produce behavior that corresponds with our expectations, see Chapter 3, pages 87–89, and Chapter 5, pages 176–178.

ideology blinds them to the truth. Of course, our opponents are viewing us in the same way. As a result, neither side understands the other's perceptions or intentions, and, as Figure 13.5 illustrates, conflict may continue to escalate.

The Special Competitiveness of Groups: People Expect Groups to Be Supercompetitive, So They React in Kind. Biased and extreme perceptions of out-groups are yet another reason why groups act more competitively than individuals. People expect groups to be highly competitive and hostile (Hoyle, Pinkley, & Insko, 1989). To demonstrate this, Nilanjana Dasgupta and her colleagues (Dasgupta, Banaji, & Abelson, 1997) showed students drawings of novel humanoid creatures called "Gs" and asked the students to judge how likely the Gs were to behave in various ways toward other creatures, "Hs." Two aspects of the pictures were varied. If the Gs were all the same color (compared to different colors) or if they were standing close together (rather than scattered apart), the participants thought that they would be more likely to perform negative actions such as threatening the Hs. In other words, the more these cues of similarity and proximity suggested that the Gs were a group rather than separate individuals, the more negative their actions were expected to be (Abelson, Dasgupta, Park, & Banaji, 1998). And in the real world, of course, this expectation has a self-fulfilling quality (Hoyle and others, 1989). If you think your opponents will act competitively, you will probably try to beat them to it, either to deter them or at least to defend yourself (Insko, Schopler, Hoyle, Dardis, & Graetz, 1990).

"Final Solutions": Eliminating the Out-Group

Ultimately, conflict may escalate into an attempt at total domination or destruction of the out-group. When power differences exist between the groups and the out-group is morally excluded, one group may try to eliminate the other.

Intense conflicts may escalate to the point where groups seek to completely dominate or even destroy the out-group. The processes described above cause intergroup attitudes to harden and mutual misperceptions to become oversimplified and overwhelmingly negative. An initially realistic conflict over valuable resources can then become a battle for social supremacy in which the primary concern is not gaining resources, but dominating, exploiting, enslaving, or even exterminating the out-group (Allport, 1954b; Kaplowitz, 1990). Three factors seem particularly important in pushing a group to seek a "final solution" to intergroup differences once the groundwork of intergroup hostility and conflict has been laid.

1. *A difference in power between the groups translates desire into action.* Without power, no group can turn prejudice into discrimination, or discrimination into domination. But power gives a group the ability to attain its goals without fear of interference or retaliation, thereby increasing its ability and motivation to discriminate, dominate, and, possibly, eradicate a weaker opponent (Sachdev & Bourhis, 1985, 1991). As history shows, political repression, religious inquisitions, slavery, and genocide often follow (Opotow, 1990).

2. *Moral exclusion blocks moral outrage.* When we discussed moral exclusion in Chapters 6 and 10, we noted that biased perceptions of out-group inferiority can make one group indifferent to the plight of out-group members. If we place out-group members outside the boundaries of moral principles, regarding them as less than human, they can be treated in whatever way the in-group finds convenient or profitable (Opotow, 2012). Research suggests that moral exclusion is particularly likely when people harm others under orders from their in-group authorities (Bandura and others, 1996).

3. *Routinization produces desensitization.* As we saw in Chapter 10, many who carry out crimes of politically and socially sanctioned evil begin with small, morally questionable deeds that gradually escalate into unthinkable acts (Kelman & Hamilton, 1989; Staub, 1989). Those in the Milgram experiments, for example, began by inflicting only a mild, relatively painless shock to the victim. Over time, they gradually gave shocks of increasing severity, until many of them inflicted what they thought was an extremely painful jolt. Repetition of individual actions becomes routine, until, at the extreme, even heinous acts like torture and murder become mundane. Such desensitization numbs the horror that naturally inhibits such brutality, allowing social atrocities to continue.

The Special Competitiveness of Groups: Groups Offer Social Support for Competitiveness. This point constitutes another reason for the greater competitiveness of groups than individuals. Groups offer a rich soil for rationalizing negative acts that are motivated by greed or by fear of the out-group. Taking advantage of others, putting our own self-interest above others' good, discriminating against or even massacring those whom we hate—these and similar actions rank high on the "don't do" list that parents, teachers, or religious figures teach to most of us. But in a group, competing with or even exploiting out-groups can be rationalized as a form of group loyalty—a motive that fits well with people's general tendency to look out for "me and mine." Those who harm or exploit members of the out-group may even view themselves as performing noble acts of altruism and self-sacrifice: After all, they are putting their own lives on the line for the sake of their valued in-group (Schopler and others, 1993).

As Roy Baumeister (1997) commented, "When someone kills for the sake of promoting a higher good, he may find support and encouragement if he is acting as part of a group of people who share that belief. If he acts as a lone individual, the same act is likely to brand him as a dangerous nut" (p. 190). So through history, nations as well as religious and political movements have defended their acts in the name of the most exalted and worthy goals. Invasion of a less powerful neighbor nation is cloaked as self-defense, and murder of those who follow a different creed is obedience to God's revealed will. Individuals who participate in such acts of aggression have no need to formulate their own rationalizations for their evil acts, for their identification with the group does it for them. The power of groups to define norms for their members—to establish as unquestionably right what the group declares to be right—is the most fundamental reason that groups are so often more aggressive than individuals.

Final Solutions in History. The effects of these forces can be seen in the events culminating in the Holocaust in Nazi Germany. Many of the conditions that set the stage for a "final solution" were already in place. Germany's defeat in the First World War led to terrible economic lives in the 1930s. The situation was ripe for a scapegoat: an enemy who, by bearing the blame for Germany's defeat and material ills, could enhance in-group cohesion and solidify leaders' power. Nazi ideologists drew on centuries of European anti-Semitism to emphasize supposed distinctions between in-group Aryans (racially "pure" Germanic folk) and out-group Jews. Negative perceptions and attitudes toward Jews flourished, and German Jews were blamed for the nation's problems.

The three forces that make "final solutions" possible were also operating. First, Nazis held all the high cards, particularly after Hitler's election as Chancellor in 1933. Their control over the media, government, and military enabled them to enforce rules about every aspect of their victims' social, political, religious, and economic lives. Jews as a group held little political power within Germany, and their appeals to other nations for rescue went largely unanswered. Second, the Nazis dehumanized the Jews, labeling them "worms" and "vermin," thereby excluding them from the sphere in which fair, just, or human treatment could be expected or demanded. Third, killers became desensitized to their acts through routine and repetition. For example, the special police squads who traveled through occupied Poland to round up and kill Jews reacted with shock and horror to their first participation in a massacre (C. R. Browning, 1992). They experienced strong emotions, drank heavily afterwards, and suffered from nightmares. But, eventually, killing people became no more than an unpleasant duty, and at the end of the day the men could sit around, laughing and joking over games of cards.

The Nazi Holocaust was unique in many respects, but the social-psychological processes that allowed it to happen are not. They can be found whenever one powerful group oppresses a weaker opponent. They are at work in the unfolding conflict that began in 2011 in Syria where pro-government forces are attacking and killing opposition protestors and civilians, and they were at work in the genocidal attacks by Arab militias on Black residents in the Darfur region of Sudan in 2003–2005, the massacres of Tutsi and dissident Hutus by the Hutu-dominated government of Rwanda in 1994, massacres of Armenians by the Ottoman Turks early in the 20th century, and White Americans'

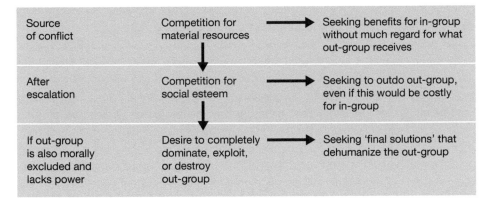

Figure 13.6 Two shifts in conflict
Conflicts often begin with realistic competition over material resources. If escalation occurs, groups may turn from seeking to do well for themselves to seeking to outdo their opponents. Winning, not prospering, then becomes the goal. In a context where the out-group is morally excluded and the groups have differential power, further escalation may result in a final shift in which the goal changes from outdoing the out-group to completely dominating or eliminating it.

and Europeans' capture and enslavement of Africans. When one group holds power over another and begins to dominate or exploit them, negative stereotypes shade into dehumanization, and moral exclusion of the out-group is not far behind. Ultimately, as the processes shown in Figure 13.6 operate, enslavement and genocide become acceptable actions justified by the superiority of the dominant group.

The social-psychological study of intergroup conflict yields many significant lessons, but perhaps the most important is that each of us is psychologically capable of hatred, dehumanization, and violence toward out-group members. Many of the New England ship captains who transported Africans to slavery in the Americas were regular church-goers, fine family men, and respected leaders within their own communities (Deutsch, 1990). And as we noted in Chapter 10, Nazi leaders viewed themselves as no more than ordinary citizens who cared about their families and did their job to protect them. Yet when groups are in conflict, social and cognitive processes—the same processes that sometimes produce empathy, bravery, altruism, and self-sacrifice—can conspire to produce extraordinary evil.

REDUCING INTERPERSONAL AND INTERGROUP CONFLICT AND AGGRESSION

When we left the Rattlers and the Eagles at Robbers Cave State Park, they were thoroughly at odds with each other. Of course, their war did not spiral out of control like many international conflicts, but as childhood conflicts go, the hostility was pretty bad. Moreover, they displayed many of the earmarks of conflict discussed in the previous sections. The groups' negative feelings about each other escalated: "Those guys" became, in the slang of the day, "bums," "bad guys," "those damn campers," and "stinkers." The groups felt powerful: As the athletic tournament began, each team was supremely confident of winning. Group norms were strictly enforced. Anyone wanting to be friends or even seen speaking with a member of the other team was branded a traitor and ruthlessly brought into line with threats of bodily harm or ostracism.

How could this hostility be resolved? Reducing conflict and aggression, whether at the interpersonal or intergroup level, may be possible if we draw on what we know about their causes. You will see that many of the processes that increase aggression and conflict can be turned around to help reduce it (Deutsch, 1973; Pruitt, 1998). Efforts at reducing aggression often involve altering people's immediate perceptions of others or the situational cues that may increase aggression. Some conflict-resolution strategies focus on reconciling the parties' concrete goals and aspirations, for example, by finding material outcomes that satisfy both individuals or groups. Other strategies encourage cooperation, to make former adversaries part of a new and more inclusive in-group. Our very ability to make this list offers some hope: Knowledge about the causes of aggression can now be recruited into the struggle to reduce it.

It's interesting that task and social interdependence, the main issues that must be solved to reduce intergroup conflict, are the same issues that must be handled for a single group to perform effectively, as discussed in Chapter 11.

Altering Perceptions and Reactions

Approaches to reducing aggression and conflict include promoting norms of non-aggression, minimizing or removing the cues that often cause individuals to commit aggressive acts, and encouraging careful interpretation and identification with others.

Whether conflicts are between individuals or groups, an irrevocable line is crossed when one person first throws a punch or draws a gun. Acts that precipitate aggression can be discouraged by promoting norms of non-aggression, controlling situational cues, and by encouraging people to reinterpret the situation and empathize with others.

Promote Norms of Non-Aggression. We discussed earlier that many norms promote aggression. But many groups and societies maintain and teach some norms that limit and inhibit aggression. "Pick on someone your own size," like many other norms, forbids aggression against the weak and helpless. And although "an eye for an eye, a tooth for a tooth" seems to be a formula for revenge, its original purpose was to prevent retaliation from spiraling out of control.

Some groups have developed norms that effectively counteract aggression. Anthropological reports indicate that among the Inuit of the Arctic, the Pygmies of Africa, and the Zuni and Blackfoot peoples of North America, controversy and conflict are avoided, physical violence is rare, and war is nonexistent (Gorer, 1968). Japanese social norms also dictate that it is often better to yield than fight, as reflected in the expression *Makeru ga kachi* "to lose is to win" (Alcock, Carment, & Sadava, 1988; Triandis, Bontempo, Villareal, Asai, & Lucca, 1988).

Norms are usually most effective in limiting aggression against other in-group members. Thus, similarity reduces aggression, and it does so for two reasons. First, as we have seen in Chapter 6, shared group membership breeds liking, and positive feelings for another person are incompatible with aggression (P. A. Miller & Eisenberg, 1988). Second, the norms of most groups proscribe or strictly control aggression within the group so that cohesion can be maintained and group goals achieved. In-group members are protected by a norm that appears to warn, "Don't hurt me. I'm one of us."

Minimize Cues for Aggression. Some cues activate aggressive thoughts and feelings, making overt acts of aggression more likely. Many in the United States believe that the ready availability of weapons deters aggression, but the evidence suggests just the opposite. When firearms are unavailable, aggression not only is less deadly but also less likely. When Jamaica implemented strict gun control and censored gun scenes from television and movies beginning in 1974, robbery and shooting rates dropped dramatically (Diener & Crandall, 1979). When Washington, DC, passed a handgun-control law, the numbers of homicides and suicides involving guns decreased substantially. Importantly, there was no offsetting increase in other methods of murder or suicide (Loftin, McDowall, Wiersema, & Cottey, 1991). Even if those inclined to murder simply pick up a knife or a lead pipe if no gun is handy, the outcome is not as deadly. Perhaps the most dramatic illustration of the effectivenss of gun control laws comes from Australia. In 1996, Martin Bryant shot over 50 people, killing 35, in that country's worst mass shooting incident. Shortly after, the government passed more restrictive gun laws and organized a massive gun buyback program. Since then, the risk of death by shooting is down over 50%, and no other mass shootings have occurred (Schifrin, 2012).

Not only the removal of negative cues such as guns but also the presence of more positive cues may reduce the likelihood of aggression. For example, the receipt of a gift, a kind and gentle response, the presence of an infant, and even laughter in a tense situation can cue thoughts and feelings that are incompatible with aggression (P. A. Bell & Baron, 1990; Berkowitz, 1984; Miron, Brummett, Ruggles, & Brehm, 2008). And, remember that exposure to violent media has been shown to increase aggressive behavior? Recent research shows that media can promote peace as well. In one study, students were assigned to either play a prosocial video game, a neutral game, or a violent game. Later, they selected the volume of noise that another person would have to endure. Showing again that violent cues increase aggression, those who played the violent game selected louder, more painful noise than did those who played the neutral game. But equally importantly, those who played the prosocial game selected lower volume than those in the neutral condition (Greitemeyer and others, 2012).

Interpret, and Interpret Again. Aggression is sometimes an immediate, almost unthinking response to a provocation that sparks intense anger. But it can also occur as a result of extensive consideration, weighing the relevant norms and the pros and cons of an aggressive action. So neither quick, heuristic processing nor systematic, extensive thought is a sure pathway to avoiding aggression. However, research described above shows that the factors that make it difficult for people to think carefully, such as alcohol use, high emotion, or limited time to think, generally increase aggressive behavior. Thus, in most cases systematic thought seems to be helpful in preventing aggression. The old advice to "count to 10" before taking any action when you are angry is very sound. When you feel provoked, think hard about the other person's intentions: Perhaps he or she did not mean the action the way you took it. Kenneth Dodge's research shows that children who have problems processing social cues tend to display a bias in their reactions to ambiguous harmful actions. They tend to automatically treat the actions as intentionally hostile, and as a result they act more aggressively in retaliation. But while their immediate reactions display this bias, their more considered reactions do not (Dodge & Newman, 1981). We can all learn from this finding. When a situation looks like a cause for angry retaliation or an opportunity for advantage through aggression, we should try to see it in a different light before we respond.

Engaging in what researchers call self-distancing might help us achieve this aim. Students in one experiment were first provoked by the experimenter during an initial task. Some were then randomly assigned to think about the task again from a first-person perspective, which is what most people naturally do. Others were assigned to take a "distant" view on those events, re-living them from a third-party perspective. Yet others were given no specific instructions. After this, the researchers measured participants' angry emotions and hostile thoughts. Those in the distancing condition showed lower levels of both anger and hostile thoughts compared to students in the other conditions. Moreover, in a follow-up study using similar methods, those in the distancing condition exhibited less aggression as well (Mischkowski, Kross, & Bushman, 2012). Taking a more third-party perspective on provocative events may allow us to interpret the provocation differently, which reduces aggressive reactions.

Promote Empathy with Others. Self-distancing encourages people to move away from their own perspective. Empathy, by encouraging people to move closer to another person's perspective, may have similar effects. Aggression is easiest when victims are distanced and dehumanized. Thus, it is tempting to place one's enemies outside the realm of human sympathy, eliminating normative and moral restraints. To avoid this temptation, we need to intentionally reflect on their humanity and thus on the things they share with us. Indeed, both feelings of empathy and perspective taking play important roles in reducing conflict (Galinsky, Gilin, & Maddux, 2011). For example, Norma Feshbach and Seymour Feshbach (1982) trained elementary schoolchildren to put themselves in other children's shoes, to recognize others' feelings, and to try to share their emotions. Compared with children in control groups, the children who engaged in this empathy training were much less aggressive in everyday playground activities. Empathy is fellow feeling, and fellow feeling is incompatible with aggression (Eisenberg, Eggum, & Di Giunta, 2010).

Resolving Conflict Through Negotiation

Conflict resolution also involves the parties in trying to find mutually acceptable solutions, which requires understanding and trust. When direct discussion is unproductive, third parties can intervene to help the parties settle their conflict.

Types of Solutions. A key part of any long-range approach to conflict resolution involves seeking solutions for the concrete disagreements that separate two individuals or groups. Sometimes solutions are dictated by one party, as when one nation overwhelms another by force or one person prevails in a lawsuit over another. In such cases, the conflict is resolved by an imposed solution. Not surprisingly, those who lose are usually dissatisfied with the outcome, and such solutions are rarely successful in ending conflict (Burke, 1970). Historians often point to the harsh terms of defeat imposed on Germany by the victors in the First World War as one of the factors that contributed to the rise of the Nazis and Germany's later aggression. Other conflicts are settled by distributive solutions, which involve mutual compromise or concessions that carve up a fixed-size pie.

Examples of such solutions include international treaties that divide territory under dispute or union–management contracts that set workers' raises somewhere between the union's demands and management's proposals (R. Fisher & Ury, 1981). Compromise and concession mean that all parties must give up something they wanted, but the loss may be tolerable, particularly when compared to the cost of continued conflict.

Integrative solutions are the best solutions because one side's gain is not necessarily the other's loss. These solutions are often termed win–win solutions because both sides can benefit simultaneously (Pruitt & Rubin, 1986). Imagine, for example, a resolution in which labor and management agree to split the increased profits from a new way of organizing production so that both sides come out ahead (Kimmel, Pruitt, Maganau, Konar-Goldband, & Carnevale, 1980; Pruitt & Lewis, 1977). One strategy that can lead to integrative solutions is log-rolling, in which each party gives up on issues that it considers less important but that the other group views as crucial (Pruitt, 1986). Although each party gets only some of its demands, it wins on the issues it considers most important. In an industry where employment is dropping as a result of foreign competition, for example, the union may accept limited pay raises to get guarantees of job security. Management's concessions on job security enable it to maintain wage scales that allow competitive pricing.

Finding an integrative solution generally requires creative thinking and an understanding of each party's interests, values, goals, and costs. Identifying an integrative solution is more difficult than just locating some halfway point between the parties' demands. Integrative solutions attempt to satisfy the parties' underlying motives, rather than their explicit demands (R. Fisher & Ury, 1981), and they may offer the only way out of some difficult international conflicts. For example, relations between Iran and the United States have been quite tense over the past decade, in large part because of Iran's desire to enrich uranium and have a nuclear program. Iran argues that the program is for peaceful civilian energy production. The United States and other countries, fearing that Iran is planning to produce and possibly use a nuclear weapon, have repeatedly insisted that Iran stop its program, and Iran has faced international sanctions because of its refusal to desist. Some have argued that a solution could be reached in which Iran is allowed to have its nuclear program, satsifying its need to have soveignty over its own energy production, in return for strenuous and frequent international inspections that could verify that they are not producing a bomb, which might ease the security concerns of the U.S. and others. Compared with solutions based on compromise, integrative solutions result in better outcomes for both parties, are more enduring, and produce better interparty relationships (Pruitt, 1986; L. Thompson, 1993).

Achieving Solutions: The Negotiation Process. Finding a solution to a conflict, particularly an integrative solution, requires the parties to communicate. **Negotiation** is reciprocal communication designed to reach agreement in situations in which some interests are shared and some are in opposition (R. Fisher & Ury, 1981; J. Z. Rubin & Brown, 1975). Diplomatic negotiations have successfully resolved international disputes over arms control, territory, and trade. Of course, not all negotiation is large-scale and formal. We all negotiate with others virtually every day: when we discuss what movie to see with our friends, split up tasks with our classmates on a group project, or debate bedtime with our children.

negotiation
the process by which parties in conflict communicate and influence each other to reach agreement

Photo 13.4 Negotiation. Negotiation is one way to find solutions that reduce interpersonal or intergroup conflict. When there is sufficient time and the parties involved can build trust, negotiation can be quite effective.

Successful resolution of conflict on small or large scales requires sufficient time for negotiation. Studies have shown that when parties are under time pressure, they reach less integrative solutions (Harinck & De Dreu, 2004). One reason may be that time pressure leads people to use stereotypes about the other parties to make judgments, rather than considering the situation systematically (De Dreu, 2005; Kray, Reb, Galinsky, & Thompson, 2004).

When adequate time is available, the fundamental goal of negotiators is to help each party understand how the other interprets and evaluates the issues. Unfortunately, conflicts often lead the parties to misperceive each other's position and goals, usually exaggerating their disagreement (L. Thompson & Hastie, 1990b). In one study demonstrating this point, 85% of the participants failed to realize, even after a period of negotiations, that they and their opponents agreed perfectly on one issue in contention (L. Thompson & Hastie, 1990a). These negative expectations regarding adversaries lower the chances of finding an integrative solution.

Building Trust. One of the priorities in negotiation is to build trust, so that parties will abandon their search for negative motives within each other's proposals. This is not easily accomplished because a history of bitter conflict is a poor foundation for trust. Even a sincere offer may be seen as a trick, a subterfuge designed to lull the opponent into a false sense of security. In such situations, trust must be built up by repeated displays of consistency between words and behavior (Lindskold, 1978; Weber, Malhotra, & Murnigham, 2005).

Negotiators usually try to break conflicts into sets of small, manageable issues. By focusing on specific issues rather than just repeatedly stating their overall conflicting goals, negotiation can reverse the decline of trust that occurs during the commitment and escalation phases of the conflict. This reversal occurs because when one party successfully negotiates an issue with the opponent, liking and trust for the other party increase, perhaps making later issues easier to settle (L. Thompson, 1993). In fact, negotiators who have reached successful agreements in the past are more likely to be able to agree again in the future, whereas past disagreements are more likely to lead to impasse. Because trust is such an important outcome, good negotiators tend to think of negotiations as ongoing relationships rather than one-time interactions (O'Connor, Arnold, & Burris, 2005).

Mediation and Arbitration: Bringing in Third Parties. Direct communication is not always the best way to resolve conflicts. When opponents are too angry to discuss issues rationally or negotiators run out of ideas for resolving an impasse, third-party intervention may offer the best hope for a solution. The United Nations Security Council, baseball labor arbitrators, divorce mediators, moderators at a debate, and parents intervening in their children's squabbles are all third parties attempting to inhibit, regulate, or help resolve conflicts. Some negotiations involve mediators who help the opponents

SOCIAL PSYCHOLOGY AND CULTURE: NEGOTIATING ACROSS CULTURAL LINES

Pervasive differences among cultures influence the way people negotiate just as they influence other types of social interaction (M. White, Härtel, & Panipucci, 2005). As we have seen many times before, whether individuals come from individually oriented or collectivist cultures can make a big difference to the motives that people bring to interactions. One recent meta-analysis of 36 empirical studies found that negotiators from individualist cultures preferred competitive strategies such as demanding concessions. In contrast, negotiators from collectivist cultures were more likely to prefer problem solving, compromising, or even withdrawing from the negotiation as a means of trying to reach agreement (Adair & Brett, 2005; Holt & Devore, 2005). Training in differing cultural styles and expectations for negotiation could be a valuable preparation for those who bargain with members of other cultures.

Another factor that comes into play when parties to a negotiation come from different groups is a greater emphasis on outcomes rather than perceptions of fairness (Tyler and others, 1998). When members of a common in-group negotiate, they are concerned not only about how they stand in the final outcome, but also about being treated fairly and respectfully (Tyler & Lind, 1992). Thus, when conflict takes place within a group, fair treatment, politeness, and respect for all may win assent for an agreement, even if all cannot get what they want in terms of the concrete resources at stake. However, when negotiations cross group lines, concerns about fairness and respect recede, leaving the parties more interested in simply what they can get—potentially complicating the resolution of their dispute.

focus their discussion on the issues and reach a voluntary agreement. In arbitration, the third party has the power to hand down a decision after hearing the disputants present their arguments and information.

Third-party intervention has several advantages. First, mediators or arbitrators can arrange meeting agendas, times, and places so that these details do not themselves become sources of conflict (Raven & Rubin, 1976). Second, skillful intervention—mediation, in particular—can improve intergroup relationships. In one case, third parties were called in to mediate a dispute between public housing tenants and private homeowners in a small Canadian community. As a result of their work, intergroup attitudes improved, as did understanding of the complexity of each side's position (R. Fisher & White, 1976). Moreover, research suggests that intergroup negotiations are particularly competitive and therefore third-party intervention can be helpful in settling disputes, in part, because it reduces the competitive element (Loschelder & Trotschel, 2010). A third advantage of third-party intervention is that, because outsiders bring fresh ideas, they may be able to offer more creative integrative solutions than those proposed by people deeply enmeshed in the conflict (R. Fisher & Ury, 1981). Finally, a skilled third party can leave room for graceful retreat and face-saving when disputants lock themselves into positions they themselves realize are untenable (Pruitt, 1981). Third-party intervention may allow both sides to accept concessions without embarrassment. By doing so, it is more likely to lead to a mutually acceptable outcome than are unaided negotiations (J. Z. Rubin, 1980). It is also more likely to reduce stress and frustration for the parties locked in ongoing conflict (Giebels & Janssen, 2005). Overall, then, third-party interventions can be quite effective. Indeed, an analysis of hundreds of international crises revealed that agreements were much more likely to be reached when a mediator was used (Wilkenfeld, Young, Asal, & Quinn, 2003).

Intergroup Cooperation: Changing Social Identity

Conflict resolution can also be facilitated by having groups cooperate toward shared goals that can be attained only if both groups work together. Under the proper conditions, cooperative intergroup interaction reduces conflict.

After an athletic contest that marked the height of the Robbers Cave conflict, the researchers decided to see whether joint participation in some pleasant activity could reduce hostilities. They arranged for the boys to have meals at the same time and to watch a movie together. If you recall our discussion in Chapter 5 of the conditions under which contact improves intergroup attitudes, you will not be surprised that the group contact did not help. Rather than providing the opportunity for consistently friendly interaction that disconfirmed stereotypes—the key to changing negative group perceptions—this kind of contact increased hostilities. The boys found that the shared meals provided perfect opportunities for food fights.

superordinate goals

shared goals that can be attained only if groups work together

Superordinate Goals. When simple contact failed, the researchers tried a different strategy. They engaged the groups in the pursuit of **superordinate goals,** which are goals that can be attained only if groups work cooperatively as a team. Examples of superordinate goals in political life are cooperation between agricultural and urban interests to increase the water supply for all, and cooperation between nations to reduce greenhouse gases in the atmosphere to stop global warming. At Robbers Cave, the superordinate goals were a series of problems that could be solved only if the teams worked together. For example, the staff staged a breakdown of the water supply, and the boys worked together to trace the water pipeline back into the hills. A movie was

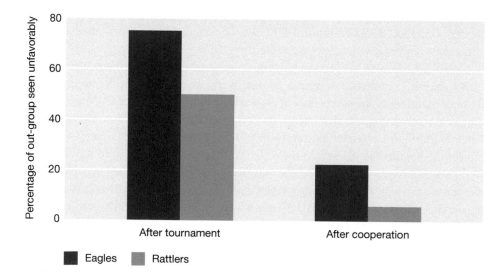

Figure 13.7 Cooperation cures conflict
In the Robbers Cave experiment, hostility between Eagles and Rattlers reached a peak right after an athletic tournament. Researchers then arranged for the two groups to work together to achieve a series of superordinate goals that neither could attain alone. As the boys cooperated, intergroup hostility greatly declined. (Data from M. Sherif & Sherif, 1953.)

too expensive for either group alone to rent, so all the boys pooled their funds to pay the rental fee. Finally, after finding that the camp truck had broken down, they figured out how to restart the truck by pulling on a rope attached to its bumper. In contrast to the earlier competitive tug-of-war contests, the boys literally had to pull together, and, thanks to the driver's carefully calibrated foot pressure on the brake, it took the efforts of all the boys from both groups to get the truck moving.

Superordinate goals improved intergroup relationships, but not overnight. After repairing the water supply, the two groups mingled good-naturedly, but they capped the day off with a food fight. They rented the movie with pooled resources, but the two groups sat on opposite sides of the dining hall to watch it. After 6 days of cooperation, however, their previous hostilities were greatly decreased, as can be seen in Figure 13.7. In fact, when it was time to leave, they asked if they could travel home together on one bus. As the boys took their seats on the bus, the camp staff noticed that a Rattler was just as likely to sit next to an Eagle as to another Rattler (M. Sherif & Sherif, 1953). Superordinate goals have had similar success in eliminating other forms of experimentally induced conflict (Diab, 1970).

Why Does Intergroup Cooperation Work? Intergroup cooperation is not a foolproof cure for conflict. But when the right conditions exist, intergroup cooperation undermines many processes that contribute to conflict and it encourages positive interaction and even friendship, which can ultimately reduce prejudice (Allport, 1954b; Pettigrew, 1997, 1998; Pettigrew & Tropp, 2006). What are the circumstances that make it most effective?

- *Cooperation should be for a valued common goal, which eliminates competition for material and social resources.* Rather than battling for pocket knives or bragging rights, the campers at Robbers Cave pooled their talents and resources to reach mutually desired goals (Gaertner and others, 2000).
- *Cooperation should provide repeated opportunities to disconfirm out-group stereotypes.* Remember that intergroup conflict arises from group differences as well as from competition over resources. As we saw at Robbers Cave, it took several bouts of cooperation to bring the Rattlers and Eagles together. Similar results are found in laboratory studies: A single cooperative episode often has quite limited effects (Lockhart & Elliot, 1981; Wilder & Thompson, 1980).
- *Cooperation should produce successful results.* If groups fail while working together, each is likely to blame the other, and hostility may even increase (Worchel, 1979; Worchel & Norvell, 1980). In contrast, success helps the intergroup climate, in part by allowing friendships to grow up across group lines (Pettigrew, 1997).
- *Cooperation should take place between equals, at least for the task at hand.* The Rattlers and the Eagles were all equally capable of pulling the bus and donating to the film fund.
- *Cooperation should be supported and promoted by social norms.* The goal of peaceable and respectful coexistence needs official institutional endorsement (Allport, 1954b; Amir, 1969). A few instances of cooperation cannot overwhelm intergroup hostility that is culturally ingrained and institutionally supported. Thus, for example, brief programs that bring together Israeli Jews and Palestinian Arabs will not change intergroup perceptions if segregated communities continue to isolate one group from the other.

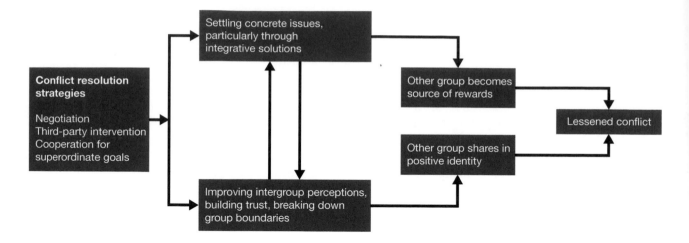

Figure 13.8 Processes in conflict resolution

Just as social and cognitive processes can help escalate conflict, the processes involved in conflict resolution can build on themselves. Interventions that either help the groups settle the concrete issues in dispute or improve their feelings about each other can set the tone for further reductions in conflict.

Intergroup cooperation resolves conflicts over concrete resources because it makes the out-group a source of rewards rather than punishments. Cooperation also resolves problems of esteem and status by creating friendships across group lines and eventually fusing the warring parties into one new and improved in-group (Gaertner & Dovidio, 2000; Gaertner and others, 1989, 1990; Pettigrew, 1997). Figure 13.8 portrays this idea. Indeed, while cooperating, the two separate groups must act as "one"—at least temporarily re-categorizing themselves as one unit instead of two opposing groups. Therefore, cooperation may help transcend or eliminate group categorizations entirely, which may account for why it is successful in eliminating group-based hostilties. Laboratory demonstrations using experimentally created minimal groups have confirmed that blurring boundaries can coalesce groups into one larger overarching structure, thereby reducing bias and discrimination (Nier and others, 2001). Samuel Gaertner and his colleagues (Gaertner, Mann, Murrell, & Dovidio, 1989) found, for example, that intergroup relations were improved when members of two subgroups were placed at alternating seats around a table and when they gave the joint group a new and separate name.

As "we" and "they" become just "we," the new, larger group membership can be a source of self-esteem and a positive social identity (S. Feshbach & Singer, 1957; Gaertner & Dovidio, 2000, 2012). Even more importantly, "we" feelings decrease competition. In an experimental demonstration of this point, Roderick Kramer (1989) had small groups of participants play a game simulating an arms race. To create in-group feelings, some participants were reminded that all the groups had some features in common. Compared with participants not receiving the reminder, those with "we" feelings were much less likely to stockpile weapons. Similarly, in a study in which two groups of participants drew from a common resource pool, each took large amounts and quickly depleted the resource (Kramer & Brewer, 1984). However, when participants were reminded of their joint membership in a larger shared group, both groups cooperated more and used less of the resource.

Forming a new and more inclusive in-group works best in solving intergroup conflict if the original groups retain some measure of distinctiveness rather than merging completely (Condor & Brown, 1988; Crisp, Stone, & Hall, 2006). For example, each group might perform distinct roles and tasks that contribute to the overall good (R. Brown, Condor, Matthews, Wade, & Williams, 1986; Deschamps & Brown, 1983; Hornsey & Hogg, 2000). When the subgroups retain their identity in some manner, this highlights that the contact between members is truly intergroup, that one is dealing with a representative of an out-group. This may be valuable, because the positive views that form toward those out-group members may then generalize to the out-group as a whole, that is, to other group members not directly involved with the contact (Brown & Hewstone, 2005). In this way, each group maintains its own cultural distinctiveness and its positive identity, but cooperating toward a greater goal improves its view of other groups (D. M. Taylor & Simard, 1979). The real ideal of a multicultural society is a tossed salad, not a melting pot, with every group's contribution valued and respected for itself rather than as an indistinguishable part of a uniform whole. Cultural differences then become opportunities for learning and mutual enrichment rather than bases for conflict (Deutsch, 1993; Wolsko and others, 2000).

Some favor a "melting pot" approach over the "tossed salad" because they worry that an emphasis on group differences may foster intergroup hostility and prejudice. This sort of concern helped make the so-called color-blind ideology popular with some as a means to reduce racial group conflicts. As we discussed in Chapter 6, this view argues that people should not see race and that racial differences should be ignored. However, color-blind ideology has important disadvantages. First, in schools and many other settings, including even the workplace, the values of getting to know about other cultures and learning to live and work alongside culturally different individuals are important, perhaps as important as individual task performance. Janet Schofield (1986) found that color-blind ideology impeded such learning, for example, by keeping schoolchildren and teachers from capitalizing on their cultural diversity to enrich their perspectives. Second, color-blind ideology desensitizes members of a dominant group to the value placed on group membership by members of minority or disadvantaged groups. Charles Judd and his colleagues (Judd, Park, Ryan, Brauer, & Kraus, 1995) found that many White Americans professed color-blindness, refusing with apparent sincerity even to acknowledge that Whites and Blacks differ in important ways. Yet the Blacks in the same study regarded their group membership as quite meaningful and important to them. From their perspective, color-blindness denies an important social identity and may even translate into a demand for assimilation, that is, for members of minority groups to adopt the values and customs of the dominant White group. Clearly, a balance is required. Members of different groups can share common goals and work together, while simultaneously maintaining their own group memberships as sources of identity and esteem (Condor & Brown, 1988; Eller & Abrams, 2004).

Under the right conditions, intergroup cooperation not only leads group members to think of themselves in terms of a higher-level common identity, but also encourages them to get to know out-group members as individuals (Bettencourt, Brewer, Croak, & Miller, 1992; Brewer, 1999). Over time, as out-group members become friends, reductions in bias should result (Davies, Tropp, Aron, Pettigrew, & Wright, 2011; Pettigrew, 1997; Pettigrew & Tropp, 2006). Thus, cooperation works at multiple levels: increasing the salience of a new and more inclusive in-group and also decreasing the salience of group memberships in general as relationships become more friendly and personalized. Because many real-world intergroup situations involve many and varied sources of

For more detail on the nature and consequences of this way of thinking about group differences, check out Chapter 6, pages 224–225.

conflict—such as competing group interests, historical wrongs committed by each group against the other, negative stereotypes, segregation, and limited opportunity for contact —the fact that intergroup cooperation can work in multiple ways is perhaps its strongest advantage (Hewstone, Rubin, & Willis, 2002).

Intergroup cooperation for superordinate goals holds the promise of true conflict resolution, rather than conflict management (S. P. Cohen & Arnone, 1988). Conflict resolution turns groups' basic strivings for mastery and connectedness toward positive ends. Previously hostile groups find ways to enhance their identities by cooperating, for example, in creating a truly multicultural society, rather than by outdoing one another. New symbols are created that reflect pride and respect for both sides, and the groups' old symbols of intransigence and hatred are allowed to slip into history. Just as conflict can build on itself and escalate, each step toward conflict resolution—whether aimed at task or social interdependence—can help to further reduce conflict, as Figure 13.8 shows. Peaceful relations will ultimately be possible when the world community finds ways to accommodate the needs of groups and nations not only for physical security and material resources, but also for positive and distinctive identities.

CONCLUDING COMMENTS

Whenever someone commits aggression, it is a safe bet that he or she sees it as reasonable, justified, even necessary. A man who kills in a barroom brawl sees himself as retaliating against the previous punch thrown by his victim or as defending his honor against an intolerable insult or slur. Muggers and robbers see themselves as taking what they need from those who have too much and whose losses will be covered by insurance in any case. It is worth repeating the eloquent statement by Martin Luther King, Jr. (1967), which we already quoted in Chapter 5: "It seems to be a fact of life that human beings cannot continue to do wrong without eventually reaching out for some rationalization to clothe their acts in the garments of righteousness" (p. 72). The clothing is often so complete that people do not even feel guilty about their acts that harm others.

When individuals make their own interpretations of reality, they are deeply vulnerable to rationalizing their self-interest in these ways. As Chapter 9 discussed, seeking consensus from others often helps us see situations clearly. For those who fail to rely on others' perceptions to check their own possibly skewed opinions, the result in all too many cases is the aggressive behavior of the outlaw: the petty bully, mugger, or murderer.

When groups commit aggression, they, too, rationalize their acts with high-sounding words and ideas. Exploiting, repressing, even massacring other groups are considered necessary to fulfill the glorious in-group's historical destiny or to redress past wrongs. Those outsiders are in any case less than fully human, so they do not deserve moral consideration.

When groups interpret reality for their members, they, too, are vulnerable to rationalizing their own self-interested desires for mastery of resources or for respect and esteem. Conformity and groupthink can mean that no group members dare to speak out, even if they are capable of seeing things differently. The result in all too many cases is the aggressive behavior of groups of true believers: fanatical Nazis, Bosnian Serbs bent on "ethnic cleansing," or Rwandan Hutus whipped by self-serving political leaders into a murderous frenzy against Tutsis.

Which is worse, a lone outlaw or a group of true believers? True believers are probably more dangerous. The civilized world thought it had put genocide behind it with the defeat of Nazi Germany and the Nuremberg war crimes trials, only to see intergroup conflict and massacre re-emerge within a few years in India and Pakistan, Africa, and central Europe. Our opinion that true believers are probably a greater threat than outlaws is supported by the research reviewed in this chapter, showing that groups are more aggressive than individuals.

But perhaps we need not choose between these two depressing alternatives. There is no single easy answer that works for every time and situation. Individuals cannot stand independent and reject group consensus without becoming easy prey for rationalized self-interest: That way lies the outlaw. Neither can individuals unthinkingly accede to the siren song of group consensus, which may rationalize and glorify group interests while dehumanizing opponents: That produces true believers. But each of us can try to balance our own individual perceptions and group consensus, applying plenty of thought—unclouded by strong emotion or immediate responses to threat. We must beware particularly of group-induced and group-sanctioned actions that victimize out-groups. History shows that group consensus that calls for aggressive action against outsiders, even when portrayed as necessary self-defense or a well-justified response to past injustices, requires the most searching moral scrutiny.

SUMMARY

The Nature of Aggression and Conflict. Aggression, defined by people's immediate intention to hurt others, is often set in motion by **conflict** or incompatible goals. There are two types of aggression—hostile and instrumental. **Hostile aggression** is often driven by anger due to insult, disrespect, or other threats to self-esteem or identity. **Instrumental aggression** is in service of mastery needs.

Humans have evolved to compete effectively for food and mates. Although the capacity to act aggressively may have helped, aggression has no special place in "human nature." Aggression is just one strategy among many others that humans use to attain rewards and respect in accordance with individual perceptions and social norms. Aggression can be difficult to study experimentally because people are often unwilling to act aggressively when they are being observed. Researchers have used a variety of techniques to get around these problems.

Interpersonal Aggression. Aggression is triggered by a variety of factors. Some aggression is a result of mastery needs. Potential rewards make this kind of aggression more likely and costs or risks make it less likely. Sometimes, however, perceived provocation such as a threat to self-esteem or connectedness produces anger, which can also set off aggression. As suggested by **frustration-aggression theory**, frustration can make aggression more likely, and many negative emotions do so as well. Norms too can promote aggressive behavior. Other people's aggressive actions, including portrayals in

CHAPTER 13 THEMES

■ **Construction of Reality**
Aggression and conflict are often driven by people's perceptions of others.

■ **Pervasiveness of Social Influence**
Social norms and people's group memberships dramatically influence aggression and conflict.

■ **Striving for Mastery**
The prospect of concrete rewards frequently triggers instrumental aggression and group conflict.

■ **Seeking Connectedness**
Disrespect and other threats to feelings of connectedness frequently trigger emotional aggression and group conflict.

■ **Valuing Me and Mine**
Valuing a group can lead to downgrading others, exacerbating conflicts.

■ **Conservatism**
Conflict is often self-perpetuating.

■ **Superficiality Versus Depth**
In-depth processing can diminish aggression by allowing people to think of alternative solutions to conflict.

the media, may indicate that aggression is appropriate. Cues in a specific situation, such as the presence of guns or other weapons, may also increase the accessibility of thoughts related to aggression. Both of these types of factors therefore make aggression more likely to occur.

Situations that favor superficial thinking often favor aggression. Thinking carefully can reduce aggression, but many factors interfere with people's motivation and ability to process information carefully and evenhandedly, increasing the likelihood of aggression. All these factors and the ways they interact to produce interpersonal aggression are summarized in the **General Aggression Model**.

Intergroup Conflict. Groups are generally even more competitive and aggressive than individuals. Group conflict often stems from competition for valued material resources, according to **realistic conflict theory**, or for social rewards like respect and esteem. Groups in conflict are often more attuned to social rewards than to material ones. Individuals and groups use social comparisons to determine acceptable levels of resources, as described by **relative deprivation theory**.

Once conflict starts, poor communication can make it worse. In-group interaction hardens in-group opinion, threats are directed at the out-group, each group retaliates more and more harshly, sometimes engaging in acts of **vicarious retribution**, and other parties choose sides and potentially engage in **coalition formation**. All of these processes tend to escalate the conflict.

As escalation continues, the in-group sees the out-group as totally evil and sees itself in unrealistically positive terms. These biases show themselves, for example, in **reactive devaluation** of proposals made by out-groups. Emotion and arousal make these biases even worse.

Ultimately, conflict may escalate into an attempt at total domination or destruction of the out-group. When power differences exist between the groups and the out-group is morally excluded, one group may try to eliminate the other.

Reducing Interpersonal and Intergroup Conflict and Aggression. Approaches to reducing aggression and conflict include promoting norms of non-aggression, minimizing or removing the cues that often cause individuals to commit aggressive acts, and encouraging careful interpretation and identification with others.

Conflict resolution also involves the parties in trying to find mutually acceptable solutions through **negotiation**, which requires understanding and trust. When direct discussion is unproductive, for example, because of cultural differences, third parties can intervene to help the parties settle their conflict.

Conflict resolution can also be facilitated by having groups cooperate toward **superordinate goals**, shared goals that can be attained only if both groups work together. Under the proper conditions, cooperative intergroup interaction reduces conflict.

HELPING AND COOPERATION

SOCIAL DILEMMA
NEGATIVE-STATE RELIEF
BYSTANDER
PROSOCIAL BEHAVIOR
DIFFUSION   ALTRUISM INFLUENCE
SUPERFICIALITY DEPTH   RESPONSIBILITY
EMPATHY-ALTRUISM
COOPERATION   TRUST

As social beings, we often act, alone or in groups, to benefit other people. Some of these kindnesses are quite ordinary—we give blood, drop some spare change into a charity collection box, or pool our resources and skills for a morning to build a playground in a rundown neighborhood. At other times we give generously of our effort and energy, volunteering to help battered women, delivering hot meals to the homebound, or organizing the collection and shipping of medical supplies to those affected by hurricanes, earthquakes, and tsunamis. And sometimes, people even risk their own health and safety for others, as with heroic rescuers in the U.S. and Canada who are recognized by awards from the Carnegie Hero Commission. In 2012, an award went to college student Joshua Steed, who was working in an office when a gunman entered and repeatedly shot an officemate who was at the front desk. Steed managed to throw a chair at the gunman and then jump on him, disarming him. New York City firefighters willingly put their own lives in jeopardy attempting to save trapped occupants of the World Trade Center on September 11, 2001, with horrific consequences. And despite constant intimidation, arrests, and executions at the hands of their own Vichy government, the people of the French village of Le Chambon-sur-Lignon worked tirelessly together between 1937 and 1943 to hide and protect no fewer than 5,000 refugees, among them 3,500 Jews, from the systematic persecutions of the Third Reich.

Social psychologists call both everyday kindnesses as well as inspiring acts of heroism **prosocial behavior**: behavior whose immediate goal is to help or benefit others. As is the case with aggressive behavior, it is the intention with which action is carried out, rather than its consequences, that defines behavior as prosocial. At times people act in a prosocial way not just toward a single individual, but for the benefit of larger groups. **Cooperation** involves two or more people working together toward a common goal that will benefit all involved. While helping usually involves an asymmetry (with one person helping and another being helped), cooperation usually depends on contributions from all parties.

In studying helping and cooperation, social psychologists have looked at many kinds of behavior: giving aid in everyday situations, dramatic responses to emergencies, and long-term commitments of time, effort, and even personal risk (Penner, Dovidio, Piliavin,

prosocial behavior
behavior intended to help someone else

cooperation

two or more people working together toward a common goal that will benefit all involved

& Schroeder, 2005). In laboratory studies, for instance, they have allowed participants to divide money in any way they wish between themselves and an anonymous stranger (Shariff & Norenzayan, 2007) or to volunteer to take the place of someone scheduled to receive painful electric shocks (Batson, Duncan, Ackerman, Buckley, & Birch, 1981). Researchers have examined how much of their own money members of laboratory groups will sacrifice to provide a monetary bonus that will benefit all group members equally (Brewer & Kramer, 1986). Outside the laboratory, researchers have investigated why people volunteer for community service organizations (Omoto & Snyder, 1995), who goes above and beyond their formal job description to help co-workers (Joireman and others, 2006), and what circumstances affect responses to staged emergencies (Cramer, McMaster, & Bartell, 1988). This variety of research approaches means that researchers' conclusions about prosocial behavior often have high construct validity and good generalizability. What have they learned?

As you will see, helping and cooperation depend on how people interpret social situations as well as the social influences acting on them. We begin this chapter by exploring when people help. Indeed, it seems that for every example of heartwarming generosity, there are also examples of people turning away, failing to render much-needed aid, or ignoring and deflecting pleas for assistance. Understanding the individual and social forces that lead people to help also uncovers the circumstances in which people don't help, even when others seem to be in need.

We then turn to the tricky question of what motivates prosocial behavior. We often label behaviors such as sending money to support starving children, biking to work to help improve the community's air quality, or delivering care parcels to the needy as altruism. But this term has a more specific meaning, referring to one possible motive for helping: **Altruism** refers to prosocial behavior motivated by the desire to benefit others for their own sake, rather than for personal rewards (Batson, 1991, 2002). Consider the following example. Walking with a friend down the street, you donate $10 to someone collecting money for a homeless shelter. You intended to help the homeless but also wanted to impress your companion with your generosity. Your intention to help makes this an example of prosocial behavior. Is it also altruism? No, because part of the intention involved personal gain.

Of course, as is the case with aggression, multiple motives often influence any single prosocial act. For this reason, we will see that it is often difficult to know whether a particular incident of helping or cooperation is altruistically motivated. In fact, some argue that pure altruism doesn't exist—that helping is always in one way or another driven by **egoism**, the desire to obtain personal rewards, if only in the form of positive feelings about having helped. Can people never think, feel, or act for the greater good of others without any consideration of self-interest? To answer this question, we need to go beyond the issue of when people act prosocially and probe why they do so. Is the tendency to help part of our genetic make-up? What motivates people to help others in distress or need? And what spurs people to cooperate for group goals, when seeking individual benefits is often more personally profitable? After we discuss these intriguing issues, we will consider how people make decisions about helping and cooperating, whether under the time pressure and stress of a sudden emergency or with leisure to reflect and consider.

Understanding prosocial behavior provides a foundation for considering a very practical question: How can we promote more caring, helpful, and cooperative communities?

altruism

behavior intended to help someone else without any prospect of personal rewards for the helper

egoism

behavior motivated by the desire to obtain personal rewards

In the last part of the chapter, we will see what suggestions for increasing the level of prosocial behavior in groups and in society emerge from social-psychological research.

WHEN DO PEOPLE HELP?

Imagine walking back home from a trip to the neighborhood store one evening, carrying a half-gallon of milk. You notice a car stopped at the curb. You can hear fruitless attempts to start the motor. Although you glance repeatedly at the car, the elderly driver does not wave or gesture for help. After a pause, the attempts to start the engine begin again and then cease. You see another pedestrian further down the street. After a casual glance over his shoulder at the sound of the sputtering engine, he walks on.

Even in this common, everyday situation, the questions that might run through your mind as you decide whether or not to help are the very same ones that determine helping in the most extreme emergencies. If you are like most people, you first wonder whether help is actually needed. Social situations in which helping might be necessary are often ambiguous: Does the driver need help or not? Other questions soon follow: What should be done? And should you be the one to do it? Whether people are responding to an emergency, giving casual aid, or making a long-term commitment as a caregiver, helping behavior is affected by the same social and cognitive factors that influence all social behavior. Helping is crucially dependent on people's interpretation of a situation, but such perceptions don't take place in a social vacuum. As we saw in Chapters 9 and 10, the actions of others are often crucially important to whether we act or not.

Is Help Needed and Deserved?

Helping is dependent on people's perception of someone as both needing and deserving help. The ability and motivation to pay attention to others' needs influence whether people think help is needed. People are more likely to help those not held responsible for their own need.

Perceiving Need. Several factors influence the judgment that someone needs help. Imagine walking through your quiet neighborhood in the evening and hearing the motorist's repeated attempts to start the stranded car. Now imagine jostling your way down a busy city street, trying to tune out the roar of traffic and the honking of taxicabs. In this situation, the driver's need would be much harder to notice. Becoming aware of a need is usually the first step in the helping chain of events (Darley & Latané, 1968), and busy or noisy surroundings reduce the likelihood of people noticing that someone needs help (Korte, Ypma, & Toppen, 1975). Anything that distracts potential helpers from their surroundings—even being in a hurry (Darley & Batson, 1973)—makes noticing need less likely. No doubt this is one reason that people are more likely to help others in quiet, rural areas than in crowded cities (R. V. Levine, Reysen, & Ganz, 2008).

In contrast, being in a positive mood increases people's sensitivity to others. Indeed, happy people seem to pay more attention to others around them and are more likely to notice others' needs than sad people (Schaller & Cialdini, 1990). It is no wonder, then, that positive thinking often translates into positive actions. In an early study demonstrating this point, researchers put one group of students in a good mood by telling them they had succeeded on a task, whereas another group were put in a bad mood by learning they had failed (Isen & Levin, 1972). When a confederate dropped a stack of books nearby, the happy students were more likely to help than the unhappy ones. Happy participants also remembered much more about the confederate and her actions, demonstrating that happy people's attention is turned outward. For this reason, they are more attuned to others' needs for help.

Judging Deservingness. Even if you noticed a stranded motorist, a panhandler asking for change on a street-corner, or a person slumped in a doorway, would you offer help? Helping depends on whether we think help is deserved, and groups typically develop norms that dictate who does and does not deserve help (Caporael & Brewer, 1991). The **norm of social responsibility**, for example, suggests that those able to take care of themselves have a duty and obligation to assist those who cannot: the old, young, sick, helpless, or dependent (Berkowitz, 1972; Berkowitz & Daniels, 1963). Sometimes people who believe that they have more than their fair share give valued resources to others or take less than they could (Nettle, Colléony, & Cockerill, 2011). In close relationships, norms dictate communal sharing of resources with others based on their need (M. S. Clark & Mills, 1979). This norm is also prevalent in cohesive groups. Among the Moose people of West Africa, for example, even the most valuable resources, such as land and water in time of drought, are shared freely with anyone who asks for them (A. P. Fiske, 1991).

Especially in the individualist cultures of the West, deservingness also depends on the attributions we make about controllability. If we think people are in need "through no fault of their own" (that is, due to an uncontrollable cause), we are more motivated to help. If, on the other hand, we perceive people as having "brought it on themselves" (a controllable cause), we think they don't deserve help and we are less likely to offer it (Marjanovic and others, 2009; Weiner, Osborne, & Rudolph, 2011). Thus, helping a person unconscious on the sidewalk seems more appropriate when the victim is ill than when he or she is drunk. Stereotypes of social groups often influence judgments about controllability and deservingness (Fiske, Cuddy, Glick, & Xu, 2002). For example, groups such as the elderly or disabled

norm of social responsibility
a norm that those able to take care of themselves have a duty and obligation to assist those who cannot

The ways we treat others in close relationships, such as by sharing resources with them, are described in Chapter 12.

Photo 14.1 Lending a helping hand. Would you ask this distressed-looking man if he needed any help? If not, is it because you think he might be dangerous, or because he can handle the situation himself? Decisions to help are often based on perceptions of whether the person in trouble needs and deserves help.

people may be stereotyped as unable to help themselves through no fault of their own, and offered help driven by feelings of pity and sympathy. In contrast, groups such as welfare recipients are often stereotyped as intentionally exploiting the system, so people may oppose help for them based on feelings of contempt or anger.

Should I Help?

People sometimes help because social norms, their own standards, or the behavior of others show them that it is appropriate to do so. However, sometimes the presence of other potential helpers can diminish the pressures to help. While some norms work against helping, others dictate that certain people should receive help.

Even when people think that helping is both needed and deserved, action doesn't always follow. Jayna Murray was brutally attacked and killed by a co-worker in a Lululemon Athletica store in a Bethesda, Maryland mall in 2011. Two employees in an adjoining store could clearly hear the attack taking place and the victim crying for help. Yet they did nothing, eventually returning to work without calling the police (Johnson, Nov. 4, 2011). Why didn't the employees help? What could have made them act differently?

Social psychologists began asking these questions following national news reports of a similarly tragic event that took place in Queens, New York, early one March morning in 1964 (Latané & Darley, 1970). Kitty Genovese was attacked by Winston Moseley as she returned to her apartment from her night job. Bleeding from multiple stab wounds, Genovese staggered to a street corner, where she cried out for help. As lights in the surrounding apartments went on, her assailant returned and stabbed her again, this time fatally. Reports at the time claimed that at least 38 people heard her cries for help or saw part of the attack without responding even by phoning the police, and portrayed their inaction as reflecting a shocking level of apathy.

This version of the events persists in most textbooks to this day and certainly was what inspired social psychologists John Darley and Bibb Latané (1968) to begin their groundbreaking program of research on bystander intervention. (In fact, the first paragraph of their article recounts the story of the Genovese murder.) However, recent historical investigation has found significant inaccuracies in the initial reports (Manning, Levine, & Collins, 2007). There were likely fewer than 38 bystanders, most of whom only heard the attack—evidence suggests that only three of them actually saw Moseley and Genovese together. The second and fatal attack took place in a building stairwell, out of view of any witnesses. Most important, some of the bystanders did act: one shouted out the window, driving Moseley away after his first attack, and at least one did call the police, who arrived before Genovese died.

Despite the inaccuracies in media reports, the fact remains that a number of people who potentially could have prevented Genovese's murder failed to do anything. Darley and Latané doubted whether their inaction could be simply attributed to apathy and so were inspired to begin an important program of research.

Is Helping Up to Me? Diffusion of Responsibility. One of the first factors that Darley and Latané (1968) considered as a possible cause of the bystanders' inactivity was, ironically, the fact that so many other onlookers were present. How might this have affected people's decisions about whether they should help? They decided to study this aspect of the helping situation in the laboratory.

Participants in Darley and Latané's study thought they had signed up for a group discussion about problems of college life. Supposedly to guarantee anonymity, each participant was seated alone in an intercom-equipped cubicle. Each person was told that his or her microphone would be activated for 2 minutes at a time, giving each person in turn a chance to talk while the other group members—but not the experimenter—listened. In reality, all of this was stage management. Only one person participated at a time, believing that one, two, or five other group members, represented by audio recordings, were also present.

Then came the emergency. The participant heard one of the other "group members," who had previously mentioned a susceptibility to epilepsy, suddenly begin to have a seizure. Speaking with increasing difficulty, he asked for help and then lapsed into silence. How did people react? As Figure 14.1 shows, the more other people the participants believed to be present, the less likely they were to help and the longer they delayed before seeking aid. Of those who thought that four other potential helpers were present, only 62% ever came to the victim's aid. Don't assume the passive majority didn't care, however. Most were in the grip of anxiety and indecision, caught between behaving inappropriately by helping and behaving inappropriately by not helping.

Darley and Latané concluded that the number of participants in the group made a difference because of the **diffusion of responsibility**: when other people are present, responsibility is divided and each person feels less responsible for helping than when

diffusion of responsibility

the effect of other people present on diminishing each individual's perceived responsibility for helping; one explanation for the bystander effect

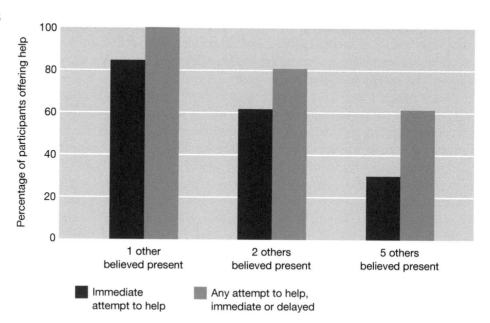

Figure 14.1 Diffusion of responsibility: Lost in the crowd

In this experiment, participants heard another participant having a "seizure" in what they believed was a group of two, three, or six people. (They actually heard recordings of other voices.) The more people participants believed to be present, the less likely the real participants were to help. (Data from Darley & Latané, 1968.)

alone. A massive study conducted in 36 cities across the United States confirmed this conclusion by testing six different types of helping (including helping a blind person with a white cane cross a street and donating to the United Way). Helping was systematically lower in cities with higher population densities, suggesting that diffusion of responsibility also affects helping at the level of communities (R. V. Levine and others, 1994).

Since Darley and Latané's pioneering work, studies involving over 7,700 participants confirm the existence of the **bystander effect**, the finding that the presence of more bystanders consistently decreases the likelihood of any one person giving help (Fischer and others, 2011). Not only the physical presence of others but even the thought of the presence of others can have this effect. One clever study primed the presence of others and examined the effect on donations to charity. Stephen Garcia and his colleagues (Garcia, Weaver, Moskowitz, & Darley, 2002) asked students to imagine winning a dinner in a restaurant for themselves and 30 other people, 10 other people, or one other person. When the students were later asked to make a donation to charity, those who had imagined a larger number of people contributed less money.

There are some circumstances, however, in which people help regardless of how many others are present. For example, when the situation is perceived as dangerous (for example, when someone has been injured by gunfire and the shooter is still at large), the presence of bystanders does not diminish helping very much (Fischer and others, 2011). Shortly, we will describe one possible reason for this pattern.

When Norms Make Helping Inappropriate. Besides the sheer number of other potential helpers, other people's reactions can influence whether any one individual decides to help. No one wants to foolishly rush to help in a case that may not be an emergency after all. In fact, people sometimes fail to act because they fear appearing foolish in front of others (Latané, Nida, & Wilson, 1981). So we usually keep calm and check to see what others present are doing. Perhaps in the example of the stalled car, the fact that the other passerby did not seem concerned would have made you less likely to help. Of course, if everyone else is also keeping calm while they check the reactions of others, everyone will conclude that help is not needed or that norms make helping inappropriate. In one series of studies, experimenters arranged for smoke to pour into a laboratory room in which students were sitting completing questionnaires (Latané & Darley, 1968). When the students were alone, their concern at the unusual situation soon led them to seek help. But when two confederates in the room showed no reaction to the smoke, participants also did nothing. When people notice that bystanders and passersby are unresponsive, that observation reduces the likelihood that they will help (R. E. Smith, Vanderbilt, & Callen, 1973). Thus, one way that the presence of bystanders can influence helping is by suggesting that helping is contrary to norms.

Other norms can make entire categories of people unlikely to receive help. Estimates suggest that in the United States alone, each year as many as 2.3 million women are physically assaulted or raped by a current or former intimate partner, and almost a quarter of women will be victimized by such an assault during her adult life (*The Violence Against Women Act of 2005, Summary of Provisions*. National Network to End Domestic Violence. Retrieved 2011-11-20.). Norms that make intervening socially inappropriate in certain situations contribute to women's victimization. The norm of family privacy, for example, makes people reluctant to intervene when they observe family violence,

bystander effect
the finding that the presence of more bystanders consistently decreases the likelihood of any one person giving help

You may recognize this as a state of pluralistic ignorance, discussed in detail in Chapter 9, pages 336–337.

whether that violence involves a mother angrily slapping her child in a supermarket aisle, a man verbally abusing his wife on the street, or a grown child impatiently shaking an aging or forgetful parent. To demonstrate this point, Lance Shotland and Margaret Straw (1976) staged a physical attack by a man on a woman in front of bystanders. Half the bystanders heard the woman say, "I don't know you!" whereas half heard her say, "I don't know why I ever married you!" Fully 65% of the bystanders tried to prevent the stranger's assault, compared to only 19% who intervened in the husband's attack. Why were people so reluctant to intervene in a family affair? People think wives would be embarrassed and upset by such intervention and that husbands would likely turn on the would-be helper! Perhaps an increased awareness of and sensitivity to spousal abuse and date rape will gradually change norms that currently inhibit intervention in violence among intimates.

> The unwillingness of bystanders to intervene in what they regard as a "family dispute" may contribute to the huge social costs of domestic violence, described in Chapter 12, page 473.

When Norms Make Helping Appropriate. Norms do not always inhibit helping, however. We have already mentioned the norm of social responsibility, which is activated when people are given leadership or other special roles ("If you are seated in the exit row of this aircraft, you must be willing and able to . . ."). This norm increases helping in emergency situations (Baumeister, Chesner, Senders, & Tice, 1988). And if one person rushes to offer help, many more may also do so: The first person serves as a model or example, implicitly defining helping as an appropriate response as we rely on others to help us understand what is happening and what we should do (Bandura, 1977b; Staub, 1978). When one group of researchers sought ways to increase the money contributed to worthy causes, they discovered that indicating that others had found giving to be an appropriate response—"We've already received contributions ranging from a penny up"—doubled the frequency of giving compared to a control condition (Cialdini & Schroeder, 1976). Even video games portraying prosocial behavior constitute models that make game-players more likely to help (Greitemeyer & Osswald, 2010). These findings provide further evidence of the power of social norms: In ambiguous situations, the way that other people act has a big impact on our own behavior.

The importance of norms became even clearer when social psychologists asked why some individuals have strong personal feelings of obligation that lead them to help others in unusual, costly, or dangerous ways (Schwartz, 1977). Why do such people help in situations in which others turn away? They often have been deeply influenced by personal examples, particularly their parents who may teach norms that encourage helping others (Staub, 2002). Studies of heroic helpers, such as committed civil-rights workers in the segregated Southern United States in the 1960s and Gentiles who sheltered Jews from the Nazis during the Third Reich, have found that they often identify strongly with a parent who exemplified norms of concern for others (Oliner & Oliner, 1988; Rosenhan, 1970).

Photo 14.2 The norm of helping. Norms such as social responsibility and reciprocity often play a role in motivating helping behavior. When thousands of people—old and young, healthy and sick—turn out for walkathons to help raise money for charitable causes, the decision to participate is influenced by social norms as well as personal desires.

HOT TOPICS IN SOCIAL PSYCHOLOGY: RELIGION AND PROSOCIAL BEHAVIOR

Since every major world religion teaches some version of "love your neighbor" as a norm, do religious people act more prosocially than others? While you might expect a clear positive answer, the evidence is mixed. In a classic study, Darley and Batson (1973) arranged for participants, who were students preparing for the ministry, to pass someone slumped in an alley, potentially needing help. Measures of the participants' religious beliefs or orientations failed to predict whether they stopped to help. And students who were expecting to give a speech about the Bible's parable of the Good Samaritan—who stopped to help an out-group member when others did not—did not help any more than those planning a speech about an irrelevant topic. All that mattered was whether the participants were in a hurry because they had been told they were late for their speech. On the other hand, recent studies find that priming positive religious words (such as heaven or Christmas) activates prosocial thoughts and leads to more prosocial acts among students at a Catholic university (Pichon and others, 2007). And religious primes cause students to divide money between themselves and an anonymous stranger in a fairer, less selfish way (Shariff & Norenzayan, 2007).

To make sense of such mixed findings, Preston and others (2010) propose that a person's religious orientation involves two separate dimensions. One, termed the religious principle, involves identification with a religious denomination as an in-group. This principle attunes people to the welfare of others beyond the self, but might increase prosocial behavior mainly to in-group others. The second, termed the supernatural principle, involves belief in a God or other supernatural agent that cares whether people do good or evil. This principle orients people toward moral virtue and may increase prosocial behavior more generally. Testing these ideas, these researchers subliminally primed participants with the word "Religion," "God," or a control word. Those primed with "Religion" subsequently cooperated more with an in-group member than those in the other conditions, but the "God" prime led to the most cooperation with an out-group member. Additional supportive evidence comes from a large-scale survey of U.S. residents (Einolf, 2011). Those who reported more daily spiritual experiences, such as a profound sense of caring for others or a feeling of deep inner peace, also reported more volunteering, charitable giving, and other forms of helping. Spiritual experiences were especially strongly related to helping in participants who were not part of a religious congregation. Other research found that feelings of compassion, whether self-reported or experimentally manipulated, increase prosocial behavior, but more strongly for people who report a weaker religious identity (Saslow and others, 2013). These findings are consistent with the ideas of Preston and others (2010). Spiritual experiences and compassion appear more closely tied to the supernatural principle than to the religious principle, and so they should lead to prosocial behavior even among those without a formal religious affiliation.

Does the situation in which you passed the stranded motorist look a little more complicated now? The fact that the driver did not ask for help, and the unconcerned response of the other passerby, may have suggested that help was not appropriate. Yet, with the departure of the other pedestrian, the entire responsibility for providing help fell to you. The elderly driver may not have been able to make even minor repairs himself and might have been afraid to venture out of the car to seek assistance. Would you help or not? As in every social situation, many pieces of information may need to be woven together before an appropriate response can be made.

WHY DO PEOPLE HELP? HELPING AND COOPERATION FOR MASTERY AND CONNECTEDNESS

Decades of research have provided some answers about when and how people will or will not act prosocially. But it is the bigger question that really intrigues social psychologists: Even if others clearly needed help, even if they were deserving, even if norms suggested that help was appropriate, people still would not help unless they were somehow motivated to do so. What are the fundamental motives behind helping and cooperation? Why do we spend time, effort, and money, and sometimes even risk our lives, to benefit others?

Biological Perspectives: Is Prosocial Behavior in Our Genes?

Evolutionary principles suggest that some forms of helping, such as reciprocal helping or helping kin, have been naturally selected because they increase survival of specific genes. In humans, cognitive and social processes mediate such biologically based helping.

One possible answer is that helping, or the lack thereof, is determined by our evolutionary history. From one perspective it would seem that any kind of helping or cooperation that has costs to the helper could not become common in an evolving population. Surely, behaviors that reduce the likelihood that an organism will survive and reproduce, such as sharing food with others or diving into a lake to rescue a drowning child, should be selected against, and individuals with inherited tendencies to do such things would soon vanish from the population. In fact, some evolutionary scientists have argued that evolution has shaped humans, like other animals, to be fundamentally and unalterably selfish (Lorenz, 1966). But more sophisticated modern evolutionary theory holds that selection occurs at the level of the gene and not the organism that bears the gene (W. D. Hamilton, 1964). Some types of prosocial behavior might enhance the likelihood that genes (though not necessarily the individual carrying them) will survive, and therefore these behaviors could be favored by evolution (Barrett, Dunbar, & Lycett, 2002; Nowak, 2006). There are several ways in which helping others could benefit the survival of the helper's genes.

First, helping kin may be like helping oneself. When individuals help relatives who share their genes, the genes have a better chance of survival, even if each individual carrier of them does not (W. D. Hamilton, 1964). For example, female ground squirrels often cry out in alarm when they notice a predator and do so more often if they are living with close kin rather than unrelated animals (P. W. Sherman, 1977). No doubt making an alarm call is riskier than quietly hiding, but if the alarm saves the lives of offspring, brothers, sisters, nieces, and nephews, then the squirrel's genes will survive to the next generation. Like ground squirrels, humans tend to help kin more than non-kin (Kruger, 2003). For example, cross-cultural studies show that grandmothers, aunts, and other relatives are the most likely to adopt a child whose mother dies or is incapable of child rearing (Kurland, 1979). It is possible that our tendency to help emotionally close others originally evolved to encourage us to help kin, because emotional closeness and genetic relatedness often go together (Korchmaros & Kenny, 2001). But we tend to help kin more than non-kin, even when the degree of emotional closeness is the same (Curry, Roberts, & Dunbar, 2013). Such helping clearly illustrates people's general motive to value "me and mine," in this case by helping relatives.

Second, help given to another may be reciprocated at a later time. Reciprocal helping can evolve in species where individuals can remember other individuals who helped them in the past—or failed to do so (Trivers, 1971). Of course, reciprocal helping is common in humans: As we noted in Chapter 10, we often feel compelled to repay favors to those who have helped us. When helping engenders payback helping, those who help may improve their own chance of survival.

Third, entire groups may prosper and flourish when they include cooperative members, perhaps at the expense of groups that include more selfish members (Nowak, 2006). How can this be? People who put their group's interests ahead of their personal interests by, for example, sharing food within the group or defending the group against outsiders, help perpetuate the group's existence (Sober & Wilson, 1999). Even if the cooperative individual perishes in the process, the advantage to the group (which probably includes many members related to the cooperator) may help ensure the survival of genes that promote cooperation.

Fourth, helping or cooperation may ultimately produce more indirect rewards, as others learn of the prosocial behavior and spread the word, creating a positive reputation for the helper within the group (McAndrew, 2002; Nowak, 2006). Takahashi (2000) developed a model of individuals who choose whether or not to help others based on those others' reputations for helpfulness. If individuals help those who have themselves been helpful in the past, even purely selfish agents will end up being helpful because help they provide to others will be rewarded. The reward comes not from the specific recipient (as in reciprocal helping) but from the general population, based on the agent's positive reputation. Consistent with this idea, Beersma and Van Kleef (2011) found that prosocial contributions to a group were higher when they were public, especially when people believed that the group members were likely to gossip, spreading information about each member's reputation. And another study found that the presence of a webcam on the experimental computer, which increased participants' self-awareness, actually led to more helping when more bystanders were believed to be present—reversing the typical bystander effect (van Bommel and others, 2012). Self-awareness in the presence of others presumably activated concerns about norms and about what others would think, that is, about one's reputation.

Thus, current evolutionary psychology supports the idea that evolution can favor prosocial tendencies, even when they are costly or dangerous to the helper. In humans, helping and other types of behavior are not genetically "hard-wired" and inflexible, but are the result of flexible cognitive and emotional processes that guide our behavior in diverse and changing environments (Batson, 1998). Prosocial behavior in humans is likely to be the result of a naturally selected predisposition, or motivation, that can be activated and influenced by social or cognitive processes (M. L. Hoffman, 1981; Korchmaros & Kenny, 2001). Thus, even as we accept the idea that natural selection contributes to human helping and cooperation, this line of thinking returns us to the real question of interest: What motivates people to help? As we will see, the answer involves the same basic motives as all other forms of social behavior: our desires for mastery and concrete rewards, and for connectedness with others.

The norm of reciprocity and its powerful effect on behaviors was reviewed in Chapter 10, pages 364–368.

You may recall that we discussed similar issues regarding the evolutionary basis of aggression in Chapter 13, pages 484–485. Both helping and aggression are motivated by mastery and connectedness.

Helping for Mastery: The Personal Rewards and Costs of Helping

Help may be motivated by perceived rewards or deterred by perceived costs or risks. These rewards and risks can be emotional: People sometimes help to alleviate their own distress at the victim's suffering.

Rewards and Costs of Helping. The desire to help often depends on perceptions of the consequences of helping—on its potential rewards and costs. The upside of helping is its many rewards. One review listed 11 material, social, or personal rewards that could be gained from helping and 9 material, social, or personal punishments that could be avoided by giving help (Batson, 1998). These benefits are often quite concrete: the gratitude of the victim, the cheers of a crowd of onlookers, or the thrill of making the evening news. And just as the evolutionary theorists noted, helping often occurs because we expect to receive reciprocated help at some future date.

But other potential consequences of helping can stop acts of generosity in their tracks. The costs of helping likely explain why, in the study described earlier, students who thought they were a little late for their appointment with the experimenter were less likely to stop and assist an apparently ill confederate than those who thought they had plenty of time. The costs of helping can be many and varied: lost time, effort, embarrassment, money, social disapproval, or physical danger. Even when the need is clear and the victim seems deserving, people may not help if the costs appear too high.

However, specific circumstances can lower the costs of helping. The more helping skills a person has, the lower the costs of helping. People with relevant abilities or training, for example, those with water-rescue or first aid skills, are more likely to offer direct help (Cramer and others, 1988). Perhaps someone with mechanical skills, confident of his or her ability to start a balky engine, would have been more likely to offer help to the stranded motorist we described earlier. Those who are generally high in self-efficacy, the confidence that one's actions are likely to be successful, are also helpful (Graziano & Eisenberg, 1997). Self-efficacy is related to long-term patterns of volunteering as well as to small and short-term forms of help, as Colby and Damon (1992) found in a study of 22 lifelong altruists. The presence of others who have useful helping skills or who are likely to assist also lowers the costs of helping. This explains one exception to the general principle that bystanders reduce helping: People are more likely to help in the presence of bystanders who can offer potential support for a helping action, for example, because they are known to have relevant skills, or when they are a group of friends rather than strangers (Fischer and others, 2011).

The importance of perceived ability to help may explain Alice Eagly and Maureen Crowley's (1986) meta-analysis showing that in studies of bystander intervention in emergencies, men are more likely to help than women. In contrast, women help more within relationships, such as by caring for children or elderly relatives (Eagly, 2009). This is because men perceive themselves as better able to help in the situations typically studied in bystander intervention studies, such as assisting a motorist with a disabled car or carrying someone to safety—tasks requiring technical skills or physical strength. In contrast, women see themselves as more skilled in relationships (Eagly & Crowley, 1986). Thus, perceived abilities influence helping. Of course, the abilities that men and women think they have partially reflect gender stereotypes, roles, and norms, so as those change, so too will men and women's patterns of helping. Interestingly, in real disasters (rather than milder experimentally simulated emergencies) men may not use their skills and strength to help others. In shipwrecks, despite the well-known norm of "women and children first," men are more likely to survive than women, and captains and crew survive at a higher rate than passengers (Elinder & Erixson, 2012).

Although costs and rewards are usually important influences on people's decisions about helping, their effects are not always equally powerful. According to Jack Dovidio and his colleagues (1991), intense emotional arousal makes individuals more likely to intervene regardless of rewards or costs. As we mentioned earlier, Fischer and others (2011) found in their meta-analysis that in clear emergencies or obviously dangerous situations such as a victim having been injured by an attacker who is still present, the negative effect of the number of bystanders on helping was reduced. Presumably this is because emergencies generate higher levels of arousal in potential helpers, motivating them to act regardless of other considerations such as the number of other bystanders.

Emotional Rewards of Helping. Although helping sometimes leads to concrete rewards, more often helping is its own reward: We feel good about ourselves because we helped others. Such internal rewards can be an even more powerful motivator of helping than external ones.

Because helping makes us feel good, people sometimes help to keep their spirits high (Isen, 1970). In one study, for example, participants who were happy because they "happened" to find some money were asked to help the experimenter by reading a series of positive, upbeat or negative, depressing statements (Isen & Simmonds, 1978). Compared to people in a neutral mood, happy participants were more willing to help by reading the positive sentences—and stay in a good mood—but were less willing to read the negative sentences that might make them feel blue. Thus, people who want to stay in a good mood may be particularly prone to good works, but only the kinds of good works that keep them feeling good.

People can also help to escape from a bad mood. Thus, guilty people, like happy people, are often helpful (Nelissen and others, 2007). The most successful donation collector for the entire international network of Save the Children agencies works the pavement Saturdays outside the local supermarket of one of your authors. As every passerby tries to maneuver into the market, he waves the pictures of hungry children and reminds us, quite correctly, that we don't know how lucky we are. The ploy works. In experimental studies of the effects of guilt on helping, researchers have induced participants to break little rules or to tell little lies and then given them the opportunity to make up for their wrongdoing by helping. For example, some students in one study were made to feel guilty because another participant in an experimental game was punished for the participant's own errors. These students allocated more money to the unknown person who would play the next game and also made larger anonymous donations to an anti-AIDS charity (Hooge, Nelissen, Breugelmans, & Zeelenberg, 2011). A clever field study of guilt makes the same point: Roman Catholics were solicited for donations to a worthy cause either on their way into confession or on their way out (M. B. Harris, Benson, & Hall, 1975). It's not hard to guess that those going in gave more than those coming out.

You may recall from Chapter 13, page 490, that feeling bad can also make people commit aggressive acts. Can you think of other cases we have described in which the same inner state can have diverse effects on a person's behavior, depending on the way the person interprets the situation?

Photo 14.3 Guilt and giving. Seeing other people suffer can be unpleasant and doing something to remove that unpleasantness—handing money to someone less fortunate than ourselves, for example—can be as rewarding for the giver as for the recipient.

negative-state relief model

the theory that most people hate to watch others suffer, so the ultimate goal of their help is not to aid the person in need for his or her sake, but to reduce the helper's own distress

Is Helping Pure Egoism? The fact that helping others can make people feel better raises an intriguing question. Might people help simply to maintain their own positive feelings or to relieve their own negative feelings, meaning that helping is self-interested rather than truly altruistic? The **negative-state relief model of helping** answers this question with a solid "Yes" (Schaller & Cialdini, 1988). This theory begins with the assumption that most people hate to watch others suffer. So the ultimate goal of their help is not to aid the person in need for his or her sake but to reduce the helper's own distress. Certainly, the evidence we described above, showing that people feeling guilty may help in an effort to feel better, is consistent with the negative-state relief model. The model also explains why people sometimes choose to walk away rather than help. Putting the victim "out of sight, out of mind" may be the easiest way to reduce distress. In fact, people who know that they will soon have a distracting experience—say, watching a comedy film—tend to be less helpful (Schaller & Cialdini, 1988). Distressed by the sight of starving refugees on a TV news program, will we write a check to a relief agency—or turn quickly to a variety show on another channel?

However, other findings suggest that the negative-state relief model is an incomplete explanation for helping. Although some negative emotions such as guilt do increase helping, others do not. In particular, sad people generally are not helpful people. One reason is that deep depression and profound grief disengage their sufferers from the social world and replace social concern with self-absorption (Carlson & Miller, 1987). If grief

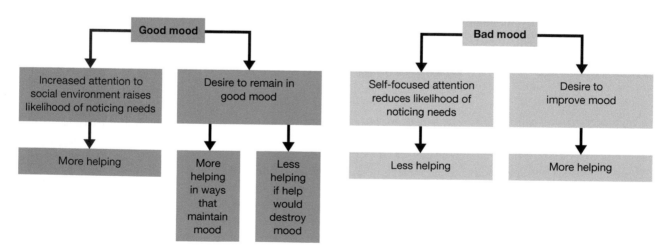

Figure 14.2 Multiple effects of mood on helping
The effects of a positive or a negative mood on helping vary because they occur through several different processes. Both positive and negative moods have the ability to increase or decrease helping, depending on the circumstances.

makes us think only of ourselves, it may keep us from using the warm glow of helping to cheer ourselves up. For this reason, people do not always use helping as a way of relieving their own negative emotional states.

In summary, emotional costs and rewards can influence helping in several different ways. The ways in which positive or negative feelings can either increase or decrease helping are summarized in Figure 14.2. When helping results from personal rewards or costs (either cognitive or emotional), as postulated by the negative-state relief model, helping is motivated by the need for mastery. Does this mean that all helping is ultimately driven by egoism? Are people capable of true altruism, helping another for that person's own sake?

Helping for Connectedness: Empathy and Altruism

People are often motivated by a feeling of empathy to relieve another's suffering, regardless of personal rewards and costs.

"OK, Mr. Altruism, real fast, name three selling points of loyalty that don't involve food."

Daniel Batson and his co-workers have conducted a number of clever studies that attempt to demonstrate the existence of true altruism, helping others not for personal rewards but as an end in itself (Batson, 2002). Imagine that you are a participant who has just arrived in their research laboratory. You learn that a second participant, Elaine, will be receiving mild electric shocks as she performs a task in another room. Your job will be to observe her performance through a window. As you watch, Elaine (who is, of course, actually a confederate) is hooked up to some equipment and the shocks apparently begin. Obviously upset after two shocks, she asks for a glass of water and tells the experimenter that she's been frightened of electricity ever since a childhood accident when a horse threw her into an electric fence. The experimenter hesitates. Perhaps Elaine shouldn't continue. The experiment could be canceled . . . or perhaps you (the real participant) would be willing to trade places with Elaine and take the remaining shocks for her? Would you suffer for someone else?

Batson and his colleagues (1981), who designed this scenario, expected participants' responses to depend on how they reacted emotionally to the woman's plight. Their **empathy-altruism model** suggests that people can experience two types of emotion when they see someone in trouble: personal distress, including alarm, anxiety, and fear, or empathic concern, including sympathy, compassion, and tenderness. Personal distress motivates either egoistic helping—aimed at reducing the observer's own negative feelings—or escape, just as the negative-state relief model predicts. In contrast, feelings of empathic concern lead to altruistic behavior: helping designed to relieve the victim's suffering. When this motive predominates, people will help even if they could easily escape from the situation.

empathy-altruism model
the theory that feelings of empathic concern lead to a motive to help someone in need for his or her own sake

To test these ideas, the researchers manipulated participants' emotional responses to the situation and their ease of escape. To vary empathic concerns, they told half of the participants that Elaine's personal values and interests were very similar to their own, information designed to lead these participants to empathize with Elaine. The other half of the participants were told that she was quite different from them. To vary ease of escape, half of the participants (in the easy escape condition) were told they had to observe only two shocks, so when the experimenter asked them about changing places, the participants knew they could simply leave. The other half of the participants (in the difficult escape condition) were told they had to watch Elaine go through a series of 10 shocks.

The results of the experiment, as Figure 14.3 shows, were consistent with the empathy-altruism model. Participants who were not led to feel empathy acted differently depending on the ease of escape. A high percentage of those who could not escape—who knew they had to watch all 10 shocks—volunteered to take Elaine's place, presumably to avoid the distress of watching her suffer. However, most of their low-empathy peers who could walk out the door took advantage of the escape hatch, leaving Elaine to suffer out of their view. In contrast, participants who empathized with Elaine helped altruistically: Even when escape was easy, most offered to stay and take the shocks for her.

Although not all researchers agree (Maner and others, 2002), a good deal of evidence supports the conclusion that helping can be motivated by a true concern for and identification with the person in need (Batson, 2002; Batson and others, 1991; Batson, Dyck, Brandt, & Batson, 1988; Dovidio, Allen, & Schroeder, 1990; A. P. Fiske, 1991). Studies

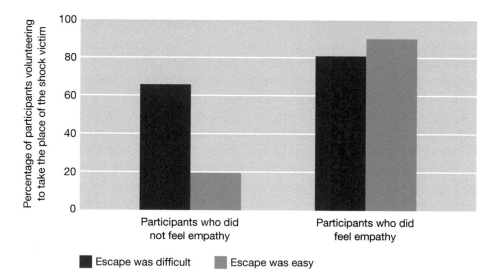

Figure 14.3 Does altruism exist?
For participants who did not empathize with Elaine, helping was a matter of avoiding personal distress. When escape was difficult—when participants could not simply leave the experiment—most volunteered to receive shocks in Elaine's place. But when an easy escape was available, most of the low-empathy participants left Elaine to suffer alone. In contrast, almost all those who empathized with Elaine volunteered to help her, regardless of the ease of escape. Their help must have been motivated by a focus on Elaine's feelings rather than by a desire to reduce their own distress. (Data from Batson and others, 1981.)

show that participants induced to feel empathy with someone in need continue to feel bad if their attempts to help are unsuccessful, even if the lack of success is fully justified (Batson & Weeks, 1996). And people who generally tend to empathize with others and to be concerned for others' welfare naturally tend to be more emotionally moved by others' suffering, and therefore more motivated to help in large as well as small ways (Davis and others, 1999; Goetz, Keltner, & Simon-Thomas, 2010; Penner and others, 1995). Indeed, Oliner and Oliner (1988) found that heroic rescuers of Jews in the Third Reich tended to be more empathetic than others. It even appears that people can be trained to feel more compassionate, actually increasing their altruistic behavior (Weng, and others, 2013).

These findings should not surprise us, however. We already know that when people identify with other people and feel connected to them, they pay attention to those others' outcomes as well as to their own. Even a minimal social connection between two individuals can turn a bystander into a likely helper. One study found that people who had given their name to a researcher, made eye contact with her, or joined her in a trivial conversation, were more likely than total strangers to help her at a later time (Solomon and others, 1981). Another study by Dutch researchers (Van Baaren, Holland, Kawakami, & Van Knippenberg, 2004) showed that when people are mimicked—that is, when their gestures are subtly copied by an interaction partner—they are more likely to help not only the person doing the mimicking, but also other people they may encounter. The researchers explain these results by arguing that being mimicked tends to increase liking, enhance empathy, and facilitate social interactions. Thus, many subtle factors may create a social connection that in turn facilitates helping. As connections grow stronger still, people are even more likely to feel empathy for the other and more likely to help. It is no wonder, then, that people are more likely to help a friend or family member than to help a stranger (Curry & Dunbar, 2013).

When empathy motivates helping, however, it can have a strange effect: By focusing us on a specific individual, it may lead us to ignore the number of people needing help. A depiction of a poor orphan in South Sudan may induce empathy and a willingness to donate to an aid organization, but a depiction of twenty such orphans may produce the same degree of empathy and generosity—or even less! This surprising result has been found in studies showing that people report less compassion and donate less money when they consider multiple victims than when they consider just one (Dunn & Ashton-James, 2008). Fortunately, Christopher Hsee and his colleagues (2013) recently proposed a method to avoid this tendency: they ask donors to indicate an amount that they would hypothetically be willing to donate to one victim, before asking how much they will give to aid all the victims. This technique works. In one study, donors who were asked to help 70 needy individuals donated more than 4 times as much when questioned in this way than when simply asked how much they were willing to give in total.

All these results contradict the notion that helpful actions are motivated simply by mastery motives: the prospect of maximizing personal rewards and minimizing personal costs. Of course, most actions involve multiple motives—a person might offer help while thinking both about the potential benefit for the person in need and also about the prospect of winning status and respect from observers. But this research suggests that true altruism—acting with the goal of benefiting another—is part of the repertoire of human behavior. Such actions depend on, and are often triggered by, a cognitive and

HOT TOPICS IN SOCIAL PSYCHOLOGY: HELPING AND HAPPINESS

We have discussed several ways in which happiness influences helping. But prosocial behavior helps meet basic needs for mastery and connectedness, and having basic needs met usually makes people happy. Is there evidence that helping increases happiness? Elizabeth Dunn and her colleagues (2008) tested this idea by giving participants either $5 or $20 in the morning, instructing them to spend it that day. They were randomly assigned either to spend it on a personal expense or gift for themselves, or on a gift for a friend or a charitable donation. When participants were called at the end of the day and asked how happy they were, those who had spent the money on others were happier. And $5 created just as much happiness as $20.

In this study, perhaps giving a gift to a friend was not purely prosocial; the gift might strengthen the relationship, or the friend might reciprocate in the future. So in another study, Aknin and others (2013) gave participants from Canada and South Africa the opportunity to buy a bag of treats, either for themselves or to be anonymously delivered to a sick child in a local hospital. In this condition, the donor and recipient would not know each other or be able to meet. Still, those who were assigned to buy the gift for others reported greater happiness than those who bought it for themselves.

The effect of prosocial actions on psychological well-being may be universal. Aknin and colleagues (2013) used survey data from over 200,000 people in 136 countries to show that those who reported having donated money to charity within the past month had higher life satisfaction than those who had not, even when household income was controlled for. This was true for respondents from poor as well as from rich countries. The authors conclude that the "warm glow of giving" may be a universal feature of human psychology.

emotional connection with another person. Among the many consequences of such connections is the motivation to increase another person's happiness and welfare regardless of the costs or benefits of such actions for the self.

Mastery and Connectedness in Cooperation

In a social dilemma, rewards for each individual are in direct conflict with what is best for the group. However, people can be motivated by changes in rewards or costs, by trust for other group members, and by feelings of group connectedness, to act for the good of the group. When group identification increases commitment to shared goals and norms, social dilemmas can be successfully resolved.

Cooperation, in contrast to most helping, involves benefiting an entire group of people. To begin considering the issues, imagine a group of roommates sharing an apartment. Each one finds it easier not to bother cleaning up the kitchen after preparing dinner and to leave towels thrown on the bathroom floor after showering. But if all the roommates act in that way, the apartment will become and remain a mess. Or consider residents of a city, who find it convenient to drive to work rather than taking public transportation. But as all make this individually reasonable choice, traffic congestion and air pollution decrease the quality of life for all. When and why will people act cooperatively in situations such as these? As with all types of social behavior, the answers depend on fundamental motives involving both mastery and connectedness.

Social Dilemmas: Self-Interest Versus Group Interest.
Situations such as these offer fascinating insights into the
nature of human helping and cooperation, because individual self-interest is directly opposed to the best interests
of the group. Such situations are **social dilemmas**, in which
failing to cooperate is tempting for each individual group
member because it yields better outcomes for the individual, but all members of the group are better off if they
all cooperate (Van Lange and others, 2013). Often the
temptation of non-cooperation is even greater because
individual rewards are usually immediate, while the group
benefits may be evident only in the long term. For example,
fishermen can catch fish and sell them for immediate profit.
But if all catch as many fish as possible, there will eventually
be no fish left for anyone. This is an example of a resource
depletion dilemma. Individuals benefit personally by harvesting some of the resource. If enough of the resource is
left untouched, it can reproduce and replenish itself, so that
harvesting can continue indefinitely. If too much of the
resource is taken, however, reproduction cannot replenish
the stock, and the resource disappears. A different type of dilemma, a public goods
dilemma, is posed by problems like maintaining unpolluted air, a strong national defense,
or viewer-supported public broadcasting stations. A public good is one that has to be
provided for everybody or nobody; it cannot be given to some and withheld from others.
For this reason "free riders," like those who ride a city bus without paying the fare, are
tempted to use public goods without paying for them. If everyone watches public
television without contributing to its support, public television stations must ultimately
go off the air. Although social life is always characterized by tensions between individual
and group goals, social dilemmas directly pit the individual against the group.

   To study behavior in such situations, social psychologists have recreated them in
the laboratory. In resource depletion dilemmas, for example, groups of participants might
play the roles of fishermen making repeated decisions about whether to take many fish
for personal benefit or to maintain the resource as long as possible (Messick and others,
1983). And in public goods dilemmas, participants are assigned to groups and asked to
contribute money that can earn a bonus for all members of the group, if enough members
of the group contribute, as illustrated in Table 14.1. If too few people decide to contribute,

Photo 14.4 Failing to solve a social dilemma. Individual convenience motivates each person to drive to work, instead of walking,
biking, or taking public transportation. But when everyone drives,
traffic delays as well as air pollution and smog result. When everyone
makes this self-interested choice, there is a cost to the whole group
or society. Here, we see massive air pollution in Beijing. Getting individual people and businesses to act for the good of society as a whole
will be necessary to fix this social dilemma.

social dilemma
a form of interdependence in which
the most rewarding action for each
individual will, if chosen by all
individuals, produce a negative
outcome for the entire group

You may recognize social
loafing, which we
discussed in Chapter 11,
pages 413–416, as a kind
of free riding. In that
case every individual is
probably better off not
expending effort, but
if no one does so, the
group task does not get
accomplished. In the
next few pages you'll see
that many of the
conditions that make
social loafing better or
worse work the same way
for social dilemmas.

TABLE 14.1 Possible Outcomes in an Experimental Social Dilemma

Individual action	Keep $5	Donate $5
Result if most others keep their $5	End up with $5	End up with nothing
Result if most others donate their $5	End up with $15	End up with $10

In this example of a laboratory social dilemma, participants are put in groups of 7 and each given $5.
They individually and anonymously choose whether to keep that money or to contribute it to a public good.
If a majority of group members contribute, everyone (even those who did not contribute) is awarded a $10
bonus. What would you do if you were in this situation?

no bonus is provided and the contributors lose their money (Caporael, Dawes, Orbell, & Van de Kragt, 1989). Although these studies never mimic all the complexities of actual large-scale dilemmas, they can offer insight into the social-psychological processes that come into play.

Mastery Motives in Social Dilemmas: Rewards and Costs. Faced with dilemmas like these, what do people do? Often they quite reasonably, but disastrously, follow their individual interests. Left to their own devices, almost every individual faced with a resource depletion dilemma makes the same decision: to harvest as much as possible, even though the resource is rapidly depleted (Weber, Kopelman, & Messick, 2004). Self-interest usually wins the day in public-goods dilemmas too. For example, only about 50% of participants in one study (Caporael and others, 1989) donated toward the group bonus, so only a few experimental groups collected the bonus. And when groups make repeated decisions in public goods dilemmas, the level of cooperation almost invariably declines over time (Fehr & Schmidt, 1999; Ledyard, 1995).

These behaviors reflect the rewards and costs built into the dilemma itself, so one obvious way to change behavior is to change the rewards and costs that group members face—for example, by rewarding those who cooperate or fining those who do not cooperate. Thus, in the apartment scenario described above, other roommates might punish one who leaves the apartment messy, informally by criticizing him or more formally, by instituting a system of monetary fines.

In larger-scale dilemmas, rewards and fines are most often implemented by centralized authorities (Kerr, 1992). For example, a standard solution to a public-goods dilemma is to levy taxes to pay for provision of the good: If everyone benefits, everyone should pay. In a resource-depletion dilemma, solutions usually involve setting quotas so that users can't deplete the resource. For example, international fishery commissions restrict the number of fish of different species that can be caught every year. Unfortunately, such structural solutions to dilemmas can generate about as many problems as they try to solve. First, they require an authority to impose them. Experimenters can easily set sanctions in laboratory game playing, but who has the accepted authority to regulate use and misuse of the world's atmosphere or the proliferation of biological weapons? Second, people often resist such externally imposed solutions. For example, fishermen often resist the establishment of catch limits intended to allow the regrowth of fish stocks, including prawn fishers in Australia's Gulf of Carpentaria (http://www.abc.net.au/news/2013-08-12/npf-fishers-oppose-prawn-quota-plan/4880832). Third, group members' resistance necessitates a system for monitoring compliance, with no guarantee of successful enforcement (Kameda, Takezawa, & Hastie, 2003; Yamagishi, 1986). Centralized structural solutions do not seem to be the answer for many of our most intractable global dilemmas.

Rewards and punishments can be more effective if they are internally imposed, by the group itself (Balliet, Mulder, & Van Lange, 2011). In a typical study, researchers have group members make their decisions on the dilemma, then all group members learn of everyone's decision and have an opportunity to anonymously reward or punish other individuals. This could be free, with members simply allowed to choose, for example, to "Take away $3 from member D, who did not cooperate." Or giving a reward or punishment could be costly, with members allowed to spend $1 of their own earnings to take away $3 from a non-cooperator. Costly incentives are more effective than free ones, perhaps because they more clearly signal that group members who issue rewards or fines are truly committed to the ideal of cooperation.

Work by the late Nobel Prize-winning political scientist Elinor Ostrom points in the same direction. Ostrom and her colleagues have made worldwide studies of informal arrangements designed to promote cooperation in small-scale social dilemmas (Ostrom, Gardner, & Walker, 2003). For example, a number of farmers with adjacent fields may cooperate to maintain the irrigation ditches on which they all depend, a situation in which each farmer has an incentive to free ride. Ostrom's work shows that the small to moderate size and stable membership of these groups allow both local monitoring (as other members readily find out who is free riding) and informal enforcement. Enforcement is likely to be graduated, beginning with gentle reminders designed mainly to shame the violator, but potentially escalating to stronger economic or physical punishments if the free riding persists. Such systems are organized by the group members themselves rather than being imposed by an outside authority. Local monitoring of others' behavior and informal enforcement operate to sustain cooperation over time.

The benefits of self-organization for cooperation help explain why group size is so crucial for cooperation. On the one hand, free riding is easier in large groups than in small groups because monitoring members' actions is more difficult. On the other hand, larger groups will on average have more resources, some of which they can devote to monitoring and punishing free riders. It is no wonder then that past laboratory research has shown mixed effects of group size. A recent real-world study examined a forest preserve in China that is an important habitat for giant pandas (Yang and others, 2013). The research looked at the effects of group size, defined as the number of families who were responsible for protecting a specific area of forest, for example, by watching out for illegal logging. Findings showed that intermediate group sizes were best. They contributed the most effort to caring for the forest and saw the largest resulting increase in forest health. The largest groups produced more free riding, harming their performance. The smallest groups had little within-group enforcement of norms against free riding. The intermediate-size groups had the overall advantage due to the balance of these opposing trends (Yang and others, 2013).

The Role of Trust. Although internally imposed reward and punishment is effective, the development of norms that support cooperation and mutual trust that others will follow them is even more essential. **Trust**, defined as the expectation that others will act in a prosocial way during a social interaction, is a central factor in determining one's own behavior in dilemmas. Trust increases cooperation, and the more strongly people's interests are in conflict, the more important trust becomes (Balliet & Van Lange, 2012). Trusting that the other will cooperate means that you do not have to worry that the other will exploit your own cooperation. In contrast, thinking that others will follow their own self-interest or actually seeing them do so makes people even more likely to act selfishly themselves (Messick and others, 1983). After all, continuing to sacrifice when others are taking a free ride would make you feel like a sucker. What can be done to increase trust when cooperation is necessary?

One solution is to increase communication among group members. When members of a group are allowed to discuss a dilemma before making their decisions, cooperation increases, especially in face-to-face groups (Balliet, 2010). For example, only 47% of

trust
the expectation that others will act prosocially during a social interaction

SOCIAL PSYCHOLOGY AND CULTURE: CULTURE, TRUST, AND PUNISHMENT

We have just described research showing that the possibility of punishment usually increases cooperation in social dilemmas and that trust likewise increases cooperation. Recent findings show a surprising interplay between these two factors when examined in different cultures. Punishment affects cooperation in quite different ways across cultures. In some countries punishment strongly increases cooperation, but the effect is absent in other countries. A meta-analysis by Balliet and Van Lange (2013) suggests that the reason is cultural differences in the general tendency to trust others. In high-trust cultures such as the Netherlands and Israel, people act according to norms that encourage both cooperation and the punishment of free riders. Even if someone does free ride in such a society, punishment will create guilt and encourage future adherence to the norm. So punishment is highly effective in encouraging cooperation in high-trust societies. In contrast, in low-trust cultures there is no normative support for cooperation, so attempts to punish non-cooperation produce only resentment rather than prosocial behavior. This pattern is found in nations such as Russia, Greece, and Saudi Arabia. In low-trust cultures, in fact, people sometimes use punishment to enforce norms of non-cooperation—by punishing cooperators rather than free riders (Gintis, 2008; Stavrova and others, 2013). Thus cultural norms related to trusting others play an important role in what behaviors will be punished and therefore whether punishment will support or undermine cooperation.

In Chapter 9, we described the processes of consensus formation in a group and the reasons individuals come to accept the group consensus as a norm.

participants in one study donated to a public good when no discussion was permitted, but discussion raised the figure to 84% (Caporael and others, 1989). What did group members talk about? Mostly they worked on forming consensus around a norm for appropriate behavior, defining the meaning of deviance from the norm, and making promises to stick to the norm. Group discussion committed members to promises of cooperation and sharing (Bouas & Komorita, 1996; Kerr & Kaufman-Gilliland, 1993), allowing other members to trust that they would follow through. In fact, even imagining the group discussing and coming to consensus on such issues increases cooperation (Meleady, Hopthrow, & Crisp, 2013).

Cooperation can also be increased by ensuring equal opportunities and outcomes among group members. If all group members use the same amount of a resource, that level of consumption becomes a norm for group members (Messick and others, 1983). Inequality of resource use reduces people's trust that others will act fairly, weakens prosocial norms, and makes people wonder if they are being exploited. Thus, it's not surprising that inequality has a detrimental effect on cooperation (Van Lange and others, 2013). Inequality is a major roadblock to solving current global problems of pollution and resource depletion (Simons, 1992). The poorer nations wonder why environmental considerations should require them to use fewer resources than the already developed nations do. Why should they give up the promise of prosperity when the developed nations literally took the quick and dirty route to wealth?

Connectedness Motives in Social Dilemmas: Social Identification. What could increase trust that others will adhere to group norms, will treat you as well as you treat them, and will look out for the greater good? We hope that you will recognize that identification with the group could help do so. When group belonging becomes uppermost in people's minds, cooperation can be motivated by social identification, promoting the desire to benefit the group as a whole regardless of outcomes for the self. That is, individuals become concerned for "not me or thee but we" (Dawes, Van de Kragt, & Orbell, 1988; Klandersman, 2000; Van Vugt & Hart, 2004). In a classic study illustrating this point, Marilynn Brewer and Roderick Kramer (1986) created a resource depletion dilemma in the laboratory. Students sat in individual cubicles with computers but were led to believe that they were part of either a small 8-member group or a large 32-member group. In addition, some people in each condition were encouraged to develop group identification and some were not. The manipulation was subtle: Participants in the group identification condition were simply told that their payment for experimental participation would be decided for the group as a whole, rather than separately for each individual. Sharing a common fate in this way was enough to change their behavior, significantly lowering the amount of resources participants drew from the common pool.

When individuals identify with groups, three changes usually take place. First, the greater good of the group becomes the top priority (Caporael and others, 1989; Swann and others, 2012). Behaviors like contributing to a common good, which might appear foolish or naive from an individual point of view, instead seem loyal, trustworthy, and generous from the perspective of the group (P. E. Tetlock, 1989). For example, one study found that people who themselves identified and cooperated with a group rated others who also cooperated as more intelligent than noncooperators (Van Lange & Liebrand, 1991).

Second, when the group thinks and works together as one, people are likely to trust that other group members will also be helping, rather than hurting, the group effort. There is no longer any need to worry that others will free ride while you exercise self-control, nor will you take the opportunity to free ride while others act responsibly (Caporael and others, 1989). In fact, when Caporael and her colleagues questioned people who contributed in their experimental groups, these participants said that they thought most others would contribute as well. As we just discussed, trust that others will cooperate is a powerful factor motivating cooperation (Balliet & Van Lange, 2012), and trust is itself increased by shared group identification.

Third, group norms favoring cooperation become salient guides for individual action. Individuals in Caporael's study who thought that most others would contribute must have realized that they could refrain from contributing to the public good, while still collecting the bonus earned by others' contributions! Still, these individuals preferred to follow what they saw as a group norm of contributing rather than to maximize their individual earnings. The norm of commitment can have such a powerful effect that individuals who vow to cooperate during group discussion actually do so (Hopthrow & Hulbert, 2005). They do this even if they know their behavior is unlikely to solve the dilemma effectively (N. L. Kerr & Kaufman-Gilliland, 1993). Even nonconscious priming of cooperative norms can increase people's level of cooperation (Smeesters, Warlop, Van Avermaet, Corneille, & Yzerbyt, 2003).

For all these reasons, shared group identity increases cooperative behavior in social dilemmas. In fact, group identification can even overcome some of the negative consequences of group size. In one study, when group membership was primed, group members were more likely to help in line with the norms and values of the group when the group was said to be large rather than small (Levine, Cassidy, & Jentzsch, 2010). These effects should not surprise you given the many important changes, described in

You may recognize these social identification and norm-based solutions to the problems of large-scale social dilemmas to be very similar to the conditions that help work groups function more smoothly, see Chapter 11.

Chapter 6, that can occur when people identify strongly with a group. Whereas empathy tends to motivate people to benefit a single other individual, as we described earlier in the chapter, group identification can dictate helping all members of any size group. In fact, feeling empathy for a single other member of a group involved in a social dilemma may—just like selfish motivations—damage the outcomes for the group as a whole, by inducing people to allocate more resources to the favored individual (Batson and others, 1995, 1999). Thus empathy seems quite distinct from group identification, which seems necessary to solve social dilemmas. From work and sports teams, communities, and villages, to political parties, ethnic groups, and nations, group identification can be a powerful motivator of helping and cooperation.

social value orientation

stable differences in the ways people act in social dilemmas (such as competitive or prosocial)

Individual Differences in Cooperation. People show stable differences in their **social value orientation**, which affects the ways they act in social dilemmas (Van Lange, 1999). Those with an individualist orientation try to maximize their own outcomes regardless of how others fare, and those with a competitive orientation try to "win" over other players in a dilemma. In contrast to both of these, those with a prosocial orientation seek to maximize outcomes for the group as a whole and also tend to favor equal outcomes (Van Lange and others, 2013). One interesting study shows that priming thoughts about "smart" behavior increases cooperation among people with a prosocial orientation, but makes those with individualist or competitive orientations act more selfishly (Utz, Ouwerkerk, & Van Lange, 2004). In other words, it seems that everyone regards acting consistently with their orientation as just being smart! Social value orientation influences many types of behavior, extending far beyond simple laboratory dilemma situations. For example, prosocials are more willing to donate to charities and to engage in proenvironmental behavior (Joireman and others, 2001; McClintock & Allison, 1989).

Researchers have also examined gender differences, usually expecting to find more cooperation from women because of their greater emphasis on connectedness with others. A meta-analysis of over 50 years of research on social dilemmas showed that, overall, men and women cooperate to the same extent (Balliet, Li, Macfarlan, & Van Vugt, 2011). However, subsets of the studies showed intriguing patterns. In same-sex interactions, men are more cooperative than women; however, in mixed-sex interactions women cooperate more then men. The authors' interpretation of this finding is that gender stereotypes that portray women as cooperative and relationship-oriented are activated more strongly in mixed-sex than in same-sex interactions.

Now that we know who tends to cooperate and why they do so, these insights suggest ways of increasing cooperation. Of course, neither changing group members' rewards and costs through monitoring and punishment of free riders, nor increasing identification with a group to motivate cooperation, is a perfect solution. As we have seen, such efforts to increase cooperation in social dilemmas are not always feasible, and they tend to be more effective in some situations than in others. In addition, as we saw in Chapter 6, identification with one group can often go hand in hand with rejection of other groups. When we think of out-group members as dissimilar from ourselves, we may morally exclude them, placing them outside the scope of norms and moral standards that might encourage helping and cooperation. And despite the promise of group identification for solving global resource dilemmas, the groups involved are often enormous in size, have

Problems in solving social dilemmas	Motivation problems *Individuals seek personal rewards, undermining group benefits.*	Coordination problems *Individuals are unaware of others' choices. Individuals cannot trust others to cooperate.*
Remedies for social dilemmas	Task interdependence solutions: Change incentives for individuals. *Individuals seeking personal rewards now benefit group.*	Social interdependence solutions: Individuals communicate and agree on appropriate actions. *Individuals assume others will cooperate.*
	Social interdependence solutions: Individuals identify with group norms. *Individuals seek to act in ways that benefit the group.*	Social interdependence solutions: Individuals follow group norms. *Norm of commitment keeps individuals cooperating.*
Contribution of group cohesion to cohesion	Individuals adopt group goals as their own.	Group exercises social influence over individuals.

Figure 14.4 Social dilemmas: Problems and remedies
Social dilemmas are situations in which individual goals are opposed to group goals. Conditions that realign individual motivation with the group's good and coordinate individual effort for the good of the group offer the best hope of solving such dilemmas.

little in common, do not communicate, and are notably unequal in resource usage. These factors mean that it is difficult to create the sense of common group membership that may be the best hope of solving such dilemmas.

Nevertheless, as Figure 14.4 shows, feeling themselves to be part of a community can make people act more cooperatively, value group outcomes above individual ones, and forgo self-interest in helping others for the benefit of the group as a whole. The future of our human group may depend on creating and maintaining that shared feeling of belonging.

ROLE OF SUPERFICIAL OR SYSTEMATIC PROCESSING IN HELPING AND COOPERATION

The Impact of Processing

When desires and norms conflict, various factors may be considered superficially or thought through extensively before a decision about helping is made. Emotions can play a role in this process, for strong emotion disrupts extensive processing. When helping is a considered decision, it can result in a long-term commitment. In general, however, quicker decisions tend to be more prosocial than considered ones.

Sometimes it's relatively easy to decide whether or not to help or cooperate, but more often we experience conflict over what to do. We may desperately want to come to the aid of a mugging victim but fear the risks and costs to ourselves. We may want to conserve water by taking shorter showers but fear being made a sucker by those who will free ride on our contributions. The final decision to act or to turn away is influenced by how these various facilitators or inhibitors of helping are processed. Sometimes the decision about whether to help or cooperate has to be made quickly and impulsively. At other times it is the product of extensive processing.

Superficial Processing, Spontaneous Helping. Emergencies are heart-stopping, adrenaline-pumping, sweaty-palm situations. The suffering of others causes anguish, distress, empathy, sadness, and guilt, and these strong emotions can motivate us to action, including helpful action (Penner and others, 2005). However, strong emotions also limit our ability to think things through carefully. In addition, emergencies usually don't allow much time for thought. The combination of arousal, emotions, and split-second timing usually leads people to respond to emergencies quickly and impulsively. When arousal is high and time for reflection is limited, people act on the basis of the most accessible motives or norms. In such cases, onlookers' empathy for those in need or the activation of feelings of social responsibility often outweigh thoughts of discomfort and danger. And as we saw earlier in this chapter, in a clear and dangerous emergency situation, the negative effect of the number of bystanders on helping is reduced (Fischer and others, 2011). In fact, although official emergency workers are usually primary responders to routine events such as vehicle crashes or house fires, in mass casualty events (such as plane crashes or building collapses due to earthquake), bystanders are most often the first responders. Research finds that their quick action is usually highly effective (McNulty, 2012).

When people process superficially, the most readily accessible mental representations will be the most likely to influence behavior. Therefore, priming manipulations that intentionally change the accessibility of thoughts can affect the likelihood of helping. Greitemeyer and Osswald (2010), for example, had participants play prosocially oriented video games, such as Lemmings, in which the player must protect small creatures from dangers and guide them to the exit. Playing such games (compared to neutral games such as the block-stacking game Tetris) activated prosocial thoughts and led to increased helping, such as picking up "accidentally" spilled pencils, volunteering to help with further studies without compensation, and intervening in a staged incident of sexual harassment.

Systematic Processing, Planned Helping. In some circumstances a would-be helper may give careful—even agonized—consideration to the available information. Someone may reflect on the victim's need, then on the possible cost and danger, then on feelings of personal responsibility and ability to help. Extensive thought can even reverse a first, quick reaction. When a Dutch couple with four children were asked to shelter a Jewish infant from the Nazis, they immediately reacted negatively. "This is going too far," they said. "We have given money to support and hide Jews—but we don't need a Jewish kid in the house!" (Oliner & Oliner, 1988, p. 69). Reflection, however, produced a change of heart. By the next morning they had made plans to save the infant: For example, the wife would pretend to be pregnant for a time to allay neighbors' suspicions about the sudden appearance of a new child.

One of the most typical forms of planned helping is volunteering, where people provide voluntary, sustained, and ongoing benefits to others, often for long periods of time (J. Wilson, 2000). Both the initial decision to help and the decision to continue volunteering may result from considerable thought. As we have pointed out many times, decisions based on extensive thought produce long-lasting commitments that are not easily changed. When people repeatedly help others, they come to see themselves as helpful and altruistic, and these self-perceptions reinforce further helping (Grant &

Dutton, 2012). This process explains why people who give blood a few times tend to become regular blood donors, for example (Piliavin and others, 1982). Repeated helping also builds perceptions of self-efficacy, the sense that one's actions are effective and meaningful. Self-efficacy also increases the likelihood that helpful attitudes and norms will be translated into helpful actions (Graziano & Eisenberg, 1997).

Volunteering can be motivated by a number of different goals (Clary and others, 1998; Trudeau & Devlin, 1996). Research has identified six distinct goals, which serve mastery needs (gaining understanding, new knowledge, and skills; obtaining career benefits; helping solve personal problems), connectedness needs (socializing with friends and earning their approval; expressing personal values related to humanitarian concern for others), or self-esteem needs (enhancing self-esteem and personal growth; Clary and others, 1998). These motives include egoistic concerns, for volunteering provides many material, social, and emotional benefits. But many volunteers are also motivated by altruistic concerns for others and the opportunity to do something worthwhile for them. Group identification also motivates helping when volunteers help out of a sense of social responsibility, or in order to create a better society in general or to improve the condition of their group. Some research even suggests that volunteering for other-oriented reasons, rather than selfish ones, brings important health benefits (Konrath, Fuhrel-Forbis, Lou, & Brown, 2012). The decision to volunteer, which often involves extensive thought, may involve more and different motivations than the decision to help in an emergency, where thought is often limited by time pressure and emotional arousal (Penner and others, 2005).

More Helping from Impulse or from Deliberation? By now, you can see how many factors play a role in determining whether helping occurs or not. The decision to help may involve extensive thought, or just a quick snap judgment when cognitive capacity is low, time is short, or emotional arousal is high. Do snap judgments or extensive thought produce more prosocial behavior in general? To answer this question, Rand, Greene,

SOCIAL PSYCHOLOGY IN PRACTICE: HELPING IN ORGANIZATIONS

Employees who "go the extra mile" in the workplace provide another example of cooperative behavior. Researchers have investigated so-called organizational citizenship behaviors (OCBs), which are helpful efforts — like lending a hand to fellow workers faced with an urgent deadline — that go beyond a worker's formal job description (Brief & Weiss, 2002). As with many forms of helping, the question arises: Are helpful employees motivated by the selfish desire to look especially good in the eyes of their bosses, or are they driven by a genuine desire to help? Research by Marcia Finkelstein and Louis Penner (2004) suggests that motives to help co-workers or the organization as a whole are more strongly related to OCB than are motives concerned with creating a good impression. The researchers also found that those who strongly identified as a "citizen" of the organization tended to display higher levels of OCB. Those who chronically experience more empathy with others are also more likely to perform OCBs, especially when they expect to remain with the organization for a long time (Joireman and others, 2006). Thus, the workplace is another arena in which prosocial efforts are often motivated by altruistic concerns for co-workers and for the organization as a whole.

and Nowak (2012) looked at how long players took to make their allocation decisions in a number of social dilemma experiments using both college students in the lab and volunteers using an online system. In these public goods dilemmas, people participate with several anonymous others and choose how much of their own funds to allocate toward earning a group bonus that will be equally shared among all group members. A consistent pattern emerged: Decisions made more quickly tended to be more prosocial. For example, in one study those who made their decisions in 10 seconds or less allocated an average of 65% of their funds toward a public good, compared to only about 50% among those who were slower to respond. In another study, participants were randomly assigned to decide quickly on each trial (in less than 10 seconds) or to deliberate for at least 10 seconds before responding. Again, those under time pressure were more cooperative. All these results suggest that superficial processing resting on people's quick intuitions leads to more prosocial behavior, compared to systematic, deliberative processing. The researchers propose that this pattern arises because most people's general life experiences involve mostly interactions with familiar others, where cooperation is encouraged by rewards, punishments, internalized norms, and concerns for our reputation. Because of these experiences, people's automatic first response is usually to cooperate. Consistent with this idea, the researchers found that faster responses were more cooperative only among participants who report that their interactions in daily life are mostly cooperative; among those who report the opposite, fast and slow responses were about equally cooperative (Rand and others, 2012). Given the cultural differences in general levels of trust and cooperation highlighted earlier in this chapter, we may speculate that people from low-trust cultures might actually show the reverse of the typical pattern, with faster, less deliberative responses being less cooperative than slower, more reasoned responses.

Prosocial behavior is influenced by many different personal and social forces, including perceptions of other people and the situation, activated norms, other people's actions that serve as models, and so on. As this research shows, the way people integrate all these factors to come up with a decision—especially whether they do so with little thought or much deliberation—becomes crucial in determining whether or not helping or cooperation will result.

PROSOCIAL BEHAVIOR IN SOCIETY

Help That Helps; Help That Hurts

Receiving help can have negative as well as positive consequences, especially if recipients cannot reciprocate because of an unequal power relationship between helper and helped, or because receiving help makes them look and feel less competent.

Helpers usually feel good about themselves (Aknin and others, 2013). But how does it feel to receive help? It depends on the recipient's need and on how being helped affects self-esteem. Help that relieves physical suffering or mental anguish—a hot meal on an empty stomach, a safe escort across a busy street, or rescue from a house fire—is always welcome. Help that creates a positive relationship between helper and helped is welcome too. Cooperation builds trust and respect and helpers feel protective and proud of the person they benefited. Those on the receiving end of help and cooperation typically feel gratitude.

However, receiving help is not always positive. First, help can make people feel that they owe a favor and that can be a problem for those who are unable to reciprocate. People who cannot return a favor may resent the help and derogate their helper (J. D. Fisher, Nadler, & Whitcher-Alagner, 1982).

Second, helping can send a mixed message. Though help can convey a positive message of caring, it also implies that the helper is more powerful, more able, or more in control than the recipient. For this reason, receiving help may trigger feelings of gratitude only when the individual who received help feels at least partially in control, responsible for his or her own successful outcomes (Chow & Lowery, 2010). Effects of these opposing messages have been investigated by comparing people's reactions to receiving what are termed dependency-oriented versus autonomy-oriented help, the distinction between "giving a man a fish" versus "teaching him to fish" in the old proverb. Dependency-oriented help provides a solution to the immediate problem, without teaching how to solve future problems. Autonomy-oriented help provides tools or knowledge to solve problems on one's own. Katherina Alvarez and Esther Van Leeuwen (2011) gave students one of these forms of help, supposedly from a peer (another student) or an expert (a professor), while they solved difficult mathematical and logical puzzles. Autonomy-oriented help led recipients to feel more competent and respected overall, because this form of help increases feelings of self-efficacy. But even autonomy-oriented help wasn't completely positive. When it came from a fellow student—but not from a professor—autonomy-oriented help made recipients feel angry and distrustful of the helper, even though they also felt more competent. The researchers believe that peers providing autonomy-oriented help violated expectations, reducing trust and respect. Such results demonstrate that it is not always easy to provide help that elicits only positive reactions and that the most appropriate strategy depends on the situation and the relationships involved.

In Chapter 10, page 370, we described how some people (especially from collectivist cultures) are so sensitive to the norm of reciprocity that they will avoid receiving a favor in the first place.

Photo 14.5 Autonomy-oriented help. Learning how to solve math problems, instead of just being given the answers to the problems, is a form of autonomy-oriented helping. Such help can give students confidence in their abilities to solve future math problems on their own.

Increasing Prosocial Behavior in Society

Helping in society can be increased by making needs clear, teaching and activating helping norms, fostering helpful self-concepts, focusing rather than diffusing responsibility, and promoting connectedness to engender empathy, altruism, and group identification.

For social psychologists, understanding helping and cooperation is more than just a theoretical concern. Helping is essential to group life and social functioning, and insights from multiple lines of research can show us how to increase both the giving of help and our chances of receiving it when we are in need.

1. ***Reduce ambiguity: Make the need for help and cooperation clear.*** If you are injured in a fall, don't rely on the fact that passersby can see that you are bleeding. Make your need obvious—by calling out, for example—to increase your chances of receiving aid (R. D. Clark & Word, 1972). The benefits of making the need for help clear have been demonstrated in studies of why people report crimes (Bickman, 1979; Bickman & Rosenbaum, 1977). Participants in these studies witnessed a staged shoplifting, which an experimental confederate labeled for one group of participants ("Say, look at her. She's shoplifting. She put that in her purse.") while remaining silent with the other group. Participants who had the event interpreted for them were more likely to report the crime than those who did not.

2. ***Increase internal attributions for helping and cooperation.*** If you need your friends to donate blood for a family member who is seriously ill, one way to encourage their generosity is to foster a helpful self-concept, so motivation is internal rather than external (Grant & Dutton, 2012). Daniel Batson and his colleagues have shown that people doing good deeds for their own sake rather than for external rewards are likely to see themselves as genuinely altruistic people and to get hooked on helping (Batson, Fultz, Schoenrade, & Paduano, 1987). In their experiment, the researchers led people to attribute a helpful act either to external factors ("I guess we have no choice") or to their own compassion ("The guy really needed help"). When later asked to help on an unrelated task, more than twice as many of the participants who had labeled themselves as compassionate actually volunteered. Similarly, linking individual efforts to the outcome of the group allows people a sense of self-efficacy, making it more likely that they will act on the group's behalf again.

3. ***Teach norms that support helping and cooperation.*** Families and schools can reinforce norms supporting social responsibility and prosocial behavior both by explicit teaching and by personal examples or models (Choi, Johnson, & Johnson, 2011). Research on the impact of the media on behavior confirms that seeing promotes doing (Greitemeyer, 2011).

4. ***Activate prosocial norms.*** Social norms that support helping have to be brought to mind before they can guide behavior. In an emergency situation, directions like, "That small child needs help" or "That elderly man needs a coat over him" can activate norms of social responsibility to the old, young, and weak. In one condition of Bickman's crime-reporting study, the observer commented: "We saw the shoplifting. We should report it. It's our responsibility." Activating the norm boosted reporting of the incident to store management (Bickman, 1979; Bickman & Rosenbaum, 1977). And a recent study found that having the ability to "fly" in a virtual reality computer game (compared to virtually riding in a helicopter) increased children's prosocial behavior. The researchers believe that flying activated norms and behaviors associated with well-known superheroes such as Superman (Rosenberg, Baughman, & Bailenson, 2013).

5. ***Infuse, don't diffuse, responsibility.*** Directions that activate norms are not particularly useful if they are broadcast to the world at large, because diffusing responsibility among many people lessens each one's feelings of obligation to help. Focusing

responsibility on specific people makes normative pressures to help more insistent. To get help, therefore, make it clear whom you want help from (Moriarty, 1975). If you are lying bleeding in the street, don't just shout, "Help me!"—such a general request might allow most people to convince themselves that someone else will do so. Focus on a particular individual and specifically ask that person to help: "You there, in the red jacket! Help me now!"

6. *Promote identification with those who need help and cooperation.* No matter what the need—emergency or long term—a feeling of connectedness with the person in need breeds empathy and increases willingness to help. This principle—that we help others to whom we are connected as if we were helping ourselves—works with kin, friends, and in-groups. Connectedness is what motivates helping even if no personal rewards are involved. Weng and others (2013) demonstrated that training people to feel compassion for individual others produced increases in helping behavior. Perhaps interventions of this sort, applied to children or adults, might help people expand the number of others they are willing to help or cooperate with.

The diversity of these recommendations reflects the large number of factors that can influence prosocial behavior, but the diversity should come as no real surprise. Helping is a microcosm of human behavior: a series of judgments influenced by what we see and who we are, by our groups and our norms, by what we think and how we feel, until judgment culminates in action.

HOT TOPICS IN SOCIAL PSYCHOLOGY: GLOBAL-SCALE SOCIAL DILEMMAS REQUIRE GLOBAL COOPERATION

We are used to thinking about helping and cooperating among those who meet face to face or interact on the street, on the job, in families, or in communities. We ordinarily don't reflect on the fact that almost every aspect of our lives, even our long-term survival, also depends on actions of others we never see. The rapid destruction of the global environment is less a failure of technology than a failure to solve large-scale social dilemmas. Because humans are producing unprecedented amounts of carbon dioxide and other greenhouse gases, the composition of the atmosphere is changing, leading geoscientists virtually unanimously to predict massive global climate changes over the coming centuries. Can the processes outlined in this chapter also contribute to cooperation in global-scale dilemmas such as this one?

We know that identification with others may contribute to cooperation, but are there people who identify with others on a global scale? To find out, researchers have asked questions such as: "When they are in need, how much do you want to help (a) people in my community, (b) Americans [or the participant's own country], (c) people all over the world?" (McFarland, Webb, & Brown, 2012, p. 833). Those who give the (c) response across several such questions report more concern for global human rights and humanitarian needs (McFarland and others, 2012) and are more willing to contribute to a global-level (not just local) public good (Buchan and others, 2011). For very large groups where monitoring, communication, and other facilitators of cooperation in small groups are impossible, cooperation based on identification is key.

■ ■ ■

■■■

Global dilemmas such as climate change also have a temporal dimension. Solutions to this dilemma must involve people currently alive sacrificing some material wealth and convenience to limit greenhouse gas production, to limit devastating climate effects for generations yet unborn. Can people be motivated to sacrifice for nameless, faceless future others? At first glance the prospects seem slim. The current generation has total power over these decisions; future generations have no say in the health of the planet they will be born into. The current generation will depart over time, so they cannot expect any reciprocation from future generations. Yet Kimberly Wade-Benzoni and Leigh Tost (2009) believe that people can still be motivated to sacrifice for future generations. First, absolute power creates strong feelings of social responsibility which may motivate prosocial behavior. Second, reciprocity in the usual sense cannot apply between generations, but more generally, reciprocity simply means treating others as you would like to be treated. Thus, people can reflect that they themselves inherited a beautiful, habitable planet and resolve to "pay it forward," leaving future generations the same. Third, thoughts about the reality of death often drive people to seek symbolic immortality (Greenberg, Pyszczynski, & Solomon, 1986). Improving the situation of people in the future can be considered as a meaningful legacy that serves this function. Finally, Wade-Benzoni and Tost (2009) describe feelings of "affinity," a combination of empathy, perspective taking, and perceived oneness with future generations, somewhat parallel to identification with all humanity as just described. Affinity makes people feel outcomes for future generations as immediate and personal, motivating prosocial behavior (Wade-Benzoni, 2008).

Today we all have to learn to identify with larger groups so that our motives and abilities to benefit others extend beyond the local sphere. Our current state of global interdependence is historically recent, and our sense of common purpose has not yet caught up to this situation. We have yet to learn that our choices to help and cooperate—as individuals and as nations—have implications beyond our private well-being and our group and national interests.

CONCLUDING COMMENTS

When people provide help and benefits to other people, their activities inevitably reflect the same social and cognitive processes that you have seen exemplified in every other chapter of this book. Whether we deliver aid in an emergency situation or remain on the sidelines, whether we make charitable and philanthropic activities part of our lives or go about our own daily business depends vitally on our construction of reality. How we interpret cues and signs that help is needed, and how others around us interpret those signals, work together to determine whether helping seems appropriate and achievable. Going out of our way to benefit others fulfills our fundamental need to be connected to others, but because it can bring a variety of rewards in return, it also makes us feel more competence and mastery of our environment. Research has often focused on the kinds of helping decisions that need to be made on the basis of rapid and superficial processing. Perhaps, though, the kinds of helping that make an enduring difference to communities are more likely to result from long-term, extensive weighing of the pros and cons of getting involved.

Because helping and cooperation reflect the same principles as all other types of social behavior, we must interpret with caution statements that self-sacrifice is the essence of what it means to be a social being. In fact, we hope that as you've read this chapter

TABLE 14.2 Parallels Between Prosocial and Aggressive Behavior

Parallel in:	Prosocial Behavior	Aggressive Behavior
Construction of reality	Many (sometimes conflicting) pieces of information (cues, attitudes, norms) influence whether helping occurs.	Many (sometimes conflicting) pieces of information (cues, attitudes, norms) influence whether aggression occurs.
Pervasive social influence	When situations are ambiguous, people sometimes look to others to see if helping is appropriate.	When situations are ambiguous, people sometimes look to others to see if aggression is appropriate.
	Norms—like the norm of reciprocity or the norm of "minding your own business"—can encourage or discourage helping.	Norms—like the norm of reciprocity or the norm "pick on someone your own size"—can encourage or discourage aggression.
Motivational principles	People sometimes help others purely for the rewards it brings them.	Instrumental aggression and realistic conflict often occur as people strive for rewards.
	Because of connectedness needs, people often help others with whom they empathize or identify without regard to the costs involved.	When connectedness or respect is threatened, hostile aggression and intergroup conflict occur without regard to the costs involved.
	Empathy and identification are more likely when the person needing help is an in-group rather than an out-group member.	Aggression and competition over positive identity are more likely when the provokers are out-group rather than in-group members.
Processing principles	Information relevant to helping can be dealt with superficially or in great depth.	Information relevant to aggression and conflict can be dealt with superficially or considered in great depth.
	Factors that limit systematic processing—emotion or time constraints—make only the most salient cues likely to be used.	Factors that limit systematic thinking—emotion, alcohol, distracting stressors—increase the influence of salient cues.
	Systematic processing sometimes increases prosocial behavior by increasing the impact of multiple pieces of information like accurate interpretation of need, empathy, and prosocial norms. At other times, people's immediate decisions, based on their immediate impulses, are more cooperative than more considered decisions.	Systematic thinking often decreases aggression by increasing the impact of multiple pieces of information like accurate interpretation of provocation, nonaggressive norms, or alternative solutions, and by decreasing anger. At other times, aggression can emerge as a result of thoughtful consideration rather than immediate impulse.

the many parallels between our propensity to help and our propensity to hurt, discussed in the previous chapter, have struck you. Examine Table 14.2 to see many of these parallels for yourself.

Seeing the connections between helping and cooperation and other forms of social behavior also makes it clear that prosocial behavior is not alone in having moral implications. Almost all aspects of social behavior involve issues of right and wrong, including how people handle conflicts in close relationships (Chapter 12), whether they obey or disobey destructive authorities (Chapter 10), whether they stand up for their own views or go along with the majority in the case of groupthink (Chapter 9), and whether they let their own group's self-interest dictate unjust treatment of others (Chapter 6), to mention just some examples. At the heart of all these different behaviors lie the issues of responsibility and choice, which often involve difficult balances between serving one's own and others' interests.

CHAPTER 14 THEMES

■ **Construction of Reality**
Interpretations of others' situations, not their actual needs, influence helping and cooperation.

■ **Pervasiveness of Social Influence**
Helping and cooperation are fundamentally shaped by social norms.

■ **Striving for Mastery**
Helping and cooperation are often motivated by the prospect of concrete rewards for the helper.

■ **Seeking Connectedness**
Helping and cooperation often flow from feelings of identification and connectedness with others.

■ **Valuing Me and Mine**
We are likely to treat fellow in-group members with cooperation and altruism.

■ **Accessibility**
The accessibility of norms can increase their impact on helping.

■ **Superficiality versus Depth**
In-depth processing can promote long-term, committed helping.

SUMMARY

When Do People Help? **Prosocial behavior**, behavior intended to help another person or group, can take different forms. Helping involves giving aid to a specific person or persons. In contrast, **cooperation** involves two or more people acting together in an attempt to benefit all involved. Prosocial behavior may reflect different underlying motives. **Altruism** is helping motivated by the desire to benefit others for their own sake, while helping driven by personal rewards to the helper is termed **egoism**. Offering help is crucially dependent on people's perception of someone as both needing and deserving help. The ability and motivation to pay attention to others' needs influence whether people think help is needed. People are more likely to help those they see as deserving because they are not responsible for their own need.

People sometimes help because social norms or the behavior of others show them that it is appropriate to do so. However, the presence of other potential helpers can make each individual less likely to help, termed the **bystander effect**. One reason for this effect is **diffusion of responsibility**, where the presence of others diminishes each individual's sense that he or she is required to help. While some norms work against helping, others such as the **norm of social responsibility** dictate that certain people should receive help.

Why Do People Help? Helping and Cooperation for Mastery and Connectedness. Evolutionary principles suggest that some forms of helping, such as reciprocal helping or helping kin, have been naturally selected because they increase survival. In humans, however, cognitive and social processes mediate such biologically based helping.

Help may be motivated by perceived rewards for the helper or deterred by perceived costs or risks. These rewards and risks can be emotional: People sometimes help to alleviate their own distress at the victim's suffering. In these cases helping is motivated by egoism, as described by the **negative-state relief model**.

People are often motivated by a feeling of empathy to relieve another's suffering, regardless of personal rewards and costs. This helping is consistent with the **empathy-altruism model**, because it is not motivated by even indirect or emotional rewards for the helper.

In a **social dilemma**, rewards for each individual are in direct conflict with what is best for the group. However, people can be motivated to cooperate by feelings of group connectedness or by **trust** for other group members, regardless of personal costs or benefits. Individuals' **social value orientations** influence the ways they think about and act in social dilemmas. When group identification increases commitment to shared goals and norms, social dilemmas can be successfully resolved.

Role of Superficial or Systematic Processing in Helping and Cooperation. When desires and norms conflict, various factors may be considered superficially or thought through extensively before a decision about helping is made. Emotions can play a role in this process, for strong emotion disrupts extensive processing. When helping is a considered decision, it can result in a long-term commitment. In some cases, however, quicker decisions tend to be more prosocial than considered ones.

Prosocial Behavior in Society. Receiving help can have negative as well as positive consequences, especially if recipients cannot reciprocate because of an unequal power relationship between helper and helped or because receiving help makes them look and feel less competent.

Helping in society can be increased by making needs clear, teaching and activating helping norms, fostering helpful self-concepts, focusing rather than diffusing responsibility, and promoting connectedness to engender empathy, altruism, and group identification.

EPILOGUE

Now that we are at the end of our journey, we hope you have come to appreciate the incredible diversity of exciting ideas and findings that make up social psychology. These are what have kept your three authors coming into our laboratories every day for several decades now, and every day we learn once again how intriguing, compelling, sometimes frustrating, but often downright satisfying the study of social behavior can be. We also hope that you noticed a few key ideas coming up again and again as we described such diverse topics as impression formation, intergroup conflict, close relationships, and attitude change. In fact, just as a limited number of chemical elements can be combined to form millions of different substances, so a set of basic principles can be seen to underlie all social behavior. It is this orderliness underlying diversity that makes social psychology a unified field instead of a random collection of interesting topics.

CORE PRINCIPLES OF SOCIAL PSYCHOLOGY

The principles we highlighted throughout this text are those we see as most important for understanding the findings and theories of social psychology. Let's take a final look at how we can use these eight principles to help understand the wide range of social behavior we encounter in everyday life.

- ■ Whether we are alone or with others, we **construct social reality** as we form impressions of other people and groups (Chapters 3 and 5) and as we act in ways that reflect our own attitudes and group norms (Chapters 8 and 10). This is why we so often react to unexpected, unusual, or ambiguous events by immediately turning to others and asking, "Do you smell gas?" or "Was that an earthquake?" or "So what have *you* heard about Bill?"
- ■ The **pervasive effects of social influence** are evident when we conform to the opinions of important groups (Chapter 9) and cooperate or compete with others (Chapters 13 and 14). Next time you find yourself caught up in the latest clothing fad, realize

that you just said something your dad always used to say, or feel uncomfortable about expressing your political views, remind yourself of the power and pervasiveness of social influence.

■ Our *strivings for mastery* explain why we want to form accurate opinions and attitudes about ourselves and others (Chapters 4 and 7) and why we are capable of helping or harming others in order to gain rewards (Chapters 13 and 14). This principle offers insights into why we work so hard to find out what instructors want in test answers, why group efforts can be more successful than any one person's efforts (Chapter 11), and why we spend so much time trying to learn who we really are.

■ We *seek connectedness with others* when we conform to group norms (Chapters 9 to 11) and when we form close relationships with others (Chapter 12). This principle explains why many people feel empty and incomplete when they lack intimate relationships, why the support of a good friend seems to make daily hassles as well as big crises easier to cope with, and why our memberships in groups and our relationships with others are some of the most important aspects of human life.

■ Our desire to *value me and mine* is evident in our efforts to feel good about ourselves as individuals and as members of groups (Chapters 4 and 6). It also helps explain why we act against out-group members while often behaving with kindness and altruism toward members of the in-group (Chapters 13 and 14). Perhaps understanding the me and mine principle will alert you to the moments when your group puts others down just to make yourselves feel better. It may also help explain why news of an earthquake in a nearby state elicits more donations than news of a similar tragedy in some distant place.

■ The processing principle of *accessibility* is responsible for our using easily grasped information to form our impressions of other people and our attitudes (Chapters 3 and 7) and for the times we find ourselves conforming to accessible norms (Chapters 6 and 10). After staring blankly at the rows of breakfast cereal in the supermarket, have you ever just grabbed the first one you could remember hearing about? Have you ever realized that you'd felt compelled to exchange gifts with someone you don't really like? Accessibility may have been at work.

■ The principle of *conservatism* accounts for the persistence of first impressions, well established attitudes, and stereotypes (Chapters 3, 5, and 7) and also for the difficulties minorities experience in swaying a majority's opinion (Chapter 9). If conservatism were not such a powerful influence on our thinking, advertisers wouldn't have to spend so much money trying to persuade us, and friends wouldn't have to work so hard to change our mistaken snap judgments.

■ Finally, the principle of *superficial versus extensive processing* operates when we decide how much thought to devote to understanding a member of a stereotyped group (Chapter 5), being persuaded by an ad or an appeal (Chapter 7), or to acting in accordance with our attitudes (Chapter 8). This principle helps explain why we often make snap judgments when the stakes are low but give considerable thought to matters of importance.

Of course, these are just a few examples of the principles at work, and as you review or reread the chapters, you will think of others. We hope these principles will help you take a fresh look at events in your own lives. Perhaps you now see why making a good first impression at a job interview is important (conservatism), why you feel so good when your favorite team wins (me and mine), or why the whole world looks bleak when you're feeling low (accessibility). You may be better able to understand why people care so much about the majority point of view (connectedness) but also how the majority's opinion can sometimes be changed by minority dissent (systematic processing). If these ideas help you make sense of the world in which you live, our goals for this book have been achieved.

HOW THE PRINCIPLES INTERRELATE

Although we have described the eight principles separately so that you can see how they operate, we do not mean to suggest that they are unrelated to each other. They operate together, usually in a harmonious fashion.

Part of the reason we construct reality, for example, is because we want to master the environment, and part of the reason we influence others and accept social influence is because we seek connectedness. Social influence is important because we want to construct an appropriate and correct reality, and we need other people to do so. Accessibility helps us make judgments quickly and efficiently, which in turn helps us to master the environment we construct. It also means that we pay most attention to those closest to us, which helps us achieve connectedness and makes possible the give and take of social influence. The principle of conservatism, on the other hand, helps us maintain a stable view of the world—how would we be able to master the environment or form relationships with others if our views of them changed from minute to minute? Superficial versus systematic processing is the moderating principle, the fulcrum that keeps us balanced between the stability of conservatism and the flux of accessibility. For example, receiving unexpected or inconsistent information from those connected to us makes us think hard, opening the way for change.

Although the principles usually operate together to produce positive outcomes, they sometimes can result in conflicts and paradoxes. For example, the short cuts we use to make inferences are often efficient routes to the right answer, but they sometimes lead us astray (Chapter 3). Relying on social consensus often helps people master the environment and achieve connectedness, but it also can lead to mindless acceptance of a dangerous status quo (Chapter 9). Thus, depending on the circumstances, the same motives and processes produce useful and valuable outcomes or misleading and destructive ones. In fact, almost every aspect of social behavior has an up side and a down side, whether that behavior is adherence to norms like obedience and reciprocity (Chapter 10) or the biased thinking we use to elevate our self-esteem, sometimes by disparaging other people and groups (Chapters 4 and 6).

These examples of ways in which the principles work with and against one another are not a complete list. We hope you have found other meaningful interrelationships that link different types and forms of social behavior.

AN INVITATION TO SOCIAL PSYCHOLOGY

When you first picked up this textbook, you probably expected it to tell you how much social psychologists know. Were you surprised to discover how many things we *don't* know? Our understanding of social behavior still has many gaping holes and many unresolved issues because research in social psychology, like research in all fields of human knowledge, has been shaped by its historical development and social context. In the late 1800s, when researchers were just beginning to ask social-psychological questions, nobody could have written down the list of principles we just presented or used them to guide research. (Correspondingly, 20 years from now, the set of principles that social psychologists think are most important may have changed again.) Instead, as we have said, specific events have inspired and guided researchers' questions. The most important events for North American social psychology were the Nazi domination of Europe and the Second World War, which gave rise to research areas involving persuasion, prejudice, obedience to authority, and conformity.

As research traditions grew up around socially significant and culturally relevant issues, other areas were relatively neglected. For instance, the social effects of drug use, heterogeneity in the workforce, and variations in family composition were not widespread enough to gain scientists' attention 50 years ago, but they certainly are today. Many important issues involving group identification, kin and friend relationships, and social stability and change have been neglected, perhaps because so much social-psychological research to date has been done in the individually oriented United States. As social psychology becomes a global enterprise, questions of more concern to non-Western societies may come to the fore. For example, the effects of social change are of particular importance to social psychologists in developing countries, who underscore that social psychology should be even more active as a positive force in bringing about and guiding such change. And though much is known about how people form and change attitudes on the basis of information, much less is known about the impact of values, ethics, and religious convictions on people's social behavior. These are just a few of the many areas in which social psychology needs to grow and develop.

We mention these gaps in knowledge and opportunities for development because we want you to understand that social psychology is a young science. One unfortunate characteristic that is almost inherent in the nature of textbooks is that they convey the impression that everything worth learning has already been learned: that all the *i*s have been dotted, all the *t*s have been crossed, and everyone agrees about everything. How boring social psychology would be if this were true. But it is not true; social psychologists are well aware of how much we still need to know about human social behavior. We guarantee that as you read these words, whatever the day or time, social psychologists somewhere—in their offices, laboratories, schools, businesses, hospitals, or out on the streets—are planning or carrying out research or reporting new findings. If that idea appeals to you and if you find yourself interested in the topics and issues social psychologists study, we invite you to consider becoming a social psychologist. You could help to shape the future of our science and contribute to what we know about the endlessly fascinating forms of human social behavior.

PHOTO AND CARTOON CREDITS

GLOSSARY

Accessibility. The ease and speed with which information comes to mind and is used.

Accessibility principle. The processing principle that the information that is most readily available generally has the most impact on thoughts, feelings, and behavior.

Accommodation. The processes of responding to a negative action by the partner.

Actor–observer effect. The idea that we attribute our own behaviors to situational causes while seeing others' acts as due to their inner characteristics.

Aggression. Behavior intended to harm someone else.

Altruism. Behavior intended to help someone else without any prospect of personal rewards for the helper.

Ambivalent attitude. An attitude based on conflicting negative and positive information.

Appraisal. An individual's interpretation of a self-relevant event or situation that directs emotional responses and behavior.

Archival measures. Those based on examining traces of past behavior.

Assimilation effect. An effect of a comparison standard or prime that makes the perceiver's judgment more similar to the standard.

Association. A link between two or more mental representations.

Attachment styles. People's basic securely attached, avoidant, or anxious orientation toward others in close relationships.

Attitude. A mental representation that summarizes an individual's evaluation of a particular person, group, thing, action, or idea.

Attitude change. The process by which attitudes form and change by the association of positive or negative information with the attitude object.

Authoritarian personality. Based on Freudian ideas, people who are prejudiced because they cannot accept their own hostility, believe uncritically in the legitimacy of authority, and see their own inadequacies in others.

Automatic. Refers to processes that operate spontaneously (without the perceiver's deliberate intent) and often efficiently and without awareness.

BIRG (Bask In Reflected Glory). A way of boosting self-esteem by identifying oneself with the accomplishments or good qualities of fellow in-group members.

Bystander effect. The finding that the presence of more bystanders consistently decreases the likelihood of any one person giving help.

Causal attribution. A judgment about the cause of a behavior or other event.

Classical conditioning. A form of learning in which a previously neutral stimulus, when paired with a stimulus that elicits an emotion or other response, itself comes to generate that response.

Close relationship. A relationship involving strong and frequent interdependence in many domains of life.

Coalition formation. When two or more parties pool their resources to obtain a mutual goal they probably could not achieve alone.

Cognitive dissonance. An unpleasant state caused by people's awareness of inconsistency among important beliefs, attitudes, or actions.

Cognitive processes. The ways in which our memories, perceptions, thoughts, emotions, and motives influence our understanding of the world and guide our actions

Collectivist cultures. Those in which people tend to think of themselves as linked to others, and to define themselves in terms of their relationships to others.

Commitment. The combined forces that hold the partners together in an enduring relationship.

Communal relationship. A relationship in which people reward their partner out of direct concern and to show caring.

Confederate. A research assistant playing a specific role in the study such as pretending to be just another participant.

Conflict. A perceived incompatibility of goals between two or more parties.

Conformity. The convergence of individuals' thoughts, feelings, or behavior toward a social norm.

Conservatism principle. The processing principle that individuals' and groups' views of the world are slow to change and prone to perpetuate themselves.

Construct validity. The extent to which the independent and dependent variables used in research correspond to the theoretical constructs under investigation.

Construction of reality. The axiom that each person's view of reality is a construction, shaped both by cognitive processes (the ways our minds work) and by social processes (input from others either actually present or imagined).

Constructs. Abstract and general concepts that are used in theories and that are not directly observable.

Contact hypothesis. The theory that certain types of direct contact between members of hostile groups will reduce stereotyping and prejudice.

Contingency theories of leadership. Theories holding that leader behaviors can differ and that different behaviors are most effective in specific leadership situations.

Contrast effect. An effect of a comparison standard or prime that makes the perceiver's judgment more different from the standard.

Cooperation. Two or more people working together toward a common goal that will benefit all involved.

Correspondence bias. The tendency to infer an actor's personal characteristics from observed behaviors, even when the inference is unjustified because other possible causes of the behavior exist.

Correspondent inference. The process of characterizing someone as having a personality trait that corresponds to his or her observed behavior.

Debriefing. Informing research participants—as soon as possible after the completion of their participation in research—about the purposes, procedures, and scientific value of the study, and discussing any questions participants may have.

Deception. Keeping participants uninformed or actively misleading them about particular aspects of a study.

Deindividuation. The psychological state in which group or social identity completely dominates personal or individual identity so that group norms become maximally accessible.

Demand characteristics. Cues in a research setting that lead participants to make inferences about what researchers expect or desire and that therefore bias how the participants act.

Dependent variable. A concrete measurement of a construct that is thought to be an effect of other constructs

Descriptive social norms. Agreed-upon mental representations of what a group of people think, feel, or do.

Diffusion of responsibility. The effect of other people present on diminishing each individual's perceived responsibility for helping; one explanation for the bystander effect.

Discounting. Reducing a belief in one potential cause of behavior because there is another viable cause.

Discrimination. Any positive or negative behavior directed toward a social group and its members.

Door-in-the-face technique. A technique in which the influencer makes an initial request so large that it will be rejected, and follows it with a smaller request that looks like a concession, making it more likely that the other person will concede in turn.

EEG (electro-encephalographic) measures. Measures that use electrical signals on the scalp to very accurately detect the times at which specific neural events occur.

Effort Justification effect. Attitude change that occurs to reduce the dissonance caused by freely choosing to exert considerable effort or suffering to achieve a goal.

Egoism. Behavior motivated by the desire to obtain personal rewards.

Elaboration. The generation of favorable or unfavorable reactions to the content of a persuasive appeal.

Elaboration Likelihood Model (ELM). A model of persuasion that claims that attitude change occurs through either a peripheral route or a central route that involves elaboration, and that the extent of elaboration depends on motivation and capacity.

Emotion-focused coping. Dealing with the negative emotions aroused by threats or stressors, often by suppressing emotions or distraction.

Empathy-altruism model. The theory that feelings of empathic concern lead to a motive to help someone in need for his or her own sake.

Evaluative conditioning. The process by which positive or negative attitudes are formed or changed by association with other positively or negatively valued objects.

Exchange relationship. A relationship in which people offer rewards in order to receive benefits in return.

Experimental research design. A research design in which researchers randomly assign participants to different groups and manipulate one or more independent variables.

Explicit attitude. The attitude that people openly and deliberately express about an attitude object in self-report or by behavior.

External validity. The extent to which research results can be generalized to other appropriate people, times, and settings.

False consensus effect. The tendency to overestimate others' agreement with one's own opinions, characteristics, and behaviors.

Field research. Research that takes place outside the laboratory.

fMRI (functional magnetic resonance imaging). Indirectly measures the activation levels of specific brain regions.

Foot-in-the-door technique. A technique for increasing compliance with a large request by first asking people to go along with a smaller request, engaging self-perception processes.

Frustration-aggression theory. A theory holding that any frustration—defined as the blocking of an important goal—inevitably triggers aggression.

General Aggression Model. A theory that person and situation factors influence people's cognition, emotions, and arousal, which in turn influence interpretations of the situation and decisions about aggression.

Group polarization. The process by which a group's initial average position becomes more extreme following group interaction.

Group socialization. The cognitive, affective, and behavioral changes that occur as individuals join and leave groups.

Groupthink. Group decision making that is impaired by the drive to reach consensus regardless of how the consensus is formed.

Habit. A repeated behavior automatically triggered in a particular situation.

Hostile aggression. Aggression that is driven by anger due to insult, disrespect, or other threats to self-esteem or social identity.

Hypocrisy effect. Change in behavior that occurs to reduce the dissonance caused by freely choosing to publicly advocate a behavior that one does not actually perform oneself.

Ideal self. A person's sense of what he or she would ideally like to be.

Illusory correlation. A perceived association between two characteristics that are not actually related.

Implementation intention. A plan to carry out a specific goal-directed behavior in a specific situation.

Implicit attitude. Automatic and uncontrollable positive or negative evaluation of an attitude object.

Implicit measures. Alternatives to self-report measures, such as priming measures or the IAT, which are based on difficult-to-control aspect of people's performance, such as their response speed or accuracy.

Impression management function. The way an attitude contributes to connectedness by smoothing interactions and relationships.

Independent variable. A concrete manipulation or measurement of a construct that is thought to cause other constructs.

Individual mobility. The strategy of individual escape, either physical or psychological, from a stigmatized group.

Individualist cultures. Those in which people are particularly likely to think of themselves as separate from other people and to define themselves in terms of their uniqueness.

Informational influence. The process by which group norms are privately accepted to achieve or maintain mastery of reality.

Informed consent. Consent voluntarily given by an individual who decides to participate in a study after being told what will be involved in participation.

Injunctive social norms. Agreed upon mental representations of what people in a group should think, feel, or do.

Instrumental aggression. Aggression serving mastery needs, used as a means to an end, to control other people, or to obtain valuable resources.

Instrumental function. The way an attitude contributes to mastery by guiding our approach to positive objects and our avoidance of negative objects.

Insufficient justification effect. Attitude change that occurs to reduce dissonance caused by attitude-discrepant behavior that cannot be attributed to external reward or punishment.

Intention. A commitment to reach a desired outcome or desired behavior.

Interdependence. Each group member's thoughts, emotions, and behaviors influence the others'.

Internal validity. The extent to which it can be concluded that changes in the independent variable actually caused changes in the dependent variable in a research study.

Interventions. Practical steps taken to change people's behavior or to solve social problems.

Intimacy. A positive emotional bond that includes understanding and support.

Knowledge function. The way an attitude contributes to mastery by organizing, summarizing, and simplifying experience with an attitude object.

Leadership. A process in which one or more group members are permitted to influence and motivate others to help attain group goals.

Love. Thoughts, feelings, and actions that occur when a person wishes to enter or maintain a close relationship with a specific person.

Low-ball technique. A technique in which the influencer secures agreement with a request but then increases the cost of honoring the commitment.

Manipulate. Intentionally varying some factor as the independent variable in an experimental research design.

Mental representation. A body of knowledge that an individual has stored in memory.

Mere exposure. Exposure to a stimulus without any external reward, which creates familiarity with the stimulus and generally makes people feel more positively about it.

Meta-analysis. A systematic technique for locating studies on a particular topic and summarizing their results.

Metacognition. Thoughts about thoughts or about thought processes.

Minimal intergroup situation. A research situation in which people are categorized, on an arbitrary or trivial basis, into groups that have no history, no conflicts of interest, and no stereotypes.

Moral exclusion. Viewing out-groups as subhuman and outside the domain in which the rules of morality apply.

Negative-state relief model. The theory that most people hate to watch others suffer, so the ultimate goal of their help is not to aid the person in need for his or her sake, but to reduce the helper's own distress.

Negotiation. The process by which parties in conflict communicate and influence each other to reach agreement.

Nonexperimental research design. A research design in which both the independent and dependent variables are measured.

Norm of obedience to authority. The shared view that people should obey those with legitimate authority.

Norm of reciprocity. The shared view that people are obligated to return to others the goods, services, and concessions they offer to us.

Norm of social commitment. The shared view that people are required to honor their agreements and obligations.

Norm of social responsibility. A norm that those able to take care of themselves have a duty and obligation to assist those who cannot.

Normative influence. The process by which group norms are privately accepted to achieve or maintain connectedness and a valued social identity.

Observational measures. Those based on directly watching and recording people's behavior, including online behavior.

Ostracism. Being ignored and excluded from a group.

Ought self. A person's sense of what he or she is obligated to be, or should be.

Out-group homogeneity effect. The tendency to see the out-group as relatively more homogeneous and less diverse than the in-group.

Performance measures. Those that ask participants to perform some task as well as they can.

Perseverance bias. The tendency for information to have a persisting effect on our judgments even after it has been discredited.

Persuasion. The process of forming, strengthening, or changing attitudes by communication.

Persuasion heuristic. Association of a cue that is positively or negatively evaluated with the attitude object, allowing the attitude object to be evaluated quickly and without much thought.

Pervasiveness of social influence. The axiom that other people influence virtually all of our thoughts, feelings, and behavior, whether those others are physically present or not.

Physiological measures. Those based on measurement of some physiological process such as heart rate or muscle movements.

Pluralistic ignorance. Occurs when everyone publicly conforms to an apparent norm that no one in fact privately accepts.

Post-decisional regret effect. Attitude change that occurs to reduce the dissonance caused by freely making a choice or decision.

Power. The ability to provide or withhold rewards or punishments from others.

Prejudice. A positive or negative evaluation of a social group and its members.

Primacy effect. A pattern in which early-encountered information has a greater impact than subsequent information; an example of the principle of cognitive conservatism.

Priming. The activation of a mental representation to increase its accessibility and thus the likelihood that it will be used.

Private conformity. Private acceptance of social norms.

Problem-focused coping. Dealing with threats or stressors directly, often by reappraising the situation or by directly removing the threat.

Prosocial behavior. Behavior intended to help someone else.

Public conformity. Overt behavior consistent with social norms that are not privately accepted.

Random assignment. The procedure of assigning participants to different experimental groups so that every participant has exactly the same chance as every other participant of being in any given group.

Reactance. The motive to protect or restore a threatened sense of behavioral freedom.

Reactive devaluation. Perceiving a proposed solution to a conflict negatively simply because the out-group offers it.

Realistic conflict theory. The theory that intergroup hostility arises from competition among groups for scarce but valued material resources.

Reference group. Those people accepted as an appropriate source of information for a judgment because they share the attributes relevant for making that judgment.

Regulatory focus theory. A theory that people typically have either a promotion or prevention focus, shaping the ways they self-regulate to attain positive outcomes versus avoiding negative outcomes.

Relative deprivation theory. The theory that feelings of discontent arise from the belief that other individuals or other groups are better off.

Replication. Conducting new studies in an effort to provide evidence for the same theoretically predicted relations found in prior research.

Research design. A plan that specifies how research participants will be selected and treated.

Romantic love. Involves sexual feelings, a sense of intense longing for the partner, euphoric feelings of fulfillment and ecstasy when the relationship goes well, and anxiety and despair when it does not.

Salience. The ability of a cue to attract attention in its context.

Scientific Theory. A statement that satisfies three requirements: It is about constructs; it describes causal relations; and it is general in scope, although the range of generality differs for different theories.

Seeking connectedness. The motivational principle that people seek support, liking, and acceptance from the people and groups they care about and value.

Self-affirmation. Any action or event that enhances or highlights one's own sense of personal integrity, such as affirming one's most important values.

Self-aspects. Summaries of a person's beliefs about the self in specific domains, roles, or activities.

Self-awareness. A state of heightened awareness of the self, including our internal standards and whether we measure up to them.

Self-categorization. The process of seeing oneself as a member of a social group.

Self-complexity. The extent to which a person possesses many and diverse self-aspects.

Self-concept. All of an individual's knowledge about his or her personal qualities.

Self-enhancing bias. Any tendency to gather or interpret information concerning the self in a way that leads to overly positive evaluations.

Self-esteem. An individual's positive or negative evaluation of himself or herself.

Self-evaluation maintenance. A theory outlining the conditions under which people's self-esteem will be maintained or will suffer based on social comparisons to close or distant others.

Self-expression. A motive for choosing behaviors that are intended to reflect and express the self-concept.

Self-fulfilling prophecy. The process by which one person's expectations about another become reality by eliciting behaviors that confirm the expectations.

Self-handicapping. Seeking to avoid blame for an expected poor performance, either by claiming an excuse in advance or by actively sabotaging one's own performance (for example, by failing to practice).

Self-monitoring. A personality characteristic defined as the degree to which people are sensitive to the demands of social situations and shape their behaviors accordingly.

Self-perception theory. The theory that we make inferences about our personal characteristics on the basis of our overt behaviors when internal cues are weak or ambiguous.

Self-presentation. A motive for choosing behaviors intended to create in observers a desired impression of the self.

Self-regulation. Efforts to control one's behavior in line with internal standards (self-guides) or external standards.

Self-report measures. Those based on asking the individual about his or her thoughts, feelings, or behaviors.

Self-schema. Core characteristics that a person believes characterize him or her across situations.

Social categorization. The process of identifying individual people as members of a social group because they share certain features that are typical of the group.

Social change. The strategy of improving the overall societal situation of a stigmatized group.

Social comparison theory. The theory that people learn about and evaluate their personal qualities by comparing themselves to others.

Social compensation. One group member working especially hard to compensate for another's low level of effort or performance.

Social competition. The strategy of directly seeking to change the conditions that disadvantage the in-group, for example, by building group solidarity and challenging the out-group.

Social creativity. The strategy of introducing and emphasizing new dimensions of social comparison, on which a negatively regarded group can see itself as superior.

Social desirability response bias. People's tendency to act in ways that they believe others find acceptable and approve of.

Social dilemma. A form of interdependence in which the most rewarding action for each individual will, if chosen by all individuals, produce a negative outcome for the entire group.

Social facilitation. An increase in the likelihood of highly accessible responses, and a decrease in the likelihood of less accessible responses, due to the presence of others.

Social group. Two or more people who share some common characteristic that is socially meaningful for themselves or for others.

Social identity. Those aspects of the self-concept that derive from an individual's knowledge and feelings about the group memberships he or she shares with others.

Social identity function. The way an attitude contributes to connectedness by expressing important self and group identities and values.

Social identity theory. The theory that people's motivation to derive self-esteem from their group memberships is one driving force behind in-group bias.

Social interdependence. Reliance on other members of the group for feelings of connectedness, social and emotional rewards, and a positive social identity.

Social loafing. The tendency to exert less effort on a task when an individual's efforts are an unidentifiable part of a group than when the same task is performed alone.

Social norms. Generally accepted ways of thinking, feeling, or behaving that people in a group agree on and endorse as right and proper.

Social processes. The ways in which input from the people and groups around us affect our thoughts, feelings, and actions.

Social psychology. The scientific study of the effects of social and cognitive processes on the way individuals perceive, influence, and relate to others

Social support. Emotional and physical coping resources provided by other people.

Social value orientation. Stable differences in the ways people act in social dilemmas (such as competitive or prosocial).

Stereotype. A mental representation or impression of a social group that people form by associating particular characteristics and emotions with the group.

Stereotype threat. The fear of confirming others' negative stereotype of your group.

Stigmatized. Negatively evaluated by others.

Striving for mastery. The motivational principle that people seek to understand and predict events in the social world in order to obtain rewards.

Strong attitude. A confidently-held extremely positive or negative evaluation that is persistent and resistant and that influences information processing and behavior.

Subliminal. Presentation of stimuli in such a way (usually with a very brief duration) that perceivers are not consciously aware of them.

Subtype. A narrower and more specific social group, such as housewife or feminist, that is included within a broad social group, like women.

Superficial processing. Relying on accessible information to make inferences or judgments, while expending little effort in processing.

Superficiality versus depth. The processing principle that people ordinarily put little effort into dealing with information, but at times are motivated to consider information in more depth

Superordinate goals. Shared goals that can be attained only if groups work together.

Systematic processing. Giving thorough, effortful consideration to a wide range of information relevant to a judgment.

Task interdependence. Reliance on other members of a group for mastery of material outcomes that arise from the group's task.

Terror Management Theory. A theory stating that reminders of one's own mortality lead individuals to reaffirm basic cultural worldviews, which can have both positive and negative effects.

Theory of planned behavior. The theory that attitudes, social norms, and perceived control combine to influence intentions and thus behavior.

Theory of reasoned action. The theory that attitudes and social norms combine to produce behavioral intentions, which in turn influence behavior.

Transformational leadership. Leaders who inspire extreme devotion and emotional identification on the part of their followers, allowing them to have profound effects on their followers.

Trust. The expectation that others will act prosocially during a social interaction.

Valuing "me and mine." The motivational principle that people desire to see themselves, and other people and groups connected to themselves, in a positive light

Vicarious retribution. Members of a group who were not themselves directly harmed by an attack retaliating against members of the offending group.

REFERENCES

Aaker, J. L., & Schmitt, B. (2001). Culture-dependent assimilation and differentiation of the self: Preferences for consumption symbols in the United States and China. *Journal of Cross-Cultural Psychology, 32*, 561–576.

Aarts, H., & Dijksterhuis, A. (2003). The silence of the library: Environment, situational norm, and social behavior. *Journal of Personality and Social Psychology, 84*, 18–28.

Abele, S., & Stasser, G. (2008). Coordination success and interpersonal perceptions: Matching versus mismatching. *Journal of Personality and Social Psychology, 95*, 576–592.

Abelson, R. P., Dasgupta, N., Park, J., & Banaji, M. R. (1998). Perceptions of the collective other. *Personality and Social Psychology Review, 2*, 243–250.

Abelson, R. P., Kinder, D. R., Peters, M. D., & Fiske, S. T. (1982). Affective and semantic components in political person perception. *Journal of Personality and Social Psychology, 42*, 619–630.

Aboud, F. E. (1976). Self-evaluation: Information seeking strategies for interethnic social comparisons. *Journal of Cross Cultural Psychology, 7*, 289–300.

Aboud, F. E., & Taylor, D. M. (1971). Ethnic and role stereotypes: Their relative importance in person perception. *Journal of Social Psychology, 85*, 17–27.

Abramovitch, I. (1997, Aug. 12). Rap or rock? For dorm mates that may not be an easy negotiation. *The New York Times*, p. B3.

Abrams, D. (2009). Social identity on a national scale: Optimal distinctiveness and young people's self-expression through musical preference. *Group Processes & Intergroup Relations, 12*, 303–317.

Abrams, D. (2013). Social identity and groups. In J. M. Levine (Ed.), *Group processes* (pp. 267–295). New York: Psychology Press.

Abrams, D., Wetherell, M., Cochrane, S., Hogg, M. A., & Turner, J. C. (2001). Knowing what to think by knowing who you are: Self-categorization and the nature of norm formation, conformity and group polarization. In M. A. Hogg & D. Abrams (Eds.), *Intergroup relations: Essential readings. Key readings in social psychology* (pp. 270–288). Philadelphia, PA: Psychology Press.

Abrams, J. (1991, Aug. 31). Survey cites racism in housing. *Santa Barbara News Press*, p. A5.

Abramson, L. Y., Seligman, M. E. P., & Teasdale, J. (1978). Learned helplessness in humans: Critique and reformulation. *Journal of Abnormal Psychology, 87*, 49–74.

Achtziger, A., Gollwitzer, P. M., & Sheeran, P. (2008). Implementation intentions and shielding goal striving from unwanted thoughts and feelings. *Personality and Social Psychology Bulletin, 34*, 381–393.

Ackerman, J. M., Griskevicius, V., & Li, N. P. (2011). Let's get serious: Communicating commitment in romantic relationships. *Journal of Personality & Social Psychology, 100*, 1079–1094.

Ackerman, J. M., Kenrick, D. T., & Schaller, M. (2007). Is friendship akin to kinship? *Evolution and Human Behavior, 28*, 365–374.

Ackerman, J. M., Nocera, C. C., & Bargh, J. A. (2010). Incidental haptic sensations influence social judgments and decisions. *Science, 328*, 1712–1715.

Adair, W. L., & Brett, J. M. (2005). The negotiation dance: Time, culture, and behavioral sequences in negotiation. *Organization Science, 16*(1), 33–51.

Addessi, E., Galloway, A. T., Visalberghi, E., & Birch, L. L. (2005). Specific social influences on the acceptance of novel foods in 2–5-year-old children. *Appetite, 45*, 264–271.

Adelmann, P. K., & Zajonc, R. B. (1989). Facial efference and the experience of emotion. *Annual Review of Psychology, 40*, 249–280.

Adorno, T. W., Frenkel-Brunswik, E., Levinson, D. J., & Sanford, R. N. (1950). *The authoritarian personality*. New York: Harper.

African American chairman & CEO's of Fortune 500 companies. (n.d.). Retrieved from http:// www.blackentrepreneur profile.com/fortune-500-ceos/

Agiesta, J. (2013, June 16). Most men aspire to be dads, poll finds. *USA Today*. Retrieved from http://www.usatoday.com

Agnew, C. R. (2000). Cognitive interdependence and the experience of relationship loss. In J. H. Harvey & E. D. Miller (Eds.), *Loss and trauma: General and close relationship perspectives* (pp. 385–398). Philadelphia, PA: Brunner-Routledge.

Agnew, C. R., van Lange, P. A. M., Rusbult, C. E., & Langston, C. A. (1998). Cognitive interdependence: Commitment and the mental representation of close relationships. *Journal of Personality and Social Psychology, 74,* 939–954.

Aguilar-Luzon, M. C., Garcia-Martinez, J. M. A., Calvo-Salguero, A., & Salinas, J. M. (2012). Comparative study between the theory of planned behavior and the value-belief-norm model regarding the environment, on Spanish housewives' recycling behavior. *Journal of Applied Social Psychology, 42,* 2797–2833.

Aiello, J. R., & Douthitt, E. A. (2001). Social facilitation from Triplett to electronic performance monitoring. *Group Dynamics, 5,* 163–180.

Aiello, J. R., & Kolb, K. J. (1995). Electronic performance monitoring and social context: Impact on productivity and stress. *Journal of Applied Psychology, 80,* 339–353.

Ailes, R. (1988). *You are the message.* New York: Doubleday.

Ainsworth, M., Blehar, M., Waters, E., & Wall, S. (1978). *Patterns of attachment.* Hillsdale, NJ: Lawrence Erlbaum Associates.

Ainsworth, S. E., & Maner, J. K. (2012). Sex begets violence: Mating motives, social dominance, and physical aggression in men. *Journal of Personality & Social Psychology, 103,* 819–829.

Ajzen, I. (1991). The theory of planned behavior. *Organizational Behavior and Human Decision Processes, 50,* 179–211.

Ajzen, I. (1996). The directive influence of attitudes on behavior. In P. M. Gollwitzer, & J. A. Bargh (Eds.), *The psychology of action: Linking cognition and motivation to behavior* (pp. 385–403). New York, NY: Guilford Press.

Ajzen, I., & Cote, N. G. (2008). Attitudes and the prediction of behavior. In W. D. Crano & R. Prislin (Eds.), *Attitudes and attitude change* (pp. 289–311). New York, NY: Psychology Press.

Ajzen, I., & Fishbein, M. (1977). Attitude-behavior relations: A theoretical analysis and review of empirical research. *Psychological Bulletin, 84,* 888–918.

Ajzen, I., & Fishbein, M. (1980). *Understanding attitudes and predicting social behavior.* Englewood Cliffs, NJ: Prentice-Hall.

Ajzen, I., & Madden, T.J. (1986). Prediction of goal-directed behavior: Attitudes, intentions, and perceived behavioral control. *Journal of Experimental Social Psychology, 22,* 453–474.

Aknin, L. B., Barrington-Leigh, C. P., Dunn, E., Helliwell, J. F., Burns, J., & Norton, M. (2013). Prosocial spending and well-being: Cross-cultural evidence for a psychological universal. *Journal of Personality and Social Psychology.* doi:10.1037/a0031578.supp

Albarracín, D., & Kumkale, G. T. (2003). Affect as information in persuasion: A model of affect identification and discounting. *Journal of Personality and Social Psychology, 84,* 453–469.

Albarracín, D., & McNatt, P. S. (2005). Maintenance and decay of past behavior influences: Anchoring attitudes on beliefs following inconsistent actions. *Personality and Social Psychology Bulletin, 31*(6), 719–733.

Albarracín, D., & Wyer, R. S., Jr. (2000). The cognitive impact of past behavior: Influences on beliefs, attitudes, and future behavioral decisions. *Journal of Personality and Social Psychology, 79*(1), 5–22.

Alcock, J. E., Carment, D. W., & Sadava, S. W. (1988). *A textbook of social psychology.* Scarborough, Ontario: Prentice-Hall.

Alderfer, C. P. (2011). *The practice of organizational diagnosis: Theory and methods.* New York, NY: Oxford University Press.

Allen, K. M., Blascovich, J., Tomaka, J., & Kelsey, R. M. (1991). Presence of human friends and pet dogs as moderators of autonomic responses to stress in women. *Journal of Personality and Social Psychology, 61,* 582–589.

Allen, V. L. (1965). Situational factors in conformity. In L. Berkowitz (Ed.), *Advances in experimental social psychology* (vol. 8, pp. 133–175). New York: Academic Press.

Allen, V. L. (1975). Social support for non-conformity. In L. Berkowitz (Ed.), *Advances in experimental social psychology* (vol. 18, pp. 2–43). New York: Academic Press.

Allen, V. L., & Bragg, B.W. (1965). The generalization of non-conformity within a homogeneous content dimension. Cited in V. L. Allen (1975).

Allen, V. L. & Wilder, D. A. (1972). Social support in absentia: effect of an absentee partner on conformity. Cited in V. L. Allen (1975).

Allen, V. L. & Wilder, D. A. (1979). Group categorization and belief similarity. *Small Group Behavior, 10,* 73–80.

Allison, S.T., Mackie, D.M., Muller, M.M., & Worth, L.T. (1993). Sequential correspondence biases and perceptions of change: The Castro studies revisited. *Personality and Social Psychology Bulletin, 19,* 151–157.

Allison, S. T., & Messick, D. M. (1985). The group attribution error. *Journal of Experimental Social Psychology, 21,* 563–579.

Allison, S. T., Messick, D. M., & Goethals, G. R. (1989). On being better but not smarter than others: The Muhammad Ali effect. *Social Cognition, 7,* 275–295.

Alloy, L. B., & Abramson, L. Y. (1979). Judgment of contingency in depressed and nondepressed students: Sadder but wiser? *Journal of Experimental Psychology: General, 108,* 441–485.

Allport, F. H. (1924). *Social psychology.* Boston: Houghton Mifflin.

Allport, F. H., & Lepkin, M. (1945). Wartime rumors of waste and special privilege: Why some people believe them. *Journal of Abnormal and Social Psychology, 40,* 3–36.

Allport, G. W. (1935). Attitudes. In *Handbook of social psychology* (pp. 798–844). Worcester, MA: Clark University Press.

Allport, G. W. (1954a). The historical background of modern social psychology. In G. Lindzey (Ed.), *The handbook of social psychology* (vol. 1, pp. 3–56). Cambridge, MA: Addison-Wesley.

Allport, G. W. (1954b). *The nature of prejudice.* New York: Addison-Wesley.

Allport, G. W. (1958). *The nature of prejudice.* Garden City, NY: Doubleday Anchor.

Aloise, P. A. (1993). Trait confirmation and disconfirmation: The development of attribution biases. *Journal of Experimental Child Psychology, 55*, 177–193.

Alós-Ferrer, C., Granić, D., Shi, F., & Wagner, A. K. (2012). Choices and preferences: Evidence from implicit choices and response times. *Journal of Experimental Social Psychology, 48*(6), 1336–1342.

Altemeyer, B. (1981). *Right-wing authoritarianism*. Winnipeg, MB: University of Manitoba Press.

Alter, A. L., Aronson, J., Darley, J. M., Rodriguez, C., & Ruble, D. N. (2010). Rising to the threat: Reducing stereotype threat by reframing the threat as a challenge. *Journal of Experimental Social Psychology, 46*, 166–171.

Alterovitz, S. S.-R., & Mendelsohn, G. A. (2011). Partner preferences across the life span: Online dating by older adults. *Psychology of Popular Media Culture, 1*, 89–95.

Altman, I., & Taylor, D. A. (1973). *Social penetration*. New York: Holt, Rinehart, Winston.

Alvarez, K., & van Leeuwen, E. (2011). To teach or to tell? Consequences of receiving help from experts and peers. *European Journal of Social Psychology, 41*(3), 397–402. doi:10.1002/ ejsp.789

Alvaro, E. M., & Crano, W. D. (1996). Cognitive responses to minority- or majority-based communications: Factors that underlie minority influence. *British Journal of Social Psychology, 35*, 105–121.

Alvaro, E. M., & Crano, W. D. (1997). Indirect minority influence: Evidence for leniency in source evaluation and counterargumentation. *Journal of Personality and Social Psychology, 72*, 949–964.

Amato, P. R., & Previti, D. (2003). People's reasons for divorcing: Gender, social class, the life course, and adjustment. *Journal of Family Issues, 24*, 602–626.

Ambady, N., Bernieri, F. J., & Richeson, J. A. (2000). Toward a histology of social behavior: Judgmental accuracy from thin slices of the behavioral stream. In M. P. Zanna (Ed.), *Advances in experimental social psychology* (vol. 32, pp. 201–271). San Diego, CA, US: Academic Press.

Ambady, N., & Rosenthal, R. (1993). Half a minute: Predicting teacher evaluations from thin slices of nonverbal behavior and physical attractiveness. *Journal of Personality & Social Psychology, 64*, 431–441.

Amir, Y. (1969). Contact hypothesis in ethnic relations. *Psychological Bulletin, 71*, 319–342.

Amodio, D. M., Devine, P. G., & Harmon-Jones, E. (2008). Individual differences in the regulation of intergroup bias: The role of conflict monitoring and neural signals for control. *Journal of Personality & Social Psychology, 94*, 60–74.

Amodio, D. M., & Frith, C. D. (2006). Meeting of minds: the medial frontal cortex and social cognition. *Nature Reviews Neuroscience, 7*, 268–277.

Andersen, S. M. (1984). Self-knowledge and social inference: II. The diagnosticity of cognitive/ affective and behavioral data. *Journal of Personality and Social Psychology, 46*, 294–307.

Andersen, S. M., & Klatsky, R. L. (1987). Traits and social stereotypes: Levels of categorization in person perception. *Journal of Personality and Social Psychology, 53*, 235–246.

Anderson, C. A. (2001). Heat and violence. *Current Directions in Psychological Science, 10*, 33–38.

Anderson, C. A., Anderson, K. B., & Deuser, W. E. (1996). Examining an affective aggression framework: Weapon and temperature effects on aggressive thoughts, affect, and attitudes. *Personality and Social Psychology Bulletin, 22*, 366–376.

Anderson, C. A., & Bushman, B. J. (1997). External validity of "trivial" experiments: The case of laboratory aggression. *Review of General Psychology, 1*, 19–41.

Anderson, C. A., & Bushman, B. J. (2002). Human aggression. *Annual Review of Psychology, 53*, 27–51.

Anderson, C. A., Carnagey, N. L., & Eubanks, J. (2003). Exposure to violent media: The effects of songs with violent lyrics on aggressive thoughts and feelings. *Journal of Personality and Social Psychology, 84*(5), 960–971.

Anderson, C. A., Carnagey, N. L., Flanagan, M., Benjamin, A. J., Eubanks, J., & Valentine, J. C. (2004). Violent video games: Specific effects of violent content on aggressive thoughts and behavior. *Advances in Experimental Social Psychology, 36*, 199–249.

Anderson, C. A., & DeLisi, M. (2011). Implications of global climate change for violence in developed and developing countries. In J. P. Forgas, A. W. Kruglanski, & K. D. Williams (Eds.), *The psychology of social conflict and aggression* (vol. 13, pp. 249–265). New York: Psychology Press.

Anderson, C. A., Deuser, W. E., & DeNeve, K. M. (1995). Hot temperatures, hostile affect, hostile cognition, and arousal: Tests of a general model of affective aggression. *Personality & Social Psychology Bulletin, 21*, 434–448.

Anderson, C. A., & Dill, K. E. (2000). Video games and aggressive thoughts, feelings, and behavior in the laboratory and in life. *Journal of Personality and Social Psychology, 78*(4), 772–790.

Anderson, C. A., & Godfrey, S. S. (1987). Thoughts about actions: The effects of specificity and availability of imagined behavioral scripts on expectations about oneself and others. *Social Cognition, 5*, 238–258.

Anderson, C.A., Jennings, D. L., & Arnoult, L. H. (1988). Validity and utility of the attributional style construct at a moderate level of specificity. *Journal of Personality and Social Psychology, 55*, 979–990

Anderson, C. A., Shibuya, A., Ihori, N., Swing, E. L., Bushman, B. J., Sakamoto, A., Rothstein, H. R., & Saleem, M. (2010). Violent video game effects on aggression, empathy, and prosocial behavior in eastern and western countries: A meta-analytic review. *Psychological Bulletin, 136*, 151–173.

Andreoli, V., & Worchel, S. (1978). Effects of media, communicator, and message position on attitude change. *Public Opinion Quarterly, 42*, 59–70.

Angier, N. (1990). Anger can ruin more than your day. *New York Times*, Dec. 13.

Anthony, T., Copper, C., & Mullen, B. (1992). Cross-racial facial identification: A social cogntive integration. *Personality and Social Psychology Bulletin, 18*, 296–301.

Antonakis, J., & Dalgas, O. (2009). Predicting elections: Child's play! *Science, 323*, 1183.

Anzures, G., Mondloch, C. J., & Lackner, C. (2009). Face adaptation and attractiveness aftereffects in 8-year-olds and adults. *Child Development, 80*, 178–191.

APA (2010). *Ethical principles of psychologists and code of conduct.* Washington, DC: American Psychological Association.

Apicella, C. L., Little, A. C., & Marlowe, F. W. (2007). Facial averageness and attractiveness in an isolated population of hunter-gatherers. *Perception, 36*, 1813–1820.

Aramovich, N. P., Lytle, B. L., & Skitka, L. J. (2012). Opposing torture: Moral conviction and resistance to majority influence. *Social Influence, 7*, 21–34.

Archer, J. (2002). Sex differences in physically aggressive acts between heterosexual partners: A meta-analytic review. *Aggression and Violent Behavior, 7*, 313–351.

Archer, J. (2004). Sex differences in aggression in real-world settings: A meta-analytic review. *Review of General Psychology, 8*, 291–322.

Archer, J. (2013). Can evolutionary principles explain patterns of family violence? *Psychological Bulletin, 139*, 403–440.

Archer, J., & Coyne, S. (2005). An integrated review of indirect, relational, and social aggression. *Personality and Social Psychology Review, 9*, 212–230.

Archer, R. L. (1980). Self-disclosure. In D. M. Wegner & R. R. Vallacher (Eds.), *The self in social psychology.* New York: Oxford University Press.

Arendt, H. (1965). *Eichmann in Jerusalem: A report on the banality of evil.* New York: Viking Press.

Ariyanto, A., Hornsey, M. J., & Gallois, C. (2010). United we stand: Intergroup conflict moderates the intergroup sensitivity effect. *European Journal of Social Psychology, 40*(1), 169–177.

Arkes, H. R., Hackett, C., & Boehm, L. (1989). The generality of the relation between familiarity and judged validity. *Journal of Behavioral Decision Making, 2*, 81–94.

Arkin, R. M. (1981). Self-presentation styles. In J. T. Tedeschi (Ed.), *Impression management theory and social psychological research* (pp. 311–333). New York: Academic Press.

Armitage, C. J., & Conner, M. (2001). Efficacy of the theory of planned behaviour: A meta-analytic review. *British Journal of Social Psychology, 40*, 471–499.

Armitage, C. J., & Reidy, J. G. (2008). Use of mental simulations to change theory of planned behaviour variables. *British Journal of Health Psychology, 13*(3), 513–524.

Arnold, M. B. (1960). *Emotion and personality.* New York: Columbia University Press.

Aron, A., & Aron, E. N. (1991). Love and sexuality. In K. McKinney & S. Sprecher (Eds.), *Sexuality in close relationships* (pp. 25–48). Hillsdale, NJ: Lawrence Erlbaum Associates.

Aron, A., Aron, E. N., Tudor, M., & Nelson, G. (1991). Close relationships as including other in the self. *Journal of Personality and Social Psychology, 60*, 241–253.

Aron, A., Norman, C. C., Aron, E. N., McKenna, C., & Heyman, R. E. (2000). Couples' shared participation in novel and arousing activities and experienced relationship quality. *Journal of Personality & Social Psychology, 78*, 273–284.

Aron, A., Paris, M., & Aron, E. N. (1995). Falling in love: Prospective studies of self-concept change. *Journal of Personality and Social Psychology, 69*, 1102–1112.

Aron, E. N., & Aron, A. (1996). Love and expansion of the self: The state of the model. *Personal Relationships, 3*, 45–58.

Aronson, E. (1961). The effect of effort on the attractiveness of rewarded and unrewarded stimuli. *Journal of Abnormal and Social Psychology, 63*, 375–380.

Aronson, E., & Mills, J. (1959). The effect of severity of initiation on liking for a group. *Journal of Abnormal and Social Psychology, 59*, 177–181.

Aronson, E., & Worchel, S. (1966). Similarity versus liking as determinants of interpersonal attractiveness. *Psychonomic Science, 5*, 157–158.

Arriaga, X. B., & Agnew, C. R. (2001). Being committed: Affective, cognitive, and conative components of relationship commitment. *Personality and Social Psychology Bulletin, 27*, 1190–1203.

Asch, S. E. (1946). Forming impressions of personality. *Journal of Abnormal and Social Psychology. 41*, 258–290.

Asch, S.E. (1951). Effects of group pressure upon the modification and distortion of judgment. In H. Guetzkow (Ed.), *Groups, leadership, and men.* Pittsburgh, PA: Carnegie University Press.

Asch, S. E. (1955). Studies of independence and conformity: A minority of one against a unanimous majority. *Psychology Monographs, 70*, 1–70.

Asch, S. E. (1956). Opinions and social pressure. *Scientific American, 193*(5), 31–35.

Asch, S. E., & Zukier, H. (1984). Thinking about persons. *Journal of Personality and Social Psychology, 46*, 1230–1240.

Ashburn-Nardo, L., Knowles, M. L., & Monteith, M. J. (2003). Black Americans' implicit racial associations and their implications for intergroup judgment. *Social Cognition, 21*, 62–87.

Ashmore, R. D. (1981). Sex stereotypes and implicit personality theory. In D. L. Hamilton (Ed.), *Cognitive processes in stereotyping and intergroup behavior* (pp. 37–81). Hillsdale, NJ: Erlbaum.

Ashmore, R. D., & Del Boca, F. K. (1981). Conceptual approaches to stereotypes and stereotyping. In D. L. Hamilton (Ed.), *Cognitive processes in stereotyping and intergroup behavior* (pp. 1–36). Hillsdale, NJ: Erlbaum.

Askenasy, H. (1978). *Are we all Nazis?* Secaucus, NJ: Lyle Stuart.

Aubrey, J. S. (2004). Sex and punishment: An examination of sexual consequences and the sexual double standard in teen programming. *Sex Roles, 50*, 505–514.

Avolio, B. J., Zhu, W., Koh, W., & Bhatia, P. (2004).

Transformational leadership and organizational commitment: Mediating role of psychological empowerment and moderating role of structural distance. *Journal of Organizational Behavior, 25,* 951–968.

Axsom, D., & Cooper, J. (1985). Cognitive dissonance and psychotherapy: The role of effort justification in inducing weight loss. *Journal of Experimental Social Psychology, 21*(2), 149–160.

Axsom, D., Yates, S., & Chaiken, S. (1987). Audience response as a heuristic cue in persuasion. *Journal of Personality and Social Psychology, 53,* 30–40.

Azar, B. (1994, September). Teams that wear blinders are often the cause of tragic errors. *APA Monitor,* p. 23.

Back, M. D., Schmukle, S. C., & Egloff, B. (2008). Becoming friends by chance. *Psychological Science, 19,* 439–440.

Back, M. D., Stopfer, J. M., Vazire, S., Gaddis, S., Schmukle, S. C., Egloff, B., & Gosling, S. D. (2010). Facebook profiles reflect actual personality, not self-idealization. *Psychological Science, 21,* 372–374.

Bahns, A. J., Pickett, K. M., & Crandall, C. S. (2012). Social ecology of similarity: Big schools, small schools and social relationships. *Group Processes & Intergroup Relations, 15,* 119–131.

Bailenson, J. N., Garland, P., Iyengar, S., & Yee, N. (2006). Transformed facial similarity as a political cue: A preliminary investigation. *Political Psychology, 27,* 373–385.

Bailenson, J. N., & Yee, N. (2005). Digital chameleons: Automatic assimilation of nonverbal gestures in immersive virtual environments. *Psychological Science, 16,* 814–819.

Balcetis, E., & Dunning, D. (2007). Cognitive dissonance and the perception of natural environments. *Psychological Science, 18*(10), 917–921.

Balcetis, E., & Dunning, D. (2010). Wishful seeing: Desirable objects are seen as closer. *Psychological Science, 21,* 147–152.

Baldry, A. C., Pagliaro, S., & Porcaro, C. (2013). The rule of law at time of masculine honor: Afghan police attitudes and intimate partner violence. *Group Processes & Intergroup Relations, 16,* 363–374.

Baldwin, M. W., & Fehr, B. (1995). On the instability of attachment style ratings. *Personal Relationships, 2*(3), 247–261.

Baldwin, M. W., & Sinclair, L. (1996). Self-esteem and "if . . . then" contingencies of interpersonal acceptance. *Journal of Personality and Social Psychology, 71,* 1130–1141.

Bales, R. F. (1953). The equilibrium problem in small groups. In T. Parsons, R. F. Bales, & E. A. Shils (Eds.), *Working papers in the theory of action* (pp. 111–162). Glencoe, IL: Free Press.

Bales, R. F., Cohen, S. P., & Williamson, S. A. (1979). *SYMLOG: A system for the multiple level observation of groups.* New York: Free Press.

Balliet, D. (2010). Communication and cooperation in social dilemmas: A meta-analytic review. *Journal of Conflict Resolution, 54*(1), 39–57. doi:10.1177/0022002709352443

Balliet, D., Li, N. P., Macfarlan, S. J., & Van Vugt, M. (2011). Sex differences in cooperation: A meta-analytic review of social dilemmas. *Psychological Bulletin, 137*(6), 881–909. doi:10.1037/a0025354

Balliet, D., Mulder, L. B., & Van Lange, P. A. M. (2011). Reward, punishment, and cooperation: A meta-analysis. *Psychological Bulletin, 137*(4), 594–615. doi:10.1037/a0023489

Balliet, D., & Van Lange, P. A. M. (2012). Trust, conflict, and cooperation: A meta-analysis. *Psychological Bulletin.* doi:10.1037/a0030939

Balliet, D., & Van Lange, P. A. M. (2013). Trust, punishment, and cooperation across 18 societies: A meta-analysis. *Perspectives on Psychological Science, 8*(4), 363–379. doi:10.1177/174569 1613488533

Baltes, B. B., Dickson, M. W., Sherman, M. P., Bauer, C. C., & LaGanke, J. S. (2002). Computer-mediated communication and group decision making: A meta-analysis. *Organizational Behavior and Human Decision Processes, 87,* 156–179.

Bandura, A. (1973). *Aggression: A social learning analysis.* Englewood Cliffs, NJ: Prentice-Hall.

Bandura, A. (1977a). Self-efficacy: Toward a unifying theory of behavioral change. *Psychological Review, 84,* 191–215.

Bandura, A. (1977b). *Social learning theory.* Englewood Cliffs, NJ: Prentice-Hall.

Bandura, A. (1982). Self-efficacy: Mechanism in human agency. *American Psychologist, 37,* 122–147.

Bandura, A. (1986). The explanatory and predictive scope of self-efficacy theory. Special Issue: Self-efficacy theory in contemporary psychology. *Journal of Social and Clinical Psychology, 4,* 359–373.

Bandura, A., Barbaranelli, C., Caprara, G. V., & Pastorelli, C. (1996). Mechanisms of moral disengagement in the exercise of moral agency. *Journal of Personality and Social Psychology, 71,* 364–374.

Bandura, A., Ross, D., & Ross, S. A. (1961). Transmission of aggression through imitation of aggressive models. *Journal of Abnormal and Social Psychology, 63,* 575–582.

Bandura, A., Ross, D., & Ross, S. A. (1963). Imitation of film-mediated aggressive models. *Journal of Abnormal and Social Psychology, 66,* 3–11.

Banuazizi, A., & Movahedi, S. (1975). Interpersonal dynamics in a simulated prison: A methodological analysis. *American Psychologist, 30,* 152–160.

Barchia, K., & Bussey, K. (2011). Individual and collective social cognitive influences on peer aggression: Exploring the contribution of aggression efficacy, moral disengagement, and collective efficacy. *Aggressive Behavior, 37,* 107–120.

Barden, J., & Petty, R. E. (2008). The mere perception of elaboration creates attitude certainty: Exploring the thoughtfulness heuristic. *Journal of Personality & Social Psychology, 95,* 489–509.

Barelds, D. P. H., & Dijkstra, P. (2011). Positive illusions about a partner's personality and relationship quality. *Journal of Research in Personality, 45,* 37–43.

Bargh, J. A. (1994). The four horsemen of automaticity:

Awareness, intention, efficiency, and control in social cognition. In R. S. Wyer, Jr., & T. K. Srull (Eds.), *Handbook of social cognition* (2nd ed., pp. 1–40). Hillsdale, NJ: Erlbaum.

Bargh, J. A., Bond, R. N., Lombardi, W. J., & Tota, M. E. (1986). The additive nature of chronic and temporary sources of construct accessibility. *Journal of Personality and Social Psychology, 50,* 869–878.

Bargh, J. A., Chaiken, S., Raymond, P., & Hymes, C. (1996). The automatic evaluation effect: Unconditional automatic attitude activation with a pronunciation task. *Journal of Experimental Social Psychology, 32,* 104–128.

Bargh, J. A., & Gollwitzer, P. M. (1994). Environmental control of goal-directed action: Automatic and strategic contingencies between situations and behavior. In W. D. Spaulding (Ed.), *Integrative views of motivation, cognition, and emotion* (pp. 71–124). Lincoln: University of Nebraska Press.

Bargh, J. A., & Pietromonaco, P. (1982). Automatic information processing and social perception: The influence of trait information presented outside of conscious awareness on impression formation. *Journal of Personality and Social Psychology, 43,* 437–449.

Bargh, J. A., & Thein, R. D. (1985). Individual construct accessibility, person memory, and the recall-judgment link: The case of information overload. *Journal of Personality and Social Psychology, 49,* 1129–1146.

Barnet, R. (1971, November). The game of nations. *Harper's, 243,* 53–59.

Baron, R. A. (1972). Aggression as a function of ambient temperature and prior anger arousal. *Journal of Personality and Social Psychology, 21,* 183–189.

Baron, R. A. (1983a). The control of human aggression: An optimistic perspective. *Journal of Social and Clinical Psychology, 1,* 97–119.

Baron, R. A., Baron, P., & Miller, N. (1973). The relation between distraction and persuasion. *Psychological Bulletin, 80,* 310–323.

Baron, R. S. (1986). Distraction-conflict theory: Progress and problems. In L. Berkowitz (Ed.), *Advances in experimental social psychology* (vol. 19, pp. 1–40). New York: Academic Press.

Baron, R. S. (2005). So right it's wrong: Groupthink and the ubiquitous nature of polarized group decision making. In M. P. Zanna (Ed.), *Advances in experimental social psychology* (vol. 37, pp. 219–253). San Diego, CA: Elsevier Academic Press.

Baron, R. S., & Roper, G. (1976). Reaffirmation of social comparison views of choice shift: averaging and extremitization in an auto-kinetic situation. *Journal of Personality and Social Psychology, 35,* 521–530.

Baron, R. S., Vandello, J. A., & Brunsman, B. (1996). The forgotten variable in conformity research: impact of task importance on social influence. *Journal of Personality & Social Psychology, 71,* 915–927.

Barrett, L., Dunbar, R., & Lycett, J. (2002). *Human evolutionary psychology.* Princeton, NJ: Princeton University Press.

Barriger, M., & Velez-Blasini, C. J. (2013). Descriptive and injunctive social norm overestimation in hooking up and their role as predictors of hook-up activity in a college student sample. *Journal of Sex Research, 50,* 84–94.

Barsade, S. G. (2002). The ripple effects: Emotional contagion and its influence on group behavior. *Administrative Science Quarterly, 47,* 644–675.

Barsade, S. G., & Gibson, D. E. (2012). Group affect: Its influence on individual and group outcomes. *Current Directions in Psychological Science, 21,* 119–123.

Bartel, C. A., & Saavedra, R. (2000). The collective construction of work group moods. *Administrative Science Quarterly, 45,* 197–231.

Barth, J., Schneider, S., & von Känel, R. (2010). Lack of social support in the etiology and the prognosis of coronary heart disease: A systematic review and meta-analysis. *Psychosomatic Medicine, 72,* 229–238.

Bartholomew, K., & Horowitz, L. M. (1991). Attachment styles among young adults: A test of a four-category model. *Journal of Personality and Social Psychology, 61,* 226–244.

Bartholow, B. D., Anderson, C. A., Carnagey, N. L., & Benjamin, A. J. (2005). Interactive effects of life experience and situational cues on aggression: The weapons priming effect in hunters and nonhunters. *Journal of Experimental Social Psychology, 41,* 48–60.

Bartis, S., Szymanski, K., & Harkins, S. G. (1988). Evaluation and performance: A two-edged knife. *Personality and Social Psychology Bulletin, 14,* 242–251.

Bass, B. M. (1985). *Leadership and performance beyond expectations.* New York: Free Press.

Bass, B. M. (1990). *Bass and Stogdill's handbook of leadership: Theory, research, and managerial applications* (3rd ed.). New York: Free Press.

Bass, B. M. (1997). Does the transactional-transformational leadership paradigm transcend organizational and national boundaries? *American Psychologist, 52,* 130–139.

Bass, B. M., & Riggio, R. E. (2006). *Transformational leadership* (2nd ed.). Mahwah, NJ: Lawrence Erlbaum Associates.

Bassili, J. N. (2003). The minority slowness effect: Subtle inhibitions in the expression of views not shared by others. *Journal of Personality and Social Psychology, 84,* 261–276.

Bastian, B., Loughnan, S., Haslam, N., & Radke, H. R. M. (2012). Don't mind meat? The denial of mind to animals used for human consumption. *Personality & Social Psychology Bulletin, 38,* 247–256.

Batson, C. D. (1991). *The altruism question: Toward a social-psychological answer.* Hillsdale, NJ: Erlbaum.

Batson, C. D. (1998). Altruism and prosocial behavior. In D. T. Gilbert, S. T. Fiske, & G. Lindzey (Eds.), *Handbook of social psychology* (4th ed., vol. 2, pp. 282–315). New York: McGraw-Hill.

Batson, C. D. (2002). Addressing the altruism question experimentally. In S. G. Post & L. G. Underwood (Eds.),

Altruism and altruistic love: Science, philosophy, & religion in dialogue (pp. 89–105). London: Oxford University Press.

Batson, C. D., Ahmad, N., Yin, J., Bedell, S. J., Johnson, J. W., Templin, C. M., & Whiteside, A. (1999). Two threats to the common good: Self-interested egoism and empathy-induced altruism. *Personality and Social Psychology Bulletin, 25,* 3–16.

Batson, C. D., Batson, J. G., Slingsby, J. K., Harrell, K. L., Peekna, H. M., & Todd, R. M. (1991). Empathic joy and the empathy-altruism hypothesis. *Journal of Personality and Social Psychology, 61,* 413–426.

Batson, C. D., Batson, J. G., Todd, M., Brummett, B. H., Shaw, L. L., & Aldeguer, C. M. R. (1995). Empathy and the collective good: Caring for one of the others in a social dilemma. *Journal of Personality and Social Psychology, 68,* 619–631.

Batson, C. D., Duncan, B. D., Ackerman, P., Buckley, T., & Birch, K. (1981). Is empathic emotion a source of altruistic motivation? *Journal of Personality and Social Psychology, 40,* 290–302.

Batson, C. D., Dyck, J. L., Brandt, J. R., & Batson, J. G. (1988). Five studies testing two new egoistic alternatives to the empathy-altruism hypothesis. *Journal of Personality and Social Psychology, 55,* 52–77.

Batson, C. D., Fultz, J., Schoenrade, P. A., & Paduano, A. (1987). Critical self-reflection and self-perceived altruism: When self-reward fails. *Journal of Personality and Social Psychology, 53,* 594–602.

Batson, C. D., & Weeks, J. L. (1996). Mood effects of unsuccessful helping: Another test of the empathy-altruism hypothesis. *Personality and Social Psychology Bulletin, 22,* 148–157.

Baumeister, R. F. (1997). *Evil: Inside human cruelty and violence.* New York: W. H. Freeman.

Baumeister, R. F. (1998). The self. In D. T. Gilbert, S. T. Fiske, & G. Lindzey (Eds.), *Handbook of social psychology* (4th ed., vol. 1, pp. 680–740). Boston: McGraw-Hill.

Baumeister, R. F., Bratslavsky, E., Finkenauer, C., & Vohs, K. D. (2001). Bad is stronger than good. *Review of General Psychology, 5,* 323–370.

Baumeister, R. F., Campbell, J. D., Krueger, J. I., & Vohs, K. D. (2003). Does high self-esteem cause better performance, interpersonal success, happiness, or healthier lifestyles? *Psychological Science in the Public Interest, 4,* 1–44.

Baumeister, R. F., Chesner, S. P., Senders, P. S., & Tice, D. M. (1988). Who's in charge here? Group leaders do lend help in emergencies. *Personality and Social Psychology Bulletin, 14,* 17–22.

Baumeister, R. F., & Leary, M. R. (1995). The need to belong: Desire for interpersonal attachments as a fundamental human motivation. *Psychological Bulletin, 117,* 497–529.

Baumeister, R. F., Muraven, M., & Tice, D. M. (2000). Ego depletion: A resource model of volition, self-regulation, and controlled processing. *Social Cognition, 18,* 130–150.

Baumeister, R. F., & Newman, L. S. (1994). How stories make sense of personal experiences: Motives that shape auto-biographical narratives. *Personality and Social Psychology Bulletin, 20,* 676–690.

Baumeister, R. F., Smart, L. & Boden, J. M. (1996). Relation of threatened egotism to violence and aggression: The dark side of high self-esteem. *Psychological Review, 103,* 5–33.

Baumgardner, A. H., & Brownlee, E. A. (1987). Strategic failure in social interaction: Evidence for expectancy disconfirmation process. *Journal of Personality and Social Psychology, 52,* 525–535.

Baumrind, D. (1964). Some thoughts on ethics of research: After reading Milgram's "Behavioral Study of Obedience." *American Psychologist, 19,* 421–423.

Baxter, L. A. (1986). Gender differences in the heterosexual relationship rules embedded in break-up accounts. *Journal of Social and Personal Relationships, 1,* 29–48.

Baxter, T. L., & Goldberg, L. R. (1987). Perceived behavioral consistency underlying trait attributions to oneself and another: An extension of the actor-observer effect. *Personality and Social Psychology Bulletin, 13,* 437–447.

Bazarova, N. N., Walther, J. B., & McLeod, P. L. (2012). Minority influence in virtual groups: A comparison of four theories of minority influence. *Communication Research, 39,* 295–316.

Beach, S. R. H., Tesser, A., Fincham, F. D., Jones, D. J., Johnson, D., & Whitaker, D. J. (1998). Pleasure and pain in doing well, together: An investigation of performance-related affect in close relationships. *Journal of Personality and Social Psychology, 74,* 923–938.

Beal, D. J., Cohen, R. R., Burke, M. J., & McLendon, C. L. (2003). Cohesion and performance in groups: A meta-analytic clarification of construct relations. *Journal of Applied Psychology, 88,* 989–1004.

Beasley, R. K., & Joslyn, M. R. (2001). Cognitive dissonance and post-decision attitude change in six presidential elections. *Political Psychology, 22,* 521–540.

Beauvois, J. L., & Joule, R. V. (1996). A radical dissonance theory. *European Monographs in Social Psychology.* Philadelphia, PA: Taylor & Francis.

Bechtold, A., Naccarato, M.E. & Zanna, M.P. (1986). Need for structure and the prejudice-discrimination link. Paper presented at the annual meeting of the Canadian Psychological Association, Toronto.

Bechtoldt, M. N., De Dreu, C. K. W., Nijstad, B. A., & Choi, H.-S. (2010). Motivated information processing, social tuning, and group creativity. *Journal of Personality and Social Psychology, 99,* 622–637.

Becker, J. C. (2012). The system-stabilizing role of identity management strategies: Social creativity can undermine collective action for social change. *Journal of Personality & Social Psychology, 103,* 647–662.

Beersma, B., & Van Kleef, G. A. (2011). How the grapevine keeps you in line: Gossip increases contributions to the group. *Social Psychological and Personality Science.* doi:10.1177/194855 0611405073

Beersma, B., & Van Kleef, G. A. (2012). Why people gossip: An empirical analysis of social motives, antecedents, and consequences. *Journal of Applied Social Psychology, 42,* 2640–2670.

Beggan, J. K. (1992). On the social nature of nonsocial perception: The mere ownership effect. *Journal of Personality and Social Psychology, 62,* 229–237.

Bell, D. A. (1973). Racism in American courts: Cause for Black disruption or despair? *California Law Review, 761,* 165–203.

Bell, P. A., & Baron, R. A. (1990). Affect and aggression. In B. S. Moore & A. M. Isen (Eds.), *Affect and social behavior: Studies in emotion and social interaction* (pp. 64–88). New York: Cambridge University Press.

Bellah, R.N. and others. (1985). *Habits of the heart: Individualism and commitment in American life.* Berkeley: University of California Press.

Bellezza, S., Gino, F., & Keinan, A. (2014). The Red Sneakers effect: Inferring status and competence from signals of nonconformity. *Journal of Consumer Research, 41*(1), 35–54.

Belmore, S. M., & Hubbard, M. L. (1987). The role of advance expectancies in person memory. *Journal of Personality and Social Psychology, 53,* 61–70.

Bem, D. J. (1967). Self-perception: An alternative interpretation of cognitive dissonance phenomena. *Psychological Review, 74,* 183–200.

Bem, D. J. (1972). Self-perception theory. In L. Berkowitz (Ed.), *Advances in experimental social psychology* (vol. 6). New York: Academic Press.

Bem, S. (1981). Gender schema theory: A cognitive account of sex typing. *Psychological Review, 88,* 354–364.

Bentler, P.M., & Speckart, G. (1979). Models of attitude-behavior relations. *Psychological Review, 86,* 452–464.

Berg, J. H. (1984). Development of friendship between roommates. *Journal of Personality and Social Psychology, 46,* 346–356.

Berg, J. H., & Archer, R. L. (1980). Disclosure or concern: A second look at liking for the norm-breaker. *Journal of Personality, 48,* 245–257.

Berg, J. H., & McQuinn, R. D. (1986). Attraction and exchange in continuing and noncontinuing dating relationships. *Journal of Personality and Social Psychology, 50,* 942–952.

Berger, J., & Heath, C. (2008). Who drives divergence? Identity signaling, outgroup dissimilarity, and the abandonment of cultural tastes. *Journal of Personality & Social Psychology, 95,* 593–607.

Berglas, S., & Jones, E. E. (1978). Drug choice as a self-handicapping strategy in response to noncontingent success. *Journal of Personality and Social Psychology, 36,* 405–417.

Bergsieker, H. B., Shelton, J. N., & Richeson, J. A. (2010). To be liked versus respected: Divergent goals in interracial interactions. *Journal of Personality & Social Psychology, 99,* 248–264.

Berkowitz, L. (1972). Social norms, feelings, and other factors affecting helping behavior and altruism. In L. Berkowitz (Ed.), *Advances in experimental social psychology* (vol. 6). New York: Academic Press.

Berkowitz, L. (1984). Some effects of thoughts on anti- and prosocial influences of media events: A cognitive-neoassociationist analysis. *Psychological Bulletin, 95,* 410–427.

Berkowitz, L. (1989). The frustration-aggression hypothesis: An examination and reformulation. *Psychological Bulletin, 106,* 59–73.

Berkowitz, L. (1993). *Aggression: Its causes, consequences, and control.* New York: McGraw-Hill.

Berkowitz, L., & Daniels, L. R. (1963). Responsibility and dependency. *Journal of Abnormal and Social Psychology, 66,* 429–436.

Berkowitz, L., & Harmon-Jones, E. (2004). Toward an understanding of the determinants of anger. *Emotion, 4*(2), 107–130.

Berkowitz, L., & LePage, A. (1967). Weapons as aggression-eliciting stimuli. *Journal of Personality and Social Psychology, 7,* 202–207.

Bernache-Assollant, I., Laurin, R., Bouchet, P., Bodet, G., & Lacassagne, M.-F. (2010). Refining the relationship between ingroup identification and identity management strategies in the sport context: The moderating role of gender and the mediating role of negative mood. *Group Processes & Intergroup Relations, 13,* 639–652.

Bernstein, M., & Crosby, F. (1980). An experimental examination of relative deprivation theory. *Journal of Experimental Social Psychology, 16,* 442–456.

Bernstein, M. J., & Claypool, H. M. (2012). Social exclusion and pain sensitivity: Why exclusion sometimes hurts and sometimes numbs. *Personality and Social Psychology Bulletin, 38,* 185–196.

Bernstein, M. J., Young, S. G., Brown, C. M., Sacco, D. F., & Claypool, H. M. (2008). Adaptive responses to social exclusion: Social rejection improves detection of real and fake smiles. *Psychological Science, 19,* 981–983.

Bernstein, M. J., Young, S. G., & Hugenberg, K. (2007). The cross-category effect: Mere social categorization is sufficient to elicit an own-group bias in face recognition. *Psychological Science, 18,* 706–712.

Berry, D. S., & Brownlow, S. (1989). Were the physiognomists right? Personality correlates of facial babyishness. *Personality and Social Psychology Bulletin, 15,* 266–279.

Berry, D. S., & McArthur, L. Z. (1985). Some components and consequences of a babyface. *Journal of Personality and Social Psychology, 48,* 312–323.

Berscheid, E. (1988). Some comments on love's anatomy: Or, whatever happened to old-fashioned lust? In R. Sternberg & M. Barnes (Eds.), *The psychology of love* (pp. 359–374). New Haven, CT: Yale University Press.

Berscheid, E. & Reis, H. T. (1998). Attraction and close relationships. In D. T. Gilbert, S. T. Fiske, & G. Lindzey (Eds.), *Handbook of social psychology* (4th ed., vol. 2, pp. 193–281). Boston: McGraw-Hill.

Berscheid, E., Snyder, M., & Omoto, A. M. (1989). The Relationship Closeness Inventory: Assessing the closeness of interpersonal relationships. *Journal of Personality and Social Psychology, 57,* 792–807.

Bersoff, D. M. (1999). Why good people sometimes do bad things: Motivated reasoning and unethical behavior. *Personality and Social Psychology Bulletin, 25,* 28–39.

Bettencourt, B. A., Brewer, M. B., Croak, M. R., & Miller, N. (1992). Cooperation and the reduction of intergroup bias: The role of reward structure and social orientation. *Journal of Experimental Social Psychology, 28,* 301–319.

Bettencourt, B. A., Charlton, K., Dorr, N., & Hume, D. L. (2001). Status differences and in-group bias: A meta-analytic examination of the effects of status stability, status legitimacy, and group permeability. *Psychological Bulletin, 127*(4), 520–542.

Bickman, L. (1971). The effect of another bystander's ability to help on bystander intervention in an emergency. *Journal of Experimental Social Psychology, 7,* 367–379.

Bickman, L. (1974). The social power of a uniform. *Journal of Applied Social Psychology, 4,* 47–61.

Bickman, L. (1979). Interpersonal influence and the reporting of a crime. *Personality and Social Psychology Bulletin, 5,* 32–35.

Bickman, L., & Rosenbaum, D. P. (1977). Crime reporting as a function of bystander encouragement, surveillance, and credibility. *Journal of Personality and Social Psychology, 35,* 577–586.

Biernat, M., & Manis, M. (1994). Shifting standards and stereotype-based judgments. *Journal of Personality and Social Psychology, 66,* 5–20.

Billig, M. (1976). *Social psychology and intergroup relations.* New York: Academic Press.

Billig, M., & Tajfel, H. (1973). Social categorization and similarity in intergroup behavior. *European Journal of Social Psychology, 3,* 27–52.

Binder, A. R., Dalrymple, K. E., Brossard, D., & Scheufele, D. A. (2009). The soul of a polarized democracy: Testing theoretical linkages between talk and attitude extremity during the 2004 presidential election. *Communication Research, 36,* 315–340.

Binning, J. F., Goldstein, M. A., Garcia, M. F., & Scatteregia, J. H. (1988). Effects of preinterview impressions on questioning strategies in same- and opposite-sex employment interviews. *Journal of Applied Psychology, 73,* 30–37.

Binning, K. R., Sherman, D. K., Cohen, G. L., & Heitland, K. (2010). Seeing the other side: Reducing political partisanship via self-affirmation in the 2008 presidential election. *Analyses of Social Issues and Public Policy, 10*(1), 276–292.

Birchler, G. R., & Webb, L. J. (1977). Discriminating interaction behavior in happy and unhappy marriages. *Journal of Consulting and Clinical Psychology, 45,* 494–495.

Birt, C. M., & Dion, K. L. (1987). Relative deprivation theory and responses to deprivation in a gay male and lesbian sample. *British Journal of Social Psychology, 26,* 139–145.

Blair, I. V. (2002). The malleability of automatic stereotypes and prejudice. *Personality and Social Psychology Bulletin, 6,* 242–261.

Blair, I. V., & Banaji, M. R. (1996). Automatic and controlled processes in stereotype priming. *Journal of Personality and Social Psychology, 70,* 1142–1163.

Blair, I. V., Ma, J. E., & Lenton, A. P. (2001). Imagining stereotypes away: The moderation of implicit stereotypes through mental imagery. *Journal of Personality and Social Psychology, 81,* 828–841.

Blake, R. R., and Mouton, J. S. (1979). Intergroup problem solving in organizations: From theory to practice. In W. G. Austin & S. Worchel (Eds.), *The social psychology of intergroup relations* (pp. 19–32). Monterey, CA: Brooks/Cole.

Blake, R. R., & Mouton, J. S. (1980). *The versatile manager: A Grid profile.* Homewood, IL: Dow Jones-Irwin.

Blake, R.R., & Mouton, J.S. (1984). *Solving costly organizational conflicts.* San Francisco, CA: Jossey-Bass.

Blankenship, K. L., Wegener, D. T., & Murray, R. A. (2012). Circumventing resistance: Using values to indirectly change attitudes. *Journal of Personality & Social Psychology, 103,* 606–621.

Blanton, H., Crocker, J., & Miller, D. T. (2000). The effects of in-group versus out-group social comparison on self-esteem in the context of a negative stereotype. *Journal of Experimental Social Psychology, 36*(5), 519–530.

Blascovich, J. (2008). Challenge, threat, and health. In J. Y. Shah & W. L. Gardner (Eds.), *Handbook of motivation science* (pp. 481–493). New York: Guilford Press.

Blascovich, J., & Tomaka, J. (1996). The biopsychosocial model of arousal regulation. In M.P. Zanna (Ed.), *Advances in experimental social psychology* (vol. 28, pp. 1–51). New York: Academic Press.

Blascovich, J., Wyer, N. A., Swart, L. A., & Kibler, J. L. (1997). Racism and racial categorization. *Journal of Personality and Social Psychology, 72,* 1364–1372.

Blass, T. (2000). *Obedience to authority: Current perspectives on the Milgram paradigm.* Mahwah, NJ: Lawrence Erlbaum Associates.

Blass, T. (2012). A cross-cultural comparison of studies of obedience using the Milgram paradigm: A review. *Social and Personality Psychology Compass, 6,* 196–205.

Bleske-Rechek, A., Remiker, M. W., & Baker, J. P. (2009). Similar from the start: Assortment in young adult dating couples and its link to relationship stability over time. *Individual Differences Research, 7,* 142–158.

Bless, H., Clore, G. L., Schwarz, N., Golisano, V., Rabe, C., & Wolk, M. (1996). Mood and the use of scripts: Does a happy mood really lead to mindlessness? *Journal of Personality and Social Psychology, 71,* 665–679.

Bloom, P. N., McBride, C. M., Pollak, K. I., Schwartz-Bloom, R. D., & Lipkus, I. M. (2006). Recruiting teen smokers in shopping malls to a smoking-cessation program using the foot-in-the-door technique. *Journal of Applied Social Psychology, 36,* 1129–1144.

Blumstein, P., & Schwartz, P. (1983). *American couples: Money, work, sex*. New York: William Morrow.

Bocchiaro, P., Zimbardo, P. G., & Van Lange, P. A. M. (2012). To defy or not to defy: An experimental study of the dynamics of disobedience and whistle-blowing. *Social Influence, 7*, 35–50.

Bodenhausen, G. V. (1990). Stereotypes as judgmental heuristics: Evidence of circadian variations in discrimination. *Psychological Science, 1*, 319–322.

Bodenhausen, G. V. (1993). Emotions, arousal and stereotyping judgments: A heuristic model of affect and stereotyping. In D. M. Mackie & D.L. Hamilton (Eds.), *Affect, cognition, and stereotyping: Interactive processes in group perception* (pp. 13–37). San Diego: Academic Press.

Bodenhausen, G. V., & Lichtenstein, M. (1987). Social stereotypes and information-processing strategies: The impact of task complexity. *Journal of Personality and Social Psychology, 52*, 871–880.

Bodenhausen, G. V., Schwarz, N., Bless, H., & Wanke, M. (1995). Effects of atypical exemplars on racial beliefs: Enlightened racism or generalized appraisals? *Journal of Experimental Social Psychology, 31*, 48–63.

Bodenhausen, G. V., Sheppard, L. A., & Kramer, G. P. (1994). Negative affect and social judgement: The differential impact of anger and sadness. Special Issue: Affect on social judgements and cognition. *European Journal of Social Psychology, 24*, 45–62.

Boer, D., & Fischer, R. (2013). How and when do personal values guide our attitudes and sociality? Explaining cross-cultural variability in attitude–value linkages. *Psychological Bulletin, 139*(5), 1113–1147.

Bohlen, C. (1992, Oct. 20). Irate Russians demonize traders from Caucasus. *The New York Times*, p. A3.

Bohner, G., Dykema-Engblade, A., Tindale, R. S., & Meisenhelder, H. (2008). Framing of majority and minority source information in persuasion: When and how "consensus implies correctness." *Social Psychology, 39*, 108–116.

Bohner, G., Einwiller, S., Erb, H.-P., & Siebler, F. (2003). When small means comfortable: Relations between product attributes in two-sided advertising. *Journal of Consumer Psychology, 13*, 454–463.

Bolger, N., Zuckerman, A., & Kessler, R. C. (2000). Invisible support and adjustment to stress. *Journal of Personality and Social Psychology, 79*, 953–961.

Bond, C. F., & Atoum, A. O. (2000). International deception. *Personality and Social Psychology Bulletin, 26*, 385–395.

Bond, C. F., & DePaulo, B. M. (2006). Accuracy of deception judgments. *Personality & Social Psychology Review, 10*, 214–234.

Bond, C. F., Jr, & Brockett, D. R. (1987). A social context-personality index theory of memory for acquaintances. *Journal of Personality and Social Psychology, 52*, 1110–1121.

Bond, M. H. (1988). *The cross-cultural challenge to social psychology*. Newbury Park, CA: Sage Publications.

Bond, M. H. (2004). Culture and aggression: From context to coercion. *Personality & Social Psychology Review, 8*(1), 62–78.

Bond, R. (2005). Group size and conformity. *Group Processes & Intergroup Relations, 8*, 331–354.

Bond, R., & Smith, P. B. (1996). Culture and conformity: A meta-analysis of studies using Asch's (1952b, 1956) line judgment task. *Psychological Bulletin, 119*, 111–137.

Boninger, D., Krosnick, J. A., & Berent, M. K. (1995). Origins of attitude importance: Self-interest, social identification, and value relevance. *Journal of Personality and Social Psychology, 68*, 61–80.

Booth-Kewley, S., & Friedman, H. S. (1987). Psychological predictors of heart disease: A quantitative review. *Psychological Bulletin, 101*, 343–362.

Bornstein, G. (2003). Intergroup conflict: Individual, group, and collective interests. *Personality and Social Psychology Review, 7*, 129–145

Bornstein, R. F. (1989). Exposure and affect: Overview and meta-analysis of research, 1968–1987. *Psychological Bulletin, 106*, 265–289.

Bornstein, R. F., Leone, D. R., & Galley, D. J. (1987). The generalizability of subliminal mere exposure effects: Influence of stimuli perceived without awareness on social behavior. *Journal of Personality and Social Psychology, 53*, 1070–1079.

Boster, F. J., Fediuk, T. A., & Kotowski, R. (2001). The effectiveness of an altruistic appeal in the presence and absence of favors. *Communication Monographs, 68*, 340–346.

Bothwell, R.K., Brigham, J.C., & Malpass, R.S. (1989). Cross-racial identification. *Personality and Social Psychology Bulletin, 15*, 19–25.

Bouas, K. S., & Komorita, S. S. (1996). Group discussion and cooperation in social dilemmas. *Personality and Social Psychology Bulletin, 22*, 1144–1150.

Bourhis, R. Y., Giles, H., Leyens, J. P., & Tajfel, H. (1978). Psychological distinctiveness: language divergence in Belgium. In H. Giles & R. St Clair (Eds.), *Language and social psychology* (pp. 158–185). Oxford: Blackwell.

Bowers, C. A., Weaver, J. L., & Morgan, B. B., Jr. (1996). Moderating the performance effects of stressors. In J. E. Driskell & E. Salas (Eds.), *Stress and human performance* (pp. 163–192). Mahwah, NJ: Lawrence Erlbaum Associates.

Bowlby, J. (1969). *Attachment and loss*: vol. 1. *Attachment*. New York: Basic Books.

Bowman, J. M., & Wittenbaum, G. M. (2012). Time pressure affects process and performance in hidden-profile groups. *Small Group Research, 43*, 295–314.

Boyanowsky, E. O., & Griffiths, C. T. (1982). Weapons and eye contact as instigators or inhibitors of aggressive arousal in police-citizen interaction. *Journal of Applied Social Psychology, 12*, 398–407.

Boyle, P. J., Hanlon, D., & Russo, E. (2012). The value of task conflict to group decisions. *Journal of Behavioral Decision Making, 25*, 217–227.

Bradbury, T. N., & Fincham, F. D. (1990). Attributions in

marriage: Review and critique. *Psychological Bulletin, 107,* 3–33.

Bradley, B. H., Postlethwaite, B. E., Klotz, A. C., Hamdani, M. R., & Brown, K. G. (2012). Reaping the benefits of task conflict in teams: The critical role of team psychological safety climate. *Journal of Applied Psychology, 97,* 151–158.

Brandt, A. C., Vonk, R., & van Knippenberg, A. (2011). Augmentation and discounting in impressions of targets described by third parties with ulterior motives. *Social Cognition, 29,* 210–220.

Branscombe, N. R. (1998). Thinking about one's gender group's privileges or disadvantages: Consequences for well-being in women and men. *British Journal of Social Psychology, 37,* 167–184.

Branscombe, N. R., & Wann, D. L. (1994). Collective self-esteem consequences of outgroup derogation when a valued social identity is on trial. *European Journal of Social Psychology, 24,* 641–657.

Branscombe, N. R., Wann, D. L., Noel, J. G., & Coleman, J. (1993). In-group or out-group extremity: Importance of the threatened social identity. *Personality and Social Psychology Bulletin, 19,* 381–388.

Brauer, M., Judd, C. M., & Gliner, M. D. (1995). The effects of repeated expressions on attitude polarization during group discussions. *Journal of Personality and Social Psychology, 68,* 1014–1029.

Brauer, M., Judd, C. M., & Jacquelin, V. (2001). The communication of social stereotypes: The effects of group discussion and information distribution on stereotypic appraisals. *Journal of Personality and Social Psychology, 81,* 463–475.

Brawley, L. R., Carron, A. V., & Widmeyer, W. N. (1987). Assessing the cohesion of teams: Validity of the Group Environment Questionnaire. *Journal of Sport Psychology, 9,* 275–294.

Brawley, L. R., Carron, A. V., & Widmeyer, W. N. (1988). Exploring the relationship between cohesion and group resistance to disruption. *Journal of Sport and Exercise Psychology, 10,* 199–213.

Bray, R. M., Johnson, D., & Chilstrom, J. T., Jr., (1982). Social influence by group members with minority opinions: A comparison of Hollander and Moscovici. *Journal of Personality and Social Psychology, 43,* 78–88.

Breckler, S. J., & Wiggins, E. C. (1989). Affect versus evaluation in the structure of attitudes. *Journal of Experimental Social Psychology, 25,* 253–271.

Brehm, J. W. (1956). Post-decision changes in desirability of alternatives. *Journal of Abnormal and Social Psychology, 52,* 384–389.

Brehm, J. W. (1966). *A theory of psychological reactance.* New York: Academic Press.

Brennan, K. A., Clark, C. L., & Shaver, P. R. (1998). Self-report measurement of adult attachment: An integrative overview. In J. A. Simpson & W. S. Rholes (Eds.), *Attachment theory and close relationships* (pp. 46–76). New York: Guilford Press.

Brewer, M. B. (1979). In-group bias in the minimal intergroup situation: A cognitive-motivational analysis. *Psychological Bulletin, 86,* 307–324.

Brewer, M. B. (1988). A dual process model of impression formation. In T. Srull & R. Wyer (Eds.), *Advances in social cognition* (vol. 1, pp. 177–183). Hillsdale, NJ: Erlbaum.

Brewer, M. B. (1991). The social self: On being the same and different at the same time. *Personality and Social Psychology Bulletin, 17,* 475–482.

Brewer, M. B. (1999). The psychology of prejudice: Ingroup love or outgroup hate? *Journal of Social Issues, 55,* 429–444.

Brewer, M. B. (2001). Ingroup identification and intergroup conflict: When does ingroup love become outgroup hate? In R. D. Ashmore & L. Jussim (Eds.), *Social identity, intergroup conflict, and conflict reduction* (vol. 3, pp. 17–41). New Brunswick, NJ: Rutgers University Press.

Brewer, M. B., & Campbell, D. T. (1976). *Ethnocentrism and intergroup attitudes: East African evidence.* New York: Halstead Press.

Brewer, M. B., Dull, V., & Lui, L. (1981). Perceptions of the elderly: Stereotypes as prototypes. *Journal of Personality and Social Psychology, 41,* 656–670.

Brewer, M. B., & Kramer, R. M. (1986). Choice behavior in social dilemmas: Effects of social identity, group size, and decision framing. *Journal of Personality and Social Psychology, 50,* 543–549.

Brewer, M. B., & Silver, M. (1978). Ingroup bias as a function of task characteristics. *European Journal of Social Psychology, 8,* 393–400.

Brewer, M. B., & Weber, J. G. (1994). Self-evaluation effects of interpersonal versus intergroup social comparison. *Journal of Personality and Social Psychology, 66,* 268–275.

Brickman, P., Coates, D., & Janoff-Bulman, R. (1978). Lottery winners and accident victims: Is happiness relative? *Journal of Personality and Social Psychology, 36,* 917–927.

Brickner, M. A., Harkins, S. G., & Ostrom, T. M. (1986). Effects of personal involvement: Thought-provoking implications for social loafing. *Journal of Personality and Social Psychology, 51,* 763–770.

Brief, A. P., Dietz, J., Cohen, R. R., Pugh, S. D., & Vaslow, J. B. (2000). Just doing business: Modern racism and obedience to authority as explanations for employment discrimination. *Organizational Behavior and Human Decision Processes, 81,* 72–97.

Brief, A. P., & Weiss, H. M. (2002). Organizational behavior: Affect in the workplace. *Annual Review of Psychology, 53,* 279–307.

Brigham, J. C. (1971). Ethnic stereotypes. *Psychological Bulletin, 76,* 15–33.

Briñol, P., & Petty, R. E. (2003). Overt head movements and persuasion: A self-validation analysis. *Journal of Personality & Social Psychology, 84,* 1123–1139.

Briñol, P., & Petty, R. E. (2009). Source factors in persuasion: A self-validation approach. *European Review of Social Psychology, 20,* 49–96.

Brooks, C. M., & Ammons, J. L. (2003). Free riding in group projects and the effects of timing, frequency, and specificity of criteria in peer assessments. *Journal of Education for Business, 78,* 268–272.

Brooks, D. (2004, June 29.). Age of political separation. *New York Times.*

Brown, E. R., Diekman, A. B., & Schneider, M. C. (2011). A change will do us good: Threats diminish typical preferences for male leaders. *Personality and Social Psychology Bulletin, 37,* 930–941.

Brown, J. D. (1986). Evaluations of self and others: Self-enhancing biases in social judgment. *Social Cognition, 4,* 353–376.

Brown, J. D. (2010). High self-esteem buffers negative feedback: Once more with feeling. *Cognition & Emotion, 24,* 1389–1404.

Brown, J. D., & Smart, S. A. (1991). The self and social conduct: Linking self-representations to prosocial behavior. *Journal of Personality and Social Psychology, 60,* 368–375.

Brown, R., Condor, S., Matthews, A., Wade, G., & Williams, J. A. (1986). Explaining intergroup differentiation in an industrial organization. *Journal of Occupational Psychology, 59,* 273–286.

Brown, R., & Hewstone, M. (2005). An integrative theory of intergroup contact. In M. P. Zanna (Ed.), *Advances in experimental social psychology* (vol. 37, pp. 255–343). San Diego, CA: Elsevier Academic Press.

Brown, R. P., Osterman, L. L., & Barnes, C. D. (2009). School violence and the culture of honor. *Psychological Science, 20,* 1400–1405.

Brown, S. L., Brown, R. M., House, J. S., & Smith, D. M. (2008). Coping with spousal loss: Potential buffering effects of self-reported helping behavior. *Personality and Social Psychology Bulletin, 34,* 849–861.

Browning, C. R. (1992). *Ordinary men.* New York: HarperCollins.

Bryan, A. D., Webster, G. D., & Mahaffey, A. L. (2011). The big, the rich, and the powerful: Physical, financial, and social dimensions of dominance in mating and attraction. *Personality & Social Psychology Bulletin, 37,* 365–382.

Bryan, J. H., & Test, M. A. (1967). Models and helping: Naturalistic studies in aiding behavior. *Journal of Personality and Social Psychology, 10,* 222–226.

Buchan, N. R., Brewer, M. B., Grimalda, G., Wilson, R. K., Fatas, E., & Foddy, M. (2011). Global social identity and global cooperation. *Psychological Science : A Journal of the American Psychological Society / APS, 22*(6), 821–828. doi:10.1177/0956797611409590

Budescu, D. V., Rapoport, A., & Suleiman, R. (1990). Resource dilemmas with environmental uncertainty and asymmetric players. *European Journal of Social Psychology, 20,* 475–487.

Bui, K.-V. T., Peplau, L. A., & Hill, C. T. (1996). Testing the Rusbult model of relationship commitment and stability in a 15-year study of heterosexual couples. *Personality and Social Psychology Bulletin, 22,* 1244–1257.

Buller, D. J. (2005). *Adapting minds: Evolutionary psychology and the persistent quest for human nature.* Cambridge, MA: MIT Press.

Bulman, R., & Wortman, C. (1977). Attributions of blame and coping in the "real world:" Severe accident victims respond to their lot. *Journal of Personality and Social Psychology, 35,* 351–363.

Bureau of Labor Statistics. (2012). *Household data annual averages.* Retrieved from http://www. bls.gov/cps/cpsaat11.htm

Burger, J. M. (1999). The foot-in-the-door compliance procedure: A multiple-process analysis and review. *Personality & Social Psychology Review, 3,* 303–325.

Burger, J. M. (2009). Replicating Milgram: Would people still obey today? *American Psychologist, 64,* 1–11.

Burger, J. M., & Caldwell, D. F. (2003). The effects of monetary incentives and labeling on the foot-in-the-door effect: Evidence for a self-perception process. *Basic and Applied Social Psychology, 25,* 235–241.

Burger, J. M., Ehrlichman, A. M., Raymond, N. C., Ishikawa, J. M., & Sandoval, J. (2006). Reciprocal favor exchange and compliance. *Social Influence, 1,* 169–184.

Burger, J. M., Girgis, Z. M., & Manning, C. C. (2011). In their own words: Explaining obedience to authority through an examination of participants' comments. *Social Psychological and Personality Science, 2,* 460–466.

Burger, J. M., & Shelton, M. (2011). Changing everyday health behaviors through descriptive norm manipulations. *Social Influence, 6,* 69–77.

Burke, C. S., Stagl, K. C., Salas, E., Pierce, L., & Kendall, D. (2006). Understanding team adaptation: A conceptual analysis and model. *Journal of Applied Psychology, 91,* 1189–1207.

Burke, R. J. (1970). Methods of resolving superior-subordinate conflict; The constructive use of subordinate differences and disagreements. *Organizational Behavior and Human Performance, 5,* 393–411.

Burkley, E., Anderson, D., & Curtis, J. (2011). You wore me down: Self-control strength and social influence. *Social and Personality Psychology Compass, 5,* 487–499.

Burleson, B. R. (2003). The experience and effects of emotional support: What the study of cultural and gender differences can tell us about close relationships, emotion and inter-personal communication. *Personal Relationships, 10,* 1–23.

Burnette, J. L., Davisson, E. K., Finkel, E. J., Van Tongeren, D. R., Hui, C. M., & Hoyle, R. H. (2014). Self-control and forgiveness: A meta-analytic review. *Social Psychological and Personality Science, 5,* 443–450.

Burns, J. M. (2003). *Transformational leadership.* New York: Atlantic Monthly Press.

Burns, J. M., & Sorenson, G. J. (2000). *Dead center: Clinton-Gore leadership and the perils of moderation.* New York: Scribner.

Burnstein, E., & Vinokur, A. (1977). Persuasive argumentation and social comparison as determinants of attitude polarization. *Journal of Experimental Social Psychology, 13,* 315–332.

Bushman, B. J. (2005). Violence and sex in television programs do not sell products in advertisements. *Psychological Science, 16,* 702–708.

Bushman, B. J., & Anderson, C. A. (2001a). Is it time to pull the plug on hostile versus instrumental aggression dichotomy? *Psychological Review*, 108(1), 273–279.

Bushman, B. J., & Anderson, C. A. (2001b). Media violence and the American public: Scientific facts versus media misinformation. *American Psychologist*, 56, 477–489.

Bushman, B. J., & Anderson, C. A. (2002). Violent video games and hostile expectations: A test of the general aggression model. *Personality & Social Psychology Bulletin*, 28(12), 1679–1686.

Bushman, B. J., & Baumeister, R. F. (1998). Threatened egotism, narcissism, self-esteem, and direct and displaced aggression: Does self-love or self-hate lead to violence? *Journal of Personality and Social Psychology*, 75, 219–229.

Bushman, B. J., Baumeister, R. F., & Stack, A. D. (1999). Catharsis, aggression, and persuasive influence: Self-fulfilling or self-defeating prophecies? *Journal of Personality & Social Psychology*, 76(3), 367–376.

Bushman, B. J., & Cooper, H. M. (1990). Effects of alcohol on human aggression: An integrative research review. *Psychological Bulletin*, 107, 341–354.

Bushman, B. J., & Geen, R. G. (1990). Role of cognitive-emotional mediators and individual differences in the effects of media violence on aggression. *Journal of Personality and Social Psychology*, 58, 156–163.

Bushman, B. J., & Gibson, B. (2011). Violent video games cause an increase in aggression long after the game has been turned off. *Social Psychological and Personality Science*, 2, 29–32.

Bushman, B. J., Wang, M. C., & Anderson, C. A. (2005). Is the curve relating temperature to aggression linear or curvilinear? Assaults and temperature in Minneapolis reexamined. *Journal of Personality & Social Psychology*, 89, 62–66.

Buss, A. (1961). *The psychology of aggression*. New York: Wiley.

Buss, D. M. (1984). Marital assortment for personality dispositions: Assessment with three different data sources. *Behavior Genetics*, 14, 111–123.

Buss, D. M. (1989). Sex differences in human mate preferences: Evolutionary hypotheses tested in 37 cultures. *Behavioral and Brain Sciences*, 12, 1–49.

Buss, D. M. (1994). The strategies of human mating. *American Scientist*, 82, 238–249.

Buss, D. M., & Barnes, M. (1986). Preferences in human mate selection. *Journal of Personality and Social Psychology*, 50, 559–570.

Buss, D. M., & Kenrick, D. T. (1998). Evolutionary social psychology. In D. T. Gilbert, S. T. Fiske, & G. Lindzey (Eds.), *Handbook of social psychology* (3rd edn, vol. 2, pp. 982–1026). Boston: McGraw-Hill.

Buunk, B. P., Gibbons, F. X., & Visser, A. (2002). The relevance of social comparison processes for prevention and health care. *Patient Education and Counseling*, 47, 1–3.

Byrne, D. (1971). *The attraction paradigm*. New York: Academic Press.

Cacioppo, J. T., Berntson, G. G., & Decety, J. (2011). A history of social neuroscience. In A. W. Kruglanski & W. Stroebe (Eds.), *Handbook of the history of social psychology*. New York: Psychology Press

Cacioppo, J. T., Cacioppo, S., Gonzaga, G. C., Ogburn, E. L., & VanderWeele, T. J. (2013). Marital satisfaction and break-ups differ across on-line and off-line meeting venues. *Proceedings of the National Academy of Sciences*, 110, 10135–10140.

Cacioppo, J. T., & Hawkley, L. C. (2005). People thinking about people: The vicious cycle of being a social outcast in one's own mind. In K. D. Williams, J. P. Forgas, & W. von Hippel (Eds.), *The social outcast: Ostracism, social exclusion, rejection, and bullying* (pp. 91–108). New York: Psychology Press.

Cacioppo, J. T., Hughes, M. E., Waite, L. J., Hawkley, L. C., & Thisted, R. A. (2006). Loneliness as a specific risk factor for depressive symptoms: Cross-sectional and longitudinal analyses. *Psychology & Aging*, 21, 140–151.

Cacioppo, J. T., & Patrick, W. (2008). *Loneliness: Human nature and the need for social connection*. New York: W. W. Norton & Co.

Cacioppo, J. T., & Petty, R. E. (1979). Attitudes and cognitive responses: An electro-physiological approach. *Journal of Personality and Social Psychology*, 37, 2181–2199.

Cacioppo, J. T., & Petty, R. E. (1982). The need for cognition. *Journal of Personality and Social Psychology*, 42, 116–131.

Cacioppo, J. T., & Petty, R. E. (1984). The need for cognition: Relationship to attitudinal processes. In R. McGlynn, J. Maddux, C. Stoltenberg, & J. Harvey (Eds.), *Social perception in clinical and counseling psychology*. Lubbock, TX: Rexas Tech Press.

Cacioppo, J. T., Petty, R. E., Feinstein, J. A., Jarvis, W., & Blair, G. (1996). Dispositional differences in cognitive motivation: The life and times of individuals varying in need for cognition. *Psychological Bulletin*, 119, 197–253.

Cacioppo, J. T., Petty, R. E., Losch, M. E., & Kim, H. S. (1986). Electromyographic activity over facial muscle regions can differentiate the valence and intensity of affective reactions. *Journal of Personality and Social Psychology*, 50, 260–268.

Cahill, J. B. (1999, October 4). Here's the pitch: How Kirby persuades uncertain consumers to buy $1,500 vacuum—the door-to-door hard sell brings profits, criticism, to Berkshire Hathaway—'pushiest people I ever saw'. *The Wall Street Journal*, p. A.1.

Calvert, S. L. (2008). Children as consumers: Advertising and marketing. *The Future of Children*, 18, 205–234.

Camodeca, M., & Goossens, F. A. (2005). Aggression, social cognitions, anger and sadness in bullies and victims. *Journal of Child Psychology and Psychiatry*, 46, 186–197.

Campbell, A., Converse, P. E., & Rodgers, W. L. (1976). *The quality of American life*. New York: Russell Sage Foundation.

Campbell, D.T. (1963). Social attitudes and other aquired behavioral dispositions. In S. Koch (Ed.), *Psychology: A study of a science* (vol. 6, pp. 94–172). New York: McGraw-Hill.

Campbell, D. T. (1965). Ethnocentric and other altruistic motives.

In D. Levine (Ed.), *Nebraska Symposium on motivation* (vol. 13, pp. 283–311). Lincoln: University of Nebraska Press.

Campbell, D. T. (1967). Stereotypes and the perception of group differences. *American Psychologist, 22,* 817–829.

Campbell, J. D. (1990). Self-esteem and clarity of the self-concept. *Journal of Personality and Social Psychology, 59,* 538–549.

Campbell, J. D., Chew, B., & Scratchley, L. S. (1991). Cognitive and emotional reactions to daily events: The effects of self-esteem and self-complexity. *Journal of Personality, 59,* 473–505.

Campbell, J. D., & Fairey, P. (1985). Effects of self-esteem, hypothetical explanations, and verbalization of expectancies on future performance. *Journal of Personality and Social Psychology, 48,* 1097–1111.

Campbell-Meiklejohn, D. K., Bach, D. R., Roepstorff, A., Dolan, R. J., & Frith, C. D. (2010). How the opinion of others affects our valuation of objects. *Current Biology, 20,* 1165–1170.

Cantor, N., & Kihlstrom, J. F. (1987). *Personality and social intelligence.* Englewood Cliffs, NJ: Prentice-Hall.

Cantor, N., & Malley, J. (1991). Life tasks, personal needs, and close relationships. In G. Fletcher & F. Fincham (Eds.), *Cognition in close relationships* (pp. 101–126). Hillsdale, NJ: Lawrence Erlbaum Associates.

Caporael, L. (1997). The evolution of truly social cognition: The core configurations model. *Personality and Social Psychology Review, 1,* 276–298.

Caporael, L. R., & Brewer, M. B. (1991). Reviving evolutionary psychology: Biology meets society. *Journal of Social Issues, 47*(3), 187–195.

Caporael, L. R., Dawes, R. M., Orbell, J. M., & Van de Kragt, A. J. C. (1989). Selfishness examined: Cooperation in the absence of egoistic incentives. *Behavioral and Brain Sciences, 12,* 683–699.

Caprariello, P. A., Cuddy, A. J. C., & Fiske, S. T. (2009). Social structure shapes cultural stereotypes and emotions: A causal test of the stereotype content model. *Group Processes & Intergroup Relations, 12,* 147–155.

Carli, L. (1990). Gender, language, and influence. *Journal of Personality and Social Psychology, 59,* 941–951.

Carli, L. L., & Leonard, J. B. (1989). The effect of hindsight on victim derogation. *Journal of Social and Clinical Psychology, 8,* 331–343.

Carlson, M., Marcus-Newhall, A., & Miller, N. (1989). Evidence for a general construct of aggression. *Personality and Social Psychology Bulletin, 15,* 377–389.

Carlson, M., & Miller, N. (1987). Explanation of the relation between negative mood and helping. *Psychological Bulletin, 102,* 91–108.

Carlston, D. E. (1994). Associated systems theory: A systematic approach to cognitive representations of persons. In T. K. Srull & R. S. Wyer (Eds.), *Advances in social cognition* (vol. 7, pp. 1–78). Hillsdale, NJ: Erlbaum.

Carlston, D. E., & Skowronski, J. J. (1986). Trait memory and behavior memory: The effects of alternative pathways on

impression judgment response times. *Journal of Personality and Social Psychology, 50,* 5–13.

Carlston, D. E., & Skowronski, J. J. (1994). Savings in the relearning of trait information as evidence for spontaneous inference generation. *Journal of Personality and Social Psychology, 66,* 840–856.

Carnagey, N. L., & Anderson, C. A. (2005). The effects of reward and punishment in violent video games on aggressive affect, cognition, and behavior. *Psychological Science, 16,* 882–889.

Carney, D. R., Cuddy, A. J. C., & Yap, A. J. (2010). Power posing: Brief nonverbal displays affect neuroendocrine levels and risk tolerance. *Psychological Science, 21,* 1363–1368.

Carothers, B. J., & Reis, H. T. (2013). Men and women are from earth: Examining the latent structure of gender. *Journal of Personality & Social Psychology, 104,* 385–407.

Carr, D. (2002, Nov. 18). On covers of many magazines, a full racial palette is still rare. *The New York Times,* p. C1.

Carré, J. M., Putnam, S. K., & McCormick, C. M. (2009). Testosterone responses to competition predict future aggressive behaviour at a cost to reward in men. *Psychoneuroendocrinology, 34,* 561–570.

Carrere, S., Buehlman, K. T., Gottman, J. M., Coan, J. A., & Ruckstuhl, L. (2000). Predicting marital stability and divorce in newlywed couples. *Journal of Family Psychology, 14,* 42–58.

Carroll, J. M., & Russell, J. A. (1996). Do facial expressions signal specific emotions? Judging emotion from the face in context. *Journal of Personality and Social Psychology, 70,* 205–218.

Carter, S. (1991). *Reflections of an affirmative action baby.* New York: Basic Books.

Carter-Sowell, A. R., Chen, Z., & Williams, K. D. (2008). Ostracism increases social susceptibility. *Social Influence, 3,* 143–153.

Cartwright, D. (1979). Contemporary social psychology in historical perspective. *Social Psychology Quarterly, 42,* 82–93.

Carver, C. S., & Scheier, M. F. (1981). *Attention and self-regulation: A control theory approach to human behavior.* New York: Springer-Verlag.

Carver, C. S., & Scheier, M. F. (1990). Origins and functions of positive and negative affect: A control-process view. *Psychological Review, 97,* 19–35.

Cary, L. (1992, June 29). As plain as black and white. *Newsweek,* p. 53.

Castano, E. (2008). On the perils of glorifying the in-group: Intergroup violence, in-group glorification, and moral disengagement. *Social and Personality Psychology Compass, 2,* 154–170.

Cate, R. M., & Lloyd, S. A. (1988). Courtship. In S. Duck (Ed.), *Handbook of personal relationships: Theory, relationships, and interventions.* Chichester: Wiley.

Centerbar, D. B., & Clore, G. L. (2006). Do approach-avoidance actions create attitudes? *Psychological Science, 17,* 22–29.

Cesario, J., Corker, K. S., & Jelinek, S. (2013). A self-regulatory framework for message framing. *Journal of Experimental Social Psychology*, 49, 238–249.

Cesario, J., & Jonas, K. J. (in press). Replicability and models of priming: What a resource computation framework can tell us about expectations of replicability. *Social Cognition*.

Chacko, T.I. (1982). Women and equal employment opportunity: Some unintended effects. *Journal of Applied Psychology*, 67, 119–123.

Chaiken, S. (1979). Communicator physical attractiveness and persuasion. *Journal of Personality and Social Psychology*, 37, 1387–1397.

Chaiken, S. (1980). Heuristic versus systematic information processing and the use of source versus message cues in persuasion. *Journal of Personality and Social Psychology*, 39, 752–756.

Chaiken, S. (1987). The heuristic model of persuasion. In M. P. Zanna, J. M. Olson, & C. P. Herman (Eds.), *Social influence: The Ontario Symposium* (vol. 5, pp. 3–40). Hillsdale, NJ: Erlbaum.

Chaiken, S., & Baldwin, M. W. (1981). Affective-cognitive consistency and the effect of salient behavioral information on the self-perception of attitudes. *Journal of Personality and Social Psychology*, 41, 1–12.

Chaiken, S., Giner-Sorolla, R., & Chen, S. (1996). Beyond accuracy: Defense and impression motives in heuristic and systematic information processing. In P. M. Gollwitzer & J. A. Bargh (Eds.), *The psychology of action: Linking cognition and motivation to behavior* (pp. 553–578). New York: Guilford Press.

Chaiken, S., & Maheswaran, D. (1994). Heuristic processing can bias systematic processing: Effects of source credibility, argument ambiguity, and task importance on attitude judgement. *Journal of Personality and Social Psychology*, 66, 460–473.

Chaiken, S., & Trope, Y. (Eds.). (1999). *Dual-process theories in social psychology*. New York: Guilford Press.

Chan, A. C.-Y., & Au, T. K.-F. (2011). Getting children to do more academic work: Foot-in-the-door versus door-in-the-face. *Teaching and Teacher Education*, 27, 982–985.

Chapman, J. (2006). Anxiety and defective decision making: An elaboration of the groupthink model. *Management Decision*, 44, 1391–1404.

Charters, W. W., & Newcomb, T. M. (1958). Some attitudinal effects of experimentally increased salience of a membership group. In E. E. Maccoby, T. M. Newcomb, & E. L. Hartley (Eds.), *Readings in social psychology* (pp. 276–281). New York: Holt.

Chartrand, T. L., & Bargh, J. A. (1999). The chameleon effect: The perception-behavior link and social interaction. *Journal of Personality & Social Psychology*, 76, 893–910.

Chartrand, T. L., & van Baaren, R. (2009). Human mimicry. In M. P. Zanna (Ed.), *Advances in experimental social psychology* (vol. 41, pp. 219–274). New York: Academic Press.

Chebat, J.-C., El Hedhli, K., Gelinas-Chebat, C., & Boivin, R. (2007). Voice and persuasion in a banking telemarketing context. *Perceptual & Motor Skills*, 104, 419–437.

Cheetham, M., Pedroni, A. F., Antley, A., Slater, M., & Jancke, L. (2009). Virtual Milgram: Empathic concern or personal distress? Evidence from functional MRI and dispositional measures. *Frontiers in Human Neuroscience*, 3. doi: 10.3389/neuro.09.029.2009

Chen, F. F., Jing. Y. & Lee, J. M. (2012). "I" value competence but "we" value social competence: The moderating role of voters' individualistic and collectivistic orientation in political elections. *Journal of Experimental Social Psychology*, 48, 1350–1355.

Chen, G., & Klimoski, R. J. (2003). The impact of expectations on newcomer performance in teams as mediated by work characteristics, social exchanges, and empowerment. *Academy of Management Journal*, 46, 591–607.

Chen, M. K., & Risen, J. L. (2010). How choice affects and reflects preferences: Revisiting the free-choice paradigm. *Journal of Personality and Social Psychology*, 99, 573–594.

Chen, S., & Chaiken, S. (1999). The heuristic-systematic model in its broader context. In S. Chaiken & Y. Trope (Eds.), *Dual-process theories in social psychology* (pp. 73–96). New York: Guilford Press.

Chen, S., Shechter, D., & Chaiken, S. (1996). Getting at the truth or getting along: Accuracy- versus impression-motivated heuristic and systematic processing. *Journal of Personality and Social Psychology*, 71, 262–275.

Cherlin, A. J., and others. (1991). Longitudinal studies of effects of divorce on children in Great Britain and the United States. *Science*, 252, 1386–1389.

Chih-Mao, H., & Park, D. (2013). Cultural influences on Facebook photographs. *International Journal of Psychology*, 48, 334–343.

Chiu, C.-Y., Gelfand, M. J., Yamagishi, T., Shteynberg, G., & Wan, C. (2010). Intersubjective culture: The role of intersubjective perceptions in cross-cultural research. *Perspectives on Psychological Science*, 5, 482–493.

Chiu, C.-Y., Morris, M. W., Hong, Y.-y., & Menon, T. (2000). Motivated cultural cognition: The impact of implicit cultural theories on dispositional attribution varies as a function of need for closure. *Journal of Personality & Social Psychology*, 78, 247–259.

Cho, J. C., & Knowles, E. D. (2013). I'm like you and you're like me: Social projection and self-stereotyping both help explain self–other correspondence. *Journal of Personality and Social Psychology*, 104(3), 444–456. doi:10.1037/a0031017

Choi, I., & Choi, Y. (2002). Culture and self-concept flexibility. *Personality and Social Psychology Bulletin*, 28, 1508–1517.

Choi, I., Dalal, R., Kim-Prieto, C., & Park, H. (2003). Culture and judgment of causal relevance. *Journal of Personality and Social Psychology*, 84, 46–59.

Choi, J., Johnson, D. W., & Johnson, R. (2011). Relationships among cooperative learning experiences, social interdependence, children's aggression, victimization, and prosocial behaviors. *Journal of Applied Social Psychology*, *41*(4), 976–1003. doi:http://dx.doi.org/10.1111/j.1559–1816.2011.00744.x

Chow, R. M., & Lowery, B. S. (2010). Thanks, but no thanks: The role of personal responsibility in the experience of gratitude. *Journal of Experimental Social Psychology*, *46*(3), 487–493. doi:http://dx.doi.org/10.1016/j.jesp.2009.12.018

Christakis, N. A., & Fowler, J. H. (2007). The spread of obesity in a large social network over 32 years. *The New England Journal of Medicine*, *357*, 370–379.

Christakis, N. A., & Fowler, J. H. (2011). *Connected: The surprising power of our social networks and how they shape our lives. How your friends' friends' friends affect everything you feel, think, and do*. New York, NY: Back Bay Books.

Christensen, P. N., Rothgerber, H., Wood, W., & Matz, D. C. (2004). Social norms and identity relevance: A motivational approach to normative behavior. *Personality and Social Psychology Bulletin*, *30*, 1395–1309.

Christensen, U., Schmidt, L., Budtz-Jorgensen, E., & Avlund, K. (2006). Group cohesion and social support in exercise classes: Results from a Danish intervention study. *Health Education & Behavior*, *33*, 677–689.

Chu, D., & McIntyre, B. T. (1995). Sex role stereotypes on children's TV in Asia: A content analysis of gender role portrayals in children's cartoons in Hong Kong. *Communication Research Reports*, *12*, 206–219.

Chun, W. Y., Spiegel, S., & Kruglanski, A. W. (2002). Assimilative behavior identification can also be resource dependent: The unimodel perspective on personal-attribution phases. *Journal of Personality and Social Psychology*, *83*, 542–555.

Cialdini, R. B. (1984). Principles of automatic influence. In J. Jacoby & G. S. Craig (Eds.), *Personal selling* (pp. 1–27). Lexington, MA: Lexington Books.

Cialdini, R. B. (1993). *Influence: Science and practice* (3rd ed.). New York: HarperCollins.

Cialdini, R. B. (2003). Crafting normative messages to protect the environment. *Current Directions in Psychological Science*, *12*, 105–109.

Cialdini, R. B., Borden, R. J., Thorne, A., Walker, M. R., Freeman, S., & Sloan, L. R. (1976). Basking in reflected glory: Three (football) field studies. *Journal of Personality and Social Psychology*, *34*, 366–375.

Cialdini, R. B., Cacioppo, J. T., Bassett, R., & Miller, J. A., (1978). Lowball procedure for producing compliance: Commitment then cost. *Journal of Personality and Social Psychology*, *36*, 463–476.

Cialdini, R. B., Darby, B. L., & Vincent, J. E. (1973). Transgression and altruism: A case for hedonism. *Journal of Experimental Social Psychology*, *9*, 502–516.

Cialdini, R. B., & Kenrick, D. T. (1976). Altruism as hedonism: A social development perspective on the relationship of negative mood state and helping. *Journal of Personality and Social Psychology*, *34*, 907–914.

Cialdini, R. B., Reno, R. R., & Kallgren, C. A. (1990). A focus theory of normative conduct: Recycling the concept of norms to reduce littering in public places. *Journal of Personality and Social Psychology*, *58*, 1015–1026.

Cialdini, R. B., & Schroeder, D. A. (1976). Increasing compliance by legitimizing paltry contributions: When even a penny helps. *Journal of Personality and Social Psychology*, *34*, 599–604.

Cialdini, R. B., Vincent, J. E., Lewis, S. K., Catalan, J., Wheeler, D., & Darby, B.L. (1975). Reciprocal concessions procedure for inducing compliance: The door in the face technique. *Journal of Personality and Social Psychology*, *31*, 206–215.

Cicero, L., Bonaiuto, M., Pierro, A., & van Knippenberg, D. (2008). Employees' work effort as a function of leader group prototypicality: The moderating role of team identification. *European Review of Applied Psychology*, *58*, 117–124.

Clark, A. E., & Kashima, Y. (2007). Stereotypes help people connect with others in the community: A situated functional analysis of the stereotype consistency bias in communication. *Journal of Personality & Social Psychology*, *93*, 1028–1039.

Clark, K. B. (1965). *Dark ghetto: Dilemmas of social power*. New York: Harper & Row.

Clark, L. F., & Collins, J. E. (1993). Remembering old flames: How the past affects assessments of the present. *Personality and Social Psychology Bulletin*, *19*, 399–408.

Clark, M. S., & Mills, J. (1979). Interpersonal attraction in exchange and communal relationships. *Journal of Personality and Social Psychology*, *37*, 12–24.

Clark, N. K., Stephenson, G. M., & Kniveton, B. H. (1990). Social remembering: Quantitative aspects of individual and collaborative remembering by police officers and students. *British Journal of Psychology*, *81*, 73–94.

Clark, R. D., & Word, L. E. (1972). Why don't bystanders help? Because of ambiguity. *Journal of Personality and Social Psychology*, *24*, 392–400.

Clarkson, J. J., Tormala, Z. L., & Rucker, D. D. (2008). A new look at the consequences of attitude certainty: The amplification hypothesis. *Journal of Personality & Social Psychology*, *95*, 810–825.

Clary, E. G., & Orenstein, L. (1991). The amount and effectiveness of help: The relationship of motives and abilities to helping behavior. *Personality and Social Psychology Bulletin*, *17*, 58–64.

Clary, E. G., Snyder, M., Ridge, R. D., Copeland, J., Stukas, A. A., Haugen, J., & Miene, P. (1998). Understanding and assessing the motivations of volunteers: A functional approach. *Journal of Personality and Social Psychology*, *74*, 1516–1530.

Cleary, A. M., Ryals, A. J., & Nomi, J. S. (2009). Can déjà vu result from similarity to a prior experience? Support for the similarity hypothesis of déjà vu. *Psychonomic Bulletin and Review*, *16*, 1082–1088.

Clement, R. W., & Krueger, J. (1998). Liking persons versus liking groups: A dual-process hypothesis. *European Journal of Social Psychology*, *28*, 457–470.

Clevering, J. B. (2009). The beholder's eye: Vision and perception in afterimage studies of attitude change. *Social and Personality Psychology Compass, 3*, 339–350.

Clifford, M. M. (1975). Physical attractiveness and academic performance. *Child Study Journal, 5*, 201–209.

Codaccioni, C., & Tafani, E. (2011). Advertising effectiveness as a function of numerical support: From majority compliance to minority conversion. *European Review of Applied Psychology, 61*, 77–87.

Codol, J. P. (1975). On the so-called "superior conformity of the self" behavior: Twenty experimental investigations. *European Journal of Social Psychology, 5*, 457–501.

Cohen, A. (1957). Need for cognition and order of communication as determinants of opinion change. In C. Hovland (Ed.), *The order of presentation in persuasion.* New Haven, CT: Yale University Press.

Cohen, D., & Gunz, A. (2002). As seen by the other . . .: Perspectives on the self in the memories and emotional perceptions of Easterners and Westerners. *Psychological Science, 13*, 55–59.

Cohen, D., & Nisbett, R. E. (1994). Self-protection and the culture of honor: Explaining southern violence. *Personality and Social Psychology Bulletin, 20*, 551–567.

Cohen, F. (1984). Coping. In J. D. Matarazzo et al. (Eds.), *Behavioral health* (pp. 261–274). New York: Wiley.

Cohen, G. L. (2003). Party over policy: The dominating impact of group influence on political beliefs. *Journal of Personality and Social Psychology, 85*, 808–822.

Cohen, G. L., & Garcia, J. (2008). Identity, belonging, and achievement: A model, interventions, implications. *Current Directions in Psychological Science, 17*, 365–369.

Cohen, S. (2004). Social relationships and health. *American Psychologist, 59*, 676–684.

Cohen, S., Doyle, W.J., Skoner, D. P. & Fireman, P. (1995). State and trait negative affect as predictors of objective and subjective symptoms of respiratory viral infections. *Journal of Personality and Social Psychology, 68*, 159–169.

Cohen, S. P., & Arnone, H. C. (1988). Conflict resolution as the alternative to terrorism. *Journal of Social Issues, 44*(2), 175–190.

Colasanto, D. (1989, Nov.). Americans show commitment to helping those in need. *Gallup Report,* No. 290, 17–24.

Colby, A., & Damon, W. (1992). *Some do care.* New York: Free Press.

College Board. (1976–77). *Student descriptive questionnaire.* Princeton, NJ: Educational Testing Service.

Collins, E. C., Biernat, M., & Eidelman, S. (2009). Stereotypes in the communication and translation of person impressions. *Journal of Experimental Social Psychology, 45*, 368–374.

Collins, N. L., Ford, M. B., Guichard, A. C., & Allard, L. M. (2006). Working models of attachment and attribution processes in intimate relationships. *Personality & Social Psychology Bulletin, 32*, 201–219.

Collins, N. L., & Miller, L. C. (1994). Self-disclosure and liking: A meta-analytic review. *Psychological Bulletin, 116*, 457–475.

Collins, N. L., & Read, S. J. (1990). Adult attachment, working models, and relationship quality in dating couples. *Journal of Personality and Social Psychology, 58*, 644–663.

Colvin, C. R., Block, J. & Funder, D. C. (1995). Overly positive self-evaluations and personality: Negative implications for mental health. *Journal of Personality and Social Psychology, 68*, 1152–1162.

Condon, J. W., & Crano, W. D. (1988). Inferred evaluation and the relation between attitude similarity and interpersonal attraction. *Journal of Personality and Social Psychology, 54*, 789–797.

Condor, S., & Brown, R. (1988). Psychological processes in intergroup conflict. In W. Stroebe, A.W. Kruglanski, D. Bar-Tal, & M. Hewstone (Eds.), *The social psychology of intergroup conflict* (pp. 3–26). New York: Springer-Verlag.

Conner, M., & Higgins, A. R. (2010). Long-term effects of implementation intentions on prevention of smoking uptake among adolescents: A cluster randomized controlled trial. *Health Psychology, 29*, 529–538.

Conway, M. A., & Pleydell-Pearce, C. W. (2000). The construction of autobiographical memories in the self-memory system. *Psychological Review, 107*, 261–288.

Cook, S. W. (1985). Experimenting on social issues: The case of school desegregation. *American Psychologist, 40*, 452–460.

Cook, T. D., & Campbell, D. T. (1979). *Quasi-experimentation.* Chicago: Rand McNally.

Cooke, A., Kavussanu, M., McIntyre, D., & Ring, C. (2011). Effects of competition on endurance performance and the underlying psychological and physiological mechanisms. *Biological Psychology, 86*, 370–378.

Cooke, R., & Sheeran, P. (2004). Moderation of cognition-intention and cognition-behaviour relations: A meta-analysis of properties of variables from the theory of planned behaviour. *British Journal of Social Psychology, 43*, 159–186.

Cooley, D. H. (1902). *Human nature and the social order.* New York: Scribners.

Cooper, H. (1990). Meta-analysis and the integrative research review. In C. Hendrick & M. S. Clark (Eds.), *Review of personality and social psychology* (vol. 11, pp. 142–163). Newbury Park, CA: Sage Publications.

Cooper, H., & Good, T. (1983). *Pygmalion grows up: Studies in the expectation communication process.* New York: Longman.

Cooper, J., & Fazio, R. H. (1984). A new look at dissonance theory. In L. Berkowitz (Ed.), *Advances in experimental social psychology* (vol. 17). New York: Academic Press.

Cooper, P. A., & Maurer, D. (2008). The influence of recent experience on perceptions of attractiveness. *Perception, 37*, 1216–1226.

Cornil, Y., & Chandon, P. (2013). From fan to fat? Vicarious losing increases unhealthy eating, but self-affirmation is an effective remedy. *Psychological Science: A Journal of the American Psychological Society/APS.* doi:10.1177/0956797613481232

Correll, J., Park, B., Judd, C. M., & Wittenbrink, B. (2002). The police officer's dilemma: Using ethnicity to disambiguate potentially threatening individuals. *Journal of Personality and Social Psychology, 83,* 1314–1329.

Correll, J., Park, B., Judd, C. M., Wittenbrink, B., Sadler, M. S., & Keesee, T. (2007). Across the thin blue line: Police officers and racial bias in the decision to shoot. *Journal of Personality & Social Psychology, 92,* 1006–1023.

Cosmides, L. (1989). The logic of social exchange: Has natural selection shaped how humans reason? Studies with the Wason selection task. *Cognition, 31,* 187–276.

Cosmides, L., Tooby, J., & Kurzban, R. (2003). Perceptions of race. *Trends in Cognitive Sciences, 7*(4), 173–179. doi:http://dx.doi.org/10.1016/S1364-6613(03)00057-3

Costarelli, S., & Colloca, P. (2007). The moderation of ambivalence on attitude—intention relations as mediated by attitude importance. *European Journal of Social Psychology 37,* 923–933.

Cottrell, C. A., & Neuberg, S. L. (2005). Different emotional reactions to different groups: a sociofunctional threat-based approach to "prejudice." *Journal of Personality and Social Psychology, 88,* 770–789.

Cousins, S. (1989). Culture and selfhood in Japan and the U.S. *Journal of Personality and Social Psychology, 56,* 124–131.

Cox, D. S., Cox, A. D., Sturm, L., & Zimet, G. (2010). Behavioral interventions to increase HPV vaccination acceptability among mothers of young girls. *Health Psychology, 29,* 29–39.

Cramer, R. E., McMaster, M. R., & Bartell, P. A. (1988). Subject competence and minimization of the bystander effect. *Journal of Applied Social Psychology, 18,* 1133–1148.

Crandall, C. S., & Cohen, C. R. (1994). The personality of the stigmatizer: Cultural world view, conventionalism, and self-esteem. *Journal of Research in Personality, 28,* 461–480.

Crandall, C. S., & Eshleman, A. (2003). A justification-suppression of the expression and experience of prejudice. *Psychological Bulletin, 129,* 414–446.

Crandall, C. S., & Stangor, C. (2005). Conformity and prejudice. In J. F. Dovidio, P. Glic, & L. A. Rudman (Eds.), *On the nature of prejudice: Fifty years after Allport* (pp. 295–309). Malden, MA: Blackwell.

Crandall, C. S., Tsang, J.-A., Harvey, R. D., & Britt, T. W. (2000). Group identity-based self-protective strategies: The stigma of race, gender, and garlic. *European Journal of Social Psychology, 30*(3), 355–381.

Crano, W. D. (2012). *The rules of influence: Winning when you're in the minority.* New York, NY: St Martin's Press.

Crano, W. D., & Alvaro, E. M. (1998). The context/comparison model of social influence: Mechanisms, structure, and linkages that underlie indirect attitude change. In W. Stroebe & M. Hewstone (Eds.), *European review of social psychology* (vol. 8, pp. 175–202). Chichester: John Wiley and Sons, Inc.

Crano, W. D., Gorenflo, D. W., & Shackelford, S. L. (1988). Overjustification, assumed consensus, and attitude change: Further investigation of the incentive-aroused ambivalence

hypothesis. *Journal of Personality and Social Psychology, 55,* 12–22.

Crick, N. R., & Dodge, K. A. (1994). A review and reformulation of social information-processing mechanisms in children's social adjustment. *Psychological Bulletin, 115,* 74–101.

Crisp, R. J., Stone, C. H., & Hall, N. R. (2006). Recategorization and subgroup identification: Predicting and preventing threats from common ingroups. *Personality and Social Psychology Bulletin, 32,* 230–243.

Crocker, J., Hannah, D. B., & Weber, R. (1983). Personal memory and causal attributions. *Journal of Personality and Social Psychology, 44,* 55–66.

Crocker, J., & Major, B. (1989). Social stigma and self-esteem: The self-protective properties of stigma. *Psychological Review, 96,* 608–630.

Crocker, J., Major, B., & Steele, C. M. (1998). Social stigma. In D. T. Gilbert, S. T. Fiske, & G. Lindzey (Eds.), *Handbook of social psychology* (4th ed., vol. 2, pp. 504–553). Boston: McGraw-Hill.

Crocker, J., Voelkl, K., Testa, M., & Major, B. (1991). Social stigma: The affective consequences of attributional ambiguity. *Journal of Personality and Social Psychology, 60,* 218–228.

Croizet, J.-C., Despres, G. R., Gauzins, M.-E., Huguet, P., Leyens, J.-P., & Meot, A. (2004). Stereotype threat undermines intellectual performance by triggering a disruptive mental load. *Personality & Social Psychology Bulletin, 30*(6), 721–731.

Crosby, F. (1976). A model of egoistic relative deprivation. *Psychological Review, 83,* 85–113.

Crosby, F. J., Pufall, A., Snyder, R. C., O'Connell, M., & Whalen, P. (1989). The denial of personal disadvantage among you, me, and all the other ostriches. In M. Crawford & M. Gentry (Eds.), *Gender and thought: Psychological perspectives* (pp. 79–99). New York: Springer-Verlag.

Croyle, R., & Cooper, J. (1983). Dissonance arousal: Physiological evidence. *Journal of Personality and Social Psychology, 45,* 782–791.

Crutchfield, (1955). Conformity and character. *American Psychologist, 10,* 191–198.

Cruwys, T., Platow, M. J., Angullia, S. A., Chang, J. M., Diler, S. E., Kirchner, J. L., . . . Wadley, A. L. (2012). Modeling of food intake is moderated by salient psychological group membership. *Appetite, 58,* 754–757.

Csikszentmihalyi, M., & Figurski, T. J. (1982). Self-awareness and aversive experience in everyday life. *Journal of Personality, 50,* 15–28.

Cuddy, A. J. C., Fiske, S. T., & Glick, P. (2007). The BIAS map: Behaviors from intergroup affect and stereotypes. *Journal of Personality & Social Psychology, 92,* 631–648.

Cullum, J., O'Grady, M., Armeli, S., & Tennen, H. (2012). The role of context-specific norms and group size in alcohol consumption and compliance drinking during natural drinking events. *Basic and Applied Social Psychology, 34,* 304–312.

Cundiff, J. L. (2012). Is mainstream psychological research

"womanless" and "raceless"? an updated analysis. *Sex Roles, 67*(3–4), 158–173. doi:http://dx.doi.org/10.1007/s11199-012-0141-7

Cunha, M., & Caldieraro, F. (2009). Sunk-cost effects on purely behavioral investments. *Cognitive Science, 33,* 105–113.

Curhan, J. R., Neale, M. A., & Ross, L. (2004). Dynamic valuation: Preference changes in the context of face-to-face negotiation. *Journal of Experimental Social Psychology, 40*(2), 142–151.

Curry, O., & Dunbar, R. I. M. (2013). Do birds of a feather flock together?: The relationship between similarity and altruism in social networks. *Human Nature, 24*(3), 336–347. doi: http://dx.doi.org/10.1007/s12110-013-9174-z

Curry, O., Roberts, S. G. B., & Dunbar, R. I. M. (2013). Altruism in social networks: Evidence for a 'kinship premium'. *British Journal of Psychology, 104*(2), 283–295. doi:http://dx.doi.org/10.1111/j.2044-8295.2012.02119.x

Cutrona, C. E. (1982). Transition to college: Loneliness and the process of social adjustment. In L. A. Peplau & D. Perlman (Eds.), *Loneliness.* New York: Wiley Interscience.

Cutrona, C. E. (1996). *Social support in couples: Marriage as a resource in times of stress.* Thousand Oaks, CA: Sage Publications.

Dalcourt, P. (1996). Les stereotypes sexuels dans la publicité québecoise télévisée: le maintien d'une tradition. *Revue Québecoise de Psychologie, 17,* 29–42.

Daly, M., Salmon, C., & Wilson, M. (1997). Kinship: The conceptual hole in psychological studies of social cognition and close relationships. In J. A. Simpson & D. T. Kenrick (Eds.), *Evolutionary social psychology* (pp. 265–296). Hillsdale, NJ: Lawrence Erlbaum Associates.

Darke, P. R., & Chaiken, S. (2005). The pursuit of self-interest: Self-interest bias in attitude judgment and persuasion. *Journal of Personality & Social Psychology, 89,* 864–883.

Darley, J. M., & Batson, C. D. (1973). From Jerusalem to Jericho: A study of situational and dispositional variables in helping behavior. *Journal of Personality and Social Psychology, 27,* 100–108.

Darley, J. M., & Fazio, R. H. (1980). Expectancy confirmation processes arising in the social interaction sequence. *American Psychologist, 35,* 867–881.

Darley, J. M., & Gross, P. H. (1983). A hypothesis-confirming bias in labelling effects. *Journal of Personality and Social Psychology, 44,* 20–33.

Darley, J. M., & Latané, B. (1968). Bystander intervention in emergencies: Diffusion of responsibility. *Journal of Personality and Social Psychology, 8,* 377–383.

Darwin, C. (1871/1909). *The descent of man.* New York: Appleton.

Dasgupta, N., Banaji, M. B., & Abelson, R. P. (1997, March). Beliefs and attitudes toward cohesive groups. Paper presented at Midwestern Psychological Association, Chicago.

David, B., & Turner, J. C. (1996). Studies in self-categorization and minority conversion: Is being a member of the outgroup an advantage? *British Journal of Social Psychology, 35,* 179–199.

Davidson, A. R. & Jaccard, J. J. (1979). Variables that moderate the attitude-behavior relation: results of a longitudinal survey. *Journal of Personality and Social Psychology, 37,* 1364–76.

Davies, K., Tropp, L. R., Aron, A., Pettigrew, T. F., & Wright, S. C. (2011). Cross-group friendships and intergroup attitudes: A meta-analytic review. *Personality and Social Psychology Review, 15,* 332–351.

Davis, M. H. (1983). Empathic concern and muscular dystrophy telethon: Empathy as a multidimensional construct. *Personality and Social Psychology Bulletin, 9,* 223–229.

Davis, M. H., Mitchell, K. V., Hall, J. A., Lothert, J., Snapp, T., & Meyer, M. (1999). Empathy, expectations, and situational preferences: personality influences on the decision to volunteer helping behaviors. *Journal of Personality, 67,* 469–503.

Davis, S. N., Greenstein, T. N., & Marks, J. P. G. (2007). Effects of union type on division of household labor: Do cohabiting men really perform more housework? *Journal of Family Issues, 28,* 1246–1272.

Dawes, R. M. (1980). Social dilemmas. *Annual Review of Psychology. 31,* 169–193.

Dawes, R. M., & Smith, T. L. (1985). Attitude and opinion measurement. In G. Lindzey & E. Aronson (Eds.), *The handbook of social psychology* (3rd ed., vol. 1, pp. 509–566). New York: Random House.

Dawes, R. M., Van de Kragt, A. J., & Orbell, J. M. (1988). Not me or thee but we: The importance of group identity in eliciting cooperation in dilemma situations: Experimental manipulations. *Acta Psychologica, 68,* 83–97.

Day, R.S. (2006). Comprehension of prescription drug information: Overview of a research program. *Proceedings of the American Association for Artificial Intelligence. Argumentation for Consumer Healthcare,* www.aaai.org.

De Cremer, D. (2002). Charismatic leadership and cooperation in social dilemmas: A matter of transforming motives? *Journal of Applied Social Psychology, 32,* 997–1016.

De Cremer, D. & van Knippenberg, D. (2004). Leader self-sacrifice and leadership effectiveness: The moderating role of leader self-confidence. *Organizational Behavior and Human Decision Processes, 95,* 140–155.

De Cremer, D. & Van Vugt, M. (2002). Intergroup and intragroup aspects of leadership in social dilemmas: A relational model of cooperation. *Journal of Experimental Social Psychology, 38,* 126–136.

De Dreu, C. K. W. (2005). A PACT against conflict escalation in negotiation and dispute resolution. *Current Directions in Psychological Science, 14*(3) 149–152

De Dreu, C. K. W., & Beersma, B. (2010). Team confidence, motivated information processing, and dynamic group decision making. *European Journal of Social Psychology, 40,* 1110–1119.

De Dreu, C. K. W., Nijstad, B., Baas, M., & Bechtoldt, M. (2008). The creating force of minority dissent: A motivated information processing perspective. *Social Influence, 3,* 267–285.

De Dreu, C. K. W., & Weingart, L. R. (2003). Task versus relationship conflict, team performance and team members satisfaction: A meta-analysis. *Journal of Applied Psychology, 88*, 741–749.

De Hoog, N., Stroebe, W., & de Wit, J. B. F. (2005). The impact of fear appeals on processing and acceptance of action recommendations. *Personality and Social Psychology Bulletin, 31*, 24–33.

De Hooge, I. E., Nelissen, R. M. A., Breugelmans, S. M., & Zeelenberg, M. (2011). What is moral about guilt? Acting "prosocially" at the disadvantage of others. *Journal of Personality and Social Psychology, 100*(3), 462–473. doi:http://dx.doi.org/10.1037/a0021459

De Hoogh, A. H. B., den Hartog, D. N., Koopman, P. L., Thierry, H., van den Berg, P. T., van der Weide, J. G., & Wilderom, C. P. M. (2004). Charismatic leadership, environmental dynamism, and performance. *European Journal of Work and Organizational Psychology, 13*, 447–471.

De Jong, M. G., Pieters, R., & Stremersch, S. (2012). Analysis of sensitive questions across cultures: An application of multigroup item randomized response theory to sexual attitudes and behavior. *Journal of Personality and Social Psychology, 103*, 543–564.

De Jong, P. J., van den Hout, M. A., Rietbroek, H., & Huijding, J. (2003). Dissociations between implicit and explicit attitudes toward phobic stimuli. *Cognition & Emotion, 17*, 521–545.

De Kwaadsteniet, E. W., Homan, A. C., van Dijk, E., & van Beest, I. (2011). Social information as a cue for tacit coordination. *Group Processes & Intergroup Relations, 15*, 257–271.

De Kwaadsteniet, E. W., & van Dijk, E. (2010). Social status as a cue for tacit coordination. *Journal of Experimental Social Psychology, 46*, 515–524.

De Kwaadsteniet, E. W., & van Dijk, E. (2012). A social-psychological perspective on tacit coordination: How it works, when it works, (and when it does not). *European Review of Social Psychology, 23*, 187–223.

De Lange, M. A., Debets, L. W., Ruitenburg, K., & Holland, R.W. (2012). Making less of a mess: Scent exposure as a tool for behavioral change. *Social Influence, 7*, 90–97.

De Rivera, J. (1977). *A structural theory of the emotions*. New York: International Universities Press.

De Wit, F. R. C., Greer, L. L., & Jehn, K. A. (2012). The paradox of intragroup conflict: A meta-analysis. *Journal of Applied Psychology, 97*, 360–390.

Deaux, K., & Emswiller, T. (1974). Explanations of successful performance on sex-linked tasks: What is skill for the male is luck for the female. *Journal of Personality and Social Psychology, 29*, 80–85.

Deaux, K., & Hanna, R. (1984). Courtship in the personals column: The influence of gender and sexual orientation. *Sex Roles, 11*, 363–375.

Deaux, K., & Lewis, L. L. (1983). Components of gender stereotypes. *Psychological Documents, 13*, 25–34.

Deaux, K., & Lewis, L. L. (1984). Structure of gender stereotypes: Interrelationships among components and gender label. *Journal of Personality and Social Psychology, 46*, 991–1004.

DeBono, K. G., & Harnish, R. (1988). Source expertise, source attractiveness, and processing of persuasive information: A functional approach. *Journal of Personality and Social Psychology, 55*, 541–546.

DeBono, K. G., & Snyder, M. (1995). Acting on one's attitudes: The role of a history of choosing situations. *Personality and Social Psychology Bulletin, 21*, 629–636.

DeBruine, L. M. (2004). Resemblance to self increases the appeal of child faces to both men and women. *Evolution and Human Behavior, 25*, 142–154.

Deci, E. L. (1971). Effects of externally mediated rewards on intrinsic motivation. *Journal of Personality and Social Psychology, 18*, 105–115.

Deci, E. L. (1975). *Intrinsic motivation*. New York: Plenum Press.

DeCoster, J., & Claypool, H. M. (2004). A meta-analysis of priming effects on impression formation supporting a general model of informational biases. *Personality and Social Psychology Review, 8*, 2–27.

DeJong, W. (1979). An examination of self-perception mediation on the foot-in-the-door effect. *Journal of Personality and Social Psychology, 37*, 2221–2239.

DeMarree, K. G., Petty, R. E., & Brinol, P. (2007). Self and attitude strength parallels: Focus on accessibility. *Social & Personality Psychology Compass, 1*, 441–468.

DePaulo, B. M., Lassiter, G. D., & Stone, J. I. (1982). Attentional determinants of success at detecting deception and truth. *Personality and Social Psychology Bulletin, 8*, 273–279.

Derlega, V. J., Wilson, M., & Chaikin, A. L. (1976). Friendship and disclosure reciprocity. *Journal of Personality and Social Psychology, 34*, 578–587.

Derlega, V. J., Winstead, B. A., Wong, P. T. P., & Hunter, S. (1985). Gender effects in an initial encounter: A case where men exceed women in disclosure. *Journal of Social and Personal Relationships, 2*, 25–44.

Deschamps, J. C., & Brown, R. (1983). Superordinate goals and intergroup conflict. *British Journal of Social Psychology, 22*, 189–195.

Desforges, D. M., Lord, C. G., Ramsey, S. L., Mason, J. A., Van Leeuwen, M. D., West, S. C., & Lepper, M. R. (1991). Effects of structured cooperative contact on changing negative attitudes toward stigmatized social groups. *Journal of Personality and Social Psychology, 60*, 531–544.

Desmond, E. W. (1987, Nov. 30). Out in the open. *Time*, 80–90.

Deters, F. G., & Mehl, M. R. (2013). Does posting Facebook status updates increase or decrease loneliness? An online social networking experiment. *Social Psychological and Personality Science, 4*, 579–586.

Deutsch, M. (1949). An experimental study of the effects of cooperation and competition upon group process. *Human Relations, 2*, 199–231.

Deutsch, M. (1973). *The resolution of conflict*. New Haven, CT: Yale University Press.

Deutsch, M. (1990). Psychological roots of moral exclusion. *Journal of Social Issues, 46*(1), 21–25.

Deutsch, M. (1993). Educating for a peaceful world. *American Psychologist, 48*, 510–517.

Deutsch, M., & Collins, M. E. (1951). *Interracial housing: A psychological evaluation of a social experiment.* Minneapolis, MN: University of Minnesota Press.

Deutsch, M. & Gerard, H.B. (1955). A study of normative and informational social influence upon individual judgment. *Journal of Abnormal and Social Psychology, 51*, 629–636.

Deutsch, M. and Krauss, R. M. (1960). The effect of threat upon interpersonal bargaining. *Journal of Abnormal and Social Psychology, 61*, 181–189.

Devine, D. J. (2012). *Jury decision making: The state of the science.* New York, NY: New York University Press.

Devine, P. G. (1989). Stereotypes and prejudice: Their automatic and controlled components. *Journal of Personality and Social Psychology, 56*, 5–18.

Devine, P. G., Tauer, J. M., Barron, K. E., Elliot, A. J., & Vance, K. M. (1999). Moving beyond attitude change in the study of dissonance related processes. In E. Harmon-Jones & J. Mills (Eds.), *Cognitive dissonance: Progress on a pivotal theory in social psychology* (pp. 297–323). Washington, DC: American Psychological Association.

Devos, T., Silver, L. A., Mackie, D. M., & Smith, E. R. (2002). Experiencing intergroup emotions. In D. M. Mackie & E. R. Smith (Eds.), *From prejudice to intergroup emotions* (pp. 111–134). New York: Psychology Press.

DeWall, C. N. (2010). Forming a basis for acceptance: Excluded people form attitudes to agree with potential affiliates. *Social Influence, 5*, 245–260.

DeWall, C. N., Anderson, C. A., & Bushman, B. J. (2011). The general aggression model: Theoretical extensions to violence. *Psychology of Violence, 1*, 245–258.

DeWall, C. N., Maner, J. K., & Rouby, D. A. (2009). Social exclusion and early-stage interpersonal perception: Selective attention to signs of acceptance. *Journal of Personality & Social Psychology, 96*, 729–741.

Diab, L. N. (1970). A study of intragroup and intergroup relations among experimentally produced small groups. *Genetic Psychology Monographs, 82*(1), 49.

Diamond, L. M. (2003). What does sexual orientation orient? A biobehavioral model distinguishing romantic love and sexual desire. *Psychological Review, 110*(1), 173–192. doi:http:// dx.doi.org/10.1037/0033-295X.110.1.173

Dickerson, S. S., Gruenewald, T. L., & Kemeny, M. E. (2004). When the social self is threatened: Shame, physiology, and health. *Journal of Personality, 72*, 1191–1216.

Dickerson, S. S., Gruenewald, T. L., & Kemeny, M. E. (2009). Psychobiological responses to social self threat: Functional or detrimental? *Self & Identity, 8*, 270–285.

Diehl, M., & Stroebe, W. (1991). Productivity loss in idea-generating groups: Tracking down the blocking effect. *Journal of Personality and Social Psychology, 61*, 392–403.

Diener, E., & Crandall, R. (1979). An evaluation of the Jamaican anticrime program. *Journal of Applied Social Psychology, 9*, 135–146.

DiFonzo, N., Bourgeois, M. J., Suls, J., Homan, C., Stupak, N., Brooks, B. P., Ross, D. S., & Bordia, P. (2013). Rumor clustering, consensus, and polarization: Dynamic social impact and self-organization of hearsay. *Journal of Experimental Social Psychology, 49*, 378–399.

Dijker, A. J. M. (1987). Emotional reactions to ethnic minorities. *European Journal of Social Psychology, 47*, 1105–1117.

Dindia, K., & Allen, M. (1992). Sex differences in self-disclosure: A meta-analysis. *Psychological Bulletin, 112*, 106–122.

Dion, K. K. (2002). Cultural perspectives on facial attractiveness. In G. Rhodes & L. A. Zebrowitz (Eds.), *Facial attractiveness: Evolutionary, cognitive, and social perspectives* (pp. 239–259). Westport, CT: Ablex.

Dion, K. K., Berscheid, E., & Walster, E. (1972). What is beautiful is good. *Journal of Personality and Social Psychology, 24*, 285–290.

Dion, K. L., & Dion, K. K. (1988). Romantic love: Individual and cultural perspectives. In R. Sternberg & M. Barnes (Eds.), *The psychology of love* (pp. 264–289). New Haven, CT: Yale University Press.

Dixon, N. F. (1976). *On the psychology of military incompetence.* London: Jonathan Cape.

Dixon, T. L., & Linz, D. (2000). Overrepresentation and underrepresentation of African Americans and Latinos as lawbreakers on television news. *Journal of Communication, 50*, 131–154.

Dodge, K., & Coie, J. D. (1987). Social-information-processing factors in reactive and proactive aggression in children's peer groups. *Journal of Personality and Social Psychology, 53*, 1146–1158.

Dodge, K. A., Bates, J. E., & Pettit, G. S. (1990). Mechanisms of the cycle of violence. *Science, 250*, 1678–1683.

Dodge, K. A., & Newman, J. P. (1981). Biased decision-making processes in aggressive boys. *Journal of Abnormal Psychology, 90*, 375–379.

Dodge, K. A., & Somberg, D. R. (1987). Hostile attributional biases among aggressive boys are exacerbated under conditions of threat to the self. *Child Development, 58*, 213–224.

Doise, W. (1978). *Groups and individuals: Explanations in social psychology.* Cambridge: Cambridge University Press.

Doise, W., & Sinclair, A. (1973). The categorization process in intergroup relations. *European Journal of Social Psychology, 3*, 145–157.

Doise, W., & Weinberger, M. (1973). Représentations masculines dans différentes situations de rencontre mixtes. *Bulletin de Psychologie, 26*, 649–657.

Dolan, K. (2010). The impact of gender stereotyped evaluations on support for women candidates. *Political Behavior, 32*, 69–88.

Dolinski, D. (2000). On inferring one's beliefs from one's attempt and consequences for subsequent compliance. *Journal of Personality and Social Psychology, 78*, 260–272.

Dolinski, D. (2012). The nature of the first small request as a decisive factor in the effectiveness of the foot-in-the-door technique. *Applied Psychology: An International Review, 61,* 437–453.

Dollard, J., Doob, L. W., Miller, M. E., Mowrer, O. H., & Sears, R. R. (1939). *Frustration and aggression.* New Haven, CT: Yale University Press.

Don, B. P., & Mickelson, K. D. (2012). Paternal postpartum depression: The role of maternal postpartum depression, spousal support, and relationship satisfaction. *Couple and Family Psychology: Research and Practice, 1,* 323–334.

Donnellan, M. B., Trzesniewski, K. H., Robins, R. W., Moffitt, T. E., & Caspi, A. (2005). Low self-esteem is related to aggression, antisocial behavior, and delinquency. *Psychological Science, 16,* 328–335.

Donnerstein, E., Linz, D., & Penrod, S. (1987). *The question of pornography: Research findings and policy implications.* New York: Free Press.

Doosje, B., Branscombe, N. R., Spears, R., & Manstead, A. S. R. (1998). Guilty by association: When one's group has a negative history. *Journal of Personality and Social Psychology, 75,* 872–886.

Doosje, B., Ellemers, N., & Spears, R. (1995). Perceived intragroup variability as a function of group status and identification. *Journal of Experimental Social Psychology, 31,* 410–436.

Douglas, K. M., Sutton, R. M., & Stathi, S. (2010). Why I am less persuaded than you: People's intuitive understanding of the psychology of persuasion. *Social Influence, 5,* 133–148.

Dovidio, J. F., Allen, J. L., & Schroeder, D. A. (1990). Specificity of empathy-induced helping: Evidence for altruistic motivation. *Journal of Personality and Social Psychology, 59,* 249–260.

Dovidio, J. F., & Fazio, R. H. (1992). New technologies for the direct and indirect assessment of attitudes. In J. M. Tanur and others (Eds.), *Questions about questions: Inquiries into the cognitive bases of surveys* (pp. 204–237). New York: Russell Sage Foundation.

Dovidio, J. F. & Gaertner, S. L. (1993). Stereotypes and evaluative intergroup bias. In D. M. Mackie & D. L. Hamilton (Eds.), *Affect, cognition, and stereotyping: Interactive processes in group perception* (pp. 167–193). San Diego, CA: Academic Press.

Dovidio, J. F., Kawakami, K., & Gaertner, S. L. (2002). Implicit and explicit prejudice and interracial interaction. *Journal of Personality and Social Psychology, 82,* 62–68.

Dovidio, J. F., Piliavin, J. A., Gaertner, S. L., Schroeder, D. A., & Clark, R. D. (1991). The arousal: cost-reward model and the process of intervention: A review of the evidence. In M. S. Clark (Ed.), *Prosocial behavior* (pp. 86–118). Newbury Park, CA: Sage Publications.

Dovidio, J. F., Saguy, T., & Shnabel, N. (2009). Cooperation and conflict within groups: Bridging intragroup and intergroup processes. *Journal of Social Issues, 65,* 429–449.

Downey, G., & Feldman, S. (1996). Implications of rejection sensitivity for intimate relationships. *Journal of Personality and Social Psychology, 70,* 1327–1343.

Downey, G., Feldman, S., & Ayduk, O. (2000). Rejection sensitivity and male violence in romantic relationships. *Personal Relationships, 7,* 45–61.

Downs, A. C., & Lyons, P. M. (1991). Natural observations of the links between attractiveness and initial legal judgments. *Personality and Social Psychology Bulletin, 17,* 541–547.

Drigotas, S. M., & Rusbult, C. E. (1992). Should I stay or should I go? A dependence model of breakups. *Journal of Personality and Social Psychology, 62,* 62–87.

Drummond, P. D., & Quah, S. H. (2001). The effect of expressing anger on cardiovascular reactivity and facial blood flow in Chinese and Caucasians. *Psychophysiology, 38,* 190–196.

Dubrovsky, V. J., Kiesler, S., & Sethna, B. N. (1991). The equalization phenomenon: Status effects in computer-mediated and face-to-face decision-making groups. *Human Computer Interaction, 6,* 119–146.

Duckitt, J., & Mphuthing, T. (1998). Group identification and intergroup attitudes: A longitudinal analysis in South Africa. *Journal of Personality and Social Psychology, 74,* 80–85.

Duckworth, K. L., Bargh, J. A., Garcia, M., & Chaiken, S. (2002). The automatic evaluation of novel stimuli. *Psychological Science, 13,* 513–519.

Duke, L., & Morin, R. (1992, Mar. 8). Focusing on race: Candid dialogue, elusive answers. *The Washington Post,* p. A35.

Duncan, L. A., Schaller, M., & Park, J. H. (2009). Perceived vulnerability to disease: Development and validation of a 15-item self-report instrument. *Personality and Individual Differences, 47,* 541–546.

Dunn, E., & Ashton-James, C. (2008). On emotional innumeracy: Predicted and actual affective responses to grand-scale tragedies. *Journal of Experimental Social Psychology, 44*(3), 692–698. doi:10.1016/j.jesp.2007.04.011

Dunn, E. W., Aknin, L. B., & Norton, M. I. (2008, March 21). Spending money on others promotes happiness. *Science, 319,* 1687–1688. doi: 10.1126/science.1150952

Dunton, B. C., & Fazio, R. H. (1997). An individual difference measure of motivation to control prejudiced reactions. *Personality and Social Psychology Bulletin, 23,* 316–326.

Durantini, M. R., Albarracin, D., Mitchell, A. L., Earl, A. N., & Gillette, J. C. (2006). Conceptualizing the influence of social agents of behavior change: A meta-analysis of the effectiveness of HIV-prevention interventionists for different groups. *Psychological Bulletin, 132,* 212–248.

Durkheim, E. (1898). *The rules of sociological method.* New York: Free Press.

Dutton, D. G. (1996). *The domestic assault of women.* Vancouver: University of British Columbia Press.

Duval, S., Duval, V. H., & Neely, R. (1979). Self-focus, felt responsibility, and helping behavior. *Journal of Personality and Social Psychology, 37,* 1769–1778.

Duval, S., & Wicklund, R. A. (1972). *A theory of objective self-awareness.* New York: Academic Press.

Dweck, C. S. (1986). Motivational processes affecting learning. *American Psychologist, 41*, 1040–1048.

Dweck, C. S., & Leggett, E. L. (1988). A social-cognitive approach to motivation and personality. *Psychological Review, 95*, 256–273.

Eagly, A. H. (1974). Comprehensibility of persuasive arguments as a determinant of opinion change. *Journal of Personality and Social Psychology, 29*, 758–773.

Eagly, A. H. (1987). *Sex differences in social behavior: A social role interpretation.* Hillsdale, NJ: Lawrence Erlbaum Associates.

Eagly, A. H. (1995). The science and politics of comparing women and men. *American Psychologist, 50*, 145–158.

Eagly, A. H. (2009). The his and hers of prosocial behavior: An examination of the social psychology of gender. *American Psychologist, 64*(8), 644–658. doi:http://dx.doi.org/10.1037/0003-066X.64.8.644

Eagly, A. H., & Carli, L. L. (2003). The female leadership advantage: An evaluation of the evidence. *Leadership Quarterly, 14*, 807–834.

Eagly, A. H., & Chaiken, S. (1993). *The psychology of attitudes.* San Diego: Harcourt, Brace, Jovanovich.

Eagly, A. H., Chaiken, S., & Wood, W. (1981). An attributional analysis of persuasion. In J. H. Harvey, W. J. Ickes, & R. F. Kidd (Eds.), *New directions in attribution research* (vol. 3). Hillsdale, NJ: Erlbaum.

Eagly, A. H., & Crowley, M. (1986). Gender and helping behavior: A meta-analytic review of the social psychological literature. *Psychological Bulletin, 100*, 283–308.

Eagly, A. H., & Johnson, B. T. (1990). Gender and leadership style: A meta-analysis. *Psychological Bulletin, 108*, 233–256.

Eagly, A. H., & Karau, S. J. (1991). Gender and the emergence of leaders: A meta-analysis. *Journal of Personality and Social Psychology, 60*, 685–710.

Eagly, A. H., Karau, S. J., & Makhijani, M. G. (1995). Gender and the effectiveness of leaders: A meta-analysis. *Psychological Bulletin, 117*, 125–145.

Eagly, A. H., & Kite, M. E. (1987). Are stereotypes of nationalities applied to both women and men? *Journal of Personality and Social Psychology, 53*, 451–462.

Eagly, A.H., & Makhijani, M. (1991). What is beautiful is good, but . . .: A meta-analytic review of research on the physical attractiveness stereotype. *Psychological Bulletin, 110*, 109–128.

Eagly, A. H., Makhijani, M. G., & Klonsky, B. G. (1992). Gender and the evaluation of leaders: A meta-analysis. *Psychological Bulletin, 111*, 3–22.

Eagly, A. H., & Mladinic, A. (1989). Gender stereotypes and attitudes toward women and men. *Personality and Social Psychology Bulletin, 15*, 543–558.

Eagly, A. H., & Steffen, V.J. (1984). Gender stereotypes stem from the distribution of women and men into social roles. *Journal of Personality and Social Psychology, 46*, 735–754.

Eagly, A. H., & Wood, W. (2011). Feminism and the evolution of sex differences and similarities. *Sex Roles, 64*, 758–767.

Eagly, A. H., Wood, W., & Chaiken, S. (1978). Causal inferences about communicators and their effect on opinion change. *Journal of Personality and Social Psychology, 36*, 424–435.

Earley, P. C. (1989). Social loafing and collectivism: A comparison of the United States and the People's Republic of China. *Administrative Science Quarterly, 34*, 565–581.

Easterbrook, J. A. (1959). The effect of emotion on cue utilization and the organization of behavior. *Psychological Review, 66*, 183–201.

Eastwick, P. W., & Finkel, E. J. (2008). Sex differences in mate preferences revisited: Do people know what they initially desire in a romantic partner? *Journal of Personality & Social Psychology, 94*, 245–264.

Eastwick, P. W., & Gardner, W. L. (2009). Is it a game? Evidence for social influence in the virtual world. *Social Influence, 4*, 18–32.

Eastwick, P. W., Luchies, L. B., Finkel, E. J., & Hunt, L. L. (in press). The predictive validity of ideal partner preferences: A review and meta-analysis. *Psychological Bulletin.*

Eberhard, J. L., & Fiske, S. T. (1996). Motivating individuals to change: What is a target to do? In C. N. Macrae, C. Stangor, & M. Hewstone (Eds.), *Stereotypes and stereotyping* (pp. 369–418). New York: Guilford Press.

Echterhoff, G., Higgins, E. T., & Levine, J. M. (2009). Shared reality: Experiencing commonality with others' inner states about the world. *Perspectives on Psychological Science, 4*, 496–521.

Eckes, T. (1994). Explorations in gender cognition: Content and structure of female and male subtypes. *Social Cognition, 12*, 37–60.

Eckes, T., & Six, B. (1994). Fact and fiction in research on the relationship between attitude and behavior: A meta-analysis. *Journal of Social Psychology, 25*, 253–271.

Edelson, M., Sharot, T., Dolan, R. J., & Dudai, Y. (2011). Following the crowd: Brain substrates of long-term memory conformity. *Science, 333*, 108–111.

Edney, J. J. (1980). The commons problem: Alternative perspectives. *American Psychologist, 35*, 131–150.

Edwards, K., & Smith, E. (1996) A disconfirmation bias in the evaluation of arguments. *Journal of Personality and Social Psychology, 71*, 5–24.

Edwards, K., & von Hippel, W. (1995). Hearts and minds. The priority of affective versus cognitive actors in person perception. *Personality and Social Psychology Bulletin, 21*, 996–1011.

Egan, L. C., Santos, L. R., & Bloom, P. (2007). The origins of cognitive dissonance: Evidence from children and monkeys. *Psychological Science, 18*, 978–983.

Eibach, R. P., & Mock, S. E. (2011). Idealizing parenthood to rationalize parental investments. *Psychological Science, 22*, 203–208.

Einolf, C. J. (2011). Daily spiritual experiences and prosocial behavior. *Social Indicators Research, 110*(1), 71–87. doi:10.1007/s11205-011-9917-3

Eisenberg, N. (1991). Meta-analytic contributions to the literature on prosocial behavior. *Personality and Social Psychology Bulletin, 17,* 273–282.

Eisenberg, N., Eggum, N. D., & Di Giunta, L. (2010). Empathy-related responding: Associations with prosocial behavior, aggression, and intergroup relations. *Social Issues and Policy Review,* 4: 143–180. doi: 10.1111/j.1751-2409.2010.01020.x

Eisenberg, N., Guthrie, I. K., Cumberland, A., Murphy, B. C., Shepard, S. A., et al. (2002). Prosocial development in early adulthood: A longitudinal study. *Journal of Personality and Social Psychology, 78,* 136–157.

Eisenberger, N. I., Lieberman, M. D., & Williams, K. D. (2003). Does rejection hurt? An fMRI study of social exclusion. *Science, 302,* 290–292.

Eisenstat, R. A. (1990). Compressor team start-up. In J. R. Hackman (Ed.), *Groups that work (and those that don't)* (pp. 411–426). San Francisco: Jossey-Bass.

Eiser, J. R., & Fazio, R. H. (2008). How approach and avoidance decisions influence attitude formation and change. In A. J. Elliot (Ed.), *Handbook of approach and avoidance motivation* (pp. 323–340). New York: Psychology Press.

Eiser, J. R., Fazio, R. H., Stafford, T., & Prescott, T. J. (2003). Connectionist simulation of attitude learning: Asymmetries in the acquisition of positive and negative evaluations. *Personality and Social Psychology Bulletin, 29,* 1221–1235.

Eiser, J. R., & Sutton, S. R. (1977). Smoking as a subjectively rational choice. *Addictive Behaviors, 2,* 129–134.

Eiser, J. R., & van der Pligt, J. (1986). Smoking cessation and smokers' perceptions of their addiction. *Journal of Social and Clinical Psychology, 4,* 60–70.

Eiser, J. R., van der Pligt, J., Raw, M., & Sutton, S. R. (1985). Trying to stop smoking: Effects of perceived addiction, attributions for failure and expectancy of success. *Journal of Behavioral Medicine, 8,* 321–341.

Ekman, P. (1992). Facial expressions of emotion: New findings, new questions. *Psychological Science, 3,* 34–38.

Ekman, P., & Friesen, W. V. (1974). Detecting deception from the body or face. *Journal of Personality and Social Psychology, 29,* 288–298.

Ekman, P., Friesen, W. V., & Ellsworth, P. (1972). *Emotion in the human face.* Elmsford, NY: Pergamon Press.

Ekman, P., and others. (1987). Universals and cultural differences in the judgments of facial expressions of emotion. *Journal of Personality and Social Psychology, 53,* 712–717.

Elinder, M., & Erixson, O. (2012). Gender, social norms, and survival in maritime disasters. *Proceedings of the National Academy of Sciences, 109,* 13220–13224.

Elizur, Y., & Mintzer, A. (2003). Gay males' intimate relationship quality: The roles of attachment security, gay identity, social support, and income. *Personal Relationships, 10,* 411–435.

Ellemers, N. (2001). Individual upward mobility and the perceived legitimacy of intergroup relations. In J. T. Jost & B. Major (Eds.), *The psychology of legitimacy: Emerging perspectives on ideology, justice, and intergroup relations* (pp. 205–222). New York: Cambridge University Press.

Ellemers, N., de Gilder, D., & Haslam, S. A. (2004). Motivating individuals and groups at work: A social identity perspective on leadership and group performance. *Academy of Management Review, 29,* 459–478.

Ellemers, N., Spears, R., & Doosje, B. (1997). Sticking together or falling apart: In-group identification as a psychological determinant of group commitment versus individual mobility. *Journal of Personality and Social Psychology, 72,* 617–626.

Ellemers, N., Spears, R., & Doosje, B. (2002). Self and social identity. *Annual Review of Psychology, 53*(1), 161–186.

Ellemers, N., & van Knippenberg, A. (1997). Stereotyping in social context. In R. Spears & P. J. Oakes (Eds.), *The social psychology of stereotyping and group life* (pp. 208–235). Oxford: Blackwell.

Eller, A., & Abrams, D. (2004). Come together: Longitudinal comparisons of Pettigrew's reformulated intergroup contact model and the common ingroup identity model in Anglo-French and Mexican-American contexts. *European Journal of Social Psychology, 34*(3), 229–256.

Elliot, A. J., & Devine, P. G. (1994). On the motivational nature of cognitive dissonance: Dissonance as psychological discomfort. *Journal of Personality & Social Psychology, 67,* 382–394.

Elliot, A. J., Kayser, D. N., Greitemeyer, T., Lichtenfeld, S., Gramzow, R. H., Maier, M. A., & Liu, H. (2010). Red, rank, and romance in women viewing men. *Journal of Experimental Psychology: General, 139,* 399–417.

Engelhardt, C. R., Bartholow, B. D., Kerr, G. T., & Bushman, B. J. (2011). This is your brain on violent video games: Neural desensitization to violence predicts increased aggression following violent video game exposure. *Journal of Experimental Social Psychology, 47,* 1033–1036.

English, T., & Chen, S. (2007). Culture and self-concept stability: Consistency across and within contexts among Asian Americans and European Americans. *Journal of Personality & Social Psychology, 93,* 478–490.

Ennis, R., & Zanna, M. P. (2000). Attitude function and the automobile. In G. R. Maio & J. M. Olson (Eds.), *Why we evaluate: Functions of attitudes* (pp. 1–36). Mahwah, NJ: Lawrence Erlbaum Associates.

Epley, N. (2008). Solving the (real) other minds problem. *Social & Personality Psychology Compass, 2,* 1455–1474.

Epstein, S. (1992). Coping ability, negative self-evaluation, and overgeneralization: Experiment and theory. *Journal of Personality and Social Psychology, 62,* 826–836.

Epstein, Y. M., Suedfeld, P., & Silverstein, S. J. (1973). The experimental contract: Subjects' expectations of and reactions to some behaviors of experimenters. *American Psychologist, 28,* 212–221.

Epstude, K., & Roese, N. J. (2008). The functional theory of counterfactual thinking. *Personality & Social Psychology Review, 12,* 168–192.

Erb, H. P., & Bohner, G. (2001). Mere consensus effects in

minority and majority influence. In C. K. W. De Dreu & N. K. De Vries (Eds.), *Group consensus and minority influence: Implications for innovation* (pp. 40–59). Malden, MA: Blackwell Publishers.

Erb, H.-P., Bohner, G., Schmalzle, K., & Rank, S. (1998). Beyond conflict and discrepancy: Cognitive bias in minority and majority influence. *Personality and Social Psychology Bulletin, 24,* 620–633.

Erceg-Hurn, D. M., & Steed, L. G. (2011). Does exposure to cigarette health warnings elicit psychological reactance in smokers? *Journal of Applied Social Psychology, 41,* 219–237.

Erdley, C. A., & Asher, S. R. (1996). Children's social goals and self-efficacy perceptions as influences on their responses to ambiguous provocation. *Child Development, 67,* 1329–1344.

Erickson, B., Lind, E. A., Johnson, B. C., O'Barr, W. M. (1978). Speech style and impression formation in a court setting: The effects of "powerful" and "powerless" speech. *Journal of Experimental Social Psychology, 14,* 266–279.

Esposo, S. R., Hornsey, M. J., & Spoor, J. R. (2013). Shooting the messenger: Outsiders critical of your group are rejected regardless of argument quality. *British Journal of Social Psychology, 52,* 386–395.

Esses, V. M, Haddock, G., & Zanna, M. P. (1993). Values, stereotypes, and emotions as determinants of intergroup attitudes. In D. M. Mackie & D. L. Hamilton (Eds.), *Affect, cognition, and stereotyping: Interactive processes in group perception* (pp. 137–166). San Diego, CA: Academic Press.

Evans, G. W. (1979). Behavioral and physiological consequences of crowding in humans. *Journal of Applied Social Psychology, 9,* 27–46.

Evans, L. M., & Petty, R. E. (2003). Self-guide framing and persuasion: Responsibly increasing message processing to ideal levels. *Personality & Social Psychology Bulletin, 29,* 313–324.

Falbo, T., & Peplau, L. A. (1980). Power strategies in intimate relationships. *Journal of Personality and Social Psychology 38,* 618–628.

Farvid, P., & Braun, V. (2006). 'Most of us guys are raring to go anytime, anyplace, anywhere': Male and female sexuality in *Cleo* and *Cosmo. Sex Roles, 55,* 295–310.

Fast, N. J., Heath, C., & Wu, G. (2009). Common ground and cultural prominence: How conversation reinforces culture. *Psychological Science, 20,* 904–911.

Fazio, R. H. (1986). How do attitudes guide behavior? In R. Sorrentino & E. Higgins (Eds.), *Handbook of motivation and cognition: Foundations of social behavior* (pp. 204–243). New York: Guilford Press.

Fazio, R. H. (1989). On the power and functionality of attitudes: The role of attitude accessibility. In A. R. Pratkanis, S. J. Breckler, & A. G. Greenwald (Eds.), *Attitude structure and function* (pp. 153–179). Hillsdale, NJ: Erlbaum Associates.

Fazio, R. H. (1990). Multiple processes by which attitudes guide behavior: The MODE model as an integrative framework. In M. P. Zanna (Ed.), *Advances in experimental social psychology,* (vol. 23, pp. 75–109). New York: Academic Press.

Fazio, R. H. (1995). Attitudes as object-evaluation associations: Determinants, consequences, and correlates of attitude accessibility. In R. E. Petty & J. A. Krosnick (Eds.), *Attitude strength: Antecedents and consequences* (pp. 247–282). Hillsdale, NJ: Lawrence Erlbaum.

Fazio, R. H. (2000). Accessible attitudes as tools for object appraisal: Their costs and benefits. In G. R. Maio & J. M. Olson (Eds.), *Why we evaluate: Functions of attitudes* (pp. 1–36). Mahwah, NJ: Lawrence Erlbaum Associates.

Fazio, R. H. (2001). On the automatic activation of associated evaluations: An overview. *Cognition & Emotion. Special automatic affective processing, 15,* 115–141.

Fazio, R. H., Blascovich, J., & Driscoll, D. M. (1992). On the functional value of attitudes: The influence of accessible attitudes upon the ease and quality of decision-making. *Personality and Social Psychology Bulletin, 18,* 388–401.

Fazio, R. H., Chen, J., McDonel, E., & Sherman, S. J. (1982). Attitude accessibility, attitude-behavior consistency, and the strength of the object-evaluation association. *Journal of Experimental Social Psychology, 18,* 339–357.

Fazio, R. H., Effrein, E. A., & Falender, V. J. (1981). Self-perceptions following social interactions. *Journal of Personality and Social Psychology, 41,* 232–242.

Fazio, R. H., Jackson, J. R., Dunton, B. C., & Williams, C. J. (1995). Variability in automatic activation as an unobstrusive measure of racial attitudes: A bona fide pipeline? *Journal of Personality and Social Psychology, 69,* 1013–1027.

Fazio, R. H., Ledbetter, J. E., & Towles-Schwen, T. (2000). On the costs of accessible attitudes: Detecting that the attitude object has changed. *Journal of Personality and Social Psychology, 78,* 197–210.

Fazio, R. H., & Olson, M. A. (2003). Implicit measures in social cognition research: Their meaning and uses. *Annual Review of Psychology, 54,* 297–327.

Fazio, R. H., & Zanna, M. P. (1981). Direct experience and attitude behavior consistency. In L. Berkowitz (Ed.), *Advances in experimental social psychology* (vol. 14, pp. 161–202). New York: Academic Press.

Fazio, R. H., Zanna, M. P., & Cooper, J. (1977). Dissonance and self-perception: An integrative view of each theory's proper domain of application. *Journal of Experimental Social Psychology, 13,* 464–479.

Federal Bureau of Investgation. (2003). *Crime in the United States,* Uniform Crime Reporting Program. Washington, DC: FBI.

Feeney, J. A. (2002). Attachment-related dynamics: What can we learn from self-reports of avoidance and anxiety? *Attachment & Human Development, 4,* 193–200.

Fehr, E., & Schmidt, K. M. (1999). A theory of fairness, competition, and cooperation. *Quarterly Journal of Economics, 114*(3), 817–868.

Fein, S., & Hilton, J. L. (1992). Attitudes toward groups and behavioral intentions toward individual group members: The impact of nondiagnostic information. *Journal of Experimental Social Psychology, 28,* 101–124.

Fein, S., & Spencer, S. J. (1997). Prejudice as self-image maintenance: Affirming the self through derogating others. *Journal of Personality and Social Psychology, 73*, 31–44.

Feinberg, M., & Willer, R. (2013). The moral roots of environmental attitudes. *Psychological Science, 24*, 56–62.

Feingold, A. (1990). Gender differences in effects of physical attractiveness on romantic attraction: A comparison across five research paradigms. *Journal of Personality and Social Psychology, 59*, 981–993.

Feingold, A. (1992a). Gender differences in mate selection preferences: A test of the parental investment model. *Psychological Bulletin, 112*, 125–139.

Feingold, A. (1992b). Good-looking people are not what we think. *Psychological Bulletin, 111*, 304–341.

Felson, R. B. (1989). Parents and the reflected appraisal process: A longitudinal analysis. *Journal of Personality and Social Psychology, 56*, 965–971.

Felson, R. B., & Staff, J. (2010). The effects of alcohol intoxication on violent versus other offending. *Criminal Justice and Behavior, 37*, 1343–1360.

Ferguson, C. J. (2013). *Adolescents, crime, and the media: A critical analysis.* New York: Springer.

Feshbach, N., & Feshbach, S. (1982). Empathy training and the regulation of aggression: Potentialities and limitations. *Academic Psychology Bulletin, 4*, 399–413.

Feshbach, S. & Singer, R. (1957). The effects of personality and shared threats upon social prejudice. *Journal of Abnormal and Social Psychology, 54*, 411–416.

Festinger, L. (1950). Informal social communication. *Psychological Review, 57*, 271–282.

Festinger, L. (1954). A theory of social comparison processes. *Human Relations, 7*, 117–140.

Festinger, L. (1957). *A theory of cognitive dissonance.* Stanford, CA: Stanford University Press.

Festinger, L., & Carlsmith, J. M. (1959). Cognitive consequences of forced compliance. *Journal of Abnormal and Social Psychology, 58*, 203–210.

Festinger, L., Schachter, S., & Back, K. (1950). *Social pressures in informal groups: A study of human factors in housing.* Stanford, CA: Stanford University Press.

Feygina, I., Jost, J. T., & Goldsmith, R. (2010). System justification, the denial of global warming, and the possibility of "system-sanctioned change." *Personality and Social Psychology Bulletin, 36*, 326–338.

Fiedler, F. (1964). A contingency model of leadership effectiveness. In L. Berkowitz (Ed.), *Advances in experimental social psychology* (vol. 1, pp. 149–190). New York: Academic Press.

Fiedler, K. (1991). The tricky nature of skewed frequency tables: An information loss account of distinctiveness-based illusory correlations. *Journal of Personality and Social Psychology, 60*, 24–36.

Fiedler, K., & Bluemke, M. (2005). Faking the IAT: Aided and unaided response control on the Implicit Association Tests. *Basic & Applied Social Psychology, 27*, 307–316.

Fiedler, K., Messner, C., & Bluemke, M. (2006). Unresolved problems with the "I", the "A", and the "T": A logical and psychometric critique of the Implicit Association Test (IAT). *European Review of Social Psychology, 17*, 74–147.

Fincham, F. D., & Beach, S. R. H. (2001). Forgiving in close relationships. In F. Columbus (Ed.), *Advances in psychology research* (vol. 7, pp. 163–197). Hauppauge, NY: Nova Science Publishers.

Fink, B., Neave, N., & Seydel, H. (2007). Male facial appearance signals physical strength to women. *American Journal of Human Biology, 19*, 82–87.

Finkel, E. J., DeWall, C. N., Slotter, E. B., Oaten, M., & Foshee, V. A. (2009). Self-regulatory failure and intimate partner violence perpetration. *Journal of Personality & Social Psychology, 97*, 483–499.

Finkel, E. J., & Eastwick, P. W. (2008). Speed-dating. *Current Directions in Psychological Science, 17*, 193–197.

Finkel, E. J., Slotter, E. B., Luchies, L. B., Walton, G. M., & Gross, J. J. (2013). A brief intervention to promote conflict reappraisal preserves marital quality over time. *Psychological Science, 24*, 1595–1601.

Finkelstein, M. A., & Penner, L. A. (2004). Predicting organizational citizenship behavior: Integrating the functional and role identity approaches. *Social Behavior and Personality, 32*, 383–398.

Fischer, P., & Greitemeyer, T. (2006). Music and aggression: The impact of sexual-aggressive song lyrics on aggression-related thoughts, emotions, and behavior toward the same and the opposite sex. *Personality and Social Psychology Bulletin, 32*, 1165–1176.

Fischer, P., & Greitemeyer, T. (2010). A new look at selective-exposure effects: An integrative model. *Current Directions in Psychological Science, 19*, 384–389.

Fischer, P., Krueger, J. I., Greitemeyer, T., Vogrincic, C., Kastenmüller, A., Frey, D., et al. (2011). The bystander-effect: A meta-analytic review on bystander intervention in dangerous and non-dangerous emergencies. *Psychological Bulletin, 137*(4), 517–537. doi:10.1037/a0023304

Fishbach, A., Dhar, R., & Zhang, Y. (2006). Subgoals as substitutes or complements: The role of goal accessibility. *Journal of Personality and Social Psychology, 91*, 232–242.

Fishbein, M., & Ajzen, I. (1975). *Belief, attitude, intention, and behavior: An introduction to theory and research.* Reading, MA: Addison-Wesley.

Fisher, J. D., Nadler, A., & Whitcher-Alagner, S. (1982). Recipient reactions to aid. *Psychological Bulletin, 91*, 27–54.

Fisher, M. (2012, December 14). Chart: The U.S. has far more gun-related killings than any other developed country. *The Washington Post.* Retrieved from http://www.washingtonpost.com/

Fisher, R., & Ury, W. L. (1981). *Getting to YES: Negotiating agreement without giving in.* Boston: Houghton Mifflin.

Fisher, R., & White, J. H. (1976). Intergroup conflicts resolved by outside consultants. *Journal of Community Development, 7*, 88–98.

Fiske, A. P. (1991). The cultural relativity of selfish individualism. In M. S. Clark (Ed.), *Prosocial behavior* (pp. 176–214). Newbury Park, CA: Sage Publications.

Fiske, A. P. (1992). The four elementary forms of sociality: Framework for a unified theory of social relations. *Psychological Review, 99,* 689–723.

Fiske, A. P., Kitayama, S., Markus, H. R., & Nisbett, R. E. (1998). The cultural matrix of social psychology. In D. T. Gilbert, S. T. Fiske, & G. Lindzey (Eds.), *Handbook of social psychology* (4th ed., vol. 2, pp. 915–981). Boston: McGraw-Hill.

Fiske, S. T. (1993a). Controlling other people: The impact of power on stereotyping. *American Psychologist, 48,* 621–628.

Fiske, S. T. (1993b). Social cognition and social perception. *Annual Review of Psychology, 44,* 155–194.

Fiske, S. T. (2002). What we know about bias and intergroup conflict, the problem of the century. *Current Directions in Psychological Science, 11*(4), 123–128.

Fiske, S. T., Cuddy, A. J. C., Glick, P., & Xu, J. (2002). A model of (often mixed) stereotype content: Competence and warmth respectively follow from perceived status and competition. *Journal of Personality and Social Psychology, 82*(6), 878–902. doi:10.1037//0022-3514.82.6.878

Fiske, S. T., & Neuberg, S. L. (1990). A continuum of impression formation, from category-based to individuating processes: Influences of information and motivation on attention and interpretation. In M. P. Zanna (Ed.), *Advances in experimental social psychology* (vol. 23, pp. 1–74). New York: Academic Press.

Fiske, S. T., and others. (1991). Social science research on trial: Use of sex stereotyping research in Price Waterhouse v. Hopkins. *American Psychologist, 46,* 1049–1060.

Fitness, J., & Fletcher, G. J. O. (1993). Love, hate, anger, and jealousy in close relationships. *Journal of Personality and Social Psychology, 65,* 942–958.

Fitzsimmons, D. (2004). What are we trying to measure? Rethinking approaches to health outcome assessment for the older person with cancer. *European Journal of Cancer Care, 13,* 416–423.

Fleming, I., Baum, A., & Weiss, L. (1987). Social density and perceived control as mediators of crowding stress in high-density residential neighborhoods. *Journal of Personality and Social Psychology, 52,* 899–906.

Fleming, M. A. (2009). Group-based brand relationships and persuasion: Multiple roles for identification and identification discrepancies. In D. J. MacInnis, C. W. Park, & J. R. Priester (Eds.), *Handbook of brand relationships* (pp. 151–169). Armonk, NY: M. E. Sharpe.

Fletcher, G. J. O., & Fincham, F. D. (1991). Attribution processes in close relationships. In G. Fletcher & F. Fincham (Eds.), *Cognition in close relationships* (pp. 7–36). Hillsdale, NJ: Lawrence Erlbaum Associates.

Flink, C., & Park, B. (1991). Increasing consensus in trait judgments through outcome dependency. *Journal of Experimental Social Psychology, 27,* 453–467.

Flynn, F. J., Reagans, R. E., Amanatullah, E. T., & Ames, D. R. (2006). Helping one's way to the top: Self-monitors achieve status by helping others and knowing who helps whom. *Journal of Personality & Social Psychology, 91,* 1123–1137.

Foa, U. G., & Foa, E. B. (1974). *Societal structures of the mind.* Oxford: Charles C. Thomas.

Fointiat, V., Somat, A., & Grosbras, J.-M. (2011). Saying, but not doing: Induced hypocrisy, trivialization, and misattribution. *Social Behavior and Personality, 39,* 465–476.

Folkman, S. (1984). Personal control and stress and coping processes: A theoretical analysis. *Journal of Personality and Social Psychology, 46,* 839–852.

Ford, M. B., & Collins, N. L. (2010). Self-esteem moderates neuroendocrine and psychological responses to interpersonal rejection. *Journal of Personality & Social Psychology, 98,* 405–419.

Ford, T. E. (2000). Effects of sexist humor on tolerance of sexist events. *Personality and Social Psychology Bulletin, 26,* 1094–1107.

Ford, T. E., & Thompson, E. P. (2000). Preconscious and postconscious processes underlying construct accessibility effects: An extended search model. *Personality and Social Psychology Review, 4,* 317–336.

Forgas, J. P. (1995). Mood and judgment: The Affect Infusion Model (AIM). *Psychological Bulletin, 117,* 39–66.

Förster, J. (2004). How body feedback influences consumers' evaluation of products. *Journal of Consumer Psychology, 14,* 415–425.

Forsyth, D. R. (1999). *Group dynamics* (3rd edn). Pacific Grove, CA: Brooks/Cole.

Forsyth, D. R., Schlenker, B. R., Leary, M. R., & McCown, N. E. (1985). Self-presentational determinants of sex differences in leadership behavior. *Small Group Behavior, 16,* 197–210.

Fournier, A. K., Hall, E., Ricke, P., & Storey, B. (2013). Alcohol and the social network: Online social networking sites and college students' perceived drinking norms. *Psychology of Popular Media Culture, 2,* 86–95.

Foushee, H. C. (1984). Dyads and triads at 35,000 feet: Factors affecting group process and aircrew performance. *American Psychologist, 39,* 885–893.

Frable, D.E.S. (1989). Sex typing and gender ideology: Two facets of the individual's gender psychology that go together. *Journal of Personality and Social Psychology, 56,* 95–108.

Frable, D. E. S. (1997). Gender, racial, ethnic, sexual, and class identities. *Annual Review of Psychology, 48,* 139–162.

Fraley, R. C., Roisman, G. I., Booth-LaForce, C., Owen, M. T., & Holland, A. S. (2013). Interpersonal and genetic origins of adult attachment styles: A longitudinal study from infancy to early adulthood. *Journal of Personality & Social Psychology, 104,* 817–838.

Frank, M. G., & Gilovich, T. (1988). The dark side of self- and social perception: Black uniforms and aggression in professional sports. *Journal of Personality and Social Psychology, 54,* 74–85.

Frattaroli, J. (2006). Experimental disclosure and its moderators: A meta-analysis. *Psychological Bulletin, 132,* 823–865.

Freedman, J. L., & Fraser, S. C. (1966). Compliance without pressure: The foot-in-the-door technique. *Journal of Personality and Social Psychology, 4,* 195–202.

Freedman, J. L., & Sears, D. O. (1965). Warning, distraction and resistance to influence. *Journal of Personality and Social Psychology, 1,* 262–266.

Freijy, T., & Kothe, E. J. (2013). Dissonance-based interventions for health behaviour change: A systematic review. *British Journal of Health Psychology, 18,* 310–337.

Freitas, A. L., & Higgins, E. T. (2002). Enjoying goal-directed action: The role of regulatory fit. *Psychological Science, 13,* 1–6.

Freund, T., Kruglanski, A. W., & Shpitzajsen, A. (1985). The freezing and unfreezing of impression primacy: Effects of need for structure and the fear of invalidity. *Personality and Social Psychology Bulletin, 11,* 479–487.

Friedman, H. S., Riggio, R. E., & Casella, D. F. (1988). Nonverbal skill, personal charisma, and initial attraction. *Personality and Social Psychology Bulletin, 14,* 203–211.

Friesen, J. P., Kay, A. C., Eibach, R. P., & Galinsky, A. D. (2014). Seeking structure in social organization: Compensatory control and the psychological advantages of hierarchy. *Journal of Personality and Social Psychology, 106,* 590–609.

Friess, S. (2002). The power of peer pressure. *Newsweek,* December 23.

Frijda, N. H. (1986). *The emotions.* Cambridge: Cambridge University Press.

Frijda, N. H., Kuipers, P., & ter Schure, E. (1989). Relations among emotion, appraisal, and emotional action readiness. *Journal of Personality and Social Psychology, 57,* 212–228.

Froming, W. J., Walker, G. R., & Lopyan, K. J. (1982). Public and private self awareness: When personal attitudes clash with societal expectations. *Journal of Experimental Social Psychology, 18,* 476–487.

Frost, J. H., Chance, Z., Norton, M. I., & Ariely, D. (2008). People are experience goods: Improving online dating with virtual dates. *Journal of Interactive Marketing, 22,* 51–61.

Fuglestad, P. T., & Snyder, M. (2010). Status and the motivational foundations of self-monitoring. *Social & Personality Psychology Compass, 4,* 1031–1041.

Fujita, K., & Han, H. A. (2009). Moving beyond deliberative control of impulses: The effect of construal levels on evaluative associations in self-control conflicts. *Psychological Science, 20,* 799–804.

Fujita, K., Henderson, M. D., Eng, J., Trope, Y., & Liberman, N. (2006). Spatial distance and mental construal of social events. *Psychological Science, 17,* 278–282.

Fujita, K., Trope, Y., Liberman, N., & Levin-Sagi, M. (2006). Construal levels and self-control. *Journal of Personality & Social Psychology, 90,* 351–367.

Funder, D. C., & Colvin, C. R. (1988). Friends and strangers: Acquaintanceship, agreement, and the accuracy of personality judgments. *Journal of Personality and Social Psychology, 55,* 149–158.

Furnham, A., & Baguma, P. (1994). Cross-cultural differences in the evaluation of male and female body shapes. *International Journal of Eating Disorders, 15,* 81–89.

Furnham, A., & Gunter, B. (1984). Just world beliefs and attitudes towards the poor. *British Journal of Social Psychology, 23,* 265–269.

Gable, S. L., Reis, H. T., Impett, E. A., & Asher, E. R. (2004). What do you do when things go right? The intrapersonal and interpersonal benefits of sharing positive events. *Journal of Personality & Social Psychology, 87,* 228–245.

Gabrenya, W. K., Wang, Y., & Latané, B. (1985). Social loafing on an optimizing task: Cross-cultural differences among Chinese and Americans. *Journal of Cross Cultural Psychology, 16,* 223–242.

Gaertner, L., Iuzzini, J., & O'Mara, E. M. (2008). When rejection by one fosters aggression against many: Multiple-victim aggression as a consequence of social rejection and perceived groupness. *Journal of Experimental Social Psychology, 44,* 958–970.

Gaertner, L., Iuzzini, J., Witt, M. G., & Orina, M. M. (2006). Us without them: Evidence for an intragroup origin of positive in-group regard. *Journal of Personality & Social Psychology, 90,* 426–439.

Gaertner, L., & Schopler, J. (1998). Perceived ingroup entitativity and intergroup bias: An interconnection of self and others. *European Journal of Social Psychology, 28,* 963–980.

Gaertner, S. L., & Dovidio, J. F. (2000). *Reducing intergroup bias: The common ingroup identity model.* New York, NY: Psychology Press.

Gaertner, S. L., & Dovidio, J. F. (2012). The common ingroup identity model. In P. A. M. van Lange, A. W. Kruglanski, & E. T. Higgins (Eds.), *Handbook of theories of social psychology* (vol. 2, pp. 439–457). Thousand Oaks, CA: Sage Publications.

Gaertner, S. L., Dovidio, J. F., Anastasio, P. A., Bachman, B. A., & Rust, M. C. (1993). The common ingroup identity model: Recategorization and the reduction of intergroup bias. In W. Stroebe & M. Hewstone (Eds.), *European review of social psychology* (vol. 4, pp. 1–26). Chichester: John Wiley & Sons, Ltd.

Gaertner, S. L., Dovidio, J., Banker, B., S., Houlette, M., Johnson, K. M., & McGlynn, E. A. (2000). Reducing intergroup conflict: From superordinate goals to decategorization, recategorization, and mutual differentiation. *Group Dynamics, 4,* 1089–1099.

Gaertner, S. L., Mann, J., Murrell, A., & Dovidio, J. F. (1989). Reducing intergroup bias: The benefits of recategorization. *Journal of Personality and Social Psychology, 57,* 239–249.

Gaertner, S.L., Mann, J., Dovidio, J.F., Murell, A., & Pomare, M. (1990). How does cooperation reduce intergroup bias? *Journal of Personality and Social Psychology, 59,* 692–704.

Gagnon, A., & Bourhis, R. Y. (1996). Discrimination in the

minimal group paradigm: Social identity or self-interest? *Personality and Social Psychology Bulletin, 22,* 1289–1301.

Gaines, S. O., & Henderson, M. C. (2002). Impact of attachment style on responses to accommodative dilemmas among same-sex couples. *Personal Relationships, 9,* 89–93.

Galinsky, A. D., Gilin, D., & Maddux, W. W. (2011). Using both your head and your heart: The role of perspective taking and empathy in resolving social conflict. In J. P. Forgas, A. W. Kruglanski, & K. D. Williams (Eds.), *The psychology of social conflict and aggression* (vol. 13, pp. 103–118). New York: Psychology Press.

Galinsky, A. D., Hall, E. V., & Cuddy, A. J. C. (2013). Gendered races: implications for interracial marriage, leadership selection, and athletic participation. *Psychological Science, 24*(4), 498–506. doi:10.1177/0956797612457783

Galinsky, A. D., Magee, J. C., Gruenfeld, D. H., Whitson, J. A., & Liljenquist, K. A. (2008). Power reduces the press of the situation: Implications for creativity, conformity, and dissonance. *Journal of Personality and Social Psychology, 95,* 1450–1466.

Galinsky, A. D., & Moskowitz, G. B. (2000). Counterfactuals as behavioral primes: Priming the simulation heuristic and consideration of alternatives. *Journal of Experimental Social Psychology, 36,* 384–409.

Gallo, I. S., Keil, A., McCulloch, K. C., Rockstroh, B., & Gollwitzer, P. M. (2009). Strategic automation of emotion regulation. *Journal of Personality and Social Psychology, 96,* 11–31.

Gallup. (2013). *State of the American workplace: Employee engagement insights for U.S. business leaders.* Retrieved from http://www.gallup.com/strategicconsulting/163007/state-american-workplace.aspx

Gallupe, R. B., Cooper, W. H., Grise, M.-L., & Bastianutti, L. M. (1994). Blocking electronic brainstorms. *Journal of Applied Psychology, 79,* 77–86.

Galton, F. (1879). Composite portraits, made by combining those of many different persons into a single resultant figure. *Journal of the Anthropological Institute of Great Britain & Ireland, 8,* 132–144.

Gamson, W. A. (1992). The social psychology of collective action. In A. D. Morris & C. M. Mueller (Eds.), *Frontiers in social movement theory* (pp. 53–76). New Haven, CT: Yale University Press.

Gamson, W. A., Fireman, B., & Rytina, S. (1982). *Encounters with unjust authority.* Homewood, IL: Dorsey Press.

Gangestad, S. W., & Snyder, M. (2000). Self-monitoring: Appraisal and reappraisal. *Psychological Bulletin, 126,* 530–555.

Gangestad, S. W., Garver-Apgar, C. E., Simpson, J. A., & Cousins, A. J. (2007). Changes in women's mate preferences across the ovulatory cycle. *Journal of Personality and Social Psychology, 92,* 151–163.

Garcia, S. M., Weaver, K., Moskowitz, G. B., Darley, J. M. (2002). Crowded minds: The implicit bystander effect. *Journal of Personality and Social Psychology, 83,* 843–853.

Gardikiotis, A. (2011). Minority influence. *Social and Personality Psychology Compass, 5,* 679–693.

Gardikiotis, A., Martin, R., & Hewstone, M. (2004). The representation of majorities and minorities in the British press: A content analytic approach. *European Journal of Social Psychology, 34,* 637–646.

Gardikiotis, A., Martin, R., & Hewstone, M. (2005). Group consensus in social influence: Type of consensus information as a moderator of majority and minority influence. *Personality and Social Psychology Bulletin, 31,* 1163–1174.

Gardner, R. C., Lalone, R. N., Nero, A. M., & Young, M. Y. (1988). Ethnic stereotypes: Implications of measurement strategy. *Social Cognition, 6,* 40–60.

Gardner, W. L., Gabriel, S., & Lee, A. Y. (1999). "I" value freedom, but "we" value relationships: Self-construal priming mirrors cultural differences in judgment. *Psychological Science, 10,* 321–326.

Gardner, W. L., & Knowles, M. L. (2008). Love makes you real: Favorite television characters are perceived as "real" in a social facilitation paradigm. *Social Cognition, 26,* 156–168.

Gardner, W. L., Pickett, C. L., & Brewer, M. B. (2000). Social exclusion and selective memory: How the need to belong influences memory for social events. *Personality and Social Psychology Bulletin, 26,* 486–496.

Gates, G. J. (2011). *How many people are lesbian, gay, bisexual and transgender?* Retrieved from University of California Los Angeles, Williams Institute website: http://williamsinstitute.law.ucla.edu/research/census-lgbt-demographics-studies/how-many-people-are-lesbian-gay-bisexual-and-transgender/

Gaucher, D., Friesen, J., & Kay, A. C. (2011). Evidence that gendered wording in job advertisements exists and sustains gender inequality. *Journal of Personality and Social Psychology, 101,* 109–128.

Gawronski, B. (2012). Back to the future of dissonance theory: Cognitive consistency as a core motive. *Social Cognition, 30,* 652–668.

Gawronski, B., Deutsch, R., Mbirkou, S., Seibt, B., & Strack, F. (2008). When "just say no" is not enough: Affirmation versus negation training and the reduction of automatic stereotype activation. *Journal of Experimental Social Psychology, 44,* 370–377.

Gay and Lesbian Alliance Against Defamation. (2011). *Where we are on TV report: 2011–2012 season.* Retrieved from http://www.glaad.org/publications/whereweareontv11

Geary, D. C. (2007). Evolution of fatherhood. In C. A. Salmon & T. K. Shackelford (Eds.), *Family relationships: An evolutionary perspective* (pp. 115–144). New York: Oxford University Press.

Geen, R. G. (1991). Social motivation. *Annual Review of Psychology, 42,* 377–391.

Geen, R. G. (1998). Aggression and antisocial behavior. In D. T. Gilbert, S. T. Fiske, & G. Lindzey (Eds.), *Handbook of social psychology* (3rd ed., vol. 2, pp. 317–356). Boston: McGraw-Hill.

Geer, J. H., Judice, S., & Jackson, S. (1994). Reading times for erotic material: The pause to reflect. *Journal of General Psychology, 121*, 345–352.

Geis, F. L., Brown, V., Jennings, J., & Porter, N. (1984). TV commercials as achievement scripts for women. *Sex Roles, 10*, 513–525.

Gelles, R. J. (1972). *The violent home: A study of physical aggression between husband and wife*. Beverly Hills, CA: Sage.

Gelles, R. J. (1997). *Intimate violence in families* (3rd ed.). Beverly Hills, CA: Sage.

Gerard, H. B., & Rabbie, J. M. (1961). Fear and social comparison. *Journal of Abnormal and Social Psychology, 62*, 586–592.

Gersick, C. J. (1989). Marking time: Predictable transitions in task groups. *Academy of Management Journal, 32*, 274–309.

Giancola, P. R., Josephs, R. A., Parrott, D. J., & Duke, A. A. (2010). Alcohol myopia revisited: Clarifying aggression and other acts of disinhibition through a distorted lens. *Perspectives on Psychological Science, 5*, 265–278.

Giancola, P. R., & Parrott, D. J. (2008). Further evidence for the validity of the Taylor aggression paradigm. *Aggressive Behavior, 34*, 214–229.

Gibbons, F. X., Eggleston, T. J., & Benthin, A. C. (1997). Cognitive reactions to smoking relapse: The reciprocal relation between dissonance and self-esteem. *Journal of Personality and Social Psychology, 72*, 184–195.

Gibbons, F. X., & Wicklund, R. A. (1982). Self-focused attention and helping behavior. *Journal of Personality and Social Psychology, 43*, 462–474.

Giebels, E. & Janssen, O. (2005). Conflict stress and reduced well-being at work: The buffering effect of third-party help. *European Journal of Work and Organizational Psychology, 14*, 137–155.

Giessner, S. R., van Knippenberg, D., & Sleebos, E. (2009). License to fail? How leader group prototypicality moderates the effects of leader performance on perceptions of leadership effectiveness. *The Leadership Quarterly, 20*, 434–451.

Gilbert, D. T. (1991). How mental systems believe. *American Psychologist, 46*, 107–119.

Gilbert, D. T. (1998). Ordinary personology. In D. T. Gilbert, S. T. Fiske, & G. Lindzey (Eds.), *Handbook of social psychology* (4th ed., vol. 2, pp. 89–150). Boston: McGraw-Hill.

Gilbert, D. T., & Jones, E. E. (1986). Perceiver-induced constraint: Interpretations of self-generated reality. *Journal of Personality and Social Psychology, 50*, 269–280.

Gilbert, D. T., Krull, D. S., & Malone, P. S. (1990). Unbelieving the unbelievable: Some problems in the rejection of false information. *Journal of Personality and Social Psychology, 59*, 601–613.

Gilbert, D. T., & Osborne, R. E. (1989). Thinking backward: Some curable and incurable consequences of cognitive busyness. *Journal of Personality and Social Psychology, 57*, 940–949.

Gilbert, D. T., Pelham, B. W., & Krull, D. S. (1988). On cognitive busyness: When person perceivers meet persons perceived. *Journal of Personality and Social Psychology, 54*, 733–740.

Giles, L. C., Glonek, G. F. V., Luszcz, M. A., & Andrews, G. R. (2005). Effect of social networks on 10 year survival in very old Australians: The Australian longitudinal study of aging. *Journal of Epidemiology and Community Health, 59*, 574–579.

Gillespie, N. A., & Mann, L. (2004). Transformational leadership and shared values: The building blocks of trust. *Journal of Managerial Psychology, 19*, 588–607.

Giner-Sorolla, R. (1999). Affect in attitude: Immediate and deliberative perspectives. In S. Chaiken & Y. Trope (Eds.), *Dual-process theories in social psychology*. (pp. 441–461). New York, NY: Guilford Press.

Gintis, H. (2008, March 7). Punishment and cooperation. *Science, 319*, 1345–1346. doi:10.1126/ science.1155333

Girandola, F. (2002). Sequential requests and organ donation. *Journal of Social Psychology, 142*, 171–178.

Glasman, L. R., & Albarracín, D. (2006). Forming attitudes that predict future behavior: A meta-analysis of the attitude-behavior relation. *Psychological Bulletin, 132*, 778–822.

Glick, P., & Fiske, S. T. (1996). The Ambivalent Sexism Inventory: Differentiating hostile and benevolent sexism. *Journal of Personality and Social Psychology, 70*, 491–512.

Glick, P., and others. (2000). Beyond prejudice as simple antipathy: Hostile and benevolent sexism across cultures. *Journal of Personality and Social Psychology, 79*, 763–775.

Glynn, C. J., Hayes, A. F., & Shanahan, J. (1997). Perceived support for one's opinion and willingness to speak out. *Public Opinion Quarterly, 61*, 452–463.

Goel, S., Mason, W., & Watts, D. J. (2010). Real and perceived attitude agreement in social networks. *Journal of Personality and Social Psychology, 99*, 611–621.

Goethals, G. R. (2005). Presidential leadership. *Annual Review of Psychology, 56*, 545–570.

Goethals, G.R., Cooper, J., & Nacify, A. (1979). Role of foreseen, foreseeable, and unforeseeable behavioral consequences in the arousal of cognitive dissonance. *Journal of Personality and Social Psychology, 37*, 1179–1185.

Goethals, G. R., Messick, D. M., & Allison, S. T. (1991). The uniqueness bias: Studies of constructive social comparison. In J. Suls & T. A. Wills (Eds.), *Social comparison: Contemporary theory and research* (pp. 149–176). Hillsdale, NJ: Lawrence Erlbaum Associates.

Goethals, G. R. & Nelson, R. E. (1973). Similarity in the influence process: The belief-value distinction. *Journal of Personality and Social Psychology, 25*, 117–122.

Goetz, J. L., Keltner, D., & Simon-Thomas, E. (2010). Compassion: An evolutionary analysis and empirical review. *Psychological Bulletin, 136*(3), 351–374. doi:http://dx.doi.org/10.1037/a0018807

Goff, P. A., Thomas, M. A., & Jackson, M. C. (2008). "Ain't I a woman?": Towards an intersectional approach to person perception and group-based harms. *Sex Roles, 59*, 392–403.

Goffman, E. (1959). *The presentation of self in everyday life*. Garden City, NY: Doubleday.

Goldberg, C. (1997, Feb. 25). Real-space meetings fill in the cyberspace gaps. *The New York Times*, p. A8.

Goldin, C. (1990). *Understanding the gender gap*. New York: Oxford University Press.

Goldstein, J. H. (1982). Sports violence. *National Forum*, 62(1), 9–11.

Goldstein, N. J., Cialdini, R. B., & Griskevicius, V. (2008). A room with a viewpoint: Using social norms to motivate environmental conservation in hotels. *Journal of Consumer Research*, 35, 472–482.

Gollwitzer, P. M. (1996). The volitional benefits of planning. In P. M. Gollwitzer & J. A. Bargh (Eds.), *The psychology of action: Linking cognition and motivation to behavior* (pp. 287–312). New York, NY: Guilford Press.

Gollwitzer, P. M. (1999). Implementation intentions: Strong effects of simple plans. *American Psychologist*, 54, 493–503.

Gollwitzer, P. M., & Moskowitz, G. B. (1996). Goal effects on action and congnition. In E. T. Higgins & A. W. Kruglanski (Eds.), *Social psychology: Handbook of basic principles* (pp. 361–399). New York, NY: Guilford Press.

Gollwitzer, P. M., & Schaal, B. (1998). Metacognition in action: The importance of implementation intentions. *Personality and Social Psychology Review*, 2, 124–136.

Gollwitzer, P. M., & Sheeran, P. (2006). Implementation intentions and goal achievement: A meta-analysis of effects and processes. In M. P. Zanna (Ed.), *Advances in experimental social psychology* (vol. 38, pp. 69–119). San Diego, CA: Elsevier Academic Press.

Goncalo, J. A., Polman, E., & Maslach, C. (2010). Can confidence come too soon? Collective efficacy, conflict and group performance over time. *Organizational Behavior and Human Decision Processes*, 113, 13–24.

Gonsalkorale, K., & Williams, K. D. (2007). The KKK won't let me play: Ostracism even by a despised outgroup hurts. *European Journal of Social Psychology*, 37, 1176–1186.

Gonzaga, G. C., Campos, B., & Bradbury, T. (2007). Similarity, convergence, and relationship satisfaction in dating and married couples. *Journal of Personality and Social Psychology*, 93, 34–48.

Goodfriend, W., & Agnew, C. R. (2008). Sunken costs and desired plans: Examining different types of investments in close relationships. *Personality and Social Psychology Bulletin*, 34, 1639–1652.

Goodman, M. (1952). *Race awareness in young children*. Cambridge, MA: Addison-Wesley.

Goodnough, A. (2005, Oct. 16). A favorite Florida fish is off the menu till next year. *The New York Times*,

Goodwin, R. (1999). *Personal relationships across cultures*. New York: Routledge.

Goodwin, S. A., Gubin, A., Fiske, S. T., & Yzerbyt, V. Y. (2000). Power can bias impression processes: Stereotyping subordinates by default and by design. *Group Processes and Intergroup Relations*, 3, 227–256.

Goranson, R.E., & Berkowitz, L. (1966). Reciprocity and responsibility reactions to prior help. *Journal of Personality and Social Psychology*, 3, 227–232.

Gordijn, E. H., De Vries, N. K., & De Dreu, C. K. W. (2002). Minority influence on focal and related attitudes: Change in size, attributions and information processing. *Personality and Social Psychology Bulletin*, 28, 1315–1326.

Gordijn, E. H., Wigboldus, D. I., & Yzerbyt, V. (2001). Emotional consequences of categorizing victims of negative outgroup behavior as ingroup or outgroup. *Group Processes & Intergroup Relations*, 4(4), 317–326.

Gordon, R. A., & Anderson, K. S. (1995). Perceptions of race-stereotypic and race-nonstereotypic crimes: The impact of response-time instructions on attributions and judgments. *Basic and Applied Social Psychology*, 16, 455–470.

Gore, J. S., Cross, S. E., & Morris, M. L. (2006). Let's be friends: Relational self-construal and the development of intimacy. *Personal Relationships*, 13, 83–102.

Gorenflo, D. W., & Crano, W. D. (1989). Judgmental subjectivity/objectivity and locus of choice in social comparison. *Journal of Personality and Social Psychology*, 57, 605–614.

Gorer, G. (1968). Man has no "killer" instinct. In M. F. A. Montagu (Ed.), *Man and aggression* (pp. 27–36). New York: Oxford University Press.

Gorn, G. (1982). The effects of music in advertising on choice behavior: A classical conditioning approach. *Journal of Marketing Research*, 46, 94–101.

Gosling, S. D., Gaddis, S., & Vazire, S. (2008). First impressions based on the environments we create and inhabit. In N. Ambady & J. J. Skowronski (Eds.), *First impressions* (pp. 334–356). New York: Guilford.

Gosling, S. D., Ko, S. J., Mannarelli, T., & Morris, M. E. (2002). A room with a cue: Personality judgments based on offices and bedrooms. *Journal of Personality and Social Psychology*, 82, 379–398.

Gottfredson, M. R., & Hirschi, T. (1990). *A general theory of crime*. Stanford, CA: Stanford University Press.

Gottman, J., Notarius, C., Markman, H., Bank, S., Yoppi, S., & Rubin, M. (1976). Behavior exchange theory and marital decision making. *Journal of Personality and Social Psychology*, 34, 14–23.

Gottman, J. M. (1993). The roles of conflict engagement, escalation, and avoidance in marital interaction: A longitudinal view of five types of couples. *Journal of Consulting and Clinical Psychology*, 61, 6–15.

Gould, S. J. (1978). Morton's ranking of races by cranial capacity. *Science*, 200, 503–509.

Gould, S. J. (1991). *Bully for Brontosaurus*. New York: W. W. Norton & Co.

Gouldner, A.W. (1960). The norm of reciprocity: A preliminary statement. *American Sociological Review*, 25, 161–178.

Goumas, C. (2013). Home advantage and crowd size in

soccer: A worldwide study. *Journal of Sport Behavior, 36,* 387–399.

Graham, J. M., & Barnow, Z. B. (2013). Stress and social support in gay, lesbian, and heterosexual couples: Direct effects and buffering models. *Journal of Family Psychology, 27,* 569–578.

Graham, K., Bernards, S., Osgood, D. W., & Wells, S. (2006). Bad nights or bad bars? Multi-level analysis of environmental predictors of aggression in late-night large-capacity bars and clubs. *Addiction, 101,* 1569–1580.

Graham, K., Bernards, S., Wilsnack, S. C., & Gmel, G. (2011). Alcohol may not cause partner violence but it seems to make it worse: A cross-national comparison of the relationship between alcohol and severity of partner violence. *Journal of Interpersonal Violence, 26,* 1503–1523.

Gramzow, R. H., Gaertner, L., & Sedikides, C. (2001). Memory for in-group and out-group information in a minimal group context: The self as an informational base. *Journal of Personality and Social Psychology, 80*(2), 188–205.

Grant, A., & Dutton, J. (2012). Beneficiary or benefactor: Are people more prosocial when they reflect on receiving or giving? *Psychological Science, 23*(9), 1033–1039. doi:http://dx.doi.org/10.1177/0956797612439424

Grant, T., & Dajee, K. (2003). Types of task, types of audience, types of actor: Interactions between mere presence and personality type in a simple mathematical task. *Personality and Individual Differences, 35,* 633–639.

Gray, P. B., Yang, C.-F. J., & Pope, H. G. (2006). Fathers have lower salivary testosterone levels than unmarried men and married non-fathers in Beijing, China. *Proceedings of the Royal Society B, 273,* 333–339.

Graziano, W. G., & Eisenberg, N. (1997). Agreeableness: Dimension of personality. In R. Hogan, J. Johnson, & S. Briggs (Eds.), *Handbook of personality* (pp. 795–825). San Diego, CA: Academic Press.

Graziano, W. G., Habashi, M., Sheese, B. E., & Tobin, R. (2004). Feeling compassion and helping the unfortunate: A social motivational analysis. Manuscript submitted for publication.

Greenberg, J., & Pyszczynski, T. (1985). The effect of an over-heard ethnic slur on evaluations of the target: How to spread a social disease. *Journal of Experimental Social Psychology, 21,* 61–72.

Greenberg, J., Pyszczynski, T., & Solomon, S. (1986). The causes and consequences of a need for self-esteem: A terror management theory. In R. F. Baumeister (Ed.), *Public self and private self* (pp. 189–212). New York: Springer-Verlag.

Greene, G. (1980). *Ways of escape.* New York: Simon & Schuster.

Greenwald, A. G. (1968). Cognitive learning, cognitive response to persuasion, and attitude change. In A. Greenwald, T. Brock, & T. Ostrom (Eds.), *Psychological foundations of attitudes* (pp. 148–170). New York: Academic Press.

Greenwald, A. G. (1980). The totalitarian ego: Fabrication and revision of personal history. *American Psychologist, 35,* 603–618.

Greenwald, A. G., McGhee, D. E., & Schwartz, J. L. K. (1998). Measuring individual differences in implicit cognition: The implicit association test. *Journal of Personality & Social Psychology, 74,* 1464–1480.

Greenwald, A. G., Poehlman, T. A., Uhlmann, E. L., & Banaji, M. R. (2009). Understanding and using the Implicit Association Test: III. Meta-analysis of predictive validity. *Journal of Personality & Social Psychology, 97,* 17–41.

Greenwald, A. G., & Ronis, D. L. (1978). Twenty years of cognitive dissonance: Case study of the evolution of a theory. *Psychological Review, 85,* 53–57.

Greitemeyer, T. (2005). Receptivity to sexual offers as a function of sex, socioeconomic status, physical attractiveness, and intimacy of the offer. *Personal Relationships, 12,* 373–386.

Greitemeyer, T. (2011). Effects of prosocial media on social behavior: When and why does media exposure affect helping and aggression? *Current Directions in Psychological Science, 20*(4), 251–255. doi:http://dx.doi.org/10.1177/0963721411415229

Greitemeyer, T., Agthe, M., Turner, R., & Gschwendtner, C. (2012). Acting prosocially reduces retaliation: Effects of prosocial video games on aggressive behavior. *European Journal of Social Psychology, 42,* 235–242.

Greitemeyer, T., & Osswald, S. (2010). Effects of prosocial video games on prosocial behavior. *Journal of Personality and Social Psychology, 98*(2), 211–221. doi:10.1037/a0016997

Greitemeyer, T., Schulz-Hardt, S., & Frey, D. (2009). The effects of authentic and contrived dissent on escalation of commitment in group decision making. *European Journal of Social Psychology, 39,* 639–647.

Gromet, D. M., Kunreuther, H., & Larrick, R. P. (2013). Political ideology affects energy-efficiency attitudes and choices. *Proceedings of the National Academy of Sciences of the United States of America, 110,* 9314–9319.

Gross, A. E., & Latané, J. G. (1974). Receiving help, reciprocation, and interpersonal attraction. *Journal of Applied Social Psychology, 4,* 210–223.

Gross, J. J., Halperin, E., & Porat, R. (2013). Emotion regulation in intractable conflicts. *Current Directions in Psychological Science, 22*(6), 423–429. doi:10.1177/0963721413495871

Grossman, R. P., & Till, B. D. (1998). The persistence of classically conditioned brand attitudes. *Journal of Advertising, 27,* 23–31.

Grube, J. A., & Piliavin, J. A. (in press). Role identity, organizational commitment, and volunteer performance. *Personality and Social Psychology Bulletin.*

Gruenfeld, D. H., Thomas-Hunt, M. C., & Kim, P. H. (1998). Cognitive flexibility communication strategy, and integrative complexity in groups: Public versus private reactions to majority and minority status. *Journal of Experimental Social Psychology, 34,* 202–226.

Guadagno, R. E., & Cialdini, R. B. (2010). Preference for consistency and social influence: A review of current research findings. *Social Influence, 5,* 152–163.

Guala, F., & Mittone, L. (2010). Paradigmatic experiments: The dictator game. *The Journal of Socio-Economics, 39,* 578–584.

Guéguen, N. (2002). Foot-in-the-door technique and computer-mediated communication. *Computers in Human Behavior*, *18*, 11–15.

Guéguen, N., & DeGail, M. (2003). The effect of smiling on helping behavior: Smiling and Good Samaritan behavior. *Communication Reports*, *16*, 133–140.

Guéguen, N., Marchand, M., Pascual, A., & Lourel M. (2008). The effect of the foot-in-the-door technique on a courtship request: A field experiment. *Psychological Reports*, *103*, 529–534.

Guéguen, N., Pascual, A., & Dagot, L. (2002). Low-ball and compliance to a request: An application in a field setting. *Psychological Reports*, *91*, 81–84.

Guenther, C. L., & Alicke, M. D. (2010). Deconstructing the better-than-average effect. *Journal of Personality and Social Psychology*, *99*, 755–770.

Guerin, B. (1986). The effects of mere presence on a motor task. *Journal of Social Psychology*, *126*, 399–401.

Guimond, S., & Dube-Simard, L. (1983). Relative deprivation theory and Quebec Nationalist Movement: The cognitive-emotion distinction and the personal-group deprivation issue. *Journal of Personality and Social Psychology*, *44*, 526–535.

Guinote, A. (2007a). Behaviour variability and the situated focus theory of power. *European Review of Social Psychology*, *18*, 256–295.

Guinote, A. (2007b). Power affects basic cognition: Increased attentional inhibition and flexibility. *Journal of Experimental Social Psychology*, *43*, 685–697.

Guinote, A. (2007c). Power and goal pursuit. *Personality and Social Psychology Bulletin*, *33*, 1076–1087.

Gully, S. M., Devine, D. J., & Whitney, D. J. (2012). A meta-analysis of cohesion and performance: Effects of level of analysis and task interdependence. *Small Group Research*, *43*, 702–725.

Gupta, U., & Singh, P. (1982). An exploratory study of love and liking and type of marriages. *Indian Journal of Applied Psychology*, *19*, 92–97.

Gurr, T. (1970). *Why men rebel*. Princeton, NJ: Princeton University Press.

Hackenbracht, J., & Gasper, K. (2013). I'm all ears: The need to belong motivates listening to emotional disclosure. *Journal of Experimental Social Psychology*, *49*, 915–921.

Hacker, H. M. (1951). Women as a minority group. *Social Forces*, *30*, 60–69.

Hackman, J. R. (1987). The design of work teams. In J. Lorsch (Ed.), *Handbook of organizational behavior* (pp. 315–342). Englewood Cliffs, NJ: Prentice-Hall.

Hackman, J. R. (1992). Group influences on individuals in organizations. In M. D. Dunnette & L. M. Hough (Eds.), *Handbook of industrial and organizational psychology* (2nd ed., vol. 3, pp. 199–267). Palo Alto, CA: Consulting Psychologists Press.

Hackman, J. R. (1993). Teams, leaders, and organizations: New directions for crew-oriented flight training. In E. Wiener, B. Kanki, & R. L. Helmreich (Eds.), *Cockpit resource management* (pp. 47–69). San Diego, CA: Academic Press.

Hadden, S. B., & Brownlow, S. (1991). The impact of facial structure and assertiveness on dating choice. Paper presented at the annual meeting of the Southeastern Psychological Association, New Orleans, March 20–24.

Hafer, C. L., & Begue, L. (2005). Experimental research on just-world theory: Problems, developments, and future challenges. *Psychological Bulletin*, *131*, 128–167.

Hafer, C. L., Reynolds, K. L., & Obertynski, M. A. (1996). Message comprehensibility and persuasion: Effects of complex language in counterattitudinal appeals to laypeople. *Social Cognition*, *14*, 317–337.

Hahlweg, K., Markman, H. J., Thurmaier, F., Engl, J., & Eckert, V. (1998). Prevention of marital distress: Results of a German prospective longitudinal study. *Journal of Family Psychology*, *12*, 543–556.

Haines, H., & Vaughan, G. M. (1979). Was 1898 a "great date" in the history of experimental social psychology? *Journal of the History of Behavioral Sciences*, *15*, 323–332.

Haines, M., & Spear, S. F. (1996). Changing the perception of the norm: A strategy to decrease binge drinking among college students. *Journal of American College Health*, *45*, 134–140.

Hains, S. C., Hogg, M. A., & Duck, J. M. (1997). Self-categorization and leadership: Effects of group prototypicality and leader stereotypicality. *Personality and Social Psychology Bulletin*, *23*, 1087–1099.

Hall, P. A., Zehr, C. E., Ng, M., & Zanna, M. P. (2012). Implementation intentions for physical activity in supportive and unsupportive environmental conditions: An experimental examination of intention–behavior consistency. *Journal of Experimental Social Psychology*, *48*, 432–436.

Halperin, E. (2008). Group-based hatred in intractable conflict in Israel. *Journal of Conflict Resolution*, *52*, 713–736.

Halverson, S. K., Holladay, C. L., Kazama, S. M., & Quiñones, M. A. (2004). Self-sacrificial behavior in crisis situations: The competing roles of behavioral and situational factors. *Leadership Quarterly*, *15*, 263–275.

Hamermesh, D. S., & Biddle, J. E. (1993, Nov.). Beauty and the Labor Market. NBER Working Paper No. W4518. NBER.

Hamilton, D. L. (1981). Stereotyping and intergroup behavior: Some thoughts on the cognitive approach. In D.L. Hamilton (Ed.), *Cognitive processes in stereotyping and intergroup behavior* (pp. 333–354). Hillsdale, NJ: Lawrence Erlbaum Associates.

Hamilton, D. L., Driscoll, D., & Worth, L. T. (1989). *Journal of Personality and Social Psychology*, *57*, 925–939.

Hamilton, D. L., & Gifford, R. K. (1976). Illusory correlation in interpersonal perception: A cognitive basis for stereotypic judgments. *Journal of Experimental Social Psychology*, *12*, 392–407.

Hamilton, D. L., Katz, L. B., & Leirer, V. (1980). Organizational processes in impression formation. In R. Hastie, T. M. Ostrom, E. B. Ebbesen, R. S. Wyer, D. L. Hamilton, & D. E. Carlston (Eds.), *Person memory* (pp. 121–153). Hillsdale, NJ: Lawrence Erlbaum Assoc.

Hamilton, D. L. & Mackie, D. M. (1990). Specificity and generality in the nature and use of stereotypes. In T. Srull & R. S. Wyer, Jr., (Eds). *Advances in Social Cognition: Content and process specificity in the effects of prior experiences* (vol. 3, pp. 99–110). Hillsdale, NJ: Erlbaum.

Hamilton, D. L., & Rose, T. L. (1980). Illusory correlation and the maintenance of stereotypic beliefs. *Journal of Personality and Social Psychology, 39,* 832–845.

Hamilton, D. L., & Sherman, S. J. (1989). Illusory correlations: Implications for stereotype theory and research. In D. Bar-Tal, C. F. Graumann, A. W. Kruglanski, & W. Stroebe (Eds.), *Stereotypes and prejudice: Changing conceptions* (pp. 59–82). New York: Springer-Verlag.

Hamilton, D. L., & Sherman, S. J. (1996). Perceiving persons and groups. *Psychological Review, 103,* 336–355.

Hamilton, D. L., Stroessner, S. J., & Mackie, D. M. (1993). The influence of affect on stereotyping: The case of illusory correlations. In D. M. Mackie & D. L. Hamilton (Eds.), *Affect, cognition, and stereotyping: Interactive processes in group perception* (pp. 39–61). San Diego, CA: Academic Press.

Hamilton, M. A. (2012). Verbal aggression: Understanding the psychological antecedents and social consequences. *Journal of Language and Social Psychology, 31,* 5–12.

Hamilton, V. L., & Sanders, J. (1992). *Everyday justice: Responsibility and the individual in Japan and the United States.* New Haven, CT: Yale University Press.

Hamilton, V. L., & Sanders, J. (1995). Crimes of obedience and conformity in the workplace: Surveys of Americans, Russians, and Japanese. *Journal of Social Issues, 51,* 67–88.

Hamilton, W. D. (1964). The genetical evolution of social behavior, I & II. *Journal of Theoretical Biology, 7,* 1–52.

Hamman, W. R. (2004). The complexity of team training: What we have learned from aviation and its applications to medicine. *Quality & Safety in Health Care, 13,* i72–i79.

Hammond, K. R. (1948). Measuring attitudes by error-choice: An indirect method. *Journal of Abnormal and Social Psychology, 43,* 38–48.

Han, H. A., Czellar, S., Olson, M. A., & Fazio, R. H. (2010). Malleability of attitudes or malleability of the IAT? *Journal of Experimental Social Psychology, 46,* 286–298.

Han, S, & Shavitt, S. (1993). Persuasion and culture: Advertising appeals in individualistic and collectivistic societies. Unpublished manuscript, University of Illinois.

Haney, C., Banks, C., & Zimbardo, P. (1973). Interpersonal dynamics in a simulated prison. *International Journal of Criminology and Penology, 1,* 69–97.

Hansen, J., & Wanke, M. (2009). Liking what's familiar: The importance of unconscious familiarity in the mere-exposure effect. *Social Cognition, 27,* 161–182.

Hansson, R. O., Stroebe, M. S., & Stroebe, W. (1988). In conclusion: Current themes in bereavement and widowhood research. *Journal of Social Issues, 44*(3), 207–216.

Harackiewicz, J. M. (1979). The effects of reward contingency and performance feedback on intrinsic motivation. *Journal of Personality and Social Psychology, 37,* 1352–1363.

Harber, K. D. (1998). Feedback to minorities: Evidence of a positive bias. *Journal of Personality and Social Psychology, 74,* 622–628.

Hardy, C., & Latané, B. (1986). Social loafing on a cheering task. *Social Science, 71,* 165–172.

Hare-Mustin, R. T., & Marecek, J. (1988). The meaning of difference: Gender theory, postmodernism, and psychology. *American Psychologist, 43,* 455–464.

Harinck, F., & De Dreu, C. K. W. (2004). Negotiating interests or values and reaching integrative agreements: The importance of time pressure and temporary impasses. *European Journal of Social Psychology, 34*(5), 595–611.

Haritos-Fatouros, M. (1988). The official torturer: A learning model for obedience to the authority of violence. *Journal of Applied Social Psychology, 18,* 1107–1120.

Harkins, S. G., & Petty, R.E. (1983). Social context effects in persuasion: The effects of multiple sources and multiple targets. In P. Paulus (Ed.). *Basic group processes.* New York: Springer-Verlag.

Harkins, S. G., & Petty, R. E. (1987). Information utility and the multiple source effect. *Journal of Personality and Social Psychology, 52,* 260–268.

Harkins, S. G., & Szymanski, K. (1989). Social loafing and group evaluation. *Journal of Personality and Social Psychology, 56,* 934–941.

Harmon-Jones, C., Schmeichel, B. J., Inzlicht, M., & Harmon-Jones, E. (2011). Trait approach motivation relates to dissonance reduction. *Social Psychological and Personality Science, 2,* 21–28.

Harmon-Jones, E., Amodio, D. M., & Harmon-Jones, C. (2009). Action-based model of dissonance: A review, integration, and expansion of conceptions of cognitive conflict. In M. P. Zanna (Ed.), *Advances in experimental social psychology* (vol. 41, pp.119–166). San Diego, CA: Elsevier Academic Press.

Harmon-Jones, E., & Harmon-Jones, C. (2008). Cognitive dissonance theory: An update with a focus on the action-based model. In J. Y. Shah & W. L. Gardner (Eds.), *Handbook of motivation science* (pp. 71–83). New York: Guilford Press.

Harries, T., Eslambolchilar, P., Stride, C., Rettie, R., & Walton, S. (2013). Walking in the wild – Using an always-on smartphone application to increase physical activity. In P. Kotze, G. Marsden, G. Lindgaard, J. Wesson, & M. Winckler (Eds.), *Human-computer interaction – INTERACT 2013* (pp. 19–36). New York: Springer.

Harris, C. R. (2004). The evolution of jealousy. *American Scientist, 92,* 62–71.

Harris, M. B., Benson, S. M., & Hall, C. L. (1975). The effects of confession on altruism. *Journal of Social Psychology, 96,* 187–192.

Harris, M. J. (1991). Controversy and cumulation: Meta-analysis and resaerch on interpersonal expectancy effects. *Personality and Social Psychology Bulletin, 17,* 316–322.

Harris, M. J., & Rosenthal, R. (1985). Mediation of interpersonal expectancy effects: 31 meta-analyses. *Psychological Bulletin, 97,* 363–386.

Hart, J. W., Bridgett, D. J., & Karau, S. J. (2001). Coworker ability and effort as determinants of individual effort on a collective task. *Group Dynamics, 5,* 181–190.

Hart, J. W., Karau, S. J., Stasson, M. F., & Kerr, N. A. (2004). Achievement motivation, expected coworker performance, and collective task motivation: Working hard or hardly working? *Journal of Applied Social Psychology, 34,* 984–1000.

Hart, W., & Albarracín, D. (2009). The effects of chronic achievement motivation and achievement primes on the activation of achievement and fun goals. *Journal of Personality & Social Psychology, 97,* 1129–1141.

Hart, W., Ottati, V. C., & Krumdick, N. D. (2011). Physical attractiveness and candidate evaluation: A model of correction. *Political Psychology, 32,* 181–203.

Harvey, J. H., & Omarzu, J. (1997). Minding the close relationship. *Personality and Social Psychology Review, 1,* 224–240.

Harvey, J. H., Wells, G. L., & Alvarez, M. D. (1978). Attribution in the context of conflict and separation in close relationships. In J. H. Harvey, W. Ickes, & R. F. Kidd (Eds.), *New directions in attribution research* (vol. 2, pp. 235–260). Hillsdale, NJ: Lawrence Erlbaum Associates.

Hasan, Y., Begue, L., & Bushman, B. J. (2012). Viewing the world through "blood-red tinted glasses": The hostile expectation bias mediates the link between violent video game exposure and aggression. *Journal of Experimental Social Psychology, 48,* 953–956.

Haslam, N., & Fiske, A. P. (1999). Relational models theory: A confirmatory factor analysis. *Personal Relationships, 6,* 241–250.

Haslam, S. A., Oakes, P. J., Turner, J. C., & McGarty, C. (1995). Social categorization and group homogeneity: Changes in the perceived applicability of stereotype content as a function of comparative context and trait favourableness. *British Journal of Social Psychology, 34,* 139–160.

Haslam, S. A., & Reicher, S. D. (2004). A critique of the role-based explanation of tyranny: Thinking beyond the Stanford prison. *Revista de Psicología Social, 19,* 115–122.

Haslam, S. A., & Reicher, S. D. (2012a). Contesting the "nature" of conformity: What Milgram and Zimbardo's studies really show. *PloS Biology, 10,* e1001426.

Haslam, S. A., & Reicher, S. D. (2012b). When prisoners take over the prison: A social psychology of resistance. *Personality and Social Psychology Review, 16,* 154–179.

Hastie, R. (1984). Causes and effects of causal attribution. *Journal of Personality and Social Psychology, 46,* 44–56.

Hastie, R., & Kumar, P. A. (1979). Person memory: Personality traits as organizing principles in memory for behaviors. *Journal of Personality and Social Psychology, 37,* 25–38.

Hastie, R., & Park, B. (1986). The relationship between memory and judgment depends on whether the judgment task is memory-based or on-line. *Psychological Review, 93,* 258–268.

Hastie, R., Penrod, S. D., & Pennington, N. (1983). *Inside the jury.* Cambridge, MA: Harvard University Press.

Hastorf, A., & Cantril, H. (1954). They saw a game: A case study. *Journal of Abnormal and Social Psychology, 49,* 129–134.

Hatfield, E. (1988). Passionate and companionate love. In R. Sternberg & M. Barnes (Eds.), *The psychology of love* (pp. 191–217). New Haven, CT: Yale University Press.

Hatfield, E., & Rapson, R. L. (1993). *Love, sex, and intimacy.* New York: HarperCollins.

Hatfield, E., Sprecher, S., Pillemer, J. T., Greenberger, D., & Wexler, P. (1989). Gender differences in what is desired in the sexual relationship. *Journal of Psychology and Human Sexuality, 1,* 39–52.

Haugtvedt, C. P., & Wegener, D. T. (1994). Message order effects in persuasion: An attitude strength perspective. *Journal of Consumer Research, 21,* 205–218.

Haun, D. B. M., van Leeuwen, E. J. C., & Edelson, M. G. (2013). Majority influence in children and other animals. *Developmental Cognitive Neuroscience, 3,* 61–71.

Hausenblas, H. A., Campbell, A., Menzel, J. E., Doughty, J., Levine, M., & Thompson, J. K. (2013). Media effects of experimental presentation of the ideal physique on eating disorder symptoms: A meta-analysis of laboratory studies. *Clinical Psychology Review, 33,* 168–181.

Hausmann, L. R. M., Levine, J. M., & Higgins, E. T. (2008). Communication and group perception: Extending the 'saying is believing' effect, *Group Processes & Intergroup Relations, 11,* 539–554.

Havas, D. A., Glenberg, A. M., Gutowski, K. A., Lucarelli, M. J., & Davidson, R. J. (2010). Cosmetic use of botulinum toxin-a affects processing of emotional language. *Psychological Science, 21,* 895–900.

Hawkley, L. C., & Cacioppo, J. T. (2010). Loneliness matters: A theoretical and empirical review of consequences and mechanisms. *Annals of Behavioral Medicine, 40,* 218–227.

Hawkley, L. C., Preacher, K. J., & Cacioppo, J. T. (2010). Loneliness impairs daytime functioning but not sleep duration. *Health Psychology, 29,* 124–129.

Hays, R. B. (1984). The development and maintenance of friendship. *Journal of Social and Personal Relationships, 1,* 75–98.

Hazan, C., & Shaver, P. (1987). Romantic love conceptualized as an attachment process. *Journal of Personality and Social Psychology, 52,* 511–524.

Heatherton, T. F., & Polivy, J. (1991). Development and validation of a scale for measuring state self-esteem. *Journal of Personality & Social Psychology, 60,* 895–910.

Heerdink, M. W., van Kleef, G. A., Homan, A. C., & Fischer, A. H. (2013). On the social influence of emotions in groups: Interpersonal effects of anger and happiness on conformity versus deviance. *Journal of Personality and Social Psychology, 105,* 262–284.

Heider, F. (1944). Social percpetion and phenomenal causality. *Psychological Review, 51*, 358–374.

Heider, F. (1958). *The psychology of interpersonal relations.* New York: Wiley.

Heilman, M. E., Battle, W. S., Keller, C. E., & Lee, R. A. (1998). Type of affirmative action policy: A determinant of reactions to sex-based preferential selection? *Journal of Applied Psychology, 83*, 190–205.

Heilman, M. E., Simon, M. C., & Repper, D. P. (1987). Intentionally favored, unintentionally harmed? Impact of sex-based preferential selection on self-perceptions and self-evaluations. *Journal of Applied Psychology, 72*, 62–68.

Heilman, M. E., & Stopek, M. H. (1985). Attractiveness and corporate success: Different causal attributions for males and females. *Journal of Applied Psychology, 70*, 379–388.

Heine, S. J. (2005). Where is the evidence for pancultural self-enhancement? A reply to Sedikides, Gaertner, and Toguchi (2003). *Journal of Personality & Social Psychology, 89*, 531–538.

Heine, S. J., Kitayama, S., & Hamamura, T. (2007). Which studies test whether self-enhancement is pancultural? Reply to Sedikides, Gaertner, and Vevea, 2007. *Asian Journal of Social Psychology, 10*, 198–200.

Heine, S. J., & Lehman, D. R. (1997). Culture, dissonance, and self-affirmation. *Personality and Social Psychology Bulletin, 23*, 389–400.

Heitland, K., & Bohner, G. (2010). Reducing prejudice via cognitive dissonance: Individual differences in preference for consistency moderate the effects of counter-attitudinal advocacy. *Social Influence, 5*, 164–181.

Helgeson, V. S. & Mickelson, K. D. (1995). Motives for social comparison. *Personality and Social Psychology Bulletin, 21*, 1200–1209.

Hemstrom, O. (1996). Is marriage dissolution linked to differences in mortality risks for men and women? *Journal of Marriage and the Family, 58*, 366–378.

Henderson-King, E. I., & Nisbett, R. E. (1996). Anti-black prejudice as a function of exposure to the negative behavior of a single black person. *Journal of Personality and Social Psychology, 71*, 654–664.

Hendrick, S., Hendrick, C., & Adler, N. L. (1988). Romantic relationships: Love, satisfaction, and staying together. *Journal of Personality and Social Psychology, 54*, 980–988.

Henrich, J. (2008) A cultural species. In M. Brown (Ed.), *Explaining culture scientifically* (pp. 184–210). Seattle: University of Washington Press.

Henrich, J., Heine, S. J., & Norenzayan, A. (2010). The weirdest people in the world? *Behavioral and Brain Sciences, 33*(2–3), 61–83. doi:10.1017/S0140525X0999152X

Henry, D. B., Kobus, K., & Schoeny, M. E. (2011). Accuracy and bias in adolescents' perceptions of friends' substance use. *Psychology of Addictive Behaviors, 25*, 80–89.

Henslin, J. M. (2003). Doing the unthinkable: Eating your friends is the hardest: The survivors of the F-227. *Down to earth sociology: Introductory readings* (12th ed., pp. 261–270). New York: Free Press.

Herlocker, C. E., Allison, S. T., Foubert, J. D., & Beggan, J. K. (1997). Intended and unintended overconsumption of physical, spatial, and temporal responses. *Journal of Personality and Social Psychology, 73*, 992–1004.

Herrett-Skjellum, J., & Allen, M. (1996). Television programming and sex stereotyping: A meta-analysis. In B. R. Burleson (Ed.), *Communication yearbook 19* (pp. 157–185). Thousand Oaks, CA: Sage Publications.

Hersey, P., & Blanchard, K. H. (1982). *Management of organizational behavior* (4th ed.). Englewood Cliffs, NJ: Prentice-Hall.

Hertel, G. & Kerr, N. L. (2001). Priming in-group favoritism: The impact of normative scripts in the minimal group paradigm. *Journal of Experimental Social Psychology, 37*, 316–324.

Hertel, G., Kerr, N. L., & Messe, L. A. (2000). Motivation gains in performance groups: Paradigmatic and theoretical developments on the Kohler effect. *Journal of Personality and Social Psychology, 79*, 580–601.

Hewstone, M., Jaspars, J., & Lalljee, M. (1982). Social representations, social attribution and social identity: The intergroup images of "public" and "comprehensive" schoolboys. *European Journal of Social Psychology, 12*, 241–269.

Hewstone, M., Rubin, M., & Willis, H. (2002). Intergroup bias. *Annual Review of Psychology, 53*(1), 575–604.

Higgins, E. T. (1987). Self-discrepancy: A theory relating self and affect. *Psychological Review, 94*, 319–340.

Higgins, E. T. (1996a). Knowledge activation: Accessibility, applicability, and salience. In E. T. Higgins & A. W. Kruglanski (Eds.), *Social psychology: Handbook of basic principles* (pp. 133–168). New York: Guilford Press.

Higgins, E. T. (1996b). The "self digest": Self-knowledge serving self-regulatory functions. *Journal of Personality and Social Psychology, 71*, 1062–1083.

Higgins, E. T. (1997). Beyond pleasure and pain. *American Psychologist, 52*, 1280–1300.

Higgins, E. T., & Bargh, J. A. (1987). Social cognition and social perception. *Annual Review of Psychology, 38*, 369–425.

Higgins, E. T., King, G. A., & Mavin, G. H. (1982). Individual construct accessibility and subjective impressions and recall. *Journal of Personality and Social Psychology, 43*, 35–47.

Higgins, E. T., & McCann, C. D. (1984). Social encoding and subsequent attitudes, impressions, and memory: "Context-driven" and motivational aspects of processing. *Journal of Personality and Social Psychology, 47*, 26–39.

Higgins, E. T., & Rholes, W. S. (1978). Saying is believing: Effects of message modification on memory and liking for the person described. *Journal of Experimental Social Psychology, 14*, 363–378.

Higgins, E. T., Rholes, W. S., & Jones, C. R. (1977). Category accessibility and impression formation. *Journal of Experimental Social Psychology, 13*, 141–154.

Hill, C. T., Rubin, Z., & Peplau, L. A. (1976). Breakups before marriage: The end of 103 affairs. *Journal of Social Issues, 32*(1), 147–168. ·

Hill, R. A., & Barton, R. A. (2005). Red enhances human performance in contests. *Nature, 435,* 293.

Hilton, J. L., & Darley, J. M. (1985). Constructing other persons: A limit on the effect. *Journal of Experimental Social Psychology, 21,* 1–18.

Hinsz, V. B., & Davis, J. H. (1984). Persuasive arguments theory, group polarization, and choice shifts. *Personality and Social Psychology Bulletin, 10,* 260–268.

Hirokawa, R. Y. (1990). The role of communication in group decision-making efficacy: A task-contingency perspective. *Small Group Research, 21,* 190–204.

Hiroto, D. S. (1974). Locus of control and learned helplessness. *Journal of Experimental Psychology, 102,* 187–193.

Hirst, G., van Dick, R., & van Knippenberg, D. (2009). A social identity perspective on leadership and employee creativity. *Journal of Organizational Behavior, 30,* 963–982.

Hirt, E. R., McCrea, S. M., & Boris, H. I. (2003). 'I know you self-handicapped last exam': Gender differences in reactions to self-handicapping. *Journal of Personality and Social Psychology, 84,* 177–193.

Hodgins, H. S., & Zuckerman, M. (1993). Beyond selecting information: Biases in spontaneous questions and resultant conclusions. *Journal of Experimental Social Psychology, 29,* 387–407.

Hoelter, J. W. (1985). The structure of self-conception: Conceptualization and measurement. *Journal of Personality and Social Psychology, 49,* 1392–1407.

Hoffman, C. & Hurst, N. (1990). Gender stereotypes: perception or rationalization? *Journal of Personality and Social Psychology, 58,* 197–208.

Hoffman, M. L. (1981). Is altruism part of human nature? *Journal of Personality and Social Psychology, 40,* 121–137.

Hoffman, M. L. (1986). Affect, cognition, motivation. In R. M. Sorrentino & E.T. Higgins (Eds.), *Handbook of motivation and cognition: Foundations of social behavior* (vol. 1, pp. 244–280). New York: Guilford Press.

Hofling, C. K., Brotzman, E., Dalrymple, S., Graves, N., & Pierce, C. M. (1966). An experimental study in nurse-physician relationships. *Journal of Nervous and Mental Disease, 143,* 171–180.

Hofmann, W., Friese, M., & Roefs, A. (2009). Three ways to resist temptation: The independent contributions of executive attention, inhibitory control, and affect regulation to the impulse control of eating behavior. *Journal of Experimental Social Psychology, 45,* 431–435.

Hofmann, W., & Windschitl, P. D. (2008). Judging a group by sampling members: How the subdivision of a minority affects its perceived size and influence. *The Journal of Social Psychology, 148,* 91–104.

Hogan, R., Curphy, G. J., & Hogan, J. (1994). What we know about leadership: Effectiveness and personality. *American Psychologist, 49,* 493–504.

Hogg, M. (1987). Social identity and group cohesiveness. In J. C. Turner (Ed.), *Rediscovering the social group: A self-categorization theory* (pp. 89–116). Oxford: Basil Blackwell.

Hogg, M. A. (1996). Social identity, self-categorization, and the small group. In E. H. Witte & J. A. Davis (Eds.), *Understanding group behavior,* vol. 2: *Small group processes and interpersonal relations* (pp. 227–253). Mahwah, NJ: Lawrence Erlbaum Associates.

Hogg, M. A. (2012). Social identity and the psychology of groups. In M. R. Leary & J. P. Tangney (Eds.), *Handbook of self and identity* (2nd ed., pp. 502–519). New York: Guilford Press.

Hogg, M. A. (2013). Leadership. In J. M. Levine (Ed.), *Group processes* (pp. 241–266). New York: Psychology Press.

Hogg, M. A., & Abrams, D. (1988). *Social identifications.* London: Routledge.

Hogg, M. A., & Abrams, D. (1993). Toward a single-process uncertainty-reduction model of social motivation in groups. In M. A. Hogg & D. Abrams (Eds.), *Group motivation: Social psychological perspectives* (pp. 173–190). London: Harvester Wheatsheaf.

Hogg, M. A., Abrams, D., Otten, S., & Hinkle, S. (2004). The social identity perspective: Intergroup relations, self-conception, and small groups. *Small Group Research, 35,* 246–276.

Hogg, M. A., Cooper-Shaw, L., & Holzworth, D. W. (1993). Group prototypicality and depersonalized attraction in small interactive groups. *Personality and Social Psychology Bulletin, 19,* 452–465.

Hogg, M. A., & Hardie, E. A. (1991). Social attraction, personal attraction, and self-categorization: A field study. *Personality and Social Psychology Bulletin, 17,* 175–180.

Hogg, M. A., & Turner, J. C. (1987). Intergroup behavior, self-stereotyping and the salience of social categories. *British Journal of Social Psychology, 26,* 325–340.

Hogg, M. A., van Knippenberg, D., & Rast, D. E. (2012). The social identity theory of leadership: Theoretical origins, research findings, and conceptual developments. *European Review of Social Psychology, 23,* 258–304.

Hoigaard, R., Safvenbom, R., & Tonnessen, F. E. (2006). The relationship between group cohesion, group norms, and perceived social loafing in soccer teams. *Small Group Research, 37,* 217–232.

Holbrook, A. L., Berent, M. K., Krosnick, J. A., Visser, P. S., & Boninger, D. S. (2005). Attitude importance and the accumulation of attitude-relevant knowledge in memory. *Journal of Personality & Social Psychology, 88,* 749–769.

Holland, R. W., de Vries, M., Hermsen, B., & van Knippenberg, A. (2012). Mood and the attitude-behavior link: The happy act on impulse, the sad think twice. *Social Psychological and Personality Science, 3,* 356–364.

Holland, R. W., Verplanken, B., & van Knippenberg, A. (2002). On the nature of attitude-behavior relations: The strong guide, the weak follow. *European Journal of Social Psychology, 32,* 869–876.

Hollander, E.P. (1958). Conformity, status, and idiosyncrasy credit. *Psychological Review, 65*, 117–127.

Hollingshead, A. B. (2004). Communication technologies, the internet, and group research. In M. B. Brewer & M. Hewstone (Eds), *Applied social psychology: Perspectives on social psychology* (pp. 301–317). Malden, MA: Blackwell.

Holsti, O. R., & North, R. (1965). The history of human conflict. In E. B. McNeil (Ed.), *The nature of human conflict* (pp. 155–171). Englewood Cliffs, NJ: Prentice-Hall.

Holt, J. L., & DeVore, C. J. (2005). Culture, gender, organizational role, and styles of conflict resolution: A meta-analysis. *International Journal of Intercultural Relations, 29*(2), 165–196.

Holt-Lunstad, J., Smith, T. B., & Layton, J. B. (2010). Social relationships and mortality risk: A meta-analytic review. *PLOS Medicine, 7*(7): e1000316

Homan, A. C., & Greer, L. L. (2013). Considering diversity: The positive effects of considerate leadership in diverse teams. *Group Processes & Intergroup Relations, 16*, 105–125.

Honour Based Violence Awareness Network. (2013). *Statistics & Data*. Retrieved from www.hbv-awareness.com/statistics-data/

Hoover, C. W., Wood, E. E., & Knowles, E. S. (1983). Forms of social awareness and helping. *Journal of Experimental Social Psychology, 19*, 577–590.

Hopthrow, T., & Hulbert, L. G. (2005). The effect of group decision making on cooperation in social dilemmas. *Group Processes & Intergroup Relations, 8*, 89–100.

Horcajo, J., Petty, R. E., & Briñol, P. (2010). The effects of majority versus minority source status on persuasion: A self-validation analysis. *Journal of Personality and Social Psychology, 99*, 498–512.

Hornsey, M. J., & Hogg, M. A. (2000). Subgroup relations: A comparison of mutual intergroup differentiation and common ingroup identity models of prejudice reduction. *Personality and Social Psychology Bulletin, 26*, 242–256.

Hornsey, M. J., & Jetten, J. (2004). The individual within the group: Balancing the need to belong with the need to be different. *Personality & Social Psychology Review, 8*(3), 248–264.

Hornstein, H. A. (1975). Social psychology as social intervention. In M. Deutch & H. A. Hornstein (Eds.), *Applying social psychology: Implications for research, practice, and training* (pp. 211–234). Hillsdale, NJ: Lawrence Erlbaum Associates.

Horowitz, M. J. (1987). *States of mind*. New York: Plenum.

Horwitz, M., & Rabbie, J. M. (1982). Individuality and membership in the intergroup system. In H. Tajfel (Ed.), *Social identity and intergroup relations* (pp. 241–274). New York: Cambridge University Press.

Hoshino-Browne, E. (2012). Cultural variations in motivation for cognitive consistency: Influences of self-systems on cognitive dissonance. *Social and Personality Psychology Compass, 6*, 126–141.

Houben, K., Havermans, R. C., & Wiers, R. W. (2010). Learning to dislike alcohol: Conditioning negative implicit attitudes toward alcohol and its effect on drinking behavior. *Psychopharmacology, 211*, 79–86.

House, R. J., & Shamir, B. (1993). Toward the integration of transformational, charismatic, and visionary theories. In M. M. Chemers & R. Ayman (Eds.), *Leadership theory and research: Perspectives and directions* (pp. 81–107). San Diego, CA: Academic Press.

Housley, M. K., Claypool, H. M., Garcia-Marques, T., & Mackie, D. M. (2010). "We" are familiar but "it" is not: Ingroup pronouns trigger feelings of familiarity. *Journal of Experimental Social Psychology, 46*, 114–119.

Hovland, C. I., Janis, I. L., & Kelley, H. H. (1953). *Communication and persuasion*. New Haven, CT: Yale University Press.

Hovland, C. I., Lumsdaine, A., & Sheffield, F. (1949). *Experiments on mass communication*. Princeton, NJ: Princeton University Press.

Hovland, C. I., & Weiss, W. (1951). The influence of source credibility on communication effectiveness. *Public Opinion Quarterly, 15*, 635–650.

Howard, D. J. (1997). Familiar phrases as peripheral persuasion cue. *Journal of Experimental Social Psychology, 33*, 231–243.

Howland, M., & Simpson, J. A. (2010). Getting in under the radar: A dyadic view of invisible support. *Psychological Science, 21*, 1878–1885.

Hoyle, R. H., Pinkley, R. L., & Insko, C. A. (1989). Perceptions of social behavior: Evidence of differing expectations for interpersonal and intergroup interaction. *Personality and Social Psychology Bulletin, 15*, 365–376.

Hoyt, C. L. (2010). Women, men, and leadership: Exploring the gender gap at the top. *Social and Personality Psychology Compass, 4*, 484–498.

Hsee, C. K., Zhang, J., Lu, Z. Y., & Xu, F. (2013). Unit asking: A method to boost donations and beyond. *Psychological Science*. doi:10. 1177/0956797613482947

Hsu, F. L. K. (1983). *Rugged individualism reconsidered*. Knoxville: University of Tennessee Press.

Huang, J.-W. (2013). The effects of transformational leadership on the distinct aspects development of social identity. *Group Processes & Intergroup Relations, 16*, 87–104.

Huckfeldt, R., & Sprague, J. (2000). Political consequences of inconsistency: The accessibility and stability of abortion attitudes. *Political Psychology, 21*, 57–79.

Huddy, L., & Feldman, S. (2011). Americans respond politically to 9/11: Understanding the impact of the terrorist attacks and their aftermath. *American Psychologist, 66*, 455–467.

Huesmann, L. R. (1986). Psychological processes promoting the relation between exposure to media violence and aggressive behavior by the viewer. *Journal of Social Issues, 42*(3), 125–139.

Huesmann, L. R., & Eron, L. D. (1984). Cognitive processes and the persistence of aggressive behavior. *Aggressive Behavior, 10*, 243–251.

Huesmann, L. R., & Eron, L. D. (1986). *Television and aggressive child: A cross-national comparison*. Hillsdale, NJ: Lawrence Erlbaum Associates.

Hugenberg, K., & Bodenhausen, G. V. (2003). Facing prejudice: Implicit prejudice and the perception of facial threat. *Psychological Science, 14*, 640–643.

Hugenberg, K., Miller, J., & Claypool, H. M. (2007). Categorization and individuation in the cross-race recognition deficit: Toward a solution to an insidious problem. *Journal of Experimental Social Psychology, 43*, 334–340.

Hugenberg, K., & Sacco, D. F. (2008). Social categorization and stereotyping: How social categorization biases person perception and face memory. *Social & Personality Psychology Compass, 2*, 1052–1072.

Hugenberg, K., Young, S. G., Bernstein, M. J., & Sacco, D. F. (2010). The categorization-individuation model: An integrative account of the other-race recognition deficit. *Psychological Review, 117*, 1168–1187.

Huguet, P., Galvaing, M. P., Monteil, J. M., & Dumas, F. (1999). Social presence effects in the Stroop task: Further evidence for an attentional view of social facilitation. *Journal of Personality and Social Psychology, 77*, 1011–1025.

Hull, J. G. (1981). A self-awareness model of the causes and effects of alcohol consumption. *Journal of Abnormal Psychology, 90*, 586–600.

Hullett, C. R. (2005). The impact of mood on persuasion: A meta-analysis. *Communication Research, 32*, 423–442.

Humphrey, R. (1985). How work roles influence perception: Structural-cognitive processes and organizational behavior. *American Sociological Review, 50*, 242–252.

Hunter, C. E., & Ross, M. W. (1991). Determinants of health-care workers' attitudes toward people with AIDS. *Journal of Applied Social Psychology, 21*, 947–956.

Hurtz, W., & Durkin, K. (1997). Gender role stereotyping in Australian radio commercials. *Sex Roles, 36*, 103–114.

Hyatt, D. E., & Ruddy, T. M. (1997). An examination of the relationship between work group characteristics and performance: Once more into the breech. *Personnel Psychology, 50*, 553–585.

Hyde, J. S. (1979). *Understanding human sexuality*. New York: McGraw-Hill.

Hyde, J. S. (1984). How large are gender differences in aggression? A developmental meta-analysis. *Developmental Psychology, 20*, 722–736.

Iacono, W. G. (2008). Polygraph testing. In E. Borgida & S. T. Fiske (Eds.), *Beyond common sense: Psychological science in the courtroom* (pp. 219–235). Hoboken, NJ: Wiley-Blackwell.

Ickes, W., & Simpson, J. A. (1997). Managing empathic accuracy in close relationships. In W. J. Ickes (Ed.). *Empathic accuracy* (pp. 218–250). New York: Guilford Press.

Ilgen, D.R., Hollenbeck, J.R., Johnson, M., & Jundt, D. (2005). Teams in organizations: From Input-Process-Output models to IMOI models. *Annual Review of Psychology, 56*, 517–43.

Insko, C. A. (1981). Balance theory and phenomenology. In R. Petty, T. Ostrom, & T. Brock (Eds.), *Cognitive responses and persuasion*. Hillsdale, NJ: Erlbaum.

Insko, C. A., & Schopler, J. (1987). Categorization, competition, and collectivity. In C. Hendrick (Ed.), *Group processes* (vol. 8, pp. 213–251). New York: Sage.

Insko, C. A., & Schopler, J. (1998). Differential distrust of groups and individuals. In C. Sedikides, J. Schopler, & C. Insko (Eds.), *Intergroup cognition and intergroup behavior* (pp. 75–108). Mahwah, NJ: Erlbaum.

Insko, C. A., Schopler, J., Hoyle, R.H., Dardis, G. J., & Graetz, K. A. (1990). Individual-group discontinuity as a function of fear and greed. *Journal of Personality and Social Psychology, 58*, 68–79.

Insko, C. A., Thompson, V. D., Stroebe, W., Shaud, K. F., Pinner, B. E., & Layton, B. D. (1973). Implied evaluation and the similarity-attraction effect. *Journal of Personality and Social Psychology, 25*, 297–308.

Insko, C. A., & Wilson, M. (1977). Interpersonal attraction as a function of social interaction. *Journal of Personality and Social Psychology, 35*, 903–911.

Insko, S. A., Dreenan, S., Soloman, M. R., Smith, R. & Wade, T. J. (1983). Conformity as a function of the consistency of positive self-evaluation with being liked and being right. *Journal of Experimental Social Psychology, 19*, 341–358.

IPCC. (2001). *Climate change 2001: The scientific basis*. Contribution of Working Group I to the Third Assessment Report of the Intergovernmental Panel on Climate Change, edited by J. T. Houghton et al. Cambridge: Cambridge University Press.

Isen, A. (1970). Success, failure, attention, and reaction to others: The warm glow of success. *Journal of Personality and Social Psychology, 15*, 294–301.

Isen, A., & Simmonds, S. F. (1978). The effect of feeling good on a helping task that is incompatible with good mood. *Social Psychology, 41*, 345–349.

Isen, A.M. (1987). Positive affect, cognitive processes, and social behavior. In L. Berkowitz (Ed.), *Advances in experimental social psychology* (vol. 20, pp. 203–253). New York: Academic Press.

Isen, A. M., & Levin, P. F. (1972). The effect of feeling good on helping: Cookies and kindness. *Journal of Personality and Social Psychology, 21*, 384–388.

Islam, M. R., & Hewstone, M. (1993). Intergroup attributions and affective consequences in majority and minority groups. *Journal of Personality and Social Psychology, 64*, 936–950.

Ito, T. A., Larsen, J. T., Smith, N. K., & Cacioppo, J. T. (1998). Negative information weighs more heavily on the brain: The negativity bias in evaluative categorizations. *Journal of Personality & Social Psychology, 75*, 887–900.

Ito, T. A., Miller, N., & Pollock, V. E. (1996). Alcohol and aggression: A meta-analysis on the moderating effects of inhibitory cues, triggering events, and self-focused attention. *Psychological Bulletin, 120*, 60–82.

Iyer, A., Leach, C. W., & Crosby, F. J. (2003). White guilt and racial compensation: The benefits and limits of self-focus. *Personality and Social Psychology Bulletin, 29*(1), 117–129.

Izuma, K., Matsumoto, M., Murayama, K., Samejima, K., Sadato, N., & Matsumoto, K. (2010). Neural correlates of cognitive dissonance and choice-induced preference change. *Proceedings of the National Academy of Sciences, 107,* 22014–22019.

Jackson, L. A., Sullivan, L. A., Harnish, R., & Hodge, C. N. (1996). Achieving positive social identity: Social mobility, social creativity, and permeability of group boundaries. *Journal of Personality and Social Psychology, 70,* 241–254.

Jackson, L. A., & Sullivan, L. A. (1989). Cognition and affect in evaluations of stereotyped group members. *Journal of Social Psychology, 129,* 659–672.

Jackson, L. M., & Esses, V. M. (1997). Of scripture and ascription: The relation between religious fundamentalism and intergroup helping. *Personality and Social Psychology Bulletin, 23,* 893–906.

Jacob, C., & Guéguen, N. (2013). The effect of employees' verbal mimicry on tipping. *International Journal of Hospitality Management, 35,* 109–111.

Jacobson, R. P., Mortensen, C. R., & Cialdini, R. B. (2011). Bodies obliged and unbound: Differentiated response tendencies for injunctive and descriptive social norms. *Journal of Personality and Social Psychology, 100,* 433–448.

Jacoby, J., Hoyer, W. D., & Sheluga, D. A. (1980). *Miscomprehension of televised communications.* New York: American Association of Advertising Agencies.

Jaffe, E. (2005, September). How random is that? *APS Observer, 18,* 20–30.

James, W. (1884). What is an emotion? *Mind, 9,* 188–205.

Janicik, G. A., & Bartel, C. A. (2003). Talking about time: Effects of temporal planning and time awareness norms on group coordination and performance. *Group Dynamics: Theory, Research, and Practice, 7,* 122–134.

Janis, I. (1972). *Victims of groupthink.* Boston: Houghton Mifflin.

Janis, I. (1982). *Groupthink* (2nd ed.). Boston: Houghton Mifflin.

Janis, I. L. (2007). Groupthink. In R. P. Vecchio (Ed.), *Leadership: Understanding the dynamics of power and influence in organizations* (2nd ed., pp. 157–169). Notre Dame, IN: University of Notre Dame Press.

Janis, I. L., Kaye, D., & Kirschner, P. (1965). Facilitating effects of "eating while reading" on responsiveness to persuasive communications. *Journal of Personality and Social Psychology, 1,* 181–186.

Janssen, L., Fennis, B. M., & Pruyn, A. T. H. (2010). Forewarned is forearmed: Conserving self-control strength to resist social influence. *Journal of Experimental Social Psychology, 46,* 911–921.

Janssen, L., Fennis, B. M., Pruyn, A. T. H., & Vohs, K. D. (2008). The path of least resistance: Regulatory resource depletion and the effectiveness of social influence techniques. *Journal of Business Research, 61,* 1041–1045.

Jassawalla, A., Sashittal, H., & Malshe, A. (2009). Students' perceptions of social loafing: Its antecedents and consequences in undergraduate business classroom teams. *Academy of Management Learning & Education, 8,* 42–54.

Jennings, J., Geis, F. L., & Brown, V. (1980). Influence of television commercials on women's self-confidence and independent judgment. *Journal of Personality and Social Psychology, 38,* 203–210.

Jensen-Campbell, L. A., Graziano, W. G., & West, S. G. (1995). Dominance, prosocial orientation, and female preferences: Do nice guys really finish last? *Journal of Personality and Social Psychology, 68,* 427–440.

Jeong, S.-H., Cho, H., & Hwang, Y. (2012). Media literacy interventions: A meta-analytic review. *Journal of Communication, 62,* 454–472.

Jepson, C., & Chaiken, S. (1990). Chronic issue-specific fear inhibits systematic processing of persuasive communications. *Journal of Social Behavior and Personality, 2,* 61–84.

Jervis, R. (1976). *Perception and misperception in international politics.* Princeton, NJ: Princeton University Press.

Jetten, J., Branscombe, N. R., Schmitt, M. T., & Spears, R. (2001). Rebels with a cause: Group identification as a response to perceived discrimination from the mainstream. *Personality and Social Psychology Bulletin, 27*(9), 1204–1213.

Jetten, J., Hornsey, M. J., Spears, R., Haslam, S. A., & Cowell, E. (2010). Rule transgressions in groups: The conditional nature of newcomers' willingness to confront deviance. *European Journal of Social Psychology, 40,* 338–348.

Jetten, J., Postmes, T., & McAuliffe, B. J. (2002). "We're all individuals": Group norms of individualism and collectivism, levels of identification and identity threat. *European Journal of Social Psychology, 32,* 189–207.

Ji, L.-J., Nisbett, R. E., & Su, Y. (2001). Culture, change, and prediction. *Psychological Science, 12,* 450–456.

Johar, G. V., & Roggeveen, A. L. (2007). Changing false beliefs from repeated advertising: The role of claim-refutation alignment. *Journal of Consumer Psychology, 17,* 118–127.

Johnson, B. T., & Eagly, A. H. (1989). Effects of involvement on persuasion: A meta-analysis. *Psychological Bulletin, 106,* 290–314.

Johnson, D. W., Maruyama, G., Johnson, R. T., Nelson, D., & Skon, L. (1981). The effects of cooperative, competitive, and individualistic goal structures on achievement: A meta-analysis. *Psychological Bulletin, 89,* 47–62.

Johnson, E. J., & Tversky, A. (1983). Affect, generalization, and the perception of risk. *Journal of Personality and Social Psychology 45,* 20–31.

Johnson, K. L., Freeman, J. B., & Pauker, K. (2011). Race is gendered: How covarying phenotypes and stereotypes bias sex categorization. *Journal of Personality and Social Psychology, 102,* 116–131.

Johnson, R. D., & Downing, L. L. (1979). Deindividuation and valence of cues: Effects on prosocial and antisocial behavior. *Journal of Personality and Social Psychology, 37,* 1532–1538.

Johnson, S. K. (2008). I second that emotion: Effects of emotional contagion and affect at work on leader and follower outcomes. *The Leadership Quarterly, 19,* 1–19.

Johnson, S. K. (2009). Do you feel what I feel? Mood contagion and leadership outcomes. *The Leadership Quaterly, 20,* 814–827.

Johnson, S. K., Bettenhausen, K., & Gibbons, E. (2009). Realities of working in virtual teams: Affective and attitudinal outcomes of using computer-mediated communication. *Small Group Research, 40,* 623–649.

Johnson, S. K., Podratz, K. E., Dipboye, R. L., & Gibbons, E. (2010). Physical attractiveness biases in ratings of employment suitability: Tracking down the "beauty is beastly" effect. *The Journal of Social Psychology, 150,* 301–318.

Johnston, L., & Hewstone, M. (1992). Cognitive models of stereotype change. 3. Subtyping and the perceived typicality of disconfirming group members. *Journal of Experimental Social Psychology, 28,* 360–386.

Johnston, L., & Macrae, C. N. (1994). Changing social stereotypes: The case of the information seeker. *European Journal of Social Psychology, 24,* 581–592.

Joireman, J., Kamdar, D., Daniels, D., & Duell, B. (2006). Good citizens to the end? It depends: Empathy and concern with future consequences moderate the impact of a short-term time horizon on organizational citizenship behaviors. *Journal of Applied Psychology, 91*(6), 1307–1320. doi:10.1037/0021-9010.91.6.1307

Joireman, J. A., Lasane, T. P., Bennett, J., Richards, D., & Solaimani, S. (2001). Integrating social value orientation and the consideration of future consequences within the extended norm activation model of proenvironmental behavior. *British Journal of Social Psychology, 40,* 133–155.

Jonas, E., Sullivan, D., & Greenberg, J. (2013). Generosity, greed, norms, and death: Differential effects of mortality salience on charitable behavior. *Journal of Economic Psychology, 35,* 47–57.

Jones, E. E. (1985). Major developments in social psychology during the last five decades. In G. Lindzey & E. Aronson (Eds.), *Handbook of social psychology* (vol. I, pp. 47–107). New York: Random House.

Jones, E. E. (1990a). Constrained behavior and self-concept change. In J. M. Olson & M. P. Zanna (Eds.), *Self-inference processes: The Ontario Symposium* (vol. 6, pp. 69–86). Hillsdale, NJ: Lawrence Erlbaum Associates.

Jones, E. E. (1990b). *Interpersonal perception.* New York: Freeman.

Jones, E. E., Brenner, K., & Knight, J. G. (1990). When failure elevates self-esteem. *Personality and Social Psychology Bulletin, 16,* 200–209.

Jones, E. E., Carter-Sowell, A. R., Kelly, J. R., & Williams, K. D. (2009). 'I'm out of the loop': Ostracism through information exclusion. *Group Processes and Intergroup Relations, 12,* 157–174.

Jones, E. E., & Davis, K. E. (1965). A theory of correspondent inferences: From acts to dispositions. In L. Berkowitz (Ed.), *Advances in experimental social psychology* (vol. 2, pp. 219–266). New York: Academic Press.

Jones, E. E., & Harris, V. A. (1967). The attribution of attitudes. *Journal of Experimental Social Psychology, 3,* 1–24.

Jones, E. E., & Kelly, J. R. (2007). Contributions to a group discussion and perceptions of leadership: Does quantity always count more than quality? *Group Dynamics: Theory, Research, and Practice, 11,* 15–30.

Jones, E. E., & Nisbett, R. E. (1972). The actor and the observer: Divergent perceptions of the causes of behavior. In E. E. Jones, D. E. Kanouse, H. H. Kelley, R. E. Nisbett, S. Valins, & B. Weiner (Eds.), *Attribution: Perceiving the causes of behavior* (pp. 79–94). Morristown, NJ: General Learning Press.

Jones, E. E., & Pittman, T. S. (1982). Toward a general theory of strategic self-presentation. In J. Suls (Ed.), *Psychological perspectives on the self* (vol. 1, pp. 231–262). Hillsdale, NJ: Lawrence Erlbaum Associates.

Jones, E. E., Rhodewalt, F., Berglas, S., & Skelton, J. A. (1981). Effects of strategic self-presentation on subsequent self-esteem. *Journal of Personality and Social Psychology, 41,* 407–421.

Jones, E. E., Rock, L., Shaver, K. G., Goethals, G. R., & Ward, L. M. (1968). Pattern of performance and ability attribution: An unexpected primacy effect. *Journal of Personality and Social Psychology, 10,* 317–340.

Jones, J. T., Pelham, B. W., Carvallo, M., & Mirenberg, M. C. (2004). How do I love thee? Let me count the Js: Implicit egotism and interpersonal attraction. *Journal of Personality and Social Psychology, 87,* 665–683.

Jones, R. A., & Brehm, J. W. (1970). Persuasiveness of one-sided and two-sided communications as a function of the awareness that there are two sides. *Journal of Experimental Social Psychology, 6,* 47–56.

Jordan, C. H., Spencer, S. J., Zanna, M. P., Hoshino-Browne, E., & Correll, J. (2003). Secure and defensive high self-esteem. *Journal of Personality & Social Psychology, 85*(5), 969–978.

Josephs, R. A., Larrick, R. P., Steele, C. M., & Nisbett, R. E. (1992). Protecting the self from the negative consequences of risky decisions. *Journal of Personality and Social Psychology, 62,* 26–37.

Josephs, R. A., Markus, H. R., & Tafarodi, R. W. (1992). Gender and self-esteem. *Journal of Personality and Social Psychology, 63,* 391–402.

Jost, J. T., & Banaji, M. R. (1994). The role of stereotyping in system-justification and the production of false consciousness. *British Journal of Social Psychology, 33,* 1–27.

Jost, J. T., & Hamilton, D. L. (2005). Stereotypes in our culture. In J. F. Dovidio, P. Glic, & L.A. Rudman (Eds.), *On the nature of prejudice: Fifty years after Allport* (pp. 208–224). Malden, MA: Blackwell.

Jost, J. T., Kivetz, Y., Rubini, M., Guermandi, G., & Mosso, C. (2005). System-justifying functions of complementary regional and ethnic stereotypes: Cross-national evidence. *Social Justice Research, 18,* 305–333.

Joule, R. V., & Beauvois, J. L. (1998). Cognitive dissonance theory: A radical view. In W. Stroebe, & M. Hewstone (Eds.), *European review of social psychology* (pp. 1–32). New York: John Wiley & Sons, Inc.

Joule, R. V., & Martinie, M.-A. (2008). Forced compliance, mis-attribution and trivialization. *Social Behavior and Personality*, *36*, 1205–1212.

Judd, C. M., & Park, B. (2005). Group differences and stereotype accuracy. In J. F. Dovidio, P. Glic, & L. A. Rudman (Eds.), *On the nature of prejudice: Fifty years after Allport* (pp. 123–138). Malden, MA: Blackwell.

Judd, C. M., Park, B., Ryan, C. S., Brauer, M., & Kraus, S. (1995). Stereotypes and ethnocentrism: Diverging interethnic perceptions of African American and White American youth. *Journal of Personality and Social Psychology*, *69*, 460–481.

Judge, T. A., & Cable, D. M. (2004). The effect of physical height on workplace success and income: Preliminary test of a theoretical model. *Journal of Applied Psychology*, *89*, 428–441.

Judge, T. A., & Piccolo, R. F. (2004). Transformational and transactional leadership: A meta-analytic test of their relative validity. *Journal of Applied Psychology*, *89*, 755–768.

Judge, T. A., Piccolo, R. F., & Ilies, R. (2004). The forgotten ones? The validity of consideration and initiating structure in leadership research. *Journal of Applied Psychology*, *89*, 36–51.

Jussim, L. (2005). Accuracy in social perception: Criticisms, controversies, criteria, components, and cognitive processes. *Advances in Experimental Social Psychology*, *37*, 1–93.

Jussim, L., & Harber, K. (2005). Teacher expectations and self-fulfilling prophecies: Knowns and unknowns, resolved and unresolved controversies. *Personality and Social Psychology Review*, *9*, 131–155.

Kachadourian, L. K., Fincham, F., & Davila, J. (2004). The tendency to forgive in dating and married couples: The role of attachment and relationship satisfaction. *Personal Relationships*, *11*, 373–393.

Kafetsios, K., & Nezlek, J. B. (2002). Attachment styles in everyday social interaction. *European Journal of Social Psychology*, *32*, 719–735.

Kahneman, D., & Miller, D. T. (1986). Norm theory: Comparing reality to its alternatives. *Psychological Review*, *93*, 136–153.

Kaighobadi, F., Shackelford, T. K., & Goetz, A. T. (2009). From mate retention to murder: Evolutionary psychological perspectives on men's partner-directed violence. *Review of General Psychology*, *13*, 327–334.

Kaiser, C. R., & Miller, C. T. (2001). Stop complaining! The social costs of making attributions to discrimination. *Personality & Social Psychology Bulletin*, *27*, 254–263.

Kaiser, F. G., Byrka, K., & Hartig, T. (2010). Reviving Campbell's paradigm for attitude research. *Personality and Social Psychology Review*, *14*, 351–367.

Kalin, R., & Berry, J. W. (1982). The social ecology of ethnic attitudes in Canada. *Canadian Journal of Behavioral Science*, *14*, 97–109.

Kallgren, C. A., Reno, R. R., & Cialdini, R. B. (2000). A focus theory of normative conduct: When norms do and do not affect behavior. *Personality and Social Psychology Bulletin*, *26*, 1002–1012.

Kalven, H. Jr., & Zeisel, H. (1966). *The American jury*. Chicago: University of Chicago Press.

Kameda, T., Ohtsubo, Y., & Takezawa, M. (1997). Centrality in sociocognitive networks and social influence: An illustration in a group decision-making context. *Journal of Personality and Social Psychology*, *73*, 296–309.

Kameda, T., Takezawa, M., & Hastie, R. (2003). The logic of social sharing: An evolutionary game analysis of adaptive norm development. *Personality and Social Psychology Review*, *7*, 2–19.

Kammrath, L. K., & Dweck, C. (2006). Voicing conflict: Preferred conflict strategies among incremental and entity theorists. *Personality and Social Psychology Bulletin*, *32*, 1497–1508.

Kandler, C., Bleidorn, W., & Riemann, R. (2012). Left or right? Sources of political orientation: The roles of genetic factors, cultural transmission, assortative mating, and personality. *Journal of Personality & Social Psychology*, *102*, 633–645.

Kanter, R. (1977). *Men and women of the corporation*. New York: Basic Books.

Kaplan, M. F. & Miller, C. E. (1987). Group decision making and normative versus informational influence: Effects of type of issue and assigned decision rule. *Journal of Personality and Social Psychology*, *53*, 306–313.

Kaplan, M. F., & Wilke, H. (2001). Cognitive and social motivation in group decision making. In J. P. Forgas, & K. D. Williams (Eds.), *The social mind: Cognitive and motivational aspects of interpersonal behavior*. New York: Cambridge University Press.

Kaplowitz, N. (1990). National self-images, perception of enemies, and conflict strategies: Psychopolitical dimensions of international relations. *Political Psychology*, *11*, 39–82.

Karabenick, S. A., Lerner, R. M., & Beecher, M. D. (1973). Relation of political affiliation to helping behavior on election day, November 7, 1972. *Journal of Social Psychology*, *91*, 223–227.

Karau, S. J., & Williams, K. D. (1997). The effects of group cohesiveness on social loafing and social compensation. *Group Dynamics*, *1*, 156–168.

Karau, S. J., & Kelly, J. R. (1992). The effects of time scarcity and time abundance on group performance quality and interaction process. *Journal of Experimental Social Psychology*, *28*, 542–571.

Karau, S. J., & Williams, K. D. (1993). Social loafing: A meta-analytic review and theoretical integration. *Journal of Personality and Social Psychology*, *65*, 681–706.

Kardes, F. R., Sanbonmatsu, D. M., Voss, R. T., & Fazio, R. H. (1986). Self-monitoring and attitude accessibility. *Personality and Social Psychology Bulletin*, *12*, 468–474.

Karpinski, A., Steinman, R.B., & Hilton, J. L. (2005). Attitude importance as a moderator of the relationship between implicit and explicit attitude measures. *Personality and Social Psychology Bulletin*, *31*, 949–962.

Karremans, J. C., & Aarts, H. (2007). The role of automaticity in determining the inclination to forgive close others. *Journal of Experimental Social Psychology*, *43*, 902–917.

Karremans, J. C., & Van Lange, P. A. M. (2008). The role of forgiveness in shifting from "me" to "we". *Self and Identity*, 7, 75–88.

Kaschak, M. P., & Maner, J. K. (2009). Embodiment, evolution, and social cognition: An integrative framework. *European Journal of Social Psychology*, 39(7), 1236–1244. doi:10.1002/ejsp.664

Kasser, T. & Ryan, R. M. (1996). Further examining the American dream: Differential correlates of intrinsic and extrinsic goals. *Personality and Social Psychology Bulletin*, 22, 280–287.

Kassin, S. M., & Gudjonsson, G. H. (2004). The psychology of confessions. *Psychological Science in the Public Interest*, 5, 33–67.

Kassin, S. M., & Kiechel, K. L. (1996). The social psychology of false confessions: Compliance, internalization, and confabulation. *Psychological Science*, 7, 125–128.

Katz, D. (1960). The functional approach to the study of attitudes. *Public Opinion Quarterly*, 24, 163–204.

Katz, D. (1965). Nationalism and strategies of international conflict resolution. In H. C. Kelman (Ed.), *International behavior: A social psychological analysis* (pp. 354–390). New York: Holt, Rinehart & Winston.

Katz, D., & Braly, K. W. (1933). Racial stereotypes of 100 college students. *Journal of Abnormal and Social Psychology*, 28, 280–290.

Katz, I. (1981). *Stigma: A social psychological analysis*. Hillsdale, NJ: Earlbaum.

Katz, I., & Hass, R. G. (1988). Racial ambivalence and American value conflict: Correlational and priming studies of dual cognitive structures. *Journal of Personality and Social Psychology*, 55, 893–905.

Keating, C. F., Pomerantz, J., Pommer, S. D., Ritt, S. J. H., Miller, L. M., & McCormick, J. (2005). Going to college and unpacking hazing: A functional approach to decrypting initiation practices among undergraduates. *Group Dynamics: Theory, Research, and Practice*, 9, 104–126.

Keller, R. T. (1986). Predictors of the performance of project groups in R & D organizations. *Academy of Management Journal*, 29, 715–726.

Kellermanns, F. W., Walter, J., Floyd, S. W., Lechner, C., & Shaw, J. C. (2011). To agree or not to agree? A meta-analytical review of strategic consensus and organizational performance. *Journal of Business Research*, 64, 126–133.

Kelley, H. H. (1950). The warm-cold variable in first impressions of persons. *Journal of Personality*, 18, 431–439.

Kelley, H. H. (1952). Two functions of reference groups. In G. E. Swanson, T. M. Newcomb, & E. L. Hartley (Eds.), *Readings in social psychology*. New York: Henry Holt.

Kelley, H. H. (1967). Attribution theory in social psychology. In D. Levine (Ed.), *Nebraska symposium on motivation* (vol. 15, pp. 192–241). Lincoln: University of Nebraska Press.

Kelley, H. H. (1972). Attribution in social interaction. In E. E. Jones and others (Eds.), *Attribution: Perceiving the causes of behavior* (pp. 1–26). Morristown, NJ: General Learning Press.

Kelley, H. H. (1979). *Personal relationships: Their structures and processes*. Hillsdale, NJ: Lawrence Erlbaum Associates.

Kelley, H. H., Berscheid, E., Christensen, A., Harvey, J. H., Huston, T. L., Levinger, G., McClintock, E., Peplau, L. A., & Peterson, D. L. (Eds.). (1983). *Close relationships*. San Francisco, CA: Freeman.

Kelly, A. E., & Rodriguez, R. R. (2006). Publicly committing oneself to an identity. *Basic & Applied Social Psychology*, 28, 185–191.

Kelly, J. R., Jackson, J. W., & Hutson-Comeaux, S. L. (1997). The effects of time pressure and task differences on influence modes and accuracy in decision-making groups. *Personality and Social Psychology Bulletin*, 23, 10–22.

Kelly, J. R., & Karau, S. J. (1999). Group decision making: The effects of initial preferences and time pressure. *Personality and Social Psychology Bulletin*, 25, 1342–1354.

Kelly, J. R., & Loving, T. J. (2004). Time pressure and group performance: Exploring underlying processes in the Attentional Focus Model. *Journal of Experimental Social Psychology*, 40, 185–198.

Kelly, J. R., & Spoor, J. R. (2013). Affective processes. In J. M. Levine (Ed.), *Group processes* (pp. 33–53). New York: Psychology Press.

Kelman, H. C. (1961). Processes of opinion change. *Public Opinion Quarterly*, 25, 57–78.

Kelman, H. C. (1973). Violence without moral restraint: Reflections on the dehumanization of victims and victimizers. *Journal of Social Issues*, 29, 25–61.

Kelman, H. C., & Hamilton, V. L. (1989). *Crimes of obedience: Toward a social psychology of authority and responsibility*. New Haven, CT: Yale University Press.

Kelman, H. C., & Hovland, C. I. (1953). "Reinstatement" of the communicator in delayed measurement of opinion change. *Journal of Abnormal and Social Psychology*, 48, 327–335.

Keltner, D., Ellsworth, P.C. & Edwards, K. (1993). Beyond simple pessimism: Effects of sadness and anger on social perception. *Journal of Personality and Social Psychology*, 64, 740–752.

Keltner, D., Gruenfeld, D. H., & Anderson, C. (2003). Power, approach, and inhibition. *Psychology Review*, 110, 265–284.

Kenny, D. A. (1991). A general model of consensus and accuracy in interpersonal perception. *Psychological Review*, 98, 155–163.

Kenny, D. A. (1994). Using the social relations model to understand relationships. In R. Erber & R. Gilmour (Eds.), *Theories for the study of relationships* (pp. 111–127). Hillsdale, NJ: Lawrence Erlbaum Associates.

Kenworthy, J. B., Miller, N., Collins, B. E., Read, S. J., & Earleywine, M. (2011). A trans-paradigm theoretical synthesis of cognitive dissonance theory: Illuminating the nature of discomfort. *European Review of Social Psychology*, 22, 36–113.

Kenworthy, J. B., Turner, R. N., Hewstone, M., & Voci, A. (2005). Intergroup contact: When does it work, and why? In J. F. Dovidio, P. Glic, & L. A. Rudman (Eds.), *On the nature of prejudice: Fifty years after Allport* (pp. 278–292). Malden, MA: Blackwell.

Kernis, M. H., & Goldman, B. M. (2003). Stability and variability in self-concept and self-esteem. In M. R. Leary & J. P. Tangney (Eds.), *Handbook of self and identity* (pp. 106–127). New York: Guilford Press.

Kernis, M. H., Grannemann, B. D., & Barclay, L. C. (1989). Stability and level of self-esteem as predictors of anger arousal and hostility. *Journal of Personality and Social Psychology, 56*, 1013–1022.

Kerr, N. L. (1992). Efficacy as a causal and moderating variable in social dilemmas. In W. Liebrand, D. Messick, & H. Wilke (Eds.), *A social psychological approach to social dilemmas*. New York: Pergamon Press.

Kerr, N. L., & Bruun, S. (1983). The dispensability of member effort and group motivation losses: Free rider effects. *Journal of Personality and Social Psychology, 44*, 78–94.

Kerr, N. L., & Hertel, G. (2011). The Kohler group motivation gain: How to motivate the 'weak links' in a group. *Social and Personality Psychology Compass, 5*, 43–55.

Kerr, N. L., & Kaufman-Gilliland, C. M. (1993). Communication, commitment, and cooperation in social dilemmas. Unpublished paper, Michigan State University.

Kerr, N. L., MacCoun, R. J., Hansen, C. H., & Hymes, J. A. (1987). Gaining and losing social support: Momentum in decision making groups. *Journal of Experimental Social Psychology, 23*, 119–145.

Kerr, N. L., MacCoun, R. J., & Kramer, G. P. (1996). Bias in judgment: Comparing individuals and groups. *Psychological Review, 103*, 687–719.

Kerr, N. L., & Tindale, R. S. (2004). Group performance and decision making. *Annual Review of Psychology, 55*, 623–655.

Key, W. B. (1992). *The age of manipulation: The con in confidence, the sin in sincere.* Madison, WI: Madison Books.

Khan, R., Misra, K., & Singh, V. (2013). Ideology and brand consumption. *Psychological Science, 24*, 326–333.

Kiecolt-Glaser, J. K., Fisher, L. D., & Ogrocki, P. (1987). Marital quality, marital disruption, and immune function. *Psychosomatic Medicine, 49*, 13–34.

Kiecolt-Glaser, J. K., & Glaser, R. (1988). Psychological influences on immunity: Implications for AIDS. Special Issue: Psychology and AIDS. *American Psychologist, 43*, 892–898.

Kierein, N. M., & Gold, M. A. (2000). Pygmalion in work organizations: A meta-analysis. *Journal of Organizational Behavior, 21*, 913–928.

Kiesler, C. A. & Kiesler, S. B. (1969). *Conformity.* Reading, MA: Addison-Wesley.

Kille, D. R., Forest, A. L., & Wood, J. V. (2013). Tall, dark, and stable: Embodiment motivates mate selection preferences. *Psychological Science, 24*, 112–114.

Kim, H., & Markus, H. R. (1999). Deviance or uniqueness, harmony or conformity? A cultural analysis. *Journal of Personality and Social Psychology, 77*, 785–800.

Kim, H. S. (2002). We talk, therefore we think? A cultural analysis of the effect of talking on thinking. *Journal of Personality and Social Psychology, 83*, 828–842.

Kim, H-S., & Baron, R. S. (1988). Exercise and the illusory correlation: Does arousal heighten stereotypic processing? *Journal of Experimental Social Psychology, 24*, 366–380.

Kim, H. S., & Sherman, D. K. (2007). "Express yourself": Culture and the effect of self-expression on choice. *Journal of Personality & Social Psychology, 92*, 1–11.

Kim, J., & Paek, H.-J. (2009). Information processing of genetically modified food messages under different motives: An adaptation of the multiple-motive heuristic-systematic model. *Risk Analysis, 29*, 1793–1806.

Kimel, S. Y., Grossmann, I., & Kitayama, S. (2012). When gift-giving produces dissonance: Effects of subliminal affiliation priming on choices for one's self versus close others. *Journal of Experimental Social Psychology, 48*, 1221–1224.

Kimmel, M. J., Pruitt, P. G., Maganau, J. M., Konar-Goldband, E., Carnevale, P. J. D. (1980). Effects of trust, aspiration, and gender on negotiation tactics. *Journal of Personality and Social Psychology, 38*, 9–22.

Kinder, D. R. (1986). The continuing American dilemma: White resistance to racial change 40 years after Myrdal. *Journal of Social Issues, 42*(2), 151–171.

Kinder, D. R., & Sears, D. O. (1985). Public opinion and political action. In G. Lindzey & E. Aronson (Eds.), *Handbook of social psychology* (vol. II, pp. 659–742). New York: Random House.

King, M. L. (1967). *Where do we go from here? Chaos or community.* New York: Harper & Row.

Kitayama, S., Ishii, K., Imada, T., Takemura, K., & Ramaswamy, J. (2006). Voluntary settlement and the spirit of independence: Evidence from Japan's "northern frontier." *Journal of Personality and Social Psychology, 91*, 369–384.

Kitayama, S., & Karasawa, M. (1997). Implicit self-esteem in Japan: Name letters and birthday numbers. *Personality and Social Psychology Bulletin, 23*, 736–742.

Kitayama, S., Markus, H. R., & Matsumoto, H. (1995). Culture, self, and emotion: A cultural perspective on "self conscious" emotions. In J. P. Tangney & K. W. Fischer (Eds.), *Self-conscious emotions: The psychology of shame, guilt, embarrassment, and pride* (pp. 366–383). New York, NY: Guilford Press.

Kitayama, S., Markus, H. R., Matsumoto, H. & Norasakkunkit, V. (1997). Individual and collective processes in the construction of the self: Self-enhancement in the United States and self-criticism in Japan. *Journal of Personality and Social Psychology, 72*, 1245–1267.

Kitayama, S., Snibbe, A. C., Markus, H. R., & Suzuki, T. (2004). Is there any "free" choice? Self and dissonance in two cultures. *Psychological Science, 15*, 527–533.

Kitayama, S., Takagi, H., & Matsumoto, H. (1995). Cultural psychology of Japanese self: I. Causal attribution of success and failure. *Japanese Psychological Research, 38*, 247–280.

Kitayama, S., & Uskul, A. K. (2011). Culture, mind, and the brain: Current evidence and future directions. *Annual Reviews in*

Psychology, 62(1), 419–449. doi:10.1146/annurev-psych-120709-145357

Kito, M. (2005). Self-disclosure in romantic relationships and friendships among American and Japanese college students. *The Journal of Social Psychology, 145*, 127–140.

Kiviniemi, M. T., Synder, M., & Omoto, A. M. (2002). Too many of a good thing? The effects of multiple motivations on stress, cost, fulfillment and satisfaction. *Personality and Social Psychology Bulletin, 28*, 732–743.

Klama, J. [pseudonym for John Durant, Peter Klopfer, and Susan Oyama] (1988). *Aggression: The myth of the beast within.* New York: John Wiley & Sons.

Klandersman, B. (2000). Identity and protest: How group identification helps to overcome collective action dilemmas. In M. Van Vugt, M. Snyder, T. Tyler, & A. Biel (Eds.), *Cooperating in modern society: Promoting the welfare of communities, states, and organizations* (pp. 162–183). London: Routledge.

Klein, S. B. & Loftus, J. (1993). Behavioral experience and trait judgments about the self. *Personality and Social Psychology Bulletin, 19*, 740–745.

Klein, W. M., & Kunda, Z. (1992). Motivated person perception: Constructing justifications for desired beliefs. *Journal of Experimental Social Psychology, 28*, 145–168.

Klineberg, O. (1986). SPSSI and race relations in the 1950's and after. *Journal of Social Issues, 42*(4), 53–60.

Kluegel, J. R., & Smith, E. R. (1986). *Beliefs about inequality: Americans' views of what is and what ought to be.* Hawthorne, NY: Aldine de Gruyter.

Knapp, M. L. (1978). *Nonverbal communication in human interaction.* New York: Holt, Rinehart, Winston.

Knee, C. R. (1998). Implicit theories of relationships: Assessment and prediction of romantic relationship initiation, coping, and longevity. *Journal of Personality and Social Psychology, 74*, 360–370.

Knee, C. R., & Bush, A. L. (2008). Relationship beliefs and their role in romantic relationship initiation. In S. Sprecher, A. Wenzel, & J. Harvey (Eds.), *Handbook of relationship initiation* (pp. 471–485). New York: Psychology Press.

Knee, C. R., Patrick, H., & Lonsbary, C. (2003). Implicit theories of relationships: Orientations toward evaluation and cultivation. *Personality and Social Psychology Review, 7*, 41–55.

Kniffin, K. M., & Wilson, D. S. (2004). The effect of nonphysical traits on the perception of physical attractiveness: Three naturalistic studies. *Evolution and Human Behavior, 25*, 88–101.

Knudson, R. M., Sommers, A. A., & Golding, S. L. (1980). Interpersonal perception and mode of resolution in marital conflict. *Journal of Personality and Social Psychology, 38*, 751–763.

Kobak, R. R., & Hazan, C. (1991). Attachment in marriage: Effects of security and accuracy of working models. *Journal of Personality and Social Psychology, 60*, 861–869.

Kobrynowicz, D., & Biernat, M. (1997). Decoding subjective evaluations: How stereotypes provide shifting standards. *Journal of Experimental Social Psychology, 33*, 579–601.

Koenig, A. M., Eagly, A. H., Mitchell, A. A., & Ristikari, T. (2011). Are leader stereotypes masculine? A meta-analysis of three research paradigms. *Psychological Bulletin, 137*, 616–642.

Komorita, S. S., & Meek, D. D. (1978). Generality and validity of some theories of coalition formation. *Journal of Personality and Social Psychology, 36*, 392–404.

Konrath, S., Fuhrel-Forbis, A., Lou, A., & Brown, S. (2012). Motives for volunteering are associated with mortality risk in older adults. *Health Psychology, 31*(1), 87.

Koo, M., & Fishbach, A. (2010). Climbing the goal ladder: How upcoming actions increase level of aspiration. *Journal of Personality and Social Psychology, 99*, 1–13.

Koole, S. L., Dijksterhuis, A., & van Knippenberg, A. (2001). What's in a name?: Implicit self-esteem and the automatic self. *Journal of Personality and Social Psychology, 80*, 669–685.

Korchmaros, J. D., & Kenny, D. A. (2001). Emotional closeness as a mediator of the effect of genetic relatedness on altruism. *Psychological Science, 12*, 262–265.

Koriat, A. (2012). When are two heads better than one and why? *Science, 336*, 360–362.

Koriat, A., & Adiv, S. (2011). The construction of attitudinal judgments: Evidence from attitude certainty and response latency. *Social Cognition, 29*, 577–611.

Korte, C., Ypma, I., & Toppen, A. (1975). Helpfulness in Dutch society as a function of urbanization and environmental input level. *Journal of Personality and Social Psychology, 32*, 996–1003.

Kotkin, J. (1986). The "SMART-TEAM" at Compaq Computer. *Inc.*, Feb., 48–56.

Koudenburg, N., Postmes, T., & Gordijn, E. H. (2013). Resounding silences: Subtle norm regulation in everyday interactions. *Social Psychology Quarterly, 76*, 224–241.

Krackow, A., & Blass, T. (1995). When nurses obey or defy inappropriate physician orders: Attributional differences. *Journal of Social Behavior and Personality, 10*, 585–594.

Kramer, R. M. (1989). Windows of vulnerability or cognitive illusions? Cognitive processes and the nuclear arms race. *Journal of Experimental Social Psychology, 25*, 79–84.

Kramer, R. M., & Brewer, M. B. (1984). Effects of group identity on resource use in a simulated commons dilemma. *Journal of Personality and Social Psychology, 46*, 1044–1057.

Kraus, S. J. (1995). Attitudes and the prediction of behavior: A meta-analysis of the empirical literature. *Personality and Social Psychology Bulletin, 21*, 58–75.

Krauss, R. M., Freyberg, R., & Morsella, E. (2002). Inferring speakers' physical attributes from their voices. *Journal of Experimental Social Psychology, 38*, 618–625.

Kravitz, D. A., & Martin, B. (1986). Ringelmann rediscovered: The original article. *Journal of Personality and Social Psychology, 50*, 936–941.

Kray, L. J., Reb, J., Galinsky, A. D., & Thompson, L. (2004). Stereotype reactance at the bargaining table: The effect of stereotype activation and power on claiming and creating value. *Personality & Social Psychology Bulletin, 30*(4), 399–411.

Kray, L. J., & Thompson, L. (2005). *Gender stereotypes and negotiation performance: An examination of theory and research.* Greenwood, CT: Elsevier Science/JAI Press.

Krebs, D. L. (1970). Altruism—an examination of the concept and review of the literature. *Psychological Bulletin, 73*, 258–303.

Kredentser, M. S., Fabrigar, L. R., Smith, S. M., & Fulton, K. (2012). Following what people think we should do versus what people actually do: Elaboration as a moderator of the impact of descriptive and injunctive norms. *Social Psychology and Personality Science, 3*, 341–347.

Kroese, F. M., Adriaanse, M. A., Evers, C., & De Ridder, D. T. D. (2011). "Instant success": Turning temptations into cues for goal-directed behavior. *Personality & Social Psychology Bulletin, 37*, 1389–1397.

Krosnick, J. A., Betz, A. L., Jussim, L. J., & Lynn, A. R. (1992). Subliminal conditioning of attitudes. *Personality and Social Psychology Bulletin, 18*, 152–162.

Krosnick, J. A., Boninger, D. S., Chuang, Y. C., Berent, M. K., & Carnot, C. G. (1993). Attitude strength: One construct or many related constructs? *Journal of Personality & Social Psychology, 65*, 1132–1151.

Krueger, A. B. (2002, Dec. 12). Economic scene. *The New York Times*, p. C2.

Krueger, J., & Rothbart, M. (1990). Contrast and accentuation effects in category learning. *Journal of Personality and Social Psychology, 59*, 651–663.

Krueger, J. I. (2007). From social projection to social behaviour. *European Review of Social Psychology, 18*, 1–35. doi:10.1080/10463280701284645

Kruger, D. J. (2003). Evolution and altruism: Combining psychological mediators with naturally selected tendencies. *Evolution and Human Behavior, 24*, 118–125.

Kruger, J. (1999). Lake Wobegon be gone! The "below-average effect" and the egocentric nature of comparative ability judgments. *Journal of Personality & Social Psychology, 77*, 221–232.

Kruger, J., Epley, N., Parker, J., & Ng, Z.-W. (2005). Egocentrism over e-mail: Can we communicate as well as we think? *Journal of Personality and Social Psychology, 89*, 925–936.

Kruglanski, A. W. (1975). The human subject in the psychology experiment: Fact and artifact. In L. Berkowitz (Ed.), *Advances in experimental social psychology* (vol. 8, pp. 101–147). New York: Academic Press.

Kruglanski, A. W., & Freund, T. (1983). The freezing and unfreezing of lay-inferences. Effects of impressional primacy, ethnic stereotyping, and numerical anchoring. *Journal of Experimental Social Psychology, 19*, 448–468.

Kruglanski, A., & Mackie, D. M. (1990). Majority and minority influence: A judgmental process integration. In W. Stroebe & M. Hewstone (Eds.), *Advances in European social psychology*, (vol. 1, pp. 229–262). Chichester: John Wiley & Sons.

Kruglanski. A.W., Thompson, E.P., & Spiegel, S. (1999). Separate or equal: Bimodal notions of persuasion and a single process "unimodal". In S. Chaiken & Y. Trope (Eds.), *Dual-process theories in social psychology* (pp. 441–461). New York: Guilford Press.

Krull, D. S. (1993). Does the grist change the mill? The effect of the perceiver's inferential goal on the process of social inference. *Personality and Social Psychology Bulletin, 19*, 340–348.

Krupp, D. B., Debruine, L. M., & Barclay, P. (2008). A cue of kinship promotes cooperation for the public good. *Evolution & Human Behavior, 29*, 49–55.

Ku, H.-H., Kuo, C.-C., & Kuo, T.-W. (2012). The effect of scarcity on the purchase intentions of prevention and promotion motivated consumers. *Psychology & Marketing, 29*, 541–548.

Kuhlman, D. M., Brown, D., & Teta, P. (1992). Judgments of cooperation and defection in social dilemmas: The moderating role of judges' social orientation. In W. B. G. Liebrand & D. M. Messick (Eds.), *Social dilemmas: Theoretical issues and research findings* (pp. 111–132). Oxford: Pergamon Press.

Kuhn, D. & Lao, J. (1996). Effects of evidence on attitudes: Is polarization the norm? *Psychological Science, 7*, 115–121.

Kuhn, M. H. & McPartland, T. (1954). An empirical investigation of self attitudes. *American Sociological Review, 19*, 68–76.

Kumkale, G. T., Albarracin, D., & Seignourel, P. J. (2010). The effects of source credibility in the presence or absence of prior attitudes: Implications for the design of persuasive communication campaigns. *Journal of Applied Social Psychology, 40*, 1325–1356.

Kunda, Z. (1990). The case for motivated reasoning. *Psychological Bulletin, 108*, 480–498.

Kurdek, L. A. (1991). Sexuality in homosexual and heterosexual couples. In K. McKinney & S. Sprecher (Eds.), *Sexuality in close relationships* (pp. 177–192). Hillsdale, NJ: Lawrence Erlbaum Associates.

Kurland, J. A. (1979). Paternity, mother's brother, and human sociality. In N. A. Chagnon & W. Irons (Eds.), *Evolutionary biology and human social behavior: An anthropological perspective*. North Scituate, MA: Duxbury Press.

Kwang, T., Crockett, E. E., Sanchez, D. T., & Swann, W. B. (2013). Men seek social standing, women seek companionship: Sex differences in deriving self-worth from relationships. *Psychological Science, 24*, 1142–1150.

Kypri, K., Paschall, M. J., Langley, J., Baxter, J., Cashell-Smith, M., & Bordeaux, B. (2009). Drinking and alcohol-related harm among New Zealand university students: Findings from a national web-based survey. *Alcoholism: Clinical & Experimental Research, 33*, 307–314.

LaBrie, J. W., Hummer, J. F., Neighbors, C., & Pedersen, E. R. (2008). Live interactive group-specific normative feedback reduces misperceptions and drinking in college students: A randomized cluster trial. *Psychology of Addictive Behaviors, 22,* 141–148.

Laeng, B., Vermeer, O., & Sulutvedt, U. (2013). Is beauty in the face of the beholder? *PLoS ONE, 8,* e68395.

Lagerquist, R. (1992, Aug. 15). Band's not pretty, but the money's lovely. *Santa Barbara News Press,* p. B3.

Lakin, J. L., Jefferis, V. E., Cheng, C. M., & Chartrand, T. L. (2003). The chameleon effect as social glue: Evidence for the evolutionary significance of nonconscious mimicry. *Journal of Nonverbal Behavior, 27,* 145–162.

Lally, P., Bartle, N., & Wardle, J. (2011). Social norms and diet in adolescents. *Appetite, 57,* 623–627.

Lalonde, R. N. (1992). The dynamics of group differentiation in the face of defeat. *Personality and Social Psychology Bulletin, 18,* 336–342.

Lang, A., Newhagen, J., & Reeves, B. (1996). Negative video as structure: Emotion, attention, capacity, and memory. *Journal of Broadcasting & Electronic Media, 40,* 460–477.

Langer, E. J. (1975). The illusion of control. *Journal of Personality and Social Psychology, 32,* 311–328.

Langer, E. J., Blank, A., & Chanowitz, B. (1978). The mindlessness of ostensibly thoughtful action. *Journal of Personality and Social Psychology, 36,* 635–642.

Langlois, J. H., Kalakanis, L., Rubenstein, A. J., Larson, A., Hallam, M., & Smoot, M. (2000). Maxims or myths of beauty? A meta-analytic and theoretical review. *Psychological Bulletin, 126,* 390–423.

Langlois, J. H., & Roggman, L. A. (1990). Attractive faces are only average. *Psychological Science, 1,* 115–121.

Lansford, J. E., Skinner, A. T., Sorbring, E., Di Giunta, L., Deater-Deckard, K., Dodge, K. A., . . . Chang, L. (2012). Boys' and girls' relational and physical aggression in nine countries. *Aggressive Behavior, 38,* 298–308.

LaPiere, R. T. (1934). Attitudes vs. actions. *Social Forces, 13,* 230–237.

LaPiere, R. T. (1936). Type-rationalizations of group antipathy. *Social Forces, 15,* 232–237.

Larrick, R. P., Timmerman, T. A., Carton, A. M., & Abrevaya, J. (2011). Temper, temperature, and temptation: Heat-related retaliation in baseball. *Psychological Science, 22,* 423–428.

Larson, J. R. Jr., Christensen, C., Abbott, A. S., & Franz, T. M. (1996). Diagnosing groups: Charting the flow of information in medical decision-making teams. *Journal of Personality & Social Psychology, 71,* 315–330.

Larwood, L., & Whittaker, W. (1977). Managerial myopia: Self-serving biases in organizational planning. *Journal of Applied Psychology, 62,* 194–198.

Lassiter, G. D., Geers, A. L., Munhall, P. J., Handley, I. M., & Beers, M. J. (2001). Videotaped confessions: Is guilt in the eye of the camera? In M. P. Zanna (Ed.), *Advances in experimental social psychology* (vol. 33, pp. 189–254). San Diego, CA: Academic Press.

Latané, B., & Darley, J. M. (1968). Group inhibition of bystander intervention in emergencies. *Journal of Personality and Social Psychology, 10,* 215–221.

Latané, B., & Darley, J. M. (1970). *The unresponsive bystander: Why doesn't he help?* New York: Appleton-Crofts.

Latané, B., Nida, S. A., & Wilson, D. W. (1981). The effects of group size on helping behavior. In J. P. Rushton & R. M. Sorrentino (Eds.), *Altruism and helping behavior.* Hillsdale, NJ: Lawrence Erlbaum Associates.

Latané, B., Williams, K., & Harkins, S. (1979). Many hands make light the work: The causes and consequences of social loafing. *Journal of Personality and Social Psychology, 37,* 822–832.

Lau, R. R., & Russell, D. (1980). Attributions in the sports pages. *Journal of Personality and Social Psychology, 39,* 29–38.

Laughlin, P. R. (1980). Social combination processes of cooperative problem solving groups on verbal intellective tasks. In M. Fishbein (Ed.), *Progress in social psychology.* Hillsdale, NJ: Erlbaum.

Laughlin, P. R., Hatch, E. C., Silver, J. S., & Boh, L. (2006). Groups perform better than the best individuals on letters-to-numbers problems: Effects of group size. *Journal of Personality and Social Psychology, 90,* 644–651.

Laughlin, P. R., VanderStoep, S. W., & Hollingshead, A. B. (1991). Collective versus individual induction: Recognition of truth, rejection of error, and collective information processing. *Journal of Personality and Social Psychology, 61,* 50–67.

Laumann, E. O., Gagnon, J. H., Michael, R. T., & Michaels, S. (1994). *The social organization of sexuality.* Chicago: University of Chicago Press.

Laurin, K., Kay, A. C., & Fitzsimons, G. J. (2012). Reactance versus rationalization: Divergent responses to policies that constrain freedom. *Psychological Science, 23,* 205–209.

Lavine, H., & Snyder, M. (1996). Cognitive processing and the functional matching effect in persuasion: The mediating role of subjective perceptions of message quality. *Journal of Experimental Social Psychology, 32,* 580–604.

Lawler, E. J., Ford, R. S., & Bleger, M. A. (1988). Coercive capability in conflict: A test of bilateral deterrence versus conflict spiral theory. *Social Psychology Quarterly, 51,* 93–107.

Le, B., & Agnew, C. R. (2003). Commitment and its theorized determinants: A meta-analysis of the Investment Model. *Personal Relationships, 10,* 37–57.

Leaper, C., Breed, L., Hoffman, L., & Perlman, C. A. (2002). Variations in the gender-stereotyped content of children's television cartoons across genres. *Journal of Applied Social Psychology, 32,* 1653–1662.

Leary, M. R. (1995). *Self-presentation: Impression management and interpersonal behavior.* Madison, WI: Brown & Benchmark.

Leary, M. R., Barners, B. D., & Griebel, C. (1986). Cognitive, affective, and attributional effects of potential threats to self-esteem. *Journal of Social and Clinical Psychology, 4,* 461–474.

Leary, M. R., Kowalski, R. M., Smith, L., & Phillips, S. (2003). Teasing, rejection, and violence: Case studies of the school shootings. *Aggressive Behavior*, 29, 202–214.

Leary, M. R., Tambor, E. S., Terdal, S. K., & Downs, D. L. (1995). Self-esteem as an interpersonal monitor: The sociometer hypothesis. *Journal of Personality and Social Psychology*, 68, 518–530.

LeBon, G. (1895/1947). *The crowd: A study of the popular mind.* London: Ernest Benn.

LeBon, G. (1903). *The crowd.* London: Unwin.

Lebow, R. N., & Stein, J. G. (1987). Beyond deterrence. *Journal of Social Issues*, 43(4), 5–71.

Ledgerwood, A., & Chaiken, S. (2007). Priming us and them: Automatic assimilation and contrast in group attitudes. *Journal of Personality and Social Psychology*, 93, 940–956.

Ledgerwood, A., Mandisodza, A. N., Jost, J. T., & Pohl, M. J. (2011). Working for the system: Motivated defense of meritocratic beliefs. *Social Cognition*, 29, 322–340.

Ledyard, J. (1995). Public goods: A survey of experimental research. In J. H. Kagel & A. E. Roth (Eds.), *Handbook of experimental economics.* Princeton, NJ: Princeton University Press, pp. 111–194.

Lee, A. Y., & Aaker, J. L. (2004). Bringing the frame into focus: The influence of regulatory fit on processing fluency and persuasion. *Journal of Personality and Social Psychology*, 86, 205–218.

Leersnyder, J., Boiger M., & Mesquita, B. (2013) Cultural regulation of emotion: individual, relational, and structural sources. *Frontiers in Psychology*, 4:55. doi: 10.3389/fpsyg. 2013. 00055

Legault, L., & Inzlicht, M. (2013). Self-determination, self-regulation, and the brain: Autonomy improves performance by enhancing neuroaffective responsiveness to self-regulation failure. *Journal of Personality and Social Psychology*, 105, 123–138.

Leidner, B., Castano, E., Zaiser, E., & Giner-Sorolla, R. (2010). Ingroup glorification, moral disengagement, and justice in the context of collective violence. *Personality and Social Psychology Bulletin*, 36, 1115–1129.

Leigh, B. C. (1989). Reasons for having and avoiding sex: Gender, sexual orientation, and relationship to sexual behavior. *Journal of Sex Research*, 26, 199–209.

Lemaine, G. (1974). Social differentiation and social originality. *European Journal of Social Psychology*, 4, 17–52.

Lemay, E. P., & Clark, M. S. (2008). "Walking on eggshells": How expressing relationship insecurities perpetuates them. *Journal of Personality and Social Psychology*, 95, 420–441.

Lemyre, L., & Smith, P. M. (1985). Intergroup discrimination and self-esteem in the minimal group paradigm. *Journal of Personality and Social Psychology*, 49, 660–670.

Leonardelli, G. J., Pickett, C. L., & Brewer, M. B. (2010). Optimal distinctiveness theory: A framework for social identity, social cognition, and intergroup relations. *Advances in Experimental Social Psychology*, 43, 63–113.

Lepore, L., & Brown, R. (1997). Category and stereotype activation: Is prejudice inevitable? *Journal of Personality and Social Psychology*, 72, 275–287.

Lepper, M. R., Greene, D., & Nisbett, R. E. (1973). Undermining children's intrinsic interest with extrinsic reward: A test of the "overjustification" hypothesis. *Journal of Personality and Social Psychology*, 28, 129–137.

Lerner, M. J. (1980). *The belief in a just world: A fundamental delusion.* New York: Plenum.

Lerner, M.J., & Miller, D.T. (1978). Just world research and the attribution process: Looking back and ahead. *Psychological Bulletin*, 85, 1030–1051.

Lerner, M. J., & Simmons, C. H. (1966). Observers' reaction to the "innocent victim:" Compassion or rejection? *Journal of Personality and Social Psychology*, 4, 203–210.

Levav, J., & Fitzsimons, G. J. (2006). When questions change behavior: The role of ease of representation. *Psychological Science*, 17, 207–213.

Leventhal, H. (1970). Findings and theory in the study of fear communications. In L. Berkowitz (Ed.), *Advances in experimental social psychology* (vol. 5). New York: Academic Press.

Leventhal, H., Singer, R. P., & Jones, F. (1965). Effects of fear and specificity of recommendations upon attitudes and behavior. *Journal of Personality and Social Psychology*, 2, 20–29.

Levine, J. M., & Moreland, R. L. (1991). Culture and socialization in work groups. In L. B. Resnick, J. M. Levine, & S. D. Teasley (Eds.), *Perspectives on socially shared cognition* (pp. 257–279). Washington, DC: American Psychological Association.

Levine, J. M., & Moreland, R. L. (1998). Small groups. In D. L. Gilbert, S. T. Fiske, & G. Lindzey (Eds.), *Handbook of social psychology* (4th ed., vol. 2, pp. 415–469). Boston: McGraw-Hill.

Levine, J. M., & Prislin, R. (2013). Majority and minority influence. In J. M. Levine (Ed.), *Group processes* (pp. 135–163). New York, NY: Psychology Press.

Levine, M., Cassidy, C., & Jentzsch, I. (2010). The implicit identity effect: Identity primes, group size, and helping. *British Journal of Social Psychology*, 49(4), 785–802.

Levine, M., Prosser, A., Evans, D., & Reicher, S. (2005). Identity and emergency intervention: How social group membership and inclusiveness of group boundaries shape helping behavior. *Personality and Social Psychology Bulletin*, 31, 443–453.

LeVine, R. A., & Campbell, D. T. (1972). *Ethnocentrism: Theories of conflict, ethnic attitudes and group behavior.* New York: Wiley.

LeVine, R. A., LeVine, S., Leiderman, P. H., Brazelton, T. B., Dixon, S., Richman, A., & Keefer, C. H. (1994). *Child care and culture: Lessons from Africa.* New York: Cambridge University Press.

Levine, R. V., Martinez, T. S., Brase, G., & Sorenson, K. (1994). Helping in 36 U.S. cities. *Journal of Personality and Social Psychology*, 67, 69–82.

Levine, R. V., Reysen, S., & Ganz, E. (2008). The kindness of strangers revisited: A comparison of 24 US cities. *Social Indicators Research, 85,* 461–481.

Levinger, G. (1991). Commitment vs. cohesiveness: Two complementary perspecvtives. In W. H. Jones & D. Perlman (Eds.), *Advances in personal relationships* (vol. 3, pp. 145–150). London: Jessica Kingsley.

Levinger, G., & Schneider, D. (1969). Test of the "risk is a value" hypothesis. *Journal of Personality and Social Psychology, 11,* 165–169.

Lewandowsky, S., Ecker, U. K. H., Seifert, C. M., Schwarz, N., & Cook, J. (2012). Misinformation and its correction: Continued influence and successful debiasing. *Psychological Science in the Public Interest, 13*(3), 106–131.

Lewicki, P. (1984). Self-schema and social information processing. *Journal of Personality and Social Psychology, 47,* 1177–1190.

Lewin, K. (1936). *Principles of topological psychology.* New York: McGraw-Hill.

Lewin, K. (1943). Forces behind food habits and methods of change. *Bulletin of the National Research Council, 108,* 35–65.

Lewin, K. (1947). Group decision and social change. In T. M. Newcomb & E. L. Hartley (Eds.), *Readings in social psychology* (pp. 330–344). New York: Henry Holt & Co.

Lewin, K. (1948). *Solving social conflicts.* New York: Harper & Brothers.

Lewin, K. (1951). Problems of research in social psychology. In D. Cartwright (Ed.), *Field theory in social science* (pp. 155–169). New York: Harper & Row.

Lewis, A. C., & Sherman, S. J. (2010). Perceived entitativity and the black-sheep effect: When will we denigrate negative ingroup members? *The Journal of Social Psychology, 150,* 211–225.

Lewis, C. C. (1995). *Educating hearts and minds.* New York: Cambridge University Press.

Li, N. P., & Kenrick, D. T. (2006). Sex similarities and differences in preferences for short-term mates: What, whether, and why. *Journal of Personality and Social Psychology, 90,* 468–489.

Lickel, B., Hamilton, D. L., & Sherman, S. J. (2001). Elements of a lay theory of groups: Types of groups, relationship styles, and the perception of group entitativity. *Personality and Social Psychology Review, 5,* 129–140.

Lickel, B., Miller, N., Stenstrom, D. M., Denson, T. F., & Schmader, T. (2006). Vicarious retribution: The role of collective blame in intergroup aggression. *Personality & Social Psychology Review, 10,* 372–390.

Lieberman, S. (1956). The effects of changes in roles on the attitudes of role occupants. *Human Relations, 9,* 385–402.

Liebert, R. M., & Sprafkin, J. (1988). *The early window: Effects of television on children and youth* (3rd ed.). New York: Pergamon Press.

Liebrand, W. B., & Van Run, G. J. (1985). The effects of social motives on behavior in social dilemmas in two cultures. *Journal of Experimental Social Psychology, 21,* 86–102.

Liljenquist, K. A., Galinsky, A. D., & Kray, L. J. (2004). Exploring the rabbit hole of possibilities by myself or with my group: The benefits and liabilities of activating counterfactual mindsets for information sharing and group coordination. *Journal of Behavioral Decision Making, 17,* 263–279.

Linder, D. E., Cooper, J., & Jones, E. E. (1967). Decision freedom as a determinant of the role of incentive magnitude in attitude change. *Journal of Personality and Social Psychology, 6,* 245–254.

Lindsay, J. J., & Anderson, C. A. (2000). From antecedent conditions to violent actions: A general affective aggression model. *Personality and Social Psychology Bulletin, 26,* 533–547.

Lindskold, S. (1978). Trust development, the GRIT proposal and the effects of conciliatory acts on conflict and cooperation. *Psychological Bulletin, 85,* 772–793.

Lingle, J. H., & Ostrom, T. M. (1979). Retrieval selectivity in memory-based impression judgments. *Journal of Personality and Social Psychology, 37,* 180–194.

Linville, P. W. (1985). Self-complexity and affective extremity: Don't put all of your eggs in one cognitive basket. Special Issue: Depression. *Social Cognition, 3,* 94–120.

Linville, P. W. (1987). Self-complexity as a cognitive buffer against stress-related illness and depression. *Journal of Personality and Social Psychology, 52,* 663–676.

Linville, P. W., Fisher, G. W., & Salovey, P. (1989). Perceived distributions of the characteristics of ingroup and outgroup members. *Journal of Personality and Social Psychology, 57,* 165–188.

Lippmann, W. (1922). *Public opinion.* New York: Harcourt, Brace.

Lisitsa, E. (2013, April 24). The four horsemen: Recognizing criticism, contempt, defensiveness, and stonewalling. http://www.gottmanblog.com/2013/04/the-four-horsemen-recognizing-criticism.html

Liska, A. E. (1984). A critical examination of the causal structure of the Fishbein/Ajzen attitude-behavior model. *Social Psychology Quarterly, 47,* 61–74.

Litt, D. M., Stock, M. L., & Lewis, M. A. (2012). Drinking to fit in: Examining the need to belong as a moderator of perceptions of best friends' alcohol use and related risk cognitions among college students. *Basic and Applied Social Psychology, 34,* 313–321.

Little, A. C., Apicella, C. L., & Marlowe, F. W. (2007). Preferences for symmetry in human faces in two cultures: Data from the UK and the Hadza, an isolated group of hunter-gatherers. *Proceedings of the Royal Society B, 274,* 3113–3117.

Little, A. C., Burt, D. M., & Perrett, D. I. (2006). What is good is beautiful: Face preference reflects desired personality. *Science Direct, 41,* 1107–1118.

Little, A. C., & Hill, R. A. (2007). Attribution to red suggests special role in dominance signalling. *Journal of Evolutionary Psychology, 5,* 161–168.

Little, A. C., & Jones, B. C. (2006). Attraction independent of detection suggests special mechanisms for symmetry preferences in human face perception. *Proceedings of the Royal Society B, 273,* 3093–3099.

Little, A. C., Penton-Voak, I. S., Burt, D. M., & Perrett, D. I. (2003). Investigating an imprinting-like phenomenon in humans: Partners and opposite-sex parents have similar hair and eye colour. *Evolution and Human Behavior, 24,* 43–51.

Littlepage, G. E. (1991). Effects of group size and task characteristics on group performance: A test of Steiner's model. *Personality and Social Psychology Bulletin, 17,* 449–456.

Littlepage, G. E., Schmidt, G. W., Whisler, E. W., & Frost, A. G. (1995). An input-process-output analysis of influence and performance in problem-solving groups. *Journal of Personality and Social Psychology, 69,* 877–889.

Livingstone, A. G., Haslam, S. A., Postmes, T., & Jetten, J. (2011). "We are, therefore we should": Evidence that in-group identification mediates the acquisition of in-group norms. *Journal of Applied Social Psychology, 41,* 1857–1876.

Locher, P., Unger, R., Sociedade, P., & Wahl, J. (1993). At first glance: Accessibility of the physical attractiveness stereotype. *Sex Roles, 28,* 729–743.

Lockhart, W. H., & Elliot, R. (1981). Changes in the attitudes of young offenders in an integrated assessment centre. In J. Harbison & J. Harbison (Eds.), *A society under stress.* Somerset: Open Books.

Loewenstein, G. F., Thompson, L., & Bazerman, M. H. (1989). Social utility and decision making in interpersonal contexts. *Journal of Personality and Social Psychology, 57,* 426–441.

Loftin, C., McDowall, D., Wiersema, B., & Cottey, T. J. (1991). Effects of restrictive licensing of handguns on homicide and suicide in the District of Columbia. *New England Journal of Medicine, 325,* 1615–1620.

Loftus, E. F. (1974). The incredible eyewitness. *Psychology Today, 8*(7), 116–119.

Lopes, D., Vala, J., & Garcia-Marques, L. (2007). Social validation of everyday knowledge: Heterogeneity and consensus functionality. *Group Dynamics: Theory, Research, and Practice, 11,* 223–239.

Lord, C., & Lepper, M. R. (1999). Attitude representation theory. In M. P. Zanna (Ed.), *Advances in experimental social psychology* (vol. 31). San Diego, CA: Academic Press.

Lord, C. G., Lepper, M. R., & Mackie, D. (1984). Attitude prototypes as determinants of attitude-behavior consistency. *Journal of Personality and Social Psychology, 46,* 1254–1266.

Lord, C. G., Lepper, M. R., & Preston, E. (1984). Considering the opposite: A corrective strategy for social judgment. *Journal of Personality and Social Psychology, 47,* 1231–1243.

Lord, C. G., Ross, L., & Lepper, M. (1979). Biased assimilation and attitude polarization: The effects of prior theories on subsequently considered evidence. *Journal of Personality and Social Psychology, 37,* 2098–2109.

Lorenz, K. (1966). *On aggression.* New York: Harcourt Brace Jovanovich.

Losch, M. E., & Cacioppo, J. T. (1990). Cognitive dissonance may enhance sympathetic tonus, but attitudes are changed to reduce negative affect rather than arousal. *Journal of Experimental Social Psychology, 26,* 289–304.

Loschelder, D. D., & Trotschel, R. (2010). Overcoming the competitiveness of an intergroup context: Third-party intervention in intergroup negotiations. *Group Processes & Intergroup Relations, 13,* 795–815.

Lowenstein, J. A., Blank, H., & Sauer, J. D. (2010). Uniforms affect the accuracy of children's eyewitness identification decisions. *Journal of Investigative Psychology and Offender Profiling, 7,* 59–73.

Lowery, B. S., Hardin, C. D., & Sinclair, S. (2001). Social influence effects on automatic racial prejudice. *Journal of Personality and Social Psychology, 81,* 842–855.

Lu, L., Yuan, Y. C., & McLeod, P. L. (2012). Twenty-five years of hidden profiles in group decision making: A meta-analysis. *Personality and Social Psychology Review, 16,* 54–75.

Lucas, M., Koff, E., Grossmith, S., & Migliorini, R. (2011). Sexual orientation and shifts in preferences for a partner's body attributes in short-term versus long-term mating contexts. *Psychological Reports, 108,* 699–710.

Luckinbill, D. (1977). Criminal homicide as a situated trans-action. *Social Problems, 25,* 176–186.

Luckow, A., Reifman, A., & McIntosh, D. N. (1998, August). Gender differences in coping: A meta-analysis. Paper presented at Annual Convention of the American Psychological Association, San Francisco.

Luhtanen, R., Blaine, B., & Crocker, J. (1991, April). Personal and collective self-esteem and depression in African-American and White students. Paper presented at Eastern Psychological Association, New York.

Luhtanen, R., & Crocker, J. (1992). A collective self-esteem scale: Self-evaluation of one's social identity. *Personality and Social Psychology Bulletin, 18,* 302–318.

Lun, J., Sinclair, S., Whitchurch, E. R., & Glenn, C. (2007). (Why) do I think what you think? Epistemic social tuning and implicit prejudice. *Journal of Personality and Social Psychology, 93,* 957–972.

Lundgren, D. C., & Knight, D. J. (1978). Sequential stages of development in sensitivity training groups. *Journal of Applied Behavioral Science, 14,* 204–222.

Lydall, E. S., Gilmour, G., & Dwyer, D. M. (2010). Rats place greater value on rewards produced by high effort: An animal analogue of the "effort justification" effect. *Journal of Experimental Social Psychology, 46,* 1134–1137.

Lydon, J. E., Jamieson, D. W., & Holmes, J. G. (1997). The meaning of social interactions in the transition from acquaintanceship to friendship. *Journal of Personality and Social Psychology, 73,* 536–548.

Lykken, D. T. (1985). The probity of the polygraph. In S. Kassin & L. Wrightsman (Eds.), *The psychology of evidence and trial procedure* (pp. 95–123). Beverly Hills, CA: Sage Publications.

Lykken, D. T. (1998). *A tremor in the blood: Uses and abuses of the lie detector.* New York, NY: Plenum Press.

Maass, A. (1999). Linguistic intergroup bias: Stereotype perpetuation through language. In M. P. Zanna (Ed.), *Advances in experimental social psychology* (vol. 31, pp. 79–122). San Diego, CA: Academic Press.

Maass, A., Salvi, D., Arcuri, L., & Semin, G. (1989). Language use in intergroup contexts: The linguistic intergroup bias. *Journal of Personality and Social Psychology, 57*, 981–993.

Maccoby, E. E. (1980). *Social development: Psychological growth and the parent-child relationship*. New York: Harcourt Brace Jovanovich.

MacCoun, R. J. (2012). The burden of social proof: Shared thresholds and social influence. *Psychological Review, 119*, 345–372.

MacDonald, T. K., Fong, G. T., Zanna, M. P., & Martineau, A. M. (2003). *Alcohol myopia and condom use: Can alcohol intoxication be associated with more prudent behavior?* New York, NY: Psychology Press.

MacDonald, T. K., Zanna, M. P., & Fong, G. T. (1995). Decision making in altered states: Effects of alcohol on attitudes toward drinking and driving. *Journal of Personality & Social Psychology, 68*, 973–985.

MacDonald, T. K., Zanna, M. P., & Fong, G. T. (1996). Why common sense goes out the window: Effects of alcohol on intentions to use condoms. *Personality & Social Psychology Bulletin, 22*, 763–775.

Mack, R. W., & Snyder, R. C. (1957). The analysis of social conflict- Toward an overview and synthesis. *Journal of Conflict Resolution, 1*, 212–248.

Mackie, D. (1984). Social comparison in high- and low-status groups. *Journal of Cross-Cultural Psychology, 15*, 379–398.

Mackie, D. (1986). Social identification effects in group polarization. *Journal of Personality and Social Psychology, 50*, 720–728.

Mackie, D. M., Asuncion, A. G., & Rosselli, F. (1992). The impact of positive affect on persuasion processes. In M. S. Clark (Ed.), *Emotion and social behavior: Review of personality and social psychology* (pp. 247–270). Newbury Park, CA: Sage Publications.

Mackie, D. M., Devos, T., & Smith, E. R. (2000). Intergroup emotions: Explaining offensive action tendencies in an intergroup context. *Journal of Personality and Social Psychology, 79*(4), 602–616.

Mackie, D. M., Gastardo-Conaco, C. M., & Skelly, J. J. (1992). Knowledge of the advocated position and the processing of in-group and out-group persuasive messages. *Personality and Social Psychology Bulletin, 18*, 145–151.

Mackie, D. M. & Hamilton, D. L. (Eds.). (1993). *Affect, cognition, and stereotyping: Interactive processes in group perception*. San Diego, CA: Academic Press.

Mackie, D. M., Smith, E. R., & Ray, D. G. (2008). Intergroup emotions and intergroup relations. *Social and Personality Psychology Compass, 2*, 1866–1880.

Mackie, D. M., Worth, L. T., & Asuncion, A. G. (1990). The processing of persuasive ingroup messages. *Journal of Personality and Social Psychology, 58*, 812–822.

MacLachlan, J., & Siegel, M. H. (1980). Reducing the costs of TV commercials by use of time compressions. *Journal of Marketing Research, 17*, 52–57.

Macours, K. (2010). Increasing inequality and civil conflict in Nepal. *Oxford Economic Papers, 63*, 1–26.

Macrae, C. N., Bodenhausen, G. V., & Milne, A. B. (1998). Saying no to unwanted thoughts: Self-focus and the regulation of mental life. *Journal of Personality and Social Psychology, 74*, 578–589.

Macrae, C. N., Bodenhausen, G. V., Milne, A. B., & Jetten, J. (1994). Out of mind but back in sight: Stereotypes on the rebound. *Journal of Personality and Social Psychology, 67*, 808–817.

Macrae, C. N., Bodenhausen, G. V., Milne, A. B., Thorn, T. M., & Castelli, L. (1997). On the activation of social stereotypes: Moderating role of processing objectives. *Journal of Experimental Social Psychology, 33*, 471–489.

Magdol, L. (2002). Is moving gendered? The effects of residential mobility on the psychological well-being of men and women. *Sex Roles, 47*, 553–560.

Magdol, L., & Bessel, D. R. (2003). Social capital, social currency, and portable assets: The impact of residential mobility on exchanges of social support. *Personal Relationships, 10*, 149–169.

Magee, J. C., Gruenfeld, D. H., Keltner, D. J., & Galinsky, A. D. (2005). Leadership and the psychology of power. In D. M. Messick & R. M. Kramer (Eds.), *The psychology of leadership: New perspectives and research* (pp. 275–293). Mahwah, NJ: Lawrence Erlbaum Associates.

Magee, J. C., & Tiedens, L. Z. (2006). Emotional ties that bind: The roles of valence and consistency of group emotion in inferences of cohesiveness and common fate. *Personality and Social Psychology Bulletin, 32*, 1703–1715.

Magnusson, S. (1981). *The flying Scotsman*. London: Quartet Books.

Maheswaran, D., & Chaiken, S. (1991). Promoting systematic processing in low-motivation settings: Effect of incongruent information on processing and judgment. *Journal of Personality and Social Psychology, 61*, 13–33.

Maheswaran, D., Mackie, D. M., & Chaiken, S. (1992). Brand name as a heuristic cue: The effects of task importance and expectancy confirmation on consumer judgments. *Journal of Consumer Psychology, 1*, 317–336.

Maio, G. R., & Olson, J. M. (Eds.). (2000). *Why we evaluate: Functions of attitudes*. Mahwah, NJ: Lawrence Erlbaum Associates.

Maison, D., Greenwald, A. G., & Bruin, R. H. (2004). Predictive validity of the Implicit Association Test in studies of brands, consumer attitudes, and behavior. *Journal of Consumer Psychology, 14*, 405–415.

Maitner, A. T., Mackie, D. M., Claypool, H. M., & Crisp, R. J. (2010). Identity salience moderates processing of group-relevant information. *Journal of Experimental Social Psychology, 46*, 441–444.

Major, B. (1994). From social inequality to personal entitlement: The role of social comaprisons, legitimacy appraisals, and group membership. In M. P. Zanna (Ed.), *Advances in experimental social psychology* (vol. 26, pp. 293–348). San Diego, CA: Academic Press.

Major, B., Kaiser, C. R., & McCoy, S. K. (2003). It's not my fault: When and why attributions to prejudice protect self-esteem. *Personality & Social Psychology Bulletin, 29,* 772–781.

Ma-Kellams, C., & Blascovich, J. (2012). Inferring the emotions of friends versus strangers: The role of culture and self-construal. *Personality and Social Psychology Bulletin, 38,* 933–945.

Malle, B. F. (1999). How people explain behaviour: A new theoretical framework. *Personality and Social Psychology Review, 3,* 23–48.

Malle, B. F. (2006). The actor-observer asymmetry in attribution: A (surprising) meta-analysis. *Psychological Bulletin, 132,* 895–919.

Manago, A. M., Taylor, T., & Greenfield, P. M. (2012). Me and my 400 friends: The anatomy of college students' facebook networks, their communication patterns, and well-being. *Developmental Psychology, 48*(2), 369–380. doi:http://dx.doi.org/10.1037/a0026338

Maner, J. K., DeWall, C. N., Baumeister, R. F., & Schaller, M. (2007). Does social exclusion motivate interpersonal reconnection? Resolving the "porcupine problem." *Journal of Personality and Social Psychology, 92,* 42–55.

Maner, J. K., & Kenrick, D. T. (2010). Evolutionary social psychology. In R. F. Baumeister & E. J. Finkel (Eds.), *Advanced social psychology: The state of the science* (pp. 613–653). New York: Oxford University Press.

Maner, J. K., Luce, C. L., Neuberg, S. L., Cialdini, R. B., Brown, S., & Sagarin, B. J. (2002). The effects of perspective taking on motivations for helping: Still no evidence for altruism. *Personality and Social Psychology Bulletin, 28,* 1601–1610.

Manis, M., Nelson, T. E., & Shedler, J. (1988). Stereotypes and social judgment: Extremity, assimilation and contrast. *Journal of Personality and Social Psychology, 55,* 28–36.

Mannes, A. E., Larrick, R. P., & Soll, J. B. (2012). The social psychology of the wisdom of crowds. In J. I. Krueger (Ed.), *Social judgment and decision making* (pp. 227–242). New York, NY: Psychology Press.

Mannetti, L., Brizi, A., Giacomantonio, M., & Higgins, E.T. (2013). Framing political messages to fit the audience's regulatory orientation: how to improve the efficacy of the same message content. *PLoS ONE 8,*10.

Manning, R., Levine, M., & Collins, A. (2007). The Kitty Genovese murder and the social psychology of helping: The parable of the 38 witnesses. *American Psychologist, 62*(6), 555–562. doi:10.1037/0003-066X.62.6.555

Manstead, A. S. R., & van Eekelen, S. A. M. (1998). Distinguishing between perceived behavioral control and self-efficacy in the domain of academic achievement intentions and behaviors. *Journal of Applied Social Psychology, 28,* 1375–1392.

Maoz, I., & McCauley, C. (2008). Threat, dehumanization, and support for retaliatory aggressive policies in asymmetric conflict. *Journal of Conflict Resolution, 52,* 93–116.

Maoz, I., Ward, A., Katz, M., & Ross, L. (2002). Reactive devaluation of an "Israeli" vs. "Palestinian" peace proposal. *Journal of Conflict Resolution, 46*(4), 515–546.

Marigold, D. C., Holmes, J. G., & Ross, M. (2010). Fostering relationship resilience: An intervention for low self-esteem individuals. *Journal of Experimental Social Psychology, 46,* 624–630.

Marjanovic, Z., Greenglass, E. R., Struthers, C. W., & Faye, C. (2009). Helping following natural disasters: A social-motivational analysis. *Journal of Applied Social Psychology, 39*(11), 2604–2625. doi:http://dx.doi.org/10.1111/j.1559-1816.2009.00540.x

Markman, H. J. (1981). Prediction of marital distress: A five-year follow up. *Journal of Consulting and Clinical Psychology, 49,* 760–762.

Markus, H. (1977). Self-schemata and processing information about the self. *Journal of Personality and Social Psychology, 35,* 63–78.

Markus, H., & Kitayama, S. (1991). Culture and the self: Implications for cognition, emotion, and motivation. *Psychological Review, 98,* 224–253.

Markus, H., Kitayama, S., & Heiman, R. J. (1996). Culture and basic psychological principles. In E. T. Higgins & A. W. Kruglanski (Eds.), *Social psychology: Handbook of basic principles* (pp. 857–914). New York: Guilford.

Markus, H., Kitayama, S., & VandenBos, G. R. (1996). The mutual interactions of culture and emotion. *Psychiatric Services, 47,* 225–226.

Markus, H., & Nurius, P. (1986). Possible selves. *American Psychologist, 41,* 954–969.

Markus, H., Smith, J., & Moreland, R. L. (1985). Role of the self-concept in the perception of others. *Journal of Personality and Social Psychology, 49,* 1494–1512.

Markus, H., & Wurf, E. (1987). The dynamic self-concept: A social psychological perspective. *Annual Review of Psychology, 38,* 299–337.

Marques, J. M., & Yzerbyt, V. Y. (1988). The black sheep effect: Judgmental extremity towards ingroup members in inter- and intra-group situations. *European Journal of Social Psychology, 18,* 287–292.

Marques, J. M., Yzerbyt, V. Y., & Rijsman, J. B. (1988). Context effects on intergroup discrimination: In-group bias as a function of experimenter's provenance. *British Journal of Social Psychology, 27,* 301–318.

Martin, C. L. (1987). A ratio measure of sex stereotyping. *Journal of Personality and Social Psychology, 52,* 489–499.

Martin, G. N., & Gray, C. D. (1996). The effects of audience laughter on men's and women's responses to humor. *Journal of Social Psychology, 136,* 221–231.

Martin, L. L., Seta, J. J., & Crelia, R. (1990). Assimilation and contrast as a function of people's willingness and ability to expend effort in forming an impression. *Journal of Personality and Social Psychology, 59*, 27–37.

Martin, L. L., Ward, D. W., Achee, J. W., & Wyer, R. S. (1993). Mood as input: People have to interpret the motivational implications of their moods. *Journal of Personality and Social Psychology, 64*, 317–326.

Martin, P. Y., Laing, J., Martin, R., & Mitchell, M. (2005). Caffeine, cognition, and persuasion: Evidence for caffeine increasing the systematic processing of persuasive messages. *Journal of Applied Social Psychology, 35*, 160–182.

Martin, R., & Hewstone, M. (2001). Determinants and consequences of cognitive processes in majority and minority influence. In J. P. Forgas & K. D. Williams (Eds.), *Social influence: Direct and indirect processes* (pp. 315–330). New York: Psychology Press.

Martin, R., & Hewstone, M. (2008). Majority versus minority influence, message processing and attitude change: The source-context-elaboration model. In M. P. Zanna (Ed.), *Advances in experimental social psychology* (vol. 40, pp. 237–326). San Diego, CA: Elsevier Academic Press.

Martin, R., Hewstone, M., & Martin, P. Y. (2007). Systematic and heuristic processing of majority- and minority-endorsed messages: The effects of varying outcome relevance and levels of orientation on attitude and message processing. *Personality and Social Psychology Bulletin, 33*, 43–56.

Martin, R., Martin, P. Y., Smith, J. R., & Hewstone, M. (2007). Majority versus minority influence and prediction of behavioral intentions and behavior. *Journal of Experimental Social Psychology, 43*, 763–771.

Martinie, M.-A., Olive, T., & Milland, L. (2010). Cognitive dissonance induced by writing a counterattitudinal essay facilitates performance on simple tasks but not on complex tasks that involve working memory. *Journal of Experimental Social Psychology, 46*, 587–594.

Marx, D. M., & Roman, J. S. (2002). Female role models: Protecting women's math test performance. *Personality and Social Psychology Bulletin, 28*(9), 1183–1193.

Mashek, D. J., Aron, A., & Boncimino, M. (2003) Confusions of self with close others. *Personality and Social Psychology Bulletin, 29*, 382–392.

Masi, C. M., Chen, H.-Y., Hawkley, L. C., & Cacioppo, J. T. (2011). A meta-analysis of interventions to reduce loneliness. *Personality and Social Psychology Review, 15*, 219–266.

Mast, M. S., & Hall, J. A. (2004). Who is the boss and who is not? Accuracy of judging status. *Journal of Nonverbal Behavior, 28*, 145–165.

Mastro, D. E., & Behm-Morawitz, E. (2005). Latino representation on primetime television. *Journalism & Mass Communication Quarterly, 82*, 110–130.

Mattes, K., Spezio, M., Kim, H., Todorov, A., Adolphs, R., & Alvarez, R. M. (2010). Predicting election outcomes from positive and negative trait assessments of candidate images. *Political Psychology, 31*, 41–58.

Matz, D. C., & Wood, W. (2005). Cognitive dissonance in groups: The consequences of disagreement. *Journal of Personality and Social Psychology, 88*, 22–37.

Mayadas, N., & Glasser, P. (1985). Termination: A neglected aspect of social group work. In M. Sundel, P. Glasser, R. Sarri, & R. Vinter (Eds.), *Individual change through small groups* (2nd ed., pp. 251–261). New York: Free Press.

Mayer, N. D., & Tormala, Z. L. (2010). "Think" versus "feel" framing effects in persuasion. *Personality & Social Psychology Bulletin, 36*, 443–454.

McAdams, D. P. (2001). The psychology of life stories. *Review of General Psychology, 5*, 100–122.

McAdams, D. P., & Bryant, F. B. (1987). Intimacy motivation and subjective mental health in a nationwide sample. *Journal of Personality, 55*, 395–414.

McAlister, A., Perry, C., Killen, J., Slinkard, L. A., & Maccoby, N. (1980). Pilot study of smoking, alcohol and drug abuse prevention. *American Journal of Public Health, 70*, 719–721.

McAndrew, F. T. (2002). New evolutionary perspectives on altruism: Multilevel-selection and costly-signaling theories. *Current Directions in Psychological Science, 11*, 79–82.

McArthur, L. Z. (1981). What grabs you? The role of attention in impression formation and causal attribution. In E. T. Higgins, C. P. Herman, & M. P. Zanna (Eds.), *Social cognition: The Ontario Symposium* (vol. 1, pp. 201–246). Hillsdale, NJ: Erlbaum.

McArthur, L. Z., & Berry, D. S. (1987). Cross-cultural agreement in perceptions of babyfaced adults. *Journal of Cross Cultural Psychology, 18*, 165–192.

McArthur, L. Z., & Post, D. L. (1977). Figural emphasis and person perception. *Journal of Experimental Social Psychology, 13*, 520–535.

McCann, S. J. H. (2001). Height, societal threat, and the victory margin in presidential elections (1824–1992). *Psychological Reports, 88*, 741–742.

McClintock, C. G., & Allison, S. T. (1989). Social value orientation and helping behavior. *Journal of Applied Social Psychology, 19*, 353–362.

McClintock, C. G., & Liebrand, W. B. (1988). Role of interdependence structure, individual value orientation, and another's strategy in social decision making: A transformational analysis. *Journal of Personality and Social Psychology, 55*, 396–409.

McConnell, A. R. (2011). The multiple self-aspects framework: Self-concept representation and its implications. *Personality & Social Psychology Review, 15*, 3–27.

McConnell, A. R., & Brown, C. M. (2010). Dissonance averted: Self-concept organization moderates the effect of hypocrisy on attitude change. *Journal of Experimental Social Psychology, 46*, 361–366.

McCrae, R. R., & Costa, P. T. (1988). Psychological resilience among widowed men and women: A 10-year follow-up of a national sample. *Journal of Social Issues, 44*(3), 129–142.

McCrea, S. M. (2008). Self-handicapping, excuse making, and counterfactual thinking: Consequences for self-esteem and future motivation. *Journal of Personality & Social Psychology, 95*, 274–292.

McCullough, M. E., Worthington, E. L., & Rachal, K. C. (1997). Interpersonal forgiving in close relationships. *Journal of Personality and Social Psychology, 73*, 321–336.

McFarland, S., Webb, M., & Brown, D. (2012). All humanity is my ingroup: A measure and studies of identification with all humanity. *Journal of Personality and Social Psychology, 103*(5), 830–853. doi:10.1037/a0028724

McGill, A. L. (1989). Context effects in judgments of causation. *Journal of Personality and Social Psychology, 57*, 189–200.

McGrath, J. E. (1984). *Groups: Interaction and performance.* Englewood Cliffs, NJ: Prentice-Hall.

McGrath, J. E., Kelly, J. R., & Rhodes, J. E. (1993). A feminist perspective on research methodology: Some metatheoretical issues, contrasts, and choices. In S. Oskamp & M. Costanzo (Eds.), *Gender issues in contemporary society* (pp. 19–37). Newbury Park, CA: Sage Publications.

McGrath, J. E., & Tschan, F. (2004). Group development and change. In J. E. McGrath & F. Tschan (Eds.), *Temporal matters in social psychology: Examining the role of time in the lives of groups and individuals* (pp. 99–120). Washington, DC: American Psychological Association.

McGregor, H. A., Lieberman, J. D., Greenberg, J., Solomon, S., Arndt, J., Simon, L., & Pyszczynski, T. (1998). Terror management and aggression: Evidence that mortality salience motivates aggression against worldview-threatening others. *Journal of Personality and Social Psychology, 74*(3), 590–605.

McGuire, T. W., Kiesler, S., & Siegel, J. (1987). Group and computer-mediated discussion effects in risk decision making. *Journal of Personality and Social Psychology, 52*, 917–930.

McGuire, W. J. (1964). Inducing resistance to persuasion: Some contemporary approaches. In L. Berkowitz (Ed.), *Advances in experimental social psychology* (vol. 1). New York: Academic Press.

McGuire, W. J. (1969). The nature of attitudes and attitude change. In G. Lindzey & E. Aronson (Eds.), *Handbook of social psychology* (2nd, ed., vol. 3). Reading, MA: Addison-Wesley.

McGuire, W. J. (1985). Attitudes and attitude change. In G. Lindzey & E. Aronson (Eds.), *Handbook of social psychology* (3rd ed., vol. 2, pp. 233–346). New York: Random House.

McGuire, W. J., & McGuire, C. V. (1981). The spontaneous self-concept as affected by personal distinctiveness. In M. D. Lynch, A. A. Norem-Hebeisen, & K. J. Gergen (Eds.), *Self-concept: Advances in theory and research* (pp. 147–171). Cambridge, MA: Ballinger.

McGuire, W. J., McGuire, C. V., Child, P., & Fujioka, T. (1978). Salience of ethnicity in the spontaneous self-concept as a function of one's ethnic distinctiveness in the social environment. *Journal of Personality and Social Psychology, 36*, 511–520.

McGuire, W. J., McGuire, C. V., & Winton, W. (1979). Effects of household sex composition on the salience of one's gender in the spontaneous self-concept. *Journal of Experimental Social Psychology, 15*, 77–90.

McGuire, W. J., & Padawer-Singer, A. (1978). Trait salience in the spontaneous self-concept. *Journal of Personality and Social Psychology, 33*, 743–754.

McIntyre, M., Gangestad, S. W., Gray, P. B., Chapman, J. F., Burnham, T. C., O'Rourke, M. T., & Thornhill, R. (2006). Romantic involvement often reduces men's testosterone levels – but not always: The moderating role of extrapair sexual interest. *Journal of Personality and Social Psychology, 91*, 642–651.

McIntyre, R. B., Paulson, R. M., Lord, C. G., & Lepper, M. R. (2004). Effects of attitude action identification on congruence between attitudes and behavioral intentions toward social groups. *Personality and Social Psychology Bulletin, 30*, 1151–1164.

McKenna, K. Y. A., & Bargh, J. A. (1998). Coming out in the age of the Internet: Identity "demarginalization" through virtual group participation. *Journal of Personality and Social Psychology, 75*, 681–694.

McMillen, R., Ritchie, L., Frese, W., & Cosby, A. (2000). Smoking in America: 35 years after the Surgeon General's Report. A report on the 2000 National Social Climate Survey (November 1, 2000). Tobacco Control. Surveys and Program Evaluations. Paper MSCI, Mississippi State University.

McNatt, D. B. (2000). Ancient Pygmalion joins contemporary management: A meta-analysis of the result. *Journal of Applied Psychology, 85*, 314–322.

McNulty, E. (2012). The role of bystanders in mass casualty events: Lessons from the 2010 Haiti earthquake. *Journal of Defense Studies and Resource Management, 1*, 2.

McNulty, J. K., & Karney, B. R. (2001). Attributions in marriage: Integrating specific and global evaluations of a relationship. *Personality and Social Psychology Bulletin, 27*, 943–955.

McNutt, M. (2014, 17 January). Reproducibility. *Science, 343*, 229.

Medvec, V. H., Madey, S. F. & Gilovich, T. (1995). When less is more: Counterfactual thinking and satisfaction among Olympic medalists. *Journal of Personality and Social Psychology, 69*, 603–610.

Meeus, H. J., & Raaijmakers, Q. A. W. (1995). Obedience in modern society: The Utrecht studies. *Journal of Social Issues, 51*, 155–176.

Meeus, W. H., & Raaijmakers, Q.A.W. (1986). Administrative obedience: Carrying out orders to use psychological-administrative violence. *European Journal of Social Psychology, 16*, 311–324.

Mehrabian, A. (1972). *Nonverbal communication.* Chicago: Aldine.

Meier, B. P., & Hinsz, V. B. (2004). A comparison of human aggression committed by groups and individuals: An inter-individual-intergroup discontinuity. *Journal of Experimental Social Psychology, 40*(4), 551–559.

Meleady, R., Hopthrow, T., & Crisp, R. J. (2013). Simulating social dilemmas: Promoting cooperative behavior through imagined group discussion. *Journal of Personality and Social Psychology, 104*(5), 839–853. doi:10.1037/a0031233

Merali, N. (2012). Arranged and forced marriage. In M. A. Paludi (Ed.), *The psychology of love* (vol. 1–4, pp. 143–168). Santa Barbara, CA: Praeger.

Merton, R. (1948). The self-fulfilling prophecy. *Antioch Review, 8*, 193–210.

Messick, D. M., & Brewer, M. B. (1983). Solving social dilemmas: A review. In L. Wheeler & P. Shaver (Eds.), *Review of personality and social psychology* (vol. 4, pp. 11–44). Beverly Hills, CA: Sage.

Messick, D. M., et al. (1983). Individual adaptations and structural change as solutions to social dilemmas. *Journal of Personality and Social Psychology, 44*, 294–309.

Messner, M., Reinhard, M.-A., & Sporer, S. L. (2008). Compliance through direct persuasive appeals: The moderating role of communicator's attractiveness in interpersonal persuasion. *Social Influence, 3*, 67–83.

Meyers, S. A., & Berscheid, E. (1997). The language of love: The difference a preposition makes. *Personality and Social Psychology Bulletin, 23*, 347–362.

Michaels, J. W., Blommel, J. M., Brocato, R. M., Linkous, R. A., & Rowe, J. S. (1982). Social facilitation and inhibition in a natural setting. *Replications in Social Psychology, 2*, 21–24.

Mickelson, K. D., Kessler, R. C., & Shaver, P. R. (1997). Adult attachment in a nationally representative sample. *Journal of Personality and Social Psychology, 73*, 1092–1106.

Mikula, G. (1980). *Justice and social interaction*. New York: Springer-Verlag.

Milburn, T. W. (1977). The nature of threat. *Journal of Social Issues, 33*(1), 126–139.

Miles, L. K., Lumsden, J., Richardson, M. J., & Macrae, C. N. (2011). Do birds of a feather move together? Group membership and behavioral synchrony. *Experimental Brain Research, 211*, 495–503.

Milfont, T.L., Richter, I., Sibley, C. G., Wilson, M. S., & Fischer, R. (2013). Environmental consequences of the desire to dominate and be superior. *Personality and Social Psychology Bulletin, 39*, 1127–1138.

Milgram, S. (1963). The behavioral study of obedience. *Journal of Abnormal and Social Psychology, 67*, 467–472.

Milgram, S. (1964). Issues in the study of obedience: A reply to Baumrind. *American Psychologist, 19*, 848–852.

Milgram, S. (1974). *Obedience to authority*. New York: Harper & Row.

Milgram, S. (1977). Subjects' reactions: The neglected factor in the ethics of experimentation. *Hastings Center Report*, October, 19–23.

Millar, M. (2002a). Effects of a guilt induction and guilt reduction on door in the face. *Communication Research, 29*, 666–680.

Millar, M. (2002b). The effectiveness of the door-in-the-face compliance strategy on friends and strangers. *Journal of Social Psychology, 142*, 295–304.

Millar, M. G., & Millar, K. U. (1996). The effects of direct and indirect experience on affective and cognitive responses and the attitude-behavior relation. *Journal of Experimental Social Psychology, 32*, 561–579.

Millar, M. G., Millar, K. U., & Tesser, A. (1988). The effects of helping and focus of attention on mood states. *Personality and Social Psychology Bulletin, 14*, 536–543.

Millar, M. G., & Tesser, A. (1986). Thought-induced attitude change: The effects of schema structure and commitment. *Journal of Personality and Social Psychology, 51*, 259–269.

Miller, D.T. & McFarland, C. (1987). Pluralistic ignorance: When similarity is interpreted as dissimilarity. *Journal of Personality and Social Psychology, 53*, 298–305.

Miller, D. T., & Morrison, K. R. (2009). Expressing deviant opinions: Believing you are in the majority helps. *Journal of Experimental Social Psychology, 45*, 740–747.

Miller, D. T., & Ross, M. (1975). Self-serving biases in the attribution of causality: Fact or fiction? *Psychological Bulletin, 82*, 213–225.

Miller, D. T., & Turnbull, W. (1986). Expectancies and interpersonal processes. *Annual Review of Psychology, 37*, 233–256.

Miller, G. (2011). Why loneliness is hazardous to your health. *Science, 331*, 138–140.

Miller, G., Chen, E., & Cole, S. W. (2009). Health psychology: Developing biologically plausible models linking the social world and physical health. *Annual Review of Psychology, 60*, 501–524.

Miller, J. G. (1984). Culture and the development of everyday social explanation. *Journal of Personality and Social Psychology, 46*, 961–978.

Miller, J. G., Bersoff, D. M., & Harwood, P. L. (1997). Perceptions of social responsibilities in India and the United States: Moral imperatives or personal decisions. In L. A. Peplau & S. E. Taylor (Eds.), *Sociocultural perspectives in social psychology* (pp. 113–144). Upper Saddle River, NJ: Prentice-Hall.

Miller, N., & Brewer, M.B. (1986). Categorization effects on ingroup and outgroup perception. In J. F. Dovidio & S. L. Gaertner (Eds.), *Prejudice, discrimination, and racism* (pp. 209–230). Orlando, FL: Academic Press.

Miller, N. E. (1941). The frustration-aggression hypothesis. *Psychological Review, 48*, 337–342.

Miller, P. A., & Eisenberg, N. (1988). The relation of empathy to aggressive and externalizing/ antisocial behavior. *Psychological Bulletin, 103*, 324–344.

Miller, R. L., Brickman, P., & Bolen, D. (1975). Attribution versus persuasion as a means for modifying behavior. *Journal of Personality and Social Psychology, 31*, 430–441.

Miller, R. L., Seligman, C., Clark, N. T., & Bush, M. (1976). Perceptual contrast versus reciprocal concessions as mediators of induced compliance. *Canadian Journal of Behavioral Science, 8*, 401–409.

Miller, R. S. (1997). Inattentive and contented: Relationship commitment and attention to alternatives. *Journal of Personality and Social Psychology, 73*, 758–766.

Miller, S. M., & Mangan, C. E. (1983). Interacting effects of information and coping style in adapting to gynecologic stress: Should the doctor tell all? *Journal of Personality and Social Psychology, 45*, 223–236.

Mills, J., Clark, M. S., Ford, T. E., & Johnson, M. (2004). Measurement of communal strength. *Personal Relationships, 11*, 213–230.

Milyavsky, M., Hassin, R. R., & Schul, Y. (2012). Guess what? Implicit motivation boosts the influence of subliminal information on choice. *Consciousness and Cognition, 21*, 1232–1241.

Minson, J. A., & Monin, B. (2012). Do-gooder derogation: Disparaging morally motivated minorities to defuse anticipated reproach. *Social Psychological and Personality Science, 3*, 200–207.

Minson, J. A., & Mueller, J. S. (2012). The cost of collaboration: Why joint decision making exacerbates rejection of outside information. *Psychological Science, 23*, 219–224.

Mintzberg, H. (1980). *The nature of managerial work* (2nd ed.). Englewood Cliffs, NJ: Prentice-Hall.

Miron, A. M., Brummett, B., Ruggles, B., & Brehm, J. W. (2008). Deterring anger and anger-motivated behaviors. *Basic and Applied Social Psychology, 30*, 326–338.

Mischkowski, D., Kross, E., & Bushman, B. J. (2012). Flies on the wall are less aggressive: Self-distancing "in the heat of the moment" reduces aggressive thoughts, angry feelings and aggressive behavior. *Journal of Experimental Social Psychology, 48*, 1187–1191.

Misumi, J. (1995). The development in Japan of the Performance-Maintenance (PM) Theory of Leadership. *Journal of Social Issues, 51*, 213–228.

Moghaddam, F. M., Taylor, D. M., & Wright, S. C. (1993). *Social psychology in cross-cultural perspective*. New York: W.H. Freeman & Company.

Mojzisch, A., Grouneva, L., & Schulz-Hardt, S. (2010). Biased evaluation of information during discussion: Disentangling the effects of preference consistency, social validation, and ownership of information. *European Journal of Social Psychology, 40*, 946–956.

Mojzisch, A., & Schulz-Hardt, S. (2010). Knowing others' preferences degrades the quality of group decisions. *Journal of Personality and Social Psychology, 98*, 794–808.

Mok, A., & Morris, M. W. (2010). An upside to bicultural identity conflict: Resisting groupthink in cultural ingroups. *Journal of Experimental Social Psychology, 46*, 1114–1117.

Monahan, J. L., Murphy, S. T., & Zajonc, R. B. (2000). Subliminal mere exposure: Specific, general, and diffuse effects. *Psychological Science, 11*, 462–466.

Monteith, M. J., Sherman, J. W., & Devine, P. G. (1998). Suppression as a stereotype control strategy. *Personality and Social Psychology Review, 2*, 63–82.

Montoya, R. M. (2008). I'm hot, so I'd say you're not: The influence of objective physical attractiveness on mate selection. *Personality and Social Psychology Bulletin, 34*, 1315–1331.

Montoya, R. M., & Horton, R. S. (2013). A meta-analytic investigation of the processes underlying the similarity-attraction effect. *Journal of Social and Personal Relationships, 30*, 64–94.

Montoya, R. M., Horton, R. S., & Kirchner, J. (2008). Is actual similarity necessary for attraction? A meta-analysis of actual and perceived similarity. *Journal of Social and Personal Relationships, 25*, 889–922.

Montoya, R. M., & Insko, C. A. (2008). Toward a more complete understanding of the reciprocity of liking effect. *European Journal of Social Psychology, 38*, 477–498.

Mook, D. G. (1980). In defense of external invalidity. *American Psychologist, 38*, 379–388.

Moon, H., Hollenbeck, J. R., Humphrey, S. E., Ilgen, D. R., West, B. J., Ellis, A. P. J., & Porter, C. O. L. (2004). Asymmetric adaptability: Dynamic team structures as one-way streets. *Academy of Management, 47*, 681–695.

Moons, W. G., & Mackie, D. M. (2007). Thinking straight while seeing red: The influence of anger on information processing. *Personality & Social Psychology Bulletin, 33*, 706–720.

Moons, W. G., Mackie, D. M., & Garcia-Marques, T. (2009). The impact of repetition-induced familiarity on agreement with weak and strong arguments. *Journal of Personality & Social Psychology, 96*, 32–44.

Moore, D. A., & Small, D. A. (2007). Error and bias in comparative judgment: On being both better and worse than we think we are. *Journal of Personality & Social Psychology, 92*, 972–989.

Moore, D. L., Hausknecht, D., & Thamodaran, K. (1986). Time compression, response opportunity, and persuasion. *Journal of Consumer Research, 13*, 85–99.

Moreland, R. L. (1987). The formation of small groups. In C. Hendrick (Ed.), *Group processes* (pp. 80–110). Beverly Hills, CA: Sage.

Moreland, R. L., & Beach, S. R. (1992). Exposure effects in the classroom: The development of affinity among students. *Journal of Experimental Social Psychology, 28*, 255–276.

Moreland, R. L., & Levine, J. M. (1988). Group dynamics over time: Development and socialization in small groups. In J. E. McGrath (Ed.), *The social psychology of time: New perspectives* (pp. 151–181). Newbury Park, CA: Sage.

Moreland, R. L., & Levine, J. M. (2001). Socialization in organizations and work groups. In M. E. Turner (Ed.), *Groups at work: Theory and research* (pp. 69–112). Mahwah, NJ: Lawrence Erlbaum.

Moreland, R. L., & Zajonc, R. B. (1982). Exposure effects in person perception: Familiarity, similarity, and attraction. *Journal of Experimental Social Psychology, 18*, 395–415.

Morelli, G. A., & Rothbaum, F. (2007). Situating the child in context: Attachment relationships and self-regulation in different cultures. In S. Kitayama & D. Cohen (Eds.), *Handbook of cultural psychology* (pp. 500–527). New York: Guilford Press.

Morgan, P. M. (1983). *Deterrence: A conceptual analysis.* Beverly Hills, CA: Sage.

Morgan, S. E., & Reichart, T. (1999). The message is in the metaphor: Assessing the comprehension of metaphors in advertisements. *Journal of Advertising, 28,* 1–12.

Moriarty, T. (1975). Crime, commitment, and the responsive bystander: Two field experiments. *Journal of Personality and Social Psychology, 31,* 370–376.

Morling, B., & Lamoreaux, M. (2008). Measuring culture outside the head: A meta-analysis of individualism-collectivism in cultural products. *Personality & Social Psychology Review, 12,* 199–221.

Morris, M. W., & Peng, K. (1994). Culture and cause: American and Chinese attributions for social and physical events. *Journal of Personality & Social Psychology, 67,* 949–971.

Morrison, K. R., & Matthes, J. (2011). Socially motivated projection: Need to belong increases perceived opinion consensus on important issues. *European Journal of Social Psychology, 41,* 707–719.

Morton, T. L. (1978). Intimacy and reciprocity of exchange: A comparison of spouses and strangers. *Journal of Personality and Social Psychology, 36,* 72–81.

Moscovici, S. (1980). Toward a theory of conversion behavior. In L. Berkowitz (Ed.), *Advances in experimental social psychology* (vol. 13, pp. 209–239). New York: Academic Press.

Moscovici, S., & Lage, E. (1976). Studies in social influence. III: Majority versus minority influence in a group. *European Journal of Social Psychology, 6,* 149–174.

Moscovici, S., Lage, S., & Naffrechoux, M. (1969). Influence of a consistent minority on the responses of a majority in a color perception task. *Sociometry, 32,* 365–380.

Moscovici, S., & Zavalloni, M. (1969). The group as a polarizer of attitudes. *Journal of Personality and Social Psychology, 12,* 125–135.

Moseley, R. (1998, April 5). Anti-foreigner bias sparks violent attacks. *Santa Barbara News Press,* p. A15.

Moskos, C. C. Jr. (1969). Why men fight: American combat soldiers in Vietnam. *Transaction, 7*(1), 13–23.

Moss-Racusin, C. A., Dovidio, J. F., Brescoll, V. L., Graham, M. J., & Handelsman, J. (2012). Science faculty's subtle gender biases favor male students. *Proceedings of the National Academy of Sciences, 109,* 16474–16479.

Mucchi-Faina, A., Pacilli, M. G., & Pagliaro, S. (2010). Minority influence, social change, and social stability. *Social and Personality Psychology Compass, 4,* 1111–1123.

Mucchi-Faina, A., Pacilli, M. G., & Pagliaro, S. (2011). Automatic reactions to the labels "minority" and "majority" are asymmetrical: Implications for minority and majority influence. *Social Influence, 6,* 181–196.

Mugny, G. (1975). Negotiations, image of the other, and the process of minority influence. *European Journal of Social Psychology, 5,* 209–228.

Mugny, G., & Papastamous, S. (1980). When rigidity does not fail: individualization and psychologization as resistances to the diffusion of minority innovations. *European Journal of Social Psychology, 10,* 43–62.

Mullan, B., Wong, C., & Kothe, E. (2013). Predicting adolescent breakfast consumption in the UK and Australia using an extended theory of planned behaviour. *Appetite, 62,* 127–132.

Mullen, B., Brown, R., & Smith, C. (1992). Ingroup bias as a function of salience, relevance, and status: An integration. *European Journal of Social Psychology, 22,* 103–122.

Mullen, B., & Hu, L. (1989). Perceptions of ingroup and outgroup variability: A meta-analytic integration. *Basic and Applied Social Psychology, 10,* 233–252.

Mullen, B., & Riordan, C. A. (1988). Self-serving attributions for performance in naturalistic settings: A meta-analytic review. *Journal of Applied Social Psychology, 18,* 3–22.

Mullen, B., & Smyth, J. M. (2004). Immigrant suicide rates as a function of ethnophaulisms: Hate speech predicts death. *Psychosomatic Medicine, 66,* 343–348.

Muller, D., Atzeni, T., & Butera, F. (2004). Coaction and upward social comparison reduce the illusory conjunction effect: Support for distraction-conflict theory. *Journal of Experimental Social Psychology, 40,* 659–665.

Mummendey, A., Simon, B., Dietze, C., Grunert, M., Haeger, G., Kessler, S., Lettgen, S., & Schaferhoff, S. (1992). Categorization is not enough: Intergroup discrimination in negative outcome allocations. *Journal of Experimental Social Psychology, 28,* 125–144.

Munro, G. D., & Ditto, P. H. (1997). Biased assimilation, attitude polarization, and affect in reactions to stereotyped-relevant scientific information. *Personality and Social Psychology Bulletin, 23*(6), 636–653.

Munro, G. D., Ditto, P. H., Lockhart, L. K., Fagerlin, A., Gready, M., & Peterson, E. (2002). Biased assimilation of sociopolitical arguments: Evaluating the 1996 U.S. presidential debate. *Basic & Applied Social Psychology, 24,* 15–26.

Murray, S. L., Derrick, J. L., Leder, S., & Holmes, J. G. (2008). Balancing connectedness and self-protection goals in close relationships: A levels-of-processing perspective on risk regulation. *Journal of Personality and Social Psychology, 94,* 429–459.

Murray, S. L., & Holmes, J. G. (1997). A leap of faith? Positive illusions in romantic relationships. *Personality and Social Psychology Bulletin, 23,* 586–604.

Murray, S. L., Holmes, J. G., Bellavia, G., Griffin, D. W., & Dolderman, D. (2002). Kindred spirits? The benefits of egocentrism in close relationships. *Journal of Personality and Social Psychology, 82,* 563–581.

Murray, S. L., Holmes, J. G., & Collins, N. L. (2006). Optimizing assurance: The risk regulation system in relationships. *Psychological Bulletin, 132,* 641–666.

Murray, S. L., Holmes, J. G., & Griffin, D. W. (1996). The self-fulfilling nature of positive illusions in romantic relationships: Love is not blind, but prescient. *Journal of Personality and Social Psychology, 71,* 1155–1180.

Mussweiler, T., & Bodenhausen, G. V. (2002). I know you are, but what am I? Self-evaluative consequences of judging in-group and out-group members. *Journal of Personality and Social Psychology, 82*(1), 19–32.

Mussweiler, T., Gabriel, S., & Bodenhausen, G. V. (2000). Shifting social identities as a strategy for deflecting threatening social comparisons. *Journal of Personality and Social Psychology, 79*(3), 398–409.

Mussweiler, T., Ruter, K., & Epstude, K. (2004). The ups and downs of social comparison: Mechanisms of assimilation and contrast. *Journal of Personality & Social Psychology, 87,* 832–844.

Myers, D. G. (2000). The funds, friends, and faith of happy people. *American Psychologist, 55,* 56–67.

Myers, D. G., & Bishop, G. D. (1971). The enhancement of dominant attitudes in group discussion. *Journal of Personality and Social Psychology, 20,* 386–391.

Myers, D. G., & Kaplan, M. F. (1976). Group-induced polarization in simulated juries. *Personality and Social Psychology Bulletin, 2,* 63–66.

Nadler, A. (2002). Inter-group helping relations as power relations: Maintaining or challenging social dominance between groups through helping. *Journal of Social Issues, 58,* 487–502.

Nadler, A., & Fisher, J. D. (1986). The role of threat to self-esteem and perceived control in recipient reactions to help: Theory development and empirical validation. In L. Berkowitz (Ed.), *Advances in experimental social psychology* (vol. 19, pp. 81–122). New York: Academic Press.

Nahemow, L., & Lawton, M. P. (1975). Similarity and propinquity in friendship formation. *Journal of Personality and Social Psychology, 32,* 205–213.

Naroll, R., Bullough, V. L., & Naroll, F. (1974). *Military deterrence in history: A pilot cross-historical survey.* Albany: State University of New York Press.

Narula, T., Ramprasad, C., Ruggs, E. N., & Hebl, M. R. (2014). Increasing colonoscopies? A psychological perspective on opting in versus opting out. *Health Psychology,* Dec 2.

Nasco, S. A., & Marsh, K. L. (1999). Gaining control through counterfactual thinking. *Personality & Social Psychology Bulletin, 25,* 557–569.

National Research Council (2003). *The polygraph and lie detection.* Washington, DC: The National Academies Press.

Neal, D. T., Wood, W., & Drolet, A. (2013). How do people adhere to goals when willpower is low? The profits (and pitfalls) of strong habits. *Journal of Personality and Social Psychology, 104,* 959–975.

Neal, D. T., Wood, W., Labrecque, J. S., & Lally, P. (2012). How do habits guide behavior? Perceived and actual triggers of habits in daily life. *Journal of Experimental Social Psychology, 48,* 492–498.

Neal, D. T., Wood, W., & Quinn, J. M. (2006). Habits—a repeat performance. *Current Directions in Psychological Science, 15,* 198–202.

Neal, D. T., Wood, W., Wu, M., & Kurlander, D. (2011). The pull of the past: When do habits persist despite conflict with motives? *Personality and Social Psychology Bulletin, 37,* 1428–1437.

Neighbors, C., Jensen, M., Tidwell, J., Walter, T., Fossos, N., & Lewis, M. A. (2011). Social-norms interventions for light and nondrinking students. *Group Processes & Intergroup Relations, 14,* 651–669.

Neisser, U. (1967). *Cognitive psychology.* New York: Appleton-Century-Crofts.

Nelissen, R. M. A., Dijker, A. J. M., & deVries, N. K. (2007). How to turn a hawk into a dove and vice versa: Interactions between emotions and goals in a give-some dilemma game. *Journal of Experimental Social Psychology, 43*(2), 280–286. doi:http://dx.doi.org/10.1016/j.jesp. 2006.01.009

Nelissen, R. M. A., & Mulder, L. B. (2013). What makes a sanction "stick"? The effects of financial and social sanctions on norm compliance. *Social Influence, 8,* 70–80.

Nelson, L. J., & Miller, D. T. (1995). The distinctiveness effect in social categorization: You are what makes you unusual. *Psychological Science, 6,* 246–249.

Nelson, L. D., & Morrison, E. L. (2005). The symptoms of resource scarcity: Judgments of food and finances influence preferences for potential partners. *Psychological Science, 16,* 167–173.

Nemeth, C. (1977). Interactions between jurors as a function of majority vs. unanimity decision rules. *Journal of Applied Social Psychology, 7,* 38–56.

Nemeth, C. J. (1995). Dissent as driving cognition, attitudes, and judgments. *Social Cognition, 13,* 273–291.

Nemeth, C. J. (2012). Minority influence theory. In P. A. M. Van Lange, A. W. Kruglanski, & E. T. Higgins (Eds.), *Handbook of theories of social psychology* (vol. 2, pp. 362–378). Thousand Oaks, CA: Sage Publications.

Nemeth, C. J., & Chiles, C. (1988). Modelling courage: the role of dissent in fostering independence. *European Journal of Social Psychology, 18,* 275–280.

Nemeth, C. J., Connell, J. B., Rogers, J. D., & Brown, K. S. (2001). Improving decision making by means of dissent. *Journal of Applied Social Psychology, 31,* 48–58.

Nemeth, C. J., & Kwan, J. L. (1987). Minority influence, divergent thinking and detection of correct solutions. *Journal of Applied Social Psychology, 17,* 788–799.

Nemeth, C. J., & Wachtler, J. (1983). Consistency and the modification of judgments. *Journal of Experimental Social Psychology, 9,* 65–79.

Nemeth, C. J., Wachtler, J., & Endicott, J. (1977). Increasing the size of the minority: Some gains and losses. *European Journal of Social Psychology, 7,* 15–27.

Neto, F., & Pinto, M. C. (2013). The satisfaction with sex life across the adult life span. *Social Indicators Research, 114,* 767–784.

Nettle, D., Colléony, A., & Cockerill, M. (2011). Variation in cooperative behaviour within a single city. *PLoS One, 6.*10: e26922.

Nettles, E. J., & Loevinger, J. (1983). Sex role expectations and ego level in relation to problem marriages. *Journal of Personality and Social Psychology, 45,* 676–687.

Neuberg, S. L. (1989). The goal of forming accurate impressions during social interactions: Attenuating the impact of negative expectancies. *Journal of Personality and Social Psychology, 56,* 374–386.

Neuberg, S. L., & Cottrell, C. A. (2002). Intergroup emotions: A biocultural approach. In D. M. Mackie & E. R. Smith (Eds.), *From prejudice to intergroup emotions* (pp. 265–284). New York: Psychology Press.

Neuberg, S. L., & Fiske, S. T. (1987). Motivational influences on impression formation: Outcome dependency, accuracy-driven attention, and individuating processes. *Journal of Personality and Social Psychology, 53,* 431–444.

Newcomb, T. M. (1961). *The acquaintance process.* New York: Holt, Rinehart, & Winston.

Newsweek. (1990). Perspectives. May 21, p. 17.

Niedenthal, P. M. (1990). Implicit perception of affective information. *Journal of Experimental Social Psychology, 26,* 505–527.

Niedenthal, P. M. (2007). Embodying emotion. *Science, 316,* 1–5.

Niedenthal, P. M., & Cantor, N. (1986). Affective responses as guides to category-based inferences. *Motivation and Emotion, 10,* 217–232.

Nields, D. (1991, May 27). The dirt on Shakespeare. *Newsweek,* p. 8.

Nienhuis, A. E., Manstead, A. S. R., & Spears, R. (2001). Multiple motives and persuasive communication: Creative elaboration as a result of impression motivation and accuracy motivation. *Personality & Social Psychology Bulletin, 27,* 118–132.

Nier, J. A., Gaertner, S. L., Dovidio, J. F., Banker, B. S., Ward, C. M., & Rust, M. C. (2001). Changing interracial evaluations and behavior: The effects of a common group identity. *Group Processes & Intergroup Relations, 4*(4), 299–316.

Nijstad, B. A. (2013). Performance. In J. M. Levine (Ed.), *Group processes* (pp. 193–213). New York: Psychology Press.

Nijstad, B. A., & Stroebe, W. (2006). How the group affects the mind: A cognitive model of idea generation in groups. *Personality and Social Psychology Review, 10,* 186–213.

Nijstad, B. A., Stroebe, W., & Lodewijkx, H. F. M. (2006). The illusion of group productivity: A reduction of failures explanation. *European Journal of Social Psychology, 36,* 31–48.

Nisbett, R. E. (1987). Lay personality theory: Its nature, origin, and utility. In N. E. Grunberg, R. E. Nisbett, J. Rodin, & J. E. Singer (Eds.), *A distinctive approach to psychological research: The influence of Stanley Schacter* (pp. 87–117). Hillsdale, NJ: Erlbaum.

Nisbett, R. E. (2003). *The geography of thought: How Asians and Westerners think differently . . . and why.* New York: Free Press.

Nisbett, R. E., & Cohen, D. (1996). *Culture of honor: The psychology of violence in the South.* Boulder, CO: Westview Press.

Nisbett, R. E., & Wilson, T. D. (1977). Telling more than we can know: Verbal reports on mental processes. *Psychological Review, 84,* 231–259.

Noller, P., & Ruzzene, M. (1991). Communication in marriage: The influence of affect and cognition. In G. Fletcher & F. Fincham (Eds.), *Cognition in close relationships* (pp. 203–234). Hillsdale, NJ: Lawrence Erlbaum Associates.

Norenzayan, A., & Nisbett, R. E. (2000). Culture and causal cognition. *Current Directions in Psychological Science, 9,* 132–135.

North, A. C., & Tarrant, M. (2004). The effects of music on helping behavior. *Environment and Behavior, 36,* 266–275.

North, R. C., Brody, R. A., & Holsti, O. R. (1964). Some empirical data on the conflict spiral. *Peace Research Society International Papers, 1,* 1–14.

Nosek, B. A., Smyth, F. L., Sriram, N., Linder, N. M., Devos, T., Ayala, A., . . . Greenwald, A. G. (2009). National differences in gender-science stereotypes predict national sex differences in science and math achievement. *Proceedings of the National Academy of Sciences, 106,* 10593–10597.

Nowak, M. A. (2006). Five rules for the evolution of cooperation. *Science (New York, NY), 314*(5805), 1560–1563. doi:10.1126/science.1133755

Nuttin, J. M. (1987). Affective consequences of mere ownership: The name letter effect in twelve European languages. *European Journal of Social Psychology, 17,* 381–402.

O'Connor, K. M., Arnold, J. A., & Burris, E. R. (2005). Negotiators' bargaining histories and their effects on future negotiation performance. *Journal of Applied Psychology, 90*(2) 350–362.

O'Donnell, A. T., Jetten, J., & Ryan, M. K. (2010). Watching over your own: How surveillance moderates the impact of shared identity on perceptions of leaders and follower behaviour. *European Journal of Social Psychology, 40,* 1046–1061.

O'Gorman, R., Wilson, D. S., & Miller, R. R. (2008). An evolved cognitive bias for social norms. *Evolution and Human Behavior, 29,* 71–78.

O'Keefe, D. J., & Figgé, M. (1999). Guilt and expected guilt in the door-in-the-face technique. *Communication Monographs, 66,* 312–324.

O'Keefe, D. J., & Hale, S. L. (2001). An odds-ratio-based meta-analysis of research on the door-in-the-face influence strategy. *Communication Reports, 14,* 31–38.

O'Leary, M. B., & Mortensen, M. (2010). Go (con)figure: Subgroups, imbalance, and isolates in geographically dispersed teams. *Organization Science, 21,* 115–131.

Oakes, P., Haslam, S. A., & Turner, J. C. (1998). The role of prototypicality in group influence and cohesion: Contextual variation in the graded structure of social categories. In S. Worchel, J. F. Morales, D. Paez, & J.-C. Deschamps (Eds.), *Social identity: International perspectives* (pp. 75–92). Thousand Oaks, CA: Sage Publications.

Oakes, P. J., & Turner, J. C. (1980). Social categorization and intergroup behaviour: Does minimal intergroup discrimination make social identity more positive? *European Journal of Social Psychology, 10,* 295–301.

Oates, C., Blades, M., & Gunter, B. (2002). Children and television advertising: When do they understand persuasive intent? *Journal of Consumer Behaviour, 1*, 238–245.

Ogilvy, D. (1983). *Ogilvy on advertising.* New York: Vintage Books.

Oh, S. H. (2013). Do collectivists conform more than individualists? Cross-cultural differences in compliance and internalization. *Social Behavior and Personality, 41*, 981–994.

Ohlert, J., & Kleinert, J. (2013). Social loafing during preparation for performance situations: The preloafing effect. *Social Psychology, 44*, 231–237.

Ohtsubo, Y., Miller, C. E., Hayashi, N., & Masuchi, A. (2004). Effects of group decision rules on decisions involving continuous alternatives: The unanimity rule and extreme decisions in mock civil juries. *Journal of Experimental Social Psychology, 40*, 320–331.

Oishi, S., Graham, J., Kesebir, S., & Galinha, I. C. (2013). Concepts of happiness across time and cultures. *Personality and Social Psychology Bulletin, 39*(5), 559–577.

Oishi, S., Krochik, M., & Akimoto, S. (2010). Felt understanding as a bridge between close relationships and subjective well-being: Antecedents and consequences across individuals and cultures. *Social and Personality Psychology Compass, 4*, 403–416.

Oliner, S. P., & Oliner, P. M. (1988). *The altruistic personality.* New York: Free Press.

Oliver, M. B., & Hyde, J. S. (1993). Gender differences in sexuality: A meta-analysis. *Psychological Bulletin, 114*, 29–51.

Olivola, C.Y., & Todorov, A. (2010). Elected in 100 milliseconds: Appearance-based trait inferences and voting. *Journal of Nonverbal Behavior, 34*, 83–110

Olson, C. K., Kutner, L. A., Warner, D. E., Almerigi, J. B., Baer, L., Nicholi, A. M., & Beresin, E. V. (2007). Factors correlated with violent video game use by adolescent boys and girls. *Journal of Adolescent Health, 41*, 77–83.

Olson, J. M. (1990). Self-inference processes in emotion. In J. M. Olson & M. P. Zanna (Eds.), *Self-inference processes: The Ontario Symposium* (vol. 6, pp. 17–42). Hillsdale, NJ: Lawrence Erlbaum Associates.

Olson, J. M., Roese, N. J., & Zanna, M. P. (1996). Expectancies. In E. T. Higgins & A. W. Kruglanski (Eds.), *Social Psychology: Handbook of basic principles* (pp. 211–238). New York: Guilford.

Olson, J. M., Vernon, P. A., Harris, J. A., & Jang, K. L. (2001). The heritability of attitudes: A study of twins. *Journal of Personality & Social Psychology, 80*, 845–860.

Olson, M. A., & Fazio, R. H. (2002). Implicit acquisition and manifestation of classically conditioned attitudes. *Social Cognition, 20*, 89–104.

Olson, M. A., & Fazio, R. H. (2004). Reducing the influence of extrapersonal associations on the Implicit Association Test: personalizing the IAT. *Journal of Personality and Social Psychology, 86*, 653–667.

Omoto, A. M., & Snyder, M. (2002). Considerations of community: The context and process of volunteerism. *American Behavioral Scientist, 45*, 846–886.

Oosterhof, N. N., & Todorov, A. (2008). The functional basis of face evaluation. *Proceedings of the National Academy of Sciences of the USA, 105*, 11087–11092.

Opotow, S. (1990). Moral exclusion and injustice: An introduction. *Journal of Social Issues, 46*(1), 1–20.

Opotow, S. (2012). The scope of justice, intergroup conflict, and peace. In L. R. Tropp (Ed.), *The Oxford handbook of intergroup conflict* (pp. 72–86). New York: Oxford University Press.

Orbell, J. M., van de Kragt, A. J. C., & Dawes, R. M. (1988). Explaining discussion-induced cooperation. *Journal of Personality and Social Psychology, 54*, 811–819.

Orne, M. T. (1962). On the social psychology of the psychological experiment: With particular reference to demand characteristics and their implications. *American Psychologist, 17*, 776–783.

Osborn, A. F. (1953). *Applied imagination.* New York: Scribner.

Oskamp, S., & Hartry, A. (1968). A factor-analytic study of the double standard in attitudes toward U.S. and Russian actions. *Behavioral Science, 13*, 178–188.

Ostrom, E. (2012). Experiments combining communication with punishment options demonstrate how individuals can overcome social dilemmas. *Behavioral and Brain Sciences, 35*, 33–34. doi:10.1017/S0140525X11001282

Ostrom, E., Gardner, R., & Walker, J. (2003). *Rules, games, and common-pool resources.* Ann Arbor: University of Michigan Press.

Ostrom, T. M. (1969). The relationship between the affective, behavioral, and cognitive components of attitude. *Journal of Experimental Social Psychology, 5*, 12–30.

Oswald, D. L., Clark, E. M., & Kelly, C. M. (2004). Friendship maintenance: An analysis of individual and dyad behaviors. *Journal of Social and Clinical Psychology, 23*, 413–441.

Oswald, F. L., Mitchell, G., Blanton, H., Jaccard, J., & Tetlock, P. E. (2013). Predicting ethnic and racial discrimination: A meta-analysis of IAT criterion studies. *Journal of Personality & Social Psychology, 105*, 171–192.

Otten, S., & Mummendey, A. (2000). Valence-dependent probability of ingroup favouritism between minimal groups: An integrative view on the positive-negative asymmetry in social discrimination. In D. Capozza (Ed.), *Social identity processes: Trends in theory and research* (pp. 33–48). London: Sage Publications Ltd.

Otten, S., Mummendey, A., & Blanz, M. (1996). Intergroup discrimination in positive and negative outcome allocations: Impact of stimulus valence, relative group status, and relative group size. *Personality and Social Psychology Bulletin, 22*, 568–581.

Otten, S., & Wentura, D. (2001). Self-anchoring and in-group favoritism: An individual profiles analysis. *Journal of Experimental Social Psychology, 37*(6), 525–532.

Ouellette, J. A., & Wood, W. (1998). Habit and intention in everyday life: The multiple processes by which past behavior predicts future behavior. *Psychological Bulletin, 124*, 54–74.

Overbeck, J. R., & Park, B. (2001). When power does not corrupt: Superior individuation processes among powerful perceivers. *Journal of Personality & Social Psychology, 81,* 549–565.

Owen, J. J., Rhoades, G. K., Stanley, S. M., & Fincham, F. D. (2010). "Hooking up" among college students: Demographic and psychosocial correlates. *Archives of Sexual Behavior, 39,* 653–663.

Oyserman, D., Coon, H. M., & Kemmelmeier, M. (2002). Rethinking individualism and collectivism: Evaluation of theoretical assumptions and meta-analyses. *Psychological Bulletin, 128,* 3–72.

Pachucki, M. A., Jacques, P. F., & Christakis, N. A. (2011). Social network concordance in food choice among spouses, friends, and siblings. *American Journal of Public Health, 101,* 2170–2177.

Packer, D. J., & Chasteen, A. L. (2010). Loyal deviance: Testing the normative conflict model of dissent in social groups. *Personality and Social Psychology Bulletin, 36,* 5–18.

Paladino, M.-P., Leyens, J.-P., Rodriguez, R., Rodriguez, A., Gaunt, R., & Demoulin, S. (2002). Differential association of uniquely and non uniquely human emotions with the ingroup and the outgroup. *Group Processes & Intergroup Relations, 5*(2), 105–117.

Paleari, F. G., Regalia, C., & Fincham, F. (2005). Marital quality, forgiveness, empathy, and rumination: A longitudinal analysis. *Personality and Social Psychology Bulletin, 31,* 368–378.

Pallak, S. R. (1983). Salience of a communicator's physical attractiveness and persuasion: A heuristic versus systematic processing interpretation. *Social Cognition, 2,* 156–168.

Paluck, E. L. (2010). Is it better not to talk? Group polarization, extended contact, and perspective taking in eastern Democratic Republic of Congo. *Personality and Social Psychology Bulletin, 36,* 1170–1185.

Paluck, E. L., & Shepherd, H. (2012). The salience of social referents: A field experiment on collective norms and harassment behavior in a school social network. *Journal of Personality and Social Psychology, 103,* 899–915.

Pape, H. (2012). Young people's overestimation of peer substance use: An exaggerated phenomenon? *Addiction, 107,* 878–884.

Paquette, L., Bergeron, J., & Lacourse, E. (2012). Self regulation, risky sporting practices and consumption of psychotropic drugs among adolescent adepts of sliding sports. *Canadian Journal of Behavioural Science, 44,* 308–318.

Park, B. (1986). A method for studying the development of impressions of real people. *Journal of Personality and Social Psychology, 51,* 907–917.

Park, B., & Judd, C. M. (1990). Measures and models of perceived group variability. *Journal of Personality and Social Psychology, 59,* 173–191.

Park, B., & Rothbart, M. (1982). Perception of out-group homogeneity and levels of social categorization: Memory for the subordinate attributes of in-group and out-group members. *Journal of Personality and Social Psychology, 42,* 1051–1068.

Parke, R. D., Berkowitz, L., Leyens, J.-P., West, S. G., & Sebastian, R. J. (1977). Some effects of violent and nonviolent movies on the behavior of juvenile delinquents. In L. Berkowitz (Ed.), *Advances in experimental social psychology* (vol. 10, pp. 135–172). New York: Academic Press.

Parker, K. A., Ivanov, B., & Compton, J. (2012). Inoculation's efficacy with young adults' risky behaviors: Can inoculation confer cross-protection over related but untreated issues? *Health Communication, 27,* 223–233.

Pascual, A., & Gueguen, N. (2005). Foot-in-the-door and door-in-the-face: A comparative meta-analytic study. *Psychological Reports, 96,* 122–128.

Pashler, H., & Wagenmakers, E. J. (2012). Editors' introduction to the special section on replicability in psychological science: a crisis of confidence? *Perspectives on Psychological Science, 7*(6), 528–530. doi:10.1177/1745691612465253

Pataki, S. P., Shapiro, C., & Clark, M. S. (1994). Children's acquisition of appropriate norms for friendships and acquaintances. *Journal of Social and Personal Relationships, 11,* 427–442.

Patterson, M. L., Churchill, M. E., Burger, G. K., & Powell, J. L. (1992). Verbal and nonverbal modality effects on impressions of political candidates: Analysis from the 1984 Presidential debates. *Communication Monographs, 59,* 231–242.

Paulson, R. M., Lord, C. G., Taylor, C. A., Brady, S. E., McIntyre, R. B., & Fuller, E. W. (2012). A matching hypothesis for the activity level of actions involved in attitude-behavior consistency. *Social Psychological and Personality Science, 3,* 40–47.

Paulus, P. B. (1988). *Prison crowding: A psychological perspective.* New York: Springer-Verlag.

Paulus, P. B., Annis, A. B., Seta, J. J., Schkade, J. K., & Matthews, R. W. (1976). Density does affect task performance. *Journal of Personality and Social Psychology, 34,* 248–253.

Paulus, P. B., & Coskun, H. (2013). Creativity. In J. M. Levine (Ed.), *Group processes* (pp. 215–239). New York: Psychology Press.

Payne, B. K. (2001). Prejudice and perception: The role of automatic and controlled processes in misperceiving a weapon. *Journal of Personality & Social Psychology, 81*(2), 181–192.

Payne, B. K., Lambert, A. J., & Jacoby, L. L. (2002). Best laid plans: Effects of goals on accessibility bias and cognitive control in race-based misperceptions of weapons. *Journal of Experimental Social Psychology, 38,* 384–396.

Pearsall, M. J., Christian, M. S., & Ellis, A. P. J. (2010). Motivating interdependent teams: Individual rewards, shared rewards, or something in between? *Journal of Applied Psychology, 95,* 183–191.

Pelham, B. (1991). On confidence and consequence: The certainty and importance of self-knowledge. *Journal of Personality and Social Psychology, 60,* 518–530.

Pendleton, M. G., & Bateson, C. D. (1979). Self-presentation and the door-in-the-face technique for inducing compliance. *Personality and Social Psychology Bulletin, 5,* 77–81.

Peng, K., & Nisbett, R. E. (1999). Culture, dialectics, and reasoning about contradiction. *American Psychologist, 54*, 741–754.

Penke, L., Bates, T. C., Gow, A. J., Pattie, A., Starr, J. M., Jones, B. C., Perrett, D. I., & Deary, I. J. (2009). Symmetric faces are a sign of successful cognitive aging. *Evolution and Human Behavior, 30*, 429–437.

Pennebaker, J. W. (1997). Writing about emotional experiences as a therapeutic process. *Psychological Science, 8*, 162–166.

Pennebaker, J. W., Kiecolt-Glaser, J. K., & Glaser, R. (1988). Disclosure of traumas and immune function: Health implications for psychotherapy. *Journal of Consulting and Clinical Psychology, 56*, 239–245.

Penner, L. A. (2002). The causes of sustained volunteerism: An interactionist perspective. *Journal of Social Issues, 58*, 447–467.

Penner, L. A., Dovidio, J. F., Piliavin, J. A., & Schroeder, D. A. (2005). Prosocial behavior: Multilevel perspectives. *Annual Review of Psychology, 56*, 365–392.

Penner, L. A., & Finkelstein, M. A. (1998). Dispositional and structural determinants of volunteerism. *Journal of Personality and Social Psychology, 74*, 525–537.

Penner, L. A., Fritzsche, B. A., Craiger, J. P., & Freifeld, T. R. (1995). Measuring the prosocial personality. In J. Butcher & C. D. Spielberger (Eds.), *Advances in personality assessment* (vol. 10, pp. 147–163). Hillsdale, NJ: Erlbaum.

Peplau, L. A., & Conrad, E. (1989). Beyond nonsexist research: The perils of feminist methods in psychology. *Psychology of Women Quarterly, 13*, 379–400.

Peplau, L. A., & Fingerhut, A. W. (2007). The close relationships of lesbians and gay men. *Annual Review of Psychology, 58*, 405–424.

Perdue, C. W., Dovidio, J. F., Gurtman, M. B., & Tyler, R. B. (1990). Us and them: Social categorization and the process of intergroup bias. *Journal of Personality and Social Psychology, 59*, 475–486.

Perillo, J. T., & Kassin, S. M. (2011). Inside interrogation: The lie, the bluff, and false confessions. *Law and Human Behavior, 35*, 327–337.

Perkins, H. W., Linkenbach, J. W., Lewis, M. A., & Neighbors, C. (2010). Effectiveness of social norms media marketing in reducing drinking and driving: A statewide campaign. *Addictive Behaviors, 35*, 866–874.

Perlow, L., & Weeks, J. (2002). Who's helping whom? Layers of culture and workplace behavior. *Journal of Organizational Behavior, 23*, 345–361.

Perrett, D. I., Burt, D. M., Penton-Voak, I. S., Lee, K. J., Rowland, D. A., & Edwards, R. (1999). Symmetry and human facial attractiveness. *Evolution and Human Behavior, 20*, 295–307.

Perry, D. G., Perry, L. C., & Rasmussen, P. (1986). Cognitive social learning mediators of aggression. *Child Development, 57*, 700–711.

Peterson, C., Seligman, M. E. & Vaillant, G. E. (1988). Pessimistic explanatory style is a risk factor for physical illness: A thirty-five-year longitudinal study. *Journal of Personality and Social Psychology, 55*, 23–27.

Peterson, R. S. (1997). A directive leadership style in group decision making can be both virtue and vice: Evidence from elite and experimental groups. *Journal of Personality and Social Psychology, 72*, 1107–1121.

Pettigrew, T. F. (1968). Race relations: Social and psychological aspects. In D. L. Sills (Ed.), *The international encyclopedia of the social sciences* (vol 13, pp. 277–282). New York: The Macmillan Company.

Pettigrew, T. F. (1979). The ultimate attribution error: Extending Allport's cognitive analysis of prejudice. *Personality and Social Psychology Bulletin, 5*, 461–476.

Pettigrew, T. F. (1980). Prejudice. In S. Thernstrom (Ed.), *Harvard encyclopedia of American ethnic groups*. Cambridge, MA: Harvard University Press.

Pettigrew, T. F. (1997). Generalized intergroup contact effects on prejudice. *Personality and Social Psychology Bulletin, 23*, 173–185.

Pettigrew, T. F. (1998). Intergroup contact theory. *Annual Review of Psychology, 49*, 65–85.

Pettigrew, T. F. (2009). Secondary transfer effect of contact: Do intergroup contact effects spread to noncontacted outgroups? *Social Psychology, 40*, 55–65.

Pettigrew, T. F., & Martin, J. (1987). Shaping the organizational context for black American inclusion. *Journal of Social Issues, 43*, 41–78.

Pettigrew, T. F., & Tropp, L. R. (2006). A meta-analytic test of intergroup contact theory. *Journal of Personality & Social Psychology, 90*, 751–783.

Petty, R. E., Brinol, P., Loersch, C., & McCaslin, M. J. (2009). The need for cognition. In M. R. Leary & R. H. Hoyle (Eds.), *Handbook of individual differences in social behavior* (pp. 318–329). New York: Guilford Press.

Petty, R. E., & Cacioppo, J. T. (1981). *Attitudes and persuasion: Classic and contemporary approaches.* Dubuque, IA: Wm. C. Brown.

Petty, R. E., & Cacioppo, J. T. (1984). The effects of involvement on responses to argument quantity and quality: Central and peripheral routes to persuasion. *Journal of Personality and Social Psychology, 46*, 69–81.

Petty, R. E., & Cacioppo, J. T. (1986). *Communication and persuasion: Central and peripheral routes to attitude change.* New York: Springer-Verlag.

Petty, R. E., Cacioppo, J. T., & Goldman, R. (1981). Personal involvement as a determinant of argument-based persuasion. *Journal of Personality and Social Psychology 41*, 847–855.

Petty, R. E., Haugtvedt, C. P., & Smith, S. M. (1995). Elaboration as a determinant of attitude strength: Creating attitudes that are persistent, resistant, and predictive of behavior. In R. E. Petty & J. A. Krosnick (Eds.), *Attitude strength: Antecedents and consequences* (pp. 93–130). Mahwah, NJ: Lawrence Erlbaum Associates.

Petty, R. E., Schumann, D. W., Richman, S. A., & Strathman, A. J. (1993). Positive mood and persuasion: Different roles for affect under high- and low-elaboration conditions. *Journal of Personality and Social Psychology, 64,* 5–20.

Petty, R. E., Tormala, Z. L., Brinol, P., & Jarvis, W. B. G. (2006). Implicit ambivalence from attitude change: An exploration of the PAST model. *Journal of Personality & Social Psychology, 90,* 21–41.

Petty, R. E., & Wegener, D. T. (1998a). Attitude change: Multiple roles for persuasion variables. In D. T. Gilbert, S. T. Fiske, & G. Lindzey (Eds.), *The handbook of social psychology* (4th ed., pp. 323–390). Boston, MA: McGraw-Hill.

Petty, R. E., & Wegener, D. T. (1998b). Matching versus mismatching attitude functions: Implications for scrutiny of persuasive messages. *Personality & Social Psychology Bulletin, 24,* 227–240.

Petty, R. E., & Wegener, D. T. (1999). The elaboration likelihood model: Current status and controversies. In S. Chaiken & Y. Trope (Eds.), *Dual-process theories in social psychology* (pp. 37–72). New York: Guilford Press.

Petty, R. E., Wells, G. L., & Brock, T. C. (1976). Distraction can enhance or reduce yielding to propaganda: Thought disruption versus effort justification. *Journal of Personality and Social Psychology, 34,* 874–884.

Pew Research Center (2009, October). *Support for abortion slips.* Retrieved from http://www. pewforum.org/2009/10/01/support-for-abortion-slips/

Pfaff, E., & Huddleston, P. (2003). Does it matter if I hate teamwork? What impacts student attitudes toward teamwork. *Journal of Marketing Education, 25,* 37–45.

Phelps, E. A., O'Connor, K. J., Cunningham, W. A., Funayama, S., Gatenby, J. C., Gore, J. C., & Banaji, M. R. (2000). Performance on indirect measures of race evaluation predicts amygdala activation. *Journal of Cognitive Neuroscience, 12,* 729–738.

Phillips, A. P., & Dipboye, R. L. (1989). Correlational tests of predictions from a process model of the interview. *Journal of Applied Psychology, 74,* 41–52.

Phillips, K. W., Liljenquist, K. A., & Neale, M. A. (2009). Is the pain worth the gain? The advantages and liabilities of agreeing with socially distinct newcomers. *Personality and Social Psychology Bulletin, 35,* 336–350.

Pichon, I., Boccato, G., & Saroglou, V. (2007). Nonconscious influences of religion on prosociality: a priming study. *European Journal of Social Psychology, 37*(5), 1032–1045. doi:10.1002/ ejsp.416

Pickert, K. (2008, May). Do consumers understand drug ads? *Time.* Retrieved from www.time. com.

Pierro, A., Mannetti, L., Kruglanski, A. W., Klein, K., & Orehek, E. (2012). Persistence of attitude change and attitude-behavior correspondence based on extensive processing of source information. *European Journal of Social Psychology, 42,* 103–111.

Pietromonaco, P. R., & Feldman Barrett, L. (1997). Working models of attachment and daily social interactions. *Journal of Personality and Social Psychology, 73,* 1409–1423.

Pietromonaco, P. R., Uchino, B., & Dunkel-Schetter, C. (2013). Close relationship processes and health: Implications of attachment theory for health and disease. *Health Psychology, 32,* 499–513.

Piliavin, J. A., Callero, P. L., & Evans, D. E. (1982). Addiction to altruism? Opponent-process theory and habitual blood donation. *Journal of Personality and Social Psychology, 43,* 1200–1213.

Piliavin, J. A., Dovidio, J. F., Gaertner, S. L., & Clark, R. D. III (1981). *Emergency intervention.* New York: Academic Press.

Pine, K. J., & Nash, A. (2002). Dear Santa: The effects of television advertising on young children. *International Journal of Behavioral Development, 26,* 529–539.

Pines, A. M., Aronson, E., & Kafry, D. (1981). *Burnout: From tedium to personal growth.* New York: Freeman.

Pinquart, M., & Duberstein, P. R. (2010). Associations of social networks with cancer mortality: A meta-analysis. *Critical Reviews in Oncology/Hematology, 75,* 122–137.

Pittman, T. S. (1975). Atribution of arousal as a mediator of dissonance reduction. *Journal of Experimental Social Psychology, 11,* 53–63.

Plakoyiannaki, E., Mathioudaki, K., Dimitratos, P., & Zotos, Y. (2008). Images of women in online advertisements of global products: Does sexism exist? *Journal of Business Ethics, 83,* 101–112.

Plaks, J. E., & Higgins, E. T. (2000). Pragmatic use of stereotyping in teamwork: Social loafing and compensation as a function of inferred partner-situation fit. *Journal of Personality and Social Psychology, 79,* 962–974.

Plant, E. A., & Devine, P. G. (1998). Internal and external motivation to respond without prejudice. *Journal of Personality & Social Psychology, 75,* 811–832.

Platow, M. J., Haslam, S. A., Both, A., Chew, I., Cuddon, M., Goharpey, N., Maurer, J., et al. (2005). "It's not funny if they're laughing": Self-categorization, social influence, and responses to canned laughter. *Journal of Experimental Social Psychology, 41,* 542–550.

Platt, J. (1973). Social traps. *American Psychologist, 28,* 641–651.

Platz, S. J., & Hosch, H. M. (1988). Cross-racial/ethnic eyewitness identification: A field study. *Journal of Applied Social Psychology, 18,* 972–984.

Pond, R. S., DeWall, C. N., Lambert, N. M., Deckman, T., Bonser, I. M., & Fincham, F. D. (2012). Repulsed by violence: Disgust sensitivity buffers trait, behavioral, and daily aggression. *Journal of Personality & Social Psychology, 102,* 175–188.

Pool, G. J., Wood, W., & Leck, K. (1998). The self-esteem motive in social influence: Agreement with valued majorities and disagreement with derogated minorities. *Journal of Personality and Social Psychology, 75,* 967–975.

Postmes, T., Haslam, S. A., & Swaab, R. I. (2005). Social influence in small groups: An interactive model of social identity formation. *European Review of Social Psychology, 16,* 1–42.

Postmes, T., & Spears, R. (1998). Deindividuation and antinormative behavior: A meta-analysis. *Psychological Bulletin, 123,* 1–22.

Postmes, T., Spears, R., & Cihangir, S. (2001). Quality of decision making and group norms. *Journal of Personality and Social Psychology, 80,* 918–930.

Postmes, T., Spears, R., Lee, A. T., & Novak, R. J. (2005). Individuality and social influence in groups: Inductive and deductive routes to group identity. *Journal of Personality and Social Psychology, 89,* 747–763.

Postmes, T., Spears, R., Sakhel, K., & de Groot, D. (2001). Social influence in computer-mediated communication: The effects of anonymity on group behavior. *Personality and Social Psychology Bulletin, 27,* 1243–1254.

Powell, A. (2009). Wendy's vandalism prank on West Bank leads to arrest of Texas teenager. *The Time Picayune,* Sept. 9, http://www.nola.com/crime/index.ssf/2009/09/jpso_announces_arrest_in_broke.html

Pranulis, M., Dabbs, J., & Johnson, J. (1975). General anesthsia and the patient's attempts at control. *Social Behavior and Personality, 3,* 49–54.

Pratto, F., Sidanius, J., Stallworth, L. M., & Malle, B. F. (1994). Social dominance orientation: A personality variable predicting social and political attitudes. *Journal of Personality and Social Psychology, 67,* 741–763.

Prentice, D. A. (1990). Familiarity and differences in self- and other-representations. *Journal of Personality and Social Psychology, 59,* 369–383.

Prentice, D. A., & Carranza, E. (2002). What women and men should be, shouldn't be, are allowed to be, and don't have to be: The contents of prescriptive gender stereotypes. *Psychology of Women Quarterly, 26,* 269–281.

Prentice, D. A., & Miller, D. T. (1993). Pluralistic ignorance and alcohol use on campus: Some consequences of misperceiving the social norm. *Journal of Personality and Social Psychology, 64,* 243–256.

Prentice, D. A., & Miller, D. T. (2002). The emergence of homegrown stereotypes. *American Psychologist, 57*(5), 352–359.

Preston, J. L., Ritter, R. S., & Ivan Hernandez, J. (2010). Principles of religious prosociality: A review and reformulation. *Social and Personality Psychology Compass, 4*(8), 574–590. doi:10.1111/j.1751-9004.2010.00286.x

Preston, J. L., Ritter, R. S., & Wegner, D. M. (2011). Action embellishment: An intention bias in the perception of success. *Journal of Personality and Social Psychology, 101,* 233–244.

Price, V. (1989). Social identification and public opinion: Effects of communicating group conflict. *Public Opinion Quarterly, 53,* 197–224.

Priester, J. R., & Petty, R. E. (2001). Extending the bases of subjective attitudinal ambivalence: Interpersonal and intrapersonal antecedents of evaluative tension. *Journal of Personality & Social Psychology, 80,* 19–34.

Priester, J. R., Cacioppo, J. T., & Petty, R. E. (1996). The influence of motor processes on attitudes toward novel versus familiar semantic stimuli. *Personality and Social Psychology Bulletin, 22,* 442–447.

Pronin, E. (2008). How we see ourselves and how we see others. *Science, 320,* 1177–1180.

Pronin, E., Berger, J., & Molouki, S. (2007). Alone in a crowd of sheep: Asymmetric perceptions of conformity and their roots in an introspection illusion. *Journal of Personality & Social Psychology, 92,* 585–595.

Proulx, T., Inzlicht, M., & Harmon-Jones, E. (2012). Understanding all inconsistency compensation as a palliative response to violated expectations. *Trends in Cognitive Sciences, 16,* 285–291.

Pruitt, D. G. (1981). *Negotiation behavior.* New York: Academic Press.

Pruitt, D. G. (1986). Achieving integrative agreements in negotiation. In R. K. White (Ed.), *Psychology and the prevention of nuclear war* (pp. 463–478). New York: New York University Press.

Pruitt, D. G. (1998). Social conflict. In D. T. Gilbert, S. T. Fiske, & G. Lindzey (Eds.), *Handbook of social psychology* (3rd ed., vol. 2, pp. 470–503). Boston: McGraw-Hill.

Pruitt, D. G., & Kimmel, M. J. (1977). Twenty years of experimental gaming: Critique, synthesis, and suggestions for the future. *Annual Review of Psychology, 28,* 3–39.

Pruitt, D. G., & Lewis, S. A. (1977). The psychology of integrative bargaining. In D. Druckman (Ed.), *Negotiations: A social-psychological analysis* (pp. 161–192). New York: Halstead.

Pruitt, D. G., & Rubin, J. Z. (1986). *Social conflict: Escalation, stalemate, and settlement.* New York: Random House.

Pyszczynski, T., & Greenberg, J. (1987). Self-regulatory perseveration and the depressive self-focusing style: A self-awareness theory of reactive depression. *Psychological Bulletin, 102,* 122–138.

Quigley-Fernandez, B., & Tedeschi, J. T. (1978). The bogus pipeline as lie detector: Two validity studies. *Journal of Personality and Social Psychology, 36,* 247–256.

Quist, M. C., DeBruine, L. M., Little, A. C., & Jones, B. C. (2012). Integrating social knowledge and physical cues when judging the attractiveness of potential mates. *Journal of Experimental Social Psychology, 48,* 770–773.

Rabbie, J. M. & Bekkers, F. (1978). Threatened leadership and intergroup competition. *European Journal of Social Psychology, 8,* 9–20.

Rabinovich, A., Morton, T. A., Postmes, T., & Verplanken, B. (2012). Collective self and individual choice: The effects of inter-group comparative context on environmental values and behavior. *British Journal of Social Psychology, 51,* 551–569.

Rafferty, A. E., & Griffin, M. A. (2004). Dimensions of transformational leadership: Conceptual and empirical extensions. *Leadership Quarterly, 15,* 329–354.

Rains, S. A. (2013). The nature of psychological reactance revisited: A meta-analytic review. *Human Communication Research, 39,* 47–73.

Rand, D. G., Greene, J. D., & Nowak, M. A. (2012). Spontaneous giving and calculated greed. *Nature*, *489*(7416), 427–430. doi:10.1038/nature11467

Rank, S. J., & Jacobsen, C. K. (1977). Hospital nurses' compliance with medication overdose orders: A failure to replicate. *Journal of Health and Social Behavior*, *18*, 188–193.

Rapoport, A., & Bornstein, G. (1987). Intergroup competition for the provision of binary public goods. *Psychological Review*, *94*, 291–299.

Rapoport, A., & Eshed-Levy, D. (1989). Provision of step-level public goods: Effects of greed and fear of being gypped. *Organizational Behavior and Human Decision Processes*, *44*.

Rasinski, K. A., Crocker, J., & Hastie, R. (1985). Another look at sex stereotypes and social judgments: An analysis of the social perceiver's use of subjective probabilities. *Journal of Personality and Social Psychology*, *49*, 317–326.

Raven, B. H., & Rubin, J. Z. (1976). *Social psychology: People in groups*. New York: Wiley.

Reber, R., Schwarz, N., & Winkielman, P. (2004). Processing fluency and aesthetic pleasure: Is beauty in the perceiver's processing experience? *Personality and Social Psychology Review*, *8*, 364–382.

Reed, M. B., Lange, J. E., Ketchie, J. M., & Clapp, J. D. (2007). The relationship between social identity, normative information, and college student drinking. *Social Influence*, *2*, 269–294.

Reeves, B., & Nass, C. (1996). *The media equation*. New York: Cambridge University Press.

Regan, D. T. (1971). Effects of a favor and liking on compliance. *Journal of Experimental Social Psychology*, *7*, 627–639.

Regan, P. C., Levin, L., Sprecher, S., Christopher, F. S., & Cate, R. (2000). Partner preferences: What characteristics do men and women desire in their short-term sexual and long-term romantic partners? *Journal of Psychology and Human Sexuality*, *12*, 1–21.

Rehm, J., Steinleitner, J., & Lilli, W. (1987). Wearing uniforms and aggression: A field experiment. *European Journal of Social Psychology*, *17*, 357–360.

Reiber, C., & Garcia, J. R. (2010). Hooking up: Gender differences, evolution, and pluralistic ignorance. *Evolutionary Psychology*, *8*, 390–404.

Reicher, S. D. (1987). Crowd behavior as social action. In J. C. Turner (Ed.), *Rediscovering the social group: A self-categorization theory*. Oxford: Blackwell.

Reicher, S., & Haslam, S. A. (2006). Rethinking the psychology of tyranny: The BBC prison study. *British Journal of Social Psychology*, *45*, 1–40.

Reicher, S., Haslam, S. A., & Hopkins, N. (2005). Social identity and the dynamics of leadership: Leaders and followers as collaborative agents in the transformation of social reality. Special Issue: Leadership, Self, and Identity, *Leadership Quarterly*, *16*, 547–568.

Reicher, S., Haslam, S. A., & Rath, R. (2008). Making a virtue of evil: A five-step social identity model of the development of collective hate. *Social and Personality Psychology Compass*, *2*, 1313–1344.

Reicher, S. D., Haslam, S. A., & Smith, J. R. (2012). Working toward the experimenter: Reconceptualizing obedience within the Milgram paradigm as identification-based followership. *Perspectives on Psychological Science*, *7*, 315–324.

Reid, A. E., & Aiken, L. S. (2013). Correcting injunctive norm misperceptions motivates behavior change: A randomized controlled sun protection intervention. *Health Psychology*, *32*, 551–560.

Reis, H. T. (1986). Gender effects in social participation: Intimacy, loneliness, and the conduct of social interaction. In R. Gilmour & S. Duck (Eds.), *The emerging field of personal relationships* (pp. 91–108). Hillsdale, NJ: Lawrence Erlbaum Associates.

Reis, H. T., Clark, M. S., & Holmes, J. G. (2004). Perceived partner responsiveness as an organizing construct in the study of intimacy and closeness. In D. J. Mashek & A. P. Aron (Eds.), *Handbook of closeness and intimacy* (pp. 201–225). Mahwah, NJ: Lawrence Erlbaum Associates.

Reis, H. T., Gable, S. L. (2003). Toward a positive psychology of relationships. In C. L. M. Keyes & J. Haidt (Eds.), *Flourishing: Positive psychology and the life well-lived* (pp. 129–159). Washington, DC: American Psychological Association.

Reis, H. T., Maniaci, M. R., Caprariello, P. A., Eastwick, P. W., & Finkel, E. J. (2011). Familiarity does indeed promote attraction in live interaction. *Journal of Personality & Social Psychology*, *101*, 557–570.

Reis, H. T., & Patrick, B. C. (1996). Attachment and intimacy: Component processes. In E. T. Higgins & A. W. Kruglanski (Eds.), *Social psychology: Handbook of basic principles* (pp. 523–563). New York: Guilford Press.

Reis, H. T., Senchak, M., & Solomon, B. (1985). Sex differences in the intimacy of social interaction. *Journal of Personality and Social Psychology*, *48*, 1204–1217.

Reisenzein, R. (1983). The Schacter theory of emotion: Two decades later. *Psychological Bulletin*, *94*, 239–264.

Reiss, I. L. (1986). A sociological journey into sexuality. *Journal of Marriage and the Family*, *48*, 233–242.

Reiss, I. L., & Lee, G. R. (1988). *Family systems in America* (4th ed.). New York: Holt, Rinehart, & Winston.

Renaud, T. (2010). The biggest bully in the room. *The Jury Expert*, *22*, 23–26.

Rhodes, G. (2006). The evolutionary psychology of facial beauty. In S. T. Fiske, A. E. Kazdin, & D. L. Schacter (Eds.), *Annual review of psychology* (vol. 57, pp. 199–226). Palo Alto, CA: Annual Reviews.

Rhodes, G., Yoshikawa, S., Clark, A., Lee, K., McKay, R., & Akamatsu, S. (2001). Attractiveness of facial averageness and symmetry in non-Western cultures: In search of biologically based standards of beauty. *Perception*, *30*, 611–625.

Rhodewalt, F., & Agustsdottir, S. (1986). Effects of self-presentation on the phenomenal self. *Journal of Personality and Social Psychology*, *50*, 47–55.

Rholes, W. S., & Pryor, J. B. (1982). Cognitive accessibility and causal attributions. *Personality and Social Psychology Bulletin, 8*, 719–727.

Richards, J. M., & Gross, J. J. (2000). Emotion regulation and memory: The cognitive costs of keeping one's cool. *Journal of Personality and Social Psychology, 79*, 410–424.

Richards, M., Hardy, R., & Wadsworth, M. (1997). The effects of divorce and separation on mental health in a national UK birth cohort. *Psychological Medicine, 27*, 1121–1128.

Ridgeway, J. (1991, Apr. 28). A meeting with haters. *Parade*, p. 5.

Rim, S., Hansen, J., & Trope, Y. (2013). What happens why? Psychological distance and focusing on causes versus consequences of events. *Journal of Personality and Social Psychology, 104*(3), 457–472. doi:10.1037/a0031024

Ringelmann, M. (1913). Recherches sur les moteurs animés: Travail de l'homme. *Annales de l'Institute National Agronomique*, 2nd series, vol. xii, 1–40.

Rink, F. A., & Ellemers, N. (2009). Temporary versus permanent group membership: How the future prospects of newcomers affect newcomer acceptance and newcomer influence. *Personality and Social Psychology Bulletin, 35*, 764–775.

Rink, F., & Ellemers, N. (2010). Benefiting from deep-level diversity: How congruence between knowledge and decision rules improves team decision making and team perceptions. *Group Processes & Intergroup Relations, 13*, 345–359.

Rios, K. (2012). Minority opinions: Antecedents and benefits of expression. *Social and Personality Psychology Compass, 6*, 392–401.

Robberson, M. R., & Rogers, R. W. (1988). Beyond fear appeals: Negative and positive persuasive appeals to health and self esteem. *Journal of Applied Social Psychology, 18*, 277–287.

Robbins, J. M., & Krueger, J. I. (2005). Social projection to ingroup and outgroups: A review and meta-analysis. *Personality and Social Psychology Review, 9*, 32–47.

Robies, T. F., Slatcher, R. B., Trombello, J. M., & McGinn, M. M. (2014). Marital quality and health: A meta-analytic review. *Psychological Bulletin, 140*, 140–187.

Robinson, E., & Higgs, S. (2012). Liking food less: The impact of social influence on food liking evaluations in female students. *PLoS ONE, 7*, e48858.

Robinson, J., & McArthur, L. Z. (1982). Impact of salient vocal qualities on causal attribution for a speaker's behavior. *Journal of Personality and Social Psychology, 43*, 236–247.

Robinson, R. & Bell, W. (1978). Equality, success, and social justice in England and the United States. *American Sociological Review, 43*, 125–143.

Rochat, F., & Modigliani, A. (1995). The ordinary quality of resistance: From Milgram's laboratory to the village of Le Chambon. *Journal of Social Issues, 51*, 195–210.

Rocheleau, C. A. (2013). Organ donation intentions and behaviors: Application and extension of the theory of planned behavior. *Journal of Applied Social Psychology, 43*, 201–213.

Rodin, J., & Salovey, P. (1989). Health psychology. *Annual Review of Psychology, 40*, 533–579.

Rodin, M. J. (1987). Who is memorable to whom: A study of cognitive disregard. *Social Cognition, 5*, 144–165.

Roethlisberger, F. J., & Dickson, W. J. (1939). *Management and the worker*. Cambridge, MA: Harvard University Press.

Rogers, R. W. (1983). Cognitive and physiological processes in fear appeals and attitude change: A revised theory of protection motivation. In J. T. Cacioppo & R. E. Petty (Eds.), *Social psychophysiology: A sourcebook*. New York: Guilford Press.

Rogers, T. B. (1981). A model of the self as an aspect of the human information processing system. In N. Cantor & J. F. Kihlstrom (Eds.), *Personality, cognition, and social interaction* (pp. 193–214). Hillsdale, NJ: Lawrence Erlbaum Associates.

Rohrer, J. H., Baron, S. H., Hoffman, E. L., & Schwander, D. V. (1954). The stability of autokinetic judgments. *Journal of Abnormal and Social Psychology, 49*, 595–597.

Roisman, G. I., Clausell, E., Holland, A., Fortuna, K., & Elieff, C. (2008). Adult romantic relationships as contexts of human development: A multimethod comparison of same-sex couples with opposite-sex dating, engaged, and married dyads. *Developmental Psychology, 44*, 91–101.

Romer, D., Jamieson, K. H., & de Coteau, N. J. (1998). The treatment of persons of color in local television news: Ethnic blame discourse or realistic group conflict? *Communication Research, 25*, 286–305.

Ronay, R., Greenaway, K., Anicich, E. M., & Galinsky, A. D. (2012). The path to glory is paved with hierarchy: When hierarchical differentiation increases group effectiveness. *Psychological Science, 23*, 669–677.

Ronis, D. L., & Kaiser, M. K. (1989). Correlates of breast self-examination in a sample of college women: Analyses of linear structural relations. *Journal of Applied Social Psychology*.

Rook, K. S., & Peplau, L. A. (1982). Perspectives on helping the lonely. In L. A. Peplau & D. Perlman (Eds.), *Loneliness*. New York: Wiley Interscience.

Rosander, M., & Eriksson, O. (2012). Conformity on the Internet: The role of task difficulty and gender differences. *Computers in Human Behavior, 28*, 1587–1595.

Roseman, I. J., Spindel, M. S., & Jose, P. E. (1990). Appraisals of emotion-eliciting events: Testing a theory of discrete emotions. *Journal of Personality and Social Psychology, 59*, 899–915.

Rosenbaum, M. E. (1986). The repulsion hypothesis: On the nondevelopment of relationships. *Journal of Personality and Social Psychology, 51*, 1156–1166.

Rosenberg, M. (1956). Cognitive structure and attitudinal affect. *Journal of Abnormal and Social Psychology, 53*, 367–372.

Rosenberg, M. (1965). *Society and the adolescent self-image*. Princeton, NJ: Princeton University Press.

Rosenberg, M. (1969). The conditions and consequences of evaluation apprehension. In R. Rosenthal & R. L. Rosnow (Eds.), *Artifact in behavioral research* (pp. 279–349). New York: Academic Press.

Rosenberg, M. (1979). *Conceiving the self*. New York: Basic Books.

Rosenberg, M., & Simmons, R. B. (1971). *Black & white*

self-esteem: The urban school child. Washington, DC: The American Sociological Association.

Rosenberg, R. S., Baughman, S. L., & Bailenson, J. N. (2013). Virtual superheroes: Using superpowers in virtual reality to encourage prosocial behavior. *PLoS One, 8*.

Rosenberg, S., Nelson, C., & Vivekananthan, P. S. (1968). A multidimensional approach to the structure of personality impressions. *Journal of Personality and Social Psychology, 9*, 283–294.

Rosenfeld, P., Giacalone, R., & Tedeschi, J.T. (1984). Cognitive dissonances and impression management explanations for effort justification. *Personality and Social Psychology Bulletin, 10*, 394–401.

Rosenfield, D., and Stephan, W. G. (1981). Intergroup relations among children. In S. Brehm, S. Kassin, & F. Gibbons (Eds.), *Developmental social psychology* (pp. 271–297). New York: Oxford University Press.

Rosenhan, D. (1970). The natural socialization of altruistic autonomy. In J. Macaulay & L. Berkowitz (Eds.), *Altruism and helping behavior*. New York: Academic Press.

Rosenhan, D. L. (1973). On being sane in insane places. *Science, 179*, 250–258.

Rosenthal, R. (1969). Interpersonal expectations: Effects of the experimenter's hypothesis. In R. Rosenthal & R. L. Rosnow (Eds.), *Artifact in behavioral research* (pp. 181–277). New York: Academic Press.

Rosenthal, R. (1985). From unconscious experimenter bias to teacher expectancy effects. In J. B. Dusek, V. C. Hall, & W. J. Meyer (Eds.), *Teacher expectancies* (pp. 37–66). Hillsdale, NJ: Lawrence Erlbaum Associates.

Rosenthal, R. (1991). Meta-analysis: A review. *Psychosomatic Medicine, 53*, 247–271.

Rosenthal, R., & Fode, K. L. (1963). Three experiments in experimenter bias. *Psychological Reports, 12*, 491–511.

Rosenthal, R., & Jacobson, L. (1968). *Pygmalion in the classroom*. New York: Holt, Rinehart, & Winston.

Rosette, A. S., Leonardelli, G. J., & Phillips, K. W. (2008). The white standard: Racial bias in leader categorization. *Journal of Applied Psychology, 93*, 758–777.

Rosette, A. S., & Livingston, R. W. (2012). Failure is not an option for Black women: Effects of organizational performance on leaders with single versus dual-subordinate identities. *Journal of Experimental Social Psychology, 48*, 1162–1167.

Roskos-Ewoldsen, D. R., & Fazio, R. H. (1992). On the orienting value of attitudes: Attitude accessibility as a determinant of an object's attraction of visual attention. *Journal of Personality & Social Psychology, 63*, 198–211.

Ross, A. S., & Braband, J. (1973). Effect of increased responsibility on bystander intervention: II. The cue value of a blind person. *Journal of Personality and Social Psychology, 25*, 254–258.

Ross, L., Greene, D., & House, P. (1977). The "false consensus effect": An egocentric bias in social perception and attribution processes. *Journal of Experimental Social Psychology, 13*, 279–301.

Ross, L., Lepper, M. R., & Hubbard, M. (1975). Perseverance in self-perception and social perception: Biased attributional processes in the debriefing paradigm. *Journal of Personality and Social Psychology, 32*, 880–892.

Ross, L., & Nisbett, R. E. (1990). *The person and the situation*. New York: McGraw-Hill.

Ross, L. D., Amabile, T. M., & Steinmetz, J. L. (1977). Social roles, social control, and biases in social-perception processes. *Journal of Personality and Social Psychology, 35*, 485–494.

Ross, M., & Conway, M. (1986). Remembering one's own past: The construction of personal histories. In R. Sorrentino & E. T. Higgins (Eds.), *Handbook of motivation and cognition* (pp. 122–144). New York: Guilford Press.

Ross, M., & Sicoly, F. (1979). Egocentric biases in availability and attribution. *Journal of Personality and Social Psychology, 37*, 322–336.

Ross, M., McFarland, C., & Fletcher, G. J. O. (1981). The effect of attitude on recall of past histories. *Journal of Personality and Social Psychology, 40*, 627–634.

Ross, S. I., & Jackson, J. M. (1991). Teachers' expectations for black males' and black females' academic achievement. *Personality and Social Psychology Bulletin, 17*, 78–82.

Rosselli, F., Skelly, J. J., & Mackie, D. M. (1995). Processing rational and emotional messages: The cognitive and affective mediation of persuasion. *Journal of Experimental Social Psychology, 31*, 163–190.

Rothbart, M. (1981). Memory processes and social beliefs. In D. L. Hamilton (Ed.), *Cognitive processes in stereotyping and intergroup behavior* (pp. 145–182). Hillsdale, NJ: Erlbaum.

Rothbart, M., Dawes, R., & Park, B. (1984). Stereotyping and sampling biases in intergroup perception. In J. R. Eiser (Ed.), *Attitudinal judgment* (pp. 109–134). New York: Springer-Verlag.

Rothbart, M., Evans, M., & Fulero, S. (1979). Recall for confirming events: Memory processes and the maintenance of social stereotyping. *Journal of Experimental Social Psychology, 15*, 343–355.

Rothbart, M., Fulero, S., Jensen, C., Howard, J., & Birrel, P. (1978). From individual to group impressions: Availability heuristics in stereotype formation. *Journal of Experimental Social Psychology, 14*, 237–255.

Rothbart, M., & Hallmark, W. (1988). In-group-out-group differences in the perceived efficacy of coercion and conciliation in resolving social conflict. *Journal of Personality and Social Psychology, 55*, 248–257.

Rothbart, M., & John, O. P. (1985). Social categorization and behavioral episodes: A cognitive analysis of the effects of intergroup contact. *Journal of Social Issues, 41*, 81–104.

Rothbart, M., & Park, B. (1986). On the confirmability and disconfirmability of trait concepts. *Journal of Personality and Social Psychology, 50*, 131–142.

Rothenberg, R. (1991, July 23). Blacks are found to be still scarce in advertisements in major magazines. *The New York Times*, p. A7.

Rozin, P., & Royzman, E. B. (2001). Negativity bias, negativity dominance, and contagion. *Personality and Social Psychology Review, 5,* 296–320.

Rubin, J. Z. (1980). Experimental research on third-party intervention in conflict: Toward some generalizations. *Psychological Bulletin, 87,* 379–391.

Rubin, J. Z., & Brown, B. R. (1975). *The social psychology of bargaining and negotiation.* New York:Academic Press.

Rubin, M. (2012). Current problems and resolutions: Group status is related to group prototypicality in the absence of social identity concerns. *Journal of Social Psychology, 152,* 386–389.

Rubin, M., & Hewstone, M. (1998). Social identity theory's self-esteem hypothesis: A review and some suggestions for clarification. *Personality and Social Psychology Review, 2,* 40–62.

Rubin, Z. (1970). Measurement of romantic love. *Journal of Personality and Social Psychology, 16,* 265–273.

Rubin, Z., Hill, C. T., Peplau, L. A., & Dunkel-Schetter, C. (1980). Self-disclosure in dating couples: Sex roles and the ethic of openness. *Journal of Marriage and the Family, 42,* 305–317.

Rucker, D. D., & Petty, R. E. (2004). When resistance is futile: Consequences of failed counterarguing for attitude certainty. *Journal of Personality & Social Psychology, 86,* 219–235.

Rudman, L. A. (2005). Rejection of women? Beyond prejudice as antipathy. In J. F. Dovidio, P. Glic, & L. A. Rudman (Eds.), *On the nature of prejudice: Fifty years after Allport* (pp. 106–120). Malden, MA: Blackwell.

Rudman, L. A., & Bordiga, E. (1995). The afterglow of construct accessibility: The behavioral consequences of priming men to view women as sexual objects. *Journal of Experimental Social Psychology, 31,* 493–517.

Rule, N. O., & Ambady, N. (2008). Inferences from chief executive officers' appearance predict company profits. *Psychological Science, 19,* 109–111.

Rule, N. O., Krendl, A. C., Ivcevic, Z., & Ambady, N. (2013). Accuracy and consensus in judgments of trustworthiness from faces: Behavioral and neural correlates. *Journal of Personality and Social Psychology, 104*(3), 409–426. doi:10.1037/a0031050

Runciman, W. G. (1966). *Relative deprivation and social justice.* Berkeley, CA: University of California Press.

Rusbult, C. E. (1983). A longitudinal test of the investment model: The development (and deterioration) of satisfaction and commitment in heterosexual involvements. *Journal of Personality and Social Psychology, 45,* 101–117.

Rusbult, C. E., Arriaga, X. B., & Agnew, C. R. (2001). Interdependence in close relationships. In G. J. O. Fletcher & M. S. Clark (Eds.), *Blackwell handbook of social psychology,* vol. 2: *Interpersonal processes* (pp. 359–387). Oxford: Blackwell.

Rusbult, C. E., Martz, J. M., & Agnew, C. R. (1998). The Investment Model Scale: Measuring commitment level, satisfaction level, quality of alternatives, and investment size. *Personal Relationships, 5,* 357–391.

Rusbult, C. E., Van Lange, P. A. M., Wildschut, T., Yovetich, N. A., & Verette, J. (2000). Perceived superiority in close relationships: Why it exists and persists. *Journal of Personality and Social Psychology, 79,* 521–545.

Rusbult, C. E., Verette, J., Whitney, G. A., Slovik, L. F., & Lipkus, I. (1991). Accommodation processes in close relationships: Theory and preliminary empirical evidence. *Journal of Personality and Social Psychology, 60,* 53–78.

Rusbult, C. E., Yovetich, N. A., & Verette, J. (1996). An interdependence analysis of accommodation processes. In G. J. O. Fletcher & J. Fitness (Eds.), *Knowledge structures in close relationships: A social psychological approach* (pp. 63–90). Mahwah, NJ: Erlbaum.

Rushton, J. P., & Bons, T. A. (2005). Mate choice and friendship in twins: Evidence for genetic similarity. *Psychological Science, 16,* 555–559.

Ruskin, J. (1907/1963). *The seven lamps of architecture.* London: Everyman's Library.

Russell, C. A. (2002). Investigating the effectiveness of product placements in television shows: The role of modality and plot connection congruence on brand memory and attitude. *Journal of Consumer Research, 29,* 306–318.

Russell, J. A. (1994). Is there universal recognition of emotion from facial expressions? A review of the cross-cultural studies. *Psychological Bulletin, 115,* 102–141.

Russell, J. A. (2003). Core affect and the psychological construction of emotion. *Psychological Review, 110,* 145–172.

Russock, H. I. (2011). An evolutionary interpretation of the effect of gender and sexual orientation on human mate selection preferences, as indicated by an analysis of personal advertisements. *Behaviour, 148,* 307–323.

Rutchick, A. M. (2010). Deus ex machina: The influence of polling place on voting behavior. *Political Psychology, 31,* 209–225.

Rutter, D. R., & Robinson, B. (1981). An experimental analysis of teaching by telephone. In G. M. Stephenson & J. H. Davis (Eds.), *Progress in applied social psychology* (vol. 1, pp. 345–374). New York: Wiley.

Ryan, C. S. (1996). Accuracy of black and white college students' in-group and out-group stereotypes. *Personality and Social Psychology Bulletin, 22,* 1114–1127.

Ryan, C. S., & Bogart, L. M. (1997). Development of new group members' in-group and out-group stereotypes: Changes in perceived group variability and ethnocentrism. *Journal of Personality and Social Psychology, 73,* 719–732.

Ryan, R. M., & Grolnick, W. S. (1986). Origins and pawns in the classroom: Self-report and projective assessments of individual differences in children's perceptions. *Journal of Personality and Social Psychology, 50,* 550–558.

Rydell, R. J., & McConnell, A. R. (2010). Consistency and inconsistency in implicit social cognition: The case of implicit and explicit measures of attitudes. In B. Gawronski & B. K. Payne (Eds.), *Handbook of implicit social cognition: Measurement, theory, and applications* (pp. 295–310). New York: Guilford Press.

Rydell, R. J., McConnell, A. R., & Beilock, S. L. (2009). Multiple social identities and stereotype threat: Imbalance, accessibility, and working memory. *Journal of Personality & Social Psychology, 96*, 949–966.

Ryen, A. H., & Kahn, A. (1975). The effects of intergroup orientation on group attitudes and proxemic behavior. *Journal of Personality and Social Psychology, 31*, 302–310.

Sachdev, I., & Bourhis, R. Y. (1985). Social cateogrization and power differentials in group relations. *European Journal of Social Psychology, 15*, 415–434.

Sachdev, I., & Bourhis, R. Y. (1991). Power and status differentials in minority and majority group relations. *European Journal of Social Psychology, 21*, 1–24.

Sadri, G., & Lees, B. (2001). Developing corporate culture as a competitive advantage. *Journal of Management Development, 20*, 853–859.

Safire, W. (1992, Aug. 27). God bless us. *The New York Times*, p. A15.

Sagar, H. A., & Schofield, J. W. (1980). Racial and behavioral cues in black and white children's perceptions of ambiguously aggressive acts. *Journal of Personality and Social Psychology, 39*, 590–598.

Sagarin, B. J., Cialdini, R. B., Rice, W. E., & Serna, S. B. (2002). Dispelling the illusion of invulnerability: The motivations and mechanisms of resistance to persuasion. *Journal of Personality & Social Psychology, 83*, 526–541.

Sagi, A., & Friedland, N. (2007). The cost of richness: The effect of the size and diversity of decision sets on post-decision regret. *Journal of Personality and Social Psychology, 93*, 515–524.

Saguy, T., Tausch, N., Dovidio, J. F., & Pratto, F. (2009). The irony of harmony: Intergroup contact can produce false expectations for equality. *Psychological Science, 20*, 114–121.

Said, C. P., & Todorov, A. (2011). A statistical model of facial attractiveness. *Psychological Science, 22*, 1183–1190.

Sakai, H. (1999). A multiplicative power-function model of cognitive dissonance: Toward an integrated theory of cognition, emotion, and behavior after Leon Festinger. In E. Harmon-Jones, & J. Mills (Eds.), *Cognitive dissonance: Progress on a pivotal theory in social psychology* (pp. 267–294). Washington, DC: American Psychological Association.

Salancik, G. R., & Conway, M. (1975). Attitude inference from salient and relevant cognitive content about behavior. *Journal of Personality and Social Psychology, 32*, 829–840.

Salas, E., Nichols, D. R., & Driskell, J. E. (2007). Testing three team training strategies in intact teams: A meta-analysis. *Small Group Research, 38*, 471–488.

Salas, E., Wilson, K. A., Burke, C. S., & Wightman, D. C. (2006). Does crew resource management training work? An update, an extension, and some critical needs. *Human Factors, 48*, 392–412.

Salganik, M. J., Dodds, P. S., & Watts, D. J. (2006). Experimental study of inequality and unpredictability in an artificial cultural market. *Science, 311*, 854–856.

Salmon, C. A., & Shackelford, T. K. (Eds.) (2007). *Family relationships: An evolutionary perspective*. New York: Oxford University Press.

Salovey, P., & Rodin, J. (1984). Some antecedents and consequences of social-comparison jealousy. *Journal of Personality and Social Psychology, 47*, 780–792.

Salovey, P., & Rodin, J. (1989). Envy and jealousy in close relationships. In C. Hendrick (Ed.), *Close relationships* (pp. 221–246). Beverly Hills, CA: Sage.

Salovey, P., Rothman, A. J., & Rodin, J. (1998). Health behavior. In D. T. Gilbert, S. T. Fiske, & G. Lindzey (Eds.), *Handbook of social psychology* (4th ed., vol. 2, pp. 633–683). Boston: McGraw-Hill.

Salwen, J. K., & O'Leary, K. D. (2013). Adjustment problems and maladaptive relational style: A mediational model of sexual coercion in intimate relationships. *Journal of Interpersonal Violence, 28*, 1969–1988.

Samuelson, C. D. (1991). Perceived task difficulty, causal attributions, and preferences for structural change in resource dilemmas. *Personality and Social Psychology Bulletin, 17*, 181–187. doi:10.1177/ 014616729101700210

Samuelson, C. D., Messick, D. M., Rutte, C. G., & Wilke, H. (1984). Individual and structural solutions to resource dilemmas in two cultures. *Journal of Personality and Social Psychology, 47*, 94–104.

Sande, G. N., Goethals, G. R., & Radloff, C. E. (1988). Perceiving one's own traits and others': The multifaceted self. *Journal of Personality and Social Psychology, 54*, 13–20.

Sanitioso, R., Kunda, Z., & Fong, G. T. (1990). Motivated recruitment of autobiographical memory. *Journal of Personality and Social Psychology, 59*, 229–241.

Sanna, L. J., & Shotland, R. L. (1990). Valence of anticipated evaluation and social facilitation. *Journal of Experimental Social Psychology, 26*, 82–92.

Saslow, L. R., Willer, R., Feinberg, M., Piff, P. K., Clark, K., Keltner, D., & Saturn, S. R. (2013). My brother's keeper?: Compassion predicts generosity more among less religious individuals. *Social Psychological and Personality Science, 4*(1), 31–38. doi:10.1177/1948550612444137

Sassenberg, K. & Boos, M. (2003). Attitude change in computer-mediated communication: Effects of anonymity and category norms. *Group Processes Intergroup Relations, 6*, 405–422.

Sassenberg, K., Matschke, C., & Scholl, A. (2011). The impact of discrepancies from ingroup norms on group members' well-being and motivation. *European Journal of Social Psychology, 41*, 886–897.

Sato, K. (1987). Distribution of the cost of maintaining common resources. *Journal of Experimental Social Psychology, 23*, 19–31.

Sattler, D. N., & Kerr, N. L. (1991). Might versus morality explored: Motivational and cognitive bases for social motives. *Journal of Personality and Social Psychology, 60*, 756–765.

Sauter, D. A., Eisner, F., Ekman, P., & Scott, S. K. (2010). Cross-cultural recognition of basic emotions through nonverbal emotional vocalizations. *Proceedings of the National Academy of Sciences, 107*, 2408–2412.

Saxe, L., Dougherty, D., & Cross, T. (1985). The validity of polygraph testing: Scientific analysis and public controversy. *American Psychologist, 40*, 355–366.

Schachter, S. (1951). Deviation, rejection and communication. *Journal of Abnormal and Social Psychology, 46*, 190–207.

Schachter, S. (1959). *The psychology of affiliation.* Stanford, CA: Stanford University Press.

Schachter, S., & Singer, J. (1962). Cognitive, social, and physiological determinants of the emotional state. *Psychological Review, 69*, 379–399.

Schaller, M., & Cialdini, R. B. (1988). The economics of empathic helping: Support for a mood management motive. *Journal of Experimental Social Psychology, 24*, 163–181.

Schaller, M., & Cialdini, R. B. (1990). Happiness, sadness, and helping: A motivational integration. In E. T. Higgins & R. M. Sorrentino (Eds.), *Handbook of motivation and cognition* (vol. 2, pp. 265–296). New York: Guilford.

Scheib, J. E., Gangestad, S. W., & Thornhill, R. (1999). Facial attractiveness, symmetry, and cues of good genes. *Proceedings of the Royal Society B, 266*, 1913–1917.

Scheier, M. F., & Carver, C. S. (1977). Self-focused attention and the experience of emotion: Attraction, repulsion, elation, and depression. *Journal of Personality and Social Psychology, 35*, 625–636.

Schein, V. E., Mueller, R., Lituchy, T., & Liu, J. (1996). Think manager-think male: A global phenomenon? *Journal of Organizational Behavior, 17*, 33–41.

Scheinkman, M., & Werneck, D. (2010). Disarming jealousy in couples relationships: A multidimensional approach. *Family Process, 49*, 486–502.

Schell, T. L., Klein, S. B. & Babey, S. H. (1996). Testing a hierarchical model of self-knowledge. *Psychological Science, 7*, 170–173.

Schifrin, N. (2012, December 19). Will lessons from Down Under stem the undertaker here? *ABC News.* Retrieved from http://abcnews.go.com

Schiller, J. C. F. (1882). *Essays, esthetical and philosophical, including the dissertation on the "Connexions between the animal and the spiritual in man."* London: Bell.

Schlenker, B. R. (1985). Identity and self-identification. In B. R. Schlenker (Ed.), *The self and social life* (pp. 65–100). New York: McGraw-Hill.

Schlenker, B.R., & Forsyth, D.R. (1977). On the ethics of psychological research. *Journal of Experimental Social Psychology, 13*, 369–396.

Schmader, T., & Johns, M. (2003). Converging evidence that stereotype threat reduces working memory capacity. *Journal of Personality and Social Psychology, 85*(3), 440–452.

Schmader, T., Johns, M., & Forbes, C. (2008). An integrated process model of stereotype threat effects on performance. *Psychological Review, 115*, 336–356.

Schmalz, J. (1992, Oct. 11). Gay politics goes mainstream. *The New York Times Magazine*, pp. 18–21, 29, 41.

Schmeichel, B. J., & Vohs, K. (2009). Self-affirmation and self-control: Affirming core values counteracts ego depletion. *Journal of Personality & Social Psychology, 96*, 770–782.

Schmid Mast, M. (2010). Interpersonal behaviour and social perception in a hierarchy: The interpersonal power and behaviour model. *European Review of Social Psychology, 21*, 1–33.

Schmidt, M. F. H., & Tomasello, M. (2012). Young children enforce social norms. *Current Directions in Psychological Science, 21*, 232–236.

Schmidt, W. E. (1990, Dec. 13). White men get better deals on cars, study finds. *The New York Times.*

Schmitt, B. H., Gilovich, T., Goore, N., & Joseph, L. (1986). Mere presence and social facilitation: One more time. *Journal of Experimental Social Psychology, 22*, 242–248.

Schmitt, D. P., Alcalay, L., Allik, J., Ault, L., Austers, I., Bennett, K. L., . . . Zupanèiè, A. (2003). Universal sex differences in the desire for sexual variety: Tests from 52 nations, 6 continents, and 13 islands. *Journal of Personality and Social Psychology, 85*, 85–104.

Schmitt, D. P., Jonason, P. K., Byerley, G. J., Flores, S. D., Illbeck, B. E., O'Leary, K. N., & Qudrat, A. (2012). A reexamination of sex differences in sexuality: New studies reveal old truths. *Current Directions in Psychological Science, 21*, 135–139.

Schmitt, M. T., & Branscombe, N. R. (2001). The good, the bad, and the manly: Threats to one's prototypicality and evaluations of fellow in-group members. *Journal of Experimental Social Psychology, 37*(6), 510–517.

Schmutte, G. T., & Taylor, S. P. (1980). Physical aggression as a function of alcohol and pain feedback. *Journal of Social Psychology, 110*, 235–244.

Schnall, S., Benton, J., & Harvey, S. (2008). With a clean conscience: Cleanliness reduces the severity of moral judgments. *Psychological Science, 19*, 1219–1222.

Schneider, D. J. (1973). Implicit personality theory: A review. *Psychological Bulletin, 79*, 294–309.

Schneider, I. K., Eerland, A., van Harreveld, F., Rotteveel, M., van der Pligt, J., van der Stoep, N., & Zwaan, R. A. (2013). One way and the other: The bidirectional relationship between ambivalence and body movement. *Psychological Science, 24*, 319–325.

Schoenrade, P. A., Batson, C. D., & Brandt, J. R. (1986). Attachment, accountability, and motivation to benefit another not in distress. *Journal of Personality and Social Psychology, 51*, 557–563.

Schofield, J. W. (1986). Causes and consequences of the colorblind perspective. In J. F. Dovidio & S. L. Gaertner (Eds.), *Prejudice, discrimination, and racism* (pp. 231–254). Orlando, FL: Academic Press.

Scholten, L., van Knippenberg, D., Nijstad, B. A., & De Dreu, C. K. W. (2007). Motivated information processing and group decision-making: Effects of process accountability on information processing and decision quality. *Journal of Experimental Social Psychology, 43,* 539–552.

Schopler, J., Insko, C. A., Graetz, K. A., Drigotas, S., Smith, V. A., & Dahl, K. (1993). Individual-group discontinuity: Further evidence for mediation by fear and greed. *Personality and Social Psychology Bulletin, 19,* 419–431.

Schrift, R. Y., & Parker, J. R. (2014). Staying the course: The option of doing nothing and its impact on post-choice persistence, *Psychological Science, 25,* 772–780.

Schroeder, D. A., and others. (1983). The actions of others as determinants of behavior in social trap situations. *Journal of Experimental Social Psychology, 19,* 522–539.

Schubert, T. W. (2005). Your highness: Vertical positions as perceptual symbols of power. *Journal of Personality and Social Psychology, 89,* 1–21.

Schug, J., Yuki, M., & Maddux, W. (2010). Relational mobility explains between- and within-culture differences in self-disclosure to close friends. *Psychological Science, 21,* 1471–1478.

Schulz-Hardt, S., Mojzisch, A., & Vogelgesang, F. (2008). Dissent as a facilitator: Individual- and group-level effects on creativity and performance. In C. K. W. De Dreu & M. J. Gelfand (Eds.), *The psychology of conflict and conflict management in organizations* (pp. 149–177). New York, NY: Lawrence Erlbaum Associates.

Schuster, J. R. (1985). Compensation plan design. *Management Review,* May, 21–25.

Schwartz, S. H. (1977). Normative influences on altruism. In L. Berkowitz (Ed.), *Advances in experimental social psychology* (vol. 10, pp. 221–279). New York: Academic Press.

Schwartz, S. H., & Gotleib, A. (1980). Bystander anonymity and reaction to emergencies. *Journal of Personality and Social Psychology, 39,* 418–430.

Schwarz, N. (1999). Self-reports: How the questions shape the answers. *American Psychologist, 54,* 93–105.

Schwarz, N., Bless, H., & Bohner, G. (1991). Mood and persuasion: Affective states influence processing of persuasive communications. In M. P. Zanna (Ed.), *Advances in experimental social psychology* (vol. 24, pp. 161–199). San Diego, CA: Academic Press.

Schwarz, N., & Clore, G. L. (1983). Mood, misattribution, and judgments of well-being: Informative and directive functions of affective states. *Journal of Personality and Social Psychology, 45,* 513–523.

Schwarz, N., & Clore, G. L. (1988). How do I feel about it? Informative functions of affective states. In K. Fiedler & J. Forgas (Eds.), *Affect, cognition, and social behavior* (pp. 44–62). Toronto: Hogrefe.

Schwarz, N., Groves, R. M., & Schuman, H. (1998). Survey methods. In D. T. Gilbert, S. T Fiske., & G. Lindzey (Eds.), *The handbook of social psychology* (143–189). New York: McGraw-Hill.

Schwarzer, R., & Leppin, A. (1989). Social support and health: A meta-analysis. *Psychology and Health, 3,* 1–15.

Scott, K. A., & Brown, D. J. (2006). Female first, leader second? Gender bias in the encoding of leadership behavior. *Organizational Behavior and Human Decision Processes, 101,* 230–242.

Sczesny, S. & Kühnen, U. (2004). Meta-cognition about biological sex and gender-stereotypic physical appearance: Consequences for the assessment of leadership competence. *Personality and Social Psychology Bulletin, 30,* 13–21.

Sear, R., & Marlowe, F. W. (2009). How universal are human mate choices? Size does not matter when Hadza foragers are choosing a mate. *Biology Letters, 5,* 606–609.

Sears, D. O., (1988). Symbolic racism. In P. Katz & D. Taylor (Eds.), *Eliminating racism: Profiles in controversy* (pp. 53–84). New York: Plenum.

Sears, D. O., & McConahay, J. B. (1973). *The politics of violence: The new urban blacks and the Watts riot.* Boston: Houghton Mifflin.

Sedek, G., & Kofta, M. (1990). When cognitive exertion does not yield cognitive gain: Toward an informational explanation of learned helplessness. *Journal of Personality and Social Psychology, 58,* 729–743.

Sedikides, C., Gaertner, L., & Toguchi, Y. (2003). Pancultural self-enhancement. *Journal of Personality and Social Psychology, 84,* 60–79.

Sedikides, C., Gaertner, L., & Vevea, J. L. (2005). Pancultural self-enhancement reloaded: A meta-analytic reply to Heine (2005). *Journal of Personality & Social Psychology, 89,* 539–551.

Sedikides, C., Gaertner, L., & Vevea, J. L. (2007). Evaluating the evidence for pancultural self-enhancement. *Asian Journal of Social Psychology, 10,* 201–203.

Sedikides, C., & Skowronski, J. J. (1993). The self in impression formation: Trait centrality and social perception. *Journal of Experimental Social Psychology, 29,* 347–357.

See, Y. H. M., Petty, R. E., & Fabrigar, R. L. (2013). Affective–cognitive meta-bases versus structural bases of attitudes predict processing interest versus efficiency. *Personality and Social Psychology Bulletin, 39,* 1111–1123.

Segal, M. W. (1974). Alphabet and attraction: An unobtrusive measure of the effect of propinquity in a field setting. *Journal of Personality and Social Psychology, 30,* 654–657.

Seidel, M.-D. L., Polzer, J. T., & Stewart, K. J. (2000). Friends in high places: The effects of social networks on discrimination in salary negotiations. *Administrative Science Quarterly, 45,* 1–24.

Sekaquaptewa, D., Waldman, A., & Thompson, M. (2007). Solo status and self-construal: Being distinctive influences racial self-construal and performance apprehension in African American women. *Cultural Diversity and Ethnic Minority Psychology, 13*(4), 321–327. doi:http://dx.doi. org/10.1037/1099-9809.13.4.321

Selfhout, M., Denissen, J., Branje, S., & Meeus, W. (2009). In the eye of the beholder: Perceived, actual, and peer-rated similarity in personality, communication, and friendship intensity during the acquaintanceship process. *Journal of Personality and Social Psychology, 96,* 1152–1165.

Seligman, C. L., Becker, J., & Darley, J. M. (1981). Encouraging residential energy conservation through feedback. In A. Baum & J. Singer (Eds.), *Advances in environmental psychology* (vol. 3, pp. 53–91). Hillsdale, NJ: Lawrence Erlbaum Associates.

Seligman, M. E. P. (1975). *On depression, development, and death.* San Francisco: Freeman.

Seligman, M. E. P., & Maier, S. F. (1967). Failure to escape traumatic shock. *Journal of Experimental Psychology, 74,* 1–9.

Sell, J., Lovaglia, M. J., Mannix, E. A., Samuelson, C. D., & Wilson, R. K. (2004). Investigating conflict, power, and status within and among groups. *Small Group Research, 35,* 44–72.

Sénémeaud, C., & Somat, A. (2009). Dissonance arousal and persistence in attitude change. *Swiss Journal of Psychology, 68,* 25–31.

Senneker, P., & Hendrick, C. (1983). Androgyny and helping behavior. *Journal of Personality and Social Psychology, 45,* 916–925.

Sexton, J. D., & Pennebaker, J. W. (2009). The healing powers of expressive writing. In S. B. Kaufman & J. C. Kaufman (Eds.), *The psychology of creative writing* (pp. 264–273). New York: Cambridge University Press.

Seyranian, V., Atuel, H., & Crano, W. D. (2008). Dimensions of majority and minority groups. *Group Processes & Intergroup Relations, 11,* 21–37.

Shackelford, T. K., Schmitt, D. P., & Buss, D. M. (2005). Universal dimensions of human mate preferences. *Personality and Individual Differences, 39,* 447–458.

Shamir, B., House, R. J., & Arthur, M. B. (1993). The motivational effects of charismatic leadership: A self-concept based theory. *Organization Science, 4,* 577–594.

Shanab, M. E., & Yahra, K. A. (1977). A behavioral study of obedience in children. *Journal of Personality and Social Psychology, 35,* 530–536.

Shariff, A. F., & Norenzayan, A. (2007). God is watching you: Priming God concepts increases prosocial behavior in an anonymous economic game. *Psychological Science, 18,* 803–809.

Sharot, T., Fleming, S. M., Yu, X., Koster, R., & Dolan, R. J. (2012). Is choice-induced preference change long lasting? *Psychological Science, 23,* 1123–1129.

Sharpsteen, D. J., & Kirkpatrick, L. A. (1997). Romantic jealousy and adult romantic attachment. *Journal of Personality and Social Psychology, 72,* 627–640.

Shaver, P., & Hazan, C. (1985). Incompatibility, loneliness, and "limerence." In W. Ickes (Ed.), *Compatible and incompatible relationships* (pp. 163–186). New York: Springer-Verlag.

Shaver, P., Schwartz, J., Kirson, D., & O'Connor, C. (1987). Emotion knowledge: Further exploration of a prototype approach. *Journal of Personality and Social Psychology, 52,* 1061–1086.

Shaver, P. R., & Mikulincer, M. (2009). Attachment styles. In M. R. Leary & R. H. Hoyle (Eds.), *Handbook of individual differences in social behavior* (pp. 62–81). New York: Guilford Press.

Shavitt, S., Lee, A. Y., & Johnson, T. P. (2008). Cross-cultural consumer psychology. In C. P. Haugtvedt, P. M. Herr, & F. R. Kardes (Eds.), *Handbook of consumer psychology* (vol. 4, pp. 1103–1131). New York: Lawrence Erlbaum Associates.

Shavitt, S., & Nelson, M. R. (2000). The social-identity function in person perception: Communicated meanings of product preferences. In G. R. Maio & J. M. Olson (Eds.), *Why we evaluate: Functions of attitudes* (pp. 37–57). Mahwah, NJ: Lawrence Erlbaum Associates.

Shaw, M. E. (1976). *Group dynamics: The psychology of small group behavior* (2nd ed.). New York: McGraw-Hill.

Sheeran, P. (2002). Intention–behavior relations: A conceptual and empirical review. *European Review of Social Psychology, 12,* 1–36.

Shen, H., Wan, F., & Wyer, R. S. (2011). Cross-cultural differences in the refusal to accept a small gift: The differential influence of reciprocity norms on Asians and North Americans. *Journal of Personality and Social Psychology, 100,* 271–281.

Sheppard, B. H., Hartwick, J., Warshaw, P. R. (1988). The theory of reasoned action: A meta-analysis of past research with recommendations for modifications and future research. *Journal of Consumer Research, 15,* 325–343.

Sherif, C. W. (1979). Bias in psychology. In J. A. Sherman & E. T. Beck (Eds.), *The prism of sex: Essays in the sociology of knowledge* (pp. 93–133). Madison, WI: University of Wisconsin Press.

Sherif, M. (1936). *The psychology of social norms.* New York: Harper.

Sherif, M. (1966). *In common predicament: Social psychology of intergroup conflict and cooperation.* Boston: Houghton-Mifflin.

Sherif, M., Harvey, O. J., White, B. J., Hood, W. E., & Sherif, C. W. (1961). *Intergroup conflict and cooperation: The Robbers Cave experiment.* Norman, OK: University of Oklahoma Press/Book Exchange.

Sherif, M., & Sherif, C. W. (1953). *Groups in harmony and tension.* New York: Harper.

Sherman, D. K., Gangi, C., & White, M. L. (2010). Embodied cognition and health persuasion: Facilitating intention-behavior consistency via motor manipulations. *Journal of Experimental Social Psychology, 46,* 461–464.

Sherman, J. W., Gawronski, B., Gonsalkorale, K., Hugenberg, K., Allen, T. J., & Groom, C. J. (2008). The self-regulation of automatic associations and behavioral impulses. *Psychological Review, 115,* 314–335.

Sherman, J. W., & Klein, S. B. (1994). Development and representation of personality impressions. *Journal of Personality and Social Psychology, 67,* 972–983.

Sherman, P. W. (1977). Nepotism and the evolution of alarm calls. *Science, 197,* 1246–1253.

Shields, A., & Cicchetti, D. (1998). Reactive aggression among maltreated children: The contributions of attention and emotion dysregulation. *Journal of Clinical Child Psychology*, 27(4), 381–395.

Shih, M., Pittinsky, T. L., & Ambady, N. (1999). Stereotype susceptibility: Identity salience and shifts in quantitative performance. *Psychological Science*, 10, 80–83.

Shils, E. A., & Janowitz, M. (1948). Cohesion and disintegration in the Wehrmacht in World War II. *Public Opinion Quarterly*, 12, 280–315.

Shook, N. J., & Fazio, R. H. (2008). Interracial roommate relationships: An experimental field test of the contact hypothesis. *Psychological Science*, 19, 717–723.

Shotland, R. L., & Heinold, W. D. (1985). Bystander response to arterial bleeding: Helping skills, the decision-making process, and differentiating the helping response. *Journal of Personality and Social Psychology*, 49, 347–356.

Shotland, R. L., & Straw, M. K. (1976). Bystander response to an assault: When a man attacks a woman. *Journal of Personality and Social Psychology*, 34, 990–999.

Showers, C. (1992). Compartmentalization of positive and negative self-knowledge: Keeping bad apples out of the bunch. *Journal of Personality and Social Psychology*, 62, 1036–1049.

Shu, L. L., Gino, F., & Bazerman, M. H. (2011). Dishonest deed, clear conscience: When cheating leads to moral disengagement and motivated forgetting. *Personality & Social Psychology Bulletin*, 37, 330–349.

Sia, T. L., Lord, C. G., Blessum, K. A., Ratcliff, C. D., & Lepper, M. R. (1997). Is a rose always a rose? The role of social category exemplar change in attitude stability and attitude-behavior consistency. *Journal of Personality and Social Psychology*, 72, 501–514.

Sieverding, M., Decker, S., & Zimmermann, F. (2010). Information about low participation in cancer screening demotivates other people. *Psychological Science*, 21, 941–943.

Sieverding, M., Matterne, U., & Ciccarello, L. (2010). What role do social norms play in the context of men's cancer screening intention and behavior? Application of an extended theory of planned behavior. *Health Psychology*, 29, 72–81.

Signorielli, N. (2009). Minorities representation in prime time: 2000 to 2008. *Communication Research Reports*, 26, 323–336.

Silka, L. (1989). *Intuitive judgments of change*. New York: Springer-Verlag.

Silver, M., & Geller, D. (1978). On the irrelevance of evil: The organization and individual action. *Journal of Social Issues*, 34, 125–136.

Silverstein, L. (1965). *Defense of the poor in criminal cases in American state courts*. Chicago: American Bar Foundation.

Simon, B. (1992). The perception of ingroup and outgroup homogeneity: Reintroducing the intergroup context. In W. Stroebe & M. Hewstone (Eds.), *European Review of Social Psychology* (vol. 3, pp. 1–30). Chichester: John Wiley & Sons.

Simon, B. (1998). Individuals, groups, and social change: On the relationship between individual and collective self-interpretations and collective action. In C. Sedikides & J. Schopler (Eds.), *Intergroup cognition and intergroup behavior* (pp. 257–282). Mahwah, NJ: Lawrence Erlbaum Associates, Inc.

Simon, B., & Brown, R. (1987). Perceived homogeneity in minority-majority contexts. *Journal of Personality and Social Psychology*, 53, 703–711.

Simon, B., Loewy, M., Sturmer, S., Weber, U., Freytag, P., Habig, C., Kampmeier, C., & S. Pahlinger, P. (1998). Collective identification and social movement participation. *Journal of Personality and Social Psychology*, 74, 646–658.

Simon, H. A. (1990). A mechanism for social selection and successful altruism. *Science*, 250, 1665–1668.

Simon, S., & Hoyt, C. L. (2013). Exploring the effect of media images on women's leadership self-perceptions and aspirations. *Group Processes & Intergroup Relations*, 16, 232–245.

Simons, M. (1992, Mar. 17). North-South chasm is threatening search for environmental solutions. *The New York Times*, A5.

Simpson, J. A. (1987). The dissolution of romantic relationships: Factors involved in relationship stability and emotional distress. *Journal of Personality and Social Psychology*, 53, 683–692.

Simpson, J. A. (1990). Influence of attachment styles on romantic relationships. *Journal of Personality and Social Psychology*, 59, 971–980.

Simpson, J. A., Campbell, B., & Berscheid, E. (1986). The association between romantic love and marriage: Kephart (1967) twice revisited. *Personality and Social Psychology Bulletin*, 12, 363–372.

Simpson, J. A., Gangestad, S. W., & Lerma, M. (1990). Perception of physical attractiveness: Mechanisms involved in the maintenance of romantic relationships. *Journal of Personality and Social Psychology*, 59, 1192–1201.

Simpson, J. A., Ickes, W., & Blackstone, T. (1995). When the head protects the heart: Empathic accuracy in dating relationships. *Journal of Personality and Social Psychology*, 69, 629–641.

Simpson, J. A., Rholes, W. S., & Nelligan, J. S. (1992). Support seeking and support giving within couples in an anxiety-provoking situation: The role of attachment styles. *Journal of Personality and Social Psychology*, 62, 434–446.

Simpson, J. A., Rholes, W. S., & Phillips, D. (1996). Conflict in close relationships: An attachment perspective. *Journal of Personality and Social Psychology*, 71, 899–914.

Sinaceur, M., Thomas-Hunt, M. C., Neale, M. A., O'Neill, O. A., & Haag, C. (2010). Accuracy and perceived expert status in group decisions: When minority members make majority members more accurate privately. *Personality and Social Psychology Bulletin*, 36, 423–437.

Singelis, T. M. (1994). The measurement of independent and interdependent self-construals. *Personality and Social Psychology Bulletin*, 20(5), 580–591.

Singer, J. L., & Singer, D. G. (1981). *Television, imagination, and aggression: A study of preschoolers*. Hillsdale, NJ: Lawrence Erlbaum Associates.

Singh, R., Yeo, S. E.-L., Lin, P. K. F., & Tan, L. (2007). Multiple mediators of the attitude similarity-attraction relationship: Dominance of inferred attraction and subtlety of affect. *Basic and Applied Social Psychology, 29*, 61–74.

Skaalvik, E. M. (1986). Sex differences in global self-esteem. *Scandinavian Journal of Educational Research, 30*, 167–179.

Skitka, L. J., Liu, J. H.-F., Yang, Y., Chen, H., Liu, L., & Xu, L. (2013). Exploring the cross-cultural generalizability and scope of morally motivated intolerance. *Social Psychological and Personality Science, 4*, 324–331.

Skowronski, J. J., & Carlston, D. E. (1989). Negativity and extremity biases in impression formation: A review of explanations. *Psychological Bulletin, 105*, 131–142.

Skurnik, I., Yoon, C., Park, D. C., & Schwarz, N. (2005). How warnings about false claims become recommendations. *Journal of Consumer Research, 31*, 713–724.

Slatcher, R. B. (2010). Marital functioning and physical health: Implications for social and personality psychology. *Social and Personality Psychology Compass, 4*, 455–469.

Slater, M., Antley, A., Davison, A., Swapp, D., Guger, C., Barker, C., Pistrang, N., & Sanchez-Vives, M. V. (2006). A virtual reprise of the Stanley Milgram obedience experiments. *PLoS ONE, 1*, e39.

Smeesters, D., Warlop, L., Van Avermaet, E., Corneille, O., & Yzerbyt, V. (2003). Do not prime hawks with doves: The interplay of construct activation and consistency of social value orientation on cooperative behavior. *Journal of Personality and Social Psychology, 84*, 972–987.

Smith, A., Lyons, A., Ferris, J., Richters, J., Pitts, M., Shelley, J., & Simpson, J. M. (2011). Sexual and relationship satisfaction among heterosexual men and women: The importance of desired frequency of sex. *Journal of Sex & Marital Therapy, 37*, 104–115.

Smith, C. A., Konik, J. A., & Tuve, M. V. (2011). In search of looks, status, or something else? Partner preferences among butch and femme lesbians and heterosexual men and women. *Sex Roles, 64*, 658–668.

Smith, C. M. (2008). Adding minority status to a source of conflict: An examination of influence processes and product quality in dyads. *European Journal of Social Psychology, 38*, 75–83.

Smith, D., Wright, C., Allsopp, A., & Westhead, H. (2007). It's all in the mind: PETTLEP-based imagery and sports performance. *Journal of Applied Sport Psychology, 19*, 80–92.

Smith, E. R. (1977). Single-sex colleges and sex-typing. *Journal of Social Issues, 33*, 197–199.

Smith, E. R. (1991). Illusory correlation in a simulated exemplar-based memory. *Journal of Experimental Social Psychology, 27*, 107–123.

Smith, E. R. (1993). Social identity and social emotions: Toward new conceptualizations of prejudice. In D. M. Mackie & D. L. Hamilton (Eds.), *Affect, cognition, and stereotyping: Interactive processes in group perception* (pp. 297–316). San Diego: Academic Press.

Smith, E. R. (1998). Mental representation and memory. In D. Gilbert, S. T. Fiske, & G. Lindzey (Eds.), *Handbook of social psychology* (4th ed., vol. 1, pp. 391–445). Boston: McGraw-Hill.

Smith, E. R., Coats, S., & Walling, D. (1999). Overlapping mental representations of self, in-group, and partner: Further response time evidence and a connectionist model. *Personality and Social Psychology Bulletin, 25*, 873–882.

Smith, E. R., & Collins, E. C. (2009). Contextualizing person perception: Distributed social cognition. *Psychological Review, 116*, 343–364.

Smith, E. R., & Ho, C. (1999). Prejudice as intergroup emotion: Integrating relative deprivation and social comparison explanations of prejudice. In I. Walker & H. Smith (Eds.), *Relative deprivation: Specification, development, and integration*. Boulder, CO: Westview Press.

Smith, E. R., & Kluegel, J. R. (1982). Cognitive and social bases of emotional experience: Outcome, attribution, and affect. *Journal of Personality and Social Psychology, 43*, 1129–1141.

Smith, E. R., & Mackie, D. M. (2005). Aggression, hatred, and other emotions. In J. F. Dovidio, P. Glic, & L. A. Rudman (Eds.), *On the nature of prejudice: Fifty years after Allport* (pp. 361–376). Malden, MA: Blackwell.

Smith, E. R., Miller, D. A., Maitner, A. T., Crump, S. A., Garcia-Marques, T., & Mackie, D. M. (2006). Familiarity can increase stereotyping. *Journal of Experimental Social Psychology, 42*, 471–478.

Smith, E. R., Seger, C. R., & Mackie, D. M. (2007). Can emotions be truly group level? Evidence regarding four conceptual criteria. *Journal of Personality & Social Psychology, 93*, 431–446.

Smith, E. R., & Zárate, M. A. (1992). Exemplar-based model of social judgment. *Psychological Review, 99*, 3–21.

Smith, H. J., Pettigrew, T. F., Pippin, G. M., & Bialosiewicz, S. (2012). Relative deprivation: A theoretical and meta-analytic review. *Personality & Social Psychology Review, 16*, 203–232.

Smith, H. J., & Spears, R. (1996). Ability and outcome evaluations as a function of personal and collective (dis)advantage: A group escape from individual bias. *Personality and Social Psychology Bulletin, 22*, 690–704.

Smith, H. J., & Tyler, T. R. (1997). Choosing the right pond: The impact of group membership on self-esteem and group-oriented behavior. *Journal of Experimental Social Psychology, 33*, 146–170.

Smith, J. R., & Hogg, M. A. (2008). Social identity and attitudes. In W. D. Crano & R. Prislin (Eds.), *Attitudes and attitude change* (pp. 337–360). New York: Psychology Press.

Smith, J. R., Louis, W. R., Terry, D. J., Greenaway, K. H., Clarke, M. R., & Cheng, X. (2012). Congruent or conflicted? The impact of injunctive and descriptive norms on environmental intentions. *Journal of Environmental Psychology, 32*, 353–361.

Smith, M. B., Bruner, J. S., & White, R. W. (1956). *Opinions and personality*. New York: Wiley.

Smith, P. B., & Bond, M. H. (1993). *Across cultures.* Boston, MA: Allyn & Bacon.

Smith, P. B., & Tayeb, M. (1989). Organizational structure and processes. In M. Bond (Ed.), *The cross-cultural challenge to social psychology.* Newbury Park, CA: Sage.

Smith, R. E., & Smoll, F. L. (1996). *Way to go, Coach! A scientifically validated approach to coaching effectiveness.* Portola Valley, CA: Warde Publishers.

Smith, R. E., & Smoll, F. L. (1997). Coaching the coaches: Youth sports as a scientific and applied behavioral setting. *Current Directions in Psychological Science, 6,* 16–21.

Smith, R. E., Vanderbilt, K., & Callen, M. B. (1973). Social comparison and bystander intervention in emergencies. *Journal of Applied Social Psychology, 3,* 186–196.

Smith, S. M., & Shaffer, D. R. (1995). Speed of speech and persuasion: Evidence for multiple effects. *Personality and Social Psychology Bulletin, 21,* 1051–1060.

Smith, S. S., & Richardson, D. (1983). Amelioration of deception and harm in psychological research: The important role of debriefing. *Journal of Personality and Social Psychology, 44,* 1075–1082.

Smith, W. P., & Anderson, A. J. (1975). Threats, communication and bargaining. *Journal of Personality and Social Psychology, 32,* 76–82.

Snyder, C. R., & Higgins, R. L. (1988). Excuses: Their effective role in the negotiation of reality. *Psychological Bulletin, 104,* 23–35.

Snyder, C. R., Lassegard, M. A., & Ford, C. E. (1986). Distancing after group success and failure: Basking in reflected glory and cutting off reflected failure. *Journal of Personality and Social Psychology, 51,* 382–388.

Snyder, C. R., Smith, T. W., Augelli, R. W., & Ingram, R. E. (1985). On the self-serving function of social anxiety: Shyness as a self-handicapping strategy. *Journal of Personality and Social Psychology, 48,* 970–980.

Snyder, M. (1974). The self-monitoring of expressive behavior. *Journal of Personality and Social Psychology, 30,* 526–537.

Snyder, M., & Gangestad, S. (1982). Choosing social situations: Two investigations of self-monitoring processes. *Journal of Personality and Social Psychology, 43,* 123–135.

Snyder, M., & Haugen, J. A. (1995). Why does behavioral confirmation occur? A functional perspective on the role of the target. *Personality and Social Psychology Bulletin, 21,* 963–974.

Snyder, M., & Omoto, A. M. (1992). Volunteerism and society's response to the HIV epidemic. *Current Directions in Psychological Science, 1,* 113–116.

Snyder, M., & Swann, W. B. (1978). Behavioral confirmation in social interaction: From social perception to social reality. *Journal of Personality and Social Psychology, 36,* 1202–1212.

Snyder, M., & Swann, W. B., Jr. (1976). When actions reflect attitudes: The politics of impression management. *Journal of Personality and Social Psychology, 34,* 1034–1042.

Snyder, M., Tanke, E. D., & Berscheid, E. (1977). Social perception and interpersonal behavior: On the self-fulfilling nature of social stereotypes. *Journal of Personality and Social Psychology, 35,* 656–666.

Sober, E., & Wilson, D. S. (1999). *Unto others: The evolution and psychology of unselfish behavior.* Cambridge, MA: Harvard University Press.

Solomon, H., Solomon, L. Z., Arnone, M. M., Maur, B. J., Reda, R. M., & Rother, E. O. (1981). Anonymity and helping. *Journal of Social Psychology, 113,* 37–43.

Solomon, S., Greenberg, J., & Pyszczynski, T. (2000). Pride and prejudice: Fear of death and social behavior. *Current Directions in Psychological Science, 9*(6), 200–204.

Sommers, S. (2011). *Situations matter: Understanding how context transforms your world.* New York, NY: Riverhead Books.

Song, H., & Schwarz, N. (2009). If it's difficult to pronounce, it must be risky: Fluency, familiarity, and risk perception. *Psychological Science, 20,* 135–138.

Song, Z., Foo, M.-D., Uy, M. A., & Sun, S. (2011). Unraveling the daily stress crossover between unemployed individuals and their employed spouses. *Journal of Applied Psychology, 96,* 151–168.

Son Hing, L. S., Chung-Yan, G. A., Hamilton, L. K., & Zanna, M. P. (2008). A two-dimensional model that employs explicit and implicit attitudes to characterize prejudice. *Journal of Personality & Social Psychology, 94,* 971–987.

Sorrentino, R. M., & Field, N. (1986). Emergent leadership over time: The functional value of positive motivation. *Journal of Personality and Social Psychology, 50,* 1091–1099.

Spangenberg, E. R., Crowley, A. E., & Henderson, P. W. (1996). Improving the store environment: Do olfactory cues affect evaluations and behaviors? *Journal of Marketing, 60,* 67–80.

Spears, R., Doosje, B., & Ellemers, N. (1997). Self-stereotyping in the face of threats to group status and distinctiveness: The role of group identification. *Personality and Social Psychology Bulletin, 23,* 538–553.

Special, W. P., & Li-Barber, K. T. (2012). Self-disclosure and student satisfaction with Facebook. *Computers in Human Behavior, 28,* 624–630.

Spence, J. T., Deaux, K., and Helmreich, R.L. (1985). Sex roles in contemporary American society. In G. Lindzey & E. Aronson (Eds.), *Handbook of social psychology* (3rd ed., vol. 2, pp. 149–178). New York: Random House.

Spencer, S. J. (1994). The effect of stereotype vulnerability on women's math performance. *Dissertation Abstracts International: Section B: the Sciences & Engineering, 54*(7-B), 3903. Department of Psychology, University of Michigan.

Spencer-Rodgers, J., Williams, M. J., & Peng, K. (2010). Cultural differences in expectations of change and tolerance for contradiction: A decade of empirical research. *Personality & Social Psychology Review, 14,* 296–312.

Spielmann, S. S., Joel, S., MacDonald, G., & Kogan, A. (2013). Ex appeal: Current relationship quality and emotional attachment to ex-partners. *Social Psychological and Personality Science, 4,* 175–180.

Spink, K. S., Wilson, K. S., & Odnokon, P. (2010). Examining the relationship between cohesion and return to team in elite athletes. *Psychology of Sport and Exercise, 11,* 6–11.

Spisak, B. R., Homan, A. C., Grabo, A., & van Vugt, M. (2012). Facing the situation: Testing a biosocial contingency model of leadership in intergroup relations using masculine and feminine faces. *The Leadership Quarterly, 23,* 273–280.

Sprague, J., & Quadagno, D. (1989). Gender and sexual motivation: An exploration of two assumptions. *Journal of Psychology and Human Sexuality, 2,* 57–76.

Sprecher, S. (1999). "I love you more today than yesterday": Romantic partners' perceptions of changes in love and related affect over time. *Journal of Personality and Social Psychology, 76,* 46–53.

Sprecher, S. (2002). Sexual satisfaction in premarital relationships: Associations with satisfaction, love, commitment, and stability. *The Journal of Sex Research, 39,* 190–196.

Sprecher, S., Treger, S., Wondra, J. D., Hilaire, N., & Wallpe, K. (2013). Taking turns: Reciprocal self-disclosure promotes liking in initial interactions. *Journal of Experimental Social Psychology, 49,* 860–866.

Srull, T. K. (1981). Person memory: Some tests of associative storage and retrieval models. *Journal of Experimental Psychology: Human Learning and Memory, 7,* 440–463.

Srull, T. K., & Brand, J. F. (1983). Memory for information about persons: The effect of encoding operations upon subsequent retrieval. *Journal of Verbal Learning and Verbal Behavior, 22,* 219–230.

Srull, T. K., Lichtenstein, M., & Rothbart, M. (1985). Associative storage and retrieval processes in person memory. *Journal of Experimental Psychology: Learning, Memory, and Cognition, 11,* 316–345.

Stallen, M., De Dreu, C. K. W., Shalvi, S., Smidts, A., & Sanfey, A. G. (2012). The herding hormone: Oxytocin stimulates in-group conformity. *Psychological Science, 23,* 1288–1292.

Stallen, M., Smidts, A., & Sanfey, A. G. (2013). Peer influence: Neural mechanisms underlying in-group conformity. *Frontiers in Human Neuroscience, 7.* doi: 10.3389/fnhum.2013.00050

Stangor, C., Lynch, L., Duan, C., & Glass, B. (1992). Categorization of individuals on the basis of multiple social features. *Journal of Personality and Social Psychology, 62,* 207–218.

Stangor, C., & Schaller, M. (1996). Stereotypes as individual and collective representations. In C. N. Macrae, C. Stangor, & M. Hewstone (Eds.), *Stereotypes and stereotyping* (pp. 3–40). New York: Guilford Press.

Stanley, D., Phelps, E., & Banaji, M. (2008). The neural basis of implicit attitudes. *Current Directions in Psychological Science, 17,* 164–170.

Starzyk, K. B., Fabrigar, L. R., Soryal, A. S., & Fanning, J. J. (2009). A painful reminder: The role of level and salience of attitude importance in cognitive dissonance. *Personality and Social Psychology Bulletin, 35,* 126–137.

Stasser, G., Abele, S., & Parsons, S. V. (2012). Information flow and influence in collective choice. *Group Processes & Intergroup Relations, 15,* 619–635.

Stasser, G., Taylor, L. A., Hanna, C. (1989). Information sampling in structured and unstructured discussions of three- and six-person groups. *Journal of Personality and Social Psychology, 57,* 67–78.

Staub, E. (1978). *Positive social behavior and morality.* New York: Academic Press.

Staub, E. (1989). *The roots of evil: The origins of genocide and other group violence.* Cambridge: Cambridge University Press.

Staub, E. (2002). Emergency helping, genocidal violence, and the evolution of responsibility and altruism in children. In R. J. Davidson & A. Harrington (Eds.), *Visions of compassion: Western scientists and Tibetan Buddhists examine human nature* (pp. 165–181). Oxford: Oxford University Press.

Stavrova, O., Schlosser, T., & Fetchenhauer, D. (2013). Are virtuous people happy all around the world? Civic virtue, antisocial punishment, and subjective well-being across cultures. *Personality and Social Psychology Bulletin, 39(7),* 927–942. doi:10.1177/0146167213485902

Staw, B. M., & Ross, J. (1987). Behavior in escalation situations: Antecedents, prototypes, and solutions. *Research in Organizational Behavior, 9,* 39–78.

Steele, C. M. (1988). The psychology of self-affirmation: Sustaining the integrity of the self. In L. Berkowitz (Ed.), *Advances in experimental social psychology* (vol. 21, pp. 261–302). San Diego, CA: Academic Press.

Steele, C. M. (1992, April). Race and the schooling of black Americans. *Atlantic, 269(4),* 68–78.

Steele, C. M., & Aronson, J. (1995). Stereotype threat and the intellectual test performance of African Americans. *Journal of Personality and Social Psychology, 69,* 797–811.

Steele, C. M., & Josephs, R. A. (1990). Alcohol myopia: Its prized and dangerous effects. *American Psychologist, 45,* 921–933.

Steele, C. M., & Southwick, L. (1985). Alcohol and social behavior I: The psychology of drunken excess. *Journal of Personality and Social Psychology, 48,* 18–34.

Steele, C. M., Southwick, L. L., & Critchlow, B. (1981). Dissonance and alcohol: Drinking your troubles away. *Journal of Personality and Social Psychology, 41,* 831–846.

Steele, C. M., Spencer, S. J., & Lynch, M. (1993). Self-image resilience and dissonance: The role of affirmational resources. *Journal of Personality and Social Psychology, 64,* 885–896.

Steiner, I. (1972). *Group process and productivity.* New York: Academic Press.

Stephan, C. W., & Stephan, W. G. (1984). The role of ignorance in intergroup relations. In N. Miller & M. Brewer (Eds.), *Groups in contact: The psychology of desegregation* (pp. 229–255). New York: Academic Press.

Stephan, W. G. (1987). The contact hypothesis in intergroup relations. In C. Hendrick (Ed.), *Review of personality and social psychology* (vol. 9, pp. 13–40). Newbury Park, CA: Sage.

Stephan, W. G., & Renfro, C. L. (2002). The role of threat in intergroup relations. In D.M. Mackie & E. R. Smith (Eds.), *From prejudice to intergroup emotions* (pp. 191–208). New York: Psychology Press.

Stephan, W. G., & Stephan, C. W. (1985). Intergroup anxiety. *Journal of Social Issues, 41*, 157–175.

Stephens, N. M., Townsend, S. S. M., Markus, H. R., & Phillips, L. T. (2012). A cultural mismatch: Independent cultural norms produce greater increases in cortisol and more negative emotions among first-generation college students. *Journal of Experimental Social Psychology, 48*, 1389–1393.

Steptoe, A., Shankar, A., Demakakos, P., & Wardle, J. (2013). Social isolation, loneliness, and all-cause mortality in older men and women. *Proceedings of the National Academy of Sciences, 110*, 5797–5801.

Stern, J. (2013, June 27). Flooded with support for gay marriage, Facebook releases new pride emoticon. *ABC News*. Retrieved from http://abcnews.go.com/

Stern, P. C. (1992). Psychological dimensions of global environmental change. *Annual Review of Psychology, 43*, 269–302.

Sternberg, R. J. (1988). Triangulating love. In R. J. Sternberg & M. L. Barnes (Eds.), *The psychology of love* (pp. 119–138). New Haven, CT: Yale University Press.

Sternberg, R. J., & Grajek, S. (1984). The nature of love. *Journal of Personality and Social Psychology, 47*, 312–329.

Sterngold, J. (1992, May 21). Japan cuts back on fingerprinting. *The New York Times*, p. A4.

Sternthal, B., Dholakia, R., & Leavitt, C. (1978). The persuasive effect of source credibility: A test of cognitive response analysis. *Journal of Consumer Research, 4*, 252–260.

Stevens, L. E., & Fiske, S. T. (2000). Motivated impressions of a powerholder: Accuracy under task dependency and misperception under evaluation dependency. *Personality & Social Psychology Bulletin, 26*, 907–922.

Stewart, D. D., & Stasser, G. (1995). Expert role assignment and information sampling during collective recall and decision making. *Journal of Personality and Social Psychology, 69*, 619–628.

Stewart, J. E. (1985). Appearance and punishment: The attraction-leniency effect in the courtroom. *Journal of Social Psychology, 125*, 373–378.

Stice, E., Marti, C. N., Spoor, S., Presnell, K., & Shaw, H. (2008). Dissonance and healthy weight eating disorder prevention programs: Long-term effects from a randomized efficacy trial. *Journal of Consulting and Clinical Psychology, 76*, 329–340.

Stock, R. W. (1995, Oct. 19). Wearing the gray badge of courage. *The New York Times*, p. B5.

Stockton, P. (2004, November 30) Supervisors strip-search workers after phony calls: Caller dupes managers by claiming to be a cop. *The Patriot Ledger*.

Stogdill, R. M. (1963). *Handbook for the leader behavior description questionnaire: Form XII*. Columbus, OH: Ohio State University.

Stok, F. M., de Ridder, D. T. D., de Vet, E., & de Wit, J. B. F. (2012). Minority talks: The influence of descriptive social norms on fruit intake. *Psychology & Health, 27*, 956–970.

Stone, J. (2002). Battling doubt by avoiding practice: The effects of stereotype threat on self-handicapping in white athletes. *Personality and Social Psychology Bulletin, 28*(12), 1667–1678.

Stone, J., & Cooper, J. (2001). A self-standards model of cognitive dissonance. *Journal of Experimental Social Psychology, 37*, 228–243.

Stone, J., & Focella, E. (2011). Hypocrisy, dissonance and the self-regulation processes that improve health. *Self and Identity, 10*, 295–303.

Stone, J., Wiegand, A. W., Cooper, J., & Aronson, E. (1997). When exemplification fails: Hypocrisy and the motive for self-integrity. *Journal of Personality and Social Psychology, 72*, 54–65.

Stoner, J. A. (1961). A comparison of individual and group decisions involving risk. Unpublished master's thesis, MIT.

Stonewall. (n.d.). *Unseen on screen: Gay people on youth TV*. Retrieved from http://www.stonewall.org.uk/media/current_releases/4510.asp

Storch, E. A., & Storch, J. B. (2003). Academic dishonesty and attitudes towards academic dishonest acts: Support for cognitive dissonance theory. *Psychological Reports, 92*, 174–176.

Storck, J., & Sproull, L. (1995). Through a glass darkly: What do people learn in videoconferences? *Human Communication Research, 22*, 197–219.

Storms, M. D. (1973). Videotape and the attribution process: Reversing actors' and observers' points of view. *Journal of Personality and Social Psychology, 27*, 165–175.

Stouffer, S. A. (1949). *The American soldier*. Princeton, NJ: Princeton University Press.

Stouffer, S. A., Suchman, E. A., DeVinney, L. C., Star, S. A., & Williams, R. M., Jr. (1949). *The American soldier: Adjustment during army life* (vol. 1). Princeton, NJ: Princeton University Press.

Strack, F., Martin, L. L., & Stepper, S. (1988). Inhibiting and facilitating conditions of the human smile: A nonobtrusive test of the facial feedback hypothesis. *Journal of Personality and Social Psychology, 54*, 768–777.

Strahan, E. J., Spencer, S. J., & Zanna, M. P. (2002). Subliminal priming and persuasion: Striking while the iron is hot. *Journal of Experimental Social Psychology, 38*, 556–568.

Strauman, T. J., Lemieux, A. M., & Coe, C. L. (1993). Self-discrepancy and natural killer cell activity: Immunological consequences of negative self-evaluation. *Journal of Personality and Social Psychology, 64*, 1042–1052.

Straus, M. A. (1991). Family violence in American families: Incidence rates, causes, and trends. In D. D. Knudsen & J. L. Miller (Eds.), *Abused and battered: Social and legal responses of family violence. Social institutions and social change* (pp. 17–34). Hawthorne, NY: Aldine de Gruyter.

Streufert, S., & Streufert, S. C. (1986). The development of international conflict. In S. Worchel & W. G. Austin (Eds.), *Psychology of intergroup relations* (2nd ed., pp. 134–152). Chicago: Nelson-Hall.

Stroebe, M., Schut, H., & Stroebe, W. (2007). Health outcomes of bereavement. *The Lancet, 370,* 1960–1973.

Stroebe, W., & Diehl, M. (1991). You can't beat good experiments with correlational evidence: Mullen, Johnson, and Sala's meta-analytic misinterpretations. *Journal of Basic and Applied Social Psychology, 12,* 25–32.

Stroebe, W., Stroebe, M. S., & Domittner, G. (1988). Individual and situational differences in recovery from bereavement: A risk group identified. *Journal of Social Issues, 44*(3), 143–158.

Stroessner, S. J., & Mackie, D. M. (1992). The impact of induced affect on the perception of variability in social groups. *Personality and Social Psychology Bulletin, 18,* 546–554.

Strube, M. J., & Garcia, J. E. (1981). A meta-analytic investigation of Fiedler's contingency model of leadership effectiveness. *Psychological Bulletin, 90,* 307–321.

Struch, N., & Schwartz, S. H. (1989). Intergroup aggression: Its predictors and distinctness from in-group bias. *Journal of Personality and Social Psychology, 56,* 364–373.

Sturmer, S., Snyder, M., & Omoto, A. M. (2005). Prosocial emotions and helping: The moderating role of group membership. *Journal of Personality and Social Psychology, 88,* 532–546.

Suedfeld, P. (1992). Bilateral relations between countries and the complexity of newspaper editorials. *Political Psychology, 13,* 601–632.

Suedfeld, P., & Tetlock, P. (1977). Integrative complexity of communications in international crises. *Journal of Conflict Resolution, 21,* 169–184.

Suedfeld, P., Tetlock, P. E., & Ramirez, C. (1977). War, peace, and integrative complexity: UN speeches on the Middle East problem. *The Journal of Conflict Resolution, 21,* 427–442.

Sugarman, D. B., & Hotaling, G. T. (1989). Violent men in intimate relationships: An analysis of risk markers. *Journal of Applied Social Psychology, 19,* 1034–1048.

Suls, J., Martin, R., & Wheeler, L. (2002). Social comparison: Why, with whom, and with what effect? *Current Directions in Psychological Science, 11,* 159–163.

Sumner, W. G. (1906). *Folkways.* New York: Ginn.

Sunnafrank, M., & Ramirez, A. (2004). At first sight: Persistent relational effects of get-acquainted conversations. *Journal of Social and Personal Relationships, 21,* 361–379.

Surowiecki, J. (2004). *The wisdom of crowds: Why the many are smarter than the few and how collective wisdom shapes business, economies, societies, and nations.* New York: Doubleday & Co.

Surra, C. A., & Longstreth, M. (1990). Similarity of outcomes, interdependence, and conflict in dating relationships. *Journal of Personality and Social Psychology, 59,* 501–516.

Sutcliffe, A., Dunbar, R., Binder, J., & Arrow, H. (2012). Relationships and the social brain: Integrating psychological and evolutionary perspectives. *British Journal of Psychology, 103,* 149–168.

Svenson, O. (1981). Are we all less risky and more skillful than our fellow drivers? *Acta Psychologica, 47,* 143–148.

Swaab, R. I., Phillips, K. W., Diermeier, D., & Medvec, V. H. (2008). The pros and cons of dyadic side conversations in small groups: The impact of group norms and task type. *Small Group Research, 39,* 372–390.

Swami, V., Frederick, D. A., Aavik, T., Alcalay, L., Allik, J., Anderson, D., . . . Zivcic-Becirevic, I. (2010). The attractive female body weight and female body dissatisfaction in 26 countries across 10 world regions: Results of the international body project I. *Personality and Social Psychology Bulletin, 36,* 309–325.

Swami, V., Furnham, A., Chamorro-Premuzic, T., Akbar, K., Gordon, N., Harris, T., Finch, J., & Tovee, M. J. (2010). More than just skin deep? Personality information influences men's ratings of the attractiveness of women's body sizes. *The Journal of Social Psychology, 150,* 628–647.

Swann, W. B., & Ely, R. J. (1984). A battle of wills: Self-verification versus behavioral confirmation. *Journal of Personality and Social Psychology, 46,* 1287–1302.

Swann, W. B., Hixon, J. G., & de la Ronde, C. (1992). Embracing the bitter "truth:" Negative self-concepts and marital commitment. *Psychological Science, 3,* 118–121.

Swann, W. B., Jetten, J., Gómez, A., Whitehouse, H., & Bastian, B. (2012). When group membership gets personal: A theory of identity fusion. *Psychological Review, 119*(3), 441–456. doi:10.1037/a0028589

Swann, W. B., & Read, S. J. (1981). Acquiring self-knowledge: The search for feedback that fits. *Journal of Personality and Social Psychology, 41,* 1119–1128.

Sy, T., Cote, S., & Saavedra, R. (2005). The contagious leader: Impact of the leader's mood on the mood of group members, group affective tone, and group processes. *Journal of Applied Psychology, 90,* 295–305.

Symons, C. S., & Johnson, B. T. (1997). The self-reference effect in memory: A meta-analysis. *Psychological Bulletin, 121,* 371–394.

Tait, R., & Silver, R.C. (1989). Coming to terms with major negative life events. In J. S. Uleman & J. A. Bargh (Eds.), *Unintended thought* (pp. 351–382). New York: Guilford.

Tajfel, H. (1972). La categorization sociale. In S. Moscovici (Ed.), *Introduction à la psychologie sociale* (vol. 1, pp. 272–302). Paris: Larousse.

Tajfel, H. (1978). *Differentiation between social groups: Studies in the social psychology of intergroup relations.* London: Academic Press.

Tajfel, H., Billig, M. G., Bundy, R. P., & Flament, C. (1971). Social categorization and intergroup behavior. *European Journal of Social Psychology, 1,* 149–178.

Tajfel, H., & Turner, J. C. (1979). An integrative theory of intergroup conflict. In W. G. Austin & S. Worchel (Eds.), *The social psychology of intergroup relations* (pp. 33–48). Monterey, CA: Brooks-Cole.

Tajfel, H., & Wilkes, A. L. (1963). Classification and quantitative judgment. *British Journal of Psychology, 54,* 101–114.

Takahashi, N. (2000). The emergence of generalized exchange 1. *American Journal of Sociology*, *10*(4), 1105–1134.

Takemura, K., & Yuki, M. (2007). Are Japanese groups more competitive than Japanese individuals? A cross-cultural validation of the interindividual-intergroup discontinuity effect. *International Journal of Psychology*, *42*, 27–35.

Tam, K.-P., Lee, S.-L., Kim, Y.-H., Li, Y., & Chao, M. M. (2012). Intersubjective model of value transmission: Parents using perceived norms as reference when socializing children. *Personality and Social Psychology Bulletin*, *38*, 1041–1052.

Tannen, D. (1990). *You just don't understand*. New York: Ballantine Books.

Tanner, R. J., Ferraro, R., Chartrand, T. L., Bettman, J. R., & Van Baaren, R. (2008). Of chameleons and consumption: The impact of mimicry on choice and preferences. *Journal of Consumer Research*, *34*, 4–66.

Täuber, S., & Sassenberg, K. (2012). Newcomer conformity: How self-construal affects the alignment of cognition and behavior with group goals in novel groups. *Social Psychology*, *43*, 138–147.

Tausch, N., Becker, J. C., Spears, R., Christ, O., Saab, R., Singh, P., Siddiqui, R. N. (2011). Explaining radical group behavior: Developing emotion and efficacy routes to normative and nonnormative collective action. *Journal of Personality and Social Psychology*, *101*, 129–148

Taylor, C. A., Lord, C. G., & Bond, C. F. (2009). Embodiment, agency, and attitude change. *Journal of Personality & Social Psychology*, *97*, 946–962.

Taylor, C. R., & Stern, B. B. (1997). Asian-Americans: Television advertising and the "model minority" stereotype. *Journal of Advertising*, *26*, 47–61.

Taylor, D. A., & Moriarty, B. F. (1987). Ingroup bias as a function of competition and race. *Journal of Conflict Resolution*, *31*, 192–199.

Taylor, D. M., Doria, J., & Tyler, J. K. (1983). Group performance and cohesiveness: An attribution analysis. *Journal of Social Psychology*, *119*, 187–198.

Taylor, D. M., & Jaggi, V. (1974). Ethnocentrism and causal attribution in a south Indian context. *Journal of Cross Cultural Psychology*, *5*, 162–171.

Taylor, D. M., & Simard, L. M. (1979). Ethnic identity and inter-group relations. In D. J. Lee (Ed.), *Emerging ethnic boundaries* (pp. 155–174). Ottawa: University of Ottawa Press.

Taylor, D. M., Wright, S. C., Moghaddam, F. M., & Lalonde, R. N. (1990). The personal/group discrimination discrepancy: Perceiving my group, but not myself, to be a target for dis-crimination. *Personality and Social Psychology Bulletin*, *16*, 254–262.

Taylor, S. E. (1975). On inferring one's attitude from one's behavior: Some delimiting conditions. *Journal of Personality and Social Psychology*, *31*, 126–131.

Taylor, S. E. (1981). A categorization approach to stereotyping. In D. L. Hamilton (Ed.), *Cognitive processes in stereotyping and intergroup behavior* (pp. 83–114). Hillsdale, NJ: Lawrence Erlbaum Associates.

Taylor, S. E. (1983). Adjustment to threatening events: A theory of cognitive adaptation. *American Psychologist*, *38*, 1161–1173.

Taylor, S. E., & Brown, J. D. (1988). Illusion and well-being: A social psychological perspective on mental health. *Psychological Bulletin*, *103*, 193–210.

Taylor, S. E., Falke, R. L., Shoptaw, S. J., & Lichtman, R. R. (1986). Social support, support groups, and the cancer patient. *Journal of Consulting and Clinical Psychology*, *54*, 608–615.

Taylor, S. E., & Fiske, S. T. (1975). Point of view and perceptions of causality. *Journal of Personality and Social Psychology*, *32*, 439–445.

Taylor, S. E., Fiske, S. T., Etcoff, N. L., & Ruderman, A. J. (1978). Categorical and contextual bases of person memory and stereotyping. *Journal of Personality and Social Psychology*, *36*, 778–793.

Taylor, S. E., Kemeny, M. E., Reed, G. M., Bower, J. E., & Gruenewald, T. L. (2000). Psychological resources, positive illusions, and health. *American Psychologist*, *55*, 99–109.

Taylor, S. E., Klein, L. C., Lewis, B. P., Gruenewald, T. L., Gurung, R. A. R., & Updegraff, J. A. (2000). Biobehavioral responses to stress in females: Tend-and-befriend, not fight-or-flight. *Psychological Review*, *107*, 411–429.

Taylor, S. E., & Lobel, M. (1989). Social comparison activity under threat: Downward evaluation and upward contacts. *Psychological Review*, *96*, 569–575.

Taylor, S. P., Gammon, C. B., & Capasso, D. R. (1976). Aggression as a function of alcohol and threat. *Journal of Personality and Social Psychology*, *34*, 938–941.

Tedeschi, J. T. (Ed.). (1981). *Impression management theory and social psychological research*. New York: Academic Press.

Tedeschi, J. T., & Felson, R. B. (1994). *Violence, aggression, and coercive actions*. Washington, DC: American Psychological Association.

Tedeschi, J. T., Gaes, G. G., & Rivera, A. N. (1977). Aggression and the use of coercive power. *Journal of Social Issues*, *33*(1), 101–125.

Tellis, G. J., Prabhu, J. C., & Chandy, R. K. (2009). Radical innovation across nations: The preeminence of corporate culture. *Journal of Marketing*, *73*, 3–23.

Tennen, H., & Afflect, G. (1993). The puzzles of self-esteem: A clinical perspective. In R. F. Baumeister (Ed.), *Self-esteem: The puzzle of low self-esteem* (pp. 241–262). New York: Plenum.

Tennov, D. (1979). *Love and limerence: The experience of being in love*. New York: Stein and Day.

Ten Velden, F. S., Baas, M., Shalvi, S., Preenen, P. T. Y., & De Dreu, C. K. W. (2012). In competitive interaction displays of red increase actors' competitive approach and perceivers' withdrawal. *Journal of Experimental Social Psychology*, *48*, 1205–1208.

Terkel, S. (1992). *Race*. New York: The New Press.

Terry, D. J., & Hogg, M. A. (1996). Group norms and the attitude-behavior relationship: A role for group identification. *Personality and Social Psychology Bulletin, 22,* 776–793.

Tesser, A. (1988). Toward a self-evaluation maintenance model of social behavior. In L. Berkowitz (Ed.), *Advances in experimental social psychology* (vol. 21, pp. 181–227). San Diego, CA: Academic Press.

Tesser, A. (1993). The importance of heritability in psychological research: The case of attitudes. *Psychological Review, 100,* 129–142.

Tesser, A., & Collins, J. E. (1988). Emotion in social reflection and comparison situations: Intuitive, systematic, and exploratory approaches. *Journal of Personality and Social Psychology, 55,* 695–709.

Tetlock, P. E. (1988). Monitoring the integrative complexity of American and Soviet policy rhetoric: What can be learned? *Journal of Social Issues, 44*(2), 101–131.

Tetlock, P. E. (1989). The selfishness-altruism debate: In defense of agnosticism. *Behavioral and Brain Sciences, 12,* 723–724.

Tetlock, R. E. (1985). Integrative complexity of American and Soviet foreign policy rhetoric: A time-series analysis. *Journal of Personality and Social Psychology, 49,* 1565–1585.

Themnér, L., & Wallensteen, P. (2012). Armed conflicts, 1946–2011. *Journal of Peace Research, 49,* 565–575.

The New York Times. (1992, March 25). Plenty of fish in sea? Not anymore. p. A8.

The New York Times. (1992, June 28). Turning the tables: A reverse questionnaire. p. F23.

The New York Times Magazine. (1995, Aug. 13). The romance of science. p. 16.

Thibaut, J. J., & Kelley, H. H. (1959). *The psychology of groups.* New York: Wiley.

Thiel, C., Alemanno, A., Scarcella, G., Zubaryeva, A., & Pasaoglu, G. (2012). Attitude of European car drivers towards electric vehicles: A survey. Retrieved from European Commission Joint Research Centre website: http://publications.jrc.ec. europa.eu/repository/bitstream/111111111/26995/1/eur%2 025597%20scientific%20report%20on%20ev%20attitudes _online.pdf

Thomas, E. F., McGarty, C., & Mavor, K. I. (2009). Aligning identities, emotions, and beliefs to create commitment to sustainable social and political action. *Personality and Social Psychology Review, 13,* 194–218.

Thombs, D. L., Dotterer, S., Olds, R. S., Sharp, K. E., & Raub, C. G. (2004). A close look at why one social norms campaign did not reduce student drinking. *Journal of American College Health, 53,* 61–68.

Thombs, D. L., Olds, R. S., Osborn, C. J., Casseday, S., Glavin, K., & Berkowitz, A. D. (2007). Outcomes of a technology-based social norms intervention to deter alcohol use in freshman residence halls. *Journal of American College Health, 55,* 325–332.

Thompson, L. (1993). The impact of negotiation on intergroup relations. *Journal of Experimental Social Psychology, 29,* 304–325.

Thompson, L., & Hastie, R. (1990a). Judgment tasks and biases in negotiation. In B. H. Sheppard, M. H. Bazerman, & R. J. Lewicki (Eds.), *Research in negotiation in organizations* (vol. 2, pp. 31–54). Greenwich, CT: JAI Press.

Thompson, L., & Hastie, R. (1990b). Social perception in negotiation. *Organization Behavior and Human Decision Processes, 47,* 98–123.

Thompson, L. F., Sebastianelli, J. D., & Murray, N. P. (2009). Monitoring online training behaviors: Awareness of electronic surveillance hinders e-learners. *Journal of Applied Social Psychology, 39,* 2191–2212.

Thompson, M. S., Judd, C. M., & Park, B. (2000). The consequences of communicating social stereotypes. *Journal of Experimental Social Psychology, 36,* 567–599.

Thompson, T. L., & Zerbinos, E. (1995). Gender roles in animated cartoons: Has the picture changed in 20 years? *Sex Roles, 32,* 651–673.

Thompson, W. C., Cohen, A. N., & Rosenhan, D. L. (1980). Focus of attention mediates the impact of negative affect on altruism. *Journal of Personality and Social Psychology, 38,* 291–300.

Thompson, W. C., Fong, G. T., & Rosenhan, D. L. (1981). Inadmissible evidence and juror verdicts. *Journal of Personality and Social Psychology, 40,* 453–463.

Thoresen, C. E., & Low, K. G. (1990). Women and the Type A behavior pattern: Review and commentary. *Journal of Social Behavior and Personality, 5,* 117–133.

Thorley, C., & Dewhurst, S. A. (2009). False and veridical collaborative recognition. *Memory, 17,* 17–25.

Thornhill, R., & Gangestad, S. W. (2006). Facial sexual dimorphism, developmental stability, and susceptibility to disease in men and women. *Evolution and Human Behavior, 27,* 131–144.

Tiedens, L. Z. (2001). Anger and advancement versus sadness and subjugation: The effect of negative emotion expressions on social status conferral. *Journal of Personality and Social Psychology, 80,* 86–94.

Tiedens, L. Z., & Fragale, A. R. (2003). Power moves: Complementarity in dominant and submissive nonverbal behavior. *Journal of Personality and Social Psychology, 84,* 558–568.

Tiedens, L. Z., & Linton, S. (2001). Judgment under emotional certainty and uncertainty: The effects of specific emotions on information processing. *Journal of Personality and Social Psychology, 81,* 973–988.

Tindale, R. S., Smith, C. M., Dykema-Engblade, A., & Kluwe, K. (2012). Good and bad group performance: Same process – different outcomes. *Group Processes & Intergroup Relations, 15,* 603–618.

Ting-Toomey, S. (1991). Intimacy expressions in three cultures: France, Japan, and the United States. *International Journal of Intercultural Relations, 15,* 29–46.

Todd, J., & Mullan, B. (2011). Using the theory of planned behaviour and prototype willingness model to target binge drinking in female undergraduate university students. *Addictive Behaviors, 36,* 980–986.

Todd, P. M., Penke, L., Fasolo, B., & Lenton, A. P. (2007). Different cognitive processes underlie human mate choices and mate preferences. *Proceedings of the National Academy of Sciences, 104,* 15011–15016.

Todorov, A., Mandisodza, A. N., Goren, A., & Hall, C. C. (2005). Inference of competence from faces predict election outcomes. *Science, 308,* 1623–1626.

Tomaka, J., Blascovich, J., Kibler, J., & Ernst, J.M. (1997). Cognitive and physiological antecedents of threat and challenge appraisal. *Journal of Personality and Social Psychology, 73,* 63–72.

Tommasini, A. (1996, April 9). Music history: One woman wielding a baton. *The New York Times,* p. B1.

Tong, E. M. W., Tan, C. R. M., Latheef, N. A., Selamat, M. F. B., & Tan, D. K. B. (2008). Conformity: Moods matter. *European Journal of Social Psychology, 38,* 601–611.

Tormala, Z. L., Clarkson, J. J., & Petty, R. E. (2006). Resisting persuasion by the skin of one's teeth: The hidden success of resisted persuasive messages. *Journal of Personality & Social Psychology, 91,* 423–435.

Tormala, Z. L., & DeSensi, V. L. (2009). The effects of minority/majority source status on attitude certainty: A matching perspective. *Personality and Social Psychology Bulletin,35,* 114–125.

Tormala, Z. L., & Petty, R. E. (2004). Resistance to persuasion and attitude certainty: The moderating role of elaboration. *Personality and Social Psychology Bulletin, 30,* 1446–1457.

Tourangeau, R., & Rasinski, K. A. (1988). Cognitive processes underlying context effects in attitude measurement. *Psychological Bulletin, 103,* 299–314.

Trafimow, D., & Finlay, K. A. (1996). The importance of subjective norms for a minority of people: Between-subjects and within-subjects analyses. *Personality and Social Psychology Bulletin, 22,* 820–828.

Trafimow, D., & Finlay, K. A. (2001). The importance of traits and group memberships. *European Journal of Social Psychology, 31*(1), 37–43.

Trafimow, D., & Fishbein, M. (1994a). The importance of risk in determining the extent to which attitudes affect intentions to wear seat belts. *Journal of Applied Social Psychology, 24,* 1–11.

Trafimow, D., & Fishbein, M. (1994b). The moderating effect of behavior type on the subjective norm-behavior relationship. *Journal of Social Psychology, 134,* 755–763.

Trafimow, D., Triandis, H. C., & Goto, S. G. (1991). Some tests of the distinction between the private self and the collective self. *Journal of Personality and Social Psychology, 60,* 649–655.

Trautmann-Lengsfeld, S. A., & Herrmann, C. S. (2013). EEG reveals an early influence of social conformity on visual processing in group pressure situations. *Social Neuroscience, 8,* 75–89.

Trawalter, S., Adam, E. K., Chase-Lansdale, P. L., & Richeson, J. A. (2012). Concerns about appearing prejudiced get under the skin: Stress responses to interracial contact in the moment and across time. *Journal of Experimental Social Psychology, 48,* 682–693.

Triandis, H. C. (1980). Values, attitudes, and interpersonal behavior. In H. Howe & M. Page (Eds.), *Nebraska Symposium on motivation* (vol. 27). Lincoln: University of Nebraska Press.

Triandis, H. C. (1994). Major cultural syndromes and emotion. In S. Kityama & H. R. Markus (Eds.), *Handbook of industrial and organizational psychology* (2nd ed., vol. 4, pp. 285–308). Palo Alto, CA: Consulting Psychologists Press, Inc.

Triandis, H. C., Bontempo, R., Villareal, M. J., Asai, M., & Lucca, N. (1988). Individualism and collectivism: Cross-cultural perspectives on self-ingroup relaitonships. *Journal of Personality and Social Psychology, 54,* 323–338.

Tripathi, R.C., & Srivasta, R. (1981). Relative deprivation and intergroup attitudes. *European Journal of Social Psychology, 11,* 313–318.

Triplett, N. (1898). The dynamogenic factors in pacemaking and competition. *American Journal of Psychology, 9,* 507–533.

Trivers, R. L. (1971). The evolution of reciprocal altruism. *Quarterly Review of Biology, 46,* 35–57.

Trivers, R. L. (1972). Parental investment and sexual selection. In B. Campbell (Ed.), *Sexual selection and the descent of man, 1871–1971* (pp. 136–172). Chicago: Aldine.

Trope, Y. (1986). Identification and inferential processes in dispositional attribution. *Psychological Review, 93,* 239–257.

Trope, Y., Bassok, M., & Alon, E. (1984). The questions lay interviewers ask. *Journal of Personality, 52,* 90–106.

Trope, Y., & Fishbach, A. (2000). Counteractive self-control in overcoming temptation. *Journal of Personality and Social Psychology, 79,* 493–506.

Trope, Y., & Gaunt, R. (2000). Processing alternative explanations of behavior: Correction or integration? *Journal of Personality and Social Psychology, 79,* 344–354.

Trope, Y., & Liberman, N. (2010). Construal-level theory of psychological distance. *Psychological Review, 117,* 440–463.

Trope, Y., & Mackie, D. M. (1987). Sensitivity to alternatives in social hypothesis-testing. *Journal of Experimental Social Psychology, 23,* 445–459.

Trope, Y., & Thompson, E. P. (1997). Looking for truth in all the wrong places? Asymmetric search of individuating information about stereotyped group members. *Journal of Personality and Social Psychology, 73,* 229–241.

Tropp, L. R., & Pettigrew, T. F. (2005). Differential relationships between intergroup contact and affective and cognitive dimensions of prejudice. *Personality and Social Psychology Bulletin, 31,* 1145–1158.

Trost, M. R., Cialdini, R. B., & Maass, A. (1989). Effects of an international conflict simulation of perceptions of the Soviet Union: A FIREBREAKS backfire. *Journal of Social Issues, 45,* 139–158.

Trudeau, K. J., & Devlin, A. S. (1996). College students and community service: Who, with whom, and why? *Journal of Applied Social Psychology, 26,* 1867–1888.

Tsapelas, I., Aron, A., & Orbuch, T. (2009). Marital boredom now predicts less satisfaction 9 years later. *Psychological Science, 20,* 543–545.

Tuckman, B. W. (1965). Developmental sequences in small groups. *Psychological Bulletin, 63,* 384–399.

Turnbull, W., Miller, D.T., & McFarland, C. (1990). Population-distinctiveness, identity, and bonding. In J. M. Olson & M. P. Zanna (Eds.), *Self-inference processes: The Ontario Symposium* (vol. 6, pp. 115–133). Hillsdale, NJ: Lawrence Erlbaum Associates.

Turner, C. W., Simons, L. S., Berkowitz, L., & Frodi, A. (1977). The stimulating and inhibiting effects of weapons on aggressive behavior. *Aggressive Behavior, 3,* 355–378.

Turner, J. C. (1980). Fairness or discrimination in intergroup behavior? A reply to Braithwaite, Doyle, and Lightbrown. *European Journal of Social Psychology, 10,* 131–147.

Turner, J. C. (1981). The experimental social psychology of intergroup behavior. In J. C. Turner & H. Giles (Eds.), *Intergroup behavior* (pp. 66–101). Chicago: University of Chicago Press.

Turner, J.C. (1982). Towards a cognitive redefinition of the social group. In H. Tajfel (Ed.), *Social identity and intergroup relations.* Cambridge: Cambridge University Press.

Turner, J. C. (1991). *Social influence.* Belmont, CA: Wadsworth Publishing.

Turner, J. C., Hogg, M. A., Oakes, P. J., Reicher, S. D., & Wetherell, M. S. (1987). *Rediscovering the social group: A self-categorization theory.* Oxford: Blackwell.

Turner, J. C., Sachdev, I., & Hogg, M. A. (1983). Social categorization interpersonal attraction and group formation. *British Journal of Social Psychology, 22,* 227–239.

Turner, M. E., Pratkanis, A. R., & Struckman, C. K. (2007). Groupthink as social identity maintenance. In A. R. Pratkanis (Ed.), *The science of social influence: Advances and future progress* (pp. 223–246). New York, NY: Psychology Press.

Turner, R. N., Crisp, R. J., & Lambert, E. (2007). Imagining intergroup contact can improve intergroup attitudes. *Group Processes & Intergroup Relations, 10,* 427–441.

Twenge, J. M., Baumeister, R. F., Tice, D. M., & Stucke, T. S. (2001). If you can't join them, beat them: Effects of social exclusion on aggressive behavior. *Journal of Personality and Social Psychology, 81,* 1058–1069.

Twenge, J. M., & Campbell, W. K. (2003). "Isn't it fun to get the respect that we're going to deserve?" Narcissism, social rejection, and aggression. *Personality & Social Psychology Bulletin, 29*(2), 261–272.

Twenge, J. M., & Crocker, J. (2002). Race and self-esteem: Meta-analyses comparing Whites, Blacks, Hispanics, Asians, and American Indians and comment on Gray-Little and Hafdahl (2000). *Psychological Bulletin, 128*(3), 371–408.

Tyler, T., & Lind, E. A. (1992). A relational model of authority in groups. In M. P. Zanna (Ed.), *Advances in experimental social psychology* (vol. 25, pp. 115–191). New York: Academic Press.

Tyler, T., Lind, E. A., Ohbuchi, K.-I., Sugawara, I., & Huo, Y. J. (1998). Conflict with outsiders: Disputing within and across cultural boundaries. *Personality and Social Psychology Bulletin, 24,* 137–146.

Tyler, T. R., & Smith, H. J. (1998). Social justice and social movements. In D. T. Gilbert, S. T. Fiske, & G. Lindzey (Eds.), *The handbook of social psychology* (4th ed., vol. 2, pp. 595–629). New York: McGraw-Hill.

Uchino, B. N. (2009). Understanding the links between social support and physical health: A life-span perspective with emphasis on the separability of perceived and received support. *Perspectives on Psychological Science, 4,* 236–255.

Uchino, B. N., Bosch, J. A., Smith, T. W., Carlisle, M., Birmingham, W., Bowen, K. S., Light, K. C., Heaney, J., & O'Hartaigh, B. (2013). Relationships and cardiovascular risk: Perceived spousal ambivalence in specific relationship contexts and its links to inflammation. *Health Psychology, 32,* 1067–1075.

Uchino, B. N., Cacioppo, J. T., & Kiecolt-Glaser, J. K. (1996). The relationship between social support and physiological processes: A review with emphasis on underlying mechanisms and implications for health. *Psychological Bulletin, 119,* 488–531.

Uleman, J. S., Saribay, S. A., & Gonzalez, C. M. (2008). Spontaneous inferences, implicit impressions, and implicit theories. *Annual Review of Psychology, 59,* 329–360.

Unnever, J. D., & Cullen, F. T. (2012). White perceptions of whether African Americans and Hispanics are prone to violence and support for the death penalty. *Journal of Research in Crime and Delinquency, 49,* 519–544.

U.S. Department of Justice. (2012). *Intimate partner violence, 1993–2010.* Retrieved from http:// www.bjs.gov/

U.S. Department of Labor. (2011). *Women in the labor force: A databook.* Retrieved from http:// www.bls.gov/cps/wlf-databook2011.htm

Uskul, A. K., & Oyserman, D. (2010). When message-frame fits salient cultural-frame, messages feel more persuasive. *Psychology & Health, 25,* 321–337.

Utz, S., Ouwerkerk, J. W., & Van Lange, P. A. M. (2004). What is smart in a social dilemma? Differential effects of priming competence on cooperation. *European Journal of Social Psychology, 34,* 317–332.

Vachon, M. L., and others. (1982). Predictors and correlates of adaptation to conjugal bereavement. *American Journal of Psychiatry, 139,* 998–1002.

Vaes, J., Paladino, M. P., Castelli, L., Leyens, J.-P., & Giovanazzi, A. (2003). On the behavioral consequences of infrahumanization: The implicit role of uniquely human emotions in intergroup relations. *Journal of Personality and Social Psychology, 85*(6), 1016–1034.

Vail, K. E., Juhl, J., Arndt, J., Vess, M., Routledge, C., & Rutjens,

B. T. (2012). When death is good for life: Considering the positive trajectories of terror management. *Personality & Social Psychology Review, 16,* 303–329.

Vaish, A., Grossmann, T., & Woodward, A. (2008). Not all emotions are created equal: The negativity bias in social-emotional development. *Psychological Bulletin, 134,* 383–403.

Vala, J., Drozda-Senkowska, E., Oberlé, D., Lopes, D., & Silva, P. (2011). Group heterogeneity and social validation of everyday knowledge: The mediating role of perceived group participation. *Group Processes & Intergroup Relations, 14,* 347–362.

Van Baaren, R. B., Holland, R. W., Kawakami, K., Van Knippenberg, A. (2004). Mimicry and prosocial behavior. *Psychological Science, 15,* 71–74.

Van Beest, I., Williams, K. D., & van Dijk, E. (2011). Cyberbomb: Effects of being ostracized from a death game. *Group Processes & Intergroup Relations, 14,* 581–596.

Van Bommel, M., van Prooijen, J.-W., Elffers, H., & Van Lange, P. A. M. (2012). *Journal of Experimental Social Psychology, 48*(4), 926–930. doi:10.1016/j.jesp.2012.02.011

Van Dijk, H., van Engen, M. L., & van Knippenberg, D. (2012). Defying conventional wisdom: A meta-analytical examination of the differences between demographic and job-related diversity relationships with performance. *Organizational Behavior and Human Decision Processes, 119,* 38–53.

Van Dillen, L. F., Papies, E. K., & Hofmann, W. (2013). Turning a blind eye to temptation: How cognitive load can facilitate self-regulation. *Journal of Personality and Social Psychology, 104,* 427–443.

Van Egeren, L. F. (1979). Cardiovascular changes during social competition in a mixed-motive game. *Journal of Personality and Social Psychology, 37,* 858–864.

Van Engen, M. L., & Willemsen, T. M. (2004). Sex and leadership styles: A meta-analysis of research published in the 1990s. *Psychological Reports, 94,* 3–18.

Van Gyn, G. H., Wenger, H. A., & Gaul, C. A. (1990). Imagery as a method of enhancing transfer from training to performance. *Journal of Sport and Exercise Psychology, 12,* 366–375.

Van Harreveld, F., van der Pligt, J., & de Liver, Y. N. (2009). The agony of ambivalence and ways to resolve it: Introducing the MAID model. *Personality & Social Psychology Review, 13,* 45–61.

Van Kleef, G. A., Homan, A. C., Beersma, B., & van Knippenberg, D. (2010). On angry leaders and agreeable followers: How leaders' emotions and followers' personalities shape motivation and team performance. *Psychological Science, 21,* 1827–1834.

Van Knippenberg, D., De Dreu, C. K. W., & Homan, A. C. (2004). Work group diversity and group performance: An integrative model and research agenda. *Journal of Applied Psychology, 89,* 1008–1022.

Van Lange, P. A., & Liebrand, W. B. (1991). Social value orientation and intelligence: A test of the Goal Prescribes Rationality Principle. *European Journal of Social Psychology, 21,* 273–292.

Van Lange, P. A. M. (1999). The pursuit of joint outcomes and equality in outcomes: An integrative model of social value orientation. *Journal of Personality and Social Psychology, 77,* 337–349.

Van Lange, P. A. M., De Bruin, E. M. N., Otten, W., & Joireman, J. A. (1997). Development of prosocial, individualistic, and competitive orientations: Theory and preliminary evidence. *Journal of Personality and Social Psychology, 73,* 733–746.

Van Lange, P. A. M., Joireman, J., Parks, C. D., & van Dijk, E. (2013). The psychology of social dilemmas: A review. *Organizational Behavior and Human Decision Processes, 120*(2), 125–141. doi:10.1016/j.obhdp.2012.11.003

Van Lange, P. A. M., Rusbult, C. E., Drigotas, S. M., Arriaga, X. B., Witcher, B. S., & Cox, C. L. (1997). Willingness to sacrifice in close relationships. *Journal of Personality and Social Psychology, 72,* 1373–1395.

Van Leeuwen, F., Park, J. H., & Penton-Voak, I. S. (2012). Another fundamental social category? Spontaneous categorization of people who uphold or violate moral norms. *Journal of Experimental Social Psychology, 48,* 1385–1388.

Van Leeuwen, M. L., Veling, H., van Baaren, R. B., & Dijksterhuis, A. (2009). The influence of facial attractiveness on imitation. *Journal of Experimental Social Psychology, 45,* 1295–1298.

Van Osch, Y., Breugelmans, S. M., Zeelenberg, M., & Boluk, P. (2013). A different kind of honor culture: Family honor and aggression in Turks. *Group Processes & Intergroup Relations, 16,* 334–344.

Van Veen, V., Krug, M. K., Schooler, J. W., & Carter, C. S. (2009). Neural activity predicts attitude change in cognitive dissonance. *Nature Neuroscience, 12,* 1469–1474.

Van Vugt, M., & De Cremer, D. (1999). Leadership in social dilemmas: The effects of group identification on collective actions to provide public goods. *Journal of Personality and Social Psychology, 76,* 587–599.

Van Vugt, M., & Hart, C. M. (2004). Social identity as social glue: The origins of group loyalty. *Journal of Personality and Social Psychology, 86,* 585–598.

Van Vugt, M., Jepson, S. F., Hart, C. M., & De Cremer, D. (2004). Autocratic leadership in social dilemmas: A threat to group stability. *Journal of Experimental Social Psychology, 40,* 1–13.

Van Vugt, M., & Spisak, B. R. (2008). Sex differences in the emergence of leadership during competitions within and between groups. *Psychological Science, 19,* 854–858.

Van Zomeren, M., Leach, C. W., & Spears, R. (2012). Protesters as "passionate economists": A dynamic dual pathway model of approach coping with collective disadvantage. *Personality and Social Psychology Review, 16*(2), 180–199. doi:10.1177/1088868311430835

Van Zomeren, M., Postmes, T., & Spears, R. (2008). Toward an integrative social identity model of collective action: A quantitative research synthesis of three socio-psychological perspectives. *Psychological Bulletin, 134*(4), 504–535. doi:10.1037/0033-2909.134.4.504

Van Zomeren, M., Spears, R., Fischer, A. H., & Leach, C. W. (2004). Put your money where your mouth is! Explaining collective action tendencies through group-based anger and group efficacy. *Journal of Personality and Social Psychology, 87,* 649–664.

vanDellen, M. R., Campbell, W. K., Hoyle, R. H., & Bradfield, E. K. (2011). Compensating, resisting, and breaking: A meta-analytic examination of reactions to self-esteem threat. *Personality & Social Psychology Review, 15,* 51–74.

Vandello, J. A., & Cohen, D. (2003). Male honor and female fidelity: Implicit cultural scripts that perpetuate domestic violence. *Journal of Personality and Social Psychology, 84,* 997–1010.

Vanman, E. J., & Miller, N. (1993). Applications of emotion theory and research to stereotyping and intergroup relations. In D. M. Mackie & D. L. Hamilton (Eds.) *Affect, cognition, and stereotyping: Interactive processes in group perception* (pp. 213–238). New York: Academic Press.

Vanman, E. J., Paul, B. Y., Ito, T. A., & Miller, N. (1997). The modern face of prejudice and structural features that moderate the effect of cooperation on affect. *Journal of Personality and Social Psychology, 73,* 941–959.

Vargas, P. T., von Hippel, W., & Petty, R. E. (2004). Using partially structured attitude measures to enhance the attitude-behavior relationship. *Personality and Social Psychology Bulletin, 30,* 197–211.

Vauclair, C., & Fischer, R. (2011). Do cultural values predict individuals' moral attitudes? A cross-cultural multilevel approach. *European Journal of Social Psychology, 41*(5), 645–657.

Vazire, S., & Gosling, S. D. (2004). e-Perceptions: Personality impressions based on personal websites. *Journal of Personality & Social Psychology, 87,* 123–132.

Vecsey, G. (Feb. 2, 2003). England battles racism that infests soccer. *The New York Times,* Section 8, pp. 1, 4.

Verkuyten, M., & Maliepaard, M. (2013). A further test of the "party over policy" effect: Political leadership and ethnic minority policies. *Basic and Applied Social Psychology, 35,* 241–248.

Verrier, D. B. (2012). Evidence for the influence of the mere-exposure effect on voting in the Eurovision Song Contest. *Judgment and Decision Making, 7,* 639–643.

Voisin, D., Stone, J., & Becker, M. (2013). The impact of the antitobacco norm on the selected mode of cognitive dissonance reduction. *Journal of Applied Social Psychology, 43,* 57–67.

Vonk, R. (1995). Effects of inconsistent behaviors on person impressions: A multidimensional study. *Personality and Social Psychology Bulletin, 21,* 674–685.

Vroom, V. H. (1976). Leadership. In M. D. Dunnette (Ed.), *Handbook of industrial and organizational psychology* (pp. 1527–1552). Chicago: Rand McNally.

Vroom, V. H., & Jago, A. G. (2007). The role of the situation in leadership. *American Psychologist, 62,* 17–24.

Waddell, B. D., Roberto, M. A., & Yoon, S. (2013). Uncovering hidden profiles: Advocacy in team decision making. *Management Decision, 51,* 321–340.

Wade-Benzoni, K. A. (2008). Maple trees and weeping willows: The role of time, uncertainty, and affinity in intergenerational decisions. *Negotiation and Conflict Management Research, 1,* 220–245.

Wade-Benzoni, K. A., & Tost, L. P. (2009). The egoism and altruism of intergenerational behavior. *Personality and Social Psychology Review, 13*(3), 165–193. doi:10.1177/1088868309339317

Wagner, B. C., Brinol, P., & Petty, R. E. (2012). Dimensions of metacognitive judgment: Implications for attitude change. In P. Brinol & K. DeMarree (Eds.), *Social metacognition* (pp. 43–61). New York: Psychology Press.

Wakslak, C. J. (2012). The experience of cognitive dissonance in important and trivial domains: A construal-level theory approach. *Journal of Experimental Social Psychology, 48,* 1361–1364.

Walker, A. (2001). British psychology students' perceptions of group-work and peer assessment. *Psychology Learning and Teaching, 1,* 28–36.

Walker, I., & Mann, L. (1987). Unemployment, relative deprivation, and social protest. *Personality and Social Psychology Bulletin, 13,* 275–283.

Walker, R. (2005, March). Sticky success. *The New York Times Magazine.* Retrieved from www. nytimes.com

Walster, E., Aronson, V., Abrahams, D., & Rottman, L. (1966). The importance of physical attractiveness in dating behavior. *Journal of Personality and Social Psychology, 4,* 508–516.

Walster, E., & Festinger, L. (1962). The effectiveness of "overheard" persuasive communications. *Journal of Abnormal and Social Psychology, 65,* 395–402.

Walther, E. (2002). Guilty by mere association: Evaluative conditioning and the spreading attitude effect. *Journal of Personality & Social Psychology, 82,* 919–934.

Walton, G. M. (2014). The new science of wise psychological interventions. *Current Directions in Psychological Science, 23*(1), 73–82. doi:10.1177/0963721413512856

Walton, G. M., & Cohen, G. L. (2011). A brief social-belonging intervention improves academic and health outcomes among minority students. *Science, 331,* 1447–1451.

Walton, G. M., Cohen, G. L., Cwir, D., & Spencer, S. J. (2012). Mere belonging: The power of social connections. *Journal of Personality and Social Psychology, 102*(3), 513–532. doi:10.1037/a0025731

Walumbwa, F. O., Wang, P., Lawler, J. J., & Shi, K. (2004). The role of collective efficacy in the relations between transformational leadership and work outcomes. *Journal of Occupational and Organizational Psychology, 77,* 515–530.

Walzer, M. (1970). *Obligations.* Cambridge, MA: Harvard University Press.

Warburton, W. A., Williams, K. D., & Cairns, D. R. (2006). When ostracism leads to aggression: The moderating effects of control deprivation. *Journal of Experimental Social Psychology, 42,* 213–220.

Was, C. A. (2010). The persistence of content-specific memory operations: Priming effects following a 24-h delay. *Psychonomic Bulletin and Review, 17*(3), 362–368. doi:10.3758/PBR. 17.3.362

Watson, D. (1982). The actor and the observer: How are their perceptions of causality divergent? *Psychological Bulletin, 92,* 304–314.

Watson, D., & Pennebaker, J. W. (1989). Health complaints, stress, and distress: Exploring the central role of negative affectivity. *Psychological Review, 96,* 234–254.

Weaver, K., Garcia, S. M., Schwarz, N., & Miller, D. T. (2007). Inferring the popularity of an opinion from its familiarity: A repetitive voice can sound like a chorus. *Journal of Personality and Social Psychology, 92,* 821–833.

Weber, B., & Hertel, G. (2007). Motivation gains of inferior group members: A meta-analytical review. *Journal of Personality and Social Psychology, 93,* 973–993.

Weber, J. M., Kopelman, S., & Messick, D. M. (2004). A conceptual review of decision making in social dilemmas: Applying a logic of appropriateness. *Personality and Social Psychology Review, 8,* 281–307.

Weber, J. M., Malhotra, D., & Murnighan, J. K. (2005). *Normal acts of irrational trust: Motivated attributions and the trust development process.* Greenwood, CT: Elsevier Science/JAI Press.

Weber, M. (1921/1946). The sociology of charismatic authority. In H. H. Gertz & C. W. Mills (Trans. & Eds.), *From Max Weber: Essays in sociology* (pp. 245–252). New York: Oxford University Press.

Weber, R., & Crocker, J. (1983). Cognitive processes in the revision of stereotypic beliefs. *Journal of Personality and Social Psychology, 45,* 961–977.

Wegener, D. T., & Petty, R. E. (1995). Flexible correction processes in social judgment: The role of naive theories in corrections for perceived bias. *Journal of Personality and Social Psychology, 68,* 36–51.

Wegener, D. T., & Petty, R. E. (1997). The flexible correction model: The role of naive theories of bias in bias correction. In M. P. Zanna (Ed.), *Advances in experimental social psychology* (vol. 29, pp. 141–208). Mahwah, NJ: Lawrence Erlbaum Associates.

Wegener, D. T., & Petty, R. E. (2001). Understanding effects of mood through the elaboration likelihood and flexible correction models. In L. L. Martin, & G. L. Clore (Eds.), *Theories of mood and cognition: A user's guidebook* (pp. 177–210). Mahwah, NJ: Lawrence Erlbaum Associates.

Wegener, D. T., Petty, R., & Smith, S. M. (1995). Positive mood can increase or decrease message scrutiny: The hedonic contingency view of mood and message processing. *Journal of Personality and Social Psychology, 69,* 5–15.

Wegner, D. (1987). Transactive memory: A contemporary analysis of the group mind. In B. Mullen & G. R. Goethals (Eds.), *Theories of group behavior* (pp. 185–208). New York: Springer.

Wegner, D. M. (1994). Ironic processes of mental control. *Psychological Review, 101,* 34–52.

Wegner, D. M., & Vallacher, R. R. (1986). Action identification. In R. M. Sorrentino & E. T. Higgins (Eds.), *Handbook of motivation and cognition: Foundations of social behavior* (pp. 550–582). New York: Guilford Press.

Weide, J. G., & Wilderom, C. P. M. (2004). Charismatic leadership, environmental dynamism, and performance. *European Journal of Work and Organizational Psychology, 13,* 447–471.

Weiner, B., Osborne, D., & Rudolph, U. (2011). An attributional analysis of reactions to poverty: The political ideology of the giver and the perceived morality of the receiver. *Personality and Social Psychology Review, 15*(2), 199–213. doi:http://dx.doi.org/10.1177/1088868310387615

Weinstein, N. D. (1987). Unrealistic optimism about susceptibility to health problems: Conclusions from a community-wide sample. *Journal of Behavioral Medicine, 10,* 481–500.

Weisbuch, M., Ivcevic, Z., & Ambady, N. (2009). On being liked on the web and in the "real world": Consistency in first impressions across personal webpages and spontaneous behavior. *Journal of Experimental Social Psychology, 45,* 573–576.

Weisbuch, M., & Mackie, D. (2009). False fame, perceptual clarity, or persuasion? Flexible fluency attribution in spokesperson familiarity effects. *Journal of Consumer Psychology, 19,* 62–72.

Welbourne, J. L. (2001). Changes in impression complexity over time and across situations. *Personality and Social Psychology Bulletin, 27,* 1071–1085.

Weldon, E., & Mustari, E. L. (1988). Felt dispensability in groups of coactors: The effects of shared responsibility and explicit anonymity on cognitive effort. *Organizational Behavior and Human Decision Processes, 41,* 330–351.

Wellesley College Center for Research on Women. (1992). *How schools shortchange girls: The AAUW Report.* Washington, DC: American Association of University Women Educational Foundation.

Wells, G. L., & Gavanski, I. (1989). Mental simulation of causality. *Journal of Personality and Social Psychology, 56,* 161–169.

Wells, G. L., & Petty, R. E. (1980). The effects of overt head movements on persuasion: Compatibility and incompatibility of responses. *Basic and Applied Social Psychology, 1,* 219–230.

Weng, H. Y., Fox, A. S., Shackman, A. J., Stodola, D. E., Caldwell, J. Z. K., Olson, M. C., . . . Davidson, R. J. (2013). Compassion training alters altruism and neural responses to suffering. *Psychological Science, 24*(7), 1171–1180. doi:http://dx.doi.org/10.1177/0956797612469537

Wenzel, M. (2004). Social identification as a determinant of concerns about individual-, group-, and inclusive-level justice. *Social Psychology Quarterly, 67*(1), 70–87.

Werch, C. E., Lundstrum, R. H., & Moore, A. (1989). Bogus-pipeline effects on self-reported college student drug use, problems, and attitudes. *The International Journal of the Addictions, 24,* 1003–1010.

Wetherell, M. S. (1987). Social identity and group polarization. In J. C. Turner (Ed.), *Rediscovering the social group: A self-categorization theory.* London: Basil Blackwell.

Wheatley, T., & Haidt, J. (2005). Hypnotic disgust makes moral judgments more severe. *Psychological Science, 16,* 780–784.

Wheelan, S. A. (1994). *Group processes: A developmental perspective.* Boston, MA: Allyn & Bacon.

Wheelan, S. A., Davidson, B., & Tilin, F. (2003). Group development across time: Reality or illusion? *Small Group Research, 34,* 223–245.

White, G. L., Fishbein, S., & Rutstein, J. (1981). Passionate love: The misattribution of arousal. *Journal of Personality and Social Psychology, 41,* 56–62.

White, M., Härtel, C. E. J., & Panipucci, D. (2005). *Understanding cross-cultural negotiation: A model integrating affective events theory and communication accommodation theory.* Mahwah, NJ: Lawrence Erlbaum Associates.

White, R. K. (1965). Images in the context of international conflict: Soviet perceptions of the U.S. and the U.S.S.R. In H. C. Kelman (Ed.), *International behavior: A social-psychological analysis* (pp. 236–276). New York: Holt, Rinehart & Winston.

White, R. K. (1977). Misperception in the Arab-Israeli conflict. *Journal of Social Issues, 33,* 190–221.

White, R. K. (1984). *Fearful warriors: A psychological profile in U.S.-Soviet relations.* New York: Free Press.

White, R. K. (1987). Underestimating and overestimating others' fear. *Journal of Social Issues, 43*(4), 105–110.

White, R. W. (1959). Motivation reconsidered: The concept of competence. *Psychological Review, 66,* 297–333.

Whittington, J. L., Goodwin, V. L., & Murray, B. (2004). Transformational leadership, goal difficulty, and job design: Independent and interactive effects on employee outcomes. *Leadership Quarterly, 15,* 593–606.

Wicker, A. W. (1969). Attitudes versus actions: The relationship of verbal and overt behavioral responses to attitude objects. *Journal of Social Issues, 25,* 41–78.

Widom, C. S. (1989). The cycle of violence. *Science, 244,* 160–166.

Wierzbicka, A. (1994). Emotion, language, and cultural scripts. In S. Kitayama, & H. R. Markus (Eds.), *Emotion and culture: Empirical studies of mutual influence* (pp. 133–196). Washington, DC: American Psychological Association.

Wilder, D. (1977). Perception of groups, size of opposition, and social influence. *Journal of Experimental Social Psychology, 13,* 253–268.

Wilder, D. A. (1981). Perceiving persons as a group: Categorization and intergroup relations. In D. L. Hamilton (Ed.), *Cognitive processes in stereotyping and intergroup behavior* (pp. 213–258). Hillsdale, NJ: Lawrence Erlbaum Associates.

Wilder, D. A. (1984). Intergroup contact: The typical member and the exception to the rule. *Journal of Experimental Social Psychology, 20,* 177–194.

Wilder, D. A. (1986). Social categorization: Implications for creation and reduction of intergroup bias. In L. Berkowitz (Ed.), *Advances in experimental social psychology* (vol. 19, pp. 291–355). New York: Academic Press.

Wilder, D. A. (1990). Some determinants of the persuasive power of in-groups and out-groups: Organization of information and attribution of independence. *Journal of Personality and Social Psychology, 59,* 1202–1213.

Wilder, D. A., & Shapiro, P. N. (1984). Role of out-group cues in determining social identity. *Journal of Personality and Social Psychology, 47,* 342–348.

Wilder, D. A., & Shapiro, P. N. (1988). Role of competition-induced anxiety in limiting the beneficial impact of positive behavior by out-group members. *Journal of Personality and Social Psychology, 56,* 60–69.

Wilder, D. A., & Shapiro, P. (1991). Facilitation of outgroup stereotypes by enhanced ingroup identity. *Journal of Experimental Social Psychology, 27,* 431–452.

Wilder, D. A., & Thompson, J. E. (1980). Intergroup contact with independent manipulations of in-group and out-group interaction. *Journal of Personality and Social Psychology, 38,* 589–603.

Wildschut, T., & Insko, C. A. (2007). Explanations of interindividual-intergroup discontinuity: A review of the evidence. *European Review of Social Psychology, 18,* 175–211.

Wilke, H., & Lanzetta, J. T. (1970). The obligation to help: The effects of amount of prior help on subsequent helping behavior. *Journal of Experimental Social Psychology, 6,* 488–493.

Wilke, H., & Lanzetta, J. T. (1982). The obligation to help: Factor affecting response to help received. *European Journal of Social Psychology, 12,* 315–319.

Wilkenfeld, J., Young, K., Asal, V., & Quinn, D. (2003). Mediating international crises: Cross-national and experimental perspectives. *Journal of Conflict Resolution, 47,* 279–301.

Willard, J., Madon, S., Guyll, M., Scherr, K. C., & Buller, A. A. (2012). The accumulating effects of shared expectations. *European Journal of Social Psychology, 42,* 497–508.

Williams, E. (1977). Experimental comparisons of face-to-face and mediated communication: A review. *Psychological Bulletin, 84,* 963–976.

Williams, J. E., & Best, D. L. (1982). *Measuring sex stereotypes: A thirty-nation study.* Beverly Hills, CA: Sage Publications.

Williams, K. D. (2007). Ostracism. *Annual Review of Psychology, 58,* 425–452.

Williams, K. D. (2009). Ostracism: A temporal need-threat model. In M. P. Zanna (Ed.), *Advances in experimental social psychology* (vol. 41, pp. 275–314). San Diego, CA: Elsevier Academic Press.

Williams, K. D., Cheung, C. K. T., & Choi, W. (2000).

Cyberostracism: Effects of being ignored over the Internet. *Journal of Personality and Social Psychology, 79*, 748–762.

Williams, K. D., Harkins, S., & Latané, B. (1981). Identifiability as a deterrent to social loafing: Two cheering experiments. *Journal of Personality and Social Psychology, 40*, 303–311.

Williams, L. (1991, Nov. 30). In a 90's quest for black identity, intense doubts and disagreement. *The New York Times*, pp. A1, A7.

Williams, L. E., & Bargh, J. A. (2008). Experiencing physical warmth promotes interpersonal warmth. *Science, 322*, 606–607.

Williamson, G. M., & Clark, M. S. (1989). Providing help and desired relationship type as determinants of changes in moods and self-evaluations. *Journal of Personality and Social Psychology, 56*, 722–734.

Willis, G. B., & Guinote, A. (2011). The effects of social power on goal content and goal striving: A situated perspective. *Social and Personality Psychology Compass, 5*, 706–719.

Wilson, D. S., Van Vugt, M., & O'Gorman, R. (2008). Multilevel selection theory and major evolutionary transitions implications for psychological science. *Current Directions in Psychological Science, 17*(1), 6–9.

Wilson, J. (2000). Volunteering. *Annual Review of Sociology, 26*, 215–240.

Wilson, T. D., & Dunn, D. S. (1986). Effects of introspection on attitude-behavior consistency. Analyzing reasons versus focusing on feelings. *Journal of Experimental Social Psychology, 22*, 249–263.

Wilson, T. D., Gilbert, D. T., & Wheatley, T.P. (1998). Protecting our minds: The role of lay beliefs. In V. Yzerbyt, G. Lories, & B. Dardenne (Eds.), *Metacognition: Cognitive and social dimensions* (pp. 171–201). New York: Sage.

Wilson, T. D., Houston, C. E., & Meyers, J. M. (1998). Choose your poison: Effects of lay beliefs about mental processes on attitude change. *Social Cognition, 16*, 114–132.

Wilson, T. D., Laser, P. S., & Stone, J. I. (1982). Judging the predictors of one's own mood: Accuracy and the use of shared theories. *Journal of Experimental Social Psychology, 18*, 537–549.

Wilson, T. D., Lindsey, S., & Schooler, T. Y. (2000). A model of dual attitudes. *Psychological Review, 107*, 101–126.

Wilson, T. D., Lisle, D. J., Schooler, J. W., Hodges, S. D., Klaaren, K. J., & LaFleur, S. J. (1993). Introspecting about reasons can reduce post-choice satisfaction. *Personality and Social Psychology Bulletin, 19*, 331–339.

Wiltermuth, S. (2012). Synchrony and destructive obedience. *Social Influence, 7*, 78–89.

Winkielman, P., Berridge, K. C., & Wilbarger, J. L. (2005). *Emotion, behavior, and conscious experience: Once more without feeling.* New York, NY: Guilford Press.

Wittenbaum, G. M., Shulman, H. C., & Braz, M. E. (2010). Social ostracism in task groups: The effects of group composition. *Small Group Research, 41*, 330–353.

Wittenbaum, G. M., Stasser, G., & Merry, C. J. (1996). Tacit coordination in anticipation of small group task completion. *Journal of Experimental Social Psychology, 32*, 129–152.

Wittenbrink, B., Judd, C. M., & Park, B. (2001). Evaluative versus conceptual judgments in automatic stereotyping and prejudice. *Journal of Experimental Social Psychology, 37*, 244–252.

Wojcieszak, M. (2011). Deliberation and attitude polarization. *Journal of Communication, 61*, 596–617.

Wolfgang, M., & Strohm, R. B. (1956). The relationship between alcohol and criminal homicide. *Quarterly Journal of Studies on Alcohol, 17*, 411–425.

Wolpe, P. R., Foster, K. R., & Langleben, D. D. (2010). Emerging neurotechnologies for lie-detection: Promises and perils. *The American Journal of Bioethics, 10*, 40–48.

Wolsko, C., Park, B., Judd, C. M., & Bachelor, J. (2003). Intergroup contact: Effects on group evaluations and perceived variability. *Group Processes & Intergroup Relations, 6*, 93–110.

Wolsko, C., Park, B., Judd, C. M., & Wittenbrink, B. (2000). Framing interethnic ideology: Effects of multicultural and color-blind perspectives on judgments of groups and individuals. *Journal of Personality and Social Psychology, 78*, 635–654.

Wong, E., Tschan, F., Messerli, L., & Semmer, N. K. (2013). Expressing and amplifying positive emotions facilitate goal attainment in workplace interactions. *Frontiers in Psychology, 4.* doi: 10.3389/fpsyg.2013.00188

Wood, J. V. (1989). Theory and research concerning social comparisons of personal attributes. *Psychological Bulletin, 106*, 231–248.

Wood, J. V., Taylor, S. E., & Lichtman, R. R. (1985). Social comparison in adjustment to breast cancer. *Journal of Personality and Social Psychology, 49*, 1169–1183.

Wood, W., Christensen, P. N., Hebl, M. R., & Rothgerber, H. (1997) Conformity to sex-typed norms, affect, and the self-concept. *Journal of Personality and Social Psychology, 73*, 523–535.

Wood, W., & Eagly, A. H. (2002). A cross-cultural analysis of the behavior of women and men: Implications for the origins of sex differences. *Psychological Review, 128*, 699–727.

Wood, W., Lundgren, S., Ouellette, J. A., Busceme, S., & Blackstone, T. (1994). Minority influence: A meta-analytic review of social influence processes. *Psychological Bulletin, 115*, 323–345.

Wood, W., Pool, G. J., Leck, K., & Purivs, D. (1996). Self-definition, defensive processing, and influence: The normative impact of majority and minority groups. *Journal of Personality and Social Psychology, 71*, 1181–1193.

Wood, W., & Quinn, J. M. (2003). Forewarned and forearmed? Two meta-analysis syntheses of forewarnings of influence appeals. *Psychological Bulletin, 129*, 119–138.

Wood, W., Quinn, J. M., & Kashy, D. A. (2002). Habits in everyday life: Thought, emotion, and action. *Journal of Personality and Social Psychology, 83*, 1281–1297.

Wood, W., Rhodes, N., & Beik, M. (1995). Working knowledge and attitude strength: An information processing analysis. In R. E. Petty & J. A. Krosnick (Eds.), *Attitude strength: Antecedents and consequences* (pp. 283–313). Hillsdale, NJ: Erlbaum.

Wood, W., Tam, L., & Witt, M. G. (2005). Changing circumstances, disrupting habits. *Journal of Personality and Social Psychology, 88*, 918–933.

Wood, W., Wong, F., & Chachere, J. (1991). Effects of media violence on viewers' aggression in unconstrained social interaction. *Psychological Bulletin, 109*, 371–383.

Worchel, S. (1979). Cooperation and the reduction of intergroup conflict: Some determining factors. In W. G. Austin & S. Worchel (Eds.), *The social psychology of intergroup conflict* (pp. 262–273). Monterey, CA: Brooks/Cole.

Worchel, S., Lee, J., & Adewole, A. (1975). Effects of supply and demand on ratings of object value. *Journal of Personality and Social Psychology, 32*, 906–914.

Worchel, S., & Norvell, N. (1980). Effect of perceived environmental conditions during cooperation on intergroup attraction. *Journal of Personality and Social Psychology, 38*, 264–272.

Word, C. O., Zanna, M. P., & Cooper, J. (1974). The nonverbal mediation of self-fulfilling prophecies in interracial interaction. *Journal of Experimental Social Psychology, 10*, 109–120.

Workman, P. (2013, Sept. 4). The 'other' Syrian war. *CTV NEWS.* http://www.ctvnews.ca/ctv-national-news/the-other-syrian-war-visiting-the-violent-street-that-has-divided-lebanon-s-tripoli-1.1440425

Worringham, C. J., & Messick, D. M. (1983). Social facilitation of running: An unobtrusive study. *Journal of Social Psychology, 121*, 23–29.

Worth, L. T., & Mackie, D. M. (1987). Cognitive mediation of positive affect in persuasion. *Social Cognition, 5*, 76–94.

Wortman, C., Adesman, P., Herman, E., & Greenberg, R. (1976). Self-disclosure: An attributional perspective. *Journal of Personality and Social Psychology, 33*, 184–191.

Wosinska, W., Cialdini, R. B., Petrova, P. K., Barrett, D. W., Gornik-Durose, M., Butner, J., & Griskevicius, V. (2009). Resistance to deficient organizational authority: The impact of culture and connectedness in the workplace. *Journal of Applied Social Psychology*, *39*, 834–851.

Wright, P. H. (1982). Men's friendships, women's friendships and the alleged inferiority of the latter. *Sex Roles, 8*, 1–20.

Wright, Q. (1965). Escalation of international conflicts. *Journal of Conflict Resolution, 9*, 434–449.

Wright, S. C., Aron, A., McLaughlin-Volpe, T., & Ropp, S. A. (1997). The extended contact effect: Knowledge of cross-group friendships and prejudice. *Journal of Personality and Social Psychology, 73*, 73–90.

Wright, S. C., Taylor, D. M., & Moghaddam, F. M. (1990). Responding to membership in a disadvantaged group: From acceptance to collective protest. *Journal of Personality and Social Psychology, 58*, 994–1003.

Wrosch, C., Scheier, M. F., Miller, G. E., Schulz, R., & Carver, C. S. (2003). Adaptive self-regulation of unattainable goals: Goal disengagement, goal reengagement, and subjective well-being. *Personality & Social Psychology Bulletin, 29*, 1494–1508.

Wundt, W. (1916). *Elements of folk psychology: Outlines of a psychological history of the development of mankind.* London: Allen and Unwin.

Wyer, R. S., & Srull, T. K. (1989). *Memory and cognition in its social context.* Hillsdale, NJ: Lawrence Erlbaum Associates.

Xu, A. J., & Wyer, R. S. (2010). Puffery in advertisements: The effects of media context, communication norms, and consumer knowledge. *Journal of Consumer Research, 37*, 329–343.

Xu, F., Wu, D., Toriyama, R., Ma, F., Itakura, S., & Lee, K. (2012). Similarities and differences in Chinese and Caucasian adults' use of facial cues for trustworthiness judgments. *PloS ONE, 7*, e34859.

Xygalatas, D., Mitkidis, P., Fischer, R., Reddish, P., Skewes, J., Geertz, A. W., Roepstorff, A., & Bulbulia, J. (2013). Extreme rituals promote prosociality. *Psychological Science, 24*, 1602–1605.

Yamagishi, T. (1986). The provision of a sanctioning system as a public good. *Journal of Personality and Social Psychology, 51*, 110–116.

Yang, W., Liu, W., Viña, A., Tuanmu, M.-N., He, G., Dietz, T., & Liu, J. (2013). Nonlinear effects of group size on collective action and resource outcomes. *Proceedings of the National Academy of Sciences of the United States of America.* doi:10.1073/pnas.1301733110/-/DCSupplemental.

Yaniv, I., & Choshen-Hillel, S. (2012). Exploiting the wisdom of others to make better decisions: Suspending judgment reduces egocentrism and increases accuracy. *Journal of Behavioral Decision Making, 25*, 427–434.

Yoo, B., & Donthu, N. (2005). The effect of personal cultural orientation on consumer ethnocentrism: Evaluations and behaviors of U.S. consumers toward Japanese products. *Journal of International Consumer Marketing, 18*, 7–44.

Yoshida, E., Peach, J. M., Zanna, M. P., & Spencer, S. J. (2012). Not all automatic associations are created equal: How implicit normative evaluations are distinct from implicit attitudes and uniquely predict meaningful behavior. *Journal of Experimental Social Psychology, 48*, 694–706.

Young, A. I., & Fazio, R. H. (2013). Attitude accessibility as a determinant of object construal and evaluation. *Journal of Experimental Social Psychology, 49*, 404–418.

Young, A. I., Ratner, K. G., & Fazio, R. H. (2013). Political attitudes bias the mental representation of a presidential candidate's face. *Psychological Science Online First*, doi:10.1177/0956797613510717

Young, S. D., & Jordan, A. H. (2013). The influence of social networking photos on social norms and sexual health behaviors. *Cyberpsychology, Behavior, and Social Networking, 16*, 243–247.

Young, S. G., Sacco, D. F., & Hugenberg, K. (2011). Vulnerability to disease is associated with a domain-specific preference for symmetrical faces relative to symmetrical non-face stimuli. *European Journal of Social Psychology, 41*, 558–563.

Yovetich, N. A., & Rusbult, C. E. (1994). Accommodative behavior in close relationships: Exploring transformation of motivation. *Journal of Experimental Social Psychology, 30*, 138–164.

Yzerbyt, V., Rocher, S., & Schadron, G. (1997). Stereotypes as explanations: A subjective essentialistic view of group perception. In R. Spears, P. J. Oakes, N. Ellemers, & S. A. Haslam (Eds.), *The social psychology of stereotyping and group life* (pp. 20–50). Oxford: Blackwell.

Zaccaro, S. J. (1984). Social loafing: The role of task attractiveness. *Personality and Social Psychology Bulletin, 10*, 99–106.

Zaccaro, S. J., Foti, R. J., & Kenny, D. A. (1991). Self-monitoring and trait-based variance in leadership: An investigation of leader flexibility across multiple group situations. *Journal of Applied Psychology, 76*, 308–315.

Zadro, L., Williams, K. D., & Richardson, R. (2004). How low can you go? Ostracism by a computer is sufficient to lower self-reported levels of belonging, control, self-esteem, and meaningful existence. *Journal of Experimental Social Psychology, 40*, 560–567.

Zajonc, R. B. (1965). Social facilitation. *Science, 149*, 269–274.

Zajonc, R. B. (1968). Attitudinal effects of mere exposure. *Journal of Personality and Social Psychology, 9*, Monograph Suppl. No. 2, part 2.

Zajonc, R. B. (1980). Feeling and thinking: Preferences need no inferences. *American Psychologist, 35*, 151–175.

Zajonc, R. B. (1998). Emotions. In D. T. Gilbert, S. T. Fiske, & G. Lindzey (Eds.), *Handbook of social psychology* (4th ed., vol. 1, pp. 591–634). Boston: McGraw-Hill.

Zajonc, R. B. (2001). Mere exposure: A gateway to the subliminal. *Current Directions in Psychological Science, 10*, 224–228.

Zaki, J., Schirmer, J., & Mitchell, J. P. (2011). Social influence modulates the neural computation of value. *Psychological Science, 22*, 894–900.

Zanna, M. P., & Rempel, J. K. (1988). Attitudes: A new look at an old concept. In D. Bar-Tal & A. Kruglanski (Eds.), *The social psychology of knowledge* (pp. 315–334). New York: Cambridge University Press.

Zárate, M. A., & Smith, E. R. (1990). Person categorization and stereotyping. *Social Cognition, 8*, 161–185.

Zayas, V., Mischel, W., Shoda, Y., & Aber, J. L. (2011). Roots of adult attachment: Maternal caregiving at 18 months predicts adult peer and partner attachment. *Social Psychological and Personality Science, 2*, 289–297.

Zebrowitz, L. A., Franklin, R. G., Jr., Hillman, S. & Boc, H. (2013). Older and younger adults' first impressions from faces: Similar in agreement but different in positivity. *Psychology and Aging, 28*, 202–212.

Zebrowitz, L. A., Hall, J. A., Murphy, N. A., & Rhodes, G. (2002). Looking smart and looking good: Facial cues to intelligence and their origin. *Personality and Social Psychology Bulletin, 28*, 238–249.

Zebrowitz, L. A., & Montepare, J. (2006). The ecological approach to person perception: Evolutionary roots and contemporary offshoots. In M. Schaller, J. A. Simpson, & D. T. Kenrick (Eds.), *Evolution and social psychology* (pp. 81–113). Madison, CT: Psychosocial Press.

Zebrowitz, L. A., Tenenbaum, D. R., & Goldstein, L. H. (1991). The impact of job applicants' facial maturity, sex, and academic achievement on hiring recommendations. *Journal of Applied Social Psychology, 21*, 525–548.

Zebrowitz, L. A., White, B., & Wieneke, K. (2008). Mere exposure and racial prejudice: Exposure to other-race faces increases liking for strangers of that race. *Social Cognition, 26*, 259–275.

Zentall, T. R. (2010). Justification of effort by humans and pigeons: Cognitive dissonance or contrast? *Current Directions in Psychological Science, 19*, 296–300.

Zhang, J. (2010). The persuasiveness of individualistic and collectivistic advertising appeals among Chinese generation-X consumers. *Journal of Advertising, 39*, 69–80.

Zhou, E. S., Penedo, F. J., Lewis, J. E., Rasheed, M., Traeger, L., Lechner, S., & Antoni, M. H. (2010). Perceived stress mediates the effects of social support on health-related quality of life among men treated for localized prostate cancer. *Journal of Psychosomatic Research, 69*, 587–590.

Zillmann, D. (1979). *Hostility and aggression*. Hillsdale, NJ: Lawrence Erlbaum Associates.

Zou, X., Tam, K.-P., Morris, M. W., Lee, S.-L., Lau, I. Y.-M., & Chiu, C.-Y. (2009). Culture as common sense: Perceived consensus versus personal beliefs as mechanisms of cultural influence. *Journal of Personality and Social Psychology, 97*, 579–597.

Zuckerman, M. (1979). *Sensation seeking: Beyond the optimal level of arousal*. Hillsdale, NJ: Lawrence Erlbaum Associates.

AUTHOR INDEX

SUBJECT INDEX